The Law of American Business Organizations:

An Environmental Approach

Business Law Textbooks from John Wiley and Sons

Atteberry, Pearson, and Litka: REAL ESTATE LAW, 3rd
Cataldo, Kempin, Stockton, and Weber: INTRODUCTION TO LAW AND
THE LEGAL PROCESS, 3rd
Delaney and Gleim: CPA REVIEW: AUDITING
Delaney and Gleim: CPA REVIEW: BUSINESS LAW
Delarey and Gleim: CPA REVIEW: THEORY AND PRACTICE
Dunfee and Gibson: LEGAL ASPECTS OF
GOVERNMENT REGULATION OF BUSINESS, 3rd
Dunfee, Gibson, Lamber, and McCarty: MODERN BUSINESS LAW:
INTRODUCTION TO THE LEGAL ENVIRONMENT OF BUSINESS
Dunfee and Gibson: AN INTRODUCTION TO CONTRACTS, 2nd
Erickson, Dunfee, and Gibson: ANTITRUST AND TRADE REGULATION:
CASES AND MATERIALS
Gleim and Delaney: CPA EXAMINATION REVIEW: VOLUME I
OUTLINES AND STUDY GUIDE
Gleim and Delaney: CPA EXAMINATION REVIEW: VOLUME II
PROBLEMS AND SOLUTIONS
Griffith, LEGAL ENVIRONMENT OF BUSINESS
Henszey and Friedman: REAL ESTATE LAW, 2nd
Inman, THE REGULATORY ENVIRONMENT OF BUSINESS
Litka and Inman: LEGAL ENVIRONMENT OF BUSINESS, PUBLIC AND
PRIVATE LAWS, 3rd
Litka and Jennings: BUSINESS LAW, 3rd
Rothenberg and Blumenkrantz: PERSONAL LAW
Walder: PASS THIS BAR

The Law of American Business Organizations:
An Environmental Approach

Arthur D. Wolfe

Member of the Ohio, Indiana, Virgin Islands,
and Federal Bars
Associate Professor of Business Law
Michigan State University

Frederick J. Naffziger

Member of the Illinois, District of Columbia,
Texas, and Federal Bars
Professor of Business Law
Indiana University

John Wiley & Sons

New York   Chichester   Brisbane   Toronto   Singapore

Library of Congress Cataloging in Publication Data:

Wolfe, Arthur D.
　The law of American business organizations.

　Includes index.
　1. Corporation law—United States.　2. Partnership—
United States.　3. Securities—United States.
4. Agency (Law)—United States.　I. Naffziger,
Frederick J.　II. Title.
KF1355.W59　1984　　346.73′066　　83-19777
ISBN 0-471-86936-8　　347.30666

Printed in the United States of America

10 9 8 7 6 5 4 3 2 1

This book is dedicated to our children,
Wendy, Becky, and Jane Wolfe and
Susan, John, Ann, and Ellen Naffziger

Preface

Most new textbooks are motivated by a perceived gap between the real world and the knowledge of that world provided by current instructional materials. In *The Law of American Business Organizations: An Environmental Approach,* formerly entitled *Legal Perspectives of American Business Associations,* we attempt to close that gap by proceeding in three ways, all of which help to distinguish this book from others on the same material. First, most textbooks focus primarily on the formation and control of business corporations under state law. They neglect the strong federal influence exerted on business corporations through federal regulation of the issuance and trading of securities. Over one-fifth of this text is devoted to a comprehensive treatment of federal securities regulation.

Second, the title includes the words, "An Environmental Approach." These words reflect both substantive ideas and matters of form. Business students, undergraduates especially, have a strong urge to seek out hard-and-fast rules. This is a result of the kind of information and pedagogy that exists in almost all business-college instruction. But law, like life, *cannot and should not be reduced to a mere presentation and then memorization of rules.* Almost all rules have exceptions, rough or vague edges, and even voids. The exceptions, the vagueness, and the voids are understood only if the rules are presented in a broader context that includes at least history and present-day policy and political ideas and forces. Substantively, the material in this book in all the major areas covered includes information on the history of the rules or exceptions and the policy reasons for them.

As a matter of form, we realize that a convenient starting point for the study of law is with the rules. The critical question for authors is, which rules are important? Often students are presented with massive doses of rules and they cannot discern the important rules from the less important rules. We focus on fewer rules. What we believe to be the more important ones in the areas of law are covered and then explained, analyzed, and evaluated in a thorough manner. Also, as a matter of form, the cases are a bit longer than those found in comparable texts. This requires the student to analyze a factual pattern as he or she must do when confronting a problem outside the classroom. The review questions following the cases focus the readers' attention on our purpose for including the case in the text. At the end of each chapter, and in the appendix, are a series of review questions, some of which are from past CPA exams. These require the student to analyze the facts, correctly recall and apply one or more legal principles, and, finally, synthesize an answer by, in some cases, considering both legal and policy issues.

Third, we demonstrate how business organizations do not operate merely within the sometimes too-narrow confines of a legal environment. There exist social, political, ethical, and international forces that affect the management of a business. An enterprise may operate legally and profitably yet encounter serious problems if society believes that its activities are harming the social fabric of the nation. Some social beliefs, such as the view that discrimination against an individual on account of race, religion, sex, or national origin is wrong, eventually are enacted into law. Others, no less real, exist in an unwritten form within the collective conscience of a country. Readers of this text are made aware that the consideration of such nonlegal factors is a significant part of the management process.

The book is intended for two types of courses: (1) the undergraduate course in business organizations, particularly that taken by accounting majors and (2) the graduate MBA course that deals with the legal environment of business.

The student in the business organization course will find not only the traditional material on agency, partnership, and corporation law, but also, the law of federal securities. Excerpts from the Model Business Corporation Act are integrated into the text. The accounting student will also find worthwhile Chapter 17, Accountants and the Securities Law, for it also contains a discussion of accountants' liability under common law. The CPA examination law questions in both the review problems at the end of most chapters and the appendix should be a major aid to those considering taking the CPA examination.

MBA students will find the text illustrating the legal environment within which the business organization operates relevant, as well as illuminating. The emphasis on the most important rules, policy questions, and issues of social responsibility that confront management provide for graduate students a thorough introduction to the law and legal environment of business organizations.

The text is divided into six parts followed by an appendix and glossary.

Part One of the book is written with the assumption that the student has never taken a law course. We realize this assumption may not be accurate, but we believe it is better to be thorough than incomplete. Students who have had a previous business law course my wish to skip Chapter 1, which presents the process of rule creation by legislatures, individuals, and judges. This chapter gives special emphasis to the studying and briefing of appellate cases. In Chapter 2 we present an overview of the most prominent forms of American business organizations, as well as "S" (formerly subchapter S) corporations and franchises.

Part Two discusses the law of agency. These chapters, and the ones that follow, are not burdened with the terse statements of all the possible rules on agency law. Rather, the textual material emphasizes the fundamental rules of agency: the nature of the fiduciary relationship, the concepts of contractual authority and vicarious liability, and the growing uses of apparent authority.

Part Three combines text and appellate cases, together with sections of the Uniform Partnership Act, in order to analyze and evaluate partnership law. The presentation uses a typical partnership agreement as an orgnizational guide. Topics included are partnership formation, the duties owed by partners to each other and the partnership, partnership property, the contractual and tort liabilities of the partners and the partnership, and the liability of incoming partners and other issues created by partnership dissolution.

Part Four focuses on corporation law. Corporate documents, the MBCA and statutes from various states, as well as text and appellate cases are used in these chapters to illustrate the circumstances in which courts apply corporate law. The chapters cover the formation and personality of corporations; the relationship of the shareholder to both the large and closely held corporation; the role of the directors and officers in managing the corporation and their liability for crimes, torts, and the breach of their fiduciary duties; and the alteration or dissolution of the corporate structure.

Part Five presents federal securities law. The increasing importance of this area of law for business persons is manifested not only by the increasing number of major CPA examination questions on the topic, but also by the increased litigation spawned under these federal statutes. The analysis of this area begins with a chapter that provides an overview of securities regulation and is followed by one devoted to the issues raised by the insider trading laws. Next we discuss the liability of directors and attorneys involved in securities transactions. The explosive growth of litigation against accountants under these statutes has resulted in a longer chapter on accountants' liability, including an explanation of the Foreign Corrupt Practices Act. Coverage of the proxy and tender offer process ends this portion of the book.

Part Six explores the business organization's duties to employees and the public. The discussion of such legal issues also involves issues of a social and ethical nature. The relationship of the employer to the employees is examined not only in the traditional labor law context, but also within the milieu of the laws against discrimination in employment. The social responsibilities of business are examined within the context of products liability and environmental protection laws. Finally, the role of the corporation in the political process is explored and its role in the international business environment is considered.

We wish to note the extensive contributions of the judges who authored the opinions reproduced herein. Without their careful analysis and lucid prose this work would suffer significantly. Also we gratefully acknowledge the kind contributions of Thomas H. Corson, Chairman of Coachmen Industries, Inc., for the use of a Coachmen stock certificate; the American Institute of Certified Public Accountants for the use of CPA examination questions; Professor Keith Knauss for permission to reprint portions of a chapter from a book that he coauthored; and Matthew Bender and Company, Inc., for the use of a partnership agreement.

Appreciation also goes to professors James R. Bliss of Western Michigan University, Donald L. Boren of Bowling Green State University, Michael D. Engber of Ball State University, Richard A. Mann of the University of North Carolina, and David Reitzel of California State University, Fresno, for the many helpful suggestions they provided in the review process. Legal discussions with Robert Schlifke, attorney-at-law of South Bend, Indiana, have also been productive. We note also the special contribution of Professor Thomas Dunfee of the Wharton School, University of Pennsylvania, to the previous edition of this book. Finally, we express our gratitude to Lucille H. Sutton, business law editor at John Wiley & Sons. Her encouragement, patience, and suggestions aided us immensely. Authors cannot have a better editor than Lucille.

As authors the final responsibility for the book rests with us. We are responsible for the views presented and the accuracy of the information. Professor Wolfe is primarily responsible for the material in chapters 1–8 and 21. Professor Naffziger is primarily responsible for the material in chapters 14–20 and 22. Chapters 9–13 reflect a blending of efforts.

We welcome suggestions and comments from those who use the text.

Arthur D. Wolfe
Frederick J. Naffziger

Contents

List of Cases   xxvii

Introduction to the Study of Law and American Business   **PART ONE**
  Organizations   1

1   **Introduction to the Study of Law**   3

Definition of the Law   3

Rule Creation   3
  Legislative Rule Creation—Federal   4
  Legislative Rule Creation—State   4
  Individual Rule Creation   5
  Judicial Rule Creation   6
    The Common Law   6
    Equity Law or Equitable Principles   6

Rule Application   7
  Types of Rules   8
  Criminal and Civil Rules Distinguished   8
  Judicial Systems   9
    The Federal Court System   10
    The State Court System   10
    The Overlap Between the Two Court Systems   10
  The Civil Trial Process   11
    The Complaint   11
    Serving the Complaint   16
    Answer   16
    Class Actions   16
    Trial Motions   17
    Discovery   17

Judgment on the Pleadings or Summary Judgment   *18*
The Civil Jury Trial   *19*
Presenting the Evidence   *20*
Motion for a Directed Verdict   *20*
Judges' Instructions to the Jury   *20*
Motion for a Judgment N.O.V.   *21*
The Appellate Process   **21**
Appellate Court Action   **22**

Analysis, Recall, Evaluation, and Synthesis as Educational
Objectives   23

The Study of Appellate Cases   24

Briefing Appellate Cases   26
Parties   **27**
Facts   **27**
Cause of Action   **27**
Court's Decision and Reasoning   **28**
**Concluding Remarks About the Study of Appellate
Cases**   **28**

Structure and Method of this Book   30

**2   An Overview of Business Organizations and Their
Regulation   32**

Restraints on State Governments for the Formation and Regulation
of Business Organizations   32
Issues of Federalism   **32**
The Police Power of States   **33**
Limitations on the Use of the Police Power   **34**
**Typical State-Level Restraints on Business
Organizations**   **39**
Licensing   *39*
Trade-Name Registration   *39*
Regulation of Banks and Insurance Companies   *40*

Restraints on the Federal Government in Regulating Business
Conduct   41

Summary of Restraints on Governments to Regulate   45

Types of American Business Organizations   46
Agency   **48**
**Unincorporated Associations, Clubs, and Other Informal
Forms of Organization**   **49**
The Organization as a Separate Legal Entity   *50*
Liability of the Members   *50*

Proprietorships   54
Partnerships   56
Limited Partnerships   57
Joint Ventures   58
Corporations   58
    Subchapter S Corporations   *60*
    Public Versus Private Corporations   *60*
    Restrictions on the Use of the Corporate Form   *61*
Cooperatives   63
Franchises   67
Business Organizations Formed for Illegal Purposes   69

Review Problems   72

Agency Law   75   **PART TWO**

3   The Mutual Legal Duties of Principal and Agent   77

Creation of the Agency Relationship   79
  Creation of Agency by Contract   80
  Creation of Agency by Ratification   80
  Creation of Agency by Estoppel   80
  Creation of Agency by Operation of Law   81

Duties of the Agent to the Principal   84
  **Reconciling the Conflicting Interests of the Principal and the
    Agent**   85
  **Fiduciary Duties and the Nature of the Employment
    Relationship**   85
    Patent and Trade Secret Law   *90*
    Restrictive Covenants   *95*

Remedies for Breach of the Fiduciary Duty   99
  Recovery of Property or Opportunities Taken   99
  Injunction Against the Employee   100
  Discharging the Employee   100
  **The Corporate Value Structure, The Duty of Loyalty, and the
    Individual Conscience**   103

Duties of the Principal to the Agent   104

Capacity   106
  Husband and Wife as Principal and Agent   106

Review Problems   108

4   Contractual Liability of Principals and Agents to Third Parties   113

Contract and Tort Liability Distinguished   113

Contractual Liability of Principals to Third Parties   114
   Actual Authority—Express or Implied   114
   Circumstantial Authority—Apparent Authority, Estoppel, and Inherent Authority   119
      Apparent Authority   120
      Estoppel   123
      Inherent Authority   127
   Ratification   130

Contractual Liability of the Agent to Third Parties   134

Review Problems   139

5   Tort Liability of Principal and Agent to Third Parties   143

Tort Liability   143

Tort Liability of a Principal to a Third Party   144
   Principal Negligent with Respect to Hiring an Agent or Entrusting Property to the Agent   145
   Vicarious Liability of the Principal   147
      Basic Distinctions: Master, Servant, Independent Contractor   151
      The Difference Between a Master-Servant Relationship and a Principal-Nonservant Agent Relationship   157
      Liability for Damage Caused While Doing Personal Business on Company Time   161
      Intentional Torts and the Scope of Employment   162
   Apparent Authority and Vicarious Liability   167
   Ratification of an Agent's Torts and Other Rules Creating Vicarious Liability for a Principal   172
      Liability of Principal to Third Parties Based on Public Policy or Statutory Law   173
      Contractual Duty to Act Carefully to Third Parties   174
      Tort Liability of Principal for Representations by Agent   174

Review Problems   176

6   Agency Operation and Termination   182

Agency Operation   182
   Notice, Knowledge, and Payment   182
   Subagents   186

Delegation of Agency Duties   190
Loaned or Borrowed Servants   191

Agency Termination   195
Agency Coupled with an Interest   196
Termination by Consent   196
Termination by Events   198
Termination of the Agent's Authority as Perceived by Third
Parties   199

Review Problems   201

Partnership Law   205   **PART THREE**

**7   The Partnership Form of Organization: Creation and Partnership
Property   207**

The Uniform Partnership Act   207

Definition and Legal Character of a Partnership   208
A Partnership as a Separate Legal Entity   208
The Legal Character of a Partner   208
The Legal Capacity of a Partner   209
The Meaning of Co-owners   210
Business Organizations Formed for Profit   210

Partnership Creation   211
The Need for a Written Partnership Agreement   211
A Partner's Right to an Action to "Account"   215
Partnership by Estoppel   215
A Typical Partnership Agreement   216

Partnership Property and a Partner's Interest   220
Partnership Capital   220
A Partner's Rights in Partnership Property   220
A Partner's Interest in the Partnership   223
A Partner's Right to Manage   223
Expelling a Partner   224
Additional Rights of a Partner   224
A Partner's Duties   225
Problems with Corporations as Partners   225

Other Forms of Partnerships   229
Joint Ventures   229
Limited Partnerships   229
Filing Requirement   230
Control by a Limited Partner   230

Limited Partnership with Corporate General Partner   *232*
Other Legal Characteristics of a Limited Partnership   *233*
Dissolution of a Limited Partnership   *233*

Review Problems   234

8   Partnership Operation and Dissolution   239

Partnership Operation: Contract Liability   239
    **Trading and Nontrading Partnerships: The Traditional
    Approach   240**
    The Agency Analysis: The Modern Approach   240

Partnership Operation: Tort Liability   243
    Master-Servant Analysis   243
    Principal-Nonservant Agent Analysis   243
    **Partnership Liability for the Negligent Operation of an
    Auto   247**
    **Partnership Liability for Willful or Intentional Torts and
    Crimes   251**

Incoming Partners   255

Ending the Partnership   257
    Dissolution of the Partnership   257
        A Typical Partnership Dissolution   *257*
        Valuing a Partner's Interest   *257*
        Dissolution in the Absence of an Agreement   *258*
        Dissolution and Partnership Creditors   *258*
        The Nature of a Partner's Interest on Dissolution   *258*
    Causes of Dissolution   261
    Winding Up the Partnership Business   261
    Distribution of the Assets of a Limited Partnership   262
    **Liquidation of Partnership Property—A Distinction Between
    Real and Personal Property   262**
    A Partner's Liability on Dissolution and Winding Up   263
    Joint and Several Liability on Dissolution   264
    Dissolution Notice to Third Parties   264

Review Problems   267

PART FOUR   Corporation Law   271

**9   Corporations: Introduction, Formation, and Corporate
    Personality   273**

Corporations as Major Institutions in Our Society   273
    The Focus of State-Based Corporation Law   275
    The Nature of Corporation Law   275

State-Based Corporation Law: A Historical Note 276
The Model Business Corporation Act 281

The Legal Nature of Corporations: Constitutional Law   281

Whether to Incorporate: Advantages and Disadvantages   286

The Process of Incorporation   287
Where to Incorporate   287
How to Incorporate   287
Promoters   287
Watered Stock   288
Promoters' Contracts   289

Articles of Incorporation   292
Beginning Corporate Life   295
Beginning Corporate Business   295

Defectively Formed Corporations   296

Disregarding the Corporate Entity   297
**Suits by Corporate Creditors Against Shareholders
    (Humans)**   297
**Suits by Corporate Creditors Against Shareholders
    (Corporations)**   298
**Suits Alleging the Abuse of the Corporate Form to
    Intentionally Evade Statutory, Judicial, or Contractual
    Obligations**   303
Subordination of Shareholder Debts   304
Summary: Piercing the Corporate Veil   304

Foreign Corporations   304

Formal, Legal Powers and Purposes of a Corporation   308
Ultra Vires   309
Corporate Purposes   310

Review Problems   316

10 Shareholders and the Corporate Capital Structure   321

The Shareholder   321
An Overview of Share Ownership   322
Shareholder Liability   323

Corporate Capital Structure: Financing the Corporation   323
Debt Financing   323
Equity Financing   324
Types of Shares   324
Common and Preferred Stock   326

Shareholder Meetings   331
   Cumulative Voting   332
   Proxies   334
   Voting Trusts   335
   Preemptive Rights   336

Close Corporations   337
   Shareholder Agreements   341
   Close Corporation Statutes   343

Shareholders' Remedial Rights   345
   Right to Inspect Corporate Books and Records   345
   Shareholders' Derivative Suits   348

Review Problems   352

11   Managing the Corporation: The Role of the Directors and Officers   355

Directors   355
   Board Authority and Meetings: Managing the Corporation   358
   Shareholder Removal of Directors   359
   Special Committees of the Board   360
     The Executive Committee   360
     The Audit Committee   360
   Director Dissent   362
   Director Qualification   362

Declaration of Dividends   363
   Sources of Dividends   363
     What Is "Earned Surplus"?   365
     Directors' Liability for Impermissible Dividends   366
   Types of Dividends   367
   Directors' Discretion in Dividend Matters   368

Officers   373
   Officers' and Agents' Authority   374
   A Corporation's Tort Liability   380

Executive Compensation   380

Review Problems   385

12   The Liability of Management for Corporate Crimes and Torts, for Mismanagement, and for Breach of Fiduciary Duty   389

The Liability of Management and Employees for Corporate Crimes   389
   A Typical Prosecution for a Corporate Crime   390

Corporate Criminal Prosecutions and the Fifth Amendment's Privilege Against Self-Incrimination   391
Defenses of Individual Defendants   392
Summary of a Corporation's and Management's Criminal Liability   396

The Liability of Directors and Management for Breach of Duty—The Business Judgment Defense   397
    The Exercise of Due Care and the Business Judgment Defense   397
    Statutory Duties   398
    Lack of Causation   408
    Breach of Duty in Special Circumstances   410

Indemnification of Directors and Officers   414
    Director and Officer (D&O) Insurance   416

Dealing with the Corporation: Potential Conflicts of Interest   417
    Interlocking Directorates   419
    Using Corporate Assets for Self-Benefit   422
    Corporate Opportunities   427
    Corporate Opportunities When They Have Been Rejected by a Vote of the Board   431

Sale of Control   433

Review Problems   439

13   Altering the Corporate Structure and Dissolution   445

Amending the Articles   446

Merger, Consolidation, and Sale of Assets   446
    The Rights of a Dissenting Shareholder   447
    Short Form Mergers   454
    The Appraisal Process   454
    The Fiduciary Duty of Directors and Others in Corporate Reorganizations, Mergers, and Other Changes in the Corporate Structure   459

A Note on Close Corporations and the Liability of Majority Shareholders for "Freezeouts" or the Oppression of Minority Interests   462

Dissolution   464
    Voluntary Dissolution   464
    Involuntary Dissolution   465
    Corporate Existence After Dissolution   469

Review Problems   470

PART FIVE   Business Organizations and the Securities Laws   475

14   Securities Regulation   477

Blue Sky Laws   477

Federal Securities Regulation   478
   The Securities Act of 1933   479
   The Securities Exchange Act of 1934   480

The Securities and Exchange Commission   480

Going Public   481

What Is a Security?   483

Public Sale of Securities   488
   Underwriting   489
   Shelf Registration   489

Involuntarily Going Public   490

Securities Exempt from Registration   490

Rule 144: Persons Deemed Not to Be Engaged in a Distribution
   and Therefore Not Underwriters   493

Rule 147: The Intrastate Offering Exemption   495

Regulation A and Regulation D Exemptions   495

What Constitutes The Same Issue?   496

Application of the Laws' Antifraud Provisions   496

Securities Investor Protection Corporation   498

Commodity Futures Trading Commission   499

Review Problems   500

15   Insider Trading   504

Short-Swing Profits: Section 16(b) of the '34 Act   504

Section 10(b) of the '34 Act and Rule 10b-5   510

Materiality   513

Tipper and Tippee Liability   522

Who Is an Insider for Purposes of Section 10(b)?   523

SEC Enforcement of the Insider Trading Prohibitions   526

Who May Recover for Section 10(b) and Rule 10b-5
   Violations?   527

The Burden of Proof in Securities Litigation   534

Other Fraudulent Activities   535

Review Problems   537

16   **Liability of Directors and Attorneys Under the Securities Law   541**

Liability of the Board of Directors   541

A Federal Securities Checklist for Directors   551

Corporate Reporting   552

Attorney's Liability   553

Statutory Liability for Securities Law Violations   556

Review Problems   557

17   **Accountants and the Securities Law   560**

Accountants' Liability Under Common Law   560

Accountants and the Federal Securities Law   561

Accounting Standards and Securities Liability   562

Accountants and Section 10(b) of the '34 Act   569

Accountants' Liability to the Securities Investors Protection Corporation   573

Liability of a Negligent Accountant to a Negligent Client   575

Watchdog Audit Committees of Outside Directors   578

The Foreign Corrupt Practices Act   578
    The Antibribery Provisions   579
    The Accounting Provisions   579
    Enforcement of the Law   580
    Controversy over the Law   581

Review Problems   581

18   **Regulation of the Proxy Process and Tender Offers   585**

Proxy Regulation   585
    Shareholder Proposals   587
    Improper Shareholder Proposals   587
    Proxy Expenses   588

False or Misleading Proxy Statements   589

Tender Offers   590

Acquisition of 5 Percent or More of a Company's
Securities   591

Regulation of Tender Offers   592
**Communications by Management During the Tender
Offer   592**
Withdrawal and Proration   593
Fraudulent, Deceptive or Manipulative Practices   593
Issuer's Tender Offer for Its Own Securities   593

Corporate Takeovers   593

Defensive Strategies to Avoid a Takeover   596

Anatomy of a Complex Corporate Takeover   598

State Anti-takeover Statutes   597

Securities and the Uniform Commercial Code   601
Transfer   601
Restrictions on Transfer   602
Warranties   602
Wrongful Transfers   602
Registration   603

Review Problems   603

**PART SIX   A Business Organization's Duties to Its Employees and the
Public   607**

19   The Employer-Employee Relationship   609

Historical Background of Labor Law   609

The National Labor Relations Act   610

Employee Rights and Union Elections   610

The Duty of Fair Representation   612

Right-to-Work Laws   613

Employer Unfair Labor Practices   614

The Taft-Hartley Act   616

Union Unfair Labor Practices   617

The Obligation to Bargain   617

Strikes   620

Secondary Activity   621

Consumer Boycotts   622

Occupational Safety and Health   623

The Employment Retirement Income Security Act of 1974   630

Review Problems   632

20 Discrimination in Employment   634

Religious and National Origin Discrimination   635

Sex Discrimination   635

Pregnancy and Sex Discrimination   637

Race and Color Discrimination   639

Bona Fide Occupational Qualifications   642

Quotas, Goals and Reverse Discrimination   643

Seniority Systems and Civil Rights   647

Assorted Provisions   649

The Equal Employment Opportunity Commission   649

The Equal Pay Act   650

Age Discrimination   652

Discrimination Against the Handicapped   657

Office of Federal Contract Compliance Programs   658

Review Problems   659

21 Business Organization Duties to the Public   661

Products Liability Law   662
  Contract Liability Through Warranty: State Law   662
  Exclusion or Modification of Warranties   664
  Federal Warranty Legislation   670
  **Tort Liability Through Negligent Design and Strict
    Liability   673**
  **Recent Judicial Developments in Product Liability Law: The
    Sindell Case   679**
  Summary of *Sindell* and Related Theories   684

Recent State and Federal Legislation on Product Safety   685
Proposed Legislation   686
Existing Consumer Product Safety Legislation:
Introduction   688
Summary of Consumer Law   703

Recent Federal Environmental Protection Laws   703
The National Environmental Policy Act   704
Council on Environmental Quality   707
Environmental Protection Agency   708
Clean Air Legislation   711
Clean Water Legislation   712
Solid Waste, Pesticides, Radiation, and Noise Legislation   713

Social Responsibilities of American Business Organizations   713
The Reserve Mining Litigation   715
Ford Motor Company and the Pinto Gas-Tank Litigation   722
An Analysis of the "Social Responsibility" Debate   724
On the Significance of Conventional Wisdom   724
Conventional Wisdom and the Rise of the Modern Corporation   726
Confronting the Modern Corporation   728

Review Problems   730

22 American Business Organizations in the Political and International Environment   735

Business Organizations and the Political Process   735
The First Amendment and the Corporation   735
Commercial Speech and Corporations   738
Corporate Lobbying   739
The Freedom of Information Act   740
Lobbying and the Judiciary   740
The Corporation and Political Contributions   741

The Corporation and the International Business Environment   743
International Business Risks   743
Foreign Risk or "Political Risk" Insurance   744

The Legal Complexities of International Business   744
A Comparative Legal View   747

Corporate Responsibility and the Employee's Duty of Loyalty and Obedience: A Preliminary Inquiry   749   APPENDIX A

Uniform Partnership Act   761   APPENDIX B

Selected Portions of the Uniform Limited Partnership Act   771   APPENDIX C

Selected Portions of the Uniform Limited Partnership Act (1976)   776   APPENDIX D

Selected Portions of the Model Business Corporation Act   784   APPENDIX E

Review Problems   817   APPENDIX F

Glossary of Legal Terms   836   APPENDIX G

Index   845

List of Cases

Aaron v. S.E.C.   573

Adamski v. Tacoma Gen. Hosp.   158

Adler v. Epstein   86

ADT v. Grinnell   369

Albermarle Paper Co. v. Moody   640

Allenberg Cotton v. Pittman   306

Aluma Kraft Mfg. Co. & Solmica, Inc. v. Fox &
   Co.   25

American Smelting and Refining Co. v. OSAHRC
   627

American Soc. of Mech. Eng. Inc. v. Hydrolevel
   Corp.   171

App'l of Delaware Racing Assoc.   455

Bancroft Whitney v. Glen   425

Barber Agency v. Co-operative Barrel Co.   190

Barnes v. Andrews   409

Berger v. CBS   301

Bird v. Penn Central   183

Blau v. Lehman   507

Blue Chip Stamps v. Manor Drug   531

Bowe v. Colgate-Palmolive   636

Bowen v. U.S. Postal Service   613

Bradley v. Brabham Agcy.   132

Brantman, In re   369

Bremen v. Zapata   745

Buckley v. Valeo   741

Burch v. Americus Grocery Co.   200

Cady, Roberts & Co., In re   512

Calif. Brewers v. Bryant   648

Calvert Cliffs' v. A.E.C.   705

Cenco v. Seidman & Seidman   575

Central Hudson Gas v. Public Service Comm.   738

Channon v. Channon   369

Chiarella v. U.S.   523

Chrysler v. Dept. of Transportation   699

Citizens Against Rent Control v. Berkeley   737

Clement v. Clement   226

Cleveland Bd. Ed. v. LaFleur   639

Coblentz v. Riskin   118

Consolidated Edison v. Public Service Comm.   736

Consolidated Sun Ray, Inc., v. Oppenstein   299

Co. of Wash. v. Gunther   652

Cooper v. Cooper   107

Corning Glass v. Brennan   652

Cote Bros. Inc., v. Granite Lake Realty   376

Cox v. Bowling   198

Crouse-Hinds v. Internorth   462

Davidsville First National Bank v. St. John's
   Church   116

Dempsey v. Chambers   173

Diaz v. Pan Am   642

Dirks v. SEC   524

Dodge v. Ford Motor Co.   311

Donahue v. Permacel Tape Corp.   96

Dothard v. Rawlinson   636

Dow Chemical v. E.P.A.   709

Edgar v. Mite   599

E.E.O.C. v. Brown & Root   636

E.E.O.C. v. Wyoming   656

Ellingson v. Walsh, O'Connor & Barneson   255

Ernst & Ernst v. Hochfelder   570

Escott v. Barchris Construction Corp.   542

Essex Universal Corp. v. Yates   438

Farris v. Glen Alden Corp.   450

First National Bank of Boston v. Bellotti   736
First National Maintenance v. NLRB   618
Foremost-McKesson, Inc. v. Provident Securities
   Co.   506
Franks v. Bowman Trans.   647
Fullilove v. Klutznick   645
Gall v. Exxon   403
Galler v. Galler   337
Gizzi v. Texaco   168
Globe Woolen Co. v. Utica Gas & Elec. Co.   419
Goldenberg v. Bartell Broadcasting   377
Gottfried v. Gottfried   370
Gratz v. Claughton   505
Greenman v. Yuba Power Prod. Inc.   676
Griggs v. Duke Power   639
Guth v. Loft   422
Heart of Atlanta Motel v. U.S.   42
Heckel v. Cranford Country Club   121
Henningsen v. Bloomfield Motors   666
Herman & MacLean v. Huddleston   534
Hobbs v. U.S.   423
Hodge v. Garrett   240
Hodgson v. Approved Personnel   655
Hodgson v. 1st Fed. S & L   655
Hodgson v. Greyhound   654
Hodgson v. Robert Hall   651
Holzman v. De Escamilla   231
Houghton v. McDonnell Douglas   654
Humphrey v. Virginian Ry. Co.   174
Irving Trust Co. v. Deutsch   431
Johnson v. Greene   427
Kaiser Aluminum v. Weber   644
Kelley v. Comm'r I.R.S.   328
Kelsey-Seybold Clinic v. Maclay   244
Kewanee Oil v. Bicron   91
Lamb v. Leroy   447
Larsen v. General Motors   674
Lind v. Schenley Industries Inc.   128
Litwin v. Allen   410
Lyons v. American Legion Post No. 650   52
Malloy v. Fong   187
Manufacturing Trust Co. v. Becker   432
Marshall v. Barlow's   624
Mass. Bd. Ret. v. Murgia   655
Massey v. Tube Art Display   152

Mayer v. Adams   350
McDonnell Douglas v. Green   649
McClennen v. Comm'r of I.R.S.   259
Miller v. AT&T   406
Minnesota v. Clove Leaf Creamery   36
Miss. Univ. for Women v. Hogan   645
Mitchell v. Vulture Min. & Mill Co.   196
Murray v. Modoc State Bank   145
Myzel v. Fields   496
Nashville Gas v. Satty   639
NLRB v. Business Machine   622
NLRB v. Fruit Packers   622
NLRB v. Hendricks   615
Nye v. Lovelace   83
Panter v. Marshall Field   594
Patton v. Nicholas   369
People v. Smithtown Gen. Hosp.   253
Percival v. General Motors   101
Perlman v. Feldman   434
Philipsborn v. Suson   289
Phillips v. Cook   248
Phillips v. Martin-Marietta   639
Pierce v. Commonwealth   333
Poretta v. Superior Dowel Company   136
Principe v. McDonald's   68
Radom & Neidorff, In re   467
Reliance Elec. Co. v. Emerson Elec. Co.   506
Rockwell v. Stone   192
Rogers v. Hill   381
Rosenfeld v. Fairchild Engine   589
Sandman v. Hagan & Striegel   163
Santa Fe Industries v. Green   541
Schein v. Chasen   528
School Dist. of Phila. v. Frankford Grocery Co.   64
S.E.C. v. Aminex Resources   580
S.E.C. v. Capital Gains Research Bureau   536
S.E.C. v. Howey   484
S.E.C. v. Int. Systems & Controls   580
S.E.C. v. Koscot Interplanetary Inc.   487
S.E.C. v. National Student Marketing   554
S.E.C. v. Ralston Purina Co.   491
S.E.C. v. Sloan   557
S.E.C. v. Texas Gulf Sulphur   515
Shapiro v. Merrill Lynch   522
Sheldon v. Little   213

Shultz v. *Wheaton Glass* 651

Sinclair Oil v. *Levien* 369

Sindell v. *Abbott Laboratories* 679

Smith Mfg. Co. v. *Barlow* 314

Smolowe v. *Delendo Corp.* 505

Solomon v. *Kirkwood* 265

Southland Mower v. *Consumer Product Safety Comm.* 691

Southwestern Portland Cement v. *Beavers* 125

State v. *Elsbury* 221

State ex. rel. Pillsbury v. *Honeywell Inc.* 346

Stockwell v. *Morris* 155

Teamsters v. *Daniel* 487

Teamsters v. *U.S.* 647

Thomas v. *McBride Exp. Co.* 162

Touche Ross v. *Redington* 574

Treadway v. *Care* 459

TSC Industries v. *Northway* 589

TWA v. *Hardison* 635

U of CA Regents v. *Bakke* 644

Ultramares v. *Touche* 560

U.S. v. *Naftalin* 535

U.S. v. *Natelli* 566

U.S. v. *Park* 393

U.S. v. *Reserve Mining Co.* 717, 721

U.S. v. *Simon* 562

U.S. Liability Ins. Co. v. *Haidinger-Hayes Inc.* 400

Von Au v. *Magenhemer* 369

Vrabel v. *Acri* 252

Washington v. *Davis* 642

Wellington Print Works v. *Magid* 423

Wheeling Steel v. *Glander* 282

Whirlpool v. *Marshall* 629

Winkleman v. *General Motors Corp.* 384

Zajac v. *Harris* 212

Introduction to the Study of Law and American Business Organizations

Part One

Introduction to the Study of Law

1

If laws were unchanging and if human behavior were simple, then the study of law would be a matter of memorization—of fixed rules and of the situations they govern. The student of law would merely master the constitutions and statute books of federal, state, and local legislation, the rulings of administrative agencies, and the opinions of the courts. But the body of society has the complex vitality of a living organism, and its legal system has the energy of process rather than the inert mass of fixed rules.

Definition of the Law

To perceive law as a process, as activity, we must observe its rules at work in a complex and changing social, economic, political, and moral environment. The focus of law study must include not only the written rules, but also the activity of law application. A working definition of law must include these minimum descriptions: (1) the rules, written and unwritten, generated by the sovereign or other rule source; (2) how these rules are applied; (3) how persons and institutions respond to rule applications; and (4) how the rule-making bodies change old rules and generate new ones.

Our discussion of law begins with the creation of rules and then expands to the judicial process of the application of rules by the court system. Through such a course of study, we can begin to learn to predict with some certainty when and how the rules will be enforced and how those affected will react. This development of the ability to predict when and how laws will be applied is the primary objective of law study; memorization of some rules is simply a convenient starting point.

Rule Creation

The basic source of rules in American law is the U.S. Constitution. This document proclaims that it is the supreme law of the land and that any other law or "legal" activity that conflicts with it is unconstitutional or illegal.

Legislative Rule Creation—Federal

The federal Constitution creates our three, coequal branches of government: the legislature whose prime responsibility is to pass the laws; the executive whose prime responsibility is to implement and enforce the laws; and the judiciary whose responsibility is to adjudicate; that is, to provide a framework for deciding if there has been a violation of law.

Since the U.S. Constitution delegates to the Congress the duty to pass laws, any law passed by Congress that is consistent with the powers delegated to Congress by the U.S. Constitution is the supreme law of the land and forms the second level in our scheme of legislative rule creation.

Congress, like state legislatures, may delegate some of its rule-making powers to other governmental units called administrative agencies. For example, the Sixteenth Amendment to the U.S. Constitution gives Congress the authority to levy a tax on incomes. After Congress passed income tax legislation (the most recent comprehensive law is the Internal Revenue Code of 1954), it delegated the authority to enforce the code to the Secretary of the Treasury. Congress further provided that the President, with the advice and consent of the Senate, should appoint a Commissioner of Internal Revenue who ". . . shall be in the Department of the Treasury,"[1] and that the Secretary or his or her delegate (usually the Commissioner) shall prescribe all necessary rules and regulations for the enforcement of the Internal Revenue Code.[2] So both the Secretary of the Treasury and the Commissioner of Internal Revenue have substantial rule-making authority. There are numerous federal administrative agencies; some may be "independent" such as the Federal Trade Commission, some more directly controlled by Congress such as the Internal Revenue Service, and some controlled by the President, such as the Department of Labor. All of these administrative agencies make rules, formally called "regulations," which are applied by the agency itself. See Figure 1-1.

Legislative Rule Creation—State

The Tenth Amendment to the U.S. Constitution provides that those powers not expressly given (or necessarily implied in) the grant of authority given to the federal government are reserved to the states. The rule-creating power within each state follows the same general pattern as that of the federal government. Each state has a constitution that creates the basic rights, duties, and privileges of the residents of the state as well as organizes the state system of government. The legislature, one of three branches of state government, is the primary rule-making body, and any rules made by it that are consistent with the state constitution's fundamental guidelines are the supreme law of the state. State rules that are consistent with state constitutional provisions are valid unless they conflict with a federal rule made by Congress and consistent with the U.S. Constitution.

Sixteenth Amendment to the U.S. Constitution

(authority to levy a
tax on incomes)

↓

U.S. Congress

(the 1954
Internal Revenue Code)

↓

Secretary of the Treasury

appointed by the President
(Department of Treasury)

↓

Commissioner of Internal Revenue

appointed by the President
prescribes rules and regulations

↓

Rules and regulations for application
of the Internal Revenue Code
applied by IRS agents

**FIGURE 1-1 Example of legislative delegation
of power to create rules.**

If state-made rules or the official acts of a state agency conflict with a
federal statute or the U.S. Constitution, those state rules or activities are
unconstitutional or illegal.

State legislatures may also create administrative agencies; state departments of welfare, taxation, and education that have rule-making authority are just a few examples. Moreover, a state may also delegate some
of its rule-making authority to local governments such as county and city
governments, which enact ordinances.

Individual Rule Creation

Another major source of our rules comes from individuals who voluntarily make rules to govern a transaction between themselves. These rules
form the body of our contract law. Contract law is rule creation in every
sense of the term because the rules are recognized by the courts as enforceable obligations. This means that on a violation of them, one party
may be compelled through our court system to pay damages to the injured party.

Other examples of individual or institutional rule creation, such as the rules adopted by a particular religion or fraternal group or the rules adopted and followed in sporting or competitive events, are generally not considered "legal" rules because the breach of them is not punishable by a *court-imposed* damage award, fine, or loss of freedom. This is not to say that the infraction of these rules might not be severely punished; indeed, they may be, and those arguing for a very broad definition of law would probably include these rules. We believe, however, that convenient and useful classification of individual rule creation is limited to those rules for which the judiciary provides a remedy.

Judicial Rule Creation

The role of the judiciary (court system) in rule creation may be divided into two broad categories. First, the judiciary in applying (and in this process interpreting) legislative rules inevitably creates rules of its own. These rules, whether in the form of an exception to the rule or otherwise, become part of the meaning of the legislative rules.

Second, and more applicable to this section, the judiciary may create substantive duties and rights where none existed in the statutory law. Generally, the rules of the law of negligence are made by the judiciary, as well as the rules regarding agency law, the subject of the first portion of this book. The entire body of the law of contracts was created by the judiciary, but recently the rules regarding contracts for the sale of goods were enacted by almost all of the state legislatures in the Uniform Commercial Code, Article 2, thus becoming part of the legislative rule scheme.

The Common Law. This second class of rules, which is separate from legislative enactments and which derives its authority from custom as adopted and recognized by the courts, is often referred to as the common law. The common law of this country is determined only after reading decision after decision in which judges have attempted to describe the substantive rules in areas in which the legislatures have not acted and in which rules are needed to govern activity. To bring some uniformity into our system of common law, legal scholars have collected and codified what they believe to be the best judicially created rules on a subject. These scholars publish and, from time to time, revise these rules in volumes entitled *Restatements of the Law*. In the chapters following we will discuss the *Restatement of the Law of Agency*, which, although stated in the form of a comprehensive code, remains nonlegislative.

Equity Law or Equitable Principles. Another important source of judicially created rules that is not usually thought of as part of the common law but as a distinct body of judicially generated rules is called equity law. Since equity law or equitable principles will be discussed throughout this book we must provide a brief overview of how this body of law developed.

The word "equity" is derived from the Latin word "aequitas," which means equality or justice. Like much of our law this body of rules comes from England. As the English sovereigns began to gather legislative power to themselves in the thirteenth and fourteenth centuries, the "law" became more and more the very word of the sovereign. The law became rigid and inflexible, and often a very literal application of the law had such severe repercussions that the effect of its application served to defeat the intent of the rule. To create flexibility in the application of law the English sovereign (beginning about 1350) allowed his immediate subordinate, the Chancellor, to hear grievances arising because of the harsh application of the law or where no remedy existed in the sovereign's law. The Chancellor would hear only those cases he believed to be worthy and would decide each case according to his conscience and sense of justice. In short, he was to provide equity when the literal application of the law failed in some respect.

Thus, equity law became a supplementary set of rules or principles that operated only when the established legal system of the sovereign would not provide that which in good conscience should be done. The Tudor and Stuart sovereigns and the Puritan Revolution somewhat confined the powers of the Chancellor, but by the colonial period, there were still two discernible legal systems: that based on the word of the sovereign (by then the Parliament), enforced in "courts of law," and that based on principles of what was fair given the circumstances, enforced in "courts of equity."

During and after colonization the American legal system continued to provide separate "law" and "equity" courts, but by the middle of the nineteenth century the two separate courts were made one and a single judge administered both bodies of rules. Today the federal system and all of the states have but one system of courts, but the judges presiding may from time to time invoke certain "equitable" principles in those situations where the remedies provided by the law (or, today, the legislative and individual rules) are either inadequate to do "justice" or work an "injustice" by their direct application. These equitable rules are still applied at the discretion of the judge and remain supplementary in nature. Two examples of present day "equitable" principles are the remedies of the issuance of an injunction (a court order prohibiting activity) or the decree of specific performance (a court order directing that certain activity take place). Both of these remedies are given to a party in a lawsuit where the traditional remedy at law of awarding money damages would be insufficient to compensate the injured party.

Rule Application

Learning the circumstances in which rules are applied is at the heart of the instructional process in law. However, before we examine the process of rule application we must distinguish between the types of rules that are applied.

	Criminal Rules	*Civil Rules*
1. Who prosecutes	Only federal or state governmental agents	Private persons and federal and state governmental agents
2. Standard of proof	The elements of the crime exist beyond a reasonable doubt	It is more likely than not that the elements of the civil wrong exist
3. Potential punishment or remedy	Imposition of a fine or imprisonment	Award of money damages or an equitable remedy

FIGURE 1-2

Types of Rules

The types of rules generated by the three primary sources discussed above, the legislature, private persons, and the judiciary, are divided into two broad categories: criminal and civil. Neither the judiciary nor private persons can create criminal rules. These are created only by the federal and state legislatures. The criminal law is distinguished from the civil law primarily by: (1) who initiates the prosecution process after a violation; (2) the standard of proof; and (3) the potential punishment or remedy.

Criminal and Civil Rules Distinguished

A crime is an illegal act, the prosecution of which is initiated by a federal, state, or county prosecutor; the person being tried for the crime (the defendant) is tried on behalf of and in the name of the federal or state government. The civil law is usually "enforced" by private persons or by a governmental unit suing for the breach of a civil rule. The "wrong" involved in a criminal prosecution is one which usually manifests an "evil" intent. It is the purpose of the criminal law to punish this evil intent. If the defendant does not plead guilty, punishment may be imposed only after a trial by a jury (unless trial by jury is waived by the defendant, in which case the judge acts as a jury). In some less significant crimes (traffic violations, for example) there is no trial by jury.

In a criminal case, the government has the burden of proving guilt beyond a reasonable doubt. This differs substantially from the standard of proof in a civil case. In the latter instance, the plaintiff must prove that it is more probable than not that the defendant committed the act complained of. Obviously, this standard of proof is less than that required in criminal cases.

Finally, in the prosecution of a criminal case the action sought (by the court and jury) is the imposition of a fine or imprisonment. In a civil case, the law seeks to compensate the injured party, not punish the defendant. Thus, the plaintiff seeks money damages for compensation or an equitable decree.

The criminal law is usually subdivided into two more categories: felonies and misdemeanors. A felony is a crime of a serious nature and is defined by the federal and state legislatures as an offense, the punishment for which may be a penitentiary sentence of over one year, or in some states, over six months. A misdemeanor, a less serious crime, is usually punishable by fine or imprisonment for less than one year or six months in some states. Since the state legislatures have the duty of creating rules for the health and welfare of the residents of the state, most of the commonly known criminal rules are created by state legislatures.

Most of the rules in this book about business organizations are civil in nature and not criminal. Therefore, you will find that a person such as an individual, a partnership, or a corporation and not a governmental unit initiates the prosecution, suing for damages. If it is found by the jury (or the judge sitting as a jury) that it is more probable than not that the one being sued did the act complained of, and that the act of the defendant breached a duty owed to the plaintiff, and that the damages requested will compensate for the injury done, then the court will award a judgment to the one bringing the suit.

Judicial Systems

Since the U.S. Constitution and all the state constitutions create judicial systems for the redress of the breach of a rule, there are 51 different systems: 1 federal system and 50 state systems. The federal system is nationwide and is composed of three levels of courts. The courts on the initial level, the trial courts, are called the federal district courts. Each state is divided into districts, and there may be as many federal district courts in each district as Congress deems adequate.

If a litigant in the federal system believes an error was committed at the trial stage, an appeal may be taken to the second level of the system, the federal circuit court of appeals. Currently there are 11 appellate circuits in the federal system, plus a separate appellate circuit for the District of Columbia. An appeal from the circuit court level goes to the third level, the U.S. Supreme Court, composed of nine justices sitting in Washington, D.C. Usually, appeals will be heard by the Supreme Court if four justices vote to hear the case. That is, almost all appeals to the Supreme Court are heard at the discretion of the court and very few appeals are heard as a matter of right.

Generally, the various state systems are also of a three-level nature. There is an initial trial court, an appellate court level, and a final appellate court, usually called the supreme court of the state. This basic scheme may be varied by adding township, city, or small claims courts in which the amount in dispute may not exceed a given amount (usually $500) or by adding courts of special jurisdiction such as those limited to probate, juvenile, or domestic relations. Nevertheless, the general scheme is similar to the federal scheme: one trial court level followed by two appellate levels.

The Federal Court System.   The state and federal judicial systems are administered separately. The application of the criminal law provides the best example of the division of duties between the two systems. Prosecutions for the breach of the criminal rules generated by Congress must take place in the federal system. This is necessary to secure a uniform application of the federal criminal laws. The action must begin at the federal district court level and is prosecuted by a federal official, the U.S. Attorney for the district, or the U.S. Attorney's staff. These U.S. Attorneys are agents of the U.S. Department of Justice under the U.S. Attorney General.

The State Court System.   Most crimes such as murder, assault and battery, and larceny, are defined by state legislatures. The prosecution of these crimes must begin at the trial court level in the state. These prosecutions are initiated by a state or, usually, a county prosecutor who may be elected or, in some cases, appointed.

The judicial system selected by a *civil* litigant is determined by which legislative source, federal or state, created the rule that is the subject of the complaint. For example, if a violation of the Clayton Act is alleged (adopted by Congress in 1914) and damages are sought, the suit must begin in the federal judiciary. If the failure to meet some rule standard created by the state legislature is the subject of the case, it usually begins in the state judicial system. The reason for this is, again, the necessity to preserve the uniformity of the rule application.

The Overlap Between the Two Court Systems.   The two judicial systems overlap in at least two important respects. First, to alleviate the local prejudice that might be present when a resident of one state is suing a resident of another in the state court system (usually in the state of the defendant's residence), Congress has created federal power (jurisdiction) to hear the case if the amount in controversy exceeds $10,000. In most of the cases based on this type of federal jurisdiction, called "diversity jurisdiction" because the parties in the case must be residents of different states, the rule source sued on is usually created by state-level sources. It is assumed that local prejudice will be minimized in the federal district courts because the judges are appointed by the President, not a local political body, and serve until they voluntarily retire or are impeached. They need not stand for election as do some state or county judges. Moreover, the federal district is usually geographically larger than that of the state trial court; hence the jury members in the federal court are picked from a wider area, again minimizing the chance for local prejudice to influence the matter.

In summary, a private civil litigant may use the federal system if the subject matter of the case primarily involves the breach of a federally created rule or, in the case of a rule created by state-level sources, if:

1. The parties to the case are from different states *and*

2. The amount in controversy exceeds $10,000.

A second major area of overlap between the federal and state judicial systems involves appeals from the state system to the federal. In a state-level trial, if either party raises issues of the state substantive or procedural law conflicting with the U.S. Constitution, then, after appeals raising these same issues are taken through the highest state court that can hear the case, the party may appeal from that court to the U.S. Supreme Court.

The U.S. Supreme Court has the final word on all interpretations of the U.S. Constitution whether or not the case originated on the state or federal level. This does not mean, however, that the U.S. Supreme Court must hear a case appealed to it from the federal or state system; in matters of this sort, the Supreme Court has discretion whether to hear the case.

The Civil Trial Process

Rule application takes place at many levels. Administrative agencies and individuals apply rules made by them everyday, but ultimately the judiciary has the formal task of adjudicating or declaring whether the activity complained of violates the rules. Knowledge of this formal process of rule application or adjudication is absolutely necessary to understanding most rules because it illustrates how those in charge of enforcing the rules do, in fact, enforce them. Remember that the real value in studying the law is to be able to predict when and how rules will be applied. The process of rule application, then, as manifested by the judicial process of adjudication is at the heart of the study of the law.

Below is presented the broad outlines of the trial of a civil case. The processes used may vary slightly from state to state, but, in general, the definition of the terms below are widely accepted.

The Complaint. A civil suit is initiated by the plaintiff who files several documents in a trial court of general jurisdiction (usually a county court located in the county government building). The document of greatest importance is called the complaint, which is filed by the plaintiff. The complaint must contain the following information.

1. The names of the parties to the case, the plaintiff(s), and defendant(s).

2. A statement sufficient to show that the court has jurisdiction to hear the matter.

3. A short and plain statement of the facts that indicates:
   (a) The existence of a legal duty.
   (b) The breach of this duty.
   (c) A claim for relief in the form of a request for a given amount of money damages and/or a claim for equitable relief such as a request for an injunction or an order for specific performance.

Following is a copy of the complaint filed by the plaintiffs, Aluma Kraft Manufacturing Company Inc. and Solmica, Inc., for the first appellate case you will read later in this chapter. It is here reproduced almost entirely so that you can see that it is the complaint that sets the outline of the case. Search the complaint (called "Petition" in Missouri) for the assertion of the existence of a legal duty and allegations that indicate a breach of this duty. The assertion of the legal duty and its breach are often referred to as the *cause of action*.

STATE OF MISSOURI
COUNTY OF ST. LOUIS

IN THE CIRCUIT COURT OF THE COUNTY OF ST. LOUIS
STATE OF MISSOURI

ALUMA KRAFT MANUFACTURING COMPANY a corporation, and SOLMICA, INC, a corporation,	Filed May 20, 1971
Plaintiffs, vs.	
ELMER FOX & COMPANY, Certified Public Accountants, a partnership . . . Clayton, Missouri, comprising, H. LEE SCHNURE, JR., RICHARD F. ASH, M. GUY HARDIN and VICTOR JACQUEMIN, III.	Cause No. <u>321920</u> Division _____
Defendants	

Petition

Plaintiffs, for their claim for relief, state as follows:

1. That at the times herein mentioned, plaintiff, ALUMA KRAFT MANUFACTURING COMPANY, ("ALUMA KRAFT") was and is a corporation duly

organized and existing according to law with its principal office in the City of Manchester, St. Louis County, Missouri, and the plaintiff, SOLMICA, INC., ("SOLMICA") was and is a corporation duly organized and existing according to law with its principal office in the City of St. Louis, Missouri . . . .

2.   That defendant, ELMER FOX & COMPANY, is a partnership of certified public accountants engaged in the general practice of accountancy . . . .

3.   That the defendant auditors, at the times herein mentioned and for many years prior thereto, had been regularly and routinely engaged by the plaintiff, ALUMA KRAFT, to perform general accounting and auditing services for it, and that in connection therewith, prepared plaintiff ALUMA KRAFT's financial statements, balance sheets and tax returns.

4.   That on and prior to the 1st day of August, 1969, one T.J. BOTTOM ("BOTTOM") was the President, chief executive officer, principal director and the owner of substantially all of the issued and outstanding shares of ALUMA KRAFT: that on or about the 29th day of April 1969, negotiations were entered into between BOTTOM and SOLMICA whereby SOLMICA would acquire from BOTTOM eighty percent (80%) of the issued and outstanding capital stock of ALUMA KRAFT, the remaining twenty percent (20%) to be retained by BOTTOM, and BOTTOM would then continue to manage the affairs of ALUMA KRAFT as chief executive officer; that the negotiations culminated in a contract on August 1, 1969, ...

5.   That pursuant to the said contract of August 1, 1969, SOLMICA acquired eighty percent (80%) of the issued and outstanding shares of stock of ALUMA KRAFT . . . , for which plaintiff SOLMICA paid the sum of Two Hundred and Twenty-Nine Thousand Ninety and 40/100 Dollars ($229,090.40). . . . .

6.   That in contemplation of the Agreement for Purchase and in accordance with the provisions thereof, the plaintiff, ALUMA KRAFT, engaged its regular auditors, ELMER FOX & COMPANY, the defendant auditors herein, to perform the services required in preparing the financial statements.

7.   Thereafter, on August 5, 1969, the defendant auditors furnished to the plaintiff, ALUMA KRAFT, its formal report setting forth the scope and opinion of the audit as follows:

The Board of Directors
Aluma Kraft Manufacturing Company
Manchester, Missouri

We have examined the balance sheet of Aluma Kraft Manufacturing Company as of June 30, 1969. Our examination was made in accordance with generally accepted auditing standards and accordingly included such tests of the accounting records and such other auditing procedures as we considered necessary in the circumstances.

In our opinion, the accompanying balance sheet presents fairly the financial position of Aluma Kraft Manufacturing Company at June 30, 1969 in conformity with generally accepted accounting principles.

/s/ Elmer Fox & Company

8.   In reliance upon the said report, the plaintiff SOLMICA closed on the transaction at the sale price computed in accordance with the balance sheet as determined by the defendant auditors in its formal statement.

9.   The plaintiffs state that the defendant auditors, in truth and in fact, failed to conduct their examination in accordance with "generally accepted auditing standards" and failed to furnish an opinion in conformity to "generally accepted accounting principles" and that both the scope and opinion of the said audit were false, erroneous, inaccurate and misleading and were made in disregard of the professional standards required of certified public accountants. Plaintiffs further state that the audit report was so sloppy that the defendant auditors failed to include as a liability on their audit the amounts due and unpaid to themselves by the plaintiff, ALUMA KRAFT, as of the date of the audit.

10.   The failures of the defendant auditors, ELMER FOX & COMPANY, as hereinabove alleged, to conform to generally accepted auditing standards and to furnish an opinion in accordance with generally accepted accounting principles in the said audit were, amongst others, the following:*

Item 4.

Prepaid advertising was carried at $4,000.00. There was no substantiation of this item and no inventory record, and it covered obsolete literature. There was no proper evaluation of the item and it was an unverified estimate. The entire sum amounted to an overstatement of valuation in the amount of $4,000.00

Item 6.

Reynolds Metals was one of the principal suppliers and creditors of Aluma Kraft. No attempt was made to properly verify the amounts due either as payables or by shrinkage of consignment inventory:

(a) Invoices submitted by this supplier prior to June 30, 1969, were not recorded on the books as a liability in the amount of $3,934.79

(b) Reynolds Metals inventory shortage as of June 30, 1969 . . . . $26,496.69

Reynolds Metals—Total $30,431.48

*Author's note: Many of the "Items" set out under paragraph 10 were deleted. Only a selection of those stated were reproduced to show the reader the type of items included.

Item 7.
Accrued vacation pay not disclosed on the books. No attempt was made to determine this liability and the obligations of Aluma Kraft to its Union staff. The liability was understated in the amount of $2,070.10

Item 10.
Skillform equipment was carried on the books at a cost of $59,292.58, less depreciation of $32,116.25. This was useless and obsolete junk and not used by Aluma Kraft for many years. Fifty-nine machines were originally built; thirteen of the machines are still at the Aluma Kraft factory; five machines are believed to be in the field; and forty-one machines are unaccounted for. No attempt was made to verify the physical assets or economic value of these assets, and the assets were overstated in the amount of $27,176.33

Item 13.
In addition to the Skillform equipment, a parts inventory for the Skillform equipment in the amount of $12,594.49 was likewise carried as an asset, which was obsolete and useless junk. The overstatement of the assets $12,594.49

The total of these specific items aggregates the sum of $106,584.91
. . .

11. The plaintiffs state that the defendant auditors knew that the said audit was being prepared for the purpose of determining the amounts which plaintiff SOLMICA would pay for the ALUMA KRAFT shares, and that the plaintiff SOLMICA would rely upon the said audit. Plaintiff SOLMICA states that it was entitled to rely and did in fact rely on the said audit, all to its damage in the sum of $150,000.00.

12. The plaintiff, ALUMA KRAFT, states that the audit furnished by the defendant auditors was useless, valueless and misleading; that plaintiff, ALUMA KRAFT, paid the defendant auditors the sum of $4,100.00 and is entitled to a refund of said fees.

13. Plaintiffs state that the conduct of the audit by the defendant auditors was handled in a willfully careless and wantonly negligent manner in disregard of the professional standards required to be exercised by the defendant auditors, and that by reason thereof, the plaintiffs are entitled to exemplary damages in addition to their actual damages.

WHEREFORE . . . the plaintiff, SOLMICA, INC., prays for judgment against the defendants for actual damages in the sum of $150,000.00 and exemplary damages in the sum of $150,000.00; and the plaintiff, ALUMA KRAFT MANUFACTURING COMPANY, prays for judgment against the defendants in the amount of $4,100.00, together with the costs of the plaintiffs herein expended.

ACKERMAN, SCHILLER & SCHWARTZ
By: Gideon H. Schiller
Attorneys for Plaintiffs
7701 Forsyth Boulevard
Clayton, Missouri 63105
863-4654

Serving the Complaint.   The complaint is filed together with a summons which directs the server of the papers (usually a county sheriff if the case is filed in state court or a federal marshal if the case is filed in the federal court) to the last known address of the defendant. A copy of the complaint is included for the purpose of this "service." When the server of the papers locates the defendants or, in some states, when the server locates the permanent residence of the defending parties, the papers are left with someone of suitable age and discretion residing therein. The server then files a sworn statement with the court, often called a "return," in which the server swears that the defendants were served.

Answer.   The defendants may file a document with the court responding to the complaint, called an "answer" within a given time period, usually 20 to 30 days. A copy of the answer is given to the plaintiff. The answer may admit all or part of the facts as alleged in the complaint and may admit or deny any or all of the legal consequences. In addition, the answer may include a claim for relief against the plaintiff, called a counterclaim, if the grounds exist.

If it appears that a party not originally a plaintiff or defendant may be liable to either of these parties as a result of the pleadings (the collective designation given to the complaint, answer, counterclaims, and motions) or that this party has a claim against either the plaintiffs or defendants arising from the subject of the lawsuit, then this party may be "joined" as a party to the suit and must be served with all of the pleadings and must respond.

The general rule defining those persons who may be plaintiffs or defendants is that they must have a direct interest in the subject matter of the suit; that is, they must be directly affected by the outcome. This rule has been expanded somewhat recently by permitting "class action" suits.

Class Actions.   Class action suits were first widely used on the federal level, but gradually states have been adopting procedures that provide for this type of litigation. The class action procedural rules provide that one or more members of a class may sue or be sued *as representatives of a class of persons if:* (1) the class is so numerous that joinder of all members of the class is not practicable; (2) there are questions of law or fact that are common to all members of the class; (3) the claims or defenses of the parties representing the class are typical of the claims or defenses of the class; and (4) the representatives of the class will fairly protect the interests of the class. Judicial interpretation has now added a fifth prerequisite, which is that all the members of the class must be identifiable (within reason). In addition to these prerequisites the court must find that the class action is superior to other available methods for the fair and efficient adjudication of the controversy. While the matter of class action remains the subject of controversy, you should be aware that this procedure exists and, in some cases, represents the most effective remedy available.

If a party is properly served with the complaint and fails to file an answer within the time period provided by law, then the plaintiff may ask the court to enter a "default" judgment. If such is entered, the court is making a judgment that the plaintiff is entitled to the relief claimed in the complaint.

Trial Motions.   As stated earlier, a defendant may "answer" or the defendant may challenge the plaintiff's case by "motion" before the issue is formally tried. There are several motions the parties may use to challenge the legal arguments of the other party asserted through the pleadings filed with the court. The first such opportunity is presented to the defendant, who may make a motion to the court—in this case the motion is made by filing a document labeled "Motion" with the court—to dismiss the complaint for failure to state a claim on which relief may be granted. This motion achieves the same result that was accomplished by the filing of a "demurrer." Today, however, the word demurrer is no longer used by the federal courts or many state courts to designate formal pleadings.

The filing of the "Motion to Dismiss for Failure to State a Claim" by the defendant requires the judge to rule on whether the plaintiff has stated the existence and breach of a legal duty. The judge must consider the complaint and the facts stated therein and resolve every inference created by the facts in favor of the plaintiff. When this is done, and the judge determines that the complaint presents no legal claim, the court will grant the motion to dismiss.

Discovery.   If the defendants file an answer, the litigation moves into a phase of the process generally called the discovery stage. Generally, the objectives of this pretrial procedure are to: (1) simplify the issues; (2) obtain admissions of fact to avoid unnecessary arguments and avoid surprise; (3) limit the number of expert witnesses; and (4) otherwise expedite the trial. In order to accomplish these objectives, several procedures are allowed that should be familiar to a student of the law of business organizations.

The following legal devices permit an adverse party to "discover" almost all business records, communications, documents, and other relevant material. The best-known discovery device is the deposition. A deposition is a sworn statement of any person, including a party to the action (the plaintiffs or defendants) or any witness, that is made in response to questions from the attorneys for the opposing side. The deposition is used to discover physical evidence, what a witness will say at trial, or any other matter relevant to the subject of the case. A deposition is usually taken in front of attorneys for both parties and is transcribed by a court reporter. The final copy is signed as a true statement by the one being deposed and is filed with the court. This signed statement may be used at the trial to challenge the testimony of a witness if his or her testimony varies from that in the deposition.

If the party or witness cannot be interviewed in person, a series of written questions may be sent and must be answered under oath. These written questions are called interrogatories.

To supplement depositions and interrogatories, a party may ask the court to order another party, if good cause is shown, to produce documents and other items of evidence for inspection, copying, or photographing. The subject of this order may be books, papers, accounts, letters, photographs, objects or tangible things, or other items that constitute evidence relating to the subject of the suit. The court may also order any party to permit entry on designated land or other property in the control of the party for the purpose of measuring, inspecting, surveying, or photographing the property. If the mental or physical condition of the party is in controversy, the court may order the party to submit to a physical or mental examination by a physician if good cause is shown. This latter method of "discovery" is used in many cases where personal injury is the subject of the case.

Courts in the various states adopted many of these discovery procedures in the 1960s, so they are viewed as relatively new. Their adoption has resulted in many more cases being settled out of court because the procedures allow a party to discover almost all of the relevant evidence of the opposing party. The only evidence not obtainable by an opposing party are those materials designated "privileged." Generally, such materials are an attorney's work product (thoughts and research on a case). Because of these procedures the attorneys for the parties can more accurately assess their chances for success if the matter should proceed to trial.

Judgment on the Pleadings or Summary Judgment.   If the parties decide to settle the case out of court, the attorneys ask the permission of the judge to dismiss the case. If this dismissal is done "with prejudice" it means that a party will be barred from filing the suit again. If the pretrial procedures do not result in settlement, the parties usually ask the judge to rule on another series of motions challenging the legal assertions of the adverse parties. After the pleadings are all filed either party may make a motion to dismiss the claims of an adverse party and enter judgment for the moving party by moving for a "judgment on the pleadings" or "summary judgment." Some procedural systems make a distinction between these two motions, but in essence they are the same. Like the initial motion to dismiss or the demurrer, described above, these motions require the judge to consider the arguments made in all of the pleadings, resolve every reasonable inference against the moving party, and make a finding as to whether the arguments made and facts asserted warrant submission of the case to the jury. Generally, if the judge finds that the legal arguments and facts presented could lead to but one reasonable conclusion, and that is in favor of the moving party, the motion must be granted. If there are issues of fact present that would lead reasonable minds to differ, the motion should be overruled.

If a court grants or sustains a motion to dismiss, or a motion for judgment on the pleadings or for summary judgment, the aggrieved party may appeal this decision. The first appellate decision in the book, for example, the *Aluma Kraft* case, concerns whether a trial court properly entered a judgment dismissing the complaint of the plaintiff. If the judge does not grant the motion, the trial process proceeds.

The Civil Jury Trial. A matter may be tried before a jury or a judge alone. If a party in a civil suit desires a jury trial it must be demanded, usually during the initial pleading phase. In federal courts, the U.S. Constitution guarantees a trial by jury in all civil actions at common law where the value of the controversy exceeds $20. The Constitution does not guarantee the right of a trial by jury in civil cases in state courts. However, the constitutions of the states usually provide that there is a right to trial by jury in cases where the common law gave such a right at the time the state constitution was adopted. Practically speaking, this means that almost all matters involving judgments of fact and requests for money damages may be tried before a jury. Usually negligence cases and other personal injury cases are thus tried. On the other hand, case involving the equity powers of the court, cases involving very complex issues such as antitrust suits or breaches of industrial contracts, and other cases where evaluation of the evidence requires rigorous analysis and expertise are usually tried before the judge alone. In very exceptional cases, the judge may appoint a master or referee to hear some of the evidence and make findings of fact.

The process of questioning prospective jurors to determine which of them will be permitted to sit by the court and adverse parties is called voire dire. This phrase is French in origin and means "to speak the truth." The voire dire procedure allows the court and parties to reject a prospective juror if, after questioning, it is revealed that the juror might be prejudiced or unable to render an impartial judgment. Usually, each party is given three challenges to use for any reason they so determine, and additional challenges can be made for sufficient cause.

Presenting the Evidence.   At the trial, the plaintiff, through the attorney representing the plaintiff's interests, presents its side of the evidence. After each witness is sworn and directly examined by the plaintiff's attorney, the defendant's attorney may cross-examine the witness on matters brought out on direct examination. We wish to emphasize that the process by which the facts are "found" is the process of direct examination of a witness by one side followed by a cross-examination by the attorneys for the other side. The jury or the judge, by watching the witnesses respond to the questions asked, must determine if they are telling the truth or accurately recalling an event. Not only the witness's answers, but the witness's demeanor (facial expressions and hand movements) all go into the factfinders' final determination of whether the witness is credible.

Following the plaintiff's version of the facts in the case, the defendant presents the evidence relevant to its side.

Motion for a Directed Verdict.   During the trial itself, a party may challenge the entire case of an adverse party by moving for a directed verdict. Either party may move this, and it requires the judge to rule on whether there are still issues of fact present that warrant the continuation of the trial. If reasonable minds could differ about the interpretation or existence of certain crucial facts, or of the inferences to be drawn from the facts, the court will overrule the motion and the trial will proceed.

Judges' Instructions to the Jury.   At the close of the defendant's case, both sides make summary arguments emphasizing the aspects of the testimony and other evidence they believe most pertinent to their arguments. Before the jury retires to make its finding of fact, the judge instructs the jury as to the appropriate rules of law to apply. Below is an example of the type of "instruction" the judge may give to the jury in a negligence case.

> Negligence is lack of ordinary care. It is a failure to exercise that degree of care which a reasonably prudent person would have exercised under the same circumstances. It may arise from doing an act which a reasonably prudent person would not have done under the same circumstances, or, on the other hand, from failing to do an act which a reasonably prudent person would have done under the circumstances.[3]

In applying this statement of the law, each juror must decide by using his or her own life experience as a guide whether the defendant acted as a "reasonably prudent person" would have, given the circumstances.

The judge gives the jury instructions on each matter of law argued in the case. After the instructions, the jury retires to the jury room where they apply all the rules stated by the judge to the facts as presented to them at the trial by the parties, witnesses and attorneys. The jury reaches a verdict both as to liability—was the defendant legally at fault for a breach of a rule?—and damages—if the defendant was liable, what is the appropriate amount of damages that will compensate the plaintiff for the breach of the rule?

Motion for a Judgment N. O. V.   A motion for "judgment notwithstanding the verdict"—formally called a judgment non obstante veredicto or judgment N. O. V.—may be made by a party against whom the verdict has been announced. This motion requires the judge to rule on whether the jury could reasonably have reached the verdict they did given the evidence and the court's instructions. This motion is granted only when the judge believes that the jury reached a verdict by ignoring the judge's instructions, or where, after hearing and seeing all of the evidence, the jury could not logically have reached the verdict they did. This motion, like the one for summary judgment or the one for a directed verdict, essentially challenges the legal sufficiency of a party's case. It must not be confused with a motion for a new trial, which may be made after a verdict is reached but is granted only where substantial errors in the trial process occurred.

The Appellate Process

If either of the parties believe that there was an error during the trial and this error caused an unfavorable verdict, he or she may appeal. The error must be one in the process of introducing evidence, or in the statement of the law or in the application of the rule to the facts. Parties usually cannot appeal the finding of a fact. For example, if the jury finds that as a matter of fact the defendant did sign the agreement in question on a given date, then this may not be appealed. However, a party may appeal the issue of whether signing the agreement did legally bind the party. This latter conclusion is one which is a mixture of fact finding and law application and is appropriate for appeal. The reason for this is that a party should get only one chance to introduce the evidence the party deems appropriate. Therefore, the trial courts are set up to take evidence; all the procedures at this level are adopted to insure the fairness of the evidence producing process. The right to cross examination, the right to demand and examine other evidence, and the right to object to the introduction of irrelevant or excessively prejudicial evidence all exist at the trial level.

Appellate courts are not equipped to hear testimony or inspect evidence. Appellate courts are composed of three or more judges who hear the arguments of the appealing parties as to why the statements of the rules in the trial court were erroneous or why the process of rule application was erroneous.

An appeal may be initiated by either party. The one appealing is called the appellant or, in some courts, the petitioner. The one answering the appeal is the appellee or the respondent. At the trial stage, the case is given a name or "style" (in legal language), and almost always this is done by putting the name of the plaintiff first followed by the name of the defendant. However, on appeal some courts, but not all, put the name of the appellant first when reporting the case. So, if the defendant appeals, this name goes first in the official report. You should note that the appellate case's style does not reveal who is the plaintiff or defendant in the original trial of the matter. This may only be determined by reading the appellate opinion.

The appellant must file with the appellate court at least two documents. One is the transcribed version of the trial court testimony. During the trial a court reporter took down all of the testimony, all objections and motions, and other relevant happenings in a special form of shorthand. This shorthand version of the trial is not transcribed into prose unless it is requested and paid for by one of the parties. Together with this transcript, the appellant files a legal brief which contains the legal arguments of the party. The appellate court considers the trial transcript, the written legal arguments (briefs) of both parties, and in many cases allows attorneys for the parties to appear before it to orally answer questions asked by the appellate court and, in general, to argue the merits of the issues advanced. For the reasons stated above the appellate court does not consider additional evidence, cannot call new or recall the old witnesses, and, generally, cannot view the evidence again. The facts as found by the trial court must be taken as given.

The appellate court then takes the matter into consideration, does considerable legal research on the matter, votes, and writes its opinion. If some of the judges do not agree with the majority of the court, they may write dissenting opinions stating their reasons. This appellate opinion usually is published and is available to all. The numbers after the name of the cases reprinted in this text indicate the volume of case reports that contains the opinion.

If either party is still of the belief that a substantial error was made in the statement of the rule or in the application of the rule to the facts by either the trial or intermediate appellate court, the party may appeal the case to the next higher level, the supreme court of the state or federal system, which is usually the highest level. Again, the party appealing this is called the appellant or petitioner and the answering party is the appellee or respondent. The name of the appellant is usually placed first again. The same general practice is followed in filing the appeals papers and hearing the arguments except that additional arguments are made either supporting or attacking the decision of the first appellate court.

Appellate Court Action.   An appellate court (either intermediate or supreme court) may do one of three things with the case before it. It may affirm the holding of the trial court (or intermediate appellate court) and state its reasons for affirming the holding. If it affirms the decision, the same party who won the case in the trial court wins again.

The appellate court may reverse the decision being appealed and enter its own judgment, giving the reasons. The third option is to order all or part of the case tried again using the interpretation of the law as stated by the appellate court. In this case, if the parties so desire, the case will be tried again.

This concludes the presentation of material on the trial and appeal of a civil case. The terms defined above and the processes outlined are crucial to our understanding of how to study law because the published opinions of appellate judges are the best source available to indicate how the law is applied. For this reason much of the information about the law in this text will come from reading the appellate opinions reproduced herein. We have made an attempt to edit the irrelevant portions out of these opinions, and to leave in enough information so that you may discern the complete outlines of how the dispute developed and how the legal rules were applied to solve the dispute.

Analysis, Recall, Evaluation, and Synthesis as Education Objectives

As we stated at the beginning of this chapter, the study of law has little permanent value if rule memorization is the sole objective. The intellectual activity of memorizing and then recalling numerous rules is the easiest of the cognitive activities and should be thought of as necessary for the study of law, but not the ultimate objective. The prediction of when and with what results a rule will be enforced by those in charge of rule enforcement should be a central objective. Essentially this involves a detailed assessment of rule application. Rule application involves the process of analyzing, recalling, evaluating, and synthesizing. These intellectual or cognitive skills therefore should be the central focus of the instructional process in the study of law.

More specifically, law application involves, first, the precise comprehension of a factual pattern. This means you should be able to segregate the essential elements of a communication into parts that are recognized as familiar and parts that are, at first, unfamiliar or cannot be grouped together. Once this is done, the familiar parts of the factual pattern should call forth some abstraction, principle, or, in the case of law study, rule, that will be used if a solution to the factual problem is needed or if relationships between the facts are to be discerned. This recall of principles or rules is the second cognitive element in law application. When recalling the principles and rules used in the past to solve similar factual problems, you may find that several alternative rules are presented. When this is true, you must evaluate which rule is the best one to apply in the circumstances. Finally, you must be able to synthesize (create) an answer to the question of when and with what result rules will be applied.

Law application demonstrates that the law is not a static phenomenon, but a relation; it cannot exist in a vacuum as a mere statement of a rule—rather, it is relative to time, place, and persons. Assessing the legal rules relative to time, place and persons develops, we believe, an intellectual pattern that may have educational significance for you beyond the objectives of this course and this text. The process of analyzing, recalling, evaluating, and synthesizing is one in which we all engage when asked to render a judgment. It should be pointed out that this process is not completely described by a series of steps; it is more accurately portrayed, we believe, as circular in nature. For example, when one is presented with a factual pattern some facts may immediately stand out as relevant to an ultimate decision. However, when the principles or rules are recalled and evaluated, they may suggest facts necessary to the proper application of the principle that were initially discarded as irrelevant. One may actually alternate from analyzing (mentally dissecting and arranging) to recalling and synthesizing and then back to analyzing (rearranging) before an acceptable solution is synthesized.

The Study of Appellate Cases

The process of rule application is best illustrated in the published reports of appellate cases. You will note that in these appellate cases a judge has analyzed a factual pattern, isolated similar or "pertinent" facts, recalled several possible rules that could be applied, evaluated their application, selected one or more to apply, integrated the pertinent facts with the proper principle, and thereby resolved the dispute. You are encouraged to take note of this analytical process in each case presented by making a brief outline. At first this process of "briefing" a case will appear clumsy, time consuming, and of no apparent value. However, over the course of a term notice how the ability to brief a case develops; how the ability to spot the "pertinent" facts becomes almost instinctive and how the ability to critically assess the opinion develops. There is no reason to doubt that if analysis of an appellate opinion improves, analysis of other forms of written communication also improves.

Following we have printed portions of an appellate decision and followed it with an explanation of how we suggest you take notes or brief the case. We suggest you first read the opinion and the briefing instructions that follow, then reread the case making a brief of it according to the instructions.

*ALUMA KRAFT MANUFACTURING
COMPANY & SOLMICA, INC. v. ELMER
FOX AND COMPANY*
493 SW2d 378 (1973)

SIMEONE, Judge
Plaintiff Solmica, Incorporated (hereinafter Solmica), appeals from the judgment of the Circuit Court of St. Louis County entered April 18, 1972, dismissing with prejudice Solmica's amended petition against defendants Elmer Fox & Company, certified public accountants, a partnership, (hereinafter Fox). . . .

The issue presented, one of first impression in this state, is whether the defendants, certified public accountants, are under a duty to exercise due care to protect a third party from economic injury and are liable for damages caused by their alleged negligence, even though there is a lack of privity of contract. . . .

Solmica contends that the defendants, certified public accountants, having negligently performed an audit and having rendered an unqualified opinion, are liable to it without regard to contractual privity. . . .

On the other hand, the defendants urge that the long-standing rule of privity should be retained and that ". . . an accounting firm is liable only to the person or firm with which it is in contractual privity when the claimed liability is based on ordinary negligence" when such alleged negligence causes harm to intangible economic interests.

In determining whether the petition filed states a claim, we assume as true all facts well pleaded and give the appellant the benefit of every favorable inference to be drawn from the facts pleaded. . . .

The precise issue to be determined under these facts is whether an accounting firm may be liable to a third party not in privity when it is alleged that the public accountant knows the audit would be utilized and relied upon by the plaintiff, and knows the audit was being performed for the purpose of determining the price the plaintiff would pay for the shares of stock.

The accountant's liability to a third person not in privity with him for ordinary negligence, as distinguished from fraud, begins with the well-known decision by Mr. Justice Cardozo in *Ultramares Corp.* v. *Touche*, 174 N. E. 441. The New York Court of Appeals held that the firm of accountants could be held responsible for fraud but rejected the accountants' liability for ordinary negligence. Discussing the question as to whether the accountants were under a duty to third persons, Justice Cardozo stated:

". . . If liability for negligence exists (to third parties), a thoughtless slip or blunder . . . may expose accountants to liability in an indeterminate amount for an indeterminate time to an indeterminate class. . . . Liability for negligence is one that is bounded by the contract, and is to be enforced between the parties by whom the contract has been made." The court held (in Ultramares) that since ". . . public accountants are public only in the sense that their services are offered to any one who chooses to employ them," privity or a bond so close so as to approach privity is essential to impose liability upon the public accountant.

The necessity of privity of contract when a petition is based on ordinary negligence was decided recently by our Supreme Court in *Westerhold* v. *Carroll*, Mo., 419 S. W. 2d 73. An action was brought by an indemnitor of a surety on a performance bond against an architect for incorrectly certifying the amount of material furnished and work performed in the construction of a church. There was no privity between the defendant architect and the indemnitor or surety. The Supreme Court rejected the rule requiring privity and held that the petition stated a claim against the architect.

While not abandoning the doctrine of privity under all circumstances, Westerhold held that the extension of limits of liability should be done on a "case-to-case basis" and where the third party is known, the requirement of privity is not applicable.

The liability of the accountant has been discussed in recent years. The view that the rule of privity is to be rejected as to those third persons for whose benefit and guidance the accountant intends to supply such information to a limited class of persons, has been upheld in recent decisions and has been adopted by the *Restatement of the Law, Second, Torts,* § 552, *Tentative Draft No. 12.[1]*

We also reject the privity requirement when, as alleged in the petition, the accountant knows the audit is to be used by the plaintiff for its benefit and guidance, or knows the recipient intends to supply the information to prospective users such as the plaintiff here. Therefore, we hold that a third party in such situations, although not in privity, has a claim for the alleged negligence of an accountant who renders an unqualified opinion upon which the third person relies to its detriment.

The allegations of the amended petition filed by Solmica bring this case within our holding and the decisions of Westerhold . . . , supra. The allegations are that the defendants knew the financial statement and opinion would be utilized by the plaintiff Solmica. The petition stated that ". . . in contemplation that (the report) would be utilized by plaintiff . . . the defendant auditors furnished . . . its formal report setting forth the scope and opinion of the audit. . . ." The petition further stated that the ". . . auditors knew that the said audit was being prepared for the purpose of determining the amounts which plaintiff . . . would pay for the ALUMA KRAFT shares, and that the plaintiff . . . would rely upon the said audit." These allegations are sufficient to show that Fox knew its opinion would be utilized by the plaintiff, knew a purchase of the stock was contemplated, knew the purchase price was to be computed based upon the audit, and knew the audit would be furnished to the purchasers, Solmica. Therefore, these allegations are sufficient to state a claim for relief.

We have examined the cases cited by the respondents and do not believe they control this case.

In conclusion, we hold the amended petition filed by Solmica states a claim for relief against respondents Fox & Company although there is no privity of contract between Solmica and the respondents.

Therefore, the judgment of the Circuit Court is reversed and remanded for further proceedings.

---

[1] *Restatement of the Law, Second, Torts, Tentative Draft, No. 12* § 552, p. 14 "(1) One who, in the course of his business, profession or employment, or in a transaction in which he has a pecuniary interest, supplies false information for the guidance of others in their business transactions, is subject to liability for pecuniary loss caused to them by their justifiable reliance upon the information, if he fails to exercise reasonable care or competence in obtaining or communicating the information. (2) Except as stated in subsection (3) the liability stated in subsection (1) is limited to loss suffered (a) by the person for whose benefit and guidance he intends to supply the information, or knows that the recipient intends to supply it; and (b) through reliance upon it in a transaction which he intends the information to influence, or knows that the recipient so intends, or in a substantially similar transaction. (3) The liability of one who is under a public duty to give the information extends to loss suffered by any of the class of persons for whose benefit the duty is created in any of the transactions in which it is intended to protect them."

Briefing Appellate Cases The traditional starting point for briefing an appellate case is a statement of the legal position of the parties before the court. That is, it is stated who, at the trial court level, was the plaintiff and who the defendant and what, at the appellate court level, is the status of the litigation. A typical brief, then, has four main components. These are short statements about (1) the parties, (2) the facts, (3) the cause of action or legal issue, and (4) the court's decision and reasoning.

Parties

Plaintiff. Aluma Kraft Manufacturing Co., and Solmica, Inc. (The "Inc." is important and should be noted because it indicates the nature of the legal entity suing, a corporation).

Defendant. Elmer Fox & Co., a CPA accounting firm (partnership), and individual partners.

Trial Court. The plaintiff Solmica alleged that the defendant was negligent in preparing an audit of Aluma Kraft. The trial court dismissed the petition of Solmica without a hearing on the evidence. Solmica appeals.

After the parties to the suit are identified and the current posture of the litigation identified, a brief explanation of the "facts" of the case is presented.

Facts

Solmica negotiated with T. J. Bottom, president and principal owner of Aluma Kraft, concerning the purchase of 80 percent of the stock of Aluma Kraft. They negotiated a contract in which Solmica was to purchase 80 percent of Aluma paying a purchase price based on the book value of the shares of Aluma as of June 30, 1969. Aluma was to prepare a financial statement showing the financial condition of the business. Aluma engaged (contracted with) Fox to prepare the audit, and Fox knew the reasons for the audit. Relying on the audit, Solmica purchased 80 percent of Aluma and later purchased the remaining 20 percent of the firm. Solmica alleges that Fox, the defendant, made errors that resulted in an overstatement of the book value of Aluma's stock.

Cause of Action

The plaintiff alleges that the defendant has committed a negligent act, as defined by the common law of the state, and that the defendant is therefore liable to the plaintiff for damages.

The defendant alleges that it is not liable to any legal person with whom it has not contracted, that this bond between contracting parties (called "privity") is a necessary element of the plaintiff's case.

The legal question or issue presented is stated succinctly by the court: ". . . is . . . an accounting firm . . . liable to a third party not in privity (with it) when it is alleged that the public accountant knows the audit would be utilized and relied upon by the (third party) plaintiff . . ."

Court's Decision and Reasoning

The court relies on *Westerhold* and the *Restatement* and holds that where it is alleged that a CPA knows that a third party will rely on an audit, and it is alleged that the audit was negligently prepared, then the third party may bring a cause of action against the CPA where it relied on the audit to its detriment even though the third party and the CPA never directly contracted for the audit. The court reversed the decision of the trial court and remanded the case to the trial court. Presumably a trial on the merits will follow.

1. The established law directly pertinent to this case is stated in the *Ultramares Corp.* case (a New York case) in which it was held that liability for negligence is bounded by contract; that is, one not a party to the contract with the alleged wrongdoer (tortfeasor) cannot recover for negligence.

2. But, the court apparently rejects the reasoning of *Ultramares* and relies instead on the *Westerhold* case (a Missouri case) in which it was held that a party not in contract with an architect could sue the architect for negligence when the architect knew the third party might rely on assertions made by the architect.

3. The court also relies on the *Restatement of the Law*, which provides that if a person in the course of business supplies false information for the guidance of others in their business, he or she is subject to liability for loss caused by the justifiable reliance on the information.

Concluding Remarks About the Study of Appellate Cases

Studying appellate cases to sharpen one's analytical skills and, just as important, to learn the circumstances under which some of the major rules governing business organizations are applied is not without some drawbacks. Appellate cases are not a perfect instructional tool.

Sometimes an appellate court will not clearly define exactly what the trial court held. One might think that an appellate court would clearly outline the posture of the case before it, but some courts seem to assume the reader already knows or can pick out by inference or deduction what the trial court did. Another somewhat confusing aspect of reading appellate cases is that in a case involving many parties the style or title of the case may not reveal all of the names. Some reporters may arrange several plaintiffs or defendants alphabetically and then select only the first name in each list as the title to the case. Thus, a particular named plaintiff or defendant referred to in the àppellate decision may not be mentioned in the style of the case.

One will find that some questions presented by the factual pattern will often remain unanswered. Generally, they remain unanswered because the appellate court has not deemed them relevant to the issue before it. For example, in the *Solmica* case one may be left wondering how a CPA firm can make what is alleged to be such a gross error.

Be careful not to read more into the case than is presented in the opinion. Judge Simeone said nothing about what constitutes negligence in the preparation of an audit, nor did he indicate whether the plaintiffs would ultimately prevail. The "rule" of this case is that in Missouri a CPA firm now owes a legal duty to persons with whom it has not contracted when it furnishes an opinion and knows that a specific third person might reasonably rely on it to its detriment. The plaintiffs may now pursue the case in the trial court and proceed to obtain a judgment on the merits of the case if they can prove negligence.

If you believe several or, perhaps, numerous issues are presented in an appellate case you may narrow these by considering the chapter heading and subheading in the text which immediately precede the case. These will provide some guide as to what our objectives are in presenting a case. For example, the *Solmica* case may have been used to accomplish many possible objectives: the case illustrates the phenomenon of judicial rule creation; it illustrates the use of case precedent (the court followed the holding in *Westerhold* and rejected the holding in *Ultramares* even though the facts of *Ultramares* were more like the ones in *Solmica*); it also illustrates one use of the *Restatement of Law* and, finally, it provides a concise statement of one of the rules of law which may at some time be of value to the student. While all of these potential uses of the case exist, our objective here is rather narrow: it is important that you carefully read the case and clearly understand the process of briefing the decision.

Most of the cases reproduced in this text were chosen for their instructional value. That is, they probably illustrate the "classic" factual outlines of the conflict under discussion or explain thoroughly the rationale for the application of a given principle. Since these were our criteria for case selection, the age of the case is not important. For purposes of illustrating the circumstances under which a rule will be applied by officials or illustrating the reasons why a rule is so applied, an 1890s opinion by Oliver Wendell Holmes may be just as instructive as a 1980s case.

**Structure and
Method of
This Book**

At the beginning of this chapter we stated that the definition of law is a statement of: (1) the rules written or unwritten generated by one of the rule sources; (2) how those rules are applied by those persons in charge of rule application; (3) how persons and institutions respond to the application; and (4) how the old rules are changed or new ones generated.

Within the chapters that follow we have presented four different kinds of material that represent the four aspects of law study stated above. First, there is textual material that presents a statement of the general rules of law applicable to business organizations. These rules are both legislative and judicial in origin. Where the law varies from state to state, this will be noted by pointing out that most states take one approach (the "majority" rule) while fewer take a different approach (the "minority" rule).

However, presenting the written rules is only a starting point. A second type of information illustrates how some of the important rules are applied by those in charge of rule application, either the state or federal governments or private individuals. This rule application is illustrated by presenting long excerpts from appellate case opinions. These case opinions demonstrate how the abstract statements presented by the written rules are applied to reality. The cases literally breathe life into the rules and are absolutely necessary to an understanding of how the law "works." Much of the information in the text is contained in these appellate opinions; therefore, you are encouraged to read them carefully and make notes on them as described earlier.

A third kind of material is presented that assesses how the persons and institutions respond to a given rule and how the rule should be changed. This information is usually in the form of an excerpt from an article written by a recognized expert in the field or from an article written by a law professor or law student who has done research in the area.

Fourth, we have presented at the end of some appellate cases and at the end of most chapters review questions and review problems, which are another source of material requiring you to integrate several of the rules discussed and to assess whether or not a rule should be the way that it is. Some of these review problems were created by us, so they should be reviewed as not portraying an actual factual pattern.

A final word about footnoting. The footnotes within the appellate cases and articles have been renumbered to conform to our editing of the material. These footnotes have been numbered in italics and placed at the bottom of the page because they add to an understanding of the case or article. Footnotes substantiating assertions we make in the text appear at the end of the chapter as endnotes.

Review Problems

1. In the *Aluma Kraft* case, why wasn't T.J. Bottom, President of Aluma Kraft, made a defendant? According to the information presented in the complaint and the appellate decision, did T.J. Bottom have any legal duties that ran to Solmica and that were breached?

2. Summarize the holding of the appellate court in the *Solmica* case in a few concise sentences. Should this holding include the statement that the CPA firm has a duty of care only to those it knew would rely on the audit? Can an argument be made that the holding should not be so limited? Read the *Restatement,* Section 552, quoted in the case. Didn't the court rely on this in forming its judgment?

3. In your opinion, why did the court reject the reasons and holding in the *Ultramares* case and follow the *Westerhold* and *Restatement* rationales? When are appellate courts likely to change the law?

4. Below are some terms that will be used repeatedly throughout the text. They appear in the approximate order in which they were discussed in this chapter. You should be able to recall and write down the definition of each term and explain its use in the context where the term was discussed. If you cannot, then reread this chapter or refer to the glossary of terms at the end of the text. Another alternative is to refer to *Black's Law Dictionary,* 4th ed., which should be available in your library.

law, study of	class action cases
statute, statutory law	default judgment
administrative agency	motion to dismiss for failure to
ordinance	state a claim
breach of duty	discovery procedures/devices
Restatement of the Law	deposition
common law	interrogatories
equity law, equitable principles	dismissal with prejudice
injunction	judgment on the pleadings
specific performance	summary judgment
appellate court	verdict
criminal law/civil law	voire dire
defendant	direct verdict
plaintiff	judge's instructions
felony/misdemeanor	judgment notwithstanding the
diversity jurisdiction	verdict
complaint	judgment N.O.V.
cause of action	intermediate appellate court
summons	appellant/petitioner
service of process	appellee/respondent
answer	trial transcript
pleadings	appellate brief
counterclaim	

Endnotes

1. 26 USCA §7802.

2. 26 USCA §7805.

3. 1 *New York Pattern Jury Instruction—Civil 126* (2nd ed. 1974).

2

An Overview of Business Organizations and Their Regulation

Our study of American business organizations begins with an explanation of the powers of the state and federal governments to regulate the form and conduct of these organizations. Although people are free to create whatever type of business organization suits their purpose, they usually must gain recognition of the organization from the state. This is true of corporations, all of which are created by state law. It is less true of partnerships, which may be created just by the intention of the partners.

The definitions and explanations of the most prominent forms of business organizations used in this country today are discussed in the last half of this chapter. More comprehensive definitions of agency, partnerships, limited partnerships, joint ventures, and corporations are found in the following pages.

In addition to these definitions, you should be aware of the relative advantages of using each form of organization. A table contrasting the various organization types is given at the end of this chapter.

Restraints on State Governments for the Formation and Regulation of Business Organizations

In very general terms, the U.S. Constitution gives express powers to the federal government to regulate some activity while delegating to the states the power and authority to act in most areas in which the federal government cannot or has not acted. Discussions of the constitutional division of the power to govern between Congress and the state legislatures are referred to as issues or questions of *federalism*.

Issues of Federalism

The balance of various powers between Congress and state legislatures is constantly changing. Most currently, for example, President Reagan has sought a "new federalism," in an attempt to return some of the power of the federal government to the state governments.

Issues of federalism can be thought of as involving four essential questions:[1]

1. Which of the legislative powers mentioned in the U.S. Constitution are exclusive to the federal government? Generally, the power to coin money, to establish post offices, to declare war, and to borrow money are part of the usual answer.
2. Which of the powers may also be exercised by the states if the federal government *does not* legislate? Generally, the regulation of local commerce that affects commerce among other states is part of the answer to this question.
3. Which powers are overlapping so that both federal and state governments may exercise them? The power to tax and, more recently, the power to legislate to protect the environment would, together with other powers, be part of the answer to this question.
4. Which powers are clearly outside those expressed in the Constitution and are not prohibited to the states? The power to regulate private legal remedies for wrongs to another person, property, reputation, or business relation (torts), as well as the power to define crimes, help answer this question.

{ *business regulations are state laws* }

The regulation of business conduct is a task shared by the federal and state governments. The legal mechanism that defines the power of the federal government to regulate business conduct is Article I, Section 8 of the U.S. Constitution. This article will be discussed later in this chapter.

The Police Power of States

The regulation of the *forms* of business organizations is a task that is accomplished almost entirely by state law. When state legislatures act to define a type of business organization or to limit business in one way or another they are relying on their *police power.* The police power of states is even more fundamental than the powers to act derived from state constitutions. Very generally, the police power of a state is an essential attribute of sovereignty that implies the power to legislate, to protect, and promote the health, safety, and welfare of the residents of the state.

The police power is as old as governments themselves and is the very reason governments exist. The governmental units that existed in America before the present Constitution was adopted had this power; thus, in a technical sense, the power exists independently of constitutional powers.[2]

The "real" foundation of the police power is a matter better left for discussions in political philosophy. For our purposes, its foundation may be thought of as a combination of two widely recognized western moral precepts. The first, expressed in Latin as *sic utere tuo ut alienum non laedas,* means "so use your own that you do not injure that of another"—a probable variant of the Golden Rule. The other is more related to the writings of western philosophers and is expressed as *salus populi suprema lex est,* or "the welfare of the people is the highest law."[3]

Limitations on the Use of the Police Power

The police power is usually thought of as the fundamental right of *state legislatures* to act, but state-level executive and judicial branches may also claim its use. Regardless of the branch of state government relying on it, it is subject to limitation. However, the police power should be subject to only very general restraints because the potential of government to control business conduct and form must be adequate to respond to changing social, political, and economic conditions.

Usually there are three classifications of limitations: first, the governmental unit acting must have a *purpose* that is consistent with the traditional use of the power; second, its use must be *reasonable;* and third, the *means* chosen to affect the result must be appropriate. The overriding consideration here is usually the reasonableness of the governmental activity.

The chief sources that are construed as limitations on the use of the police power of states are the federal and state constitutions. The Fourteenth Amendment to the U.S. Constitution in particular is the most frequently cited source of limitations. This amendment provides, in part: "[N]or shall any state deprive any person of life, liberty or property without due process of law; nor deny to any person within its jurisdiction the equal protection of the laws."

The U.S. Supreme Court has used these two clauses—called the "due process" clause and the "equal protection" clause, respectively—to impose the central requirement of reasonableness on the use of the states' police power. In very general terms, when a state attempts to regulate business conduct or form and, in the process of this, seems to impinge on a person's property right, the aggrieved person may argue that the regulation is unconstitutional because it denies him or her due process of law. More particularly, the regulation may be unconstitutional if it does deprive a person of a property right and the regulation is not *reasonably related* to the protection of the public health, safety, and welfare.

An example of an unconstitutional use of the police power can be found in the case of *Liggett Co.* v. *Baldridge,* 278 U.S. 105 (1928). The State of Pennsylvania attempted to regulate the dispensing of drugs and passed a statute that required all stockholders in corporations owning drug stores to be registered pharmacists. The Supreme Court held that this statute was an unreasonable restriction upon individuals' property right to own stock in a corporation. It was unreasonable since the requirement as to ownership of stock bore no reasonable relation to the public health.

This "reasonable relationship" test is not easy to define or to apply. In broad terms it does require some kind of factual cause-and-effect relationship between the statute and the genuine protection of other people. The test described in the *Liggett* case was based on substantive due process. Today issues of substantive due process are not favored by courts because applying this test casts a reviewing court in the position of a super legislature, in a way second-guessing the "reasonableness" of state legislative actions. Many courts are reluctant to accept this position.

The main source of the limitations on state police power today is the equal protection clause. This source is argued whenever a state statute or action discriminates between alternative uses, means, methods, or the like of regulating business conduct or form. Think for a minute about the great number of state statutes that discriminate between various interests and groups. State statutes usually prohibit those less than 16 years of age from driving a car; many state statutes proclaim that those persons younger than 18 or 21, depending on the state, cannot buy alcoholic beverages; similar discriminatory statutes define who can practice medicine, law, or accounting.

Under what circumstances may a state use its police power to discriminate and to regulate business conduct or form? The following case is a very recent application of the equal protection clause of the Fourteenth Amendment to an attempt by a state legislature to regulate the sale of milk containers. You can learn from this case what the most recent definition of "reasonable" is for purposes of allowing states to act.

Also, note in this case another constitutional limitation on the use of a state's police power. Article I, Section 8 states in part, "Congress shall have Power . . . to regulate Commerce with foreign Nations, and among the several States. . . ." This clause is often referred to as the "interstate commerce clause," or just the "commerce clause." A brief description of it adds to our understanding of the distribution of powers to regulate between states and the federal government. On the one hand, it means Congress cannot legally regulate commercial conduct unless the conduct regulated affects interstate commerce; on the other hand, it has also been interpreted to mean that any state regulation that exceeds state boundaries and that places an undue burden on interstate commerce is not legal because this power to regulate interstate commerce resides with Congress. This also means that commercial conduct that is only intrastate in character should be regulated by the states. The following case explores the latter interpretation of this clause, as well as the meaning of the equal protection clause.

STATE OF MINNESOTA v. *CLOVER LEAF CREAMERY*
449 U.S. 456 (1981)

. . .

In 1977, the Minnesota Legislature enacted a statute banning the retail sale of milk in plastic nonreturnable, nonrefillable containers, but permitting such sale in other nonreturnable, nonrefillable containers, such as paperboard milk cartons. . . . Respondents contend that the statute violates the Equal Protection and Commerce Clauses of the Constitution.

. . .

The Act was introduced with the support of the state Pollution Control Agency, Department of Natural Resources, Department of Agriculture, Consumer Services Division, and Energy Agency, and debated vigorously in both houses of the state Legislature. Proponents of the legislation argued that it would promote resource conservation, ease solid waste disposal problems, and conserve energy. Relying on the results of studies and other information, they stressed the need to stop introduction of the plastic nonreturnable container before it became entrenched in the market. Opponents of the Act, also presenting empirical evidence, argued that the Act would not promote the goals asserted by the proponents, but would merely increase costs of retail milk products and prolong the use of ecologically undesirable paperboard milk cartons.

After the Act was passed, respondents filed suit in Minnesota District Court, seeking to enjoin its enforcement. The Court conducted extensive evidentiary hearings into the Act's probable consequences, and found the evidence "in sharp conflict. . . ." Nevertheless, finding itself, "as fact-finder . . . obliged to weigh and evaluate this evidence," the Court resolved the evidentiary conflicts in favor of respondents, and concluded that the Act "would not succeed in effecting the Legislature's published policy goals . . . ." The Court further found that, contrary to the statement of purpose . . . the "actual basis" for the Act "was to promote the economic interests of certain segments of the local dairy and pulpwood industries at the expense of the economic interests of other segments of the dairy industry and the plastics industry. . . ." The Court therefore declared the Act "null, void and unenforceable" and enjoined its enforcement, basing the judgment on substantive due process under the Fourteenth Amendment to the United States Constitution and Art. I, § 7, of the Minnesota Constitution; equal protection under the Fourteenth Amendment; and prohibition of unreasonable burdens on interstate commerce under Art. I, § 8, of the United States Constitution. . . .

The State appealed to the Supreme Court of Minnesota, which affirmed the District Court on the federal equal protection and due process grounds, without reaching the Commerce Clause or state law issues. . . .

The parties agree that the standard of review applicable to this case under the Equal Protection Clause is the familiar "rational basis" test. . . . Moreover, they agree that the purposes of the Act cited by the legislature—promoting resource conservation, easing solid waste disposal problems, and conserving energy—are legitimate state purposes. Thus, the controversy in this case centers on the narrow issue of whether the legislative classification between plastic and nonplastic nonreturnable milk containers is rationally related to achievement of the statutory purposes.

Respondents apparently have not challenged the theoretical connection between a ban on plastic returnables and the purposes articulated by the legislature; instead, they have argued that there is no empirical connection between the two. They produced impressive supporting evidence at trial to prove that the probable consequences of the ban on plastic nonreturnable milk containers will be to deplete natural resources, exacerbate solid waste disposal problems, and waste energy, because consumers unable to purchase milk in plastic containers will turn to paperboard milk cartons, allegedly a more environmentally harmful product.

But States are not required to convince the courts of the correctness of their legislative judgments. Rather, "those challenging the legislative judgment must convince the court that the legislative facts on which the classification is apparently based could not reasonably be conceived to be true by the governmental decisionmaker. . . ."

Although parties challenging legislation under the Equal Protection Clause may introduce evidence supporting their claim that it is irrational . . . they cannot prevail so long as "it is evident from all the considerations presented to [the legislature], and those of which we may take judicial notice, that the question is at least debatable. . . ." Where there was evidence before the legislature reasonably supporting the classification, litigants may not procure invalidation of the legislation merely by tendering evidence in court that the legislature was mistaken.

. . .

The State identifies four reasons why the classification between plastic and nonplastic nonreturnables is rationally related to the articulated statutory purposes. If any one of the four substantiates the State's claim, we must reverse the Minnesota Supreme Court and sustain the Act.

First, the State argues that elimination of the popular plastic milk jug will encourage the use of environmentally superior containers. There is no serious doubt that the plastic containers consume energy resources and require solid waste disposal, nor that refillable bottles and plastic pouches are environmentally superior. . . .

. . .

The Equal Protection Clause does not deny the State of Minnesota the authority to ban one type of milk container conceded to cause environmental problems, merely because another type, already established in the market, is permitted to continue in use. Whether in fact the Act will promote more environmentally desirable milk packaging is not the question: the Equal Protection Clause is satisfied by our conclusion that the Minnesota Legislature could rationally have decided that its ban on plastic nonreturnable milk jugs might foster greater use of environmentally desirable alternatives.

Second, the State argues that its ban on plastic nonreturnable milk containers will reduce the economic dislocation foreseen from the movement toward greater use of environmentally superior containers. The State notes that plastic nonreturnables have only recently been introduced on a wide scale in Minnesota, and that, at the time the legislature was considering the Act, many Minnesota dairies were preparing to invest large amounts of capital in plastic container production. . . .

Moreover, the State explains, to ban both the plastic and the paperboard nonreturnable milk container at once would cause an enormous disruption in the milk industry because few dairies are now able to package their products in refillable bottles or plastic pouches. Thus, by banning the plastic container while continuing to permit the paperboard container, the State was able to prevent the industry from becoming reliant on the new container, while avoiding severe economic dislocation.

. . .

Third, the State argues that the Act will help to conserve energy. It points out that plastic milk jugs are made from plastic resin, an oil and natural gas derivative, whereas paperboard milk cartons are primarily composed of pulpwood, which is a renewable resource. . . .

. . .

The Minnesota Supreme Court held, in effect, that the legislature misunderstood the facts. . . .

The Minnesota Supreme Court may be correct that the Act is not a sensible means of conserving energy. But we reiterate that "it is up to legislatures, not courts, to decide on the wisdom and utility of legislation. . . ."

Fourth, the State argues that the Act will ease the State's solid waste disposal problem. Most solid consumer wastes in Minnesota are disposed of in landfills. A reputable study before the Minnesota Legislature indicated that plastic milk jugs occupy a greater volume in landfills than other nonreturnable milk containers. . . .

The Minnesota Supreme Court found that plastic milk jugs in fact take up less space in landfills and present fewer solid waste disposal problems than do paperboard containers. . . . But its ruling on this point must be rejected for the same reason we rejected its ruling concerning energy conservation: it is not the function of the courts to substitute their evaluation of legislative facts for that of the legislature.

We therefore conclude that the ban on plastic nonreturnable milk containers bears a rational relation to the State's objectives, and must be sustained under the Equal Protection Clause.

The District Court also held that the Minnesota statute is unconstitutional under the Commerce Clause because it imposes an unreasonable burden on interstate commerce. We cannot agree.

When legislating in areas of legitimate local concern, such as environmental protection and resource conservation, States are nonetheless limited by the Commerce Clause. . . . If a state law purporting to promote environmental purposes is in reality "simple economic protectionism," we have applied a "virtually per se rule of invalidity. . . ." Even if a statute regulates "even-handedly," and imposes only "incidental" burdens on interstate commerce, the courts must nevertheless strike it down if "the burden imposed on such commerce is clearly excessive in relation to the putative local benefits. . . ." Moreover, "the extent of the burden that will be tolerated will of course depend on the nature of the local interest involved, and on whether it could be promoted as well with a lesser impact on interstate activities. . . ."

Minnesota's statute does not effect "simple protectionism," but "regulates even-handedly" by prohibiting all milk retailers from selling their products in plastic, nonreturnable milk containers, without regard to whether the milk, the containers, or the sellers are from outside the State. This statute is therefore unlike statutes discriminating against interstate commerce, which we have consistently struck down. . . .

Since the statute does not discriminate between interstate and intrastate commerce, the controlling question is whether the incidental burden imposed on interstate commerce by the Minnesota Act is "clearly excessive in relation to the putative local benefits. . . ." We conclude that it is not.

The burden imposed on interstate commerce by the statute is relatively minor. Milk products may continue to move freely across the Minnesota border, and since most dairies package their products in more than one type of container, the inconvenience of having to conform to different packaging requirements in Minnesota and the surrounding States should be slight.

. . .

The judgment of the Minnesota Supreme Court is

Reversed.

. . .

1. Why could the state of Minnesota regulate the type of milk container used in the state, but the state of Pennsylvania could not regulate, in the manner they attempted to regulate, the sale of drugs? (See the Liggett case discussed in the text.)

2. The Fourteenth Amendment to the U.S. Constitution is interpreted to put restraints on the use of a state's police power. Carefully define these restraints.

3. Why did not the Minnesota statute in question violate the commerce clause of the U.S. Constitution?

Typical State-Level Restraints on Business Organizations

Licensing.   Using the police power of its legislatures, most states have adopted comprehensive regulatory schemes that affect almost all business organizations. Generally, partnerships and corporations are regulated by state statute. Also, this police power gives most states the right to promulgate licensing schemes for various professions and businesses. These licensing schemes require those rendering certain types of personal service deemed potentially dangerous to the public to comply with certain conditions in order to receive a state license. The purpose of this requirement is to control those individuals affecting public health and welfare. This type of licensing must be distinguished from licensing for tax purposes. The latter is imposed pursuant to a state's taxing power and has as its prime objective the raising of revenue. Almost all business and professional persons are subject to this latter form of taxation and are required, therefore, to buy a business license each year.

Those who are regulated under the police power of the state, such as doctors, attorneys, CPAs, real estate brokers, electricians, plumbers, barbers, and others engaged in a "profession" or business requiring special training and skill, usually need to receive only the initial license to operate; this license is good for as long as the professional remains qualified.

Practicing without a license when one is required may result in a permanent denial of the privilege to practice the profession or in the assessment of a fine. The only way to determine if a license is needed is to consult the state statutes or a professional advisor in the state of proposed activity. States vary greatly in their licensing requirements. California, Illinois, and Pennsylvania, for example, list over 160 licensed occupations, while others list less than 70.[4]

Trade-Name Registration.   A second general restraint applicable to all business organizations is the requirement that an organization using a name other than the surname of the proprietor or the partners must register the name with the secretary of state in the state where business is conducted. This name is usually called a "trade-name." Many authorities do not distinguish between trade-names and trademarks because the same principles and procedures are applicable to both. Most agree, however, that a trade-name is a broader concept referring to the designation of an entire business; a trademark is usually thought of as a distinguishable mark placed on goods for sale. For purposes of registration and protection by the state they are treated similarly, and in many states the same statute governs the registration of both.

States require registration of trade-names to protect established businesses from those who would confuse or mislead the public by adopting the same name as the established business. If confusion between a previously registered name and a proposed new business would result, then a state will refuse to register the trade-name of the new business and the owners must adopt another name. For example, most states would not permit one to use the name "General Motors" for a business producing automobiles.

Some states attempt to enforce trade-name or trademark registration by creating an enforceable right in the one who has properly registered the name. The following Indiana statute is typical:

> Improper use of registered mark or imitation-damages . . .
> [A]ny person who shall
> (a) use, without the consent of the registrant, any reproduction; counterfeit, copy or colorable imitation of a trade-mark registered under this act . . . which . . . is likely to cause confusion or mistake or to deceive as to the source or origin of such goods or services; . . . shall be liable to a civil action by the owner of such registered trade-mark. . . . (Ind. Ann. Stat. § 24-2-1-4 (Burns, 1974)

A subsequent section, 24-2-1-14, provides that the registrant may sue for an injunction to prohibit the use of the unregistered trademark as well as profits derived from its use if the illegal user did so with the intent to confuse the public.

Regulation of Banks and Insurance Companies. In addition to requiring organizations or individuals to procure licenses and register trade-names, states may, again pursuant to the police power they possess, enact comprehensive regulatory schemes for types of business invested with a vital public interest. For example, most states have enacted very complex regulatory schemes for banks or those planning to offer some banking activity to the public. Also, insurance companies, trust companies, mortgage companies, and others are regulated by special statutes; professional advice should be sought in complying with registration under these laws.

Also, partnerships and corporations must meet numerous filing requirements that are propounded by the state legislatures and regulative agencies. All such organizations should request of the secretary of state in the state(s) in which they do business a list of all such filing requirements (such as an annual report of a corporation) as well as tax filing requirements that are necessary to operate in good standing within the state.

There are numerous federal laws applicable to both individuals and business organizations that intend to engage in commerce. The authority of Congress to act comes from more than one part of the Constitution. The authority to tax income, for example, is created by the Sixteenth Amendment. Pursuant to this authority, Congress has said that every corporation must request from the Internal Revenue Service an identification number, in addition to paying a tax if the provisions of the Internal Revenue Code of 1954 and its various rules and regulations require it.

Restraints on the Federal Government in Regulating Business Conduct

Recently, however, Congress has sought to regulate business activity by relying on its authority to do so as created by the commerce clause quoted above. Except for the Federal Securities Laws, and a briefer consideration of employment discrimination, job safety, the new pension reform law, environmental legislation, and the new federal regulation of product warranties, the federal regulation of American business organizations is beyond the scope of this book. However, you should be aware that the following kinds of activity may be subject to federal law if the interstate commerce requirement is met.

1. *Anticompetitive Behavior.*   Regulated by the application of the antitrust laws: the Sherman Act; the Clayton Act, as amended; and the Federal Trade Commission Act, as amended.

2. *Employment Practices.*   Regulated by the application of the Civil Rights Acts, the Wagner Act, hours of work and minimum wage legislation, and pension reform legislation.

3. *Safety Conditions.*   Regulated by the application of the Williams-Steiger Act (referred to as the Occupational Safety and Health Act or OSHA).

4. *Environmental Activities.*   Regulated by the application of several federal environmental protection acts, as well as rules created by the Environmental Protection Agency.

5. *The Sale or Purchase of Securities of the Corporation.*   Regulated by the application of the Securities Acts of 1933 and 1934.

6. *Transportation, Banking, Insurance, Broadcasting, and Other Industries Invested with a Special Public Trust.*   Regulated by the application of numerous rules and regulations generated by the various federal regulatory agencies such as the ICC, FPC, FCC, NRC, and so on.

The Clover Leaf Creamery case excerpted above discusses a limitation on state governments imposed by the commerce clause, but does not define the words "interstate" or "commerce" which give the Congress so much of its power to act. The following case is instructive on these definitions.

HEART OF ATLANTA MOTEL, INC. v. *UNITED STATES*
379 U.S. 241 (1964)

. . .

This is a declaratory judgment action . . . attacking the constitutionality of Title II of the Civil Rights Act of 1964 . . . . In addition to declaratory relief the complaint sought an injunction restraining the enforcement of the Act and damages against appellees based on allegedly resulting injury in the event compliance was required. Appellees counterclaimed for enforcement under § 206(a) of the Act . . . .

. . .

The case comes here on admissions and stipulated facts. Appellant owns and operates the Heart of Atlanta Motel which has 216 rooms available to transient guests. The motel is located on Courtland Street, two blocks from downtown Peachtree Street. It is readily accessible to interstate highways 75 and 85 and state highways 23 and 41. Appellant solicits patronage from outside the State of Georgia through various national advertising media, including magazines of national circulation; it maintains over 50 billboards and highway signs within the State, soliciting patronage for the motel; it accepts convention trade from outside Georgia and approximately 75% of its registered guests are from out of State. Prior to passage of the Act the motel had followed a practice of refusing to rent rooms to Negroes, and it alleged that it intended to continue to do so. In an effort to perpetuate that policy this suit was filed.

The appellant contends that Congress in passing this Act exceeded its power to regulate commerce under Art. I, § 8, cl. 3, of the Constitution of the United States . . . .

The appellees counter that the unavailability to Negroes of adequate accommodations interferes significantly with interstate travel, and that Congress, under the Commerce Clause, has power to remove such obstructions and restraints . . . .

. . .

. . . No major legislation in this field had been enacted by Congress for 82 years when the Civil Rights Act of 1957 became law. It was followed by the Civil Rights Act of 1960. Three years later, on June 19, 1963, the late President Kennedy called for civil rights legislation in a message to Congress to which he attached a proposed bill. Its stated purpose was

> to promote the general welfare by eliminating discrimination based on race, color, religion or national origin in . . . public accommodations through the exercise by Congress of the powers conferred upon it . . . to enforce the provisions of the fourteenth and fifteenth amendments, to regulate commerce among the several States, and to make laws necessary and proper to execute the powers conferred upon it by the Constitution . . . .

Bills were introduced in each House of the Congress, embodying the President's suggestion, one in the Senate being S. 1732 and one in the House, H.R. 7152. However, it was not until July 2, 1964, upon the recommendation of President Johnson, that the Civil Rights Act of 1964, here under attack, was finally passed.

. . .

This Title is divided into seven sections beginning with § 201(a) which provides that:

> All persons shall be entitled to the full and equal enjoyment of the goods, services, facilities, privileges, advantages, and accommodations of any place of public accommodation, as defined in this section, without discrimination or segregation on the ground of race, color, religion, or national origin.

There are listed in § 201(b) four classes of business establishments, each of which "serves the public" and "is a place of public accommodation" within the meaning of § 201(a) "if its operations affect commerce, or if discrimination or segregation by it is supported by State action. . . ."

. . .

Section 201(c) defines the phrase "affect commerce" as applied to the above establishments. It first declares that "any inn, hotel, motel, or other establishment which provides lodging to transient guests" affects commerce per se. Restaurants, cafeterias, etc., in class two affect commerce only if they serve or offer to serve interstate travelers or if a substantial portion of the food which they serve or products which they sell have "moved in commerce." Motion picture houses and other places listed in class three affect commerce if they customarily present films, performances, etc., "which move in commerce." And the establishments listed in class four affect commerce if they are within, or include within their own premises, an establishment "the operations of which affect commerce." Private clubs are excepted under certain conditions. See § 201(e).

. . .

It is admitted that the operation of the motel brings it within the provisions of § 201(a) of the Act and that appellant refused to provide lodging for transient Negroes because of their race or color and that it intends to continue that policy unless restrained.

The sole question posed is, therefore, the constitutionality of the Civil Rights Act of 1964 as applied to these facts. The legislative history of the Act indicates that Congress based the Act on . . . its power to regulate interstate commerce under Art. I, § 8, cl. 3, of the Constitution.

. . .

While the Act as adopted carried no congressional findings the record of its passage through each house is replete with evidence of the burdens that discrimination by race or color places upon interstate commerce. . . .

This testimony included the fact that our people have become increasingly mobile with millions of people of all races traveling from State to State; that Negroes in particular have been the subject of discrimination in transient accommodations, having to travel great distances to secure the same; that often they have been unable to obtain accommodations and have had to call upon friends to put them up overnight, . . . and that these conditions had become so acute as to require the listing of available lodging for Negroes in a special guidebook which was itself "dramatic testimony to the difficulties" Negroes encounter in travel. These exclusionary practices were found to be nationwide, the Under Secretary of Commerce testifying that there is "no question that this discrimination in the North still exists to a large degree" and in the West and Midwest as well. . . . This testimony indicated a qualitative as well as quantitative effect on interstate travel by Negroes. The former was the obvious impairment of the Negro traveler's pleasure and convenience that resulted when he continually was uncertain of finding lodging. As for the latter, there was evidence that this uncertainty stemming from racial discrimination had the effect of discouraging travel on the part of a substantial portion of the Negro community. . . .

. . .

The power of Congress to deal with these obstructions depends on the meaning of the Commerce Clause. Its meaning was first enunciated 140 years ago by the great Chief Justice John Marshall in *Gibbons* v. *Ogden,* 9 Wheat. 1 (1824), in these words.

> The subject to be regulated is commerce; and . . . to ascertain the extent of the power, it becomes necessary to settle the meaning of the word. The counsel for the appellee would limit it to traffic, to buying and selling, or the interchange of commodities . . . but it is something more: it is intercourse . . . between nations, and parts of nations, in all its branches, and is regu-

lated by prescribing rules for carrying on that intercourse. . . .

. . .

To what commerce does this power extend? The constitution informs us, to commerce "with foreign nations, and among the several States, and with the Indian tribes."

It has, we believe, been universally admitted, that these words comprehend every species of commercial intercourse . . . . No sort of trade can be carried on . . . to which this power does not extend. . . .

In short, the determinative test of the exercise of power by the Congress under the Commerce Clause is simply whether the activity sought to be regulated is "commerce which concerns more States than one" and has a real and substantial relation to the national interest. Let us now turn to this facet of the problem.

That the "intercourse" of which the Chief Justice spoke included the movement of persons through more States than one was settled as early as 1849, in the Passenger Cases . . . . "That the transportation of passengers is a part of commerce is not now an open question. . . ."

. . .

The same interest in protecting interstate commerce which led Congress to deal with segregation in interstate carriers and the white-slave traffic has prompted it to extend the exercise of its power to gambling, . . . to criminal enterprises, . . . to deceptive practices in the sale of products, . . . to fraudulent security transactions, . . . to misbranding of drugs, . . . to wages and hours, . . . to members of labor unions, . . . to crop control, . . . to discrimination against shippers, . . . to the protection of small business from injurious price cutting, . . . to resale price maintenance, . . . (and) to professional football . . . .

That Congress was legislating against moral wrongs in many of these areas rendered its enactments no less valid. In framing Title II of this Act Congress was also dealing with what it considered a moral problem. But that fact does not detract from the overwhelming evidence of the disruptive effect that racial discrimination has had on commercial intercourse. It was this burden which empowered Congress to enact appropriate legislation, and, given this basis for the exercise of its power, Congress was not restricted by the fact that the particular obstruction to interstate commerce with which it was dealing was also deemed a moral and social wrong.

It is said that the operation of the motel here is of a purely local character. But, assuming this to be true, "(i)f it is interstate commerce that feels the pinch, it does not matter how local the operation which applies the squeeze. . . ."

. . .

Thus the power of Congress to promote interstate commerce also includes the power to regulate the local incidents thereof, including local activities in both the States of origin and destination, which might have a substantial and harmful effect upon that commerce. One need only examine the evidence which we have discussed above to see that Congress may—as it has—prohibit racial discrimination by motels serving travelers, however "local" their operations may appear.

. . .

We, therefore, conclude that the action of the Congress in the adoption of the Act as applied here to a motel which concededly serves interstate travelers is within the power granted it by the Commerce Clause of the Constitution, as interpreted by this Court for 140 years. It may be argued that Congress could have pursued other methods to eliminate the obstructions it found in interstate commerce caused by racial discrimination. But this is a matter of policy that rests entirely with the Congress not with the courts. How obstructions in commerce may be removed—what means are to be employed—is within the sound and exclusive discretion of the Congress. It is subject only to one caveat—that the means chosen by it must be reasonably adapted to the end permitted by the Constitution. We cannot say that its choice here was not so adapted. The Constitution requires no more.

Affirmed.

. . .

---

1. The case above illustrates that Congress sought to ban racial discrimination in certain instances. Exactly how is racial discrimination defined as "commerce" for the purposes of Article I, Section 8?

2. The late 1960s and 1970s saw attempts by Congress to regulate business conduct, attempts that have since been labeled by some as "social" regulation. Generally, the areas of conduct involving job-related race, sex, and age discrimination, environmental pollution, job safety and health, and product safety have all been subject to federal legislation. Using the definition of interstate commerce found in the case, and using the pattern of logic developed by the court, explain how interstate commerce is involved in each of these areas of regulation.

Summary of Restraints on Governments to Regulate

In this first part of the chapter, we have explained how the state and federal governments derive their power to regulate business conduct and form. The states' police power is very fundamental and comes from our western notions and traditions defining sovereignty. The federal government's power to regulate business conduct and form comes from several different parts of the U.S. Constitution.

The due process and equal protection clauses of the Fourteenth Amendment to the U.S. Constitution put limits on the states' police power. In very general terms, the states' power to act to protect the health and welfare of state residents is limited by notions of reasonableness as defined by the judicial branch of government when it applies the Fourteenth Amendment.

The federal government's authority to act to regulate business conduct and form comes primarily from the commerce clause of the U.S. Constitution. Generally, when the commercial activity involved may affect interstate commerce, Congress may act. But Congress need not act to regulate all such commercial activity.

Finally, the division of authority to regulate commercial conduct between the state and federal governments is always changing. Therefore, generalizations about the proper balance of such authority is difficult. Moreover, issues of federalism are subject to never-ending debate by policymakers. Can the state or federal government do a better job? This and related questions will be addressed in the final part of this book.

Types of American Business Organizations

Americans are a people who pride themselves on their freedom, their ability to invent and innovate, and their independence from perceived, older European ideologies. What this means for students who study American business organizations is that because of our notions of freedom and our ability to innovate, there are numerous forms of business enterprise. Moreover, because of our apparent lack of ideology or our lack of a strong belief about the way things should be, the legal system does not provide a comprehensive or integrated legal theory about business organizations. The law in this area is, generally, almost ad hoc; and the only safe generalization is that the law with regard to business organization forms is established in response to what the most creative entrepreneurs can dream up. Over time, however, business circumstances have created law and legal theory, and the latter has in turn affected the business circumstances. In a kind of alternating process, a particular business circumstance dealt with by a creative entrepreneur in a particular way can result in either case law or legislation. The case law or legislation will then be applied to a newer and slightly different business circumstance with the result that both the law and the business organization may change slightly.

Another safe generalization is that as our society becomes more complex, the number, type, and functions of organizations increase dramatically. One of the major social phenomena of the twentieth century has been and continues to be the "organizational revolution."[5] Several characteristics of this revolution are noteworthy for our purposes.

The first has already been stated. Compare the number of organizations that the average American belongs to today with the number the average American belonged to 50 years ago and you will notice a dramatic increase. A dominant feature of our life today is the sheer *number* of existing business organizations, associated labor and professional groups, social, fraternal, and sports organizations, spiritual organizations, and, finally, governmental groups and related sub-groups such as political parties and interest groups.

A second characteristic is an apparent shift in the functions among organizations. The family unit as a form of social organization has decreased in importance with regard to providing economic production, education, and spiritual or moral guidance. Economic production is now accomplished by business organizations, and the latter functions are being performed increasingly by public and private schools and various spiritual groups and churches.

Another characteristic of this revolution is the broadening of the base of participation in these organizations. In comparison with the organizations prevalent in the nineteenth century—family, established and traditional churches, and large, family-owned business enterprises—today's organizations are relatively easy to belong to. The ability to buy shares of stock in almost all large business corporations and to join numerous types of social and sporting clubs (although people are not completely free to join, they are at least more so than they were in the nineteenth century) attest to this characteristic.

A related characteristic is the ability to renounce allegiance or membership in one organization for another. Today many people will work for two, three, or four business enterprises during their working career. They may change home addresses the same number of times or more, necessitating a change in social and religious organizations. On a more political level, it seems that it is becoming fashionable for state and national politicians to switch political parties between elections.[6]

A final characteristic, and the one of most importance for our study of business organizations, is the increase in size and consequent economic, political, and social power of the largest American business corporations. The definition of what a "large" corporation is will be developed in a later chapter; for now, let us note that in 1970 there were 1.7 million corporations, and those companies belonging to the New York Stock Exchange (NYSE) represented less than 0.1% of this number.[7] Yet in 1970, those NYSE companies accounted for 94.3% of the total net income (after taxes) of all United States corporations.[8] According to *Forbes* magazine, the total 1980 sales of the 200 largest American business corporations was 64.13% of our gross national product, and those 200 firms earned 90.25% of all 1980 corporate profits.[9] Thus, today our largest business corporations resemble in size and strength, to the extent we can measure those things, some of our largest states and some of the world's oldest, and by no means smallest, countries. For example, in 1971, the combined GNP of Austria, Denmark, Finland, Greece, Ireland, Norway, Portugal, and Turkey was $97.35 billion. This was less for the same year than the total of $136 billion in sales of the *ten* largest NYSE corporations.[10]

The presence of these massive economic concentrations of power is a relatively new phenomenon for our society, and may be a major cause of much of the debate today that focuses on the "government regulation" of business. Because of our lack of ideology, or perhaps the presence of one that is essentially laissez faire,[11] *we do not have widely accepted ideas or shared beliefs about the precise role of government with respect to these large corporations.* Moreover, to the extent that we have any legal theory applicable to these large institutions it may be either inadequate or inappropriate. For example, the law treats corporations as legal individuals. So, for the purposes of the application of the Bill of Rights of the U.S. Constitution to corporations, the law assumes there is little difference between humans and corporations; they are alike in many if not most respects. This assumption and the legal traditions based on it are being questioned today. In short, is General Motors or IBM like a human? Should it have the same rights and duties as an individual? These and related questions will be explored in the chapters on corporation law.

In summary, the reality of the organizational revolution plus our

American traditions of freedom and a spirit of innovation and our apparent lack of ideology may make the study of the types of business organizations seem to be fragmented and piecemeal. Americans have very few transcendent legal principles. To the extent that we do (such as the principle that business organizations that are separate legal entities are treated in law as analogous to humans), they may not be accurate. But law reflects life, and commercial life especially. Thus, the study of the law of business organizations has value for us. Through the study of American business organizations, we learn about our American commercial life.

There are three distinctive types of business organizations with many variations and even combinations: the proprietorship, the partnership, and the corporation. These three fundamental types are compared in Figure 2-4 at the end of this chapter. Before we begin our discussion of these three types, however, we must explain the place of agency law in the general scheme of business organizations and introduce some of the basic legal principles of unincorporated organizations or clubs.

Agency

An agency form of organization exists whenever one person voluntarily consents to act on behalf of another or under another's control. It is by far the most pervasive form of voluntary organization[12] and may exist for profit or nonprofit purposes. A student who leaves a dorm party to buy another keg of beer for the guests is an agent for the group sponsoring the party. When a properly authorized employee of IBM signs a contract to lease a computer to a customer, the employee is an agent. And, when an authorized representative of the federal government signs a contract to purchase a ship for the U.S. Navy, the representative is an agent. Agency law applies to all of the types of business organizations and creates essentially two categories of legal duties. The first is that together with the law creating the business organization, it defines the duties between the employer or principal and the employee or agent. More precise definitions of employer, employee, principal, and agent will be given later. The second category of duties created by agency law defines the legal relationship between the business organization, the employer or principal, and some person neither a member of the organization nor associated with the employer or principal. The outside party is called a "third party." The agent transacting business with the third party on behalf of the principal creates legal duties. Agency law may be depicted as shown in Figure 2-1.

Although agency law is applicable to all kinds of business organizations, it is itself a form of organization when just one other person directs or controls the activities of another. The key feature of such an agency organization is that an act, and a benefit or detriment from the act, is intended to be visited on the person in control while the other party (the

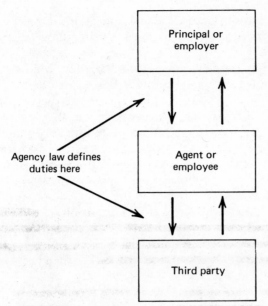

**FIGURE 2-1 Other duties may be defined
by the laws creating the form of business
organization such as corporation or
partnership law.**

one acting) is a mere instrument.[13] Most of the legal duties defined by
agency law will be explained in the following four chapters.

Unincorporated Organizations, Clubs, and Other Informal Forms of Organization

There are numerous fraternal orders (the Lions Club, the Daughters of
the American Revolution, the Rotary Club, etc.), benefit societies, religious groups, labor organizations, professional societies and other societies, syndicates, leagues, foundations, and clubs that may all engage in
commercial activity for profit. These forms of organization may not have
been created solely to make a profit, but are free to do so if such activity is
consistent with their purpose. If these organizations want to be treated as
tax-exempt, they must be committed to educational, charitable, or religious purposes and must seek tax-exempt status from the Internal Revenue Code by applying to the Internal Revenue Service (IRS). The IRS
imposes some conditions on the ability of these groups to earn a profit, but
so long as these conditions are not violated, some profit may be earned.

These forms of organization range in size and complexity from a
card-playing social group that may want to sponsor a fundraiser to assist a
retiring high school coach, to an international organization like the Rotary

Club. Generalizations about such organizations are necessarily difficult, but the following legal principles are the dominant ones.

The Organization as a Separate Legal Entity.   An unincorporated organization of people or a club has no legal existence except that which may be provided for by state statute. That is, for these types of organizations there is no common law existence apart from that of the members. If a state statute recognizes the existence of an unincorporated entity, then it has a separate organizational entity (separate from the members) and may own property, contract, sue, and be sued in its own name.

Liability of the Members.   In our American civil law there are two broad categories of legal duties and thus legal liability. Contract law creates duties and liabilities that result from an expressed or implied exchange of promises; tort law creates duties and liabilities when someone damages another's person, reputation, or property. We shall first examine the contract liability of the members.

If an unincorporated organization is recognized by state statute and if a contract is signed by an agent of the organization in the name of the organization, then the organization is primarily liable and anyone damaged by a breach of the contract should sue the organization in its name. This would be desirable from the plaintiff's point of view if the organization owned a lot of assets. However, since no limited liability feature applies to these organizations (discussed in regard to corporations, below), a person suing an organization in its name would probably also join all of the members in the original suit and, if the contract were authorized in the first place, they would all be liable for the resulting damage. Stated simply, all of the members of the organization could be liable for a breach of contract whether they knew of the contract or whether they intended it, so long as the contract was authorized. If the contract was not authorized (the issue of "authorization" will be discussed in Chapter 4), only the person signing the contract would be liable.

The presence of a state statute creating a separate organizational entity is really of little significance with regard to contract liability because in most jurisdictions the civil procedural laws allow both the organizational entity and the members to be sued. For example, assume that an amateur baseball team had $500 in assets that had some market value, such as uniforms, balls, and bats, and they wished to purchase new shirts. An authorized member signed a contract in the name of the team, and then the members decided to breach the contract. The team would be liable for the damages caused by the breach. A judgment against the team would be satisfied by selling the assets and paying what the court ordered.

What if the damages were in excess of $500? (Assume the shirts were made out of very expensive fabric with sequins sewn on them and the seller could not get rid of them after the breach.) Most jurisdictions would allow the injured plaintiff to join the other members of the team in the suit, who would then have to pay (probably dividing the judgment) for any portion of the judgment not satisfied by selling the assets. The liability of the members in cases like this is usually *joint and several*. This, a term of legal significance, means that one of the members may have to pay the entire judgment if the other members and the organization have no assets. Theoretically, then, the liability on a contract made on behalf of an unincorporated association is primarily that of the organization. But if the organization is unable to pay a judgment, the members may have to pay, and if any of them is unable to pay, the others who are solvent must pay. After the judgment has been paid to the plaintiff, the members who had to pay may seek recovery from the members who did not pay so that all share equally in the end.

With regard to tort liability, courts often first inquire into the purpose of the event out of which the damages arose. If the purpose of the event was to make a profit, some courts would treat the organization as a partnership and hold all of the members liable for the tort of just one of the members so long as the tort was done within the scope of (during the process of benefiting) the organizational purpose. If the event was not to make a profit, courts usually hold those members liable who committed the tort or who participated in it or those who were somehow responsible for setting the events in motion. The existence of a separate organizational entity does not seem to affect the outcome in this instance either.

The real impact of a statutorily created separate organizational entity is more important in shielding the assets of the organization from a member's creditors than it is in shielding a member's assets from the organization's creditors. That is, if a state statute says that any unincorporated association may own property and sue or be sued in its own behalf, a separate legal entity has been created. Say that ten friends form a canoeing club and set out to buy five special, light canoes. They each put in $500, and the canoes are bought for $2500 and owned by the club. The club now has an independent worth of $2500. If one of the members of the club is negligent while driving a car (on a trip unrelated to the club), injuring X, and X recovers a judgment for $200,000 from the member, then this judgment must be paid by the member. X cannot get at the club's $2500. However, if one of the members was negligent and injured Y while on an authorized club canoeing trip, then Y could sue the club for the full value of the injury and, if it exceeded $2500, could sue (in the same suit) the negligent member and those other members who participated in the tort. This is what we mean by saying that a statutorily created separate organizational entity is more important in shielding the assets of the organization from members' creditors than it is in shielding the members' assets from the organization's creditors.

The following case illustrates some of the legal principles just discussed.

LYONS v. AMERICAN LEGION POST NO. 650
172 Ohio St. 331; 175 N.E. 2nd 733,
(S.Ct., Ohio, 1961)

(Authors' note: William A. Lyons attended a fish fry conducted by the defendant and was injured and later died as a result of the alleged negligence of the defendant and its agents in maintaining a defective gas heater owned or leased by the defendant. Also sued as defendants were 81 members of the defendant association. The plaintiff is the administratrix of the estate of the deceased, Martha A. Lyons. The trial court and the first appellate court held that the existence of the state statute in question abolished the right to sue the members.)

ZIMMERMAN, Judge

In the cases of *Koogler et al., Trustees* v. *Koogler,* . . . 186 N.E. 725; . . . it was either indicated or held that, since a voluntary unincorporated association had no status as a legal entity, an action against it as such would not lie, and that ordinarily any action had to be brought against the individual members of such an association collectively and conjointly.

Or stating it in another way, "In the absence of an enabling statute, a voluntary association cannot be sued by its association name. It has no legal existence, and the persons composing it must be joined individually." . . . .

Then effective on September 30, 1955, the General Assembly enacted legislation which is now Sections 1745.01 through 1745.04, Revised Code. Section 1745.01 provides:

> Any unincorporated association may contract or sue in behalf of those who are members and, in its own behalf, be sued as an entity under the name by which it is commonly known and called.

Section 1745.02 reads:

> All assets, property, funds and any right or interest, at law or in equity, of such unincor-

porated association shall be subject to judgment, execution and other process. A money judgment against such unincorporated association shall be enforced only against the association as an entity and shall not be enforceable against the property of an individual member of such association. . . .

. . . Ordinarily, it is for the Legislature to determine who may sue or be sued so long as it does not interfere with vested rights, deny any remedy or transgress constitutional inhibitions. As a general rule, every state has control over the remedies it offers litigants in its courts. It may give a new and additional remedy as to a right or equity already in existence and it may abolish old remedies and substitute new. . . .

. . .

In the early case of *Darling* v. *Peck,* . . . the following statement appears:

> Where a statute gives a new remedy without impairing or denying one already known to the law, the rule is, to consider it as cumulative, allowing either the new or the old remedy to be pursued at the option of the party seeking redress. . . .

Is it the purpose and intent of the statutes quoted and referred to above to limit actions solely against unincorporated associations as entities in the names they commonly use, as determined by the two lower courts herein, or may the individual members of such associations still be sued as under the former practice? We think the new statutes are no more than cumulative and do not abrogate the right to sue the members of the associations if the suitor chooses to proceed in that way. It is to be noted that Section 1745.01, Revised Code, uses the permissive word, "may," and that, under Section 1745.02, Revised Code, when a suitor does take advantage of the enabling statutes by suing an unincorporated association by the name it uses, the collection of any judgment obtained against such association must be satisfied out of its property alone and the property of its members is immune from seizure. Surely, had the General Assembly intended to eliminate actions against the individuals composing an unincorporated association, it would have so expressed itself.

. . .

However, a recognized difference exists between an unincorporated association organized for the transaction of business and one organized for fraternal or social purposes. This is illustrated in *Azziolina* v. *Order of Sons of Italy, Conte Luigi Cadorna,* . . . 179 A. 201, 204, where it is stated in the opinion:

In the case of a voluntary association formed for the purpose of engaging in business and making profits, its members are liable, as partners, to third persons upon contracts which are within its scope and are entered into with actual or apparent authority, and a joint judgment against them is justified. . . . But when, as here, the purpose of the association is not business or profit, the liability, if any, of its members is not in its nature that of partners but that arising out of the relation of principal and agent, and only those members who authorize or subsequently ratify an obligation are liable on account of it.

The same principle is recognized in relation to torts. In *Thomas, Potentate* v. *Dunne,* . . . 279 P.2d 427, 432, the following language is found in the course of the opinion:

We cannot subscribe to the proposition that one who becomes a member of an unincorporated association such as a fraternal organization, a veterans organization or any one of numerous other societies which might be mentioned, subjects himself to liability for injuries sustained in ceremonies held under the auspices of that organization, in the absence of any allegation in the complaint against him that he took an active part in the act resulting in the injury or in some manner had knowledge of the proposed initiation rites or "stunts" to be employed and gave assent or encouragement to the use thereof.

. . . In the instant case the petition alleges that the defendants, "American Legion Post No. 650 . . . and the individual members of American Legion Post No. 650 . . . conducted or caused to be conducted within said building a social affair known as a fish fry for which they charged each person attending the sum of one dollar ($1.00)," and that "defendants, and each of them, were negligent in failing to provide a safe heating system in the building; in equipping and maintaining the building with a defective heating system; in failing to provide proper ventilation in the building; and in failing to warn invitees in the building, including decedent, of the presence of carbon monoxide fumes therein."

Such petition . . . states causes of action good as against demurrer . . . but on the trial of the action to establish liability on the part of individual defendants evidence would have to be produced linking them as active participants in the affair resulting in plaintiff's decedent's alleged injuries, and, furthermore, that they knew or in the exercise of ordinary care should have known of the defective condition of the instrumentality claimed to have caused the injury. And, of course, the other elements necessary to support recovery would have to be proved.

The judgment of the Court of Appeals is reversed, and the cause is remanded to the trial court for further proceedings.

Judgment reversed.

Case Questions

1. If a judgment were recovered against the American Legion Post No. 650 as the sole defendant, could the property of the president of the post be taken to satisfy the judgment?
2. Under what circumstances could the property of the president of the post be taken to satisfy the judgment?
3. Why would an injured plaintiff want to sue an unincorporated association as a separate entity?
4. What is the difference between the liability of a member of an unincorporated association organized for business and the liability of a member of an unincorporated association organized for social purposes?

Case Comment

In this case one may say that the opinion is not clearly written. We are not told the holding of the trial court nor the holding of the Ohio Court of Appeals. Further, the facts of the case appear at the end of the opinion, not the beginning. There is no required pattern that an appellate opinion must follow.

Proprietorships

In the mid-1970s, there were about 14.7 million business organizations that could be classified as proprietorships, partnerships, or corporations. Although proprietorships far outnumber the other forms of business organization, they earn a fraction of the total receipts of corporations.

In our explanation and analysis of these forms of organization, we wish to focus on three characteristics: control of the organization, liability of the owners of the organization for business-related debts, and the tax consequences of the organization.

A proprietorship is a business organization that is headed by one individual who owns all or most of the business property and who may hire employees to act as agents. In short, the proprietor controls the entire organization. The advantage of this form is that it is the simplest; for this reason it is the most numerous. There are ten times as many proprietorships as partnerships and five times as many proprietorships as corporations. However, proprietorships account for only about one tenth of the volume of business of all corporations.

The business liability of the proprietor cannot be separated from his or her other types of personal liability. The business assets and liabilities of the proprietorship are one and the same with the proprietor's non-business or personal assets and liabilities.

One of the disadvantages of this form of organization is that the ability to raise capital is limited to the reputation and net worth of the proprietor. In some cases, especially when one is beginning a business, this may be a substantial limiting factor.

Since the business entity and the personal affairs of the proprietor

Item	Unit	1955	1960	1965	1970	1974	1975	1976	1977	1978, prel.
Number	1,000	9,046	11,172	11,416	12,001	13,902	13,979	14,536	14,741	(NA)
Receipts	Bil. dol.	781	1,095	1,469	2,082	3,557	3,685	4,170	4,699	(NA)
Net income (less deficit)	Bil. dol.	65	73	111	109	201	196	245	283	(NA)
Proprietorships, number	1,000	8,239	9,090	9,078	9,400	10,874	10,882	11,358	11,346	12,018
Business receipts	Bil. dol.	139	171	199	238	328	339	375	394	443
Net income (less deficit)	Bil. dol.	18	21	28	33	46	45	50	51	59
Partnerships, number	1,000	(NA)	941	914	936	1,062	1,073	1,096	1,153	1,234
Total receipts	Bil. dol.	(NA)	74	75	93	139	147	160	177	219
Net income (less deficit)	Bil. dol.	(NA)	8	10	10	9	8	10	13	14
Corporations, number	1,000	807	1,141	1,424	1,665	1,966	2,024	2,082	2,242	(NA)
Total receipts	Bil. dol.	642	849	1,195	1,751	3,090	3,199	3,635	4,128	(NA)
Net income (less deficit)	Bil. dol.	47	44	74	66	146	143	185	219	(NA)

Figures are estimates based on samples for all years for proprietorships and corporations, and beginning 1960 for partnerships.
(*Source*: Statistical Abstract of the United States, 1981, page 534; U.S. Department of Commerce, Bureau of the Census.)

FIGURE 2-2   Business enterprises: proprietorships, partnerships, and corporations—number of returns, receipts, and net income: 1955 to 1978.

are not separated, the proprietor files one income tax return with the state and federal governments. Business expenses are subtracted from business income and a tax paid on the balance (if income exceeds expenses). Of course, the proprietor will receive a salary or some form of income from the business; this is treated as a business expense to the business but as income to the individual.

The proprietorship as a form of organization suffers the same fate as the owner. It stops or is incapacitated (legally) if the proprietor dies or suffers incapacity.

Partnerships

A partnership is an organization of two or more persons to carry on as coowners a business for profit. Individuals form partnerships when they wish to *share* the management, profits, or ownership of an enterprise for profit. In some instances where these aspects of coownership are intended but the partnership form was not intended, courts will nevertheless impose the partnership form on individuals. This is discussed in greater detail in the chapters on partnerships.

Partnerships are created by the contractual understanding, expressed or implied, of the partners. The usual process involves the drafting of written "articles of partnership" agreed to by all partners. Although this is the usual method of creation, a partnership can be created without a written contract.

While there is some disagreement on whether partnerships are a separate legal entity apart from the owners, we believe the best view is that it is separate for some purposes. A partnership contracts in its own name; holds the title to assets in its own name; can be sued in its own name and files income tax returns in its name; and is treated as a separate entity by the bankruptcy statutes. The Uniform Partnership Act, the act governing the rights and duties of partners adopted by most states, does not expressly state that a partnership is a separate legal entity, but would have done so had the original chief draftsman, Dean James Barr Ames, lived to complete the drafting.[14]

A key distinction between a proprietorship and a partnership is that under usual circumstances every partner has an equal say in how the business is run. This shared control of the firm is accomplished without regard to how the profits are to be divided. For example, the partnership agreement may provide that A is to contribute 75% of the capital and receive 75% of the profits while B's share of both is 25%. But each will have an equal say in the management of the firm.

In a partnership, each partner may be liable for any and all debts of the partnership acting as a business entity. That is, for the purposes of paying off those who obtain a court judgment against the partnership, the owner-partner cannot separate his or her own individual assets from those of the partnership. The partner cannot "limit" liability for partnership obligations.

This is a chief distinction between corporations and partnerships; owners of the former are able to limit their liability. This means that judgment creditors of the corporation must be paid from the corporation's assets, not the owner's assets.

Another disadvantage of the partnership form as contrasted with the corporation is the limited life of a partnership; any time a partner dies, is incapacitated, or voluntarily leaves the partnership, the old partnership is dissolved. Any time a new partner joins, the old partnership is dissolved and a new partnership is created. Also, the ability and opportunities to raise capital are not as diverse as in a corporation, because in a partnership this ability rests solely on the financial resources of the partners.

The advantages of this form of organization are its simplicity in creation and the democratic methods it offers in operation, which allow, for example, one partner to contribute cash, one to contribute technical know-how, and another to contribute manual work, and then all three to share equally their profits and management of the partnership.

A partnership must file an income tax return each year, but this return is for informational purposes only. The real income or losses of the partnership are divided in accordance with the partnership agreement and are "passed through" to each individual partner's income tax return. The partnership earnings need not have been distributed to the partners; they may be retained in the partnership, but the partners pay income tax on these earnings whether they are distributed or not. An important distinction between the tax treatment of partnerships and that of corporations is that the income of partnerships is subject to only one tax. There is no double taxation of income, as we find when a corporation pays a tax on its income and then a shareholder pays a tax on the same earnings on receiving a dividend.

Another tax advantage of the partnership is that tax rates on individual partners tend to be less than corporate rates, and partnership losses can be applied against partners' other personal ordinary income. This may also result in a carryover and a return of a prior year's taxes.

Limited Partnerships.   There are several variations of the partnership form in use today. A limited partnership is a partnership formed by two or more persons, one of whom is a general partner and one is a limited partner, who have filed with the state as a limited partnership. The Uniform Limited Partnership Act, in force in most states, requires that such partnerships file a certificate with the state that reveals all essential obligations of the partners. The limited partnership is formed once the filing is complete or there is substantial compliance in good faith with the filing requirement.

The essential characteristic of a limited partnership is that the limited partner is not liable as a general partner unless he or she takes part in the control of the business. Thus, a limited partner may contribute cash to the partnership, and his or her liability will be limited to this amount; the limited partner is an investor rather than an active partner. At present, the limited partnership is popular as a form of organization for real estate investment groups and theatrical promotions.[15]

Joint Ventures.   A joint venture is another variation of the partnership, more narrow in function and duration than a partnership. The law of partnership applies to joint ventures. The primary purpose for this form of organization is to share the risks and profits of a *specific business* undertaking.

A few state courts have found difficulty with a corporation becoming a *general partner*. The reason for this is that statutes require corporations to be managed by a board of directors; if they joined a partnership, the corporate partner would be subject to additional management authority since every partner is controlled by a vote of a majority of the partners. However, the Uniform Partnership Act defines a corporation as a person, allowing it thus to be a partner; furthermore, many states allow corporations to be partners as a matter of corporate law. Almost all states allow corporations to be a joint venturer. Indeed, today many of the large corporations combine in joint ventures to explore for oil and to develop experimental products and manufacturing facilities.

Corporations

The corporate form of business organization has three fundamental characteristics that distinguish it from proprietorships and partnerships. The first is the way it is owned and managed. Corporations traditionally issue ownership shares in the form of common stock. The owners of this stock may vote individually or combine in numerous ways to elect a board of directors who *manage* the corporation for the shareholders. Thus, at least in the case of large corporations, practical control of the corporation is removed from the owners by a board of directors. Issues raised by the method of ownership and control of corporations will be more fully explored in later chapters. The point here is that control of the organizations is usually vested in a board of directors who, in some cases, delegate this control to management.

A second characteristic of the corporate form is that it may have perpetual life. It is not dissolved on the death of the owner as are proprietorships and partnerships. This result follows from the notion that a corporation is a separate legal entity with a life of its own established by the articles of incorporation filed with the secretary of state pursuant to a general incorporation statute. Also, the owners may choose to sell or transfer their ownership freely without altering the corporate form if there is a market for the ownership shares. So, besides perpetual life, there is a measure of flexibility in the transfer of ownership not available in other forms of business organizations.

Perhaps the most important characteristic of the corporation is that it is considered to be a separate legal entity from the shareholders or owners. The corporation can own property, sue and be sued, contract to buy and sell, and be fined, all in its own name. Most importantly, however, the owners under most circumstances cannot be made to pay the debts of the corporation. That is, the liability of the owners is limited to the amount of money they have paid or promised to pay into the corporation. A few states, such as New York, make the shareholders liable for certain obligations to the employees; but the general rule is that the corporate form offers limited liability. Exceptions to this rule will be disclosed in the chapters on corporations.

One characteristic that most believe to be a disadvantage is the "double taxation" of the owners of the corporation. The corporation must pay federal income tax on its income. After income taxes are paid, some of the earnings may be distributed to the shareholders in the form of dividends, which are again taxed by the federal government as income to the shareholders. Thus, a shareholder suffers taxation twice on accretions to an initial single investment. This is not true for proprietorships and partnerships. A partnership is required to file a separate federal income tax return but usually it is for informational purposes only. The income tax is levied on the partners' distributive share of the partnership's income whether that income is received by the partners or remains in the partnership account. A sole proprietor includes all business income and deductions on his or her individual income tax return.

The disadvantage of double taxation is, in the case of large publicly held corporations, far outweighed by the advantages of shared control, limited liability, perpetual life, ease of transferability of ownership, and the ability to raise new capital by selling more stock. In the case of small corporations, those owned by one family or by a very few people, this disadvantage is minimized since the owners of these corporations are usually officers or employees of the corporation and may gain an indirect return for their investment by drawing salaries from the corporation. These amounts, which must be "reasonable," are deducted from corporate income as an expense and are paid out before determining taxable income to the corporation. The shareholder-employee, however, must pay income tax on this salary.

A final disadvantage of the corporate form is the expense of creation. Proprietorships cost very little to form; partnerships cost more because usually an attorney is paid to draw up the contractual understanding of the parties. Corporations cost the most because fees must be paid to the state (the amount varies according to the number of shares authorized) and also to an attorney to help form the corporation. The attorney usually buys a corporate minute book and arranges for the printing of stock certificates and the purchase of a seal. At a minimum, it costs $400 to $600 to form a corporation.

There are numerous variations of the corporate form, all offering the same advantages of a completely separate entity: limited liability for the owners, perpetual life, and the advantages that flow from the share ownership. Some of the more widely used variations are explained in the following pages.

Subchapter S Corporations.   One method of minimizing the disadvantages of double taxation of the corporate form as well as securing other tax advantages is provided by Subchapter S of the Internal Revenue Code (Sections 1371–1379). The code allows corporations with 35 or fewer shareholders who are individuals or estates (not partnerships or corporations) with one class of stock plus other requirements to qualify under "Subchapter S" for special tax treatment. This special status allows the *shareholders* to treat the income or loss of such a corporation as their personal income or loss. Owners of a Subchapter S corporation may, for example, offset their share of corporate losses against their personal income resulting in less individual tax liability. If a corporation elects to file under Subchapter S, the tax treatment of the corporation income and loss is very similar to that of a partnership.

As of 1983 the Subchapter S corporation is designated by new IRS rules as just an "S" corporation, and the amount of loss that may be deducted is limited to the amount of money put into the corporation plus any loans that have been made to the corporation.

Section 1244 of the Internal Revenue Code offers further tax advantages to *small* corporations that qualify. Generally, it provides that a qualifying corporation may issue stock pursuant to a plan meeting the requirements of Section 1244, and that any loss sustained by an individual shareholder on the sale of this stock will be treated as an ordinary loss of the individual and can be deducted from the shareholders ordinary income up to a maximum amount of $25,000.

Thus, Subchapter S and Section 1244 could permit, for instance, a doctor with an individual income of $75,000 per year to buy a small cattle ranch and incorporate it. The ranch would be the chief asset of the S corporation. By paying ranch hands salaries that just equalled the ranch income and by taking depreciation on buildings at the ranch, it could be run at a paper loss of say, $5,000 per year, which could be transferred through the corporation to the doctor (presumably the sole or chief shareholder) and deducted by him from his income, resulting in a $5,000 deduction from his salary before he arrived at his taxable income. This would result in a reduction of his cost basis on the buildings but would still result in a substantial present tax savings. Also, if he should sell his corporate ownership shares at a loss, he may offset as much as $25,000 from his individual income.

Do not confuse the privilege of offsetting Subchapter S corporate losses against one's individual income with limited liability. Subchapter S corporations still offer limited liability in that the shareholders cannot be made to pay out-of-pocket for corporate debts. What they are offered is the privilege of offsetting losses against their income to reduce their tax liability. They pay nothing; they receive, in essence, a credit that is a substantial benefit to them.

Public Versus Private Corporations.   The corporate form may be used to conduct any activity, unless prohibited from doing so by law. We are accustomed to the fact that *private* corporations may pursue many objectives, however, *public* corporations are often overlooked. These corporations are created primarily for purposes connected with the administration of government. Municipalities, school districts, and townships are a few examples of "municipal corporations," the name given to these public corporations. The ownership of municipal corporations is vested by state statute in the sovereign (the state), and their management is subject to a charter issued by the state. These public corporations are beyond the scope of this book.

Private corporations may be divided into those that are operated for a profit and those that are not for profit. The former, probably the most familiar to you, are the subject of the last half of this book. Corporations not for profit are created by state statutes that are separate from those governing corporations for profit and provide, generally, that organizations for religious, charitable, or educational purposes shall be issued a corporate charter on complying with several filing requirements. Thus, churches, private hospitals, private schools and universities, and philanthropic organizations may all enjoy corporate status.

Developing a classification system for private corporations for profit is beyond the scope of this book, but two types of such corporations should be mentioned. Holding companies are corporations chartered primarily for the purpose of owning the shares of other companies. Today these companies own and control a substantial number of our large manufacturing companies.

Another type of private corporation that is somewhat similar in objective is the conglomerate corporation. Although frequently the conglomerate takes the name of an established manufacturing corporation the object is to diversify the original company into both related and unrelated markets. The conglomerate owns numerous other corporations.

Restrictions on the Use of the Corporate Form.   As discussed before, a chief advantage of the corporate form is the concept of the limited liability of the owners of the corporation. Limited liability is a legal privilege for the owners bestowed by the state; this privilege may be withheld in the exercise of the state's police powers. Until recently those offering a professional service such as doctors, lawyers, dentists, and optometrists were forbidden by many states from incorporating. It was believed inappropriate for one offering a professional service to be able to separate personal assets from business assets when being sued for the negligent performance of the service offered. Patients or clients relied on the personal skill and judgment of the professional in the rendering of the service, and thus the professional should not be able to shield his or her personal assets from the risks of the profession. Another reason for denying such a professional the use of the corporate form was that it would not be appropriate for this individual to subject his or her actions and judgment to the discretion of a board of directors who, by state law, manage the business of corporations.

However, within the last decade many states have passed special statutes allowing the formation of professional corporations. This special legislation was in response to the pressure of these professionals to allow members of the profession to share in some of the special tax benefits offered by the corporate form. Although the owners of the professional corporation are subject to double taxation if they pay themselves dividends, the tax advantages for their retirement plans and insurance programs are considerable, and more than offset the double taxation disadvantage. For example, if the professional were a partner and the partnership decided to use some of its income to pay into a retirement plan or pay for insurance premiums on the life of a partner, then these payments (premiums) would be taxed as income to the partner in the year in which they were made. However, if the professional were an employee of a corporation, the corporation could make contributions to the retirement plan or insurance program of the employee which would, first, be deducted by the corporation as a business expense, and, second, would not be taxed to the owner as income when the payments to the plan were made. The owner would, of course, pay income tax on the benefits of the plan when they were distributed. These retirement plans and insurance programs, generally, allow the professional to simply postpone taxation on a portion of his or her income. At the peak income years it would be advantageous to be able to postpone some of the income to the waning years and thereby suffer less of a current tax liability. This is the central advantage of the professional corporation.

The Internal Revenue Service has argued that for the professional corporation to be taxed as a regular for-profit corporation the professional's potential liability to third parties can be no greater than that of a shareholder in a regular for-profit corporation. This view has not prevailed, however, since most state laws on professional corporations do not allow professionals to limit their personal liability for their own tortious acts or the acts of associates.[16] Thus, a professional's potential liability to third parties is much greater than that of a shareholder in a regular, for-profit corporation, yet the courts are still allowing the professionals to enjoy the tax benefits just described. In short, many states have allowed the creation of a hybrid form of corporation that permits professionals to incorporate for tax purposes but not for the purpose of limiting personal liability.

Cooperatives

A form of organization that combines the democratic management aspects of a partnership with some of the advantages of a corporation is the cooperative. Cooperatives are being popularized today at both ends of the economic spectrum. Large land developers are concentrating much of their resources into the construction of cooperative apartment buildings (and the related legal form, the condominium) and smaller organizations are forming food and consumer cooperatives. These enterprises have at least two things in common that cause them to be classified as cooperatives. First, they are organized primarily to provide the members (not the public) with an economic benefit or service and, second, each member, usually an individual, has one vote in the management of the enterprise thus resulting in substantial equality of ownership.

In addition to these two general characteristics, it should be emphasized that while a cooperative may make a profit, such is not its primary purpose. The members usually expect no monetary return for putting their money into a cooperative. What they expect is to enjoy whatever nonmonetary, but economically useful, benefits the organization provides. The emphasis on *economically useful* benefits for members distinguishes the cooperative from charitable, religious, educational, or political organizations.

Generalizations about this form of organization (used for so many different tasks) should be attempted with caution, but it has been suggested that the following are some characteristics of a cooperative:[17]

1. Control and ownership is substantially equal.

2. Members are limited to those who avail themselves of the services furnished by the cooperative.

3. Transfer of membership is prohibited or limited.

4. Capital investment receives either no return or a limited return.

5. Economic benefits pass to members on a substantially equal basis.

6. Members are not personally liable for obligations of the organization unless they agree to such liability.

7. Death, bankruptcy, or withdrawal of one or more of the members does not terminate the organization.

8. Services of the organization are furnished primarily for the use of the members.

Cooperatives are not a new form of organization. Rural communities have been served by cooperatives since the early 1900s with, first, the formation of marketing cooperatives to sell farmers' produce, and then the development of rural electrification cooperatives to furnish electricity.

Type of Organization	1965			1970			1979		
	Organi-zations	Mem-bers	Busi-ness	Organi-zations	Mem-bers	Busi-ness	Organi-zations	Mem-bers	Busi-ness
Credit unions	22,064	16,756	8,098	23,656	22,819	14,106	22,012	43,258	52,224
Electric power cooperatives	880	4,964	781	875	5,789	1,195	871	8,435	5,322
Rural telephone cooperatives	21	485	48	235	609	86	249	931	299
Independent prepaid and self-insured health plans	568	8,684	608	482	12,204	1,068	(NA)	29,107	9,353
Community consumer	45	3,400	216	40	4,691	445	(NA)	7,962	2,519
Labor and management	500	5,068	366	418	5,834	545	(NA)	18,457	5,810
Health professionals (both profit making and nonprofit plans)	19	(NA)	26	24	1,679	78	(NA)	2,688	1,024
Farmer cooperatives selling producer and consumer goods	6,763	(NA)	2,910	6,209	(NA)	3,871	5,212	(NA)	13,521
Petroleum products	2,773	(NA)	643	2,774	(NA)	862	3,062	(NA)	3,827
Meats and groceries	775	(NA)	60	717	(NA)	83	485	(NA)	184
Miscellaneous	4,800+	(NA)	356	4,800+	(NA)	527	4,500+	(NA)	1,665

Members in thousands; businesses in millions of dollars. Business refers to loans outstanding.
(*Source:* Statistical Abstract of the United States, 1981, page 554; U. S. Department of Commerce, Bureau of the Census.)

FIGURE 2-3   Consumer cooperatives and farmer cooperatives selling consumer goods, by type of organization: 1965 to 1979.

Cooperatives may be either incorporated or unincorporated organizations. With the exception of labor unions (which have generally remained unincorporated because they prefer no regulation from the state), most cooperatives do incorporate. Since the management of the cooperative is conducted by a vote of the members and not by a board of directors, the enterprise is not managed like the typical corporation. This difference in management is allowed in almost all states by the existence of special cooperative statutes that provide for the incorporation and operation of cooperatives.

The case below illustrates one set of circumstances in which individuals utilized the cooperative form of business organization to achieve their goals.

SCHOOL DISTRICT OF PHILADELPHIA v. *FRANKFORD GROCERY CO.*
376 Pa. 542; 103 A. 2d 738 (1954)

CHIDSEY, Justice

In this action . . . the School District of Philadelphia sought to recover the sum of $29,056.03 as additional tax due under a levy made in 1950 upon the gross receipts of the defendant for the calendar year 1949. . . . The defendant's gross receipts in 1949 amounted to $29,358,488.33 and it paid tax on $302,464.06 thereof, claiming that the balance of its gross receipts represented receipts from the distribution of commodities and services rendered as a purely cooperative association to its constituent members, and therefore not within the purview of the statute authorizing the tax. The case was heard by Judge Levinthal of the Common Pleas Court of Philadelphia sitting without a jury, and after a submission of briefs and oral argument to the court . . . , judgment was entered for the defendant. The School District appeals therefrom.

The history, structure and operation of the defendant are well summarized from the evidence. . . . The company originated in 1905 as the Frankford Retail Grocer Association, which name was changed to the present one in 1909. It was formed by a small group of fourteen or fifteen retailers to purchase goods in large quantities and eliminate wholesalers' profits because of chain store competition. The articles of incorporation stated that the purpose of the organization was to act as a purely cooperative enterprise of retail grocers. Every member stockholder in the corporation is obligated to buy sufficient capital stock to cover his average weekly purchases, and to deposit the stock with the company in escrow, and then to pay his bills weekly. This system eliminates credit losses. A member is not obligated to obtain all his supplies from the company. But ordinarily merchandise is distributed only to retail grocer members. Occasionally it is sold at cost to charities. In some instances a surplus of a commodity is sold on the open market in order to dispose of it. Each member receives only one weekly delivery. The company employs no salesmen and all orders are received by mail or in person on written order blanks. . . . The company provides advertising, accounting and promotion assistance to members. It operates schools to give instruction in the best methods of meat cutting and meat and produce merchandising. A construction department rebuilds stores for members, installs fixtures and display stands and equipment, and services refrigeration equipment. The company also purchases store equipment for members. It has established and promoted a

'Unity' brand name which it owns and which represents a valuable good will. . . .

Usually at the end of a fiscal year there is an excess of receipts over total costs. This fund is distributed to members in proportion to the withdrawals they have made, as a patronage dividend. . . . The company has some surplus, part of which is in the form of securities of a market value of $304,006.25. . . .

The Act of 1949 imposing the tax . . . defines "business" as follows: "Carrying on or exercising *for gain or profit* within a school district of the first class, any trade, business, including financial business as hereinafter defined, profession, vocation, or commercial activity, or making sales to persons within such school district of the first class." (Emphasis supplied.) . . .

We think it clear that business as contemplated by the Act means business for "gain or profit," that is, for (the) profit motive. . . .

The matter therefore reduces itself to the question whether the defendant in its cooperative functioning is carrying on a business for gain or profit, and therefore within the purview of the tax. We deem it important that it is incorporated under the Business Corporation Law. We are not concerned with the form but with the substance of its structure and operation in its cooperative activities. That it pays the tax on some of its activities does not prevent immunity from tax on its nonprofit activities, . . . to the same extent that a nonprofit corporation may be liable for the tax on some of its activities. . . .

We think there is a persuasive indication that the Legislature did not contemplate the inclusion of cooperatives in that double taxation would result. Each individual retail grocer member would not only pay, as he does, the tax on his gross receipts, but also on his intermediate purchasing methods. . . .

While it is true that the defendant conducts its operation as a corporation, which is the tendency of most cooperative associations today, it possesses all of the attributes of a purchasing cooperative. In their present form and mode of operation, purchasing cooperatives are of comparatively recent origin and, like all cooperatives, they are somewhat of a hybrid, partaking both of the nature of a corporation and of a partnership. But basically a purchasing cooperative acts as the joint agent of all its member principals in purchasing in bulk and distributing at costs the products sold by its members. That it also acts as such agent in supplying at cost equipment and services incidental to and in furtherance of the economic objectives of its principals, does not change its character. By means of this principle of unified action the merchants secure the advantages of quantity buying, eliminate wholesalers' profits and attain a position where they can compete on even terms with the giant grocery chains. Viewing the defendant as an enterprise separate and distinct from its members, it has what superficially resembles a profit, that is, an excess of receipts over cost of operation. Realistically, however, the apparent profit is due entirely to the fact that each cooperator has paid in more than enough to cover the cost of the products he obtains for himself. By reason of the contract between the organization and each cooperator, this money belongs to the latter. When a group of individuals enter into an agreement to pool their resources for a common purpose and state therein that their contributions to the extent not required for that purpose shall be repaid to them, it is hard to conceive how the contributions returned to them should be regarded as a gain or profit to the entity acting as their mutual agent. . . .

Conflicting views are expressed in the appellate courts of other States as to the tax status of cooperatives under the particular state statutes involved. Confining ourselves to the Pennsylvania statute here in question, we are of the opinion that the defendant in its cooperative functioning is not conducting an independent business separate and apart from its constituent members, and its receipts from them in payment for their withdrawal of merchandise purchased for their account, are not taxable. . . .

Judgment affirmed.

Case Questions   1. Why did the groceries choose the cooperative form of association?
2. Why do you suppose the Frankford Grocery was compelled to pay some taxes?

Case Comment   When competing businesses combine to form purchasing cooperatives there is a chance that the federal government through the Federal Trade Commission or the Justice Department might become interested. Can you guess why? Could Ford Motor Co. and General Motors form a purchasing cooperative? The federal antitrust laws and especially Section 1 of the Sherman Act prohibit conspiracies and combinations in restraint of trade. Generally, competitors are not permitted to "cooperate." However, the court mentions that the formation of the cooperative was to counter the competitive impact of large chain stores. So, one may conclude that the extent of cooperation allowed between competing enterprises depends on the reasons for the cooperation; that is, the competitiveness of the market, the size of the firms in the market, and the outcome or results of the cooperation are all weighed by the federal government before it takes action.

Franchises

A franchise is a popular business organization device that may exist as a corporation, partnership, or proprietorship. It is like a cooperative in that it is a form of organization that exists on top of an underlying corporate or partnership form.

Individuals who drive down the street in an automobile purchased from a General Motors dealer, fill their gasoline tank at the corner Texaco station, have lunch at McDonald's, work at a Pepsi-Cola bottling plant, live in a home purchased through a Century 21 real estate broker, and sleep in a Holiday Inn while vacationing have dealt extensively with franchises.

The franchisor develops a concept or product, the use of which is licensed to the franchisee. The franchisor protects that concept or product through the patent, copyright, or trademark law. The franchisee acquires the right to exploit the franchisor's idea by signing a franchise agreement. The franchisee is a legally separate entity from the franchisor. Each party is free to choose the form of business enterprise under which they wish to operate their respective entity. Most franchises are regulated by a Federal Trade Commission rule. The basic thrust of the rule is to require the franchisor to make full and fair disclosure concerning the terms of the franchising agreement. Violations of the rule may result in the imposition of fines or damage suits or both.

To protect their reputation, most franchisors exert tight control over the activities of their franchisees. A franchisor who spends substantial advertising dollars wants to insure that the public will recognize the franchise in both physical appearance and the quality of the products offered. Restrictions placed on the franchisee in this regard will raise antitrust problems unless it can be shown that the restrictions are reasonable and related to quality control. For example, the requirement that a franchisee of a fast food chicken outlet purchase its cooking equipment and supplies only from the franchisor is illegal. (See *Siegel* v. *Chicken Delight*, 448 F.2d 43 (1971).) It is not illegal for the franchisor to require the franchisee to purchase its supplies from either the franchisor or franchisor-approved suppliers, so long as the franchisor does not unreasonably withhold approval from outside suppliers. The following case shows how a franchisor can legally impose rather restrictive terms on a franchisee.

PRINCIPE v. McDONALD'S CORP.
631 F.2d 303 (1980)

(Authors' note: Under the franchise agreement McDonald's grants the franchisee the right to use McDonald's food preparation system and to sell food products under the McDonald's name. The franchisee pays a $12,500 franchisee fee and agrees to remit 3 percent of his or her gross sales as a royalty. The franchisee also leases the particular store premises from McDonald's. The franchisee deposits a refundable $15,000 security deposit and agrees to pay 8½ percent of the gross sales as rent. The franchisee is also responsible for building maintenance, improvements, property taxes, and other costs associated with the premises. The franchise agreement and the lease are of 20 years' duration. Principe unsuccessfully attacked the franchise agreement-lease arrangement as a violation of the antitrust laws. The plaintiff argued that the requirement that a franchisee agree to all of these arrangements to gain a franchisee constituted an illegal tying arrangement. That is, it was a restraint of trade to tie the franchise agreement and lease terms together.)

HARRY PHILLIPS, Senior Circuit Judge
Far from merely licensing franchisees to sell products under its trade name, a modern franchisor such as McDonald's offers its franchisees a complete method of doing business. It takes people from all walks of life, sends them to its management school, and teaches them a variety of skills ranging from hamburger grilling to financial planning. It installs them in stores whose market has been researched and whose location has been selected by experts to maximize sales potential. It inspects every facet of every store several times a year and consults with each franchisee about his operation's strengths and weaknesses. Its regime pervades all facets of the business, from the design of the menu board to the amount of catsup on the hamburgers, nothing is left to chance. This pervasive franchisor supervision and control benefits the franchisee

in turn. His business is identified with a network of stores whose very uniformity and predictability attracts customers. In short, the modern franchisee pays not only for the right to use a trademark but for the right to become a part of a system whose business methods virtually guarantee his success. It is often unrealistic to view a franchise agreement as little more than a trademark license.

Given the realities of modern franchising, we think the proper inquiry is not whether the allegedly tied products are associated in the public mind with the franchisor's trademark, but whether they are integral components of the business method being franchised. Where the challenged aggregation is an essential ingredient of the franchised system's formula for success, there is but a single product and no tie in exists as a matter of law.

Applying this standard to the present case, we hold the lease is not separable from the McDonald's franchise to which it pertains. McDonald's practice of developing a system of company owned restaurants operated by franchisees has substantial advantages, both for the company and for franchisees. It is part of what makes a McDonald's franchise uniquely attractive to franchisees.

First, because it approaches the problem of restaurant site selection systematically, McDonald's is able to obtain better sites than franchisees could select.

Second, McDonald's policy of owning all of its own restaurants assures that the stores remain part of the McDonald's system. McDonald's franchise arrangements are not static: franchisees retire or die; occasionally they do not live up to their franchise obligations and must be replaced.

Third, because McDonald's acquires the sites and builds the stores itself, it can select franchisees based on their management potential rather than their real estate expertise or wealth. Ability to emphasize management skills is important to McDonald's because it has built its reputation largely on the consistent quality of its operations rather than on the merits of its hamburgers. A store's quality is largely a function of its management.

Finally, because both McDonald's and the franchisee have a substantial financial stake in the success of the restaurant, their relationship becomes a sort of partnership that might be impossible under other circumstances. McDonald's spends close to half a million dollars on each new store it establishes. Each franchisee invests over $100,000 to make the store operational. Neither can afford to ignore the other's problems, complaints or ideas. . . . We decline to find that it is an illegal tie in.

Business Organizations Formed for Illegal Purposes

Agency relationships and partnerships are sometimes formed for purposes of accomplishing an illegal act. Property may be exchanged, money deposited into bank accounts, and some other apparent legal duties created. When a court is asked to apply the principles of law discussed herein to return the property or money or to enforce one of the apparent duties, it will probably dismiss the case leaving the parties without any legal remedy. Rather than acknowledging the existence of the illegal purpose, a court will back away from the matter leaving the parties where they stood before the suit.

In concluding this rather brief overview of American business organizations, we must again mention that any such presentation is far from complete. Attorneys, accountants, entrepreneurs and other creative business people are always creating new business organization forms or hybrids of the established ones to take advantage of new tax incentives or to share in the ever changing character of business risks.

Comprehensive discussions of the law of agency, partnerships and corporations are presented in the following chapters.

Case Comment

share profits + loss
somehow
key to
determination

1 owner

	Proprietorship	*Partnership*	*Corporation*
Legal basis	Common law	Express contract of owners consistent with UPA or contract implied in law by courts	State statute
Legal entity	Not separate from owner	Separate from owner for some purposes	Separate legal person
Owner's liability	Owner liable for all debts	General partner liable for all debts; limited partner liable for amounts contributed	Owners liable only to the extent of paid-in capital
Length of life	Same as owner	Agreed to by partners (usually life of any partner)	Perpetual
Management control	By owner directly	By majority vote of partners—owners manage	By vote of board of directors elected by owners—owners do not manage.
Capital	Limited to what the single owner can raise	Limited to what partners can raise—may necessitate a new partner, thus a new partnership	Sale of more ownership shares
Federal income taxes	Profits taxed to owner as individual	Profits taxed proportionately to each owner as agreed in contract, or all share equally	Profits of corporation taxed to corporation—owners pay income tax on dividends
Complexity of creation/operation	Simplest; no agreement with other individuals or filings with state required unless doing business under a name other than owner's name	Should have partnership agreement and must file partnership name if name is other than those of partners	Numerous filings required, and formalities of organization imposed by state statute must be followed

FIGURE 2-4 Comparative legal aspects of most often used business organizations.

1. We have listed more terms below that will be used repeatedly throughout the text. You should be able to recall and write down the definition of each term. If you believe the text discussion of the term is inadequate, refer to the glossary or to *Black's Law Dictionary*, 4th ed.

federalism
state police power
substantive and procedural
   due process
interstate commerce
trademark/trade name
federal law versus state
   law
agency
proprietorship
partnership
judgment creditor

limited partnership
corporation
limited liability
double taxation
Subchapter S corporation
Section 1244 stock
public versus private corporations
municipal corporation
cooperative organization
unincorporated organization
joint venture

2. In a few short sentences explain federalism.

3. When state governments regulate the business conduct of residents, they rely on the authority created by the police power of sovereign governments. What is meant by the "police power" of the states?

4. Is the police power of the states unlimited? What are the limits, if any, on the use of the police power? That is, may a state government regulate whatever it wants in whatever manner it deems appropriate?

5. The Maryland state legislature passed a statute that forbids corporations from engaging in the practice, business, or profession of funeral directing and undertaking. Another statute also provided that individuals could practice this commercial activity and that such individuals must obtain a license from the State Board of Funeral Directors and Embalmers. Brooks wishes to form a corporation to practice undertaking and embalming. He forms a corporation to do so, and the board not only refuses a license to the corporation but suspends Brooks's license. He challenges the state statute forbidding corporations from engaging in undertaking and embalming by arguing that it is unconstitutional.

    (a) Briefly state Brooks's argument.

    (b) If the state introduced evidence that undertaking and embalming almost always involved the handling of bodies that could easily develop various diseases (or diseases present before death), what relevance would this have to the issues in the case?

    (c) Decide the case brought by Brooks. See *Brooks* v. *State Board of Funeral Directors and Embalmers*, 195 A.2d 728 (1963).

6. The federal government can regulate commercial activity if the activity meets a certain condition. Describe in detail what this condition is.

7. Filburn owned and operated a small farm in Montgomery County, Ohio. He maintained a herd of dairy cattle, raised poultry, and sold both milk and eggs. He also grew a small acreage of winter wheat that he used to feed his animals, make flour for home consumption, and otherwise use for seed and related farm and home consumption. On some occasions he sold locally small quantities of his wheat. In 1938 Congress passed the Agricultural Adjustment Act which, as related to wheat, was intended to control the volume of wheat moving in interstate commerce. In July 1940, Filburn was given notice that under this act and its amendments he was to plant no more than 11.1 acres of wheat with a normal yield of 20.1 bushels an acre. Filburn planted 23 acres of wheat and harvested 239 bushels of wheat. Wickard, the Secretary of Agriculture, through his agents, notified Filburn that he would have to pay $117.11 as a fine for violating the Act. Filburn brings an action seeking to enjoin the application of the Act to him. What does he argue? Should he be successful? (*Wickard* v. *Filburn*, 317 U.S. 111 (1942).) *Filburn claims intrastate.*

8. A, B, and C were friends. They discovered that they could work well together and decided that on graduation from college they would continue to associate even though they would pursue separate career paths. They decided to promote their version of social good by helping certain self-help groups like the local food co-op or the local summer camp for disadvantaged youth by putting on fundraising events. For this they charged a nominal fee. Often they would have T-shirts made for a special event, advertise the event, stage the event, and then turn over the proceeds to the needy group. They called their group "Mutual Aid." In a few months time Mutual Aid had about $500 in assets—a typewriter, stationery, etc. A signs a contract with X, "A on behalf of Mutual Aid." Because of unanticipated events, they breach the contract.
   (a) Who can X sue? From whom can X recover damages?
   (b) Assume that B is negligent and injures Y in the staging of a performance for Mutual Aid. Who can Y sue and from whom can Y recover damages?

9. What are the characteristics of a Subchapter S corporation and under what circumstances would this form of business organization be used?

10. Assume that you and a friend wish to start a retail business selling discount merchandise, which would be ordered through catalogues available in your store. You would carry some inventory, but the main intent of the business would be to provide the customer with catalogue information and guidance in ordering, reasonable prices, and

delivery service. Besides a small store, you plan to lease warehouse space and either buy or lease a delivery truck. For the present time you do not plan to hire any employees because you and your friend can do all of the required work. You and your friend plan to furnish $2,500 each to the enterprise, and you are hoping to borrow another $2,500 from a bank. Assume you have decided to call your business the "Quality Discount Service." List the procedures for starting such a business. Which type of business organization would you choose and why?

Endnotes

1. M. Conant, *The Constitution and Capitalism,* pp. 7–8 (1974).
2. 16 *Am. Jur.* 2d § 360, p. 31, cases at fn. 66.
3. *Ibid.,* § 369, p. 46.
4. U.S. Department of Labor Manpower Administration, Manpower Research Monograph No. 11, 1969, as quoted in A.F. Conard, R.L. Knauss, and S. Siegel, *Enterprise Organization,* pp. 9–10 (1972).
5. See K.E. Boulding, *The Organizational Revolution,* pp. 3–15 (1953).
6. Some of this discussion was based on A.F. Conard, R.L. Knauss, and S. Siegel, *Enterprise Organization* (Agency, Oganizations, Employment, Licensing, Partnerships), pp. 1–4 (1972).
7. P.I. Blumberg, *The Megacorporation in American Society,* p. 16 (1975).
8. *Ibid.,* p. 17.
9. These figures were drawn from the May, 1981, issue of *Forbes* in which sales, profits, etc. for the largest 500 corporations are reported beginning at p. 215.
10. Blumberg, *supra,* p. 31.
11. The American presence or lack of ideology is explored in G.C. Lodge, *The New American Ideology* (1975).
12. Conard, *supra,* p. 4.
13. *Ibid.,* p. 5.
14. J. Crane and A. Bromberg, *Law of Partnerships,* p. 26 (1968).
15. Conard, *supra,* p. 336.
16. *Ibid.,* p. 122.
17. I. Packel, *The Organization and Operation of Cooperatives,* pp. 4–5 (1970).

Agency Law

The Mutual Legal Duties of Principal and Agent 3

Commercial activity is almost always conducted by agents of various kinds. These agents are usually individuals who are acting on behalf of other individuals, partnerships, corporations, governments, or other legal entities. The legal relationship created by an agent on behalf of a principal with a third party is defined by that body of rules referred to as agency law. Agency law is a large part of the total legal framework governing the employer-employee relationship. This law, created primarily by state judicial decisions, today remains one of the most important bodies of law still based almost entirely on the common law. Since the common law varies from state to state, studies of agency law can be very confusing. We have attempted to simplify the presentation of the most important agency rules by focusing on one widely recognized reference work, *The Restatement of Agency, 2nd,*[1] referred to hereafter as the *Restatement.* The *Restatement* was written by the legal practitioners, jurists, and scholars who comprise the American Law Institute (an organization founded in 1923 to promote the clarification and simplification of the law). Also, from time to time, we will cite material from a respected treatise on agency law by Harvard Professor Warren A. Seavey entitled, *Law of Agency.*[2] The writings of other legal scholars will also be used. You should remember that these rules do not have the force of legislative law or even of a court decision but represent a synthesis of what some legal scholars believe the law is or should be.

As we pointed out in the last chapter, agency law does not present a body of principles that define a business organization in the same sense that proprietorships, partnerships, and corporations are so defined. Neither federal or state statutes nor administrative agencies such as the Internal Revenue Service recognize agency law as creating a distinct form of business organization. In essence, agency law is just one component, although a major one, of all business organizations. For example, Section 9 of the Uniform Partnership Act provides that partners are agents of the partnership for performing partnership business. Similarly, the common law provides that all employees of a corporation who are authorized to contract with persons outside of the corporation are its agents. A knowl-

THE LAW OF EMPLOYMENT RELATIONSHIPS

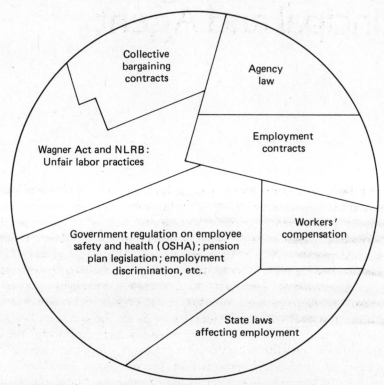

FIGURE 3-1 The law of employment relationships.

edge of agency law, then, is a logical necessity for understanding some aspects of American business organizations and most properly precedes the direct study of such organizations.

The advantages in using others (agents) to do one's work are numerous. They enable an individual or corporation or other legal person to extend his or her physical reach. One may safely negotiate a binding contract in Europe or Africa by sending an agent, properly authorized, to conduct the negotiating and contracting. Also, one's intellectual reach may be likewise extended by hiring experts or others specially trained to act for and at the direction of the employer.

Most of the legal disputes that are resolved by the application of agency law involve at least three parties and, thus, three potential pairs of legal duties.

Principal ⟷ Agent
Principal ⟷ Third party
Agent ⟷ Third party

A third party is just someone who is not part of the principal–agent relationship. Most often in the agency relationship, the agent is interacting with a third party on behalf of the principal. We may picture the various legal rights and duties like this:

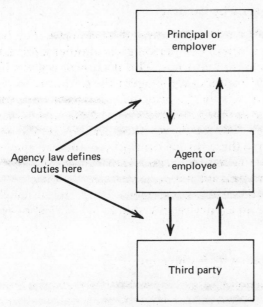

FIGURE 3-2   Other duties may be defined by the laws creating the form of business organization such as corporation or partnership law.

Although many of the agency law issues involve a third party, an essential portion of agency law involves only the principal and agent. For the sake of convenience we start by defining the agency relationship and then proceed to analyze the mutual legal duties of the principal and agent. The final portion of the chapter presents material on the rights and obligations of employers and employees, and, finally, the legal capacity of one to be an agent.

The *Restatement* (Section 1) defines an agency as follows:

Creation of the Agency Relationship

1. Agency is: The fiduciary relation which results from the manifestation of consent by one person to another that the other shall act on his behalf and subject to his control, and consent by the other so to act.
2. The one for whom action is to be taken is the principal.
3. The one who is to act is the agent.

In this instance perhaps Professor Seavey provides a clearer definition. He states: Agency is a consensual, fiduciary relation between two persons, created by law, by which one, the principal, has a right to control the conduct of the agent, and the agent has the power to affect the legal relations of the principal.[3]

Creation of Agency by Contract

Most agency relationships are created by contract. The best example of such a creation is where one person gives another a formal written document called a power of attorney. This document is given by the principal to the agent and confers on the agent the authority to perform certain specified kinds of acts for the principal. The primary purpose of a power of attorney is not so much to define the relationship between the principal and agent but to evidence the authority of the agent to third parties.

In addition to these formal contracts creating an agency relationship, there are a wide range of circumstances in which courts will create or impose an agency relationship to protect the reasonable expectations of a third party who has relied on the agent. These circumstances are referred to as creation of an agency relationship by *ratification, estoppel,* or *operation of law.*

Creation of Agency by Ratification

Ratification is action by a principal that affirms a prior unauthorized act by an agent, an act that did not bind the principal but that was done on his or her account.[4] This action of ratification by the principal then relates back to the unauthorized act so that the unauthorized act is then given effect as if originally authorized. For example, assume that Paul authorizes Angela to sell his car for him at an auction. Angela also takes along Paul's stereo, which she wrongly believes Paul would like to sell. Angela is not able to sell the car, but does sell the stereo for less than it is worth. Paul is disappointed when he learns of the sale, but accepts the money. Accepting the money is an act of ratification that relates back to the unauthorized sale and, for purposes of determining the liabilities of all of the parties, authorizes it. Technically, if Paul wanted to, he could refuse the money and sue Angela for the full fair value of the stereo. In most cases, Paul could not get the stereo back from the buyer if the buyer bought it without notice of the unauthorized sale.

Creation of Agency by Estoppel

Estoppel is a doctrine created by courts using their equity powers. As applied to agency law, it creates an agency relationship between a principal and agent when the principal intentionally or carelessly causes a third party to rely on representations by an agent that the agent is authorized to do a specific act.[5] Or, stated a little differently, if a principal allows another to act on his or her behalf and a third party changes position relying on the act and on the belief that the act is authorized, then the principal cannot deny the consequences of the action. The principal is *estopped* from denying the consequences of his or her action. One may be estopped because of a failure to act. For example, if Paul and Angela decide to go to an auction to sell Paul's stereo and if Paul is standing beside Angela when Angela tells Bob Buyer that she is authorized to sell it for $200, then the law places a duty on Paul to speak up. If Angela is unauthorized to say that, or if the sale price is $250, then Paul must tell Bob. If he does not tell Bob and Bob reasonably relies on Angela's representations, then Paul will be estopped from denying the agency relationship.

Creation of Agency by Operation of Law

In some circumstances, courts will create an agency relationship (when none was intended) to protect the reasonable expectations of the public. Courts have created an agency relationship between a husband and wife when they would not do so between strangers and when the husband and wife did not really intend it. These circumstances are examined at the end of this chapter.

The necessary elements of an agency relationship are *consent* by the principal that the agent act on the principal's behalf, a *voluntary act* by the agent for the benefit of the principal, and, usually, *reasonable reliance* on the agent's authority to act by a third party. The agent need not receive money for the action.

A good example of the circumstances that are needed for a court to create an agency relationship based on "operation of law" are found in the case of *Abresch* v. *Northwestern Bell Telephone Company*, 75 N.W. 2d 206, (1956). The plaintiff's business caught fire and he telephoned the operator at the phone company, requesting the operator to call the local fire department. Apparently the operator agreed to do this, but through negligence or some unexplained reason, failed to do so and the business burned down. The plaintiff alleged that the phone company's agent (the operator) agreed to do something and then failed to do it, so that the phone company (the principal) was liable. The phone company answered by arguing that there could be no agency relationship for the purpose of transmitting emergency messages because of a company rule that forbids employees to accept written and verbal communications from the public for transmission. Moreover, they argued, there was no business relationship between the plaintiff and the agent. All that existed was a gratuitous promise. The court held for the plaintiff and relied on a section of the *Restatement* (§ 378), which provides:

> One who, by a gratuitous promise or other conduct which he should realize will cause another reasonably to rely upon the performance of definite acts of service by him as the other's agent, causes the other to refrain from having

such acts done by other available means is subject to a duty to use care to perform such service. . . .

There are several lessons to be learned from this case. The first is that a court may create an agency relationship for a purpose not intended by the principal in order to provide a remedy to someone who reasonably relied on the agent. The second lesson is that the minimum circumstances that are needed for an agency relationship to be created are consent between the principal and agent (here there was no consent for the specific act in question but there was consent that the agent should act in other matters for the principal), an act by the agent, and reasonable reliance on that act by a third party.

Duties of the Agent to the Principal

Most of the duties of the agent to the principal are implied by describing the relationship between principal and agent as a fiduciary one. A fiduciary relationship is one that is vested with a special form of trust: A fiduciary is a person who acts as a trustee and who is required to display scrupulous good faith and candor toward the body of the trust.[6] In agency law, the agent is a fiduciary, and this imposes on the agent the following duties:

1. To act with the utmost loyalty for and on behalf of the principal.
2. To act with due care and diligence.
3. To render complete and accurate information to the principal.
4. To account for all receipts and profits.
5. To follow directions of the principal.

The fiduciary duties outlined apply to the agent only for acts conducted pursuant to the purpose of the agency. To determine if there has been a breach of the fiduciary duties the first step must usually be to determine the exact nature or scope of the agency relationship. This determination is made by inquiring about the authority of the agent, which is defined by a contract, if there is one; if there is no contract, then it is defined by the usual and normal authority of other agents in similar circumstances. The process of defining the authority or scope of agency is explained in greater detail in the following chapters. It is sufficient to say here that for an agent to be liable for a breach of a fiduciary duty, it must be found that the breach was within the ambit of employment. For example, an agent employed to buy personal property such as goods for a principal may compete with the principal for the purchase of real property (land) and not be liable.[7]

However, if an agent is instructed to buy designated property on a map provided by the principal, he may not even buy for himself property outside of that designated if it could reasonably be thought of as related to the purpose of the agency. The closer the competing opportunity taken by the agent is to the purpose of the agency, the greater the chance is that a court will hold that the agent must tender the opportunity to the principal before it is taken by the agent.

The following case illustrates a circumstance in which the agent obviously violated the special trust placed in him and therefore created liability for himself. Note carefully the arguments of the defendant and how the court reasons that what the agent took for himself really belonged to the principal.

NYE v. LOVELACE
228 F. 2d 599 (5th Cir., 1956)

(Authors' note: The express objective of the agency in this case was the procurement of mineral rights under land designated by the principal on a map of the area. One parcel of land, the Johnson tract, was entirely within the designated area. The Crosby parcel of 1,260 acres had 400 acres within the designated tract. One of the owners of the Crosby parcel, Hart, also owned the Gray parcel, no part of which was within the designated tract.)

BROWN, Circuit Judge

Appellant Nye, an Oklahoma oil investor, in the spring of 1951 made arrangements through his agent, Tom Gorton, with the appellee, Lovelace, to procure mineral interests in an area later known as the Pollard Field in Alabama. The last transaction was concluded August 16, 1951. Later on, perhaps inadvertently, Nye learned that Lovelace had purchased in his own name and held for his own account one-half of the minerals under 40 acres known as the Gray tract. . . .

The trial court held that [the Gray tract] was properly purchased by Lovelace for his own account since it lay outside the designated buying area, and its purchase was not necessary to the acquisition of interests within the area. And this, even though Gray was purchased from the same person (Hart) and simultaneously with the Crosby tract, one concededly within the agency. We cannot agree.

In the beginning Nye furnished to Gorton, and through him, to Lovelace a plat on which lines, following strictly the perpendiculars of sections, were traced outlining the area in which minerals were desired. Nye had confidential information as to the location of a test well (later dry) and the area, roughly 7 miles in width east and west and 1½ miles in depth north and south, ran generally northwest to southeast in stairstep fashion roughly paralleling the supposed location of a fault. Offsetting the well-site, in part, in the adjacent section was the Crosby tract, owned in equal one-third shares by James Hart and two other partners. . . .

The trial court placed great reliance on the fact that, since the Gray tract happened to be just outside of the lines on the plat, Nye had himself excluded it from the buying area even though he knew it was a physical, diagonal, offset to the well-site. The court recognized, however, that it could not automatically exclude from the agency all land outside of the designated buying area, since so much had been, and had to be, procured beyond it to acquire interests within it. In the trial court's view, the outside acreage was within the agency only when necessarily procured in a single transaction as a condition to acquiring acreage within the area. On this approach the court then held that these were two separate transactions, separately negotiated so that procurement of Gray was wholly unrelated to acquisition of the desired interest in Crosby. . . .

Disregarding Lovelace's subjective attitude whether this was one or two transactions and the factual conflict between Hart and Lovelace on whether the original trade was for 100 acres or something more or less, it is uncontradicted that so far as Hart was concerned, it was a common transaction, whether in one or two parts, or more, and under no circumstance would he have sold the Gray tract had not he been selling Crosby. While the trial court rejected, as Hart's conclusion, his insistence that it was one transaction, the court did not, could not, find that had Lovelace approached him solely to procure Gray, he would have made the trade for the equivalent of $180.00. Everything about the course of dealing between Lovelace and the owners of Crosby bespeaks the recognition by Lovelace that these people were not going to permit a purchaser to pick and choose the good and reject the bad. Requiring Lovelace to take 560 acres of Crosby outside the designated area to procure the interest in 400 within makes practically absolute Hart's assertion that Gray would not have been sold alone.

The trial court, we think, became so preoccupied with the notion that Hart did not require purchase of Gray as a condition precedent to delivery of Crosby, that the vital importance of Hart's unwillingness to sell Gray unless they bought Crosby completely escaped him. This meant that the opportunity to procure a valuable interest in Gray was due entirely to Lovelace's position as agent for Nye. It was not simply the case of an agent acquiring knowledge of an attractive opportunity through performance of the master's work. When the door was opened solely because of Lovelace's dealings for his principal—when the only way to exploit the collateral opportunity was to consummate concurrently the principal's transaction—he was under an obligation to tender the co-incidental benefits to his principal or at least advise him of his personal tentative interest in it. It is not for the agent to determine for the principal whether the fruits are, or are not, attractive or desired, nor is it open to the servant under his heavy obligation of high fidelity to analyze, in reverse, what must have been in his principal's mind at the time the general outline of the area was made, or to determine that, because the particular tract was separately owned under a title unrelated to the larger purchase, the principal would adhere to the strict artificial lines of the area instead of acquiring, as was otherwise frequently done, interests in the seller's outside acreage.

Here, an unfaithful servant, whose activities from the inception were in breach of his heavy duties, undertook, with circumstances strongly suggesting a studied furtiveness, to capitalize upon the information which had come to him under an obligation of trust, and in doing so, he sought to make decisions and resolve questions for his principal in which he stood to gain or lose as self-interest prevailed or was submerged. That which he has obtained by these means, he must restore.

As we think the total record is an overpowering portrayal of an agent unfaithful to his trust, the denial by the trial court of equitable relief to recapture the diverted fruits of his actions leaves us with the conviction that an injustice has been done and a mistake has been committed. . . . and the judgment, insofar as it concerns the Gray tract, must be reversed and rendered in favor of appellant, Clark C. Nye.

Reversed.

1. At issue in the *Nye* case was whether the scope of the agency should be limited to the property described in the map provided by the principal or whether it should be broader than the property so described. What did the court hold?

2. Would Lovelace be liable to the principal if he had purchased land a quarter of a mile away from that designated on the map and was unconnected from any parcel within the designated area?

3. Defining the ambit or scope of the agency may not always be easily accomplished. Often principals give general instructions to agents such as, "Sell my product in the Chicago area" or, "Manage my business." When this is how the relationship is defined, how would you go about discovering the intended scope of the agency?

Case Questions

Reconciling the Conflicting Interests of the Principal and the Agent

The case above is important because it reveals the first step in the method of analysis you must use to determine the duties of the agent. This step is to define, as clearly as possible, the real purpose and interest or the *scope* of the relationship. This scope may have physical boundaries as in the case above (the map outlining the agent's duties) or it may have limits established by working habits, trade practices, or traditions. Determining the scope of the relationship defines the powers the agent has to alter the legal relations between the principal and a third party[8] and also defines the limits of the agent's fiduciary responsibilities.[9]

Fiduciary Duties and the Nature of the Employment Relationship

In the study of agency law, a very important subject for study is the precise nature of the fiduciary relationship between the principal and agent. For purposes of this section of the chapter and a few to follow, we want to expand the focus of the material to cover the employer-employee relationship and the question of what duties the employee or agent owes to the employer or principal when that relationship appears to conflict.

From the perspective of the employee-agent, every person should have a legally protected interest in his or her own specially developed skills and talents. During the normal 40-year working life, an employee should be expected to develop an array of marketable skills. And the employee should be free to market these skills whenever he or she wishes. By the very nature of the circumstance of employment, the skills the employee has, if not used for the employer where they were learned, will probably be used for a competitor. What legal mechanisms help our commercial society to achieve a balance between what the employee can take away from the employer and call his or her own and what should remain with the employer as its own? At the most general level of analysis we find that the First and Fourteenth Amendments to the U.S. Constitution are two of these legal mechanisms.

As the case below illustrates, from the perspective of an employee, when a court orders that an employee may not advertise to compete with an employer, this may violate the employee's First Amendment and Fourteenth Amendment rights. However, the exercise of these rights does not allow the employee to interfere with the contractual rights of the employer.

ADLER, BARISH, DANIELS, LEVIN AND CRESKOFF v. ALAN B. EPSTEIN
393 Acd 1175 (S. Ct., Pa., 1978)

ROBERTS, Justice

Appellant, the law firm of Adler, Barish, Daniels, Levin and Creskoff, filed a complaint in Equity in the Court of Common Pleas in Philadelphia. It sought to enjoin appellees, former associates of Adler Barish, from interfering with existing contractual relationships between Adler Barish and its clients. The court of common pleas entered a final decree granting the requested relief, but a divided Superior Court dissolved the injunction and dismissed Adler Barish's complaint. We granted allowance of appeal. Now we reverse and direct reinstatement of the decree of the court of common pleas.

From the formation of Adler Barish in February, 1976, through March of the next year, appellees were salaried associates of Adler Barish. Appellees were under the supervision of Adler Barish partners, who directed appellees' work on cases which clients brought to the firm.

While still working for Adler Barish, appellees decided to form their own law firm and took several steps toward achieving their goal. They retained counsel to advise them concerning their business venture, sought and found office space, and early in March, 1977, signed a lease.

Shortly before leaving Adler Barish, appellees procured a line of $150,000 from First Pennsylvania Bank. As security, appellees furnished bank officials with a list of eighty-eight cases and their anticipated legal fees, several of which were higher than $25,000, and together exceeded $500,000. No case on the list, however, was appellees'. Rather, each case was an Adler Barish case on which appellees were working.

Appellee Alan Epstein's employment relationship with Adler Barish terminated on March 10, 1977. At his request, Epstein continued to use offices of Adler Barish until March 19. During this time, and through April 4, when Adler Barish filed its complaint, Epstein was engaged in an active campaign to procure business for his new law firm. He initiated contacts by phone and in person, with clients of Adler Barish with open cases on which he had worked while a salaried employee. Epstein advised the Adler Barish clients that he was leaving the firm and that they could choose to be represented by him, Adler Barish, or any other firm or attorney.

Epstein's attempt to procure business on behalf of the firm did not stop with these contacts. He mailed to the clients form letters which could be used to discharge Adler Barish as counsel, name Epstein the client's new counsel and create a contingent fee agreement. . . .

Thus, clients of Adler Barish served a dual purpose in appellees' effort to start their own law firm. First, while appellees still worked for Adler Barish, Adler Barish cases formed the basis for appellees' obtaining bank credit. Then, appellees, as they left Adler Barish, made a concentrated attempt to procure the cases which had been used to obtain credit.

Adler Barish argues that appellees' conduct constitutes an intentional interference with existing contractual relationships between Adler Barish and its clients. According to Adler Barish, appellees' conduct is "deserving of censure, not encouragement." Appellees, on the other hand, contend that their conduct was "privileged," and that therefore no right of action for intentional interference lies. Moreover, they argue that their conduct is protected under the first and fourteenth amendments to the Constitution of the United States.

Nothing in the challenged decree prohibited appellees from engaging in truthful advertising. . . . Appellees could inform the general public, including clients of Adler Barish, of the availability of their legal services, and thus the "free flow of commercial information" to the public is unimpaired. Moreover, the injunction expressly permitted appellees to announce "formation of their new professional relationship in accordance with the requirements of the Code of Professional Responsibility." Appellees therefore were permitted to mail announcements to "lawyers, clients, former clients, personal friends and relatives."

What the injunction did proscribe was appellees' "contacting and/or communicating with those persons who up to and including April 1, 1977, had active legal matters pending and were represented by the law firm of ADLER, BARISH, DANIELS, LEVIN and CRESKOFF." Our task is to decide whether the conduct of appellees is constitutionally subject to sanction.

They recommended their own employment, even though clients of Adler Barish did not seek appellees' advice "regarding employment of a lawyer."

Ohralik v. Ohio State Bar Association, 436 U.S. 447 (1978), makes plain that . . . states may constitutionally impose sanctions upon attorneys engaging in conduct which violates these disciplinary rules, even though the conduct involves "commercial speech." In *Ohralik,* the state bar association suspended an attorney who "solicited" persons injured in an automobile accident by making visits to the hospital room where the persons were recovering. Mr. Justice Powell, speaking for the Court, emphasized that commercial speech does not enjoy the same constitutional protections traditionally afforded other forms of speech.

> We have not discarded the 'commonsense' distinction between speech proposing a commercial transaction, which occurs in an area traditionally subject to government regulation, and other varieties of speech. To require a parity of constitutional protection for commercial and noncommercial speech alike could invite dilution, simply by a leveling process, of the force of the Amendment's guarantee with respect to the latter kind of speech. Rather than subject the First Amendment to such a devitalization, we instead have afforded commercial speech a limited measure of protection, commensurate with its subordinate position in the scale of First Amendment values, while allowing modes of regulation that might be impermissible in the realm of noncommercial expression. 436 U.S. 447, 455–56.

Appellees' concern for their line of credit and the success of their new law firm gave them an immediate, personally created financial interest in the clients' decisions. In this atmosphere, appellees' contacts posed too great a risk that clients would not have the opportunity to make a careful, informed decision. . . . Therefore, we must reject appellees' argument and conclude that just as in *Ohralik,* the Constitution permits regulation of their conduct.

Thus, we turn to whether the court of common pleas properly concluded that Adler Barish is entitled to relief. In *Birl v. Philadelphia Electric Co.,* 167 A.2d 472 (1961), this court adopted Section 766 of *Restatement of Torts* and its definition of the right of action for intentional interference with existing contractual relations. There, we stated:

> [T]he common law has recognized an action in tort for an intentional, unprivileged interfer-

ence with contractual relations. It is generally recognized that one has the right to pursue his business relations or employment free from interference on the part of other persons except where such interference is justified or constitutes an exercise of an absolute right. *Restatement, Torts,* § 766. The Special Note to comment m. in § 766 points out: 'There are frequent expressions in judicial opinions that "malice" is requisite for liability in the cases treated in this Section. But the context and course of decision make it clear that what is meant is not malice in the sense of ill will but merely purposeful interference without justification. . . .'

The elements of this tort of inducing breach of contract or refusal to deal, which must be averred in the complaint, are set forth in the *Restatement, Torts,* § 766, which says, '. . . one who without a privilege to do so, induces or otherwise purposely causes a third person not to (a) perform a contract with another, or (b) enter into or continue a business relation with another is liable to the other for the harm caused thereby.' In other words, the actor must act (1) for the purpose of causing this specific type of harm to the plaintiff, (2) such act must be unprivileged, and (3) the harm must actually result.

The Court constantly seeks to harmonize common law rules, principles, and doctrines with modern perceptions of social needs and responsibilities. . . .

An examination of this case in light of *Restatement (Second) of Torts,* § 766, reveals that the sole dispute is whether appellees' conduct is "improper." There is no doubt that appellees intentionally sought to interfere with the performance of the contractual relations between Adler Barish and its clients. While still at Adler Barish, appellees' behavior, particularly their use of expected fees from Adler Barish clients' cases, indicates appellees' desire to gain a segment of the firm's business. This pattern of conduct continued until the court of common pleas enjoined it. Indeed, appellees' intentional efforts to obtain a share of Adler Barish's business were successful. The record reveals that several clients signed the forms Epstein prepared on behalf of the appellees

notifying Adler Barish that the clients no longer wished the services of Adler Barish. Likewise, the record reveals that Adler Barish and its clients were parties to valid, existing contracts. We are guided, too, by Section 766 of *Restatement (Second) of Torts,* which focuses on what factors should be considered in determining whether conduct is "improper:"

> In determining whether an actor's conduct in intentionally interfering with an existing contract or a prospective contractual relation of another is improper or not, consideration is given to the following factors:
>
> (a) The nature of the actor's conduct,
> (b) The actor's motive,
> (c) The interests of the other with which the actor's conduct interferes,
> (d) The interests sought to be advanced by the actor,
> (e) The proximity or remoteness of the actor's conduct to the interference and
> (f) The relations between the parties.

We find nothing in the " 'rules of the game' which society has adopted" which sanctions appellees' conduct. Indeed, the rules which apply to those who enjoy the privilege of practicing law in this Commonwealth expressly disapprove appellees' method of obtaining clients.

Appellees' conduct adversely affected more than the informed and reliable decision-making of Adler Barish clients with active cases. Their conduct also had an immediate impact upon Adler Barish. Adler Barish was prepared to continue to perform services for its clients and therefore could anticipate receiving compensation for the value of its efforts.

It is true that, upon termination of their employment relationship with Adler Barish, appellees were free to engage in their own business venture. See *Restatement (Second) of Agency,* § 396(a) (1958) ("[u]nless otherwise agreed, after termination of the agency, the agent . . . has no duty not to compete with the principal"); but appellees' right to pursue their own business interests is not absolute. "[U]nless otherwise agreed, after the termination of the agency, the agent . . . has a duty to the principal not to take advantage of a still subsisting confidential relation created during the prior agency relation").

Appellees' contacts were possible because Adler Barish partners trusted appellees with the high responsibility of developing its clients' cases. From this position of trust and respon-

sibility, appellees were able to gain knowledge of the details, and status, of each case to which appellees had been assigned. In the atmosphere surrounding appellees' departure, appellees' contacts unduly suggested a course of action for Adler Barish clients and unfairly prejudiced Adler Barish. No public interest is served in condoning use of confidential information which has these effects. Clients too easily may suffer in the end.

Appendix to Opinion of the Court

Epstein sent the following cover letter:

>404 South Camac Street
>Philadelphia, Pennsylvania 19147
>March 25, 1977
>   re:

Dear

In confirmation of our recent conversation, I have terminated my association with the offices of Adler, Barish, Daniels, Levin and Creskoff and will be continuing in the practice of law in center city Philadelphia. As I explained, you have the right to determine who shall represent your interests and handle the above-captioned matter in the future. You may elect to be represented by my former office, me or any other attorney permitted to practice in this jurisdiction.

During our conversation, you expressed a desire to have me continue as your legal representative, and in recognition of your choice in this regard, I have enclosed two documents which must be signed and returned to me in the enclosed stamped, addressed envelope to effect this end. Copies of these documents are also enclosed for your records.

If you have any questions regarding these

materials or any other matter, feel free to call me at KI 6-5223.

>Sincerely,

>Alan B. Epstein

MANDERINO, Justice, dissenting.

I dissent.

Specifically, the majority relying on *Ohralik* concludes that appellees, former associates of the law firm Adler Barish, engaged in illegal solicitation when they mailed to the clients of Adler Barish form letters which could be executed to discharge Adler Barish as counsel, name appellees as client's new counsel and then create a contingent fee agreement.

Contrary to the majority's analysis, however, the United States Supreme Court's decision in *Ohralik* does not prohibit the type of direct solicitation which is before this court today.

One need not be a legal scholar to see the distinction for First Amendment purposes between the ambulance-chasing tactics used by the lawyer in *Ohralik* and the written communications which appellees mailed to the clients of Adler Barish. The letters sent to prospective clients which would discharge Adler Barish should the client sign on the dotted line contained no arm-twisting device pressuring clients to make an immediate response. Nor were these clients uninformed about the choices they could make in either retaining or discharging Adler Barish as legal counsel. Additionally, appellees' communication contained *no* false and misleading statements which would confuse, deceive, or mislead prospective clients. More importantly, appellees did not attempt to motivate these clients to stir up litigation as was done in *Ohralik*.

This Court today misuses its injunctive powers to prohibit not only what is a protected form of direct solicitation under the First Amendment but to prohibit an attorney from truthfully informing a client about the client's legal rights. The Order of the Superior Court should therefore be affirmed.

Case Questions

1. In a few sentences, state how the First and Fourteenth Amendments were argued in this case.

2. If the actions of the employees who quit had not interfered with the contractual relationships of the partnership, would the employees have been able to set up a competing partnership?

3. Could the new partnerships of Alan Epstein and others solicit work from the clients of the partnership with whom there had been past contracts but no *present* work or contracts?

The foregoing case illustrates the principle that an employee-agent cannot interfere with the existing contractual rights of the employer-principal. Also the First and Fourteenth Amendments to the U.S. Constitution may protect some employee rights. There are three other important legal principles used by courts and employers to help define the respective duties of employers and employees as related to the ownership or use of the employee's work product. They are, at a less general level than the U.S. Constitution, the existence of patent law and trade secret law and the use of restrictive covenants in employment contracts.

Patent and Trade Secret Law. First, as creatures of constitutional and federal law, both employers and employees have the right to enforce their exclusive right to a patent for a period of 17 years by seeking an injunction against anyone who appropriates the patent.

A patent may be granted to any person (or corporation) on any new and useful invention that is: (1) a process, (2) a machine, (3) a product, (4) a composition of matter, (5) a new and useful improvement of a prior patented invention, (6) a growing plant, or (7) a design. The patented subject must not have been (1) patented or described in any printed publication in this or any foreign country for more than one year prior to application, (2) known or in use by others in this country prior to its invention, and (3) in public use or sale in this country for more than one year prior to application. Obviously, if an employer owns the patent, an employee may not appropriate or take or use the material that is the subject of the patent. However, all patented materials are "invented" by employees. Usually, the ownership of the patent is clarified or established by an employment contract. In almost all cases, these provide that any patent resulting from work done at the place of employment or on the employee's time will belong to the employer.

Many useful devices and techniques *cannot* be patented, so another layer of legal duties protecting the creator is established by state law. The legal duties are established by the law of trade secrets. A good definition of a trade secret and the relationship between patent law and trade secret law is discussed in the following United States Supreme Court decision.

KEWANEE OIL CO. v. BICRON CORP.
416 U.S. 470 (1973)   *Patent Law Case*

MR. CHIEF JUSTICE BURGER

Harshaw Chemical Co., an unincorporated division of petitioner, is a leading manufacturer of a type of synthetic crystal which is useful in the detection of ionizing radiation. In 1949 Harshaw commenced research into the growth of this type crystal and was able to produce one less than two inches in diameter. By 1966, as the result of expenditures in excess of $1 million, Harshaw was able to grow a 17-inch crystal, something no one else had done previously. Harshaw had developed many processes, procedures, and manufacturing techniques in the purification of raw materials and the growth and encapsulation of the crystals which enabled it to accomplish this feat. Some of these processes Harshaw considers to be trade secrets.

The individual respondents are former employees of Harshaw who formed or later joined respondent Bicron. While at Harshaw the individual respondents executed as a condition of employment, at least one agreement each, requiring them not to disclose confidential information or trade secrets obtained as employees of Harshaw. Bicron was formed in August 1969 to compete with Harshaw in pro-

duction of the crystals, and by April 1970, had grown a 17-inch crystal.

Petitioner brought this . . . action in United States District Court for the Northern District of Ohio seeking injunctive relief and damages for the misappropriation of trade secrets. The District Court, applying Ohio trade secret law, granted a permanent injunction against the disclosure or use by respondents of 20 of the 40 claimed trade secrets until such time as the trade secrets had been released to the public, had otherwise generally become available to the public, or had been obtained by respondents from sources having the legal right to convey the information.

The Court of Appeals for the Sixth Circuit held that the findings of fact by the District Court were not clearly erroneous, and that it was evident from the record that the individual respondents appropriated to the benefit of Bicron secret information on processes obtained while they were employees at Harshaw. Further, the Court of Appeals held that the District Court properly applied Ohio law relating to trade secrets. Nevertheless, the Court of Appeals reversed the District Court, finding Ohio's trade secret law to be in conflict with the patent laws of the United States. The Court of Appeals reasoned that Ohio could not grant monopoly protection to processes and manufacturing techniques that were appropriate subjects for consideration . . . for a federal patent but which had been in commercial use for over one year and so were no longer eligible for patent protection. . . .

We hold that Ohio's law of trade secrets is not preempted by the patent laws of the United States, and accordingly, we reverse.

. . .

Ohio has adopted the widely relied-upon definition of a trade secret found at *Restatement of Torts* § 757, comment *b*, (1939) . . . . According to the *Restatement,*

> [a] trade secret may consist of any formula, pattern, device or compilation of information which is used in one's business, and which gives him an opportunity to obtain an advantage over competitors who do not know or use it. It may be a formula for a chemical compound, a process of manufacturing, treating or preserving materials, a pattern for a machine or other device, or a list of customers.

The subject of a trade secret must be secret, and must not be of public knowledge or of a general knowledge in the trade or business . . . . This necessary element of secrecy is not lost, however, if the holder of the trade secret reveals the trade secret to another "in confidence, and under an implied obligation not to use or disclose it." . . . These others may include those of the holder's "employees to whom it is necessary to confide it, in order to apply it to the uses for which it is intended." . . . .

The first issue we deal with is whether the States are forbidden to act at all in the area of protection of the kinds of intellectual property which may make up the subject matter of trade secrets.

Article I. § 8. cl.8. of the Constitution grants to the Congress the power

> [t]o promote the Progress of Science and useful Arts, by securing for limited Times to Authors and Inventors the exclusive right to their respective Writings and Discoveries. . . .

In the 1972 Term, in *Goldstein v. California,* 412 U.S. 546 (1973), we held that the cl. 8 grant of

power to Congress was not exclusive and that, at least in the case of writings, the States were not prohibited from encouraging and protecting the efforts of those within their borders by appropriate legislation. The States could, therefore, protect against the unauthorized re-recording for sale of performances fixed on records or tapes, even though those performances qualified as "writings" in the constitutional sense and Congress was empowered to legislate regarding such performances and could pre-empt the area if it chose to do so. This determination was premised on the great diversity of interests in our Nation—the essentially non-uniform character of the appreciation of intellectual achievements in the various States. . . .

Just as the States may exercise regulatory power over writings so may the States regulate with respect to discoveries. States may hold diverse viewpoints in protecting intellectual property relating to invention as they do in protecting the intellectual property relating to the subject matter of copyright. The only limitation on the States is that in regulating the area of patents and copyrights they do not conflict with the operation of the laws in this area passed by Congress, and it is to that more difficult question we now turn.

. . .

The question of whether the trade secret law of Ohio is void under the Supremacy Clause involves a consideration of whether that law "stands as an obstacle to the accomplishment and execution of the full purposes and objectives of Congress." . . . .

The stated objective of the Constitution in granting the power to Congress to legislate in the area of intellectual property is to "promote the Progress of Science and useful Arts." The patent laws promote this progress by offering a right of exclusion for a limited period as an incentive to inventors to risk the often enormous costs in terms of time, research, and development. The productive effort thereby fostered will have a positive effect on society through the introduction of new products and processes of manufacture into the economy, and the emanations by way of increased employment and better lives for our citizens. In return for the right of exclusion—this "reward for inventions,". . .—the patent laws impose upon the inventor a requirement of disclosure. To insure adequate and full disclosure so that upon the expiration of the 17-year period "the knowledge of the invention enures to the people, who are thus enabled without restriction to practice it and profit by its use," . . . the patent laws require that the patent application shall include a full and clear description of the invention and "of the manner and process of making and using it" so that any person skilled in the art may make and use the invention. When a patent is granted and the information contained in it is circulated to the general public and those especially skilled in the trade, such additions to the general store of knowledge are of such importance to the public weal that the Federal Government is willing to pay the high price of 17 years of exclusive use for its disclosure, which disclosure, it is assumed, will stimulate ideas and the eventual development of further significant advances in the art. . . .

The maintenance of standards of commercial ethics and the encouragement of invention are the broadly stated policies behind trade secret law. "The necessity of good faith and honest, fair dealing, is the very life and spirit of the commercial world." . . .

Having now in mind the objectives of both the patent and trade secret law, we turn to an examination of the interaction of these systems of protection of intellectual property—one established by the Congress and the other by a State—to determine whether and under what circumstances the latter might constitute "too great an encroachment on the federal patent system to be tolerated.". . . .

Congress has spoken in the areas of those discoveries which fall within one of the categories of patentable subject matter of 35 U.S.C. § 101 and which are, therefore, of a nature that would be subject to consideration for a patent. Processes, machines, manufactures, compositions of matter, and improvements thereof, which meet the tests of utility, novelty, and nonobviousness are entitled to be patented, but those which do not, are not. The question remains whether those items which are proper subjects for consideration for a patent may also have available the alternative protection accorded by trade secret law.

Certainly the patent policy of encouraging invention is not disturbed by the existence of another form of incentive to invention. In this respect the two systems are not and never would be in conflict. . . .

Trade secret law provides far weaker protection in many respects than the patent law. While trade secret law does not forbid the discovery of the trade secret by fair and honest means, *e.g.,* independent creation or reverse engineering, patent law operates "against the world," forbidding any use of the invention for whatever purpose for a significant length of time. The holder of a trade secret also takes a substantial risk that the secret will be passed on to his competitors, by theft or by breach of a confidential relationship, in a manner not easily susceptible of discovery or proof. . . . Where patent law acts as a barrier, trade secret law functions relatively as a sieve. The possibility that an inventor who believes his invention meets the standards of patentability will sit back, rely on trade secret law, and after one year of use forfeit any right to patent protection, is remote indeed.

We conclude that the extension of trade secret protection to clearly patentable inventions does not conflict with the patent policy of disclosure. . . .

Our conclusion that patent law does not pre-empt trade secret law is in accord with prior cases of this Court. . . . Trade secret law and patent law have co-existed in this country for over one hundred years. Each has its particular role to play, and the operation of one does not take away from the need for the other. Trade secret law encourages the development and exploitation of those items of lesser or different invention than might be accorded protection under the patent laws, but which items still have an important part to play in the technological and scientific advancement of the Nation. Trade secret law promotes sharing of knowledge, and the efficient operation of industry: it permits the individual inventor to reap the rewards of his labor by contracting with a company large enough to develop and exploit it. Congress, by its silence over these many years, has seen the wisdom of allowing the States to enforce trade secret protection. Until Congress takes affirmative action to the contrary, States should be free to grant protection to trade secrets.

Since we hold that Ohio trade secret law is not pre-empted by the federal patent law, the Judgment of the Court of Appeals for the Sixth Circuit is reversed, and the case is remanded to the Court of Appeals with directions to reinstate the judgment of the District Court.

It is so ordered.

Mr. Justice Douglas, with whom Mr. Justice Brennan concurs, dissenting.

The conflict with the patent laws is obvious. The decision of Congress to adopt a patent system was based on the idea that there will be much more innovation if discoveries are disclosed and patented then there will be when everyone works in secret. Society thus fosters a free exchange of technological information at the cost of a limited 17-year monopoly.

A trade secret, unlike a patent, has no property dimension. . . .

> The word property as applied to trade-marks and trade secrets is an unanalyzed expression of certain secondary consequences of the fact that the law makes some rudimentary requirements of good faith. Whether the plaintiffs have any valuable secret or not the defendant knows the facts, whatever they are, through a special confidence that he accepted. The property may be denied but the confidence cannot be. Therefore the starting point for the present matter is not property or due process of law, but that the defendant stood in confidant relations with the plaintiffs, or one of them. These have given place to hostility, and the first thing to be made sure of is that the defendant shall not fraudulently abuse the trust reposed in him. It is the usual incident of confidential relations. If there is any disadvantage in the fact that he knew the plaintiff's secrets he must take the burden with the good. 244 U.S. 100, 102.

From the findings of fact of the lower courts, the process in this litigation was unique, such a great discovery as to make its patentability a virtual certainty. Yet the Court's opinion reflects a vigorous activist anti-patent philosophy. My objection is not because it is activist. This is a problem that involves no neutral principle. The Constitution in Art. I, § 8, expresses the activist policy which we should enforce, not our individual notions of the public good.

I would affirm the judgment below.

Case Questions

1. Describe the relationship between patent law and trade secret law. Does one preempt the other? What is the test the court uses to answer this question?

2. Define a trade secret.

3. Explain the remedy given by the court. How is trade secret law enforced?

Justice Douglas's dissent in the case above returns us to the central point of this part of the chapter: An agency relationship is one based on trust; it is a fiduciary relationship. But today's business environment inevitably challenges relatively simple understandings, such as the idea that an employee-agent owes a duty of loyalty to the employer-principal. As our business-oriented society becomes more sophisticated and complex, employers are required to spend larger amounts of money to develop new methods of production, new databases, and more efficient and humane management techniques. The protection of this investment is vital if we are to expect firms to continue to engage in this type of activity.

On the other hand, all of us are employees of one kind or another. None of us want undue restrictions on our ability to earn a living. This means we should be allowed to develop our own knowledge, skills, and experiences and be able to take them with us from job to job. Our ideas of freedom and individualism are bound up with how we think of our jobs. Some, if not most, of the things we learn in an employment situation should be ours. In deciding the tough questions which arise in the grey areas between the coverage of patent law and trade secret law, a legal scholar has suggested that courts should balance the following factors in determining if an employee may use his or her "generalized knowledge" or the "confidential information" of the employer: (1) the extent of the limitation imposed on the employee's job mobility; (2) an assessment of whether the employee helped to develop the trade secret and whether he or she was hired to work on it; (3) the existence of notice to the employee that the employer would claim the work on the project was protectable as the employer's own; (4) the duration and other conditions relating to post employment restraints, if any; and (5) the amount of the employer's investment and how disclosure of the information would affect the employer's incentive to invest.[10]

Restrictive Covenants.   The designation of an agency relationship as a fiduciary one can have different meanings because agency and employment relationships cover such a wide variety of circumstances. They range from the confidential relation of attorney and client to the relatively slight fiduciary relationship that exists between a landowner and a person who sells real estate, so that the duties finally imposed by a court may vary greatly.

The fiduciary nature of the agency relationship may continue even after termination of the agency. The very essence of the relationship is one based on trust, and in some circumstances, such as the attorney-client relationship, trust implies confidentiality. Thus, even after the completion of such a relationship, the attorney may not reveal or use confidential information.

In the typical employer-employee context, the employer who exposes employees to confidential information usually attempts to guard its interest in such information by asking the employee to agree *by contract* not to use the information in a manner detrimental to the interests of the employer after the employment is terminated. Such a contractual agreement is called a "restrictive convenant." Generally, *in the absence of a restrictive covenant* limiting the right of an employee to use information gained from the work experience, or to compete with the employer after employment termination, courts will permit employees to compete with the previous employer.

In many instances, employers who use restrictive covenants draft them using such broad language that, if a court interpreted the language literally, the employee would be totally barred from using the skills and talents learned on the job. The case below explains how some courts deal with this problem.

DONAHUE v. PERMACEL TAPE CORPORATION

234 Ind. 398; 127 N.E. 2d. 235 (S. Ct. Ind., 1955)

ANCHOR, Judge

Concerned about scope

Appellee is engaged in the manufacture and sale of adhesives and adhesive tapes. Appellant was formerly a sales representative for appellee. During such employment the parties entered into a written contract, the pertinent sections of which are as follows:

1. Employee shall not divulge to others or use for his own benefit any confidential information obtained during the course of his employment with Company relating to sales, sales volume or strategy, customers, number or location of salesmen, formulae, processes, methods, machines, manufacturers, compositions, idea, improvements or invention belonging to or relating to the affairs of the company, Johnson & Johnson or its subsidiary or affiliated companies, without first obtaining Company's written permission.

2. Employee for a period of three (3) years after leaving Company's employment for any reason whatsoever, shall not, in the United States or Canada without first obtaining Company's written permission, engage in or enter the employment of or act as a sales agent or broker for the products of or as an advisor or consultant to any person, firm or corporation engaged in or about to become

engaged in the manufacture of adhesive or adhesive tapes.

Thereafter appellant terminated his employment with appellee and, without the consent of appellee, became a sales representative for a competitor. An action for temporary and permanent injunctive relief followed. A temporary restraining order was issued and it is from that decree that this appeal is prosecuted.

In support of his appeal, appellant contends, among other things, that whereas, the scope of his employment with appellee was limited to northern Indiana, the restrictive covenant contained in the contract was unreasonably restrictive in that the restricted territory (United States and Canada) encompassed too large an area, and that therefore the contract in its entirety was contrary to public policy and void. . . . It is upon these facts that the validity of the restrictive covenant in issue must be determined.

. . .

We therefore give our consideration to the covenant, the contract and the situation to which it related. While it is true that section one of the contract refers to "confidential information obtained during the course of employment" the pleadings, . . . do not allege, nor can it reasonably be inferred therefrom, that appellant obtained any "confidential information" which was of such a nature that it was related to the business of the convenantee in more than a general way outside the limited territory assigned to the covenantor as a sales representative. In fact, the express allegation of the complaint upon the subject of the breach of covenant indicates that appellee's only cause of complaint is that appellant is working for a competitor and is "soliciting trade" for it in competition with appellee. There is no allegation of fact as to the use or abuse of either "trade secrets" or "confidential information." . . .

We proceed to analyze the second class of cases which state that covenants in restraint of trade will be enforced if limited to the "area of the business involved"—those related to . . . the sale of a business or profession. The rule is well established that a vendor may enter into a valid covenant not to compete within the area of the business or profession sold. . . .

It must be noted that these cases relate to the good will, which is "the interest to be protected" in the business or profession sold, and they do not relate to the scope of the business of the buyer. For example, if the seller operated stores in cities A, B, and C, and he sells the store in city A, the cases do not hold that a negative covenant may be enforced prohibiting seller from continuing business in cities B and C, neither do they hold that the mere fact that the buyer operates a business throughout the state of Indiana that he may preclude a seller whose business was limited to a single county, from operating elsewhere within the State of Indiana. . . .

By clear analogy the precedent of these cases, when applied to employer-employee covenants, clearly supports the conclusion that such covenants will be upheld, if limited to the area in which operation of the employee's activity was related to the good will of the employer's business. Also, they provide strong precedent in support of the position that covenants which would restrict the competitive em-

ployment of an employee beyond the area of his former employment are void, unless such subsequent employment involves that use or divulgence of "trade secrets" of the former employer which are related to the scope of the latter's business throughout the "restricted area." . . .

When we look to the reported cases from other states and the authors of texts on the subject, we find that they provide strong precedent and persuasive reasoning in support of the position that (where "trade secrets" affecting the entire business are not involved), a covenant which would restrict an employee beyond the area of his prior operation are void, notwithstanding the fact that the employer's business covers a much greater area. . . .

The general principles governing the legality of a contract in restraint of trade have been stated by *Williston on Contracts*, § 1636, pp. 4580–4581:

> It is everywhere agreed that in order to be valid a promise imposing a restraint in trade or occupation must be reasonable. The question of reasonableness is for the court, not the jury; and in considering what is reasonable, regard must be paid to (a) the question whether the promise is wider than is necessary for the protection of the covenantee in some legitimate interest, (b) the effect of the promise upon the covenantor, and (c) the effect upon the public.

. . .

To what conclusion do we arrive when we apply the first above stated test to the facts in this case? Was (a) the covenant wider than was necessary for the protection of the covenantee (appellee) in some legitimate interest? There was no evidence from which the court could assume that the "confidential sales information, including ideas, customer lists and the like . . . made available" to appellant, were related (except in a general way) to appellee's business outside the limited area of his employment with appellee in northern Indiana. Therefore, the case clearly fails to meet the first test of "necessity for the protection of the covenantee" in the area prescribed,—"the United States and Canada."

Furthermore, when we consider the second test above stated, namely (b) the effect upon the covenantor, we find that the covenant also fails to meet the test of validity in this respect. We are here concerned with one of the most basic rights of man as recognized by our Judean-Anglican civilization, "that man is endowed by his Creator with the rights of life, liberty and the pursuit of happiness." We perceive that these rights are inherent and therefore inalienable—whether on the part of governments or by man individually through his own act. By way of illustration only, because we perceive that man is inherently free, our courts will not interfere even with the folly of a man who voluntarily (without mistake, fraud or duress) bargains away his property accumulated through all his past years for a consideration of grossly disproportionate value. Courts will purposely close their eyes to such transactions, as Isaac was unwittingly blinded to the folly of Esau who sold his birthright to Jacob. Our society recognizes and is committed to guard the sacredness of every human personality and to make possible its fullest possible development. Therefore, in order to guarantee that every man shall, as of now and in the future, enjoy the freedom of "life, liberty and the pursuit of happiness" our courts will zealously guard every individual against even his own commitments which would limit or thwart the greatest constructive employment and enjoyment of his faculties from this moment forward, unless the manner of his living would contravene public policy or the personal property rights of another.

This brings us to a consideration of the property rights of both the parties to this action. As an incident to his business the appellee (employer) was entitled to contract with regard to and thus to protect the good will of his business. Elements of this good will include "secret or confidential information," such as the names and addresses and requirements of customers and the advantage acquired through representative contact with the trade in the area of their application. These are property rights which the employer is entitled to protect. However, is not the same true regarding the skill . . . the employee has acquired, or the general knowledge or information he has obtained which is not directly related to the good will or value of his employer's business. Knowledge, skill and information (except trade secrets and confidential information) become a part of the employee's personal equipment. They belong to him as an individual for the transaction of any business in which he may engage, just the same as any part of the skill, knowledge, information or education that was received by him before entering the employment. Therefore, on terminating his employment he has a right to take them with him. These things cannot be taken from him, although he may forget them or abandon them. . . . An employee may contract to conditionally forego these personal attainments as a consideration for his employment only where their use adverse to his employer would result in irreparable injury to the employer. This would occur only in the area of his employment. Therefore, a covenant which would limit his employment with a competitor beyond the scope of his present employment is void. . . .

Appellant's employment with appellee was limited to northern Indiana. There is no evidence that he acquired "trade secrets" or "confidential information" from appellee, the competitive use of which was related to or could result in irreparable injury to the business of the appellee throughout the breadth of "the United States and Canada," where the covenant attempted to restrict appellant's employment. We conclude, therefore, . . . that the covenant of the contract before us was unreasonable to the extent that it attempted to restrict the gainful employment of appellant beyond the area of his former employment with appellee.

The above conclusion gives rise to the final issue in the case. It is asserted that even though the covenant of the contract may not be enforceable as to all the area interdicted, that the equities of the case require enforcement in the area of appellant's former actual employment. . . . However, we are not permitted to consider that question or the equities which might support such a decision in this case. . . . Whereas the contract before us does not describe the area of appellee's former employment but, on the contrary, the restricted territory is described in one indivisible whole—"The United States and Canada." We cannot rewrite the contract made by the parties and add to it matters which it does contain and then use the contract as rewritten as a basis for litigation, however justifiable equitable interference under the circumstances might seem to be. We conclude, therefore, the covenant of contract upon which this action is predicated, is unenforceable in its entirety. . . .

Therefore, the temporary restraining order heretofore issued is ordered dissolved.

Case Questions

1. Develop a clear statement of the circumstances in which courts will enforce restrictive covenants.

2. Assume that you work for a company which has valuable information which it wishes to protect. Write your own restrictive covenant for employees to sign.

3. Companies have a habit of writing restrictive covenants much broader than necessary. In spite of the law of the *Donahue* case and numerous others like it employers continue to use language almost identical to that used in *Donahue*. Why is this so?

Note that in the case above, the court refused to reform the contractual language and declared the covenant unenforceable. Some courts *will* reform the agreement. This is an extension of the "blue pencil" rule used in contract law, which allows courts to uphold reasonable restrictions in contracts while deleting unreasonable ones. The restrictive covenant is reformed by simply striking out some words.

Recovery of Property or Opportunities Taken

Remedies for Breach of the Fiduciary Duty

What can the employer-principal do if the employee-agent breaches the fiduciary duty of loyalty? A common remedy was that given by the court in *Nye* v. *Lovelace*. In that case, the plaintiff-principal asked the court for, and was awarded, the ownership of the Gray parcel of land. Of course, the principal would have to pay the agent what the agent had to pay for the land. The general rule is that when an agent breaches the fiduciary duty of loyalty owed to the principal by converting to his or her own use a business opportunity that belonged to the principal, then the principal may recover the ownership of that which is converted, just as if it had belonged to the principal in the first place. Moreover, if the agent sells that which he or she wrongfully purchased and realizes a profit, then the principal may recover the profit.

Injunction Against the Employee

If that which is converted by the agent cannot be traced (a legal term for "specifically identified"), or it is impossible to assess in money terms the measure of damages suffered by the principal, then the principal may ask the court for an equitable remedy such as an injunction. Remember that equitable remedies are awarded only if the court finds that the remedies at law (primarily money damages) are inadequate to fully compensate the injured plaintiff. An injunction was sought and granted by a court in the *Adler Barish* and *Kewanee* cases.

If an agent takes property of value from the principal and either destroys it or disposes of it so that tracing is impossible, then the agent is liable to the principal for the value of the thing taken.

Discharging the Employee

The most obvious remedy available to the principal for a breach of duty by the agent is to discharge the agent. In the absence of a contractual provision stating that an agent shall be employed for a given length of time, there is no duty on the part of the principal to keep the agent employed. Usually, a union contract provides protection for employees and agents against unreasonable discharge. But it has been estimated that such contracts apply to only one quarter of the work force.[11] Unless a statute applies to protect against arbitrary dismissal or an employee is subject to civil service protection, an agent or employee may be dismissed without cause. Before we create an image that the law is sometimes unjust or crude in this area, we must point out that many firms and principals have adopted internal rules and regulations, sometimes called bylaws or simply company or personnel policies, which do provide a measure of protection against arbitrary discharge. It is not our purpose here to review these; moreover, it is quite possible that a court would hold that these are not binding.

The general rule is that since an agency relationship is founded on consent, it can therefore be terminated by either party by simply withdrawing the consent. This rule does not seem harsh, but let us consider a typical situation. Assume one has worked for an employer for 10 or 15 years and has no employment contract. After this amount of time, there are reasonable expectations that one will continue to be employed and will be discharged only for something called "just cause." But this is not the rule. The general rule may be stated this way—a willful refusal to obey a reasonable company rule or employer order will justify discharge.[12] However, what is "reasonable" is almost always resolved in favor of the employer-principal. For example, in a fairly recent case,[13] a salesman for United States Steel Corporation claimed he was maliciously discharged for pointing out to his superiors the unsafe nature of the tubular products being sold to the oil and gas industry. The product was subsequently withdrawn from the market by the principal. After this discharge, he filed a claim against the principal but the complaint was dismissed on proper motion. This means the court had to accept the allegations of the complaint as true. Nevertheless, the court recognized no legal duty on the part of the principal to act "reasonably" or what might be called "in the public interest," or in any other way than in its own self-interest. In short, an employee does owe a duty of loyalty to the employer, and this duty is not usually excused because of acts that the employee believes to be right.

There are, however, a few cases that have recognized a duty not to discharge an employee arbitrarily. At this point, some have said there is a tort duty on the employer not to act unreasonably. The word "unreasonably" has been held to mean, generally, that the employer cannot act against the public's best interest. So, there is one case granting an employee a remedy where the employer has discharged the employee for disobeying company orders to testify falsely before a state legislative committee[14] and another for refusing to alter pollution control reports required by the state.[15] The basic claim of the employee or the *cause of action* looks as if it is in tort, but some scholars believe that it should be based on implied contract.[16] So far, only one court has recognized an implied contractual duty not to discharge unreasonably.[17]

But these cases are the exception and not the rule. The case below is, we believe, representative of the law in this area.

PERCIVAL v. GENERAL MOTORS CORP.
539 F.2d 1126 (8th Cir., 1976)

HENLEY, Circuit Judge

Worth H. Percival, appellant here and plaintiff below, brought this action in the United States District Court for the Eastern District of Missouri against the defendant, General Motors Corporation, to recover actual and punitive damages for allegedly wrongful discharge from his employment at an executive level. . . .

Prior to answering the complaint the defendant moved for summary judgment. . . . The motion was submitted to the district court on affidavits tendered by the defendant and on counter-affidavits submitted by plaintiff. The

motion was granted and judgment for the defendant was entered. . . . Plaintiff appeals.

The historical facts of the case are not in dispute.

Mr. Percival is a mechanical engineer by profession and holds a Master's Degree from Massachusetts Institute of Technology. He was first employed as an engineer by General Motors in 1947 and remained in that employ until the employment relationship was terminated in 1973. At the time of the termination plaintiff was the head of the defendant's Mechanical Development Department and had held that position since 1968. But for his termination he probably would have remained in the employ of the company until 1985 when he would have been eligible for retirement or might have been required to retire.

In 1973 disagreements arose between Mr. Percival and other top management personnel of General Motors. Discussions were held, and plaintiff was offered another position with the company. He was unwilling to accept that position and ultimately resigned; in connection with his resignation he accepted a cash payment. He commenced this suit in 1975.

Plaintiff contended in the district court and contends here that he was actually discharged from his employment, and that his discharge was wrongful and malicious. However, he does not contend that the alleged discharge was prohibited by any federal or state statute or by any collective bargaining agreement. He denies that his employment was at the will of the defendant, but argues that even if it was his discharge was violative of the public policy of the State of Michigan.

Specifically, plaintiff contends that he was discharged as a result of a conspiracy among his fellow executives to force him out of his employment because of his age and because he had legitimately complained about certain allegedly deceptive practices of General Motors, had refused to give the government false information although urged to do so by colleagues and superiors, and had, on the contrary, undertaken to correct certain alleged misrepresentations made to the government by the defendant. . . .

As far as this appeal is concerned, the narrow question presented is whether the district court erred in granting the defendant's motion for summary judgment.

The principles that are to be applied by a federal court in passing upon a motion for summary judgment are familiar. . . .

In passing upon such a motion the court is required to view the facts in the light most favorable to the party opposing the motion and to give to that party the benefit of all reasonable inferences to be drawn from underlying facts. . . .

In view of those principles, the district court was required to assume, and we are required to assume that the plaintiff was discharged and that he did not voluntarily resign his position, and that his discharge was arbitrary and capricious and was improperly motivated. To put it another way, it must be assumed that in 1973 Mr. Percival was still a capable and efficient employee and was running his department in a satisfactory manner, and that he lost his job simply because his superiors wanted to replace him or because he refused to give false information to the government or undertook to correct misinformation that the defendant had disseminated to the government.

The record reflects that plaintiff was actually hired on a month to month basis. It appears to us, however, that plaintiff had a right to expect to be continued in employment as long as he performed satisfactorily or until he reached retirement age, and we will assume for purposes of this case that he was employed on those terms. In Michigan such an employment is an employment at will and may be terminated by either party at any time with or without cause. . . . Whether an employee has performed satisfactorily is to be determined by the employer and not by the courts. . . . The district court characterized plaintiff's employment as having been at will, and we are satisfied that it did not err in so doing.

In applying the general rule that a person who is employed at will may be discharged at any time with or without cause and without regard to the motivation of the employer in terminating the employment relationship, the district court took note of a "newly emerging theory" advanced by plaintiff to the effect that the general rule should not be applied to a case in which the discharge violated public policy. The theory is that even if an employer has a general right to discharge an employee without cause or justification, a discharge is wrongful and actionable if it is motivated by the fact that the employee did something that public policy encourages or that he refused to do something that public policy forbids or condemns.

. . .

It may be conceded to plaintiff that there are strong policy arguments that can be made in support of the theory which he invokes; there are also strong policy arguments that can be made against it. It should be kept in mind that as far as an employment relationship is concerned, an employer as well as an employee has rights; and it should also be kept in mind that a large corporate employer such as General Motors, except to the extent limited by statute or contractual obligations, must be accorded wide latitude in determining whom it

will employ and retain in employment in high and sensitive managerial positions particularly where developments in the field of mechanical engineering are involved.

. . .

We do not think that the district court was required to predict that Michigan will adopt plaintiff's theory in general or would apply it to the facts of this particular case, and we deem it inappropriate for us to make such a prediction. We conclude that no error was committed when the district court applied the general rule that has been mentioned.

The judgment of the district court will be affirmed.

Case Questions

1. Exactly what was the holding in this case? What does it mean when an appellate court affirms a trial court's decision to grant a summary judgment?

2. This court acknowledges that some states recognize a tort cause of action for malicious discharge. Under what circumstances will these courts do this?

3. Do you believe that General Motors should have the legally protected power to do what it did in this case? Should there be any public right or a personal right to have exposed the truth of Mr. Percival's allegations?

The Corporate Value Structure, the Duty of Loyalty, and the Individual Conscience

It may be that the issues present in the above case are so complex that a single court should not create new law. There is the tradition of an almost absolute right of the employer to discharge an employee at will, the necessity—from the perspective of the employer—to demand and expect loyalty from the employee, and, finally and by no means least, the individual conscience, will, and ego of the employee. The proper balance between the collective desires, wants, and will and the individual desires, wants, and will is one that is rarely achieved.

In a 1971 *New Yorker* article, then Yale law professor Charles Reich argued that a new form of evil was perceivable in our society and that this came about, more often than not, when people were acting in accordance with what they perceived to be their duty.[18] Many if not most of the illegal acts of large corporations (involving illegal campaign contributions and bribing of foreign governmental officials to secure business, etc.) were done in the name of "the good of the corporation." That is, most of these actions were justified based on the duty of loyalty that an employee owes to an employer. Are there not limits on this duty?

The case law that would help with an answer to this question is very sparse. The *Restatement*, however, does provide a partial answer. The duty to act for the principal is stated this way in Section 385(1): "Unless otherwise agreed, an agent is subject to a duty to obey all reasonable directions in regard to the manner of performing a service that he has contracted to perform." Comment (a) qualifies this by stating, "in determining whether or not the orders of the principal to the agent are reasonable, the customs of business with regard to such agency, business or professional ethics, [and] the effect upon the agent's business . . . and other similar facts are considered." Further on, this same comment concludes, "In no event would it be implied that an agent has a duty to perform acts which, although otherwise within the scope of his duties, are illegal or unethical. . . ." The *Restatement* then provides that the duty of loyalty does not extend to engaging in unethical acts. But the precise definition of an "unethical" act is not provided, nor could it be. These actions would vary so much from business circumstance to circumstance that almost no definition would be meaningful. Moreover, this provision of the *Restatement* simply excuses the employee from performing for the principal. In a way, if adopted by a court, it states that a principal cannot sue an agent for failure to act in a way that the agent believes to be ethical. However, as we have seen, the principal may end the agency relationship. So, in some cases an agent may have to choose between keeping a job and acting ethically.

To some people it does not seem fair to put an employee or agent in this position.[19] Doing so obviously creates substantial problems for the principal-agent and employer-employee relationship.

A solution that is not court generated is to rely on federal law to develop the idea of "just cause" for a firing. This law could work in conjunction with similar state laws and could apply only when state law does not apply. The elements of "just cause" are (1) a provision for notice to employees of all appropriate work rules; (2) fair and consistent application of these rules; and (3) a system of progressive disciplinary steps with discharge as the final step.[20] The process should emphasize conciliation followed by binding arbitration.

We believe that the problems caused by the confrontation of the employer's and employee's differing notions of ethical business conduct are substantial. For further reading on this topic we have included portions of a law review article by Phillip Blumberg in the Appendix.

Duties of the Principal to the Agent

Primarily, the duties of the principal to the agent are based on the contractual understanding of the parties. Where there is no formal contract between the agent and the principal, or if there is a contract and it does not mention these duties, then the duties are based on the prior relation of the parties, the customs of the particular type of business involved, and common law.

The common law provides that in exchange for the fiduciary duties owed by the agent to the principal, the principal owes the following duties to the agent:

1. Not to interfere with the work of the agent.
2. To keep reasonably accurate records indicating the amount due to the agent.
3. To indemnify the agent for liabilities properly incurred by the agent in the scope of the agency.
4. To pay the agent a reasonable amount for the performance of the work contemplated by the subject of the agency.

Although an agency relationship may be based on consent and mere voluntary or gratuitous acts, most such relationships are created to exchange value. The agent offers a service and the principal pays for that service. Perhaps the largest single class of agents are salespeople. These salespeople represent the principal to third parties and try to sell either a service or a product.

The most frequent problems in agency law involving compensation revolve around the nature and the time at which a salesperson is entitled to a commission. The general rule is that in the absence of an agreement on when a commission is due, the commission is due when the sale is made even though it is not actually carried through or performed. For example, if you arrange with a real estate agent to sell your property and the agent procures a buyer who signs an offer form, and if the buyer meets all the conditions you put on the sale (and you meet the buyer's conditions), then the agent is entitled to be paid even if the transaction never closes. In many instances, the salesperson is entitled to the commission if the effort put forth on behalf of the principal is the effective or procuring cause for the sale, even though others were involved in completing the transaction.

Two related and important duties are not made clear by the list above. The first involves the liability of an employer-principal to the employee-agent for personal injuries sustained while performing work-related tasks. Because the circumstances of an agent's suing a principal for such injuries is often very contentious and filled with potential negative consequences for the employee (e.g., getting fired for suing), these matters are dealt with by workers' compensation acts in effect in most states. In general, the agent is compensated by a department of state government, which then adjusts insurance premiums for the employer to reflect the risk to employees working there.

A related idea is the duty of employers to provide a safe and healthy working place. This duty is created by both the common law and federal law. The existence of workers' compensation acts did not, in general, bring about safer work places. Job-related injuries cost the work force (and the economy) 250 million man-days in 1973. In that year, 14,200 employees were killed in work-related incidents and 2.5 million were permanently or temporarily disabled.[21] As a result of this record or one similar to it, and the ever-present threat of substances affecting worker health, Congress passed the Williams-Steiger Occupational Safety and Health Act of 1970. The duties created by this act are discussed elsewhere in this text, but we should note here that the duties from the employer-principal to the employee-agent created by this act are substantial.

Capacity

Legal capacity as we use the term here refers to the legal qualification of one to contract. Most states have statutes defining this legal capacity. Generally, they state that minors, persons declared insane, or those deprived of their civil rights (those in prison for a felony or aliens) lack this capacity. The common law of some states may further provide that persons so under the influence of drugs or alcohol that they cannot understand or appreciate the legal effect of their acts lack the legal capacity to accomplish the act.

In an agency relationship, it is most important that the principal have the legal capacity to act. If the principal has the capacity to give a legally operative consent, then an agent may be appointed by the principal to conduct all of those transactions that the principal could conduct if he were present.[22] This is so even if the agent lacks capacity to act for himself or herself, unless the agent is so drunk or similarly incapacitated that a third party would see that the agent did not know what he or she was doing. For example, if a state declares that those under 18 years of age lack capacity to contract, a principal of legal age may appoint a 17-year-old agent to act and will be bound by contracts made for the principal by the agent. Similarly, when the principal lacks capacity, such a person cannot appoint one who, alone, would have the capacity. When the capacity of the principal is removed, an agent who acts for the principal also lacks capacity.

Husband and Wife as Principal and Agent

Closely related to the discussion on capacity are the issues of when a husband and wife may act as agents for one another. Under common law, a wife was denied the capacity to contract. Today this is not so, but the law nevertheless does treat the contracts between husband and wife as well as those by a husband and wife with a third person for the benefit of the marriage as special. Neither the husband nor the wife has the power to contractually bind the other by virtue of the marriage relation alone.[23] However, the relation is such that circumstances which would not create an agency relationship between strangers might create an agency relationship between husband and wife. For example, consider this illustration from the *Restatement:*[24]

> P tells A, his wife, that she can open accounts for household supplies with certain designated local stores but with no others. A opens accounts in P's name with such stores and also with others; the latter accounts not being revealed to P. Modest bills for such supplies are incurred. Each month P gives A the money to pay the household bills, making no inquiries as to the creditors. At the end of six months P discovers the facts and refuses to pay the current bills of the undesignated stores. It may be found that A had apparent authority to incur such indebtedness on P's account.

In this case, the marriage relationship does create apparent authority (this concept of apparent authority is discussed in the next chapter) which would contractually bind the husband. Without additional facts, if P and A were strangers P would not be liable.

Except in the case of "necessaries" (needed food, clothing and shelter), a contract signed by one spouse does not bind the other unless there are additional circumstances indicating that one is acting on behalf of the other. Where one spouse contracts with regard to jointly owned property, then this is usually sufficient to bind the other party. Also, where one receives a benefit from jointly owned property, the recipient owns half of that received and holds the other half in trust as an agent for the other. The following case highlights this principle.

COOPER v. *COOPER*
284 S.W. 2d 617 (S.Ct. of Arkansas, 1955)

(Authors' note: An "estate by the entirety" is a legal form of joint ownership in which a husband and wife each have an equal right to possess all of the property owned and, on the death of either spouse, the remaining partner becomes owner of the entire property.)

ROBINSON, Justice

The principal issues here are the validity of a divorce granted by a court in the State of Nevada, and the wife's interest in funds received on a fire insurance policy for the loss of a house owned as an estate by the entirety. Appellant and appellee were married on August 29, 1950, in Columbia County, Arkansas, where they had lived all their lives. A son was born in January, 1952. On May 24, 1951, they purchased two acres of land as an estate by the entirety and built a house on the property. The house was insured for $2,500 against fire; later it burned and the loss was settled for $2,250 which was paid to appellant J. W. Cooper.

A short time later, he departed for the State of Nevada where it appears that he . . . filed suit for divorce. Dorothy was not notified, and he obtained a decree of divorce on March 26, 1953. Two days after this divorce was granted he returned to Arkansas and immediately married another person.

Appellee, Dorothy Cooper, then filed this suit in which she . . . asks for maintenance for herself and support for the child. She further asks that appellant be required to account to her for one-half of the proceeds from the insurance policy, . . . Cooper answered, alleging that he had been granted a valid divorce in the State of Nevada. Dorothy replied, denying the validity of the Nevada divorce. . . .

The Chancellor made a finding that the Nevada court was without jurisdiction to grant a divorce to Cooper, and ordered appellant to pay $12.50 a week for support of his child. The court also rendered a judgment against appellant for one-half of the proceeds of the insurance policy. . . .

Next is the question of the ownership of the proceeds of a policy of fire insurance. The house owned by the parties was destroyed by fire and Cooper collected and kept the insurance money. He had taken out the policy of insurance in his own name, but in doing so he was acting as agent for his wife as well as for himself.

The husband is not an agent for the wife solely by reason of the marital relationship. "But slight evidence of actual authority is sufficient proof of the agency of the husband for the wife in matters of domestic nature." . . .

And, it is said in *Restatement of Agency*, § 22: "Neither husband nor wife by virtue of the relationship has power to act as agent for the other. The relationship is of such a nature, however, that circumstances which in the case of strangers would not indicate the creation of authority or apparent authority may indicate it in the case of husband or wife." In the case at bar, the husband secured a policy of fire insurance in his name only on property which is an estate by the entirety. In these circumstances, the fact that the husband was acting as agent for his wife in addition to acting for himself is established if any reasonable inference to be deduced from the evidence leads to that conclusion.

In the case at bar, the circumstantial evidence proves that at the time Cooper obtained the policy of insurance not only was he acting for himself but he was also acting as an agent for his wife. . . .

As evidence of the fact that Cooper was acting as agent for his wife, she testified that she knew he had taken out the fire insurance policy, but she did now know that he had taken it out in his name only. She was present in the insurance company office, along with Cooper, when the settlement was agreed on, but she was not present when the check was delivered to him. In fact, she did not know that he had received the check. . . .

In the case at bar the evidence is convincing that Mrs. Cooper did not know that her husband had collected the insurance money, although there is some evidence to the contrary. Cooper held his wife's interest in the funds as trustee, and the court correctly found that he was indebted to Mrs. Cooper for one-half of the amount of the insurance he had collected on the house, . . .

The decree is affirmed.

Case Questions

1. What single fact caused the court to say that the husband was the agent of the wife?

2. The cause of action by the wife against the husband was based on the breach of what type of duty?

Review Problems

1. P, while on vacation, writes to A telling him to go to P's safe deposit vault, the key to which P encloses, to remove specified negotiable securities and to sell them on P's account. A takes the securities from the box and sells them, but fails to account for them to P. Soon after, A dies. Who owns the securities and why?

2. A falsely purports to be authorized by P to transfer some of P's property. T, a prospective purchaser, calls P on the telephone, mentions that A has contacted her about the sale. P neither admits nor denies that A was authorized to act for P. T pays A for the property, and A gives T what is purported to be a "title" to the property. As between T and P, who is entitled to the property?

3. P learns that A, who has no authority whatsoever to negotiate for P, is negotiating with Q as P's supposed agent. P does nothing about this, although he could rather easily notify Q. Q pays A for goods belonging to P. Who is entitled to the goods?

4. Falsely saying that he is acting for a "well-known Chicago wholesale house," A contracts to sell goods to T. In fact, A was intending to act for P, a small-town manufacturer of doubtful reliability. When P finds out about this, P affirms the contract. When T finds out about it, T wants out of the contract. Will T be excused from performing, or did P ratify the contract of A?

5. Ed was hired by Allen to be a drillpress operator. Eighteen years later Ed had worked his way up to chief of the production engineering department for Allen, now called the Allen Manufacturing Company, a company that made various kinds of screws. In 1956 Allen gave permission to Ed and one of his subordinates to attempt to adapt a new idea for producing screws to Allen's production process. Ed spent about $180,000 of Allen's money plus his own and his helper's time to do this. The diagrams made were not marked secret or confidential, and this new process could be seen by frequent visitors to Allen's plant. This was true even though the new process did give Allen a competitive advantage in the markets he sold in. The new process was never patented.

   Ed and his subordinate were offered a job by a competing screw manufacturer to adapt the new process to the competitor's process. Both of them quit Allen and began work for the competitor. Allen sued Ed and his helper and requested the court to grant an injunction against them forbidding disclosure of the new process. Should the court grant the injunction?

6. Kate was on the audit staff of a large certified public accounting firm. She had been with the firm for six years and was at the level of supervisor. This position was crucial in the firm because the supervisor conducted the audit (through subordinates) and was, in general, responsible for its accuracy, although a partner in the firm was the one ultimately responsible to the partnership and to the public for it. When the audit on Darth Corporation was completed, Kate was called into the partner's office. It was explained to her that a few of

her qualifying notes would have to be changed. Although her notes were thorough and accurate and changing them was not illegal, the change did not represent what she thought was a fair presentation of the client's business operation. Is she under a duty to change the audit report? Can she be sued by the CPA firm if she refuses to change it? Can she be fired if she refuses to change it? In general what are the rights and obligations of Kate and her partnership?

7. The plaintiff was hired in September, 1968 at $1.84 per hour to work on a conversion machine in the defendant's factory and was allegedly told that if she worked well she would get better jobs with better pay. After working without incident for about three months, she applied to fill an opening on a press machine at higher wages. The plaintiff testified that her foreman told her that if she wanted the job she would have to be "nice." She got the job at $2.79 per hour and claimed that her foreman then asked her to go out with him, which she refused to do because she was married and had three children. There followed a series of events in which she was, she claimed, harassed and she ultimately was fired for refusing to be "nice." Should the common law recognize a cause of action on her behalf for malicious discharge? (See *Monge* v. *Beebe Rubber Co.*, 316 A 2d 549, S.Ct., N.H., 1974.)

8. M started a small manufacturing firm in Ohio to produce and market a new form of skin protection lotion, which was formed by mixing suntan lotion with bug repellant and perfume. The advantage of using such a solution seemed so obvious to M that he was sure the firm would make a profit. He made his own suntan lotion from a combination of coconut oils and iodine and combined this with sprucewood sap and alcohol with a pinch of rosebud fragrance thrown in. M hired P to be chief production engineer, and as part of the employment contract P agreed in writing that he would not:

> . . . for a period of five years after leaving M's employment for any reason whatsoever in an area east of the Mississippi River engage in or consult with any person or firm in or about to be engaged in the manufacture of suntan lotions or bug repellants or other skin protection lotions.

M also hired S, a salesperson, to develop the market for the product in Illinois, Ohio, and surrounding states. S was to drive his own car, pay for his own gas, and determine his own route. Additionally, M hired an office staff which consisted of a secretary, G, a receptionist, R, and an office manager, O.

The firm was an overnight success and sales and profits shot skyward. The firm even began selling throughout the midwest. The idea seemed so simple M never did apply for a patent. All of the employees wondered why no one had ever tried it before. Unknown to M, the secretary he hired was a brilliant mathematician whose hobby was theoretical chemistry. She immediately discerned that it would take no great effort to make her own combination suntan-bug repellant-perfume lotion so she quit the firm taking with her the production manager, P. They set up their firm in Kentucky, but had a disagreement and P went to Florida to set up a firm of his own while G continued to develop her firm.

Neither G nor P used the same identical ingredients as M but used chemicals which could be substituted for M's substances. They did use the same proportions of materials which P and M had calculated as being a uniquely stable combination of ingredients. P had informed G of this combination.

Assume that you are M and you wish to do everything possible to protect your business. Write a short essay in which you explain how the legal arguments would be developed. First list the legal principles or rules you learned from this chapter that you believe might help your case. Next write down a complete and precise definition of these rules. Following the definition of the rules, apply the definition to the factual pattern above by integrating the facts of the case with the statement of the rule. Be sure to list the "relevant facts"; that is, list those facts that lead you to believe that the principle should be applied. If there is a question in your mind about whether or not the principle would be applied, then state the facts of the case that cause you to question the rule's applicability. Perhaps there are some facts missing that would cause you to conclude definitely that the principle is applicable. State these facts and how they would influence your decision.

Finally, based on your conclusions as to the applicability of the rules discussed in this chapter, conclude whether or not M can legally restrain P and G from operating their respective businesses.

9. In addition to the above facts in problem 8, assume that one day M could not get away from work to pick up an important package at the post office and so he asked a neighbor, N, to do so, and N agreed. Was an agency formed between M and N?

10. The office manager in the above factual pattern, O, was a very generous type and was always looking out for and protecting the interests of the office staff. O paid for a new typewriter for M's business out of his own pocket when the firm was short of cash. Also, O used his own money to pay for a color TV for employees to watch on their coffee and lunch breaks. Could M be required to reimburse O for these expenditures?

In answering this question, construct your answer in the same way you answered question 8. First state and then define the legal principle that you believe will control this case. Then integrate the facts with the principle and finally state your conclusion.

Endnotes

1. Vol.'s 1 & 2, Am. L. Inst., *The Restatement of Agency,* 2d (1958). (Hereafter referred to as "Restatement, 2nd")

2. W. A. Seavey, *Law of Agency,* 1964.

3. *Ibid.,* p. 3.

4. *Restatement,* 2nd § 82.

5. *Ibid.,* § 8B.

6. *Black's Law Dictionary,* Rev. 4th ed., 753 (1957).

7. Seavey, *Supra,* p. 243.

8. *Restatement,* 2nd § 12.

9. *Ibid.,* § 13.

10. *Developments-Competitive Torts,* 77 Harv. L. Rev. 951–953 (1964).

11. Lansing and Pegnetter, *Fair Dismissal Procedures for Non-Union Employees,* 20 Am. Bus. L. J. 75, 90 (1982).

12. *The Legality of Discharging Employees for Insubordination,* 18 Am. Bus. L. J. 371, 372 (1980).

13. See *Geary* v. *United States Steel Corporation,* 456 Pa. 171, 319 A2d 174 (1975).

14. *Peterman* v. *Teamsters Local 396,* 174 Cal. App. 2d 184, 344 P2d 25 (1959).

15. *Trombetta* v. *Detroit, T & I.R.R.,* 81 Mich. App. 489, 265 N.W. 2d 385 (1978).

16. Blackburn, *Restricted Employer Discharge Rights: A Changing Concept of Employment at Will,* 17 Am. Bus. L. J. 467 (1980).

17. See *Mange* v. *Beebe Rubber Co.,* 114 N.H. 130, 316 A2d 549 (1974).

18. Reich, The Limits of Duty, *The New Yorker,* 52 (June 19, 1971).

19. See Blumberg, Corporate Responsibility and the Employee's Duty of Loyalty and Obedience: A Preliminary Inquiry, 24 Okla. L. Rev. 279 (1971).

20. *Ibid.,* and see Lansing, *supra,* p. 90–91.

21. Ill. Inst. for Continuing L. Ed., OSHA, pp. 1–5 (1974).

22. *Restatement* 2d *supra,* p. 91.

23. *Ibid.,* p. 94.

24. *Ibid.,* p. 95.

Contractual Liability of Principals and Agents to Third Parties

4

In Chapter 3 the first two elements of the agency definition were presented. They were that (1) the relationship is a fiduciary one and (2) it is based on consent. The remainder of the agency definition presented in Chapter 3 stated that the relationship is one in which one person, the agent, shall act on behalf of the principal and subject to this person's control.

All corporations, partnerships, governmental units, and some individuals employ others to act on their behalf and subject to their control. The last part of the definition of agency implies that agents are utilized primarily to act for the principal in dealings with persons who are strangers to the agency relationship. These strangers are called "third parties." Indeed, the real heart of agency law is that body of legal principles creating legal duties that run from the principal to third parties because of the promises, representations, or acts of the agent. The circumstances in which the agent can create legal duties, that is, legally bind the principal to third parties, are the subjects of this and the following chapter.

Before proceeding with an analysis of these circumstances it would be helpful to keep in mind a basic distinction between the two central branches of the civil law. Civil duties (as opposed to criminal duties) are imposed primarily by the common law of *torts* and *contracts*.

Contract and Tort Liability Distinguished

Tort liability arises because of injury to one's person, property, reputation, or some other legally protected interest. The common torts such as negligence, battery, defamation, and so forth are defined in the next chapter along with the methods the law uses to impute the tort liability of the agent to the principal when the agent tortiously injures a third party. Generally speaking, these methods vary depending on the degree of control exercised by the principal over the agent.

Contract duties or liabilities arise because one breaches a promise or set of promises made to another party. These promises may be stated, either in writing or orally; that is, *expressed*. Or, they may be imposed on the agent or principal because of the acts of the principal or agent. These promises are *implied* by the law. Most of the circumstances in which principals will be liable to third parties based on a breach of either expressed or implied promises made by the agent are presented in this chapter.

The reader should be cautioned, however, that "compartmentalizing" the law into tort liability and contract liability for purposes of presenting this agency material is not without drawbacks. Simply stated, some factual patterns just do not neatly fit into either category. Hence, if an agent (A) is given money by a third party (T/P) for delivery to the principal (P) and A absconds with it, the act of absconding may be both a breach of contract to T/P (if P fails to deliver the goods the money was intended to pay for) as well as a tort (a conversion of T/P's money). Nevertheless, we believe the reader will be helped in understanding the agency material if a factual pattern is first read for an understanding of the basic violation of duty (either contract or tort) and then read for an understanding of the court's reasoning.

If you use this method of analysis, you will find that cases involving a breach of promise are usually resolved by applying legal principles that define *authority*, and that cases involving torts are resolved by applying legal principles that define the right of the principal to *control* the physical acts of the agent. Authority and control are the two primary distinguishing principles between contract liability for the principal and tort liability.

Contractual Liability of Principals to Third Parties

Courts will impose liability on a principal for the promises or representations made by an agent to a third party when the court finds that the principal *authorized* the agent to make the promise or representation.

Courts have defined two broad types of authority: actual authority—either express or implied; and circumstantial authority—either apparent or inherent. The doctrines of estoppel and ratification, discussed below, achieve the same result as the application of principles of authority but are not usually considered types of authority.

Actual Authority—Express or Implied

Expressed authority is defined as that authority that the principal gives either in writing or by spoken word to the agent when instructing the agent when and how to act on the principal's behalf. Express authority may take the form of a formal document such as a power of attorney, which is a sworn statement in writing that another is to act for and in the place of the principal, or it may be manifested in less formal ways such as a board of directors' resolution or a mere statement in an employment contract that the employee (agent) is to "sell the goods of the employer."

In a commercial transaction of any complexity at all, however, it is impossible for the principal to express all of the kinds of authority that may be needed by the agent to complete the transaction. Therefore, the law recognizes "implied" authority, which is that authority reasonably necessary to accomplish the act for which the express authority was given. Implied authority is found by examining the facts of the particular case, defining the express authority, and then asking whether a reasonable person familiar with the customs and ways of dealings of agents in the particular line of business could believe that the agent had the authority to act (See Figure 4.1). The key difference between implied authority and the kinds of circumstantial authority described below is that the implied authority flows from the grant of express authority and must be reasonably necessary to accomplish the purpose of the express authority. If there is no express authority, there can be no implied authority; yet, there may be circumstantial authority.

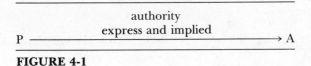

FIGURE 4-1

Since implied authority is primarily authority by necessity, it also includes the authority to act in an emergency to protect the interests of the principal when no express authority was given. Of course, if there is time to communicate with the principal, the agent must do so. But if the agent cannot communicate by any reasonable means and the circumstances appear to call for action in order to prevent loss for the principal, the agent has the authority to act as necessary. For example, a chauffeur employed only "to drive" may be authorized to have repairs made to the limousine when it breaks down on the road and the principal cannot be contacted. He may have this authority even though it was contrary to the expressed authority so long as there is a reasonable probability of further loss to the principal.[1]

Most of the cases in the remaining material on agency will involve three parties: the principal, the agent and the third party. It is essential to understand at the outset who is the plaintiff and who is the defendant and who committed the breach of duty alleged. So, when analyzing the remainder of the textual material on agency and the appellate cases, you may find it helpful to draw a diagram to clarify the identity of the parties and the rules being discussed. For example, the first case presented below could be diagrammed as shown in Figure 4-2.

The two cases that follow present factual patterns involving first, express authority and then implied authority. The first case illustrates that even though the agent is expressly authorized to contract, the third party is held to a certain standard of reasonableness. There is no absolute right to rely on the express authority of the principle.

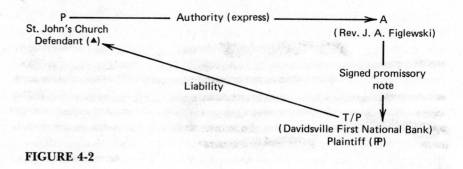

FIGURE 4-2

DAVIDSVILLE FIRST NATIONAL BANK v. ST. JOHN'S CHURCH
296 Pa. 467 (1929)

(Author's note: The trial court found for the plaintiff and defendant appeals.)

Opinion By Mr. Justice Walling:

The defendant, St. John's Church, Windber, Pa., is an unincorporated Roman Catholic Church organization, located in Somerset County, of which Rev. J. A. Figlewski was pastor or priest, and as such gave the plaintiff bank a note as follows:

> 2500.00/100 Davidsville, Pa., Nov. 30, 1925.
>
> On demand after date, we or either of us promise to pay to the order of THE FIRST NATIONAL BANK, DAVIDSVILLE, Pa., at the FIRST NATIONAL BANK, DAVIDSVILLE, Pa., Two thousand five hundred and no/100—dollars without defalcation, value received. . . .
> St. John's Church, Windber, Pa. (Seal).
> Rev. J. A. Figlewski, Pastor (Seal). . . .

In the summer of 1923, the church membership, at a properly convened meeting, decided to repair their school building and erect a convent and to secure a loan of $15,000 for that purpose. Under the rule of the church a parish like the defendant could not incur an indebtedness exceeding $500 without the consent of the bishop of the diocese. Hence, the pastor sought and obtained a permit, as follows:

> CHANCERY 1211 Thirteenth St., Altoona, Pa., July 7—23
>
> Rev. J. Figlewski:
>   St. John's Church, Windber.
>   Dear Father: At a meeting of the Diocesian Consultors you were granted permission to contract a debt of $15,000 for masonry repairs & changes to school & convent.
>   By Order of the Rt. Rev. Bishop Bernard Conlay
>
> Sec'y Consultors.

Some two years and four months after the permit was issued the pastor presented it to the plaintiff and obtained thereon a loan of $2,500, for which he gave the note in suit. There was oral testimony that he told the bank the permit was not nearly exhausted. So far as appears, he made no representations to the bank as to the action taken by the congregation. The evidence for the defendant was that the church had obtained loans to the amount of the $15,000 from two local banks shortly after the date of the permit; with which, and some $10,000 additional raised by the congregation, the specific improvements were made during 1923 and 1924. The loan in suit was the only one made by the pastor from plaintiff for defendant, although he was known to the bank and had previously done business with it. The proof tends to show that soon after making the loan in suit the pastor absconded with the $2,500. From the church funds the succeeding pastor paid the interest on this note for two years, but testified that he did so in ignorance of the true situation and without the knowledge or approval of the lay members. . . .

By law the bishop cannot create an indebtedness without the consent of the congregation nor under the canons of the church can it incur an indebtedness exceeding $500 without his permit. Each is a check upon the other.

The trial court erred in treating the mere permit and assurance of the pastor that it was not exhausted as warranting the loan. The age of the permit, nearly two and a half years, was such as to require inquiry of the congregation. The plaintiff bank and the church were close neighbors and slight inquiry by the former would doubtless have disclosed the fact that the improvements stated in the permit had been completed and paid for . . . by funds secured from other banks, to the full amount of the permit and that the congregation had refused to request a further permit. . . .

One who gives credit to a pastor on the faith of an old permit without inquiry from the congregation does so at his peril. Otherwise a pastor might bankrupt the church for his own purposes despite the limit in the permit. Happily, it is rare that a priest or pastor betrays his church. That the pastor had possession of the old permit proved nothing as to its vitality. The money having been secured from different banks, there was nothing strange in his retention of the permit, especially as it was his warrant for executing the notes. That it had been fully exhausted shortly after its date, quite clearly appeared by the evidence for the defense. . . .

Here the agency of the pastor was to borrow $15,000 for the church; when that was done and obligations given therefore, the permit was exhausted and the agency terminated. . . . "A person dealing with an agent must not act negligently, but must use reasonable diligence to ascertain whether the agent acts within the scope of his power. He is not authorized under any circumstances blindly to trust the agent's statements as to the extent of his powers:" 21 R.C.L., page 853. If this loan was valid, one for the entire $15,000 would have been. So the bishop's express limit and the like limit of the congregation would go for nought.

Had the church received the $2,500 the case would present a different aspect . . . , but there is no evidence or even averment that it received the money or any part of it, and the burden as to that was upon the plaintiff.

True, the new pastor receiving bills for interest on the note paid them for two years, supposing, as he testified, that it was a bona fide note of the church; but if done in ignorance, that would not constitute a ratification on the part of the church. In any event the burden of showing ratification was upon the plaintiff and the priest could not ratify the note without authority from the lay members. A principal can ratify the unauthorized act of an agent only when he has knowledge thereof. This may be a hard case for the bank; if so, it results from its overconfidence in the pastor, for which neither the bishop nor the congregation was blamable. . . .

The judgment is reversed. . . .

Case Questions

1. St. John's Church was an unincorporated association. Under what circumstances could it be sued in its own name?

2. In this case there was a contract signed between the old pastor, Figlewski, and the bank for the purported benefit of the church. The legal issue may be stated

in broad terms thusly: Did the signing of the contract by the pastor legally bind the church? In a few concise sentences state why or why not.

3. A third party who does business with an agent has a duty to ascertain the authority of the agent. How do you define this duty?

COBLENTZ v. RISKIN
74 Nev. 53, 322 P. 2d 905 (S. Ct. Nev., 1958)

MERRILL, Justice

The sole question upon this appeal is whether the record supports the determination of the trial court (sitting without jury) that the acts of the employee in receiving the merchandise and in executing the consignment agreement were on behalf of the defendants and were authorized by them. We have concluded that the record provides such support and that judgment should be affirmed.

Appellants are owners of the Thunderbird Jewel Shop in Clark County, Nevada. Respondent Riskin is a diamond broker and wholesale jeweler of Los Angeles, California. In August, 1955 appellants employed Hyman Davidson for services in connection with their store. In January, 1956 Davidson entered into a consignment agreement with Riskin pursuant to which he received, for purposes of retail sale, two expensive items of jewelry. In his dealings with Riskin, Davidson represented himself as manager of the jewel shop with full authority to receive merchandise on consignment. Riskin did not check these representations with appellants but did check with others in the jewelry trade and satisfied himself as to Davidson's authority. The jewelry pieces were reconsigned by Davidson without Riskin's approval or consent. The person to whom they were reconsigned has disappeared. Riskin demanded of appellants the return of the jewelry or its agreed value pursuant to the terms of the agreement. Upon failure of appellants to comply with his demand this action was brought. Judgment in favor of Riskin was given in the sum of $16,300.

Appellants contend that there is no evidence from which the trial court could have found the essentials of either actual or apparent authority to exist. . . .

In support of its conclusion of authority the court found, "That during the month of August, 1955 the defendants . . . engaged and employed one Hyman Davidson . . . as manager of the Thunderbird Jewel Shop . . . . That the said Hyman Davidson was and acted as manager of the said Thunderbird Jewel Shop at all times between August, 1955 and the beginning of March, 1956 on behalf of, for the account of and for the benefit of the said defendants and each of them. That the said Hyman Davidson, during the period aforesaid, with the knowledge, consent and approval of the defendants, and each of them, held himself out to the jewelry trade and to persons dealing with the said Thunderbird Jewel Shop as the manager of the said Thunderbird Jewel Shop, with full authority to receive merchandise on behalf of the said Thunderbird Jewel Shop on memorandum and/or consignment."

Although in many respects the evidence is in dispute the record unquestionably provides support for this finding.

Riskin testified that it was the custom in the jewelry trade to take expensive pieces of jewelry on consignment rather than by purchase at wholesale. This testimony is compellingly supported by reason when the nature of consignment transactions and the benefit to retail merchants of this commercial practice are considered. By consignment retail merchants are not financially committed to the purchase of expensive items until they have themselves resold the items. Until resale their only financial commitment is that of safekeeping. Thus there is substantial benefit to be realized at the minimum of financial commitment. It can hardly be questioned that the engaging in consignment transactions would be regarded by those in the jewelry trade as a customary, proper and necessary function of store management.

Davidson testified positively that he had been employed as manager of the store with instructions to run the store as he saw fit; . . .

Actual authority includes . . . implied authority . . . Implied authority is that which the agent reasonably believes himself to possess as a result of representations by the principal or of acts of the agent permitted by the principal over a course of time in which the principal has acquiesced. . . . (or) that which is reasonably necessary, proper and usual to carry into effect the main authority granted. . . .

The trial court has found that Davidson was employed to serve as manager and that he did so serve. The evidence we have recited presents a clear case of . . . implied authority. . . . We conclude that the trial court's determination of actual authority is supported by the record and that appellants are bound by Davidson's actions in their behalf in committing them to the consignment agreement with Riskin.

Affirmed.

Case Questions

1. In your own words define "implied authority."

2. If you hire an agent and instruct him or her to "manage" your business, what other limitations, if any, are placed on his or her authority to act for you? To help answer this question some legal scholars and courts recognize a distinction between general and special agents. A general agent is one who is employed as a permanent employee to conduct a series of transactions. A general manager is such an agent, and if a person has such a title, third parties can reasonably assume that the person has the same authority to act that most general managers in that business possess. In the above case, note that an important element of proof for the plaintiff was the fact that much of the business between jewel owners and jewel sellers or retailers was done on a consignment basis.

A special agent is one employed to conduct a specific task. Usually there is authority to conduct only one transaction. If the circumstances reveal to a third party that an employee is a special agent, the third party should inquire about the precise nature of the authority possessed. With regard to the *Davidsville* case, the pastor might well be labeled a special agent. Why?

Circumstantial Authority—Apparent Authority, Estoppel, and Inherent Authority

Circumstantial authority is authority that courts recognize and impose on an agency relationship even though there is no express or implied authority. Courts do this because the circumstances of the third party's dealing with the agent could reasonably lead a third party to believe that the agent was authorized. A key difference between actual and circumstantial authority is that the actual authority is defined by asking what measure of authority was really given to the agent by the principal, while circumstantial authority is defined by asking what measure of authority could a third party reasonably believe the agent to have under the circumstances.

Apparent Authority. Circumstantial authority is often divided into several categories or types. The most comprehensive type of circumstantial authority is called apparent authority. The *Restatement* defines apparent authority as follows:

> Apparent authority is the power to affect the legal relations of another person by transactions with third parties, professedly as agent for the other, arising from and in accordance with the other's manifestations to such third party.[2]

Generally, there are two factual elements that a court must find in order to conclude that the agent was apparently authorized. First, it must find that the *principal,* referred to in the definition above as the "other" person, not the agent, created some of the circumstances leading the third party to believe the agent was authorized, and, second, it must find that the third party reasonably relied on these circumstances. It makes no difference if the principal has expressly forbidden the agent to act, or has otherwise secretly placed restrictions on the agent's authority. So long as the court or jury can find the two basic factual elements mentioned above, they most probably will find that the agent's promise or conduct was apparently authorized.

The concept of apparent authority was created to protect the reasonable expectations of those in commerce who do business with agents. It is one of the more dynamic principles in the law of agency and today occupies a central, almost dominating position in the agency field.[3] The concept is not only growing and changing a principal's liability for an agent's contracts but, just as important, it is imposing new types of liability on the principal for the agent's tortious conduct. This will be more fully explained in the next chapter.

In some cases, apparent authority will be the proper principle to apply, but the facts of the case may suggest that either implied authority or apparent authority are proper. Given the theoretical differences between implied authority and apparent authority, rarely should they be used or applied in the same case. Remember that for the use of implied authority, you must find a grant of express authority from which the implied authority could reasonably follow. In the *Coblentz* case, Davidson was told to "manage" the jewelry store. This grant of express authority carried with it the implied authority to accept consignments. It seemed that there was no expressed limitation by the principal on the agent's authority to manage. The following case is different. Read it with a view to understanding why the court resolved the conflict in terms of apparent authority and not implied authority.

HECKEL et al. v. CRANFORD COUNTRY CLUB

97 N.J. Law 538; 117 A. 607 (1922)

KATZENBACH, J.

This action was instituted to recover the value of articles of food alleged to have been sold by the plaintiffs-respondents to the defendant-appellant. The plaintiffs were engaged in the meat and produce business in Bloomfield. The defendant was the Union County Country Club, subsequently known as the Cranford Golf Club, and later as the Echo Lake Country Club. The articles were purchased between August 1, 1918, and December 10, of the same year. They were ordered by one Roachman, who had been engaged about March 29, 1918, as manager of the club, and was known and is referred to in the testimony as the club manager or steward. Roachman was paid a salary of $200 a month, and also had the restaurant privilege of the club; that is, Roachman was to furnish the members with meals and refreshments to be supplied by him and for which they were to pay him, and the profit, if any, was to supplement his salary. Roachman was the steward during the entire period of the purchases from the plaintiffs. At the time of the first purchase, he introduced himself as the steward of the club, and as the person of whom the steward of the Baltursrol Club, which was located near the defendant's grounds, had spoken to the plaintiffs. The goods ordered by Roachman were charged by the plaintiffs to the club, delivered to the clubhouse, accompanied by charge slips addressed to the club, with each order delivered. Bills were sent by mail monthly by the plaintiffs, addressed to the club. . . . From these facts the plaintiffs contended that the club was responsible to them for the goods ordered by Roachman, and the defendant contended that Roachman was the plaintiffs' debtor, and no liability to pay the account attached to the club. There was no dispute as to the delivery of the goods or the correctness of the charges made therefor. The one question at issue was that of liability. The trial judge permitted the case to go to the jury, which rendered a verdict for the plaintiffs for the full amount of their claim. From the judgment entered upon the verdict the club has appealed.

The appellant contends that there was no evidence of Roachman's power to bind the club for the payment of the goods ordered by him, and in the absence of such evidence it was the duty of the trial court to grant either the defendant's motion for a nonsuit or for the direction of a verdict in its favor.

Mr. Justice Trenehard . . . stated the law with . . . clearness when he said:

"As between the principal and third persons the true limit of the agent's power to bind the principal is the apparent authority with which the agent is invested. The principal is bound by the acts of the agent within the apparent authority which he knowingly permits the agent to assume, or which he holds the agent out to the public as possessing. And the reason is that to permit the principal to dispute the authority of the agent in such cases would be to enable him to commit a fraud upon innocent persons. . . .

"The question in every such case is whether the principal has by his voluntary act placed the agent in such a situation that a person of ordinary prudence, conversant with business usages, and the nature of the particular business, is justified in presuming that such agent has authority to perform the particular act in question, and when the party relying upon such apparent authority presents evidence which would justify a finding in his favor, he is entitled to have the questions submitted to the jury."

The difficulty always arises in the application of the law to the facts of the given case. In the present case, did the club place Roachman in such a situation that a person of ordinary prudence, conversant with business usages and the nature of the particular business, would be justified in presuming that Roachman had authority to order provisions for the club? Did the plaintiffs present such evidence of Roachman's apparent authority as to justify the trial court in submitting to the jury the question of his authority to bind the club? We think these two questions should be answered in the affirmative.

It was admitted that the club employed Roachman as manager or steward, and paid him a salary. It is a matter of common knowledge that one of the duties of a steward of a country club is to obtain the supplies necessary to serve the members of the club with meals and refreshments. While it is true that as between Roachman and the club, Roachman was

to be responsible for the payment of the supplies ordered by him, yet by his employment as steward the club had apparently clothed Roachman with the powers usually appertaining to the position of steward, of which one was the purchase of supplies for a club. When, therefore, Roachman approached the plaintiffs, informed them of the position he held with the club, ordered provisions, which were charged to the club, delivered to the club-house, and bills therefore were mailed to the club monthly, and this course of dealing continued for approximately five months, without either repudiation of Roachman's authority or any intimation from the club that he was without authority to bind it, we feel that such evidence presented a question for the determination of the jury. . . .

The judgment is affirmed, with costs.

Case Questions   1. Exactly what did the principal do in this case to create the reasonable expectation that Roachman was authorized to contract?

2. What act or acts were the reasonable reliance which the law requires for the proper application of apparent authority?

3. In simple terms, who won the above case and why?

4. What could the principal have done in this case to protect itself from liability created by Roachman?

In the *Heckel* case, the parties could not properly argue and the court could not properly apply the principle of implied authority because it seems that as between the principal and agent, there was an understanding that the agent (Roachman) had no express authority to negotiate on behalf of the country club with third parties. Although Roachman was to manage the country club, the operation of the restaurant was entirely his. That is, with regard to the purchase and sale of the food, he was an independent contractor. An independent contractor is defined and discussed in the next chapter. Simply put, there was no expression of authority (to buy or sell food) from the principal to the agent. Implied authority would have to flow from the express authority, and since there was no express authority, the court relied on applying apparent authority. Apparent authority does present a separate legal theory from either express or implied authority. However, its difference from estoppel is less clear.

Estoppel.   The circumstances in which the courts will impose apparent authority on the agent when actual authority existed in fact are very similar to those circumstances in which some courts will invoke the doctrine of estoppel. Estoppel is a well established legal principle created from the law of equity and was discussed in the last chapter with regard to creating an agency relationship. In general terms, it means that one's own act or failure to act when a reasonable person would have, will stop or close his mouth to plead the truth.[4]

The *Restatement* provides a more elaborate definition:

1. A person who is not otherwise liable as a party to a transaction purported to be done on his account, is nevertheless subject to liability to persons who have changed their positions because of their belief that the transaction was entered into by or for him, if
    (a) he intentionally or carelessly caused such belief, or
    (b) knowing of such belief and that others might change their positions because of it, he did not take reasonable steps to notify them of the facts. . . .

        . . .

3. Change of position, as the phrase is used in the restatement, indicates the payment of money, expenditure of labor, suffering a loss or subjection to legal liability.[5]

There is some disagreement as to whether "estoppel" is a distinctly separate legal doctrine in the law of agency. Some courts believe that estoppel forms the real basis for apparent authority and therefore seem to use apparent authority in circumstances that would support the use of an estoppel argument. Other authorities such as the *Restatement* and Professor Warren Seavey assert that estoppel is more narrowly defined than apparent authority.[6] The *Restatement,* for example, admits that in most circumstances in which apparent authority exists, estoppel may also exist.[7] However, estoppel is appropriately argued when there have been (1) circumstances created by the principal that (2) cause a third party to reasonably believe the agent has authority (these two elements are identical to the elements for apparent authority) and (3) the third party has changed position. Thus estoppel is more narrow than apparent authority because it requires an additional element of proof—change in position.

Another difference that some perceive between apparent authority and estoppel is that estoppel may not be pleaded by the principal as the basis for a cause of action against a third party but apparent authority may be. That is, if an agent does not have the express authority to contract with a third party, but does so anyway, and the third party could reasonably believe the agent was authorized to contract by relying on circumstances created by the principal, most courts would allow the principal to sue the third party on a theory of apparent authority. Most courts would not apply the doctrine of estoppel to either the principal or the third party in such a case.

Perhaps an example of the different circumstances in which courts would usually apply the doctrines of apparent authority and estoppel will help in understanding the need for and use of the two principles.

Assume that P, by letter, authorizes A to sell his real property. The letter is given to A who shows it to T/P who then contracts with A for the purchase of P's real property. Assume that P telephones A and revokes the authority in the letter just before A signs the contract with T/P. Nevertheless, A signs the contract. The contract was not expressly authorized because P did revoke A's authority by telephone; therefore, there could be no implied authority to contract either. However, P would be liable to T/P on the basis of apparent authority. Without changing his position, T/P could sue P if P refused to abide by the contractual provisions. Even though P revoked the actual authority, P could also hold T/P liable if T/P breached the contract.[8] Estoppel would not be properly applied in this case because T/P suffered no change of position or out-of-pocket loss.

Now consider the following example: assume A, in the presence of P, states to T/P that he, A, is authorized by P to sell P's painting. P heard this statement of A's and said nothing. A contracts with T/P for the sale of P's painting and T/P thereby refrains from buying another painting he had an opportunity to buy. In this example, if T/P sued P for breach of contract, a court most probably would estop (not allow) P to defend on the basis of the lack of authority. In essence, the court would be reasoning that because P had a duty to speak up if A lacked authority, but did not do so, the court will not permit him to speak now. In this example, A was not actually authorized to sell the painting. Further, the use of apparent authority here would be a weak argument because of the lack of positive acts of P clothing A with authority to act. Yet, it appears that T/P has changed his position by refraining from buying another painting, which is presumably not available now, so that it would be unfair to allow P to deny he authorized the sale.

Perhaps a more realistic example is the following summary of a rather complicated commercial transaction. Southwestern Portland Cement, the plaintiff, was contacted by an agent, Adams, and asked to furnish bulk cement to Adams' plant where Adams mixed the cement into concrete. The concrete was delivered to two people, the principals, Beavers and Glasgow, who were doing business in the name of a partnership called Plains Sand and Gravel. This partnership had contracted to deliver the concrete to Wilkerson-Webb, who had a contract with Cannon

Air Force Base for a major construction job. A diagram of these parties would look like this:

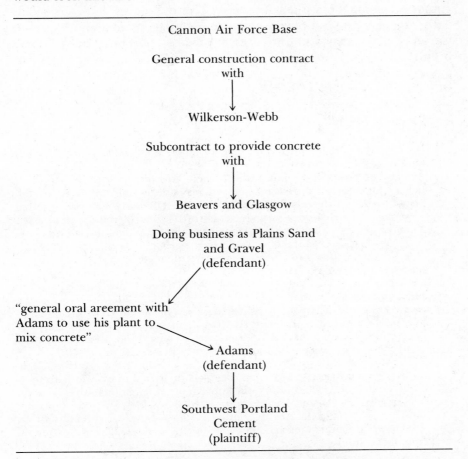

Cannon Air Force Base

General construction contract
with

Wilkerson-Webb

Subcontract to provide concrete
with

Beavers and Glasgow

Doing business as Plains Sand
and Gravel
(defendant)

"general oral areement with
Adams to use his plant to
mix concrete"

Adams
(defendant)

Southwest Portland
Cement
(plaintiff)

On two occasions, the partnership, Plains Sand and Gravel, ordered cement from Southwest and had them deliver it to Adams. Adams signed for these deliveries on behalf of Plains Sand and Gravel, and Southwest was paid by a joint check from Wilkerson-Webb to Plains Sand and Gravel and Southwest. After these two deliveries, Adams called Southwest and ordered three more shipments of cement. In the meantime, Adams' mixing equipment broke down and he was unable to deliver the cement to Plains Sand and Gravel, who then contracted with someone else to deliver the cement. Plains Sand and Gravel did not contact Southwest when it did this. Southwest sought payment for the three deliveries from Plains Sand and Gravel, saying that Adams had been authorized to order the shipment. Southwest sued both Adams and Beavers and Glasgow for the amount of payment due for the last three shipments of cement.

Assume that there are no other important circumstances tending to show that Adams was an agent for Plains Sand and Gravel. What kinds of authority should be argued for here? There is no evidence of actual authority, express or implied, for the three orders in question. Were the elements of apparent authority present? The essential question is, do two orders placed *by the partnership* for delivery to the alleged agent create apparent authority in the agent to order more? The answer was not an easy one. In an opinion that reads more like a simple balancing of the equities of the case, the court, affirming a decision for the plaintiff, Southwest, reasoned as follows.

> We cannot say that under these circumstances Southwestern acted in bad faith or without reasonable prudence in delivering the last three shipments. As between Southwestern and the partners, it is the latter's conduct which fails to meet the test of reasonable prudence, for not only did they have the responsibility for the relationship, they neglected to notify Southwestern that they had made different arrangements for delivery of the concrete when Adams' equipment broke down. If they had done this, Southwestern's delivery of the last three shipments would have been at its peril. . . .
>
> A settled course of conduct does serve to create apparent authority in the agent binding upon the principal where the acts are not timely disavowed and a third party is thereby induced to rely on the ostensible authority of the agent and does so in good faith and with reasonable prudence. The doctrine is based upon an estoppel: the principal will not be permitted to establish that the agent's authority was less than what was apparent from the course of dealing for when one of two innocent parties must suffer, the loss must fall upon the party who created the enabling circumstances. . . .
>
> It is the appellants who should bear the loss since they are responsible for a course of business with the necessary apparent authority and are now estopped to deny that authority, the appellant having reasonably relied upon it. Furthermore, balancing the positions of both sides, the appellants fall short for they could have easily averted their loss by advising Southwestern that they had made other arrangements for the concrete because of Adams' equipment failure. . . .[9]

This quote from the court reveals that some courts do see a direct link between apparent authority and estoppel. Here the court said apparent authority was really *based* on estoppel. As we noted earlier, the *Restatement* would not agree with this position. However, we believe the case is a good one to illustrate the application of estoppel. The circumstances allegedly creating apparent authority are not strong or convincing. It could not be argued with great authority that two orders placed by a principal through an alleged agent is sufficient to create apparent authority for subsequent orders. But likewise, it is not fair to hold that Southwest should suffer the loss. So an equitable doctrine, estoppel, was used. In any given factual pattern involving acts by the principal that reasonably lead a third party to believe the agent is authorized, it is sometimes difficult to predict whether a court will apply principles of apparent authority or estoppel. We believe that the best approach is to argue for the application of both.

Inherent Authority.   There is another type of authority that is neither actual authority nor apparent authority, nor is it derived from the elements of estoppel. This type of authority is called inherent authority. The *Restatement* defines it this way:

> Inherent agency power is a term used in the *Restatement* to indicate the power of an agent which is derived not from authority, apparent authority or estoppel, but solely from the agency relation and exists for the protection of persons harmed by or dealing with . . . an agent.[10]

The best example of this type of authority is the liability of the principal for the negligence or other torts and unauthorized acts committed in the scope of employment.[11] A fuller discussion of a principal's liability for the negligent acts of an agent (servant) will be found in the next chapter. This type of liability and this notion of inherent authority are based on the idea that because the principal derives a benefit from being able to do business through agents, the principal should pay when a wrongdoer (the agent) causes harm to a third party. In circumstances where this type of authority is applied, the court is usually faced with two innocent parties: a principal who intended no harm, and an injured third party. Because the principal does receive a benefit by being able to use agents and because the principal can guard against these injuries by better hiring and training of its agents, the law requires the principal to compensate the third party.[12]

We attempt to put labels on the circumstances when the principal is required to pay for injury to third parties. The existence of express and implied authority as legal doctrines is well recognized and understood. It should be obvious that circumstantial authority is less precisely defined, and that inherent authority is the least precisely defined. Nevertheless the law quests for certainty, and in this quest it has developed the related doctrines of apparent authority, estoppel, and inherent authority.

Generally, inherent authority is applied to create contractual liability for a principal in circumstances where the existence of a binding, enforceable contract between the third party and agent for the benefit of the principal are questionable; or the breach of duty being sued on is quasi-contractual (this term is usually used to designate a circumstance in which someone has unfairly benefited at the expense of someone else); or the breach of duty may look like the breach of one of the generally recognized torts but it is not; thus the other principles of circumstantial authority do not fit the factual pattern.

Inherent authority differs from implied authority in that the former is created by the circumstance of position and not the express delegation of authority. Inherent authority may exist when the principal has expressly forbidden the agent to act in certain matters, yet failed to take measures to inform third parties of this limitation, causing them to reasonably believe the position of the agent carried with it the authority asserted.

The doctrine of inherent authority is another example of courts' recognition that it is vital to protect the reasonable expectations of persons in business. To this end, the principles of apparent authority, estoppel, and inherent authority are all directed and all achieve the same practical result: in a commercial transaction where the principal stands to benefit by the utilization of agents, this principal should bear the loss as between itself, who is innocent of any intentional wrong, and a third party who is likewise innocent when it can be found reasonably that the principal created the impression that the agent was authorized.

In any given factual situation any third-party plaintiff may argue all of the types of authority. There is no inconsistency in this. If the facts reasonably lend themselves to the creation of circumstantial authority it is best to argue apparent authority, estoppel, and inherent authority. The following case illustrates the application of the doctrine of inherent authority as well as the difficulty some courts experience in attempting to delineate between the various types of circumstantial authority.

LIND v. *SCHENLEY INDUSTRIES INC.*
278 F. 2d 79 (C.C.A. 3rd, 1960)

BIGGS, Chief Judge

This is a diversity case: Lind, the plaintiff-appellant, sued Park & Tilford Distiller's Corp.,[1] the defendant-appellee, for compensation that he asserts is due him by virtue of a contract expressed by a written memorandum supplemented by oral conversations as set out hereinafter. . . . The evidence, including Lind's own testimony, taking the inferences most favorable to Lind, shows the following. Lind had been employed for some years by Park & Tilford. In July 1950, Lind was informed by Herrfeldt, then Park & Tilford's vice-president and general salesmanager, that he would be appointed assistant to Kaufman, Park & Tilford's sales-manager for metropolitan New

York. Herrfeldt told Lind to see Kaufman to ascertain what his new duties and his salary would be. Lind embarked on his new duties with Kaufman and was informed in October 1950, that some "raises" had come through and that Lind should get official word from his "boss," Kaufman. Subsequently, Lind received a communication, dated April 19, 1951, signed by Kaufman, informing Lind that he would assume the title of "District Manager." The letter went on to state: "I wish to inform you of the fact that you have as much responsibility as a State Manager and that you should consider yourself to be of the same status." The letter concluded with the statement: "An incentive plan is being worked out so that you will not only be responsible for increased sales in your district, but will benefit substantially in a monetary way." . . . In July 1951, Kaufman informed Lind that he was to receive one percent commission on the gross sales of the men under him. This was an oral communication and was completely corroborated by Mrs. Kennan,

---

[1] Park & Tilford Distiller's Corp. was merged into Schenley Industries, Inc., a Delaware corporation, before the commencement of this action, with Schenley assuming all of Park & Tilford's obligations.

Kaufman's former secretary, who was present. On subsequent occasions Lind was assured by Kaufman that he would get his money. Lind was also informed by Herrfeldt in the autumn of 1952 that he would get a one percent commission on the sales of the men under him. . . .

The court . . . requested the jury to answer the following five questions: "1. Did Kaufman offer plaintiff one percent of gross sales effected by the salesmen under plaintiff?" "2. If the answer to question 1 is yes, when was plaintiff to commence such commissions?" "3. If the answer to question 1 is yes, when was the commission arrangement to terminate?" "4. Did defendant cause the plaintiff to believe that Kaufman had authority to make the offer to plaintiff referred to in question 1?" "5. Was plaintiff justified in presuming that Kaufman had the authority to make the offer?"

The answers provided by the jury amounted to a determination that Kaufman did offer Lind a one percent commission on the gross sales of the men under him; that the agreement commenced April 19, 1951; that the agreement terminated February 15, 1952, the date of Lind's transfer to New Jersey; that Park & Tilford did cause Lind to believe that Kaufman had authority to offer him the one percent commission; and that Lind was justified in assuming that Kaufman had the authority to make the offer. . . .

[J]udgment was rendered by the jury in favor of Lind against Schenley for $36,953.10 plus interest for the commission. . . . However, the judgment was nullified by the court's decision to enter a verdict for the defendant. . . .

The decision to reverse the verdict for Lind with respect to the one percent commission was based on two alternative grounds. First, the court found that Lind had failed to prove a case of apparent authority in that the evidence did not disclose that Park & Tilford acted in such a manner as to induce Lind to believe that Kaufman had been authorized to offer him the one percent commission. Also

the court concluded that the issues of "actual" and "implied" authority had somehow been eliminated from the case. Second, the court reasoned, that even if the jury could find apparent authority, the alleged contract was not sufficiently definite nor specific to be enforceable against Park & Tilford. . . .

The problems of "authority" are probably the most difficult in that segment of law loosely termed, "Agency." Two main classifications of authority are generally recognized, "actual authority," and "apparent authority." The term "implied authority" is often seen but most authorities consider "implied authority" to be merely a sub-group of "actual" authority. Mechem, *Agency*, §§ 51–60 (4th ed. 1952). An additional kind of authority has been designated by the *Restatement*, Agency 2d, §§ 8A and 161(b) as "inherent agency." . . .

"Actual authority" means, as the words connote, authority that the principal, expressly or implicitly, gave the agent. "Apparent authority" arises when a principal acts in such a manner as to convey the impression to a third party that an agent has certain powers which he may or may not actually possess. "Implied authority" has been variously defined. It has been held to be actual authority given implicitly by a principal to his agent. Another definition of "implied authority" is that it is a kind of authority arising solely from the designation by the principal of a kind of agent who ordinarily possesses certain powers. . . .

In the case at bar Lind attempted to prove all three kinds of agency; actual, apparent, and inherent, although most of his evidence was directed to proof of "inherent" or "apparent" authority. From the evidence it is clear that Park & Tilford can be held accountable for Kaufman's action on the principle of "inherent authority." Kaufman was Lind's direct superior, and was the man to transfer communications from the upper executives to the lower. Moreover, there was testimony tending to prove that Herrfeldt, the vice-president in charge of sales, had told Lind to see Kaufman for information about his salary and that Herrfeldt himself had confirmed that one percent commission arrangement. Thus Kaufman, so far as Lind was concerned, was the spokesman for the company. . . .

Testimony was adduced by Schenley tending to prove that Kaufman had no authority to set salaries, that power being exercisable solely by the president of the corporation, and that the president had not authorized Kaufman to

offer Lind a commission of the kind under consideration here. However, this testimony, even if fully accepted, would only prove lack of actual or implied authority in Kaufman but is irrelevant to the issue of apparent authority. . . .

The judgment of the court below will be reversed and the case will be remanded . . . to reinstate the verdict and judgment in favor of Lind.

Case Questions

1. Can you pinpoint in time when the "contract" between Lind and the corporation was made?

2. Is there sufficient evidence in this case for you to feel comfortable in applying the principle of apparent authority or estoppel? What facts are there which indicate that Lind's superiors were authorized by the corporation to promise him a commission on all sales made by those under his direction?

Ratification

Ratification is another legal principle applied by courts to hold the principal liable to third parties for a promise or act that was not initially authorized by the principal. The *Restatement* defines it in this way:

> Ratification is the affirmance by a person of a prior act which did not bind him but which was done professedly on his account, whereby the act, as to some or all persons, is given effect as if originally authorized by him.[13]

Stated in the above definition are several important notions. The first is that the promise or act was not authorized either actually or circumstantially and that the promise or act was done for the benefit of the principal. This means that the promise or act must be of the kind that could have been authorized initially but was not. If the promise or act could not have been authorized initially, it cannot be ratified.

Just as important is the notion that the principal must *affirm* by some word, action, or perhaps a failure to act, the transaction in question. The principal must have *knowledge* either actual or implied—which means the principal *should have known* if he did not actually know—of the transaction being affirmed.

A classic application of the principle of ratification is found in the case of *Wilkins* v. *Waldo Lumber Co.*, 130 Me. 5; 153 A.191, S. Ct. Me. (1931). In this case, the agent, Adams, made a contract with a third party, Wilkins, for the purchase of timber. Adams said at the time of the initial agreement, and the contract itself stated, that the "contract" would have to be approved by the principal, Waldo Lumber Co., before it became binding. Adams also made an agreement with another person to haul the timber once it was cut and even contacted a purchaser for the wood once it was milled. Before the contract to purchase the wood was approved by the principal, Adams ordered that the timber be cut and hauled to the mill. The principal was informed of this. For three months timber was cut and hauled away and sold. When the agreement began to appear less profitable than at first thought, the principal told the owner of the property, Wilkins, that it was canceling the contract because it was never authorized or approved by the principal. It did appear from the evidence that Adams was *not* authorized to make these arrangements. However, the court held that the principal was liable for breach of contract because it knew that third parties were acting as if there were a contract and it accepted some of the sale proceeds. The court relied on this quote from *Mechem on Agency,* a respected treatise on agency law, to hold the principal liable:

> Ratification, like authorization of which it is the equivalent, is generally the creature of intent, but that intent may often be presumed by the law in cases where the principal, as a matter of fact, either had no express intent at all, or had an express intent not to ratify.
>
> If the principal has knowingly appropriated and enjoyed the fruits and benefits of an agent's act, he will not afterwards be heard to say that the act was unauthorized. One who voluntarily accepts the proceeds of an act done by one assuming, though without authority, to be his agent's act, he will not afterwards be heard to say that the act was unauthorized. One who voluntarily accepts the proceeds of an act done by one assuming, though without authority, to be his agent, ratifies his act and takes it as his own, with all its burdens as well as its benefits. He may not take the benefits and reject the burdens, but he must either accept them or reject them as a whole. (153 A. 191 at 193.)

In the last chapter we also discussed ratification as a means of creating an agency relationship. This circumstance differs from the case above in that the agent, Adams, was known by all parties to be an agent of the lumber company, but the specific transaction was not authorized because the written form of contract shown to the third party made it clear that it had to be approved by the principal before it was binding. This fact also made it inappropriate for the third party to argue for the application of circumstantial authority. Ratification is a legal principal that results in a principal's being bound by its own actions. Although these actions take place after the unauthorized act of the agent, they relate back to the time of the unauthorized act and result in the creation of authority as of that time.

Although most of the circumstances in which ratification is applied involve a receipt of benefits by the principal, the real heart of the doctrine is "affirmance." The *Restatement* (§ 83) defines affirmance as either:

1. A manifestation of an election by one on whose account an unauthorized act has been done to treat the act as authorized.
2. Conduct by him justifiable only if there were such an election.

The following is a more modern case emphasizing the affirmance element of ratification.

BRADLEY v. JOHN M. BRABHAM AGCY, INC.
463 F. Supp. 27 (D. Ct., S. Carolina, 1978)

The plaintiffs are husband and wife and at the times mentioned in the complaint plaintiff Roland Bradley was a sergeant in the United States Air Force assigned to Shaw Air Force Base near Sumter, South Carolina. The defendant is a corporation with its principal place of business in Sumter, South Carolina and is engaged in the business of acting as a real estate broker representing buyers and sellers of real property. Plaintiffs contend that as a result of seeing one of defendant's signs on a lot near Shaw Air Force Base, said sign indicating that the house and lot were for sale, they contacted the defendant, and one of defendant's agents, John Pate, came to their residence located on Shaw Air Force Base and after observing that they were black refused to show them the dwelling which was known as 2377 Tall Oak Road. The plaintiffs further allege that at the time of this refusal to show them the real estate they were in the market to purchase a home and have subsequently purchased a home in the Sumter area. They allege that this refusal to show the home was a violation of the Fair Housing Act and they have suffered humiliation, embarrassment and emotional distress and have incurred expenses as a result of defendant's act. Plaintiffs seek damages against the defendant and also an injunction permanently restraining and denying defendant from refusing to show, negotiate and sell real estate to plaintiffs and others in similar situations.

Defendant contends that it has not violated any provisions of the Fair Housing Act and also asserts that Pate was an independent contractor and not an agent of John M. Brabham Agency, Inc.

Findings of Fact
. . .

The following day plaintiffs reported this incident to the Shaw Air Force Base housing office and lodged a complaint against the defendant which was investigated by the housing office. . . .

[D]efendant has a real estate broker's license issued by the State of South Carolina and Pate and three or four other agents have salesman licenses and operate under defendant's broker's license. . . . Defendant contends that the real estate agents associated with defendant are independent contractors, but defendant furnishes them with an office, secretary, does all of the advertising, furnishes stationery, copies of contracts and listing agreements and receives approximately 50 percent of the commission when an agent makes a sale.

Pate had business cards printed with his name and defendant's name thereon which were used in the business of buying and selling real estate. . . . [A] day or so after July 29, 1974, Pate called Avenue Realty, the black real estate agency, and suggested to the owner thereof that he contact the plaintiffs.

[W]hen personnel from the Shaw Air Force Base housing office contacted Mr. Brabham, owner of defendant corporation, he exhibited a letter dated July 30, 1974 from Lt. Col. F. J. McKenna, Jr., owner of 2377 Tall Oak Road cancelling the listing of the property with defendant. At the same time Mr. Brabham advised the representative from the housing office that he had discussed the matter with Pate and upheld Pate's decision not to show the house to plaintiffs.

Conclusions of Law

. . .

§ 1982 provides: "All citizens of the United States shall have the same right, in every State and Territory, as is enjoyed by white citizens thereof to inherit, purchase, lease, sell, hold, and convey real and personal property."

Title 42 U.S.C. § 3604 provides in part:

"... it shall be unlawful ... (a) to refuse to sell or rent after the making of a bona fide offer, or to refuse to negotiate for the sale or rental of, or otherwise make unavailable or deny, a dwelling to any person because of race, color, religion, sex, or national origin."

[T]he provisions of the Fair Housing Act apply to the defendant, the plaintiffs herein and the dwelling located at 2377 Tall Oak Road near Sumter, South Carolina.

[T]he efforts by Mr. Pate, an agent of the defendant, to discourage plaintiffs from inspecting the dwelling in question were made because of plaintiffs' race and were in direct violation of 42 U.S.C. § 3604(a), since such actions amounted to a refusal to negotiate because of race. Also Pate's action in attempting to divert plaintiffs away from Oakland Subdivision and into Runnymede Subdivision, an all black area, and his efforts to have them contacted by Avenue Realty Co. were all in violation of the same act.

. . .

[D]efendant is liable for the actions of Pate under the principle of ratification. When defendant's president and owner approved Pate's actions in the present case in discussions with the Shaw Air Force Base housing office representative several days after the incident in question, defendant ratified these actions and is thus liable therefor.

. . .

The Court finds that an award of Two Thousand and No/100 ($2,000.00) Dollars actual damages for emotional distress is proper in this case, together with Five Thousand and No/100 ($5,000.00) Dollars for loss of plaintiffs' civil rights, and Five Hundred and No/100 ($500.00) Dollars punitive damages, making a total of Seven Thousand Five Hundred and No/100 ($7,500.00) Dollars, shall be awarded to the plaintiffs against the defendant.

IT IS, THEREFORE, ORDERED that the plaintiffs Roland Bradley and Ernesteen Bradley have judgment against defendant John M. Brabham Agency, Inc. in the amount of Seven Thousand and No/100 ($7,000.00) Dollars actual damages and Five Hundred and No/100 ($500.00) Dollars punitive damages, together with the costs of this action.

IT IS FURTHER ORDERED that the John M. Brabham Agency, Inc., its agents, servants, officers and employees be and they are hereby enjoined from any further violation of the Fair Housing Act, 42 U.S.C. § 3601 et seq. in the sale, rental or offering to sell or rent real property and shall not discriminate against any person or persons because of race, color, religion, sex or national origin.

And it is so ordered.

1. In this case, there was not a contract that was authorized by ratification. Exactly what was authorized?
2. What was the act of authorization?
3. Comment: Do you think Mr. Brabham knew that the consequences of his act of ratification would be to suffer a $7,500.00 judgment? Ignorance of the law is never an excuse from its application.

In concluding this section on the rules the law has developed to hold the principal liable to third parties for an agent's promises or representation, we wish to emphasize two points. First, remember that the agent's promises or representations to a third party cannot, *by themselves,* confer authority on the agent. No agent can create liability for a principal by a forged instrument, or other false assertion. Usually, there must be circumstances present in which it seems fair and reasonable to hold the principal liable. This means one must find that the principal is in some way responsible for creating the circumstances that lead the third party to believe the agent was authorized or otherwise accepts the benefits of the transaction.

Second, in analyzing a factual pattern involving contractual liability, you should be prepared to argue more than one, perhaps all, of the types of authority discussed herein if it is appropriate. It is seldom that a factual pattern of any complexity will yield to a direct, obvious application of just one of the authority rules. In fact almost all of the cases in this chapter contain discussions of more than one of the authority rules.

Contractual Liability of the Agent to Third Parties

Implicit in the factual patterns discussed in the first portion of this chapter is the fact that the third party knew of the existence of the principal-agent relationship at the time the transaction occurred or shortly thereafter. When an agent is contracting for a principal the contract or the circumstances usually indicate that the agent is acting in a representative capacity. One of the most common ways to indicate this representative capacity is for the agent to sign the contract as follows.

Artie Agent for Peter Principal

Peter Principal by Artie Agent

In P Corporation, by A, President

In the above examples the agent may sign both the names of the principal and agent. Of course, other circumstances, such as the use of a letterhead or the use of an office in the same building area as the principal or even the use of a company car with a name on it, may indicate that the agent is indeed acting for and on behalf of someone else.

When the contract is signed in a representative capacity, the agent is not liable to the third party unless he or she performed one of the following acts:

1. Signed a negotiable instrument (a promissory note, check, or the like) without the principal's authority and a third party took it in good faith and paid value for it.
2. Made a personal promise to perform.
3. Misrepresented his or her authority or the existence of the capacity of the principal.

Only the circumstances of each case will reveal if the contract signed was a negotiable instrument, or if a personal promise to perform was made, or if there was some misrepresentation. A very important circumstance revealing whether an agent personally promised to perform is whether the principal was disclosed to the third party, partially disclosed, or undisclosed *at the time the contract was made.*

The *Restatement* defines these classifications of principals as follows:[14]

1. If, at the time of a transaction conducted by an agent, the other party thereto has notice that the agent is acting for a principal and of the principal's identity, the principal is a disclosed principal.
2. If the other party has notice that the agent is or may be acting for a principal but has no notice of the principal's identity, the principal for whom the agent is acting is a partially disclosed principal.
3. If the other party has no notice that the agent is acting for a principal, the one for whom he acts is an undisclosed principal.

The difference between (1) and (2) above is slight. In the case of a disclosed principal, the third party can identify the principal by name; this is not so of the partially disclosed principal, yet the existence of a principal is indicated. If a principal is disclosed, the law assumes the contract signed by the agent and the promises therein are made for the benefit of the principal unless otherwise specifically indicated. Therefore, the third party may enforce the contract against the principal *but not the agent.* If the principal is partially disclosed, the law assumes that both the principal and agent may have personally promised to perform and one should carefully search the contractual language for the agent's personal promise. If such a promise is found then both principal and agent may be liable to the third party.

If a principal is undisclosed, the law assumes that the agent has personally promised to perform the contract.[15] *Therefore, the agent is liable* for the breach of the promise(s) made. But just as important is the rule that the *principal is also liable* even though its existence is not known to the third party. This result may be contrary to your natural instincts. The reason for imposing liability on the undisclosed principal is that it is the one that initiated the activities of the agent and has a right to control the agent. Since the third party may sue an undisclosed principal the law also recognizes the right of the undisclosed principal to enforce the contract against the third party so long as the agent intended that the contract benefit the principal and the agent acted within the authority possessed. This latter result is perhaps more surprising than the rule that allows a third party to sue an undisclosed principal. However, if the agent induces the third party to enter the contract by positively representing that no principal is involved or if the contract "excludes all principals," then the third party may be granted the remedy of rescission of the contract.

It should be clear at this point that even though the agent may not be liable to a third party when the principal is disclosed or partially disclosed, either the principal or the third party may compel the agent to plead in the case for purposes of determining the respective liabilities between these parties and the agent. For example, assume a principal gives his horse to an agent to sell for him, and while conducting the sale the agent promises that the horse is "a fine working horse that can plow all day." The third party buys the horse and it dies of heart failure after plowing 100 feet. If the third party sues the principal for a breach of warranty, the principal may join the agent in the case so that the liability between the three parties is worked out in one forum.

If a third party finds out about the existence of the principal after the contract is made, the best course of action for the third party who wishes to sue for the breach of the contract is to join both the principal and agent in the case. However, if either the principal or agent objects the third-party plaintiff *must elect* to continue against either one or the other and may secure a judgment only against the one whom he elects to hold.[16] If the third party knows the identity of the initially undisclosed principal and does not join the principal and recovers a judgment against the agent, the principal is discharged from liability.[17] If the third party does not know the identity of the undisclosed principal at the time of trial and recovers a judgment against the agent, the principal is not discharged from liability by such a recovery.[18]

The following case illustrates one court's reasoning on the liability of an undisclosed principal who has paid the agent for the goods the agent was directed to order. The agent did not pay the third-party seller. In this case both the undisclosed principal and the third party are innocent of any wrongdoing, causing the court to go to great lengths to explain precisely why the former should be liable and, in effect, be required to pay twice for the same goods.

PORETTA v. SUPERIOR DOWEL COMPANY
153 Me. 308, 137 A2d 361 (S. Ct., Me., 1957)

(Authors' note: In this case the plaintiff, Poretta, delivered wood worth $2,574.44 to R. H. Young &

Son, Inc. The plaintiff was not paid by R. H. Young & Son, Inc., referred to by the court as "Company," and the plaintiff brought this suit against the Superior Dowel Company, referred to by the court as "Superior," alleging that Superior was the undisclosed principal for Company. The appellate court *affirmed the finding of the referee, which was in <u>favor</u> of the plaintiff and which established that the wood was purchased by the Company in the capacity as agent for Superior and that the Company was within its scope of authority when it purchased the wood. On the final issue before the court, Superior argued that it had paid the agent, Company (presumably insolvent), and this discharged its liability.*

The issue thus raised presents a problem of novel impression in this State. The issue is:

> Is an undisclosed principal absolved from liability to his agent's vendor who has sold goods to the agent upon the credit of the agent who has received payment or advances, or a settlement of accounts from his undisclosed principal, before discovery of the undisclosed principal by the agent's vendor?

There are two different rules bearing upon the issue. The first one, which appears to be supported by the weight of authority is that an undisclosed principal is generally relieved of his liability for his agent's contracts to the extent that he has settled with his agent prior to the discovery of the agency. The other rule is, that an undisclosed principal is discharged only where he has been induced to settle with the agent by conduct on the part of the third person leading him to believe that such person has settled with the agent. . . .

The American Law Institute, as of May 4, 1933, adopted and promulgated the following rule:

> An undisclosed principal is discharged from liability to the other party to the contract if he has paid or settled accounts with an agent reasonably relying upon conduct of the other party, not induced by the agent's misrepresentations, which indicates that the agent has paid or otherwise settled the account. 1 *Am. Law Inst. Restatement of Agency,* § 208. . . .

We are, therefore, called upon to determine which rule shall become the law in this State.

Manifestly, if we adopt the rule which we have designated as the first rule, as distin-

guished from the rule laid down in the *Restatement of the Law of Agency,* then, . . . the exceptions of Superior would have to be sustained. On the other hand, if we adopt the rule laid down in the *Restatement,* then the decision of the referee was correct and Superior's exceptions should be overruled. . . .

In arriving at his conclusion that the law as now set forth in the *Restatement* was the correct law, Mr. Mechem had this to say in his Treatise on the *Law of Agency,* 2nd Ed. § 1749, Vol. II,

> [I]f a principal sends an agent to buy goods for him and on his account, it is not unreasonable that he should see that they are paid for. Although the seller may consider the agent to be the principal, the actual principal knows better. He can easily protect himself by insisting upon evidence that the goods have been paid for or that the seller with full knowledge of the facts has elected to rely upon the responsibility of the agent, and if he does not, but, except where misled by some action of the seller, voluntarily pays the agent without knowing that he has paid the seller, there is no hardship in requiring him to pay again. If the other party has the right, within a reasonable time, to charge the undisclosed principal upon his discovery,— and this right seems to be abundantly settled in the law of agency—it is difficult to see how this right of the other party can be defeated, while he is not himself in fault, by dealings between the principal and the agent, of which he had no knowledge, and to which he was not a party.

It is interesting to note that this work on Agency by Mechem was published in 1914.

We think it is pertinent at this point to record something of the establishment, organization and object of the American Law Institute. The Institute was organized on February 23, 1923. The organization meeting was attended by the Chief Justice of the United States, and other representatives of the Supreme Court, representatives of the United States Circuit Courts of Appeals, the highest courts of a majority of the States, the Association of American Law Schools, and the American and State Bar Associations. The Institute was composed of Justices of the Supreme

Court of the United States, senior judges of the United States Circuit Court of Appeals, the chief justices of the highest courts of the several States, the president and members of the Executive Committee of the American Bar Association, the presidents of certain legal societies, and the deans of member schools of the Association of American Law Schools. Its object as expressed in its charter was "to promote the clarification and simplification of the law and its better adaptation to social needs, to secure the better administration of justice and to carry on scholarly and scientific legal work."

The *Restatement* may be regarded both as the product of expert opinion and as the expression of the law by the legal profession.

The Committee on Agency which prepared the *Restatement of the Law of Agency* was composed of outstanding representatives of the leading law schools of the country. It was headed by Mr. Floyd R. Mechem, who at the time was regarded as the foremost living authority on the subject of agency. Its rule as set forth in § 208 promulgated on May 4, 1933

expounds the thinking of some of the best legal minds in the country.

The purpose of the Institute in the promotion of clarification of the law can be applied to no more needy situation than that of the question before us for determination. It is our opinion that the reasoning of Mr. Mechem in support of the doctrine promulgated in the *Restatement* is sound. The adoption of this doctrine by this court will establish a clear cut and explicit rule of law free from the confusion, complications and perplexities which have existed throughout the years.

We, therefore, adopt the rule as laid down in the *Restatement of the Law of Agency.*

Having already ruled that the Company was the duly authorized agent of Superior and that when it purchased the wood from the plaintiff, it was acting within the scope of its authority, we now rule that the referee applied the proper law and that his decision was correct and should be affirmed.

Exceptions overruled.

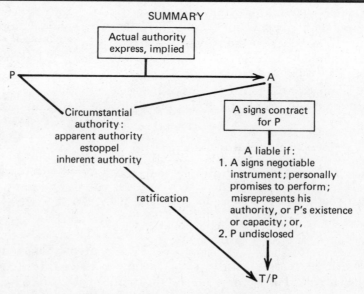

FIGURE 4-3   Contractual liability of principals and agents to third parties.

1. In this case it appears that the principal was required to pay twice for the same goods. How could the principal have protected itself against such an event?
2. On the facts of this case, could R. H. Young and Son, Inc., be liable to Poretta? Why?

1. In this chapter we have stated that a principal will be liable to third parties for the contracts made by an agent if there are circumstances present indicating that the principal authorized or ratified the contract. List and define five types of authority discussed in this chapter and, using factual patterns not similar to any of the cases in the chapter; give an example of each.

2. P made storefronts and other additions to commercial buildings and employed A to call on contractors and older commercial enterprises to promote the sales of P. A was specifically forbidden to collect payment for the erection of the storefronts and other improvements. T went to P's place of business inquiring about a new front for his store and was directed to A's office. A negotiated a contract and signed on behalf of P, and P's men began work. P did not keep very good account of his workers or accounts receivable. A pocketed the payments made by T to A and absconded. When P discovered this, since A was unavailable, he sued T to recover the payments owed to him for the work done. Can he collect?

3. Henry Wilson & Sons, Inc., manufactured and sold custom-made shoes. Henry Wilson, Sr., the president of the company, hired his grandson, James Wilson, age 17, as a salesperson during his summer vacation. James was instructed not to make any contracts in excess of $500 without first obtaining approval from his father, Frank Wilson, the vice-president of marketing. All other salespersons could make contracts up to $1500 without approval. James Wilson made numerous contracts on the corporation's behalf; two of these were for $750. Discuss whether or not James had capacity to contract on behalf of Henry Wilson & Sons, Inc., and whether the latter would be liable to those who contracted for orders of $750. (Material from the Uniform CPA Examination, copyright © 1973 by the American Institute of Certified Public Accountants, Inc. is here reprinted with permission. This is adapted from Question Number 3, E of the May 11, 1973 Exam.)

4. Explain how your arguments in the above case would change if it appeared that Frank Wilson accepted payment for the two orders for $750.

5. P employs A as the general manager of his manufacturing plant, instructing A to purchase certain materials from specifically named

suppliers and no others. A, realizing that some of the materials supplied by the designated suppliers are inferior and without consultation with P, contracts with other suppliers for better materials at a more reasonable price. The contracts with the new suppliers are written on plain paper (not letterhead), and A signs the contracts at P's headquarters in the presence of the new suppliers as follows: "A, general manager for P." Will P be bound by these contracts? Why?

6. A uses his own name in conducting a business but is in reality a general agent for P in the management of the business. He, A, contracts with T/P to buy goods that are customarily used in the business, not disclosing in any way that he is P's agent. In fact, A has been directed by P to sign contracts for the business only after P has okayed the contract. In this instance P did not okay the contract.

  Assume that A fails to pay for the goods and T/P finds out about P's existence. May T/P sue P? May T/P sue A?

7. Assume T/P fails to deliver the goods. May A sue T/P? May P sue T/P?

8. The following was taken from a local newspaper:

  A local insurance man, who has provided health insurance coverage for city employees for the past six years, admitted today that he misused premiums paid to him by the city.

  Michael Daher of M. Daher and Associates, Lakeshore Bank Building, made the admission to a newsman after Mayor Randall Miller said in a news release this morning that the city had been informed by the Golden Rule Insurance Co. that claims filed by city employees during June, July and August of this year would not be honored by the company. The mayor said that the city was informed of the company's decision last week. He said at that time the company informed city officials that insurance premiums for those three months had not been remitted to the company by Daher.

  The mayor said that the city had paid the premiums in good faith to Daher and Daher agreed that the city was not at fault. He said, "The mayor is correct, the premiums were remitted to me. The city did act in good faith." Daher went on, "I admit I have misused the funds."

  The mayor said today that during conversations with company officials the city had been informed that the company would be willing to honor the claims if the premiums ($17,000 per month) are paid. He said that the city has contacted the office of the State Insurance Commissioner in Indianapolis and that the office is sending an investigator to examine the situation. The mayor said that since the premiums have been paid to Daher, the company has a duty to honor the claims.

  He said if they continue to refuse to pay the claims we will vigorously pursue any and every course of action to insure the payment of claims to our employees including legal action against Golden Rule Insurance Co., and Mr. Daher as their agent.

  Assume that you are the investigator sent by the state to examine the situation:

(a) Clearly state the legal rules under which the Golden Rule Co. could be held liable.

(b) What kinds of evidence will you look for to substantiate your proper use of the above listed legal rules?

(c) Clearly state whether or not Mr. Daher could be liable to either the Golden Rule Insurance Co., or the city for the premiums taken.

9. Duval was the agent for Sunshine Pools, Inc. He sold pools, related equipment, and accessories for Sunshine. Holmes, president of Tilden Sporting Equipment, Inc., approached Duval and offered him an excellent deal on a commission basis if he would secretly sell their brand of diving boards and platforms instead of the Sunshine products. Duval agreed. The arrangement worked out between them was to have Duval continue to act as a general sales agent for Sunshine and concurrently act as the agent for an "undisclosed" principal in respect to Tilden diving boards. He could then sell both lines to new pool customers and go back to prior customers to solicit sales of the Tilden boards. Duval was not to mention his relationship with Tilden to the prospective customers, and of course, no mention of these facts would be made to Sunshine. Duval was told to use his discretion insofar as effectively misleading the prospective customers about whose diving board they were purchasing.

Things went smoothly for the first several months until Tilden began to manufacture and ship defective diving boards. Subsequently, Tilden became insolvent, and Holmes absconded with advance payments made by purchasers including those who had purchased from Duval.

Answer the following, setting forth reasons for any conclusions stated.

(a) What are the rights of the various customers against Duval?

(b) What are the rights of the various customers against Tilden and/or Holmes?

(c) What rights does Sunshine have against Duval?

(d) What rights does Sunshine have against Tilden and/or Holmes?

(This is CPA Exam Question #5, Business Law, taken from the November 1977 exam. © 1977 American Institute of Certified Public Accountants.)

10. Vogel, an assistant buyer for the Granite City Department Store, purchased metal art objects from Duval Reproductions. Vogel was totally without express or apparent authority to do so, but believed that his purchase was a brilliant move likely to get him a promotion. The head buyer of Granite was livid when he learned of Vogel's activities. However, after examining the merchandise and listening to

Vogel's pitch, he reluctantly placed the merchandise in the storeroom and put a couple of pieces on display for a few days to see whether it was a "hot item" and a "sure thing" as Vogel claimed. The item was neither "hot" nor "sure" and when it didn't move at all, the head buyer ordered the display merchandise repacked and the entire order returned to Duval with a letter that stated the merchandise had been ordered by an assistant buyer who had absolutely no authority to make the purchase. Duval countered with a lawsuit for breach of contract.

Answer the following, setting forth reasons for any conclusions stated.

Will Duval prevail?

(This is CPA Exam Question #5a, Business Law, taken from the May 1980 exam. © 1980, American Institute of Certified Public Accountants.)

Endnotes

1. W. A. Seavey, *Law of Agency*, 40 (1964).
2. *Restatement 2d* § 8 (1958).
3. A. Conrad, R. Knauss, and S. Siegel, *Enterprise Organization*, 418 (1972).
4. *Black's Law Dictionary* Rev. 4th Ed., 648 (1957).
5. *Restatement 2d*, § 8B.
6. Seavey, pp. 14–15.
7. *Restatement 2d*, pp. 33 and 40.
8. *Ibid.*, Illustration 7, p. 33.
9. *Southwestern Portland Cement* v. *Beavers and Glasgow*, 82 N.M. 218; 478 P2d 546 (S. Ct. New Mex., 1970).
10. *Restatement 2d*, § 8A.
11. H. Renschlein and W. Gregory, *Agency and Partnership*, 69 (1979).
12. *Restatement 2d*, pp. 36–38.
13. *Ibid.*, § 82
14. *Ibid.*, § 4.
15. Seavey, pp. 120–121.
16. *Restatement 2d*, § 210A.
17. *Ibid.*, § 210(1).
18. *Ibid.*, § 210(2).

Tort Liability of Principal and Agent to Third Parties 5

We suggested in Chapter 4 that it would be useful to divide the discussion of the principal's liability to third persons into two broad categories depending on the nature of the breach of duty sued on. We stated in Chapter 4 that when the breach of a *contract duty* is alleged the courts usually search for a principle of *authority* to apply. The second category of cases involves a principal's liability to third parties based on a breach of a *tort duty*. When the breach of a *tort duty* is alleged courts usually focus on the degree of *control* exercised by the principal over the agent's physical conduct. Precisely how and when courts use rules of *control* by the principal will be the primary subject of this chapter. A secondary subject will be an explanation and demonstration of how the law is changing. In general, we will see that in addition to focusing on circumstances of control, courts today are using ideas that look very similar to apparent or inherent authority to impose liability on a principal for an agent's torts.

Tort Liability

Before proceeding with the subject of the principal's control over the physical conduct of the agent, an understanding of the nature of tort liability is essential. A tort may be variously defined as a private or civil wrong (breach of duty) independent of contract.[1] More comprehensively, a tort is "any intentional or unintentional invasion of, or interference with property, property rights, personal rights or personal liberties causing injury without just cause or excuse."[2]

Torts are divided broadly into unintentional torts and intentional ones. The most pervasive unintentional tort is negligence, defined broadly as any conduct that falls below the standard established by law for the protection of others against unreasonable risk of harm.[3] The standard referred to is that of a reasonable person under like circumstances.[4]

Two other torts that may exist either with or without the intent of the wrongdoer (sometimes called a tortfeasor) are conversion and trespass. Conversion is the act of wrongfully exercising ownership over another's personal property. For example, if a third party (T/P) orders from a principal (P) and pays for a set of furniture and P directs an agent (A) to deliver the furniture to T/P and A wrongfully delivers it to X who absconds with it, A and P may both be liable for converting T/P's furniture.

Trespass is the unintentional or intentional interference with another's real or personal property.

Some common torts usually requiring an element of intent on the part of the tortfeasor are defined as follows:

1. Assault—an act other than the speaking of words that puts another person in apprehension of an immediate and harmful contact (e.g., threatening to strike another by raising a fist).
2. Battery—unpermitted, unprivileged, physical contact with another person (e.g., striking another with a fist).
3. False imprisonment—an unprivileged confinement of another for any time where the other is aware of the confinement (e.g., a manager closes his store thirty minutes early and locks in several customers for the night).
4. Defamation—the unprivileged publication of false matter that damages another's reputation. Defamation is subdivided into libel (written or printed defamation) and slander (spoken defamation).
5. Deceit or misrepresentation—knowingly making a misrepresentation of fact or opinion for the purpose of inducing another to act or refrain from acting.

Other less common torts are malicious prosecution, abuse of process, interference with another's right of privacy, and the intentional infliction of mental distress.

The precise definition of these common torts is beyond the scope of this book. However, pertinent to this chapter is the notion that, generally speaking, a third party injured by the intentional tortious conduct of an agent cannot usually hold the principal liable for the resulting harm unless the principal authorized the tort or the tort was committed to directly further or protect the interests of the principal. If the tortious conduct was unintentional, the injured party may hold the principal liable even though the conduct was not authorized; this result is more fully explained below.

Tort Liability of a Principal to a Third Party

A fundamental principle of law is that an individual is always liable for his or her own torts. If a person is acting as an agent and negligently operates the principal's car injuring a third party, the agent is liable to the third party. However, the agent is seldom as wealthy as the principal. Therefore, injured third parties are usually more concerned with finding a legal way to impute an agent's tortious conduct to the principal than they are in recovering a judgment against the agent. The important inquiry is, under what circumstances will the principal be liable for the torts of the agent? A corollary to this first important issue is that if the third party does succeed in recovering a judgment against the principal, the principal can then usually hold the agent liable. That is, the agent is usually required to indemnify the principal for loss suffered as a result of the agent's negligence.

Principal Negligent with Respect to Hiring an Agent or Entrusting Property to an Agent

Since one is almost always liable for one's own negligence, a principal may be liable to a third party because of his or her own negligence in hiring the agent or entrusting potentially harmful tools to the agent. This is an act of negligence independent of the agent's act. Such liability is well demonstrated in the following case.

MURRAY v. *MODOC STATE BANK*
181 Kan. 642, 313 P.2d 304 (S. Ct. Kan., 1957)

SCHROEDER, Justice

The petition in substance alleges that one Donald Breithaupt was employed as the cashier and managing officer of the defendant, The Modoc State Bank, a banking corporation at Modoc, Kansas, on January 1, 1952, and was employed continuously in that capacity until on and after March 9, 1954; that plaintiff and Breithaupt had business transactions involving plaintiff and defendant and also involving plaintiff and Breithaupt; that the relationship between plaintiff and Breithaupt was strained and angry; that Breithaupt had threatened bodily harm to the plaintiff; that once when plaintiff had gone to the defendant bank to transact business with defendant, Breithaupt had assaulted him; that the violence and antagonism of Breithaupt grew so great that plaintiff could not in safety go to the defendant bank to transact business but was compelled to do so by mail, all of which facts were known and understood by the defendant; that plaintiff was indebted to the defendant; that on or about the 9th day of March, 1954, plaintiff attempted to transact business with the defendant by mail, particularly the depositing of checks to his personal account, that Breithaupt telephonically requested plaintiff to come to

the defendant bank to discuss the transaction with him, but that plaintiff declined to do so; that thereafter and on the 9th day of March, 1954, Breithaupt went to the plaintiff's home and demanded to see the plaintiff; that plaintiff went onto the porch of his home to see Breithaupt; that Breithaupt demanded that plaintiff deposit said checks as he, Breithaupt, directed and further demanded that plaintiff execute and deliver to the defendant a property statement for the benefit of defendant; that plaintiff declined to forthwith comply with said demand, whereupon Breithaupt jerked plaintiff from the porch, struck him with his fists, threw him to the ground, and fell upon him, inflicting upon the plaintiff the injuries complained of.

The petition then specifically alleges:

That said injuries complained of were caused by and as a direct result of the negligence of the defendant in the following particulars, without which negligence the injuries would not have occurred, to wit:

1. In permitting the aforementioned Donald Breithaupt to manage and conduct the affairs of said defendant with this plaintiff. . . .

* * *

3. In continuing the aforenamed Donald Breithaupt in its employ after having notice or when it should have had notice, of his

violent, aggressive, and antagonistic disposition toward this plaintiff.

4. In directing and permitting said Donald Breithaupt to transact business with this plaintiff when it knew, or by the exercise of reasonable care, should have known, that such would reasonably result in an assault on and injury to this plaintiff. . . .

That as a result of the acts committed by this defendant, this plaintiff suffered a broken left leg, a comminuted fracture involving the upper tibia, and a comminuted fracture of the proximal end of the left tibia, one of the fracture lines entering the mid portion of the articular surface of the tibia at the left knee. That such break caused a puncture wound below the tibial tuberosity; that this plaintiff suffered a fracture of the left fibula, all of which necessitated an open reduction of said fractures and breaks, the removal of both menisci, the placement of a tibial bolt across the upper tibia with plates along both sides of the upper tibia, and the alignment and fixation of the fracture fragments by means of wire, metal bolts and two metal plates.

The petition further sets up the various items for which the plaintiff seeks damages and prays judgment for $65,822 and costs. Breithaupt was not joined in the action. The petition was filed on March 8, 1956. . . .

It will be observed that the cause of action arose on the 9th day of March, 1954, and the petition was filed March 8, 1956, which was one day less than two years.

The first question considered is whether or not the plaintiff's cause of action is outlawed by the statute of limitations.

The defendant argues that this is simply a case of assault and battery and that if an action had been brought against the servant, Breithaupt, or if the servant had been joined as a party defendant in this action, the case could have been nothing more than assault and battery. . . .

Admittedly, if this petition is construed as one charging the defendant with the assault and battery committed by Breithaupt, the managing officer of the bank, the one-year limitation . . . bars recovery by the plaintiff in that the face of the petition discloses the action was filed more than one year after the cause of action arose. However, if the petition is construed as one alleging actionable negligence against the bank, then a two-year limitation . . . applies and the plaintiff's right to maintain the action is not barred under the statute of limitations.

The defendant argues that the injury of which the plaintiff complains was occasioned and caused by the assault and battery, and his attempt to change the cause of action into a negligence action by alleging the negligence of the defendant in hiring and retaining a cashier and general manager with known violent, quarrelsome and antagonistic tendencies, is an effort to circumvent the statute of limitation. . . .

This subject has been thoroughly discussed in earlier decisions of this court and the law is now clear that the fundamental distinction between assault and battery, on the one hand, and negligence, on the other, is that the former is *intentional* and the latter is *unintentional*. . . .

It is not a necessary element of negligence that the defendant anticipate the precise injury sustained. . . .

The Restatement of Law, Torts, § 284, pp. 744, 745, defines "negligent conduct" thus:

Negligent conduct may be either:

(a) an act which the actor as a reasonable man should realize as involving an unreasonable risk of causing an invasion of an interest of another, or

(b) a failure to do an act which is necessary for the protection or assistance of another and which the actor is under a duty to do.

The precise point before this court for decision is a matter of first impression. Simply stated, the question is whether a master may be held liable for injuries to a third person proximately resulting from the incompetence or unfitness of his servant, where the master was negligent in selecting or retaining an incompetent or unfit servant. . . .

We hold that the doctrine of *respondeat superior* is not involved in the instant case. Construing the pleading most favorably to the petitioner as we must, the issue presented is whether the employer, The Modoc State Bank, was negligent in retaining its managing officer, Breithaupt, who had propensities toward violence. What the evidence will disclose upon trial of the case we are not at liberty to speculate. . . .

Some of the cases in which it was held there was sufficient showing that a master was negligent in keeping his servant in employment are: *Duckworth* v. *Apostalis,* D.C., 208 F. 936, where a guest sued to recover for injuries inflicted by an employee known by the master to have made previous assaults on guests; *Crawford* v. *Exposition Cotton Mills*, 63 Ga. App. 458, 11 S.E.2d 234, where a customer of a store sued to recover for injuries by a servant known by the master to have an unusual and abnormally high temper; *Priest* v. *F.W. Woolworth Five & Ten Cent Store,* 228 Mo. App. 23, 62 S.W.2d 926, where a customer sought recovery for injuries inflicted by a servant while he was engaged in an act of horseplay and who was known by the manager to have been guilty of previous acts; and *Hall* v. *Smathers,* 240 N.Y. 486, 148 N.E. 654, where a tenant of an apartment house sought to recover as against the master for injuries by a servant known by the master to be a drunkard and incompetent and dangerous.

The following jurisdictions have expressly or impliedly indicated that an employer may be primarily liable for a personal assault by an employee upon a customer, patron, or other invitee, if he has failed to exercise due care to avoid the selection or retention of employees who will assault such invitees: California, Dakota (sic), Georgia, Kentucky, Massachusetts, Michigan, Missouri, Mississippi, Nebraska, New York, Ohio, Pennsylvania, Washington, and several federal districts. . . .

In conclusion, we hold that the plaintiff has alleged a cause of action against The Modoc State Bank on the theory of negligence.

The ruling of the trial court in overruling the demurrer to plaintiff's petition should be and hereby is affirmed.

PRICE, Justice (dissenting).

In my opinion the decision of the court confuses form and substance. What plaintiff actually is attempting to do is to recover, under the guise of a negligence action, for an assault and battery. Despite the language in which the petition is couched, the real wrong complained of, and the real basis of his action—is the assault and battery. An action to recover for an assault and battery must be brought within one year . . . This action was brought too late. Defendant's demurrer should have been sustained. For this reason I respectfully dissent.

PARKER, C.J., joins in the foregoing dissent.

Case Questions

1. Why did not the injured plaintiff also sue Donald Breithaupt?
2. Carefully define the negligent act for which the defendant was liable.

Vicarious Liability of the Principal

Vicarious liability is a type of liability imposed on the principal for the tortious acts of the agent when the principal was not directly responsible for the tort and the tortious conduct had not been authorized. Vicarious liability of the principal is usually based on the doctrine of respondeat superior ("let the master answer"). There is no legal doctrine or principle more vital to the law of agency and more necessary to the understanding of the liability of business organizations to damaged third parties than respondeat superior. This doctrine and the reasons therefor are fully explained in the following edited article. You are asked to read the article carefully and to make a list of the reasons supporting the need for the doctrine of respondeat superior.

SPECULATIONS AS TO "RESPONDEAT SUPERIOR"

Warren Abner Seavey

(Reprinted by permission of the publisher and Harvard Law School from Harvard Legal Essays, *Written in Honor of and Presented to Joseph Henry Beale and Samuel Williston, Cambridge, Mass.: Harvard University Press, 1934; edited by the authors with some footnotes deleted. Copyright © 1934, Harvard Law School.)*

Respondeat superior, as the phrase is commonly used, summarizes the doctrine that a master or other principal is responsible, under certain conditions, for the conduct of a servant or other agent although he did not intend or direct it. In practice, it is used chiefly with reference to the liability of a master for the torts of a servant, but its principle includes, as well, the liability of one who is not a master for the undirected contracts made for him by his agent in cases in which there is not the obvious contract basis, such as exists where the agent has apparent authority. Similar reasons lie back of the rules established for both types of situation.

The entire field of vicarious liability is far broader than that of respondeat superior, but in most other cases there is at present liability for the conduct of others only where it is said that there is some fault on the part of the person made responsible, as in the case of the par-

ent who has not used care to restrain the activities of a dangerous child. That the principal is made responsible for certain injurious conduct of the agent, although the principal did not intend it and was not negligent in failing to foresee it or to control the agent, is said to make the doctrine unjust. . . .

The fact that the supposed victims of the rule, the employing class, usually powerful and vocal in the protection of their interests, have not been militant in demanding a change, and that the rule is constantly expanding without meeting substantial opposition during a time of searching analysis and self-revelation, is some evidence that it does not greatly depart from the common feeling of justice which it is the primary function of the law to satisfy.

It is quite true that we have no sure tests of the ethical basis or economic expediency of respondeat superior. We have no authoritative code of ethics, nor are the economists or psychologists likely soon to be successful in so uniting upon principles that those whom they would make the beneficiaries of their views will accept them as the basis of conduct. In the absence of such definitive information, it appears feasible only to set down some a priori reasons for my belief that respondeat superior is not out of line with our 1934 conceptions of liability or of justice to the employer; that the field of liability without either personal or "constructive" fault is rapidly widening both as to those who are within the classic categories of principal and master and as to others whom we term independent contractors and bailees.

. . .

In fact, legal fault upon which liability is based has little connection with personal morality or with justice to the individual; it is always tinctured with a supposed expediency in shifting the loss from one harmed to one who has caused the harm by acting below the standard imposed by the courts or legislators. But even this emasculated form of fault, while very important in the hierarchy of legal ideas, plays no part in many situations. It may be worthwhile briefly to indicate some of those in which it is recognized that fault is not essential to liability.

Justification for "Respondeat Superior"

[T]he predominant reason for the objective standard in contracts is the advancement of trade through the comparative certainty created by a fixed standard. In many situations, the same reason applies to the imposition of liability upon a principal for the unauthorized contracts of an agent. If the business of the world is to be done by agents, third persons in dealing with them must be relieved, so far as is possible, from uncertainty as to the extent of their authority, and it is for the general advantage of the entire class of persons acting as principals that occasionally an individual principal should be held liable for contracts which he did not authorize. . . .

Similar reasons apply to cases where an agent employed to manage a business deals in an unauthorized manner with a third person who does not know the position which the agent occupies. In many of these cases there is no basis for finding apparent authority, and hence, if the principal is liable upon the authorized contract it is not because of a "holding out," since the agent was not held out to the plaintiff, but because of a business policy which requires that third persons be reasonably protected in their dealings with those who in fact have been placed in a position of authority by the principal, although the authority has been abused. . . .

Perhaps the strongest reason which can be given for the imposition of "absolute" liability applies even more strongly in the case of vicarious liability; that is, the fact that one who is responsible for all consequences is more apt to take precautions to prevent injurious consequences from arising. If the law requires a perfect score in result, the actor is more likely to strive for that than if the law requires only the ordinary precautions to be taken; the cases where, . . . an actor is made absolutely liable for consequences indicated that this reason plays a very large part. . . .

But whether or not the law of torts has an appreciable deterrent effect upon individuals, it has important consequences where servants are employed. Without further investigation, our self-questioning inevitably leads us to believe that respondeat superior results in greater care in the selection and instruction of servants than would be used otherwise. . . .

Another reason for liability without fault in many cases is the difficulty of proving negligence. This reason is particularly cogent in imposing liability upon a master. Whether an employee was unfit at the time of the accident or whether there was improper supervision would ordinarily have to be proved by the testimony of fellow workers. Truthful testimony in such cases is difficult to obtain from the members of a well-disciplined organization. Aside from self-interest, which is obvious, only disgruntled fellow-workers are likely to subject themselves to the name commonly applied to a "tattle tale" within the organization. If the instructions of the master are such as to require acts likely to be tortious, if obeyed, ordinarily the instructions will be brought to light by the servant only in the comparatively rare case where he does so in self-protection.

Another reason not frequently acknowledged specifically by the courts is the "long purse" cynicism of Baty. The bald statement that the master should pay because he can pay may have little more than class appeal, although it is in conformity with the spirit of our times to believe that if one is successful enough either to operate a business or to employ servants, in addition to the income taxes taking off the upper layers of soft living, he should pay for the misfortunes caused others by his business or household. This, of itself, may not be a sufficiently strong reason; the liability of a master for the negligence of his domestic servants is less obvious than that of one employing his servants in business. Today, however, we realize that the loss from accident usually falls upon the community as a whole, and that a cause of action is not money in pocket. . . . The business enterprise, until it becomes insolvent, can shift losses imposed upon it because of harm to third persons to the consumers who ultimately pay, and it is not unjust to have the burden of misfortune shared by those who benefit from the work in the course of which liability occurs. It is this which is leading to the extension of absolute liability. . . .

Finally, in the situations most frequently occurring, that is, those in which a corporation or other business organization is a defendant, it is reasonably obvious that the doctrine of respondeat superior is practically a necessity. Without this, the members of the organization, normally free in any event from personal liability, would be released as to the funds contributed, not only for the harms caused by the physical negligence of servants, but also for the wrongs done by the deceit and other similar torts of the directors and other corporate executives. To permit a group of persons to organize that so without personal liability they can secure the profits resulting both from the lawful and the unlawful conduct of those in charge of the organization without having the assets subject to liability for the harm caused by the unlawful conduct, is so shocking that it

would seem to be unnecessary to do more than to state the alternatives. Whether or not the rule of respondeat superior was sustainable as a matter of justice when it originated, it is reasonably clear that in the modern world we cannot get along without it.

Spread of "Respondeat Superior"

Irrespective of its justice or injustice, its expediency or inexpediency, the doctrine of respondeat superior is spreading rapidly, both within and without the field of agency.

In the cases involving unauthorized contracts made by an agent, the liability of a principal has been widely extended, very largely through an expansion in the original meaning of "apparent authority." It is reasonably clear that where a person represents to another that his agent is authorized to do a specified class of acts, such person should be liable for what the agent does within the field as thus defined. It is becoming increasingly recognized, however, that in many cases the person who is given a cause of action against the principal has not relied upon any statement or representation for which the principal is in any way responsible. In a wide variety of situations the courts find a contract where an agent, usually a manager, has disobeyed orders in dealing with a person who had no notice of the extent of his authority. . . .

The liability of a master to a third person for the torts of a servant has been widely extended by aid of the elastic phrase "scope of the employment" which may be used to include all which the court wishes to put into it. At the beginning of the nineteenth century, the courts were cautiously expanding the master's liability beyond the field of commanded acts, liability for the main part being confined to negligent acts resulting in physical harm and to cases involving mistake by a servant as to the subject matter. Where the servant performed what was described as a "wilful act," the master was not responsible. . . . Likewise the master was not held liable for the conduct of a servant while he was going on "a frolic of his own" and the extent of the frolic was interpreted liberally in favor of the master. The expansion in this field has been rapid. In the detour case, the tendency is more and more to find that even a very extended detour is within the scope of the employment, and in many jurisdictions, at least, the servant reenters his employment, although far from his sphere of action, as soon as he decides so to do. . . .

The year 1934 is not a time for prophecies. The changes in the world are so great and so recent that to attempt a forecast concerning either the trend of legislation or of judicial opinion is an extra hazardous occupation. There would seem, however, to be an adequate basis for a guess that . . . the absence of negligence or fault . . . will play a continually smaller part, and that we are likely to revert to the primitive rule by which liability for harm, at least of certain types, is not dependent upon either legal or moral fault. Whether or not, however, this guess proves to be correct, it seems clear that until we have an entirely changed form of political organization, the principles or respondeat superior will not disappear.

1. Professor Seavey discusses at least five reasons for the doctrine of respondeat superior. What are they?

2. Professor Seavey suggests at one point that the doctrine of respondeat superior is based more on expediency than justice. Why is it not "just" that a principal-master who is in business to make a profit should be required to pay the cost incurred in conducting the business? Certainly this cost includes injury by servants to innocent third persons. Obviously, our perceptions of what is "just" change over the decades. Note that many businesses still behave as though it is "unjust" for them to bear the cost of eliminating the pollution caused by the business; or, that it is "unjust" that they should be required to provide a safe working environment for the employees.

Article Review Questions

Basic Distinctions: Master, Servant, Independent Contractor.   Mentioned throughout the article by Seavey are the terms master and servant. Some authorities believe that the law of master and servant exists independently from the law of principal and agent. However, we believe that the *Restatement* is correct when it defines master and servant as a subclassification of principal and agent. The *Restatement* provides that:[5]

1. A master is a principal who employs an agent to perform service in his affairs and who controls or has the right to control the physical conduct of the other in the performance of the service.

2. A servant is an agent employed by a master to perform service in his affairs whose physical conduct in the performance of the service is controlled or is subject to the right to control by the master.

3. An independent contractor is a person who contracts with another to do something but who is not controlled by the other nor subject to the other's right to control with respect to physical conduct in the performance of the undertaking. An independent contractor may or may not be an agent.

Examining the circumstances in which courts apply the definitions above is very important because of the legal consequences that flow from the designation of a master-servant relationship, rather than a principal-independent contractor relationship. Simply stated, these legal consequences are that a *master is liable for the torts of a servant committed while acting in the scope of employment*.[6] One who employs an independent contractor suffers *no liability based on respondeat superior for his agent's torts!* However, liability of a principal in the latter case may be imposed if the activity of the independent contractor is ultrahazardous or a state or federal statute or public policy holds that the principal shall be liable (discussed later in this chapter).

The key to understanding the above definitions is to focus on who has the *right to control the physical conduct* of the supposed servant.[7] The control need not be exercised; it is the *right* to control that is important.

The classifications of master-servant or principal-independent contractor are conceptual generalities, and sometimes the application of these generally stated principles to reality can be very difficult. We have therefore presented two cases for your analysis. The first is rather simple. It sets out in detail the factual circumstances that courts look for in guiding them to conclusions about the right to control.

Perhaps the most difficult circumstance (and certainly one of the most common) where the master-servant relationship is important involves an agent traveling by car who negligently injures a third party. Such agents are usually hired to contract for the principal and must do so in circumstances where a physical act (traveling by auto) is necessary. Should the principal be liable when the agent negligently operates an auto on a business-related trip? The answer depends on whether that agent can be classified as a servant at the moment the negligent act occurred. Such facts as the ownership of the auto, the principal's right to control the route traveled, and the right to designate who should be called on by the agent become very important. Usually if the agent owns the car and selected the route and customers, the principal will not be liable. Conversely, if the auto is owned by the principal and the principal selected the route and customers, the agent may be termed a servant, thus creating liability for the principal-master for unintentional torts. This is the subject of the second case below.

MASSEY v. TUBE ART DISPLAY, INC.
15 Wash. App. 782; 551 P2d 1387 (1976)

SWANSON, Judge
Tube Art Display, Inc. (Tube Art) appeals from a judgment entered on a jury verdict awarding $143,000 in damages to John Mas-sey, doing business as Olympic Research & Design Associates (Massey).

The facts leading to the initiation of this action are not in substantial dispute. A recently opened branch office of McPherson's Realty Company desired to move a reader board sign from its previous location to a site adjacent to its new quarters in a combination commercial-apartment building. An agreement was reached with Tube Art, the owner of the sign, to transport and re-install it on the northwest corner of the building's parking lot. On February 15, 1972, Tube Art obtained a permit from the City of Seattle for installation of the sign. On the following morning Tube Art's service manager and another employee went to the proposed site and took photographs and measurements. Later, a Tube Art employee laid out the exact size and location for the excavation by marking a 4 by 4 foot square on the asphalt surface with yellow paint. The dimensions of the hole, including its depth of 6 feet, were indicated with spray paint inside the square. After the layout was painted on the asphalt, Tube Art engaged a backhoe operator, defendant Richard F. Redford, to dig the hole.

In response to Tube Art's desire that the job be completed on the 16th of February, 1972, Redford began digging in the early evening hours at the location designated by Tube Art. At approximately 9:30 p.m. the bucket of Redford's backhoe struck a small natural gas pipeline. After examining the pipe and finding no indication of a break or leak, he concluded that the line was not in use and left the site. Shortly before 2 a. m. on the following morning, an explosion and fire occurred in the building serviced by that gas pipeline. As a result, two people in the building were killed and most of its contents were destroyed.

Tube Art's first assignment of error is directed to the following instructions given in the liability portion of the trial:

The defendants are sued as principal and agent. The defendant Tube Art Display, Inc., is the principal and the defendant Richard Redford is the agent. If you find the defendant Richard Redford liable then you must find that the defendant Tube Art Display, Inc., is also liable. However, if you do not find that Richard

Redford is liable, then you must decide whether or not Tube Art Display, Inc., is liable for its own negligence, if any, as defined elsewhere in these instructions.

Traditionally, servants and non-servant agents have been looked upon as persons employed to perform services in the affairs of others under an express or implied agreement, and who, with respect to physical conduct in the performance of those services, is subject to the other's control or right of control.

An independent contractor, on the other hand, is generally defined as one who contracts to perform services for another, but who is not controlled by the other nor subject to the other's right to control with respect to his physical conduct in performing the services.

In determining whether one acting for another is a servant or independent contractor, several factors must be taken into consideration. These are listed in Restatement (Second) of *Agency* § 220(2) (1958), as follows:

(a) The extent of control which, by the agreement, the master may exercise over the details of the work;

(b) whether or not the one employed is engaged in a distinct occupation or business;

(c) the kind of occupation, with reference to whether, in the locality, the work is usually done under the direction of the employer or by a specialist without supervision;

(d) the skill required in the particular occupation;

(e) whether the employer or the workman supplies the instrumentalities, tools, and the place of work for the person doing the work;

(f) the length of time for which the person is employed;

(g) the method of payment, whether by the time or by the job;

(h) whether or not the work is a part of the regular business of the employer;

(i) whether or not the parties believe they are creating the relation of master and servant; and

(j) whether the principal is or is not in business.

All of these factors are of varying importance in determining the type of relationship involved and, with the exception of the element of control, not all the elements need be present. It is the right to control another's physical conduct that is the essential and oftentimes decisive factor in establishing vicarious liability whether the person controlled is a servant or a nonservant agent.

In discussing the actual extent to which the element of control must be exercised, we pointed out in *Jackson v. Standard Oil Co.,* 8 Wash.App. 83, 505 P.2d 139 (1972), that the plaintiff need not show that the principal controlled or had the right to control every aspect of the agent's operation in order to incur vicarious liability. Rather,

> [i]t should be sufficient that plaintiff present substantial evidence of . . . control or right of control over those activities from whence the actionable negligence flowed. If the rule were otherwise, then a person wishing to accomplish a certain result through another could declare the other to be an independent contractor generally, and yet retain control over a particularly hazardous part of the undertaking without incurring liability for acts arising out of that part. Such a result would effectively thwart the purpose of the rule of vicarious liability.
>
> In this regard, it may be emphasized that it is not de facto control nor actual exercise of a right to interfere with or direct the work which constitutes the test, but rather, the *right to control* the negligent actor's physical conduct in the performance of the service.

In making his ruling that Tube Art was responsible as a matter of law for Redford's actions the trial judge stated,

> I think that under the undisputed evidence in this case they not only had the right to control, but they did control. They controlled the location of the spot to dig. They controlled the dimensions. They controlled the excavation and they got the building permits. They did all of the discretionary work that was necessary before he started to operate. They knew that the method of excavation was going to be by use of a backhoe rather than a pick and shovel which might have made a little difference on the exposure in this situation. They in effect created the whole atmosphere in which he worked. And the fact that even though he did not work for them all the time and they paid him on a piece-work basis for the individual job didn't impress me particularly when they used him the number of times they did. Most of the time they used him for this type of work. So I am holding as a matter of law that Redford's activities are the responsibility of Tube Art.

Our review of the evidence supports the trial court's evaluation of both the right and exercise of control even though Redford had been essentially self-employed for about 5 years at the time of trial, was free to work for other contractors, selected the time of day to perform the work assigned, paid his own income and business taxes and did not participate in any of Tube Art's employee programs. The testimony advanced at trial, which we find determinative, established that during the previous 3 years Redford had worked exclusively for sign companies and 90 percent of his time for Tube Art. He had no employees, was not registered as a contractor or subcontractor, was not bonded, did not himself obtain permits or licenses for his jobs, and dug the holes at locations and in dimensions in exact accordance with the instructions of his employer. In fact, Redford was left no discretion with regard to the placement of the excavations that he dug. Rather, it was his skill in digging holes pursuant to the exact dimensions prescribed that caused him to be preferred over other backhoe operators. We therefore find no disputed evidence of the essential factor—the right to control, nor is there any dispute that control was exercised over the most significant decisions—the size and location of the hole. Consequently, only one conclusion could reasonably be drawn from the facts presented. In such a circumstance, the nature of the relationship becomes a question of law. We find no error.

1. Recall the article by Professor Seavey and then, in general terms, explain why the principal-master should be liable to the injured third party in this case.

2. Why does the plaintiff want to sue Tube Art? Why not just sue the alleged servant?

3. What facts caused the court to conclude that the master had the right to control the physical conduct of the servant?

STOCKWELL v. MORRIS
46 Wyo. 1, 22 P.2d 189 (S. Ct. Wyo., 1933)

BLUME, Justice

In this case Morris, salesman for the Maytag Intermountain Company, was driving his automobile from Hudson to Lander and collided with the automobile of plaintiff. The latter sued the salesman, as well as his principal, for damages caused by the collision. The court directed a verdict for the company, and the sole question herein is—assuming the agent to have been negligent—as to whether or not the court's action was right. The testimony herein is uncontradicted.

Morris was a salesman for the company in selling washing machines, and had been working for it for some years. That was his only occupation. He received a commission on all sales made, and no further compensation. He made no collections, but occasionally seems to have delivered washing machines sold. He drove his own automobile in the performance of his work, and paid his own expenses. He appointed and discharged subsalesmen under him, receiving a commission on their sales, and he took them out from time to time to show them how to sell washing machines. . . . The company furnished him with no rules or regulations as to his work, except as to the terms of the contracts to be made for the sale of washing machines. The details of the work were left to him. . . . On May 27, 1930 the date of his collision above mentioned, Morris, in company with his wife, drove his automobile to Lander to see a Mr. Tyler, a salesman under him, to see if he could help him in his work. After

reaching Lander, he, at the suggestion of Tyler, and in company with him, drove to Hudson, to see Mrs. Radovitch, who had a Maytag washing machine which was out of repair, though repairs of machines were ordinarily made by a special representative of the company. Tyler discovered the trouble, fixed the machine, gratuitously, and he and Morris then drove back to Lander, and the collision occurred while doing so. Morris wrote the Maytag Company as to that fact.

Counsel for appellant argue that the Maytag Intermountain Company was the principal and Morris was its agent, and that the former is, accordingly, liable herein, and they say that the cases which hold contrary to their contention deal with the relationship of master and servant, and that such cases have no application here. But an attorney is an agent. If, then, in attempting to manage his client's case, he, without specific directions, travels in an automobile to see a man who, in his opinion, might become an important witness in his case, is his client responsible? So we have "Ford agencies," "Buick agencies," and other similar "agencies," handling products of automobile manufacturers. While today the managers of these agencies, ordinarily, perhaps, buy such products, they might handle them tomorrow on commission. They are agents, in the broad sense of that term, but should the manufacturer be held responsible for all the torts that the former might commit in disposing of these products? The Curtis Publishing Company, located at Philadelphia, every week sends its *Saturday Evening Posts* throughout the country. If a boy in Cheyenne, while on the errand of soliciting subscriptions for the magazine, or delivering it, negligently runs into another with his bicycle, should the company be held responsible? . . .

Courts in cases of the character now before us . . . have ordinarily merely attempted to determine in a particular case whether the person through whose instrumentality a negligent act was committed was a servant or ordinary agent on the one hand, or an independent contractor, or independent agent, pursuing a separate occupation, on the other. The controlling or principal test is generally stated to be as to whether or not the employer, using that term in a broad sense, has the right to control the details of the work to be done by the servant or agent, or whether the latter represents the former only as to the result to be accomplished. . . . The rules governing principal and agent are a later development in our law than those governing master and servant, and have branched off from the latter. A servant is defined as a person employed to perform personal service for another in his affairs, and who, in respect to his physical movements in the performance of the service is subject to the other's control or right to control, while an agent is defined as a person who represents another in contractual negotiations or transactions akin thereto. The reason assigned for the importance of making the distinction is that an agent who is not at the same time acting as servant cannot ordinarily make his principal liable for incidental negligence in connection with the means incidentally employed to accomplish the work intrusted to his care. . . . Of course, an agent may, as to some work performed for his principal, be a servant. But no personal service, not even the delivery of washing machines, is involved in this case, unless the driving of the automobile may be called such. And the gist of the controversy herein is as to whether the principal is liable for its agent's negligence while engaged in a more or less necessary physical act which is incidental to the performance of his general duties. . . .

One of the best statements which we have seen, particularly applicable in a case of the character now before us, is that of Professor Seavey in Tentative Draft No. 5 of the *Restatement of the Law of Agency,* page 100, where it is said: "A principal employing another to achieve a result but not controlling the details of his physical movements is not responsible for incidental negligence while such person is conducting the authorized transaction. Thus the principal is not responsible for the negligent physical conduct of an attorney, a broker, a factor or a rental agent, as such. In their movements and their control of physical forces, they are in the relation of independent contractors to the principal. It is only when to the relationship of principal and agent there is added that right to control physical details as to the manner of performance, which is characteristic of the relation of master and servant, that the person in whose service the act is done, becomes subject to liability for the physical conduct of the actor.". . .

The evidence shows that the Maytag Company furnished Morris no rules or regulations to govern him in the performance of the work but that the means and manner thereof was left to him. . . .

In the case at bar there was no express reservation of control, and none can be implied. In fact it would seem that in view of the fact that actual control of an automobile driven hundreds of miles away from the place of the employer can at best be theoretical only, even though actual control has been reserved, the right of such control should, in a case of this character, be able to be implied only from reasonably clear evidence showing it.

We think, accordingly, that the employer in this case ought not to be held liable. . . . Some criticism has been leveled at courts for their disagreement on this subject and for not finding a more decisive and clear-cut test. But it must be remembered that the rule that a master is liable for the negligence of his servant committed in the course of his employment—which is at the basis of the cases holding the employer in cases of this character liable—is founded not upon a rule of logic, but upon a rule of public policy, . . .

Every rule should, of course, have a reason. Why should we depart from the ordinary rule applicable in the case of master and servant? Is that departure, in the case at bar, based on reason? We think it is. We have, it may be noted, laid some emphasis on the fact of the ownership of the automobile in question. . . .

Practically, in a case of the character before us, the agent has the sole power of control of his automobile. He, as owner, can distribute the risk of driving it by taking out insurance better than, or at least as well as, his principal.

If he alone is held responsible for his negligence, that has a tendency to cause him to exercise care to prevent accidents. To put a man upon his own responsibility generally has that effect. And that prevention of automobile accidents is a matter of considerable, nay vital, importance today is, of course, attested by daily experience. And while this reason cannot be held to be controlling, or perhaps should not be even considered, in some cases, it furnishes at least some basis in the application of public policy.

The judgment of the trial court is, accordingly,

Affirmed.

---

1. List the circumstances in which a traveling salesperson may cause liability for a principal through the negligent operation of an auto.

2. In your opinion, would Maytag be liable to an injured third party if Morris were negligent in the process of repairing a washing machine?

Case Questions

The Difference Between a Master-Servant Relationship and a Principal-Nonservant Agent Relationship.   Generally, if the main objective of the agency is to accomplish a *physical result* such as building, destroying, or altering something in the physical environment and the principal is to direct this work, then chances are good that a master-servant relationship exists. If the main objective of the agency is to accomplish a more abstract, nonphysical or legal result such as negotiating, contracting, or auditing, then chances are that a principal-independent contractor relationship exists.

The *Restatement* distinguishes between two types of independent contractors.[8] An independent contractor may be an agent of the principal (sometimes called a nonservant agent) if he has the authority to contract for the principal (e.g., a salesman); or an independent contractor may not be an agent. For example, if an independent contractor (I/C) contracts with an owner (O) to construct a home for O, and O reserves no right of direction over I/C and I/C is not authorized to contract for O, then I/C is not an agent of O, but is properly called an independent contractor.[9] However, I/C may become an agent of O if O begins to interfere and direct the work of I/C.

In a few instances a nonservant agent or independent contractor may create tort liability for the principal based on respondeat superior or a doctrine very similar to it. These instances are the commission of a tort within the *inherent scope* of the agency; that is, those torts committed during the very act for which the agent was employed. Since most nonservant agents are hired to achieve a legal or other rather abstract, nonphysical result, the torts creating the principal's liability are usually those of a nonphysical nature. These torts are, typically, misrepresentation, fraud, deceit, conversion, and interference with contractual relations. Thus, while a principal who employs a traveling salesperson who owns the auto and selects the route and customers may not be liable to a third party for the agent's tortious operations of the auto, the principal may be liable for the agent's misrepresentations or fraud in the negotiations for an authorized contract. Similarly, if a young accountant working for a certified public accounting firm is negligent while driving his or her own car to see a client, most courts would not hold the firm liable for this act. However, if the same accountant negligently prepared an audit or misrepresented the firm's financial picture, the principal (the firm) most probably would be liable.

The case below reveals a court struggling with the older test for respondeat superior based on the right to control. The court finally abandons the test and adopts the more modern view of vicarious liability that a principal is liable to injured third parties when an agent is negligent in the performance of the very work for which the agent was hired.

ADAMSKI v. TACOMA GENERAL HOSPITAL
20 Wash. App. 98; 579 P2d. 970 (1978)

On January 9, 1974, plaintiff injured his finger while playing basketball. According to plaintiff the bone had broken and was protruding from a gash on the palmar surface of the finger. Plaintiff, aided by a friend, forced the bone back into position, applied a crude splint, covered the wound with a makeshift bandage and continued the game. Later that evening he presented himself for treatment at the emergency room of Tacoma General. Plaintiff first explained his injury to an emergency room nurse, who had his finger X-rayed, and then to the physician in charge, Dr. Tsoi. The doctor irrigated, debrided and cleansed the wound with saline solution and the cut was closed completely with nylon sutures and bandaged.

Plaintiff was told to consult his personal physician in 5 to 6 days for removal of the stitches, or sooner if swelling should occur. . . .

That evening plaintiff's hand began to swell and was somewhat tender; the next day the swelling had increased and he experienced severe pain. According to plaintiff, he called Tacoma General's emergency room for advice; plaintiff avers he talked with the nurse on duty, who told him that pain and swelling were not an unusual aftermath of his treatment. The next day, January 11, plaintiff avers he again called the Hospital and explained to the emergency room nurse that his situation had worsened and that he wished to be seen by the emergency room physician. He claims he was again told his symptoms were not unusual and that he should see his personal physician.

Plaintiff then attempted to contact Dr. R. Marx, an orthopedic specialist by whom he had previously been treated. Dr. Marx was not available, however, and his office referred plaintiff to Lakewood General Hospital, where he was examined by its emergency room physician, Dr. North, who tentatively diagnosed a deep infection of the hand and referred him to Dr. Dale Hirz, a private physician. Plaintiff told Dr. Hirz how the injury had been sustained and how he had reduced the fracture so that the bone was not exposed. Based on this history, Dr. Hirz suspected that a staphylococcus infection had entered the joint sheath and determined that immediate treatment was needed to halt the spread of infection. . . .

[D]r. Hirz surgically opened the little finger; the adjacent ring finger and wrist were also opened to permit a thorough flushing of purulent material from the infected area. The wound on the little finger was left open for drainage—it eventually healed naturally without suturing—and plaintiff was placed on specific antibiotics.

Plaintiff brought this action for damages against Dr. Tsoi, Tacoma Emergency Care Physicians, Inc., P.S. (TECP), a group of physicians who had contracted with Tacoma General, and Tacoma General, alleging as to the latter that (1) Dr. Tsoi was negligent in his diagnosis and treatment, (2) Dr. Tsoi was acting as the Hospital's agent. . . .

Tacoma General moved for summary judgment in its favor, asserting it could not be held liable for Dr. Tsoi's negligence upon the theory of respondeat superior because the doctor was not acting as its agent (employee-servant). Tacoma General argued the doctor was an independent contractor over whose actions it neither had nor exercised any right of control. . . .

On this record, the trial court concluded that Dr. Tsoi was an independent contractor and not an employee of the Hospital, and thus refused to hold the Hospital liable on a respondeat superior theory. . . .

On appeal we are asked to decide if the trial court should have submitted to the jury the issue of Dr. Tsoi's agency. . . .

We have found no Washington cases addressing the problems inherent in the application of the doctrine of respondeat superior to the hospital-physician relationship. Tacoma General argues that the ordinary rules of agency must be applied and that if this is done, Dr. Tsoi must be held to be an independent contractor for whose negligent acts the Hospital is not responsible. We are referred to the case of *Hollingbery* v. *Dunn*, . . . which adopts the criteria of the Restatement (Second) Agency § 220 (1958), and holds that the single most important factor to be considered in determining the status of one who performs services for another is the right of the latter to control the former. Tacoma General points out that nowhere in its contract with TECP does it reserve the right to exercise any control over the actual medical treatment rendered to its emergency room patients. Rather, Tacoma General argues, the only contract requirement is that the doctors must be members of Tacoma General's staff and conform to the usual and accepted professional and ethical standards of conduct.

For many years the majority of courts followed the rule espoused by Tacoma General and held that physicians, because of their skill and training in a highly technical field, were not subject to control by hospital lay boards and thus could not be servants or employees in the sense required by the doctrine of respondeat superior. Rather, physicians were classified as independent contractors with the result that the hospitals in which they labored could not be held vicariously liable for their medical mistakes. . . .

When . . . the hospital undertakes to provide medical treatment rather than merely serving as a private physician to administer to his patients, the physician employed to deliver that service for the hospital may be looked upon as an integral part of the total "hospital enterprise." In such cases, it should make no difference that the physician is compensated on some basis other than salary or that he bills his patient directly. These are artificial distinctions, the efficacy of which has long since disappeared. . . .

Turning to the case before us it can readily be seen that . . . [p]laintiff went directly to the emergency room of Tacoma General and was there given no choice respecting his physician. In fact, Dr. Tsoi had been chosen for him at the time Tacoma General contracted with TECP for emergency room staffing. It is true . . . that Dr. Tsoi does not hold a salaried position; rather, except for the guaranty, his group is dependent upon the charges it makes to patients for professional services. There is, however, substantial evidence that Dr. Tsoi was performing an inherent function of the hospital, a function without which the hospital could not properly achieve its purpose, . . . *i.e.,* he was an integral part of the total hospital function or enterprise. Clearly, when one considers all the facts and circumstances of the relationship between Tacoma General and its emergency room physicians, a substantial and genuine issue arises as to whether that relationship is that of principal and agent. It was error to resolve this issue by summary judgment.

Moreover, where a physician is found not to be the actual agent of the hospital, the latter may still be held responsible for his departures from good medical practice under the so-called "holding out" or "ostensible agent" theory. Restatement (Second) Agency § 267, p. 578 (1958) sets forth the rule as follows:

> One who represents that another is his servant or other agent and thereby causes a third person justifiably to rely upon the care or skill of such apparent agent is subject to liability to the third person for harm caused by the lack of care or skill of the one appearing to be a servant or other agent as if he were such.

In the instant case, a jury could find that Tacoma General held itself out as providing emergency care services to the public. A jury could find that plaintiff reasonably believed Dr. Tsoi *was employed by the Hospital to deliver that emergency room service.* It appears plaintiff was not advised to the contrary and, in fact, he believed he was being treated by the Hospital's agent; . . . Clearly, when the facts before the trial court and the fair inferences therefrom are viewed in a light most favorable to plaintiff, a jury could find that the emergency room personnel were "held out" as employees of the Hospital. It was error, therefore, not to submit this issue to the jury.

Case Questions

1. Why was there no master-servant relationship here?
2. In a few sentences, state the legal principle applied in this case.
3. There are really two bases for liability in this case. What are they?

If there is an emerging legal rule that holds a principal liable for torts committed by an agent who acts within the inherent scope of authority, then why worry about the right to control at all? Is not this more modern principle easier to apply? It may be, but the master-servant relationship is still very important because (1) many courts might not take the more modern approach of the *Adamski* cases; and (2) the range of circumstances in which a master will be liable for the torts of a servant is broader than the range for a principal-nonservant agent. This second idea is usually expressed this way: A master is liable for the unintentional torts of a servant committed while acting in the scope of employment plus those torts that are incidental to the scope of employment. The key here is the phrase "scope of employment." The scope of employment is defined by the authority that the principal-master gives to the agent-servant. Generally, for an act to be within the scope of employment, it must be so related in substance and time to the reasons for the employment that courts can conclude it is of the same general nature as that conduct that is authorized, and was accomplished while benefiting the principal-master.

A tort that is *incidental* to this scope of employment is one that is done during an event subordinate to or pertinent to an act that the servant is employed to perform. The action resulting in the tort must be within the overall objective of the agency relationship and of such a character that it is likely that a reasonable servant might do it. For example, if a principal hires an agent to cut weeds in his field, and carefully explains how the weeds are to be cut and provides the tools for cutting, then the agent may be classified as a servant. If the servant is negligent in lighting a fire in the field to cook his lunch and burns up a third party's crops on adjacent land, the principal-master will be liable.[10] The negligent act was not within the inherent scope of employment (cutting weeds) but was incidental to the employment.

Liability for Damage Caused While Doing Personal Business on Company Time.   In some situations, it is difficult to determine the time or the point at which action by a servant or an agent is either within the inherent scope of employment or incidental to it. Many courts therefore focus on the intent of the servant or agent. If a servant-agent is "at work" but is engaged in an activity intended to benefit only the servant, and a tort occurs while this action is underway, then the tort is beyond the scope of employment and the principal or master is not liable to an injured third party. These circumstances frequently involve a person hired to drive who then does personal errands on the employer's time. Courts would say that the servant or agent in these circumstances was engaged in a "detour" or "frolic." The beginning of the detour or frolic is relatively easy to establish. This occurs when the servant substantially departs from the established route with the intent to receive a personal benefit. While some courts have said that deviating one block or a relatively short distance is not a detour, most courts would hold that a deviation of several miles or a deviation of considerable proportion was a detour.

What if the tort occurred after the servant had accomplished his objective and was returning to the established route? In this instance the courts are divided on the definition of the "scope of employment". Some have held that the servant reenters the scope of employment at the moment of turning back; others have said that the servant reenters when he or she is relatively close to the point of departure; other courts allow recovery from the principal only when the servant is back on the authorized road.[11] Perhaps an example will clarify this. McBride Express Co. was a trucking firm that employed Smyser as a driver. Smyser made daily runs for McBride from Mattoon, Illinois, to St. Louis, Missouri. On the day in question, Smyser took his 16-year-old son with him (with McBride's permission). When he arrived in St. Louis, Smyser delivered the freight to the terminal and then put his son on a bus to visit friends while he attended a ball game. He left the game when it began to rain and returned to the terminal to pick up the truck and another load of freight. As he was leaving town, he drove four or five blocks out of his way to pick up his son. Before he picked his son up, he negligently ran into the plaintiff. The plaintiff sued the master. At the trial, it was established that the employer set the driver's route, owned the truck and, in general, controlled the activities of the employee. Thus, a master-servant relationship existed. In holding in favor of the defendant, the court said:

> The solution of the problem presented is not merely a matter of measuring the distance, the time, or the direction of the departure from what may be called the path of authorized conduct. Such circumstances may guide the judgment, but will not be suffered to control it aside from other circumstances which may characterize the intent of the transaction.
>
> A servant may in certain instances deviate from the most direct or authorized route and still be in the master's service. Thus it may be that one turns aside to avoid heavy traffic, or to seek a smoother route. There may be parallel routes leading in the direction of his ultimate destination, either of which could be said to be within his sphere of service, on the theory that it might be reasonably expected that he would, in the exercise of his best judgment, choose either while in the pursuit of his master's business; or he might turn aside to attend to necessary personal wants which are considered incidental to his employment. But any turning aside from the designated or customary route, where the sole motive is self interest, unmixed with any intent to serve the master, separates the servant from the master's service, regardless of the extent of the deviation. Any other rule would lead to inconsistencies and ultimate confusion in the law.
>
> Smyser, defendant's servant, while making the journey to the Caroline Street address to pick up his son, was performing no service for his master. He was not within his contemplated sphere of service at the time, nor performing an act which could be said to be incidental to his employment. His deviation was not made to facilitate the movement of the freight he was employed to haul. His intent was to serve a private purpose. As a matter of law, Smyser was not within the scope of his employment when the collision occurred.[12]

Intentional Torts and the Scope of Employment. Many of the cases brought by injured third parties against principals and masters are based on negligence. What if a servant commits an intentional tort such as assault and battery? The more precise question is, is an assault and battery on a third party beyond the scope of employment? The *Restatement* would answer this by stating that such conduct is within the scope of employment if the use of force is expectable by the master.[13] The *Restatement* presents the more modern view, but one may wonder under what circumstances a master ever expects a servant to be violent. This expectation may be present when a tavern owner employs a bouncer, but in the ordinary course of events, a master or employer does not normally expect a servant or employee to be violent. The court reports show no real, consistent application of a principle involving intentional torts. At this point, it seems the courts are split. The following case reveals the nature of this split.

SANDMAN v. HAGAN & STRIEGEL, d/b/a Beane Plumbing and Heating Co., and Andrew Montagne
261 La. 560, 154 N.W. 2d 113 (S.Ct. Iowa, 1967)

It appears from the record that on November 7, 1963, the plaintiff Jerry Sandman, employed by the Sioux City Sewer Department, was directed to inspect a job at 2213 Pierce Street in Sioux City, Iowa, and arrived on the job between 8 and 9 A.M. His duty that particular morning was to inspect the installation, the hookup, and the backfill of the connection to the city water system being done by Beane Plumbing and Heating Co., hereafter referred to as the employer. The defendant Montagne and two other employees of Beane Plumbing and Heating Co., Lloyd Brunssen and Martin Wilde, were doing the actual work. A hole had been dug in the street approximately three to four feet wide, five feet long, and six feet deep. The installation and hookup had been completed and the backfill operation involving the refilling of the hole was awaiting the arrival of Sandman. In this operation a small quantity of dirt is first dumped into the excavation and then this dirt must be firmly tamped beneath the water pipe and main. . . . Inspector Sandman was there to see that the dirt was properly compacted under the main by the installing workmen. . . .

Sandman testified he was observing the backfill operation from above when he noticed that dirt had not been properly compacted under the main, and he brought this to the attention of Brunssen. Not being satisfied with the results of his directions, he jumped down in the hole to show Brunssen that there was a void under the main.

Brunssen testified that Sandman had said nothing to him about improper backfilling, but rather jumped into the hole with him and began shoving dirt into a gap under the main. Both testified that no altercation or abusive language occurred until Sandman had demonstrated to Brunssen that there was indeed a gap between the main and the ground. At this point Sandman testified that Brunssen called him an s.o.b. and other derogatory names, told him to get out of the hole, and said he had no business down there. . . .

Immediately following this name-calling, a fight took place between Sandman and Brunssen. Sandman testified that to the best of his recollection he struck Brunssen only once and that the fight lasted about two minutes. Brunssen testified that he did not strike Sandman, but doubled up to protect himself and that Sandman struck him several times on the face and body, and that the fight lasted about 15 to 30 seconds.

Montagne testified that he did not hear the conversation between Sandman and Brunssen prior to the fight because the noisy air compressor was running at the time, that the first thing he knew Sandman was pounding on Brunssen and he yelled at Sandman to stop but that he did not stop, and that he (Montagne) became scared that Brunssen might be hurt. Montagne then struck Sandman on the back of the head with a shovel. Although Sandman testified he saw Montagne swing the shovel at him, he did not hear Montagne say anything to him before he got hit with the shovel. . . .

The jury returned a verdict for Sandman against all defendants. On motion by the employer, the trial court granted judgment notwithstanding the verdict for it, concluding there was insufficient evidence to sustain a finding that Montagne was acting within the scope of his employment. . . .

The sole issue presented on appeal by appellant Sandman is whether at the time in question employee Montagne was acting within the scope of his apparent authority so as to make the defendant employer liable and sustain the jury determination on that issue.

The trial court concluded there was no evidence to sustain a finding that Montagne's authority extended beyond that of putting in water lines and refilling excavations, or that his duties contemplated conflict with others, or that the assault was done in the furtherance of the employer's business or interests within the scope of his employment. We must agree.

I. It is well established in Iowa that under the common law the master and servant may each and both be liable for a servant's torts committed within the course of employment. . . .

The difficulty encountered by various courts in cases of willful torts committed by servants has resulted in irreconcilable decisions, and unless carefully scrutinized, the authorities seem to be in hopeless confusion. . . . The difficulty is in defining and applying the concept of acts within the course of employment or the scope of the servant's authority. These terms are often used loosely and not carefully analyzed. . . .

It has been said an act is "within the scope of the servant's employment" where such act is necessary to accomplish the purpose of the employment and is intended for such purpose, although in excess of the powers actually conferred on the servant by the master. . . .

It is safe to say that "within the scope of the employment" requires that the conduct complained of must be of the same general nature as that authorized or incidental to the conduct authorized. . . . The facts in the Kentucky Wood case and the Minnesota Plotkin case are not greatly different. Both result in no employer liability. In each case, after an altercation with another vehicle on the highway, the bus company driver stopped his bus and assaulted the operator of the other vehicle. Both courts recognize the rule that to determine whether an agent's act is within the scope of employment so as to make the master liable therefor, the question is whether the agent's conduct is so unlike that authorized that it is "substantially different." Both state that, to render a master liable for a servant's battery, it is not sufficient that the battery is due to anger arising from the performance of the servant's duties. . . .

II. As we have pointed out, a deviation from the employer's business, or interest to pursue the employee's own business or interest must be substantial in nature to relieve the employer from liability. . . . Here, the employer contends the assault was clearly a deviation substantial in nature, for under no theory advanced would the duty of installing water lines and digging ditches include the exercise of force upon others. It is difficult to see how his employer's business or interest would ever be furthered by such an employee attack, especially on an inspector. . . .

III. We are aware of the so-called modern trend to find liability in this class of cases on the basis that such wrongs are committed by the employee only because of the employment situation, and that since the employer has the benefit of the enterprise as between two innocent third parties, he is better able to bear the risk of loss. If he cannot altogether avoid such wrongs, he can at least minimize them. In those cases it is argued that a general sense of fairness requires that the employer, as the person interested and benefited by the business, rather than the persons who have no concern in or control over it, should bear the burden of such wrongs as incidental to such business. . . .

If employer liability is to be extended this far, we believe it should come from the legislature, and do not find that this concept has substantial support in judicial decisions.

We are satisfied here that the employee Montagne's assault on Inspector Sandman was a substantial deviation from his duties, that his act was substantially different in nature from that authorized by the employer, and that at the time thereof he was acting outside the scope of his employment. The trial court was correct in granting the employer's motion for judgment notwithstanding the verdict and must be affirmed on appellant Sandman's appeal. . . .

Affirmed.

BECKER, Justice
I dissent as to plaintiff's appeal from judgment in favor of defendant employer.

Thompson-Starrett Co. v. *Heinold* . . . involves a situation where an employee hit the employee of a subcontractor with a lead pipe when the plaintiff didn't move his equipment as ordered. "It is undisputed that in the early cases a master was held not liable for the tortious act of his servant, when the act was wanton and malicious. In later cases, the master is held liable for the wrongful act of the servant, notwithstanding its wanton and malicious character, if the act was done in the course and within the scope of his employment, and the determination of the question whether the tort was committed while the servant was acting in the course and within the scope of his employment is for the jury."

The foregoing statement is a short summation of the law as it has developed in the past thirty years. Standing alone the case would not necessarily persuade. But a careful reading of the very authorities cited by the majority; i.e., *Restatement, Second Agency* § 245,

Comment a (as amended by the Appendix, Restatement, *Second, Agency* § 245) . . . indicates the rule stated in *Thompson-Starrett Co.* v. *Heinold, supra,* is the majority view. It should be followed by this court. . . .

The change in *Restatement, Second, Agency,* § 245 as indicated in the Appendix written 23 years later should be especially noted because the change is substantial and weakens the authority upon which the majority relies. At page 389 the author of the Appendix states: "It is believed that it is now desirable to state a rule invoking a somewhat greater liability because of the cases in the intervening years. The courts of some states are more conservative in subjecting the master to liability than those of other states, but the tendency of the courts is to broaden the area within which the principal is found liable." The author then carefully reviews the history of the developments of the doctrine and cities numerous cases supporting his conclusion. . . .

In *Carr* v. *William C. Crowell Co.,* . . . Traynor, J., analyzes the problem in a closely analogous case and sets forth several principles that should govern our consideration here.

"The employer's responsibility for the tortious conduct of his employee extends far beyond his actual or possible control over the conduct of the servant. It rests on the broader ground that every man who prefers to manage his affairs through others remains bound to so manage them that third persons are not injured by any breach of legal duty on the part of such others while acting in the scope of their employment. In the present case, defendant's enterprise required an association of employees with third parties, attended by the risk that someone might be injured. The risks of such associations and conditions were risks of the employment." Cardozo, J. in *Leonbruno* v. *Champlain Silk Mills,* . . . 128 N.E. 711. . . . Such associations 'include the faults and derelictions of human beings as well as their virtues and obediences. Men do not discard their personal qualities when they go to work. Into the job they carry their intelligence, skill, habits of care and rectitude. Just as inevitably they take along also their tendencies to carelessness and camaraderie, as well as emotional makeup. In bringing men together, work brings these qualities together, causes frictions between them, creates occasions for lapses into carelessness, and for fun-making and emotional flareup. Work could not go on if men became automatons repressed in every natural expression. . . . These expressions of human nature are incidents inseparable from working together. They involve risks of injury and these risks are inherent in the working environment. . . .

. . . Here the employees' duties regularly brought them in contact with the inspector. The inspector and Montagne had had previous altercations. This fight developed over the method of performing the employer's business of laying the pipe. Montagne entered the fray on the side of the fellow employee, if not on his behalf. It is for the jury to decide whether this employee was acting within the scope of his employment or on a venture of his own. I would affirm as to defendant Montagne but would reverse and reinstate the verdict as to employer-defendants.

Case Questions

1. In your own words state:
   a. how and why the law uses the phrase, "within the scope of employment."
   b. when an act is "within the scope of employment."

2. Does the dissent suggest that as a general rule all intentional torts are within the scope of employment? Or, is the dissenting view more narrow in its statement of the rule?

3. List and define the torts that are, according to some courts, not within the scope of employment. List and define those torts that are within the scope of employment. For the purposes of this chapter you may consider willful and intentional torts as the same thing.

Case Comment

The *Sandman* majority opinion indicates that in Iowa the general rule is that intentional torts of the servant are not within the scope of employment even if they are engendered by the employment; therefore, the master will not be liable for injury caused by a servant's intentional torts. Note that the dissent states that this rule is a minority view. The authors of the *Restatement* and the noted California authority, Judge Traynor, both would reach a decision for the plaintiff here. Note especially the *reasoning* of Judge Traynor cited in the dissent. Although he does not state it explicitly, it appears his reasons for the principal's liability in cases such as *Sandman* bear a distinct similarity to the reasons why some courts invoke the doctrine of inherent authority in quasi-contract cases.

In concluding this section on vicarious liability we wish to point out that utilizing the concepts of master-servant, principal-nonservant agent, and independent contractor is not as simple or easy as you might at first think. Do not think of the term servant as denoting an agent who does only menial or manual work. Many servants perform work requiring mental effort rather than physical effort. Corporate officers, highly skilled engineers, interns in hospitals, and most of those other employees who are employed to achieve a physical result and to give their time rather than their product to their employees may be servants.[14] Moreover, it may be possible for one person to be an independent contractor for some tasks and a servant for others.

For resolving complex issues in this area we suggest you look first for a precise definition of the conduct or work being performed for the principal at the time of the tortious conduct. Second, confine your focus to this circumstance and ask what was the purpose of the agency and what degree of control was exercised or was exercisable by the principal over the physical conduct of the agent? If the purpose of the agency was to achieve a physical result and there was a high degree of control over the physical conduct of the agent, a master-servant relationship might exist. Third, if a master-servant relationship exists, you must then determine if, with regard to this specific act, it was within the scope of the agency or was incidental to the agency or beyond the scope of the agency.

Adopting an ironclad rule in this matter is impossible. Definitions of the scope of the agency relationship and matters of control are presented in terms of degrees. An agency relationship and a principal's control are dynamic, always changing. It might be best to think of control on a scale where the legal result varies as you vary the control (see Fig. 5-1).

Apparent Authority and Vicarious Liability

In the first part of this chapter, we said that the vicarious liability of the principal or master is *usually* based on the doctrine of respondeat superior. That concept is more narrow than the concept of vicarious liability and represents the more traditional analytical pattern of basing liability on the *right to control*. In recent years, there have been cases imposing liability on the principal for the agent's torts based on an extension of apparent authority and the related Section 267 of the *Restatement* entitled "Reliance upon Care or Skill of Apparent Servant or Other Agent." These cases are not based on control and seem to reveal a changing emphasis in the law. Rather than present a landmark case on the extension of apparent authority, we present an edited excerpt from a law review article that discusses this development.

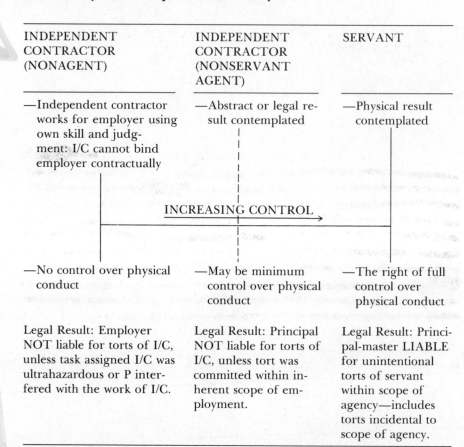

INDEPENDENT CONTRACTOR (NONAGENT)	INDEPENDENT CONTRACTOR (NONSERVANT AGENT)	SERVANT
—Independent contractor works for employer using own skill and judgment: I/C cannot bind employer contractually	—Abstract or legal result contemplated	—Physical result contemplated

INCREASING CONTROL →

—No control over physical conduct	—May be minimum control over physical conduct	—The right of full control over physical conduct
Legal Result: Employer NOT liable for torts of I/C, unless task assigned I/C was ultrahazardous or P interfered with the work of I/C.	Legal Result: Principal NOT liable for torts of I/C, unless tort was committed within inherent scope of employment.	Legal Result: Principal-master LIABLE for unintentional torts of servant within scope of agency—includes torts incidental to scope of agency.

FIGURE 5-1   An Overview of the Use of "Control" in Creating Liability for a Master

"YOU CAN TRUST YOUR CAR TO THE MAN WHO WEARS THE STAR"—OR CAN YOU? THE USE OF APPARENT AUTHORITY TO ESTABLISH A PRINCIPAL'S TORT LIABILITY
William H. Dickey, Jr.

[Reprinted with permission of the publisher; copyright ©, 1971, University of Pittsburgh Law Review. From: 33 Univ. of Pitt. L. Rev. 257 (Winter, 1971).]

(Authors' note: This article has been edited, footnotes renumbered, and citations simplified.)

Gizzi v. Texaco, Inc.

The recent Third Circuit case of *Gizzi* v. *Texaco, Inc.* 437 F. 2d 308 (3d Cir., 1971), shattered the traditional interpretation given the service station-oil company relationship. Briefly, the facts involved are as follows: A Texaco station operator in New Jersey offered for sale to one of his regular patrons a 1958 Volkswagen van. The price of $400 included the installation and complete inspection of a new master braking system. When completed, the patron paid the $400, received a Texaco receipt and departed with a friend to Philadelphia. The brakes failed to work, and the van crashed on the Schuylkill Expressway. Plaintiff brought an action against Texaco in the United States District Court for the Eastern District of Pennsylvania. . . . When that court granted defendant Texaco's motion for a direct verdict, plaintiff appealed to the Third Circuit Court of Appeals. . . .

Plaintiff's theory of liability embraced the agency concepts of apparent authority and estoppel. It was argued that Texaco had clothed the station operator with the apparent authority to make all necessary repairs and even sell the vehicle on its behalf. Moreover, since plaintiff had entered into the transaction relying on this apparent authority, Texaco was estopped from denying the existence of the agency.

> The concepts of apparent authority, and agency by estoppel are closely related. Both depend on manifestations by the alleged principal to a third person, and reasonable belief by the third person that the alleged agent is authorized to bind the principal. (*Gizzi*, cit. 309).

The court, with one judge dissenting, accepted plaintiff's argument. Vital to this acceptance was the fact that Texaco's advertising campaign, which used the famous slogan, "You Can Trust Your Car to the Man Who Wears the Star," had instilled a great degree of confidence in plaintiff concerning Texaco. Also important in the determination were the presence of the Texaco sign and certain equipment on the premises which belonged to the company.

> In order for the third person to recover against the principal, he must have relied on the indicia of authority originated by the principal, and such reliance must have been reasonable under the circumstances. (*Gizzi*, cit. 309)

. . .

The *Gizzi* Rationale

The majority in *Gizzi* placed much reliance on certain applicable sections of the *Restatement*

(Second) of Agency. Aside from the definition of apparent authority, the court's discussion revolved around the principal's manifestation to third parties.

> The manifestation of the principal may be made directly to a third person, or may be made to the community, by signs, by advertising, by authorizing the agent to state that he is authorized, or by continuously employing the agent.

When viewed in the light of the above statement, the presence of the Texaco signs and use of the slogan become crucial factors in the court's determination of liability. But another requirement for liability is reasonable reliance by the third party on the representations made by the alleged principal to the third party:

> A purported master or other principal is subject to liability for physical harm caused to others or to their belongings by their reasonable reliance upon the tortious representations of one acting within his apparent authority or apparent scope of employment.

Thus, the question becomes: Is it reasonable to assume that Texaco will indemnify a third person who, relying on signs, slogans, and ads, is injured as a result of the tort of the gas station attendant?

Simply stated, it appears that the majority in *Gizzi* put the "wagon before the horse." It had determined—almost assumed—that an agency relationship existed between the gas station operator and Texaco, and the resulting rationale was drawn from diverse factual situations in order to support the existence of apparent authority. Thus, it is not the rationale of *Gizzi* which deserves closer attention; it is the development and establishment of the apparent authority relationship in a situation which had previously been viewed in an independent context.

Why the Sudden Shift?

The facts presented in *Gizzi* offered the majority a change "to break new ground" in the

Third Circuit. The plaintiff convinced them that he actually placed a great deal of faith in the motto, "You Can Trust Your Car to the Man Who Wears the Star." But the decision can also be viewed as an attempt to bolster the standing of America's beleaguered consumer. As stated earlier, courts traditionally viewed the gas station-oil company relationship in its proper context (at least to those parties): since no effective control was exercised by the oil company over the gas station, the two were considered independent of each other in terms of day-to-day business routine. Such paraphernalia as signs, pumps, and ads were merely a part of the business. The *Gizzi* court, however, took the same facts and placed a different emphasis on them. Actual control was not a prime factor in determining Texaco's liability. Mass media advertising had bludgeoned the average consumer into believing that Texaco exercised control over every Texaco service station in the country, even though this was not necessarily a fact. Taking into account the power of advertising and the relative business ignorance of the average consumer, it became reasonable to rely on manifestations perceived through countless television commercials that the "man who wears the star" was in fact clothed with the apparent authority to act for Texaco.

Conclusion

As emphasized earlier, because of its unique factual situation, *Gizzi* does not appear to embrace all oil companies. But it is not difficult to foresee the eventual expansion of the situations to which *Gizzi* could apply. Perhaps in some instances, this expansion could be warranted. For example, Texaco has recently buttressed its advertising campaign with a commercial showing a company employee making a surprise inspection of one of its gas stations. The employee, with clipboard in hand, inspects all aspects of the service station, from its rest room cleanliness to the appearance of the station itself. The ad invited potential customers to write to the company if any Texaco station does not appear to be offering the kind of service depicted in the commercial. In this context, an injured party would have a much stronger argument for sustaining an apparent authority theory of tort liability. The element of apparent control is seemingly much more obvious. Thus, *Gizzi* can be viewed in two different extremes; at best, as a warning to oil companies that the courts will protect the average consumer when advertising techniques border on guaranteeing all aspects of service station routines; and at worst, as an unwarranted distortion of the actual relationship which exists between an oil company and a service station. The latter interpretation would open the "floodgates" for any number of possible suits under the concept of apparent authority.

Article Questions   1. In the *Sandman* case, dissenting Justice Becker quotes Judge Traynor as follows:

> The employer's responsibility for the tortious conduct of his employee extends far beyond his actual or possible control over the conduct of the servant. It rests on the broader ground that every man who prefers to manage his affairs through others remains bound to so manage them that third persons are not injured by any breach of legal duty on the part of such others' while acting in the scope of their employment. In the present case, defendant's enterprise required an association of employ-

ees with third parties, attended by the risk that someone might be injured. The risks of such associations and conditions were risks of the employment.

Do you believe that Traynor's conception of vicarious liability is so broad as to justify the holding in the *Gizzi* case? That is, can Traynor's reasoning in the *Sandman* case be used to justify the *Gizzi* result?

2. Is the author of the above article correct when he states, "Thus the question becomes: Is it reasonable (for third parties) to assume that Texaco will indemnify a third person who, relying on signs, slogans, and ads, is injured as a result of the tort of the gas station attendant?" That is, what is the precise nature of the "reasonable reliance" required of third parties for apparent authority to be applied? Must third parties rely on facts indicating the principal intends to indemnify injured third parties, or must they rely on circumstances that simply indicate that the purported agent is indeed acting as an agent and is authorized to do the act in question? Reread the definition of apparent authority in Chapter 4.

The *Gizzi* case and the article quoted from above are now over 10 years old. Since that time, the use of apparent authority to impose liability on principals for tortious and other conduct of their agents has expanded. Very recently the U. S. Supreme Court held that apparent authority could be applied by an injured competitor suing for treble damages under the antitrust laws. In this case, the American Society of Mechanical Engineers (ASME) was sued by Hydrolevel Corporation because an agent of ASME who was acting voluntarily on behalf of ASME, and who was also employed by a competitor of Hydrolevel Corporation, had "officially" interpretated a safety standard of ASME so that Hydrolevel's product appeared unsafe. This agent drafted a letter that was typed on ASME stationery, signed by the appropriate officers of ASME, and sent to Hydrolevel's competitors, who used the letter in sales efforts. This unfair and inaccurate interpretation of the standard discussed in the letter ruined Hydrolevel. Writing for a majority of the Court, Justice Blackmun said:[15]

> As the Court of Appeals observed, under general rules of agency law, principals are liable when their agents act with apparent authority and commit torts analogous to the antitrust violation presented by this case. . . . For instance, a principal is liable for an agent's fraud though the agent acts solely to benefit himself, if the agent acts with apparent authority. Similarly, a principal is liable for an agent's misrepresentations that cause pecuniary loss to a third party, when the agent acts within the scope of his apparent authority. Also, if an agent is guilty of defamation, the principal is liable so long as the agent was apparently authorized to make the defamatory statement. Finally, a principal is responsible if an agent acting with apparent authority tortiously injures the business relations of a third person.
>
> Under an apparent authority theory, liability is based upon the fact that the agent's position facilitates the consummation of the fraud, in that from the point of view of the third person, the transaction seems regular on its face and the agent appears to be acting in the ordinary course of the business confided to him.

> ASME's system of codes and interpretative advice would not be effective if the statements of its agents did not carry with them the assurance that persons in the affected industries could reasonably rely upon their apparent trustworthiness. Behind the principal's liability under an apparent authority theory, then, is "business expediency—the desire that third persons should be given reasonable protection in dealing with agents." The apparent authority theory thus benefits both ASME and the public whom ASME attempts to serve through its codes: "It is . . . for the ultimate interest of persons employing agents, as well as for the benefit of the public, that persons dealing with agents should be able to rely upon apparently true statements by agents who are purporting to act and apparently acting in the interests of the principal."

Section 267 of the *Restatement* is not of great historical significance but, like apparent authority, it has been used in very recent years to impose vicarious liability for an agent's torts on a principal. It provides that:

> One who represents that another is his servant or other agent and thereby causes a third person justifiably to rely upon the care or skill of such apparent agent is subject to liability to the third person for harm caused by the lack of care or skill of the one appearing to be a servant or other agent as if he were such.

A good example of an application of this principle is the *Adamski* case presented earlier in the chapter. In that case, the court proposed at least two justifications for holding the hospital liable. Section 267 is the second such justification.

Ratification of an Agent's Torts and Other Principles Creating Vicarious Liability for a Principal

A principal may ratify the tort of an agent just as a contract or the agency relationship itself can be ratified. Ratification is determined by searching for and finding an act of affirmance by the principal. The *Restatement* (Section 82) says:

> Ratification is the affirmance by a person of a prior act which did not bind him but which was done or professedly done on his account, whereby the act . . . is given effect as if originally authorized by him.

Section 83 of the *Restatement* states:

> Affirmance is either (a) manifestation of an election by one on whose account an unauthorized act has been done to treat the act as authorized, or (b) conduct by him justifiable only if there were such an election.

Most courts would hold that at the time of affirmance the principal must have knowledge of the tort. You cannot ratify something you do not know about. Yet, it seems specific knowledge of the wrong doing or its exact dollar damage need not be known. In a classic case involving the principle of ratification, the owner of a coal company demanded payment from a customer who had received a delivery of coal by someone who was not an agent of the owner. This person voluntarily undertook to deliver the coal and when doing so, broke a window on the customer's property. Oliver Wendell Holmes held that by demanding payment for the coal with the knowledge that the window was broken in the process of delivery, the principal had ratified the negligent act and was liable for the damage. He states:

> We have found hardly anything in the books dealing with the precise case, but we are of opinion that consistency with the whole course of authority requires us to hold that the defendant's ratification of the employment established the relation of master and servant from the beginning, with all its incidents, including the anomalous liability for his negligent acts. . . . The ratification goes to the relation, and established it [from the beginning]. The relation existing, the master is answerable for torts which he has not ratified specifically, just as he is for those which he has not commanded, and as he may be for those which he has expressly forbidden. . . . (*Dempsey* v. *Chambers*, 154 Mass. 330; 28 N.E. 279 at 281 (Sup. Ct., Mass., 1891.)

Liability of Principal to Third Parties Based on Public Policy or Statutory Law.   In a limited number of circumstances the law will impose liability on a principal for the tortious acts of an agent-employee where the act was not authorized or ratified and the doctrine of respondeat superior does not apply.

The first set of such circumstances involves an independent contractor who is hired to perform ultrahazardous activities. Ultrahazardous activities are those that pose a substantial threat of harm to the public but are not specifically illegal, because they are of benefit to society. Such activities are blasting with dynamite or other explosives, spraying noxious solutions on crops or indoors for fumigation, transporting highly toxic chemicals, or drilling for oil in a populated area. Simply stated, the law as a matter of public policy recognizes the danger in these and similar activities and therefore holds that the employer cannot avoid liability for injury caused by hiring an independent contractor.

Closely related to the circumstances just discussed are other duties of an employer that cannot be delegated to an agent either because of statute or because of public policy. For example, The Occupational Safety and Health Act (OSHA) imposes a duty on certain employers to provide a place of work free from recognized danger. If an employer subject to the act hires an independent contractor to perform work on his factory and an employee of the independent contractor is injured in the factory, the initial employer might well be liable if there are circumstances present revealing that the employer (the principal) did not provide a workplace free from recognized hazards. Both the act and court decisions have held that the duty to provide a safe and healthy workplace cannot be delegated.

Another, more traditional example is exemplified by a 1948 case in which the plaintiff's foot became caught between the boards of a railroad crossing. The plaintiff sued the railroad and its agents and independent contractors responsible for maintaining the crossing. The court held the railroad liable independent of the actions of its agents and independent contractors by first citing a state statute that provided (in part), "Whenever any railroad . . . shall cross any state road, it shall be required to keep its own roadbed . . . in proper repair . . . and the tracks of such railroad . . . at grade crossings shall be so constructed as to give a safe . . . approach to some. . . ."

The court then concluded:

> The statute here involved . . . is, in our opinion, absolute and nondelegable, and though the railroad company like a municipality or county, is not an insurer, the statute casts upon the railway company the non-assignable duty in any event to keep and maintain the crossing in a reasonably safe condition. (*Humphrey* v. *Virginian Ry. Co.*, 54 S.E. 2d 204 (S.Ct. of App., West Va., 1948).)

Contractual Duty to Act Carefully to Third Parties. If a principal promises to personally perform an act and then hires an independent contractor to help, the principal may be liable. This result is based on the assumption that the injured third party relied primarily on the principal for performance and, as a matter of public policy, should not be allowed to avoid liability by hiring an independent contractor to perform. That is, if the principal personally promised to perform certain duties, those duties cannot be delegated to others, unless, of course, the third party consents. An exact list of all of those duties that are nondelegable is beyond the scope of this book. Many such duties are peculiar to individual states, and the answer may be found only by reference to state law.

Tort Liability of Principal for Representations by Agent. Some circumstances that create tort liability for a principal fall somewhere between the liability for an agent's contracts based on authority and the liability for torts, or are parts of both. These circumstances concern liability for the misrepresentations of an agent. Misrepresentation, deceit, and fraud are all torts, but whether the principal is subject to liability is determined by the actual or circumstantial authority of the agent, or, in some cases, liability rests on inherent authority. The *Restatement* (Section 258) phrases this principle this way:

> [A] principal authorizing . . . an agent to enter into negotiations to which representations concerning the subject matter thereof are usually incident is subject to liability for loss caused to the other party to the transaction by tortious misrepresentations of the agent upon matters which the principal might reasonably expect would be the subject of representations, provided the other party has no notice that the representations are unauthorized.

A rather simple example of this is that A, agent of P, sells P's land to T, representing that a river close by does not flood onto it. A knows this to be false and has no authority to make the statement. Relying on this representation, T purchases the land. P is subject to liability to T in an action based on deceit.[16]

In concluding our discussion of the tort liability of a principal or master for the actions of an agent or servant, we stress that often the law appears as though it treats circumstances or groups of facts as discrete, separable units. Thus, we have suggested that with regard to contract liability you first think of authority, and with regard to tort liability you think of control. These suggestions are just general guides. As you learned from reading the *Adamski* case and reading about the *Gizzi* case and the U.S. Supreme Court case involving Hydrolevel Corporation, these generalizations do not always apply. In the study of law, almost all general propositions have exceptions.

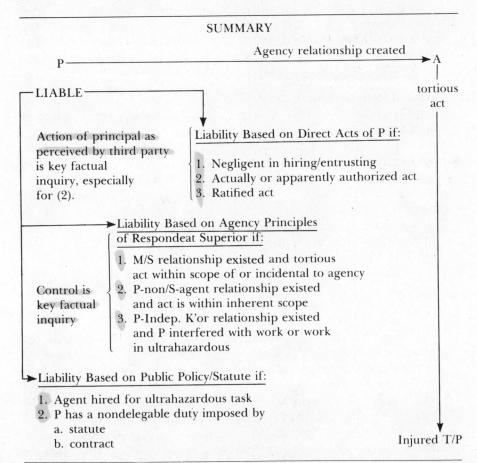

SUMMARY

Agency relationship created

P ————————————————————————————→ A

┌ LIABLE ──────────────────────────────┐   tortious act

Action of principal as perceived by third party is key factual inquiry, especially for (2).

Liability Based on Direct Acts of P if:
1. Negligent in hiring/entrusting
2. Actually or apparently authorized act
3. Ratified act

Liability Based on Agency Principles of Respondeat Superior if:
1. M/S relationship existed and tortious act within scope of or incidental to agency
2. P-non/S-agent relationship existed and act is within inherent scope
3. P-Indep. K'or relationship existed and P interfered with work or work in ultrahazardous

Control is key factual inquiry

Liability Based on Public Policy/Statute if:
1. Agent hired for ultrahazardous task
2. P has a nondelegable duty imposed by
   a. statute
   b. contract

Injured T/P

FIGURE 5-2   Tort liability of principal to third parties.

1. In this chapter we have presented material illustrating the concept of vicarious liability as applied to the agency relationship. In some circumstances the principal will be held liable for the torts of its agents when it neither authorized, ratified, nor otherwise intended that the tortious act occur. List and define these circumstances and give an example of each by using factual patterns not similar to those of the cases in this chapter.

2. Parker Drilling Company drilled for oil and employed a number of people on a full- or part-time basis to keep their equipment in good shape. Crouch was one of the people employed by Parker to do welding on the drilling equipment. Crouch owned his own truck and welding equipment, supplied his own welding materials such as rods and an arc, and maintained his own insurance, submitting invoices to Parker for work done. He was not on the payroll and could take other jobs, but worked steadily for Parker. Parker did supply drawing indicating the type of welding they wanted done, supplying the steel when needed. One of the oil-drilling derricks that Crouch welded collapsed, killing a bystander. The estate of the bystander sued Parker. State the elements of the case the estate will have to prove. Do you believe the estate will be successful?

3. The Mutual Creamery Co. was engaged in the business of buying eggs from nearby poultry raisers. Its general manager at its place of business was Morris Hanson. It also had in its employ one Sager, who two days of the week acted as salesman in selling butter, eggs, cheese, and ice cream. The other five days of the week he was employed to gather eggs from those who had eggs to sell, using his own truck for such purpose, and was paid 25 cents a case for gathering eggs for the company. Mecham in no sense was or had been in the employ of the company or in any manner connected with its business. On the late afternoon of the day in question Mecham accompanied Sager on his truck to the company's plant. When they arrived at the plant, Sager was informed that a customer, a Mrs. Robinson, had telephoned the company that she had some eggs ready to be delivered and to come and get them. It was Sager's duty to get the eggs. He and Mecham had contemplated going "to a show" that evening. Sager, learning he was to go for the eggs, stated to Mecham (not in the presence of anyone) that because of other work he could not get the eggs and go to the show, whereupon Mecham volunteered to Sager that he would go for the eggs to help him out. Sager assented to that, went inside, got a case, put it on the truck, and Mecham drove off. Hanson, the manager of the company, seeing Mecham drive away, asked Sager where Mecham was going and was told to get Mrs. Robinson's eggs. Hanson made no reply thereto. It is not made to appear that Mecham then was yet in hailing distance or that sufficient opportunity was

afforded Hanson to counterdemand what Sager in such particular had done or permitted. On the way, Mecham negligently struck and killed a small boy. After this incident, Mecham procured the eggs and delivered them to the company, which thereafter paid Mrs. Robinson for the eggs. The father of the boy sues Mutual Creamery Co. for the negligent death of his son. What theory of recovery will be alleged? Will it be successful? What additional information would you like to know?

4. On October 1, Great Puppet Shows, Inc., (The "Company") hired Mandrake as its new purchasing agent. The Company knew that Puppetland Corp. was interested in selling certain stage scenery and props but it believed that it could purchase the property for less money if it did not disclose its identity. Therefore, it instructed Mandrake to drive over to Puppetland's office the next day and negotiate for the purchase of the property in his own name without disclosing the Company's identity. Mandrake was authorized to spend up to $5,000.

   On October 2, Mandrake negotiated and signed a contract with Puppetland for the purchase of the property for $4,500 and for delivery and payment on October 15. After signing the contract Mandrake began to drive back to the Company office. On the way he stopped at a bar for a few drinks, which he knew was in violation of a Company policy that prohibited drinking of alcoholic beverages during working hours. After becoming intoxicated he left the bar and began driving to the office. Enroute he negligently struck and killed a pedestrian. On learning these facts the Company immediately discharged Mandrake, who then advised Puppetland that when he signed the contract in his own name he was really doing so for his former employer's benefit and that he wanted nothing to do with the contract.

   a. Discuss fully the liability that might arise between the Company and Mandrake on the one hand and Puppetland on the other. That is, may Puppetland enforce the contract against Mandrake? Against the Company? May the Company enforce the contract against Puppetland?

   b. Does the pedestrian's estate have a right to recover against Mandrake and the Company? State what facts you would need in order to reach an affirmative answer with regard to the Company.

   c. Does the Company have a right to recover from Mandrake if it incurs liability to the estate? (Material from the Uniform CPA Examination, copyright © 1971 by the American Institute of Certified Public Accountants, Inc., is here reprinted with permission. This is adapted from Question Number 8 of the November 5, 1971, exam.)

5. "Texas Family-Style Restaurants" was the name of a nationwide chain of restaurants. These restaurants were operated on a franchise system in which the parent organization, "Texas Family-Style Restaurants, International, Inc.," agreed to let a local owner of a restaurant use both its name and style of cooking and serving food. The local owner agreed to maintain certain standards of service and cooking in exchange for using the name, etc., and also agreed to give the parent organization a percentage of the profits earned. The parent organization also engaged in a national advertising campaign in which it made a pitch for family business and specifically emphasized that this chain of restaurants stood for unrivaled service to the public and dependable food quality.

O was the owner of a local "Texas Family-Style Restaurant" and hired primarily younger people to serve the public because he found them eager and courteous. He even sent some of them, including W, to a national school operated by the parent organization to learn the latest in the preparation and serving of food. W was captain of his high school wrestling team and had a reputation for being a very tough, almost belligerent, person.

One evening T and his family attended the restaurant for dinner and ordered the special for the evening, which was stuffed chicken. The chicken was held together with toothpicks, and some of these were buried in the chicken so that a reasonable person could not have detected them. T swallowed a toothpick and became very ill and was hospitalized for surgery.

During the commotion caused in the restaurant when T swallowed the toothpick, people became scared and rushed for the door. W, thinking that many of the persons would leave without paying, attempted to restrain them and in the process negligently struck an elderly lady, L, in the head. She also was hospitalized.

Discuss the entities which would be liable to both T and L. Against whom may they recover and why?

6. P formed a charter bus company that provided transportation for groups of 30 or more persons. P owned five buses and employed six professional drivers. P did all of the negotiating for the bus rental but left the route selection to the drivers. D was one of the drivers who had driven for P for a long time. On a trip from Chicago to Las Vegas, D became extremely agitated when a vanload of teenagers first followed him too closely and then passed him and slowed down. At a stop light in the next town D stopped in back of the van, got out and in rather unfriendly language began a discussion with the van's driver. The van driver used vile language whereupon D hit him in the head with his fist knocking the van driver out and causing the loss of five teeth.

Describe whether P will be liable for the damage caused. Discuss the possible causes of action.

7. In the question above, would the result differ if D intentionally ran *the bus* into the rear of the van at the stop light?

   a. On the facts above, could the members of the charter party be held liable?

   b. How and why would your answer change if you knew P knew that D had a very bad temper and had been arrested and convicted several times of assault and battery?

   c. What if, after striking the van driver, D resumed his travels and negligently ran into T? Explain the liability of D and P to T.

8. The deceased was given a prescription for the drug Aldactove and went to the local drug store, Union Prescription Center. Union Prescription Center was a franchise outlet (a franchise) owned by a local person, one Joseph Tochisco. The franchise agreement covered specific and detailed operation of the store, and provided that the store had to use the Union Prescription name and logo and had to accept management and marketing advice. The deceased was negligently provided with the wrong drug and died as a result shortly thereafter as a result of this negligence. His estate sues the national corporation called Union Prescription, which is the franchisor. What legal theories will the estate argue? Do you believe they will be successful?

9. Harold Watts was employed by Superior Sporting Goods as a route salesman. His territory, route, and customers were determined by Superior. He was expected to work from 9:00 AM to 5:00 PM, Monday through Friday. He received a weekly salary plus time and one-half for anything over 40 hours. He also received a small commission on sales that exceeded a stated volume. The customers consisted of sporting goods stores, department stores, athletic clubs, and large companies that had athletic programs or sponsored athletic teams. Watts used his personal car in making calls or, on occasion, making a delivery where the customer was in a rush and the order was not large. Watts was reimbursed for the use of the car for company purposes. His instructions were to assume the customer is always right and to accommodate the customer where to do so would cost little and would build goodwill for the company and himself.

   One afternoon while making a sales call and dropping off a case of softballs at the Valid Clock Company, the personnel director told Watts he was planning to watch the company's team play a game at a softball field located on the other side of town, but that his car would not start. Watts said, "Don't worry, it will be my pleasure to give you a lift and I would like to take in a few innings myself." Time was short and while on the way to the ballpark, Watts ran a light and collided with another car. The other car required $800 of repairs and the owner suffered serious bodily injury.

Answer the following, setting forth reasons for any conclusions stated.

a. What is Superior's potential liability, if any, to the owner of the other car?

b. What is Valid's potential liability, if any, to the owner of the other car?

(This is adapted from CPA Exam Question #3b, Business Law, taken from the November, 1978, exam. © American Institute of Certified Public Accountants, Inc., 1978).

10. A hired C, a contractor to build an addition to his home. Although A provided the plans for the addition and relied on C's practical skills in construction, he nevertheless went home early every day to make comments about how the job was going and to give C his impressions of the work done. C hired S to work for him. S had basic carpentry skills, but mostly did the driving, cleanup work, painting, and whatever else C told him to do.

A's house was in the city and the addition was very close to a busy sidewalk and street. When a mild rainstorm passed through the city, the frame of the new structure collapsed on the sidewalk, severely injuring P. S was sent by C to get a trailer to haul away the mess and negligently ran into Q.

Discuss the causes of action that P and Q have. Whom may they sue and will they succeed?

11. Rapid Delivery Service, Inc., hired Dolson as one of its truck drivers. Dolson was selected carefully and trained by Rapid. He was specifically instructed to obey all traffic and parking rules and regulations. One day while making a local delivery, Dolson double-parked and went into a nearby customer's store. In doing so, he prevented a car legally parked at the curb from leaving. The owner of the parked car, Charles, proceeded to blow the horn of the truck repeatedly. Charles was doing this when Dolson returned from his delivery. As a result of a combination of several factors, particularly Charles's telling him to "move it" and that he was "acting very selfishly and in an unreasonable manner," Dolson punched Charles in the nose, severely fracturing it. When Charles sought to restrain him, Dolson punched Charles again, this time fracturing his jaw. Charles has commenced legal action against Rapid.

Answer the following, setting forth reasons for any conclusions stated.

a. Will Charles prevail?

b. What liability, if any, would Dolson have?

(This is adapted from CPA Exam Question # 3a Business Law, taken from the November. 1978, exam. © American Institute of Certified Public Accountants, 1978.)

Endnotes

1. *Black's Law Dictionary*, Rev. 4th Ed., p. 1660 (1957).
2. *Green* v. *Victor Talleying Mach. Co.*, C.C.A.N.Y., 24 Fed. 378, cited as headnote definition in 86 *Corpus Juris Secundum*, p. 954.
3. *Vol. II, Restatement of the Law of Torts, Negligence,* p. 738 (1934).
4. *Ibid.*, p. 742.
5. *Restatement 2nd,* § 2.
6. *Ibid.,* § 219(1).
7. See *Ibid.,* § 220 where 10 factors establishing control are set out or see the *Massey* case in the text where they are repeated.
8. *Restatement, 2nd,* § 14.
9. *Ibid.*
10. *Bugge* v. *Brown,* High Ct. Anst., 1919, 2 Comm. L.R., p. 110.
11. W. A. Seavey, *Law of Agency* 151 (1964).
12. *Thomas* v. *McBride Express Co.*, 266 S. W. 2d 11, 13 (Ct. of App., Mo. 1954).
13. *Restatement 2d* § 245.
14. W. A. Seavey, *Law of Agency* 145–146 (1964).
15. *American Society of Mechanical Engineers, Inc.* v. *Hydrolevel Corporation,* 50 LW 4512, p. 4516 (May 17, 1982).
16. *Restatement 2d.* § 258 Comment a, Illustration 1.

6

Agency Operation and Termination

There are some important legal aspects of the agency relationship that do not conveniently fit into the discussions in the first three chapters on agency. These legal aspects we present in this chapter.

Agency Operation

Agency operation includes first of all those matters, primarily contractual or quasi-contractual in nature, in which the agent and principal are considered one and the same person. These are matters of notice, knowledge, and payment. Following a discussion of these legal principles, we will discuss the legal consequences of appointing subagents and delegating part or all of the duties of the agent imposed by the agency relationship. The last category of agency operations provides a discussion of the loaned or borrowed servant doctrine.

Notice, Knowledge, and Payment

Notice and knowledge both concern the same thing: notification of a fact. In many kinds of contractual understandings notification by a third party to a principal through an agent or vice versa is crucial to triggering certain events provided for in the contract. What happens, for example, when a large corporation (T/P) is to respond to another corporation (P) by a given date as to whether or not it will accept an alteration in their contractual understanding? A day before the given date T/P calls the vice president (A) of P to notify P of its acceptance of the alteration. A leaves that evening on a two-week vacation without telling anyone else. Was "notice" given? The *Restatement* provides:[1] . . .

> (2) A person is given notification of a fact by another if the latter
> (a) informs him of the fact by adequate or specified means or of other facts from which he has reason to know or should know the facts. . . .
> (3) A person has notice of a fact if his agent has knowledge of the fact, reason to know it or should know it. . . .

This rule from the *Restatement* makes it clear that notice was indeed legally given to the P, if the vice president was *authorized* to receive such notice. In determining issues of authority one must refer to those types of authority set out in Chapter 4. If an agent is actually, apparently, or inherently authorized to receive notice of the kind given, and if it is given to the agent but is not in fact communicated to the principal, the law assumes that it was given. .

The same assumption usually exists with regard to payment. For example, if T/P orders goods from P through A and T/P receives the goods and pays A who absconds with the payment, P will not be allowed to recover the payment from T/P. If the agent is authorized to receive payment, payment to the agent is payment to the principal. Of course, in this particular example P may sue A for a breach of A's duties as agent if A can be found.

Generally, there will be no imputation of notice or knowledge where the agent is acting adversely to the principal or beyond the scope of the agency. As we have already pointed out, the majority rule is that knowledge of an agent's intentionally dishonest acts will not be imputed to the principal (and thereby render it liable) because it is assumed such acts are beyond the scope of the agency. However, the *Restatement* would impute such knowledge to the principal if the principal benefited from the intentionally dishonest act.[2] The case below is an example of this principle.

Likewise, payment to an agent who is not authorized either actually or circumstantially to receive it will not be payment to the principal. In summary, where the agent is either actually or circumstantially authorized to give or accept notice or payment then the concept of oneness is applied if the agent does so act. If the agent is not authorized to give or accept notice or payment then courts will not hold the principal liable; however, the agent will be liable based on the fact that the agent misrepresented his or her authority.

In the following case the knowledge of an agent was imputed to the principals.

BIRD v. *PENN CENTRAL CO.*
341 F. Supp. 291 (D. Ct., E. D. Pa., 1972)

Plaintiffs in this action are certain named underwriters trading under the name of Lloyds of London. On July 2, 1968 they issued what we construe as two separate policies providing coverage for the defendants. The Directors and Officers Liability policy (hereinafter referred to as D & O policy) provides coverage for the individual defendants, all present or past officers and/or directors of the Penn Central Company. The Company Reimbursement policy provides coverage for the defendant Penn Central Company.

There was one application completed to obtain both policies. This application, which was specifically incorporated as part of the policies, was executed by defendant David C. Bevan, Chairman of the Finance Committee of the defendant corporation. It is alleged by the plaintiffs that defendant Bevan's response to

Item 10 of the application was falsely made in bad faith, was material to the risk, and was justifiably relied on so as to entitle them to rescind the policy because of fraud.

. . .

We have concluded that the Lloyds insurance package consists of two separate parts: a Company Reimbursement policy, which is a contract between Lloyds and Penn Central, and a D & O policy which is a contract between Lloyds and the directors and officers, insuring severally the distinct insurable interest of each officer and director.

. . .

The question in this case, however, does not concern the effect of one insured's breach of a condition on the rights of another insured under a valid policy, but whether the entire policy is voidable because of an alleged fraudulent act committed in the procurement of the policy.

Item 10 of the application which was the basis for both the Company Reimbursement policy and the D & O policy provides as follows:

> No person proposed for this insurance is cognizant of any act, error, or omission which he has reason to suppose might afford valid grounds for any future claim such as would fall within the scope of the proposed insurance except as follows:

Defendant Bevan's response to this, which is alleged to have been knowingly false, and which is the basis for this rescission action, was "None known." Defendant Bevan, himself, was one of the assureds under the D & O policy. Movants argue that since the answer called for a subjective response, defendant Bevan's answer, if a misrepresentation was made, was a misrepresentation only of his own state of knowledge, but was a true response in his capacity as agent for each individual officer and director (such as movants) who would have

truthfully responded "None known" to Item 10.

. . .

It is contended that defendant Bevan was acting in three capacities in signing the application: (a) as agent for Penn Central, (b) as principal for his own account as one of the assureds, and (c) as agent for each of the other individual assureds. Recognizing these various capacities, movants in effect then ask us to consider defendant Bevan's single response to Item 10 as being over sixty separate responses, his own plus one representing the knowledge of each officer and director. . . . Thus, it is urged that plaintiffs should be able to rescind the D & O policy only as to defendant Bevan, for if he answered Item 10 fraudulently it was only in his capacity as principal for his own account. If it was held that the entire D & O policy could be subject to rescission because defendant Bevan happened to be the officer who signed the insurance application, it would be manifestly unfair to the directors and officers who are completely blameless, such as movants.

While we sympathize with movants' position, and recognize that innocent officers and directors are likely to suffer if the entire policy is voidable because of one man's fraudulent response, it must be recognized that plaintiff insurers are likewise innocent parties. Defendant Bevan was not plaintiffs' agent. Movants do not deny that he was their agent in completing the application by which the policy was obtained.

. . .

The general rule in this type of situation was stated by the Pennsylvania Supreme Court over 100 years ago.

> Where the agent of the insured, in effecting an insurance, makes a false and unauthorized representation, the policy is void. Where one of two innocent persons must suffer by the fraud or negligence of a third, whichever of the two

has accredited him, ought to bear the loss . . . . Mundorff v. Wickersham, 63 Pa. 87, 89 (1870) (dictum).

That the fraud of the agent in inducing a contract is binding on an innocent principal is a well established doctrine of agency law in other jurisdictions as well.

The leading case in Pennsylvania is Gordon v. Continental Casualty Company, 319 Pa. 555, 181 A. 574 (1935). There a trust company obtained a banker's blanket bond to insure it against any loss due to the dishonesty of its officers and employees. The application which was signed by its secretary and treasurer, Ralph E. Mathews, represented that no losses had been sustained by it during the preceding five years because of employee dishonesty, and that the company had no notice or knowledge of any facts indicating that any of the officers were dishonest or unworthy of confidence. Mathews at that very time, without the trust company's knowledge, was an embezzler of the company's funds to the tune of $26,000, and was of course aware of his own misconduct. The court held that the innocent trust company could not recover on the bond because it was bound by Mathews' misrepresentations. Stated another way, recovery was barred because the knowledge of Mathews' own misdeeds was imputed to the company.

Movants wish to limit the Gordon decision strictly to its facts, arguing that the fact that a corporation is an artificial entity and can "know" only through its agents is the reason

that the trust company there was bound by the fraudulent knowledge of its agent who completed the insurance application. We do not, however, read the crucial fact in Gordon to be that the principal was a corporation, rather than an individual or a group of individuals. It is rather an application of the usual rule that a principal is bound by the fraud of his agent in procuring a contract.

> Where a principal sends forth his agent to conduct his affairs and contract for his benefit and the agent procures a contract by fraudulent or corrupt practices, although the principal may not have been privy in any way to such conduct of his agent, yet by claiming the benefits of the contract he must take it tainted as it may be by such practice. Gordon, *supra*, 319 Pa. at 566.

We do not think that the fact that defendant Bevan signed the application on behalf of numerous principals including himself alters the force of this rule. It would be extremely artificial to read defendant Bevan's response to Item 10 as being multiple separate responses on behalf of himself, the company, and each of the individual assureds under the D & O policy. No matter how the policies for Company Reimbursement insurance and D & O insurance are characterized, the simple inescapable fact is that both policies were issued on the basis of a single application, and only one response was made to Item 10 of that application. Defendant Bevan, movants' agent, made that response. . . . Therefore, the motions for summary judgment will be denied.

Case Questions

1. Who was David C. Bevan's principal? Was it Penn Central?
2. Did the court hold that all persons insured were not covered by insurance because the policy was voidable because of Bevan's alleged fraudulent act?
3. What is the holding of the court?

Subagents

The *Restatement* defines a subagent as follows:[3]

> A subagent is a person appointed by an agent empowered to do so, to perform functions undertaken by the agent for the principal, but for whose conduct the agent agrees with the principal to be primarily responsible.

It is very important to note that a subagent is appointed by the agent to work directly for the agent in accomplishing tasks for the principal. Thus, a subagent is the agent of the agent who has appointed him and the subagent of the principal. A subagent owes duties of loyalty to both the appointing agent and the principal; and, of utmost importance is that a subagent can create contract and tort liability for both the appointing agent and the principal. The *Restatement* provides:[4]

> The liability of an agent to third persons for the conduct of his servants, subservants, and other subagents is the same as that of a master or other principal for the conduct of his servants and other agents.

A third party damaged by a properly appointed subagent may sue both the appointing agent and the principal. As between the initial agent and the principal, the former should bear the loss in the absence of a contractual provision to the contrary.[5] Of course, in the case of a breach of tort duty, the subagent is the one who should ultimately bear the loss.

In order to impose liability on the agent for the tortious conduct of a subagent, the same type of analysis we used when presenting the respondeat superior doctrine must be utilized. The relationship between agent and subagent must be properly classified as a master-servant one if a tort within the scope of (or incidental to the purpose of) the agency has been committed.

An agent who hires a subagent must be distinguished from an agent whose job it is to hire employees for the employer. For example, a personnel officer for a corporation may hire employees for the corporation, but they become the agents of the corporation and not the subagents of the personnel officer. One way to determine if an agent is a subagent is to focus on the activity for which the person was hired. If the activity primarily involves functions already undertaken by the appointing agent for the principal, then this person may be a subagent.

As you read and then brief the following case, concentrate on the reasons why the court states Antisdale is liable to the plaintiff. There are at least two reasons. Be sure to note why the court holds that the Presbytery of San Francisco is liable to the plaintiff.

MALLOY v. FONG
232 P.2d 241 (Sup. Ct., Calif., 1951)

TRAYNOR, Justice

Plaintiff brought this action for damages for personal injuries allegedly caused by the concurrent negligence of defendants Holmes, Fong, and Antisdale. Plaintiff alleged that Fong and Antisdale were acting as agents of defendant Presbytery of San Francisco. The jury exonerated defendant Holmes, but returned a verdict in favor of plaintiff in the amount of $41,500 against defendants Fong, Antisdale, and the Presbytery of San Francisco. On motion of defendant Presbytery, the trial court entered a judgment notwithstanding the verdict as to it. . . .

During the summer vacation of 1943, plaintiff, then a boy of thirteen, attended a vacation Bible school conducted at the San Mateo Presbyterian Church for the children of members of the Church, then a "mission" under the jurisdiction of defendant Presbytery of San Francisco. Defendant Antisdale, pastor of the Church, was in charge of the school and gave the Bible instruction. The Bible classes were supplemented by classes in arts and crafts and by supervised recreation at a nearby playground to which the children were taken in automobiles and from which they were returned to the Church at the conclusion of the recreation period.

Antisdale became ill several days before July 1, 1943, the day plaintiff was injured, and was unable to conduct the school. It was therefore left without an instructor qualified to conduct the Bible classes. Defendant Fong, a 19-year-old divinity student, was at that time vacationing at the home of his guardian, Dr. Jones, a retired Presbyterian minister, in San Mateo. Fong agreed to conduct the Bible instruction in Antisdale's absence so that Antisdale might stay home and rest. In addition to conducting the Bible classes, Fong drove the children to the playground for their recreation period in his guardian's automobile, a Ford station wagon lent to him for that purpose.

Antisdale returned to the Church on the day of the accident, but he was occupied in his office the greater part of the morning, and Fong remained in charge of the class. At the conclusion of the Bible instruction, Fong released the children to wait outside the Church for transportation to the playground for the recreation period. Antisdale emerged from his office to see the children climbing into Fong's station wagon and several boys, including plaintiff, standing on the running boards. Antisdale then informed the children that he would take some of them in his car to relieve the congestion in the station wagon, and several of them entered the back seat of his car. . . .

During the trip the children in each vehicle were shouting and challenging the children in the other vehicle to race to the playground. Although the evidence is conflicting on this point, there is testimony that Fong and Antisdale entered into the spirit of the competition and increased the speed of their vehicles. After the vehicles turned west on Twenty-eighth Avenue, Fong pulled out to the left and endeavored to pass Antisdale, who increased the speed of his car to prevent Fong from passing. . . . The two vehicles approached the intersection of Twenty-eighth and Isabelle Avenues in that position, Fong still unsuccessfully attempting to pass Antisdale. Antisdale stopped his car at the intersection, but Fong proceeded out into the intersection at an excessive rate of speed, still on the left-hand side of the road. Defendant Holmes was driving her car north on Isabelle Avenue and had just pulled out into the intersection when Fong drove by her. The vehicles were too close for her to stop in time and, according to her testimony, Fong made no effort to stop. Her right front fender and Fong's station wagon collided, striking plaintiff standing on the left running board. As a result of the collision, plaintiff lost his left leg below the knee and sustained injuries of a permanently disabling nature to his right leg, necessitating prolonged hospitalization and medical treatment.

Plaintiff's complaint was in three counts. In the first count he alleged that Fong was the agent of Antisdale and the Presbytery, that he was a passenger in Fong's car at the time of the accident, and that the accident was caused by the concurrent negligence of defendants Fong and Holmes. In the second count he alleged that Antisdale was the agent of the Presbytery, and that his negligence was a cause of the injuries to plaintiff in that he "negligently and carelessly increased the speed of his said Chevrolet sedan automobile, so as to render it impossible for said Ford Station Wagon (driven by Fong), in which plaintiff was riding, to pass and return to the right side of the roadway. . . . In the third count, plaintiff alleged that Antisdale and Fong were negligent in failing to exercise proper care for the safety of the children for whom they were responsible in that they negligently permitted several of them, including plaintiff, to ride on the running boards of the two vehicles, and that such negligence was a proximate cause of plaintiff's injuries. . . .

The Presbytery . . . contends that Antisdale and Fong were not agents of the Presbytery.

As the judicatory in charge of all Presbyterian churches in the San Francisco Bay area, the Presbytery of San Francisco had primary responsibility for the extension of the Presbyterian movement into new localities in that region. It was the Presbytery that organized the San Mateo group in 1942 and undertook the task of transforming it into a full-fledged church. During this early period, the Presbytery not only held the Church property but was in charge of Church activities. Speaking of churches in the mission stage, an officer of the defendant Presbytery testified: "that really is the place where the presbytery does exercise control." The establishment and maintenance of religious education for children was an important part of the Presbytery's project in San Mateo. The jury could properly conclude, therefore, that the agents who conducted the Daily Vacation Bible School were the agents of the Presbytery. . . .

The Presbytery contends that even if Antisdale was engaged in work for the Presbytery, he was an independent contractor for whose negligence the Presbytery was not responsible.

Whether a person performing work for another is an agent or an independent contractor depends primarily upon whether the one for whom the work is done has the legal right to control the activities of the alleged agent. . . . The power of the principal to terminate the services of the agent gives him the means of controlling the agent's activities. . . . It is not essential that the right of control be exercised or that there be actual supervision of the work of the agent. The existence of the right of control and supervision establishes the existence of an agency relationship. . . . The evidence clearly supports the conclusion of the jury that such control existed in the present case. The right of the Presbytery to install and remove its ministers, to approve or disapprove their transfer to other jurisdictions, and to supervise and control the activities of the local churches, particularly those in the mission stage, is inconsistent with a contrary conclusion.

Although the evidence as to Antisdale's negligence is conflicting, there is substantial evidence to support the finding that he was negligent and that his negligence was a cause of the injury to plaintiff. Such a finding is supported on either of two grounds: (1) that Antisdale negligently permitted and participated in a race between his automobile and the station wagon drive by Fong, causing both vehicles to travel at an excessive speed, and forcing

Fong to enter the intersection of Twenty-eighth and Isabelle Avenues on the wrong side of the roadway, thus causing the accident; and (2) that Antisdale was negligent in permitting plaintiff among others to ride on the running boards of the vehicles, and that such negligence caused the injuries of which plaintiff complains. It is clear that Antisdale was acting in the scope of his agency at the time the tort was committed. As his principal, the Presbytery is liable for injuries to plaintiff resulting therefrom.

The verdict against the Presbytery may be supported not only on Antisdale's negligence but on that of Fong as well. Civil Code section 2351 provides: "A subagent, lawfully appointed, represents the principal in like manner with the original agent . . . ." Antisdale was an agent of the Presbytery, i.e., the "original" agent, and he lawfully appointed Fong a subagent.

An agency relationship may be informally created. No particular words are necessary, nor need there be consideration. All that is required is conduct by each party manifesting acceptance of a relationship whereby one of them is to perform work for the other under the latter's direction. . . .

There is ample evidence to support a finding that Antisdale and Fong entered into just such a relationship. Antisdale, as pastor of the Church was in charge of the Vacation Bible School. It was his responsibility to supervise and control the instruction and all activities connected with the School. He was in charge of the transportation of the children from the Church to the playground and of their return to the Church. He had authority to direct the activities of the children attending the school and to direct them into vehicles for transportation to the playground. He determined how long the children should remain at the playground and when they should be returned to the Church. . . .

The evidence that Fong, with Antisdale's knowledge and consent, performed duties for which the latter was responsible, that his performance of those duties was subject to Antisdale's supervision and control, and that his services could be terminated by Antisdale at any time, supports the conclusion that Fong was a subagent acting within the scope of his agency at the time of the accident. This conclusion is not negatived by the fact that Fong was not paid. *Restatement, Agency*, § 225. . . .

The judgment in favor of Presbytery of San Francisco is reversed, and the trial court is directed to enter judgment against Presbytery in accordance with the verdict of the jury.

Case Questions

1. It appears from the opinion that Fong was not paid for his work for the Presbytery. Was he an agent? Why?

2. Was Fong a subagent?

3. Who were the defendants in this case and against whom did the plaintiff recover?

4. Note the various possible causes of action against Antisdale and the Presbytery. Could Antisdale be vicariously liable to the plaintiff?

5. A state statute may displace or add to the common law in a state. Does the California statute cited in the opinion change the common law of subagents as we have presented it? In the absence of the state statute could the Presbytery have been liable to the plaintiff?

6. Was Antisdale a servant of Presbytery, or was he a nonservant agent?

Delegation of Agency Duties

Closely related to the subagent discussion is the delegation of the entire agency task to someone else. If the principal is aware of the delegation and consents to it, then a new agency relationship is formed. In the absence of this consent, however, an agent's power to delegate is extremely limited. It is generally recognized that an agent cannot delegate to another any task involving the exercise of judgment or discretion in the use of authority held for the principal's benefit.[6] Remember that agents are fiduciaries; thus the relationship between the parties is invested with special qualities of confidentiality. However, in some agency relationships the fiduciary quality is not nearly as strong as others. Thus, the rule that fiduciaries cannot delegate matters requiring discretion has been labeled an overstatement by some authorities.[7] Just what "discretion" means must be defined by the trade customs and usages. Clearly, there can be no delegation where a principal forbids it. Where the exercise of discretion is minimal and many principals do allow delegation, the power to delegate may be inferred. This may be true when a principal employs a corporation for a task which is not generally thought of as involving personal service. However, when a principal deals with a partnership and, in particular, where a principal selects one of the partners to deal with, the agency may not be delegated.

The following case presents the general view that an agency relationship involving one's individual skill and judgment cannot be delegated.

W.H. BARBER AGENCY CO. v. CO-OPERATIVE BARREL CO.
133 Minn. 207, 158 N.W. 38 (S. Ct. Minn., 1916)

TAYLOR, C.

Plaintiff appealed from an order sustaining a demurrer to its complaint.

The complaint sets forth that W.H. Barber was a broker and maintained an organization for the sale of commercial products; that he made a contract with defendant to have the exclusive sale, at a stated commission, for a term of years, of all the butter tubs manufactured by defendant; that after performing such contract for more than four years and establishing a large and lucrative business in the sale of such tubs, he organized the plaintiff corporation which took over all his business and his organization, and has ever since continued the same without any change in the personnel or management thereof; that defendant refused to permit the plaintiff corporation to perform the remainder of Barber's contract for the sale of its tubs; and that plaintiff has been damaged thereby in the amount of the commissions which it could have earned during the remainder of the term.

The sole question presented and argued is whether Barber could transfer his contract to the plaintiff corporation without the consent of the defendant.

Barber was defendant's sales agent, and the case is controlled by the rules governing agency, . . . The powers conferred upon an agent are based upon the confidence which the principal has in the agent's ability and integrity; and it is the universal rule that an agent cannot transfer to another powers calling for the exercise of discretion, skill or judgment. . . . It is held that, where a principal has authorized a partnership to act as his agent, the subsequent dissolution of the partnership terminates the agency, and that a partner who takes over the business cannot continue to act as such agent unless the principal authorizes him to do so. . . .

In *Meysenburg* v. *Littlefield* (C.C.) 135 Fed. 184, Meysenburg and Littlefield were selling agents for the Lorain Steel Company. We quote the opinion:

> It was the skill and diligence of Littlefield and Meysenburg, as partners, with all that term implies, which the Lorain Steel Company contracted for, and when Littlefield and Meysenburg dissolved that relation the consideration so far failed that the contract ceased to be enforceable; and the firm's action in dissolving the copartnership would be such a breach of the contract in question as to justify the steel company in subsequently ignoring it.

In *Wheaton* v. *Cadillac Automobile Co.*, 143 Mich. 21, 106 N.W. 399, the New Jersey Automobile Company, a partnership composed of two members, was defendant's selling agent in the state of New Jersey. One of the partners withdrew from the firm and assigned all his interest in the business to the other. The court held that this gave defendant the right to abrogate the contract.

In the present case, defendant made Barber its agent. He assumed to transfer to a corporation the powers conferred upon him personally. The corporation is a separate entity controlled by a board of at least three directors, and its stockholders and officers are subject to change at any time. If it acquired Barber's rights under his contract with defendant, it would retain such rights even if Barber should entirely sever his connection with it. To permit a person, employed as an agent, to transfer his duties and powers to a corporation without the consent of his principal would involve a more radical violation of the rules governing the relation of principal and agent than to permit a partnership, employed as an agent, to devolve its powers and duties upon one of its members. Barber could no more substitute plaintiff for himself as defendant's agent, without defendant's consent, than he could so substitute any other corporation or individual.

Order affirmed.

1. What is there about the structure of a corporation which caused the principal to object to the delegation of the agency in this case?
2. What could W.H. Barber have done to secure a valid delegation of authority?

Case Questions

Loaned or Borrowed Servants

Sometimes a principal-master will permit his agent-servant to work for or help someone else. A common example of this is where a building contractor leases or gratuitously provides (to another person) heavy equipment with an operator. If the operator commits a tort while working for the other person, which employer is liable? The question is answered by determining which employer had control of the servant. The *Restatement* concludes that the master exercising control over the servant at the time of the tortious act is liable.[8] It also suggests that where the issue of control is not clear a person may be a servant of two masters, thus creating liability for both to a tortiously injured third party.[9]

The liability of two masters or principals may also be established in circumstances where the tort committed is within the inherent scope of employment of the servant or agent. For example, assume P lends both his truck and his driver, A, to B and B orders A to load lumber on the truck and haul it to B's construction project. A loads the lumber negligently and as a result the truck overturns while traveling to B's project, injuring X. If loading was within the scope of A's employment, both P and B may be liable to X. In this case, control of A while loading and while driving was not directly exercised by B. In the absence of evidence of direct control, there is an inference that the agent remains in the general employment of the original principal so long as, by the service rendered to another, the agent is performing the business entrusted to it by the original principal. That is, in most cases there is no inference that because the original employer has permitted a possible division of control, control has been surrendered.[10]

The following case presents circumstances where a court has attempted to resolve factual disputes centering on the issues of control over a servant by a second master. This case is of special interest for at least two reasons. First, it illustrates that even a highly trained professional such as an anesthesiologist may be a servant. Second, it illustrates that sometimes courts may apply a well-established principle of law incorrectly. Do you agree?

ROCKWELL v. STONE
404 Pa. 574, 173 A. 2d 54 (S. Ct., Pa., 1961)

BOK, Justice

Suffice it to say that plaintiff recovered a verdict against both doctors, who have separately appealed. Dr. Kaplan, the subject of this opinion, asks judgment n.o.v. or, if he may not have it, a new trial. Both requests were refused below and this appeal is from the ensuing judgment. . . .

Dr. Kaplan's liability rests on two piers, either one of which will support it: his own negligence and his responsibility as principal for Dr. Stone's negligence, . . .

The following facts appear in the record: Dr. Kaplan said that he was "the boss of the surgical end of it and that the plaintiff was his patient; he chose the hospital and arranged the patient's admission; he chose to use a minor elective surgical procedure to remove the bursa from plaintiff's right arm, which procedure could be postponed or done at the patient's convenience; he overruled his patient, who wanted local anesthesia, and ordered a general one; if he did not choose Dr. Stone, who was the chief of the hospital's anesthesiology department, he chose Dr. Stone's hospital and was satisfied with him and with his choice of sodium pentothal as the induction agent and a gas for the general anesthesia; . . . plaintiff was presented to Dr. Kaplan for surgery fifteen minutes after the injection; . . . the injection in plaintiff's left arm missed the vein and went in or around an artery; . . . although Dr. Stone chose not to tell Dr. Kaplan of the "catastrophe" that had occurred at induction with the sodium pentothal, which is a very dangerous drug, Dr. Kaplan could and did see that the plaintiff's left arm was extended on the intravenous board when the patient entered the operating room; . . . he assumed that when the patient was presented to him in the operating room he was ready for surgery; . . . he made no inquiry about the plaintiff's reaction to the anesthesia, . . . the arm visibly deteriorated during the operation and the pulse vanished while in the recovery room afterwards; and . . . he left the operating room and the hospital without seeing the plaintiff in the recovery room. . . .

Hence the basic question of fact was whether Dr. Kaplan should have seen the condition of the arm or should have asked about it and having found out should have refused to operate until it had been taken care of. In leaving such matters generally to the jury on the ground of negligence, the trial judge gave Dr. Kaplan more than he deserved when he said:

> There is no testimony in the record that I can recall whereby such a standard of care is required under those circumstances of a surgeon in attendance. Therefore, if you find that there has been no violation of his duty in that regard there would be no basis for a finding of responsibility on the part of Dr. Kaplan on the first ground alone, namely, negligence.

There is no dispute that the misuse of sodium pentothal caused the condition of plaintiff's arm, which in turn caused its amputation. The jury needed no expert testimony of what Dr. Kaplan's duty was: it was, so far as they were concerned, to do something quickly for a dangerous condition which the evidence shows was visible and urgent. Something specific was done, though too late, . . .

Defendant's personal negligence was therefore properly left to the jury under the full range of the circumstances. . . .

As for Dr. Kaplan's responsibility for Dr. Stone's negligence, Dr. Stone testified that a surgeon could use the hospital's anesthesiologist or bring in his own. Dr. Kaplan testified

that he was "the boss of the surgical end of it," and that "as long as Dr. Stone had anything to do with the anesthesia I was perfectly satisfied." He chose the hospital in which Dr. Stone worked and chose a general rather than a local anesthetic. Dr. Stone testified that Dr. Kaplan had the authority to ask or tell him what sort of anesthesia he wanted, although it was not the practice at the Graduate Hospital to do so. Dr. Kaplan said that if it was best for his patient's safety he could discontinue the operation and tell the anesthesiologist to stop giving anesthetic, particularly in minor elective surgical procedure. His words were, on the latter point:

> Q. Suppose you felt that anesthesia should stop and the anesthetist felt that it should continue, and you felt that continuation would create a critical condition for your patient?
> A. I would stop immediately, regardless of what he had to say, if I felt strongly that this should stop, I would stop it.
> Q. And you would tell the anesthetist to stop it, wouldn't you?
> A. I would.
> Q. And he would stop, wouldn't he?
> A. I think he would have to.

The foregoing is very different from the independent contractor-like language of Dr. Kaplan's brief. We think it points clearly to the language concerning borrowed employees in *Mature* v. *Angelo*, 1953, 373 Pa. 593, 97 A. 2d 59, 60: "A servant is the employee of the person who has the *right* of controlling the manner of his performance of the work, irrespective of whether he actually *exercises* that control or not.". . .

Nor was there a conflict of evidence on the question of right of control. Dr. Kaplan and Dr. Stone did not disagree in their testimony as it has been condensed above, nor can there be doubt based on common sense that Dr. Stone acted on Dr. Kaplan's business: he had to or the surgeon could not operate. The undisputed evidence clearly shores up the instruction of the trial judge. "And in the eyes of the law, in this case, Dr. Stone was the agent for a step in the operative procedure, the anesthesia step. He was the agent of Dr. Kaplan."

It is clear, . . . that doctors are subject to the law of agency and may at the same time be agent both of another physician and of a hospital, even though the employment is not joint.

This establishes the theory of respondeat superior and also answers the heart of defendant's motion for a new trial. We have carefully read the charge and see no error in it when looked at in the round. . . .

Judgment affirmed.
   . . .

BENJAMIN R. JONES, Justice (dissenting)
Although alleged, the case at bar in my opinion presents no evidence of any *direct* negligence on the part of Dr. Kaplan and Dr. Kaplan's liability, if any, must be premised on the theory of vicarious liability. Stated otherwise, is Dr. Kaplan liable for malpractice under the doctrine of respondeat superior for an act of negligence which occurred, outside his presence and without his knowledge, during preoperative procedure involved in the administration of an anesthesia?

Certain factual circumstances must be noted. Dr. Kaplan neither requested nor exercised any choice in the selection of any particular anesthesiologist to administer the anesthesia. Although Dr. Kaplan, as any other surgeon, was at liberty to select any anesthesiologist he so desired, he simply indicated to Dr. Stone, the Chief of the Department of Anesthesiology, that he wanted a general anesthesia administered and relied upon Dr. Stone's professional competency for selection of the type of anesthesia and the person or persons to administer it. Such service was provided by the hospital and the compensation for such service would be billed by the hospital to the patient and would be paid by the latter directly to the hospital. The personnel of the Department were employed by, paid by and under the general control and direction of the hospital which had the sole power to dismiss such personnel.

When the incident occurred, as previously stated, Dr. Kaplan was not present nor was his presence required at that time and, while the injection and ensuing incident took place at approximately 9:45 a.m., Dr. Kaplan was unaware of it until approximately noon. . . .

In the case at bar, Dr. Kaplan neither prescribed nor was he advised of the use of sodium pentothal; he did not administer it, was not present when it was administered and, in fact, did not know of it until hours later. Moreover, he exercised no direction, control or authority over Drs. Stone and Jiminez, or Molnar, while in the induction room and he did not request any of them to administer this drug. Dr. Kaplan was simply using the hospital facilities and its personnel, a service for which Rockwell would be billed directly.

The sodium pentothal was administered outside of Dr. Kaplan's presence, in the induction room over which, to employ the language of McConnell, he was not the "captain of the ship:" . . . at that time *only* Dr. Stone was in command. . . .

Under such circumstances, in my opinion, Dr. Kaplan could not be held liable upon any theory of respondeat superior and the judgment as to Dr. Kaplan should be reversed and judgment . . . entered in his favor.

1. Dr. Kaplan was liable on two separate grounds. What were they?

2. Did Dr. Kaplan have the right to control at the time of the negligent act? At the time of the negligent act (before the operation) was not Dr. Stone an independent contractor?

3. Could the injured third party in this case sue the hospital and allege that Dr. Kaplan was the hospital's agent and Dr. Stone a subagent? From the facts given, would this case be successful? What additional facts, if any, would you need to know?

The agency relationship may be terminated by consent or renunciation by either party, or termination may be inferred from events. Such events as the loss of capacity (death, insanity, illegality) or impossibility, the destruction of the subject matter, lapse of time, or declarations of bankruptcy will terminate the agency relationship. When we use the term "termination," we are speaking of an end to the agency relationship, which usually involves two phases. The first phase is the end of the legal relationship between the principal and agent. The second is the end of the agent's authority as perceived by others—third parties and potential third parties.

Agency Coupled with an Interest

There is one important exception to the general rule that an agency relationship, since it is based on consent, may be terminated by either party by the withdrawal or cancellation of that consent. This exception exists when a principal creates an agency relationship for the benefit of the agent rather than for just the principal alone. In these cases the agent acquires an ownership interest in the subject matter of the agency. This legally protected *interest* is usually created by two circumstances: (1) The agency was created to secure the performance of a duty by the agent or a third person; and (2) the agency is supported by an exchange of value. This is often referred to as an *agency coupled with an interest.*

For example, assume P owns a parcel of land that she wishes to sell. She makes an agreement with A that if A advertises and improves the parcel by fixing up the house that is on it and keeping the yard trimmed, then she will convey to A a one-third interest in the parcel that is to be sold for not less that $15,000.[11] Technically, this is an irrevocable agency relationship and cannot be terminated by the principal's withdrawing consent.

This circumstance must be distinguished from one in which the principal hires an agent to sell on commission and even signs a document stating that the agency relationship is irrevocable. For example, if P appoints A to sell P's goods for a 25 percent commission and also signs a contract expressing that the agency relationship is irrevocable for one year, that is *not* an agency coupled with an interest. Essentially, it was not created to bring about a performance by the agent and to secure or otherwise benefit the agent who has performed some duty for the principal independent of the attempts to sell the property. In this case, the principal may terminate the agent's authority but may be liable for breach of contract, as is more fully explained below.

Termination by Consent

As between the principal and agent, their mutual legal duties may be terminated by mutual consent at any time, or in accordance with the terms of their agreement. This includes the completion of the authorized task. If no specific task is identified or if no time limit is set, then the relationship ends when the agent should know that the principal no longer desires him to act.

An agency relationship may end, by the expression of either party, before the date set in a contract; however, this might not relieve the parties of contractual liability. For example, a board of directors may contract with A for service as president of the corporation for a period of three years. State statutes usually provide that corporate officers may be removed at will by the board. The board then may discharge A as president at any time, but may be required to pay damages for the breach of the three-year contract. The next case illustrates the application of the principle.

MITCHELL v. VULTURE MINING & MILLING CO.
47 Az. 249; 55 P. 2d 636 (S. Ct., Ariz., 1936)

MCALISTER, Judge
This is an appeal by F. H. Mitchell from a judgment in favor of the Vulture Mining & Milling Company, a corporation, . . .

The substance of the second amended complaint on which the case was tried is that in the summer of 1930 the Vulture Mining & Milling Company, a corporation, hereinafter called defendant, owned thirty-one mining claims, patented and unpatented, near Wickenburg, Arizona. It had an authorized capital of one million shares of the par value of one dollar each, six hundred thousand of which were treasury stock it desired to sell for the purpose of raising funds to develop its mining property. F. H. Mitchell, hereinafter called plaintiff, was an experienced mining engineer and salesman who had friends in the eastern section of the United States through whom he felt he could contact prospective purchasers. So, on or about August 10, 1930, he and the defendant entered into an agreement by which he was granted for a reasonable time "the exclusive right to sell in the eastern states of the United States the treasury stock of the defendant,". . . It was agreed that the plaintiff would go to the Eastern States at his own expense and for a reasonable time devote his efforts exclusively to presenting the stock to prospective purchasers and making sales thereof at eighty cents a share and that he should receive as compensation therefor twenty-five per cent of the proceeds of the sales made by or through him. For the purpose of fulfilling this agreement the plaintiff went east on August 21, 1930, and expended large sums of money in an effort to sell the stock, the defendant being kept advised at all times of his activities and prospects. . . .

On the 29th day of October, 1930, while the plaintiff was actively endeavoring to sell the three hundred thousand shares and had reasonable prospects of completing a sale, the defendant, without advising him, granted a ten day option on the six hundred thousand shares of treasury stock to the United Verde Extension Mining Company . . . and the result of this was to disable the defendant from performing its agreement and to deprive the plaintiff of the opportunity to fulfill his and to receive compensation for his services and to reimburse himself for the monies expended by him, in the sum of $60,000, amended later, however, to read $10,000. . . .

The defendant answered, admitting the execution of the option and its exercise by the company. It denied, however, that either act was performed in the East and alleged that the option and the sale of the stock covered thereby was made, exercised and fulfilled within the state of Arizona where the company had been authorized to and had actually carried on business for more than ten years. Every other allegation, not specifically admitted, was denied. . . . According to the evidence the plaintiff and the defendant entered into an agreement by which the plaintiff was authorized to sell in the Eastern States within a reasonable time three hundred thousand shares of the defendant's treasury stock at eighty cents a share for a commission of twenty-five percent, the plaintiff agreeing to go from his home in Arizona to that section and devote his entire time and energy to making a sale of this stock, all at his own expense. Pursuant to this agreement he went East and actively endeavored to sell the stock until Octo-

ber 29, 1930, when the defendant terminated his authority in respect thereto by optioning the stock to the Verde Extension Mining Company, and the plaintiff contends that the agreement and his actual partial performance of it was sufficient to make a binding contract not revocable without rendering defendant liable for breaching it, either in damages sustained as a result thereof or for the recovery of the reasonable value of his time and efforts and the expenditures incurred by him in attempting to carry out his part of the undertaking. It occurs to us that this contention is correct, . . .

The contract being mutual, the giving of an option and thus placing it beyond the power of the defendant to live up to its terms was just as effectively a breach as a sale by the defendant of the stock in the East, the territory the plaintiff alleged to be exclusively his, would have been. The defendant, it is true, had the power to terminate it any time it saw fit but no right to do so without subjecting itself to liability for whatever damages its act may have caused the plaintiff. *Mechem on Agency,* page 405, § 568. It is utterly unthinkable that after he had entered into the agreement, gone east and, at an expense to himself of $2,000, devoted his entire time and effort for two months to selling the stock, the plaintiff's contractual status should have been such that the defendant could, before he had had a reasonable time in which to complete the undertaking, deprive him of the right to do so without rendering itself liable, at least, for the reasonable value of his services and reimbursement for expenditures made or incurred by him. The agreement specified no particular time in which he could make the sale but under all the authorities a reasonable time was implied. . . .

The judgment is reversed and the case remanded for a new trial.

Case Questions   1. Does this decision hold that the principal could not have revoked the agent's authority when it wished to do so?

2. On retrial, how do you think the court would instruct the jury as to how it should calculate the measure of damages?

Termination by Events

Generally any event that would cause the agent to reasonably believe that the principal would no longer wish him to act will cause a termination of the agent.[12] Some of the common events are the loss of capacity of the principal, impossibility, death of either party, destruction of the subject matter, or declarations of bankruptcy or illegality.

Capacity as it is used here refers to the legal capacity to conduct business transactions or contracts. Capacity is defined by state statute, and usually all persons who are of sound mind and who are over eighteen years of age have the capacity of contract. Obviously, a formal declaration of either insanity or death terminates the principal's capacity to contract, thus terminating the agent's capacity to act for the principal.

COX v. BOWLING
54 Mo. App. 289 (Kan. City Ct. of App., 1893)

GILL, J.
This is a suit for commissions for sale of real estate. Plaintiff had judgment below, and defendant appealed. The material facts are about as follows: Bowling owned a house and lot in Lamar, Missouri, which he desired to sell. He agreed with Cox, an agent, that if he, Cox, would find a purchaser for the house and lot at the price of $2,500 he would allow him $100 as commissions. Cox entered into negotiations with one Snyder, a resident of Lamar, and made an effort to sell the property to Snyder at the fixed price of $2,500. Snyder refused to give that sum and offered to purchase at a less amount, which Bowling then declined. Cox made repeated efforts to get the parties to-

gether, but to no purpose, and the negotiations then ceased. A short time thereafter the building on the lot was destroyed by fire. A few days after the fire Bowling and Snyder met on the street, and after a brief interview Bowling sold the lot (then vacant) to Snyder for $2,000. . . . [W]hen the building was destroyed and the property became materially changed (so that indeed it was not the same as when Cox was employed to sell it), Bowling and Snyder came together and a sale of the vacant lot was effected. But his was not the property that Cox was empowered to sell. There was nothing said between Bowling and Cox after the destruction of the building. So material a change in the subject-matter of the agency amounted to a revocation of Cox's authority as agent. It is well settled that the authority of the agent is terminated by the destruction of the subject-matter of the agency. . . .

Case Questions   1. Define a "material alteration" of the subject matter of the agency that will most likely result in a court's order terminating the agency relationship.

2. What if Cox made a contract to sell the property to Snyder for $2,500 after the house was materially altered but neither Cox nor the purchaser, Snyder, knew, or through the exercise of reasonable care could have known, about the alteration? Could Cox collect his commission? This is a very close question, and the outcome could go either way depending on which one of the parties, Cox or Bowling or Snyder, assumed the risk of the destruction of the subject matter. This may be established either by contract or the "usual methods and conduct of doing business." In the absence of one of the parties' assuming the risk of destruction, Cox most probably could collect his commission because he has done all that was required of him: he secured a purchaser.

3. What if Cox discovered a small uranium deposit on the land making it worth five times the $2,500 he was authorized to sell it for? Could he, without incurring liability to Bowling, sell it for $2,500 assuming that Bowling had no knowledge of the deposit?

Termination of the Agent's Authority as Perceived by Third Parties

Circumstantial authority, primarily apparent and inherent authority, was created by the common law to protect the reasonable expectations of those dealing with agents. This authority is generally not terminated when the formal actual authority between principal and agent is terminated. The general rule is that the agent's circumstantial authority continues until the third party knows or has reason to know of the termination. The *Restatement* takes the position that death or incapacity of the principal or declared illegality of the agency relationship are events of such notoriety that it will be inferred that all third parties have notice of the event.[13] Thus where the death or incapacity of a principal terminates the agency relationship and the agent subsequently contracts with a third party for the benefit of the principal and neither the agent nor the third party have actual knowledge of the death or incapacity, the contract cannot be enforced against the principal. Although this approach is theoretically sound it does work a hardship on the third party and seems to contradict (or at least be an exception to) the reasons for the creation of circumstantial authority.[14]

If the agency is not terminated by death, incapacity, or illegality, the principal is required to notify third parties of the termination of the agent's authority. In this case, the principal must proceed to give notice in one of two ways.

A third party who has contracted with or begun to contract with an agent based on the agent's apparent authority must be given actual notice of termination of the agent's authority. This is notice given to the third party personally or mailed to the party's business or posted in a place where, in view of the business customs between the parties, the third party could reasonably be expected to look for such a notice.[15]

With respect to those persons with whom the agent has not dealt prior to the termination of authority, notice of the agent's termination of apparent authority may be given by advertising the fact in a newspaper of general circulation in the place where the agency operates or by some other manner reasonably calculated to give notice to such third parties.[16]

If a third party who has dealt with an agent on the basis of apparent authority does not receive actual notice of the agency termination and enters into a contract with the agent for the apparent benefit of the principal after the actual authority is terminated, the principal is bound.

BURCH v. AMERICUS GROCERY CO.
125 Ga. 153, 53 S.E. 1008 (S. Ct., Ga., 1906)

EVANS, J.

The Americus Grocery Company sued J. B. Burch for a balance alleged to be due on open account. The only item in dispute was one of May 8, 1903, for a certain quantity of tobacco. The defendant contended that this item was purchased by his clerk, Mike Burch, after he had left his employment, and that he neither authorized nor ratified the purchase nor received the tobacco. On the other hand, the plaintiff insisted that Mike Burch was the general agent of the defendant in the management of his store, and as such, on previous occasions, had ordered goods of plaintiff on defendant's account, and that the plaintiff, without notice that Mike Burch was no longer employed by the defendant, took the order in the defendant's name and shipped the goods to the defendant, as was usual in the past transactions. . . . The plaintiff's salesman called at the commissary of the defendant and asked for Mike Burch, as he had always done, and was informed that Mike Burch was about three miles away, superintending the putting down of a sawmill. There he found him and took the order for the merchandise. It was shipped to the defendant and the bill of lading was mailed to him. The defendant testified that the goods were never received by him, but were taken possession of by Mike Burch without his knowledge, and that he never received the bill of lading for the goods. Upon these facts the

jury returned a verdict in favor of the plaintiff for the value of the goods. . . .

1. In the management of the business of the commissary, the agent, Mike Burch, had general powers. Relative to this business, he was the general agent of the defendant in the purchase of merchandise. "Whenever a general agency has been established for any purpose, all persons who have dealt with such agent, or who have known of the agency and are apt to deal with him, have a right to presume that such authority will continue until it is shown to have been terminated in one way or another; and they also have a right to anticipate that if the principal revokes such authority, they will be given due notice thereof. It is a general rule of law, therefore, upon which there seems to be no conflict of authorities, that all acts of a general agent within the scope of his authority, as respects third persons, will be binding on the principal, even though done after revocation, unless notice of such revocation has been given to those persons who have had dealings with and who are apt to have other dealings with the agent upon the strength of his former authority." 1 *Clark & Skyles on Agency*, § 173 (b). . . .

In the present case no express notice was shown, and the controlling issue was whether or not the plaintiff had "implied notice" that there had been a revocation of the agency, . . . The only circumstance upon which the defendant could rely as suggesting the necessity of making inquiry whether the agency had been terminated was that the order for the goods was given to the plaintiff's salesman three miles from the defendant's store, where the agent had been employed. The defendant was engaged in the sawmill business, and his "commissary" was run in connection with that business, as an adjunct to it, and not as a wholly independent enterprise. When the order for the goods was taken, Mike Burch, who still assumed to act as the defendant's agent, was superintending the erection of a sawmill. That it did not belong to the defendant or was not to be used in connection with his business was not self-apparent, nor was the fact that Mike Burch was not at the time engaged in his customary duties at the commissary calculated to put the plaintiff's saleman on notice that he had left the service of the defendant. Moreover, the salesman had first driven by the store of the defendant and inquired for Mike Burch, who had theretofore been in charge of it. Instead of being notified that Mike Burch was no longer in the defendant's employ, the saleman was told where Mike Burch could be found. . . . The jury, after considering all facts and circumstances brought to light at the trial, found against the contention of the defendant that

due caution and prudence on the part of the plaintiff's [agent] ought to have suggested to him the propriety of making inquiry, if he did not divine the truth. . . . The defendant was admittedly at fault, having failed to take any steps to give notice to the plaintiff, whereas the plaintiff had not omitted to perform any legal duty owing to the defendant, and the plaintiff's [agent] admittedly acted in entire good faith. . . . [A]s was pointed out by Rapallo, J., In *Clafin* v. *Lenheim*, ". . . Justice to parties dealing with agents requires that the rule requiring notice in such cases should not be departed from on slight grounds, or dubious or equivocal circumstances substituted in place of notice. If notice was not in fact given, and loss happens to the defendant, it is attributable to his neglect of a most usual and necessary precaution." The verdict of the jury appears to be in accord both with the strict law and the common justice of the case, . . .

Judgment affirmed.

Case Questions

1. Since the third party recovered from the principal in this case, could the principal recover from the agent? What must be alleged and proved for this to happen?

2. When a principal discharges an agent who has had the authority to contract with third persons, what course of conduct should the principal adopt to be sure it will be free from liability for acts of the agent after discharge?

Review Problems

1. The plaintiffs contracted with the defendant, United Van Lines, Inc., to move their household goods from Sioux City to Palo Alto. When the driver and moving van arrived to load the household goods the driver informed the plaintiffs that he would arrive in Palo Alto Friday, November 13th. The plaintiffs and their child flew from Sioux City to Palo Alto to meet the truck on its arrival. When the driver returned to the freight terminal with the plaintiffs' furnishings the truck was held up until a full load could be put on. The truck finally arrived January 3 of the next year. The plaintiffs sue the defendant alleging breach of contract. The defendant argues that its agent was not authorized to

make the statement regarding the arrival time and the notice of the plaintiffs' arrival time was never given to it. Should the plaintiffs recover for breach of contract?

2. W was a truck driver for Dixie-Ohio Express Company (D.O.X.), a common carrier. He was told by other agents of D.O.X. to pick up a load of aluminum from an ALCOA plant in Tennessee and deliver it to points in Ohio and New York. The truck was loaded by employees of ALCOA who were supervised by a foreman and a superintendant paid by ALCOA. Also present was another employee from D.O.X., who worked with the foreman from ALCOA in advising the employees of ALCOA how to load trucks with aluminum. The truck was loaded negligently; the load shifted and W was killed in the resulting crash. The estate of W sues ALCOA. Given these facts, what is ALCOA's best defense and what are its chances of succeeding?

3. Foremost Realty, Inc., is a real estate broker that also buys and sells real property for its own account. Hobson purchased a ranch from Foremost. The terms were 10 percent down with the balance payable over a 25-year period. After several years of profitable operation of the ranch, Hobson had two successive bad years. As a result, he defaulted on the mortgage. Foremost did not want to foreclose, but instead offered to allow Hobson to remain on the ranch and suspend the payment schedule until Foremost could sell the property at a reasonable price. However, Foremost insisted that it be appointed as the irrevocable and exclusive agent for the sale of the property. Although Hobson agreed, he subsequently became dissatisfied with Foremost's efforts to sell the ranch and gave Foremost notice in writing terminating the agency. Foremost has indicated to Hobson that he does not have the legal power to do so.
    Can Hobson terminate the agency?

(This is adapted from CPA Exam Question, #5b, Business Law, taken from the May, 1980, exam. © American Institute of Certified Public Accountants, Inc., 1980.)

4. The plaintiff, Beech Aircraft Corp. designs, manufactures, and sells aircraft and supporting systems. It had a government contract for the design of fuel systems for the Titan II rocket program. The Titan II was a liquid-fueled rocket, and the propellant used was extremely toxic and corrosive. Killian, an agent of the plaintiff, met with Frabbe, an agent of the defendant, Flexible Tubing Corporation, to discuss the purchase by the plaintiff of tubing that could be used for the rocket. At this meeting Killian informed Frabbe of the specific performance standards that the hose would be expected to meet. Killian responded that they could meet the intent of the specifications at that time, and that the hoses would be suitable for the particular service involved.

When Beech received the hoses it paid for them and began testing. The hoses could not stand the corrosive propellant and were rejected after thorough testing. Beech seeks to rescind the contract based on a breach of warranty, but Flexible argues that Beech purchased a standardized product designed for no particular purpose and that the contract is complete and there was no breach of warranty. Flexible also argues that it had no knowledge of any representations made by its sales agent. Can Flexible be held to the representations of its agent?

5. On October 11, 1973, John Gray, as the owner of a 50 percent interest in a government oil and gas lease, assigned 10 percent of the operating rights and working interest to John Tylle in exchange for $10,000. This money was to be used by Gray to drill and complete an oil well. If Gray wanted to, could he terminate the agency agreement at will? Was this an agency agreement?

6. O owned a small plastics manufacturing business that served the mobile home and recreational vehicle industry in north central Indiana. He employed a traveling salesman, S, who made calls on customers in the area served. S sold O's products for a period of two years and was authorized not only to sign the contracts on behalf of O but also accept payment by check from those placing orders. O became increasingly concerned with the decline in sales as a result of his customers' selling fewer of their products because of the energy crisis. He decided to change his method of selling. On September 1, 1975, he discharged S and on that date ran an advertisement in a local newspaper informing the public that:

> S, general sales agent for O, was discharged from employment as of this date, due to a new and innovative sales organization being implemented by O.

S was angry with O. He had no hopes of employment. He was desperate for money so after his discharge he went to C, a good customer of O's in the past who had not read the newspaper notice, and secured an order for $10,000 worth of plastics. S was paid by check and then cashed the check.

Also, S contracted with N, a new customer who knew of O's business but had never done business with O, and similarly took payment and absconded with it.

Of course, the plastics are never shipped to C and N and both bring suit against O for breach of contract. Should they recover? Why?

7. Would there be a difference in the outcome if O's business had filed for bankruptcy on Sept. 1, 1975, and notice of this was carried in the local newspaper?

Endnotes

1. *Restatement 2nd*, § 9 (1958).
2. *Ibid.*, § 282.
3. *Ibid.*, § 5(1).
4. *Ibid.*, § 362.
5. W. A. Seavey, *Law of Agency*, pp. 10–11 (1964).
6. *Restatement*, § 18.
7. Seavey, *supra*, p. 25.
8. *Restatement*, § 226.
9. *Ibid.*
10. *Ibid.*, § 227 Comment b.
11. *Ibid.*, § 138, Comment b, Illustration 2.
12. *Ibid.*, § 108.
13. *Ibid.*, § 134.
14. Seavey, *supra*, p. 89.
15. *Restatement*, § 136.
16. *Ibid.*
17. *Ibid.*, § 12.
18. *Ibid.*, § 14 c Comment a.

Partnership Law

Part Three

The Partnership Form of Organization: Creation and Partnership Property

7

In this chapter and the next we will present material illustrating the circumstances in which the courts will recognize the partnership form, and as a consequence will establish legal duties among partners and among the partnership, the partners, and third parties. A statement of these circumstances is called partnership law. Partnership law differs from agency law in that the former has been codified in most states in the form of partnership statutes while the latter is not in statutory form, but is based on the common law.

The National Conference of Commissioners on Uniform State Laws is a body of well-known lawyers, judges, and law professors who meet yearly to draft and make available for adoption by the various state legislatures uniform laws covering a wide variety of topics. It is believed that in some areas of the law, such as partnership law, uniformity in law application among the states is desirable. Many partnerships do business in more than one state. If such an organization were subject to a different set of laws governing the organization form in each state it would be presented with an unnecessary element of complexity. Today at least 47 states have adopted the Uniform Partnership Act with very little change in the language from that originally proposed in 1916.[1] Throughout the next two chapters, we will use the Uniform Partnership Act as a key to our presentation of material and will refer to it only as the UPA. This act is reproduced in its entirety in the Appendix.

The Uniform Partnership Act

Also, you should note that even though partnership law is mostly statutory, case law is by no means insignificant in understanding the statutory language. Appellate cases still provide, better than any other source, a statement of the circumstances in which the legal system will act to enforce either statutory, contractual, or common law duties.

At this point you might wish to refer to Chapter 2 and Figure 2-4 provided there for a list of the advantages and disadvantages of using this form of business organization.

Definition and Legal Character of a Partnership

A Partnership as a Separate Legal Entity

A partnership is defined by Section 6 of the UPA as follows:

> A partnership is an association of two or more persons to carry on as co-owners of a business for profit.

One of the unresolved issues of partnership law is presented by the use of a word "association" in the definition. The issue is whether this association is a legal entity separate from the partners. Is it like a corporation, which is a distinct legal entity, or like a proprietorship, in which the business and personal assets of the owner are not separate? The UPA does not answer this question, but, as we pointed out in Chapter 2 of this text, it is stated that the original chief draftsman of the UPA, Dean James Barr Ames of the Harvard Law School, would have defined a partnership as a legal entity had he lived to complete the drafting.[2] Today, as a general rule, the partnership is recognized by most courts as a separate legal entity for limited purposes. More specifically, a parternship can contract, own both personal and real property, and sue and be sued in its own name. Also, the Internal Revenue Laws require that partnerships file income tax returns, and bankruptcy statutes also specifically provide for partnerships.

The glaring exception to the above statements is that a partner may not shield personal assets (savings accounts, home, auto, etc.) from the business creditors of the partnership. This means that if the partnership is unable to pay its debts, the judgment creditors of the partnership may ask the court to order the sheriff to seize the partner's personal assets and sell them to satisfy the judgment. Practically speaking, most suits against partnerships also join partners as individuals so that any judgment is recovered against both. For an example of this type of joinder refer back to the complaint in the *Solmica* case (Chapter 1) and note that both the partnership, Elmer Fox & Co., and its partners were defendants.

The Legal Character of a Partner

The definition further states that a partnership "is an association of . . . persons . . . ." The UPA, Section 2 states that the word person includes "individuals, partnerships, corporations and other associations." Thus, the UPA permits humans to be partners with other humans or with any other legal form of business organization. As we noted in Chapter 2, some state legislatures in the nineteenth century did not permit a corporation to become a partner on the theory that the statutory mandate that a corporation be managed by a board of directors responsible to the shareholders was incompatible with the corporation-partner's being subject to control by a vote of the other partners. Today many legislatures and courts will allow a corporation to be a partner, especially where the power to control the partner is limited by the narrow purpose of the partnership (such as being a joint venturer) or by having its authority to act eliminated (such as being a limited partner).[3] The point to be remembered is that state partnership law does not limit those who may become partners; state corporation law, however, may.

Federal law may also have an impact on the legal character of a partner or partnership. In some cases, it is desirable to use the antifraud provisions of the federal securities laws rather than common law fraud to seek a remedy for damage caused by fraud or misrepresentation. Therefore, it is necessary that a transaction involves a security. Courts have interpreted the definition of a security very broadly. It includes not only stocks, bonds, and debentures, but also any profit-sharing agreement or *investment contract*. An investment contract is a scheme whereby a person invests money in a common enterprise and is led to expect profits solely from the efforts of a third party. (See *SEC* v. *Howey* case in the chapter on securities regulation.) A form of profit-sharing is contemplated by the investors. As you can see, the definition of an investment contract and participation in a partnership in which one contributes capital and another contributes time and management skill appear very similar. Indeed, entering into a partnership may involve the purchase of a security for purposes of the federal securities laws. The importance of this is that if the federal securities laws are applicable to a transaction, they provide another set of remedies for persons damaged because of fraud or misrepresentation. A complete elaboration of these remedies appears in the chapters on the federal securities laws.

The Legal Capacity of a Partner

Implied in the use of the term "persons" in the definition above is the principle that to be a partner one must have the legal capacity to contract. As previously noted in Chapter 3 in the section on capacity, the term is defined by state statute. Generally, minors, persons declared insane, or those deprived of their civil rights such as those in prison for a felony may lack the legal capacity to contract. In the last century many legislatures forbade married women and trustees from becoming partners, but today these restrictions have been removed almost everywhere. However, in some jurisdictions, cases in the early twentieth century held that husband-wife partnerships were not permitted because the potential for disagreement and consequent litigation was considered incompatible with the family relationship.[4] It is doubtful today if these courts would reach the same result. Similarly, older cases held it improper for a trustee to invest in a partnership because it was too risky. Today, as long as the investment is prudent, it will be allowed.

In many jurisdictions the contracts of a minor are treated differently than those of insane persons or others lacking capacity to contract.

Minors' contracts are usually voidable at the option of the minor; in the case of insane persons their contracts are usually void and unenforceable by either party. Therefore, although a minor may be a partner if he or she wishes, obligations to the partnership and its creditors may be repudiated at the minor's option in most jurisdictions.

The Meaning of Co-owners

The definition of a partnership further states that persons must "carry on as co-owners." This element of co-ownership is one of the chief features that distinguishes the partnership form of business from the proprietorship (employer-employee relationship). Often one partner may act for another or at the control of another partner, but if there is an intent to co-own, a partnership exists.

One of the surest signs of co-ownership is the sharing of profits. The UPA Section 7(4) recognizes this when it states:

> The receipt by a person of the profits of a business is prima facie evidence that he is a partner in the business, but no such inference shall be drawn if such profits were received in payment:
> a. As a debt by installment or otherwise;
> b. As wages . . . or rent. . . .
> c. As an annuity. . . .
> d. As interest on a loan, though the amount of payment may vary with the profits of the business.
> e. As the consideration for the sale of good will of a business . . . .

In addition to sharing profits, other evidence of an intent to co-own may be found in the joint ownership of property and in the joint obligation to contribute capital to the enterprise.

Business Organizations Formed for Profit

Finally, the UPA requires that the organization be one carried on for *profit*. This means that those organizations created *primarily* for charitable, religious, fraternal, or social purposes are not partnerships even though they may share in the revenue of a fundraising project or devote such revenue to further their purpose.

Although the legal definition of a partnership seems to be simple, the courts have sometimes had a difficult time applying the definition. For example, in one case a creditor lent a partnership $2.5 million in liquid securities in exchange for 40 percent of the firm's profits up to $500,000 with a guaranteed return of $100,000; in addition, the creditor had the right to (1) join the partnership; (2) obtain information pertaining to the operation of the business; (3) consult with the partners on important partnership matters; (4) veto speculative ventures; (5) limit the distribution of profits to partners; (6) demand the resignation of partners; and (7) demand other substantive legal obligations from the partnership.[5] Despite the provisions for what appears to be the sharing of profits and, in some cases, the sharing of management of the partnership, the court held that the creditor was not a partner. From this case you may conclude that the sharing of profits is not the most important indication of a partnership. In this case, the court considered the extensive loan documentation and concluded that the sharing of profits and management responsibilities (within limits) were intended to protect the creditor's loan and were not intended to be evidence of *co-ownership*.

This case may not represent the law in all jurisdictions because at least one court has held that a partnership existed where a creditor furnished financing and warehouse space to a buyer of goods and received interest on the amount financed at 6 percent plus a fixed compensation for the warehousing but did not receive a share of the profits.[6] The court, considering all of the evidence, held that the creditor was a partner because there was sufficient indication of *joint control* over the enterprise.

Holding that a creditor is a partner is a serious matter for the creditor. This exposes the creditor to business risks and possible liability to judgment creditors of the partnership. If a creditor wishes to protect its loan to a partnership, it must do so in a way that makes it clear that there was no intent to co-own the enterprise.

The Need for a Written Partnership Agreement

Partnerships may be implied in law by courts where the circumstances meet the requirements of the definition or they may be created by contract between the partners. In *some* instances a contract or a writing of some kind is required. Most states, for example, have a statute (called the Statute of Frauds) that requires agreements for the sale of an interest in real property or agreements that require performance lasting over one year to be in writing. So, if a partnership confers authority on a partner to contract in real property, such authority should be in writing. If it is not and the partner contracts with a third person to buy or sell the real property, the contract may not be enforced against or by the partnership. Also, if the partners intend the partnership to exist for longer than one year, they should place their understanding in writing.

With the exceptions noted, the general rule is that to form a partnership, a written agreement is not necessary—although it is advisable. There are many instances in which an informal business relationship may be formed for the purpose of co-owning an enterprise. Little thought may be given to the formal, legal implications of the organization until the circumstances of ownership conflict occur. Before a resolution of the conflict can be achieved courts must determine if a partnership did exist. If the facts of the case reveal the elements of a partnership as stated in the

**Partnership
Creation**

definition above, then courts will probably hold that a partnership existed; and if, as indicated before, the parties are partners rather than employer-employee, a different set of legal consequences will follow.

Following are two cases in which the issue is whether a partnership was intended. See if you can determine why the court in the first case, where there was no written agreement, concluded that there was a partnership; whereas, in the second case, where there was an agreement, the court concluded the opposite.

ZAJAC v. HARRIS
241 Ark. 737, 410 S.W. 2d 593 (S. Ct., Ark., 1967)

GEORGE ROSE SMITH, Justice

The appellee, George Harris, brought this suit to compel the appellant, Carl A. Zajac, to account for the profits and assets of a partnership that assertedly existed between the parties for some two years. Zajac denied that a partnership existed, insisting that Harris was merely an employee in a business owned by Zajac. . . .

The business association that is known in the law as a partnership is not one that can be defined with precision. To the contrary, a partnership is a contractual relationship that may vary, in form and substance, in an almost infinite variety of ways. The draftsmen of the controlling statute, the Uniform Partnership Act, tacitly acknowledged that fact by stating only in the most general language an assortment of rules that are to be considered in determining whether a partnership exists. . . .

In the case at bar there is the . . . consideration that these two laymen went into business together without consulting a lawyer or attempting to put their agreement into writing. It is apparent from the testimony that neither man had any conscious or deliberate intention of entering into a particular legal relationship. . . . Our problem is that of determining from the record as a whole whether the association they agreed upon was a partnership or an employer-employee relationship. . . .

In the salvage operation now in controversy the parties bought wrecked automobiles from insurance companies and either rebuilt them for resale or cannibalized them by reusing or reselling the parts. Harris, the plaintiff, testified that he and Zajac agreed to go into business together, splitting the profits equally—except that Harris was to receive one fourth of the proceeds from any parts sold by him. Harris borrowed $9,000 from a bank, upon the security of property that he owned, and placed the money in a bank account that he used in buying cars for the firm. The profits were divided from time to time as the cars were resold, so that Harris's capital was used and reused. He identified checks totaling more than $73,000 that he signed in making purchases for the business.

Zajac, by contrast, took the position that Harris was merely an employee working for a commission of one half the profits realized from cars that Harris himself had bought. Zajac denied that he had ever agreed that Harris would spend his own money in buying cars. "I told him, when you go out there, when you bid on a car, make a note that I will pay for it." We have no doubt, however, that Harris *did* use his own money in the venture and that Zajac knew that such expenditures were being made.

Counsel for Zajac put much stress upon their client's controlling voice in the management of the business. Zajac and his wife and their accountant had charge of the books and records. No partnership income tax return was ever filed. Harris was ostensibly treated as an employee, in that federal withholding and Social Security taxes were paid upon his share of the profits. The firm also carried workmen's compensation insurance for Harris's protection. In our opinion, however, any inferences that might ordinarily be drawn from these bookkeeping entries are effectively rebutted by the undisputed fact that Harris, apart from being able to sign his name, was unable to read or write. There is no reason to believe that he appreciated the significance of the accounting practices now relied upon by Zajac. . . .

We attach much weight to Zajac's candid admissions, elicited by the chancellor's questions, that Zajac paid Harris one half of the profits derived from cars that Zajac bought with his own money and sold by his own efforts. Zajac had insisted from the outset that Harris was working upon a commission basis,

but that view cannot be reconciled with Harris's admitted right to receive his share of the profits derived from business conducted by Zajac alone.

There is no real dispute between the parties about the governing principles of law. The ultimate question is whether the two men intended to become partners, as that term is used in the law. . . . Harris's receipt of a share of the net profits is prima facie evidence that he was a partner, unless the money was paid to him as wages. . . . He invested, as we have seen, substantial sums of his own money in the acquisition of cars for the firm. . . . When the testimony is reconciled, as we have attempted to do, it does not appear that the chancellor was wrong in deciding that a partnership existed.

Affirmed.

Case Questions

1. What facts did the court rely on in reaching its conclusion that a partnership existed?
2. Why do you think it was advantageous for Harris to establish that a partnership existed?

SHELDON v. LITTLE
111 Vt. 301, 15 A.2d 574 (S. Ct., Vt., 1940)

(Authors' note: In this case the plaintiff, Adelaide W. Sheldon, sued C. Russell Little for amounts allegedly due her. Little's motion to dismiss the case was overruled. Little argued that he and the plaintiff were partners and that no formal settlement of the partnership accounts had taken place and that the cause of action should not be one for money owed, but for an "accounting"—a legal term meaning a complete settlement of accounts. The defendant admitted that the cause of action for the money due was proper if no partnership had been formed. In the first part of the opinion, the court addressed itself to the issue of whether a partnership had been formed. This part of the opinion that affirms the dismissal of the defendant's motion is below.)

BUTTLES, Justice
On March 5, 1925, the parties executed a written agreement providing for the consolidation of their two insurance agencies. Thereafter the consolidated business was conducted in accordance with such agreement until October 1, 1932, when the parties ceased to do business together under such agreement or in any other way. During all of the time that the business was so conducted it was actively managed by the defendant who took general charge of the same, kept the books and handled the finances. Meanwhile the plaintiff was away from Fair Haven much of the time and took no active part in the business except that during the year 1932 she gave it some attention and participated in its management. At the end of each year except 1932 the defendant submitted to

the plaintiff a written report or statement purporting to give certain data regarding the business for that year. . . .

Said written agreement provided that the said agencies, after being consolidated, should be run as the property of the plaintiff and under the name as theretofore of the Sheldon Agency; that the defendant should have the supervision and management of said agency, bringing to the Sheldon office the books, files, papers, and other personal property previously used by him in his own agency and continue there the general business of the consolidated agencies, devoting his entire working time to the management and development thereof; that the plaintiff might give such time to the management of the business as she cared to give from time to time, but should be under no obligation at any time to give the same her personal attention and care; that from the gross income of the business there should be paid the running expenses including rent, heat, light, . . . and other incidental expenses usual in the conduct of such a business, and that the net profits after the payment of such expenses should be equally divided between the parties to the agreement. . . .

The question for determination is whether the plaintiff and defendant were partners or sustained some other relation to each other. Where the rights of the parties . . . are concerned, and no question as to third parties is involved, the criterion to determine whether the contract is one of partnership or not must be: What did the parties intend by the contract which they made as between themselves? . . . This intention may be shown by their express agreement or inferred from their conduct and dealings with one another. But we have here no indication of the intention of the parties other than their written agreement, so that their intention is to be ascertained by a construction of that writing.

Many definitions of partnership have been given, no one of which would, perhaps, fit all cases, and various tests for determining the existence of the partnership relation have been applied by the courts. The test most generally applied, subject to various conditions and limitations, is that of profit sharing. This Court has recently said that the indispensable constituent of a partnership is that the parties shall be jointly interested in the profits and affected by the losses of the business. . . . Such joint interest may result even though one party furnishes the capital or stock and the other contributes . . . labor and skill. . . . But there is a clear distinction between agreements whereby the parties have a specific interest in the profits themselves as profits, and agreements which give to the person sought to be charged not a specific interest in the business or profits but a stipulated proportion of the proceeds as compensation for his labor and services. The former constitute a partnership but the latter do not. . . .

In the case we are considering, by the terms of the agreement the business was to be run as the property of the plaintiff; no substantial increase in expenses of management could be incurred by the defendant as manager except with the approval of the plaintiff; the plaintiff could terminate the agreement at any time, resume control of the business and discharge the defendant as manager by paying him a sum equal to one half of the earnings for another year; the plaintiff could see the business at any time, but before selling to another she was required to offer it to the defendant at a price to be based on the business done by the agency during the year 1924; in case of plaintiff's death the defendant was to have a similar option to purchase the business from plaintiff's personal representatives. Clearly it was the intent of the parties that the plaintiff should have the sole proprietary interest in the business and in the profits resulting therefrom before they were divided. The defendant received a portion of the profits not as profits, but as compensation for his services as manager of the plaintiff's business. We hold that the parties were not partners and there was no error in the denial of the defendant's motion as made.

1. The general rule is that if the evidence reveals that the parties intended to form a partnership but never expressly agreed to do so, the courts will create one or imply one for them to protect the interests of one or more of the partners. Also, if the evidence reveals no intent to form such an association, the courts will not imply one. What evidence caused the court in this case to conclude that no partnership existed?

2. Can you reconcile the holdings of *Zajac* and *Sheldon*?

A Partner's Right to an Action to "Account"

In both of the cases presented, one of the remedies sought was for the court to order an "accounting." This term as used in partnership law designates an equitable remedy in which the court orders a comprehensive investigation of the transactions of the partnership, and a complete statement of accounts. Section 22 of the UPA provides that any partner shall have the rights to a formal account as to partnership affairs:

a. If he is wrongfully excluded from the partnership business or possession of its property by his copartners.

b. If the right exists under the terms of any agreement.

c. As provided in Section 21 (Section 21 deals with a partner receiving a partnership benefit without the consent of other partners).

d. Whenever other circumstances render it just and reasonable.

Before this remedy is available, the court must find that the party requesting the remedy is a partner. This was the issue that was before the courts in the *Zajac* and *Sheldon* cases, and is often the first issue presented in partnership litigation. Moreover, most courts hold that an action *between partners* for money owed is inappropriate. The appropriate remedy is to seek an accounting. Once a complete statement of partnership accounts has been made, then the partners and the court may more clearly decide who is owed which amounts.

Partnership by Estoppel

In addition to the circumstances discussed above where the court created a partnership, courts will also impose the duties of a partner on one under circumstances in which there may be no partnership in fact, but *third parties* are lead to believe there is one and have dealt either with the supposed partnership or one representing himself to be a partner. The circumstances under which this will occur create a partnership by estoppel. The word "estoppel" is used here in the same manner as it was used in the agency material. It is an equitable doctrine imposed on a relationship to protect the reasonable expectations of the third parties.

Section 16 of the UPA recognizes a partner by estoppel in two circumstances:

1. When a person . . . represents himself . . . as a partner in an existing partnership . . . he is liable to any . . . person to whom such representation has been made (and) who has . . . given credit to the actual or apparent partnership. . . .

2. When a person has been . . . represented to be a partner in an existing partnership, or with one or more persons not actual partners, he is an agent of the persons consenting to such representation . . . to the same extent and in the same manner as though he were a partner in fact, with respect to persons who rely upon the representation. . . .

In the first circumstance, the law recognizes a partnership when, for example, A expressly or implicitly represents he is a partner in "P Associates & Co." although in reality he is not; and a T/P extends credit to P Associates & Co., and does not directly contract with A. By recognizing a partnership in this instance, A would become liable to T/P since a court would estop A from denying he was a partner in P Associates & Co.

In the second circumstance, the law recognizes a partnership when some member or members of a partnership, P Associates & Co., allow or have knowledge that one who is not a partner, A, is holding himself out as a partner, and T/P extends credit to or otherwise contracts with A believing him to be a partner. If all partners consent to or know about the representation, then the partnership is liable. If fewer than all partners consent or know, only those who consent are liable.

The results reached in these two instances illustrate that partnership law, like agency law, will protect the reasonable expectations of third persons who deal with an apparent partner or apparent partnership to their detriment. Note that though there is liability running from the "partnership" to the third party in both cases, it is a very restricted form of partnership. Partnership by estoppel establishes an actual partnership relation between the partnership and third parties only for the purpose of providing a remedy to the injured third party. This equitable remedy does not create an actual partnership between the parties so that they can enforce other duties of partners against one another.

A Typical Partnership Agreement

The most conventional way to establish a partnership is for the parties to sign a contractual agreement declaring their intent to form a partnership. This agreement, customarily referred to as "articles of partnership," may be as complex as the parties desire. We have reproduced a rather simple partnership agreement. We suggest you read it carefully and take notes on the provisions that make the partnership form of organization distinct from other organizations. These provisions are the ones concerning capital, profit and loss, salaries, management, and termination.

Partnership Agreement

AGREEMENT made June 4, 1973, between John O'Connell and Harry Jones, both of New York, New York.

1. Name and business. The parties hereby form a partnership under the name of Ace Advertising Co. to conduct a general advertising business. The principal office of the business shall be in New York, New York.

2. Term. The partnership shall begin on June 4, 1973, and shall continue until terminated as herein provided.

3. Capital. The capital of the partnership shall be contributed in cash by the partners as follows:

    John O'Connell $20,000
    Harry Jones $20,000

   A separate capital account shall be maintained for each partner. Neither partner shall withdraw any part of his capital account. . . .
   Upon the demand of either partner, the capital accounts of the partners shall be maintained at all times in the proportions in which the partners share in the profits and losses of the partnership.

4. Profit and loss. The net profits of the partnership shall be divided equally between the partners and the net losses shall be borne equally by them. A separate income account shall be maintained for each partner. Partnership profits and losses shall be charged or credited to the separate income account of each partner. If a partner has no credit balance in his income account, losses shall be charged to his capital account.

5. Salaries and drawings. Neither partner shall receive any salary for services rendered to the partnership. Each partner may, from time to time, withdraw the credit balance in his income account. No additional share of profits shall inure to either partner by reason of his capital or income account being in excess of the capital or income account of the other.

6. Interest. No interest shall be paid on the initial contributions to the capital of the partnership or on any subsequent contributions of capital.

7. Management, duties, and restrictions. The partners shall have equal rights in the management of the partnership business, and each partner shall devote his entire time to the conduct of the business. . . . Without the consent of the other partner neither partner shall on behalf of the partnership borrow or lend money, or make, deliver or accept any commercial paper, or execute any

Source: *Current Legal Forms with Tax Analyses*, Vol. 1, Matthew Bender, 1975, p. 1–1004 Form 1.01. Copyright © 1975 by Matthew Bender & Co., Inc., and reprinted from Rabkin & Johnson *Current Legal Forms* with permission from the publisher.

mortgage, security agreement, bond, or lease, or purchase or contract to purchase, or sell or contract to sell any property for or of the partnership other than the type of property bought and sold in the regular course of its business. Neither partner shall, except with the consent of the other partner, assign, mortgage, grant a security interest in, or sell his share in the partnership or in its capital assets or property, or enter into any agreement as a result of which any person shall become interested with him in the partnership, or do any act detrimental to the best interests of the partnership or which would make it impossible to carry on the ordinary business of the partnership.

8. Banking. All funds of the partnership shall be deposited in its name in such checking account or accounts as shall be designated by the partners. All withdrawals therefrom are to be made upon checks signed by either partner.

9. Books. The partnership books shall be maintained at the principal office of the partnership, and each partner shall at all times have access thereto. The books shall be kept on a fiscal year basis, commencing July 1 and ending June 30, and shall be closed and balanced at the end of each fiscal year. An audit shall be made as of the closing date.

10. Voluntary termination. The partnership may be dissolved at any time by agreement of the partners, in which event the partners shall proceed with reasonable promptness to liquidate the business of the partnership. The partnership name shall be sold with the other assets of the business. The assets of the partnership business shall be used and distributed in the following order: (a) to pay or provide for the payment of all partnership liabilities and liquidating expenses and obligations; (b) to equalize the income accounts of the partners; (c) to discharge the balance of the income accounts of the partners; (d) to equalize the capital accounts of the partners; and (e) to discharge the balance of the capital accounts of the partners.

11. Retirement. Either partner shall have the right to retire from the partnership at the end of any fiscal year. Written notice of intention to retire shall be served upon the other partner at the office of the partner or at the office of the partnership at least three months before the end of the fiscal year. The retirement of either partner shall have no effect upon the continuance of the partnership business. The remaining partner shall have the right either to purchase the retiring partner's interest in the partnership or to terminate and liquidate the partnership business. If the remaining partner elects to purchase the interest of the retiring partner, he shall serve notice in writing of such election upon the retiring partner at the office of the partnership within two months after receipt of his notice of intention to retire.

    (a) If the remaining partner elects to purchase the interest of the retiring partner in the partnership, the purchase price and method of payment shall be the same as stated in paragraph 12 with reference to the purchase of a decedent's interest in the partnership.

    (b) If the remaining partner does not elect to purchase the interest of the retiring partner in the partnership, the partners shall proceed with reasonable promptness to liquidate the business of the partnership. The procedure as to liquidation and distribution of the assets of the partnership business shall be the same as stated in paragraph 10 with reference to voluntary termination.

12. **Death.** Upon the death of either partner, the surviving partner shall have the right either to purchase the interest of the decedent in the partnership or to terminate and liquidate the partnership business. If the surviving partner elects to purchase the decedent's interest, he shall serve notice in writing of such election, within three months after the death of the decedent, upon the executor or administrator of the decedent, or, if at the time of such election no legal representative has been appointed upon any one of the known legal heirs of the decedent at the last known address of such heir.

(a) If the surviving partner elects to purchase the interest of the decedent in the partnership, the purchase price shall be equal to the decedent's capital account as at the date of his death plus the decedent's income account as at the end of the prior fiscal year, increased by his share of partnership profits or decreased by his share of partnership losses for the period from the beginning of the fiscal year in which his death occurred until the end of the calendar month in which his death occurred, and decreased by withdrawals charged to his income account during such period. No allowance shall be made for goodwill, trade name, patents, or other intangible assets, except as those assets have been reflected on the partnership books immediately prior to the decedent's death; but the survivor shall nevertheless be entitled to use the trade name of the partnership. The purchase price shall be paid without interest in four semi-annual installments beginning six months after the end of the calendar month in which the decedent's death occurred.

(b) If the surviving partner does not elect to purchase the interest of the decedent in the partnership, he shall proceed with reasonable promptness to liquidate the business of the partnership. The surviving partner and the estate of the deceased partner shall share equally in the profits and losses of the business during the period of liquidation, except that the decedent's estate shall not be liable for losses in excess of the decedent's interest in the partnership at the time of his death. No compensation shall be paid to the surviving partner for his services in liquidation. Except as herein otherwise stated, the procedure as to liquidation and distribution of the assets of the partnership business shall be the same as stated in paragraph 10 with reference to voluntary termination. . . .

In witness whereof the parties have signed this agreement.

s/. . . . .
John O'Connell

s/. . . . .
Harry Jones

The remaining material on partnership law will be presented by using the agreement above as an organizing guide. The first two paragraphs of the partnership agreement are self-explanatory. Remember that if a partnership adopts a name that is *not* composed of the surnames of the partners, it must register such name with the state as a tradename or trademark, whichever is appropriate; additionally it must procure licenses for engaging in regulated professions and businesses.

Partnership Property and a Partner's Interest

Paragraphs 3 to 9 of the partnership agreement concern the right of a partner with regard to the property brought to the partnership and the property subsequently owned by the partnership. The nature of the partnership property will be more fully explained in the remaining portions of this chapter. Partnership operations and partnership termination (paragraphs 10 through 12 of the agreement) will be the focus of Chapter 8.

Partnership Capital

The initial capital of the enterprise is whatever the partners contribute to the partnership. It may be cash or other personal or real property. This capital is used by the partnership to buy assets for operation of the partnership. Seldom does it stay in the original form of cash or other property.

All of the property originally brought into the partnership and all of that subsequently acquired by purchase or otherwise on account of the partnership become partnership property [UPA § 8(1)]. If there is a dispute over whether a partner or the partnership owns the property the intent of the parties controls. The problem usually is in ascertaining this intent. The best evidence of intent is the articles of partnership and what it states about the property described as partnership property therein.

In the absence of an agreement, other evidence of intent must be found. If partnership funds are used to acquire property, then the law assumes, unless a contrary intention appears, that it is partnership property [UPA § 8(2)]. This is true even if the title to the property is in the name of one of the partners, not the partnership.

A Partner's Rights in Partnership Property

Once the partnership has been formed, a partner has certain rights in the partnership and its property that are unique features of a partnership. Section 24 of the UPA provides:

> The property rights of a partner are (1) his rights in specific partnership property, (2) his interest in the partnership and (3) his right to participate in the management.

The manner in which the UPA § 24(1) characterizes a partner's rights in specific partnership property may be somewhat misleading. Generally, a partner has *no* "individual" right to specific partnership property. *A partner only has an equal right shared with other partners to possess such property for the purpose of carrying out the partnership business.* That is, once the partner's capital has been committed to the enterprise, the right to repossess or control it to the exclusion of others is lost unless the partner wishes to dissolve the partnership.

This form of ownership is not unique but exists whenever persons jointly own property. Perhaps your home is jointly owned by you and your spouse, or perhaps your parents jointly own a home. This means the owners have an equal right to possess all of it; they have a right to enter any portion they wish, but so do all the owners. No specific portion may be appropriated by any one of the owners. The same is true of partnership property.

This duty to share partnership property and the right to possess partnership property for partnership purposes cannot be sold or given to someone else without the consent of all other partners, nor may an individual creditor of a partner seize this "right." That is, to a limited degree, a partner may shield personal assets from *individual creditors* by conveying some of them to a partnership and becoming a partner. To this extent a partnership does look like a distinct legal entity apart from the individuals that compose it.[7] This partnership property is subject, of course, to seizure by *partnership* creditors, and may be seized by individual creditors if the partnership is dissolved and specific partnership property is conveyed back to a partner. The right to possess partnership property for partnership purposes is accompanied by the right to repayment for the initial capital contribution on dissolution of the partnership. We will discuss this more fully in the next chapter.

The following case illustrates some of the legal implications that flow from the unique conception of partnership property.

STATE v. ELSBURY
63 Nev. 463; 175 P2d 430 (S. Ct. Nev., 1946)

Appellant was convicted of the crime of grand larceny. . . .

The information charged appellant with having stolen the sum of $1,000 from one S. L. Corsino.

The evidence shows that at the time of the alleged theft appellant and S. L. Corsino were general partners, engaged as such in operating a cafe, under written articles of partnership; that the sum of $1,000, admittedly taken and retained by appellant, constituted part of the proceeds from the business on deposit in the bank in a checking account in the firm name; and that the partnership was heavily in debt. It also shows that S. L. Corsino originally furnished the largest amount of the firm's capital.

The statute defining grand larceny reads as follows:

> Every person who shall feloniously steal, take, and carry away, lead or drive away, the personal goods or property of another, of the value of fifty dollars or more shall be deemed guilty of grand larceny, ...

Under this statute, it is essential that money which has been unlawfully taken and retained must be the "property of another." . . .

But the State relies upon section 10339, N.C.L. which provides that:

> It shall be no defense to a prosecution for larceny * * * that the money or property appropriated was partly the property of another and partly the property of the accused.

The important question to be decided, therefore, is whether this statute is applicable to a general partner who takes and retains partnership property during the existence of the partnership.

The title to partnership property is of a different class and with characteristics quite distinct from that of the title to property owned and held by individuals.

Section 24 of the Uniform Partnership Act reads:

> The property rights of a partner are (1) his rights in specific partnership property, (2) his interest in the partnership, and (3) his right to participate in the management.

By the statement that one of the property rights of a partner is his right in specific partnership property is meant simply that a partner, subject to any contrary agreement, has an equal right with his co-partners to use or possess any partnership property for any proper partnership purpose. . . .

Under section 25 of the Uniform Partnership Act, a partner is co-owner with his partners of specific partnership property holding as a tenant in partnership. The incidents of this tenancy are such that: A partner, subject to the provisions of the act and to any agreement between the partners, has an equal right with his partners to possess specific partnership property for partnership purposes, but cannot otherwise possess same without the consent of his partners. His rights in specific partnership property are not assignable except in connection with the assignment of rights of all the partners in the same property, nor are they subject to attachment or execution upon a personal claim against him. . . . On the death of a partner his right in specific partnership property vests not in the partner's personal representative but in the surviving partner. . . .

Section 26 of the same statute specifically provides:

A partner's interest in the partnership is his share of the profits and surplus, and the same in personal property.

A partner has no individual property in any specific assets of the firm. . . .

Instead, the interest of each partner in the partnership property is his share in the surplus, after the partnership debts are paid and the partnership accounts have been settled. . . .

Until that time arrives, it cannot be known what property will have to be used to satisfy the debts and, therefore, what property will remain after the debts are paid. . . .

The amounts of money invested by the partners respectively in the firm would be no criterion in determining the ownership of the partnership property, for the partner who furnished in the first instance the largest amount of capital, on final settlement might be found to have no interest whatever in the assets then on hand. . . .

When a partnership is admittedly insolvent, as was the partnership in the case at bar at the time of the alleged larceny, neither of the partners can possibly have any separate interest in the firm property. . . .

A partner's right in partnership property . . . carries with it a right to an accounting. . . .

As each partner is the ultimate owner of an undivided interest in all the partnership property, none of such property "Can be said, with reference to any partner, 'to be the property of another.' "

Therefore, it seems plain that the statute relied upon by the State does not apply where, as in this case, partnership property is appropriated by one of the partners during the existence of the partnership. . . .

The judgment of conviction and the order . . . are reversed, and the money heretofore deposited instead of bail will be refunded to the appellant.

If the $1000 did not belong to the partner who withdrew it and it was not the property of another for purposes of the application of the grand larceny statute, then to whom did it belong? This question highlights the logical bind that results when courts refuse—by implication—to recognize the partnership as a distinct, separate legal entity.

Does the decision in this case say that there was no wrongdoing here, or does it hold that the proper approach for the alleged wrongdoing is to first bring an action for an accounting and then ask a court to order a partner to pay what may be owed?

A Partner's Interest in the Partnership

The second kind of classification of partnership rights provided for in UPA § 24(2) is an "interest" in the partnership. "A partner's interest in the partnership is his share of the profits . . ." (UPA § 26). This right to an interest in profits is a property right that can be assigned (sold or given to someone else) by the partner, and that is subject to a court order directing the partner to pay it to an individual judgment creditor. Such an order is called a "charging order."

A Partner's Right to Manage.   A third property right of a partner provided for in UPA § 24(3) is the right to participate in the management. Some items of management may be delegated in the partnership agreement to specific partners. If it is not or if differences arise as to the ordinary matters connected with the partnership business, they are supposed to be settled by a majority vote of the partners. Any act that would be in violation of the partnership agreement, however, must have the consent of all partners [UPA § 18(h)]. This right to vote is given to a partner regardless of the type or amount of the capital contribution to the partnership.

Paragraph 7 of the partnership agreement in this chapter providing for "equal rights" in the management of the partnership business is typical. When partnerships are formed, the partners are usually filled with confidence in themselves and trust in one another. The general rules that ordinary partnership matters will be decided by majority vote and any act in contravention of the agreement may not be accomplished without the consent of all partners seem reasonable. But differences do arise, and some scholars have criticized the drafting of UPA Section 18 because it is possible for a majority of partners to exploit dissenting partners.[8] Section 18 states, "The rights and duties of the partners in relation to the partnership shall be determined, *subject to any agreement between them,* by the following rules:" (emphasis added). Then, paragraph (h) states that "no act in contravention of any agreement between the partners" (such as changing the nature of the partnership business, or adding or expelling partners for reasons not mentioned in the agreement) "may be done rightfully without the consent of all the partners." Because the first clause qualifies the second, a reasonable, literal interpretation of Section 18 is that so long as the partnership agreement so provides, a majority vote of the partners may determine any issue, including a change in the agreement. This could lead to a rather abrupt change of partnership affairs to the disadvantage of a few of the partners who may not vote to change. One court that has considered this issue did not interpret Section 18(h) the way it was written and held that any "fundamental change" in the partnership agreement required a unanimous vote,[9] even though the partnership agreement provided for amendment by a majority vote of the partners.

In later cases, however, this one decision may not be persuasive, and a court could hold that a vote of the majority will accomplish any legal partnership act so long as the agreement so provides.

Expelling a Partner.   A possible way to protect minority or dissenting interests in a partnership is to include provisions for expulsion in the agreement. As we will discuss in the next chapter, any partner may bring about a dissolution of the partnership by simply withdrawing. However, this approach is seldom satisfactory for the dissenting partner. There are substantial problems of valuing the goodwill of the firm and the value of a partner's interest, and these valuations are usually difficult to make. So, practitioners recommend that a partnership agreement include an expulsion clause that states the vote required to expel a partner—this should be either by unanimous vote excluding the vote of the partner to be expelled or by an 80 or 90 percent vote of the partnership—and other clauses that define the cause for which an expulsion vote may be taken.[10] It is difficult to state precisely all of the causes for expulsion (for example, "personal incompatibility" may be such a cause), but including such a provision at least puts a partner on notice that there are certain activities for which expulsion is possible. At the time a partnership is formed, some of the most important items that should be discussed are how the management of the partnership will be conducted and the conditions under which the partnership will dissolve. By raising the issue of expulsion and the issue of changing the partnership agreement to the level of explicit understanding, it is possible to protect, to a certain degree, the interests of those partners who may dissent from the majority.

Additional Rights of a Partner

In addition to the three classifications of a partner's property rights in the partnership, the UPA and most partnership agreements provide for the following rights:

1. The right to be repaid for contributions or loans (advancements) to the partnership, if there are funds available, at dissolution [§ 18(a)].

2. The right to indemnification for payments made in the ordinary course of business [§ 18(b)].

3. The right to have access and to copy the firm books (§ 19).

4. The right to an accounting (§ 22).

A Partner's Duties.   Generally, a partner is under a duty imposed by the UPA to the partnership to act as a fiduciary. Designating the relationship between the partners and the partnerships as a fiduciary one imposes on the partners all of those duties of a fiduciary discussed in the materials on agency law. The partner must act in the best interest of the partnership, and must render true and full information to the partnership of all things affecting the partnership business (UPA § 20). More specifically, this fiduciary duty includes the following:

1. Any partner who gains any advantage by fraud, misrepresentation, or the concealment of any material fact in connection with a partnership transaction must account to the other partners for the benefit received.

2. No partner shall make a profit from any transaction with the partnership or fellow partners unless it is with the consent of the copartners.

3. No partner shall make a personal profit from the use of partnership property.

4. No partner shall take a partnership business opportunity for one's individual benefit.

5. No partner shall compete with the partnership.[11]

Problems with Corporations as Partners.   There is a significant potential for a breach of a fiduciary duty when a member of the board or an officer of a corporation is also a member of a partnership that conducts business similar to that of the corporation. This may be portrayed as in Figure 7-1.

In this case, as a member of the board of X, Y, Z corporation, Person A owes a fiduciary duty to the corporation; this person also owes a fiduciary duty to the partnership. If the partnership and the corporation are in similar lines of work, then conflict would seem almost inevitable.

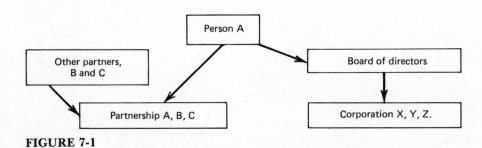

FIGURE 7-1

The solution to this is that both the corporation and the partnership should provide in their respective governing documents that all transactions between them or with competing interests be conducted openly, at market value, and in good faith. Of course, no amount of legal language will be sufficient to govern all transactions of this nature. The best solution is complete and open disclosure of all transactions.

Issues of the breach of a fiduciary relationship or other matters in which it is alleged a partner owes money to the partnership are litigated by means of a cause of action for an accounting. Economy of litigation and convenience require this. For these reasons it is usually held, as we noted earlier, that a direct lawsuit by one partner against another or the partnership against an individual partner will not be proper until an accounting has been conducted.

In addition to the duties of a partner noted, no partner is to receive interest on the capital contributed to the partnership unless it is held by the partnership after the date when it was supposed to be repaid [UPA § 18(d)] nor is a partner entitled to a salary or other fixed compensation except when the partnership is dissolved and the partner is winding up partnership affairs [UPA § 18(f)]. However, remember that the contractual understanding of the parties revealed in the Articles of Partnership create duties between parties and if it provides for salaries or guaranteed minimum income to some partner or unequal sharing of profits or unequal voting power such provisions will be enforced. The reason for the statutory provision against interest and compensation is that one type of compensation (salary) will not be inferred where another type (profit-sharing) has been expressly provided for.

An important point to remember is that in addition to the duties imposed on the partners by the articles of partnership and the UPA, partners are always under a duty to act as a fiduciary. The *Clement* case below illustrates that a court will presume that a partner acted to the detriment of the partnership when he grew relatively wealthy and could not explain the source of the wealth.

CLEMENT v. CLEMENT
436 Pa. 466, 260 A.2d 728 (S. Ct., Pa., 1970)

ROBERTS, Justice

Charles and L. W. Clement are brothers whose forty-year partnership has ended in acrimonious litigation. The essence of the conflict lies in Charles' contention that L. W. has over the years wrongfully taken for himself more than his share of the partnership's profits. Charles discovered these misdeeds during negotiations with L. W. over the sale of Charles' interest in the partnership in 1964. He then filed an action in equity, asking for dissolution of the partnership, appointment of a receiver, and an accounting. Dissolution was ordered and a receiver appointed. After lengthy hearings on the issue of the accounting the chancellor decided that L. W., who was the brighter of the two and who kept the partnership books, had diverted partnership funds. The chancellor awarded Charles a one-half interest in several pieces of property owned by L. W. and in several insurance policies on L. W.'s life on the ground that these had been purchased with partnership assets.

. . .

The court . . . then heard the case and reversed the chancellor's decree in several material respects. The reversal was grounded on two propositions: that Charles' recovery could only be premised on a showing of fraud and that this burden was not met, and that the doctrine of laches foreclosed Charles' right to complain about the bulk of the alleged misdeeds. . . .

There is a fiduciary relationship between partners. Where such a relationship exists actual fraud need not be shown. There was ample evidence of self-dealing and diversion of partnership assets on the part of L. W.—more than enough to sustain the chancellor's conclusion that several substantial investments made by L. W. over the years were bankrolled with funds improperly withdrawn from the partnership. Further, we are of the opinion that the doctrine of laches is inapplicable because Charles' delay in asserting his rights was as much a product of L. W.'s concealment and misbehavior as of any negligence on his part. In all this we are strongly motivated by the fact that the chancellor saw and heard the various witnesses for exhausting periods of time and was in a much better position than we could ever hope to be to taste the flavor of the testimony.

The Act of 1915, March 26, P.L. 18, part IV, § 21, 59 P.S. § 54, very simply and unambiguously provides that partners owe a fiduciary duty one to another. One should not have to deal with his partner as though he were the opposite party in an arms-length transaction. One should be allowed to trust his partner, to expect that he is pursuing a common

goal and not working at cross-purposes. This concept of the partnership entity was expressed most ably by Mr. Justice, then Judge, Cardozo in *Meinhard* v. *Salmon*, . . .

> Joint adventurers, like co-partners, owe to one another, while the enterprise continues, the duty of the finest loyalty. Many forms of conduct permissible in a workaday world for those acting at arm's length are forbidden to those bound by fiduciary ties. A trustee is held to something stricter than the morals of the marketplace. Not honesty alone, but the punctilio of an honor the most sensitive, is then the standard of behavior. As to this there has developed a tradition that is unbending and inveterate. Uncompromising rigidity has been the attitude of courts of equity when petitioned to undermine the rule of undivided loyalty by the 'disintegrating erosion' of particular exceptions. . . . Only thus has the level of conduct for fiduciaries been kept at a level higher than that trodden by the crowd. It will not consciously be lowered by any judgment of this court. 164 N.E. 545, 547 (1928).

It would be unduly harsh to require that one must prove actual fraud before he can recover for a partner's derelictions. Where one partner has so dealt with the partnership as to raise the probability of wrongdoing it ought to be his responsibility to negate that inference. It has been held that "where a partner fails to keep a record of partnership transactions, and is unable to account for them, every presumption will be made against him." *Bracht* v. *Connell*, . . . Likewise, where a partner co-mingles partnership funds with his own and generally deals loosely with partnership assets he ought to have to shoulder the task of demonstrating the probity of his conduct.

In the instant case L. W. dealt loosely with partnership funds. At various times he made substantial investments in his own name. He was totally unable to explain where he got the funds to make these investments. The court . . . held that Charles had no claim on the fruits of these investments because he could not trace the money that was invested therein dollar for dollar from the partnership. Charles should not have had this burden. He did show that his brother had diverted substantial sums from the partnership funds under his control. The inference that these funds provided L. W. with the wherewithall to make his investments was a perfectly reasonable one for the chancellor to make and his decision should have been allowed to stand.

The doctrine of laches has no role to play in the decision of this case. It is true that the transactions complained of cover a period of many years. However, we do not think that it can be said that Charles negligently slept on his rights to the detriment of his brother. L. W. actively concealed much of his wrongdoing. He cannot now rely upon the doctrine of laches—that defense was not intended to reward the successful wrongdoer.

The decree is vacated and the case remanded for further proceedings consistent with this opinion.

EAGEN, *Justice (dissenting)*

In 1923, L. W. Clement and his younger brother, Charles, formed a partnership for the purpose of engaging in the plumbing business under the name of Clement Brothers. They agreed to share the profits of the business equally after payment of the debts. L. W. was the more alert and aggressive of the two. He attended special training schools to upgrade his plumbing skills, and became a master plumber. He alone conducted the business here involved, and had complete control of its finances. He frequently worked nights, Sundays and holidays. Charles, on the other hand, refused to be "bothered" with the administra-

tion of the business or its finances. He insisted also on limiting his work to a regular eight-hour shift and confining his contribution to the business to the performance of various plumbing jobs assigned to him.

Over the years, L. W. accumulated assets which eventually became quite valuable. For instance, in 1945 he purchased two lots of land for $5500, and subsequently constructed a commercial building thereon. This construction was financed in most part by money secured through placing a mortgage on the property. In 1951 he purchased another piece of real estate for $3500, and in 1927, 1936, 1938, 1945, 1947, 1955, and 1965 purchased policies of life insurance on his own life. There are presently existing substantial loans against some of these policies.

In 1964, Charles for the first time accused his brother, L. W., of misusing partnership funds to gain the assets he had accumulated. Charles did not have any evidence to substantiate the accusation, but surmised something must be wrong since L. W. had so much while he had so little.

At trial, not a scintilla of evidence was introduced to establish that L. W. diverted any partnership funds to purchase any of his personal assets. In view of this, a majority of the court . . . below ruled that Charles failed to establish that he had any interest or property rights therein. With this I agree. The majority of this Court now rule, in effect, that, because of the fiduciary relationship existing, it is L. W.'s burden to prove that he did not misuse partnership funds. This I cannot accept. . . .

I dissent and would affirm the decree of the court below.

Case Questions   1. Under what circumstances will a court hold that there is sufficient evidence of a breach of a partner's fiduciary duty so that the issue of liability is one for the jury?

2. The doctrine of laches precludes a party from recovering when the party has not pursued his remedies in a timely manner. Why was not this doctrine properly asserted by the defendant in this case?

Joint Ventures

A joint venture, or joint adventure as it is sometimes called, is a business organization similar to a partnership except that it is more narrow in purpose. Usually a joint venture is formed for a single undertaking or a series of related undertakings of fairly short duration that might not involve the complete attention of the members.[12] It is a form of partnership, and the members and the organization are subject to the UPA and the court interpretations thereof.

One of the most significant reasons for distinguishing between a partnership and a joint venture is that in the few states that prohibit corporations from being general partners, courts are likely to allow them to be participants in a joint venture. This exception is based on the premise that becoming a participant in a joint venture requires less delegation of managerial authority from the board of directors to the joint ventures than participating in a general partnership requires.[13] This premise arises because of the limited nature of joint ventures.

Today, it is common for large corporations to explore new markets or ideas by forming a joint venture with another organization that may provide either expertise, capital, access to markets, or similar advantages. This may be accomplished by forming a jointly owned subsidiary that is incorporated. If the venture is risky, this method has the advantage of limiting the liability of the coventurers to the amount of capital contributed to the subsidiary.

However, this method has the disadvantage of creating the potential for a breach of the fiduciary relationship that exists between coventurers. All of the same fiduciary duties that apply to partnerships also apply to coventurers, including the duty to render true and full information. If the coventurers are engaged in similar business activities, there is, first of all, the potential for an antitrust violation (Section 1 of the Sherman Act prohibits combinations and conspiracies—by competitors—that could be restraints of trade); and, second, the probability that the nature of the joint venture would cause the coventurers to have to choose between breaching the duty to disclose or disclosing trade secrets or related information in order to achieve the purposes of the joint enterprise.[14] The matter of disclosure of information should be raised to the level of explicit understanding in the joint venture agreement.

Limited Partnerships

A limited partnership, in contrast to a joint venture and partnership, is a distinctly different form of organization. The chief distinguishing fea-

Other Forms of Partnerships

tures are in the formation and the nature of the liability of the limited partner. Limited partnerships, like corporations, can exist only where state legislatures have passed statutes providing for their formation. For this purpose, the National Conference of Commissioners on Uniform State Laws drafted the Uniform Limited Partnership Act (ULPA), which has been passed by almost all of the states since the original act was first adopted in 1916. This act was substantially revised in 1976. Very few states have adopted the revisions, because the IRS waited to give approval to some aspects of the revised act. The revised act has now been approved and widespread adoption is expected.[15] However, for purposes of this text we were faced with a dilemma. Should we discuss the older ULPA adopted and in force in most states or discuss the 1976 revised version of the UPLA—referred to by some people as the RUPLA? We have compromised. References in this text section are to the older UPLA (selected portions of which are in the appendix at the end of the book) with reference to the RUPLA where it varies substantially. Selected portions of the 1976 RUPLA are also in the appendix.

The ULPA § 1 defines a limited partnership as:

> . . . a partnership formed by two or more persons under the provisions of § 2, having as members one or more general partners and one or more limited partners.

Filing Requirement.   A limited partnership is a form of partnership, and unless the ULPA in a specific section says differently, partnership law applies. The ULPA does depart from partnership law in at least two important respects. First, Section 2 of the ULPA requires that the persons desiring to form a limited partnership sign an agreement that states, among other things:

1. The name, character, and location of the business, and the name and residence of each member including the limited partner.
2. The term of the partnership and contributions of the limited partner.
3. The right of a limited partner to withdraw or the right to add additional limited partners.

This agreement must be filed with the Secretary of State where the limited partnership does business. The reason for the filing is to make public, especially to potential creditors, the limited nature of the liability of the limited partners.

Control by a Limited Partner.   The second, and perhaps more drastic departure from partnership law is that provided by the ULPA, § 7:

> A limited partner shall not become liable as a general partner unless, in addition to the exercise of his rights and powers as a limited partner, he takes part in the control of the business.

This section is the key to understanding the differences between a limited partnership and a partnership. The next chapter explains in detail that partners are individually liable for the debts of the partnership. A limited partner is not liable beyond the amount of the contribution or that amount promised as a contribution to the firm. In one sense, then, the "limited" aspect of the partnership applies to the liability of the limited partner.

The second part of Section 7 above reveals that this limited liability may be lost if the limited partner takes control of the business. The ULPA does not define the word control, so case law must be relied on. In an important early case, two limited partners in a commercial farm were held liable (as general partners) to creditors of the business when they (1) determined in consultation with the general partner what crops should be put in; (2) visited the farm twice a week; (3) asked for and received the resignation of the general partner; and (4) could, by asking the other limited partner to countersign the checks, completely control the funds of the partnership.[16] Although the holding of this case would appear to clarify the issue of control, the ULPA further complicated the matter by providing that the following powers may be exercised by a limited partner:

1. The power to advise the general partners.

2. The power to elect or remove a general partner.

3. The power to terminate the partnership.

4. The power to amend the partnership agreement.

5. The power to veto a sale of all or substantially all the partnership assets.

6. The power to serve in the employ of the partnership.[17]

Moreover, Section 12 of the ULPA provides in part:

A person may be a general partner and a limited partner at the same time.

The uncertainty regarding the issue of control, and, thus, the crucial issue of liability for a limited partner, is probably the greatest drawback of the limited partnership form.[18]

The 1976 revision to the ULPA attempts to address this uncertainty by giving more protection to limited partners. We cannot say at this point what version of the revisions will be adopted by the states, but we can note that the general idea in the revisions is to remove the limited liability of a "limited" partner only when a third party has been misled and has relied to its detriment on the status of the limited partner. That is, if a third party has been caused to believe to its detriment that a limited partner is a general partner because of an apparent exercise of control, then courts should disregard the limited liability of the alleged limited partner.[19]

Limited Partnership with Corporate General Partner.   The advantage of the limited partnership form over the corporate form of organization is that the double federal income taxation of the corporate organization is avoided. A limited partnership is taxed as a partnership, and this has the advantage of allowing general and limited partners to pass through to themselves on a pro rata basis not only the income from the enterprise but fairly large writeoffs through accelerated depreciation.[20] So, for some commercial tasks it is desirable to have both the limited liability feature and the income tax advantage of the limited partnership form. Entrepreneurs have found that one way to take advantage of these tax advantages while at the same time limiting liability of the general partner is to list themselves as individual limited partners and to incorporate the one general partner. Recall that Section 1 of the ULPA requires at least one general partner. For example, if a group of five persons wanted to undertake a commercial venture, they could form a limited partnership with each of them as a limited partner and then incorporate, say the X, Y, Z Corporation, as the general partner with each person serving on the board of directors. (See Figure 7-2) The corporation would be liable as the general partner, but this liability would be limited to amounts contributed to the corporation or promised to it. The question then becomes, does this somehow violate the "control" limitation put on limited partners?

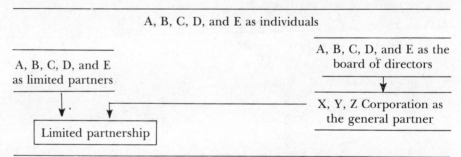

FIGURE 7-2

The courts have viewed this in one of two ways. The Texas Supreme Court has held that limited partners cannot escape personal liability when they exercise control of the limited partnership by incorporating the general partner and electing themselves as board members and officers.[21] In this case, a lease was signed by the corporate general partner, and the limited partners were held liable. This decision has been criticized because the thrust of the ULPA, and especially the 1976 revisions, is toward holding limited partners liable only where the injured third party was misled by a limited partner to believe the limited partner was a general partner.

The Washington Supreme Court has reached the opposite result, holding that limited partners who form a corporation to control the limited partnership are not liable to limited partnership creditors.[22] In this case, the court rejected or certainly minimized the "control" test in favor of a "reliance" test. It held that the dominant consideration in imposing personal liability on a limited partner is not the exercise of control by the limited partner, but the plaintiff's reliance on the appearance of general partnership status that may be created by the exercise of control.[23] The court reasoned that the limited liability of the corporate form could be pierced if there were any abuse of that form of enterprise such as under-capitalization or fraud. The more modern trend is to favor the result of the latter case, but this issue of limited partners controlling a limited partnership through incorporation is not settled.

The opposite holding of these two cases on similar facts highlights the differences between a formal and a nonformal rule.[24] A formal rule such as that adopted by the Texas court has the advantage of ease of judicial administration and certainty for planners and litigants. A nonformal rule in which courts are required to inquire into the equities of a case (Such as, was the third party misled by any representation of the limited partner?) has the advantage of flexibility for the courts, and decreased certainty for planners and litigants.

If limited partners want to control the enterprise through participation in a corporate general partner, the best advice is to avoid the appearance of undercapitalizing the corporation and to make sure the third parties dealt with realize they are dealing with a corporation as a general partner.

Other Legal Characteristics of a Limited Partnership.   The rights and liabilities of the general partner and the limited partners are determined by partnership law except to the extent that the ULPA or the limited partnership certificate change it.

The general partner or partners cannot admit other general partners without the approval of all of the limited partners, and may admit other limited partners only if the right is given in the certificate. The limited partners have a right to bring a derivative action (this is defined and discussed in the chapter on corporation law) for the benefit of the limited partnership and may, where appropriate, sue for an accounting of partnership affairs.

A requirement of the Revised Uniform Limited Partnership Act (RULPA) is that every limited partnership must use the term "limited partnership" without abbreviation as part of the partnership name.

Dissolution of a Limited Partnership.   The death or bankruptcy of a limited partner does not result in a dissolution of the partnership. Technically, the death or bankruptcy of a partner in a partnership does result in a dissolution. Also, if the general partner withdraws from the limited partnership (because of retirement or death, for example), the partnership is dissolved unless the right to continue is expressed in the certificate. The process of dissolution and the distribution of assets to the remaining partners is substantially similar (with a few exceptions) to that of a partnership. This will be explained in the following chapter.

Review Problems

1. On examining the books of account of Madison, Bradley, South & Tilson, a general partnership, you ascertain that South is in financial difficulty. He is not insolvent but has been forced to assign 90 percent of his partnership interest to his largest creditor in order to forestall legal action by the creditor. The creditor in question is particularly obnoxious and undesirable in the eyes of the other partners.

   Discuss the legal implications to the partnership, the partners, and South's creditor resulting from the above-mentioned assignment. In particular, discuss the rights of each and their relationship to one another and the partnership. (This is adapted from CPA Exam Question #6a, Business Law, taken from the May 7, 1976, exam. © American Institute of Certified Public Accountants, Inc., 1976.)

2. P went to C and told him that he had contracted for about two carloads of hogs to be delivered the next day, and he did not have the money to pay for them. P asked C to advance the money to him and take an ownership interest in the hogs in return. C refused this. P then proposed that if C would let him have the money to pay for the hogs he had bought and others he might have to buy to make two carloads, he (C) could have a security interest in the hogs that would enable C to take the hogs and sell them to repay the money advanced. In addition, C would receive half of the profits of the sale of the hogs to repay him for the risk he was taking; and in no event should C sustain any loss. C accepted this proposition and advanced $2500 to P. Shortly thereafter P bought the hogs from H on his own credit. The hogs could not be sold at a profit. C took possession of the hogs and had them sold. P still owed money to C since the sale price of the hogs did not cover the amount of the advance and P paid to C this deficiency. Meanwhile H was not paid by P for the hogs. H sues C as a partner. Was there a partnership? (*Harvey* v. *Childs,* 28 Ohio St. 319).

3. B leased land from F on which he conducted the business of a fruit farm and nursery for a period of six years. P sold fruit trees to B and received documents from time to time signed "F & B," indicating joint ownership. P also proved that advertisements for "F & B" were published in newspapers in F's area over a three-month period. B prepared and paid for these advertisements without F's consent, but F did have knowledge of them. P was not paid for the trees and B dies. P sues F as a partner of B's. F defends alleging that he merely leased some land to B and that he had no knowledge that the documents

showing a "F & B" enterprise existed and that he did not know of the advertisements until he read them in the newspaper and at that time instructed B never to do it again. Should P's cause of action be sustained? (*Flectheer* v. *Pullen*, 70 Md. 205, 16A. 887, 1889).

4. S was a young college grad who returned to his hometown to start his own business. He had never been exceptionally bright and was relatively unknown compared with his father (F), who was the recently retired football coach of the local high school. S founded a small insurance business and, with his father's permission, called it, "F & Son Insurance." As between F and S it was agreed S was the owner and would make all decisions in the business. F was employed from time to time to greet potential business clients and to seek out business in the community. He was paid a straight hourly wage for this and only worked a few days each week. When S was purchasing office furniture from P, P came to S's place of business, recognized F who happened to be there, and, primarily on the strength of F's reputation in the community as a leader and a man of his word, sold on credit $5,000 worth of furniture to "F and Son Insurance" with S signing the purchase agreement. Later S defaults. Does P have a remedy against F? Explain fully.

5. A, B, and C agree to form a business organization in which the net profits are to be split evenly. A is exceptionally bright but financially without a cent so he agrees to contribute his technical knowledge and labor, which will be used in the production phase of the business. The purpose of the business will be to develop new applications of plastic (PVC) to metal surfaces to reduce friction in fast-moving, heavy industrial machines.

    B, who is very wealthy, agrees to contribute $15,000 but will not take part in the day-to-day operation of the business. She will, however, be available to consult and vote in important managerial decisions.

    C agrees to contribute $5,000 and to work in the marketing phase of the business and will be primarily responsible for keeping the books, placing orders for suppliers, and developing new markets for their product.

    The organization becomes mildly successful. They acquire, in the firm name, "A,B,C and Associates," a small plant, several expensive materials-handling machines, and about 15 employees. One of the employees, D, is very responsible and gradually becomes a favored employee directly responsible to C. Although C was never given the actual authority to contract for the firm, C allows him to negotiate, on a preliminary basis only, some matters for the firm. In one instance, C and D were negotiating with E, with D doing most of the talking. C was called out of the meeting and shortly thereafter D initiated an agreement with E for the benefit of the firm. C was later told of this and did not object. A and B were never aware of D's representations.

Although A was a smart technician he was a very poor businessman, especially regarding his own personal affairs. He overextended himself in purchasing new home furnishings, rugs, and drapes, and was unable to pay for them when the balances became due. The seller of the furnishings, J, obtained a judgment against A that has remained uncollected.

B also suffered a severe shortage of cash. He figures since he contributed more money than the other partners he was entitled to a return on the investment in lieu of interest. He wrote a check on partnership funds for a motorcycle he needed and took title in his own name.

In a carefully worded essay describe the rights, if any, of E, J, and the partnership.

6. P and D were partners who operated a tavern in a good location of town. The partnership leased the building in which the business was conducted, and this lease expired on the same day that the partners had agreed to terminate their partnership. The partnership had spent a relatively large sum on improving the property during the life of the lease. Over one year before the expiration of the lease, D went to the owner of the property and obtained a lease in his own name to begin when the present lease and partnership were terminated. P learns of this and sues D in an attempt to have the lease declared partnership property. What breach of duty, if any, is the basis for the cause of action? Will P succeed?

7. Elwynn, Mitchell, and Grady formed a partnership to assemble and market lamps. After renting delivery trucks for several years the partnership was able to accumulate sufficient cash to purchase three delivery trucks. The title to the trucks was placed in the partnership name. Six months after the trucks were purchased, Grady sold one of the trucks and retained the proceeds on the basis that one of the three trucks belonged to him. The other partners disagreed and sought to regain title to the truck from the buyer or recover the proceeds from Grady.

    (a) Discuss the distinction between "partnership property" and a "partnership interest." Include in your discussion reasons for the legal importance of the distinction.

    (b) Under what circumstances will the partnership succeed in regaining title to the truck from the buyer?

    (c) If the partnership does not regain title to the truck from the buyer, may it recover the proceeds from Grady?

(This is adapted from CPA Exam Question #5a, Business Law, taken from the May 1977 exam. © American Institute of Certified Public Acountants, Inc., 1977.)

8. The Minlow, Richard, and Jones partnership agreement is silent on whether the partners may assign or otherwise transfer all or part of their partnership interests to an outsider. Richard has assigned his partnership interest to Smith, a personal creditor, and as a result the other partners are furious. They have threatened to remove Richard as a partner, not admit Smith as a partner, and bar Smith from access to the firm's books and records.

   Can Minlow and Jones successfully implement their threats? Discuss the rights of Richard and Smith and the effects of the assignment on the partnership.

(This is adapted from CPA Exam Question #5b, Business Law, taken from the May 1977 exam. © American Institute of Certified Public Accountants, Inc., 1977.)

9. Fletcher, Dry, Wilbert, and Cox selected the limited partnership as the form of business entity most suitable for their purpose of investing in mineral leases. Fletcher, the general partner, contributed $50,000 in capital. Dry, Wilbert, and Cox each contributed $100,000 capital and are limited partners. Necessary limited-partnership papers were duly prepared and filed clearly indicating that Fletcher was the sole general partner and that the others were limited partners.

   Fletcher managed the partnership during the first two years. During the third year, Dry and Wilbert overruled Fletcher as to the type of investments to be made, the extent of the commitments, and the major terms contained in the leases. They also exercised the power to draw checks on the firm's bank account. Finally, Fletcher withdrew and was replaced by Martin, a new and more receptive general partner. Cox did not join his fellow partners in these activities. However, his name was used without qualification and with his general knowledge and consent on the partnership stationery as part of the firm's name.

   Discuss the legal liability of Martin, Dry, Wilbert, and Cox, as individuals, to creditors of the partnership.

(This is adapted from CPA Exam Question #6b, Business Law, taken from the May 7, 1976 exam. © American Institute of Certified Public Accountants, Inc., 1976.)

10. In the question above, assume that Fletcher, Dry, Wilbert, and Cox form a corporation to be the general partner in their limited partnership. They each contribute $10,000 to the corporation in exchange for voting stock. They elect themselves to board membership and then appoint themselves officers of the corporation. After receiving a loan of $500,000 from X, Y, Z Bank, the limited partnership soon defaults. The amount owed to X, Y, Z exceeds the fair market value of the assets of the limited partnership and the corporate general partner. Discuss the remedies of X, Y, Z.

Endnotes

1. 6 *Uniform Laws Annot.*, Master Edition, p. iii; and see Mann and Roberts, *Unincorporated Business Associations: An Overview of their Advantages and Disadvantages*, 14 Tulsa L.J. 1 (1978).

2. J. Crane and A. Bromberg, *Law of Partnership*, p. 26, (1968).

3. *Ibid.*, pp. 52–54.

4. *Ibid.*, p. 48.

5. *Martin* v. *Peyton*, 246 N.Y. 213, 158 N.E. 77 (1927), analyzed in Mann, *supra*, pp. 5–6.

6. *Minute Maid Corp.* v. *United Foods, Inc.*, 291 F.2d 577 (5th Cir.), analyzed in Mann, *supra*, pp. 6–7.

7. Crane, *supra*, pp. 244–245.

8. See, "UPA Section 18(h): Majority Control, Dissenting Partners, and the Need for Reform," 13 Univ. of Calif., Davis, L. Rev. 903 (1980).

9. *McCallum* v. *Ashbury*, 238 Or. 257, 393 P.2d 774 (1964).

10. See, "The Expulsion Clause in a Partnership Agreement: A Preplanned Dissolution." 13 Univ. of Calif., Davis L. Rev., 868 (1980).

11. Mann, *supra*, pp. 10–18.

12. Crane, *supra*, p. 189.

13. *Ibid.*, p. 195.

14. See, for example, Mann, *supra*, p. 27.

15. O'Neal, "Comments on Recent Developments in Limited Partnership Law," Wash. Univ. L.Q. 669 (Fall, 1978).

16. *Halzman* v. *De Escamilla*, 86 Cal. App. 2d 858; 195 P.2d 833 (1948).

17. These are enumerated in Mann, *supra*, p. 32, and O'Neal, *supra*, pp. 680–681.

18. Crane, *supra*, p. 147.

19. O'Neal, *supra*, p. 681.

20. *Ibid.*, p. 689.

21. *Delaney* v. *Fidelity Lease Ltd.*, 526 S.W. 2d 543 (1975).

22. *Frigidaire Sales Corp.* v. *Union Properties, Inc.*, 88 Wn. 2d 400; 562 P.2d 244 (1977).

23. These two cases are analyzed in a Note, "Limited Partnership-Limited Control Through a Corporate General Partner," 53 Wash. L. Rev. 775 (1978).

24. *Ibid.*, p. 780.

Partnership Operation and Dissolution

8

In presenting the material on the liability of the partnership and partners to third parties we again believe it is convenient to divide this liability into two kinds: contract and tort liability. The law of agency is applicable to partnerships, and conflicts between the partners themselves and the partnership on the one hand, and third parties on the other, are resolved by a direct application of the same principles discussed in the chapters on agency law.

When a partner contracts on partnership business the partnership is the principal and the partner or partners acting for it are the agents. An agent will bind his or her principal contractually when the agent has the actual or circumstantial authority to act. This is expressed by Section 9 of the UPA as follows:

> Every partner is an agent of the partnership for the purpose of its business, and the act of every partner, . . . for apparently carrying on in the usual way the business of the partnership . . . binds the partnership. . . .

The articles of partnership usually state the actual authority the partners are granted. This may include the right to do any business act that may be the subject of lawful delegation of authority. In addition agents have the circumstantial authority to act in carrying on the business in the usual way. This circumstantial authority is defined by considering the business purpose or nature of the partnership, the ordinary usages and methods in which similar businesses are conducted, and the reasonable expectations of third parties. According to Section 9(3) of the UPA, this authority *does not* include extraordinary acts such as assigning partnership property in trust for creditors, disposing of the firm's good will, confessing a judgment or submitting a partnership claim to arbitration, or doing any other act that would make it impossible to carry on the ordinary business of the partnership.

Trading and Nontrading Partnerships: The Traditional Approach

Case law has developed a useful analytical device for establishing liability of the partnership when the evidence shows that no express authority existed. In cases involving the borrowing of money and the executing of negotiable instruments, some courts recognize a distinction between trading and nontrading partnerships. A trading partnership is one organized primarily to buy and sell property for profit. Those partnerships organized primarily to offer a service and in which the passage of title to property *is not* the central means of making a profit are nontrading partnerships. The latter include professional partnerships (such as doctors, lawyers, and accountants) and partnerships formed to provide a service such as to operate theatres or sell insurance. If the partnership is a trading partnership, some courts will presume that implied or circumstantial authority to obligate the partnership on a loan or other negotiable instrument exists. If the partnership is a nontrading one, some courts may require actual authority for a partner to bind the partnership on loan obligations or other negotiable instruments.

Agency Analysis: The Modern Approach

Whether this distinction should be used by most courts today is questionable.[1] With the growing diversity of activities of a single organization and the increasing variety of financing methods, this rather simplistic approach to establishing implied or circumstantial authority may not be useful. Furthermore, one may question the logical connection between buying and selling, and borrowing. The best approach is to treat the partnership as the principal, the contracting partner as the agent, the other contracting party as the "third party" and then search the facts for evidence of actual or circumstantial authority, estoppel, or ratification as those terms were defined and used in Chapter 4.

In addition to the types of authority mentioned above, a partnership may also be bound by any knowledge or notice communicated to a partner relating to partnership affairs. (UPA § 12)

The case that follows reveals how complex the issue of authority can become when a partnership apparently engages in several types of business.

HODGE v. *GARRETT*
101 Idaho 397; 614 P2d 420 (S. Ct., Idaho, 1980)

Hodge and defendant-appellant Rex E. Voeller, the managing partner of the Pay-Ont Drive-In Theatre, signed a contract for the sale of a small parcel of land belonging to the partnership. That parcel, although adjacent to the theater, was not used in theater operations except insofar as the east 20 feet were necessary for the operation of the theater's driveway. The agreement for the sale of land stated that it was between Hodge and the Pay-Ont Drive-In Theatre, a partnership. Voeller signed the agreement for the partnership, and written changes as to the footage and price were initialed by Voeller.

. . .

The trial court found that Voeller had actual and apparent authority to execute the contract on behalf of the partnership, and that the contract should be specifically enforced. The partners of the Pay-Ont Drive-In Theatre appeal, arguing that Voeller did not have authority to sell the property and that Hodge knew that he did not have that authority.

At common law one partner could not, "without the concurrence of his copartners, convey away the real estate of the partnership, bind his partners by a deed, or transfer the title and interest of his copartners in the firm real estate.". . . This rule was changed by the adoption of the Uniform Partnership Act. The relevant provisions are as follows:

> Every partner is an agent of the partnership for the purpose of its business, and the act of every partner, including the execution in the partnership name of any instrument, for apparently carrying on in the usual way the business of the partnership of which he is a member binds the partnership, unless the partner so acting has in fact no authority to act for the partnership in the particular matter, and the person with whom he is dealing has knowledge of the fact that he has no such authority.

Thus this contract is enforceable if Voeller had the actual authority to sell the property, or, even if Voeller did not have such authority, the contract is still enforceable if the sale was in the usual way of carrying on the business and Hodge did not know that Voeller did not have this authority.

As to the question of actual authority, such authority must affirmatively appear, "for the authority of one partner to make and acknowledge a deed for the firm will not be presumed . . . ." Although such authority may be implied from the nature of the business, or from similar past transactions, nothing in the record in this case indicates that Voeller had express or implied authority to sell real property belonging to the partnership. There is no evidence that Voeller had sold property belonging to the partnership in the past, and obviously the partnership was not engaged in the business of buying and selling real estate.

The next question, since actual authority has not been shown, is whether Voeller was conducting the partnership business in the usual way in selling the parcel of land, . . . i.e., whether Voeller had apparent authority. Here the evidence showed, and the trial court found:

. . .

> That at the inception of the partnership, and at all times thereafter, Rex E. Voeller was the exclusive, managing partner of the partnership and had the full authority to make all decisions pertaining to the partnership affairs, including paying the bills, preparing profit and loss statements, income tax returns and the ordering of any goods or services necessary to the operation of the business.

The court made no finding that it was customary for Voeller to sell real property, or even personal property, belonging to the partnership. Nor was there any evidence to this effect. Nor did the court discuss whether it was in the usual course of business for the managing partner of a theater to sell real property. Yet the trial court found that Voeller had apparent authority to sell the property. From this it must be inferred that the trial court believed it to be in the usual course of business for a partner who has exclusive control of the partnership business to sell real property belonging to the partnership, where that property is not being used in the partnership business. We cannot agree with this conclusion. For a theater, "carrying on in the usual way the business of the partnership," means running the operations of the theater; it does not mean selling a parcel of property adjacent to the theater. Here the contract of sale stated that the land belonged to the partnership, and, even if Hodge believed that Voeller as the exclusive manager had authority to transact all business for the firm, Voeller still could not bind the partnership through a unilateral act which was not in the usual business of the partnership. We therefore hold that the trial court erred in holding that this contract was binding on the partnership.

Judgment reversed. Costs to appellant.

. . .

SHEPARD, Justice, dissenting.

The majority, and I am sure inadvertently, neglects to include certain uncontroverted facts. . . . Some considerable time elapsed between the signing of the instrument and the decision of Voeller not to honor the contract on behalf of the partnership. During that period of time, Hodge was placed in possession of the property in question, made extensive improvements thereon, including the placement of a commercial office structure thereon which Hodge rented to a third party for the sum of $75.00 per month. . . . The majority's reversal with directions to enter judgment for the defendant effectively prevents Hodge from ever recovering any of his uncontroverted damages resulting from Voeller's breach of the contract.

It should be remembered that Voeller clearly admitted the execution of the contract of sale on behalf of the partnership. Such was not denied by the other partners, who in fact counterclaimed against Voeller for the damages the partnership might sustain by reason of the sale. It is uncontroverted that, as Hodge stated, the property involved has undergone an enormous increase in value since the execution of the contract. Undoubtedly, the trial court viewed the defense protestations of Voeller's lack of authority in that light. Indeed, Voeller testified that the sole reason the transaction was not consummated was that he later came to believe that such a sale would amount to a subdivision of the theatre property and hence result in the partnership property being brought into the city limits with a resultant increase in taxes.

. . .

Contrary to the assertions of the majority, the record reveals that the partnership had not too long before the instant transaction sold real estate in Emmett, including the entire theatre business located thereon.

I am indeed startled at the following assertion of the majority: "and obviously the partnership was not engaged in the business of buying and selling real estate." The murky and complicated history of the partnership clearly demonstrates to the contrary. As revealed in the record, what had been originally partnership property (such as three theatres in Burley, Idaho) had been somehow converted into corporate assets. . . . However, the record is clear that the partnership did purchase real property, that the partnership did sell real property, and that Voeller himself, on behalf of the partnership, engaged in the rental of property to other persons, including the leasing of the theatre operation in Lovelock, Nevada. On the basis of the above, I cannot agree with the majority's characterization of this partnership, but again would agree with the trial judge in his undoubted conclusion, albeit unstated, that the partnership failed to carry its burden of proof that the transaction in question here was outside the authority of Voeller and outside the usual and ordinary course of business of the partnership.

1. Reread Section 9 of the UPA and apply it to the facts of this case. Do you agree with the majority or the dissent? Why? Exactly how many land transactions are needed to establish a *usual* way of doing business?
2. Given what the dissenting judge points out about the improvement of the land sold, would you agree that the principle of estoppel should have been used against the position of the partnership?

The liability of a partnership to damaged third parties for the tortious acts of a partner is based on the same reasoning that supports the doctrine of respondeat superior in agency law. The principle of a partnership's vicarious liability is clearly stated by the UPA § 13:

> Where, by any wrongful act or omission of any partner acting in the ordinary course of the business of the partnership or with the authority of his copartners, loss or injury is caused to any person, not being a partner in the partnership, or any penalty is incurred the partnership is liable therefor to the same extent as the partner so acting or omitting to act.

Master-Servant Analysis

In the above provision, the key words are "acting in the ordinary course of business of the partnership or with the authority of his copartners. . . ." The basic issue then is whether the tort was within the ordinary course of business or authorized. In defining the ordinary course of business, some courts have hesitated to use the control test provided by the master-servant type of analysis of agency law because they believe that a partner who has, usually, as much management authority as every other partner cannot be a servant. Of course, an *employee* of a partnership may be a servant if the control test is met.

Principal-Nonservant Agent Analysis

Generally the tort liability of a partnership is established by using the same kind of analysis as used by courts in establishing the tort liability of a principal for the torts of a nonservant agent. In the agency material we stated that the principal is liable for the torts of a nonservant agent when the tort was committed within the inherent scope of the agency. As applied to partnership law this means that the tort must have occurred while furthering the *very purpose* of the partnership. Torts committed by a partner *incidental* to the partnership purpose do not usually create liability for the partnership.

In the case that follows, the court first uses this typical two-step analysis suggested by Section 13 of the UPA:

1. Was the wrongful conduct in the ordinary course of partnership business?

2. Was the wrongful conduct authorized somehow by the partnership?

Then the court, without specific reference to a negligent act by a partner, seems to suggest that the partnership itself could be negligent by its failure to act. This approach goes beyond what Section 13 seems to require to create a duty on the partnership as a whole to act prudently.

KELSEY-SEYBOLD CLINIC v. *MACLAY*
466 S.W. 2d 716 (S. Ct., Texas, 1971)

WALKER, Justice

This is a suit for alienation of affections in which the trial court rendered summary judgment for one of the defendants, Kelsey-Seybold Clinic, a medical partnership. (The Court of Civil Appeals . . . reversed . . . and the partnership petitioned for review.) The question to be decided is whether the Clinic established conclusively that it is not liable for the damages alleged to have been caused by the acts of one of the partners. . . .

Plaintiff alleged that Dr. Brewer and the Clinic had treated him, his wife and their children for several years; that Dr. Brewer, who is a pediatrician and one of the partners in the Clinic, was the doctor to whom his wife had taken their children; that beginning in late 1966, Dr. Brewer conceived and entered into a scheme to alienate the affections of plaintiff's wife, Mrs. Maria Maclay; that he showered his attentions and gifts upon her until April or May, 1967, when her affections were alienated as a direct result of his actions, causing her to separate from plaintiff on or about July 25, 1967.

Plaintiff further alleged that Dr. Brewer's actions designed to alienate Mrs. Maclay's affections occurred while he was acting as a medical doctor for plaintiff's family and in the course and scope of his employment as a partner in the Clinic; that various acts of undue familiarity occurred both on and off the premises of the Clinic; that prior to April, 1967, the Clinic, through Dr. Mavis Kelsey, one of the senior partners, had knowledge of Dr. Brewer's actions; that at the time this knowledge was acquired, the Clinic was providing medical treatment for plaintiff and his entire family; and that "the partnership approved of, consented to, and ratified and condoned such conduct of its partner, Brewer, and refused to come to the aid of your plaintiff or in any way attempt to halt or disapprove the actions of Brewer. . . ." Plaintiff prayed for the recovery of damages, both actual and exemplary, from Dr. Brewer and the Clinic, jointly and severally. . . .

At some time in the Spring of 1967, plaintiff complained to Dr. Kelsey that Dr. Brewer was having an affair with Mrs. Maclay. According to Dr. Kelsey's recollection of this conversation, plaintiff stated that he and his wife had separated. . . . Plaintiff did not ask him to do anything, and he had done nothing. He did not talk with Dr. Brewer about the matter until after this suit was filed. The witness did not believe that anything improper had occurred at the Clinic. If anyone had known of conduct such as that alleged by plaintiff, the partners "wouldn't put up with that." . . .

Plaintiff countered with an affidavit in which he stated that in his telephone conversation with Dr. Kelsey, he inquired whether the latter was aware that Dr. Brewer had a romantic interest or involvement with his wife. . . .

The bases of liability alleged in the petition are: (1) that Dr. Brewer's wrongful conduct was in the course and scope of the partnership business and was approved, consented to, ratified and condoned by the Clinic; and (2) that the Clinic, after notice of the alleged relationship between Dr. Brewer and Mrs. Maclay, failed to take any action. Plaintiff is thus relying upon the vicarious or partnership liability of the Clinic for the acts of one of the partners and also its liability for breach of a duty owing by the Clinic when it learned of Dr. Brewer's relationship with Mrs. Maclay. . . .

We assume for the purpose of this opinion that Dr. Brewer was not acting in the ordinary course of the Clinic's business and that his conduct was neither authorized nor ratified by the partnership. This will enable us to reach questions that may well arise at the trial of the case. . . .

We are unwilling to believe that plaintiff seriously expects to prove in a conventional trial that the acts alleged to have been committed by Dr. Brewer were in the course and scope of the partnership business or were either authorized or ratified by the Clinic.

The clinic was under a duty, of course, to exercise ordinary care to protect its patients from harm resulting from tortious conduct of persons upon the premises. A negligent breach of that duty could subject the Clinic to liability without regard to whether the tortious conduct immediately causing the harm was that of an agent or servant or was in the ordinary scope of the partnership business. For example, it might become liable, as a result of its own negligence, for damage done by a vicious employee while acting beyond the scope of his authority. . . .

We are also of the opinion that the Clinic owed a duty to the families of its patients to exercise ordinary care to prevent a tortious interference with family relations. It was not required to maintain constant surveillance over personnel on duty or to inquire into and regulate the personal conduct of partners and employees while engaged in their private affairs.

But if and when the partnership received information from which it knew or should have known that there might be a need to take action, it was under a duty to use reasonable means at its disposal to prevent any partner or employee from improperly using his position with the Clinic to work a tortious invasion of legally protected family interests. This duty relates only to conduct of a partner or employee on the premises of the Clinic or while purportedly acting as a representative of the Clinic elsewhere. Failure to exercise ordinary care in discharging that duty would subject the Clinic to liability for damages proximately caused by its negligence.

The rather meager information in the present record does not necessarily indicate that the Clinic was under a duty to act or that it could have done anything to prevent the damage when Dr. Kelsey first learned of the situation. On the other hand, it does not affirmatively and clearly appear that the Clinic could or should have done nothing. Mrs. Maclay's affections may have been alienated from her husband before anyone talked with Dr. Kelsey, but the facts in that respect are not fully developed. There is no proof as to when, where or under what circumstances the misconduct, if any, on Dr. Brewer's part occurred. Dr. Kelsey testified that he did not believe anything improper occurred at the Clinic, but the proofs do not establish as a matter of law that he was justified in not making further inquiry after his conversations with plaintiff. . . . The record does not show whether there is a partnership agreement that might have a bearing on the case, and we have no way of knowing the extent to which the Clinic might have determined which patients were to be seen by Dr. Brewer or controlled his actions while on duty. Dr. Kelsey's testimony suggests that the partners might have been in a position to prevent improper conduct by one of their number on the premises of the Clinic. In our opinion the Clinic has failed to discharge the heavy, and in a case of this character virtually impossible, burden of establishing as a matter of law at the summary judgment stage that it is not liable under any theory fairly presented by the allegations of the petition.

Judgment of Court of Civil Appeals affirmed.

GREENHILL, *Justice (dissenting).*

I am unable to agree that the partners of Dr. Brewer or the Kelsey Clinic are even potentially liable.

This suit was brought by a husband for the alienation of his wife's affections. . . .

The alleged acts involved here between Dr. Brewer and the plaintiff's wife were between consenting adults; and obviously, they were committed in secret. The majority opinion correctly finds that Dr. Brewer was acting solely for his own personal gratification; that his conduct could not benefit the clinic in any way; and it assumes that his conduct was neither authorized nor ratified by the partnership. The Uniform Partnership Act provides for liability of the partnership for wrongful acts of a partner "acting in the ordinary course of the business of the partnership. . . ." I find no such action here.

The tort of alienation of affection is not one which is universally accepted. It has been abolished in several states by legislative act.

It is not necessary here, in my opinion, to consider whether a cause of action for alienation of affection should be abolished because the suit against Dr. Brewer has been severed. But as I read the plaintiff's petition, his suit *is* one for alienation of affection; and the question is whether a cause of action for alienation of affection should be extended to each of the members of a partnership consisting of some 30 doctors, or 15 architects, or 60 lawyers, or any other type of partnership, where none of the partners are even alleged to have had anything to do with the conduct of the consenting adults involved.

The tort of alienation of affection is based on an intentional and malicious act of the defendant or defendants. It is not enough that the acts be the result of negligent conduct; i.e., as applicable here, that the other 29 partner-doctors of the Kelsey Clinic were negligent in not interfering.

In summary, as I read the pleadings and the depositions on file, there are no relevant issues of fact and no basis in law for holding the partners liable for the secret acts of a partner with a consenting adult completely outside of the business of the partnership. Negligent acts will not give rise to damages for alienation of affection, and the record, at least to me, completely negatives any intentional, malicious acts by any of the partners except Dr. Brewer, which could have been the controlling cause of the alienation of affection involved.

I would affirm the judgment of the trial court.

Case Questions

1. The issue before this appellate court was whether a motion for summary judgment made by the clinic would be proper. In answer to this question, what did the appellate court hold?

2. In a technical sense, there must be a negligent act by an agent for the principal to be liable based on the tort theory of respondeat superior. Where was the negligent act in this case (as the issues were presented to the appellate court)?

3. Is it not possible that the appellate court was hinting at the imposition of a form of strict liability in this case?

Partnership Liability for the Negligent
Operation of an Auto

An area of frequent litigation involves the liability of the partnership for the negligence of a partner when traveling by auto on partnership business. In this situation two facts are very important. The first is the ownership of the auto. If it is owned by the partnership and the partner is traveling on partnership business, liability for the partnership usually results. However, if the partner owns the auto and it is under the partner's control, and the trip is for partnership business, liability is usually determined by the second important fact, *the nature of the partnership*. While there is some conflict in the decisions in this area, we believe the best view is that unless the partnership inherently involves the delivery of goods and/or services (for example, the delivery of coal[2] or the providing of pinball repair service during the day or evening[3]), the partnership should not be held liable for the partner's negligence in the operation of an auto. This result is consistent with that of the often cited agency case of *Stockwell* v. *Morris* reproduced in the agency materials.

In the case of professional partnership such as attorneys' physicians, accountants, etc., it has been suggested that no partnership liability results when a partner negligently drives his or her own car when traveling from one business site to another.[4]

Tort liability of a partnership is treated differently procedurally from contract liability. Section 15 of the UPA provides that partners are jointly and severally liable for all wrongful acts and omissions and breaches of trust, but only jointly liable for all contractual debts. Joint and several liability means that as a procedural matter, any partner may be sued alone for the tortious acts of another partner and the other partners need not be joined. A judgment against any one partner, if it remains uncollected, is not a bar to a subsequent lawsuit against another partner for the same negligent act. The law in this instance seeks to protect the injured third party by providing a remedy against any one of the partners once it has been determined that the tort was within the scope of the partnership.

If a tort judgment is recovered against the partnership or one of the partners who *did not in fact cause* the tort then, as between the partners, the one who *did in fact cause* the tort must indemnify the partnership or other partners for their loss.

This, of course, assumes that it is possible to establish clearly which partner committed the tort. On February 3, 1982, *The Wall Street Journal* (p. 23, col. 3) reported that a federal jury in New York had ordered the partnership of Arthur Andersen & Co., one of the "big eight" accounting firms, to pay $80 million to the shareholders of a firm because Andersen,

**Joint and Several
Tort Liability of
Partners**

it was alleged, committed the tort of fraud. Andersen, it seems, had failed to disclose a fraudulent scheme of intentionally undervaluing property that it knew or should have known about. It seems that the partners and agents of Andersen used the established audit procedures and may have known of the undervaluation but were, they argued, under a separate duty not to disclose this. The point is that if this verdict stands after appeal and assuming that the partnership was not insured against an award that large, the partners of Andersen will be individually liable for the judgment. Under these circumstances, it will be extremely difficult to establish which one of the more than 1,400 partners should be responsible.

Joint liability for contractual obligations means that all partners must be joined in the suit. If they are not, then a judgment recovered against fewer than all the partners cannot be enforced against those not joined. Practically this means that all the partners must be made individual defendants and the court must have jurisdiction over all of them. This is needed only for securing a judgment against the individual partners. If the partnership is named a defendant and there is proper service of process on a partner as agent of the partnership, then a judgment creditor may attach partnership assets.

One of the best cases illustrating the circumstances when a court will hold a partnership liable for a partner's negligent operation of an auto is the *Phillips* v. *Cook* case. When reading this case try to discern the facts that the court thinks are important in deciding to impose liability on the partnership. Also, note the difference between partnership and partner liability for torts and contracts.

PHILLIPS v. COOK
239 Md. 215; 210 A. 2d 743 (Ct. of App., Md., 1965)

MARBURY, Judge

This is an appeal by Daniel Phillips individually, and trading as "Dan's Used Cars," one of the defendants below, from a judgment in favor of Delores Cook and Marshall Cook, her husband, plaintiffs below, entered upon the verdict of a jury in favor of the plaintiffs against the defendants. Isadore Harris and Daniel Phillips, individually and as co-partners trading as Dan's Used Cars, in the Superior Court of Baltimore City. . . .

The Cooks sued Harris and Phillips, individually, and as co-partners trading as Dan's Used Cars. The accident in question occurred

on January 7, 1960, at about 6:50 p.m., when a partnership automobile operated by Harris struck the rear of a vehicle driven by one Smith, which in turn hit an automobile operated by Delores Cook. . . . Harris was on his way home from the used car lot when the accident occurred. He was using the most direct route from the partnership lot and was only five blocks from his home at the time of the incident.

In October 1959, Harris and Phillips entered into a partnership on an equal basis under the name of "Dan's Used Cars" for the purpose of buying and selling used automobiles. Phillips owned the lot and a gas station adjacent to it. He went into the partnership with Harris because the latter had the experience and money which he did not have to put into the business. This partnership agreement was oral and it was agreed between the partners that each would have an equal voice in the conduct and management of the business.

Neither of the partners owned a personal automobile or had one titled in his individual name. It was agreed as a part of the partnership arrangement that Harris would use a partnership vehicle for transportation to and from his home. Under this agreement, he was authorized to demonstrate and sell such automobiles, call on dealers for the purpose of seeing and purchasing used cars, or go to the Department of Motor Vehicles on partnership business after leaving the lot in the evening and before returning the next day. Both Harris and Phillips could use a partnership automobile as desired. Such vehicles were for sale at any time during the day or night and at various times and places they had "for sale" signs on the windshields. Harris had no regular hours to report to the used car lot but could come and go as he saw fit. . . .

If there was any evidence, no matter how slight, viewed in the light most favorable to appellees, that Harris, in using the partnership vehicle, was acting within the scope of the partnership agreement and business, i.e., the use was of some benefit or incidental to the partnership arrangement, then the question was for the jury's determination. Appellant contends that because Harris was on his way home from the used car lot at the time of the accident, the evidence was insufficient to support a finding by the jury that he was acting within the scope of the partnership arrangement or that such use of the vehicle was of benefit to the partnership. . . .

The test of the liability of the partnership and of its members for the torts of any one partner is whether the wrongful act was done within what may reasonably be found to be the scope of the business of the partnership and for its benefit. The extent of the authority of a partner is determined essentially by the same principles as those which measure the scope of an agent's authority. . . . Partnership cases may differ from principal and agent and master and servant relationships because in the non-partnership cases, the element of control or authorization is important. This is not so in the case of a partnership for a partner is also a principal, and control and authorization are generally within his power to exercise. . . .

Here, the fact that the defendant partners were in the used car business; that the very vehicle involved in the accident was one of the partnership assets for sale at all times, day or night, at any location; that Harris was on call by Phillips or customers at his home—he went back to the lot two or three times after going home; that he had no set time and worked irregular hours, coupled with the fact that he frequently stopped to conduct partnership business on the way to and from the lot; . . . requires that the question of whether the use of the automobile at the time of the accident was in the partnership interest and for its benefit be submitted to the jury. We find that the lower court did not err in refusing to grant appellant's motions for a directed verdict as to him in the capacity of a co-partner trading as Dan's Used Cars. . . .

Phillips contends that . . . he could not be held liable as an individual because partnership assets must first be used in the payment of partnership liabilities and the individual assets in the payment of individual liabilities, although, concededly, a partner's individual assets may be held liable for the payment of partnership debts where partnership assets are insufficient.

The principal prevails both at common law and under the Uniform Partnership Act when suit is brought on an alleged contractual obligation of the partnership. . . . The rule is otherwise, however, both at common law and under the Uniform Partnership Act, where the claim is based upon an alleged tortious act committed in the course of the partnership business. . . .

It has been held that the language of the Uniform Partnership Act, in making all partners jointly and severally liable for tortious acts chargeable to the partnership . . . reaffirms the common law doctrine. . . . We agree with the reasoning of these cases that in tort actions, as contrasted with contractual claims, each member of the partnership may be held personally liable. . . . If the tortious act may reasonably be found to be done within the scope of the business of the partnership, the individual partner against whom judgment is obtained may have a right of contribution from the partnership and from the other partners, but that right does not limit the remedy of the plaintiff to proceed against the members of the partnership as individuals as well as co-partners.

The motions of the appellant for directed verdicts in his favor as an individual were properly denied.

Judgment affirmed: Costs to be paid by appellant.

HAMMOND, *Judge (dissenting)*.

I dissent because I think the evidence conclusively rebutted the presumption that the operator of a motor vehicle owned by another is the agent or servant of the owner, acting within the scope of the owner's business, and left no room for the jury to find the partnership liable. The holding of the majority extends the liability of a partnership for the tortious acts of a partner to new and, to me, unjustified lengths.

There was no contradiction or impeachment of, or reason to doubt, the testimony that Harris had left the used car lot on the evening of the accident for the day and was driving home to eat supper and spend the evening. He planned to remain at home and to drive back to the used car lot the next morning. It is undisputed that both Harris and Phillips were free to treat vehicles owned by the partnership as their own for personal trips and uses. In the months that the partnership had existed, Harris had returned to the used car lot, after he had gone home, only two or three times. He never kept a car at home for sale, always on the partnership lot. The car he drove he had paid for although it was titled in the name of the partnership. He did not solicit business away from the lot and apparently had not sold a car away from there, but if someone had asked him to sell the car he was driving he would have done so at the right price. . . .

Restatement, Second, Agency, Sec. 238, Comment b of that section says:

> The mere fact that the master habitually allows the servant to use the instrumentality, or even that the master maintains the instrumentality entirely for the use of the servant, does not of itself subject the master to liability. The master is liable only when the instrumentality is being used by the servant for the purpose of advancing the employer's business or interests, as distinguished from the private affairs of the servant. Thus, a master who purchases an automobile for the convenience of his servants is not subject to liability when a servant is using it for his own purposes; . . . .

The test is not whether the servant on another occasion or at another time might use the instrumentality in furtherance of the master's business or interests or within the scope of the business of the partnership, it is whether at the time the servant causes harm he then reasonably could be found to be so acting. If the servant's activities at the time of the infliction of the harm were for his own purposes, or in his own behalf, the master is not liable. It matters not that earlier he had acted for his master or that later he would again act for him; at the time of the harm the immediately predominating purpose of the servant must have some significant relation to the business of the master, if the master is to be held liable. . . .

The fact that Harris would have sold the car for a price if some purchaser had flagged him down while he was en route home or telephoned him at home, does not make his purpose in driving home to supper and an evening of television and sleep less predominantly personal and unmixed with business than that of a lawyer driving home from his office with a briefcase full of files (which he may or may not open). If the lawyer negligently injures some-

one while driving home, his partners certainly would not be liable because of the briefcase or because a client involved in a street accident might flag him down en route or another client call him at home for advice. . . .

The defendant's prayer for an instructed verdict should have been granted.

---

1. Does this case stand for the legal principle that whenever a partner commits a tort while on partnership business, the partnership will be liable? Isn't this statement too broad?

2. List the facts that caused the court to conclude that the plaintiffs had stated a good cause of action against the partnership. That is, what circumstances establish that the negligent partner was operating the vehicle in the ordinary course of the business?

3. Do you agree with the majority or the dissent? Should not the majority have focused on the intent and purpose of the very trip that was taken? Was not the partner going home for the evening?

4. Note that the court does not discuss the elements of control needed to establish liability in a master-servant case. The analysis here is very similar to that used by courts in an agency case where it is alleged that the relationship of principal-nonservant agent existed.

5. Must liability for a partner's tort be satisfied first out of partnership property; or, may the negligent partner be required to directly pay the injured party? Who ultimately bears the loss?

Case Questions

In the *Phillips* v. *Cook* case the majority thought the ordinary course of business, selling autos, could be conducted anywhere and, therefore, even though one partner was on his way home for the evening, there was still a potential to conduct business. Usually the "ordinary course of business" is easier to define. It should be obvious that the negligent preparation of an audit by a partner will subject a CPA partnership to liability,[5] even though the other partners did not participate; the same is true of a partnership of physicians when one of them negligently treats a patient.[6]

Partnership Liability for Willful or Intentional Torts and Crimes

Generally, a partnership is not liable on the basis of respondeat superior for the willful or malicious torts or crimes of a partner not intended to further partnership business. In these cases the intent to commit the act is necessary and intent will not be imputed to those who did not engage in or authorize the act. However, some state and federal regulatory laws describe acts that are criminal and intent may not be an element. When this is the case, the partnership may be liable.[7] An example of this may be criminal penalties for polluting the environment.

If a partner commits one of the so-called intentional torts of trespass, fraud, deceit, or misrepresentation and there are facts indicating that the commission was in the course of partnership business, then partnership and a partner's liability may result. However, if the tort is an assault and/or a battery and there is not much evidence that it was committed to further the business of the partnership, then the partnership will not be liable. The following case takes the standard approach to the circumstance.

VRABEL v. ACRI

156 Ohio St. 467; 103 N.E.2d 564 (S. Ct., Ohio, 1952)

ZIMMERMAN, J.

It will be noted that the amended petition seeks to fix the liability of defendant to plaintiff for his injuries on the theory of negligence. Plaintiff contends that defendant and Michael Acri were joint proprietors of the Acri Cafe and that defendant, as a joint proprietor, was negligent in failing to exercise ordinary measures and precautions to protect patrons of the cafe from unprovoked attacks by Michael Acri, a person known to the defendant to be vicious and irresponsible.

The evidence presented on the trial supports the claims in the amended petition as to the manner in which plaintiff was injured. It shows that, while plaintiff and his companion were sitting quietly at the bar of the Acri Cafe on the night of February 17, 1947, partaking of alcoholic beverages, Michael Acri, for no apparent cause, shot and killed plaintiff's companion and afterwards viciously attacked plaintiff. Evidence was also introduced which might justify the conclusion that at the time of plaintiff's injuries Michael Acri and the defendant, then husband and wife, were joint proprietors of the Acri Cafe which had been started in 1933, although defendant herself denied any such relationship. . . .

It also appears from the evidence that plaintiff secured a judgment for $10,000 against Michael Acri for the injuries received at Acri's hands, and that Acri is now serving a life sentence in the Ohio Penitentiary for killing plaintiff's companion.

For the purpose of the discussion which follows, we shall accept plaintiff's claim, supported by some evidence, that defendant and Michael Acri were joint proprietors of the Acri Cafe at the time plaintiff was assaulted by Acri.

The authorities are in agreement that whether a tort is committed by a partner or a joint adventurer, the principles of law governing the situation are the same. So, where a partnership or a joint enterprise is shown to exist, each member of such project acts both as principal and agent of the others as to those things done within the apparent scope of the business of the project and for its benefit. . . .

However, it is equally true that where one member of a partnership or joint enterprise commits a wrongful and malicious tort not within the actual or apparent scope of the agency or the common business of the particular venture, to which the other members have not assented, and which has not been concurred in or ratified by them, they are not liable for the harm thereby caused. . . .

We cannot escape the conclusion, therefore, that the above rules, relating to the nonliability of a partner or joint adventurer for wrongful and malicious torts committed by an associate outside the purpose and scope of the business, must be applied in the instant case. The willful and malicious attack by Michael Acri upon the plaintiff in the Acri Cafe cannot reasonably be said to have come within the scope of the business of operating the cafe, so as to have rendered the absent defendant, assuming her joint proprietorship of the cafe, accountable.

Since the liability of one partner or of one engaged in a joint enterprise for the acts of his associates is founded upon the principles of agency, the statement is in point that an intentional and willful attack committed by an agent

or employee, to vent his own spleen or malevolence against the injured person, is a clear departure from his employment and his principal or employer is not responsible therefor. . . .

Therefore, under the evidence in this case, we entertain the view that the trial court should have directed a verdict for the defendant at the close of the evidence, in response to her motion. The judgments of the Court of Common Pleas and of the Court of Appeals are reversed and final judgment is rendered for the defendant.

Judgment reversed.

Case Questions

1. If the plaintiff in this case could prove that the other member of the partnership knew or should have known about the violent tendencies of Michael Acri, would the result have been the same?

2. If a partnership did exist in this case and if Michael Acri were negligent in merely throwing a patron out of the cafe who was causing a disturbance, should the partnership be liable? (See the dissent in the *Sandman* case in Chapter 5.)

A concise statement about the criminal liability of a partnership is not possible, because state courts have not all decided that a partnership is a distinct and separate entity from the partners for the purposes of establishing this liability. Some courts have recognized partnerships as separate legal entities. When this has been done and when there are compelling societal needs for the establishment of criminal liability, then a court may state that a partnership may be criminally liable. The following case presents a modern view that when the public may be threatened, courts will view partnerships as potentially liable for crimes one of their partners or agents caused.

PEOPLE v. *SMITHTOWN GENERAL HOSPITAL*
399 N.Y. S.2d 993 (1977)

The position of the defendant is that it is not an entity separate and apart from the aggregate of the individuals who are members of the partnership. It urges that the doctrine of "re-

spondeat superior" does not apply . . . and therefore the partnership cannot be indicted in the absence of culpable intent on the part of each of the 42 partners.

The defendant operates a proprietary hospital and is charged, in effect, with permitting an unauthorized person to participate in a surgical procedure upon an uninformed, non-consenting patient and falsifying its records to conceal that crime. The indictment is couched in terms appropriate to Penal Law Section 120.05(5) and Penal Law Section 175.10 which respectively provides as follows:

Section 120.05:

A *person* is guilty of assault in the second degree when:

5. For a purpose other than lawful therapeutic treatment, he intentionally causes stupor, unconsciousness or other physical impairment or injury to another person by administering to him, without his consent, a drug, substance or preparation capable of producing the same.

P.L. Section 175.10:

A *person* is guilty of falsifying business records in the first degree when he commits the crime of falsifying business records in the second degree, and when his intent to defraud includes an intent to commit another crime or to aid or conceal the commission thereof.

Person is defined in P.L. Section 10.00, subd. 7, as a "human being, and *where appropriate*, a public or private corporation . . . a *partnership* . . ." (Emphasis added.)

. . .

While the criminal liability of corporations and of individuals acting in the name of a corporation is expressly set forth in the Penal Law (Sections 20.20 and 20.25) no similar provision is found with respect to partnerships and no reported case has been found in this State which deals directly with this issue.

The legislative pattern is probably grounded upon common law concepts of a partnership as opposed to that of the entity known as a corporation. But the definition of "person" in the Penal Law and the mandate of that law (Section 5.00) that it be liberally construed provide an opportunity for rationalization in the interests of promoting justice and effecting the objects of the law.

. . .

The partnership can be either an entity or an aggregate of its members depending upon the nature of its activities and in the case of criminal law depending also upon the nature of the infraction.

. . .

The concept of a partnership as an entity liable for certain of its criminal activities independent of culpability by its respective members was expressly considered in *United States* v. *A & P Trucking Co.,* 358 U.S. 121, . . . Two partnerships were charged, as entities, with violations of 18 U.S.C. § 835 which makes it a crime to knowingly violate some Interstate Commerce Commission regulations. . . .

The Supreme Court, relying upon a definition of person . . . similar to that found in P.L. Section 10.00, subd. 7, held that impersonal entities can be guilty of knowing or wilful violations of regulatory statutes through the doctrine of respondeat superior and that a partnership may be considered an entity separate and apart from the aggregate of its members.

The operation of a hospital is so intertwined with the public interest as to legally justify the imposition of extensive controls by all levels of government. The applicable regulatory statutes and implementing regulations not only involve care and services, but relate to the creation and ownership of those institutions and to every aspect of its internal affairs including limitations as to costs and charges.

. . .

The counts in the respective indictments relating first to the anesthetization of a patient without his consent for a purpose other than lawful medical or therapeutic treatment and secondly to the records maintained with respect thereto have that apparent nexus to the regulatory provisions controlling a hospital as to bring this case within the orbit of the principles enunciated in *United States* v. *A & P Trucking,* supra. . . .

In civil law, two or more persons conducting a partnership may sue or be sued in the partnership name. I now hold that this defendant may be charged in an indictment as an entity with the commission of crimes related to the discharge of its primary obligations as a general hospital even though there is no showing of culpability on the part of the individual's partners.

The motion to dismiss the indictment against Smithtown General Hospital is denied.

(Authors' note: on appeal the indictment for assault was dismissed for lack of proof of intent but the indictment for falsifying business records was affirmed thus affirming the central point of the case that partnerships may be indicted for crimes. See 402 N.S. Supp. 2d 318 (1978).)

Case Questions

1. Based on some of the information in this case that defines criminal conduct, is it a crime to serve cake or brownies to dinner guests if marijuana has been added to the cake?

2. Did this case hold that the partnership and all 42 of its partners are liable for the criminal conduct alleged or did it hold that following the indictment, a criminal trial with the partnership as a defendant would be proper?

Incoming Partners

The addition of new partners is an essential part of partnership operation. Unless the articles of partnership provide otherwise, the consent of all partners is needed to expand the partnership. A new partner is given a form of limited liability in that his or her *personal assets* cannot be attached by a partnership judgment creditor for a partnership obligation which arose before admission (UPA § 17). Only property brought to the partnership and the partner's interest therein is subject to attachment for such obligations. The next case illustrates this principle and provides an explanation for the unique obligation created by leasing property.

ELLINGSON v. WALSH, O'CONNOR & BARNESON
15 Cal. 2d 673, 104 P. 2d 507
(S. Ct. Cal, 1940)

GIBSON, Chief Justice
This is an action against a partnership and its members for rent due under a written lease. . . . Judgment was rendered against the partnership and all general partners, and from this judgment Lionel T. Barneson, one of the general partners, appeals. Appellant admits his liability for rent, but contends that the obligation therefor arose before his admission to the partnership, and that . . . liability must be satisfied only out of partnership property.

On October 4, 1929, the First National Corporation, as lessor, let the premises in question to Walsh, O'Connor & Company, a special partnership, as lessee, for a period of ten years, at a total rental of $66,000, payable in monthly installments of various amounts. . . .

On April 21, 1931, H. J. Barneson withdrew as a general partner. On April 28, 1931, appellant Lionel T. Barneson was taken in as a general partner, and ever since has enjoyed all of the rights and privileges and assumed the obligations as a general partner of said partnership. . . . During the period between April, 1931, and March, 1932, the partnership paid the full rent due under the lease to the lessor. The judgment herein is for rent claimed to be due for the period commencing March 1, 1932, and ending January 25, 1933, in the sum of $2,374.13, after deducting certain credits and payments. The judgment was a general one against all defendants, with no proviso restricting its enforcement or satisfaction against appellant.

The issue in this case is not the liability of the partnership as such, nor the liability of its assets. There is no doubt whatever that the plaintiff may satisfy his claim against the partnership out of any of its properties. The sole question is whether the appellant's liability as an incoming partner may be satisfied by resort to his personal assets.

Section 2411 of the Civil Code (sec. 17 of the Uniform Partnership Act) provides: "A person admitted as a partner into an existing partnership is liable for all the obligations of the partnership arising before his admission as though he had been a partner when such obligations were incurred, except that this liability shall be satisfied only out of partnership property." It is this section upon which appellant relies, and the interpretation urged by appellant is the sole basis of his case. Appellant contends that since the lease was executed before he became a partner, the obligation of the lease arose before his admission, and therefore his liability can only be satisfied out of partnership property.

This contention would be sound if the only obligation of the partnership in this transaction was one which arose prior to appellant's admission to the firm. For example, if a promissory note had been executed by the partnership for a consideration then passing to it, the obligation would have arisen at the time of execution of the note and the case would plainly be within the statute. But appellant's contention overlooks the fact that a tenant of real property is not liable for rent solely by reason of the contract of lease. Tenancies in property need not necessarily be created . . . by leases. One may become a tenant at will or a periodic tenant under an invalid lease, or without any lease at all, by occupancy with consent. Such tenancies carry with them the incidental obligation of rent, and the liability therefore arises not from contract but from the relationship of landlord and tenant. . . .

Both liabilities exist simultaneously. . . .

Under the above principles, the first partnership, which did not include appellant as a member, was bound by these dual obligations; that is, . . . it was bound in contract and also by reason of its tenancy. When appellant became a member, the first partnership was, in legal theory, dissolved and a new partnership came into being composed of the old members and appellant. This second partnership did not expressly assume the obligations of the lease, but it occupied the premises. Whether it was liable contractually on the lease is immaterial; it became liable for rent as a tenant. . . .

The only remaining question is whether the section of the Uniform Partnership Act, quoted above, has changed the rule. Appellant's theory is that he, as a member of the second partnership, may receive the benefits of years of occupancy under the lease, but that his personal assets cannot be reached in satisfaction of liability therefor if the lease was executed before he became a member of the partnership. The statute, however, neither contemplates nor accomplished any such result. . . . Under the general law the obligation of a tenant arising from occupation of the premises is a continuing one; that is, it arises and binds him continually throughout the period of his occupation. This obligation on the part of appellant first arose when the new partnership, of which he was a member, occupied the premises as a tenant. It follows that his obligation as a tenant arose after his admission to the partnership and the immunity given by section 2411 does not apply.

The judgment is affirmed.

1. If the liability in this case had arisen from the signing of a promissory note before Barneson was admitted as a partner, would the result have been the same?

2. Develop your own definition of partnership property. What facts or circumstances will you look for in developing this definition?

Dissolution of the Partnership

Ending the partnership organization is achieved by a two-part process. First is the dissolution of the partnership. This is defined as "a change in the relation of the partners caused by any partner ceasing to be associated in the carrying on . . . of the business (UPA § 29). In essence, dissolution dissolves the authority of the partners to act for the partnership in the ordinary course of business. The partnership and a partner's authority continues for purposes of liquidating the partnership assets and paying partnership obligations. This process of liquidation is called winding up and is the second step in ending the organization. When the winding up is completed, the partnership has been terminated. You should be careful to distinguish between these three legal terms: dissolution, winding up, and termination, the first two of which represent a two-phase process of ending the partnership organization.

A Typical Partnership Dissolution. Before proceeding to a full discussion of dissolution and winding up, we wish to point out what happens when one of the partners dies, retires, or withdraws and the surviving or continuing partners wish to continue to do business as before. Perhaps this is the most often occurring form of dissolution, although it is only a technical dissolution.

In many of the large law and accounting partnerships, for example, partners withdraw and new ones are added yearly. Technically, this is a dissolution of the partnership because there is a "change in the relation of the partners." Indeed, a new organization, either plus or minus one or more partners, results. However, the partnership does not end its business activity. If the partners are prudent, this type of dissolution will be one of the most important items covered in the articles of partnership.

Valuing a Partner's Interest. Generally, under the provisions of the articles of partnership, on the retirement or death of a partner, the partner's *interest in the partnership* is valued. At this point it would be beneficial to refer to paragraphs 11–12 of the partnership agreement provided in the last chapter. This partnership interest is composed of both a right to the return of some property in exchange for that brought to the partnership and a right to profits, if any, plus, if the agreement so provides, a right to a payment for a contribution to the good will of the firm. The entire interest is valued, perhaps somewhat arbitrarily by a preset formula, and the partner is paid this value, usually out of the revenues of the firm. We assume here that the partnership was a solvent, going enterprise at dissolution. In those cases where the partnership is insolvent and does not have the funds to pay the partners or the creditors, the partners on dissolution may have to contribute more to the partnership to pay the creditors.

Dissolution in the Absence of an Agreement. If there is *no partnership agreement* and one of the partners retires or dies and if the members of the partnership wish to continue then Section 42 of the UPA provides in part that the retiring partner or the estate of the deceased partner:

> may have the value of his interest at the date of dissolution ascertained, and shall receive as an ordinary creditor an amount equal to the value of his interest in the dissolved partnership with interest, or, at his option, . . . in lieu of interest, the profits attributable to the use of his right in the property of the dissolved partnership; provided that the creditors of the dissolved partnership as against separate creditors . . . of the retired or deceased partner, shall have priority on any claim arising under this Section, as provided by Section 41 (8) of this act.

Dissolution and Partnership Creditors. Section 41 (8) provides for the prior right of partnership creditors over individual creditors on the dissolution of the old partnership and the continuation of business as a new partnership. They also have a prior right over the claim of the retiring partner or his or her estate for sums advanced to the partnership as loans.

Even though, technically, the old organization has been dissolved, the creditors of the old organization become creditors of the partnership continuing the business. (UPA § 41). The retiring partner or, in the case of death, the partner's estate, remains liable to creditors of the partnership for obligations incurred before dissolution and even in some cases after dissolution where the creditor has no notice of the dissolution. A partner is discharged from partnership liability existing at time of dissolution by an agreement to that effect between the retired or deceased partner, the surviving partners, and the creditors [UPA § 36 (2)]. An agreement between only the retiring or deceased partner and the surviving partners will not discharge the former from partnership obligations to third-party creditors existing at dissolution.

The Nature of a Partner's Interest on Dissolution. We have provided a case that demonstrates the application of some of the legal rules just discussed. In the *McClennen* v. *Commissioner of Internal Revenue* decision the issue, broadly stated, was the nature of a partner's interest in the partnership when he died. The representatives of the estate treated this interest as income and not a return of capital and thus did not include the partnership interest as part of the deceased's estate when filing the federal estate tax return. The IRS took a different view, arguing that although the interest in the partnership was to be paid out of partnership revenues, it was a return of property brought to the partnership and was therefore includable in the gross estate at death as part of the property owned by the deceased.

McCLENNEN v. COMMISSIONER OF INTERNAL REVENUE
131 F2d 165 (C.C.A. 1st, 1942)

MAGRUDER, Circuit Judge

George R. Nutter had been a partner in the firm of Nutter, McClennen & Fish, practicing law in Boston, Massachusetts. The firm kept its accounts on the cash receipts and disbursements basis. Its receipts were derived solely from personal services. Under the partnership agreement Mr. Nutter's share of the firm's net profits was 8 percent. The agreement also contained the following provision:

> On the retirement of a partner or on his death—the other continuing the business—the retiring partner or his estate in the case of his death shall, in addition to his percentage of net profits of the Firm received by it in cash up to the date of such death or retirement, also receive the same percentage of net profits of the Firm received by it in cash until the expiration of the eighteen (18) calendar months next after such retirement, or death, and this shall be in full of the retiring or deceasing member's interest in the capital, the assets, the receivables, the possibilities of the Firm. The continuing members shall have the right to the good will and the use of the Firm name except that the deceasing or retiring member's name shall not be used without his written consent or that of his estate. . . .

After the death of George R. Nutter the other partners continued the business. Eight percent of the net profits of the firm for the 18 calendar months next after the death, computed on the basis of cash receipts and disbursements, amounted to $34,069.99, which amount was paid over to the petitioners as executors. Of this amount $28,069.46 represented 8 percent of the net profits for the period of the year next after the death, and the remainder represented 8 percent of the net profits for the last six months of the agreed 18-month period. . . .

In his notice of deficiency the Commissioner determined that $34,069.99 should have been included in the gross estate as the value of decedent's "interest in partnership Nutter, McClennen & Fish." The Board has upheld the Commissioner in this determination. We think the Board was right.

In the absence of a controlling agreement in the partnership articles the death of a partner dissolves the partnership. The survivors have the right and duty, with reasonable dispatch, to wind up the partnership affairs, to complete transactions begun but not then finished, to collect the accounts receivable, to pay the firm debts, to convert the remaining firm assets into cash, and to pay in cash to the partners and the legal representative of the deceased partner the net amounts shown by the accounts to be owing to each of them in respect of capital contributions and in respect of their shares of profits and surplus. The representative of a deceased partner does not succeed to any right to specific partnership property. In substance the deceased partner's interest, to which his representative succeeds, is a chose in action, a right to receive in cash the sum of money shown to be due him upon a liquidation and accounting. . . . The same substantive results are reached under the Uniform Partnership Act which, in form at least, proceeds on the aggregate theory. . . . That act, which is law in Massachusetts, conceives of the partner as a "co-owner with his partners of specific partnership property holding as a tenant in partnership;" but provides that on the death of a partner "his right in specific partnership property vests in the surviving partner or partners." Another enumerated property right of a partner, "his interest in the partnership," is described as "his share of the profits and surplus, and the same is personal property," regardless of whether the firm holds real estate or personalty or both. . . .

This chose in action to which the representative of the deceased partner succeeds, the right to receive payment of a sum of money shown to be due upon a liquidation and accounting, is of course a part of the deceased partner's wealth, and includable in the decedent's gross estate, for purposes of computing the estate tax. . . . This is none the less true even though the net amount thus shown to be due to the estate is derived in whole or in part from past earnings or profits of the partnership resulting from personal services—profits which the decedent, if he had lived, would have had to report as income. . . .

In the case at bar, if there had not been the controlling provision in the partnership articles, above quoted, or if the survivors had not come to some agreement otherwise with the executors of Mr. Nutter, the survivors would have had to proceed to wind up the affairs of the partnership, to conclude all unfinished legal business on hand at the date of the death, to realize upon all of the assets of the firm, tangible or intangible, to pay the debts, to return to Mr. Nutter's estate his contribution of capital, if any, and to pay to his estate in cash the amount shown to be due in respect of his "interest in the partnership," that is, his "share of the profits and surplus," as determined upon an accounting. Among other things to be

taken into account, "the earned proportion of the unfinished business" would have had "to be valued to determine the decedent's interest in the partnership assets." . . .

To obviate the necessity of a liquidation, or to eliminate accounting difficulties in determining the value of the deceased partner's interest, partners often make specific provision in the partnership articles. . . .

In the case at bar the partnership agreement contains [a] familiar arrangement, whereby no liquidation and final accounting will ever be necessary in order to satisfy the claim of the deceased partner. In place of the chose in action to which Mr. Nutter's executor would have succeeded in the absence of specific provision in the partnership articles, that is, a right to receive payment in cash of the amount shown to be due the deceased partner upon a complete liquidation and accounting, a different right is substituted, a right of the estate to receive a share of the net profits of the firm for 18 calendar months after the partner's death. . . .

In the present case the Commissioner valued Mr. Nutter's interest in the partnership at the sum of $34,069.99, which happened to be the exact amount received by the executors from the survivors as representing 8 percent of the net profits of the partnership for the 18 calendar months after the death. There is no contention that this was an overvaluation. . . .

The decision of the Board of Tax Appeals is affirmed.

Case Question   1. Valuing a partner's contribution to the goodwill of a partnership and the present value of his or her initial capital contribution are considerable problems and should be discussed when the partnership is formed. No formula is perfect. Reread the provisions for valuing the interest of a retiring or deceased partner in the partnership agreement (paragraph 12 a) reproduced in Chapter 7. How does it differ from the provisions of the agreement that were the subject of the case above?

Causes of Dissolution

The Articles of Partnership usually cover most circumstances resulting in a dissolution. In addition to retirement and death, many agreements provide that dissolution may be caused by the termination of the partnership term, by the express will of one or more of the partners before the end of the term, or the expulsion of any partner from the business in accordance with such a power conferred by the articles.

If the articles do not provide for dissolution or if there is no agreement then the UPA provides that a partnership is dissolved by one or more of the following:

1. The express will of any partner at any time where the circumstances do not permit a dissolution under any other provision of § 31 [UPA § 31(2)].
2. The illegality of the partnership business [UPA § 31 (3)].
3. The death of any partner [UPA § 31 (4)].
4. The bankruptcy of any partner or bankruptcy of the partnership [UPA § 31 (5)].
5. The decree of court under § 32 [UPA § 31 (6)].

Any of the circumstances set out above is sufficient to cause a dissolution of the partnership without further acts of the partners. Section 32 of the UPA adds to this list but requires a judicial declaration of the existence of the circumstances. It provides that a court shall declare dissolution on the application by or for a partner when one of the following is proved:

1. A partner is incapacitated by insanity or is in any other way incapable of performing his or her part of the agreement.
2. A partner has been guilty of conduct that affects prejudicially the partnership business so that it is not reasonably practicable to carry on the business.
3. The business can only be carried on at a loss.
4. Other circumstances exist that render a dissolution equitable.

Winding Up the Partnership Business

If the surviving partner or partners do not wish to continue the business, then, at dissolution, the authority of all partners to act for the others in the ordinary course of business ends (UPA § 33) and the partners wind up the business. Winding up involves selling the firm's assets, paying the firm's obligations to third parties, and then distributing the remaining amounts to the partners. More specifically, Section 40 of the UPA provides for distribution of the remaining assets in the following order:

1. Those owing to creditors other than partners.

2. Those owing to partners other than for capital and profits (advancements or loans).

3. Those owing to partners in respect of capital.

4. Those owing to partners in respect of profits.

Distribution of the Assets of a Limited Partnership

The ULPA provides for a slightly different order for the payment of limited partnership liabilities. The assets of a limited partner are protected ahead of those of a general partner but behind the protection of firm creditors. The order in which limited partnership liabilities is paid is as follows:

1. Firm creditors other than limited partners as to their capital contributions.

2. Limited partners as to their share of profits.

3. Limited partners as to their capital contribution.

4. General partners as to loans and other debts.

5. General partners as to profits.

6. General partners as to capital contributions.

Liquidation of Partnership Property— A Distinction Between Real and Personal Property

The sections of the UPA providing for the distribution of property after dissolution make no special distinction between personal and real property, thus greatly simplifying a matter of considerable historical complexity. Some courts still refuse to free their analysis of partnership property from the historical analysis, so we present here just a brief recounting of how the law treated partnership ownership of real property.

English law recognized a distinction between real and personal property on the owner's death by providing that the ownership of the real property vested in the eldest son. Ownership of personal property vested in a living representative of the "estate," who was to pay the deceased's debts and then distribute the remainder to the "next of kin."[8] This fundamental distinction between real and personal property (the former being regarded as "the" standard of wealth) manifests itself in many areas of our law. For a long time, courts refused to recognize a partnership as a distinct legal person and held, therefore, that real property could not be owned by a partnership, but only by the partners. A conveyance of real property at common law was held either to vest title in the partners as individuals or to be a nullity. This result was changed by § 8(3) of the UPA, which allows:

Any estate in real property may be acquired in the partnership name. Title so acquired can be conveyed only in the partnership name.

This section clearly indicates that a partnership, as a separate entity, may own real property, but the custom of treating real property as unique continued in other respects. On dissolution of the partnership caused by death, some courts distinguished between real and personal property by holding that the personal property must be sold first to liquidate partnership debts. The ownership of real estate used in the partnership business passed not to the partners but to the heirs of the deceased. The parties did have an equitable right to sell the real property, but only to pay partnership debts if the personal property was inadequate. Thus, courts asserting this view held there was an equitable conversion of the real property for the payment of partnership debts. This view introduced many problems as to the point at which this "conversion" begins and ends.[9] The UPA appears to clarify this by providing, as we noted in Chapter 7, that a partner's right to occupy specific partnership property is not assignable and, on the partner's death, this right vests in the surviving partner or partners [UPA § 25(2)(d)]. Again, note that this section makes no distinction between real and personal property. Despite the clear intent and wording of the UPA some courts may still give deference to this historical distinction between real and personal property, causing a lingering view that personal property is to be sold first to liquidate a partnership's assets.

A Partner's Liability on Dissolution and Winding Up

Section 40(d) of the UPA is one of the most important since it is the section that states the nature of the unlimited liability of a partner. It states:

> The partners shall contribute . . . the amount necessary to satisfy the liabilities; but if any, but not all, of the partners are insolvent, or, not being subject to process, refuse to contribute, the other partners shall contribute their share of the liability, . . .

This provision provides that creditors of the firm will be paid if some of the partners are insolvent but others are able to pay. If a firm suffers a loss at dissolution, then, as between the partners, this loss should be adjusted so that they bear the loss according to their share in profits. When partners contribute equal amounts to the partnership and share profits equally the loss distribution is easily determined. However, the matter is complicated where different amounts were contributed. Using Figure 8-1 as an example, assume that the partners contributed cash as indicated and agreed that they would share profits (and therefore, losses) equally. At dissolution, the assets are sold and only $6,700 remains. This means that the partnership suffered a loss of $3,300. This amount must be shared

Cash Contributed	Dissolution	Individual Loss
A. $ 5,000	$10,000 owed to partners	$3,300 divided
B. $ 4,000	6,700 available to pay	by 3, equals
C. $ 1,000	partners	$1,100
$10,000	loss $ 3,300	

Payment of Dissolution

Payment to A. $5,000 minus $1,100 is $3,900
Payment to B. $4,000 minus $1,100 is $2,900
C. paid only $1,000 and must pay $100 more to suffer loss of $1,100

FIGURE 8-1

equally by the three partners, requiring partner C to contribute more cash to the partnership.

Further, each partner must suffer the loss caused by his own wrongful conduct; and, the partnership must indemnify each partner for amounts reasonably expended in the ordinary course of business. Moreover, if one or more of the partners caused the dissolution of the partnership in violation of the partnership agreement, they may be liable [UPA Section 38(2)(a)(II)] for the damages caused by such a breach to the other partners. This amount of damages must be calculated or figured into the respective distributions.

Joint and Several Liability on Dissolution

If a partnership is going to dissolve and then wind up its affairs, creditors should be wary. They should act promptly to receive payment for partnership obligations. If not, many problems could arise. Many states have differing procedural requirements as to joinder of parties. Because some states may cling to the old notion that a partnership is not a distinct legal entity apart from the partners, the best course of action when suing a partnership on a partnership obligation at dissolution or otherwise is not only to name the partnership as a defendant, but also to join as defendants and serve the proper papers on all partners. If only a partner is named defendant and is served with the proper papers then a judgment based on a claim arising from the breach of contractual duty against this partner distinguishes the obligation of other partners. Moreover, if only the partnership is named as a defendant and a judgment is recovered, this judgment, in most states, may be satisfied only out of partnership assets.

Dissolution Notice to Third Parties

Dissolution ends the actual authority of a partner to act for the partnership unless he or she is winding up. However, third parties who knew of the partnership in the past, who contracted with or otherwise dealt with a partner within the scope of past partnership authority after dissolution, and who have no notice of the dissolution, may hold the partnership liable on the basis of the partner's apparent authority or estoppel.

Such apparent authority may be terminated only by notice to the third parties. More specifically, Section 35(1)(b)(I) of the UPA requires that a third party who has *given credit* to the partnership *prior to dissolution* is entitled to be given actual notice of the dissolution. This type of notice must be communicated directly to the third party or its agent. If such notice is not given and the third party does not have knowledge of the dissolution, then a partner acting in the ordinary course of business (as established before dissolution) binds the partnership.

If the third party had not extended credit to the partnership but only knew of the partnership, then constructive notice is sufficient to terminate a partner's apparent authority. Such notice may be given by publishing the fact of dissolution in a newspaper of general circulation in the place where the partnership business was regularly carried on.

Section 35(3) of the UPA provides that no notice is needed where dissolution is caused by the partnership business being declared illegal, or the bankruptcy of a *partner*. Note that when dissolution is caused by the death of a partner, the UPA does not declare this event so notorious as to negate the necessity of notice. Thus the UPA provides a change from the *Restatement of Agency* for the requirements of notice in the case of death. Remember that the *Restatement* said that in the case of the death of the principal, no notice to third parties who had dealt with the agent was required.

We present an old case that illustrates some basic common law notions about the nature of partnerships and the kind of notice requirement that must be met by a partnership on dissolution. These notions were incorporated in the UPA.

FREDERICK M. SOLOMON v. CHARLES H. KIRKWOOD AND THEODORE HOLLANDER

55 Mich. 256 (1884)

(Authors' note: The trial court found for the defendants. This appellate court affirmed this judgment with respect to the two issues discussed below, but reversed with regard to an issue not here important.)

COOLEY, C.J.

The plaintiffs, who are, in the city of Chicago, dealers in jewelry, seek to charge the defendants, as partners, upon a promissory note for

seven hundred and ninety-one, 92/100 dollars, bearing date Nov. 9, 1882, and signed "Hollander & Kirkwood." The note was given by the defendant Hollander, but Kirkwood denies that any partnership existed between the defendants at the date of the note.

The evidence on the trial tends to show that on July 6, 1882, Hollander & Kirkwood entered into a written agreement for a partnership for one year from the first day of the next ensuing month, in the business of buying and selling jewelry, clocks, watches, etc., and in repairing clocks, watches and jewelry, at Ishpeming, Michigan. Business was begun under this agreement, and continued until the latter part of October, 1882, when Kirkwood, becoming dissatisfied, locked up the goods and excluded Hollander altogether from the business. He also caused notice to be given to all persons with whom the firm had had dealings that the partnership was dissolved, and had the following inserted in the local column of the paper published at Ishpeming: "The co-partnership heretofore existing between Mr. C. H. Kirkwood and one Hollander, as jewelers, has ceased to exist, Mr. Kirkwood having purchased the interest of the latter." This was not signed by any one.

A few days later Hollander went to Chicago, and there, on November 9, 1882, he bought, in the name of Hollander & Kirkwood, all of the plaintiffs goods in their line amounting to $791.92, and gave to the plaintiffs therefor the promissory note now in suit. The note was made payable December 15, 1882, at a bank in Ishpeming. When the purchase was completed Hollander took away the goods in his satchel. The plaintiffs had before had no dealings with Hollander & Kirkwood, but they had heard there was such a firm, and were not aware of its dissolution. They claim to have made the sale in good faith, and in the belief that the firm was still in existence. . . .

The questions principally contested on the trial were—First, whether the acts of Kirkwood amounted to a dissolution of the partnership; and second, whether sufficient notice of dissolution was given; . . . The trial judge, in submitting the case to the jury, instructed them that Kirkwood, notwithstanding the written agreement, had a right to withdraw from the partnership at any time, leaving matters between him and Hollander to be adjusted between them amicably or in the courts; and for the purpose of this case it made no difference whether Kirkwood was right or wrong in bringing the partnership to an end: if wrong, he might be liable to Hollander in damages for the breach of his contract. Also, that when

partners are dissatisfied, or they cannot get along together, and one partner withdraws, the partnership is then at an end as to the public and parties with whom the partnership deals, and neither partner can make contracts in the future to bind the partnership, provided the retiring partner gives the proper notice. Also, that if they should find from the evidence that there was trouble between Hollander and Kirkwood prior to the sale of the goods and the giving of the note; that Kirkwood informed Hollander, in substance, that he would have no more dealings with him as partner; that he took possession of all the goods and locked them up, and from that time they ceased to do business,—then the partnership was dissolved. Further, that whether sufficient notice had been given of the dissolution was a question for the jury. Kirkwood was not bound to publish notice in any of the Chicago papers; he was only bound to give actual notice to such parties there as had dealt with the partnership. But Kirkwood was bound to use all fair means to publish as widely as possible the fact of a dissolution. Publication in a newspaper is one of the proper means of giving notice, but it is not absolutely essential; and on this branch of the case the question for the jury was whether Kirkwood gave such notice of the dissolution as under the circumstances was fair and reasonable. If he did, then he is not liable on the note: if he did not, he would still continue liable. . . .

I. We think the judge committed no error in his instructions respecting the dissolution of the partnership. The rule on this subject is thus stated in an early New York case. The right of a partner to dissolve, it is said, "is a right inseparably incident to every partnership. There can be no such thing as an indissoluble partnership. Every partner has an indefeasible right to dissolve the partnership as to all future contracts by publishing his own volition to that effect; and after such publication the other members of the firm have no capacity to bind him by any contract. Even where partners covenant with each other that the partnership shall continue seven years, either partner may dissolve it the next day by proclaiming his determination for that purpose; the only consequence being, that he thereby subjects himself to a claim for damages for a breach of his covenant. The power given by one partner to another to make joint contracts for them both, is not only a revocable power, but a man can do no act to divest himself of the capacity to revoke it." . . . When one partner becomes dissatisfied there is commonly no legal policy to be subserved by compelling a continuance of the relation, and the fact that a contract will be broken by the dissolution is no argument against the right to dissolve. Most contracts may be broken at pleasure, subject however to responsibility in damages. And that responsibility would exist in breaking a contract of partnership as in other cases.

II. The instruction respecting notice was also correct. No court can determine for all cases what shall be sufficient notice and what shall not be: the question must necessarily be one of fact. Publication of notice of dissolution in a local newspaper is common, but it is not the only method in which notice can be given. The purpose of the notice is to make notorious in the local community the fact that a dissolution has taken place; and publication of a notice may or may not be the most effectual means for that purpose. Very few persons in any community probably read all the advertisements published in the local papers; and matters of local importance which are advertised are quite as likely to come to them from other sources as from the published notices. . . .

One who derives knowledge of the fact from public notoriety is sufficiently notified; . . . and probably in many small communities a fact would sooner be made notorious by a notice in the local column of the county or village paper than in any other way. In a large city it might be otherwise. But all that can be required in any case is that such notice be given as is likely to make the fact generally known locally. . . . When that is done the party giving the notice has performed his duty, and any one contemplating for the first time to open dealings with the partnership must at his peril ascertain the facts. This, in effect, was the instruction given. . . .

Case Question

1. Distinguish between actual and constructive notice. In many of the large law and accounting partnerships, partnerships are technically dissolved every year on the addition of new partners or the death or retirement of a partner. Are these partnerships required to send notice of dissolution every year to those who extend credit to them?

Review Problems

1. P owned a small farm, a part of which he leased to E and F who jointly operated a small pig-raising business. E and F split profits and jointly managed the business. Later, the city prevented use of the land for such a purpose. E went to the premises to remove some lumber, some fencing, and the pigs. An altercation with P developed over his right to remove the lumber and fencing, and E intentionally struck and injured P. Immediately before the fight E negligently allowed most of the pigs to escape confinement into P's cornfield. They trampled and

ate some of P's crop. A few days after the altercation, while P was still in the hospital, E returned for the lumber, the fencing and the wandering pigs. E leaves town. P sues F for the bodily injury caused by E, the damage to his crop, and the conversion of his lumber and fencing. Will F be liable? Explain.

Your client, Williams, Watkins, and Glenn, is a general partnership engaged primarily in the real estate brokerage business; however, in addition, it buys and sells real property for its own account. Williams and Watkins are almost exclusively responsible for the brokerage part of the business, and Glenn devotes almost all of his time to partnership acquisitions and sales of real estate. The firm letterhead makes no distinction along these functional lines, and all members are listed as licensed real estate brokers. Normally acquisitions are made in the firm name; although for convenience or other reason, Glenn occasionally takes title in his own name for and on behalf of the firm.

The partnership agreement contains, among other provisions, the following:

- No partner shall reduce the standard real estate commission charged (6%) without the consent of at least one other partner.
- No partner shall purchase or sell real property for or on behalf of the partnership without the consent of all other partners. Title to real property so acquired shall be taken exclusively in the partnership name, unless otherwise agreed to by all the partners.
- All checks received that are payable to the partnership and all checks and cash received for or on behalf of the partnership shall be deposited intact in one of the partnership's bank accounts.

Part A.   Watkins showed a magnificent $350,000 ranch estate, listed for over a year with the firm by John Foster, to numerous prospective purchasers. The firm's exclusive listing had recently expired and Watkins was afraid the firm would lose the sale. Foster's price was firm, and he had repeatedly refused to negotiate with interested parties or accept an offer below $350,000. The most recent prospective buyer offered $340,000 but would not budge from that price. Watkins, fearing that a rival broker might obtain a buyer and cause him to lose the commission, agreed to lower the commission to $11,000, which was acceptable to Foster. Watkins did this without the consent of either of the other partners.

2. Can Williams, Watkins, and Glenn or Williams and Glenn recover from Foster the $10,000 reduction in the commission granted by Watkins to Foster? Explain.

3. What recourse does the partnership or the other partners have against Watkins? Explain.

Part B.   During your firm's annual examination of the financial statements of Williams, Watkins, and Glenn, the staff auditor discovered that Glenn had recently engaged in a series of questionable transactions affecting the firm's financial position. Following is a description of these transactions.

First, Glenn sold a tract of land to Bill Sparks for $18,500. Title to the land was held in the name of the partnership. Spark's check was payable to the partnership and was cashed by Glenn at the First City Bank, which handled the firm's checking account. Glenn indorsed the firm name "Per Donald Glenn, Partner" and took the cash. Obtaining this amount of cash at the First City Bank was not an uncommon practice for the partnership because the firm paid its substantial weekly payroll and commissions in cash.

Glenn's second series of transactions involved the sale of the firm's former office building for $38,000 to Charles Whitmore. Whitmore was formerly associated with the firm but had left to establish his own real estate business and was currently a tenant in the firm's old offices. Whitmore was cognizant of the express limitations on the partners' authority contained in the Williams, Watkins, and Glenn partnership agreement. However, Whitmore was assured by Glenn that the requisite consent for his individual actions had been obtained from the other partners regarding the sale in question. Glenn also persuaded Whitmore, "for convenience's sake," to make the check payable to his individual order. Glenn cashed the check at one of the savings banks in which the firm had a balance in excess of $50,000.

Glenn's third series of transactions began when he acquired a tract of land for $55,000 from Arthur Douglas. Glenn paid for the land with a partnership check but took record title in his own name. A few days later, two days before leaving for vacation, Glenn closed the sale of this property to Frank Carlson and received a certified check for $58,500 payable to his own order. The proceeds of this sale were not deposited in any of the firm's bank accounts. Glenn has not returned from his vacation. In fact, he is five days overdue and has not communicated with the firm. It was subsequently learned that he cashed the check and retained the funds for his personal use.

4. What rights does the partnership or Williams and Watkins have against Bill Sparks or First City Bank? Explain.

5. What rights does the partnership or Williams and Watkins have against Charles Whitmore? Explain.

6. What rights does the partnership or Williams and Watkins have against Frank Carlson? Explain.

(Questions 2 through 7 are adapted from CPA Exam Question #7, Uniform CPA, taken from the November 7, 1975, exam. © American Institute of Certified Public Accountants, Inc., 1975.)

7. What rights does the partnership or Williams and Watkins have against Glenn?

8. X, Y, and Z each contributed $75,000 in capital to their partnership, in which each partner was to share equally in all profits and losses. X elected to withdraw from the partnership because his personal assets were depleted. An accounting was ordered. It was found that X had advanced to the firm an additional $10,000 several years before the dissolution and this remained unpaid. Y had drawn out $25,000 of his capital before dissolution and Z had drawn out the whole of his, and owed the firm $2,000 which remains unpaid. After selling all of the assets, the partnership had $141,000 but owed $18,000 to firm creditors, and $2,000 to Y for services rendered in winding up the business. Shortly before dissolution P recovered a $12,000 judgment against X as an individual. What amounts should be distributed, if any, at the time of the final distribution? Will P recover anything? If so, when and how much?

9. Dowling, a partner of Lazor, Bassett, Dowling, & Lamb, died on February 2, 1976. The four partners were equal partners in all respects (i.e., capital accounts, profit and loss sharing, etc.). The partnership agreement was silent on the question of the rights of a deceased partner on his death. Dowling's Last Will and Testament bequeathed his entire estate to his "beloved wife." His widow is now claiming the right to 25% of all partnership property. What rights does Dowling's widow have in respect to specific partnership property or against the partnership or surviving partners? Explain.

10. How would a "buy-out" agreement affect your answer to the question above? Explain.

(Questions 9 and 10 are adapted from CPA Exam Question #6c, Business Law, taken from the May 7, 1976, exam. © American Institute of Certified Public Accountants, Inc., 1976.)

Endnotes

1. J. Crane and A. Bromberg, *Law of Partnership* 280 (1968).
2. See *Dixon* v. *Haynes*, 146 Wash. 163; 262 P. 119 (1927).
3. See *Melosevich* v. *Cichy*, 30 Wash. 2d. 702, 193 P. 2d 342 (1948).
4. Crane, *supra*, p. 309.
5. See, annot. at 54 ALR 2d 330.
6. See, *Hyrne* v. *Erwin*, 23 S.C. 226, 55 Am. Rep. 15 (1885).
7. Crane, *supra*, p. 319.
8. A. Conard, R. Knauss & S. Siegel, *Enterprise Organization*, 645 (1972).
9. *Ibid.*, p. 646.

Corporations

Part Four

Corporations: Introduction, Formation, and Corporate Personality

9

Thinking and studying about corporations is very difficult for at least two major reasons. The first is that corporations are an extremely diverse group of enterprises. Consider just the element of size. In some states a single person may incorporate a business. This person may be the only shareholder, the only director, and the only officer and employee. Thinking about such an enterprise is relatively easy. It is just one person (or, in some cases, a very few) who is acting alone and as an individual would act. Contrast this with the very large corporations or megacorporations[1] of today that have millions of shareholders, hundreds of thousands of employees, and sell goods worth billions of dollars every year. These very large American corporations are one of the dominating forces in the nation's and world's economy. Indeed, together with our laws creating and protecting property rights, they are a major tool of capitalism and deserve to be treated as one of the most significant legal innovations in the development of the Western political economy. Over 50 years ago, one of the most distinguished legal scholars who wrote about and studied large American business corporations said:

> The corporation has, in fact, become both a method of property tenure and a means of organizing economic life. Grown to tremendous proportions, there may be said to have evolved a "corporate system"—as there once was a feudal system—which has attracted to itself a combination of attributes and powers, and has attained a degree of prominence entitling it to be dealt with as a major social institution.[2]

We can easily conceive of single-person or small corporations, but thinking about these megacorporations and assessing their influence and power, their impact on our lives and our civilization is very difficult. The best analogy may be not to an individual but to a large state government. For example, the following was reported in 1973 about General Motors, which is one of the world's largest manufacturing corporations:

Corporations as Major Institutions in our Society

273

That corporation by itself gives work to 750,000 employees who turn out over 28×10^9 worth of goods, yielding a net profit of 1.9×10^9 in 1971, and from that revenue paying 9.8×10^8 of dividends to its shareholders. G.M.'s production is greater than the budget of the Federal Republic of Germany; together with 19 other U.S. companies its sales would surpass that country's GNP. Its revenues are 1/5 those of the U.S. Government, 50 times Nevada's and 8 times New York's.[3]

Another source characterizes the sheer size of some megacorporations this way:

Of *Fortune's* top 1,000 corporations, the ten largest firms had 16 percent of the workforce, 20 percent of the profits, and 23 percent of the assets. Exxon had greater sales in 1974 than each of the GNP's of Austria, Denmark and South Africa. General Motors employs more people (in 1974)—734,000—than are employed in the states of California, New York, Pennsylvania, and Michigan combined.[4]

Megacorporations are each certainly powerful and significant elements of our commercial society, but when considered as a group their impact is even more awesome. In 1980, the 200 largest manufacturing companies had total assets that were just short of 60% of the assets of all manufacturing corporations;[5] and, according to *Forbes* magazine, the total sales of the 200 megacorporations for 1980 were 64.13% of the American gross national product and they earned 90.25% of all corporate profits.

Corporations range not only from small to almost unimaginable proportions, but they also engage in every conceivable type of legal profit making or even government activities. Towns and villages, churches, schools, YMCAs, and the Girl Scouts may be incorporated. This diversity makes any discussion of corporations necessarily very general and subject to numerous exceptions.

A second impediment that especially compounds the difficulty in thinking and studying about corporations and megacorporations is that there exists no tradition of systematic inquiry, analysis and evaluation of corporations and megacorporations,[6] as the significant and powerful actors that they are. Unlike the other power centers in our society, government and organized religion, there exists no formalized study of megacorporations themselves. By "formalized study," we mean a systematic course of instruction in high schools or universities of the type found for instruction in government and how it operates. We recognize that instruction in the other power center in our society, organized religion, exists in the respective religious institutions, but the nature of the power relationship between people and the state and organized religion is examined on a systematic basis in our educational system. This instruction provides a shared conceptual base from which we gain knowledge about these institutions.

The reasons that we have no formalized instruction in megacorporations, portraying them as the powerful actors they are, may be mostly beyond the scope of this book, but should be mentioned briefly here since this book is, in part, about corporations and megacorporations. The first reason is that there is a perception that when we formalize instruction about "business" (e.g., accounting, management, marketing), especially at the college level, we are providing instruction about megacorporations. This is no more true of megacorporations than it is true that instruction about the techniques of public sector budgeting inform us about the rights that people have vis-a-vis government.

A second and more perplexing reason for the lack of any organized body of knowledge about megacorporations and their impact on our society is that our American social science base (and a large part of Western philosophy as well) is premised on individual, human action, not group action. The megacorporation is assumed to act as a rational individual would. This view totally ignores the very collective, group-oriented nature of the megacorporation. Because of our American traditions and ideology of individualism that define how we see and understand complex social phenomena, the group nature of the megacorporation has escaped our view.

The Focus of State-Based Corporation Law

It is important when you study this material that you have an image of the corporation in mind roughly equivalent to that contemplated by state legislatures as they pass and amend state corporation statutory schemes. If you can imagine a spectrum with a one-person corporation at one end and the megacorporations at the other, we believe the proper focus for understanding state statutory corporation law is on the nine-tenths of the corporations that stretch out from the one-person corporation. See Figure 9-1. In 1977 there were about 2.25 million corporations in this country (see figure 2-2 in Chapter 2), so we are focusing on, very generally stated, over two million of them.

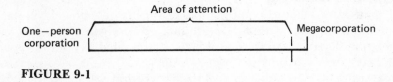

FIGURE 9-1

The Nature of Corporation Law

Corporation law, as we use that term in this book and as legal scholars and practitioners use the term, refers to the state level, mostly statutory law that is, in essence, the structural (or, as one scholar put it, the "constitutional"[7]) law of corporate existence. For the corporations that are the subject of our focus, corporation law prescribes how the shareholders relate to one another and to the directors and to the corporation. It governs corporate shareholder and board meetings and defines how power is to be distributed or circumscribed in corporations. Although megacorporations are supposedly subject to the same laws as all other corporations, it seems reasonable to conclude that the larger the corporation the more complex the structure and the more difficult it becomes (if not simply impractical) to apply any single state's law. Generally, the larger the corporation, the greater the likelihood that federal law (primarily, the federal securities laws) will be applicable to govern primarily the rights of shareholders. Also, the larger the corporation, the greater the likelihood that it can affect state legislative action. Therefore, to understand thoroughly state corporation law, we suggest the division mentioned above. In most circumstances the material discussed in this unit on corporation law is applicable to all corporations, but the reality is that some are more immune to it than others.

To round out a presentation on most of the law applicable to corporations (as opposed to "corporation law") we follow this unit on state-based corporation law with one on federal securities laws. These laws are best understood in their application to megacorporations and the corporations on the right of our suggested scale. The same may be said of the labor laws and other federal-level employment laws.[8]

State-Based Corporation Law: A Historical Note

Prior to the middle of the nineteenth century, corporate existence *was created* by a specific legislative act. The key features of corporate existence—limited liability for the owners, unlimited length of life (perpetual existence), and the size of the corporation and its purpose—were thought to be privileges and were bestowed, in theory, when the recipients could convince the legislature that in exchange for these privileges, a public purpose would be served. Thus, many of the early corporations were toll road companies, canal companies, and a few manufacturing companies. Banks and insurance companies were more severely limited in the grant of these privileges. Often the life of banks was limited to a period from 12 to 25 years and their purposes were limited strictly to receiving deposits, loaning money, discounting bills of exchange, and issuing drafts. Manufacturing companies and public utilities were encouraged by, in some cases, the award of a corporate charter with an unlimited life. Indeed, a primary legislative activity of the state legislatures until the middle of the nineteenth century was the granting of these corporate charters. For example, in the state of Ohio in 1845 there were 53 corporations created to accomplish the following purposes:[9]

Type		Number
Manufacturing		4
Public utilities		42
Railroad	8	
Water	1	
Bridge	2	
Turnpikes	30	
Misc.	1	
Banks		1
Insurance		1
Real estate		5

There were several disadvantages to granting corporate charters by specific act. Foremost was the complaint that some of these grants also carried with them the award of a monopoly. Another was that those who wished to enter business might not have the political strength nor the right kinds of information necessary to seek a legislative grant of the charter. The system of granting a corporate charter by individual legislative enactment was, in short, a matter of intense political interest.

By the time of the election of Andrew Jackson (1829), the political debate about corporate charters focused on whether corporations, with the key features mentioned above, would be abolished altogether or would be freely available to everyone. This debate was resolved in favor of "General Incorporation Laws" that set out basic requirements which, if compliance was promised by those applying for a charter, granted to any individual a corporate charter. These general laws were adopted first on the East Coast and spread to the Midwest by the 1850s. So, the first historical phase of corporation law was a movement from the creation of business corporations by individual legislative act to general incorporation laws. Under these laws, a charter was granted on the filing of the appropriate papers and the payment of a fee.

As manufacturing grew in importance, especially in Massachusetts, New York, and New Jersey, a second phase of the history of corporation law began to unfold. As corporations began doing business in states other than the state in which they were chartered, they realized that some states would treat them more favorably than others. So they began to shop around for the most "convenient state" in which to incorporate.

New Jersey was the first state to officially notice that corporations could be attracted by enacting favorable corporation laws. In the early 1890s, New Jersey was experiencing a severe financial crisis and officially went into the chartering "business" by first repealing its antitrust law and by 1896 passing the General Revision Act, which contains the essential elements of most twentieth-century state corporation statutes. Today, these elements do not seem overly attractive, but against a historical background of suspicion and extreme legislative caution in chartering corporations, these "revisions" were radical.

There were three themes to the New Jersey approach.[10] The first was to allow unlimited corporate size and life and it added that anyone could incorporate for any lawful purpose. The second was a revision of the capitalization requirements that allowed undervalued or watered stock. This permitted one company to purchase another company by payment in its own stock, and the value of the stock received was to be established by the directors of the acquired company. Thus putative monopolists could gain control of competing corporations without paying a cent. They merely offered the owners of the acquired corporation quantities of stock at prices that were irresistible. A third theme was the evisceration of the notion of shareholder control by permitting stockholders to be classified as preferred or common and then giving them unequal power. This enabled the organizers of a corporation to sell large quantities of nonvoting stock to the public while retaining all of the voting stock. This act also allowed the distribution of voting stock to everyone while giving directors the right to amend bylaws without the consent of the shareholders.[11]

New Jersey's approach worked. During the early twentieth century there was a competition between the industrial states of the East for this apparently available industrial base; the winner was the state of Delaware. As one scholar put it, "What began as a tragedy in New Jersey was institutionalized as a farce in Delaware."[12] Delaware retained the most attractive features of the New Jersey laws but expanded and liberalized those laws permitting economic concentration through "stock pyramiding." This allowed a financier to have control of a subsidiary corporation through a parent and to reduce personal investment in the controlling stock to a small amount by selling off most of the parent's equity in nonvoting stock. This could be repeated at several levels, so that multimillion dollar combinations resulted with control in persons who had less than one percent of the total ownership value. This is illustrated in figure 9-2 and described below.

The numbers outside of the box indicate the percent of voting control held by the Van Swearingen brothers and the numbers inside the box indicate the percent of ownership capital contributed by them. In the case of the Hocking Valley Railroad, the Van Swearingen brothers controlled 81% of the voting shares, yet contributed 0.25% of the ownership capital. Stated differently, 99.75% of the ownership capital was contributed by persons not in control of the corporation. Nonowners were controlling the corporation. Today the separation of ownership and control in the megacorporations is a reality seldom mentioned, analyzed, or evaluated in textbooks on corporation law, and represents another reason for separat-

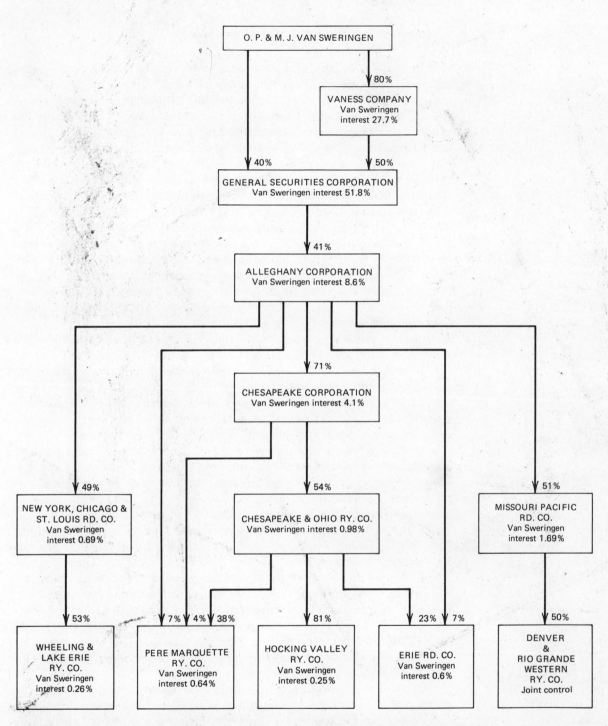

FIGURE 9-2 Major elements in the control of the Van Sweringen system of railroads.

[*Source:* A. Berle and G. Means, The Modern Corporation and Private Property, 75 (1932).]

ing the study of megacorporations from smaller ones. Most often, megacorporations are owned by thousands and millions of people, but they are controlled not by these owners but by their management. It was the collapse of the substance of state corporation law that helped make possible this separation of ownership and control.

From time to time other states have tried to "out-Delaware" Delaware, but have not succeeded. Delaware corporation law is so favorable to management (usually at the expense of the shareholders and the public) that as of 1974, it chartered 448 of the 1000 largest American corporations—including 52 of the largest 100 and 251 out of the largest 500.[13] These 448 corporations accounted for over 52% of the sales of the 1000 largest manufacturers.

In very simple terms, what this means is that should a dispute arise between a shareholder or a small group of shareholders and the management of a megacorporation that is chartered in Delaware, that state law, relative to the state law that has developed elsewhere, will probably favor management. In addition, in a state that uses its corporation law as a means to attract corporations (and thus raise state revenues), there are numerous other instances in which the law does not adequately confront the inevitable tension between corporate management on the one hand and shareholders, employees, and the public on the other.

Thus, some scholars have noted a third historical phase in the development of the law as applied to corporations implicitly recognizing the inconsequential nature of state-based law applicable to megacorporations especially. This phase is the one begun in the mid-1960s by the passage of comprehensive federal statutory schemes. This law is particularly applicable to megacorporations and deals with employment discrimination, environmental pollution, employee safety and health, and product safety. These statutory schemes together with new duties of management imposed through the application of the federal securities laws (beginning with the *Texas Gulf Sulphur* case in 1968) comprises the material for the last two parts of this book.

In this section we have traced the development of state-based corporation law from its beginnings where each corporation was chartered individually by a state legislature and those receiving the charter had to prove public benefit as a condition for chartering, through the widespread state adoption of general incorporation laws to the dimly perceived third phase of response by the federal government. This is but an overview and has been very generally stated.

Most of the approximately two million corporations that remain the focus of this part of the book could not afford or were not inclined to all incorporate in Delaware. All states do have general incorporation laws that apply to these small and midsized corporations, and it is to these laws that we now turn our attention.

The Model Business Corporation Act

The interstate nature of much of our country's business has necessitated the creation of either uniform acts (such as the Uniform Commercial Code that applies to the sale of goods, the extension of credit for the purchase of goods, etc.) or model acts. Uniform acts are urged for adoption by all states so that business will have but one set of legal principles to recognize in an area of commerce. Model acts are not urged for adoption but are offered by recognized bodies of legal practitioners, scholars, and jurists as the best statement of the law.

The Model Business Corporation Act (hereafter MBCA) was conceived in 1946 and first published in 1950. In 1960 the first edition of the Model Business Corporation Act Annotated was published under the auspices of the American Bar Foundation, following a draft prepared by scholars and practitioners who worked on the Committee On Corporate Laws, which is a section of the Corporation, Banking, and Business Law arm of the American Bar Association. Since that time 20 states have adopted the MBCA substantially in whole and 10 additional states have adopted it in a "large part."[14] This act is in the appendix of this book. The original MBCA was patterned on the Illinois Business Corporation Act of 1933, so court interpretations of it are necessarily influenced by Illinois state court opinions and subsequent Illinois legislative revisions. Because of the widespread recognition of the MBCA we will use it as our primary source for the statement of corporation law together with various state court decisions and, from time to time, we will cite Illinois law and cases. The state corporation law in your state may vary slightly, or in a few circumstances, in a major way, but it is our judgment that this source is the single best source of the law. Unlike Delaware law, the MBCA attempts to strike a balance embracing the interests of the state, shareholders, and management.[15]

As you study the corporation law presented here you should be aware that most states have entirely separate statutory schemes that apply to nonprofit corporations, banks, insurance companies, cooperatives, and various governmental units that incorporate. So, these entities are excluded from the principles discussed hereafter.

The Legal Nature of Corporations: Constitutional Law

In some sense, this entire unit is about the legal nature of corporations. Primarily it is about how corporations are created, managed, and controlled through state corporation law. But underpinning this layer of law is the constitutional law applicable to corporations. To what extent do our notions of fundamental fairness implied and explicit in the "due process" and "equal protection" clauses of the Fourteenth Amendment (applicable to state governments) and the Fifth Amendment (applicable to the federal government) apply to corporations? In the eyes of the law, is a corporation entitled to the same constitutional protections as a human being? The answer to this question is, yes!, generally, but there are some exceptions.

The most fundamental proposition is that corporations are persons for purposes of the due process and equal protection clauses of both the Fourteenth and Fifth Amendments to the U. S. Constitution. This means that most of the basic American rights and privileges are extended to corporations. It seems that the application of these rights and privileges to corporations was accomplished without much debate and discussion. The excerpts from the case below reveal this and they also reveal that there is some judicial discomfort about this lack of thoughtful discussion in treating corporations almost equally with natural persons.

WHEELING STEEL CORP. v. GLANDER
337 U.S. 562 at 574 (1949)

(Author's note: The merits of this case involved whether certain corporations not chartered by the state of Ohio (foreign corporations) but which were authorized to do business there and did do business there had to pay an ad valorem *tax on their accounts receivable derived from the sales of goods manufactured within the state. These accounts receivable were not used in the conduct of the business in Ohio. Accounts receivable of identical nature that were owned by residents and domestic corporations were exempt from the tax. The U.S. Supreme Court held that this tax unfairly discriminated against these foreign corporations and thus denied to them the equal protection of the law in violation of the Fourteenth Amendment.*

Mr. Justice Jackson wrote the opinion for the majority of the court. Nowhere in the opinion did he explain why he believed the Fourteenth Amendment was applicable to corporations. He assumed it to be applicable. However, two dissenting Justices chided Justice Jackson for this. Apparently, Justice Jackson felt compelled to respond and, in an unusual move, wrote a personal note that followed his opinion for the majority. Below are two excerpts from this exchange between the dissenters and Justice Jackson.)

BY MR. JUSTICE JACKSON
The writer of the Court's opinion deems it necessary to complete the record by pointing out why, in writing by assignment for the Court, he assumed without discussion that the protections of the Fourteenth Amendment are available to a corporation. It was not questioned by the State in this case, nor was it considered by the courts below. It has consistently been held by this Court that the Fourteenth Amendment assures corporations equal protection of the laws, at least since 1886, *Santa Clara County* v. *Southern Pacific R. Co.,* 118 U. S. 394, 396, and that it entitles them to due process of law, at least since 1889, *Minneapolis & St. L. R. Co.* v. *Beckwith,* 129 U. S. 26, 28.

It is true that this proposition was once challenged by one Justice. . . . But the challenge did not commend itself, even to such consistent liberals as Mr. Justice Brandeis and Mr. Justice Stone, and I had supposed it was no longer pressed. . . .

Without pretending to a complete analysis, I find that in at least two cases during this current term the same question was appropriate for consideration, as here. In *Railway Express Agency* v. *New York,* 336 U. S. 106, a corporation claimed to be deprived of both due process and equal protection of the law, and in *Ott* v. *Mississippi Barge Line,* 336 U. S. 169, a corporation claimed to be denied due process of law. At prior terms, in many cases the question was also inherent, for corporations made similar claims under the Fourteenth Amendment. . . . Although the author of the present dissent was the writer of each of the cited Court's opinions, it was not intimated therein that there was even doubt whether the corporations had standing to raise the questions or were entitled to protection of the Amendment. Instead, in each case the author, as I have done in this case, proceeded to discuss and dispose of the corporation's contentions on their merits. . . .

MR. JUSTICE DOUGLAS, *with whom* MR. JUSTICE BLACK *concurs, dissenting.*

It has been implicit in all of our decisions since 1886 that a corporation is a "person" within the meaning of the Equal Protection Clause of the Fourteenth Amendment. *Santa Clara County* v. *Southern Pac. R. Co.,* 118 U. S. 394, 396, so held. The Court was cryptic in its decision. It was so sure of its ground that it wrote no opinion on the point, Chief Justice Waite announcing from the bench:

> "The court does not wish to hear argument on the question whether the provision in the Fourteenth Amendment to the Constitution, which forbids a State to deny to any person within its jurisdiction the equal protection of the laws, applies to these corporations. We are all of opinion that it does."

There was no history, logic, or reason given to support that view. Nor was the result so obvious that exposition was unnecessary.

The Fourteenth Amendment became a part of the Constitution in 1868. In 1871 a corporation claimed that Louisiana had imposed on it a tax that violated the Equal Protection Clause of the new Amendment. Mr. Justice Woods (then Circuit Judge) held that "person" as there used did not include a corporation and added, "This construction of the section is strengthened by the history of the submission by congress, and the adoption by the states of the 14th amendment, so fresh in all minds as to need no rehearsal." *Insurance Co.* v. *New Orleans,* 1 Woods 85, 88.

What was obvious to Mr. Justice Woods in 1871 was still plain to the Court in 1873. Mr. Justice Miller in the *Slaughter-House Cases,* 16 Wall. 36, 71, adverted to events "almost too recent to be called history" to show that the purpose of the Amendment was to protect human rights—primarily the rights of a race which had just won its freedom. And as respects the Equal Protection Clause he stated, "The existence of laws in the States where the newly emancipated negroes resided, which discriminated with gross injustice and hardship against them as a class, was the evil to be remedied by this clause, and by it such laws are forbidden." p. 81.

Moreover what was clear to these earlier judges was apparently plain to the people who voted to make the Fourteenth Amendment a part of our Constitution. For as MR. JUSTICE BLACK pointed out in his dissent in *Connecticut General Co.* v. *Johnson,* 303 U. S. 77, 87, the submission of the Amendment to the people was on the basis that it protected human beings. There was no suggestion in its submission that it was designed to put negroes and corporations into one class and so dilute the police power of the States over corporate affairs. Arthur Twining Hadley once wrote that "The Fourteenth Amendment was framed to protect the negroes from oppression by the whites, not to protect corporations from oppression by the legislature. It is doubtful whether a single one of the members of Congress who voted for it had any idea that it would touch the question of corporate regulation at all."[1]

---

[1] The Constitutional Position of Property in America, 64 Independent 834, 836 (1908). He went on to say that the *Dartmouth College* case (4 Wheat. 518) and the construction given the Fourteenth Amendment in the *Santa Clara* case "have had the effect of placing the modern industrial corporation in an almost impregnable constitutional position." *Id.,* p. 836.

As to whether the framers of the Amendment may have had such an undisclosed purpose, see Graham, The "Conspiracy Theory" of the Fourteenth Amendment, 47 Yale L. J. 371.

Both MR. JUSTICE WOODS in *Insurance Co.* v. *New Orleans, supra,* p. 88, and MR. JUSTICE BLACK in his dissent in *Connecticut General Co.* v. *Johnson, supra,* pp. 88–89, have shown how strained a construction it is of the Fourteenth Amendment so to hold. Section 1 of the Amendment provides:

> All *persons* born or naturalized in the United States, and subject to the jurisdiction thereof, are *citizens* of the United States and of the State wherein they reside. No State shall make or enforce any law which shall abridge the privileges or immunities of *citizens* of the United States; nor shall any State deprive any *person* of life, liberty, or property, without due process of law; nor deny to any *person* within its jurisdiction the equal protection of the laws. (Italics added.)

"Persons" in the first sentence plainly includes only human beings, for corporations are not "born or naturalized."

Corporations are not "citizens" within the meaning of the first clause of the second sentence. *Western Turf Assn.* v. *Greenberg,* 204 U. S. 359, 363; *Selover, Bates & Co.* v. *Walsh,* 226 U. S. 112, 126.

It has never been held that they are persons whom a State may not deprive of "life" within the meaning of the second clause of the second sentence.

"Liberty" in that clause is "the liberty of natural, not artificial, persons." *Western Turf Assn.* v. *Greenberg, supra,* p. 363.

But "property" as used in that clause has been held to include that of a corporation since 1889 when *Minneapolis & St. L. R. Co.* v. *Beckwith,* 129 U. S. 26, was decided.

It requires distortion to read "person" as meaning one thing, then another within the same clause and from clause to clause. It means, in my opinion, a substantial revision of the Fourteenth Amendment. As to the matter of construction, the sense seems to me to be with Mr. Justice Woods in *Insurance Co.* v. *New Orleans, supra,* p. 88, where he said, "The plain and evident meaning of the section is, that the persons to whom the equal protection of the law is secured are persons born or naturalized or endowed with life and liberty, and consequently natural and not artificial persons."

History has gone the other way. Since 1886 the Court has repeatedly struck down state legislation as applied to corporations on the ground that it violated the Equal Protection Clause. Every one of our decisions upholding legislation as applied to corporations over the objection that it violated the Equal Protection Clause has assumed that they are entitled to the constitutional protection. But in those cases it was not necessary to meet the issue since the state law was not found to contain the elements of discrimination which the Equal Protection Clause condemns. But now that the question is squarely presented I can only conclude that the *Santa Clara* case was wrong and should be overruled.

One hesitates to overrule cases even in the constitutional field that are of an old vintage. But that has never been a deterrent heretofore and should not be now.

We are dealing with a question of vital concern to the people of the nation. It may be most desirable to give corporations this protection from the operation of the legislative process. But that question is not for us. It is for the people. If they want corporations to be treated as humans are treated, if they want to grant corporations this large degree of emancipation from state regulation, they should say so. The Constitution provides a method by which they may do so. We should not do it for them through the guise of interpretation.

1. What were the original reasons given by the U.S. Supreme Court for extending the Fourteenth Amendment to corporations? What sort of reasoned reflection and discussion has there been on this issue since the first time the Fourteenth was so applied?

2. In your own mind, reflect for a few minutes whether corporations, especially megacorporations, *should* be treated by the law in the same way that individual humans are. What are the reasons justifying similar treatment? What are the reasons justifying dissimilar treatment?

3. Imagine that the issue of the application of the Fourteenth and Fifth Amendments to corporations was to come up today and that you were asked to write the opinion. If you were inclined to analogize the corporation to something other than a human being, what would it be?

We said that there are some exceptions to the general rule. The Fourteenth Amendment also prohibits states from enforcing laws that abridge the "privileges" or "immunities" of citizens of the United States. Within this context, corporations are not "citizens." A good example of this is that a corporation chartered in one state is not as free as a human from that same state to go into a neighboring state and do business. It must first register and qualify with the state as a foreign corporation. Yet, a corporation is a citizen of its state of incorporation for diversity citizenship purposes.

Another major exception to the general rule that corporations are like humans for purposes of constitutional law is that the Fifth Amendment protects people from being compelled to be a witness against themselves. This privilege against self-incrimination is *not* available to a corporation. A corporate agent can be forced to produce documents and records that are incriminating to it. As you can see, it is not entirely safe to generalize about when a corporation qualifies as a person or citizen for purposes of the application of constitutional law.

Until recently corporations were prevented from engaging in a learned profession, such as law or medicine. Licenses to practice such professions are granted to individual human beings. A corporation cannot qualify for such a license. The corporation was also barred from practicing such a profession through its shareholders or employees who were properly licensed. To permit such activity was viewed as being inappropriate, unethical, and against public policy, primarily because the professionals would be able to avail themselves of limited liability. State legislatures simply believed it unwise to allow professionals to shield themselves from personal liability by incorporating. Thus, members of the medical and legal profession were forced to be solo practitioners or to form a partnership. This put them at a disadvantage for some income tax purposes. After a great deal of lobbying by the various professions, many states enacted special incorporation statutes. These statutes permit members of a profession to incorporate and to engage in their profession through that corporation. This allows them to enjoy the tax benefits of corporations—primarily deferring income in years of large earnings to years of less earnings. At the same time the statutes are designed to protect the interests of the public that deal with these professions. Protection of the public is accomplished by not allowing the professionals who incorporate under these statutes to limit their liability for their acts or for the tortious acts of fellow associates.

Whether to Incorporate: Advantages and Disadvantages

The entrepreneur can operate the enterprise as a sole proprietorship, partnership, or corporation. The biggest advantage inherent in the corporate form is the limited liability that is extended to the owners. The shareholder limits the risk to the amount of the investment; a shareholder bears no unlimited personal liability as does the sole proprietor or general partner. This limitation of liability for the owners of a corporation is accomplished by Section 25 of the MBCA, which provides (in part):

> A holder or subscriber to shares of a corporation shall be under no obligation to the corporation or its creditors with respect to such shares other than the obligation to pay to the corporation the full consideration for which such shares were issued or to be issued.

Consider just a simple example. A, B, and C decide to incorporate and each contributes $5,000 to the enterprise, which is properly chartered as the ABC Corporation. In the first month of its existence, an agent of ABC is negligent and injures D. D sues ABC and recovers a judgment of $25,000. The recovery of the judgment (which can be for more than the corporation is worth because the judgment reflects the extent of the injury) will be limited to the value of the corporation ($15,000). That is, the judgment may be for $25,000 but only $15,000 of it will be collectable. The other assets of the shareholder-owners cannot be attached or otherwise affected. There are a few exceptions to this, which will be discussed later in the chapter.

Other advantages are the continuity of existence of the enterprise regardless of additions, withdrawals, or death of the owners; the freedom with which ownership interests can be transferred, and the ability to raise capital through the sale of stock.

The greatest potential disadvantage is the double taxation—the fact that the corporation pays tax on its profits and, in turn, when these profits are distributed in the form of dividends it constitutes taxable income to the shareholders. However, taxes constitute a two-sided coin, as the corporate form does offer certain tax advantages. For instance, reasonable salaries paid to employee-shareholders are deductible from gross income, and a corporation may reasonably accumulate earnings. A partnership does not deduct partners' salaries as a business expense, and a partner is

taxed on his or her share of partnership profits whether they are distributed or not.

Another disadvantage of the corporate form is that the necessary
corporate formalities of board meetings, shareholder meetings, etc. are
more cumbersome and restrictive than the operating procedures in a
partnership. See Table 2-1 in Chapter 2, *supra,* for a complete outline of
the pros and cons of the alternate forms of business organizations.

Where to Incorporate

An individual is free to incorporate in any geographical location. It is not
necessary to have the corporate headquarters, manufacturing facilities, or
warehouse in the state of incorporation. It may not even be necessary to
do business in the state of incorporation; although it may be necessary to
have a registered agent and office located in the state. It is usually just
practical for small and medium-sized corporations to incorporate in the
state where they do their primary business. Different considerations are
present for the larger corporation, which often has a complex capital
structure and engages in business in many states. The corporation statutes
can vary in important respects from state to state. Certain features of a
given law might be unattractive, such as the Illinois prohibition (contained
in Section 28) against nonvoting stock. Another state may permit a type of
management flexibility that is inviting.

The decision of where to incorporate is based on self-interest. One
selects the location that is most favorable. A state's tax advantages, its
degree of management flexibility and the powers granted to shareholders, the obstacles it places in front of those attempting a corporate
takeover, etc. are some of the factors to be weighed. What constitutes an
important factor to one group considering incorporation can be relatively
unimportant to another group with different needs and interests.

How to Incorporate

A corporation doesn't simply blossom into existence. Someone must perform the work necessary to breathe corporate life into an enterprise.
Planning and work must be done before the required incorporation documents are filed. The design of the corporation must be formulated. Subscriptions for its shares of stock must be solicited, property acquired and
employees contacted, and all the other necessary items leading up to
incorporation performed. The individuals that occupy this role are usually called "promoters."

Promoters

Naturally the promotion process involves certain expenses. The promoter
will desire reimbursement of these expenses and possibly compensation

**The Process of
Incorporation**

for services as a promoter. The MBCA provides that corporations may be promoters, but does not otherwise deal with promoters.

The promoter will be paid if: the state's business corporation statute makes the corporation responsible for the reasonable expenses of its promotion; the articles of incorporation specify payment; or the corporation, once formed, agrees to pay. Whether promotion expenses will be paid is not usually a problem. The promoter typically will also be an influential shareholder, incorporator, and director of the resulting corporation, so he or she will be in a position to seek payment.

Legal issues can arise over the amount or form taken by such compensation. The fiduciary duties created by an agency-principal relationship occupy a significant position in corporation law. The promoter stands in a fiduciary relationship to the corporation and the initial group of shareholders. Thus, while one is permitted to make a profit, one cannot make a secret profit. A promoter can legitimatize a profit pursuing one of four courses: (1) by providing an independent board of officers in no respect directly or indirectly under the promoter's control, and making full disclosure to the corporation through them; (2) by making a full disclosure of all material facts to each original subscriber of shares in the corporation; (3) by producing a ratification of the contract allowing a profit after disclosing its circumstances by vote of the stockholders of the completely established corporation; or (4) by the promoter being the real subscriber of all the shares of the capital stock. [*Old Dominion Copper Mining & Smelting Co.* v. *Bigelow,* 89 N.E. 193 (1909)]. The promoter does not owe a fiduciary duty towards persons who subsequently acquire the stock from the original shareholders. However, these subsequent shareholders can rely on the state and federal securities laws to provide them with some degree of protection against fraud.

Watered Stock

In the booming speculative investment days of the late 1800s and early 1900s, a common method of fleecing the public was through "watered stock." A promoter might have shares issued to him or her as fully paid when, in fact, full value had not been paid. A promoter might greatly inflate the value of his services and then take his payment in stock. Or, he might sell property, of slight or dubious value, to the corporation at an inflated price taking payment either in cash or stock. Suppose the promoter received $1000 worth of stock in return for property whose value did not exceed $100. That corporation has $900 of watered stock; it has issued $900 worth of stock for which it has received no assets or services. A subsequent investor would become an owner of a company whose true assets were below those reflected on its books because the stock would be worth less than the value paid. The individual receiving watered stock is liable to the corporation for the unpaid value of his stock. Today, stock watering is a rare occurrence.

Promoters' Contracts

Oftentimes, it will be necessary for the promoter to make contracts during the promotion process. The corporation is not liable on the preincorporation contract unless, after it was incorporated, it incurred liability through its action or inaction. For example, the board might pass a resolution accepting the contract; it might start making installment payments under the contract; or it may refrain from taking action but accept the benefits of the contract. In such instances, the corporation is said to have "adopted" the contract. Adoption is the functional equivalent of ratification in agency law. The corporation is not liable on the contract in the first instance because it was not in existence when the contract was made. Although the promoter made the contract for the future benefit of the corporation, the promoter was not acting for a principal. One cannot be an agent for a nonexistent principal.

What of the promoter's personal contract liability? The promoter is not automatically relieved of liability simply because the corporation has adopted the contract. The general rule is that the promoter is liable on such preincorporation contracts unless: (1) the contract provides that he is relieved of personal liability; or (2) a novation occurs (the promoter, corporation, and the contracting third party all agree to release the promoter from liability). The *Philipsborn* v. *Suson* case that follows breaks new ground on the question of promoter's contract liability. The Illinois Supreme Court holds that the intentions of the parties, at the time the contract was made, determines the promoter's liability. Whether this legal position gains widespread acceptance remains to be seen.

H.F. PHILIPSBORN & CO. v. *SUSON*
322 N.E. 2d 45 (1974) (S. Ct. Ill.)

The testimony shows that plaintiff was an Illinois corporation engaged in the business of mortgage banking and that it had previously financed two apartment projects for Suson, a real estate developer. Following several discussions between Suson and officials of plaintiff concerning financing for a proposed real estate development, an application in the name of Estates, for a construction and mortgage loan, was prepared by plaintiff. The application, prepared on a printed form, was signed "North Shore Estates, Inc., by Morris Suson Pres." It stated that Estates applied for a "construction and permanent first mortgage loan" in the amount of $5,488,000. The following words were printed on one line of the loan application form: "Title to be in the name of." In a space following those words there was typed "Trust to be formed." Immediately following, printed in ink, appeared the words "or corporation to be formed." The parties agree that this last addition was printed by Suson. The application also provided that acceptance by plaintiff within 60 days "shall constitute a binding contract to make said loan" and that "In such event we agree to pay you a commission equal to 2 percent of the loan."

The testimony shows that while the parties were discussing a performance bond and other matters relating to the loan Suson applied to another mortgage banker for a construction and mortgage loan on the same project. This application was for a larger principal amount at a lower interest rate. This second application was accepted, and sometime thereafter, when plaintiff sent Estates the mortgage documents and the note to be executed, they were returned unsigned. . . .

The judgment in the amount of $109,760 was entered on the count in plaintiff's complaint which sought to recover the 2 percent commission due upon acceptance of the loan. . . .

Plaintiff concedes that it intended Estates to be the obligor on the loan application and that the application, of itself, imposed no individual liability on Suson for the payment of its commission. It contends, however, that Estates, which purportedly applied for the loan, did not, at the time of the application, exist as a corporate entity, and that plaintiff, at that time, was not aware of that fact. The record shows that on September 17, 1963, when the application was signed, there was no corporate entity named North Shore Estates, Inc. It was incorporated on November 12, 1963, with a paid-in capital of $1,000 and with Suson as the sole shareholder and director. The corporate minutes reflect that the Board of Directors "approved and adopted all acts of Morris Suson to date and assumed liability therefor."

It is plaintiff's theory "that in the absence of a knowing agreement to the contrary" Suson, as the promoter of Estates, "is personally liable on a pre-incorporation contract and is not released by subsequent incorporation and ratification of the contract." It argues that "The general rule concerning promoters' contracts is that the promoter will be personally liable on contracts signed on behalf of a nonexistent corporation unless the contract provides to the contrary." The record shows that the circuit court admitted testimony on the question whether plaintiff knew that Estates was not in existence when the application was executed. This testimony was admitted on the theory that the language "or corporation to be formed" which appeared on the line on which were printed the words "Title to be in the name of" was ambiguous as to whether the corporation to be formed was North Shore Estates, Inc., the applicant for the loan, or a corporate titleholder mortgagor. Plaintiff contends that the question whether it was unaware of the nonexistence of Estates was properly submitted to the jury and that the appellate court erred in holding that the verdict was against the manifest weight of the evidence.

The parties to this appeal appear to be in agreement that, unless the parties to the transaction agree otherwise, an individual who conducts the ordinary affairs of a business in the name of a nonexistent corporation is personally liable, both at common law . . . and by statute . . . on contracts made in connection with the business. However, the authorities dealing with a promoter's personal liability on contracts made for the benefit of a proposed corporation present a wide array of factual situations and many so-called general rules. . . . A number of the decisions of this court and the appellate court are relevant to the liability of persons who exercise corporate powers without authority . . . but none deal with the precise issue here presented. A number of the decisions of the courts of review of other jurisdictions state that where a promoter had become liable on a pre-incorporation contract, he was not, in the absence of an agreement to that effect, discharged from liability merely because the corporation was later organized and ratified the contract. . . .

We find the facts of *Whitney* v. *Wyman,* 101

U.S. 392 (1879) . . . similar to those of this case and the reasoning more persuasive. In that case a letter was sent to Baxter Whitney stating, "Our company being so far organized, by direction of the officers, we now order from you . . . ." certain machinery and was signed "Charles Wyman, Edward P. Ferry, Carlton L. Storrs, Prudential Committee Grand Haven Fruit Basket Co." Baxter, in a letter addressed to the Grand Haven Fruit Basket Co., accepted the order for the machinery. The machinery was delivered but Baxter's sight draft on Wyman, Ferry and Storrs was protested because it was addressed to them individually. The letters of order and acceptance were dated February 1, 1869, and February 10, 1869, respectively, which was before the articles of incorporation were filed with the Secretary of State and the county clerk and, therefore, before the corporation was authorized to do business. Whitney filed an action against Wyman, Ferry and Storrs, individually, to recover the value of the machinery.

The rule applied by the court was that whether liability will be imposed upon the promoter depends upon the intent of the parties. It found from the exchange of letters "that both parties understood and meant that the contract was to be and, in fact, was with the corporation and not with the defendants individually." (101 U.S. at 396) . . . In response to the argument that his intent could not be given effect because the corporation was forbidden to do any business when the letters were written, the court said: "The corporation subsequently ratified the contract by recognizing and treating it as valid. This made it in all respects what it would have been if the requisite corporate power had existed when it was entered into." . . .

In our opinion, insofar as the loan commission . . . executed by Suson and delivered in lieu of the standby fee were concerned, the question whether there was acceptance of the loan application, and one other issue discussed later in this opinion, were the only issues of fact for determination by the jury. A contract is to be construed to give effect to the intent of the parties, . . . and effect must be given to the contract as written and any documents executed contemporaneously therewith. . . . In this transaction, so far as this record reflects, plaintiff required no showing of Estates' assets nor did it make any inquiry concerning its solvency. Estates was organized within 60 days of the execution of the loan application, and upon its approval and adoption of Suson's acts to date, and its assumption of liability for those acts, plaintiff had received everything for which it had bargained. The record shows that when the loan application was signed Suson had an option to acquire, but did not own, the land on which the proposed project was to be built, and that upon acquisition title was to be taken in either a trust or corporation, in either event, not in existence, but "to be formed." Clearly, under these circumstances, plaintiff looked only to Estates for its commission, and the fact that Estates had not at that time been formed furnished no basis for the imposition of personal liability on Suson for the payment of the loan commission. . . . On this record we hold that whether or not Estates existed as a corporate entity at the time the application was executed, or whether plaintiff knew that it was not, was not controlling, and that although we do not agree with its rationale, the appellate court correctly reversed the judgement entered against Suson in the amount of $109,760. . . .

Affirmed in part and reversed in part.

Case Questions

1. On the basis of the limited factual pattern sketched in this decision, what does the intention of the parties appear to have been?

2. Is it more pragmatic to impose liability by retroactive speculation as to the parties' intent or by applying a mechanical rule that the promoter is liable unless the contract provides to the contrary? Which is the more equitable rule?

Articles of Incorporation

To actually incorporate a business, one must comply with the statutory formalities of the particular state. A document referred to variously as the "articles of incorporation," "certificate of incorporation" or corporate "charter" is either purchased from a store that sells legal forms, or is picked up at a lawyer's office or the Secretary of State in the state in which one desires to incorporate. The form is filled in and then filed with the Secretary of State. It is signed by the "incorporators." Many times the promoters will also be the incorporators. The information required in the articles is fairly standardized. The Illinois articles of incorporation that follow provide a good illustration. The amount of the required filing fees is indicated at the end of the form.

The undersigned.

Name	Number	Street	Address City	State
. . . .				
. . . .				
. . . .				
. . . .				

being one or more natural persons of the age of twenty-one years or more or a corporation, and having subscribed to shares of the corporation to be organized pursuant hereto, for the purpose of forming a corporation under "The Business Corporation Act" of the State of Illinois, do hereby adopt the following Articles of Incorporation:

Article One

The name of the corporation hereby incorporated is: . . . .

. . . .

Article Two

The *address* of its initial registered office in the State of Illinois is: ....

.... Street, in the .... of ....

.................(.................) County of ....
                                    (Zip Code)
and the *name* of its initial Registered Agent at *said address* is: ....

....

Article Three

The duration of the corporation is: ....

Article Four

The purpose or purposes for which the corporation is organized are:

Article Five

Paragraph 1: The aggregate number of shares which the corporation is authorized to issue is ...., divided into .... classes. The designation of each class, the number of shares of each class, and the par value, if any, of the shares of each class, or a statement that the shares of any class are without par value, are as follows:

	Series	Number of	Par value per share or statement
Class	(If any)	Shares	that shares are without par value

Paragraph 2: The preferences, qualifications, limitations, restrictions and the special or relative rights in respect of the shares of each class are:

Article Six

The class and number of shares which the corporation proposes to issue without further report to the Secretary of State, and the consideration (expressed in dollars) to be received by the corporation therefor, are:

		Total consideration to be
Class of shares	Number of shares	received therefor:
		$ ....
		$ ....

Article Seven

The corporation will not commence business until at least one thousand dollars has been received as consideration for the issuance of shares.

Article Eight

The number of directors to be elected at the first meeting of the shareholders is: . . . .

Article Nine

Paragraph 1: It is estimated that the value of all property to be owned by the corporation for the following year wherever located will be $ . . . .
Paragraph 2: It is estimated that the value of the property to be located within the State of Illinois during the following year will be $ . . . .
Paragraph 3: It is estimated that the gross amount of business which will be transacted by the corporation during the following year will be $ . . . .
Paragraph 4: It is estimated that the gross amount of business which will be transacted at or from places of business in the State of Illinois during the following year will be $ . . . .

NOTE: If all the property of the corporation is to be located in this State and all of its business is to be transacted at or from places of business in this State, or if the incorporators elect to pay the initial franchise tax on the basis of its entire stated capital and paid-in surplus, then the information called for in Article Nine need not be stated.

. . . .

. . . .

Incorporators

. . . .

. . . .

NOTE: There may be one or more incorporators. Each incorporator shall be either a corporation, domestic or foreign, or a natural person of the age of twenty-one years or more. If a corporation acts as incorporator, the name of the corporation and state of incorporation shall be shown and the execution must be by its President or Vice-President and verified by him, and the corporate seal shall be affixed and attested by its Secretary or an Assistant Secretary.

OATH AND ACKNOWLEDGMENT . . .

The following fees are required to be paid at the time of issuing the certificate of corporation: Filing fee, $75.00; Initial license fee of 50¢ per $1,000.00 or 1/20th of 1% of the amount of stated capital and paid-in surplus the corporation proposes to issue without further report (Article Six); Initial franchise tax of 1/10th of 1% of the issued, as above noted. However, the minimum initial franchise tax is $100.00.

Beginning Corporate Life

Once the articles are filed the Secretary of State checks them to ascertain if they comply with all the formal statutory requirements. If they do, and if all the required fees have been paid, the Secretary will file one copy in the office and return the other copy to the incorporators accompanied by a certificate of incorporation. Many states also require the incorporators to then file a copy of the articles and certificate of incorporation in the county of the corporation's principal place of business. Although the enterprise now has a corporate existence, it must be organized before beginning business.

Beginning Corporate Business

Organization of a corporation is a two-step process. The first step is a meeting of the subscribers to the corporation's shares and the incorporators. They elect the directors and adopt a set of bylaws. The articles are very general in nature. The bylaws are rather detailed and contain the specifics for regulating the internal affairs of the corporation. For example, the articles will specify the number of directors but will be silent as to their qualifications, term of office, compensation, etc. These latter matters are covered in the bylaws. The bylaws also cover such items as: the time and place of shareholders' and directors' meetings; the percentage of affirmative votes for approval of a measure; quorum requirements and notice provisions for meetings; the selection and removal process for directors and officers; and the officers and their respective duties. The power to alter, amend, or repeal the bylaws rests with either the directors or shareholders depending on the particular state's law. Occasionally a conflict may exist between the provisions of the bylaws, articles, or state statute. Which document is supreme and will control? The bylaws are subordinate to the articles, which in turn are subordinate to the business corporation statute.

Suppose a corporation complies with all the statutory requirements and then the state amends the statute? Can the state force the corporation to alter its articles to conform with the amendment? In 1819 the Supreme Court in *Dartmouth College* v. *Woodward,* 4 Wheat 518, held that when a state grants a charter to a corporation it is entering a contract with that corporation. The U.S. Constitution prohibits the enactment of legislation that would impair the obligations of a contract. Therefore, a state cannot amend its statute and force corresponding alterations in a corporate charter unless it reserves this right to itself in the business corporation statute. For practical reasons most states do reserve this power in their legislative branch (See § 162 Illinois statute.)

The second step in the organization process is the first formal meeting of the board of directors. It usually follows immediately after the meeting of the subscribers. The directors proceed to elect the officers, accept stock subscription agreements, adopt the form of the share certificate, accept contracts, and perform any other actions necessary to get the corporation underway.

Defectively Formed Corporations

A "de jure" corporation is a legal, validly formed corporation. If a corporation has not been perfectly formed, yet is in substantial compliance with the business corporation statute, it is said to be a "de facto" corporation. This simply means that the state of incorporation can challenge its existence as a corporation in a quo warranto proceeding. (A quo warranto proceeding is a legal action compelling a corporation to show by what authority it is transacting business). The state can force the corporation to comply with the law or, if it refuses, force it to cease doing business as a corporation. But, until such a challenge by the state, it is a corporation "in fact."

Once a corporation has been perfectly formed, it must continue to comply with the statutory requirements. In some states if a corporation does not file the required reports and pay its franchise tax the state attorney general can force its involuntary dissolution.

There is a third category of corporation that is no corporation at all. For lack of a better name it is called a "defectively formed" corporation. It is carrying on business as a corporation without substantial compliance with the state's corporation statute. The owners of this business are personally liable for the debts of the alleged corporation. Where does one draw the line between a de facto and a defectively formed corporation? What constitutes substantial compliance with the business corporation statute? At one time such questions provoked litigation. Today, the problem is almost nonexistent because of statutes like the following one in Illinois:

§ 49. EFFECT OF ISSUANCE OF CERTIFICATE OF INCORPORATION.

Upon the issuance of the certificate of incorporation by the Secretary of State, the corporate existence shall begin, and such certificate of incorporation shall be conclusive evidence, except as against the State, that all conditions precedent required to be performed by the incorporators have been complied with and that the corporation has been incorporated under this Act.

Such a statute operates to make all corporations receiving a certificate of incorporation at the very least de facto corporations.

In a few cases, courts have created a corporation by estoppel. We saw in the partnership materials that a partnership may be created by estoppel, and the same is true of corporations. If a party has dealt with a corporation as if it were properly formed, and if permitting the party to later allege that it was improperly formed would *operate unjustly,* then the party will be estopped from making such an allegation. In a way, although the court did not discuss estoppel, the *H. F. Philipsborn* case is an example of this type of reasoning. Although the corporation in the case was not in existence at the time of the contract, the bank acted as if it were in existence and was so bound by this action.

Disregarding the Corporate Entity

After enunciating the general proposition that a corporation is an entity separate and distinct from its shareholders, and that the shareholders enjoy a limited liability let us now examine some exceptions. Under certain circumstances a court will "disregard the corporate entity" or "pierce the corporate veil" and hold the owner or owners liable for the actions of the corporation. The power to pierce the corporate veil is one created by courts and their equitable powers and is designed to prevent the evasion of statutes, perpetration of frauds, or any other activity that is against public policy.

The circumstances when courts allow piercing of the corporate veil may be conveniently divided into at least four categories. These categories are not rigid and any given circumstance may involve more than one category, but, generally speaking, they present an overview of this important exception to the doctrine of limited liability.

Suits by Corporate Creditors Against Shareholders (Humans)

The typical case of piercing involves suits by corporate creditors against shareholders for debts not paid by the corporation. On a very general level, courts will talk about allowing piercing in order to "prevent fraud or injustice." What they require as elements of proof of this is *either* that the corporate entity was used as a mere appendage or "alter ego" of the shareholders and was not *in fact* separate *or* that the corporation was undercapitalized at the time the debt was incurred. We will examine each of these circumstances separately.

The alter ego approach is usually found in cases where there were very few shareholders; this may include a parent corporation which wholly owns a subsidiary. Some of the elements of proof of a corporation as an alter ego are (1) the commingling of shareholder and corporate assets—using corporate funds to pay individual debts, using corporate assets for private purposes or vice versa; (2) the lack of observance of basic corporate formalities such as issuing stock, failing to elect directors or appoint officers, failing to hold shareholder or director meetings, or not keeping separate corporate records (this second element of proof may be rebutted in some states by a showing that a corporation has elected to call itself a "close corporation" and thus enjoy a status recognized by statutory corporation laws—such as California—which allow a relaxation of basic corporate formalities); and (3) any other circumstance that tends to show that as a matter of everyday operation of the corporation, the shareholders treated the corporate entity as their business conduit, instrumentality, or agency.

The second major grouping of elements of proof involve evidence of undercapitalization. The focus here is on whether the shareholders should reasonably have anticipated that the corporation would be unable to pay the debts it was incurring. In some states, undercapitalization is but one element of proof tending to show fraud, misrepresentation, or an abuse of the state's statutory scheme, but in other states such as California,[16] the single fact of undercapitalization may be sufficient to pierce the corporate veil.

Suits by Corporate Creditors Against Shareholders (Corporations)

A similar set of circumstances is presented when a corporate creditor sues a parent corporation for the debts of a subsidiary or, perhaps, vice versa. A subsidiary corporation is one that has a majority of its stock owned by another corporation, called the parent corporation. If the parent owns 100 percent of the stock it is called a "wholly owned" subsidiary. Subsidiaries are very common and are formed for a large number of legitimate reasons. Perhaps a new venture is highly risky and success is speculative. A corporation may want to engage in the venture and simultaneously limit its liability. It can achieve this by forming a subsidiary to conduct the venture. Or, maybe a corporation exports raw materials from other countries and one of those countries enacts a higher tax on exports by foreign corporations. The corporation then incorporates a subsidiary in that country to export the material and qualify for the lower tax rate.

Usually the directors and officers of the parent will serve in the same capacity for the subsidiary. The respective corporate headquarters may be in the same building. These factors, in and of themselves, do not automatically make the parent liable for the contracts or torts of its subsidiary. The courts examine the degree to which the corporate formalities are honored and the manner in which the parent controls the subsidiary. Generally, the elements of the plaintiff's case are the same as for the first category discussed in the preceding section but the reason for the liability is slightly different. In the first category of cases, liability is imposed because the plaintiff was somehow unjustly misled as to the true character of the corporation that caused the damage complained of. In this second category, the reason for the liability is that affiliated corporate entities should not so fragment their business that an injustice results.

Before we move on to the final two categories of shareholder liability, we present excerpts from two cases, one in which piercing was permitted and the other in which it was not. By contrasting these two cases, you should learn when courts will pierce the corporate veil.

CONSOLIDATED SUN RAY, INC. v.
OPPENSTEIN, et al.
335 F 2d. 801 (8th Cir., 1964)   *[Parent responsible]*

VOGEL, Circuit Judge

This suit, . . . sought a declaratory judgment by Michael Oppenstein against appellant Consolidated Sun Ray, Inc., (Consolidated) and Berkson Brothers, Inc., (Berkson), with respect to a lease entered into on December 4, 1939, by Oppenstein and his since deceased brothers as Lessors and Berkson as Lessee. Oppenstein asked judgment declaring Consolidated liable under the lease on the theory that Berkson was the wholly owned subsidiary of Consolidated, under its complete domination and control beginning in June 1955 and continuing thereafter, and was accordingly the alter ego of Consolidated and as a result thereof Consolidated was liable on the lease as though it were in fact a named lessee. . . .

On April 5, 1963, the court made its Findings of Fact and Conclusions of Law and, based thereon, entered a declaratory judgment holding Consolidated also liable on the lease. Such judgment was entered on that date against both Berkson and Consolidated. . . . On October 24, 1963, the case . . . (as to damages) went to trial before a jury and on October 25, 1963, the jury returned a verdict in favor of Oppenstein and against Consolidated and Berkson in the sum of $102,674.73 as appellee's damages to July 1, 1963, plus attorneys' fees in the sum of $10,000. Judgment of $112,674.73 was entered thereon, from which judgment Consolidated and Berkson noticed appeals to this court. . . .

Appellant Consolidated bases this appeal upon the following grounds.

1. The District Court erred in holding that the separate corporate entity of Berkson should be disregarded and that Berkson was the alter ego of Consolidated. . . .

The District Court, in its Findings of Fact, . . . found that all of the stock of Berkson was owned by Consolidated; that on December 4, 1939, Oppenstein leased certain property to Berkson for a term of 26 years and 11 months ending June 30, 1967; . . . that after June or July 1955 Consolidated made certain changes in its dealings with its wholly-owned subsidiary Berkson, such as (a) eliminated Berkson's control of money received from its retail store which was operated at the leased premises and reserved to Consolidated alone the right to issue checks on the bank account deposited in the Commerce Trust Company in Kansas City; (b) in 1959 closed the bank account, opening a new one in Consolidated's name so that thereafter Berkson operated without an account in its own name; (c) pledged Berkson's accounts receivable as security for a loan Consolidated negotiated for itself. . . . (d) took from Berkson its former independent buying discretion and merchandising policies, buying merchandise for Berkson in New York and warehousing it in its own building in New York and directed complete retail price details; (e) changed fire and liability insurance on the leased premises from the name of Berkson to Consolidated; (f) prepared in New York and completely controlled all advertising; (g) arranged so that the directors and officers of Berkson were persons employed by Consolidated and were the same persons who were directors or officers of Consolidated, and no director or officer of Berkson lived in the Kansas City, Missouri trade area, and the local store manager was not a director or officer of Berkson; (h) charged against Berkson a share of the cost of Consolidated's accounting and warehousing operations; (i) in 1956, just after the change-over, Consolidated entered into a Chapter XI Reorganization Plan under the Bankruptcy Laws. . . . (k) many of the corporate minutes of Berkson were printed forms apparently used by Consolidated for all of its subsidiaries, with the name "Berkson's" typed in; (1) all correspondence pertaining to the business of the lessee under the lease, whether written to the lessor, to third parties or to agent of Consolidated, was on Consolidated's letterhead and was for the most part signed "Consolidated Retail Stores by;" in such correspondence Consolidated referred to the lease, the leasehold estate and the demised premises as "its lease," "its property" and "its rent;" (m) Consolidated employed a realty firm and in letters exchanged between the two companies and third parties, efforts were made for Consolidated to sell the leasehold estate for a consideration to be paid to Consolidated; (n) in October 1961 the retail store on the leased premises was closed and the inventory was sold to Macy's; the consideration therefor was paid to and kept by Consolidated, no part being made available to apply on the rent due Oppenstein for November 1961 or thereafter; (o) Consolidated operated Berkson the same as if it were one of the division stores of Consolidated rather than a wholly-owned subsidiary; (p) Consolidated did maintain substantially all the legal formalities required of Berkson as a separate corporation, such as filing necessary papers, reports and corporate tax returns.

The court also found there was a default in the payment of rent beginning November 1961 with notices, etc. From these findings the District Court made its Conclusions of Law.

1. That Consolidated had complete and absolute control over the actions and rights of Berkson from and after July 1955; that Consolidated used its power and control for the benefit of Consolidated and not for the benefit of Berkson;

2. That from June or July 1955 Consolidated did not respect the separateness of the corporate entity of Berkson, treating Berkson as a division, department, or adjunct of Consolidated; caused Berkson's assets to be intermingled with its own, making Berkson the alter ego of Consolidated;

3. That the use by Consolidated of Berkson as a division, conduit or instrumentality of Consolidated and Berkson's loss of control of its own destiny and inability to protect its own assets and the imposition of excessive financial burdens on Berkson was an injustice to Oppenstein, who sustained damage thereby;

4. That Consolidated should be held liable for the actions and obligations of Berkson, the same as though they were the acts and obligations of Consolidated. . . .

From the evidence in this case there can be no reasonable doubt but that Consolidated did completely control and use Berkson as a mere conduit, instrumentality or adjunct of Consolidated itself. The ultimate fact question for determination, then, was Consolidated purpose in so doing. If that purpose was unlawful or improper or for some illegitimate purpose which might result in damage to Oppenstein, then the court has the power to look behind Berkson, the alter ego, and hold Consolidated liable for Berkson's obligations. This necessitates a determination by the trier of the facts. Here the court, with the aid of an advisory jury, found against Consolidated on that issue. The law of Missouri is that, where the subsidiary is a mere conduit, instrumentality, or adjunct through which the parent corporation achieves some improper end, its own corporate entity will be disregarded. . . .

"* * * It does seem, however, that the determination of whether there is a case for equitable relief could and should be decided by the test of whether or not the arrangement involved is being used for a proper purpose. Should not all these other suggested tests be used only as aids for determining the true purpose of the arrangement? *Making a corporation a supplemental part of an economic unit and operating it without sufficient funds to meet obligations to those who must deal with it would be circumstantial evidence tending to show either an improper purpose or reckless disregard of the rights of others.* . . .

We hold here that Consolidated's complete and absolute control over Berkson, making Berkson a supplemental part of Consolidated's economic unit, and operating Berkson without sufficient funds to meet its obligations to its creditors, constituted circumstantial evidence from which the advisory jury and the court, as the finders of the facts, could reasonably draw the inference that Consolidated's purpose was improper and was detrimental to Oppenstein. Such inference is sustained by substantial evidence. It may not be disturbed here on appeal. . . .

As to the first issue wherein the court and jury held Consolidated liable, this case is affirmed. . . .

Case Questions

1. In view of the high degree of control that Consolidated exerted over Berkson, why did it bother to form Berkson as a subsidiary?

2. Did the amount involved, $112,674.73, justify an appeal by Consolidated? Is it possible that a factor in deciding to appeal was that other creditors of Berkson, and possibly of other subsidiaries as well, were watching the ultimate outcome of this litigation?

BERGER v. COLUMBIA BROADCASTING SYSTEM
453 F.2d 991 (1972)

No proof of "alter ego"

(Author's note: The plaintiff, Berger, contracted with CBS Films, Inc. (hereafter "Films"), a wholly owned subsidiary of the defendant, Columbia Broadcasting System, Inc., to acquire and distribute film footage of the plaintiff's International Fashion Festival for the year 1965 and the exclusive right of first refusal to license the festival for the next nine years. Shortly after this, Films also contracted with a rival fashion show producer. The plaintiff's festival was never broadcast by CBS, so he sued the parent company, Columbia Broadcasting System, Inc., alleging that the much smaller corporate unit, Films, was an alter ego of the parent company. The trial court found in favor of the plaintiff and awarded a judgment of $200,000 against the parent for breach of contract. On appeal, the parent argued that piercing the corporate veil was not proper.)

It is elemental jurisprudence that a corporation is a creature of the law, endowed with a personality separate and distinct from that of its owners, and that one of the principal purposes for legal sanctioning of a separate corporate personality is to accord stockholders an opportunity to limit their personal liability. There does exist, however, a large class of cases in which the separateness of a corporate entity has been disregarded and a parent corporation held liable for the acts of its subsidiary because the subsidiary's affairs had been so controlled as to render it merely an instrument or agent of its parent. . . . But the dual personality of parent and subsidiary is not lightly disregarded, since application of the instrumentality rule operates to defeat one of the principal purposes for which the law has created the corporation. . . . Therefore, to justify judicial derogation of the separateness of a corporate creature, an aggrieved party must prove something more than a parent's mere ownership of a majority or even all of the capital stock and the parent's use of its power as an incident of its stock ownership to elect officers and directors of the subsidiary. . . . In Lowendahl v. Baltimore & O. R.R., 1936, 247 App. Div. 144, 287 N.Y.S. 62, aff'd, 272 N.Y. 360, 6 N.E.2d 56, a New York court analyzed the various terms and legal theories and concluded that the instrumentality rule furnished the most practical theory for toppling a parent corporation's immunity. The court in *Lowendahl* then postulated the following three elements as the quantum of proof necessary to sustain application of the instrumentality rule:

> (1) Control, not mere majority or complete stock control, but complete domination, not only of finances, but of policy and business practice in respect to the transaction attacked so that the corporate entity as to this transaction had at the time no separate mind, will or existence of its own; and
>
> (2) Such control must have been used by the defendant to commit fraud or wrong, to perpetrate the violation of a statutory or other positive legal duty, or a dishonest and unjust act in contravention of plaintiff's legal rights; and
>
> (3) The aforesaid control and breach of duty must proximately cause the injury or unjust loss complained of. 287 N.Y.S. at 76.

Applying these three elements to the relationship between the defendant and Films in the case at bar, we first turn to the lower court's factual determinations. The district court held that at all relevant times Films was merely an instrumentality of the defendant based on the following findings: (1) the board of directors of Films consisted solely of employees of the defendant; (2) the organization chart of CBS, Inc. included Films; and (3) all lines of employee authority from Films passed through employees of the defendant and other subsidiaries to the chairman of the board of CBS, Inc. In addition, the trial judge was greatly influenced by the fact that several witnesses, including a comptroller of one of the defendant's subsidiaries, testified that Films was a "division" of CBS, Inc. Comparing these several facts to the requisite quantum of proof necessary to satisfy *Lowendahl's* "control" element, we think it is obvious that these factual determinations, standing alone, are insufficient to sustain application of the instrumentality rule. Moreover, an independent examina-

tion of the record in this case convinces us that the evidence adduced below concerning the relationship between the defendant and Films could not sustain any finding that the defendant completely dominated not only the finances, but the policy and business practice of Films. . . .

In our opinion complete stock ownership, common officers and directors, and the use of organizational charts illustrating lines of authority are all business practices common to most parent-subsidiary relationships, and such proof of a parent's potential to dominate its subsidiary is precisely the kind of evidence that New York courts have consistently rejected as insufficient in proving a community of management between corporations. . . . Furthermore, with respect to the testimony concerning Films' status as a division of the defendant, we think this evidence under New York law is equally unpersuasive. Affixing labels to corporate relationships for purposes of showing a parent's complete domination of a subsidiary is a dangerous business. . . .

The only evidence concerning the corporate relationship during the period in which the transaction involved herein occurred negates any assertion that Films was being operated as the alter ego of the defendant. The uncontradicted testimony of Mr. Sam Cook Digges, former administrative vice president of Films, is as follows:

> Q What was the relationship of CBS Films, Inc. to CBS Television Network?
>
> A Many of the programs that were telecast on the CBS Television Network eventually went into distribution through CBS Films. . . .
>
> Q For what period of time did you act as the administrative vice-president or operational head of CBS Films, Inc.?
>
> A From 1959 to 1967.
>
> Q In this eight-year period, Mr. Digges, did you ever sell a program from CBS Films, Inc., to CBS for network broadcast?
>
> A Yes, we did. We sold many of the Terry-Toon products in the Saturday morning kid block.

We also sold a program when we were in the production end of the business also producing shows called Angel. This was a program that was produced by Jess Oppenheimer, who developed the Lucy series. Angel was on the CBS Television Network for one year. . . .

Q Did you make any sales to CBS?

A Not except for the Angel show.

Q Did you make any sales to any other network?

A Yes. The sale was made prior to the time I joined CBS, but the show was still running when I was there. That was a program called Navy Log, which was sold to ABC.

We also sold a show called the Children's Doctor, which is a five-minute medical series, a pediatrician, to the ABC Television Network.

Q Is there any contractual commitment for the network to broadcast any product that is produced by CBS Films, Inc.?

A No, there isn't. My life would have been easier if there had been such an arrangement.

Q Of the properties that CBS Films, Inc., would be distributing, was there any obligation on the part of CBS Films, Inc., to sell it to the CBS Television Network?

A No, there was not.

Faced with both this testimony and the total absence of any evidence showing the defendant's actual domination of its subsidiary Films during the period in which the plaintiff's contract was executed and allegedly breached, this court has no alternative but to reverse the decision of the district court on the simple basis that plaintiff has failed to prove, in accordance with New York law, that Films was the alter ego of the defendant.

Reversed.

Case Questions

1. Why would almost any plaintiff try to sue a parent corporation?

2. Why would the parent want to create a subsidiary to do what Films did in the case?

3. Contrast the *Consolidated* case with the *Berger* case and make a list of factual elements that must be proved in order to argue successfully that the corporate veil should be pierced.

Suits Alleging the Abuse of the Corporate Form to Intentionally Evade Statutory, Judicial, or Contractual Obligations

This third category of piercing cases usually results in some equitable decree against the shareholders, not money judgments. For example, if a closed or family-held corporation is ordered by a court to cease and desist from an activity, the owners cannot avoid the prohibition by doing it themselves. Even though the court order would technically be against the corporation, a court would apply it also against the owners. The basic test here seems to be whether the statute, judicial act, or contract applies to an action by any person or just to a corporation. If it applies to any person, then a corporation cannot avoid the application by having the shareholder do it. For example, it would violate Section 7 of the Clayton Act for a corporation to sell its assets to a competitor; it would also be a violation for the shareholders to sell their shares to a competitor. It is a "substantial lessening of competition" that Section 7 outlaws, and this activity will be restrained regardless of what legal form attempts it.

Subordination of Shareholder Debts

Another form of shareholder liability is imposed in some states when a corporation becomes insolvent owing debts not only to ordinary business creditors but to shareholders as well. If there is evidence of bad faith, insider dealing, or conscious undercapitalization that adversely affects the corporation's ability to pay the creditors, the debts of the shareholders may be subordinated to those of the creditors. The effect of this equitable remedy, sometimes called *shareholder subordination,* is to order the payment of the debts owing to shareholders after payment to ordinary business creditors.

Summary: Piercing the Corporate Veil

Reliance on any one test or one set of facts to pierce the corporate veil and hold shareholders liable for the debts of the corporation is not wise. Each case must be viewed on its own facts. If a jury or court is presented with a preponderance of the evidence tending to prove that the shareholders intended to create nothing more than an extension of their own business interests and that the corporation as a separate legal entity serves no real business purpose other than insulating the owners from liability while they personally sought to advance themselves, then a court may pierce this corporate veil.

Some of the facts that a court would consider when urged to pierce would be that the corporation was formed to (1) conceal misrepresentation, fraud, insider deals, or other illegality; (2) aid in the working of an injustice; (3) provide a mere conduit, instrumentality, or alter ego of dominant shareholders—whether other corporations or humans; (4) present a potential for harm to creditors or the public because of undercapitalization or the indiscriminate commingling of assets; or (5) do any other acts that aid in the accomplishment of an injustice to those who relied on the corporate form.[17]

Foreign Corporations

A corporation operating within the state of its incorporation is called a domestic corporation. In all other states and countries it is called a foreign corporation. Each state has the power to regulate foreign corporations that are doing business within its borders. Before legally commencing business, the corporation must first qualify to do business as a foreign corporation. Qualification usually involves filing certain routine information with the Secretary of State and payment of a fee. The primary purpose behind the qualification requirement is to facilitate the assessment and collection of various taxes. Failure to qualify can result in the imposition of monetary penalties and/or criminal misdemeanor charges. Also, some states deny access to their courts to any corporation that has failed to properly qualify.

The MBCA § 106 sets out the basic rights of a state over foreign corporations. It provides:

> No foreign corporation shall have the right to transact business in this State until it shall have procured a certificate of authority so to do from the Secretary of State. No foreign corporation shall be entitled to procure a certificate of authority under the Act to transact in this State any business which a corporation organized under this Act is not permitted to transact. A foreign corporation shall not be denied a certificate of authority by reason of the fact that the laws of the state or country under which such corporation is organized governing its organization and internal affairs differ from the laws of this State, and nothing in this Act contained shall be construed to authorize this State to regulate the organization or the internal affairs of such corporation.

The difficult issue is determining whether or not a foreign corporation is doing business within a given state in sufficient degree to give the state the authority to require its registration as a foreign corporation. Article 1, Section 8, of the U.S. Constitution (commonly referred to as the "commerce clause") provides that "Congress shall have power . . . to regulate commerce . . . among the several states . . ." Thus, if a foreign corporation is engaged in purely interstate commerce, the states lack the authority to subject it to their qualification statutes. However, if a foreign corporation is engaged in doing "some" business within a state or is engaged in intrastate commerce, then it is doing business within that state and is subject to state regulation. In deciding whether a corporation is engaged in interstate or intrastate commerce, the courts examine a variety of factors. The presence or absence of any one of these factors is generally not conclusive. Many times, the test is a balancing one as some factors indicate an interstate nature while others are of an intrastate character. Among the examined factors are: (1) Presence of an office. Is the office maintained for the benefit of the corporate employees, such as furnishing salestaff with a place to use the telephone and complete paperwork? If so, this is not the type of activity that constitutes doing business. Or, is the office utilized for holding corporate meetings or for the storage of a stock of goods to fill the small emergency orders of customers? The latter will require the corporation to qualify as a foreign corporation. (2) Property ownership. For what purpose is the property held, mere investment or the fulfillment of corporate objectives within that state? (3) Solicitation of business. The solicitation of orders from within a state that are then accepted outside the state and filled from an inventory located outside the state is interstate in nature. Likewise, it is interstate commerce to sell or purchase goods within a state if these goods are to be delivered outside that state. However, the solicitation, acceptance, and delivery of goods all within one state is clearly doing business within that state. (4) Frequency of business. The consummation of a single or isolated business transaction is not doing business within that state. Section 106 of the MBCA (see the appendix) also sets out some circumstances to be considered in the control of foreign corporations. But, setting out such standards and applying them are two different matters.

The *Allenberg Cotton Co.* v. *Pittman* case that follows demonstrates the complexities involved in judging the interstate or intrastate nature of a business venture. Also note that the issue arises in a state that denies the use of its courts to foreign corporations that fail to qualify.

ALLENBERG COTTON CO., INC. v. PITTMAN
419 U.S. 20 (1974)

MR. JUSTICE DOUGLAS *delivered the opinion of the Court.*

This is an appeal from a judgment of the Supreme Court of Mississippi, 276 So. 2d 678 (1973), which held that under the applicable Mississippi statute appellant might not recover damages for breach of a contract to deliver cotton because of its failure to qualify to do business in the State. Appellant claims that that Mississippi statute as applied to the facts of this case is repugnant to the Commerce Clause of the Constitution. . . .

The Supreme Court of Mississippi held that appellant's transactions with Mississippi farmers were wholly intrastate in nature, being completed upon delivery of the cotton at the warehouse, and that the fact that appellant might subsequently sell the cotton in interstate commerce was irrelevant to the federal question "as the Mississippi transaction had been completed and the cotton then belonged exclusively to Allenberg, to be disposed of as it saw fit, at its sole election and discretion," . . . Under the contract which Covington negotiated with appellee, Pittman, the latter was to plant, cultivate, and harvest a crop of cotton on his land, deliver it to a named company in

Marks, Miss., for ginning, and then turn over the ginned cotton to appellant at a local warehouse. The suit brought by appellant alleged a refusal of Pittman to deliver the cotton and asked for injunctive relief and damages. One defense tendered by Pittman was that appellant could not use the courts of Mississippi to enforce its contracts, as it was doing business in the State without the requisite certificate. The Supreme Court of Mississippi sustained that plea, reversing a judgment in favor of appellant, and dismissed the complaint.

Appellant's arrangements with Pittman and the broker, Covington, are representative of a course of dealing with many farmers whose cotton, once sold to appellant, enters a long interstate pipeline. That pipeline ultimately terminates at mills across the country or indeed around the world, after a complex sorting and matching process designed to provide each mill with the particular grade of cotton which the mill is equipped to process. . . .

We deal here with a species of control over an intricate interstate marketing mechanism. . . . In *Dahnke-Walker Milling Co.* v. *Bondurant,* 257 U.S. 282 (1921), wheat raised in Kentucky was purchased by a miller in Tennessee, payment and delivery to a common carrier being made in Kentucky. There, as here, a suit against the farmer in Kentucky court was defended on the grounds that the buyer had not qualified to do business in Kentucky and that, therefore, the contract was unenforceable. The Court held that the Kentucky statute could not be applied to defeat this transaction which, though having intrastate aspects, was in fact "a part of interstate commerce," . . . The same observation is pertinent here. Delivery of the cotton to a warehouse, taken in isolation, is an intrastate transaction. But that delivery is also essential for the completion of the interstate transaction, for sorting and classification in the warehouse are essential before the precise interstate destination of the cotton, whether in this country or abroad, is determined. The determination of the precise market cannot indeed be made until the classification is made. . . .

[W]e have found appellant's transactions, when viewed against the background of customary trade practices in the cotton market, to be indistinguishable from the activities in Dahnke-Walker in any significant regard.

The Mississippi Supreme Court, as noted, ruled that appellant was doing business in Mississippi. Appellant, however, has no office in Mississippi, nor does it own or operate a warehouse there. It has no employees soliciting business in Mississippi or otherwise operating there on a regular basis; its contracts are arranged through an independent broker, whose commission is paid either by appellant or by the farmer himself and who has no authority to enter into contracts on behalf of appellant. . . . There is no indication that the cotton which makes up appellant's "perpetual inventory" in Mississippi is anything other than what appellant has claimed it to be, namely, cotton which is awaiting necessary sorting and classification as a prerequisite to its shipment in interstate commerce.

In short, appellant's contacts with Mississippi do not exhibit the sort of localization or intrastate character which we have required in situations where a State seeks to require a foreign corporation to qualify to do business. Whether there were local tax incidents of those

contacts which could be reached is a different question on which we express no opinion. Whether the course of dealing would subject appellant to suits in Mississippi is likewise a different question on which we express no view. We hold only that Mississippi's refusal to honor and enforce contracts made for interstate or foreign commerce is repugnant to the Commerce Clause.

The judgment is reversed and the cause remanded for proceedings not inconsistent with this opinion. . . .

MR. JUSTICE REHNQUIST, *dissenting.*

The question in this case is whether Mississippi may require appellant, a Tennessee corporation, to qualify as a foreign corporation under Mississippi law before it may sue in the courts of Mississippi to enforce a contract. The Supreme Court of Mississippi summarized the facts of the transaction, which it stated were "without substantial dispute," as follows:

> It is apparent that these transactions of Allenberg in each case, including that with Pittman, took place wholly in Mississippi. The contract was negotiated in Mississippi, executed in Mississippi, the cotton was produced in Mississippi, delivered to Allenberg at the warehouse in Mississippi, and payment was made to the producer in Mississippi. All interest of the producer in the cotton terminated finally upon delivery to Allenberg at the warehouse in Marks. The fact that afterward Allenberg might or might not sell the cotton in interstate commerce is irrelevant to the issue here, as the Mississippi transaction had been completed and the cotton then belonged exclusively to Allenberg. . . .

The Supreme Court of Mississippi might have added that through an exclusive agent, who was a Mississippi resident, Allenberg entered into over 20 similar contracts in 1971 with farmers in Quitman County alone, contracts covering cotton production from over 9,000 acres in this one county. Allenberg's total

1971 purchases of cotton grown in Mississippi under substantially identical contracts exceeded 25,000 bales. . . .

For reasons which are not entirely clear to me, the Court holds that Mississippi may not require Allenberg to qualify as a foreign corporation as a condition of using Mississippi courts to enforce its contract with appellee Pittman.

Mississippi's qualification statute is concededly not discriminatory. Domestic corporations organized under her laws must submit themselves to her taxing jurisdiction, to service of process within the State, and to a number of other incidents of corporate existence which state law may impose. . . . The qualification statute also serves an important informational function making available to citizens of the State who may deal with the foreign corporation details of its financing and control. Although the result of Allenberg's failure to comply with the qualification statute is a drastic one, our decisions hold that the burden imposed on interstate commerce by such statutes is to be judged with reference to the measures required to comply with such legislation, and not to the sanctions imposed for violation of it. . . . The steps necessary in order to comply with this statute are not unreasonably burdensome. . . .

I would affirm the judgment of the Supreme Court of Mississippi.

Case Questions

1. Did Mr. Justice Douglas or Rehnquist author the more persuasive opinon?

2. The court stated that delivery of cotton to a warehouse, taken in isolation, is an intrastate transaction. Should not that conclusion have been determinative of the issue?

3. Since the disputed events took place in Mississippi, why did the court shift its focus to the interstate aspects of cotton distribution?

4. Does the legal reasoning in this case usurp states rights and give the federal government undue control over intrastate transactions?

Note.   Qualifying to do business in Mississippi as a foreign corporation does not present a difficult obstacle. Certain information must be filed with the Mississippi Secretary of State accompanied by a fee of between $20 and $500. The amount of the fee is determined by the amount of the corporation's capital. Miss. Code. Ann. 79-3-219 and 79-3-255(q) (1972).

Formal, Legal Powers and Purposes of a Corporation

The articles of incorporation are the fundamental instrument of corporation law. Most state laws and the MBCA (§ 54) provide that the articles shall set forth: (1) the name of the corporation; (2) the period or duration, which may be perpetual; (3) the purpose or purposes for which the corporation is organized, which may be stated to be, or to include, the transaction of *any or all lawful business for which corporations may be incorporated under this Act* (emphasis added); and other provisions. So, the purposes of the corporation must be set out, but they may be "any or all lawful business." The last part of Section 54 provides: "It shall not be necessary to set forth in the articles of incorporation any of the corporate powers enumerated in this Act." Section 4 of the MBCA is the one that enumerates the "General Powers" of corporation (see the Appendix) and this includes 16 specific grants of power including the power "to be a promoter, partner, member, associate, or manager of any partnership, joint venture, trust or other enterprise." To digress for a short moment, the MBCA clearly permits a corporation to be a partner; thus it runs counter to some states, which do not encourage this, as we noted in the chapter on partnership law.

However, the point here is that the final paragraph of Section 4 provides that a corporation shall have the power "to have and exercise all powers necessary or convenient to effect its purpose." What this means is that the powers of a corporation may be any lawful means needed to effectuate its purpose, and its purpose then may be any or all lawful business for which corporations may be incorporated under the state's corporation act. Obviously, this is an extremely broad grant of powers. Almost all corporations take advantage of it by stating their purposes as broadly and as generally as possible.

There are only three qualifications usually found in state corporation acts. They are that the corporation be one for *profit* and that a corporation not engage in banking or insurance. In short, corporate powers can include any lawful act that individual humans have (maybe more) that is intended to make a profit and that is not banking or insurance activity.[18] Thus the purposes and powers of a corporation are almost as diverse and as vast as human activity.

Ultra Vires

In the past, some states recognized a cause of action against corporations for actions that were *ultra vires,* or beyond the purposes or powers of the corporation. And, in nineteenth-century cases, some courts allowed ultra vires as a defense to a tort claim against the corporation. For example, if an agent of X Corporation committed an intentional tort such as a battery against a third party (T/P), and if T/P sued X, some states allowed the defense that the act was ultra vires. In essence, the corporation did not have the power to commit the battery; thus it could not be liable. Today the issues in the example just cited are resolved not by the application of corporation law, but by agency law and the test of "scope of employment."

Most states have severely limited the defense of ultra vires, and corporate actions are assumed to be intra vires (within the corporate powers) unless special circumstances are alleged. Section 7 of the MBCA provides:

> No act of a corporation . . . shall be invalid by reason of the fact that the corporation was without capacity or power to do such act. . . .

There are only three exceptions to this, all of which may be said to involve corporate wrongdoing or corporate actions that depart substantially from a corporation's pattern of commercial conduct and thus usually threaten minority shareholder expectations. The MBCA's Section 7 (a), (b), and (c) allow a shareholder, the corporation, or the Attorney General of the state in which a corporation is chartered to assert corporate lack of capacity or power when, respectively, a corporation has entered into a contract, equitable relief is sought, and all parties to the contract are before the court; when the corporation sues a former officer or director for breach of duty; or when the Attorney General sues to enjoin illegal activity. So, the use of the legal assertion of ultra vires has changed substantially. When first used in the nineteenth century, it was as a legal defense by corporations enabling them to avoid liability for an agent's actions that were beyond the normal scope of operations of the corporation. Today it is used, generally, against corporations or management to protect the normal expectations of shareholders. It can result in the reformation of a contract to which the corporation is a party; it can be used by the corporation when suing management for causing the corporation to do something that deviated from normal patterns of commercial conduct with resulting damage to the corporation; or it can be used by the Attorney General of the state chartering a corporation to police corporate conduct. However, these uses of ultra vires are not found very often today.

Corporate Purposes

The purpose of almost all corporations chartered under the provisions of the MBCA and statutes like it is to use any legal means to make a profit. If the purpose is not to make a profit but to engage in charitable, religious, educational, or social service activities then in many states a different statutory authority is used; moreover, tax-exempt status must be sought from the IRS.

In today's business environment characterized by unemployment, inflation, dwindling natural resources, and substantial competition from corporations chartered in other countries, are there any limits on the central corporate purpose of profit making? The answer is no. Should there be limits on the amount of profit a corporation may make? The answer to this second question is subject to debate today.

Below we have presented two cases, both classics in the area of corporation law. The *Dodge* case presents some interesting facts and conclusions and represents the highwater mark of American capitalism. As between the well-recognized rights of the shareholders to a profit and the nonexistent rights of the employees or consumers to a measure of return because of the corporation's success, the court says that management should opt to serve the former. This case still represents the dominant view, or most of the elements of the dominant view.

The second case below reveals a crack in the rigid edifice of nineteenth-century American capitalism. Today it is generally accepted that corporations can (if not should) engage in some charitable or civic activities. The Internal Revenue Code allows up to 10 percent of the corporation's taxable income for donations to charity and other nonprofit making activities. However, most corporations do not exercise this right fully. Of the 1.4 million corporations that had positive income in 1977, only 36 percent made charitable contributions, and most of these were large corporations.[19] The 36 percent that made gifts had 86 percent of the assets and 84 percent of the net income reported; only 9 of the largest 100 corporations gave nothing. Although the 1980 charitable contributions from corporations amounted to $2.7 billion, which was a 10 percent increase over 1979, respectable studies conclude that there is room for growth.[20]

DODGE v. FORD MOTOR CO.
204 Mich. 459; 170 N.W. 668 (1919)

Action by John F. Dodge and Horace E. Dodge against the Ford Motor Company and others. Decree for plaintiffs, and defendants appeal. Affirmed in part and reversed in part. . . .

The parties in the first instance associating, who signed the articles, included Henry Ford, whose subscription was for 255 shares, John F. Dodge, Horace E. Dodge, the plaintiffs, Horace H. Rackham and James Couzens, who each subscribed for 50 shares, and several other persons. The company began business in the month of June, 1903. . . .

The business of the company continued to expand. The cars it manufactured met a public demand, and were profitably marketed, so that, in addition to regular quarterly dividends equal to 5 percent monthly on the capital stock of $2,000,000, its board of directors declared and the company paid . . . a total of $41,000,000 in special dividends. . . .

The surplus above capital stock was on September 30, 1912, $14,745,095.67, . . . July 31, 1916, it was $111,960,907.53. Originally, the car made by the Ford Motor Company sold for more than $900. From time to time, the selling price was lowered and the car itself improved until in the year ending July 31, 1916, it sold for $440. Up to July 31, 1916, it had sold 1,272,986 cars at a profit of $173,895,416.06. . . . For the year beginning August 1, 1916, the price of the car was reduced $80 to $360. . . .

No special dividend having been paid after October, 1915 . . . the plaintiffs, who together own 2,000 shares, or one-tenth of the entire capital stock of the Ford Motor Company, on the 2nd of November, 1916, filed in the circuit court for the county of Wayne, . . . their bill of complaint, . . . in which bill they charge that since 1914 they have not been represented on the board of directors of the Ford Motor Company, and that since that time the policy of the board of directors has been dominated and controlled absolutely by Henry Ford, the president of the company, who owns and for several years has owned 58 percent of the entire capital stock of the company; . . . [o]n the 31st of July, 1916, the end of its last fiscal year, the said Henry Ford gave out for publication a statement of the financial condition of the company (the same as hereinabove set out), that for a number of years a regular dividend, payable quarterly, equal to 5 percent monthly upon the authorized capital stock, and the special dividends hereinbefore referred to, had been paid, it is charged that notwithstanding the earnings for the fiscal year ending July 31, 1916, the Ford Motor Company has not since that date declared any special dividends:

> And the said Henry Ford, president of the company, has declared it to be the settled policy of the company not to pay in the future any special dividends, but to put back into the business for the future all of the earnings of the company, other than the regular dividend of five percent (5%) monthly upon the authorized capital stock of the company—two million dollars ($2,000,000).

This declaration of the future policy, it is charged in the bill, was published in the public press in the city of Detroit and throughout the United States in substantially the following language:

> "My ambition," declared Mr. Ford, "is to employ still more men; to spread the benefits of this industrial system to the greatest possible number, to help them build up their lives and their homes. To do this, we are putting the greatest share of our profits back into the business."

It is charged further that the said Henry Ford stated to plaintiffs personally, . . . that as all the stockholders had received back in dividends more than they had invested they were not entitled to receive anything additional to the regular dividend of 5 percent a month, and that it was not his policy to have larger dividends declared in the future, and that the profits and earnings of the company would be put back into the business for the purpose of extending its operations and increasing the number of its employees, and that, inasmuch as the profits were to be represented by investment in plants and capital investment, the stockholders would have no right to complain. . . .

Plaintiffs ask for an injunction to restrain the carrying out of the alleged declared policy of Mr. Ford and the company, for a decree requiring the distribution to stockholders of at least 75 percent of the accumulated cash surplus, and for the future that they be required to distribute all of the earnings of the company except such as may be reasonably required for emergency purposes in the conduct of the business.

The answer of the Ford Motor Company, which was filed November 28, 1916, admits most of the allegations in the plaintiffs' bill of complaint, ... It denies that Henry Ford forced upon the board of directors his policy of reducing the price of cars by $80, and says that the action of the board in that behalf was unanimous and made after careful consideration. . . .

The cause came on for hearing in open court on the 21st of May, 1917. A large volume of testimony was taken, with the result that a decree was entered December 5, 1917, in and by which it is decreed that within 30 days from the entry thereof the directors of the Ford Motor Company declare a dividend upon all of the shares of stock in an amount equivalent to one-half of, and payable out of, the accumulated cash surplus of said Ford Motor Company, on hand at the close of the fiscal year ending July 31, 1916. . . .

Defendants have appealed, plaintiffs have not appealed, from the decree. In the briefs, appellants state and discuss the following propositions: . . .

> (4) The management of the corporation and its affairs rests in the board of directors, and no court will interfere or substitute its judgment so long as the proposed actions are not ultra vires or fraudulent. They may be ill advised, in the opinion of the court, but this is no ground for exercise of jurisdiction.
>
> (5) The board has full power over the matter of investing the surplus and as to dividends so long as they act in good faith. . . .
>
> (9) Motives of a humanitarian character will not invalidate or form the basis of any relief so long as the acts are within the lawful powers of the board, if believed to be for the permanent welfare of the community. . . .

The record, and especially the testimony of Mr. Ford, convinces us that he has to some extent the attitude towards shareholders of one who has dispensed and distributed to them large gains and that they should be content to take what he chooses to give. His testimony creates the impression, also, that he thinks the Ford Motor Company has made too much money, has had too large profits and that, although large profits might be still earned, a sharing of them with the public, by reducing the price of the output of the company, ought to be undertaken. We have no doubt that certain sentiments, philanthropic and altruistic, creditable to Mr. Ford, had large influence in determining the policy to be pursued by the Ford Motor Company—the policy which has been herein referred to. . . .

There should be no confusion (of which there is evidence) of the duties which Mr. Ford conceives that he and the stockholders owe to the general public and the duties which in law he and his codirectors owe to protesting, minority stockholders. A business corporation is organized and carried on primarily for the profit of the stockholders. The powers of the directors are to be employed for that end. The discretion of directors is to be exercised in the choice of means to attain that end, and

does not extend to a change in the end itself, to the reduction of profits, or to the non-distribution of profits among stockholders in order to devote them to other purposes. . . .

It is said by appellants that the motives of the board members are not material and will not be inquired into by the court so long as their acts are within their lawful powers. As we have pointed out, and the proposition does not require argument to sustain it, it is not within the lawful powers of a board of directors to shape and conduct the affairs of a corporation for the merely incidental benefit of shareholders and for the primary purpose of benefiting others, and no one will contend that, if the avowed purpose of the defendant directors was to sacrifice the interests of shareholders, it would not be the duty of the courts to interfere. . . .

The decree of the court below fixing and determining the specific amount to be distributed to stockholders is affirmed. In other respects, except as to the allowance of costs, and said decree is reversed. Plaintiffs will recover interest at 5 percent per annum upon their proportional share of said dividend from the date of the decree of the lower court.

Case Questions

1. Does the fact that a corporation is organized and carried on primarily for the profit of its stockholders justify profits of any magnitude? During the 1973–1974 Arab oil embargo, the major U.S. oil companies dramatically increased their profits over the previous year. In some instances the profit increases reached 400 percent. Some individuals labeled these profits "obscene." What are obscene profits?

2. Would the decision have differed if Ford had justified his price reduction policy on stimulating demand to such a degree that even greater profits would be generated despite the lower per unit profit margin?

3. Do you believe the Dodge shareholders had a valid complaint in view of the fact that regular dividends were being paid in the amount of 5 percent monthly on the authorized capital stock of two million dollars?

Case Note

Subsequent to this litigation Henry Ford bought out the minority interests of the two Dodge brothers. The Dodges then used this money to develop what became the rival Chrysler Corporation.

A. P. SMITH MFG. CO. v. BARLOW
13 N.J. 145, 98 A.2d 581 (S. Ct. N.J., 1953)

JACOBS, J.

The Chancery Division, in a well-reasoned opinion by Judge Stein, determined that a donation by the plaintiff The A.P. Smith Manufacturing Company to Princeton University was intra vires. Because of the public importance of the issues presented, the appeal duly taken to the Appellate Division has been certified directly to this court. . . .

The company was incorporated in 1896 and is engaged in the manufacture and sale of valves, fire hydrants and special equipment, mainly for water and gas industries. Its plant is located in East Orange and Bloomfield and it has approximately 300 employees. Over the years the company has contributed regularly to the local community chest and on occasions to Upsala College in East Orange and Newark University, now part of Rutgers, the State University. On July 24, 1951 the board of directors adopted a resolution which set forth that it was in the corporation's best interests to join with others in the 1951 Annual Giving to Princeton University, and appropriated the sum of $1,500 to be transferred by the corporation's treasurer to the university as a contribution towards its maintenance. When this action was questioned by stockholders the corporation instituted a declaratory judgment action in the Chancery Division and trial was had in due course.

Mr. Hubert O'Brien, the president of the company, testified that he considered the contribution to be a sound investment, that the public expects corporations to aid philanthropic and benevolent institutions, that they obtain good will in the community by so doing, and that their charitable donations create favorable environment for their business operations. In addition, he expressed the thought that in contributing to liberal arts institutions, corporations were furthering their self-interest in assuring the free flow of properly trained personnel for administrative and other corporate employment. Mr. Frank W. Abrams, chairman of the board of the Standard Oil Company of New Jersey, testified that corporations are expected to acknowledge their public responsibilities in support of the essential elements of our free enterprise system. He indicated that it was not "good business" to disappoint "this reasonable and justified public expectation," nor was it good business for corporations "to take substantial benefits from their membership in the economic community while avoiding the normally accepted obligations of citizenship in the social community." Mr. Irving S. Olds, former chairman of the board of the United States Steel Corporation, pointed out that corporations have a self-interest in the maintenance of liberal education as the bulwark of good government. He stated that "Capitalism and free enterprise owe their survival in no small degree to the existence of our private, independent universities" and that if American business does not aid in their maintenance it is not "properly protecting the long-range interest of its stockholders, its employees and its customers." . . .

The objecting stockholders have not disputed any of the foregoing testimony nor the showing of great need by Princeton and other private institutions of higher learning and the important public service being rendered by them for democratic government and industry alike. . . . Nevertheless, they have taken the position that . . . the plaintiff's certificate of incorporation does not expressly authorize the contribution and under common-law principles the company does not possess any implied or incidental power to make it. . . .

In this discussion of the early history of business corporations Professor Williston refers to a 1702 publication where the author stated flatly that "The general intent and end of all civil incorporations is for better government." And he points out that the early corporate charters, particularly their recitals, furnish additional support for the notion that the corporate object was the public one of managing and ordering the trade as well as the private one of profit for the members. . . . However, with later economic and social developments and the free availability of the corporate device for all trades, the end of private profit became generally accepted as the controlling one in all businesses other than those classed broadly as public utilities. . . . As a concomitant the common-law rule developed that those who managed the corporation could not disburse any corporate funds for philanthropic or other worthy public cause *unless* the expenditure would benefit the corporation. . . . During the 19th Century when corporations were relatively few and small and did not dominate the country's wealth, the common-law rule did not significantly interfere with the public interest. But the 20th Century has presented a different climate. . . . Control of economic wealth has passed largely from individual entrepreneurs to dominating corporations, and calls upon the corporations for reasonable philanthropic donations have come to be made with increased public support. In many instances such contributions have been sustained by the courts within the common-law doctrine upon liberal findings that the donations tended reasonably to promote the corporate objectives. . . .

Over 20 years ago Professor Dodd, . . . 45 Harv. L. Rev., at 1159, 1160, cited the views of Justice Letton in State ex rel. *Sorensen* v. *Chicago B. & Q. R. Co.,* . . . with seeming approval and suggested the doctrine that corporations may properly support charities which are important to the welfare of the communities where they do business as soundly representative of the public attitude and actual corporate practice. Developments since he wrote leave no doubts on this score.

When the wealth of the nation was primarily in the hands of individuals they dis-

charged their responsibilities as citizens by donating freely for charitable purposes. With the transfer of most of the wealth to corporate hands and the imposition of heavy burdens of individual taxation, they have been unable to keep pace with increased philanthropic needs. They have therefore, with justification, turned to corporations to assume the modern obligations of good citizenship in the same manner as humans do. . . . In actual practice corporate giving has correspondingly increased. Thus, it is estimated that annual corporate contributions throughout the nation aggregate over 300 million dollars, with over 60 million dollars thereof going to universities and other educational institutions. Similarly, it is estimated that local community chests receive well over 40 percent of their contributions from corporations. . . .

More and more they have come to recognize that their salvation rests upon a sound economic and social environment which in turn rests in no insignificant part upon free and vigorous nongovernmental institutions of learning. It seems to us that just as the conditions prevailing when corporations were originally created required that they serve public as well as private interests, modern conditions require that corporations acknowledge and discharge social as well as private responsibilities as members of the communities within which they operate. Within this broad concept there is no difficulty in sustaining, as incidental to their proper objects and in aid of the public welfare, the power of corporations to contribute corporate funds within reasonable limits in support of academic institutions. But even if we confine ourselves to the terms of the common-law rule in its application of current conditions, such expenditures may likewise readily be justified as being for the benefit of the corporation; indeed, if need be the matter may be viewed strictly in terms of actual survival of the corporation in a free enterprise system. . . .

We find that it was a lawful exercise of the

corporation's implied and incidental powers under common-law principles and that it came within the express authority of the pertinent state legislation. . . . Clearly then, the appellants, as individual stockholders whose private interests rest entirely upon the well-being of the plaintiff corporation, ought not be permitted to close their eyes to present day realities and thwart the long-visioned corporate action in recognizing and voluntarily discharging its high obligations as a constituent of our modern social structure.

The judgment entered in the Chancery Division is in all respects

Affirmed.

Case Questions

1. When their resolution created questions with the shareholders, the directors held their decision in abeyance pending a judicial resolution of the issue. Is such a course of action appropriate or practical in every instance where stockholders object to board actions?

2. Is the purpose of a corporation to earn maximum profits or to be a social "do-gooder?" If the purpose is a blend of these two elements, in what proportion are they to be mixed?

Review Problems

1. Bigelow and Lewisohn formed the Old Dominion Corporation in July 1895. Its authorized stock was 150,000 shares of $25 par value for a total capitalization of $3,750,000. During May and June of 1895 Lewisohn and Bigelow acquired certain mining property at a cost of $1,000,000. The market value of the property did not exceed $2,000,000. They sold this property to Old Dominion in return for 130,000 shares of stock valued at $3,250,000. They completely dominated the Old Dominion board of directors. Thereafter the remaining 20,000 shares were sold to the public to raise working capital. The shares were sold at par, raising $500,000, but the subscribers did not know of the Lewisohn and Bigelow secret profit. Several years later, when the profit comes to light, the corporation sues to recover the secret profit alleging a breach of trust by the two promoters. What results? [*Old Dominion Copper Mining & Smelting Co.* v. *Lewisohn*, 210 U.S. 206 (1908); contra, *Old Dominion Copper Mining & Smelting Co.* v. *Bigelow,* 89 N.E. 193 (Mass S. Ct. 1908), aff'd 225 U.S. 111 (1912)].

2. Seminole, a California corporation, operated a public swimming pool that it leased from its owner. The plaintiffs' daughter drowned in the pool and they won a $10,000 wrongful death action. The judgment remained unsatisfied. The plaintiffs now attempt to hold Cavaney personally liable for the judgment against Seminole. Cavaney was a director and secretary-treasurer of Seminole. He was not a shareholder. At one point in time Seminole sought to issue three shares of stock; one of them to go to Cavaney. This effort was abandoned and no shares were ever issued. Seminole had no assets by Cavaney's own

admission. He also stated that "The corporation was duly organized but never functioned as a corporation." Seminole used Cavaney's office for a time to keep records and receive mail. Cavaney contends that this evidence does not support a determination that he is an alter ego of the corporation and therefore personally liable for Seminole's debts. Should the court disregard the corporate entity and hold the defendant liable? [*Minton* v. *Cavaney,* 364 P. 2d 473 (Cal. S. Ct. 1961)].

not a fraud, but who's responsible
alter ego was Cavaney.

3. The plaintiff has been run down and injured by a negligently operated taxicab. The cab is owned by Seon Cab Corporation. Seon has only two cabs and carries only the legally required minimum automobile liability insurance ($10,000) on each cab. The defendant, Carlton, is a stockholder in ten corporations, including Seon. Each corporation has only two cabs and carries the minimum amount of insurance. The plaintiff alleges that the stockholders are personally liable for his damages because the multiple corporate structure constitutes an unlawful attempt to defraud members of the general public who might be injured by the cabs. The defendant argues that the law permits taxi owner-operators to form such corporations and corporations are designed to permit the owners to escape personal liability. Furthermore, he points out that he has complied with the legislative branch's insurance mandates. What decision? [*Walkovszky* v. *Carlton,* 223 N.E. 2d 6 (N.Y. Ct. App. 1966)].

No, complied ī. law — but caused the law to be changed.

NY City — common — lots of corp; few cabs

4. The plaintiff is injured by the negligent operation of a taxicab. It is owned and operated by one of four corporations affiliated with Terminal. Terminal is not a stockholder in any of the four operating corporations. For the most part, the individuals that own Terminal also own the four corporations. Terminal actually serviced, inspected, repaired, and dispatched all the taxis of the four corporations. The Terminal name was conspicuously displayed on the sides of all the taxis used in the enterprise. Should the veil of the operating company, whose cab injured the plaintiff, be pierced to hold Terminal liable? [*Mangan* v. *Terminal Transp. System,* 286 N.Y.S. 666].

✓
yes

5. Should the results in the above two cases differ because in one an attempt is made to hold an individual liable whereas, in the other, the plaintiff seeks to hold liable another corporation?

No — facts differ

6. Grace Dawson was actively engaged in the promotion of a new corporation to be known as Multifashion Frocks, Inc. On January 3, 1978, she obtained written commitments for the purchase of shares totaling $600,000 from a group of 15 potential investors. She was also assured orally that she would be engaged as the president of the corporation upon the commencement of business. Helen Banks was the principal investor, having subscribed to $300,000 of the shares of Multifashion. Dawson immediately began work on the incorporation of Multifash-

ion, made several contracts for and on its behalf, and made cash expenditures of $1,000 in accomplishing these goals. On February 15, 1978, Banks died and her estate has declined to honor the commitment to purchase the Multifashion shares. At the first shareholders' meeting on April 5, 1978, the day the corporation came into existence, the shareholders elected a board of directors. With shareholder approval, the board took the following actions.

(a) Adopted some but not all of the contracts made by Dawson.

(b) Authorized legal action, if necessary, against the Estate of Banks to enforce Banks' $300,000 commitment.

(c) Declined to engage Dawson in any capacity (Banks had been her main supporter). *Yes – oral – not contract*

(d) Agreed to pay Dawson $750 for those cash outlays which were deemed to be directly beneficial to the corporation and rejected the balance. *No, must pay if done on behalf of corp.*

Discuss the legal implications of the above actions taken by the board.

(This is adapted from CPA Exam Question #4, taken from the May 1978 exam. © American Institute of Certified Public Accountants, Inc., 1978.)

7. During the course of your year-end audit for a new client, Otis Corporation, you discover the following facts. Otis was incorporated in 1974 and is owned 94 percent by James T. Parker, President; 1 percent by his wife; and 5 percent by Wilbur Chumley. These three individuals were incorporators and are officers and directors of the corporation.

Otis manufactures and sells telephonic equipment. In 1974 it sold approximately $350,000 of its various products almost exclusively in the state of its incorporation. In 1975 it began to branch out and sold $550,000 of its products throughout that state and $50,000 of its products in a neighboring state. Otis expanded rapidly, and 1976 was a banner year with sales of $1,250,000 and profits of $175,000. Otis constructed a small office building on a tract of land it had purchased for expansion purposes in the neighboring state and used the top floor to establish a regional sales office and rented the balance of the building.

During the course of your audit for the year 1976, you discover that Parker commingles his personal funds with those of the corporation, keeps very few records of board and shareholder meetings, and at his convenience disregards corporate law regarding separateness of personal and corporate affairs. The corporation had 1976 sales in excess of $300,000 in the neighboring state. The corporation has not filed any papers with the Secretary of State of that state in connection with these operations.

In light of the above discoveries, it was deemed prudent to examine the original incorporation papers which were filed by Parker in 1974. The following irregularities were discovered. The powers and purposes clause states that the geographical territory in which the newly created corporation was to do business was solely the state of incorporation. Next, a certified copy of the corporate charter was not obtained and filed in the county in which the corporation's principal place of business is located, as required by state law. Additionally, Mr. Chumley and Mrs. Parker did not sign the articles of incorporation, and prior to the effective date of incorporation, a lease was taken out and a car purchased in the corporate name.

Is there a valid corporate entity in existence?

8. In the situation outlined above, what is the effect of doing business in the neighboring state without having first qualified to do business there?

9. What is the effect of doing business outside the state of incorporation when the corporate charter does not permit business outside the state (under the facts outlined two problems above)?

(Questions 7, 8, and 9 are adapted from CPA Exam Question #6a, taken from the November 1977 exam. © American Institute of Certified Public Acountants, Inc., 1977.)

10. Should a corporation determine which charities will receive corporate contributions by polling the shareholders as to their choices?

Endnotes

1. The term "megacorporation" came to our attention through the writing of Philip Blumberg. See P. Blumberg, *The Megacorporation in American Society,* 1975; he attributed the use of the term megacorporation to Melvin Eisenberg and Sanford Rose.
2. A. Berle and G. Means, *The Modern Corporation and Private Property,* 1 (1932).
3. D. F. Vagts, *Basic Corporation Law,* 5 (1973).
4. R. Nader, M. Green, and J. Seligman, *Taming the Giant Corporation,* 16 (1976).
5. U. S. Department of Commerce, *Statistical Abstract of the United States,* 1981, Figure No. 917, p. 541.
6. Hereafter in this material, the word megacorporations will refer to the largest 200 corporations as ranked by yearly sales.
7. See Vagts, *supra,* p. 10.
8. In 1970, 75 percent of the employees working in manufacturing worked for the top 500 companies. Nader, *supra,* p. 27.
9. G. H. Evans, *Business Incorporations in the United States, 1900–1943,* p. 18 (1948).
10. Nader, *supra,* p. 45.
11. *Ibid.,* p. 46.
12. *Ibid.,* p. 50.
13. *Ibid.,* p. 57.
14. American Bar Foundation, Model Business Corporation Act, Vol. I., p. XIII, (1971).

15. *Ibid.*, p. 4.

16. See, for example, *Gordon* v. *Aztec Brewing*, 33 Cal. 2d 514 (1949).

17. See G. Ashe, *Lifting the Corporation Veil: Corporate Entity in the Modern Day Court*, 78 Commercial Law Journal 121 (1973).

18. Note that § 4(i) of the MBCA permits a corporation to lend money for its corporate purposes. Generally this means it may lend money to a subsidiary or, in some cases, to management.

19. The Conference Board, Annual Survey of Corporate Contributions, p. 3, 1982 Edition, (using 1980 income data).

20. *Ibid.*, p. 4.

Shareholders and the Corporate Capital Structure

10

Legally it is the shareholders who exercise ultimate control of the corporation. We will later observe that the board of directors possess the exclusive authority to manage the corporation, but it is the shareholders who select the directors. It is also the shareholders who approve any basic changes in the corporation's structure. The shareholders are the owners of the corporation. True, the corporation, as a separate entity distinct from the shareholders, holds title to the corporate assets. Yet the shareholders own the corporation and indirectly its assets. This, at least, is the orthodox theory of corporation law. There is another perspective to the issue—a perspective that applies to megacorporations and regards the theory of shareholder control and shareholder democracy as fiction. (As used here, the term shareholder democracy refers to the idea that shareholders control corporate affairs through the exercise of their voting rights.)

The Shareholder

In 1932, A. Berle and G. Means published their classic book, *The Modern Corporation and Private Property*. In their book they noted that within the realm of corporations, ownership was being separated from control. Control was shifting out of the hands of the shareholder into the hands of the professional manager. Today, some individuals would regard the shift as having been completely consummated with management able to perpetuate itself in office and dominate corporate affairs.

Wherein does the truth lie? Somewhere in between, depending on the size of corporation involved. If one is discussing the closely held corporations, shareholder democracy is alive and working. The corporation will be of a family or partnership nature. The shareholders either will be the managers or will carefully follow the details of the corporate operation. Numerically, these corporations compose a large percentage of the total 2.25 million corporations. In the middle of the spectrum are the corporations that, while not close corporations, are not corporate giants. Those corporations are also substantial in number. It is difficult to generalize about these. A corporation may have 500 shareholders who have an active interest in corporate affairs. Under such circumstances management is probably directly responsible to the shareholders. Yet, the same corporation could have a substantial number of nonchalant shareholders who merely rubber stamp all management proposals. Finally, we come to the megacorporations, corporate giants that dominate industries and whose shares are widely distributed. Although they are an important force in the corporate scheme, they are relatively few in number. Let us pause briefly and take a closer look at these immense corporations.

American Telephone & Telegraph Company (AT&T) is the largest corporation in terms of both outstanding shares and number of shareholders. At the end of 1982 AT&T had approximately 815.1 million outstanding shares held by about 3.0 million shareholders. A selection of other publicly traded corporations follow.

Corporation	Outstanding Shares (in millions)	Shareholders
Sears Roebuck	347.88	354,050
Pan Am	71.19	133,685
Polaroid	32.86	37,951

An Overview of Share Ownership

In 1972 there were 32.5 million shareholders. This represents about 15 percent of the 1972 population. According to New York Stock Exchange figures, the number of individual shareholders had declined to 25.2 million in 1975. As of mid 1971 individual Americans owned an estimated $780 billion in stock. Although the value of the stock and the number of shareholders are large, ownership is concentrated in the wealthiest segment of the population. In 1971 the wealthiest 1 percent of the population owned 51 percent of the market value of all stock held by families and received 47 percent of all dividend income. The wealthiest 10 percent owned 74 percent of the market value and received 71 percent of the dividend income. In 1973, financial institutions held 24 percent of the market value of all noninvestment company outstanding stock. Bank-administered personal trusts accounted for 10 percent.[1]

After an examination of the tremendous number of shares issued by the large corporation, their wide distribution and, at the same time, concentrated ownership within a wealthy but small population, it strains one's credulity to suggest that the average shareholder exerts control over corporate affairs. Shortly we will discuss the proxy process, which is designed to allow the shareholder to vote on various matters. Theoretically, it is shareholder democracy in action. Yet, in the large corporation the process favors management. Management selects its nominees for the board of directors and proposes various shareholder resolutions, both of which will be voted on by proxy. The corporation, and indirectly the shareholders, bear the proxy solicitation expense (printing, postage, etc.). If a shareholder wishes to mount a challenge to management, one must bear the financial burden alone while corporate lawyers and funds oppose the effort. If the shareholder surmounts these barriers and elects a board majority then the corporation will pay the expenses. However, it is an extremely rare event when an insurgent group succeeds in winning a proxy fight against an entrenched management.

Generally if a shareholder dislikes corporate policy, this protest takes the form of selling the stock. The large institutional investors usually vote their stock in support of management or refrain entirely from voting. There are some slight indications that institutional investors are beginning to reappraise this traditional passive role. Keep these various ideas in mind when reading the material in this chapter on shareholder control devices.

Shareholder Liability

Generally the shareholder enjoys limited liability, placing only the initial investment at risk. But, as we have learned, there can be exceptions to the general rule of limited shareholder liability. If the shareholder has failed to pay the subscription price of shares, liability for the unpaid balance is quite clear. The shareholder made a contract with the corporation for those shares and so the shareholder must pay the corporation. Suppose a shareholder has not paid in full for shares when the corporation topples into bankruptcy. Can the shareholder escape payment? No! The creditors look to the shareholder's investment as support for their extension of credit to the corporation. If the corporation does not pay, the creditor can look to the corporate assets for payment. If there are insufficient assets, but there are unpaid shareholder subscriptions, an unsatisfied judgment creditor of the corporation can usually pursue and collect the unpaid balance.

Many states permit an enterprise to be incorporated with only $1000 of capital. Naturally, the corporation will require continued infusions of funds as it continues to grow. Where are the sources for such funds and in what forms can capital be raised?

There are two basic sources for financing the new corporation: (1) the issuance and sale of bonds, called debt financing, and (2) the issuance and sale of stock, called equity financing.

Debt Financing

A bond is simply a written promise by the corporation to pay a stated sum of money at a specific date accompanied by a stated interest rate. The

Corporate Capital Structure: Financing the Corporation

bondholder is a creditor of the corporation. The corporation has borrowed money from the lender with the promise to pay interest in the interim with repayment of the principal to occur at a future maturity date. Generally the corporation will reserve the right to redeem the bonds prior to the maturity date.

Bonds can assume a variety of forms. Usually bonds will be issued in series and secured by a lien or a mortgage making the bondholder a secured creditor. A debenture is a debt instrument that is unsecured. A bond can be convertible into shares of stock of the corporation. The issuance and sale of bonds is a source of long-term borrowing that is usually only available to the large corporation.

Equity Financing

Normally the only method of raising capital available to the new corporation is through the sale of stock. The stockholder or shareholder is an owner of the corporation and not a creditor. The ownership of the corporation is represented by a stock certificate. As an example, Coachmen Industries, Inc. has graciously granted permission to reprint its stock certificate (shown in Figure 10-1).

If an individual wishes to purchase stock in an existing corporation it can be bought from two sources. Usually the individual will purchase the stock from a shareholder that desires to sell some stock. The other method is to enter into a postincorporation stock subscription agreement. This is simply a contract whereby the individual agrees to buy a particular number and type of shares at a specified price when issued by the corporation. Or, the individual may buy shares of a new issue by the corporation.

usually through broker

Preincorporation stock subscriptions are used by the promoters to finance the soon to be created corporation. When the corporation is formed, the board of directors accepts the subscription, issues the stock, and collects the money. Problems can arise over the questions of whether subscribers can revoke their subscription and what constitutes acceptance by the corporation. To settle the first question, a number of states have provided by statute that a preincorporation stock subscription shall be irrevocable for a stated period. The Illinois Business Corporation Act § 16 sets this period at six months. In regard to what constitutes acceptance, the courts require either an express acceptance or some act that implies acceptance.

Types of Shares

Authorized shares are the number of shares that the Articles permit the corporation to issue. The number of authorized shares can be increased or decreased by amending the Articles. Issued shares are the shares that

FIGURE 10-1

the corporation has actually distributed to shareholders (or has reacquired and is holding as treasury shares). Treasury shares are shares of the corporation that have been issued and subsequently acquired by the corporation. Although they belong to the corporation, they cannot be voted by management at a shareholders' meeting and they are not paid dividends. Treasury shares are issued shares but are not "outstanding" on the corporate books.

Prior to 1912 all stock had a stated par value and consequently was called par stock. The board of directors would fix the par value of the shares, which could not be issued for less than the stated par value. If they were issued for less than par this was considered to work a fraud on the corporate creditors. The creditors had the legal right to assume that the corporation received money, property, or services equal to the total par value of the issued shares. These assets would then be available to the creditor if it were not paid.

Par value created a number of problems. For instance, what is a corporation to do when the market price of its stock drops below its par value? If the corporation cannot issue shares, it cannot secure financing, and it cannot sell shares at less than par. To avoid problems like this, the various states began to allow no par stock starting in 1912. No par stock lacks a stated value. However, it does have an inherent monetary value since it represents the shareholder's proportionate interest in the corporation. This value will be measured by the stock's market value. Although no par stocks lack a stated value, the corporation must receive consideration or value when it issues them.

Voting and nonvoting stock is aptly described by those designations. The shareholder will either have the right to vote his or her shares or will not, depending on the type of stock. Nonvoting stock is a device to keep control of the corporation within a certain group and, at the same time, secure financing. The nonvoting and voting stock are sold to the public while the control group retains all, or a majority of, the voting stock. Some states will not permit nonvoting stock because it is assumed that as an owner, the shareholder deserves a say in corporate affairs.

The MBCA in Section 33 provides in part that:

> Each outstanding share, regardless of class, shall be entitled to one vote on each matter submitted to a vote at a meeting of shareholders, except as may be otherwise provided in the articles of incorporation.

This section would permit the issuance of nonvoting shares if the power to issue such shares was given in the articles. Why would a purchaser be interested in nonvoting shares? Today, shareholders in moderately sized corporations and megacorporations do not usually plan to vote their shares. They plan on receiving a return on their shares by way of dividends or by selling the share for more than their purchase price.

If a corporation has issued nonvoting shares on which it is obliged to pay a dividend, can corporate management suspend the dividend or, indeed, cancel it? This might require a shareholder meeting because it may fundamentally alter the capital structure of the corporation, but what good would this do if the class of shares being affected could not vote? The MBCA, Section 60, and most state statutes provide that nonvoting shares may vote when their class of shares may be affected by a change in designation, preferences, limitations or relative rights, and in other cases. In this case, this class of nonvoting shares votes as a class (i.e., their votes are not counted with the votes of other classes) on the proposed change in their shareholder status.

Common and Preferred Stock

Now that we have defined some terms applied to stock let us examine the two basic types of stock: common and preferred. Common stock is the most frequently issued type of stock. The common shareholders usually control the corporation since common stock traditionally is voting stock. They receive their portion of the corporate profits in the form of dividends. On dissolution they share in any assets that remain after payment of the creditors. The common shareholder assumes the biggest risk and can enjoy the largest benefits. Preferred stockholders are entitled to certain preferences over the common shareholders. Generally they enjoy the right to receive dividends at a specified rate before any dividends can be distributed to the common shareholders. In practice this will sometimes mean that the preferred shareholders will receive dividends and the common shareholders will not. The preferred shareholders are also given a preference over the holders of common stock to assets of the corporation on dissolution. Usually preferred shareholders will be denied voting privileges. Sometimes there will be an exception allowing the preferred shareholders to vote if no dividends have been paid for a certain number of years.

Some preferred stock can enjoy a preference over other preferred stock. For example, two classes of preferred stock may be issued with one class having a preference over the other in certain matters, such as sharing in the assets on dissolution. If the difference is in the amount of dividends, the preferred is said to be issued in "series" not "classes." Series A might be entitled to eight percent dividends whereas Series B receives dividends in the amount of six percent.

It is possible to have convertible preferred. This allows the preferred shareholder to convert the preferred stock into common stock. The rate at which it can be converted into other shares and under what conditions it may be converted will be specified when issued.

Preferred stock can also be either cumulative or noncumulative. If dividends are not paid on cumulative preferred stock in a given year, those dividends will cumulate. In other words, the shareholders will be entitled to the payment of all dividend arrearages before any dividends can be paid to the common shareholders. With noncumulative stock, if the dividends are not paid in a given year, the dividends will be forever lost. The next year all the corporation need do is pay the current dividend to the preferred shareholder and then it may pay dividends to the common shareholders. Preferred stock is cumulative unless specifically indicated otherwise.

Preferred stock will also be either nonparticipating or participating. If it is nonparticipating, once it has been paid its dividends the remaining surplus may be distributed among the common shareholders in any amount. With participating preferred, once it has received its dividends and an equal amount has been distributed to the common, it and the common can both share in the remaining funds. Of course, it is the unusual corporation that enjoys such a surplus of profits so as to face this issue. For preferred to be participating, it must be explicitly so indicated.

In their pure form it is easy to distinguish a stock from a bond or a share of common stock from a preferred share. But all securities do not have definite attributes exclusive of a debt security or an equity security.

Oftentimes an element of a bond will be combined with an element of a stock as a lawyer tailors a hybrid security to fit the requirements of a specific corporation. Sometimes these hybrid securities will almost defy classification. The *John Kelley Co. v. Commissioner of IRS* case that follows involves such hybrid securities. Notice how in each situation, the attributes of a stock are blended with the attributes of a debt so as to blur the dividing line. This case is important because it shows the Supreme Court's deference for IRS determinations in matters involving the corporate capital structure. It also reveals that when it comes to corporate finance, some lawyers and accountants can be very creative.

JOHN KELLEY CO. v. COMM'R OF I.R.S.
326 U.S. 521 (1946)

Opinion of the Court by MR. JUSTICE REED, *announced by* MR. JUSTICE FRANKFURTER.

These writs of certiorari were granted to examine the deductibility as interest of certain payments which the taxpayer corporations made to holders of their corporate obligations. Although the obligations of the two taxpayers had only one striking difference, the noncumulative in one and the cumulative quality in the other of the payments reserved under the characterization of interest, the Tax Court . . . held that the payments under the former, the Kelley Company case, were interest and under the Talbot Mills were dividends. The Circuit Court of Appeals reversed the Tax Court in the Kelley case and another circuit affirmed the Talbot Mills decision. On account of the diversity of approach in the Tax Court and the reviewing courts, we granted certiorari.

In the Kelley case, a corporation, all of whose common and preferred stock was owned directly or as trustee by members of a family group, was reorganized by authorizing the issue of $250,000 income debenture bearer bonds, issued under a trust indenture, calling for 8 percent interest, noncumulative. They were offered only to shareholders of the taxpayer but were assignable. The debentures were payable in twenty years, December 31, 1956, with payment of general interest conditioned upon the sufficiency of the net income to meet the obligation. The debenture holders had priority of payment over stockholders but were subordinated to all other creditors. The debentures were redeemable at the taxpayer's option and carried the usual acceleration provisions for specific defaults. The debenture holders had no right to participate in management. Other changes not material here were made in the corporate structure. Debentures were issued to the amount of $150,000 face value. The greater part, $114,648, was issued in exchange for the original preferred, with six percent cumulative guaranteed dividends, at its retirement price and the balance sold to stockholders at par, which was eventually paid with sums obtained by the purchasers from common stock dividends. Common stock was owned in the same proportions by the same stockholders before and after the reorganization.

In the Talbot Mills case the taxpayer was a corporation which, prior to its recapitalization, had a capital stock of five thousand shares of the par value of $100 or $500,000. All of the stock with the exception of some qualifying shares was held by members, through blood or marriage, of the Talbot family. In an effort to adjust the capital structure to the advantage of the taxpayer, the company was recapitalized just prior to the beginning of the fiscal year in question, by each stockholder surrendering four-fifths of his stock and taking in lieu thereof registered notes in aggregate face value equal to the aggregate par value of the stock retired. This amounted to an issue of $400,000 in notes to the then stockholders. These notes were dated October 2, 1939, and were payable to a specific payee or his assignees on December 1, 1964. They bore annual interest at a rate not to exceed 10 percent nor less than 2 percent, subject to a computation that took into consideration the net earnings of the corporation for the fiscal year ended last previous to the annual interest paying date. There was, therefore, a minimum amount of 2 percent and a maximum of 10 percent due annually and between these limits the interest payable varied in accordance with company earnings. The notes were transferable only by the owner's endorsement and the notation of the transfer by the company. The interest was cumulative and payment might be deferred until the note's maturity when "necessary by reason of the condition of the corporation." Dividends could not be paid until all then due interest on the notes was satisfied. . . . For the fiscal year in question the maximum payment of 10 percent was made on the notes. . . .

Both corporations deducted the payments as interest from their reports of gross income. . . . The Commissioner asserted deficiencies because the payments were considered dividends and not interest. . . .

From the foregoing statements of facts, it appears that the characteristics of all the obligations in question and the surrounding circumstances were of such a nature that it is reasonably possible for determiners to reach the conclusion that the secured annual payments were interest to creditors in one case and dividends to stockholders in the other case. In the

Kelley case there were sales of the debentures as well as exchanges of preferred stock for debentures, a promise to pay a certain annual amount, if earned, a priority for the debentures over common stock, the debentures were assignable without regard to any transfer of stock, and a definite maturity date in the reasonable future. These indicia of indebtedness support the Tax Court conclusion that the annual payments were interest on indebtedness. On the other hand, in the Talbot Mills case, the Tax Court found the factors there present of fluctuating annual payments with a two percent minimum, the limitation of the issue of notes to stockholders in exchange only for stock, to be characteristics which distinguish the Talbot Mills notes from the Kelley Company debentures. Upon an appraisal of all the facts, the Tax Court reached the conclusion that the annual payments by Talbot Mills were in reality dividends and not interest.

We think these conclusions should be accepted by the Circuit Courts of Appeals and by ourselves. . . .

These cases now under consideration deal with well understood words as used in the tax statutes—"interest" and "dividends." They need no further definition. . . . The Tax Court is fitted to decide whether the annual payments under these corporate obligations are to be classified as interest or dividends. The Tax Court decisions merely declare that the undisputed facts do or do not bring the payments under the definition of interest or dividends. The documents under consideration embody elements of obligations and elements of stock. There is no one characteristic, not even exclusion from management, which can be said to be decisive in the determination of whether the obligations are risk investments in the corporations or debts. So-called stock certificates may be authorized by corporations which are really debts, and promises to pay may be executed which have incidents of stock. . . .

This leads us to affirm the Talbot Mills decree and to reverse the Kelley judgment.

It is so ordered.

MR. JUSTICE RUTLEDGE (*concurring in part, dissenting in part*).

I think the judgments in both cases should be affirmed. On the records presented, I can see no satisfactory basis for deciding one case one way and the other differently. And I agree with the Courts of Appeals that, on the substantially identical facts, the payments were dividends and not interest. . . .

There were some highly technical differences in the two types of "security" which were devised to replace the pre-existing preferred stock issues. But in both instances the original stock and the replacing security were closely held. There was no substantial change in the distribution after the "reorganization." The difference between the stock and the substituted security was so small, in its effect upon the holders' substantial rights, that for all practical purposes it was negligible. . . .

Tax liability should depend upon the subtle refinements of corporate finance no more than it does upon the niceties of conveyancing. Sheer technicalities should have no more weight to control federal tax consequences in one instance than in the other. The taxing statute draws the line broadly between "interest" and "dividend." This requires one who would claim the interest deduction to bring himself clearly within the class for which it was intended. That is not done when the usual signposts between bonds and stock are so obliterated that they become invisible or point equally in both directions at the same time.

"Dividend" and "interest," "stock" and "bond," "debenture" or "note," are correlative and clearly identifiable conceptions in their simpler and more traditional exemplifications. But their distinguishing features vanish when astute manipulation of the broad permissions of modern incorporation acts results in a "security device" which is in truth neither stock nor bond, but the halfbreed offspring of both. At times only the label enables one to ascertain what the manipulator intended to bring forth. But intention clarified by label alone is not always legally effective for the purpose in mind. And there is scarcely any limit to the extent or variety to which this kind of intermingling of the traditional features of stock and bonds or other forms of debt may go, as the books abundantly testify. The taxpayer should show more than a label or a hybrid security to escape his liability. He should show at the least a substantial preponderance of fact pointing to "interest" rather than "dividends." . . .

Case Questions

1. If there is no one characteristic that can be said to be decisive in the determination of whether securities are equity or debt, on what exactly did the Supreme Court base its decision?

2. Whose reasoning do you find more persuasive, that of the Court or of Mr. Justice Rutledge? The case certainly drew diverse reactions from the various Justices: five agreed on all issues, three agreed on some issues while disagreeing on others, and one did not take part in the decision.

3. Is the result in the Kelley case an example of an ingenious draftsman slipping a corporation through a tax loophole? Tax evasion is illegal; tax avoidance is legal.

We suggested above that shareholders have ultimate theoretical power over the management of the corporation. We say "theoretical" power because state corporation laws provide for shareholder election of the board of directors and then provide that the board shall manage the business of the corporation. However, over time, as the board comes to rely on the information provided to it by the management, a dependency develops. So, as we discuss later, in the larger corporations the ultimate power over management of the corporation is exercised by management itself or, at best, and depending on the corporation involved, ultimate power may be shared by management, the board, and to a lesser extent the shareholders. Generalizing about who has the power to control medium to large groups of people is always subject to conjecture and, when a general rule is announced, subject to exception.

Shareholder Meetings

State laws provide that the power of a shareholder be exercised only in a properly called shareholder meeting. Obviously, if you are a shareholder of IBM, you cannot walk into corporate headquarters and demand to meet the president of the corporation or use the executive dining room. Some corporations have more than one shareholder meeting per year, but most state laws require at least one meeting annually.

The bylaws provide the time and place of the meeting as well as the manner of calling the meeting. The state statute will indicate what percentage of shares, represented in person or by proxy, will constitute a quorum. Oftentimes the statute will prescribe a minimum quorum requirement but allow the corporation to establish a higher requirement if it so desires. If the corporation is granted flexibility in this regard, it should not establish a quorum requirement so high as to make it difficult to hold a meeting nor so low as to allow a small minority to dominate shareholder affairs. The statute will also provide for the closing of the stock transfer books for a stated period (usually mandating a maximum and minimum number of days) to determine the shareholders entitled to notice of or to vote at a meeting. The notice of a regular meeting does not have to contain an agenda for the meeting.

Whenever a special meeting is called, the notice to the shareholder must specify the time, place, and purpose of the meeting. Who has the power to call a special shareholders' meeting? Typically the statute will permit the president, board of directors, or such other officers or persons as provided in the articles or bylaws to call a special meeting. Some states allow the holders of a specified number of shares to call a special meeting. Illinois Business Corporation Act § 26 permits the holders of not less than one fifth of all the outstanding shares to call a meeting.

Delaware's corporation law (§ 228) contains a unique feature. It allows the shareholders to take action without holding an annual or special meeting. It also dispenses with the requirement of prior notice and a vote.

If the shareholders holding the minimum number of votes necessary to authorize the action at a meeting consent in writing to that action, a meeting is not necessary. The shareholders that did not consent must be furnished prompt notice of the action. This provision will permit, in effect, a stockholders meeting to be held by mail. Publicly held corporations incorporated in Delaware have not used this device to avoid hostile questioning by various shareholder groups at the annual meeting. Why? The New York Stock Exchange requires that all companies with stock listed on the Big Board hold annual meetings. Thus, even though management may wish to avoid the annual meeting, and legally may do so, practical obstacles can prevent it.

Cumulative Voting

The most important item of business at a shareholder meeting is the election of directors. If this election were presented to the shareholders as an ordinary business item and if the bylaws provided that ordinary business items were to be decided by majority vote, then a majority of the shareholders could elect the entire board closing out any minority-shareholder representation. For example, assume Corporation X has 3000 shares outstanding and 2400 are expected to be present at a shareholders meeting, 1500 are owned by a group that was management or associated with management, and 900 are owned by nonmanagement interests. If five directors are to be elected, then using a method of straight voting (one vote per share) and assuming the election for each position is a separate business item, the outcome would look like this:

	Management Board				
People	A	B	C	D	E

	Nonmanagement Board				
People	F	G	H	I	J

In the first election, A would stand against F and win by a vote of 1500 to 900. The next election would proceed the same way. This is obviously an undesirable outcome because A, B, C, D, and E would be automatically elected. The owners of the 900 shares are entitled to some representation, but just how much? This is a very difficult question. The solution has been to devise a system allowing shareholders to cumulate their votes.

Cumulative voting is designed to enable a minority group of shareholders to gain representation on the board of directors. The representatives of the majority shareholders will dominate board affairs, but the minority board members will have an input and gain first-hand knowledge of corporate affairs. Typically, management will oppose cumulative voting. The stated reason for such opposition will usually be that the board is to represent the best interests of the corporation and that representatives of special interests have no place in the corporate scheme. The "real" reason for opposition is probably management's desire to avoid having its policies vigorously questioned by segments of the board. Since cumulative voting does preserve majority rule, and since even minority shareholders are owners of the corporation, valid objections to cumulative voting are absent.

Cumulative voting allows a shareholder to multiply the number of votes owned by the number of directors to be elected. The shareholder can cast all votes for a single director candidate or allocate them among several candidates. From a tactical standpoint, the minority shareholder or shareholders will desire to cumulate their votes so as to elect the greatest possible number of directors. How is this to be achieved? A formula is available to determine the most advantageous distribution of the cumulative votes.[2] Under the formula: Let X = number of shares needed to elect a given number of directors; Y = total number of shares at the meeting; N^1 = number of directors desired to elect; and N = total number of directors to be elected. The formula assumes that each share is entitled to one vote.

$$X = \frac{Y \times N^1}{N + 1} + 1$$

Let us now examine the formula in operation. Using the same example above and assuming a dissident group of shareholders desires to get one individual elected to the board, how many shares, if cumulated, will be necessary?

$$X = \frac{2400 \times 1}{5 + 1} + 1$$

$$X = 401 \text{ shares}$$

Thus, for the minority shareholders to place one person on the board of directors, they will need 401 shares if cumulated. To place two individuals on the board will require 801 shares. The five individuals receiving the highest number of votes will be elected. In our example then, the non-management shareholders will be able to elect two of five board members, thus ensuring some representation.

It is mathematically possible for a minority to use cumulative voting and seize control of the board if the majority errs. Such an error can result from sloppy majority cumulation or a failure to cumulate. In *Pierce* v. *Commonwealth*, 104 Pa. 150 (1883), the minority cumulated its votes, distributing them among four candidates, while the majority failed to cumulate its votes while distributing them evenly among six candidates. The result was that the four minority candidates were elected to a six-person board. The court upheld the result.

Staggering the terms of the directors is a method of circumventing the effect of cumulative voting. For example, if a corporation's board is composed of three members serving staggered three-year terms, only one will be elected annually. The majority shareholders will always be victorious in such an election, thereby frustrating the intent of cumulative voting. Such a result will not be permitted in a state that mandates, either constitutionally or by statute, cumulative voting.[3] In slightly less than one half the states cumulative voting is mandatory.[4]

Generally, the larger the corporation the less cumulative voting is used. Megacorporations have chosen to incorporate in states that do not require cumulative voting; thus it has been estimated that approximately 90 percent of all large industrial corporations do not require cumulative voting.[5] Indeed, to lure corporations, the trend in many states is away from requiring cumulative voting. Between 1955 and 1972, five states changed from mandatory to permissive cumulative voting. Today Delaware and 32 other states do not require it but permit it if the Articles provide for it.[6]

Proxies

In a large publicly held corporation one would not expect a large number of shareholders to personally attend shareholder meetings. The time and expense necessary to attend the meeting can be substantial. Yet this lack of attendance raises two potential problems. First, if shareholders desire to attend but are unable, they will be denied their suffrage. Second, a quorum is necessary at the meeting for shareholder action to be valid. In 1973, Bank of America had 268 shareholders attend its annual meeting, Chrysler 450, and Westinghouse 200 (in 1956 shareholder attendance was 1600).[7] How were these corporations able to legally conduct these meetings? The proxy system provides the solution. A proxy is the shareholder's equivalent of the absentee ballot. The shareholder casts a vote without attending the meeting and, at the same time, the shares are counted towards the requirements of a quorum.

The shareholder appoints an agent, called a proxy, (which is not to be confused with the written instrument creating the agency relationship, also called a proxy), to vote the shares at the meeting. Each share has one vote (except for nonvoting stock). The shareholder can limit the authority of the proxy to voting the shares in a specified manner. Or, the shareholder can delegate general authority to the proxy permitting a vote according to the judgment of the proxy. Figure 10-2 shows a sample of a proxy instrument. The proxy cannot vote for fundamental corporate changes (i.e., mergers, dissolution, basic amendments to the articles, etc.), unless the shareholder specifically delegates such authority.

The law of agency governs proxies. Thus, a proxy is revocable by the shareholder–principal. The shareholder may revoke the proxy by per-

GM

P R O X Y

GENERAL MOTORS CORPORATION

Proxy Solicited by Board of Directors for Annual Meeting of Stockholders
Fisher Building, Detroit, Michigan, Friday, May 20, 1983, 9:00 A.M. Local Time

The undersigned authorizes Roger B. Smith, F. James McDonald, Howard H. Kehrl and F. Alan Smith, and each of them as the Proxy Committee, to vote the common stock of the undersigned upon the nominees for Director (A. L. Armstrong, C. B. Cleary, J. T. Connor, J. D. deButts, J. H. Evans, W. A. Fallon, C. T. Fisher, III, M. L. Goldberger, R. S. Hatfield, R. H. Herzog, J. J. Horan, R. R. Jensen, H. H. Kehrl, F. J. McDonald, W. E. McLaughlin, T. A. Murphy, E. C. Patterson, E. T. Pratt, Jr., J. G. Smale, F. A. Smith, R. B. Smith, L. H. Sullivan, C. H. Townes), upon the other Items shown below and on the reverse side, *which are described and page referenced in the Table of Contents (page i) to the Proxy Statement*, and upon all other matters which may come before the 1983 Annual Meeting of Stockholders of General Motors Corporation, or any adjournment thereof.

You are encouraged to specify your choices by marking the appropriate boxes below, but you need not mark any boxes if you wish to vote in accordance with the Board of Directors' recommendations. The Proxy Committee cannot vote your shares unless you sign and return this card.

The Board of Directors Recommends a Vote **FOR** *the following Board of Directors Proposals:*

	For	Withheld			For	Against	Abstain
Item No. 1	☐	☐		Item No. 2	☐	☐	☐

For, except vote withheld from the following nominee(s):

This proxy will be voted "FOR" Items 1 and 2 if no choice is specified.   SEE REVERSE SIDE ▶

---

1 37 33- 06 5528 332

GM

P R O X Y

The Items shown below are described and page referenced in the Table of Contents (page i) to the Proxy Statement.
The Board of Directors Recommends a Vote **AGAINST** *the following Stockholder Proposals:*

	For	Against	Abstain		For	Against	Abstain		For	Against	Abstain
Item No. 3	☐	☐	☐	Item No. 4	☐	☐	☐	Item No. 5	☐	☐	☐

This proxy will be voted "AGAINST" Items 3 through 5 if no choice is specified.

FRED J NAFFZIGER & CAROL A
NAFFZIGER JT TEN
124 S GREENLAWN AVE
SOUTH BEND IND   46617

Dated: _____ , 1983

_____
Signature of Stockholder

Please add your title if you are signing as Attorney, Administrator, Executor, Guardian, Trustee, or in any other representative capacity.

PLEASE MARK, SIGN, DATE AND RETURN THIS PROXY CARD PROMPTLY USING THE ENCLOSED ENVELOPE.

FIGURE 10-2

sonally attending the meeting and voting the shares. Subsequently granting a proxy to another individual will revoke the first proxy. However, a proxy coupled with an interest is irrevocable. For example, if A sells his shares to B after the record date for the shareholders' meeting and gives his proxy to B, that proxy is irrevocable. A has coupled his proxy with B's interest in those shares.

The Securities Exchange Act of 1934 subjects the process of proxy solicitation to vigorous regulation. It is unlawful to solicit proxies without complying with the requirements of the 1934 Act. These requirements are discussed in detail in Chapter 18.

Voting Trusts

A voting trust is created when any number of shareholders transfer their shares to a trustee for voting purposes. Legal title accompanied by the voting rights to the shares is vested in the trustee. The trustee issues "voting trust certificates" to the shareholders to indicate their respective proportionate share in the voting trust. The shareholders retain beneficial ownership of the stock and the trustee forwards any dividends to them. A voting trust agreement sets out the terms and conditions of the voting trust. A voting trust is not to be confused with a proxy, which is revocable. Once established, a voting trust is irrevocable. Typically, the agreement will be limited by statute to a duration of ten years. See MBCA § 34.

The most famous example of a voting trust is probably the one involving Howard Hughes, at one time the majority shareholder of TWA. During 1960, Hughes attempted to borrow funds to finance the purchase of jet aircraft for TWA's fleet. The banks and insurance companies disliked his method of managing TWA and refused to lend the funds unless he placed his shares in a voting trust. The trust was to have three trustees, two of which were to be named by the financial institutions. Hughes resisted until, finally, on December 30, 1960, he agreed to the voting trust arrangement. The financial institution's two trustees installed a new management team in TWA. Shortly after the expiration of the voting trust agreement Hughes sold his 75.18 percent interest at approximately $86 per share. After the deduction of brokerage fees and expenses he received $546,549,711.

Preemptive Rights

In some circumstances, a shareholder has the right to purchase a pro rata share of any newly authorized and issued shares of the corporation. This right, called the preemptive right, was developed by the common law to enable a shareholder to maintain a proportionate interest in the corporation. The shares must be offered to the shareholder before they can be offered to other prospective purchasers. It is the shareholders' choice to exercise this right. The right does not exist in shares issued for property,[8] in connection with a merger,[9] or for payment of debts.[10]

The preemptive right doctrine is easily applied in the closely held corporation that has only one class of common stock. Shareholders in such a corporation will likewise be concerned that their voting and financial interest not be diluted by the issuance of shares to other individuals. The situation is quite different in a publicly held corporation. The typical shareholder will have only a small fractional ownership interest in the corporation and thus, will be unconcerned with the small dilution to the proportionate voting and dividend rights brought about by a new issue of stock. The administrative burden and expense (paper, postage, secretarial time, etc.) involved in offering preemptive rights to a large number of shareholders can be heavy.

Preemptive rights also pose a delay in securing financing. The shareholders are entitled to a reasonable period of time to consider and accept the offer. In the interim, the public market for such securities may decline. Finally, the widely held corporation may have both common and preferred shares and several different classes within each that have different legal rights. Such a situation can present a legal morass in determining which shareholders are entitled to preemptive rights and in what amounts.

Since preemptive rights can prove to be troublesome, may a corporation dispense with them? Yes. The states take two approaches. At one end of the spectrum is the elimination of preemptive rights unless the articles specifically call for them, i.e., Ind. Corp. Act § 25-502 (i) and the MBCA § 26. The opposite position is to permit preemptive rights unless they are limited or denied in the articles. See Ill. § 24. In actual operation preemptive rights tend to be confined to close corporations.

Close Corporations

Both case law and state statutory corporation law have recognized a distinction between different sizes of corporations. The recognition has come because of the desire of many businesspersons and small businesses to treat their corporations as partnerships or even proprietorships and yet enjoy the limited liability feature of corporations. Just how far can family members or friends or a few business associates go in varying state corporation law to serve their own needs? The case below is another classic in corporation law because it addresses this question. We begin this section with this case, which gives insight into the operation and need for special treatment for small, family-held or close corporations. Following the case we will explain how some state laws treat the close corporation.

GALLER v. GALLER
32 Ill. 2d 16, 203 N.E. 2d 577 (S. Ct., Ill., 1964)

UNDERWOOD, Justice

There is no substantial dispute as to the facts in this case. From 1919 to 1924, Benjamin and Isadore Galler, brothers, were equal partners in the Galler Drug Company, a wholesale drug concern. In 1924 the business was incorporated under the Illinois Business Corporation Act, each owning one half of the outstanding 220 shares of stock. In 1945 each contracted to sell 6 shares to an employee, Rosenberg, at a price of $10,500 for each block of 6 shares, payable within 10 years. . . .

In March, 1954, Benjamin and Isadore, on the advice of their accountant, decided to enter into an agreement for the financial protection of their immediate families and to assure their families, after the death of either brother, equal control of the corporation. In

June, 1954, while the agreement was in the process of preparation by an attorney-associate of the accountant, Benjamin suffered a heart attack. . . . During his brother's illness, Isadore asked the accountant to have the shareholders' agreement put in final form in order to protect Benjamin's wife, and this was done by another attorney employed in the accountant's office. On a Saturday night in July, 1955, the accountant brought the agreement to Benjamin's home, and 6 copies of it were executed there by the two brothers and their wives. . . . It appears from the evidence that some months after the agreement was signed, and defendants Isadore and Rose Galler and their son, the defendant, Aaron Galler sought to have the agreements destroyed. The evidence is undisputed that the defendants had decided prior to Benjamin's death they would not honor the agreement, but never disclosed their intention to plaintiff or her husband.

On July 21, 1956, Benjamin executed an instrument creating a trust naming his wife as trustee. The trust covered, among other things, the 104 shares of Galler Drug Company stock and the stock certificates were endorsed by Benjamin and delivered to Emma. When Emma presented the certificates to defendants for transfer into her name as trustee, they sought to have Emma abandon the 1955 agreement or enter into some kind of a noninterference agreement as a price for the transfer of the shares. Finally, in September, 1956, after Emma had refused to abandon the shareholders' agreement, she did agree to permit defendant Aaron to become president for one year and agreed that she would not interfere with the business during that year. The stock was then reissued in her name as trustee. During the year 1957 while Benjamin was still alive, Emma tried many times to arrange a meeting with Isadore to discuss business matters but he refused to see her.

Shortly after Benjamin's death, Emma went to the office and demanded the terms of the 1955 agreement be carried out. Isadore told her that anything she had to say could be said to Aaron, who then told her that his father would not abide by the agreement. He offered a modification of the agreement by proposing the salary continuation payment but without her becoming a director. When Emma refused to modify the agreement and sought enforcement of its terms, defendants refused and this suit followed.

During the last few years of Benjamin's life both brothers drew an annual salary of $42,000. Aaron, whose salary was $15,000 as manager of the warehouse prior to September, 1956, has since the time that Emma agreed to his acting as president drawn an annual salary of $20,000. In 1957, 1958, and 1959 a $40,000 annual dividend was paid. Plaintiff has received her proportionate share of the dividend. . . .

The essential features of the contested portions of the agreement are substantially as set forth in the opinion of the Appellate Court: (2) that the bylaws of the corporation will be amended to provide for a board of four directors; that the necessary quorum shall be three directors; and that no directors' meeting shall be held without giving ten days notice to all directors. (3) The shareholders will cast their votes for the above named persons (Isadore, Rose, Benjamin, and Emma) as directors at said special meeting and at any other meeting held for the purpose of electing directors. (4,5) In the event of the death of either brother his wife shall have the right to nominate a director in place of the decedent. (6) Certain annual dividends will be declared by the corporation. The dividend shall be $50,000 payable out of the accumulated earned surplus in excess of $500,000. If 50% of the annual net profits after taxes exceeds the minimum $50,000, then the directors shall have discretion to declare a dividend up to 50% of the annual net profits. If the net profits are less than $50,000, nevertheless the minimum $50,000 annual dividend shall be declared, providing the $500,000 surplus is maintained. (9) The certificates evidencing the said shares of Benjamin Galler and Isadore Galler shall bear a legend that the shares are subject to the terms of this agreement. (10) A salary continuation agreement shall be entered into by the corporation which shall authorize the corporation upon the death of Benjamin Galler or Isadore Galler, or both, to pay a sum equal to twice the salary of such officer, payable monthly over a five-year period. Said sum shall be paid to the widow during her widowhood, but should be paid to such widow's children if the widow remarries within the five-year period. (11,12) . . . In the event either Benjamin or Isadore decides to sell his shares he is required to offer them first to the remaining shareholders and then to the corporation at book value, according each six months to accept the offer.

The Appellate Court found the 1955

agreement void because "the undue duration, stated purpose and substantial disregard of the provisions of the Corporation Act outweigh any considerations which might call for divisibility" and held that "the public policy of this state demands voiding this entire agreement."

While the conduct of defendants towards plaintiff was clearly inequitable, the basically controlling factor is the absence of an objecting minority interest, together with the absence of public detriment. . . .

At this juncture it should be emphasized that we deal here with a so-called close corporation. Various attempts at definition of the close corporation have been made. . . . For our purposes, a close corporation is one in which the stock is held in a few hands, or in a few families, and wherein it is not at all, or only rarely, dealt in by buying or selling. . . . Moreover, it should be recognized that shareholder agreements similar to that in question here are often, as a practical consideration, quite necessary for the protection of those financially interested in the close corporation. While the shareholder of a public-issue corporation may readily sell his shares on the open market should management fail to use, in his opinion, sound business judgment, his counterpart of the close corporation often has a large total of his entire capital invested in the business and has no ready market for his shares should he desire to sell. He feels, understandably, that he is more than a mere investor and that his voice should be heard concerning all corporate activity. Without a shareholder agreement, specifically enforceable by the courts, insuring him a modicum of control, a large minority shareholder might find himself at the mercy of an oppressive or unknowledgeable majority. Moreover, as in the case at bar, the shareholders of a close corporation are often also the directors and officers thereof. With substantial shareholding interests abiding in each member of the board of directors, it is often quite impossible to secure, as in the large public-issue

corporation, independent board judgment free from personal motivations concerning corporate policy. For these and other reasons too voluminous to enumerate here, often the only sound basis for protection is afforded by a lengthy, detailed shareholder agreement securing the rights and obligations of all concerned. . . .

As the preceding review of the applicable decisions of this court points out, there has been a definite, albeit inarticulate, trend toward eventual judicial treatment of the close corporation as sui generis. Several shareholder-director agreements that have technically "violated" the letter of the Business Corporation Act have nevertheless been upheld in the light of the existing practical circumstances, i.e., no apparent public injury, the absence of a complaining minority interest, and no apparent prejudice to creditors. However, we have thus far not attempted to limit these decisions as applicable only to close corporations and have seemingly implied that general considerations regarding judicial supervision of all corporate behavior apply. . . .

Courts have long ago quite realistically, we feel, relaxed their attitudes concerning statutory compliance when dealing with close corporate behavior, permitting "slight deviations" from corporate "norms" in order to give legal efficacy to common business practice. . . .

Numerous helpful textual statements and law review articles dealing with the judicial treatment of the close corporation have been pointed out by counsel. One article concludes with the following: "New needs compel fresh formulation of corporate 'norms'. There is no reason why mature men should not be able to adapt the statutory form to the structure they want, so long as they do not endanger other stockholders, creditors, or the public, or violate a clearly mandatory provision of the corporation laws. In a typical close corporation the stockholders' agreement is usually the result of careful deliberation among all initial investors.

In the large public-issue corporation, on the other hand, the 'agreement' represented by the corporate charter is not consciously agreed to by the investors; they have no voice in its formulation, and very few ever read the certificate of incorporation. Preservation of the corporate norms may there be necessary for the protection of the public investors." Hornstein, "Stockholders' Agreements in the Closely Held Corporation," 59 Yale L. Journal, 1040, 1056. . . .

We now, in the light of the foregoing, turn to specific provisions of the 1955 agreement.

The Appellate Court correctly found many of the contractual provisions free from serious objection, and we need not prolong this opinion with a discussion of them here. That court did, however, find difficulties in the stated purpose of the agreement as it relates to its duration, the election of certain persons to specific offices for a number of years, the requirement for the mandatory declaration of stated dividends (which the Appellate Court held invalid), and the salary continuation agreement.

Since the question as to the duration of the agreement is a principal source of controversy, we shall consider it first. The parties provided no specific termination date. . . . In view of the history of decisions of this court generally upholding, in the absence of fraud or prejudice to minority interests or public policy, the right of stockholders to agree among themselves as to the manner in which their stock will be voted, we do not regard the period of time within which this agreement may remain effective as rendering the agreement unenforceable.

The clause that provides for the election of certain persons to specified offices for a period of years likewise does not require invalidation. . . .

We turn next to a consideration of the effect of the stated purpose of the agreement upon its validity. The pertinent provision is:

"The said Benjamin A. Galler and Isadore A. Galler desire to provide income for the support and maintenance of their immediate families." Obviously, there is no evil inherent in a contract entered into for the reason that the persons originating the terms desired to so arrange their property as to provide postdeath support for those dependent upon them. . . .

The terms of the dividend agreement require a minimum annual dividend of $50,000, but this duty is limited by the subsequent provision that it shall be operative only so long as an earned surplus of $500,000 is maintained. It may be noted that in 1958, the year prior to commencement of this litigation, the corporation's net earnings after taxes amounted to $202,759 while its earned surplus was $1,543,270, and this was increased in 1958 to $1,680,079 while earnings were $172,964. The minimum earned surplus requirement is designed for the protection of the corporation and its creditors, and we take no exception to the contractual dividend requirements as thus restricted. . . .

The salary continuation agreement is a common feature, in one form or another, of corporate executive employment. It requires that the widow should receive a total benefit, payable monthly over a five-year period, aggregating twice the amount paid her deceased husband in one year. . . .

We hold defendants must account for all monies received by them from the corporation since September 25, 1956, in excess of that theretofore authorized.

Accordingly, the judgment of the Appellate Court is reversed. . . . The cause is remanded to the circuit court of Cook County with directions to proceed in accordance herewith.

Affirmed in part and reversed in part, and remanded with directions.

1. What exactly is "public policy" and who ascertains its dictates? Doesn't the legislature establish the public policy toward corporations when it enacts the Business Corporation Act?
2. Is different judicial treatment of the close corporation vis-à-vis the public corporation justifiable?
3. Does the decision reflect sympathy for Emma Galler, sound judicial reasoning, or both?

Shareholder Agreements

Two of the most fundamental notions of corporation law are that the board of directors (*not* the shareholders) should manage the corporation; and that the board should be free to declare or not declare dividends payable to the shareholders. The *Galler* case intrudes on both of these notions. Why does the law support these two basic ideas? In a business setting numerous tensions and pressures must be balanced. Consider the typical small corporation and its real constituents. First there are the shareholders who must be paid a return on their investment in the form of dividends; there is management that must be paid a salary; and, just as important, there are creditors who must be paid and customers who must be served. Often these various constituents present competing claims to the corporation, and someone or somebody must decide how the resources of the corporation are to be divided. This body is the board of directors. The board, so the theory goes, should not be compelled by previous agreement to serve or decide any issue in favor of one of the constituents. This was the central issue in the *Galler* case. Could shareholders not only compel the election to the board of various named persons, but compel by agreement the board to pay out dividends and to pay a sort of benefit in the event of the death of one of the shareholders? These provisions violate the corporation-law theory because such payments, it is assumed, may jeopardize the interests of the creditors, the customers, or the public.

In the *Galler* case, the court decided that "New needs compel fresh formulation of corporate 'norms.' There is no reason why mature men (and women) should not be able to adapt the statutory form to the structure they want, so long as they do not endanger other stockholders, creditors, or the public, or violate a clearly mandatory provision of the corporation laws." So, as long as the shareholder agreement was knowingly entered into and as long as the minority shareholders, the creditors, and the public are not harmed, shareholders may try to manage the corporation as a partnership.

The *Galler* case has been followed in other jurisdictions, and some state legislatures have also responded to the need to vary the corporation-law norms.

Delaware provides a modern view of statutory treatment of closely held corporations. In 1967, it added a number of special provisions to govern the close corporation, which is defined as one having 30 or fewer shareholders. Among the more significant provisions of the Delaware General Corporation Law on close corporations are the following:

§ 350. Agreements Restricting Discretion of Directors

A written agreement among the stockholders of a close corporation holding a majority of the outstanding stock entitled to vote, whether solely among themselves or with a party not a stockholder, is not invalid, as between the parties to the agreement, on the ground that it so relates to the conduct of the business and affairs of the corporation as to restrict or interfere with the discretion or powers of the board of directors. The effect of any such agreement shall be to relieve the directors and impose upon the stockholders who are parties to the agreement the liability for managerial acts or omissions which is imposed on directors to the extent and so long as the discretion or powers of the board in its management of corporate affairs is controlled by such agreement.

§ 351. Management by Stockholders

The certificate of incorporation of a close corporation may provide that the business of the corporation shall be managed by the stockholders of the corporation rather than by a board of directors. So long as this provision continues in effect:

1. No meeting of stockholders need be called to elect directors;
2. Unless the context clearly requires otherwise, the stockholders of the corporation shall be deemed to be directors for purposes of applying provisions of this chapter; and
3. The stockholders of the corporation shall be subject to all liabilities of directors.

Such a provision may be inserted in the certificate of incorporation by amendment if all incorporators and subscribers or all holders of record of all of the outstanding stock, whether or not having voting power, authorize such a provision. An amendment to the certificate of incorporation to delete such a provision shall be adopted by a vote of the holders of a majority of all outstanding stock of the corporation, whether or not otherwise entitled to vote. If the certificate of incorporation contains a provision authorized by this section, the existence of such provision shall be noted conspicuously on the face or back of every stock certificate issued by such corporation.

§ 354. Operating Corporation as Partnership

No written agreement among stockholders of a close corporation, nor any provision of the certificate of incorporation or of the bylaws of the corporation, which agreement or provision relates to any phase of the affairs of such corporation, including but not limited to the management of its business or declaration and payment of dividends or other division of profits or the election of directors or officers or the employment of stockholders by the corporation or the arbitration of disputes, shall be invalid on the ground that it is an attempt by the parties to the agreement or by the stockholders of the corporation to treat the corporation as if it were a partnership or to arrange relations among the stockholders or between the stockholders and the corporation in a manner that would be appropriate only among partners.

§ 355. Stockholders' Option to Dissolve Corporation

(a) The certificate of incorporation of any close corporation may include a provision granting to any stockholder, or to the holders of any specified number or percentage of shares of any class of stock, an option to have the corporation dissolved at will or upon the occurrence of any specified event or contingency. Whenever any such option to dissolve is exercised, the stockholders exercising such option shall give written notice thereof to all other stockholders. After the expiration of thirty days following the sending of such notice, the dissolution of the corporation shall proceed as if the required number of stockholders having voting power had consented in writing to dissolution of the corporation as provided by § 228 of this title.

(b) If the certificate of incorporation as originally filed does not contain a provision authorized by subsection (a), the certificate may be amended to include such provision if adopted by the affirmative vote of the holders of all the outstanding stock, whether or not entitled to vote, unless the certificate of incorporation specifically authorizes such an amendment by a vote which shall be not less than two thirds of all the outstanding stock whether or not entitled to vote.

Close Corporation Statutes

In addition to Delaware the states of Florida, New York, California, Illinois, Pennsylvania, Texas, and others have special close corporation statutes. In November of 1981, the Committee on Corporation Laws of the American Bar Association published a statutory Close Corporation Supplement to the Model Business Corporation Act. At this time, this supplement is offered for comments from practitioners and scholars and has not been formally proposed as a model act. All of these close corporation acts have several key features, which we will summarize here.

1. *Definition of a close corporation.*

There is no one definition of a close corporation, but these factual elements seem to be present: the number of shareholders is limited to a small number, usually not over 50 and most often between 1 and 10; the shareholders are personally known to one another and some or most of them are active in management; there is a restriction on the transfer of shares to others and there is no established market for the sale of the shares; and the retained earnings of the firm are usually a major source of income to the shareholders-managers.

relationship of s/Hers. mainly importance.

2. *Operation of the close corporation.*

The articles of incorporation should include the phrase "a statutory corporation," and in some cases the restrictions on share transfer must be noted on the shares themselves. Some states forbid the corporation from making a public offering for the stock.

The management of the corporation may reside in the shareholders so long as a certain percentage of the shareholders agree to this in writing. The proposed supplement to the MCBA requires unanimous written agreement by the shareholders if the shareholders are to control the management of the corporation. Some statutes allow the elimination of the board; the shareholders elect management, and in exchange for this measure of control the shareholders also agree to be liable in the place of the board. This means they are to suffer the liability of the board for mismanagement, but this liability, as we discuss in the following chapters, is rarely established.

3. *Majority versus minority shareholders: the right to cause dissolution.*

A minority shareholder in a close corporation (one not a member of management or the family or group that has control) is in a particularly vulnerable position because he or she cannot withdraw from the enterprise by selling shares on the open market.[11] To protect this person or small group most states provide them the power to cause the dissolution of the corporation. The proposed model act states that the articles of incorporation *may grant* to any shareholder an option to have the corporation dissolved at will on the happening of any specified event. This power is crucial to the fair operation of a close corporation and is one completely consistent with the idea that a close corporation is somewhat like a partnership in operation and concept. Recall that any partner may cause the dissolution of a partnership and that one of the central parts of any partnership agreement is the rights of a partner on dissolution.

Some states counter this power of a minority shareholder with the right of the corporation to buy this person out.

In summary, we can see a trend, started in the 1960s and accelerated in the 1970s, to treat very small corporations or close corporations more like partnerships than corporations but retaining the idea of limited shareholder liability. We would expect this trend to continue.

Shareholders' Remedial Rights

As the owners of the corporation, the shareholders legally can control the corporation through election of the board of directors. Yet at times the right to vote for directors may be insufficient to protect the shareholders' interests. The shareholders' power may be thwarted if information regarding director and officer impropriety does not come to their attention, or if they have no weapon to halt such abuses. We will explore two shareholder remedies for combating improper activities: the right to inspect the corporate books and shareholder derivative suits.

Right to Inspect Corporate Books and Records

Common law grants to a shareholder the right to inspect the corporate books and records for a legitimate purpose. The shareholder can select another, such as an attorney or accountant, to perform this inspection.

The requirement of a legitimate purpose is designed to protect the corporation, and its other shareholders, from harrassment or other abuses. For example, an officer of a chemical manufacturer who is also a shareholder of a competing enterprise could not see the competitor's books to learn trade secrets or obtain customer lists. However, a dissident shareholder could obtain a list of shareholders in order to solicit their proxies for an attempt to remove current management. Such an effort constitutes a proper purpose, as does an inspection of the records to discover relevant evidence for a lawsuit against the directors and officers. Other legitimate purposes include a determination of the corporation's financial position or its ability to pay dividends and the investigation of possible mismanagement. This is not an all-inclusive listing of proper reasons for access to the books. A shareholder can inspect the books and records for any reason so long as a court is convinced that it is necessary to protect the interests of the corporation and the shareholder. It should go without saying that the shareholder must conduct the inspection in a reasonable manner and at a reasonable time.

What books and records are available for inspection? At common law, the answer is any and all the records relevant to the shareholder's inquiry. Some statutes specifically list the books and records available to the shareholder. The right to inspect records not named on that list is generally protected by common law right. Some statutes will require that the shareholder either have owned the stock of a specified period of time or own a certain minimum percentage of the outstanding stock before the examination of the books. The Illinois law, § 45, specifies either a six-month period of ownership or ownership of at least 5 percent of the stock.

A wrongful refusal to produce the records for inspection will subject the wrongdoer to liability for damages caused the shareholder. A computation of actual damages will usually be difficult, if not impossible. This shortcoming is provided for in some statutes by establishing arbitrary penalties. For instance, § 45 of the Illinois Act sets as a penalty 10 percent of the value of the shares owned by the shareholder in addition to any other damages.

For large corporations various federal and state statutes have reduced the significance of shareholder inspection rights by requiring the disclosure of certain types of information. The most comprehensive of these statutes is the Securities Exchange Act of 1934, which requires complete disclosure of financial and even general product information and other *material* information. State laws also require annual reports that are available to the public.

Federal and most state laws require that an annual report containing a balance sheet and an income statement be sent to shareholders.

The case below discusses what is a proper purpose for a shareholder demand for corporate books and information.

STATE EX REL. PILLSBURY v. HONEYWELL, INC.
191 N.W.2d 406 (S. Ct., Minn., 1971)

KELLY, Justice

Petitioner attended a meeting on July 3, 1969, of a group involved in what was known as the "Honeywell Project." Participants in the project believed that American involvement in Vietnam was wrong, that a substantial portion of Honeywell's production consisted of munitions used in that war, and that Honeywell should stop this production of munitions. Petitioner had long opposed the Vietnam war, but it was at the July 3rd meeting that he first learned of Honeywell's involvement. He was shocked at the knowledge that Honeywell had a large government contract to produce anti-personnel fragmentation bombs. Upset be-

cause of knowledge that such bombs were produced in his own community by a company which he had known and respected, petitioner determined to stop Honeywell's munitions production.

On July 14, 1969, petitioner ordered his fiscal agent to purchase 100 shares of Honeywell. He admits that the sole purpose of the purchase was to give himself a voice in Honeywell's affairs so he could persuade Honeywell to cease producing munitions. Apparently not aware of that purpose, petitioner's agent registered the stock in the name of a Pillsbury family nominee—Quad & Co. Upon discovering the nature of the registration, petitioner bought one share of Honeywell in his own name on August 11, 1969. . . .

Prior to the instigation of this suit, petitioner submitted two formal demands to Honeywell requesting that it produce its original shareholder ledger, current shareholder ledger, and all corporate records dealing with weapons and munitions manufacture. Honeywell refused.

On November 24, 1969, a petition was filed for writs of mandamus ordering Honeywell to produce the above mentioned records. In response, Honeywell answered the petition and served a notice of deposition on petitioner, who moved that the answer be stricken as procedurally premature and that an order be issued to limit the deposition. After a hearing, the trial court denied the motion, and the deposition was taken on December 15, 1969.

In the deposition petitioner outlined his beliefs concerning the Vietnam war and his purpose for his involvement with Honeywell. He expressed his desire to communicate with other shareholders in the hope of altering Honeywell's board of directors and thereby changing its policy. To this end, he testified, business records are necessary to insure accuracy.

A hearing was held on January 8, 1970, during which Honeywell . . . conceded all material facts stated therein, and argued that petitioner was not entitled to any relief as a matter of law. . . . On April 8, 1970, the trial court dismissed the petition, holding that the relief requested was for an improper and indefinite purpose. Petitioner contends in this appeal that the dismissal was in error.

Honeywell is a Delaware corporation doing business in Minnesota. Both petitioner and Honeywell spent considerable effort in arguing whether Delaware or Minnesota law applies. The trial court, applying Delaware law, determined that the outcome of the case rested upon whether or not petitioner has a proper purpose germane to his interest as a shareholder. . . .

Under the Delaware statute the shareholder must prove a proper purpose to inspect corporate records other than shareholder lists. . . .

. . .

The trial court ordered judgment for Honeywell, ruling that petitioner had not demonstrated a proper purpose germane to his interest as a stockholder. Petitioner contends that a stockholder who disagrees with management has an absolute right to inspect corporate records for purposes of soliciting proxies. He would have this court rule that such solicitation is per se a "proper purpose." Honeywell argues that a "proper purpose" contemplates concern with investment return. We agree with Honeywell.

This court has had several occasions to rule on the propriety of shareholders' demands for inspection of corporate books and records. . . . While inspection will not be permitted for purposes of curiosity, speculation, or vexation, adverseness to management and a desire to gain control of the corporation for economic benefit does not indicate an improper purpose.

Several courts agree with petitioner's contention that a mere desire to communicate with other shareholders is, per se, a proper purpose. Lake v. Buckeye Steel Castings Co., 2 Ohio St.2d 101, 206 N.E.2d 566 (1965). This would seem to confer an almost absolute right to inspection. We believe that a better rule would allow inspections only if the shareholder has a proper purpose for such communication. This rule was applied in McMahon v. Dispatch Printing Co., 101 N.J.L. 470, 129 A. 425 (1925), where inspection was denied because the shareholder's objective was to discredit politically the president of the company, who was also the New Jersey secretary of state.

. . .

The act of inspecting a corporation's shareholder ledger and business records must be viewed in its proper perspective. In terms of the corporate norm, inspection is merely the act of the concerned owner checking on what is in part his property. In the context of the large firm, inspection can be more akin to a weapon in corporate warfare.

. . .

That one must have proper standing to demand inspection has been recognized by statutes in several jurisdictions. Courts have also balked at compelling inspection by a shareholder holding an insignificant amount of stock in the corporation.

Petitioner's standing as a shareholder is quite tenuous. He only owns one share in his own name, bought for the purposes of this suit. He had previously ordered his agent to buy 100 shares, but there is no showing of investment intent.

. . .

Petitioner had utterly no interest in the affairs of Honeywell before he learned of Honeywell's production of fragmentation bombs. Immediately after obtaining this knowledge, he purchased stock in Honeywell for the sole purpose of asserting ownership privileges in an effort to force Honeywell to cease such production.

. . .

But for his opposition to Honeywell's policy, petitioner probably would not have bought Honeywell stock, would not be interested in Honeywell's profits and would not desire to communicate with Honeywell's shareholders. His avowed purpose in buying Honeywell stock was to place himself in a position to try to impress his opinions favoring a reordering of priorities upon Honeywell management and its other shareholders. Such a motivation can hardly be deemed a proper purpose germane to his economic interest as a shareholder.

. . .

We do not mean to imply that a shareholder with a bona fide investment interest could not bring this suit if motivated by concern with the long- or short-term economic effects on Honeywell resulting from the production of war munitions. Similarly, this suit might be appropriate when a shareholder has a bona fide concern about the adverse effects of abstention from profitable war contracts on his investment in Honeywell.

In the instant case, however, the trial court, in effect, has found from all the facts that petitioner was not interested in even the long-term well-being of Honeywell or the enhancement of the value of his shares. His sole purpose was to persuade the company to adopt his social and political concerns, irrespective of any economic benefit to himself or Honeywell. This purpose on the part of one buying into the corporation does not entitle the petitioner to inspect Honeywell's books and records.

The order of the trial court denying the writ of mandamus is affirmed.

Case Questions
1. Given the holding of this case, if a shareholder believes the corporation in which he or she owns shares is engaged in immoral conduct, what is the proper remedy? Is selling the shares the only remedy?
2. What could the petitioner have alleged to state a good case?

Shareholder Derivative Suits

What is a shareholder to do if a director or officer is violating his or her fiduciary duties thereby damaging the corporation, and the directors refuse to halt the activity and seek reimbursement? Institute a *shareholders' derivative suit* to call the corporate managers to account.

A shareholders' derivative or representative suit is brought by the plaintiff shareholder against the wrongdoing directors or officers and the corporation. Actually, the lawsuit is brought on behalf of the corporation. Despite its legal status as a defendant, the corporation is the real party at interest while the shareholder only serves as the nominal plaintiff. If the lawsuit is successful and results in a monetary award, those funds (minus the plaintiff's attorney's fees and costs) will go into the corporate treasury. A derivative action will be proper where (1) a valid claim exists on which the corporation could sue and (2) the corporation has refused to proceed after suitable demand, unless excused by extraordinary circumstances.

It is important to distinguish a derivative suit from both a direct private action and a class action. In a derivative suit, the shareholder derives the right to sue from the corporation itself and seeks to remedy a wrong done to the corporation. In a direct private action the shareholder is suing because of a personal wrong. In a class action the plaintiff is suing for all others similarly situated. For example, suppose a shareholder sues the directors and the corporation to recover funds embezzled by a director. Such a lawsuit is derivative in nature. The corporation will suffer, or has suffered, the wrongful act, and the shareholder is suing on behalf of the corporation. However, if the shareholder has instituted legal action against an officer and the corporation because the officer, while in the course of his employment, collided with the shareholder's automobile, that is a direct action. The shareholder is suing because of a personal wrong. If, however, the shareholder was accompanied by guests, who were also injured in the collision, and he now sues the corporation for damages done to all the car's occupants, it is a class action. The shareholder is suing for a personal injury to himself and for all others who themselves suffered injuries. Derivative suits and class actions can be easily confused since, in each, the plaintiff represents the legal interests of, and brings the suit on behalf of, many other persons.

Oftentimes management will regard derivative suits as a legalized form of extortion. Since defending against a derivative suit is both expensive and time consuming, an out-of-court settlement is not uncommon. Management sometimes feels that the shareholder's claim is frivolous and is brought only for its nuisance value. Nuisance value means that the corporation will find it cheaper to pay the shareholder a sum to settle the lawsuit than to conduct a full-blown successful defense. A derivative suit that lacks merit is frequently called a "strike suit." In an effort to eliminate strike suits some states have enacted security for costs statutes. Such legislation requires certain categories of shareholders to post security for costs as a condition to maintaining their derivative action. If the plaintiff shareholders are unsuccessful in their suit, the defendants may be able to gain reimbursement for expenses incurred in their defense.

The first and most famous of the security for costs (or expenses) statutes is § 627 of the New York Business Corporation Law. It provides that plaintiffs who hold less than 5 percent of the outstanding shares of any class of stock, unless the market value of their stock exceeds $50,000, must furnish security on request by the corporation. The request can be made at any time during the legal proceedings prior to final judgment. When computing the reasonable expenses for which security must be posted, attorneys' fees are included. California has taken a different approach in § 834 (b) of its corporation code. The defendant must move for the posting of security within 30 days after service of process. Then, if his motion is to prevail, he must show that there is no reasonable possibility that the derivative action will benefit the corporation and shareholders.

How do the shareholder plaintiffs finance their portion of the derivative suit? Generally the attorney will accept the suit based on the expectation of victory. If the attorney is victorious, the courts award his or her fees from the corporation. The courts are not tightfisted in awarding such fees. The judiciary recognizes worthwhile legal and social purposes in a suit that protects a corporation and its shareholders. The generous award of attorneys' fees in such cases guarantees that they will continue to be instituted whenever appropriate. If the derivative suit fails to benefit the corporation, the attorney will typically receive no fee. This serves as an economic incentive to accept only legitimate cases and reject cases of a strike suit nature.

Let us turn to an actual derivative action. The *Mayer* v. *Adams* case that follows deals with the issue of what constitutes extraordinary circumstances excusing a shareholder's demand that the board or shareholders authorize a suit against the corporation prior to instituting a derivative suit. We have already observed that a derivative suit can only be brought where: (1) the corporation has a valid legal claim and (2) the corporation declined to proceed after suitable demand, unless excused by the presence of exceptional conditions.

MAYER v. ADAMS
141 A. 2d 458, (S. Ct., Del. 1958)

SOUTHERLAND, Chief Justice
The case concerns Rule 23 (b) of the Rules of the Court of Chancery, Del. C. Ann. relating to stockholders' derivative suits. The second sentence of paragraph (b) provides:

> The complaint shall also set forth with particularity the efforts of the plaintiff to secure from the managing directors or trustees and, if necessary, from the shareholders such action as he desires, and the reasons for his failure to obtain such action or the reasons for not making such effort.

The question is:
Under what circumstances is a preliminary demand on shareholders necessary?
Plaintiff is a stockholder of the defendant

Phillips Petroleum Company. She brought an action to redress alleged frauds and wrongs committed by the defendant directors upon the corporation. They concern dealings between Phillips and defendant Ada Oil Company, in which one of the defendant directors is alleged to have a majority stock interest.

The amended complaint set forth reasons why demand on the directors for action would be futile and the sufficiency of these reasons was not challenged. It also set forth reasons seeking to excuse failure to demand stockholder action. The principal reasons were 1) that fraud was charged, which no majority of stockholders could ratify; and 2) that to require a minority stockholder to circularize more than 100,000 stockholders—in effect, to engage in a proxy fight with the management —would be an intolerably oppressive and unreasonable rule, and in any event would be a futile proceeding. . . .

In the view we take of the case, the issue between the litigants narrows itself to this:

If the ground of the derivative suit is fraud, is demand for stockholder action necessary under the rule?

When it is said that a demand on stockholders is necessary in a case involving fraud, the inquiry naturally arises: demand to do what?

Let us suppose that the objecting stockholder submits to a stockholders' meeting a proposal that a suit be brought to redress alleged wrongs. He may do so either by attending the meeting, or, if the regulations of the Securities and Exchange Commission are applicable, by requiring the management to mail copies of the proposal to the other stockholders. . . .

Let us suppose . . . that the proposal is disapproved by the majority stockholders—as common knowledge tells us it will ordinarily be. What of it? They cannot ratify the alleged fraud. . . .

If the foregoing is a correct analysis of the matter, it follows that the whole process of stockholder demand in a case of alleged fraud is futile and avails nothing. . . .

We hold that if a minority stockholders' complaint is based upon an alleged wrong committed by the directors against the corporation, of such a nature as to be beyond ratification by a majority of the stockholders, it is not necessary to allege or prove an effort to obtain action by the stockholders to redress the wrong.

The question may be asked: In what circumstances is such demand necessary? Obviously the rule contemplates that in some cases a demand is necessary; otherwise, it would have not been adopted.

We are not called upon in this case to attempt to enumerate the various circumstances in which demand on stockholders is excused; and likewise we do not undertake to enumerate all the cases in which demand is necessary. It seems clear that one instance of necessary demand is a case involving only an irregularity or lack of authority in directorate action. . . .

The cause is remanded to the Court of Chancery for New Castle County, with instructions to vacate the judgment of October 8, 1957, and to take such further proceedings as may not be inconsistent with this opinion.

---

1. Is the court here "interpreting" the law or is it "making" law?

2. Why didn't the court enumerate the various circumstances in which a demand on stockholders is necessary or is excused? If the court had done so, it would probably avoid the necessity of future litigation over such questions.

3. Is the demand-on-stockholders requirement superfluous?

Case Questions

Review Problems

*Watergate cases –
3M*

successful

*all proper
s/Her activities
Pres. has NP
discretion.*

*Yes, restrictions
part of articles!*

just interested in $

1. An officer of a corporation makes an illegal $100,000 contribution of corporate funds to a candidate for federal office. When this fact is discovered, the corporation hires legal counsel and expends $50,000 in an unsuccessful defense of the resulting criminal charge. The corporation is fined $5,000 for the violation. If the directors refuse to seek recovery of the funds from the officer, would a derivative suit be available? If so, should it seek to have the corporation reimbursed for the $100,000 plus interest from the date of contribution, the $50,000 in legal fees, and the $5,000 fine?

2. The bylaws of a corporation provide that it shall be the duty of the president to call a special meeting whenever requested in writing to do so by stockholders owning a majority of the stock. The holders of slightly more than 55 percent of the stock request such a meeting in writing. The president refuses to call the meeting and so the shareholders institute court proceedings to force him to make the call. The purpose of the meeting is to: (a) endorse the administration of the prior president, whom the board removed; (b) amend the articles and bylaws to permit the shareholders to fill board vacancies; (c) hear preferred charges against four directors, determine whether their conduct was inimical to the corporation, and, if so, vote on their removal and for the election of their successors. Will the court order the calling of a special meeting? [*Auer* v. *Dressel,* 118 N.E. 2d 590 (1954)]. *Yes*

3. A corporation issues two classes of stock. The articles provide that "none of the shares of Class B stock shall be entitled to dividends either on voluntary or involuntary dissolution or otherwise." The shares had voting rights, but the plaintiffs claim that the Class B shares do not in fact constitute stock because they are deprived of the economic incidents of stock, or of the proportionate interest in the corporate assets. The defense contends that ownership of stock may consist of one or more of the rights to participate in the control of the corporation, in its surplus or profits, or in the distribution of its assets. Do the Class B shares represent valid stock? [*Stroh* v. *Blackhawk Holding Corporation* 272 N.E. 2d 1 (1971)].

4. Why would an individual be willing to purchase nonvoting securities?

5. A corporation has a 13-member board split into two equal factions plus a neutral director. Subsequently four directors resign leaving one faction (the Vogel faction) with four directors and the other faction (the Tomlinson faction) with five directors. The Vogel faction is led by the president. Seven directors are needed for a quorum. The president then calls a special stockholders' meeting to (a) fill the director vacancies; (b) increase the board size to 19 and a quorum to 10

and elect these directors; (c) remove two of the directors of the Tomlinson faction and fill these vacancies. Naturally, the president proposes a slate of nominees for the vacancies. The bylaws provide that the president shall have power to call special meetings of the stockholders for any purpose or purposes.

The Tomlinson faction seeks to prohibit the meeting. They allege that the president lacks the power to call a special meeting for such a purpose and, alternatively, that the shareholders have no power to remove directors from office even for cause. If directors can be removed for cause, they argue that the directors must be afforded a reasonable opportunity to be heard by the stockholders on the charges made. They seek an injunction to prevent the Vogel faction from using corporate funds, employees, and facilities for the solicitation of proxies. They also seek to have it made clear in the solicitation process that the Vogel group, although representing current corporate policy and administration, is not representing a majority of the board. How should this legal can of worms be solved? [*Campbell* v. *Loew's Inc.*, 134 A. 2d 852 (1957)].

6. The United States Justice Department commenced a criminal action against Sky Manufacturing Corporation and its president, Masterson, for conspiring to fix prices on the sale of certain heavy industrial machinery. Both the corporation and Masterson denied the allegations. After a lengthy trial, the jury found that although a conspiracy did exist among certain manufacturers, neither Sky nor Masterson were parties to the illegal conspiracy. The cost to the corporation to defend the action against it was $500,000. Masterson's individual legal fees and expenses amounted to $250,000, of which Sky has paid $50,000 directly. Masterson seeks indemnification for the remaining $200,000.

Heinz, a dissenting shareholder of Sky, advised the board of directors that payment by the corporation of any of Masterson's expenses was improper. In the event no action is taken to recover the $50,000 already advanced, Heinz will commence a shareholder derivative action against Masterson. Furthermore, unless the board unequivocally promises not to indemnify Masterson for the unpaid balance of his legal expenses, Heinz will seek injunctive relief. What rights and limitations apply to Sky's payment of Masterson's legal fees and expenses?

(This is adapted from Exam Question #2c, taken from the May 1976 exam. © American Institute of Certified Public Accountants, Inc., 1976.)

7. Should the law require that a shareholder first get the approval of the outside directors before being allowed to file a shareholder derivative suit?

8. Steve gave his written proxy to his business agent. The agent was going to attend a stockholders' meeting where a matter of extreme importance to Steve is scheduled for discussion and a vote. Prior to the meeting, Steve learns that his agent has been stealing from him. Consequently, Steve fires the agent. Steve then attends the stockholders' meeting and discovers that his former agent is in attendance and claims the right to vote Steve's shares. Should the corporation allow Steve to vote the shares or honor Steve's earlier written proxy?

[handwritten: Yes revocable]

9. The founder of a company intends to leave the controlling interest in her company to a devoted friend and only a minority interest to her two children. The founder fears that on her death the children will begin legal action to challenge her will. The founder does not believe that the lawsuit will be successful, but is concerned as to the management and stability of her company during that legal action. The founder is considering placing her stock in a voting trust and naming the devoted friend as the trustee. Is a voting trust a possible solution to the founder's problem?

[handwritten: Yes, during will contesting; after end of voting trust (could be 10 yrs.)]

10. The majority shareholder in a closely held corporation convinces all of the minority shareholders to sign a shareholder agreement. The majority owner argues that the agreement will enable the corporation to be managed in a more cost-effective manner. One provision in the agreement provides that the stockholders waive their right to inspect the corporate books. One shareholder begins to suspect that the majority stockholder is cheating the corporation. When a request to inspect the books is made, the majority owner refuses and gives as an explanation the clause in the agreement. Should a court uphold such a provision in a shareholders' agreement of a close corporation?

[handwritten: No, based on fraud & the inducement; fundamental rite.]

Endnotes

1. These figures on stock ownership are taken from Blume, Crockett, and Friend, *Stock-ownership in the U.S.; Characteristics and Trends, Survey of Current Business,* Nov. 1974, Vol. 54, No. 11.

2. Williams, *Cumulative Voting for Directors*, pp. 40–46, (1951).

3. *Erie Technological Products Inc.* v. *Erie Technological Products,* 248 F. Supp. 380 (1965).

4. N. Lattin, *Lattin On Corporations* (2nd Ed. 1971) § 91 p. 374.

5. R. Nader, M. Green, and J. Seligman, *Taming the Giant Corporation,* 88 (1976).

6. *Ibid.,* p. 89.

7. *Wall Street Journal,* April 19, 1973, p. 1, col. 5.

8. *Thom* v. *Baltimore Trust Co.,* 148 A 234 (1930).

9. *Musson* v. *N.Y. & Queens Elect.,* 247 N.Y.S. 406 (1931).

10. *Dunlay* v. *Ave. M Garage & Repair,* 170 N.E. 917 (1930).

11. For a fuller discussion of the issues of control of close corporations, see A.B.A., *Selected Articles on Closely Held Enterprises,* 1971, especially pp. 443–515, "Problems of Control."

Managing the Corporation: The Role of the Directors and Officers

11

After our scrutiny of the shareholders' role in the corporate structure, we shift our focus to the directors and officers. It is not the shareholders who formulate corporate policy, nor do they execute this policy on a day-to-day basis. The directors fulfill the former function while the officers accomplish the latter task. In a close corporation, an individual may wear three hats, that of a shareholder, a director, and an officer. The law judges the authority and obligations of such an individual according to the specific capacity within which he or she is operating. Let us now examine, in turn, the role occupied by directors and officers.

Directors

Before discussing the directors' position within the corporate hierarchy we will first sketch the legal backdrop against which they operate. Carefully read the following statutory excerpts keeping in mind that the powers of a board of directors are determined by the relevant state's business corporation statute, the articles of incorporation, the bylaws, and any other formal grants of authority found, for example in shareholders' agreements or the minutes of the shareholders or board meetings.

MODEL BUSINESS CORPORATION ACT

§ 35. Board of Directors

All corporate powers shall be exercised by or under authority of, and the business and affairs of a corporation shall be managed under the direction of, a board of directors except as may be otherwise provided in this Act or the articles of incorporation. If any such provision is made in the articles of incorporation, the powers and duties conferred or imposed upon the board of directors by this Act shall be exercised or performed to such extent and by such person or persons as shall be provided in the articles of incorporation. Directors need not be residents of this State or shareholders of the corporation unless the articles of incorporation or by-laws so require. The articles of incorporation or by-laws may prescribe other qualifications for directors. The board of directors shall have authority to fix the compensation of directors unless otherwise provided in the articles.

§ 36. Number and Election of Directors

The board of directors of a corporation shall consist of one or more members. The number of directors shall be fixed by, or in the manner provided in, the articles of incorporation or the by-laws, except as to the number constituting the initial board of directors, which number shall be fixed by the articles of incorporation. . . .

§ 37. Classification of Directors

When the board of directors shall consist of nine or more members, in lieu of electing the whole number of directors annually, the articles of incorporation may provide that the directors be divided into either two or three classes, each class to be as nearly equal in number as possible, the term of office of directors of the first class to expire at the first annual meeting of shareholders after their election, that of the second class to expire at the second annual meeting after their election, and that of the third class, if any, to expire at the third annual meeting after their election. . . .

§ 38. Vacancies

Any vacancy occurring in the board of directors may be filled by the affirmative vote of a majority of the remaining directors though less than a quorum of the board of directors. A director elected to fill a vacancy shall be elected for the unexpired term of his predecessor in office. Any directorship to be filled by reason of an increase in the number of directors may be filled by the board of directors for a term of office continuing only until the next election of directors by the shareholders.

§ 39. Removal of Directors

At a meeting of shareholders called expressly for that purpose, directors may be removed in the manner provided in this section. Any director or the entire board of directors may be removed, with or without cause, by a vote of the holders of a majority of the shares then entitled to vote at an election of directors.

In the case of a corporation having cumulative voting, if less than the entire board is to be removed, no one of the directors may be removed if the votes cast against his removal would be sufficient to elect him if then cumulatively voted at an election of the entire board of directors, or, if there be classes of directors, at an election of the class of directors of which he is a part.

Whenever the holders of the shares of any class are entitled to elect one or more directors by the provisions of the articles of incorporation, the provisions of this section shall apply, in respect to the removal of a director or directors so elected, to the vote of the holders of the outstanding shares of that class and not to the vote of the outstanding shares as a whole.

§ 40. Quorum of Directors

A majority of the number of directors fixed by or in the manner provided in the by-laws or in the absence of a by-law fixing or providing for the number of directors, then of the number stated in the articles of incorporation, shall constitute a quorum for the transaction of business unless a greater number is required by the articles of incorporation or the by-laws. The act of the majority of the directors present at a meeting at which a quorum is present shall be the act of the board of directors, unless the act of a greater number is required by the articles of incorporation or the by-laws.

§ 42. Executive and Other Committees

If the articles of incorporation or the by-laws so provide, the board of directors, by resolution adopted by a majority of the full board of directors, may designate from among its members an executive committee and one or more other committees each of which, to the extent provided in such resolution or in the articles of incorporation or the by-laws of the corporation, shall have and may exercise all the authority of the board of directors, except that no such committee shall have authority to (i) declare dividends or distributions, (ii) approve or recommend to shareholders actions or proposals required by this Act to be approved by shareholders, (iii) designate candidates for the office of director, for purposes of proxy solicitation or otherwise, or fill vacancies on the board of directors or any committee thereof, (iv) amend the by-laws, (v) approve a plan of merger not requiring shareholder approval, (vi) reduce earned or capital surplus, (vii) authorize or approve the reacquisition of shares unless pursuant to a general formula or method specified by the board of directors, or (vii) authorize or approve the issuance or sale of, or any contract to issue or sell, shares. . . .

Neither the designation of any such committee, the delegation thereto of authority, nor action by such committee pursuant to such authority shall alone constitute compliance by any member of the board of directors, not a member of the committee in question, with his responsibility to act in good faith, in a manner he reasonably believes to be in the best interests of the corporation, and with such care as an ordinarily prudent person in a like position would use under similar circumstances.

§ 43. Place and Notice of Directors' Meetings

Meetings of the board of directors, regular or special, may be held either within or without this State. . . .

§ 44. Action by Directors Without a Meeting

Unless otherwise provided by the articles of incorporation or by-laws, any action required by this Act to be taken at a meeting of the directors of a corporation, or any action which may be taken at a meeting of the directors or of a committee, may be taken without a meeting if a consent in writing, setting forth the action so taken, shall be signed by all of the directors, or all of the members of the committee, as the case may be. Such consent shall have the same effect as a unanimous vote.

Board Authority and Meetings: Managing the Corporation

Each state repeats the very fundamental idea expressed in Section 35, above, that the "business and affairs of a corporation shall be managed under the direction of a board of directors. . . ." The theory is that the board of directors is to set the broad policy goals of the corporation and then "manage" it by hiring officers who may have the authority to hire other agents to carry out the policy of the board. In the absence of a provision in the articles or a shareholder agreement or qualification under a close corporation statute, the shareholders lack any right or authority to establish management policy by direct action. However, since the company does "belong" to the shareholders, there are some matters that must, by law, be submitted (for their approval) at a shareholders' meeting. These matters are those management-related transactions that would fundamentally alter what some scholars have called the "shareholder contract."

In smaller corporations especially, the shareholder invests money because of a belief in the success of the proposed or going enterprise. There is a judgment and expectation that the operation will do well and return to the shareholder some of the investment. So, the shareholder's expectation that the corporation stay in the same type of business is important.

In general terms, the full nature of the understanding between the shareholder and the corporation may be found in one of the following items listed in decreasing order of legal importance:

The "Shareholder Contract"
$\left\{ \begin{array}{l} \text{The State Corporation Law} \\ \text{The Articles of Incorporation} \\ \text{Bylaws} \\ \text{Formal, Written Shareholder Agreements} \\ \quad \text{including terms written on the individual} \\ \quad \text{shares} \\ \text{Minutes of Shareholder and Board Meetings} \end{array} \right.$

These items to the right, above, when read together, represent a statement of the fundamental purpose of the corporate enterprise and the basic understanding between the shareholder and the legal entity of the corporation. Any attempt by the board of directors to alter this understanding is *not* an item of ordinary management and must be submitted to the shareholders for a vote. Typically, these types of changes would include any attempts at a merger, a consolidation, or a change in the corporate charter; any alteration of stock rights or capital structure; or any sale or lease of substantially all of the corporate assets. These kinds of changes are labeled by some corporation law statutes as "special corporate transactions," and will be more fully treated in the final chapter on corporations. *Any matter that is not one of these fundamental types of changes may be an item of "management"* that the board may decide without consultation with the shareholders.

Most items of "management" of the corporate enterprise are established by business traditions, and practice and any substantial variation of that tradition and practice should be approved by the shareholders. For example, if a corporation owned five retail hardware stores and one was doing poorly because of its location, and the board wanted to sell it but continue the business, then shareholder approval would not be needed to close and sell the business. However, if the board wanted to sell the inventory of three of the five stores and invest in video-game outlets, then shareholders approval should be sought.

Implicit in the above statutory scheme is the idea that the directors exercise their authority only as a group. The board acts collectively; acting separately as individuals has no legal effect. This idea embodies the traditional wisdom that two heads are better than one. Ideally, the best decision will result from the give-and-take of a meeting where several individuals offer different perspectives. Consistent with this ideal is the general rule that a director cannot vote by proxy.

Shareholder Removal of Directors

Several other ideas embodied in the above statutory excerpts need emphasis. Directors may be removed *with* or *without* cause by an election of the shareholders. All corporations must have a shareholder meeting once per year, but are meetings more often possible? The answer is yes. Section 28 of the MBCA provides that:

> Special meetings of the shareholders may be called by the directors, the holders of not less than one-tenth of all the shares entitled to vote at the meeting, or such other persons as may be authorized in the articles of incorporation or the by-laws.

This section does give shareholders some power to "police" board action by calling a meeting on their own initiative. Note that the second paragraph of Section 39, above, protects the minority shareholders by providing, in essence, that a director cannot be removed (by a vote of the majority shares, one assumes) if the votes cast against the removal would be sufficient to elect the director at a meeting to elect the entire board using cumulative voting.

Special Committees of the Board

The Executive Committee.   Two more of the above MBCA provisions also demand special emphasis. An executive committee of the board may be elected and may have the same authority as the full board except that it cannot adopt a "special corporate transaction" as defined above or engage in special and fundamental changes even if the full board is so authorized. This section is one that recognizes that some board members are more interested in the corporation than others. Although the executive committee may have the authority of the full board in ordinary management matters, if the articles or bylaws so provide, the full board is not relieved of "responsibility imposed by law." Also, there are notice and quorum requirements for executive committee meetings.

Section 44, Action by Directors Without a Meeting, was intended for use in emergency situations and for matters not requiring deliberation of the full board. This section may be utilized when directors live in areas of the country far from the place of director meetings.

The Audit Committee.   A very recent phenomenon that is certain to become more important to students of corporation law is the creation of audit committees within the boards of directors of large corporations. In 1974, the SEC put great emphasis on the creation of these committees by requiring the disclosure in proxy statements of the existence of an audit committee and its composition. In 1977, the New York Stock Exchange adopted a listing requirement that each domestic company with listed common stock establish an audit committee composed solely of board members that were independent of management and free from any relationships that would interfere with the exercise of independent judgment. This was to be accomplished no later than June 30, 1978. It is expected by some observers that this requirement will become widespread and that a failure to establish an audit committee (for even medium-sized corporations) *may* become some evidence of negligence and may become a ground for assessing personal liability for board members.[1]

In 1978, the Special Committee on Audit Committees of the American Institute of Certified Public Accountants endorsed the creation of audit committees. This push for the creation of these committees comes from the perception that in many cases, the management of a large corporation controls selection to the board (because of its power over the proxy machinery, discussed later in this text) as well as the information that goes to the board. The crucial base for enlightened decisionmaking is accurate, unbiased information—financial information especially. To help insure this, audit committees were urged. Essentially, these committees are composed of members of the board of directors who are "outsiders." This means they are not officers or a part of management or related to such persons, and their general charge is to report to the board on financial matters of the corporation that are reported to them by independent auditors. More specifically, the audit committees are to perform the following acts:

1. Nominate or select the independent auditors.
2. Review the arrangements and scope of the independent auditors' examination.
3. Review the compensation of the independent auditors.
4. Consider the results of the independent auditors' review of internal accounting control and suggestions for improvements.
5. Discuss matters of concern to the independent auditors resulting from the audit.
6. Review internal accounting procedures with the company's financial and accounting staff.
7. Review the activities and recommendations of the company's internal auditors.[2]

In addition to these basic functions, the following have been added by one scholar:

1. Engage in the appropriate follow-up recommendations in the management letter. (This is the letter from the CPA firm to management offering suggestions on operations and information flow and how they can be made more efficient.)
2. Determine that appropriate action is taken with regard to all irregularities uncovered by the CPA's audit.
3. Report to the board of directors on the activities and findings of the committee and make recommendations to the board based on these findings.[3]

The push for the creation of audit committees of the board of directors for large corporations is just beginning. It is difficult to assess whether these committees are in fact insuring the accuracy of information and follow-up work or whether they are "paper" committees. In all probability, the function of these committees depends on the seriousness with which management views them.

In addition to executive and audit committees, corporations may form other committees. During 1975, Sears, Roebuck & Company had the following board committees: executive, finance, salary and supplemental compensation, audits, nominating and proxy, and public issues.

There is usually a minimum board size prescribed by statute, but, otherwise, it is a matter of discretion for the shareholders or the board. The board may be composed of inside directors (corporate employees, usually officers), outside directors (nonemployees), or both. During 1975 Pan Am had 18 directors of which 14 were outside directors, while Sears, Roebuck & Company had 23 directors only 10 of whom were outside directors (2 of which are former corporate officials). Directors are not entitled to compensation for their duties unless authorized by statute, articles, or bylaws. Common practice is to pay the outside board members a set fee for each meeting attended plus expenses or an annual fee. The 1975 outside director fees of Sears, Roebuck & Company consisted of an annual fee of $7500; $500 for each meeting attended; and $500 for each committee meeting attended ($200 on days when the board also met).

Director Dissent

If a director wishes to dissent from a vote taken at a meeting of the board, then positive action is required. The Illinois Business Corporation Act provides in Section 42.9:

> A director of a corporation who is present at a meeting of its board of directors at which action on any corporate matter is taken shall be conclusively presumed to have assented to the action taken unless his dissent shall be entered in the minutes of the meeting or unless he shall file his written dissent to such action with the person acting as the secretary of the meeting before the adjournment thereof or shall forward such dissent by registered mail to the secretary of the corporation immediately after the adjournment of the meeting. Such right to dissent shall not apply to a director who voted in favor of such action.

Director Qualification

A director need not be a shareholder or a resident of the state unless the statute, charter, or bylaws so require. A director must be of legal age and meet other qualifications established in the bylaws. The usual term of office is one year or until a successor takes office.

One of the most important functions of the board of directors is to determine and then declare and authorize payment of a dividend. A corporation pays dividends when it distributes its assets to the shareholders in respect to their stock holdings. Dividends can take the form of cash, property (including stock of another corporation), or the corporation's own shares. Typically, dividends are paid from the corporation's "profits" or "surplus." However, under some circumstances it is possible to pay a liquidating dividend thereby invading the corporation's "capital."

The three potentially conflicting interests of the shareholders, the corporation, and the creditors must be reconciled in matters of dividend distribution. The shareholders want income. In a close corporation dividends will frequently be a significant or even a primary source of income to the shareholders. The average shareholder in the publicly traded corporation also desires income. The investment is based on the expectation of income, not on any desire for corporate control. Of course the shareholders can disagree among themselves as to what form this income should assume. Depending on their tax bracket, etc. they may desire their income in the form of current dividends or prefer that it take the form of capital gains.

The directors have a different perspective. The law has given them the responsibility of managing the corporation. The best interests of the corporation can differ from the stockholder's desire for high dividends. The directors may wish to finance plant expansion from earnings rather than borrowing funds in the money markets. Or, there may be some other sound basis for retaining a large amount of the earnings.

The corporate creditors are governed by their own economic self-interest. They do not want to see the corporate assets depleted before they are paid. Since the shareholders have no personal liability for the debts of the corporation, the corporate assets are the creditors' only recourse if they are not paid.

Declaration of Dividends

Sources for Dividends

The dividends provisions of the various business corporation statutes are designed to protect the corporate creditors. These statutory provisions vary among jurisdictions but they all have the aim of preserving the corporation's capital for the benefit of creditors. In order to understand the proper declaration and payment of dividends, you should know the following definitions. These are from the MBCA § 2, Definitions.

> (i) "Net assets" means the amount by which the total assets of a corporation exceed the total debts of the corporation.
> (j) "Stated capital" means, at any particular time, the sum of (1) the par value of all shares of the corporation having a par value that have been issued, (2) the amount of the consideration received by the corporation for all

shares of the corporation without par value that have been issued, except such part of the consideration therefor as may have been allocated to capital surplus in a manner permitted by law, and (3) such amounts not included in clauses (1) and (2) of this paragraph as have been transferred to stated capital of the corporation, whether upon the issue of shares as a share dividend or otherwise, minus all reductions from such sum as have been effected in a manner permitted by law. Irrespective of the manner of designation thereof by the laws under which a foreign corporation is organized, the stated capital of a foreign corporation shall be determined on the same basis and in the same manner as the stated capital of a domestic corporation, for the purpose of computing fees, franchise taxes and other charges imposed by the Act.

(k) "Surplus" means the excess of the net assets of a corporation over its stated capital.

(l) "Earned surplus" means the portion of the surplus of a corporation equal to the balance of its net profits, income, gains and losses from the date of incorporation, or from the latest date when a deficit was eliminated by an application of its capital surplus or stated capital or otherwise, after deducting subsequent distributions to shareholders and transfer to stated capital and capital surplus to the extent such distributions and transfers are made out of earned surplus. Earned surplus shall include also any portion of surplus allocated to earned surplus in mergers, consolidations or acquisitions of all or substantially all of the outstanding shares or of the property and assets of another corporation, domestic or foreign.

(m) "Capital surplus" means the entire surplus of a corporation other than its earned surplus.

(n) "Insolvent" means inability of a corporation to pay its debts as they become due in the usual course of its business.

In addition, § 45 of the MBCA makes two important statements about dividends: (1) it is the board of directors that declares the dividends, and the declaration is proper except when the corporation would be rendered insolvent by the dividend payment or if it violates a provision of the Articles; and (2) the dividends should be paid in cash or property only out of the *unreserved* and *unrestricted earned surplus* of the corporation. There are a few exceptions to this, and they are discussed below.

The basic idea here is that the original capital contributed by the shareholders (stated capital) should remain at risk in the corporation for payment to creditors or others (employees) and that except for regulated transfers from capital surplus to earned surplus or regulated distributions from capital surplus, the shareholders are to be paid dividends only out of the surplus (earned surplus) that the corporation generates as it does business.

The complexity of questions involved in dividend distributions cannot be overstressed. As previously mentioned, the statutes vary among jurisdictions. Not only do the statutory provisions vary, but also the definition of basic terms. Indeed, accountants may use different definitions in their work. For example, accountants use the term "retained earnings" to refer to earned surplus. The form that the dividend distribution is to take can also vary widely. While most dividends are distributed as cash, other methods of payment are possible. The rights of the stockholders of different classes must be recognized. The accountants and the SEC must be satisfied that the nature and result of the distribution be accurately reported. The provisions of the internal revenue code must be met. The IRS will be concerned both that excessive earnings not be retained and that dividends (nondeductible by the corporation and taxable income to the shareholder) be properly reported as such. Sometimes the IRS will challenge the validity of interest payments or the amount of corporate salaries as being a mere disguise for a dividend distribution.

What Is Earned Surplus?   In addition to the determination of when a "surplus" is available to pay a dividend, questions can arise as to which items are properly taken into account in the computation of a surplus. Corporate goodwill is not normally included as an asset. Arriving at a reasonable valuation for goodwill is usually impossible, except where something like a trademark is purchased in an arms-length transaction.

What of appreciating and depreciating assets? These also present questions of valuation. How does one know that "true" amount of unrealized appreciation when that asset has not been sold or lacks an established market value? The availability of accepted depreciation methods and schedules for tax purposes can lessen, but not completely eliminate, the asset valuation questions involved in depreciation. It is not wise to generalize whether appreciation and depreciation of assets may or must be taken into account in surplus determination. The given state's statute or court opinions must be examined. Illinois, Section 41(c) provides that "no dividend except a dividend payable in its own shares, shall be declared or paid out of surplus arising from unrealized appreciation in value, or revaluation, of assets."

Then there is the "nimble dividend" situation. Suppose a corporation has suffered through several years of losses and now has a deficit of $100,000. The corporation then enjoys a return to prosperity and for the current year shows a profit of $20,000. A surplus remains absent, but is that $20,000 nonetheless available for dividends? The majority of states do not permit "nimble dividend" distributions. The concept is that only the corporation's net profits from its entire existence should be available for dividends. The MBCA and a handful of states permit nimble dividends. Section 45 of the MBCA provides:

> [Alternative] (a) Dividends may be declared and paid in cash or property only out of the unreserved and unrestricted earned surplus of the corporation, or out of the unreserved and unrestricted net earnings of the current fiscal year and the next preceding fiscal year taken as a single period, except as otherwise provided in this section.

Is "capital surplus" or "paid-in surplus" available as a dividend source? Earned surplus is the profit derived from the operation of the corporation. Capital surplus or paid-in surplus is derived from the sale of stock at a price in excess of its par or stated value, from a reduction in the par or stated value after issuance, or the profits received by the corporation from the purchase and sale of its own stock.

Most states place some form of restriction upon the use of capital surplus for dividend distributions. Frequently it can only be used to pay dividends on preferred stock, and then the stockholder must be told the source of dividends. This notice requirement should alert the shareholder that the corporation is not paying the dividends from ordinary corporate profits. For example, Section 46 of the MBCA provides:

> The board of directors of a corporation may also, from time to time, distribute to the holders of its outstanding shares having a cumulative preferential right to receive dividends, in discharge of their cumulative dividend rights, dividends payable in cash out of the capital surplus of the corporation, if at the time the corporation has no earned surplus and is not insolvent and would not thereby be rendered insolvent. Each such distribution when made, shall be identified as a payment of cumulative dividends out of capital surplus.

Finally, let us examine the matter of dividends in partial liquidation of the corporation. The declaration of a liquidating dividend is an extraordinary matter that usually requires specific stockholder approval by a two-thirds majority vote of the outstanding shares of each class. Illinois protects the corporate creditors by limiting liquidating dividends in Section 41(a)(d) as follows:

> No such distribution shall be made at a time when the corporation is insolvent or its net assets are less than its stated capital, or when such distribution would render the corporation insolvent or reduce its net assets below its stated capital.

Dividends are declared by a resolution of the board of directors. Shareholders cannot declare dividends, even by a unanimous vote. The board resolution will specify the amount of dividend per share declared to shareholders of record on a given future date. The dividends will then be payable on a specified date subsequent to the record date.

It is possible that a shareholder may sell his shares after the record date but prior to the date of payment. Is the buyer or seller entitled to the dividends? The seller. This problem is easily handled on the national securities exchanges. The shares are traded "ex dividend" or without the dividend. The price of ex dividend stock will be reduced to reflect the absence of the dividend.

Directors' Liability for Impermissible Dividends. Most statutes impose *civil liability* on directors who vote for or assent to the declaration and distribution of a dividend from an improper source. The directors will have joint and several liability and be entitled to contribution from the other assenting directors. Illinois' Section 42.8 imposes *criminal liability* on directors who vote for or assent to payment of an illegal dividend. Several other states also impose criminal sanctions in this situation.

Oftentimes a state will exempt from liability a director who acted in good faith in declaring the illegal dividend. Section 42.10 of the Illinois Business Corporation Act is typical:

> A director shall not be liable under . . . this section relating to the declaration of dividends and distribution of assets if he relied and acted in good faith upon a balance sheet and profit and loss statement of the corporation represented to him to be correct by the president or the officer of such corporation having charge of its books of account, or certified by an independent public or certified public accountant or firm of such accountants to fairly reflect the financial condition of such corporation, nor shall he be so liable if in good faith in determining the amount available for any such dividend or distribution he considered the assets to be of their book value.

What of the shareholders that receive the illegal dividends; are they permitted to retain them? Some statutes are silent on the matter. In such cases it would appear that if the shareholders innocently received the dividends, and if the corporation is solvent, the dividends may be retained. If the corporation was insolvent the dividends would constitute a fraudulent conveyance and could be recovered. Section 48(c) of the MBCA and Section 42.11 of the Illinois statute make the recipient shareholders liable through contribution to the liable directors if the shareholders knowingly accepted or received an illegal dividend.

Types of Dividends

The most common form for dividends is a cash distribution. Another popular type is a stock dividend, paying the shareholders a dividend with stock of the distributing corporation. In one sense, it is no dividend at all. Consider the following:

> Shareholder A owns ten shares of Corporation X's common stock. X has only 100 issued and outstanding shares. Thus A is a 10 percent shareholder and his shares represent one tenth of the value of the corporation. The directors then declare and pay a 20 percent stock dividend. A now owns 12 shares out of X's 120 shares. A now owns more shares but their value and percentage ownership remain static.

Despite these facts, stock dividends are of value to the shareholder. In a publicly traded corporation the per-share price frequently will not drop far enough to accurately reflect each share's reduced ownership ratio. If the corporation continues to be a financial success it will not take long for the per-share price to climb back up to or exceed the quoted predividend market price. The corporation need not part with any cash when it distributes a stock dividend. The corporation will be required to make a transfer from earned surplus to the capital account. What amount is to be transferred is open to some debate. Legally all that is required to be transferred is the par or stated value multiplied by the number of distributed shares. However, from an accounting standpoint, a good argument can be made that the transfer should reflect the fair market value of the distributed shares.

Do not confuse a stock dividend with a stock split; legally they are two entirely different actions. A stock split is designed to reduce the per share market price of a stock thereby both increasing demand and further broadening the number of shareholders. Suppose stock is selling at $400 per share. For most individuals that is a prohibitive price. If a four-for-one stock split occurs the price will drop to $100 per share and four shares of stock will be distributed for each one share of the previous stock. The articles will require amending, either by the board or the shareholders as the case may be, to approve a commensurate reduction in the par or stated value of each share. This is not necessary for a stock dividend. However, with both stock dividends and stock splits, it will be necessary to amend the articles if there are an insufficient number of authorized shares to effectuate the dividend or split.

It is possible to have a reverse stock split. Suppose the per-share price is only $2. Under the current margin requirements an investor cannot borrow funds to purchase stock priced below $5 per share. Thus, the $2 price can harm the attractiveness of the stock. So, the directors declare a one-for-four reverse stock split. For each four $2 shares they issue one $8 share (also multiplying the par or stated value by four).

Property dividends are a rarity, but they can fulfill a useful purpose. E.I. du Pont de Nemours & Company once held a 23 percent stock interest in General Motors. In 1957 the Supreme Court held this ownership constituted a violation of the antitrust laws. It was ordered to divest itself of the GM stock within 10 years. The stock had a $3.4 billion value and represented about 63 million shares of approximately 281 million GM shares then outstanding. Du Pont faced a myriad of problems. It couldn't just sell in one lump sum. Dumping six million shares annually for the next decade would severely depress the value of the stock. At that time the typical yearly GM trading volume did not approach six million shares. Du Pont solved its problem by distributing the GM shares as dividends to its own shareholders. Standard Oil of Indiana distributed its shares in Standard Oil of New Jersey in a similar antitrust divestiture.

Directors' Discretion in Dividend Matters

The directors decide whether a dividend is to be paid and, if so, in what amount and in what form. The courts will not interfere with the directors' discretion in these matters unless there is a showing of bad faith, abuse of discretion, unreasonableness, or willful neglect on the part of the directors. The declaration of dividends is a classic example of the application of the business judgment rule discussed in the next chapter.

Because of the deference afforded the directors' business judgment, successful shareholder suits to compel dividends are sparse. Following we review just a few of the successful cases. In *Patton v. Nicholas*, 302 S.W. 2d 441 (1957), a 61 percent stockholder maliciously suppressed the payment of any dividends for a 10-year period. The court ordered $112,000 in dividends to be paid. In *Channon v. Channon Co.*, 218 Ill. App. 397 (1920), an Illinois court held it to be an abuse of discretion where the dominant shareholder-director who was the father of the plaintiff, stated that no further dividends would be declared for as long as he lived. In *Von Au v. Magenheimer*, 89 N.E. 1114, dividends were ordered because they had been withheld in an effort to freeze out the minority shareholders. The directors, in an effort to depress the value of the stock and then buy it for less than its true value, declared low dividends, inflated salaries, and represented to the minority shareholders that the company had suffered financial reverses. Dividends have also been ordered where the directors, acting in collusion with a bankrupt shareholder, fraudulently withheld dividends to prevent the shareholder's creditors from obtaining them, *In re Brantman*, 244 F. 101 (1917). Added to this list must be the *Dodge v. Ford Motor Co.* case in chapter 9. In that case there was some evidence that Henry Ford desired to engage in his altruistic ventures just to oppose the Dodge brothers' interests.

Strange as it may seem, shareholders have complained to the courts of excessive dividends. The shareholder was unsuccessful in the following two instances. In *Sinclair Oil Co. v. Levien*, 280 A. 2d 717 (Del. S. Ct. 1971) the shareholder alleged that the subsidiary was paying out excessive dividends to the parent to finance the parent's expansion. In *ADT v. Grinnell*, 306 N.Y.S. 2d 209 (1969) a shareholder complained that a subsidiary was paying unreasonable and excessive dividends. It was argued that the parent, who owned 80 percent of the stock, was attempting to milk the corporation prior to being forced to divest the subsidiary for antitrust violations.

Lawsuits in equity to compel the declaration of dividends usually arise within the context of a close corporation. The case that follows illustrates the extreme reluctance of courts to interfere in the business judgment of the board in the declaration of dividends, as well as giving insight into the operation of a close corporation. Some states such as California have special statutes regulating dividend declaration in close corporations. A section of the California code requires directors to justify their refusal to pay less than one third of the annual net profits in dividends when holders of 20 percent or more of the shares complain. Such a statute would have resolved the problem in the next case.

GOTTFRIED v. GOTTFRIED
73 N.Y.S.2d 692 (1947)

CORCORAN, Justice

This action was brought in the early part of 1945 by minority stockholders of Gottfried Baking Corporation (hereinafter called "Gottfried"), to compel the Board of Directors of that corporation to declare dividends on its common stock. The defendants are Gottfried itself, its directors, and Hanscom Baking Corporation (hereinafter called "Hanscom"), a wholly owned subsidiary of Gottfried. Gottfried is a closely held family corporation. All of its stockholders, with minor exceptions, are children of the founder of the business, Elias Gottfried, and their respective spouses. . . .

The action is predicated upon the claim that the policy of the Board of Directors with respect to the declaration of dividends is animated by considerations other than the best welfare of the corporations or their stockholders. The plaintiffs claim that bitter animosity on the part of the directors, who own the controlling stock, against the plaintiff minority stockholders, as well as a desire to coerce the latter into selling their stock to the majority interests at a grossly inadequate price, and the avoidance of heavy personal income taxes upon any dividends that might be declared, have been the motivating factors that have dominated the defendants. Plaintiffs contend, moreover, that the defendants by excessive salaries, bonuses and corporate loans to themselves or some of them, have eliminated the immediate need of dividends insofar as they were concerned, while at the same time a starvation dividend policy with respect to the minority stockholders—not on the payroll—operates designedly to compel the plaintiffs to sacrifice their stock by sale to the defendants.

There is no essential dispute as to the principles of law involved. If an adequate corporate surplus is available for the purpose, directors may not withhold the declaration of dividends in bad faith. But the mere existence of an adequate corporate surplus is not sufficient to invoke court action to compel such a dividend. There must also be bad faith on the part of the directors. . . .

There are no infallible distinguishing earmarks of bad faith. The following facts are relevant to the issue of bad faith and are admissible in evidence: Intense hostility of the controlling faction against the minority; exclusion of the minority from employment by the corporation; high salaries, or bonuses or corporate loans made to the officers in control; the fact that the majority group may be subject to high personal income taxes if substantial dividends are paid; the existence of a desire by the controlling directors to acquire the minority stock interests as cheaply as possible. But if they are not motivating causes they do not constitute "bad faith" as a matter of law.

The essential test of bad faith is to determine whether the policy of the directors is dictated by their personal interests rather than the corporate welfare. Directors are fiduciaries. . . . Circumstances such as those above mentioned and any other significant factors, appraised in the light of the financial condition and requirements of the corporation, will determine the conclusion as to whether the directors have or have not been animated by personal, as distinct from corporate, considerations.

The court is not concerned with the direction which the exercise of the judgment of the Board of Directors may take, provided only that such exercise of judgment be made in good faith. It is axiomatic that the court will not substitute its judgment for that of the Board of Directors.

It must be conceded that closely held corporations are easily subject to abuse on the part of dominant stockholders, particularly in the direction of action designed to compel minority stockholders to sell their stock at a sacrifice. But close corporation or not, the court will not tolerate directorate action designed to achieve that or any other wrongful purpose. Even in the absence of bad faith, however, the impact of dissension and hostility among stockholders falls usually with heavier force in a closely held corporation. In many such cases, a large part of a stockholder's assets may be tied up in the corporation. It is frequently contemplated by the parties, moreover, that the respective stockholders receive their major livelihood in the form of salaries resulting from employment by the corporation. If such employment be terminated, the hardship suffered by the minority stockholder or stockholders may be very heavy. Nevertheless, such situations do not in themselves form a ground for the interposition of a court of equity.

There is no doubt that in the present case bitter dissension and personal hostility have existed for a long time between the individual plaintiffs and defendants. The plaintiffs Charles Gottfried and Harold Gottfried have both been discontinued from the corporate payrolls.

It is true too that several of the defendants have in recent years received as compensation substantial sums. In the case of Maurice K. Gottfried this has taken the form of ten percent of the gross annual profits of Hanscom before corporate income taxes. During the period from January 1, 1943 to December 21, 1946, he received, in addition to a fixed salary of $15,600, an aggregate sum of $220,528.91, or an average of $45,105.78 per annum. The evidence in this connection discloses, however, that he has been the chief executive officer of Hanscom since its acquisition by Gottfried in 1933. The stock of Hanscom had been purchased in 1933 at a cost of $10,000 plus the assumption of liabilities amounting to $18,000. At that time Hanscom had 12 retail stores, a basement bakery, and volume of sales around $300,000. By way of contrast, for the year 1945

its net sales aggregated $4,614,000. For the year 1946, they had increased to $5,907,500. The number of stores had grown to 63, and operations had been expanded from the Washington Heights district of Manhattan to all the boroughs of the City of New York except Richmond. The profits before taxes and participation by Maurice Gottfried therein had increased to the large sum of $932,168.

. . .

The evidence also discloses that substantial advances or loans have been made from time to time to several of the defendants, part of which still remain outstanding. Advances and loans of this character in varying amounts likewise had been made for many years to stockholders and directors. Without passing upon the propriety or legality of these transactions, the evidence does not sustain an inference that they were made with a view to the dividend policy of the corporation. They were incurred, in large part, long before any controversy arose with respect to dividends, nor is the aggregate amount thereof of sufficient magnitude to affect in a material way the capacity of Gottfried to pay dividends.

Plaintiff Charles Gottfried testified that Benjamin Gottfried, one of the defendants, told him that he and the other minority stockholders would never get any dividends because the majority could freeze them out and that the majority had other ways than declaring dividends of getting money out of the companies. Benjamin Gottfried denied that he had ever made such statements. There is no evidence, moreover, that such statements were made by any of the other defendants. The court does not believe that this disputed testimony carries much weight upon the question of a concerted policy on the part of the directors to refrain from declaring dividends for the purpose of "freezing out" the plaintiffs.

Nor does the evidence with respect to the financial condition of the corporation and its business requirements sustain the plaintiffs' claims. The action was started in the early part of 1945. The financial condition of Gottfried at the end of the immediately preceding year is of fundamental importance in determining the validity of plaintiffs' claim at the time that suit was brought. The consolidated balance sheet for the year ended December 30, 1944 discloses current assets of $1,055,844 against current liabilities of $468,438, or a working capital of $587,407. Of the current assets, cash represented $523,691 and inventory $357,347. The ratio of current assets to current liabilities at that time was, therefore, slightly above 2 to 1. The gross volume of business done in 1944 was $8,737,475. The net working capital, therefore, was less than 7 percent of the volume of business transacted. The net earnings for this year were $174,415.28, somewhat less than those for the two preceding war years. The earned surplus was $867,141.

. . .

Under these circumstances, it may not be said that the directorate policy regarding common stock dividends at the time the suit was brought was unduly conservative. It certainly does not appear to have been inspired by bad faith.

Although the right (but not the measure) of recovery, even in equity, is usually determined as of the date that suit is brought . . . we shall consider the situation as of the date of the trial.

In 1945 the net earnings were $318,-222.72. The current assets amounted to $1,441,-408, and the current liabilities to $1,042,967, leaving a working capital of $398,441. This is less than the working capital at the end of 1944 by approximately $188,966, despite the fact that the volume of business for 1945 had increased to $9,405,726. The ratio of working capital to volume of business done was, therefore, approximately 4½ percent. This decrease in working capital at the end of 1945, as compared with the end of 1944, demonstrates fairly conclusively that maximum dividends were paid during 1945. At the end of 1945 the ratio of current assets to current liabilities was 1.38.

. . .

The testimony discloses that many general considerations affected the policy of the Board of Directors in connection with dividend payments. Some of the major factors were as follows: The recognition that earnings during the war years might be abnormal and not representative of normal earning capacity; the pressing need for heavy expenditures for new equipment and machinery, replacement of which had been impossible during the war years; heavy expenditures required to finance the acquisition and equipment of new Hanscom stores in harmony with the steady growth of the business; the increased initial cost of opening new stores because, under present conditions, it has been difficult to lease appropriate sites necessitating actual acquisition by ownership of locations; the erection of a new bakery for Hanscom at a cost of approximately $1,000,000 inasmuch as the existing plant is incapable of producing the requirements of Hanscom sales which are running at the rate of approximately $6,000,000 per annum; unstable labor conditions with actual and threatened strikes; several pending actions involving large sums of money under the Federal Fair Labor Standards Act; a general policy of financing expansion through earnings requiring long-term debt.

The plaintiffs oppose many of these policies of expansion. There is no evidence of any weight to the effect that these policies of the Board of Directors are actuated by any motives other than their best business judgment. If they are mistaken, their own stockholdings will suffer proportionately to those of the plaintiffs. With the wisdom of that policy the court has no concern. It is this court's conclusion that these policies and the expenditures which they entail are undertaken in good faith and without relation to any conspiracy, scheme or plan to withhold dividends for the purpose of compelling the plaintiffs to sell their stock or pursuant to any other sinister design.

The plaintiffs have failed to prove that the surplus is unnecessarily large. They have also failed to prove that the defendants recognized the propriety of paying dividends but refused to do so for personal reasons.

The complaint is dismissed and judgment directed for the defendants.

Case Questions

1. What courses of action are available to a minority shareholder in a close corporation who disagrees with the dividend policy of the controlling faction? Litigation is expensive. Not only did the dissidents in the instant case bear their own legal expenses but, as 38 percent shareholders, they also indirectly bore 38 percent of the cost of defending the board against their suit.

2. How does one distinguish between the directors' personal interests and the corporate welfare when the directors hold such a dominant ownership position?

3. On reading the court's opinion in this case it seems clear that the board had legitimate reasons to support its dividend policy. If the facts were so clear, why did the minority shareholders fail to recognize them and instead institute an unsuccessful lawsuit? Did their personal feelings obscure the facts? Was their lawyer stupid? Was the action motivated by vindictiveness and merely designed to harass the controlling majority? Was it a gamble, or may the facts appear clear only in retrospect?

Case Note.   In some circumstances if a court believes that an excessive amount of compensation in the form of a bonus or salary has been paid to one stockholder, it may be deemed a dividend and other shareholders may be entitled to a similar amount. See *Kohn* v. *Kohn,* 95 Cal. App. 2d 708 (1950).]

Officers

Corporate officers frequently draw handsome salaries and enjoy plush surroundings. Since the directors have the exclusive legal authority to manage the corporation, what is it that officers do to justify such a privileged existence? A great deal. The board establishes the direction in which the corporation is to go by setting overall basic policy. The officers carry on the day-to-day operations of the enterprise within that framework. There is one school of thought that views the officers as actually running the corporation while the directors merely serve as their rubber stamps. The MBCA provides:

§ 50. Officers

The officers of a corporation shall consist of a president, one or more vice presidents as may be prescribed by the by-laws, a secretary, and a treasurer, each of whom shall be elected by the board of directors at such time and in such manner as may be prescribed by the by-laws. Such other officers and assistant officers and agents as may be deemed necessary may be elected or appointed by the board of directors or chosen in such other manner as may be prescribed by the by-laws. Any two or more offices may be held by the same person, except the offices of president and secretary.

All officers and agents of the corporation, as between themselves and the corporation, shall have such authority and perform such duties in the management of the corporation as may be provided in the by-laws, or as may be determined by resolution of the board of directors not inconsistent with the by-laws.

§ 51. Removal of Officers

Any officer or agent may be removed by the board of directors whenever in its judgment the best interests of the corporation will be served thereby, but such removal shall be without prejudice to the contract rights, if any, of the person so removed. Election or appointment of an officer or agent shall not of itself create contract rights.

Section 51, above, states the common view that an officer or agent's authority to manage or act for the corporation may be removed by the board at any time. However, this may result in the corporation's being liable for breach of contract, if the contract is properly authorized. For example, if X Corporation contracts with V.P. to be its vice president of personnel for a period of three years at $40,000 per year, the authority of V.P. to act for X may be revoked at any time, but X may be liable to continue paying V.P. even though V.P. does not work for X anymore. This duty to continue paying is subject to V.P.'s duty to use good-faith efforts to look for an equivalent job. Most management positions are not subject to contractual understandings, so officers and agents can be fired or have their authority revoked or changed at any time. The trust and confidence that an enterprise needs from its officers and agents, though, is a strong, inhibiting factor in the use of the power to remove an agent's authority.

Officers' and Agents' Authority

The officers can have actual (either express or implied) authority to manage. This authority will be found in the charter, bylaws, or board resolutions. Like any agent an officer may also have apparent authority. Or, authority for an action may be absent but the directors may ratify the officer's actions. On the other hand, the board may be displeased yet coerced into ratification by the public relations or other costs inherent in rejection. A good deal of litigation exists over the degree of authority possessed by an officer by virtue of the office. At one end of the legal spectrum is the view that the office bestows no authority on an officer. The more realistic and developing position is that the president has the residual authority to enter contracts binding on the corporation that are within the ordinary course of its business. Determining what constitutes "ordinary" must be done on a case-by-case basis. It will depend on, among other factors: the industry concerned, the custom and practice within the trade, past practice, the dollar amount of the transaction relative to the corporation's financial status, the presence or absence of an emergency, etc. An officer lacks the inherent power to execute a contract of an unusual or extraordinary nature. The fact that an officer is also a director adds nothing to the officer's authority.

A third party enters contractual transactions with a corporate officer at his or her peril. It is the third party's obligation to inquire as to the officer's authority. If the bylaws do not grant the authority, the third party should request a copy of the pertinent board resolution that has been attested to by the secretary of the corporation.

The use of inherent authority allows courts to recognize the grant of a certain degree of authority to the president, by virtue of the office, acting within the scope of ordinary matters. This unwritten authority is confined to the president; it does not extend to other corporate officers. A certain amount of confusion is engendered by different companies utilizing different labels for equivalent positions. The term "president," as used here, indicates the officer of highest authority within the respective organization. Some companies will call that individual the chief executive officer, chairman of the board, chief operating officer, or general manager. The title is irrelevant. It is the individual's duties and function within the organization that determine his or her authority.

The authority of corporate officers is established by agency law, bylaws, or a specific delegation by board resolution. The vice president's duties extend to presiding in the place of the president, in the absence of this person. The secretary keeps the corporate books and records and the minutes of shareholder and directors meetings. The treasurer has the power to accept funds and give receipts on behalf of the corporation. The business corporation statutes typically provide that an individual may hold more than one office if the bylaws so provide. However, they do prohibit one from occupying both the post of the president and secretary. Sometimes corporate documents will require the signature of the president and secretary or the president's signature accompanied by the corporate seal (kept by the secretary). If two individuals occupy these offices the chances of error or fraud are minimized.

The next two cases examine an officer's authority to enter contracts binding on the corporation in the absence of express authority. The first one is a straightforward example of an officer consummating an ordinary commercial transaction with a third party. The lesson of these cases is simple. All of the principles that you learned in the material on agency laws apply to corporate officers and agents when they conduct corporate business. The idea of inherent agency power is particularly applicable to corporations because it recognizes a power to bind corporations by virtue of one's position in the corporation. The *Goldenberg* v. *Bartell Broadcasting* case illustrates a contract that contains such extraordinary terms that the officer is rendered powerless to execute it.

COTE BROTHERS, INC. v. GRANITE LAKE REALTY CORP.

105 N.H. 111, 193 A.2d 884 (S. Ct., N.H., 1963)
(The trial court entered judgment for the plaintiff)

KENISON, Chief Justice

The defendant corporation and its allied corporation, Granite Lake Camp Associates, Inc. were both small close corporations which were organized, operated and managed by the same three individuals as stockholders, officers and directors. The issue in this case is whether the defendant is liable on a mercantile claim for merchandise delivered which, it is argued, no officer of the corporation was authorized to purchase. The guide lines for deciding this issue were set forth in *Holman-Baker Company* v. *Pre-Design Company*, 104 N.H. 116, 117–118, 179 A2d 454, 455 as follows: "In the world of credit there is emerging a rule, consistent with modern business practices, under which a principal is bound by the promise to his general agent, whether or not authorized, when such promise is made within the scope of the agent's power." . . . The rule has been developed and nurtured over some period of time by an eminent authority. Seavey, "The Rationale of Agency," 29 *Yale L.J.* 859 (1920). . . . The rationale of the rule is not based on express authority, implied authority, apparent authority or estoppel 'but (is derived) solely from the agency relation and exists for the

protection of persons harmed or dealing with a servant or other agent' and is described as 'inherent agency power.' *Restatement, Second, Agency*, § 8A."

The defendant owned the premises known as Granite Lake Camp which was leased to and operated by another corporation, Granite Lake Camp Associates, Inc. The corporations were organized by three individuals for the purpose of acquiring and operating Granite Lake Camp as "a summer camp." The same three individuals (Chester Gusick, Charles Gusick and Milton Lubow) were the sole stockholders, officers and directors of both corporations. One of the three stockholders, directors, and officers, "Milton Lubow, was the man who handled the finances." At the beginning of their operation a letter was circularized to prospective merchants and suppliers signed by Milton Lubow as secretary-treasurer of Granite Lake Camp Associates, Inc. The letter, which was admitted as an exhibit over the defendants' objection, stated that the three individuals named above were the only persons authorized to order merchandise for Granite Lake Camp and that "we operate our business through Granite Lake Camp Associates, Inc., and Granite Lake Realty Corporation." During the period of time when the plaintiff's bill was due and owing rental payments were made by Granite Lake Camp Associates, Inc. to the defendant. From 1959 to 1962 the mortgage on the real estate in the original amount of $127,500 was reduced to "approximately seventy thousand dollars."

While both Chester Gusick and Charles Gusick testified that they had no knowledge of the letter sent to prospective merchants and that it was not authorized by them, it is evident that the letter was written in furtherance of the everyday business of the corporations and that it was done by Milton Lubow who was selected by the Gusick brothers as "the man who handled the finances." . . . *The Restatement (Second), Agency,* § 161 comment (a) states in part: "Commercial convenience requires that the principal should not escape liability where there have been deviations from the usually granted authority by persons who are such essential parts of his business enterprise. In the

long run it is of advantage to business, and hence to employers as a class, that third persons should not be required to scrutinize too carefully the mandates of permanent or semi-permanent agents who do no more than what is usually done by agents in similar positions." It is reasonably clear that Lubow as a stockholder, officer and financial manager of two allied close corporations had inherent agency power to purchase ordinary supplies for the business conducted through the two corporations. . . .

The Trial Court's rulings, procedural and substantive, were correct.

Judgment on the verdict.

All concurred.

Case Question

1. Did the court hold Granite liable for the debt because Lubow was one of three stockholders, directors, and officers, or because Lubow was the man who handled the finances and the purchased supplies were of an ordinary nature?

GOLDENBERG v. BARTELL BROADCASTING CORPORATION
262 N.Y.S. 2d 274 (1965)

WILFRED A. WALTEMADE, Justice

In the case on trial, the plaintiff sets forth two causes of action, both of which seek recovery of damages for an alleged breach of a written contract of employment. The first cause of action is against the defendant Bartell Broadcasting Corporation, an entity incorporated under the laws of the State of Delaware. It is alleged in substance that on or about March 16, 1961, the plaintiff and the defendant Bartell Broadcasting Corporation entered into a written contract wherein the plaintiff was engaged as an Assistant to Gerald A. Bartell, the president of the defendant Bartell Broadcasting Corporation. The plaintiff's primary duties were to en-

gage in corporate development in the field of pay television. The contract, which was for a period of three years, provided for (1) the payment to the plaintiff of $1,933.00 per month; and (2) for the delivery to plaintiff of 12,000 shares of "Free Registered" stock of defendant Bartell Broadcasting Corporation, which stock was payable in three installments of 4,000 shares each in the months of January 1962, 1963 and 1964; and (3) the payment of plaintiff's traveling and living expenses in connection with his services to the employer; and (4) that defendant Bartell Broadcasting Corporation would provide the plaintiff with a private office and proper office facilities; and (5) that the agreement would be binding on any successor corporation or any corporation with which defendant Bartell Broadcasting Corporation would merge.

This written contract was signed by the plaintiff and by Gerald A. Bartell, in his capacity as the president of Bartell Broadcasting Corporation. It is further claimed that on or about May 1961, this contract was amended to increase plaintiff's monthly compensation from $1,933.00 to $2,400.00. It is further contended that the plaintiff was not paid his monthly compensation commencing with the month of November 1961; that the defendant Bartell Broadcasting Corporation failed to deliver the 4,000 shares of stock allegedly due in January 1962; and that in July 1962, the defendant Bartell Broadcasting Corporation denied the validity of plaintiff's employment contract. . . .

The court will now turn its consideration to the first cause of action set forth in the complaint.

A corporation can only act through its directors, officers and employees. They are the conduit by and through which the corporation is given being and from which its power to act and reason springs. Therefore in every action in which a person sues a corporation on a contract executed on behalf of the corporation by one of its officers, one of the issues to be determined is whether the officer had the express, implied or apparent authority to execute the contract in question. . . .

The authority of an officer to act on behalf of a corporation may be express, implied or apparent. There has been no proof offered in this case indicating that Gerald A. Bartell, as president of the defendant Bartell Broadcasting Corporation, had express authority to enter into the agreement, dated March 16, 1961, which is the subject of the first cause of action.

Did General A. Bartell then have either *implied* or *apparent authority* to execute the contract?

Implied authority is a species of actual authority, which gives an officer the power to do the necessary acts within the scope of his usual duties. Generally, the president of a corpora-

tion has the implied authority to hire and fire corporate employees and to fix their compensation. However the president of a corporation does *not* have the implied power to execute "unusual or extraordinary" contracts of employment. . . .

The agreement of March 16, 1961 not only provides for the payment of a substantial monthly compensation, but also requires the delivery of 12,000 shares of free registered" stock of the defendant Bartell Broadcasting Corporation. While the payment of the monthly compensation would not make the contract of March 16, 1961, *"unusual or extraordinary,"* the Court is of the opinion that the inclusion in the contract of the provision requiring the delivery to plaintiff of 12,000 shares of "free registered stock," does bring the agreement within the category of being an *"unusual and extraordinary"* contract.

A consideration of the cases . . . convinces this court to conclude that the contract of March 16, 1961 was *unusual and extraordinary* and therefore beyond the scope of the implied authority of the president of the defendant Bartell Broadcasting Corporation.

In the *Gumpert* v. *Bon Ami Company* case, the plaintiff there sued on a one year employment contract under which he was to be paid $25,000 in cash and $25,000 in defendant's corporate stock. The contract was signed on behalf of the corporation's executive committee. At page 739, of 251 F.2d, the Federal court there wrote:

> *Even if Rosenberg was chief executive officer * * * it is doubtful that he would possess power to make such an arrangement as a normal incident of his position.* . . . (Emphasis supplied)

In the case of *Noyes* v. *Irving Trust Company*, the plaintiff there sued on an employment contract under which he was to be paid $400 per month together with a bonus based upon the net profits. The contract was signed on behalf of the defendant corporation by its sales manager. At pages 276, and 277 of 250 App. Div., 294 N.Y.S. page 5, the court there wrote:

> It is well settled that a contract of this character is not the usual and ordinary contract which one authorized to employ agents and servants may make. *It would require express authority. . . .*

The reason for the rule enunciated in the cases just cited, is easily discernible. Corporate stock is the sinew, muscle and bone upon which the financial structure of a corporation is constructed. Corporate stock is sold, traded or disposed of in exchange for money, labor, services or other property. Thus in this manner a corporation acquires the necessary assets needed for the fulfillment of the corporate purposes. . . .

To permit the president of a corporation, without the express authority and approval of the corporation's Board of Directors, to barter or contract away the corporation's unissued (free) stock, would not only be an express violation of the statutes, but would also make possible the denudation of a corporation's assets, and the dilution of the value of the stock already issued to the detriment and disadvantage of the corporate stockholders. It should be noted here that in the case at bar, the stock of both defendant corporations is publicly owned and traded.

Apparent authority is the authority which the principal permits the agent to represent that he possesses. Generally, persons dealing with officers of a corporation are bound to take notice that the powers of an officer are derived from statutes, by-laws and usages which more or less define the extent of the officer's authority. In a doubtful case one must at his peril acquaint himself with the exact extent of the officer's authority. . . . The right of a third party to rely on the apparent authority of a corporate officer is subject to the condition that such third person has no notice or knowledge of a limitation in such authority. . . . Al-though it is true that secret instructions or limitations upon the apparent general authority of an officer of a corporation will not affect one who deals with the officer in the general line of his authority, and knows nothing of such limitations; however, this rule is not applicable to any limitations which are provided for in statutes. Those who contract with a corporation do so with knowledge of the statutory conditions pertaining to a corporation. . . .

The plaintiff is not a naive person, uninitiated in the business world, nor is he without knowledge of corporate financing or business practices. By his own testimony he is and was a stockholder, officer and director of several corporations. There is testimony that the plaintiff has engaged in the sale of securities to the general public. . . .

With the varied and broad business experience acquired by the plaintiff in his wide business associations as evidenced by his career resume furnished to the defendants . . . and by plaintiff's own testimony, it can be truly said that he not only was presumed to have knowledge of the statutory provisions of the law pertaining to corporations, but that he apparently also had actual knowledge of such laws. It is reasonable to infer that the plaintiff was aware, or at the least, had reason to be aware, that the authority for the issuance of corporate stock rests solely within the powers of the Board of Directors of the corporation, and that in the absence of express authority, the president of a corporation does not have the implied or apparent authority to enter into an employment contract which provides for the issuance of corporate stock as compensation. . . .

Some comment is necessary relative to the legal effect of the affixing of the seal of the defendant Bartell Broadcasting Corporation to the contract of March 16, 1961.

The plaintiff's testimony establishes that the seal was not affixed on the date of the execution of the contract, but on some date thereafter. The plaintiff testified that some time after the execution of the contract, he had a conversation with Gerald A. Bartell in which he, the plaintiff, suggested that the corporate seal should be affixed to the contract; that Mr. Bartell agreed with the plaintiff's suggestion, whereupon the plaintiff procured the seal from one of the file cabinets in the corporation's offices, and he then affixed the seal. The plaintiff contends that the placement of the seal on the contract creates the rebuttable presumption that the defendant Bartell Broadcasting Corporation authorized its president to execute the contract dated March 16, 1961. There is no merit to plaintiff's contention in law or fact.

The question of the legal effect of a corporate seal upon a contract is discussed in Hornstein, *Corporate Law and Practice,* Vol. 1, section 264, where he said:

> To-day, the one significant consequence of a seal—if coupled with an acknowledgement by an officer that it was attached by proper au-

thority—is that it gives rise to a presumption (not conclusive) that the instrument to which it is attached was duly authorized by the board of directors.

Absent from the case on trial is any evidence of an acknowledgement by any officer that the seal was attached by proper authority. To the contrary, the plaintiff's own testimony is that he placed the seal on the contract, albeit, allegedly with the consent of Gerald A. Bartell.

The Court concludes, after a careful analysis of the evidence and the application of the law reviewed herein, that the plaintiff has not made out a prima facie case of express, implied or apparent authority of the president of the defendant Bartell Broadcasting Corporation to execute the contract of employment. On the basis of the findings herein stated, the cause of action against Macfadden-Bartell Corporation must also fall.

Accordingly, the motion by the defendants to dismiss the complaint against both defendants is granted.

Case Questions

1. Should the court have enforced the salary portion of the contract since it was not unusual or extraordinary?

2. The plaintiff signed the contract in March of 1961; during May the monthly compensation was increased. Salary payments did not cease until November 1961. Under such circumstances could it be said that the directors had ratified the contract?

3. If Bartell Broadcasting is a closely held corporation, do you believe the court's decision is correct?

A Corporation's Tort Liability

A corporation is liable to third parties for the torts of its officers and agents if committed within the scope of employment. All of the legal principles establishing the tort liability of a principal for the actions of an agent discussed in the agency material are applicable here.

Executive Compensation

Compensation is the carrot that stimulates corporate officers to a high level of performance. Compensation is not synonymous with cash, although salary is the primary form of corporate remuneration. Compensation can also take the form of: (1) cash bonuses based on the corporation's performance; (2) stock options granting the executive the right to purchase a given number of corporate shares within a specified future period at a specified price (frequently the market price as of the date the option is granted); (3) phantom stock when one need not buy the stock but is paid cash equal to the dividends that would be received if one did own the stock; (4) pension benefits, life insurance, health insurance, etc.; and (5) deferred compensation where the executive will be paid as a consultant after retirement when in a lower tax bracket.

Different compensation forms enjoy varying degrees of popularity depending on the current tax law provisions, the health of the stock market, and general economic conditions. When a lawyer is putting together a compensation package many interests must be balanced, even conflicting ones! The plan should be as inexpensive to the company as possible, yet sufficiently generous to attract and retain high-quality individuals. It must recognize and reward achievement. Tax liability for both the corporation and any recipient should be the absolute minimum. It cannot be so high as to attract and unduly upset the shareholders.

When shareholders do object so vehemently to the level of executive compensation as to bring a lawsuit, they usually allege the gift or waste of corporate assets. The *Rogers* v. *Hill* case is the most famous case on executive compensation. The *Winkleman* v. *General Motors* case shows the typical outcome of such a challenge—the shareholders lose. The courts have been extremely reluctant to strike down executive compensation as constituting waste. Under the Internal Revenue Code of 1954, if a salary is to be deductible as an expense from corporate revenues, it must be reasonable. In the tax realm the courts have not been hobbled by any reluctance to declare salaries so high as to be unreasonable. That is, when the government is the plaintiff attempting to get back funds deducted from a tax obligation, courts are much more likely to be sympathetic to the plaintiff than when it is a shareholder attempting recovery of an excessive salary. Why? The following cases help define the limits of executive compensation.

ROGERS v. HILL
289 U.S. 582 (1933)

MR. JUSTICE BUTLER
The American Tobacco Company is a corporation organized under the laws of New Jersey. The petitioner, plaintiff below, acquired in 1916 and has since been the owner of 200

shares of its common stock. He also has 400 shares of common stock B. In accordance with by-law XII, adopted by the stockholders at their annual meeting, March 13, 1912, the company for many years has annually paid its president and vice-president large amounts in addition to their fixed salaries and other sums allowed them as compensation for services.

Plaintiff maintains that the by-law is invalid and that, even if valid, the amounts paid under it are unreasonably large and therefore subject to revision by the courts. In March, 1931, he demanded that the company bring suit against the officers who have received such payments to compel them to account to the company for all or such part thereof as the court may hold illegal. The company, insisting that such a suit would be without basis in law or fact, refused to comply with his demand. . . .

We come to consider whether these amounts are subject to examination and revision in the district court. As the amounts payable depend upon the gains of the business, the specified percentages are not per se unreasonable. The by-law was adopted in 1912 by an almost unanimous vote of the shares represented at the annual meeting and presumably the stockholders supporting the measure acted in good faith and according to their best judgment. . . . Regard is to be had to the enormous increase of the company's profits in recent years. The 2½ percent yielded President Hill $447,870.30 in 1929 and $842,507.72 in 1930. The 1½ percent yielded to each of the vice-presidents, Neily and Riggio, $115,141.86 in 1929 and $409,495.25 in 1930 and for these years payments under the by-law were in addition to the cash credits and fixed salaries shown in the statement.

While the amounts produced by the application of the prescribed percentages give rise to no inference of actual or constructive fraud, the payments under the by-law have by reason of increase of profits become so large as to warrant investigation in equity in the interest of the company. Much weight is to be given to the action of the stockholders, and the by-law is supported by the presumption of regularity and continuity. But the rule prescribed by it cannot, against the protest of a shareholder, be used to justify payments of sums as salaries so large as in substance and effect to amount to spoliation or waste of corporate property. The dissenting opinion of Judge Swan indicates the applicable rule: "If a bonus payment has no relation to the value of services for which it is given, it is in reality a gift in part and the majority stockholders have no power to give away corporate property against the protest of the minority." 60 F. (2d) 109, 113. The facts alleged by plaintiff are sufficient to require that the district court, upon a consideration of all the relevant facts brought forward by the parties, determine whether and to what extent payments to the individual defendants under the by-law constitute misuse and waste of the money of the corporation. . . .

The statement below shows for the years specified the amounts alleged to have been paid by the company to the named defendants as salary, credits, and under by-law XII.

	Salary	Cash Credits	By-Law
Hill			
1921	—	—	$ 89,833.94
1922	—	—	82,902.61
1923	—	—	77,336.54
			Vice President
1924	—	—	88,894.26
1925	—	—	97,059.38
1926	$ 75,000	—	188,643.45
1927	75,000	—	268,761.45
1928	75,000	—	280,203.68
			President
1929	144,500	$136,507.71	447,870.30
1930	168,000	273,470.76	842,507.72
Neiley			
1929	$ 33,333.32	$ 44,897.89	$115,141.87
1930	50,000.00	89,945.52	409,495.25
Riggio			
1929	$ 33,333.30	$ 45,351.40	$115,141.86
1930	50,000.00	90,854.06	409,495.25

(Author's note: The U.S. Supreme Court decided this case on a procedural matter and held that the case was to be sent back to the district court and that an injunction was to be issued stopping payment pending a determination by the district court whether these amounts were proper.)

After the Supreme Court's ruling in *Rogers* v. *Hill,* the parties negotiated a settlement. Under the terms of the settlement the bonus base was reduced and the employee's stock subscription plan was revised. By March of 1940 these adjustments saved the corporation $8,450,000. Rogers, the plaintiff shareholder, who was an attorney and represented himself, was paid legal fees of $525,000 (after taxes he received $263,000) or less than the 8½ percent of the savings enjoyed by the corporation. Other shareholders then attacked Roger's fee alleging that he sold out the real interests of the shareholders for the payment from American Tobacco. His fee was upheld as reasonable and the judge cleared him of any wrongdoing. *Rogers* v. *Hill,* 34 F. Supp 358 (1940).

Subsequently other shareholders challenged the amount of the officers' compensation. Their suit was unsuccessful. *Heller* v. *Boylan,* 29 N.Y.S. 2d 653 (1941). The judge said that he lacked a reliable standard to measure them against and since the great majority of stockholders had approved them, he would permit them to stand.

Note.   Notice the years of the payments in dispute—the start of the depression. Speaking of these same sums in later litigation a judge, who did not reduce them, characterized them as follows:

> Now, even a high-bracketer would deem these stipends munificent. To the person of moderate income they would be princely—perhaps something unattainable; to the wage-earner ekeing out an existence, they would be fabulous, and the unemployed might regard them as fantastic, if not criminal. To others they would seem immoral, inexcusably unequal, and an indictment of our economic system. *Heller* v. *Boylan,* 29 N.Y.S. 2d 653 (1941).

To add some perspective to the disputed amount of compensation, it might be of value to examine more recent corporate compensation figures. The following figures are taken from the respective company's 1982 documents. They reflect the aggregate salary and bonus (as calculated by S.E.C. rules) for the chief executive officer of that company.

American Telephone & Telegraph	$1,145,000
Sears Roebuck & Co.	1,050,000
General Motors	549,000
Apple Computer	349,000

What factors does a court examine in determining whether an executive's compensation is matched by his or her value to the corporation or is so excessive as to constitute an impermissible gift and waste of corporate assets? The case that follows provides some indication.

WINKELMAN v. GENERAL MOTORS CORPORATION
44 F. Supp. 960 (1942)

Among the issues presented by this litigation is the propriety of the total compensation, salary plus bonus, paid to certain executives and managers of General Motors Corporation, many of whom were directors. . . . I am of the opinion that for the years 1930 to 1940 inclusive, these amounts were not in excess of the value of the services rendered by those individuals. . . .

I stated in an opinion, filed in August 1940 on the motion of the three of the defendants, Whitney, Morgan, and Prosser, for summary judgment, that there were several of the years, to wit, 1930, 1935, 1936, and 1937, where the amounts awarded were so large that they required an investigation by a court of equity in the suit brought by plaintiff stockholders. *Rogers* v. *Hill*, 289 U.S. 582, 591, . . . This investigation has been had during the course of this trial and I am now satisfied that the compensation of these executives was not excessive as to those years also.

Concerning the compensation of executives, I have made the following findings, among others:

"There has always been keen rivalry for executives in the automobile industry. For example, General Motors lost to competitors— Charles W. Nash, who became head of the Nash Motors Company; Walter P. Chrysler, who developed the Chrysler Corporation; and K.T. Keller, who is now President of the Chrysler Corporation. Offers were made by competitors to Messrs. Knudsen and Raskob. It was necessary for the Corporation to hold out attractive financial benefits to prevent the loss of valuable executives.

. . .

"General Motors earned more in the decade of the thirties than in that of the twenties although almost a third of the period 1930– 1940 was a time of severe economic depression. In 1930–1940 inclusive, it earned $1,500,000,000 upon net sales totalling more than $12,000,000,000. Return on stockholder capital averaged 14.3 percent, a performance equalled by few companies. Over this period General Motors increased its share of the total passenger car output from approximately 34 percent in 1930 to as much as 50 percent in 1941.

"A comparison of General Motors passenger car sales with those of the Ford Motors Company, the dominant automobile manufacturer in 1923, illustrates the growth in market strength of General Motors to the present day. In 1923, Ford's sales totalled approximately 1,773,000 units; General Motors sold about 774,000 cars, only 44 percent of Ford's sales. In 1940, General Motors sales totalled approximately 1,748,000 cars; Ford sold about 717,000 cars, only 41 percent of General Motors sales."

Is a $500,000 total of salary plus bonus for the chief executive of a corporation of this magnitude, in very prosperous years, so excessive that its payment should be legally condemned as a waste of corporate assets? Having heard all the testimony and considered the exhibits I am of the opinion that the directors are not chargeable with waste for having approved these payments. These executives have built up a great industry; managed it successfully; given employment to hundreds of thousands of skilled workers; earned tremendous profits for the stockholders and contributed largely to the prosperity of the nation. Although in certain instances, hereinafter discussed, some of them have taken advantage of their position of influence to the detriment of the corporation, there is no denying the competence of their business management or its value to the Corporation.

The plaintiffs offered nothing as a yard-stick or comparison for determining the reasonableness of the salaries and bonuses. On the other hand the defendants have referred the Court to several reported stockholders' suits . . . in which it was held that compensation which was about twice the amount of the highest total compensation paid to any of these executives, was not excessive. . . . [T]he salaries and bonus allotments in the present case were not excessive, . . . they were earned by the recipients. . . .

Case Questions

1. Should a court more closely scrutinize a compensation plan established by the directors, as opposed to a plan approved by the shareholders?

2. Can any man or woman be worth $1,000,000 a year?

3. If bonus compensation is to be based on the performance of the corporation, what is to be done when factors, over which officers have no control, dramatically increase or decrease corporation performance? What if car sales slump because of an oil embargo imposed by foreign producing nations? What if a favorable tax revision, coupled with a change in accounting methods, causes a nonrecurring jump in profits?

4. If the courts are unable to devise a standard against which to measure the reasonableness of executive compensation, does that mean that there will exist no limitation on such compensation?

5. The 1954 Internal Revenue Code permits a corporation to deduct reasonable compensation only as a business expense. Should the IRS challenge the deductibility of some of today's corporate salaries?

Review Problems

1. A stockholder brings a suit in equity seeking the appointment of a receiver for the defendant corporation and the dissolution of the corporation. The president and treasurer of the corporation, who was also a director, orally employed an attorney to defend the suit for $2000. The board of directors had no knowledge of the contract. When the attorney was not paid for his services, he brought suit for his fee. Will the attorney prevail? [*Kelley* v. *Citizens Finance Co.*, 28 N.E. 2d 1005 (1940)]

2. The board of directors of American Airlines, a majority of which is disinterested, approve a restricted stock option plan. The shareholders approve the plan at the annual meeting. A committee of disinterested directors issue the options to 289 employees over a two-year time span. Several shareholders bring suit seeking to cancel the options as waste and as impermissible gifts of corporate assets. The directors contend that they have determined, in the exercise of their business judgment, that the corporation will receive benefits from the grant of this type of executive compensation. What decision? [*Beard* v. *Elster*, 160 A. 2d 731 (1960)]

No

3. Would your opinion differ if the stock option plan in the problem above had been approved by an interested board? [*Gottleib* v. *Heyden Chemical*, 90 A. 2d 660, on limited reargument, 91 A. 2d 57]

No — so decentralized so no knowledge. They proved this.

4. Allis-Chalmers and four nondirector employees entered guilty pleas in the famous 1960 electrical equipment price-fixing conspiracy. Thereafter a stockholder's derivative action was brought against the directors to recover damages that Allis-Chalmers was claimed to have suffered by reason of these violations. The corporation employed in excess of 31,000 people, had 24 plants, 145 sales officers, 5000 dealers and distributors, and a sales volume in excess of $500,000,000 annually. Its operating policy was to decentralize by delegating authority to the lowest possible management level. The evidence showed that no director had actual knowledge of the antitrust violations, nor did they have actual knowledge of any facts that should have put them on notice that illegal antitrust activities were being carried out. Nonetheless, the plaintiffs contend that the directors are liable as a matter of law by reason of their failure to take action designed to learn of and prevent antitrust activity on the part of any Allis-Chalmers employees. Is liability to be fixed on the directors? [*Graham* v. *Allis Chalmers,* 188 A.2d 125 (1963)]

5. Is it realistic to believe that directors could be completely ignorant of massive antitrust violations occurring within a large industry over a period of several years?

6. Should the labor unions that represent the corporation's employees have representatives on the board of directors, as they do in West Germany?

Courts — Must go up & down. directors ok here

7. A bankruptcy trustee sues the former directors of a company to recover dividends aggregating $3,639,058. The plaintiff claims that, despite the figures shown on the corporate books, there was no surplus and that the capital was impaired by the dividend payments. The directors claim that a proper surplus did exist. The plaintiff claims that: (1) the directors improperly "wrote up" land that cost $1,526,157.30 to a value of $8,737,949.02. The difference represents unrealized appreciation. (2) The directors improperly declined to "write down" to actual value the costs of investments in and advances to subsidiaries, thereby failing to take into account unrealized depreciation. What do you think of the directors' decisions? [*Randall* v. *Bailey*, 23 N.Y.S. 2d 179 (1940)]

8. The state business corporation statute vests discretion in the directors as to dividend declarations. The corporate articles contain the follow-

ing clause: "The holders of preferred stock shall be entitled to receive, and the Company shall be bound to pay thereon, but only out of net profits of the company, a fixed yearly dividend of fifty cents per share, payable semiannually." Are the directors obligated to declare dividends on the preferred stock whenever the corporation enjoys net profits? [*Constantin* v. *Holding Corp.*, 153 A.2d 378 1959)]

9. The Decimile Corporation is a well established, conservatively managed major company. It has consistently maintained a $3 or more per-share dividend since 1940 on its only class of stock, which has a $1 par value. Decimile's board of directors is determined to maintain a $3 per-share annual dividend distribution to maintain the corporation's image in the financial community, to reassure its shareholders, and to prevent a decline in the price of the corporation's shares, which would occur if there were a reduction in the dividend rate. Decimile's current financial position is not encouraging although the corporation is legally solvent. Its cash flow position is not good, and the current year's earnings are only $0.87 per share. Retained earnings amount to $17 per share. Decimile owns a substantial block of Integrated Electronic Services stock, which it purchased at $1 per share in 1950 and which has a current value of $6.50 per share. Decimile has paid dividends of $1 per share so far this year and contemplates distributing a sufficient number of shares of Integrated to provide an additional $2 per share. May Decimile legally pay the $2 dividend in Integrated stock? As an alternative could Decimile pay the $2 dividend in its own authorized but unissued shares of stock?

(This is adapted from CPA Exam Question #3a, taken from the May 1979 exam. © American Institute of Certified Public Accountants, Inc., 1979.)

10. Clayborn is the president and director of Marigold Corporation. He currently owns 1000 shares of Marigold, which he purchased several years ago on joining the company and assuming the presidency. At that time, he received a stock option for 10,000 shares of Marigold at $10 per share. The option is about to expire but Clayborn does not have the money to exercise his option. Credit is very tight at present, and most of his assets have already been used to obtain loans. Clayborn spoke to the chairman of Marigold's board about his plight and told the chairman that he is going to borrow $100,000 from Marigold in order to exercise his option. The chairman was responsible for Clayborn's being hired as the president of Marigold and is a close personal friend of Clayborn. Fearing that Clayborn will leave unless he is able to obtain a greater financial interest in Marigold, the chairman told Clayborn: "It is okay with me and you have a green light." Clayborn authorized the issuance of a $100,000 check payable to his

*Needs authority of BOD for
this loan if it can
further corp. good.
Didn't handle this
correctly.
Pres. personally liable*

order. He then negotiated the check to Marigold in payment for the shares of stock. What are the legal implications raised by the above circumstances?

(This is adapted from CPA Exam Question #3b, taken from the May 1979 exam. © American Institute of Certified Public Accountants, Inc., 1979.)

Endnotes

1. See A. Choka, The New Role of the Audit Committee, The Practical Lawyer, pp. 54–55 (Sept. 1, 1977).

2. Special Committee on Audit Committees—AICPA, "An AICPA Requirement for Audit Committees: An Analysis of the Issues" in SEC Report to Congress on the Accounting Profession and the Commission's Oversight Role, p. 591, July, 1978.

3. Choka, *supra*, pp. 56–57.

The Liability of Management for Corporate Crimes and Torts, for Mismanagement, and for Breach of Fiduciary Duty

12

The long title to this chapter appropriately suggests that the law in the area of the liability of corporate management is varied and complex. There is no single statutory scheme or set of legal principles that apply to the misconduct of management. In this chapter we will sketch the outlines of most of the major areas of the liability of management, leaving a few of these areas for discussion in the next section on the federal securities laws.

For the sake of convenience we have divided this chapter into three main categories of liability plus we review material on the indemnification of directors and officers. The first category of liability focuses on the *criminal liability* of management. The second category arises from the duty of care and the *business judgment rule*. Here, we discuss the liability of top decision makers for mismanagement. The final category of liability arises from management's breach of the fiduciary duty owed to the corporation and, in some cases, to minority shareholders.

There is no clear definition of "corporate crimes." But, it does appear that criminal activity on behalf of corporations is a troublesome fact of our commercial life. In a major study published in 1980, *Fortune* magazine concluded that for the 10-year period of 1970 to 1980, 117 of the 1043 largest and most respected corporations in this country were found guilty of or pleaded no contest to criminal charges.[1] This is 11 percent of those top corporations. *Fortune* limited their survey of crime to five offenses, the impropriety of which is not in doubt. The five were bribery (including kickbacks and illegal rebates), criminal fraud, illegal political contributions, tax evasion, and criminal antitrust violations. Not included were crimes directed against the corporation, such as embezzlement and even

The Liability of Management and Employees for Corporate Crimes

bribery, kickbacks, and other "questionable" payments made out of the country. In addition to the finding of corporate guilt, 50 "high-level" executives from 15 corporations went to jail.[2]

Another well-respected business-oriented national magazine conducted its own survey of corporate criminal conduct from 1971 through 1980 and in September 1982 reported that, of the 500 largest corporations, 115 or 23 percent had been convicted in the last decade of at least one major crime or had paid civil penalties for "serious" misbehavior.[3] Overall the magazine estimated that corporate crime costs the American economy and thus all of us $200 billion a year; price-fixing alone is estimated to cost consumers $60 billion a year.[4]

A survey of government documents for the same 10-year period (1971–1980) revealed that 2690 corporations of all sizes were *convicted* of federal criminal offenses,[5] and this may just be the tip of the iceberg of corporate crime. A government-financed study found that more than 60 percent of the largest corporations had been involved in one or more offenses in just a two-year period (1975–1976) but this figure included both major offenses and minor regulatory offenses.[6]

What do these statistics mean; what conclusions can we draw? Does all of this mean that our commercial society and the persons who participate in it are becoming more evil? No! This conclusion does not follow if one adopts the traditional definition of evil as an intent to cause injury or a wrong. In most of the violations reported above, the human wrongdoers were not engaged in a traditional form of evil or wrong. Very few of the prosecutions reported were against individuals in management; they were against the corporation. When individuals were prosecuted, their defense most likely included the assertion that they were acting in the best interests of the corporation. This assertion is what is so perplexing about "corporate crime." Let us take a closer look at just one area of corporate misconduct in an attempt to understand how this corporate crime comes about and how the law responds to it.

A Typical Criminal Prosecution for a Crime

In almost all cases, criminal liability is established by the application of either state or federal statutory provisions. These statutory schemes may provide for criminal or civil sanctions (a fine, imprisonment, or issuance of an injunction or other equitable order) against both the corporation and an individual participant. A typical example is found in the penalty provisions of Section 1 of the Sherman Act (outlawing conspiracies in restraint of trade) and Section 2 (outlawing monopolies). These recently amended sections provide that a person may be convicted of a felony and sentenced for up to three years and fined $100,000. The fine for the corporation may be $1 million.[7]

If the Justice Department of the U.S. Attorney General's Office has evidence that two or more firms are fixing prices, how does it decide which entity to sue: the corporations, management, or both? The answer is very complex but will generally depend on the kind of proof that the Justice Department has. If the proof shows the existence of price-fixing but is not clear as to which individual authorized or participated in the actual negotiations to fix the prices, then just the corporations will be sued. In this case, as in all criminal cases, the prosecution must prove beyond a reasonable doubt that there was an intent to fix prices. How does the government prove "corporate" intent? This question highlights another of the perplexities of having fictional legal titles such as "corporation" in our society. Can corporations have intent? A more philosophical but related question is, can or do corporations have moral character? This latter question, although a very important one and one at the core of the problem of corporate criminal conduct and law enforcement, will have to be postponed for this edition of our work or addressed in classes on business ethics.

Corporate Criminal Prosecutions and the Fifth Amendment's Privilege Against Self-Incrimination

The government proves *corporate intent* by presenting evidence from the corporate management, officers, agents, and others on what the corporate conduct was. The traditional way of proving intent is to infer it from conduct. But if a corporate agent testifies as to his or her participation in a corporate price-fixing scheme, does that not violate the corporation's Fifth Amendment privilege against self-incrimination? That is, if a corporate agent, who has been granted individual immunity from prosecution, is asked on the witness stand, "Did you know about or participate in the price-fixing scheme with X Corporation?" can the agent say, "I respectfully plead the corporation's Fifth Amendment Right?" The U.S. Supreme Court has held that the Fifth Amendment *does not* apply to corporations and agents testifying on their behalf.[8] So, the agent must answer the question. In asking this type of question and by using corporate records and other documents required by law to be kept, corporate crimes are proved.

When a prosecutor has evidence that a corporate crime has taken place, the prosecutor should decide whether to prosecute the corporate agent as an individual, the corporation, or both. If the prosecutor decides to prosecute the individual agent and the corporation, the agent cannot be forced to testify. This would violate the agent's Fifth Amendment privilege. Of course, persons are free to waive this privilege and testify in their own behalf.

Defenses of Individual Defendants

Let us return to our example of the antitrust criminal prosecution. The physical evidence (corporate records and documents, etc.) against the individual and the corporation may be overwhelming. The individual defendant may request a jury trial and then attempt to prove in an indirect manner that there was no individual intent to harm anyone. The only kind or quality of intent held by the defendant was the intent to do what was best for the business enterprise. The criminal act was done in order to survive in a very competitive business world. The defendant may also attempt to show that he or she is otherwise not like a common criminal but is in fact morally honorable by participating in church groups, civic activities, and the like.[9] This information, which is not a formal legal defense and which is really irrelevant to the central issues of the prosecution, may find its way before the court or jury through the clever maneuvers of defense counsel. The prosecutor knows this. This reality makes the criminal prosecution of individual defendants for the commission of business-related crimes, and a demand for their imprisonment in particular, unlikely to succeed. As a result, only the most outrageous conduct of undoubted illegality tends to be prosecuted.[10]

The discussion above points out the substantial problems for criminal law enforcement when fictional legal entities such as corporations are involved. Our traditional notions of criminal conduct are based on an *individual* (human) intent to do evil or wrong. In the case of some criminal conduct by corporations, the resulting conduct may have been caused by an individual's intent to help or benefit the corporation. That is, as a consequence of the intent to help the business, the criminal conduct occurs. Thus in a prosecution for such a crime, basing the entire case on the individual's intent causes confusion, and in some cases may seem unfair to the defendant. This aids us in understanding why there are relatively few individuals prosecuted for corporate crimes.

There are additional problems. In today's medium to large corporations, can top management really control the entire enterprise? There is a style of management that deems it efficient to divide large corporate enterprises into various profit centers. For many purposes these profit centers are autonomous. The structure of the corporation is such that responsibility for the numerous activities of the corporation is diffused into many parts. This diffusion of authority and responsibility in the modern large business corporation, perhaps more than any other factor, may be responsible for what appears to be a growing problem of corporate misconduct. When three or four major parts of a corporation come together to cause, unintentionally, injury to consumers or others, what is to be done? For example, if the engineering department in a large car company designs a safe gas tank, but the design is not acceptable to the finance department because it makes the car cost too much and is thus changed to a less safe design; and if the marketing department causes a public expectation of a safe design; but the end result is such an unsafe design that it results in numerous deaths (and a criminal prosecution),[11] what should happen? Should the corporation be held responsible? Should one or more individuals be held responsible?

This difficult series of questions has not been directly addressed, but there is a growing judicial sensitivity to these problems. We can see this sensitivity in the following case. The central issue is what should be done or what test should be adopted for criminal liability if the intent of the defendant is not an element of the crime. The case also shows how the legal system responds to the complex issue presented by the reality of a large corporate structure. The result is individual criminal liability when the defendant did not intend the act that violated a criminal provision of a federal regulatory statute.

U.S. v. PARK
421 U.S. 658 (1975)

MR. CHIEF JUSTICE BURGER *delivered the opinion of the Court.*

Acme Markets, Inc., is a national retail food chain with approximately 36,000 employees, 874 retail outlets, 12 general warehouses, and four special warehouses. Its headquarters, including the office of the president, respondent Park, who is chief executive officer of the corporation, are located in Philadelphia, Pennsylvania. In a five-count information filed in the United States District Court for the District of Maryland, the Government charged Acme and respondent with violations of the Federal Food, Drug, and Cosmetic Act. Each count of the information alleged that the defendants had received food that had been shipped in interstate commerce and that, while the food was being held for sale in Acme's Baltimore warehouse following shipment in interstate commerce, they caused it to be held in a building accessible to rodents and to be exposed to contamination by rodents. These acts were alleged to have resulted in the food being adulterated. . . .

Acme pleaded guilty to each count of the information. Respondent pleaded not guilty. The evidence at trial demonstrated that in April 1970 the Food and Drug Administration (FDA) advised respondent by letter of unsanitary conditions in Acme's Philadelphia warehouse. In 1971 FDA found that similar conditions existed in the firm's Baltimore warehouse. An FDA consumer safety officer testified concerning evidence of rodent infestation and other unsanitary conditions discovered during a 12-day inspection of the Baltimore warehouse in November and December 1971. He also related that a second inspection of the warehouse had been conducted in March 1972. On that occasion the inspectors found that there had been improvement in the sanitary conditions, but that, "there was still evidence of rodent activity in the building and in the warehouse and we found some rodent-contaminated lots of food items."

The Government also presented testimony by the Chief of Compliance of FDA's Baltimore office, who informed respondent by letter of the conditions at the Baltimore warehouse after the first inspection. There was testimony by Acme's Baltimore division vice president, who had responded to the letter on behalf of Acme and respondent and who described the steps taken to remedy the unsanitary conditions discovered by both inspections. The Government's final witness, Acme's vice president for legal affairs and assistant secretary, identified respondent as the president and chief executive officer of the company and read a bylaw prescribing the duties of the chief executive officer. He testified that respondent functioned by delegating "normal operating duties," including sanitation, but that he retained "certain things, which are the big, broad principles of the operation of the company," and had "the responsibility of seeing that they all work together."

. . .

Respondent was the only defense witness. He testified that, although all of Acme's employees were in a sense under his general direction, the company had an "organizational structure for responsibilities for certain functions" according to which different phases of its operation were "assigned to individuals who, in turn, have staff and departments under them." He identified those individuals responsible for sanitation and related that upon receipt of the January 1972 FDA letter, he had conferred with the vice president for legal affairs, who informed him that the Baltimore division vice president "was investigating the situation immediately and would be taking corrective action and would be preparing a summary of the corrective action to reply to the letter." Respondent stated that he did not "believe there was anything [he] could have done more constructively than what [he] found was being done."

On cross-examination, respondent conceded that providing sanitary conditions for food offered for sale to the public was something that he was "responsible for in the entire operation of the company," and he stated that it was one of many phases of the company that he assigned to "dependable subordinates." Respondent was asked about and, over the objections of his counsel, admitted receiving, the

April 1970 letter addressed to him from FDA regarding unsanitary conditions at Acme's Philadelphia warehouse. . . .

At the close of the evidence, respondent's renewed motion for judgment of acquittal was denied. . . . Respondent's counsel objected to the [jury] instructions on the ground that they failed to reflect our decision in *United States* v. *Dotterweich,* 320 U.S. 277, and to define ' "responsible relationship." ' The trial judge overruled the objection. The jury found respondent guilty on all counts of the information, and he was subsequently sentenced to pay a fine of $50 on each count.

The Court of Appeals reversed the conviction and remanded for a new trial. . . .

We granted certiorari because of an apparent conflict among the courts of appeals with respect to the standard of liability of corporate officers under the Federal Food, Drug, and Cosmetic Act as construed in *United States* v. *Dotterweich,* supra, and because of the importance of the question to the Government's enforcement program. We reverse.

The questions presented by the Government's petition for certiorari in *United States* v. *Dotterweich,* supra, and the focus of this Court's opinion, was whether "the manager of a corporation, as well as the corporation itself, may be prosecuted under the Federal Food, Drug, and Cosmetic Act of 1938 for the introduction of misbranded and adulterated articles into interstate commerce.". . .

In reversing the judgment of the Court of Appeals and reinstating Dotterweich's conviction, this Court looked to the purposes of the Act and noted that they "touch phases of the lives and health of people which, in the circumstances of modern industrialism, are largely beyond self-protection." It observed that the Act is of "a now familiar type" which "dispenses with the conventional requirement for criminal conduct—awareness of some wrongdoing. In the interest of the larger good it puts the burden of acting at hazard upon a person otherwise innocent but standing in responsible relation to a public danger."

Central to the Court's conclusion that individuals other than proprietors are subject to the criminal provisions of the act was the reality that "the only way in which a corporation can act is through the individuals who act on its behalf.". . .

At the same time, however, the Court was aware of the concern which was the motivating factor in the Court of Appeals' decision, that literal enforcement "might operate too harshly by sweeping within its condemnation any person however remotely entangled in the prescribed shipment." A limiting principle, in the form of "settled doctrines of criminal law" defining those who "are responsible for the commission of a misdemeanor," was available. In this context, the Court concluded, those doctrines dictated that the offense was committed "by all who have . . . a responsible share in the furtherance of the transaction which the statute outlaws."

. . .

The rule that corporate employees who have "a responsible share in the futherance of the transaction which the statute outlaws" are subject to the criminal provision of the Act was not formulated in a vacuum. Cases under the Federal Food and Drugs Act of 1906 reflected the view both that knowledge or intent were not required to be proved in prosecutions under its criminal provision, and that responsible corporate agents could be subjected to the liability thereby imposed. Moreover, the principle had been recognized that a corporate agent, through whose act, default, or omission the corporation committed a crime, was himself guilty individually of that crime. The principle had been applied whether or not the crime required "consciousness of wrongdo-

ing," and it has been applied not only to those corporate agents who themselves committed the criminal act, but also to those who by virtue of their managerial positions or other similar relations to the act could be deemed responsible for its commission.

In the latter class of cases, the liability of managerial officers did not depend on their knowledge of, or personal participation in, the act made criminal by the statute. Rather, where the statute under which they were prosecuted dispensed with "consciousness of wrongdoing", an omission or failure to act was deemed a sufficient basis for a responsible corporate agent's liability. It was enough in such cases that, by virtue of the relationship he bore to the corporation, the agent had the power to have prevented the act complained of. . . .

. . .

"The accused, if he does not will the violation, usually is in a position to prevent it with no more care than society might reasonably expect and no more exertion than it might reasonably exact from one who assumed his responsibilities." Similarly, in cases decided after *Dotterweich*, the court of appeals have recognized that those corporate agents vested with the responsibility, and power commensurate with that responsibility, to devise whatever measures are necessary to ensure compliance with the Act bear a "responsible relationship" to, or have a "responsible share" in, violations.

The Act does not, as we observed in *Dotterweich*, make criminal liability turn on "awareness of some wrongdoing" or "conscious fraud." The duty imposed by Congress on responsible corporate agents is, we emphasize, one that requires the highest standard of foresight and vigilance, but the Act, in its criminal aspect, does not require that which is objectively impossible. The theory upon which responsible corporate agents are held criminally accountable for "causing" violations of the Act permits a claim that a defendant was "powerless" to prevent or correct the violation to "be raised defensively at a trial on the merits." If such a claim is made, the defendant has the burden of coming forward with evidence, but this does not alter the Government's ultimate burden of proving beyond a reasonable doubt the defendant's guilt, including his power, in light of the duty imposed by the Act, to prevent or correct the prohibited condition. Congress has seen fit to enforce the accountability of responsible corporate agents dealing with products which may affect the health of consumers by penal sanctions cast in rigorous terms, and the obligation of the courts is to give them effect so long as they do not violate the Constitution. . . .

Reading the entire charge satisfied us that the jury's attention was adequately focused on the issue of respondent's authority with respect to the conditions that formed the basis of the alleged violations. Viewed as a whole, the charge did not permit the jury to find guilt solely on the basis of respondent's position in the corporation; rather, it fairly advised the jury that to find guilt it must find respondent "had a responsible relation to the situation" and "by virtue of his position . . . had authority and responsibility" to deal with the situation. The situation referred to could only be "food . . . held in unsanitary conditions in a warehouse with the result that it consisted, in part, of filth or . . . may have been contaminated with filth."

. . .

We conclude that, viewed as a whole and in the context of the trial, the charge was not misleading and contained an adequate statement of the law to guide the jury's determination. . . .

Case Questions

1. What conceivable reason could Park have had for appealing a case all the way to the Supreme Court when his fine totaled only $250.00?

2. Do you think that Park or the corporation paid for his legal expenses? If the corporation financed Park's litigation, do you believe it was a wise decision when one compares a $250.00 fine to the tremendous cost of an appeal?

3. Why would the corporation plead guilty while the chief executive officer pleads innocent?

Summary of a Corporation's and Management's Criminal Liability

Crimes are defined by both state and federal statutes. If there is evidence of a violation of these statutes, a prosecution may result. Generally, individual members of management are not prosecuted unless there is substantial evidence that the individual authorized, knew about, or participated in the act. The lack of knowledge or specific intent to do wrong is a forceful factor in the decision not to prosecute individuals for corporate criminal actions. However, recent case law indicates that where a regulatory statute does not require a specific criminal intent, management may be prosecuted by showing that the defendant had the authority to do something about the criminal action or had a responsible share in the futherance of the transaction that the statute outlaws. The decision in *U.S.* v. *Park* has profound implications for criminal corporate prosecutions because it is a major exception to the general principle of founding criminal liability on a specific criminal intent. Moreover, this case is not expected to be restricted to the area of public health.[12]

Directors, management, and sometimes controlling shareholders owe various duties to the corporation and, in some cases, to the shareholders. Generally, these duties are to act intra vires, or within their corporate authority, to exercise due care and to comply with the standards of being a fiduciary. These fiduciary duties run primarily to the corporation but may, in a few instances, run to shareholders. In this section, we will examine material on the exercise of due care in management. In the next section, we will examine material on the fiduciary duties that are traditionally classified into those involving (1) possessing some property or other interest that conflicts with the corporation, (2) competing with the corporation, (3) usurping corporate opportunities, and (4) the sale of control. In the next chapter we will discuss the oppression of minority interests. This discussion does involve a breach of a fiduciary obligation, but it also is related to an altering of the corporation's capital structure, the central focus of the next chapter.

The Liability of Directors and Management for Breach of Duty— The Business Judgment Defense

The Exercise of Due Care and the Business Judgment Defense

First, we should emphasize the obvious. If a member of the board or management ("management" here means the officers of the corporation and agents who have the authority to decide matters relating to the corporate purpose) consciously go outside of their authority, then they may suffer liability if the corporation or a third party is damaged. This liability is based on agency law. Agency law imposes liability on an agent or employee for torts committed and for contracts entered into with third parties that are not within the authority of the wrongdoer. For example, if A makes a contract with T/P that purports to be made on behalf of X Corporation, but is not *authorized* as we used that term in the agency material, then on a breach T/P may hold only A liable. Or suppose that a corporate official, on learning of the candidacy of a personal enemy for the presidency of a university, sends a defamatory letter to that university. The writer's purpose is to defeat the other man's candidacy, and, to add to the letter's credibility, he has written on corporate stationery. In such an instance the corporation would not be liable. So, in a way, a first standard of care for management is to act within the framework of established authority.

Statutory Duties

A second almost equally obvious proposition is to act within the statutory framework of both the state and federal governments. There are many, many state and federal statutes imposing liability for environmental protection, for employee safety and health, for job-related race, age, and sex discrimination, etc., that establish standards of care.

Within the state corporation statutory framework, the following standards are established:

MODEL BUSINESS CORPORATION ACT

§ 48. Liabilities of Directors in Certain Cases

In addition to any other liabilities, a director shall be liable in the following circumstances unless he complies with the standard provided in this Act for the performance of the duties of directors:

(a) A director who votes for or assents to the declaration of any dividend or other distribution of the assets of a corporation to its shareholders contrary to the provisions of this Act or contrary to any restrictions contained in the articles of incorporation, shall be liable to the corporation, jointly and severally with all other directors so voting or assenting, for the amount of such dividend which is paid. . .

(b) A director who votes for or assents to the purchase of the corporation's own shares contrary to the provisions of this Act shall be liable to the corporation, jointly and severally with all other directors so voting or assenting, for the amount of consideration paid for such shares which is in excess of the maximum amount which could have been paid therefor without a violation of the provisions of this Act.

(c) A director who votes for or assents to any distribution of assets of a corporation to its shareholders during the liquidation of the corporation without the payment and discharge of, or making adequate provision for, all known debts, obligations, and liabilities of the corporation shall be liable to the corporation, jointly and severally with all other directors so voting or assenting, for the value of such assets which are distributed, to the extent that such debts, obligations and liabilities of the corporation are not therafter paid and discharged.

Any director against whom a claim shall be asserted under or pursuant to this section for the payment of a dividend or other distribution of assets of a corporation and who shall be held liable thereon, shall be entitled to contribution from the shareholders who accepted or received any such dividend or assets, knowing such dividend or distribution to have been made in violation of this Act, in proportion to the amounts received by them.

. . .

In addition to these very explicit acts creating standards of conduct, the 1977 Amendments to the MBCA provide a much more general statement:

§ 35. Board of Directors

[Second Paragraph].   A director shall perform his duties as a director, including his duties as a member of any committee of the board upon which he may serve, in good faith, in a manner he reasonably believes to be in the best interests of the corporation, and with such care as an ordinarily prudent person in a like position would use under similar circumstances. In performing his duties, a director shall be entitled to rely on information, opinions, reports or statements, including financial statements and other financial data, in each case prepared or presented by:

(a) one or more officers or employees of the corporation whom the director reasonably believes to be reliable and competent in the matters presented,

(b) counsel, public accountants or other persons as to matters which the director reasonably believes to be within such person's professional or expert competence, or

(c) a committee of the board upon which he does not serve, duly designated in accordance with a provision of the articles of incorporation or the by-laws, as to matters within its designated authority, which committee the director reasonably believes to merit confidence,

but shall not be considered to be acting in good faith if he has knowledge concerning the matter in question that would cause such reliance to be unwarranted. A person who so performs his duties shall have no liability by reason of being or having been a director of the corporation.

Language similar to this is found in almost all state corporation statutes. Only Hawaii and New Hampshire do not have specific provisions on either the standard of care for directors or the ability of directors to rely on information presented by others.[13] The first paragraph, above, reads into the state corporation law the often cited "business judgment rule." This rule sustains corporate transactions and "*immunizes management* from liability where the transaction is within the powers of the corporation (intra vires) and the authority of management, and involves the exercise of due care and compliance with applicable fiduciary duties."[14] That is, where management makes a decision that appears through hindsight to be negligent or to breach a standard of care, management will not be liable so long as the decision was made in good faith, was within the corporation's powers and management's authority, and was the result of independent discretion and judgment. In short, business decisions by directors and management that were made in good faith do not create personal liability even though on looking back they may seem to have been negligent and most certainly resulted in a loss of money to the corporation.

Every day, large and small corporations lose money, and some file bankruptcy as a result of bad business decisions. The policy position of the law is that management should be given tremendous freedom to make these judgments. Only in rare cases will a court attempt to interfere with the internal management of a corporation and substitute its judgment for that of management. The first case below is a modern–day example of the application of the business judgment rule. Although the court does not discuss the business judgment rule, it obviously applies it. Given the facts of the case, the defendant officer was certainly negligent but was "insulated" from judgment. Also, in this case, the corporation was relatively small. As corporations grow in size, the potential for damage also grows, but so too, it seems, does the complexity of the moral issues. The next two cases show a current application or attempted application of the business judgment rule in the context of a large corporation operating in the political environment. Both of these cases stand for the proposition that the business judgment defense should not be applicable if it would offend public policy.

UNITED STATES LIABIL. INS. CO. v. HAIDINGER-HAYES, INC.

83 Cal Rptr. 418, 463 P.2d 770 (S. Ct. Cal., 1970)

MC COMB, Justice

Plaintiff insurance company, an out of state corporation, entered into a general agency contract with defendant Haidinger-Hayes, Inc., a licensed California insurance agent, effective March 31, 1959. Under the terms of their agreement defendant corporation had authority to solicit and underwrite proposals for insurance, to determine the premium rate, and to issue contracts of insurance in the eleven western states in plaintiff's behalf. The consideration to it was 20 percent of the premiums paid. Numerous policies were solicited,

underwritten and issued pursuant to this agreement. It was cancelled on December 12, 1963, at the request of plaintiff because of excessive loss history under a policy of liability insurance issued to Crescent Wharf and Warehouse Company and its wholly-owned subsidiaries (hereinafter all referred to as "Crescent").

The negotiations for the Crescent policy were the responsibility of defendant V. M. Haidinger, president and principal executive officer of defendant corporation. Acting for and on behalf of the corporation he issued the policy on October 10, 1961, for a period of three years, at the premium rate of $1.05 per $100 reportable payroll. The policy covered Crescent's legal liability for claims arising out of the work, operations and other business activities of Crescent up to a limit of liability of $25,000 per claim or casualty, plus expenses of adjusting and defending such claims. The risk under this policy was "self-rated" and was not measurable by any published standard or comparable rate. The policy by its nature anticipated the occurrence of monetary claims for injuries sustained by employees of Crescent and that a premium rate was required which would produce a reasonable profit for the insurer after the settlement, defense and payment of such claims. This policy was cancelled at the request of plaintiff on February 28, 1963. . . . This action was filed November 1, 1965, for damages resulting from the Crescent risk. . . .

The complaint therein stated several causes of action. During the trial plaintiff dismissed the breach of contract cause of action. Findings were made against both defendants on the issue of negligence in issuing the policy at the premium rate of $1.05 per $100 payroll, and judgment was based solely thereon. In their favor, however, the court found that neither was guilty of failure to disclose any material fact to plaintiff with respect to this coverage; that neither willfully or intentionally placed their own interests or that of others ahead of plaintiff's; and that neither was guilty of any dishonest, fraudulent or malicious acts in connection therewith. Damages were found to have been proximately caused by defendants' negligence in the sum of $137,606.20 as of the date of the conclusion of the trial, plus an undetermined amount on open unsettled claims. . . .

The issues on appeal are: the sufficiency of the evidence to support the findings of negligence; liability to plaintiff of the individual defendant; . . .

The trial was long and the evidence was conflicting. There were discrepancies in the testimony of defendant V.M. Haidinger.

Under well-settled rules on appeal the evidence and the inferences arising therefrom must be viewed in the light most favorable to respondent plaintiff.

Question: *Does the evidence support the findings of negligence?*

Yes, as to negligence of both defendants in the computation of the premium rate. *No,* as to the finding of personal responsibility to plaintiff on the part of the individual defendant. . . .

The court found that at the time this policy was issued a "loss ratio" of a maximum of 60 percent was required in order to produce a reasonable allowance for profit to plaintiff on this coverage, and that defendant V.M. Haidinger, acting on behalf of defendant Haidinger-Hayes, Inc. should in the exercise of reasonable care have known this. The court further found that, based on information in the possession of, or readily available to, these defendants at that time it was reasonable to anticipate that Crescent's losses under the policy would be at least $85,000 per year, that its reportable payroll would not exceed $7,000,000 per year, and that it was not reasonable to anticipate that the losses of payroll would be otherwise. In the exercise of reasonable care defendants should have known, the court found, that at the premium rate of $1.05 per $100 of payroll the loss ratio was "in excess of One Hundred Ten Percent (110%) and that the policy would probably result in substantial financial loss to plaintiff. . . ."

Among the information furnished or available to defendants and which, in the exercise of reasonable care, they should have considered in determining the premium rate for this policy, was that none of the coverages issued to Crescent by other companies since October 1, 1954, had gone to expiration, each having been cancelled by prior insurers because of loss experience thereunder; that losses under prior Crescent policies had been substantial; that there had been a sharp upward trend in these losses; and that there were payroll-reducing occurrences which might affect the anticipated payroll. These included the loss by Crescent of a major customer,—and with it one-third of its anticipated payroll, and the effects of automation which had begun prior to the issuance of the policy. There was evidence that defendant V.M. Haidinger knew that the anticipated payroll would not exceed $7,000,000, that if the loss ratio was over 60 percent that plaintiff would suffer a financial loss, and that Crescent would not accept the coverage at a substantially higher premium. . . . He anticipated a reduction in the loss picture through his better efficiency in handling claims, but he did not inquire as to the facts of prior claims or the costs of defending them. . . .

The trial court found that each defendant owed a duty to plaintiff to exercise reasonable care and to make a reasonable effort to produce a profit for plaintiff; that each acted negligently toward plaintiff in this regard; and, as a conclusion of law, found that defendant V.M. Haidinger was liable to plaintiff "by reason of his personal participation as an officer and agent of defendant Haidinger-Hayes, Inc. in the tortious conduct of defendant Haidinger-Hayes, Inc."

What is negligence under a particular set of circumstances is a question for the trier of fact. Actionable negligence involves a legal duty to use due care, a breach of such legal duty, and the breach as the proximate or legal cause of the resulting injury. . . . Defendant corporation was a fiduciary to plaintiff during the existence of the agency agreement. A professional agent is required to have the particular knowledge and to exercise the particular skill and diligence expected of it. . . . If an insurance agent negligently induces an insurer to assume coverage on which it suffers a loss the agent is liable. . . . Liability is not incurred by a mere error of judgment in the exercise of discretion unless the error is based on want of care or diligence. . . . Here there was an express finding of negligence and the "business judgment" rule does not exonerate defendant corporation. . . .

The relationship of defendant V.M. Haidinger to plaintiff is somewhat different. Liability was imposed upon him for his active participation in the tortious (negligent) act of his principal which caused pecuniary harm to a third person. . . . Liability imposed upon agents for active participation in tortious acts of the principal have been mostly restricted to cases involving physical injury, not pecuniary harm, to a third person. . . . More must be shown than breach of the officer's duty *to his corporation* to impose personal liability *to a third person* upon him. Neither the evidence nor the finding support the conclusion that defendant V.M. Haidinger was personally liable to plaintiff by reason of his negligent performance of his corporate duties. . . .

Judgment against defendant Haidinger-Hayes, Inc. is affirmed . . . Judgment against defendant V.M. Haidinger is reversed.

Case Question   1. What factors, if any, support a policy of exempting officers from personal liability for their corporate torts unless a physical injury resulted?

GALL v. EXXON CORP.

418 F. Supp. 508 (D. Ct., N.Y., 1976)

ROBERT L. CARTER, District Judge

Plaintiff's complaint arises out of the alleged payment by Exxon Corporation of some $59 million in corporate funds as bribes or political payments, which were improperly contributed to Italian political parties and others during the period 1963–1974, in order to secure special political favors as well as other allegedly illegal commitments.

. . .

The complaint demands that the individual defendants be held jointly and severally liable for damages, including loss of goodwill, allegedly suffered by Exxon. It further demands, among other things, the commencement of an investigation through independent auditors in conjunction with plaintiff's counsel, the immediate election of four new members of the Board of Directors proposed by plaintiff and, within 12 months, the election of a new Chairman of the Board and President, and reconstituting the composition of the membership of the Board of Directors and Executive Committee, such that at least 55% of the Board and the Executive Committee be made up of independent outside directors.

On September 24, 1975, Exxon's Board of Directors unanimously resolved, pursuant to Article III, Section 1, of Exxon's By-Laws to establish a Special Committee on Litigation, composed of Exxon directors Jack F. Bennett, Richard P. Dobson and Edward G. Harness, and refer to the Special Committee for the determination of Exxon's action the matters raised in this and several other pending actions relating to the Italian expenditures. With respect to the matters within its mandate, the Special Committee acts as the Board of Directors of Exxon.

. . .

On January 23, 1976, after an investigation of approximately four months, including interviews with over 100 witnesses, the Special Committee issued the "Determination and Report of the Special Committee on Litigation" ("Report"), an 82-page document summarizing the Committee's findings and recommendations. . . .

. . .

The investigation . . . revealed that political contributions by Esso Italiana to various Italian political parties during the nine-year period from 1963 through 1971 totalled $27.9 million. The amounts per year were as follows:

	$ millions
1963	0.8
1964	1.1
1965	1.0
1966	2.5
1967	3.8
1968	5.8
1969	5.7
1970	3.5
1971	3.7
	$27.9

Of this amount, $13.5 million were recycled into one or more of the 40 secret bank accounts. All political contributions by Esso Italiana were ended in 1972.

It is clear that several of the Exxon directors named as defendants in this suit were aware of the existence of the political payments in Italy prior to their termination in 1972.

. . .

It is likely that the subject of political contributions was mentioned to the Audit Committee of the Exxon Board at its October, 1970, meeting. The Audit Committee at that time included defendants W. H. Franklin and E. G. Collado. The Report indicates that there was only a passing reference to the subject of political contributions in terms which did not suggest unlawfulness. There has been no report that the subject of political contributions was mentioned to the members of the Audit Committee at any other time prior to 1972.

. . .

After careful review, analysis and investigation, and with the advice and concurrence of Special Counsel, the Special Committee unanimously determined on January 23, 1976, that it would be contrary to the interests of Exxon and its shareholders for Exxon, or anyone on its behalf, to institute or maintain a legal action against any present or former Exxon director or officer. The Committee further resolved to direct and authorize the proper officers of Exxon and its General Counsel to oppose and seek dismissal of all shareholders derivative actions relating to payments made by or on behalf of Esso Italiano S.p.A., which has been filed against any present or former Exxon director or officer.

There is no question that the rights sought to be vindicated in this lawsuit are those of Exxon and not those of the plaintiff suing derivatively on the corporation's behalf. . . . Since it is the interests of the corporation which are at stake, it is the responsibility of the directors of the corporation to determine, in the first instance, whether an action should be brought on the corporation's behalf. It follows that the decision of corporate directors whether or not to assert a cause of action held by the corporation rests within the sound business judgment of the management. . . .

This principle, which has come to be known as the business judgment rule, was articulated by Mr. Justice Brandeis speaking for a unanimous Court in *United Copper Securities Co.* v. *Amalgamated Copper Co., supra,* 244 U.S. at 263–64, 37 S.Ct. at 510. In that case the directors of a corporation chose not to bring an antitrust action against a third party. Mr. Justice Brandeis said:

> "Whether or not a corporation shall seek to enforce in the courts a cause of action for damages is, like other business questions, ordinarily a matter of internal management, and is left to the discretion of the directors, in the absence of instruction by vote of the stockholders. Courts interfere seldom to control such discretion intra vires the corporation, except where the directors are guilty of misconduct equivalent to a breach of trust, or where they stand in a dual relation which prevents an unprejudiced exercise of judgment. . . ."

Similarly, in *Ash* v. *International Business Machines, Inc., supra,* 353 F.2d at 493, the Third Circuit held:

> ". . . a stockholder's derivative action, whether involving corporate refusal to bring antitrust suits or some other controversial decision concerning the conduct of corporate affairs, can be maintained only if the stockholder shall allege and prove that the directors of the corporation are personally involved or interested in the alleged wrongdoing in a way calculated to impair their exercise of business judgment on behalf of the corporation, or that their refusal to sue reflects bad faith or breach of trust in some other way."

. . .

It is clear that absent allegations of fraud, collusion, self-interest, dishonesty or other misconduct of a breach of trust nature, and absent allegations that the business judgment exercised was grossly unsound, the court should not at the instigation of a single shareholder interfere with the judgment of the corporate officers. . . .

The question remains as to the requisite showing of good faith on the part of the corporate directors sufficient to warrant a dismissal based on the business judgment rule defense. In *Swanson* v. *Traer,* 354 U.S. 114, . . . (1957), the Supreme Court noted that the classical description of those situations where a shareholder may sue on behalf of his corporation was contained in *Hawes* v. *Oakland, supra.* The *Swanson* court quoted *Hawes* as follows:

> "Some action or threatened action of the managing board of directors or trustees of the corporation which is beyond the authority conferred on them by their charter or other source of organization;
>
> "Or such a fraudulent transaction completed or contemplated by the acting managers, in connection with some other party, or among themselves, or with other shareholders as will result in serious injury to the corporation, or to the interests of the other shareholders;
>
> "Or where the board of directors, or a majority of them, are acting for their own interest, in a manner destructive of the corporation itself, or of the rights of the other shareholders;
>
> "Or where the majority of shareholders themselves are oppressively and illegally pursuing a course in the name of the corporation, which is in violation of the rights of the other shareholders, and which can only be restrained by the aid of a court of equity."
>
> 354 U.S. at 116, 77 S.Ct. at 1118.

In this regard, plaintiff challenges the independence of the Special Committee's judgment, arguing that the decision of the Special Committee was, in effect, a decision by those accused of the wrongdoing or by a body under the control of those accused of the wrongdoing. . . .

. . .

This argument clearly misses the mark. The focus of the business judgment rule inquiry is on those who actually wield the decision-making authority, not on those who might have possessed such authority at different times and under different circumstances. In no sense was the decision of the Special Committee not to sue merely an advisory one. Indeed, in carrying out its investigation and in reaching its conclusions, the Special Committee exercised the full powers of the Board.

Plaintiff next argues that the challenged political payments were illegal and that such illegality removes this case from the operation of the business judgment rule.

[E]ven assuming that the political payments in Italy were illegal where made, the business judgment rule is nonetheless applicable. The decision not to bring suit with regard to past conduct which may have been illegal is not itself a violation of law and does not result in the continuation of the alleged violation of law. Rather, it is a decision by the directors of the corporation that pursuit of a cause of action based on acts already consummated is not in the best interest of the corporation. Such a determination, like any other business decision, must be made by the corporate directors in the exercise of their sound business judgment. . . .

Moreover, this conclusion is all the more appropriate in view of the fact that there is not a scintilla of evidence on the record before me that the political payments in issue here were illegal either under the laws of the United States or of Italy. On the contrary, the Special Committee on the basis of its intensive investigation, and with the concurrence of its Special Counsel, determined that there was no basis for concluding that the Italian payments were in any way illegal.

. . .

Again, to quote Mr. Justice Brandeis,

> "Mere belief that corporate action, taken or contemplated, is illegal gives the stockholder no greater right to interfere than is possessed by any other citizen. Stockholders are not guardians of the public. The function of guarding the public against the acts deemed illegal rests with the public officials." *Ashwander* v. *Tennessee Valley Authority, supra,* 297 U.S. at 343, 56 S.Ct. at 481. . . .

. . .

. . . I am constrained to conclude that it is premature at this stage of the lawsuit to grant summary judgment. Plaintiff must be given an opportunity to test the bona fides and independence of the Special Committee through discovery and, if necessary, at a plenary hearing. . . . Issues of intent, motivation, and good faith are particularly inappropriate for summary disposition. . . .

Accordingly, defendants' motion for summary judgment is hereby denied without prejudice to its renewal after plaintiff has conducted relevant discovery. Plaintiff will be given 60 days from the date of entry of this order to conduct discovery, and if necessary to request a hearing, in order to put before the court significant probative evidence tending to support its position. . . .

So ordered.

Case Questions

1. If the persons who made the payments for Exxon or authorized them or set them up did not think the payments were illegal, why was $13.5 million recycled into one or more of the 40 secret bank accounts?

2. In your judgment, would the standard of conduct for directors be too high or too severe if the directors should be held liable for the improper payments?

MILLER v. A.T.&T.
507 F2d 759 (3rd Cir., 1974)

SEITZ, Chief Judge
Plaintiffs, stockholders in American Telephone and Telegraph Company ("AT&T"), brought a stockholders' derivative action in the Eastern District of Pennsylvania against AT&T and all but one of its directors. The suit centered upon the failure of AT&T to collect an outstanding debt of some $1.5 million owed to the company by the Democratic National Committee ("DNC") for communications services provided by AT&T during the 1968 Democratic national convention. . . .

Plaintiffs' complaint alleged that "neither the officers or directors of AT&T have taken any action to recover the amount owed" from on or about August 20, 1968, when the debt was incurred, until May 31, 1972, the date plaintiffs' amended complaint was filed. The failure to collect was alleged to have involved a breach of the defendant directors' duty to exercise diligence in handling the affairs of the corporation, to have resulted in affording a preference to the DNC in collection procedures in violation of § 202(a) of the Communications Act of 1934, 47 U.S.C. § 202(a) (1970), and to have amounted to AT&T's making a "contribution" to the DNC in violation of a federal prohibition on corporate campaign spending, 18 U.S.C. § 610 (1970).

Plaintiffs sought permanent relief in the form of an injunction requiring AT&T to collect the debt, an injunction against providing further services to the DNC until the debt was paid in full, and a surcharge for the benefit of the corporation against the defendant directors in the amount of the debt plus interest from the due date. A request for a preliminary injunction against the provision of services to the 1972 Democratic convention was denied by the district court after an evidentiary hearing.

On motion of the defendants, the district court dismissed the complaint for failure to state a claim upon which relief could be granted. . . . The court stated that collection procedures were properly within the discretion of the directors whose determination would not be overturned by the court in the absence of an allegation that the conduct of the directors was "plainly illegal, unreasonable, or in breach of a fiduciary duty . . . ." Plaintiffs appeal from dismissal of their complaint.

In viewing the motion to dismiss, we must consider all facts alleged in the complaint and every inference fairly deductible therefrom in the light most favorable to the plaintiffs. A complaint should not be dismissed unless it appears that the plaintiffs would not be entitled to relief under any facts which they might prove in support of their claim. Judging plaintiffs' complaint by these standards, we feel that it does state a claim upon which relief can be granted for breach of fiduciary duty arising from the alleged violation of 18 U.S.C. § 610.

The pertinent law on the question of the defendant directors' fiduciary duties in this diversity action is that of New York, the state of AT&T's incorporation. . . . The sound business judgment rule, the·basis of the districts court's dismissal of plaintiffs' complaint, expresses the unanimous decision of American courts to eschew intervention in corporate decision-making if the judgment of directors and officers is uninfluenced by personal considerations and is exercised in good faith. . . . Underlying the rule is the assumption that reasonable diligence has been used in reaching the decision which the rule is invoked to justify. . . .

Had plaintiffs' complaint alleged only failure to pursue a corporate claim, application of the sound business judgment rule would support the district court's ruling that a shareholder could not attack the directors' decision. . . . Where, however, the decision not to collect a debt owed the corporation is itself alleged to have been an illegal act, different rules apply. When New York law regarding such acts by directors is considered in conjunction with the underlying purposes of the particular statute involved here, we are convinced that the business judgment rule cannot insulate the defendant directors from liability if they did in fact breach 18 U.S.C. § 610, as plaintiffs have charged.

Roth v. *Robertson*, 64 Misc. 343, 118 N.Y.S. 351 (Sup.Ct.1909), illustrates the proposition that even though committed to benefit the corporation, illegal acts may amount to a breach of fiduciary duty in New York. In *Roth*, the managing director of an amusement park company had allegedly used corporate funds to purchase the silence of persons who threatened to complain about unlawful Sunday operation of the park. Recovery from the defendant director was sustained on the ground that the money was an illegal payment:

> For reasons of public policy, we are clearly of the opinion that payments of corporate funds for such purposes as those disclosed in this case must be condemned, and officers of a corporation making them held to a strict accountability, and be compelled to refund the amounts so wasted for the benefit of stockholders. . . . To hold any other rule would be establishing a dangerous precedent, tacitly countenancing the wasting of corporate funds for purposes of corrupting public morals. *Id.* at 346, 118 N.Y.S. at 353.

The plaintiffs' complaint in the instant case alleges a similar "waste" of $1.5 million through an illegal campaign contribution.

Abrams v. *Allen*, 297 N.Y. 52, 74 N.E.2d 305 (1947), reflects an affirmation by the New York Court of Appeals of the principle of *Roth* that directors must be restrained from engaging in activities which are against public policy. In *Abrams* the court held that a cause of action was stated by an allegation in a derivative complaint that the directors of Remington Rand, Inc., had relocated corporate plants and curtailed production solely for the purpose of intimidating and punishing employees for their involvement in a labor dispute. The Court of Appeals acknowledged that, "depending on the circumstances," proof of the allegations in the complaint might sustain recovery, *inter alia,* under the rule that directors are liable for corporate loss caused by the commission of an "unlawful or immoral act." *Id.* at 55, 74 N.E.2d at 306. In support of its holding, the court noted that the closing of factories for the purpose alleged was opposed to the public policy of the state and nation as embodied in the New York Labor Law and the National Labor Relations Act. *Id.* at 56, 74 N.E.2d at 307.

The alleged violation of the federal prohibition against corporate political contributions not only involves the corporation in criminal activity but similarly contravenes a policy of Congress clearly enunciated in 18 U.S.C. § 610. That statute and its predecessor reflect congressional efforts: (1) to destroy the influence of corporations over elections through financial contributions and (2) to check the practice of using corporate funds to benefit

political parties without the consent of the stockholders. . . .

. . .

Since plaintiffs have alleged actual damage to the corporation from the transaction in the form of the loss of a $1.5 million increment to AT&T's treasury, we conclude that the complaint does state a claim upon which relief can be granted sufficient to withstand a motion to dismiss.

. . .

The order of the district court will be reversed and the case remanded for further proceedings consistent with this opinion.

Case Questions

1. What is the legal effect of this decision? Did this case hold that the business judgment rule could not be used as a defense or as a complete defense?

2. If the plaintiffs can prove at trial that the failure to press collection of the debt was intended as a gift to the DNC, then what result would you expect? If AT&T can prove that the failure to collect the debt was a result of a judgment that it was no longer legally collectible, then what result would you expect?

3. If the plaintiffs win on a retrial, would you expect the director-defendants to be indemnified by AT&T?

The business judgment rule does *insulate* management, generally speaking, when business decisions are made in good faith. Exactly what is good faith? Is it simply the absence of bad faith or are there more affirmative duties that go to creating good faith? A review of the pertinent literature and a selection of cases suggest that "good faith" means simply the absence of bad faith. That is, under most circumstances, in order to recover for a breach of the duty of care, a shareholder suing on behalf of the injured corporation will have to prove bad faith in the exercise of management discretion.

Lack of Causation

There is an additional problem in this area of corporation law, and it relates to the nature of the lawsuit that is brought. These cases of "mismanagement" are essentially negligence cases, so one must prove the duty of care and its breach, *and* the fact that the breach *caused* the resulting injury or damage claimed in the complaint. If an enterprise has failed, it is very difficult to prove not only the measure of damages but that a specific act of mismanagement or lack of a duty of care caused the failure.

For example, in the classic case, *Barnes* v. *Andrews*, 298 F. 614 (1924), the court found that a director had breached his duty of care toward the corporation by failing to attend board meetings and failing to keep himself informed about corporate affairs. He made a slight attempt at keeping informed but this was only to ask a top official of the corporation how things were going. Judge Learned Hand phrased the duty as follows and then reasoned that more than the breach of duty was needed:

> It is not enough to content oneself with general answers that the business looks promising and that all seems prosperous. Andrews was bound, certainly as the months wore on, to inform himself of what was going on with some particularity, and, if he had done so, he would have learned that there were delays in getting into production which were putting the enterprise in most serious peril. It is entirely clear from his letters of April 14, 1920, and June 12, 1920, that he had made no effort to keep advised of the actual conduct of the corporate affairs, but had allowed himself to be carried along as a figurehead, in complete reliance upon Maynard [the president]. In spite of his own substantial investment in the company, which I must assume was as dear to him as it would be to other men, his position required of him more than this. Having accepted a post of confidence, he was charged with an active duty to learn whether the company was moving to production, and why it was not, and to consider, as best he might, what could be done to avoid the conflicts among the personnel, or their incompetence, which was slowly bleeding it to death.
>
>   Therefore I cannot acquit Andrews of misprision of his office, though his integrity is unquestioned. The plaintiff must, however, go further than to show that he should have been more active in his duties. This cause of action rests upon a tort, as much though it be a tort of omission as though it had rested upon a positive act. The plaintiff must accept the burden of showing that the performance of the defendant's duties would have avoided loss, and what loss it would have avoided. I pressed Mr. Alger to show me a case in which the courts have held that a director could be charged generally with the collapse of a business in respect of which he had been inattentive, and I am not aware that he has found one. . . .
>
>   When the corporate funds have been illegally lent, it is a fair inference that a protest would have stopped the loan, and the director's neglect caused the loss. But when a business fails from general mismanagement, business incapacity, or bad judgment, how is it possible to say that a single director could have made the company successful, or how much in dollars he could have saved? Before this cause can go to a master, the plaintiff must show that, had Andrews done his full duty, he could have made the company prosper, or at least could have broken its fall. He must show what sum he could have saved the company. Neither of these has he made any effort to do. [*Barnes* v. *Andrews*, 298 F. 614 at 616 (1924)]

Thus, liability for mismanagement is very difficult to establish. One writer, reflecting on the decisions in this area, has said that the applicable principles are "often loosely stated and indiscriminately combined in the same decision. Consequently . . . no decision on the subject of liability of corporate directors for negligence . . . stands for more than the result reached on the particular facts and that precedents are of little value."[15]

Breach of Duty in Special Circumstances

Courts have not been hesitant to impose liability on directors or management when the corporation involved was a bank or similar institution in which public trust is absolutely essential. One might say that the duties of due care are more pronounced and more explicit when one manages a bank or other financial institution. The following case is one of the few where liability has been imposed on management for a lack of due care. Note that not only were the corporations involved financial institutions, but the amount of the loss was fairly certain and traceable to the breach of the duty of care.

LITWIN v. *ALLEN*
25 N.Y.S. 2d667 (1940)

These actions are derivative stockholders' actions brought on behalf of persons owning 36 shares of the stock of Guaranty Trust Company of New York out of 900,000 shares outstanding. The defendants are directors and the estates of deceased directors of Guaranty Trust Company of New York (hereinafter referred to as the Bank or Trust Company) and its wholly owned subsidiary, now in liquidation, Guaranty Company of New York (hereinafter referred to as the Company or Guaranty Company), together with members of the banking firm of J.P. Morgan & Co.

I shall now proceed to consider generally the rules to be applied in determining the liability of directors. It has sometimes been said that directors are trustees. If this means that directors in the performance of their duties stand in a fiduciary relationship to the company, that statement is essentially correct. . . . "The directors are bound by all those rules of conscientious fairness, morality, and honesty in purpose which the law imposes as the guides for those who are under fiduciary obligations and responsibilities. They are held, in official action, to the extreme measure of candor,

unselfishness, and good faith. Those principles are rigid, essential, and salutary." . . .

It is clear that a director owes loyalty and allegiance to the company—a loyalty that is undivided and an allegiance that is influenced in action by no consideration other than the welfare of the corporation. Any adverse interest of a director will be subjected to a scrutiny rigid and uncompromising. He may not profit at the expense of his corporation and in conflict with its rights; he may not for personal gain divert unto himself the opportunities which in equity and fairness belong to his corporation. He is required to use his independent judgment. In the discharge of his duties a director must, of course, act honestly and in good faith, but that is not enough. He must also exercise some degree of skill and prudence and diligence.

. . .

It has been said that a director is required to conduct the business of the corporation with the same degree of fidelity and care as an ordinarily prudent man would exercise in the management of his own affairs of like magnitude and importance. General rules, however, are not altogether helpful. In the last analysis, whether or not a director has discharged his duty, whether or not he has been negligent, depends upon the facts and circumstances of a particular case, the kind of corporation involved, is size and financial resources, the magnitude of the transaction, and the immediacy of the problem presented. A director is called upon "to bestow the care and skill" which the situation demands. . . . Undoubtedly, a director of a bank is held to stricter accountability than the director of an ordinary business corporation. A director of a bank is entrusted with the funds of depositors, and the stockholders look to him for protection from the imposition of personal liability. . . . But clairvoyance is not required even of a bank director. The law recognizes that the most conservative director is not infallible, and that he will make mistakes, but if he uses that degree of care ordinarily exercised by prudent bankers he will be absolved from liability although his opinion may turn out to have been mistaken and his judgment faulty.

. . .

This transaction involves the participation by the Trust Company or Guaranty Company or both, to the extent of $3,000,000, in a purchase of Missouri Pacific Convertible debentures on October 16, 1930, through the firm of J.P. Morgan & Co. at par, with an option to the seller, Alleghany Corporation to repurchase them at the same price at any time within six months.

In the fall of 1930, the question of putting Alleghany Corporation in funds to the extent of $10,500,000 was first broached. Alleghany had purchased certain terminal properties in Kansas City and St. Joseph, Missouri, and the balance of the purchase price, amounting to slightly in excess of $10,000,000 and interest, had to be paid by October 16. Alleghany needed money to make this payment. Because of the borrowing limitation in Alleghany's charter (which limitation had been reached or exceeded in October 1930) Alleghany was unable to borrow the money. . . .

Not being able to make a loan, the way that Alleghany could raise the necessary funds was by sale of some of the securities that it held. Among them was a large block of about $23,500,000 of Missouri Pacific convertible 5½ percent debentures. . . .

The Van Sweringens suggested that $10,000,000 of these bonds be sold to J.P. Morgan & Co. for cash at par, the latter to give an option to Alleghany to buy them back within six months for the price paid. If the transaction were carried through on that basis, namely, a sale by Alleghany with an option to them to repurchase at the same price, the same purpose would be accomplished, for Alleghany at any rate, as if a loan had been made.

The defendants testified that they were informed that the Van Sweringens insisted upon the option to repurchase within six months in order that there might be no possibility of their loss of control of Missouri Pacific through Alleghany, since these bonds were convertible and the privilege to do so might be exercised by third parties in the event of a distribution of these bonds in the market; this, despite the fact that the common stock of Missouri Pacific was then quoted in the neighborhood of 44, while the conversion price was 100.

. . .

The Trust Company took delivery of the bonds on October 16, and paid for them by its check for $3,075,625, which included accrued interest. . . .

At or shortly before the time that the Trust Company made its written commitment to J.P. Morgan & Co. to participate in the bond purchase, the Guaranty Company committed itself to the Trust Company to take up the bonds from the Trust Company at the end of the six months' period, on April 16, 1931, for the same price that the Trust Company paid, that is, par and interest, if Alleghany failed to exercise its option to repurchase.

There is no evidence in this case of any improper influence or domination of the directors or officers of the Trust Company or of the Guaranty Company by J.P. Morgan & Co. . . . Moreover, there is no evidence to indicate that any of the defendants' officers or directors acted in bad faith or profited or attempted to profit or gain personally by reason of any phase of this transaction. . . .

. . .

The decline in the market continued. On October 23, 1930, when the Executive Committee of the Trust Company approved the transaction the Missouri Pacific bonds were at 103 7/8. On November 5, 1930, when the Board of Directors of the Trust Company gave its approval, the bonds sold for 102 7/8, and on November 18, 1930, when the board of the Guaranty Company approved its commitment, the bonds had dropped to 98 5/8. At the end of the six months' period, on April 16, 1931, the bonds sold at 86 high and 81 low (the quotations being for the week ending April 18), and Guaranty Company took them over from the Trust Company at par and accrued interest and carried them on its books as an investment.

. . .

Considering it a purchase by the Trust Company at par, with an option to the seller to repurchase for the same price within a period of six months, at which time if the option was not exercised the wholly owned subsidiary of the Trust Company would take over the securities at the price paid, the question is whether such option agreement was ultra vires. . . .

There is no case directly in point. Courts have passed upon the legality or enforceability of contracts under which a bank sold securities or property and gave the purchaser an option to resell such securities or property to the bank upon stated terms. . . .

In all of the foregoing cases . . . an option of resale given by a bank to a purchaser was condemned as illegal and unenforceable. . . .

The defendants contend that there is a fundamental difference between an option to compel the bank to buy back securities which the cases cited condemned as ultra vires and unenforceable against the bank and the option in this case to compel the bank to re-sell securities which it has bought and holds. They point out that the cases emphasize the impairment of the liquidity of the bank; that while the liquidity of the bank may be impaired because it is obligated to pay cash and take back securities it has previously sold, the liquidity of the bank is not impaired, in fact it is strengthened when the bank is obligated to take cash and give back the securities it has previously purchased.

. . .

Although, as I have said, there is no case precisely in point, it would seem that if it is against public policy for a bank, anxious to dispose of some of its securities, to agree to buy them back at the same price, it is even more so where a bank purchases securities and gives the seller the option to buy them back at the same price, thereby incurring the entire risk of loss with no possibility of gain other than the interest derived from the securities during the period that the bank holds them. Here, if the market price of the securities should rise, the holder of the repurchase option would exercise it in order to recover his securities from the bank at the lower price at which he sold them to the bank. If the market price should fall, the seller holding the option will not exercise it and the bank will sustain the loss. Thus, any benefit of a sharp rise in the price of the securities is assured the seller and any risk of heavy loss is inevitably assumed by the bank. . . .

. . .

Plaintiffs urge that if the purchase subject to the option is found to be ultra vires, that finding, in and of itself, imposes absolute liability upon the defendants. It is doubtful whether any such strict rule would apply where directors as here, act honestly and particularly where no violation of a statute is involved. . . .

Directors are not in the position of trustees of an express trust who, regardless of good faith, are personally liable for losses arising from an infraction of their trust deed. . . . If liability is to be imposed on these directors it should rest on a more solid foundation. I find liability in this transaction because the entire arrangement was so improvident, so risky, so unusual and unnecessary as to be contrary to fundamental conceptions of prudent banking practices. . . . Honesty alone does not suffice; the honesty of the directors in this case is unquestioned. But there must be more than honesty—there must be diligence, and that means care and prudence, as well. This transaction, it has been said, was unusual; it was unique, yet there is nothing in the record to indicate that the advice of counsel was sought. It is not surprising that a precedent cannot be found dealing with such a situation.

What sound reason is there for a bank, desiring to make an investment, short term or otherwise, to buy securities under an arrangement whereby any appreciation will inure to the benefit of the seller and any loss will be borne by the bank? The five and one-half point differential is no answer. It does not meet the fundamental objection that whatever loss there is would have to be borne by the Bank and whatever gain would go to the customer. There is more here than a question of business judgment as to which men might well differ. The directors plainly failed in this instance to bestow the care which the situation demanded. Unless we are to do away entirely with the doctrine that directors of a bank are liable for negligence in administering its affairs liability should be imposed in connection with this transaction.

. . .

Whichever way we look at this transaction, therefore, it was so improvident, so dangerous, so unusual and so contrary to ordinary prudent banking practice as to subject the directors who approved it to liability in a derivative stockholders' action.

Having determined that the transaction in litigation is such as to impose liability upon the participating defendants, the next question is what part of the loss can be attributed to the improper transaction? . . .

The real issue as to damages is whether the directors should be liable for the total loss suffered when the bonds were ultimately sold, approximately an 81 percent loss, or only for that portion of the loss which accrued within the six months option period, making allowance for a period thereafter during which defendants could make reasonable and diligent efforts to sell the bonds. . . .

I believe that as to the decline of the bonds after April 16, 1931, there is no causal connection with the option which had expired on that date. A director is not liable for loss or damage other than what was proximately caused by his own acts or omissions in breach of his duty. . . . The portion of the present transaction which is tainted with improvidence and negligence is the repurchase option. . . . Once the option had expired, there was nothing to prevent the directors of the Company, which had taken over the bonds in accordance with its agreement, from selling them. Any loss on the bonds which was incurred after the option had expired on April 16, 1931, was occasioned as a result of the directors' independent business judgment in holding them thereafter. The further loss should not be laid at the door of the improper but already expired repurchase option. . . .

Therefore, defendants are only liable for the loss attributable to the improper repurchase option itself, and this option ceased to be the motivating cause of the loss within a reasonable time after April 16, 1931. The price of the bonds for the week ending April 18, 1931, was 86 high and 81 low and closing. The matter will be referred to a Referee for assessment of damages to determine what price could have been obtained for these bonds if defendants had proceeded to sell them after April 16, 1931. . . .

Case Questions

1. Does this decision impose a more stringent standard on directors than does the *Barnes* v. *Andrews* case?

2. A director of a bank is held to a higher standard than a director of an ordinary business corporation. If the transaction in the instant case had involved not a bank but an ordinary corporation, would the directors' business judgment defense have been successful?

3. What reasons could a bank, conservative by its very nature, have for entering a transaction where it bore all the risk and the other party enjoyed all the advantages?

Indemnification of Directors and Officers

Who bears a director's or officer's expenses incurred in defending actions in a lawsuit? Are such expenses a personal risk that accompany the position? Should they be reimbursed if their defense is successful? What is to be done if an out-of-court settlement is reached, which is a common occurrence? The problem is to balance the interests of the corporation vis-à-vis its directors and officers. It seems only fair that the directors and officers should be reimbursed for their reasonable expenses if they acted in good faith and did not breach any duties owed the corporation. So, Section 5 of the MBCA provides:

§ 5. Indemnification of Officers, Directors, Employees and Agents

(a) A corporation shall have power to indemnify any person who was or is a party or is threatened to be made a party to any threatened, pending or completed action, suit or proceeding, whether civil, criminal, administrative or investigative (other than an action by or in the right of the corporation) by reason of the fact that he is or was a director, officer, employee or agent of the corporation, or is or was serving at the request of the corporation as a director, officer, employee or agent of another corporation, partnership, joint venture, trust or other enterprise, against expenses (including attorney's fees), judgments, fines and amounts paid in settlement actually and reasonably incurred by him in connection with such action, suit or proceeding if he acted in good faith and in a manner he reasonably believed to be in or not opposed to the best interests of the corporation, and, with respect to any criminal action or proceeding, had no reasonable cause to believe his conduct was unlawful. The termination of any action, suit or proceeding by judgment, order, settlement, conviction, or upon a plea of nolo contendere or its equivalent, shall not, of itself, create a presumption that the person did not act in good faith and in a manner which he reasonably believed to be in or not opposed to the best interests of the corporation, and, with respect to any criminal action or proceeding, had reasonable cause to believe that his conduct was unlawful.

. . .

(b) Any indemnification under subsections (a) or (b) (unless ordered by a court) shall be made by the corporation only as authorized in the specific case upon a determination that indemnification of the director, officer, employee or agent is proper in the circumstances because he has met the applicable standard of conduct set forth in subsections (a) or (b). Such determination shall be made (1) by the board of directors by a majority vote of a quorum consisting of directors who were not parties to such action, suit or proceeding, or (2) if such a quorum is not obtainable, or, even if obtainable a quorum of disinterested directors so directs, by independent legal counsel in a written opinion, or (3) by the shareholders.

All 50 states, the District of Columbia, Puerto Rico, and the Virgin Islands have enacted some form of statute providing for the indemnification of corporate officers and directors and, in a few instances, other corporate agents and employees.[16] In addition to state statutes, many corporations provide for indemnification in their bylaws. In 1975, Section 15 of Pan Am's bylaws read as follows:

> To the full extent permitted by law, the Corporation shall indemnify each person made or threatened to be made a party to any civil or criminal action or proceeding by reason of the fact he, or his testator or intestate, is or was a director or officer of the Corporation or served any other corporation of any type or kind, domestic or foreign, in any capacity at the request of the Corporation.

Today, there is a pronounced trend toward the liberalization of indemnification of directors and officers.[17] This liberalization has been lamented as a matter of policy and is, to some extent, controversial. One wonders at the value of a developing standard of a duty of care for management when there is a corresponding development to use the corporate treasury to pay judgments against directors and officers. One scholar has commented that:

> The objective of the 1967 revision of the Delaware statute on indemnification is apparently not to place limits on the protection of guilty management, but to make explicit the power of management to indemnify itself in situations where, under the original artless enactment of an untutored legislature, courts and commentators had questioned the propriety of indemnification.[18]

However, some scholars see this trend as good since it helps insure that talented people will continue to want to serve on boards of directors; moreover, so long as there is a trend toward the MBCA concept of allowing indemnification only where a director or officer acted in good faith and in a manner reasonably believed to be in the best interests of the corporation, there is no encouragement of undesirable management behavior.[19]

Director and Officer (D&O) Insurance

D&O insurance has become very prominent in the last 15 years. It is needed because even if a director or an officer is indemnified for a judgment, this indemnification could put a severe strain on the corporate treasury if the judgment were large. Or, bankruptcy could intervene prior to the termination of litigation.

What is contained in a typical D&O policy? The policy will be written to cover the wrongful or negligent acts of the corporate directors and named officers (of both the parent and subsidiaries). If a corporate bylaw is written in broad language reimbursing individuals outside the above category, added insurance, with its extra premium, must be purchased. The policy will typically contain exclusions for such matters as: (1) a fine or penalty imposed by law; (2) antitrust violations; (3) profits derived from violations of § 16(b) of the securities laws; and (4) defamation.[20] Of course, the policy will contain a dollar limitation and typically a deductible; also other insurance will be deemed to provide primary coverage. The latter prevents the corporation from receiving multiple recoveries on a single claim. The policy will cover claims filed during the policy life even though the wrongful act occurred prior to the commencement of the policy.

Since a D&O policy will cover claims for incidents occurring prior to the policy's starting date, what if the corporation concealed facts about a prior incident on its insurance application? Can the insurer raise this as a defense to avoid paying the claim? At this time, the answers to these questions are uncertain. These issues are currently being litigated. The D&O insurance carriers for Penn Central are attempting to rescind their policy and return the premiums. The insurers assert that the policy is null and void because of alleged fraudulent concealment of certain facts by Penn Central in procurement of the policy.

For practical reasons, D&O insurance may not be available at a reasonable cost to all corporations. The insurer obviously attempts to measure the risk involved in insuring a particular company. An established corporation with substantial assets and a good history of earnings should experience little trouble in acquiring a policy. A newly formed corporation, a closely held corporation, a corporation dominated by a small group of shareholders, or a conglomerate may face substantial difficulty. Each one presents risks that are hard to measure or risks that an insurer may not be willing to bear.

This section and the three that follow present material on the subclassifications of the major duty of directors and management to act in the best
interests of the corporation. These subclassifications are not distinct, nor
is the list here complete. The variety of circumstances in which one's
business interests may potentially conflict with another's is endless. We
have arranged these classifications from the simplest and most concrete to
the most complex and abstract circumstances in which these duties exist.

Dealing or contracting with one's own corporation does not appear to
be an unusual circumstance and would seem to be more prevalent in close
corporations. *The Wall Street Journal* reported, for example, that the president of Work Wear Corporation together with several other officials of
the company dabbled in real estate. Their group owned the corporate
headquarters, the employee parking lot, and the manufacturing plant, all
leased to Work Wear for $80,000 a year; a Cleveland laundry plant leased
at $71,200; a 70-percent-owned Philadelphia plant leased at $63,000 a
year; the Los Angeles executive office leased at $153,600 a year; and
another plant leased at $42,000.[21] This kind of transaction must be
spelled out in materials distributed to shareholders each year, but how is
one to judge whether this kind of transaction is fair? Those involved in
these types of transactions defend them on the grounds that they deal
with their corporations on a basis that is at least fair as that provided by
the market. Of course, it is always best to do business with those you know
and trust. Maybe this helps explain the prevalence of the practice. This
practice of Work Wear is, claims the *Journal*, relatively typical. "At scores
of companies, managers and their private interests regularly do business
with the companies they manage, or with companies with which the men
are closely associated."[22]

Sometimes, however, these practices can prove very embarrassing.
North American Corporation, a Columbus, Ohio, insurance holding company, noted in its proxy materials some years ago that three loans made to
companies related to a former director were in default and that certain of
the director's interests were in bankruptcy proceedings.[23]

The MBCA approves of such dealing if it is done in a certain way. It
provides three alternative ways that directors may contract with the corporation:

§ 41. Director Conflicts of Interest

No contract or other transaction between a corporation and one or more
of its directors or any other corporation, firm, organization or entity in
which one or more of its directors are directors or officers or are
financially interested, shall be either void or voidable because of such
relationship or interest or because such director or directors are present
at the meeting of the board of directors or a committee thereof which

authorizes, approves or ratifies such contract or transaction or because his or their votes are counted for such purpose, if:

(a) the fact of such relationship or interest is disclosed or known to the board of directors or committee which authorizes, approves or ratifies the contract or transaction by a vote or consent sufficient for the purpose without counting the votes or consents of such interested directors; or

(b) the fact of such relationship or interest is disclosed or known to the shareholders entitled to vote and they authorize, approve or ratify such contract or transaction by vote or written consent; or

(c) the contract or transaction is fair and reasonable to the corporation.

Common or interested directors may be counted in determining the presence of a quorum at a meeting of the board of directors or a committee thereof which authorizes, approves or ratifies such contract or transaction.

In addition to the above statutory provisions, the MBCA and some state statutes permit a corporation to lend money to an officer or director if the loan benefits the corporation. On this point, the MBCA provides:

§ 47. Loans to Employees and Directors

A corporation shall not lend money to or use its credit to assist its directors without authorization in the particular case by its shareholders, but may lend money to and use its credit to assist any employee of the corporation or of a subsidiary, including any such employee who is a director of the corporation, if the board of directors decides that such loan or assistance may benefit the corporation.

Some states do prohibit loans to directors and officers. Section 41(b) of the Illinois statute absolutely forbids loans: "No loans shall be made by a corporation to its officers or directors, and no loans shall be made by a corporation secured by its shares." Section 42.8 of the Illinois Act declares a violation of this to be a criminal offense.

These statutes handle potential conflicts of interest by requiring disclosure of all material facts or by requiring fairness and reasonableness. Reading the MBCA, Section 41, does leave some questions, though. Because the statute uses the disjunctive word "or" after each section, it may be construed to permit, so long as the board of directors votes for it, a contract between a director and the corporation (to sell some property of the director's to the corporation, for example) that may be of questionable fairness. The dominant position of state statutes today is to allow director contracts if there has been disclosure of the director's interest.[24]

Interlocking Directorates

The issue of conflicts of interest and self-dealing are complicated by the existence of interlocking directorates. Suppose Director X sits on the boards of both Company A and Company B. Companies A and B now wish to do business with each other. Not only may X have a self-interest, but fiduciary duties are now owed to two corporations that have potentially conflicting interests.

Although it is a 1918 case, *Globe Woolen Co.* v. *Utica Gas & Elec. Co.*, 121 N.E. 378, remains the leading case on interlocking directorates. An individual by the name of Maynard was a director, officer, and large shareholder of Globe. He was also a director, but not a shareholder, of Utica. Globe operated a woolen mill in Utica, where the defendant generated and sold electricity. For several years the defendant had studied the possibility of supplying electricity for the operation of the plaintiff's plants in place of steam. An agreement was reached establishing a certain per-kilowatthour price. The contracts also guaranteed the plaintiff a savings of $300 per month on its heat, light, and power as compared with the corresponding month in the year previous to the switch to electricity. The contracts had a duration of five years with a renewal option of another five years. The required plant installations cost Globe $21,000. The defendant had miscalculated Globe's power requirements; compounding the problem were changes in Globe's production methods that increased electrical consumption. As a result, by February 1911 the defendant had supplied Globe with approximately $60,000 of electricity, had received no money, and owed Globe $11,000 under its guarantee. When the defendant attempted to void the contract Globe sued for specific performance. The court refused to enforce the contract but did require that Utica reimburse Globe for its installation expenses.

When the contracts came up for approval by the respective boards, Maynard introduced the resolution but neither spoke on the matter nor voted. Globe sought to uphold the validity of the contracts on this ground. The court pointed out that the absence of his vote gave the transaction the presumption of propriety but that a challenge to it would lead to a probe beneath its surface. The court remarked that a "dominating influence may be exerted in other ways than by a vote. . . . A beneficiary, about to plunge into a ruinous course of dealing, may be betrayed by silence as well as by the spoken word." Maynard had negotiated the contract and had dealt with his subordinates in both companies. The board members knew that he had framed the transaction and, in his presence, they were assured of its justice and equitability. The court characterized the unfairness of the contracts as "startling" and their consequences as "disastrous." In the words of the court:

> The mischief consists in this: That the guaranty has not been limited by a statement of the conditions under which the mills are to be run. No matter

how large the business, no matter how great the increase in the price of labor or of fuel, no matter what the changes in the nature or the proportion of the products, no matter even though there be extensions of the plant, the defendant has pledged its word that for ten years there will be a saving of $600 a month, $300 for each mill, $7,200 a year. As a result of that pledge it has supplied the plaintiff with electric current for nothing, and owes, if the contract stands, about $11,000 for the privilege. These elements of unfairness Mr. Maynard must have known, if indeed his knowledge be material. He may not have known how great the loss would be. He may have trusted to the superior technical skill of Mr. Greenidge to compute with approximate accuracy the comparative cost of steam and electricity. But he cannot have failed to know that he held a one-sided contract which left the defendant at his mercy. He was not blind to the likelihood that in a term of ten years there would be changes in the business. The swiftness with which some of the changes followed permits the inference that they were premeditated.

In holding the contracts voidable at the election of the defendant, the opinion ended on the following note:

> We hold, therefore, that the refusal to vote does not nullify as of course an influence and predominance exerted without a vote. We hold that the constant duty rests on a trustee to seek no harsh advantage to the detriment of his trust, but rather to protest and renounce if through the blindness of those who treat with him he gains what is unfair. And, because there is evidence that in the making of these contracts that duty was ignored, the power of equity was fittingly exercised to bring them to an end.

While direct regulation of corporations is within the states' domain, a substantial amount of federal legislation interlaces with it. The antitrust, securities, labor, and tax laws all bear a significant impact on corporations. Section 8 of the Clayton Act, 15 U.S.C.A. § 19, provides:

> No person at the same time shall be a director in any two or more corporations, any one of which has capital, surplus, and undivided profits aggregating more than $1,000,000, engaged in whole or in part in commerce . . . if such corporations are or shall have been theretofore, by virtue of their business and location of operations, competitors, so that the elimination of competition by agreement between them would constitute a violation of any of the provisions of any of the antitrust laws.

Notice that the statute does not prohibit: (1) vertical interlocks between a parent and subsidiary or a supplier and a manufacturer or (2) a circuitous interlock such as: (a) Corporation A, a noncompetitor, has one of its directors on the board of Corporation B and another on Corporation C, with both B and C being competitors, or (b) B and C are competitors and each has one of its directors on the board of A, a noncompetitor.

Today, especially in large corporations, interlocking directorates are a fact of life. Figure 12-1 was taken from a 1970s study of such interlocks. Each line represents one director.

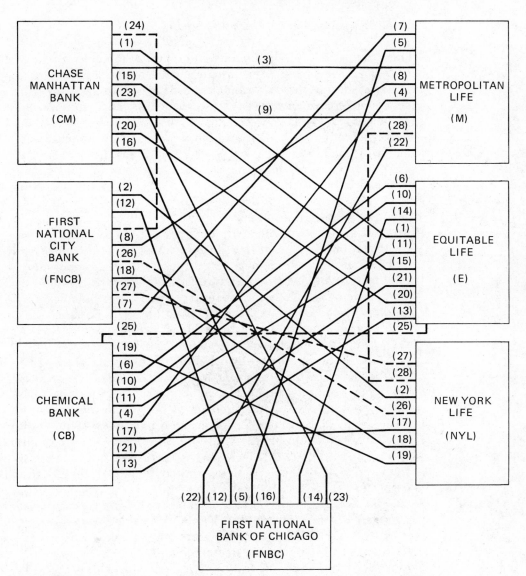

FIGURE 12-1   Interlocking directorates among the core financial institutions in the Rockefeller Group.

(*Source:* From J. Knowles, "The Rockefeller Financial Group," *Supercorporation,* R. Andreano, ed., Warner Modular Publications, Module #343.)

Using Corporate Assets for Self-Benefit

There are at least two dimensions of this part of the duty to act in the best interests of the corporation. The first is that corporate assets themselves such as cash, contracts, etc. cannot be used to benefit a director, officer, or member of management. This is so even if the corporation benefits. In the famous case of *Guth* v. *Loft,* 23 Del. Ch. 255, 5 A2d503 (1939), Guth was president of Loft, a corporation engaged in the manufacturing and selling of candies, syrups, beverages, and foodstuffs. Loft made large purchases of Coca-Cola, so management desired to obtain discounts on quantity purchases of Coke. Coke gave such discounts to other purchasers, but denied the discount to Loft. So Guth, as an officer of Loft, explored the purchase of Pepsi. He discovered that Pepsi was going bankrupt and made arrangements to buy the formula for Pepsi.

In July of 1931, Guth, as an individual, made a contract with the owner of the Pepsi trademark, Megargel, to form a corporation owned half by Guth and half by Megargel, and this company would own the Pepsi trademark. Thereafter, Megargel and Guth both were short of working capital, so from 1931 to 1935 Guth used his position as president of Loft to help the Pepsi enterprise. He used Loft's plant, facilities, materials, credit, and employees to benefit the Pepsi trademark. But, at the same time, Loft was apparently benefiting because it was buying Pepsi at a much lower price than it was buying Coke. However, Loft did begin to lose money, some of which was attributable to not serving Coke at its outlets. Ultimately, new management at Loft found out that Guth controlled or had access to the Pepsi shares through his ownership of Grace, a company to which the shares had been transferred. The Chancellor, in a suit in equity, declared that because of the use of Loft's assets, etc., the ownership of all of the Pepsi shares owned or controlled by Guth were to be put in Loft's name.

The second dimension to the problem of using corporate assets occurs when an officer or employee combines his or her own talents with the assets of the corporation to create something of value. This general issue was discussed in the agency materials and should be reviewed at this point. (See Part II.) Below we have reproduced three short cases. The first is just a definition of the shop rights doctrine. This case is followed by a longer one in which the doctrine is applied. The final case of the three examines a variation of this doctrine involving the use of confidential information. The law proscribes an employee from using confidential information for his or her own benefit. The federal securities laws, § 16(b) and Rule 10-b-5, explicitly forbid the use of such information in certain transactions involving the company's securities. The employee is also barred from passing confidential information to a competitor of the employer. If it is transferred, the employee must pay back any profit derived and the competitor will be enjoined from further use of the information, in addition to compensating the former employer for damages suffered thereby. The wrong is using the confidential information; it is irrelevant whether the corporation sustained damage. Confidential information is just that, *confidential*. It is information that is not readily available to the public. It can take numerous forms, including customer lists, salary information, trade secrets, the marketing strategy for a new product, schematic drawings for new production machinery, etc.

HOBBS v. *UNITED STATES*
376 F. 2d 488 (1967)

The classic shop rights doctrine ordains that when an employee makes and reduces to practice an invention on his employer's time, using his employer's tools and services of other employees, the employer is the recipient of an implied, nonexclusive, royalty-free license.

Shop rights generally arise only when there is a direct employer-employee relationship.

At least two considerations underlie the shop rights doctrine. First, it seems only fair that when an employee has used his employer's time and equipment to make an invention, the employer should be able to use the device without paying a royalty. Second, under the doctrine of estoppel if an employee encourages his employer to use an invention, and then stands by and allows him to construct and operate the new device without making any claim for compensation or royalties, it would not be equitable to allow the employee later to assert a claim for royalties or other compensation.

Part of the reasoning behind the first consideration is that the employer is in a position to reward the inventive employee through salary increases, promotions, bonuses and the like.

WELLINGTON PRINT WORKS, INC. v. *MAGID*
242 F. Supp. 614 (1965)

This is an action for a permanent injunction to determine whether the plaintiff, a family-owned corporation, has an ownership interest in inventions or discoveries of the defendant, a member of the family, and a former employee of the plaintiff corporation.

David B. Magid (D. B. Magid) is the father of the defendant, Eugene A. Magid. From 1955 to March 15, 1961, D. B. Magid was the principal and only shareholder of the plaintiff corporation. Eugene A. Magid was President . . . from 1955 until March 15, 1961, and D. B. Magid was Secretary-Treasurer during this period.

On March 15, 1961, D. B. Magid became President of Wellington; Eugene was appointed Treasurer, and a younger brother, Robert P. Magid, became Secretary. This arrangement continued until March 21, 1962.

Wellington had been acquired by D. B. Magid in 1949, and he sent the defendant, Eugene A. Magid, to Wellington to be his "eyes" to protect the family's interests. As previously stated, Eugene was President until 1961 with no definitely defined duties except to sign checks, audit purchase orders and settle labor disputes.

While employed at Wellington Eugene A. Magid apparently accounted to no one except his father. He set his own hours, and no one restricted his activities in the plant. Although Eugene was not a technically trained person he began to experiment with techniques for superimposing patterns on particular materials, and also, the laminating of the materials themselves.

During the year 1962, he began to devote considerable time to these experiments. Eugene submitted samples or "patches" of his work to his brother Robert and M. Danson, sales manager of Hartford. He also prepared diagrams of his inventions which reflected Wellington's machines. He also used Wellington's equipment and personnel to conduct his experiments which interrupted the normal assembly line production of the company. The time that he spent in these endeavors was not confined to the daylight hours alone, and he frequently ran samples on the machines during the two later shifts at the Wellington plant.

Initially, no one showed much interest in his samples until it became apparent that Eugene exhibited a natural talent in his inventive work. In fact, D. B. Magid expressed irritation when he was questioned by a son-in-law as to why Eugene was working such long hours. He said that if Eugene would stop playing around with the machines and do the work that he was supposed to perform, he could go home at a decent hour.

Hundreds of samples produced by Eugene were sent to the sales manager of Hartford and many of the new patterns produced by Eugene were sold. Of these numerous samples five particular discoveries which are the subject matter of this suit created great interest in Robert P. Magid. These five inventions had been submitted to Wellington's patent attorney for an opinion as to their patentability. He determined that three of the developments were patentable, and Eugene applied for patents on these discoveries.

In March of 1964, Eugene asked for commissions for the products which he had invented. Prior to this time he had not asked for

any additional compensation for his inventive efforts. Robert declined to authorize these commissions and directed Eugene to assign the patent applications on the inventions to Wellington. Eugene refused and on June 23, 1964, Robert P. Magid proffered a contract of employment to Eugene which required him to assign any patent applications to Wellington and that any future inventions would be the property of Wellington.

Eugene then met with D. B. Magid who told him to sign the contract or be fired, and also, that he must assign his patent applications to the plaintiff. Eugene refused to meet these terms, and on July 31, 1964, he was discharged.

The law is clear that absent a contrary understanding the mere existence of an employer-employee relationship does not entitle the employer to ownership of invention's of the employee even though the employee uses the time and facilities of the employer. However, if the employee does use his employer's time and facilities, the employer is entitled to a shop right in the invention. Such a shop right passes from the employee to his employer immediately upon the making of the invention by the employee. A shop right is limited to a nonexclusive right in the employer to practice the employee's invention.

The record in this case compels the conclusion that no agreement either express or implied existed between the plaintiff and the defendant, whereby the defendant was obligated to assign his inventions to the plaintiff.

However, we do conclude that because the defendant used his employer's time and facilities in developing these inventions that the plaintiff does have a non-exclusive license to practice them.

We reject the defendant's contention that because he experimented primarily on the late shifts that he was working on his own time and not Wellington's. When an employee receives a large salary of $25,000.00 a year and is an officer of a corporation his obligations do not cease at the close of normal business hours. Particularly is this true in a situation where the employer functions 24 hours a day. The method of production employed by Wellington in operating around the clock made the defendant's inventions possible.

Case Questions

1. Does the shop rights doctrine strike a fair balance between the employee-inventor and the employer?

2. Does the employer's shop right prevent the employee-inventor from granting a license to a competitor of the employer?

3. Would it be wise for a company to offer employment contracts, with a clause assigning all patent rights to the employer, to each of its employees?

4. Would the shop rights doctrine have an application to a university student who makes an important discovery during a chemistry lab experiment? Would it apply to a professor who was using the university laboratory?

BANCROFT-WHITNEY CO. v. *GLEN*
411 P.2d 921 (1966)

MOSK, Justice

During November 1961, Glen, without resigning or giving notice to plaintiff or its officers, directors, or shareholders, signed a contract with Bender Co. to become president of the contemplated western division, commencing on or about January 1, 1962. Beginning in July 1961 and thereafter, defendants joined in a concerted effort to obtain a staff of editors and other personnel for the proposed new western division and, using misrepresentations and half-truths, intentionally interfered with plaintiff's advantageous contractual relationships and surreptitiously sought to entice away carefully selected members of plaintiff's executive staff and working force. Using a full advantage the inside knowledge and confidential business information provided by Glen, who continued to occupy a position of trust with plaintiff, defendants solicited more than 20 officers, directors, and trained employees of plaintiff. On and subsequent to December 15, 1961, more than 15 persons, including officers, directors, researchers, and editors left plaintiff's employ without notice and entered the employ of the newly created western division of Bender Co. When the company qualified to do business as a foreign corporation in California on January 5, 1962, the great majority, if not all, of its employees were persons who had just previously worked for plaintiff under the supervision of Glen.

. . .

In analyzing the legal principles applicable in this case, it should be repeated that we are not concerned with the simple right of one competitor to offer the employees of another a job at more favorable terms than they presently enjoy or the right of an employee (or an officer of a corporation) to seek a better job. The question here is whether the president of a corporation is liable for the breach of his fiduciary duty because of the conduct described above relating to other employees of the corporation and whether, under these facts, those who hire the employees are guilty of unfair competition for acting in concert with the president.

Corporate officers and directors are not permitted to use their position of trust and confidence to further their private interests.

The mere fact that the officer makes preparations to compete before he resigns his office is not sufficient to constitute a breach of duty. It is the nature of his preparations which is significant.

It is beyond question that a corporate officer breaches his fiduciary duties when, with the purpose of facilitating the recruiting of the corporation's employees by a competitor, he supplies the competitor with a selective list of the corporation's employees who are, in his judgment, possessed of both ability and the personal characteristics desirable in an employee, together with the salary the corporation is paying the employee and a suggestion as to the salary the competitor should offer in order to be successful in recruitment. This conclusion is inescapable even if the information regarding salaries is not deemed to be confidential.

The *Restatement of Agency* provides that the rule prohibiting the disclosure of confidential information by an agent applies "not only to those communications which are stated to be confidential, but also to information which the agent should know his principal would not care to have revealed to others or used in competition with him. It applies to unique business methods of the employer, trade secrets, *lists of names*, and all other matters which are peculiarly known in the employer's business. It does not apply to matters of common knowledge in the community nor to special skill which the employee has acquired because of his employment." (Rest. 2d Agency, § 395, com. b.) The salaries paid by a corporation to its employees are not matters of common knowledge and, even among corporation employees, they are divulged only to those persons or organizations directly concerned with personnel matters or to responsible fiduciaries.

Defendants argue that the salary information is not confidential because the employees could have revealed their own salaries to Bender Co. or anyone else. It requires little talent to distinguish between a situation in which an individual voluntarily discloses his own salary to another and one in which the unpublished salary list of a group of prospective employees is revealed to a competitor for the purpose of facilitating the recruitment of the corporation's personnel.

It is clear from the evidence set forth above that Bender was aware of or ratified Glen's breach of his fiduciary duties in all but a few respects, that he cooperated with Glen in the breach, and that he received the benefits of Glen's infidelity. It cannot be said here, as was stated in another context . . . that Bender Co. did not "reap where it has not sown." Under all the circumstances, Bender and Bender Co. must be held liable for their part in Glen's breach of his fiduciary duties. They encouraged the sowing and reaped the benefit. They cannot now disclaim the burden.

Case Questions

1. Suppose an individual is employed in the tax department of an accounting firm. Over a period of years, because of his exposure to the tax problems of the firm's clients, he becomes an expert in the tax aspects of mergers. May he join a competing firm and put his tax expertise to work for their clients?

2. May an employee, an anticipation of taking a position with another company, solicit the business of his current employer's clients? On leaving his old employer, may he accept work from his old clients?

3. If a corporation is contemplating entering a new field or expanding its current geographic territory, is it wiser to build a staff from scratch or to raid the personnel of a competitor?

Corporate Opportunities

A slightly more abstract notion in corporation law than those presented in the sections just above is the idea that a director should not be able to take or convert a business "opportunity" that belongs to the corporation. This opportunity is not one in which the corporation has any contractual rights as such, nor is it one that accrues to the benefit of a director or officer because of the use of coporate funds. It is a circumstance from which the corporation could be expected to benefit and in which it may reasonably be expected to have an interest given its past practices and its purpose. If such an opportunity is presented to a director because of the director's position on the board, then the director should reject the opportunity. A director's fiduciary duty to the corporation requires that he or she avoid usurping or misappropriating business opportunities that the corporation should have a first right to.

Although this rule is relatively easy to state it is very difficult to apply. The following case is a classic in the field of corporate opportunities. Pay particular attention to how the court analyzes the problem. A three-step procedure is involved. First, the court defines the opportunity. Then the court attempts to define the corporate purpose, direction, or desire for being in business. Finally, it compares the opportunity to this corporate purpose. If the court had found the opportunity consistent with the corporate purpose, it probably would have declared that the opportunity was that of the corporation's.

JOHNSTON v. *GREENE*
121 A. 2d 919 (S. Ct., Del., 1956)

SOUTHERLAND, Chief Justice
The ultimate question in this case is the fairness of a transaction between a corporation and its president and dominating director. The court below held that he had appropriated for himself a corporate opportunity belonging to his corporation.

The pertinent facts, either uncontroverted or found by the Chancellor, are as follows:

Airfleets, Inc., is a Delaware corporation, organized in 1948 as a wholly owned subsidiary of Consolidated Vultee Aircraft Corporation (called "Convair"). Convair sometime thereafter distributed all of the Airfleets stock to its own stockholders. Atlas Corporation, an investment company, became Airfleets' largest single stockholder, owning about 18 percent of its stock. Upon the organization of Airfleets the defendant Odlum became and has since been its president, without compensation. Odlum is also the president of Atlas, owning or controlling about 11 percent of its stock. He is a man of varied business interests. At the time here material he also was chairman of the

Board of Directors of Convair, a director of United Fruit Company, a director of Wasatch Corporation, and a trustee of several foundations.

Airfleets was organized to finance aircraft that might be sold or leased to the air lines. This purpose was never carried out. Airfleets' first business venture was the sale of certain aircraft manufacturing plants, aircraft, and related assets that it had acquired from Convair. By the fall of 1951 it had nearly completed the sale of these assets, and was in a liquid position, with about $2,000,000 in cash. It also held marketable securities worth about $1,500,000. It was looking for investment "without any predisposition as to the type." . . . At this time, therefore, it was not a corporation with any well-defined object or purpose, other than that of employing its liquid assets for the profit of its stockholders. Certainly it was not then engaged in the business of manufacturing aircraft or aircraft accessories.

In late December of 1951 a business opportunity was brought to the attention of Mr. Odlum in the following circumstances:

Mr. Lester E. Hutson was the owner of all the stock of Nutt-Shel Company, a California corporation operating a plant in or near Los Angeles for the manufacture of self-locking nuts used in aircraft. Hutson also owned certain patents and patent applications covering the device. A license agreement was in effect, granting to Nutt-Shel exclusive rights in respect of the patents. . . .

Hutson was willing to sell the patents separately but would not sell the stock separately. He would have preferred to retain a controlling interest in the stock but Odlum said he would have to have the controlling interest. Hutson told Odlum that he had been advised by his attorney and that . . . it would be advisable to have the patents under separate ownership. The reason for this was the possibility of the disallowance of the royalty expense on renegotiation of government contracts, as pay-

ments from a wholly-owned corporation to its sole stockholder. . . .

Odlum decided to make the purchase. On February 10 he talked to Hutson by telephone and confirmed the price—"$350,000 dollars for the patents, $1,000,000 for the stock"—and told Hutson that he had decided to buy the entire deal. . . .

At about this time Odlum was advised by his tax consultant that the acquisition of Nutt-Shel might fit very well into the tax problems of Airfleets. Odlum requested further study of the matter, as a result of which he concluded to submit the proposition to Airfleets' Board of Directors.

The . . . directors reached the conclusion that the stock would be a desirable investment for Airfleets, but that it would be undesirable to acquire the patents. The reasons were two: first, the undesirability of investing the additional $350,000, or a total investment of about two-thirds of Airfleets' net assets, in one enterprise; and second, the possibility of the disallowance of royalty payments. Odlum told them that in those circumstances, in order to make it possible for the company to buy the stock, he would undertake to find buyers for the patents, and if necessary would take himself whatever interest was not so disposed of.

A formal meeting of the Board was held on January 28th. . . . The board (Odlum not voting) voted to acquire the stock but not the patents. The Chancellor found that Odlum dominated the other directors and that the decision not to acquire the patents was his. This finding we accept.

On February 8th formal contracts of sale between Hutson and Airfleets, covering the stock, and between Hutson and Odlum, covering the patents, were signed. The transaction was closed in the latter part of the month.

In the meantime Odlum had arranged for the purchase of the patents for $350,000 . . . by 37 different persons and corporations, including himself. His own retained interest is about

7½ percent. Odlum testified that he had expected to sell this interest, but after the propriety of the transaction had been questioned by an Airfleet stockholder, his position became "frozen."

The rejection of the opportunity to buy the patents is attacked as a breach of Odlum's fiduciary duty to Airfleets. The complaint charges (1) that Hutson offered to sell the patents to Airfleets for $350,000; (2) that the patents were useful and necessary to Airfleets in the conduct of the Nutt-Shel business, and the opportunity to purchase them was a valuable asset of Airfleets; (3) that the directors, under the domination of Odlum, who controlled the management of Airfleets, caused Airfleets to reject the offer, in violation of their fiduciary duty; and (4) that Odlum caused the patents to be purchased for himself and certain of his associates subject to his control.

The case made by the complaint is thus one of the unlawful diversion of a corporate opportunity for the benefit of the president and dominating director of a corporation.

The general principles of the law pertaining to corporate opportunity are settled in this state. *Guth* v. *Loft,* 23 Del. Ch. 255, 5 A.2d 503, 510. Speaking for the Supreme Court, Chief Justice Layton said:

> It is true that when a business opportunity comes to a corporate officer or director in his individual capacity rather than in his official capacity, and the opportunity is one which, because of the nature of the enterprise, is not essential to his corporation, and is one in which it has no interest or expectancy, the officer or director is entitled to treat the opportunity as his own, and the corporation has no interest in it, if, of course, the officer or director has not wrongfully embarked the corporation's resources therein.
>
> . . .
>
> On the other hand, it is equally true that, if there is presented to a corporate officer or director a business opportunity which the corporation is financially able to undertake, is, from

its nature, in the line of the corporation's business and is of practical advantage to it, is one in which the corporation has an interest or a reasonable expectancy, and, by embracing the opportunity, the self-interest of the officer or director will be brought into conflict with that of his corporation, the law will not permit him to seize the opportunity for himself.

The Chancellor found that the purchase of the patents was not essential to Airfleets' business, and assumed that it was not one in which the corporation had an expectancy. But he held that it was one in which Airfleets had an interest in the sense that through Odlum it was actively seeking valuable investments, for which it had available funds, and that it was Odlum's duty to find such opportunities.

He also found that Odlum's decision to reject the opportunity to buy the patents was taken in his own interest because by affording friends, associates, and others the opportunity to buy the patents Odlum was satisfying obligations of his own. . . .

The first important fact that appears in Hutson's offer, which was to sell the patents and at least part of the stock, came to Odlum, not as a director of Airfleets, but in his individual capacity. The Chancellor so found. The second important fact is that the business of Nutt-Shel—the manufacture of self-locking nuts—had no direct or close relation to any business that Airfleets was engaged in or had ever been engaged in, and hence its acquisition was not essential to the conduct of Airfleets' business. Again, the Chancellor so found. The third fact is that Airfleets had no interest or expectancy in the Nutt-Shel business, in the sense that those words are used in the decisions dealing with the law of corporate opportunity.

> Whether in any case an officer of a corporation is in duty bound to purchase property for the corporation, or to refrain from purchasing property for himself, depends upon whether the corporation has an interest, actual or in expectancy, in the property, or whether the purchase of the property by the officer or director

may hinder or defeat the plans and purposes of the corporation in the carrying on or development of the legitimate business for which it was created. . . . For the corporation to have an actual or expectant interest in any specific property, there must be some tie between that property and the nature of the corporate business. . . .

We accordingly find ourselves compelled to disagree with the Chancellor's decision. Recognizing that Airfleets had no expectancy in the Nutt-Shel business and that its acquisition was not essential to Airfleets, he nevertheless held that Airfleets' need for investments constituted an "interest" in the opportunity to acquire that business. Now, this is an application of the rule of corporate opportunity that requires careful examination. It is one thing to say that a corporation with funds to invest has a general interest in investing those funds; it is quite another to say that such a corporation has a specific interest attaching in equity to any and every business opportunity that may come to any of its directors in his individual capacity. This is what the Chancellor appears to have held. Such a sweeping extension of the rule of corporate opportunity finds no support in the decisions and is, we think, unsound.

We cannot find any such circumstances in this case. At the time when the Nutt-Shel business was offered to Odlum, his position was this: He was the part-time president of Airfleets. He was also president of Atlas—an investment company. He was a director of other corporations and a trustee of foundations interested in making investments. If it was his fiduciary duty, upon being offered any investment opportunity, to submit it to a corporation of which he was a director, the question arises, which corporation? Why Airfleets instead of Atlas? Why Airfleets instead of one of the foundations? So far as appears, there was no specific tie between the Nutt-Shel business and any of these corporations or foundations. Odlum testified that many of his companies had money to invest, and this appears

entirely reasonable. How, then, can it be said that Odlum was under any obligation to offer the opportunity to one particular corporation? And if he was not under such an obligation, why could he not keep it for himself? . . .

It was unnecessary to labor the point further. We are of opinion that the opportunity to purchase the Nutt-Shel business belonged to Odlum and not to any of his companies. . . .

The refusal of the directors of Airfleets to buy the patents was, under the Chancellor's finding, a transaction between the dominating director and his corporation. It is therefore subject to strict scrutiny, and the defendants have the burden of showing that it was fair. . . .

Now, as the Chancellor found, Odlum made these decisions on behalf of Airfleets. If, after making them, he had elected to keep the patents for himself, a serious question would be presented whether he had sustained the burden of establishing fairness. . . .

But Odlum did not seek to profit personally by what he had done. He promptly divested himself, prior to the closing of the transaction, of almost the entire interest in the patents. . . .

We do not think that it can be fairly said that Odlum profited personally from the sale. The Chancellor's finding that the sale of the patents was improper was, we think, based on his holding that the Nutt-Shel business, including the patents, was a corporate opportunity belonging to Airfleets. If that were so, then his conclusion would be sound, since, as he said Odlum's motive in allowing friends, associates and others to buy the patents could not justify the diversion from Airfleets of an asset belonging to it. But we are of opinion, as above stated, that this is not a case of corporate opportunity, and is to be judged by the test applicable to a transaction between the dominating director and his corporation—the test of fairness.

Our conclusions upon a careful review of this record are: first, that the opportunity to acquire the Nutt-Shel business did not belong to Airfleets second, that the transaction between Odlum and Airfleets involving the patents was fair and free of any overreaching or inequitable conduct.

It follows that the judgment of the Court of Chancery must be reversed. This cause is remanded to that court, with directions to vacate the judgment and dismiss the complaint.

Case Questions

1. Suppose Odlum sat on the board of both an aircraft manufacturer and a manufacturer of metal fasteners, including nuts and bolts. Both businesses would have a close relationship and an interest in the Nutt-Shel business. What would Odlum's obligations be in such a situation? Should he make the opportunity known to both companies and let them bid for it? If he reveals the opportunity to just one, would the other have a valid complaint? Suppose he neither seizes the opportunity for himself, nor reveals it to either company. Could both corporations successfully assert a violation of Odlum's fiduciary duties to them?

2. What difficulties does a court face in deciding whether an opportunity came to a person in his capacity as a director or as an individual? If the evidence is evenly balanced, will a court decide in favor of the corporation?

3. Do you agree that the Chancellor gave too broad a meaning to the phrase "corporate opportunity" when he held that Airfleet had an interest in Nutt-Shel because it had a need for valuable investments?

The "corporate opportunity doctrine" stripped down to its bare elements is this: if there is presented to the corporate officer or director a business opportunity that the corporation is financially able to undertake, that from its nature is in the line of the corporation's business and is of practical advantage to it, and that is one in which the corporation has an interest or a reasonable expectancy; and if, then, in embracing the opportunity the self-interest of the officer or director will be brought into conflict with that of the corporation; the law may return the opportunity to the corporation on an action of a shareholder or the corporation.[25]

Corporate Opportunities When They Have Been Rejected by a Vote of the Board

If an opportunity that comes to the board or to an officer or a director is tendered to the board of directors, and the board votes to reject the opportunity because the corporation "may" not be able to afford it, are the directors free to take the opportunity? The answer depends on whether the action to reject the opportunity was done in good faith. If the directors stood to earn a profit from taking the opportunity and they participated and voted in the decision to reject the opportunity for an alleged lack of funds, then a court may say that the opportunity should be returned to the corporation. In *Irving Trust Co. v. Duetsch*, 73 F 2d 121 (1934), the directors were not permitted to keep a substantial profit received from an opportunity that was rejected by the board because the court reasoned that if the directors were allowed to keep such a gain there would be a temptation to refrain from exerting their strongest efforts on behalf of the corporation, since if the corporation does reject the opportunity when presented, another opportunity of profit will be open to directors personally.

However, there are instances in which the directors have been allowed to keep a gain when challenged. In *Manufacturer's Trust Co.* v. *Becker, et al.*, 338 U.S. 304 (1949), the U.S. Supreme Court did not return a gain received by close relatives and "associates" of the directors of a corporation when it filed bankruptcy. In this case, when the corporation was almost insolvent and needed operating capital, the corporation and other sellers sold debentures to the defendants. The money received from this sale was used to keep the corporation going for awhile. Apparently, the proceeds from the debenture sale were the only source practically available to the corporation. Ultimately, the corporation failed. The directors and friends had purchased the debentures at a substantial discount. The question before the bankruptcy court was, should the holders of the debentures realize as much as other creditors in the bankruptcy proceeding (which was more than they paid for the debentures) or should they just receive what they paid for the debentures? In returning a gain to the defendants the court said:

> When the transaction underlying the defendant's claims here are drawn alongside a good faith standard of fiduciary obligation, they appear unobjectionable. There is no component of unfair dealing or bad faith. The findings negative any misrepresentation or deception, any utilization of inside knowledge or strategic position, or any rivalry with the corporation. During the period of the purchase the conduct of the . . . directors and of the respondents with reference to the affairs of the debtor was to its substantial benefit and to the advantage of the other debenture holders. And there is nothing to suggest that had the debentures been acquired by the Becker directors they would have been unjustly enriched. [338 U.S. 304, 311 (1949)]

Although the majority of the court held that there was a demonstration of good faith because the "true" intent of the defendants was to benefit the corporation, a strong dissent in the case would have held the standard of conduct to be somewhat higher. The dissent would have returned the gain to the corporation reasoning as follows:

> The more precarious the condition of the corporation, the more it needs the undivided loyalty of its directors. Conflicts of interest must be resolved in its favor. An example of the need for doing so arises whenever, in the face of a prospect of the corporation's liquidation, some of its directors invest in its notes at a substantial discount. An inherent conflict of interests is thereby created. It may be necessary for them to choose between a corporate policy of reorganization which might be the best for the corporation and one of liquidation which might yield more certain profits to them as noteholding directors. The fiduciary obligation of such directors to their corporation might thus conflict with their personal interest as noteholders. Their access to

confidential corporate information emphasizes the good faith expected of them. The solution lies in making them accountable to their corporation for their profits from such an investment, much as a trustee must account to his beneficiaries for his profits from dealings in the subject matter of his trust. [388 U.S. 304, 315–16 (1949)]

It makes sense that if an opportunity is rejected by the board, and if a director thereafter takes it and profits and if the director is challenged, the director should have the burden of proving that the rejection was done in absolute good faith. This may be shown by one or more of the following:

1. The real inability of the corporation to finance the opportunity.
2. The existence of any legal barriers to prevent the corporation from accepting the opportunity.
3. Proof that the transaction was beyond the powers or purposes of the corporation.
4. Proof that the corporation's charter or bylaws prevented it from accepting the opportunity or that the opportunity was against settled policy of the corporation.[26]

In short, the directors accept corporate opportunities at their own peril.

Sale of Control

A shareholder need not own an absolute majority of a corporation's voting stock to control that corporation. If the shares are sufficiently widely scattered, an individual with as little as 10 to 15 percent of the shares can elect a majority of the board of directors; such a shareholder is said to have "working control." When a controlling stockholder sells shares he or she can expect to receive more money per share than can the ordinary shareholder. Why is there a premium for controlling shares? Because the purchaser is not just acquiring the shares; the purchaser is also gaining control of the corporation. That element of control has an inherent economic value.

The question that should come to mind is whether control constitutes an asset of the corporation. Normally, the seller of a controlling block of stock is permitted to retain the premium. The idea is that the voting power is inherent in the stock and transfer of the stock transfers the voting rights. However, a controlling shareholder may not sell the stock with impunity. Sale of control is allowable in some instances and impermissible in others. The controlling shareholder does owe certain fiduciary duties to the corporation and the other shareholders.

When the sale of control is challenged, the court will focus on the legitimacy of the buyer's purpose. If the new regime intends some illegal or fraudulent activities or will cause injury to the corporation, the seller will be liable to the corporation on the grounds of a breach of duty. If a corporation enjoys a large amount of liquid assets the purchaser may intend to come in and loot the corporation of those assets. Possibly the new directors have no intention of responsibly exercising their management responsibilities. In either of these situations the seller will have breached the fiduciary obligations owed to minority shareholders if the seller knew or should have known of the plans of the purchaser not to control the corporation in its own best interests.

The *Perlman* v. *Feldman* case that follows is a famous example of the improper sale of control. It contains two unique elements. First, the sale of control is declared unallowable even though the purchasers did not engage in any illegitimate activity. Secondly, the selling shareholder must disgorge a pro rata share of the premium directly to the other shareholders and not to the corporation, as is the rule in the typical derivative suit. However, it is important to remember that one may generally sell control without liability. The Perlman case represents an exception to the general rule.

PERLMAN v. FELDMANN
219 F.2d 173 (1955)

CLARK, Chief Judge
This is a derivative action brought by minority stockholders of Newport Steel Corporation to compel accounting for, and restitution of, allegedly illegal gains which accrued to defendants as a result of the sale in August, 1950, of their controlling interest in the corporation. The principal defendant, C. Russell Feldmann, who represented and acted for the others, members of his family, was at that time not only the dominant stockholder, but also the chairman of the board of directors and the president of the corporation. Newport, an Indiana corporation, operated mills for the production of steel sheets for sale to manufacturers of steel products, . . . The buyers, a syndicate organized as Wilport Company, a Delaware corporation, consisted of end-users of steel who were interested in securing a source of supply in a market becoming ever tighter in the Korean War. Plaintiffs contend that the consideration paid for the stock included compensation for the sale of a corporate asset, a power held in trust for the corpo-

ration by Feldmann as its fiduciary. This power was the ability to control the allocation of the corporate product in a time of short supply, through control of the board of directors; and it was effectively transferred in this sale by having Feldmann procure the resignation of his own board and the election of Wilport's nominees immediately upon consummation of the sale. . . . Plaintiffs argue here, as they did in the court below, that in the situation here disclosed the vendors must account to the nonparticipating minority stockholders for that share of their profit which is attributable to the sale of the corporate power. Judge Hincks denied the validity of the premise, holding that the rights involved in the sale were only those normally incident to the possession of a controlling block of shares, with which a dominant stockholder, in the absence of fraud or foreseeable looting, was entitled to deal according to his own best interests. Furthermore, he held that plaintiffs had failed to satisfy their burden of proving that the sales price was not a fair price for the stock *per se*. Plaintiffs appeal from these rulings of law which resulted in the dismissal of their complaint.

The essential facts found by the trial judge

are not in dispute. . . . Wilport, the purchasing syndicate, consisted of geographically remote end-users of steel who were interested in buying more steel from Newport than they had been able to obtain during recent periods of tight supply. The price of $20 per share was found by Judge Hincks to be a fair one for a control block of stock, although the over-the-counter market price had not exceeded $12 and the book value per share was $17.03. But this finding was limited by Judge Hincks' statement that "[w]hat value the block would have had if shorn of its appurtenant power to control distribution of the corporate product, the evidence does not show." . . .

Both as director and as dominant stockholder, Feldmann stood in a fiduciary relationship to the corporation and to the minority stockholders as beneficiaries thereof. . . . His fiduciary obligation must in the first instance be measured by the law of Indiana, the state of incorporation of Newport. . . . Although there is no Indiana case directly in point, the most closely analogous one emphasizes the close scrutiny to which Indiana subjects the conduct of fiduciaries when personal benefit may stand in the way of fulfillment of trust obligations. . . .

In Indiana, . . . as elsewhere, the responsibility of the fiduciary is not limited to a proper regard for the tangible balance sheet assets of the corporation, but includes the dedication of his uncorrupted business judgment for the sole benefit of the corporation, in any dealings which may adversely affect it. . . . Although the [rule just cited] is particularly relevant to Feldmann as a director, the same rule should apply to his fiduciary duties as majority stockholder, for in that capacity he chooses and controls the directors, and thus is held to have assumed their liability. . . . This, therefore, is the standard to which Feldmann was by law required to conform in his activities here under scrutiny.

It is true, as defendants have been at pains to point out, that this is not the ordinary case of breach of fiduciary duty. We have here no fraud, no misuse of confidential information, no outright looting of a helpless corporation. But on the other hand, we do not find compliance with that high standard which we have just stated and which we and other courts have come to expect and demand of corporate fiduciaries. In the often-quoted words of Judge Cardozo:

> Many forms of conduct permissible in a workaday world for those acting at arm's length, are forbidden to those bound by fiduciary ties. A trustee is held to something stricter than the morals of the market place. Not honesty alone, but the punctilio of an honor the most sensitive, is then the standard of behavior. As to this there has developed a tradition that is unbending and inveterate. Uncompromising rigidity has been the attitude of courts of equity when petitioned to undermine the rule of undivided loyalty by the 'disintegrating erosion' of particular exceptions. *Meinhard* v. *Salmon*, supra, 249 N.Y. 458, 464, 164 N.E. 545, 546, 62 A.L.R. 1.

The actions of defendants in siphoning off for personal gain corporate advantages to be derived from a favorable market situation do not betoken the necessary undivided loyalty owed by the fiduciary to his principal.

The corporate opportunities of whose misappropriation the minority stockholders complain need not have been an absolute certainty in order to support this action against Feldmann. If there was possibility of corporate gain, they are entitled to recover. . . .

We do not mean to suggest that a majority stockholder cannot dispose of his controlling block of stock to outsiders without having to account to his corporation for profits or even never do this with impunity when the buyer is an interested customer, actual or potential, for the corporation's product. But when the sale necessarily results in a sacrifice of [an] element of corporate good will and consequent unusual profit to the fiduciary who has caused the sacrifice, he should account for his gains. So in a time of market shortage, where a call on a corporation's product commands an unusually large premium, in one form or another, we think it sound law that a fiduciary may not appropriate to himself the value of this premium. Such personal gain at the expense of his coventurers seems particularly reprehensible when made by the trusted president and director of his company. In this case the violation of duty seems to be all the clearer because of this triple role in which Feldmann appears, though we are unwilling to say, and are not to be understood as saying, that we should accept a lesser obligation for any one of his roles alone.

Hence to the extent that the price received by Feldmann and his codefendants included such a bonus, he is accountable to the minority stockholders who sue here. *Restatement*, Restitution §§ 190, 197 (1937); . . . And plaintiffs, as they contend, are entitled to a recovery in their own right, instead of in right of the corporation (as in the usual derivative actions), since neither Wilport nor their successors in interest should share in any judgment which may be rendered. . . . Defendants cannot well object to this form of recovery, since the only alternative, recovery for the corporation as a whole, would subject them to a greater total liability.

The case will therefore be remanded to the district court for a determination of the question expressly left open below, namely, the value of defendants' stock without the appurtenant control over the corporation's output of steel. We reiterate that on this issue, as on all others relating to a breach of fiduciary duty, the burden of proof must rest on the defendants. . . . Judgment should go to these plaintiffs and those whom they represent for any premium value so shown to the extent of their respective stock interests. . . .

SWAN, *Circuit Judge (dissenting).*

With the general principles enunciated in the majority opinion as to the duties of fiduciaries I am, of course, in thorough accord. But, as Mr. Justice Frankfurter stated in *Securities and Exchange Commission* v. *Chenery Corp.,* 318 U.S. 80, 85 . . . "to say that a man is a fiduciary only begins analysis; it gives direction to further inquiry. To whom is he a fiduciary? What obligations does he owe as a fiduciary? In what respect has he failed to discharge these obligations?" My brothers' opinion does not specify precisely what fiduciary duty Feldmann is held to have violated or whether it is a duty imposed upon him as the dominant stockholder or as a director of Newport. Without such specification I think that both the legal profession and the business world will find the decision confusing and will be unable to foretell the extent of its impact upon customary practices in the sale of stock. . . .

. . .

Judge Hincks found that Feldmann had no reason to think that Wilport would use the power of management it would acquire by the purchase to injure Newport, and that there was no proof that it ever was so used. Feldmann did know, it is true, that the reason Wilport wanted the stock was to put in a board of directors who would be likely to permit Wilport's members to purchase more of Newport's steel than they might otherwise be able to get. But there is nothing illegal in a dominant shareholder purchasing from his own corporation at the same prices it offers to other customers. That is what the members of Wilport did, and there is no proof that Newport suffered any detriment therefrom.

. . .

The final conclusion of my brothers is that the plaintiffs are entitled to recover in their own right instead of in the right of the corporation. This appears to be completely inconsistent with the theory advanced at the outset of the opinion, namely, that the price of the stock "included compensation for the sale of a corporate asset." If a corporate asset was sold, surely the corporation should recover the compensation received for it by the defendants. Moreover, if the plaintiffs were suing in their own right, Newport was not a proper party. The case of *Southern Pacific Co.* v. *Bogert,* 250 U.S. 483, 39 S.Ct. 533, 63 LEd. 1099, relied

upon as authority for the conclusion that the plaintiffs are entitled to recover in their own right, relates to a situation so different that the decision appears to me to be inapposite.

I would affirm the judgment on appeal.

Case Questions

1. Does this decision declare it to be illegal per se for a controlling shareholder to derive a premium from the sale of a controlling block of stock?

2. Is this decision relatively unimportant in that its circumstances are unique and unlikely to arise again?

3. In measuring a fiduciary's activity against the legally imposed duties does a court focus on the degree of harm caused the corporation or on the amount of advantages it was unable to secure?

4. Could a fiduciary fulfill the obligation by offering the minority shareholders the opportunity of selling a pro rata share of their holdings to the new controlling shareholder, i.e., if the new shareholder desires to purchase 40 percent ownership and the fiduciary owns 45 percent, then the fiduciary would sell 45 percent of the total number of shares necessary to constitute 40 percent ownership with the minority having the chance to sell the remaining number of shares according to their proportionate ownership?

5. Did Wilport pay a premium for control of Newport or was it actually paying a premium for Newport's steel products? Is it legally significant to know which item Wilport was purchasing at a premium?

Case Comment

The defendants sold their stock for $20 per share although the over-the-counter price had not exceeded $12. On remand the district court had the task of determining what portion of the $20 per share was attributable to its control aspects. It valued this control at $5.33 per share. The Feldmann group sold 398,927 shares to Wilport. Multiplying this times $5.33 yields a total premium of $2,126,280.91. The court, as you remember, in a somewhat unique ruling for a derivative suit, held that the recovery should not go to the corporation but to the individual minority shareholders. The Wilport shares constituted 36.99 percent of the outstanding shares of Newport. Under the ruling Wilport was barred from recovering any of the premium. Its percentage share of the premium would have been $786,511.29. After this amount was subtracted from the total premium it left $1,339,769.62 due the minority shareholders [154 F. Supp. 436 (1957)].

Another facet of the sale of control issue is that although it is permissible to sell control under most circumstances, it is not permissible to buy or sell corporate directorships. Whether a sale of shares of a corporation is the sale of control or the sale of a directorship is usually determined by the percentage of shares involved and the perceived intent of the purchaser. So, the general rule is that payment of a premium for a *clear majority* of the outstanding shares (absent evidence of intent to damage the corporation) is proper even though there is an agreement containing a provision for the resignation of directors and the election of new ones. But, if the shares sold are less than a controlling block and there is by the sale an accompanying transfer of control or what amounts to the sale of a corporate office, the transfer is unlawful.[27] In this case any premium paid for the sale of the shares is recoverable by the corporation as a bribe.

Let us examine briefly a more typical situation than the one presented in the *Feldmann* case. In *Essex Universal Corporation* v. *Yates,* 305 F. 2d 572 (2d Cir., 1962), there was a contract for the sale of 28.3 percent of the stock of Republic Pictures Corporation. The sales price was $2 above the market price. In addition to other provisions not here relevant, the contract of sale for the shares contained the following paragraph:

> 6. Resignations.
> Upon and as a condition to the closing of this transaction if requested by Buyer at least ten (10) days prior to the date of the closing:
> (a) Seller will deliver to Buyer the resignations of the majority of the directors of Republic.
> (b) Seller will cause a special meeting of the board of directors of Republic to be held, legally convened pursuant to law and the by-laws of Republic, and simultaneously with the acceptance of the directors' resignations set forth in paragraph 6(a) immediately preceding will cause nominees of Buyer to be elected directors of Republic in place of the resigned directors. [305 F2d 572, 573–4 (1962)]

The court held that the paragraph above was legal and enforceable. Explaining its reasoning, the court said:

> It is established beyond question under New York law that it is illegal to sell corporate office or management control by itself (that is, accompanied by no stock or insufficient stock to carry voting control). . . . The rationale of the rule is undisputable: persons enjoying management control hold it on behalf of the corporation's stockholders, and therefore may not regard it as their own personal property to dispose of as they wish. Any other rule would violate the most fundamental principle of corporate democracy, that management must represent and be chosen by, or at least with the consent of, those who own the corporation.
> Essex [the seller] was, however, contracting with Yates for the purchase of a very substantial percentage of Republic stock. If, by virtue of the voting power carried by this stock, it could have elected a majority of the board of directors, then the contract was not a simple agreement for the sale of an office to one having no ownership interest in the corporation. . . . Such stock voting control would incontestably belong to the owner of a majority of the voting stock, and it is commonly known that equivalent power usually accrues to the owner of 28.3 percent of the stock. . . .
> . . .

The . . . question is whether it is legal to give and receive payment for the immediate transfer of management control to one who has achieved majority share control but would not otherwise be able to convert that share control into operating control for some time. I think that it is. [305 F2d 572, 575 (1962)]

The issues in this case were, however, not so clearly and convincingly dealt with by other members of the court. In another part of the decision, another judge had the following comments:

I have no doubt that many contracts, drawn by competent and responsible counsel, for the purchase of blocks of stock from interests thought to "control" a corporation although owning less than a majority, have contained provisions like paragraph 6 of the contract. . . . However, developments over the past decades seem to me to show that such a clause violates basic principles of corporate democracy. To be sure, stockholders who have allowed a set of directors to be placed in office, whether by their vote or their failure to vote, must recognize that death, incapacity or other hazard may prevent a director from serving a full term, and that they will have no voice as to his immediate successor. But the stockholders are entitled to expect that, in that event, the remaining directors will fill the vacancy in the exercise of their fiduciary responsibility. A mass seriatim resignation directed by a selling stockholder, and the filling of vacancies by his henchmen at the dictation of a purchaser and without any consideration of the character of the latter's nominees, are beyond what the stockholders contemplated or should have been expected to contemplate. This seems to me a wrong to the corporation and the other stockholders which the law ought not countenance, whether the selling stockholder has received a premium or not. Right in this Court we have seen many cases where sudden shifts or corporate control have caused serious injury; . . . A special meeting of stockholders to replace a board may always be called, and there could be no objection to making the closing of a purchase contingent on the results of such an election. [305 F2d 572, 581 (1962)]

control

1. Keebler acquires full stock ownership of Meadors. It subsequently sells all its Meadors stock to Atlantic Services, who in turn sells the stock to Flora Mir Distributing Company. The purchase by Atlantic and Flora were financed by Meadors' own liquid assets. Certain Meadors' debenture holders now sue Keebler alleging that Keebler owed a fiduciary duty to Meadors' creditors as well as its stockholders when it sold its controlling interests. The holders allege that Keebler violated this duty by not inquiring into Atlantic's purposes behind the purchase. At the time of the sale Keebler knew the following: (1) No one from Atlantic had experience in the candy business, (2) Atlantic did not inspect the Meadors operation prior to executing the purchase agreement, (3) At the time of the closing only Atlantic's accountant had examined Meadors to any extent, and his primary interest was in the books and inventory, (4) An outsider could not accept

Review Problems

[handwritten margin note: Reasonable man would have investigated]

Meadors' profit at face value because it had no market of its own, (5) Prior to the closing, Atlantic failed to negotiate with Meadors' key employees about continuing the business. Keebler acknowledges that Atlantic looted Meadors with dispatch but argues that it must have had knowledge of the intended looting to be held liable therefor. The debenture holders argue that Keebler knew sufficient suspicious circumstances that it had the duty to investigate the prospective purchaser. What decision? [*Swinney* v. *Keebler Co.*, 329 F. Supp. 216 (1971)].

[handwritten margin note: guilty]

2. Lincoln Stores operated retail department stores in 14 cities scattered throughout several states. One store was located in Norwich, Conn. The store was successful, although it lacked sufficient space. Acquisition of additional space was frequently discussed, although in 1932 the corporation declined to exercise an option for leasing added space in the same building. It was decided that the extra sales would be outweighed by the lease expenses. Expansion was not thereafter considered until 1938. In April 1937 the Reid & Hughes department store in Norwich was put up for sale. It was on the same side of the street as the Lincoln Store and 90 feet distant but afforded it slight competition. Grant, Martin, and Haley secretly purchased it; all three were employed by Lincoln Stores. Grant and Martin were directors. Martin was the general manager of all the stores. Grant managed one store and supervised two others. Haley was a buyer. Shortly after the purchase Haley resigned to take over the Reid & Hughes store. Grant and Martin concealed their ownership interests while continuing in the employ of Lincoln Stores. The three had various meetings in several states concerning the purchase and billed their travelling expenses to the corporation. To ascertain the inventory and capital requirements of their new store, Grant used certain of the company's confidential information. The knowledge and experience they acquired in working for Lincoln Stores would be directly used in the operation of Reid & Hughes. In June 1937 Grant and Martin were discharged as employees and directors. Lincoln Stores seeks an injunction to enjoin Grant, Martin, and Haley from operating the competing store and from using information they acquired as employees. It also seeks an accounting to determine the amount of the damages it sustained through their alleged illegal activities. Later they added a petition to have a constructive trust declared on the shares owned by Grant, Martin, and Haley. What, if any, relief should be granted Lincoln Stores? [*Lincoln Stores* v. *Grant*, 34 N.E. 2d 704 (1941)].

[handwritten margin note: Not a corp. opport. — using expertise ok — taking conf. info — violation of fud. duties]

3. Seagrave Corporation proposes to merge with Fyr-Fyter Company by purchasing all of its common stock. As part of the overall plan Wetzel, who owns Post, Inc., which in turn owns Fyr-Fyter, contracts with about 30 Seagrave shareholders to purchase 35,000 shares at $20 per

share. This price is $5 or more per share higher than is available on the open market. This stock purchase is conditioned on the consummation of the merger and the delivery by the seller-stockholders of the written resignations of four Seagrave directors to Wetzel on the closing date. Seagrave had a seven-person board of directors. The selling shareholders had working control of Seagrave and elected four members of the board. Two of the selling shareholders were themselves directors. This seller-stockholder group is called the Wilkes group. The remaining three directors, called the Spain group, were also officers of Seagrave and constituted its active management. The two director groups strongly oppose each other, and the resignations of the Spain group are probable if the Wilkes group continues to dominate the board. The Spain group desires to get rid of the Wilkes group. It was Wetzel's stated intention to make no substantial changes in the operating management of Seagrave. Actually, Wetzel did not need to purchase any stock from the selling stockholders to gain a majority of Seagrave's voting stock. Minority shareholders bring a derivative suit to halt the proposed merger. They contend that the directors have placed themselves in a position of conflict of interest between their fiduciary obligation and their own private interests. Should the merger be enjoined? [*Seagrave Corp.* v. *Mount*, 212 F.2d 389 (1954)].

4. Duane Jones Company is an advertising company. The founder, Duane Jones, was the majority stockholder. In 1951 trouble arose within the company resulting in several resignations and the loss of several large advertising accounts. The company did not have employment contracts with its employees, nor was it under contract to its advertising clients. A group of directors, officers, and employees decided to make an attempt to buy out Duane Jones. During June 1951 they told Jones that if he would not sell they would leave en masse and that some of the accounts had already agreed to shift their work. Under this pressure Jones agreed, but he never completed the transaction. In August 1951 the board discharged most of this employee group. The group then formed their own advertising agency, Scheideler, Beck and Werner, Inc., which began business during September. In less than two months in excess of 50 percent of the Duane Jones Co. employees joined the new firm. A number of important advertising accounts also shifted. The new agency invited some former Duane Jones Co. accounts to make the shift. Duane Jones Co. brings suit seeking monetary damages. It alleges that the former employees breached their fiduciary duties of utmost good faith and loyalty. It argues that the defendants, while employees, determined on a course of conduct that, when carried out, resulted in benefit to themselves through destruction of the Duane Jones Co. business. Defen-

Handwritten margin notes: 1) "threat" sell to us or we'll leave — not fud. duty 2) Inducing clients to move. Tortious inter ference.

dants contend that they were fired and did not compete until after their discharge. They also argue that the advertising accounts had no contractual obligation to remain with Duane Jones Co. and were free to shift. How should this case be decided? [*Duane Jones Co.* v. *Burke*, 117 N.E. 2d 237 (1954)]. *Jones wins*

5. Towne is a prominent financier, the owner of 1 percent of the shares of Toy, Inc., and one of its directors. He is also the chairman of the board of Unlimited Holdings, Inc., an investment company in which he owns 80 percent of the stock. Toy needs land on which to build additional warehouse facilities. Toy's president, Arthur, surveyed the land sites feasible for such a purpose. The best location in Arthur's opinion from all standpoints, including location, availability, access to transportation, and price, is an eight-acre tract of land owned by Unlimited. Neither Arthur nor Towne wishes to create any legal problems in connection with the possible purchase of the land. What are the legal parameters within which this transaction may be legally consummated?

6. What are the legal ramifications if there were to be a $50,000 payment "on the side" to Towne in order that he use his efforts to "smooth the way" for the proposed acquisition described in the problem above? *Violation of fiduciary duties*

(The above two questions are adapted from CPA Exam Question #3c, taken from the May 1979 exam. © American Institute of Certified Public Accountants, Inc., 1979.)

7. Delwood is the Central American representative of Massive Manufacturing, Inc., a large diversified conglomerate listed on the New York Stock Exchange. Certain key foreign government and large foreign manufacturing company contracts were in the most important stages of bidding and negotiation. During this crucial time, Feldspar, the CEO of Massive, summoned Delwood to the company's home office for an urgent consultation. At the meeting, Feldspar told Delwood that corporate sales and profits were lagging and something definitely had to be done. He told Delwood that his job was on the line and that unless major contracts were obtained, he would have to reluctantly accept his resignation. Feldspar indicated he was aware of both the competition and the legal problems that were involved. Nevertheless, he told Delwood "do what is necessary in order to obtain the business." Delwood flew back to Central America the next day and began to implement what he believed to be the instructions he had received from Feldspar. He first contacted influential members of the ruling parties of the various countries and indicated that large discretionary contributions to their reelection campaign funds would be forthcoming if Massive's bids for foreign government contracts were approved. Next, he contacted the large foreign manufacturers and indicated

that loans were available to them on a nonrepayment basis if they placed their business with Massive. These payments were to be accounted for by charging certain nebulous accounts or by listing the payments as legitimate loans to purchasers. In any event, the true nature of the expenditures was not to be shown on the books. All this was accomplished, and Massive's sales improved markedly in Central America.

Two years later the Securities and Exchange Commission discovered the facts described above. What are the legal implications of the above for Delwood, Feldspar, and Massive Manufacturing? *Corp. get ≈ $1,000,000 fine*

(Adapted from CPA Exam Question #4a, © American Institute of Certified Public Accountants, Inc., 1981.)

8. A stock brokerage firm is expanding on the west coast. In one city it hires 12 out of 15 brokers employed by another firm. These 12 brokers resign from the other firm on Friday and on the following Monday morning open a brand new branch office for their new employer. The brokers take with them the files of the customers that have generated the bulk of commissions for their former employer. Does the former employer have a legal remedy for the predicament it finds itself in? *absolutely*

9. As a promotional effort an airline is giving each full-fare passenger a coupon that will allow the subsequent purchase of a ticket to any destination at half price. The chief financial officer of a corporation directs the travel department to book all business travel on this airline and issues an order that no employee travel voucher for business expenses will be paid unless the half-fare coupon is attached. The financial officer is going to have the travel department use the coupons to keep down travel expenses. Does the corporation have a legal claim on the coupons that are given to its employees flying on company business? *→ absolutely*

10. A corporation is on the brink of financial collapse. Its officers are very highly paid. When creditor-suppliers to the corporation are requested to cut their prices as part of an effort to save the corporation, they condition their approval on the officers' accepting an equivalent cut in pay. Do the officers have a fiduciary obligation to accept a pay cut? *No!*

Endnotes

1. I. Ross, "How Lawless Are Big Companies?" *Fortune*, p. 57 (Dec. 1, 1980).
2. *Ibid.*, p. 58.
3. "Corporate Crime, The Untold Story," *U.S. News & World Report*, p. 25 (Sept. 6, 1982).
4. *Ibid.*
5. *Ibid.*

6. *Ibid.,* p. 27.

7. Dec. 21, 1974, P.L. 93-528 § 3, 88 Stat. 1708; 15 USC §'s 1–3.

8. The Fifth Amendment provides in part that "No person . . . shall be compelled . . . to be a witness against himself. . . ." The word "person" in this sentence does *not* include corporations. See K. Davis, *Administrative Law Text,* pp. 57–60, and *Hale* v. *Henkel,* 201 U.S. 43 (1906); *Wilson* v. *United States,* 221 U.S. 361 (1911), and *U.S.* v. *White,* 332 U.S. 694 (1944).

9. See P. Areeda, *Antitrust Analysis,* 28 (1967).

10. *Ibid.*

11. See, for example, any of the materials involving the criminal prosecution of Ford Motor Co. for reckless homicide in Winamac, Indiana, in early 1980. For example, see *The Wall Street Journal,* p. 6, col. 1, Wed. Feb. 13, 1980.

12. W. Knepper, *Liability of Corporate Officers,* 3rd ed., p. 43 (1978).

13. American Bar Foundation, Model Business Corporation Act Annotated, p. 273 (1977).

14. H.G. Henn, *Law of Corporations,* p. 482 (1970).

15. See Annot., "Liability of Corporate Directors for Negligence in Permitting Mismanagement or Defalcations by Officers or Employees," 25 ALR 3d 941 at 952 (1969), quoting *Wallach* v. *Billings,* 115 N.E. 382 (1917).

16. Knepper, *supra,* p. 590.

17. *Ibid.,* p. 592.

18. *Ibid.,* quoting Professor Joseph W. Bishop in "Sitting Ducks and Decoy Ducks: New Trends in the Indemnification of Corporation Directors and Officers," 77 *Yale L. J.* 1078, 1081 (1968).

19. Knepper, *supra,* p. 593.

20. Hinsey, Delancey, Stahl & Kramer, "What Existing D&O Policies Cover," 27 *Bus. Lawyer* 153 (1972).

21. *The Wall Street Journal,* p. 1, col. 6, Aug. 8, 1972.

22. *Ibid.*

23. *Ibid.*

24. Knepper, *supra,* p. 52.

25. Annot., "What Business Opportunities Are in 'Line of Business' of Corporation for Purposes of Determining Whether a Corporate Opportunity was Presented," 77 *ALR* 3d 961 (1977).

26. Knepper, *supra,* pp. 77–78.

27. *Ibid.,* p. 139.

Altering the Corporate Structure and Dissolution

13

We have observed that the directors have the exclusive authority to manage the business and affairs of a corporation. However, certain fundamental changes in the corporate structure, i.e., mergers, consolidations, the sale or lease of virtually all the corporate assets, amendments to the articles, and dissolution, require shareholder approval. Depending on the jurisdiction involved, such action usually will require either a simple majority or a two-thirds vote of the voting shares outstanding. Thus, the shareholders have veto power over any proposed plan that would alter the basic nature of the present corporation.

Actions affecting the fundamental nature of the corporation may be subject to a complex variety of rules of law. If shareholder approval is required, then one must conform not only to the state's business corporation act but also to the federal rules on proxy solicitation. If the transaction is to be consummated through the purchase of securities, it may be necessary to comply with the 1934 Act's tender offer provisions. Insiders must be careful that their activities do not violate Section 16(b) or Rule 10b-5. One must be aware of the potential antitrust repercussions inherent in a corporate acquisition. There are the technical accounting aspects that must be surmounted. Finally, there are those inevitable tax consequences to be faced. The corporations and their respective shareholders may well desire that reorganization qualify as "tax free" under the Internal Revenue Code of 1954. The parties involved can avoid federal tax liability if the reorganization is (1) a statutory merger, (2) a statutory consolidation, (3) achieved by an exchange of stock and a minimum of 80 percent of the stock of each class of the one corporation is acquired by the other, or (4) a sale of assets for the shares of the corporation that is to survive. Occasionally the parties may desire, or be unable to avoid, a taxable reorganization with its resulting gains or losses. The typical cash tender offer is a common example. Also, state tax laws should be consulted.

In addition, issues surrounding alteration of the corporate capital and organizational structure are inextricably bound up with some of the duties of care discussed in the previous chapter. Usually such alterations are undertaken to benefit the corporation, but the definition of benefit may vary depending on one's position or vested interests in the capital or organizational structure. Thus, questions often arise about which person or group will benefit from a corporate reorganization of one type or another. These issues, usually more prevalent in close or medium-sized corporations, are discussed in the last part of this chapter. We begin the material in this chapter with an explanation of amending the articles of incorporation.

Amending the Articles

From time to time a corporation may wish to amend its articles of incorporation. It may do so in as many respects as may be desired. However, the amendments can contain only such provisions as might be lawfully contained in an original articles of incorporation made at the time of making such amendments. Section 53 of the Illinois business corporation act sets forth the typical amendment procedure. It requires that the board of directors adopt a resolution setting forth the proposed amendment and directing that it be submitted to a vote of the shareholders at either an annual or special meeting. Written or printed notice setting forth the proposed amendment or a summary of the changes to be effected thereby must be given to each shareholder of record entitled to vote at the meeting. To be adopted, the proposed amendment must receive the affirmative vote of the holders of at least two thirds of the outstanding shares entitled to vote at such meeting. If any class of shares is entitled to vote as a class, the proposed amendment must receive the affirmative vote of the holders of at least two thirds of the outstanding shares of each class of shares entitled to vote as a class and two thirds of the total outstanding shares entitled to vote at the meeting.

After the amendments have received shareholder approval, they are to be executed in duplicate and verified by the president or a vice president, and the secretary is to affix the corporate seal. Both copies are to be delivered to the Secretary of State. If the amendments conform to the law, and if all franchise taxes, fees and charges have been paid, the Secretary will file them and affix a certificate of amendment. The original will be retained in the Secretary's office and the duplicate returned to the corporation.

Merger, Consolidation, and Sale of Assets

The mechanical process involved in a merger, consolidation, sale, lease, exchange, mortgage, or other disposition of all, or substantially all, the corporate assets, other than in the regular course of business, is for the board of directors to adopt a resolution approving the transaction followed by a vote of the shareholders. In Illinois §§ 64 and 72 require the approval of at least two thirds of the outstanding shares while Delaware, § 271, requires only the approval by a majority of the outstanding stock.

A merger differs from a consolidation. In a statutory merger, Corporation A and Corporation B are combined. Corporation A will cease to exist while Corporation B, the surviving corporation, will continue in operation. In a statutory consolidation both A and B will cease to exist and will be replaced by a new Corporation C. In either a merger or consolidation, the surviving, or new, corporation will take title to all the assets and be responsible for all the liabilities of the constituent corporations. (See § 69 of the Illinois statute.)

When a corporation sells all of its assets in a bona fide transaction, the purchaser is not liable for the debts of the corporate seller. However, there are four exceptions to this general rule: (1) where the purchaser expressly or impliedly agreed to assume such debts; (2) where the transaction is really a consolidation or a merger; (3) where the purchasing corporation is merely a continuation of the selling corporation; or (4) where the transaction was fraudulently made in order to escape liability for such debts. [*Lamb* v. *Leroy Corp.*, 454 P. 2d 24 (1969)]. Caveat: a sale of assets may require compliance with the Uniform Commercial Code's Article 6, bulk transfer provisions.

Naturally, mergers, consolidations, or the sale of assets do not exhaust the list of possible forms of corporate structural changes. The methods available to combine, expand, or contract the corporate structure are limited only by man's imagination and ingenuity.

The Rights of a Dissenting Shareholder

It is not unexpected that a shareholder may oppose the merger or consolidation. Despite this opposition, the corporate reorganization may be approved. Is the position of the opposing or dissenting shareholder now untenable? What is the dissenting shareholder to do if he or she is in a close corporation that has no market for its shares? In order to protect the interests of such a shareholder the business corporation statutes contain a *dissent and appraisal remedy*. If the shareholder complies with the statutory requirements the surviving corporation must purchase the dissenter's shares.

The MBCA defines the rights of a dissenting shareholder and the buy-out procedures to be used in the sections below. These provisions are most useful to shareholders in close corporations. They do not usually apply to corporations traded on the public stock exchanges. Since a sale of corporate assets not in the regular course of business will probably result in fundamental changes in the corporate structure, we start our explanation of the rights of dissenting shareholders by presenting a partial quote of the applicable definitions and procedures for such a sale.

§ 79. Sale of Assets Other Than in Regular Course of Business

A sale, lease, exchange, or other disposition of all, or substantially all, the property and assets, with or without the good will, of a corporation, if not in the usual and regular course of its business, may be made upon such terms and conditions and for such consideration, which may consist in whole or in part of cash or other property, including shares, obligations or other securities of any other corporation, domestic or foreign, as may be authorized in the following manner:

(a) The board of directors shall adopt a resolution recommending such sale, lease, exchange, or other disposition and directing the submission thereof to a vote at a meeting of shareholders, which may be either an annual or a special meeting.

(b) Written notice shall be given to each shareholder of record, whether or not entitled to vote at such meeting, not less than twenty days before such meeting, in the manner provided in this Act for the giving of notice of meetings of shareholders, and, whether the meeting be an annual or a special meeting, shall state that the purpose, or one of the purposes is to consider the proposed sale, lease, exchange, or other disposition.

(c) At such meeting the shareholders may authorize such sale, lease, exchange, or other disposition and may fix, or may authorize the board of directors to fix, any or all of the terms and conditions thereof and the consideration to be received by the corporation therefor. Such authorization shall require the affirmative vote of the holders of a majority of the shares of the corporation entitled to vote thereon, unless any class of shares is entitled to vote thereon as a class, in which event such authorization shall require the affirmative vote of the holders of a majority of the shares of each class of shares entitled to vote as a class thereon and of the total shares entitled to vote thereon.

(d) After such authorization by a vote of shareholders, the board of directors nevertheless, in its discretion, may abandon such sale, lease, exchange, or other disposition of assets, subject to the rights of third parties under any contracts relating thereto, without further action or approval by shareholders.

§ 80. Right of Shareholders to Dissent

Any shareholder of a corporation shall have the right to dissent from any of the following corporate actions:

(a) Any plan of merger or consolidation to which the corporation is a party; or

(b) Any sale or exchange of all or substantially all of the property and assets of the corporation not made in the usual and regular course of its business, including a sale in dissolution, . . .

     . . .

This section shall not apply to the shareholders of the surviving corporation in a merger if a vote of the shareholders of such corporation is not necessary to authorize such merger. Nor shall it apply to the holders of shares of any class or series if the shares of such class or series were registered on a national securities exchange on the date fixed to determine the shareholders entitled to vote at the meeting of shareholders at which a plan of merger or consolidation or a proposed sale or exchange of property and assets is to be acted upon unless the articles of incorporation of the corporation shall otherwise provide.

§ 81. Rights of Dissenting Shareholders

Any shareholder electing to exercise such right of dissent shall file with the corporation, prior to or at the meeting of shareholders at which such proposed corporate action is submitted to a vote, a written objection to such proposed corporate action. If such proposed corporate action be approved by the required vote and such shareholder shall not have voted in favor thereof, such shareholder may, within ten days after the date on which the vote was taken . . . make written demand on the corporation, or, in the case of a merger or consolidation, on the surviving or new corporation, domestic or foreign, for payment of the fair value of such shareholder's shares, and, if such proposed corporate action is effected, such corporation shall pay to such shareholder, upon surrender of the certificate or certificates representing such shares, the fair value thereof as of the day prior to the date on which the vote was taken approving the proposed corporate action, excluding any appreciation or depreciation in anticipation of such corporate action. . . .

    . . .

Within ten days after such corporate action is effected, the corporation, or, in the case of a merger or consolidation, the surviving or new corporation, domestic or foreign, shall give written notice thereof to each dissenting shareholder who has made demand as herein provided, and shall make a written offer to each such shareholder to pay for such shares at a specified price deemed by such corporation to be the fair value thereof. Such notice and offer shall be accompanied by a balance sheet of the corporation the shares of which the dissenting shareholder holds, as of the latest available date and not more than twelve months prior to the making of such offer, and a profit and loss statement of such corporation for the twelve months' period ended on the date of such balance sheet.

If within thirty days after the date on which such corporate action was effected the fair value of such shares is agreed upon between any such dissenting shareholder and the corporation, payment therefor shall be made within ninety days after the date on which such corporate action was effected, upon surrender of the certificate or certificates representing such shares. Upon payment of the agreed value the dissenting shareholder shall cease to have any interest in such shares.

If within such period of thirty days a dissenting shareholder and the corporation do not so agree, then the corporation, within thirty days after receipt of written demand from any dissenting shareholder given within sixty days after the date on which such corporate action was effected, shall, or at its election at any time within such period of sixty days may, file a petition in any court of competent jurisdiction in the county in this State where the registered office of the corporation is located requesting that the fair value of such shares be found and determined. . . . All shareholders who are parties to the proceeding shall be entitled to judgment against the corporation for the amount of the fair value of their shares. The court may, if it so elects, appoint one or more persons as appraisers to receive evidence and recommend a decision on the question of fair value. The appraisers shall have such power and authority as shall be specified in the order of their appointment or an amendment thereof. The judgment shall be payable only upon and concurrently with the surrender to the corporation of the certificate or certificates representing such shares. Upon payment of the judgment, the dissenting shareholder shall cease to have any interest in such shares.

The judgment shall include an allowance for interest at such rate as the court may find to be fair and equitable in all the circumstances, from the date on which the vote was taken on the proposed corporate action to the date of payment.

The costs and expenses of any such proceeding shall be determined by the court and shall be assessed against the corporation, . . .

The rights given to a dissenting shareholder are substantial. In many instances, if these rights are exercised causing the corporation to pay the fair value of the shares, the corporation may not have the liquid reserves needed to consummate the proposed change. So, a crucial question in the circumstances of a corporate reorganization or other change in the corporate capital structure is whether the proposal is the kind that gives rights to dissenting shareholders. The case that follows presents an analysis of and answer to this question and also illustrates the legal complexities inherent in a corporate reorganization. Lawyers and accountants are paid to use their ingenuity to help management or the proponents of such reorganizations so that the corporations will not have to pay dissenters.

FARRIS v. GLEN ALDEN CORPORATION
393 Pa. 427; 143 A. 2d 25 (1958)

COHEN, Justice

We are required to determine on this appeal whether, as a result of a "Reorganization Agreement" executed by the officers of Glen Alden Corporation and List Industries Corporation, and approved by the shareholders of the former company, the rights and remedies of a dissenting shareholder accrue to the plaintiff.

Glen Alden is a Pennsylvania corporation engaged principally in the mining of anthracite coal and lately in the manufacture of air conditioning units and fire-fighting equipment. In recent years the company's operating revenue has declined substantially, and in fact, its coal operations have resulted in tax loss carryovers of approximately $14,000,000. In October 1957, List, a Delaware holding company owning interests in motion picture theaters, textile companies and real estate, and to a lesser extent, in oil and gas operations, warehouses and aluminum piston manufacturing, purchased through a wholly owned subsidiary 38.5 percent of Glen Alden's stock. This acquisition enabled List to place three of its directors on the Glen Alden board.

On March 20, 1958, the two corporations entered into a "reorganization agreement," subject to stockholder approval, which contemplated the following actions:

1. Glen Alden is to acquire all of the assets of List, excepting a small amount of cash reserved for the payment of List's expenses in connection with the transaction. These assets include over $8,000,000 in cash held chiefly in the treasuries of List's wholly owned subsidieries.

2. In consideration of the transfer, Glen Alden is to issue 3,621,703 shares of stock to List. List in turn is to distribute the stock to its shareholders at a ratio of five shares of Glen Alden stock for each six shares of List stock. In order to accomplish the necessary distribution, Glen Alden is to increase the authorized number of its shares of capital stock from 2,500,000 shares to 7,500,000 shares without according pre-emptive rights to the present shareholders upon the issuance of any such shares.

3. Further, Glen Alden is to assume all of List's liabilities including a $5,000,000 note incurred by List in order to purchase Glen

Alden stock in 1957, outstanding stock options, incentive stock options plans, and pension obligations.

4. Glen Alden is to change its corporate name from Glen Alden Corporation to List Alden Corporation.

5. The present directors of both corporations are to become directors of List Alden.

6. List is to be dissolved and List Alden is to then carry on the operations of both former corporations.

Two days after the agreement was executed notice of the annual meeting of Glen Alden to be held on April 11, 1958, was mailed to the shareholders together with a proxy statement analyzing the reorganization agreement and recommending its approval as well as approval of certain amendments to Glen Alden's articles of incorporation and bylaws necessary to implement the agreement. At this meeting the holders of a majority of the outstanding shares, (not including those owned by List), voted in favor of a resolution approving the reorganization agreement.

On the day of the shareholders' meeting, plaintiff, a shareholder of Glen Alden, filed a complaint in equity against the corporation and its officers seeking to enjoin them temporarily until final hearing, and perpetually thereafter, from executing and carrying out the agreement.

The gravamen of the complaint was that the notice of the annual shareholders' meeting did not conform to the requirements of the Business Corporation Law, 15 P.S. § 2852-1 et seq., in three respects: 1) It did not give notice to the shareholders that the true intent and purpose of the meeting was to effect a merger or consolidation of Glen Alden and List; 2) It failed to give notice to the shareholders of their right to dissent to the plan of merger or consolidation and claim fair value for their shares, and 3) It did not contain copies of the text of certain sections of the Business Corporation Law as required.[1]

By reason of these omissions, plaintiff contended that the approval of the reorganization agreement by the shareholders at the annual meeting was invalid and unless the carrying out of the plan were enjoined, he would suffer irreparable loss by being deprived of substantial property rights.

The defendants answered admitting the material allegations of fact in the complaint but denying that they gave rise to a cause of action because the transaction complained of was a purchase of corporate assets as to which shareholders had no rights of dissent or appraisal. For these reasons the defendants then moved for judgment on the pleadings.[2]

The court below concluded that the reorganization agreement entered into between the two corporations was a plan for a *de facto* merger and that therefore the failure of the notice of the annual meeting to conform to the pertinent requirements of the merger provisions of the Business Corporation Law rendered the notice defective and all proceedings in furtherance of the agreement void. Wherefore, the court entered a final decree denying defendant's motion for judgment on the pleadings, entering judgment upon plaintiff's complaint and granting the injunctive relief therein sought. This appeal followed.

When use of the corporate form of business organization first became widespread, it was relatively easy for courts to define a "merger" or a "sale of assets" and to label a particular transaction as one or the other. . . . But prompted by the desire to avoid the impact of adverse, and to obtain the benefits of favorable, government regulations, particularly federal tax laws, new accounting and legal techniques were developed by lawyers and accountants which interwove the elements characteristic of each, thereby creating hybrid forms of corporate amalgamation. Thus, it is no longer helpful to consider an individual transaction in the abstract and solely by reference to the various elements therein determine whether it is a "merger" or a "sale." Instead, to determine properly the nature of a corporate transaction, we must refer not only to all the provisions of the agreement, but also to the consequences of the transaction and to the purposes of the provisions of the corporation law said to be applicable. We shall apply this principle to the instant case.

Section 908, subd. A of the Pennsylvania Business Corporation Law provides: "If any shareholder of a domestic corporation which becomes a party to a plan of merger or consolidation shall object to such plan of merger or consolidation * * * such shareholder shall be entitled to * * * (the fair value of his shares upon surrender of the share certificate or certificates representing his shares)." . . .

The rationale . . . of the present section of the Business Corporation Law . . . is that when a corporation combines with another so as to lose its essential nature and alter the original fundamental relationships of the shareholders among themselves and to the corporation, a shareholder who does not wish to continue his membership therein may treat his membership in the original corporation as terminated and have the value of his shares paid to him. . . .

Does the combination outlined in the present "reorganization" agreement so fundamentally change the corporate character of Glen

---

[1] The proxy statement included the following declaration: "Appraisal Rights. In the opinion of counsel, the shareholders of neither Glen Alden nor List Industries will have any rights of appraisal or similar rights of dissenters with respect to any matter to be acted upon at their respective meetings."

[2] Counsel for the defendants concedes that if the corporation is required to pay the dissenting shareholders the appraised fair value of their shares, the resultant drain of cash would prevent Glen Alden from carrying out the agreement. On the other hand, plaintiff contends that if the shareholders had been told of their rights as dissenters, rather than specifically advised that they had no such rights, the resolution approving the reorganization agreement would have been defeated.

Alden and the interest of the plaintiff as a shareholder therein, that to refuse him the rights and remedies of a dissenting shareholder would in reality force him to give up his stock in one corporation and against his will accept shares in another? If so, the combination is a merger within the meaning of section 908, subd. A of the corporation law. . . .

If the reorganization agreement were consummated plaintiff would find that the "List Alden" resulting from the amalgamation would be a quite different corporation than the "Glen Alden" in which he is now a shareholder. Instead of continuing primarily as a coal mining company, Glen Alden would be transformed, after amendment of its articles of incorporation, into a diversified holding company whose interests would range from motion picture theaters to textile companies, Plaintiff would find himself a member of a company with assets of $169,000,000 and a long-term debt of $38,000,000 in lieu of a company of one-half that size and with but one-seventh the long-term debt.

As an aftermath of the transaction plaintiff's proportionate interest in Glen Alden would have been reduced to only two-fifths of what it presently is because of the issuance of an additional 3,621,703 shares to List which would not be subject to pre-emptive rights. In fact, ownership of Glen Alden would pass to the stockholders of List who would hold 76.5 percent of the outstanding shares as compared with but 23.5 percent retained by the present Glen Alden shareholders.

Perhaps the most important consequence to the plaintiff, if he were denied the right to have his shares redeemed at their fair value, would be the serious financial loss suffered upon consummation of the agreement. While the present book value of his stock is $38 a share after combination it would be worth only $21 a share. In contrast, the shareholders of List who presently hold stock with a total book value of $33,000,000 or $7.50 a share, would receive stock with a book value of $76,000,000 or $21 a share.

Under these circumstances it may well be said that if the proposed combination is allowed to take place with right of dissent, plaintiff would have his stock in Glen Alden taken away from him and the stock of a new company thrust upon him in its place. He would be projected against his will into a new enterprise under terms not of his own choosing. It was to protect dissident shareholders against just such a result that . . . the legislature . . . in section 908, subd. A, granted the right of dissent. And it is to accord that protection to the plaintiff that we conclude that the combination proposed in the case at hand is a merger within the intendment of section 908, subd. A.

We hold that the combination contemplated by the reorganization agreement, although consummated by contract rather than in accordance with the statutory procedure, is a merger within the protective purview of sections 908, subd. A and 515 of the corporation law. The shareholders of Glen Alden should have been notified accordingly and advised of their statutory rights of dissent and appraisal. The failure of the corporate officers to take these steps renders the stockholder approval of the agreement at the 1958 shareholders' meeting invalid. The lower court did not err in enjoining the officers and directors of Glen Alden from carrying out this agreement.

Decree affirmed at appellants' cost.

Case Questions

Court: looks for "de facto" merger. effect same as merger. look for merger. substance.

1. How can fair value be ascertained when the shares involved are in a close corporation and are not publicly traded on an exchange? What if the shares in a publicly traded corporation are selling below book value because of a severely depressed stock market?

2. Would the rationale underlying a stockholder's right of dissent or appraisal in a merger or consolidation be equally applicable in a purchase of corporate assets?

3. Could the directors of Glen Alden and List have purposely characterized the arrangement as a purchase of assets in an effort to avoid the dissent and appraisal right?

4. What is a "de facto" merger?

5. It is possible for a minority shareholder, through the successful assertion of the right of dissent, to frustrate a corporate merger when it would be unable to do so in a stockholder's vote. Does this fact open the dissent and appraisal remedy to valid criticism?

Case Comments

The Pennsylvania legislature indicated its agreement with the court ruling in *Farris* v. *Glen Alden* by codifying its result. Pa. Stat. Ann Title 15 Section 1311 (F) (1968) provides as follows:

> The shareholders of a business corporation which acquires by purchase, lease or exchange all or substantially all of the property of another corporation by the issuance of shares . . . shall be entitled to the rights and remedies of dissenting shareholders . . . if, but only if, such acquisition shall have been accomplished by the issuance of voting shares of such corporation to be outstanding immediately after the acquisition sufficient to elect a majority of the directors of the corporation.

Short Form Mergers

Some jurisdictions provide a shortcut method of merging when the merger involved a parent and subsidiary corporations. Section 253 of the Delaware General Corporation Law is a good illustration. Under its provisions, if at least 90 percent of the outstanding shares of each class of the stock of a corporation is owned by another corporation, all that is required for a merger is approval by the boards of directors. No vote by the shareholders is necessary, although they do retain their right of dissent and appraisal. These short form merger statutes are designed to give the parent corporation a means of eliminating the minority stockholders' interest in the enterprise. [See *Stauffer* v. *Standard Brands,* 187 A.2d (Del.)]. If the parent so desires, it may permit the minority to remain in the resultant going enterprise; or it may elect to force them out by paying them the value of their shareholdings.

The Appraisal Process

One of the very important areas where the law and accounting practice overlap is in the circumstance where a business enterprise must be valued.

A discussion of the rights of a dissenting shareholder inevitably highlights this area of overlap. Whether management or a court orders that an enterprise be valued, or that a share of an enterprise be valued, does not matter. The process of valuation is essentially the same. The case below presents an overview of the process of fixing the value of corporate stock. The techniques described below are not intended to be an exhaustive list. We present this case because many students of accounting will use these materials, and this important area of overlap between law and accounting deserves attention.

APPLICATION OF DELAWARE RACING ASSOCIATION

213 A.2d 203 (S. Ct. Del. 1965)

WOLCOTT, Chief Justice

This is an appeal by stockholders of Delaware Steeplechase and Race Association (Steeplechase) from a judgment of the Vice Chancellor in an appraisal proceeding fixing the value of the Steeplechase stock.

. . .

Asset Value

Both the Appraiser and the Vice Chancellor made findings as to the value of the assets of Steeplechase. The stockholders accept these findings as to the value of the assets of Steeplechase. The stockholders accept these findings but object to the deduction from the total asset value of 27 percent for obsolescence, to the refusal to include in the asset valuation a figure representing construction in progress and leasehold improvements, and to the deduction of a figure representing demolition costs from the value of the land.

Obsolescence

Delaware Park, the racing plant of Steeplechase, was built in 1937 when most of the patrons of the track arrived by railroad. At this time Delaware Park was favorably situated in close proximity to the tracks of the Pennsylvania and B. & O. Railroads. The establishment was laid out to take advantage of this then fortunate situation.

However, following the War, the pattern of transportation changed. Most, if not the greatly larger number of patrons now come to the track by automobile. The change in patron transportation habits was unfortunate from the point of view of Delaware Park. It now finds itself hemmed in by the railroad tracks which formerly served it so well. . . .

The Appraiser found these items to be incurable functional and economic obsolescence, and concluded that a deduction for such obsolescence should be made. He concluded to apply the "age-life" method in order to determine what this deduction should be. This is one of the methods generally accepted for such purpose. . . .

The Appraiser's rationale in determining the percentage factor to be applied to determine obsolescence was that the racing facility had a life expectancy of 33⅓ years which meant an age-life rate of 3 percent per year. He concluded that 1 percent of this was attributable to combined functional and economic obsolescence. Since the plant had been in existence for 27 years, he applied a 27 percent rate to the entire installation as an operational whole. This finding was approved by the Vice Chancellor.

The stockholders do not argue that no deduction should be made for obsolescence. They say, however, that the rate applied was far too high; that the rate should have been perhaps not more than 2 percent, and that in any event it should not have been applied in addition to depreciation to "equipment and personal property" and to the "newly refurbished clubhouse." They say that obsolescence is applicable only to the clubhouse and grandstand, and perhaps to the former main parking lot on Kirkwood Highway, not used at present to its former extent by reason of the change in transportation patterns.

We think, however, the stockholders misconceive what it was the Appraiser and the Vice Chancellor did. They concluded, and properly so we think upon this record, that the functional layout of Delaware Park was obsolete to a substantial degree because of the changes in the habits of the betting public, and because of the physical inability to adapt existing facilities to serve the public more efficiently.

This being so, they applied the obsolescence rate to the value of the plant as a whole, not to individual items as the stockholders would have them do. In so doing, we think they were correct for the test of the modernity of any facility to serve the public is its ability to do the job. If, by reason of the passage of time and the change of public habits, a racing plant, originally well designed for the purpose, has become less efficient to serve the purpose for which it is used, it has to some extent at least become obsolete as a whole—not merely the separate installations which together go to make up the whole plant. . . .

We affirm the application of an obsolescence rate of 27 percent to the asset value of Steeplechase.

Construction in Progress and Leasehold Improvements

The stockholders object to the refusal of the Appraiser and the Vice Chancellor to include specifically in the assets of Steeplechase the sum of $192,607.00 which, apparently, was money paid for steel for future construction and for architects' fees. The difficulty with the argument made with respect to this is that at the hearing before him the Appraiser invited the stockholders to produce proof that the items in question were not included by the Appraiser in Current Assets as Deferred Charges. No such proof was offered and we think, therefore, the argument falls.

Deduction of Demolition Cost

The real estate appraiser for Steeplechase testified that the best possible use for its land was for residential purposes. The stockholders on the other hand produced witnesses who testified that probably the land would be used for industrial purposes and put a much higher value upon it. However, the Appraiser and the Vice Chancellor accepted the valuation of $2,754,000.00 based upon residential use as the more justified. The stockholders in this appeal do not take exception to this valuation.

They do, however, argue that it was improper to deduct from that valuation the sum of $457,000.00 representing the cost of demolition of existing structures in order to make the land available for residential use. They do not object to the amount estimated for demolition cost, but do object to any deduction at all for that purpose.

We think the stockholders are wrong. The land in question is being used, not for residential purposes, but for a racing plant. Since residential use is conceded to be the best possible use, presumably the land would be more valuable for that purpose than for any other. Accordingly, a different use would necessarily discount the value of the land. Furthermore, it seems quite obvious to us that if the land were to be sold for residential use the purchaser in fixing the amount he was willing to pay would take into consideration the cost of demolishing existing structures in order to devote the land to the use intended.

It should be remembered, furthermore, that the value of the land to Steeplechase is its value as the location of a racing plant. Since we are concerned with a going concern value, we think the land value should reflect its value with respect to that going concern, and not with respect to a theoretical use. We accordingly affirm the deduction from land value of the cost of demolition of existing structures.

Market Value

The stockholders object to the Appraiser's finding, based upon the duPont offer to Steeplechase stockholders, of a market value of $1,530.00. They also object to the Vice Chancellor's use of the figure of $1,305.00 on the basis of a subsequent appraisal some year and a half after the fixing of the higher figure but reflecting the 1962 and 1963 earnings of Steeplechase. The stockholders take the position that there was no established market for Steeplechase shares and that the trading in the stock was so thin that none could be constructed.

It is, of course, axiomatic that if there is an established market for shares of a corporation the market value of such shares must be taken into consideration in an appraisal of their intrinsic value. . . . Under the circumstances, we think, a market value was established by the sale or gift of over 93 percent of Steeplechase stock over less than two years at a value of $1,530. Consequently, it was not error for the Appraiser to conclude that there was a market value at this amount.

The Vice Chancellor, however, did not accept this finding of the Appraiser. He preferred to adopt a "reconstructed market value" of $1,305 per share as of the date of the merger. The reconstructed market value as of the date of the merger was made by the same appraisers who had, in February, 1962, fixed the market value of Steeplechase stock at $1,530 per share. The reason for the reduction in amount is that by the date of the merger the 1962 and 1963 earnings of Steeplechase were known. These earnings had declined and this fact led to a reduction in the figure representing market value.

We think it was proper for the Vice Chancellor to accept this reconstructed market value related precisely to the date of merger. Since value, particularly market value, is dependent to a large extent on earnings, it is proper to take into consideration a reduction in those earnings in constructing a market value. If this is a matter entering into the realm of judgment, as we think it probably is, we can find nothing in this record to indicate an erroneous exercise of judgment by the Vice Chancellor. We therefore affirm his finding as to market value.

Earnings Value

Using an average of the five-year period 1958–1962, the Appraiser fixed the earnings per share of Steeplechase stock at $182.13. The Vice Chancellor rejected this finding and using the five-year period 1959–1963 fixed the earnings per share of Steeplechase stock at $120.19. The Appraiser in order to capitalize these earnings used a multiplier of 15.2, while the Vice Chancellor used a multiplier of 10. The stockholders except to the findings with respect to earnings value of both the Appraiser and the Vice Chancellor.

The main contention of the stockholders in this respect is a complaint against the use by Steeplechase of the sum-of-the-years digit method of depreciation which permitted Steeplechase to depreciate the major part of the cost of assets over the early years of their existence, thus reducing annual net income by a substantial amount. Accordingly, the stockholders' accountant divided Steeplechase's assets into those acquired prior to January 1, 1959 and those acquired or improved subsequent to that date. Depreciation on each of these assets was then recomputed on a basis which the accountant felt to be more proper. In so doing, the accountant materially increased the annual net earnings of Steeplechase.

Delaware law requires that earnings value be determined on the basis of historical earnings rather than on the basis of prospective earnings. . . . Average earnings over the five-year period immediately preceding the merger have ordinarily been used as the basis for determining earnings value.

We therefore are of the opinion that the Vice Chancellor was correct in averaging earnings over the five years 1959–1963, since that was the period immediately preceding the merger. Even though the merger took place on July 31, 1963, the annual race meeting of that year had terminated by that time and all of Steeplechase's 1963 earnings had been made. . . .

Dividend Value

Both the Appraiser and the Vice Chancellor found that the dividend value of Steeplechase was zero and gave it 10 percent weight. The stockholders object to this and argue that dividend value should be given no independent weight whatsoever independent of earnings. Their reason for this is that earnings and dividends are so clearly related that they largely reflect the same value factor. . . .

In the case of Steeplechase, no dividends have ever been paid on the common stock, and at the time of the merger it did not appear that the prospect of payment in the future was any brighter. This stemmed from the admittedly no-profit policy of the management, the re-

strictions imposed by the Racing Commission upon the payment of dividends on the common stock, and the plain fact that earnings in any substantial amount would not be available for the payment of dividends in the foreseeable future.

By reason of these facts, both the Appraiser and the Vice Chancellor gave the nonpayment of dividends "substantial negative recognition." . . .

Since a negative dividend value clearly is pertinent in fixing the value of stock, we cannot say that the judgment of the Appraiser and the Vice Chancellor was in error in giving it a negative weighting. We affirm that decision.

Weighting

The Vice Chancellor reversed the weighting given by the Appraiser to the various elements of value and weighted those elements according to his own judgment. His weighting was as follows:

Asset Value	25 percent
Market Value	40 percent
Earnings Value	25 percent
Dividend Value	10 percent

. . . Since the value of Steeplechase shares is not to be determined on the basis of a liquidation, we cannot say as a matter of law that the Vice Chancellor's judgment on this was clearly wrong. . . .

The question of what weight to give the various elements of value lies always within the realm of judgment. There is no precise criterion to apply to determine the question. It is a matter of discretion with the valuator. In the absence of a clear indication of a mistake of judgment or a mistake of law, we think this Court should accept the reasoned exercise of judgment of the Vice Chancellor and not substitute its own guess as to what the proper weightings should be. Since there has been no showing of an improper or arbitrary exercise of judgment by the Vice Chancellor, we accept his findings in this respect.

By reason of the foregoing, the judgment of the Vice Chancellor fixing the value of the stockholders' stock in Steeplechase at $2,321.30 per share is *affirmed.*

The Fiduciary Duty of Directors and Others in Corporate Reorganizations, Mergers, and Other Changes in the Corporate Structure

In many cases, when a corporation is reorganized or experiences a change in its capital structure, a benefit accrues to some of the shareholders and not others, so that some conflict is inevitable. In the context of such a fundamental change in the corporate structure, we see a clash of the basic rights highly valued in our commercial society. On the one hand we see asserted the political ideal of democracy. The will of the majority of shares should prevail. Recall that often less than 50 percent of the outstanding shares may be capable of exercising control of the board. In opposition to this political ideal we have an assertion by those in control that they have a property right to do with their shares what they please. So the conflict, in one way, is between people but is cast in terms of the political ideal of democracy and the rule of a majority versus the assertion of inalienable property rights. The resolution of the conflict is usually stated in terms of a fiduciary duty or some other duty that accompanies the property right. The case below is a very recent example of the tension and conflict between these two basic notions. In the absence of any overt attempt to injure the corporation or to directly injure the other shareholders, it seems that the basic rights of property prevail.

TREADWAY v. *CARE*
638 F.2d 357 (1980)

(Authors' note: Treadway is a corporation operating bowling alleys and motor inns. Cowin was a director of and financial consultant to Treadway. He was also its largest single shareholder, controlling 14 percent of its common stock. Care is another corporation. It operates health care and recreational facilities. Care had a large amount of cash and was looking for ways to invest it. Care was introduced to Cowin through an investment banker. Cowin was told that Care intended to buy Treadway stock and he was asked his opinion as to which method, either a tender

offer or purchases in the open market, would be more proper to acquire the stock. Several months later, Cowin sold the bulk of his Treadway stock to Care at a premium of 35 percent above the market price. Cowin did not tell Treadway of his intention to sell, nor did he tell it of some of his conversations with Care. He was renominated as a director about two weeks prior to his stock sale. After the sale he withdrew as a nominee and was replaced by deJourno, a Care officer. Care had been continually buying Treadway stock, a fact now known to Treadway through filings with the S.E.C. Subsequently, Browne, the chairman of Care, joined the Treadway board. At this point Care held in excess of 26 percent of the Treadway stock. Once Care had one third of the stock, it could block any merger by Treadway with another corporation, since New Jersey requires a two-thirds vote of the stockholders to approve mergers or consolidations. Treadway's chairman, Lieblich, sought out Fair Lanes as a white knight to rescue Treadway from Care's attempt at control. Care now stated its intention of taking over Treadway. The Treadway board, with deJourno and Browne dissenting, voted that a Care takeover of Treadway would not be in the best interest of its shareholders. Merger discussions continued between Treadway and Fair Lanes. The Treadway board voted its approval of a combination with Fair Lanes. As part of that combination Treadway sold 230,000 shares of Treadway stock (the shares were treasury shares and authorized but unissued shares) to Fair Lanes. Care's interest had risen to 34 percent, but this sale diluted that interest to 28 percent of the Treadway shares. At the annual meeting of Treadway, the Treadway nominees for the board defeated the Care board slate by 105,000 votes. In the interim Treadway and five of its directors sued Care, Cowin, deJourno, and Browne, seeking to divest Care of its stock and requiring all defendants to account for their profits. Care countered by seeking to set aside the stock sale to Fair Lanes as having been improperly approved by the Treadway board to perpetuate its control of the corporation. In the opinion that follows the appeals court discusses the duty of due care owed to a corporation by its directors and determines that none of the directors violated that duty in a manner requiring a legal remedy. Specifically, the court held that (1) Cowin did not breach any fiduciary duty under New Jersey law; (2) the two "Care" directors on the board of Treadway did not breach any duties they owed as directors; and (3) the action of Treadway in issuing additional shares was permissible on the basis of "business judgment.")

KEARSE, Circuit Judge

As a director of Treadway, Cowin owed that corporation a duty of due care and good faith. Treadway argues that Cowin also owed fiduciary duties to the corporation and its shareholders by reason of his positions as a major shareholder and as a paid financial consultant. Treadway asserts that Cowin breached these duties in three ways: by passing confidential information to Care; by advising Care to buy Treadway stock on the open market rather than by tender offer, and then subsequently selling his own shares to Care at a premium; and by failing to disclose to Treadway his contacts with Care and his knowledge of Care's plans regarding a takeover of Treadway. All of these contentions must be rejected.

Thus, although there were opportunities for Cowin to pass confidential information, the record is barren of evidence that he availed himself of those opportunities.

On the matter of Cowin's advising Care not to make a tender offer, the question before us reduces to whether Cowin owed a duty to the shareholders to preserve or promote the possibility that Care would purchase from them at a premium. We find no such duty. In New Jersey, as elsewhere, the directors of a corporation owe various fiduciary duties to that corporation, and, indirectly, to the corporation's shareholders insofar as the corporation's affairs are concerned. But the majority rule, followed by New Jersey, is that a director does not owe a fiduciary duty directly to the shareholders with respect to the shares of stock they own.

Treadway has pointed us to no case, and we know of none, in which a director was required, solely by reason of his status as director, to account to the shareholders for profits earned on the sale of his shares.

Nor do we find that Cowin's status as Treadway's "largest shareholder" carried with it a duty to share his premium with the other shareholders. It is true that in certain circumstances, a *controlling* shareholder may be required to account to the minority shareholders for the "control premium" he obtains upon selling his controlling shares. But Cowin was not a controlling shareholder.

Treadway's third argument is that Cowin breached the duty of good faith that he owed to Treadway as a director by failing to disclose his contacts with Care and his knowledge of Care's intentions to seek control of Treadway. Treadway places great reliance on the district court's statement that Cowin, in failing to disclose his dealings with Care, "betray[ed] . . . the trust placed in him by incumbent management." But, as the district court properly recognized, this fact has no legal significance. Management—as distinct from the corporation—had no legitimate claim to Cowin's allegiance. Rather, Cowin owned his fiduciary duties to the corporation, and through the corporation to the shareholders. Treadway has not shown that those duties were not fulfilled.

Thus, as a general matter, a director has no duty to disclose his stock dealings to the corporation and no duty to offer his shares to the corporation before he sells them to another.

Hence we decline to impose on Cowin a duty to disclose his negotiations with Care. Cowin's right to sell must imply a right to do so in a manner that will not invite Treadway to interfere.

Treadway's first, and broadest, argument is that Browne and deJourno breached the duty of good faith which they owed to Treadway as directors, in that they placed Care's interest in obtaining control of Treadway above any interest of Treadway itself. This argument assumes that Care's interests conflicted with those of Treadway. But there was certainly no theoretical conflict; it is well recognized that a director does not necessarily breach any duty owed to the corporation by promoting a change of management.

Somewhat more substantial is Treadway's third argument, that Browne and deJourno breached their duties as Treadway directors by failing to disclose and by falsely denying Care's intention to obtain control of Treadway. We need not concern ourselves with the asserted failures to disclose; Browne and deJourno had no duty to speak. But affirmative misrepresentations are another matter. There is evidence in the record that on at least two occasions after he became a Treadway director, Browne made such misrepresentations. . . . We shall assume that in making misstatements, Browne breached the duty of good faith which he owed to Treadway as a director.

Because Treadway has shown no causal link between Browne's misstatements and Care's ownership and voting of its shares, there is simply no basis for an order requiring divestiture or disenfranchisement.

Care maintains that Treadway's incumbent management caused those shares to be sold for the sole or primary purpose of retaining its control of the corporation, and that the injunction was therefore proper. Treadway counters that its directors made good faith determinations that a takeover by Care was not in Treadway's best interests, that a merger with Fair Lanes would be in Treadway's best interests, and that the stock sale was a necessary and proper step toward avoiding the former and implementing the latter. Treadway contends that its directors had no interest in the transaction, and acted in good faith, and that the stock sale must therefore be upheld under the business judgment rule. We agree that the business judgment rule, which presumes that directors have acted properly, must be applied to this case. It follows that Care, in attacking the stock sale, had the burden of proving that Treadway's directors acted in bad faith, or in furtherance of their own interests, or for some other improper purpose. We find that Care has failed to carry this burden.

Under the business judgment rule, directors are presumed to have acted properly and in good faith, and are called to account for their actions only when they are shown to have engaged in self-dealing or fraud, or to have acted in bad faith. Once a plaintiff demonstrates that a director had an interest in the transaction at issue, the burden shifts to the director to prove that the transaction was fair and reasonable to the corporation.

Once the burden has shifted, the directors must show that the transaction was fair, in the sense that it was entered into for a proper corporate purpose, and not merely for the directors' selfish purposes.

Turning to the record before us, we conclude that the evidence does not permit a finding that Care has carried that burden. The critical fact, in our view, is that the Treadway board was simply not acting to maintain its own control over the corporation. Rather, in approving the stock sale, they were moving Treadway toward a business combination with Fair Lanes. Only Lieblich had reason to anticipate that he would be given any position, or have any role to play, in the new merged entity. The district court found that the other directors expected that they would lose their positions as Treadway directors and would not be offered new ones. . . . [D]uring the negotiations Fair Lanes had requested that it be allowed to name a majority of Treadway directors immediately, and that after the proposed merger Fair Lanes would own more than 80% of Treadway's stock. Thus the consummation of the proposed business combination could not be expected to perpetuate control by these directors.

Case Questions

1. In this case, is the standard of good faith stated in terms of a lack of bad faith? That is, is good faith more than just the absence of bad faith activity?

2. What was the breach of the standard of good faith in this case?

The language in the last portion of the case seems to indicate that if the directors approved a merger with a friendly company to avoid a hostile takeover and wished to remain in office after the merger, perpetuation of control is to be presumed as their motivation. However, the court deciding the *Treadway* cases faced that issue in another case several months later. In *Crouse-Hinds* v. *InterNorth*, 634 F.2d 690 (1980), the court ruled that if the directors are to remain on the board after a merger, one is not to presume that perpetuation of control is their motive. Self-interest or bad faith on the part of directors must be demonstrated by evidence and not merely by a complaining shareholder pointing out how actions by the directors will leave them in control of the corporation.

These two decisions give the directors of a company extremely broad protection and make it quite difficult to demonstrate that their actions were based upon self-interest and not in the interests of the shareholders.

A Note on Close Corporations and the Liability of Majority Shareholders for "Freezeouts"

In some cases, the rights of a dissenting shareholder and the consequent "buyout" provisions may be so costly that management and/or controlling shareholders attempt to "freezeout" or expel minority shareholders. The word "freezeout" is established in the literature of corporation law and means the use of corporate control to (1) eliminate minority shareholders from the corporation, (2) reduce to relative insignificance their voting power or claims on corporate assets, or (3) otherwise deprive them of corporate income or advantages.[1] A purchase of shares from the minority may be part of the freezeout but it need not be.

We begin this short discussion of freezeouts with the general or majority rule that a director or officer of a corporation has no fiduciary duty to other shareholders when dealing with them for the purchase of their stock.[2] One may say that in this regard the duties of management of a close corporation to shareholders in most states are not the same as the duties of a partner in a partnership. Partners owe to one another and to the partnership the fiduciary duty to act at all times with the utmost good faith and loyalty. However, as we discuss below, the courts in a very few states have decided that since close corporations are essentially like partnerships, the same duties are owed to shareholders that partners owe to one another.

Many of the states do recognize a "special relationship" between the management and shareholders of a close corporation. The nature of this special relationship is that since management may have a superior knowledge about the corporation, there is a duty to respond to requests for information, although some courts have held that there is no duty to affirmatively disclose or volunteer information.[3] If, however, a purchase of shares is involved, Rule 10-b-5 of the SEC Act of 1934 may, if applicable, require the disclosure of material information. This rule and its application will be discussed in the following chapters.

In a leading 1981 Delaware case, a corporation that was a majority shareholder in a subsidiary acquired some of the minority shares. Some shareholders did not exchange their shares for the price offered and attacked the merger, claiming it was unfair. The majority shareholder had hired an investment banking firm to establish a "fair" price and relied on this price in offering to buy out the remaining minority shares. The court held that the majority shareholders owed no fiduciary duty to the minority shareholders.[4] Specifically, with regard to the duty of the majority shareholders and its agents, the court held that: (1) the investment banking firm had no fiduciary duty to minority shareholders and could not be liable for alleged damages in the absence of evidence of conspiracy; (2) majority shareholders owe a duty not to materially misrepresent information to minority shareholders; and (3) there was a duty of the majority to be "fair" to the minority.[5]

As we suggested above, some states are creating a duty of majority or controlling shareholders that is more beneficial to minority shareholders. In a leading 1969 California case, the majority shareholders of a savings and loan corporation, a close corporation, formed a holding company and exchanged their shares for shares in the holding company. The new holding company continued to control the original close corporation. No opportunity was given to minority shareholders to join in the holding company. Then the majority began to offer to the public the stock of the holding company. The minority shareholders claimed that the majority had essentially frozen them out of the original company and had rendered their shares unmarketable except to the holding company. The court held that the majority did owe a fiduciary duty to the minority shareholders to use control of the corporation in a fair, just, and equitable manner.[6] The creation of an artificial market to enhance the value of their majority shares breached this duty owed to the minority. More specifically, the court said:

> The increasing complex transactions of the business communities demonstrate the inadequacy of the traditional theories of fiduciary obligation as tests of majority shareholder responsibility to the minority. These theories have failed to afford adequate protection to minority shareholders and particularly to those in closely held corporations whose disadvantageous and often precarious position renders them particularly vulnerable to the vagaries of the majority. Although courts have recognized the potential for abuse or unfair advantage . . . no comprehensive rule has emerged in other jurisdictions. Nor have most commentators approached the problem from a perspective other than that of the advantage gained in the sale of control.
>
> The case before us, in which no sale or transfer of actual control is actually involved, demonstrated that the injury anticipated by these [minority shareholders] can be inflicted with impunity under the traditional rules and supports our conclusion that the comprehensive rule of good faith and inherent fairness to the minority in any transaction where control of the corporation is material properly governs controlling shareholders in this state.[7]

Although this standard is only applicable in a few states today, we expect it to spread slowly to other states.

Dissolution

Dissolution of a corporation, especially when used as a means to relieve internal shareholder tensions and disputes, is seldom a good idea. A corporation, partnership, or proprietorship all have more value as a going business enterprise than as an idle but a marketable collection of assets. So, sale of the corporation's shares is usually preferred over dissolution as a means to end a person's involvement with the corporation.

Voluntary Dissolution

Dissolution is the legal process of terminating the corporation's status as a legal entity, and is of two varieties, voluntary or involuntary. The MBCA provides for three types of voluntary dissolution. A corporation that has not commenced business and has not issued any shares may be dissolved by the incorporators by filing articles of dissolution with the Secretary of State as provided in Section 82.

A second method is dissolution by the written consent of *all* of the shareholders. A document revealing the written consent together with a statement of intent to dissolve is executed by the corporation's president and its secretary and verified by another officer. The contents of this statement are set out more fully in Section 83. This statement is then filed with the Secretary of State.

The third method of dissolution provided for by the MBCA is referred to as "Voluntary Dissolution by Act of (the) Corporation." This is a two-step process and is outlined in the following quote from Section 84:

> A corporation may be dissolved by the act of the corporation, when authorized in the following manner:
>
> (a) The board of directors shall adopt a resolution recommending that the corporation be dissolved, and directing that the question of such dissolution be submitted to a vote at a meeting of shareholders, which may be either an annual or a special meeting.
>
> (b) Written notice shall be given to each shareholder of record entitled to vote at such meeting . . . and, whether the meeting be an annual or special meeting, shall state that the purpose, or one of the purposes, of such meeting is to consider the advisability of dissolving the corporation.
>
> (c) At such meeting a vote of shareholders entitled to vote thereat shall be taken on a resolution to dissolve the corporation. Such resolution shall be adopted upon receiving the affirmative vote of the holders of a majority of the shares of the corporation entitled to vote thereon, unless any class of shares is entitled to vote thereon as a class, in which event the resolution shall be adopted upon receiving the affirmative vote of the holders of a majority of the shares of each class of shares entitled to vote thereon as a class and of the total shares entitled to vote thereon.
>
> (d) Upon the adoption of such resolution, a statement of intent to dissolve shall be executed in duplicate by the corporation by its president or a vice president and by its secretary or an assistant secretary, and verified by one of the officers signing such statement . . .

The statement referred to in section (d) above is then filed with the Secretary of State. Note that the MBCA provides for dissolution on a majority vote of the proper class of shareholders. States range all the way from specifying no percentage required to vote (Vermont requires only that the "corporation" vote to dissolve)[8] to three fourths of all stock having voting power (Hawaii), with most states requiring a two-thirds vote of all shareholders entitled to vote thereon.[9]

A corporation may also dissolve voluntarily by the expiration of its charter. While standard practice is to incorporate for perpetual life, occasionally the incorporators will specify existence for a definite period. When that period expires, so does the corporation.

Involuntary Dissolution

Involuntary dissolution may take place in one of three ways depending on the state of incorporation. Generally, involuntary dissolution may be initiated by the Attorney General, by a shareholder, or by a creditor. The MBCA Section 94 provides that a court may involuntarily dissolve a corporation in an action by the Attorney General when it is established that

(1) the corporation has failed to file its annual report or pay its franchise tax when due, (2) the corporation procured its articles of incorporation through fraud, (3) the corporation has continued to exceed or abuse the authority conferred on it by law, (4) the corporation has failed for 30 days to appoint and maintain a registered agent, or (5) the corporation failed to make other corporate document filings as specified by law. These provisions are seldom used by states' attorneys general and when they are, the offense is usually flagrant.

Involuntary dissolution on the initiative of a shareholder or creditor is considered by a court designated by the state corporation statute. In making the decision about dissolution the courts are to use the following standards (from Section 97 of the MBCA):

> The .... courts shall have full power to liquidate the assets and business of a corporation:
> (a) In an action by a shareholder when it is established:
>   (1) That the directors are deadlocked in the management of the corporate affairs and the shareholders are unable to break the deadlock, and that irreparable injury to the corporation is being suffered or is threatened by reason thereof; or
>   (2) That the acts of the directors or those in control of the corporation are illegal, oppressive or fraudulent; or
>   (3) That the shareholders are deadlocked in voting power, and have failed, for a period which includes at least two consecutive annual meeting dates, to elect successors to directors whose terms have expired or would have expired upon the election of their successors; or
>   (4) That the corporate assets are being misapplied or wasted.
> (b) In an action by a creditor:
>   (1) When the claim of the creditor has been reduced to judgment and an execution thereon returned unsatisfied and it is established that the corporation is insolvent; or
>   (2) When the corporation has admitted in writing that the claim of the creditor is due and owing and it is established that the corporation is insolvent.

Involuntary dissolution initiated by a shareholder, or in some states by a director or by a creditor, is not granted without a substantial amount of proof showing oppressive and abusive conduct by a majority of the shareholders or a controlling interest. In one of the relatively few cases to grant dissolution on a petition by the shareholders, the plaintiffs proved that they held or controlled half of the outstanding stock, that for 10 years the votes among the shareholders and directors had been evenly split, that one of the defendants had been president for 10 years and he had used his position to completely control the corporation without the effective participation of the plaintiffs, and that there had been no annual meeting for 10 years so new directors were not elected.[10]

The case below illustrates the majority approach and the extreme reluctance of courts to grant dissolution to shareholders.

In re RADOM & NEIDORFF, INC.
307 N.Y. 1, 119 N.E.2d 563, (Ct. of App., N.Y., 1954)

DESMOND, Judge

Radom & Neidorff, Inc., the proposed dissolution of which is before us here, is a domestic corporation which has for many years, conducted, with great success, the business of lithographing or printing musical compositions. For some thirty years prior to February 18, 1950, Henry Neidorff, now deceased, husband of respondent Anna Neidorff, and David Radom, brother-in-law of Neidorff and brother of Mrs. Neidorff, were the sole stockholders, each holding eighty shares. Henry Neidorff's will made his wife his executrix and bequeathed her the stock, so that, ever since his death, petitioner-appellant David Radom and Anna Neidorff, brother and sister, have been the sole and equal stockholders. Although brother and sister, they were unfriendly before Neidorff's death and their estrangement continues. On July 17, 1950, five months after Neidorff's death, Radom brought this proceeding, praying that the corporation be dissolved under section 103 of the General Corporation Law, Consol. Laws, c.23, the applicable part of which is as follows:

> "§ 103. Petition in case of deadlock
>   Unless otherwise provided in the certificate of incorporation, if a corporation has an even number of directors who are equally divided respecting the management of its affairs, or if the votes of its stockholders are so divided that they cannot elect a board of directors, the holders of one-half of the stock entitled to vote at an election of directors may present a verified petition for dissolution of the corporation as prescribed in this article. . . .

The petition here stated to the court that the corporation is solvent and its operations successful, but that, since Henry Neidorff's death, his widow (respondent here) has refused to co-operate with petitioner as president, and that she refuses to sign his salary checks, leaving him without salary, although he has the sole burden of running the business. It was alleged, too, that, because of "unresolved disagreements" between petitioner and respondent, election of any directors, at a stockholders' meeting held for that purpose in June, 1950, had proved impossible. A schedule attached to the petition showed corporate assets consisting of machinery and supplies worth about $9,500, cash about $82,000, and no indebtedness except about $17,000 owed to petitioner (plus his salary claim). Mrs. Neidorff's answering papers alleged that, while her husband was alive, the two owners had each drawn about $25,000 per year from the corporation, that, shortly after her husband's death, petitioner had asked her to allow him alone to sign all checks, which request she refused, that he had then offered her $75,000 for her stock, and, on her rejection thereof, had threatened to have the corporation dissolved and to buy it at a low price or, if she should be the purchaser, that he would start a competing business. She further alleged that she has not, since her husband's death, interfered with Radom's conduct of the business and has signed all corporate checks sent her by him except checks for his own salary which, she says, she declined to sign because of a stockholder's derivative suit brought by her against Radom, and still pending, charging him with enriching himself at this corporation's expense. . . .

From the answering papers it appears, without dispute, that for . . . three years, the corporation's profits before taxes had totaled about $242,000, or an annual average of about $71,000, on a gross annual business of about $250,000, and that the corporation had, in 1953, about $300,000 on deposit in banks. There are many other accusations and counteraccusations in these wordy papers, but the only material facts are undisputed: first, that these two equal stockholders dislike and distrust each other; second, that, despite the feuding and backbiting, there is no stalemate or impasse as to corporate policies; third, that the corporation is not sick but flourishing; fourth, that dissolution is not necessary for the corporation or for either stockholder; and, fifth, that petitioner, though he is in an uncomfortable and disagreeable situation for which he may or may not be at fault, has no grievance cognizable by a court except as to the nonpayment of his salary, hardly a ground for dissolving the corporation. . . .

The Appellate Division reversed the order (of the trial court) and dismissed the petition, pointing out, among other things, that not only have the corporation's activities not been paralyzed but that its profits have increased and its assets trebled during the pendency of this proceeding, that the failure of petitioner to receive his salary did not frustrate the corporate business and was remediable by means other than dissolution. . . .

It is worthy of passing mention, at least, that respondent has, in her papers, formally offered, and repeated the offer on the argument of the appeal before us, "to have the third director named by the American Arbitration Association, any Bar Association or any recognized and respected public body."

Clearly, the dismissal of this petition was within the discretion of the Appellate Division. . . . There is no Absolute right to dissolution under such circumstances. Even when majority stockholders file a petition because of internal corporate conflicts, the order is granted only when the competing interests "are so discordant as to prevent efficient management" and the "object of its corporate existence cannot be attained." *Hitch* v. *Hawley*, 132 N.Y. 212, 221, 30 N.E. 401, 404, see Matter of Niagara Ins. Co., 1 Paige Ch. 258. The prime inquiry is, always, as to necessity for dissolution, that is, whether judicially-imposed death "will be beneficial to the stockholders or members and

not injurious to the public." . . . Taking everything in the petition as true, this was not such a case. . . .

The order should be affirmed, with costs.

FULD, Judge (dissenting).
Section 103 of the General Corporation Law, insofar as here relevant, permits a petition for dissolution of a corporation by the holders of one half of the shares of stock entitled to vote for directors "if the votes of its stockholders are so divided that they cannot elect a board of directors." That is the precise situation in the case before us, for the petition explicitly recites that petitioner Radom and respondent Neidorff "are hopelessly deadlocked with respect to the management and operation of the corporation" and that serious disputes have developed between them with the result that "the votes of the two stockholders are so divided that they cannot elect a Board of Directors." . . .

The parties, brother and sister, are at complete loggerheads; they have been unable to elect a board of directors; dividends have neither been declared nor distributed, although the corporation has earned profits; debts of the corporation have gone unpaid, although the corporation is solvent; petitioner, who since Neidorff's death has been the sole manager of the business, has not received a penny of his salary—amounting to $25,000 a year—because respondent has refused to sign any corporate check to his order. More, petitioner's business judgment and integrity, never before questioned, have been directly attacked in the stockholder's derivative suit, instituted by respondent, charging that he has falsified the corporation's records, converted its assets and otherwise enriched himself at its expense. Negotiations looking to the purchase by one stockholder of the other's interest were begun—in an effort to end the impasse—but they, too, have failed.

In very truth, as petitioner states in his

papers, "a corporation of this type, with only two stockholders in it cannot continue to operate with incessant litigation and feuding between the two stockholders, and with differences as fundamental and wholly irreconcilable as are those of Mrs. Neidorff and myself. . . . settlement of these differences cannot be effected, while continuance on the present basis is impossible, so that there is no alternative to judicial dissolution." Indeed, petitioner avers, in view of the unceasing discord and the fact that he has had to work without salary and advance his own money to the corporation, he does not, whether or no dissolution be granted, "propose to continue to labor in and operate this business." . . .

"Dissolution will serve the interests of the shareholders as well as public policy. . . . And, if the statutory authority be deemed discretionary in essence, there is no ground for withholding its affirmative exercise here, for there is no alternative corrective remedy. . . . The dissension is such as to defeat the end for which the corporation was organized."

Here, too, the asserted dissension, the court could find, permits of no real or effective remedy but a section 103 dissolution. And that is confirmed by a consideration of the alternatives seemingly open to petitioner. He could remain as president and manager of the corporation, without compensation, completely at odds wtih his embittered sister—certainly neither a natural nor a satisfying way in which to conduct a business. Or he could carry out his present plan to quit the enterprise—and thereby risk a loss, to corporation and stockholders, far greater than that involved in terminating the business. Or he could, without quitting, set up a competing enterprise—and thereby expose himself to suit for breach of fiduciary duty to the corporation. . . . It is difficult to believe that the legislature could have intended to put one in petitioner's position to such a choice. Reason plainly indicates, and the law allows, the reasonable course of orderly dissolution pursuant to section 103. . . .

The order of the Appellate Division should be reversed. . . .

Case Questions

1. Why didn't the corporate articles or bylaws contain a provision as to a method of settling deadlocks over the selection of directors?

2. Is it conceivable that an acute situation like this could arise in a publicly traded corporation?

3. What do you think the decision would be if, instead of increasing profits and trebling assets, the corporation, although profitable, was experiencing steadily declining earnings?

4. Is the court stating, in effect, that before it will exercise its discretion and order involuntary dissolution a corporation must experience red ink?

Corporate Existence After Dissolution

Dissolution does not itself end the corporate business. Generally, on the filing of the proper documents with the Secretary of State or on the order of a court, the corporation must cease to carry on its usual business (MBCA Section 86). However, it may carry on business to liquidate or wind up its affairs. Part of this latter process is to send notice of the dissolution to creditors, sell all assets, pay creditors, and make such distributions to shareholders as are proper. Generally, the management of the corporation continues under the board of directors and the corporation remains liable on its debts. In order to expedite liquidation some statutes create a time limit within which creditors who have been given proper notice must file their claims.

Review Problems

Corp. wins not a merger. court.
wins not a Delaware

1. Bellanca Corporation is an empty shell. For many years it manufactured airplanes, but then it ceased business operations and was delisted by the American Stock Exchange. It had accumulated large losses that were available for Federal tax loss carry-over purposes. In 1961 it purchased all the capital stock of seven California corporations engaged in the egg business. The result, under the terms of the purchase agreement, was to leave the former owners of the California corporations in control of Bellanca. A Bellanca stockholder challenges the transaction. She alleges that a merger has in fact taken place without compliance with the merger provisions of the Delaware law, including the right of the dissenting shareholder to withdraw and be paid the value of his stock. The corporation argues that the state statute specifically allows one corporation to purchase all the stock of another corporation, thereby becoming a stockholder and not the owner of the assets of the other corporation. The corporation argues further that action taken in accordance with different sections of the law are acts of independent legal significance even though the end result may be the same under different sections. What decision? [*Orzeck* v. *Englehart*, 195 A.2d 375 (S. Ct. Del. 1963)].

2. Community Hotel Corporation has 2106 issued and outstanding shares of no par common stock. It also has 4335 outstanding $100 par value 6 percent cumulative preferred shares. There are 24 years of accrued but undeclared dividends on the preferred stock. This totals $645,000. Newport Hotel Corporation is incorporated with one purpose—to merge with Community. Newport would completely own the assets of Community. Each share of Community preferred would be converted into five shares of $1 par common stock, while each share of no par common stock would be converted into one share of $1 par common stock of the surviving corporation. If this recapitalization were to be accomplished by amending Community's articles, Rhode Island law would require the unanimous vote of the preferred shareholders. Under the merger statute, only a two-thirds vote is necessary. Some of the preferred shareholders object on the following grounds, inter alia: (1) the merger device has been resorted to solely to obviate the necessity of a unanimous vote, and (2) it is unfair and inequitable because, if they dissent, their dividend accruals will

unpd. div. ←

ok

must be protected in some way

not be given due consideration in the appraisal. What result? [*Bove* v. *Community Hotel Corp.*, 249 A.2d 89 (S. Ct. R.I. 1969)].

3. The usual statutory remedy for the shareholder that unsuccessfully opposes a merger is one of dissent and appraisal. Is it the exclusive remedy or may a shareholder resort to equitable relief? Should equity set a merger aside on grounds of unfairness or only on the showing of actual fraud? [*Matteson* v. *Ziebarth*, 242 P.2d 1025 (1952)].

actual fraud

4. Corporation X and Corporation Y are properly consolidated into a new Corporation CC. The holders of some of X's cumulative preferred shares, whose dividends are in arrears, sue CC. These shareholders seek the liquidation value of their shares plus the dividend arrearages. A clause in the preferred share contract states that on the voluntary dissolution of the corporation the preferred shareholders are entitled to $102.50 per share plus dividend arrearages, before any distribution of assets is made to the common shareholders. The shareholders claim that the consolidation worked a voluntary dissolution of Corporation X. CC contends that the preferred share contract's use of the term "dissolution" means a statutory dissolution. It points out that the consolidated company assumes the debts and liabilities of the constituent companies including existing dividend arrearages. CC further argues that the preferred shareholders will be fairly treated because the consolidation agreement must recognize the dividend arrearages in determining a fair basis of conversion of shares or distribution of property in lieu of shares in the consolidated corporation. Do the preferred shareholders receive the cash that they desire? [*Anderson* v. *Cleveland-Cliffs Iron Co.*, 87 N.E. 2d 384 (1948)].

No, statutory dissolution only for pref. preferences.

5. Minority shareholders petition the court for the involuntary dissolution of their corporation. They prove that prior to 1913 the company was a thriving enterprise. Its profits in 1912 were $45,465.50 and sales amounted to $310,697.23. A new president and general manager took office in 1913. Profits for 1913 amounted to only $11,617.64. In 1914 it suffered a $21,260.85 loss. The period from January 1, 1915, to March 1916 observed a loss of $52,365.00. The 1914 sales were only $164,508.45. Sales for 1915 were approximately $41,000. The four primary sales agents quit the company as a result of disagreements with the company's president. Does this situation merit the granting of a decree of involuntary dissolution? [*Goodwin* v. *Milwaukee Lithographing Co.*, 177 N.W. 618 (1920)].

Yes, flood of red-ink, beyond business judgment rule

6. The NLM Corporation owes a creditor $15,000. Subsequently, NLM sells its assets to Leroy Corporation in exchange for stock. The transaction was a bona fide sale. When approached earlier by NLM with a proposed merger, Leroy rejected it and countered with a purchase of assets proposal. While the assets did not exceed $165,000, NLM re-

ceived Leroy stock valued at approximately $700,000. Later NLM had Leroy transfer the stock from its ownership to the NLM shareholders. The shareholders then proceeded to dissolve NLM without satisfying the $15,000 debt. The creditor now brings suit against Leroy alleging that the transaction was a de facto merger and, therefore, that Leroy is responsible for NLM's liabilities. Leroy contends that the transaction was a legitimate sale of assets and fair consideration was paid. In such circumstances, the purchaser is not liable for the debts of the seller. Who will be victorious, the creditor or Leroy? [*Lamb* v. *Leroy Corporation*, 454 P.2d 24 (Nev. 1969)].

sale, $15K debt left behind

7. A corporation with in excess of $½ billion in assets has engaged a broker to sell one of its divisions. The division in question will likely have as a sales price $2.5 million. The proposed sale upsets a stockholder, who objects to the sale on sentimental grounds. The stockholder believes that a corporation may not dispose of assets without the approval of the shareholders. Thus, the objecting stockholder brings suit to prevent the sale. What chance of success does the suit have? *Not substantial. Big corp. can buy & sell 2.5 M out of ½ B?*

8. Chrysler Corporation and Internationl Harvester suffered severe financial losses during the late 1970s and early 1980s. Chrysler, in fact, obtained federal loan guarantees in its effort to survive. What attitude do you think a court would have displayed if a shareholder of either company sought their involuntary dissolution on grounds of unprofitability?

Get nowhere

9. Minority shareholders are upset at the low price the stock market has placed on their stock. They believe their stock would be worth more if the corporation were to be liquidated and sold off lock, stock, and barrel. When respected financial advisors confirm this belief, the shareholders request that the board approve liquidation. When the directors rebuff their request, the minority brings suit seeking involuntary dissolution. Will a court order dissolution?

No — No evidence of fraud.

10. A special shareholders' meeting is called to consider a proposed merger. A minority bloc of stockholders does not have sufficient voting power to prevent the merger. Nor does this group wish to exercise its dissent and appraisal remedy. However, the shares of the group are needed to meet the quorum requirements for a valid shareholders' meeting. Thus, they boycott the meeting and the merger cannot be voted on. Have these minority shareholders acted in an illegal manner? *No, s/hers don't have any fiduciary obligations except to pay for prescribed stk.*

1. O'Neal, *Close Corporations*, p. 105 (1958).

2. See, annot: "Duty and Liability of Closely Held Corporation, Its Directors, Officers, or Majority Stockholders, in Acquiring Stock of Minority Shareholder," 7 *ALR* 3d. 500 (1966).

3. See cases discussed, *ibid.*, at 504, 505.

4. *Weinberger* v. *UOP, Inc.*, 426 A2d. 1333 (1981).

5. *Ibid.*

6. *Jones* v. *Ahmanson and Company*, 460 P2d. 464 (1969).

7. *Ibid.*, at 474.

8. American Bar Foundation, Model Business Corporation Act Annotated, 2nd ed., p. 492 (1971).

9. *Ibid.*, p. 493.

10. *Gidwitz* v. *Lanzit Corrugated Box Co.*, 170 N.E. 2d. 131 (1960).

Endnotes

Business Organizations and the Securities Laws

Part
Five

Securities Regulation

14

The most dynamic and significant area of corporation law today is that of securities regulation. The past several years have observed court decisions whose effects have reverberated throughout the corporate, financial, accounting, and legal fields. Reactions to these controversial decisions have been strong and varied. At one end of the spectrum are those applauding the recent developments as the beginning of effective regulation over heretofore ignored financial shenanigans. Others perceive it as a meddling judiciary, lacking the necessary expertise, second-guessing good faith business or professional judgment. The controversy is of such intensity that the popular press occasionally gives it coverage. It is quite a change from the pre-1968 days when securities law was regarded as just another quiet, esoteric subject.

Regulation over securities transactions can come from two sources: the federal government or the states. State regulation is by statutes called "blue sky laws." The phrase received common acceptance after a judge's decision referred to "speculative schemes which have no more basis than so many feet of blue sky."[1] Prior to 1933 state statutes provided the sole regulation of securities in the United States. While these statutes vary from state to state, there are three general types.

Blue Sky Laws

The Fraud Type.   These usually proscribe as illegal the use of "fraud" in the issuance, promotion, distribution, sale, or purchase of securities. The term fraud is broadly defined but typically involves some form of deception or misrepresentation. Violations can lead to criminal prosecution for past activities and injunctions barring the future utilization of such practices.

The Dealer Type.   These mandate the registration of brokers, dealers, and sales personnel with the state. Requirements necessary to fulfill this obligation differ in the various jurisdictions.

The Registration Type.   This type of statute requires that before securities can be traded in the state, they must be first registered or "qualified." Again the specifics vary. They range from requiring the filing of only minimal information to disclosing such data as the state official deems appropriate. Finally, some states have hybrid statutes that blend together elements of the three basic types.

How important, effective, or significant are the blue sky laws within the regulatory scheme? Opinion varies. Generally, state supervision of securities transactions is regarded as less effective than federal. Federal law has the advantage of being uniform and enforceable throughout the United States. The state has only abbreviated power since it terminates at its geographical boundaries. Typically the state law will receive only perfunctory execution. Securities legislation is often not a topic of great import in a state legislature and, consequently, appropriations to the agency enforcing the law may be small. There is the attitude of "let's leave it to Uncle Sam." The minority view is that one in incorrect in downplaying the significance of such laws. Some securities are exempted from federal legislation and therefore blue sky laws are the only control. And, a few state blue sky statutes contain requirements extending beyond the federal and thus yield greater protection to the investor.

Federal Securities Regulation

The federal government did not enter the securities regulation arena until the early 1930s. Remember, this was the time of the Great Depression. The 1920s had seen great prosperity. The business of America was business, and there were no dark clouds on the horizon. Prices on the stock market reached dizzying heights as more and more people engaged in an almost euphoric speculation. Many investors lacked the requisite knowledge to prudently invest in stocks. Even worse, some went beyond investing only their own savings—they borrowed money with which to purchase stock on margin. Then in 1929 came the great stock market crash. Stock prices plummeted and citizens watched their life savings disappear. The personal despair was so great for some that they committed suicide. Men tramped the streets in search of work, farms were foreclosed with the fall of the auctioneer's hammer, banks failed, and all efforts by business to halt the economic decline proved fruitless. It was in this social, economic, and political milieu that Franklin D. Roosevelt was swept into the White House on the electoral tide of 1932. Governmental efforts to aid the economy came so swiftly that the legislative branch was dubbed the "Hundred Day" Congress. The alphabet agencies were spewed forth by Congress in a torrent. Areas traditionally regarded as being within the exclusive jurisdiction of the states were subjected to federal control. While some vehemently objected to this as a distortion of our basic governmental system, most accepted it as being necessary and proper. It was against this background that the Securities Act of 1933 (also called the '33 Act) and the Securities Exchange Act of 1934 (referred to as the '34 Act) were enacted.

The twofold objectives of the federal securities laws are disclosure and prevention of fraud. They mandate full and fair disclosure to investors of all material information, be it financial or otherwise. They also prohibit deceitful and fraudulent practices, or other acts of misrepresentation, in the sale of securities. It is important to recognize that the Securities and Exchange Commission does not make a judgment as to the merits of a securities issue when it allows their sale. If one complies with the law, one can sell the securities. If the venture is highly speculative and the enterprise's success appears dubious the individual investor must be told. Once this is done, it is the individual's decision whether or not to assume the risk and make a purchase. The Securities and Exchange Commission's approval of an issue is no guarantee that the investor will make a profit. Nor is it a warranty as to the accuracy of the information contained in the registration statement and prospectus. However, the inclusion of incomplete, deceptive, or false data can lead to civil and/or criminal penalties, and the law does provide a mechanism for the investor to recover any loss suffered thereby.

Although our primary concern will be with the '33 and '34 Acts, other federal statutes have an important impact on certain aspects of the securities field and deserve mention. They are the Public Utility Holding Company Act of 1935, the Trust Indenture Act of 1939, the Investment Company Act of 1940, the Investment Advisors Act of 1940, and Chapter X of the Bankruptcy Act as it applies to corporate reorganizations. The Securities and Exchange Commission oversees the operations of these statutes, except the latter where it serves in an advisory capacity to the federal court.

The Securities Act of 1933

The '33 Act mandates that any corporation issuing securities for sale to the public make available all material information concerning those securities. The information, which is not limited to only financial data, is supplied to the Securities and Exchange Commission in the form of a registration statement. A prospectus must be made available to the investor. A prospectus is like a coin; it has two sides. On the one side it provides information, much of which is duplicative of the registration statement, to the investor so that he or she may judge the merits of the securities. On the reverse side, a prospectus is a sales device. It makes the potential investor aware of the corporation and of the financial product that it is selling—its corporate securities. It aims to convince the investor of the wisdom of making a purchase by holding out the hope of future financial gain. The second basic element of the '33 Act is its prohibition of fraudulent, deceptive, or misleading activities in the sale of securities. Its fraud provisions apply only to sellers; the fraud provisions of the '34 Act apply to both sellers and buyers. These antifraud provisions are applicable regardless of whether registration of the securities is required.

The Securities Exchange Act of 1934

This law created the Securities and Exchange Commission (SEC). The statute requires the disclosure of specified information by companies whose securities are listed and traded on the national stock exchanges. A 1964 amendment placed these requirements on companies whose equity securities are traded over-the-counter. The disclosures required resemble those of the '33 Act. It requires the registration with the SEC of national stock exchanges and broker-dealers conducting over-the-counter activities of an interstate nature. It contains prohibitions on the use of inside information in securities transactions. It regulates the process of proxy (a shareholder's vote) solicitations and governs tender offer solicitations (corporate takeover attempts through a stock acquisition). It grants the Federal Reserve System's Board of Governors the power to establish margin requirements—the amount of credit that can be extended to purchase or carry securities. The objective is to prevent the excessive use of credit in the securities market.

The Securities and Exchange Commission

The Securities and Exchange Commission was created by Congress in 1934 to administer the various federal securities laws. It is an independent quasi-judicial agency of the federal government.

The Commission consists of five persons appointed by the President with the advice and consent of the Senate. The President designates which person shall serve as Chairman. They serve staggered five-year terms with a vacancy being created in June of each year. A Commission member is eligible for reappointment. Not more than three commissioners can be members of the same political party. However, it should be clear that a President can appoint a majority of the Commission before the expiration of his first term of office, or even sooner, if vacancies are created by death or resignation.

The SEC has enjoyed a sterling reputation for expertise, integrity, and political independence.

The Commission directs a staff that is organized along functional lines. The staff is separated into five divisions: corporation finance, market regulation, corporate regulation, investment management regulation, and enforcement. There is also an office of the general counsel and chief accountant to provide technical advice to the Commission and staff. Regional offices are maintained around the country to conduct investigations and otherwise carry out the duties of the Commission.

The Commission investigates complaints of possible violations in securities transactions. These investigations are essentially fact-finding inquiries. If there is a prima facie indication of a violation, the Commission can select from several courses of action. It may seek a civil injunction. The case can be referred to the Justice Department for criminal prosecution if fraud or other willful law violation is indicated. The Commission can impose an administrative remedy after holding an administrative hearing. Such a remedy could take the form of censuring an individual or barring him from employment with a registered firm; suspending or expelling members from the exchange; or denying, suspending or revoking the registration of broker-dealers.

It is important to remember that private individuals can bring damage actions to collect the damages they incurred because of the violations.

The Commission also promulgates rules that have the force of law. It gives public notice of suggested rules and invites comments and criticisms, which are considered in determining the nature and scope of the rules to be adopted. The operation of these rules receives regular review so as to provide pragmatic up-to-date protection for investors.

Going Public

Once an entrepreneur has successfully developed a corporation, he or she may consider taking it public. Just as the original selection of the form of business organization to be adopted involved advantages and disadvantages, so too, does the decision on going public.

Advantages of Going Public
1. Develops a new source of funds. The proceeds from the sale of the securities to the public are available to the corporation for expansion, retirement of existing debt, etc. If the corporation is successful, the public can furnish a recurring source of new funds.

2. Prestige. There is a certain degree of prestige attached to an association with a publicly owned corporation. The founders can derive a tremendous psychological feeling of achievement in the development of the corporation. The company and its products will enjoy greater visibility.

3. Enhances the capability to attract and retain high-quality personnel. The availability of publicly traded stock, with its potential for capital gains treatment, can be an important incentive to some prospective managers.

4. Establishes a ready market for the company's securities. As a private concern, there is no ready market available for trading the securities and difficulties are encountered in valuation of those securities.

5. An alternate method of financing acquisitions is created. Instead of using cash, the corporation can use its securities to purchase a desired

business. In the late 1960s many of the conglomerates were built through such stock acquisitions.

6. Going public can make the founders wealthy. They can sell off a portion of their stock, yielding a large amount of cash, while retaining a sufficiently large interest to retain corporate control.

7. It can provide the cash to pay estate taxes. Occasionally a large family concern will go public in order to raise the large amount of money necessary to pay federal estate taxes.

Disadvantages of Going Public

1. It is very expensive. The legal fees and auditors' fees can be quite large. Printing the necessary documents, such as the prospectus, can be costly. It is not uncommon for these three items to total in excess of $100,000. Added to this is the largest expense—the fee of the underwriter who is handling the issue. The underwriter typically charges a percentage commission (2 to 10 percent) based on the public offering price. Since fixed commissions were abolished on May 1, 1975, the parties negotiate the commission rate. For instance, in December 1982 AT&T sold 17.7 million shares at $60 per share for a total of $1.06 billion. It netted $1.04 billion, since its total financing costs were $1.35 per share.

2. New expenses of an ongoing nature are created. While the underwriter's commission and certain other expenses only accompany the actual issuance and distribution of securities, other expenses constantly recur. Extra legal and accounting expenses are entailed in filing required reports with the SEC. Annual shareholder reports and proxy materials involve administrative costs of preparation plus printing and mailing expenses.

3. Privacy is lost. The shareholders have access to a great deal of information on corporate activities that a private corporation would not publicly reveal.

4. Loss of independence. Managing a privately held corporation involves important differences from running a publicly held corporation. Certain actions can require approval by the shareholders or an independent board of directors. In addition to such legal requirements, there can be practical obstacles in regard to certain matters. Purchase of a corporate jet or a nepotistic hiring policy is one thing in a private corporation and quite a different matter in a public concern.

5. Accountability to the public. Required disclosure of information can involve justification for particular corporate policies. Both the shareholders and public at large may demand an explanation of a certain matter. This can demand the attention of high-level executives. If satisfactory answers are not forthcoming, the corporation may face a stockholders' derivative suit.

6. The creation of conflicting interests may be inevitable. The company founders may be in a tax bracket where they do not want dividends to be paid. Other shareholders may well desire dividend income. A particular course of action may appear highly attractive over the long run, yet would cause a plunge in the current market price of the stock. Reconciliation of such issues can prove troublesome.

7. Loss of control. In the long run, the founders may face loss of control or a severe diminution of power. Outsiders can gain progressively larger holdings if subsequent stock offerings are necessary or if a series of acquisitions occur by means of stock swaps.

Although we have been frequently using the word, we have not as yet defined "security." It has an extremely broad meaning! Section 2(1) of the '33 Act defines it thus:

What is a Security?

> The term "security" means any note, stock, treasury stock, bond, debenture, evidence of indebtedness, certificate of interest or participation in any profit-sharing agreement, collateral-trust certificate or subscription, transferable share, investment contract, voting-trust certificate, certificate of deposit for a security, fractional undivided interest in oil, gas, or other mineral rights, or, in general, any interest or instrument commonly known as a "security," or any certificate of interest or participation in, temporary or interim certificate for, receipt for, guarantee of, or warrant or right to subscribe to or purchase, any of the foregoing.

Despite this lengthy recitation, it is neither exhaustive nor all-inclusive. The definition expands to meet the ever-expanding ingenuity of promoters. As the Supreme Court has stated it will examine the substance of the transaction and not be guided merely by the form it takes. The sale of silver foxes for breeding purposes, where the seller retained possession and provided the necessary management, has been held to constitute the sale of a security.[2] So has the sale of withdrawable capital shares in a savings and loan organization[3] and the sale of memberships in a country club.[4]

The case that follows demonstrates the breadth given to the term "security." It should alert one to the fact that the securities laws apply not only to the fraudulent schemes of fly-by-night promoters but also to some commercial transactions of the legitimate enterprise. That enterprise may never even conceive that the transaction has securities consequences. One must guard against the naive concept that "security" equates only to stocks and bonds. As the court points out, the law does not excuse one who fails to abide by it, even though the person does so because of a bona fide mistake.

SEC v. HOWEY
328 U.S. 293 (1946)

MR. JUSTICE MURPHY

The Securities and Exchange Commission instituted this action to restrain the respondents from using the mails and instrumentalities of interstate commerce in the offer and sale of unregistered and non-exempt securities in violation of § 5 (a) of the Act. The District Court denied the injunction, . . . and the Fifth Circuit Court of Appeals affirmed the judgment. . . .

Most of the facts are stipulated. The respondents, W.J. Howey Company and Howey-in-the-Hills Service, Inc., are Florida corporations under direct common control and management. The Howey Company owns large tracts of citrus acreage in Lake County, Florida. During the past several years it has planted about 500 acres annually, keeping half of the grooves itself and offering the other half to the public "to help us finance additional development." Howey-in-the-Hills Service, Inc., is a service company engaged in cultivating and developing many of these groves, including the harvesting and marketing of the crops.

Each prospective customer is offered both a land sales contract and a service contract, after having been told that it is not feasible to invest in a grove unless service arrangements are made. While the purchaser is free to make arrangements with other service companies, the superiority of Howey-in-the-Hills Service, Inc., is stressed. Indeed, 85 percent of the acreage sold during the 3-year period ending May 31, 1943 was covered by service contracts with Howey-in-the-Hills Service, Inc.

The land sales contract with the Howey Company provides for a uniform purchase price per acre or fraction thereof, varying in amount only in accordance with the number of years the particular plot has been planted with citrus trees. Upon full payment of the purchase price the land is conveyed to the purchaser by warranty deed. Purchases are usually made in narrow strips of land arranged so that an acre consists of a row of 48 trees. During the period between February 1, 1941, and May 31, 1943, 31 of the 42 persons making purchases bought less than 5 acres each. These tracts are not separately fenced and the sole indication of several ownership is found in small land marks intelligible only through a plat book record.

The service contract, generally of a ten year duration without option of cancellation, gives Howey-in-the-Hills Service, Inc., a leasehold interest and "full and complete" possession of the acreage. For a specified fee plus the cost of labor and materials, the company is given full discretion and authority over the cultivation of the groves and the harvest and marketing of the crops. Without the consent of the company, the land owner or purchaser has no right of entry to market the crop; thus there is ordinarily no right to specific fruit. The company is accountable only for an allocation of the net profits based upon a check made at the time of picking. All the produce is pooled by the respondent companies, which do business under their own names.

The purchasers for the most part are non-residents of Florida. They are predominantly business and professional people who lack the knowledge, skill and equipment necessary for the care and cultivation of citrus trees. They are attracted by the expectation of substantial profits. It was represented, for example, that profits during the 1943–1944 season amounted to 20 percent and that even greater profits might be expected during the 1944–1945 season, although only a 10 percent annual return was to be expected over a ten year period. . . .

Section 2(1) of the Act defines the term "security" to include the commonly known documents traded for speculation or investment. This definition also includes . . . "investment contract." . . . The legal issue in this case turns upon a determination of whether, under the circumstances, the land sales contract, the warranty deed and the service contract together constitute an "investment contract" within the meaning of § 2(1). The lower courts, in reaching a negative answer to this problem, treated the contracts and deeds as separate transactions involving no more than an ordinary real estate sale and an agreement by the seller to manage the property for the buyer.

The term "investment contract" is undefined by the Securities Act or by relevant legislative reports. But the term was common in many state "blue sky" laws in existence prior to the adoption of the federal statute and, although the term was also undefined by the state law, it had been broadly construed by state courts so as to afford the investing public a full measure of protection. Form was disregarded for substance and emphasis was placed upon economic reality. An investment contract thus came to mean a contract or scheme for "the placing of capital or laying out of money in a way intended to secure income or profit from its employment." . . .

By including an investment contract within the scope of § 2 (1) of the Securities Act, Congress was using the term the meaning of which had been crystallized by this prior judicial interpretation. In other words, an investment contract for purposes of the Securities Act means a contract, transaction or scheme whereby a person invests his money in a common enterprise and is led to expect profits solely from the efforts of the promoter or a third party, it being immaterial whether the shares in the enterprise are evidenced by formal certificates or by nominal interests in the physical assets employed in the enterprise. . . . It embodies a flexible rather than a static principle, one that is capable of adaptation to meet the countless and variable schemes devised by those who seek the use of the money of others on the promise of profits.

The transactions in this case clearly involve investment contracts as so defined. The respondent companies are offering something more than fee simple interest in land, something different from a farm or orchard coupled with management services. They are offering an opportunity to contribute money and to share in the profits of a large citrus fruit enterprise managed and partly owned by respondents. They are offering this opportunity to persons who reside in distant localities and who lack the equipment and experience requisite to the cultivation, harvesting and marketing of the citrus products. Such persons have no desire to occupy the land or to develop it themselves; they are attacted solely by the prospects of a return on their investment. Indeed, individual development of the plots of land that are offered and sold would seldom be economically feasible due to their small size. Such tracts gain utility as citrus groves only when cultivated and developed as component parts of a larger area. A common enterprise managed by respondents or third parties with adequate personnel and equipment is therefore essential if the investors are to achieve their paramount aim of a return on their investments. Their respective shares in this enterprise are evidenced by land sales contracts and warranty deeds, which serve as a convenient method of determining the investors' allocable shares of the profits. The resulting tranfer of rights in land is purely incidental.

Thus all the elements of a profit-seeking business venture are present here. The investors provide the capital and share in the earnings and profits; the promoters manage, control and operate the enterprise. It follows that the arrangements whereby the investors' interests are made manifest involve investment contracts, regardless of the legal terminology in which such contracts are clothed. The investment contracts in this instance take the form of land sales contracts, warranty deeds and service contracts which respondents offer to prospective investors. And respondents' failure to abide by the statutory and administrative rules in making such offerings, even though the failure results from a bona fide mistake as to the law, cannot be sanctioned under the Act.

This conclusion is unaffected by the fact that some purchasers choose not to accept the full offer of an investment contract by declining to enter into a service contract with the respondents. The Securities Act prohibits the offer as well as the sale of unregistered, nonexempt securities. Hence it is enough that the respondents merely offer the essential ingredients of an investment contract. . . .

The test is whether the scheme involves an investment of money in a common enterprise with profits to come solely from the efforts of others. If that test be satisfied, it is immaterial whether the enterprise is speculative or nonspeculative or whether there is a sale of property with or without intrinsic value. The statutory policy of affording broad protection to investors is not to be thwarted by unrealistic and irrelevant formulae.

Reversed.

Case Questions

1. Does this decision reflect pragmatism on the part of the court when examining a legal issue within the context of a commercial venture?
2. Is it possible to design the sale of an orchard coupled with management services without the securities law applying to the transaction? How?
3. Is it realistic to attribute to Congress, when it enacts legislation, knowledge of various state court decisions interpreting the term "investment contract"?

Notice that in its definition of a security the Supreme Court talked of an investment of money with the expectation of "profit solely from the efforts of the promoter or a third party." Does this mean that if the investor devotes some personal effort to the enterprise that the transaction is then outside the scope of the securities laws? Consider the sale of cosmetics through a pyramid type of operation. One becomes an independent distributor called a beauty advisor by buying the product at a discount, and income is based solely on retail sales. One can become a supervisor for an investment of $1000. A supervisor gets a larger discount on the cosmetics and may sell them directly at retail or at wholesale to beauty advisors. If the supervisor introduces an individual to the program and that individual then becomes a supervisor, the supervisor who made the introduction receives $600 of the $1,000. At the peak is the position of distributor. An investment of $5,000 yields distributor status. This brings an even greater discount on cosmetics, which can then be sold to supervisors, beauty advisors, or at retail. The distributor who introduces a person to the program who becomes a distributor will receive $3,000, or if the person becomes a supervisor $600. The investor in the project gets prospects to attend a meeting where the plan is described. The prospects who attend the meeting are greeted by investors as well as employees of the company, both of whom try to project an image of affluence. The hope is to create an atmosphere where the prospect will sign a contract and become an investor. When the SEC challenged such an operation the defense was raised that the company was not selling a security because the investors themselves were contributing their own efforts to the project. The court acknowledged that a literal application of the *Howey* test would exempt such an operation from regulation by the SEC. It then went on, however, to discuss the remedial purposes of the securities statutes and noted that the Supreme Court had admonished against a rigid interpretation of the term security. It ruled that, when a promoter retains the immediate control over the essential managerial conduct of an enterprise and the investor's realization of profit is inextricably tied to the success of the promotional scheme, such a venture comes within the definition of an investment contract. The court pointed out that these pyramid operations differ significantly from the conventional franchises and that the court was not subjecting the latter to registration requirements [*SEC* v. *Koscot Interplanetary Inc.,* 497 F.2d 473 (1974)].

The next case is the most recent Supreme Court decision on the issue of what constitutes a security. In it the court determines that a common form of a pension plan does not constitute a security.

TEAMSTERS v. DANIEL
439 U.S. 551 (1979)

(Authors' note: The Teamsters and a trucking firm had a collective bargaining agreement that contained a pension plan. All contributions to the plan were made by the employer. To be eligible for a pension an employee was required to have 20 years of continuous service. Daniel, who had over 20 years' service, was denied a pension because of a break in service. He sued the union and the pension fund trustee, alleging that they had misrepresented and omitted to state material facts with respect to the pension plan and that this constituted fraud in connection with the sale of a security. The lower courts ruled that his interest in the pension fund constituted a security. The Supreme Court reversed.)

MR. JUSTICE POWELL *delivered the opinion of the Court.*

This case presents the question whether a non-contributory, compulsory pension plan constitutes a "security" within the meaning of the Securities Act of 1933 and the Securities Exchange Act of 1934.

To determine whether a particular financial relationship constitutes an investment contract, "[t]he test is whether the scheme involves an investment of money in a common enterprise with profits to come solely from the efforts of others." This test is to be applied in light of "the substance—the economic realities of the transaction—rather than the names that may have been employed by the parties."

In a pension plan such as this one . . . the purported investment is a relatively insignificant part of an employee's total and indivisible compensation package. Looking at the economic realities, it seems clear than an employee is selling his labor primarily to obtain a livelihood, not making an investment.

Respondent also argues that employer contributions on his behalf constituted his investment into the Fund. Again, it ignores the economic realities to equate employer contributions with an investment by the employee.

The Court of Appeals believed that Daniel's expectation of profit derived from the Fund's successful management and investment of its assets. To the extent pension benefits exceeded employer contributions and depended on earnings from the assets, it was thought they contained a profit element. The Fund's trustees provided the managerial efforts which produced this profit element.

As in other parts of its analysis, the court below found an expectation of profit in the pension plan only by focusing on one of its less important aspects to the exclusion of its more significant elements. It is true that the Fund, like other holders of large assets, depends to some extent on earnings from its assets. In the case of a pension fund, however, a far larger portion of its income comes from employer contributions, a source in no way dependent on the efforts of the Fund's managers.

The importance of asset earnings in relation to the other benefits received from employment is diminished further by the fact that where a plan has substantial preconditions to vesting, the principal barrier to an individual employee's realization of pension benefits is not the financial health of the fund. Rather, it is his own ability to meet the fund's eligibility requirements. When viewed in light of the to-

tal compensation package an employee must receive in order to be eligible for pension benefits, it becomes clear that the possibility of participating in a plan's asset earnings "is far too speculative and insubstantial to bring the entire transaction within the Securities Acts."

If any further evidence were needed to demonstrate that pension plans of the type involved are not subject to the Securities Acts, the enactment of ERISA in 1974 would put the matter to rest. Unlike the Securities Acts, ERISA deals expressly and in detail with pension plans.

The existence of this comprehensive legislation governing the use and terms of employee pension plans severely undercuts all arguments for extending the Securities Act to non-contributory, compulsory pension plans. Congress believed that it was filling a regulatory void when it enacted ERISA, . . .

We hold that the Securities Acts do not apply to a non-contributory, compulsory pension plan. The judgment below is therefore reversed.

Case Questions

1. In light of the importance that an individual may attach to pension benefits, does the court too casually reject Daniel's argument when it characterizes such a pension plan as a relatively insignificant part of an employee's compensation package?

2. If Congress had not passed ERISA (the pension reform law), would the court have made a different decision in this case?

3. If the pension plan was a contributory one, with Daniel contributing some of his own funds via a payroll deduction plan, would the court decision be the same?

Public Sale of Securities

Once the decision has been made to go public through the sale of securities, the registration process of the law must be complied with. The registration statement and prospectus must be prepared and filed. One cannot immediately sell the securities on filing the registration statement. The SEC must be afforded time to check the material to ascertain whether it complies with the law. While waiting for the registration statement to become effective, the issuer may circulate a copy of the preliminary prospectus but may not sell the securities. Unless the SEC requests additional information, the registration statement will become effective 20 days after its filing. Once effective, the securities may be legally sold. It is important to note again that SEC approval of a registration statement does not mean that the SEC is vouching for the accuracy of the material or the wisdom of the investment.

Underwriting

The traditional manner of handling the public sale of securities is through a process called underwriting. The underwriters handle the sale of the securities on behalf of the issuer. Normally a group of underwriting firms handle an issue, as this can lead to a wider distribution of the securities and hopefully a successful public sale. The underwriters, accountants, and legal counsel all play a role in the preparation of the registration material. When the registration statement becomes effective, the underwriters sell the securities. Some underwriters, such as Merrill Lynch White Weld Capital Markets Groups, have a wide network of retail brokerage offices related to them through which they may distribute the securities to the investing public. Others, such as Morgan Stanley & Co., lack their own retail outlets. There are two methods by which the underwriters handle the sale of an issue. Under the first method the underwriter is paid a commission on the securities it arranges to sell. Under the second, the underwriter itself purchases a specific amount of the securities and makes its profit by reselling the securities to the public at a higher price. Or at least it hopes for a higher price, because otherwise it bears the loss.

Shelf Registration

The SEC sent shudders through the securities industry when it permitted issuers to handle the public sale of securities in a second, dramatically different manner as of March 1982. Instead of registering securities each time before they are sold, a company can file one registration statement and then sell those securities "off the shelf" whenever market conditions are favorable.

The SEC adopted this experimental method in Rule 415. The rule relates to the registration of securities that are reasonably expected to be offered and sold on a delayed or continuous basis within two years. Either equity or debt may be sold under the rule. However, there are some restrictions on who may utilize the procedure. Approximately 9000 companies have securities registered with the SEC. It is believed that only about 1300 of the largest ones can qualify under the rules, as it is necessary that a company must, among other requirements, have filed all required SEC documents for at least the last three years. Naturally, a company that is initially going public cannot avail itself of the process.

The SEC originally said that it was adopting the rule on an experimental basis. Subsequently, it extended the effective date of the rule until December 31, 1983. It said that such an extension was necessary to provide sufficient data on the effectiveness of the system. The rule is controversial. Opponents argue that it does not provide the time necessary to form the traditional underwriting syndicates. Consequently, only the largest firms, with the capital, ability to absorb the risk, and the outlets to sell the securities will handle the issues. They question whether proper disclosure will be provided when an issue is registered on the shelf and then some time in the future it is taken down and quickly sold. Under such circumstances, can the underwriters and legal counsel engage in the due diligence examination required by law and will the investor be sufficiently alerted to corporate developments subsequent to the registration? Small brokerage firms and underwriting firms that lack a system of retail outlets have vehemently opposed the rule, fearing that it will mean a significant loss of business to them. Corporations have been utilizing the system. For instance, Indianapolis Power & Light registered 1.3 million shares of common; General Motors Acceptance placed $1 billion of debt on the shelf; and Exxon Finance registered $500 million in debt in the first two months the rule was effective.

Whether shelf registration will prove to be only a short-lived experiment, or whether it will come to rival the traditional underwriting method of marketing securities to the public, remains to be seen.

Involuntarily Going Public

One may believe that the decision to be a privately held concern rests solely with the corporation. While that is generally true, circumstances can force a company into the unwanted status of a publicly held concern. Under Section 12g an issuer that has $3 million in total assets and a class of securities held by 500 or more persons must file a registration statement for those securities. Thus, those concerns that wish to retain the privacy and freedom of action that accompany the nonpublic enterprise must install mechanisms designed to insure that the shareholders do not number over 499.

Securities Exempt from Registration

Some companies wish to avoid the expense of registration and forego the continuing burden of filing quarterly reports and annual reports, the latter containing audited financial statements. These reporting obligations continue indefinitely until the number of shareholders drops below 300. In such a case the reporting obligations are suspended, not eliminated. Such companies may still be able to raise funds from a sale of securities, because not every security is required to be registered under the '33 Act. There are several exemptions from the registration requirement. Some of the more important exemptions listed in Section 3 of the Act are:

1. Securities of the state or federal government or their political sub-divisions.

2. Securities of banks, charitable organizations, common carriers subject to the Interstate Commerce Act, and savings and loan associations.

3. Insurance policies, commercial paper with a maturity not exceeding nine months, and securities issued by small business investment companies.

4. Intrastate issues offered and sold only to residents within the state where the corporation is incorporated and doing business.

5. Securities not exceeding $1,500,000. (The small issue exemption under Regulation A.)

6. Transactions by an issuer not involving any public offerings, i.e., private offerings. [Section 4(2).]

7. Small issue exemptions under Rules 504, 505, and 506 of Regulation D.

One cannot forget the presence of the blue sky laws. If an issue of securities is exempt under the federal laws, it still may be necessary to comply with a state's securities laws. It is also worthwhile to again repeat the fact that the law's antifraud provisions can apply to securities offerings even though they are exempt from registration. Section 17 of the '33 Act makes it unlawful to utilize any instrumentality of interstate commerce or the mails in the fraudulent sale of securities.

Let us now examine some of these exemptions in more detail. In the *Ralston Purina* case the court provides some perspective on what constitutes an exempt private offering by holding that the arrangement in question constitutes a public offering, thus necessitating registration.

SEC v. RALSTON PURINA COMPANY
346 U.S. 119 (1953)

MR. JUSTICE CLARK *delivered the opinion of the Court.*

Section 4 (1) of the Securities Act of 1933 exempts "transactions by an issuer not involving any public offering" from the registration requirements of § 5. We must decide whether Ralston Purina's offerings of treasury stock to its "key employees" are within this exemption. . . .

At least since 1911 the company has had a policy of encouraging stock ownership among its employees; more particularly, since 1942 it has made authorized but unissued common shares available to some of them. Between 1947 and 1951, the period covered by the record in this case, Ralston Purina sold nearly $2,000,000 of stock to employees without registration and in so doing made use of the mails.

In each of these years, a corporate resolution authorized the sale of common stock "to employees . . . who shall, without any solicitation by the Company or its officers or employees, inquire of any of them as to how to purchase common stock of Ralston Purina Company.". . . Among those responding to these offers were employees with the duties of artist, bakeshop foreman, chow loading foreman, clerical assistant, copywriter, electrician, stock clerk, mill office clerk, order credit trainee, production trainee, stenographer, and veterinarian. . . .

The company bottoms its exemption claim on the classification of all offerees as "key employees" in its organization. Its position on trial was that "A key employee . . . is not confined to an organizational chart. It would include an individual who is eligible for promotion, an individual who especially influences others or who advises others, a person whom the employees look to in some special way, an individual, of course, who carries some special responsibility, who is sympathetic to management and who is ambitious and who the management feels is likely to be promoted to a greater responsibility." That an offering to all of its employees would be public is conceded.

The Securities Act nowhere defines the scope of § 4 (1)'s private offering exemption. Nor is the legislative history of much help in staking out its boundaries . . .

Decisions under comparable exemptions in the English Companies Acts and state "blue sky" laws, the statutory antecedents of federal securities legislation, have made one thing clear—to be public an offer need not be open to the whole world. In *Securities and Exchange Comm'n* v. *Sunbeam Gold Mines Co.*, 95 F 2d 699 (. . . 1938), this point was made in dealing with an offering to the stockholders of two corporations about to be merged. Judge Denman observed that:

> In its broadest meaning the term "public" distinguishes the populace at large from groups of individual members of the public segregated because of some common interest or characteristic. Yet such a distinction is inadequate for practical purposes; manifestly, an offering

of securities to all red-headed men, to all residents of Chicago or San Francisco, to all existing stockholders of the General Motors Corporation or the American Telephone & Telegraph Company, is no less "public," in every realistic sense of the word, than an unrestricted offering to the world at large. Such an offering, though not open to everyone who may choose to apply, is none the less "public" in character for the means used to select the particular individuals to whom the offering is to be made bear no sensible relation to the purposes for which the selection is made. . . .

> . . .

The design of the statute is to protect investors by promoting full disclosure of information thought necessary to informed investment decisions. The natural way to interpret the private offering exemption is in light of the statutory purpose. Since exempt transactions are those as to which "there is no practical need for (the bill's) application," the applicability of § 4 (1) should turn on whether the particular class of persons affected needs the protection of the Act. An offering to those who are shown to be able to fend for themselves is a transaction "not involving any public offering."

The Commission would have us go one step further and hold that "an offering to a substantial number of the public" is not exempt under § 4 (1). . . . But the statute would seem to apply to a "public offering" whether to few or many. It may well be that offerings to a substantial number of persons would rarely be exempt. Indeed nothing prevents the commission, in enforcing the statute, from using some kind of numerical test in deciding when to investigate particular exemption claims. But there is no warrant for superimposing a quantity limit on private offerings as a matter of statutory interpretation.

The exemption, as we construe it, does not deprive corporate employees, as a class, of the safeguards of the Act. We agree that some employee offerings may come within § 4 (1) e.g., one made to executive personnel who because of their position have access to the same kind of information that the Act would make available in the form of a registration statement. Absent such a showing of special circumstances, employees are just as much members of the investing "public" as any of their neighbors in the community. . . .

Keeping in mind the broadly remedial purposes of federal securities legislation, imposition of the burden of proof on an issuer who would plead the exemption seems to us fair and reasonable. . . . Agreeing, the court below thought the burden met primarily because of the respondent's purpose in singling out its key employees for stock offerings. But once it is seen that the exemption question turns on the knowledge of the offerees, the issuer's motives, laudable though they may be, fade into irrelevance. The focus of inquiry should be on the need of the offerees for the protections afforded by registration. The employees here were not shown to have access to the kind of information which registration would disclose. The obvious opportunities for pressure and imposition make it advisable that they be entitled to compliance with § 5.

Reversed.

Case Questions

1. Is it a valid argument to contend that "key employees" can include such personnel as a stock clerk, production trainee, and bakeshop supervisor?

2. Did the court err in not giving more weight to the fact that these employees solicited the stock on their own initiative?

3. Why did the court not hold that an offering to a substantial number of the public is not exempt?

4. Is it correct to delineate private versus public offerings on the basis of the financial sophistication of the purchaser?

Rule 144: Persons Deemed Not to Be Engaged in a Distribution and Therefore Not Underwriters

Mention should be made of an additional point of confusion involving exempt nonpublic offerings and exempt transactions by any person other than an issuer, underwriter, or dealer. The problem arises thus: an issuer sells exempt nonregistered stock to A, who purchases the stock for investment purposes. A now desires to resell the stock. Is resale permissable, absent registration of the stock? An underwriter is defined by the '33 Act as, among other things, one who purchased from an issuer with a view to distribution. Securities transactions by underwriters are not exempt from registration. So, may A legally sell? If A does sell, has the issuer also violated the Act by virtue of A's serving as a mere conduit in the transfer of those securities to the public? Lacking concrete answers to such questions, the securities industry developed the concept of "letter stock." The purchaser would sign an "investment letter" acknowledging receipt of information concerning the issuing company and attesting to the availability of any further data, their personal contact with corporate officials, their knowledge of the investment risks, and the fact that the stock was unregistered and that they were purchasing the stock with the intention of holding it for investment and not for resale. Another device designed to provide some guidance was the "change of circumstances" doctrine. If the investor purchased the nonregistered securities under one set of conditions but then experienced a "change of circumstances," this change might permit their resale. These subsequently experienced circumstances would be studied in an attempt to ascertain whether the original purchase was strictly for investment purposes. Coupled with this doctrine was the element of a time requirement. If the investor held the securities for a lengthy period of time, this could serve as an indication of his investment intentions at the time of the original purchase. No holding period was ever officially established, but a rough rule of thumb developed specifying a minimum two-year holding period. However, both the investment letter concept and the change in circumstances doctrine lacked official legal sanction. Thus, an important area of securities law was uncharted and dangerous. In 1972 the SEC ended much of the uncertainty by adopting Rule 144.

Rule 144 is not the exclusive method of meeting the statutory requirements. However, those not complying with the rule again do so at their own risk and face a substantial burden in establishing that the offers and resale are exempt from registration. The rule provides that a person who sells restricted securities is not deemed to be engaged in a distribution of the securities, and therefore is not an underwriter, if the securities are sold in accordance with the terms of the rule. The rule contains basically the following provisions: (1) the restricted securities must have been beneficially owned for a period of at least two years; (2) the amount sold cannot exceed 1 percent of the class outstanding, or if traded on an exchange, the lesser of that amount or the average weekly volume on all such exchanges during the four weeks preceding the sale; (3) the securities must be sold in brokers' transactions (the broker is restricted to only executing the order; he cannot solicit buy orders and he may be paid only the customary commission); (4) adequate information in regard to the issuer must be available to the public; and (5) the person desiring to sell the securities must file with the SEC a notice to that effect.

In conjunction with the adoption of Rule 144, the SEC made several important observations. They put all persons on notice that the "change in circumstances" concept would no longer be considered as one of the factors in determining whether a person is an underwriter. The Commission now regards that concept as failing to meet the objective of the '33 Act since the circumstances of the seller are unrelated to the need of investors for the protections afforded by registration. For restrictive securities not sold pursuant to the rule, the SEC will consider the length of time the securities have been held in deciding whether the seller is an underwriter. However, the fact that securities have been held for a particular period of time does not establish per se the availability of an exemption from registration. Finally, the Commission strongly suggests that the issuer use an appropriate legend on the stock certificates, noting the fact that they are unregistered, and provide stop-transfer instructions to stock transfer agents. It will consider these as a factor in determining whether the issuer had in fact made an initial private placement.

In 1974 the SEC adopted Rule 147 establishing guidelines for what it would consider an intrastate offering and hence exempt from registration. Like the other rules that relate to an exemption from the registration requirements, it is not the exclusive method of meeting the statutory mandate.

The rule establishes the following criteria: (1) the issuer must be a resident and doing business within the state where the securities are sold; (2) the offerees and purchasers must be residents within that state; and (3) resale of the securities must be limited for nine months after the last sale of the issue. An issuer is a resident of the state if it is a corporation incorporated there; if it is an unincorporated entity, such as a partnership; or if it is organized under the laws of that state. The SEC considers the issuer as doing business in a state if it has its principal office located there, derives 80 percent of it gross revenue from the state, has 80 percent of its assets located in the state, and will use 80 percent of the proceeds of the issue in the state. The sale of securities to a single nonresident will remove the exemption.

Using its rulemaking powers the SEC has adopted rules that allow certain issues below a specified dollar figure to be sold without the normal registration process. Regulation A allows the sale of up to $1.5 million in securities during a 12-month period. However, the issuer must prepare an offering circular and file notification with the SEC 10 business days prior to the sale of the securities. The financial statements must be in accordance with generally accepted accounting principles, but they are not required to be audited.

Effective April 15, 1982, the SEC adopted new Regulation D with six rules that exempt three types of transactions from the registration requirements of the securities laws. Under Rule 504 an issuer can sell up to $500,000 in securities in a 12-month period. There is no limit on the number of investors, but a general solicitation of investors is prohibited. Resale of the securities is restricted. Rule 505 permits the sale of $5 million in securities in a 12-month period to 35 nonaccredited investors (plus unlimited accredited investors, i.e. corporate officials and very large net-worth investors). A general solicitation for investors is prohibited and the resale of the stock is restricted. Rule 506 has no dollar limit on the size of the securities offering. The number of investors is limited to 35 nonaccredited and an unlimited number of accredited investors. As in the other two rules, a general solicitation of investors is not allowed and there are restrictions on the resale of the stock.

These rules replace exemptions that used to exist under Rules 146, 240, and 242. It is important to keep in mind that the antifraud provisions of the law apply to both registered and exempt unregistered securities. Also, the blue sky laws must be followed. Why does an issuer risk running afoul of the SEC by making a private offering? Would it not prove easier to register the securities? Typically, the answer is financial. The legal, accounting, administrative, and underwriting expenses that accompany a securities regulation can assume substantial proportions. A private placement can oftentimes be arranged more quickly than a public offering. If the securities markets are favorable, the issuing company will want to sell the securities as soon as possible to avoid an unfavorable downturn in the financial markets.

What Constitutes the Same Issue?

It has been observed that certain sales of securities can avoid the normal registration process. These sales normally have a specified dollar limit. How is it to be ascertained whether an issuer is making a number of separate issues or merely selling portions of the same issue? If it is the latter and the total amount exceeds the dollar limitation, then the issuer is in violation of the law. If the offers and sales are part of the same issue they are regarded as being "integrated." It determining whether an issue is integrated, the SEC states that the following factors may be determinative: (1) Are the offerings part of a single plan of financing? (2) Do the offerings involve the issuance of the same class of securities? (3) Are the offerings made at, or about, the same time? (4) Is the same form of consideration to be received? (5) Are the offerings made for the same general purpose?

Application of the Law's Antifraud Provisions

The following case presents an excellent illustration of what constitutes the use of an instrumentality of interstate commerce, thereby subjecting the transaction to the federal securities' laws antifraud provisions. Note two things: (1) the stock is of a closed corporation and (2) the telephone was used only on an intrastate basis.

MYZEL v. FIELDS
386 F. 2d 718 (1967)

LAY, Circuit Judge
The four cases here considered are actions brought under Securities and Exchange Commission Rule 10b-5 . . . arising out of the sale of stock of a closed corporation. Trial was held before a jury and jury verdicts totaling $441,000 were returned in favor of the plaintiff. . . . We affirm the verdicts and judgments below.

The basic issues are: (1) jurisdiction over intrastate sales. . . .

Both Section 10 of the Act [15 U.S.C. § 78j (b)] and Rule 10b-5 require as a jurisdictional basis "the use of any means or instrumentality of interstate commerce or of the mails, or of any facility of any national securities exchange."

The evidence is undisputed that the telephone was used only on an intrastate basis in the solicitation or purchase of each of the appellees' stock. Appellees claim that federal jurisdiction exists because the telephone is an "instrumentality of interstate commerce" and, therefore, the cases fall within the prohibition of the statute. Despite reasoning to the contrary,[1] we are convinced that Congress, in the

[1] See *Rosen* v. *Albern Color Research, Inc.,* 218 F. Supp, 473 (E.D. Pa. 1963). The Rosen case relies upon *Northern Trust Co.* v. *Essaness Theatres Corp.,* 103 F. Supp. 954 at 964 (N.D. Ill. 1952), wherein the district court states:

"The purpose of Section 17 (a) of the 1933 Act and Section 10(b) of the 1934 Act are similar and the phraseology employed is substantially similar."

Section 17(a) of the Securities Act of 1933, 15 U.S.C. § 77q(a), provides in part:

"It shall be unlawful for any person in the offer or sale of any securities by the use of any means or instruments of transportation or communication in interstate commerce or by the use of the mails, directly or indirectly * * *."

Judge Kraft in the Rosen opinion reasons that it is the interstate communication which is the essence of the offense. Despite the similarity there is a crucial omission from § 10(b) of the § 17(a) requirement that there be a communication in interstate commerce; the requirement of § 10(b) is "By the use of any means or instrumentality of interstate commerce." The legislative history does not serve to explain the difference in the wording of the two statutes. As we indicated in *Little* v. *United States,* 331 F. 2d 287, 292–293 (8 Cir. 1964), the use of the mails is not the gist of the offense:

"That the scheme to defraud is the evil intended to be controlled and remedied by passage of the Securities Act, supra cannot be in doubt * * *"

. . . . All the other sections of the Securities Exchange Act of 1934 incorporate similar language, as does the Act controlling investment companies. . . . In each case the language reads "use of the mails and means and instrumentalities of interstate commerce." The Supreme Court when faced with an analogous argument under Section 605 of the Communications Act of 1934, 47 U.S.C. § 605, stated:

"In making the alterations in the phraseology of the similar section of the earlier act Congress must have had some purpose." *Weiss* v. *United States,* 308 U.S. 321, 329 . . . (1939).

interest of fairly regulating interstate commerce, intended to supervise those intrastate activities in violation of Rule 10b-5 which are "inimical to the welfare and public policy of the country as a whole." . . . We hold, consequently, that intrastate use of the telephone comes within prohibition of the Act. . . . In interpreting other grants of federal power, it has long been acknowledged that Congress may regulate intrastate activity if simultaneously it is an integral part of or constitutes an instrumentality of interstate commerce. . . .

Thus, in order to protect interstate commerce, intrastate telephone messages have been placed under the statutory prohibition pertaining to unauthorized publication or use of communications under 47 U.S.C. § 605. *Weiss* v. *United States,* 308 U.S. 321 . . . (1939). We recognize that the telephone system and its voice transmission by wire is an integrated system of both intrastate and interstate commerce. . . . As such, proof of the interstate telephone message is not a prerequisite to jurisdiction over a Section 10(b) action. As long as the instrumentality itself is an integral part of an interstate system, nothing in the Constitution requires Congress to exclude intrastate activities from the regulatory control. . . .

But there exist additional grounds to sustain jurisdiction. It is the rule that where any interstate use is made to perpetuate the original fraudulent concealment or transaction, even though not part of the original solicitation or inducement of sales involved, that nevertheless the subsequent use of interstate facilities in furthering the scheme is sufficient to establish federal jurisdiction. . . .

Appellees contended that they were fraudulently induced to sell their stock to the appellants, that the purchases were made by parties (the Myzels) other than the true buyers (the Levines) and that an Illinois corporation owned by some of the appellants was used as a conduit of concealment. The transfers of the stock to the Illinois corporation, although occurring several months and even years later, involved the delivery of checks written by the Illinois corporation on Chicago, Illinois banks to a Minnesota citizen. . . . Thus, under appellees' theory, there was also sufficient evidence of interstate transactions to sustain jurisdiction.

Securities Investor Protection Corporation

In response to a number of brokerage house failures in the 1960s, and the resultant financial losses sustained by their customers, Congress passed the Securities Investor Protection Act of 1970. The Act created the Securities Investor Protection Corporation (SIPC). It is designed to protect the securities accounts of customers of broker-dealers who belong to SIPC and are liquidated under the 1970 statute.

In the case of a broker-dealer's financial failure, SIPC petitions a federal district court to appoint a trustee to supervise the liquidation of the firm. If possible, a customer's account will be transferred to another SIPC firm. The customer may then either conduct business with that firm or have the account switched to a firm of his choice. Unfortunately, liquidations do not go entirely that smoothly. The records of the failed firm may be a mess and there may be insufficient assets to pay the claims of the customers and other creditors. Under such circumstances the trustee will (1) return to customers those securities registered in their names, (2) pay the customers, on a pro rata basis, from the remaining cash and securities of customers held by the firm, and (3) utilize SIPC's funds to pay the remaining claims of a customer up to a maximum of $500,000, but only $100,000 in cash. For instance, if a customer had a claim for $700,000 ($450,000 in securities and $250,000 in cash) the trustee would pay $500,000. For a claim of $170,000 ($45,000 in securities and $125,000 in cash) the customer would receive $145,000. The customers' claims are valued as of the commencement of the proceedings, not at the date that the trustee makes the distribution to the customer. The customer is a creditor of the failed firm for the amount of the claim that remains unpaid after this three-step procedure. A customer that has several accounts with the firm in a single individual capacity will be a single customer for purposes of the SIPC limits. If a customer has multiple accounts in separate capacities, each account will be covered up to the maximum limits.

It is important to note that SIPC is designed solely to protect customers of failed firms; it does not protect investors against losses incurred by fluctuations in the prices of their securities. The law also excludes from coverage commodities accounts. Certain customers, i.e. partners, officers, directors, and 5 percent of larger stockholders in the firm, are also excluded from protection by the law.

SIPC is a nonprofit corporation, not an agency of the federal government. Its membership is made up of, with limited exceptions, all broker-dealers registered with the SEC. It operates under a seven-person board of directors, five appointed by the President, one designated by the Treasury Department, and the remaining one by the Federal Reserve Board. It is financed through assessments on its member firms. Because claims history has been small, the annual assessment of each member was set in 1979 at only $25.00. If additional funds prove necessary, assessments can be reinstituted on the gross revenues of each member firm. If SIPC funds ever prove inadequate, and the SEC determines that it is necessary for the protection of customers and the maintenance of confidence in the U.S. securities markets, SIPC can borrow up to $1 billion from the U.S. Treasury.

Although futures contracts for agricultural commodities have been traded in the United States for over a century and subject to federal regulation since the 1920s, it was not until 1974 that Congress passed comprehensive legislation governing futures trading. In that year it passed the Commodity Futures Trading Commission Act creating the Commodity Futures Trading Commission (CFTC).

Commodity Futures Trading Commission

The CFTC regulates and oversees the trading of commodity futures contracts on U.S. futures exchanges. Included under its authority are not only futures contracts in foodstuffs, grains, livestock, and related products (i.e., corn, cattle, frozen orange concentrate, frozen pork bellies, etc.), but also financial instruments, foreign currencies, and industrial materials (i.e., U.S. Treasury bills, bonds, and notes; Mexican pesos; silver; and plywood, etc.). Futures contracts legally may be bought and sold only through public outcry on exchanges licensed by the Commission. The CFTC does not regulate cash commodity transactions.

The CFTC is composed of five commissioners appointed by the President with the advice and consent of the Senate. Commission members serve staggered five-year terms. Actions such as the approval of contract market designations, the adoption of agency rules and regulations, and the authorization of enforcement actions require a majority vote of the Commission. It carries out its activities through five operating units: Enforcement, Trading and Markets, Economics and Education, General Counsel, and Executive Director. While the headquarters office of the Commission is located in Washington, D.C. it has regional offices in those cities with futures exchanges, as well as an office on the West Coast.

Participants in the futures markets are speculators who hope to profit from changes in price and who do not intend to take delivery of the commodity, as well as producers and users of the commodity that use the market as a hedging device to minimize the price risks of their operations.

Review Problems

[handwritten margin notes: making arrangements to lease living space. Not a security]

1. Purchasers of apartments in a cooperative housing project had to buy 18 shares of stock, at $25 per share, for each room desired. An information bulletin for the project estimated average monthly costs of $23.02 per room. Increased costs during construction resulted in a room cost of $39.68. A group of purchasers seeks damages, reductions in rent, and other relief in federal court. They allege violations of the fraud provisions of the securities laws. The defendant argues that the purchase of the "stock" does not mean the apartment holders have purchased a "security" under the federal law. What result? [*United Housing* v. *Forman*, 421 U.S. 837 (1975)].

2. Ann is a customer of a brokerage firm currently undergoing liquidation. When the firm failed she had $220,000 worth of bonds, $110,000 in cash, and $165,000 of stocks in the hands of the firm. On the date that the trustee is to make distribution to Ann, there remains $110,000 in cash, but the bonds have increased in value to $235,000 and the stocks have declined to $160,000 in value. The trustee proposes to give Ann assets that total $485,000. Ann claims $505,000, which is the total value of her assets on the day of distribution, or alternatively she argues for $495,000, which was their value on the day the liquidation proceedings began. What amount is Ann entitled to under the SIPC rules? *[handwritten: Date of trustee takes prices $485K. $10,000 for cash — only $100,000 can get]*

3. Which of the following statements is correct regarding qualification for the <u>private placement</u> exemption from registration under the Securities Act of 1933?

    (a) The instrumentalities of interstate commerce must *not* be used.
    (b) The securities must be offered to *not* more than 35 persons.
    (c) The minimum amount of securities purchased by each offeree must *not* be less than $100,000.
    (d) The offerees *must* <u>have access</u> to or be furnished with the kind of information that would be available in a registration statement.

(Adapted from CPA Exam Law Problem #1, Question #43, taken from the November 1980 exam. © American Institute of Certified Public Accountants, Inc., 1980.)

4. Harvey Wilson is a senior vice president, 15 percent shareholder, and a member of the Board of Directors of Winslow, Inc. Wilson has decided to sell 10 percent of his stock in the company. Which of the following methods of disposition would subject him to SEC registration requirements?

    (a) A redemption of the stock by the corporation. *[handwritten: — not sell to public]*
    (b) The sale by several brokerage houses of the stock in the ordinary course of business.

[handwritten: controlling owner — deemed to be under statute to public]

(c) The sale of the stock to an insurance company that will hold the stock for long-term investment purposes.

(d) The sale to a corporate officer who currently owns 5 percent of the stock of Winslow and who will hold the purchased stock for long-term investment. *Not to public, both insiders*

(Adapted from CPA Exam Law Problem #1, Question #48, taken from the May 1979 exam. © American Institute of Certified Public Accountants, Inc., 1979.)

5. Tweed Manufacturing, Inc., plans to issue $5 million of common stock to the public in interstate commerce after its registration statement with the SEC becomes effective. What, if anything, must Tweed do in respect to those states in which the securities are to be sold?

(a) Nothing, since approval by the SEC automatically constitutes satisfaction of any state requirements. *not necessarily*

✓(b) Make a filing in those states that have laws governing such offerings and obtain their approval.

(c) Simultaneously apply to the SEC for permission to market the securities in the various states without further clearance. *need state*

(d) File in the appropriate state office of the state in which it maintains its principal office of business, obtain clearance, and forward a certified copy of that state's clearance to all other states.

(Adapted from CPA Exam Law Problem #1, Question #43, taken from the May 1979 exam. © American Institute of Certified Public Accountants, Inc., 1979.)

6. Mr. Jackson owns approximately 40 percent of the shares of common stock of Triad Corporation. The rest of the shares are widely distributed among 2000 shareholders. Jackson needs funds for other business ventures and would like to raise about $2 million through the sale of some of his Triad shares. He accordingly approached Underwood & Sons, an investment banking house in which he knew one of the principals, to purchase his Triad shares and distribute his shares to the public at a reasonable price through its offices in the United States. Any profit on the sales could be retained by Underwood pursuant to an agreement reached between Jackson and Underwood. Would the sale of these shares constitute a public offering? *Yes controlling s/hr. Issuer in this case. Underwriter doesn't matter.*

(Adapted from CPA Exam Law Problem #1, Question #6, taken from the May 1978 exam. © American Institute of Certified Public Accountants, Inc., 1978.)

7. Issuer, Inc., a New York corporation engaged in retail sales within New York City, was interested in raising $1.6 million in capital. In this connection it approached through personal letters 88 people in New York, New Jersey, and Connecticut, and then followed up with face-to-face negotiations where it seemed promising to do so. After exten-

sive efforts in which Issuer disclosed all the information that these people requested, 19 people from these areas purchased Issuer's securities. Issuer did not limit its offer to insiders, their relatives, or wealthy or sophisticated investors. Did this constitute an exempt offering? *No — not private or interstate or insiders.*

(Adapted from CPA Exam, Law Problem #1, Question #15, taken from the May 1975 exam. © American Institute of Certified Public Accountants, Inc., 1975.)

8. Continental Tobacco is a South Carolina corporation organized for the purpose of manufacturing cigarettes. It held a series of sales presentations for prospective purchasers of its unregistered debentures at a Florida hotel. The SEC obtained preliminary injunctions halting these promotions, which the court concluded were unlawful public offerings. Shortly thereafter the company underwent a Chapter XI bankruptcy reorganization. Following its discharge from these proceedings, it sought to raise funds through the sale of unregistered common stock. Promotional meetings were held at private homes and hotels. The father and son operating Continental enlisted the aid of acquaintances in promoting the stock. A dentist, who was himself a purchaser, had his dental assistant display a brochure on the company to his patients. The stock was offered to 38 individuals, 35 of whom made purchases. The purchasers were dentists, physicians, businessmen, and housewives. They signed "investment letters" acknowledging that they knew the stock was unregistered and were purchasing it for investment purposes. The stock certificates carried a legend noting that the stock was unregistered and that a legal opinion would be required before the stock could be resold. Do the activities, subsequent to the bankruptcy proceedings, constitute a public offering? [*SEC v. Continental Tobacco*, 463 F. 2d 137 (1972)].

[margin handwritten: Too widespread — no proof of small inside group of buyers. yes]

9. Scotch whiskey warehouse receipts are being promoted for sale through direct mail and newspaper advertisements. A typical statement contained in such ads reads as follows: "Invest in Scotch Whiskey for Profit. Exceptional Capital Growth is Possible When You Buy Scotch Whiskey Reserves by the Barrel. Insured Investment for Profit and Growth in Scotch Whiskey." In addition to the phrase "Insured Investment" some ads carried the phrase "insured no loss policy." If a potential investor read a brochure prepared by the promoters he could learn that his investment was not being insured. Instead the whiskey was insured against loss from fire and cask leakage. The SEC contends that the defendants are violating the '33 Act by selling unregistered securities and the '34 Act by utilizing deceptive and fraudulent promotional advertisements. What do you think? [*SEC v. Lundy Associates*, 362 F. Supp 226 (1973)]. *Yes*

10. A mutual fund purchases Letter stock for $2 per share. That price is below the current market value. The issuer was willing to make such a private placement at less than market value in view of its need to quickly raise a large sum of money and by virtue of the savings realized by foregoing the expenses of SEC registration. Six months later the market price is $10 per share. In calculating the value of the shares of the mutual fund itself, what price should the mutual fund place on its Letter stock? What happens if the business fortunes of the company decline so greatly that it files bankruptcy while the mutual fund is legally prevented from unloading its Letter stock?

Endnotes

1. *Hall* v. *Geiger Jones & Co.*, 242 U.S. 539, 550 (1917).
2. *SEC* v. *Payne*, 35 F. Supp. 873 (1940).
3. *Tcherepnin* v. *Knight*, 389 U.S. 332 (1967).
4. *Silver Hills Country Club* v. *Sobieski*, (Cal. S.Ct.) (1961).

15

Insider Trading

When Congress held hearings on the '33 and '34 Acts it heard a great deal about gross unfairness and abuses in the securities markets resulting from persons trading on facts not available to the general investing public. Two sections of the '34 Act are designed to outlaw such activities. One section prohibits certain individuals from making a profit in stock transactions during a certain time period. The other section outlaws all transactions based on material inside information.

Short-Swing Profits: Section 16(b) of the '34 Act — Section 16 applies to every person who is directly or indirectly the beneficial owner of more than 10 percent of any class of any registered equity security, or who is a director or an officer of the issuer of such security. The word "beneficial" is extremely important. One can beneficially own securities without being the legal owner. For example, one usually will be the beneficial owner of securities legally owned by a spouse or minor children.

Section 16(b) provides:

> For the purpose of preventing the unfair use of information which may have been obtained by such beneficial owner, director, or officer by reason of his relationship to the issuer, any profit realized by him from any purchase and sale, or any sale and purchase, of any equity security of such issuer . . . within any period of less than six months, unless such security was acquired in good faith in connection with a debt previously contracted, shall inure to and be recoverable by the issuer, irrespective of any intention on the part of such beneficial owner, director, or officer in entering into such transaction of holding the security purchased or of not repurchasing the security sold for a period exceeding six months. . . . This subsection shall not be construed to cover any transaction where such beneficial owner was not such both at the time of the purchase and sale, or the sale and purchase, of the security involved, or any transaction or transactions which the Commission by rules and regulations may exempt as not comprehended within the purpose of this subsection.

The courts mechanically, yet rigorously, apply this section. It is immaterial whether one actually used inside information. The specified transactions are absolutely prohibited. If they do occur, the short-swing profits belong to the corporation. The concept is that individuals in these categories, by virtue of the positions they hold, may have access to inside information. However, if they are barred from trading at a profit in their stock, the inside information will likely become available to the investing public in the intervening six-month period. The statute has a self-enforcing mechanism. If there is a change in the stock ownership of the respective director, officer, or principal stockholder, during any month he or she must report this change to the SEC and the national securities exchange. This information is public and oftentimes is printed in financial papers such as *The Wall Street Journal.* Either the issuer of the security or a stockholder (it is not necessary that he owned stock at the time of the transaction in dispute) can sue to recover the profits for the corporation. The shareholder may bring the suit only if the issuer has failed to bring the suit within 60 days after request or has failed to diligently prosecute the suit. The shareholder does not benefit directly from any recovery. The profits go to the corporate treasury. However, the shareholder's attorney is paid a percentage of the recovered profits. The amount usually varies between 10 and 33 percent; the larger the recovery the smaller the percentage. Generally the courts are not niggardly in their allowance of attorney's fees because it serves as an important stimulus for enforcement of the law.

The statute does not give any guidance as to how a "profit" is to be calculated. In their interpretation the courts arbitrarily match purchases and sales so as to achieve the maximum profit. One cannot escape liability by showing that the specific share certificates sold (or purchased) are not the same ones purchased (or sold) during the specific six-month period. In *Smolowe* v. *Delendo Corp.,* 136 F. 2d 231 (1943), the court rejected such formulas as first in-first out and average purchase price average sales price. The court also held that any losses incurred during the six-month period cannot be set off against the profits to reduce them. If this seems harsh consider the words of the court in *Gratz* v. *Claughton,* 187 F.2d 46 (1951), ". . . [the] crushing liability of 16(b) should serve as a warning and may prove a deterrent." The application of these rules is illustrated in the following example.

Determination of what constitutes a profit under Section 16(b) is not as easy as it may appear to be at first blush. Consider the following situation:

Day 1 An insider owns 100 shares of stock.

Day 2 He purchases 10 shares at $7 per share.

Day 3 He sells 10 shares at $5 per share.

Day 4 He purchases 10 shares at $3 per share.

Day 5 He sells 10 shares at $1 per share.

The result of these transactions is to leave the insider still owning 100 shares of stock. However, since the person paid $100 for the additional purchases and only received $60 from the sales, it would appear that the insider has suffered a net loss of $40, plus commissions. Yet, amazing as it may seem, the person has made a short-swing profit in the amount of $20. This profit is arrived at by matching the purchase at $3 and the sale at $5 (keeping in mind that one cannot deduct the loss of $60 by matching the purchase at $7 and the sale at $1). Using this formula in an actual case a court concluded that the individual had made a profit in excess of $300,000 while in reality the person had suffered a loss of several hundred thousand dollars.

There had been a long-standing controversy over the interpretation of the last sentence of 16(b). The sentence provides that the section does not cover a transaction where the "beneficial owner was not such both at the time of the purchase and sale" and vice versa. The argument was over whether "at the time of purchase" means before the purchase or immediately after the purchase. In January 1976, the Supreme Court adopted the former interpretation in *Foremost-McKesson* v. *Provident Securities*, 423 U.S. 232 (1976). It decided that a purchase that makes one a 10 percent stockholder is not to be matched with a sale by the shareholder that occurred after the person had become a 10 percent holder. Foremost purchased two thirds of Provident's assets for cash and convertible debentures. When Provident received the debentures they were immediately convertible into more than 10 percent of Foremost's outstanding common stock. Provident disposed of these securities within six months. It sought a court declaration that it was not liable to Foremost for any profits under Section 16(b). The Supreme Court affirmed the grant of a declaratory judgment in Provident's favor in an opinion heavily based on legislative history. The Court acknowledged that it was creating a loophole but said that other statutory provisions against insider trading protect the investing public. Previously the Court had affirmed a ruling that a 13.2 percent shareholder, who sold 3.24 percent within six months, was liable for any profits on that sale but was now free to sell the remaining 9.96 percent within the same six-month period and retain any profits [*Reliance Elec. Co.* v. *Emerson Elec. Co.*, 404 U.S. 418 (1972)].

What time period constitutes less than six months? December 1 to the following May 30, rather than to June 1, does, for example.

The following case provides a U.S. Supreme Court interpretation of Section 16(b) within an interesting context.

BLAU v. LEHMAN
368 U.S. 403 (1962)

MR. JUSTICE BLACK *delivered the opinion of the Court.*

The petitioner Blau, a stockholder in Tide Water Associated Oil Company, brought this action in a United States District Court on behalf of the company under § 16 (b) of the Securities Exchange Act of 1934 to recover with interest "short swing" profits, that is, profits earned within a six months' period by the purchase and sale of securities, alleged to have been "realized" by respondents in Tide Water securities dealings. Respondents are Lehman Brothers, a partnership engaged in investment banking, securities brokerage and in securities trading for its own account, and Joseph A. Thomas, a member of Lehman Brothers and a director of Tide Water. The complaint alleged that Lehman Brothers "deputed . . . Thomas, to represent its interests as a director on the Tide Water Board of Directors," and that within a period of six months in 1954 and 1955 Thomas, while representing the interests of Lehman Brothers as a director of Tide Water and "by reason of his special and inside knowledge of the affairs of Tide Water, advised and caused the defendants, Lehman Brothers, to purchase and sell 50,000 shares of . . . stock of Tide Water, realizing profits thereon which did not inure to and [were] not recovered by Tide Water."

The case was tried before a district judge without a jury. The evidence showed that Lehman Brothers had in fact earned profits out of short-swing transactions in Tide Water securities while Thomas was a director of that company. But as to the charges of deputization and wrongful use of "inside" information by Lehman Brothers, the evidence was in conflict.

First, there was testimony that respondent Thomas had succeeded Hertz, another Lehman partner, on the board of Tide Water; that Hertz had "joined Tidewater Company thinking it was going to be in the interests of Lehman Brothers;" and that he had suggested Thomas as his successor partly because it was in the interest of Lehman. There was also testimony, however, that Thomas, aside from having mentioned from time to time to some of his partners and other people that he thought Tide Water was "an attractive investment" and under "good" management, had never discussed the operating details of Tide Water affairs with any member of Lehman Brothers; that Lehman had bought the Tide Water securities without consulting Thomas and wholly on the basis of public announcements by Tide Water that common shareholders could thereafter convert their shares to a new cumulative preferred issue that Thomas did not know of Lehman's intent to buy Tide Water stock until after the initial purchases had been made; that upon learning about the purchases he immediately notified Lehman that he must be excluded from "any risk of the purchase or any profit or loss from the subsequent sale;" and that this disclaimer was accepted by the firm.

From the foregoing and other testimony the District Court found that "there was no evidence that the firm of Lehman Brothers deputed Thomas to represent its interests as director on the board of Tide Water" and that there had been no actual use of inside information, Lehman Brothers having bought its Tide Water stock "solely on the basis of Tide Water's public announcements and without consulting Thomas."

On the basis of these findings the District Court refused to render a judgment, either against the partnership or against Thomas individually, for the $98,686.77 profits which it determined that Lehman Brothers had realized. . . . Despite its recognition that Thomas had specifically waived his share of the Tide Water transaction profits, the trial court nevertheless held that within the meaning of § 16 (b) Thomas had "realized" $3,893.41, his proportionate share of the profits of Lehman Brothers. The court consequently entered judgment against Thomas for that amount but refused to allow interest against him. . . .

We must therefore decide whether Lehman Brothers, Thomas or both have an absolute liability under § 16(b) to pay over all profits made on Lehman's Tide Water stock dealings even though Thomas was not sitting on Tide Water's board to represent Lehman and even though the profits made by the partnership were on its own initiative, independently of any advice or "inside" knowledge given it by director Thomas.

First. The language of § 16 does not purport to impose its extraordinary liability on any "person," "fiduciary" or not, unless he or it is a "director", "officer" or "beneficial owner of more than 10 percentum of any class of any equity security . . . which is registered on a national securities exchange." Lehman Brothers was neither an officer nor a 10 percent stockholder of Tide Water, but petitioner and the Commission contend that the Lehman partnership is or should be treated as a director under § 16 (b).

(a) Although admittedly not "literally designated" as one, it is contended that Lehman is a director. No doubt Lehman Brothers, though a partnership, could for purposes of § 16 be a "director" of Tide Water and function through a deputy, since § 3 (a) (9) of the Act provides that " 'person' means . . . partnership" and § 3 (a) (7) that "director" means any director of a corporation or any person performing similar functions with respect to any organization, whether incorporated or unincorporated." Consequently, Lehman Brothers would be a "director" of Tide Water, if as petitioner's complaint charged Lehman actually

functioned as a director through Thomas, who had been deputized by Lehman to perform a director's duties not for himself but for Lehman. But the findings of the two courts below, which we have accepted, preclude such a holding. It was Thomas, not Lehman Brothers as an entity, that was the director of Tide Water.

(b) It is next argued that the intent of § 3 (a) (9) in defining "person" as including a partnership is to treat a partnership as an inseparable entity. Because Thomas, one member of this inseparable entity, is an "insider," it is contended that the whole partnership should be considered the "insider." But the obvious intent of § 3 (a) (9), as the Commission apparently realizes, is merely to make it clear that a partnership can be treated as an entity under the statute, not that it must be. This affords no reason at all for construing the word "director" in § 16 (b) as though it read "partnership of which the director is a member." . . .

(c) Both the petitioner and the Commission contend on policy grounds that the Lehman partnership should be held liable even though it is neither a director, officer, nor a 10 percent stockholder. Conceding that such an interpretation is not justified by the literal language of § 16 (b) which plainly limits liability to directors, officers, and 10 percent stockholders, it is argued that we should expand § 16 (b) to cover partnerships of which a director is a member in order to carry out the congressionally declared purpose "of preventing the unfair use of information which may have been obtained by such beneficial owner, director, or officer by reason of his relationship to the issuer . . ."

The argument of petitioner and the Commission seems to go so far as to suggest that § 16 (b)'s forfeiture of profits should be extended to include all persons realizing "short swing" profits who either act on the basis of "inside" information or have the possibility of "inside" information. One may agree that petitioner and the Commission present persuasive policy arguments that the Act should be broadened in this way to prevent "the unfair use of information" more effectively than can be accomplished by leaving the Act so as to require forfeiture of profits only by those specifically designated by Congress to suffer those losses. But this very broadening of the categories of persons on whom these liabilities are imposed by the language of § 16 (b) was considered and rejected by Congress when it passed the Act. . . .

Congress can and might amend § 16 (b) if the Commission would present to it the policy arguments it has presented to us, but we think that Congress is the proper agency to change an interpretation of the Act unbroken since its passage, if the change is to be made.

Second. The petitioner and the Commission contend that Thomas should be required individually to pay to Tide Water the entire $98,686.77 profit Lehman Brothers realized on the ground that under partnership law he is co-owner of the entire undivided amount and has therefore "realized" it all. . . . But liability under § 16 (b) is to be determined neither by general partnership law nor by adding to the "prophylactic" effect Congress itself clearly prescribed in § 16 (b). That section leaves no room for judicial doubt that a director is to pay to his company only "any profit realized by him" from short-swing transactions. It would be nothing but a fiction to say that Thomas "realized" all the profits earned by the partnership of which he was a member. . . .

Third. It is contended that both courts below erred in failing to allow interest on the recovery of Thomas' share of the partnership profits. Section 16 (b) says nothing about interest one way or the other. . . . Both courts below denied interest here and we cannot say that the denial was either so unfair or so inequitable as to require us to upset it.

Affirmed.

MR. JUSTICE DOUGLAS, *with whom The Chief Justice concurs, dissenting.*

What the Court does today is substantially to eliminate "the great Wall Street trading firms" from the operation of § 16(b), as Judge Clark stated in his dissent in the Court of Appeals. . . . This result follows because of the wide dispersion of partners of investment banking firms among our major corporations. Lehman Brothers has partners on 100 boards. Under today's ruling that firm can make a rich harvest on the "inside information" which § 16 of the Act covers because each partner need account only for his distributive share of the firm's profits on "inside information," the other partners keeping the balance. This is a mutilation of the Act.

If a partnership can be a "director" within the meaning of § 16 (a), then "any profit realized by him," as those words are used in § 16 (b), includes all the profits, not merely a portion of them, which the partnership realized on the "inside information." There is no basis in reason for saying a partnership cannot be a "director" for the purposes of the Act. . . . Everyone knows that the investment banking-corporation alliances are consciously constructed so as to increase the profits of the bankers. . . . It is easier to make this partnership a "director" for purposes of § 16 than to hold the opposite. . . .

At the root of the present problem are the scope and degree of liability arising out of fiduciary relations. In modern times that liability has been strictly construed. The New York Court of Appeals, speaking through Chief Judge Cardozo in *Meinhard* v. *Salmon*, 249 N.Y. 458, 164 N.E. 545, held a joint adventurer to a higher standard than we insist upon today:

> Many forms of conduct permissible in the workaday world for those acting at arm's length, are forbidden to those bound by fiduciary ties. A trustee is held to something stricter than the morals of the market place. Not honesty alone,

but the punctilio of an honor the most sensitive, is then the standard of behavior. As to this there has developed a tradition that is unbending and inveterate. . . . Only thus has the level of conduct for fiduciaries been kept at a level higher than that trodden by the crowd.

We forget much history when we give § 16 a strict and narrow construction. Brandeis in *Other People's Money* spoke of the office of "director" as "a happy hunting ground" for investment bankers. He said that "The goose that lays golden eggs has been considered a most valuable possession. But even more profitable is the privilege of taking the golden eggs laid by somebody else's goose. The invest-ment bankers and their associates now enjoy that privilege." Id., at 12. . . .

What we do today allows all but one partner to share in the feast which the one places on the partnership table. They in turn can offer feasts to him in the 99 other companies of which they are directors. . . . This result is a dilution of the fiduciary principle that Congress wrote into § 16 of the Act. It is, with all respect, a dilution that is possible only by a strained reading of the law. Until now, the courts have given this fiduciary principle a cordial reception. We should not leave to Congress the task of restoring the edifice that it erected and that we tear down.

Case Question

1. Does this decision mean that a partnership, one member of which sits on the board of a corporation, can never be held liable for short-swing profits?

Section 10(b) of the '34 Act and Rule 10b-5

Section 10(b) and its accompanying Rule 10b-5 prohibit persons from trading on the basis of material inside information. The focus is not on the individual's position in the corporate hierarchy, but on whether a person possesses material inside information. If so, the person is prohibited from trading in that corporation's securities until that information has been made available to the general investing public. Material inside information is any fact that might reasonably affect the value of a corporation's securities. One is not prohibited from studying available public annual reports, quarterly reports, economic trends, etc. and on the basis of that analysis and one's own expertise making successful investment decisions. Such data is available to whoever wishes to study it. The concept behind the prohibition against trading on the basis of material inside information is to permit all investors to stand on an equal basis when it comes to access to information affecting the value of a corporate security.

Individuals are often amazed to learn that it is illegal to trade on the basis of inside information. They incorrectly regard it as being within the "rights" of a corporate executive, as simply another permissible form of executive compensation. It is not! Such trading violates both the securities laws and their fiduciary duties. This information belongs to their corporation and they may not convert it to their own personal use. The law regards the corporate employee as receiving adequate official compensation and demands in return the devotion of full efforts to the corporate welfare. The search for personal enrichment through inside trading is an unallowable distraction.

Mention should also be made of the "special circumstances" doctrine. Under this rule created by the Supreme Court, a director before purchasing the stock of other shareholders must inform them of any special circumstances that may affect the value of their stock. In one well known case a 75 percent shareholder-director purchased the interest of another shareholder without revealing that the U.S. would probably purchase certain corporate property, thereby enhancing the stock's value [*Strong* v. *Repide*, 213 U.S. 419 (1909)]. The failure to reveal this special circumstance to the seller was impermissible. Today, such legal actions would usually be brought under the federal securities laws.

Let us actually look at the provisions of Section 10(b) and Rule 10b-5, then examine two cases. *Cady Roberts* is a classic straightforward example of impermissible trading on the basis of inside information. *Texas Gulf Sulphur* is "the" famous inside trading case. It is lengthy, complex, and highly controversial.

Sec. 10.

It shall be unlawful for any person, directly or indirectly, by the use of any means or instrumentality of interstate commerce or of the mails, or of any facility of any national securities exchange—

> (b) To use or employ, in connection with the purchase or sale of any security registered on a national securities exchange or any security not so registered, any manipulative or deceptive device or contrivance in contravention of such rules and regulations as the Commission may prescribe as necessary or appropriate in the public interest or for the protection of investors.

Rule 10b-5.

It shall be unlawful for any person, directly or indirectly, by the use of any means or instrumentality of interstate commerce, or of the mails, or of any facility of any national securities exchange,

> (1) to employ any device, scheme, or artifice to defraud,
>
> (2) to make any untrue statement of a material fact or to omit a state a material fact necessary in order to make the statements made, in the light of the circumstances under which they were made, not misleading, or
>
> (3) to engage in any act, practice or course of business which operates or would operate as a fraud or deceit upon any person, in connection with the purchase or sale of any security.

IN THE MATTER OF CADY, ROBERTS & CO.

40 S.E.C. 907 (1961)

These proceedings were instituted to determine whether Cady, Roberts & Co. ("registrant") and Robert M. Gintel ("Gintel"), the selling broker and a partner of the registrant, willfully violated the "anti-fraud" provisions of Section 10(b) of the Securities Exchange Act of 1934 ("Exchange Act"), Rule 10b-5 issued under that Act, and Section 17 (a) of the Securities Act of 1923 ("Securities Act"). . . .

From November 6, through November 23, Gintel had purchased approximately 11,000 shares of Curtiss-Wright stock for about 30 discretionary accounts of customers of registrant. With the rise in the price on November 24, he began selling Curtiss-Wright shares for these accounts and sold on that day a total of 2,200 shares on the Exchange.

On the morning of November 25, the Curtiss-Wright directors, including J. Cheever Cowdin ("Cowdin")[1], then a registered representative of registrant, met to consider, among other things the declaration of a quarterly dividend. The company had paid a dividend, although not earned, of $.625 per share for each of the first three quarters of 1959. The Curtiss-Wright board, . . . approved a dividend for the fourth quarter at the reduced rate of $.375 per share. At approximately 11:00 a.m., the board authorized transmission of information of this action by telegram to the New York Stock Exchange. The Secretary of Curtiss-Wright immediately left the meeting room to arrange for this communication. There was a short delay in the transmission of the telegram because of a typing problem and the telegram, although transmitted to Western Union at 11:12 a.m., was not delivered to the Exchange until 12:29 p.m. It had been customary for the company

[1] Mr. Cowdin died in September 1960.

also to advise the Dow Jones News Ticker Service of any dividend action. However, apparently through some mistake or inadvertence, the Wall Street Journal was not given the news until approximately 11:45 a.m. and the announcement did not appear on the Dow Jones ticker tape until 11:48 a.m.

Sometime after the dividend decision, there was a recess of the Curtiss-Wright directors' meeting, during which Cowdin telephoned registrant's office and left a message for Gintel that the dividend had been cut. Upon receiving this information, Gintel entered two sell orders for execution on the Exchange, one to sell 2,000 shares of Curtiss-Wright stock for 10 accounts, and the other to sell short 5,000 shares for 11 accounts. Four hundred of the 5,000 shares were sold for three of Cowdin's customers. According to Cowdin, pursuant to directions from his clients, he had given instructions to Gintel to take profits on these 400 shares if the stock took a "run-up." These orders were executed at 11:15 and 11:18 a.m. at 40 1/4 and 40 3/8, respectively.

When the dividend announcement appeared on the Dow Jones tape at 11:48 a.m., the Exchange was compelled to suspend trading in Curtiss-Wright because of the large number of sell orders. Trading in Curtiss-Wright stock was resumed at 1:59 p.m. at 36 1/2 ranged during the balance of the day between 34 1/8 and 37, and closed at 34 7/8.

. . .

An affirmative duty to disclose material information has been traditionally imposed on corporate "insiders," particularly officers, directors, or controlling stockholders. We, and the courts have consistently held that insiders must disclose material facts which are known to them by virtue of their position but which are not known to persons with whom they deal and which, if known, would affect their investment judgment. Failure to make disclosure in these circumstances constitutes a violation of the anti-fraud provisions. If, on the other hand, disclosure prior to effecting a purchase or sale would be improper or unrealistic under the circumstances, we believe the alternative is to forego the transaction.

. . . we accordingly find that Gintel willfully violated Sections 17(a) and 10(b) and Rule 10b-5. We also find a similar violation by the registrant, since the actions of Gintel, a member of registrant, in the course of his employment are to be regarded as actions of registrant itself. It was obvious that a reduction in the quarterly dividend by the Board of Directors was a material fact which could be expected to have an adverse impact on the market price of the company's stock. The rapidity with which Gintel acted upon receipt of the information confirms his own recognition of that conclusion.

The facts here impose on Gintel the responsibilities of those commonly referred to as "insiders." He received the information prior to its public release from a director of Curtiss-Wright, Cowdin, who was associated with the registrant. Cowdin's relationship to the company clearly prohibited him from selling the securities affected by the information without disclosure. By logical sequence, it should prohibit Gintel, a partner of registrant. This prohibition extends not only over his own account, but to selling for discretionary accounts and soliciting and executing other orders. . . .

The record does not support the contention that Gintel's sales were merely a continuance of his prior schedule of liquidation. Upon receipt of the news of the dividend reduction, which Gintel knew was not public, he hastened to sell before the expected public announcement all of the Curtiss-Wright shares remaining in his discretionary accounts, contrary to his previous moderate rate of sales. In so doing, he also made short sales of securities which he then allocated to his wife's account and to the account of a customer whom he had never seen and with whom he had had no prior dealings. Moreover, while Gintel undoubtedly occupied a fiduciary relationship to his customers, this relationship could not justify any actions by him contrary to law.

Case Questions

1. If Gintel, the "tippee," had not been a partner of the same firm as Cowdin, the "tipper," would he have violated the securities law?
2. What arguments support a brokerage firm policy prohibiting members of the firm from sitting on corporate boards? What reasons support allowing a member of the firm to occupy a board seat?

Materiality

Materiality is an important concept in the securities laws. In this chapter we are examining what constitutes trading on the basis of material inside information. We will encounter the concept in upcoming chapters in relation to material misstatements and omissions in registration statements, tender offers, and proxy solicitation literature. A discussion of the concept will aid your understanding as upcoming cases are read and considered.

The law frequently judges a person's conduct by the "reasonable man" standard. If the conduct of the person in question conforms to what a reasonable person would do under the same circumstances, that conduct will normally be legal and no legal penalty will be imposed on the person. For example, it is reasonable to drive a motor vehicle at the maximum posted speed limit when the road surface is dry, the traffic volume is light, the vehicle is in good operating condition, etc. However, if one were to drive at the maximum speed in heavy traffic, fog, and on a rain-slicked highway, one's conduct would not be reasonable, but negligent or even reckless. The law utilizes this same standard of the reasonable person when it determines what is material under the securities laws. Instead of a reasonable driver, the securities law will use a reasonable investor standard.

The test of materiality is whether a reasonable person would consider the matter to be important when making investment decisions. If a fact would tend to encourage, or deter, the average prudent investor from purchasing, selling, or holding securities, the fact is material. Determining what course of conduct the reasonable investor would engage in is not, of course, subject to precision. It is a question of judgment to be exercised as best it can in light of all the relevant circumstances.

Materiality is a relative concept. For instance, would the reasonable prudent investor purchase securities if it was known that the company's earnings were actually $20,000 less than the amount stated in the prospectus? One needs more information before that question can be answered. If the earnings were stated to be $85,000, a misstatement of $20,000 would be a material misstatement. But if the earnings were reported as being $5,481, 500, an error of $20,000 would translate into an error of .0036 percent. In these circumstances such an error would not rise to the level of materiality.

Let us shift to an examination of an omission in a proxy statement. Suppose the proxy data fails to mention that one of the candidates for the board of directors has a criminal conviction in his or her background. Is this omission of any legal consequence? Again, it depends. If the director was convicted for criminal damage to property when drunk as a college student and thereafter has lived the life of a law-abiding citizen, the omission would not be a material one. If the conviction was for the embezzlement of a large sum of money from a previous employer, the omission would be material. Such a conviction will not prevent the individual from serving on the board, but the shareholders are entitled to know such an important fact prior to casting their votes for or against a candidate.

Of course, the examples cited above are easy to make a decision on because they are somewhat exaggerated and at the opposite ends of the spectrum. The law struggles with the closer decisions where it is more difficult to achieve a consensus of opinion. Let us look at another example of a criminal conviction of a director, this time for tax evasion. Some would argue that, since the conviction relates to the personal private affairs of the director, it need not be disclosed. Yet others would argue that it relates to the basic integrity of the person and it would be a material omission to fail to inform the shareholders that a candidate for the board has violated the criminal law of our country. It might also be argued that the matter is not purely personal as the conduct of corporate officials can affect the reputation of the corporation.

With this background let us take our first look at materiality in a case involving inside information. In *Texas Gulf Sulphur* a group of corporate employees purchased shares of stock in the company prior to a dramatic upswing in the price of the stock. They made their purchases with the knowledge of certain mining test results. The court must determine whether this information constitutes material inside information.

SECURITIES AND EXCHANGE COMMISSION v. TEXAS GULF SULPHUR CO. et al.
401 F.2d 833 (1968)

WATERMAN, Circuit Judge
This action was commenced in the United States District Court for the Southern District of New York by the Securities and Exchange Commission (the SEC) against Texas Gulf Sulphur Co. (TGS) and several of its officers, directors and employees, to enjoin certain conduct by TGS and the individual defendants said to violate Section 10(b) of the Act . . . and Rule 10b-5 . . . (the Rule), promulgated thereunder, and to compel the rescission by the individual defendants of securities transaction assertedly conducted contrary to law. The complaint alleged (1) that defendants Fogarty, Mollison, Darke, Murray, Huntington, O'Neill, Clayton, Crawford, and Coates had either personally or through agents purchased TGS stock or calls thereon from November 12, 1963 through April 16, 1964 on the basis of material inside information concerning the results of TGS drilling in Timmins, Ontario, while such information remained undisclosed to the investing public generally or to the particular

sellers; (2) that defendants Darke and Coates had divulged such information to others for use in purchasing TGS stock or calls[1] or recommended its purchase while the information was undisclosed to the public or to the sellers: that defendants Stephens, Fogarty, Mollison, Holyk, and Kline had accepted options to purchase TGS stock on Feb. 20, 1964 without disclosing the material information as to the drilling progress to either the Stock Option Committee or the TGS Board of Directors; and (4) that TGS issued a deceptive press release on April 12, 1964. . . .

This action derives from the exploratory activities of TGS begun in 1957 on the Canadian Shield in eastern Canada. . . . These operations resulted in the detection of numerous anomalies, i.e., extraordinary variations in the conductivity of rocks, one of which was on the Kidd 55 segment of land located near Timmins, Ontario.

On October 29 and 30, 1963, Clayton conducted a ground geophysical survey on the northeast portion of the Kidd 55 segment which confirmed the presence of an anomaly and indicated the necessity of diamond core drilling for further evaluation. Drilling of the initial hole, K-55-1, at the strongest part of the anomaly was commenced on November 8 and terminated on November 12 at a depth of 655 feet. Visual estimates by Holyk of the core of K-55-1 indicated an average copper content

---

[1] A "call" is a negotiable option contract by which the bearer has the right to buy from the writer of the contract a certain number of shares of a particular stock at a fixed price on or before a certain agreed-upon date.

of 1.15 percent and an average zinc content of 8.64 percent over a length of 599 feet. This visual estimate convinced TGS that it was desirable to acquire the remainder of the Kidd 55 segment, and in order to facilitate this acquisition TGS President Stephens instructed the exploration group to keep the results of K-55-1 confidential and undisclosed even as to other officers, directors, and employees of TGS. The hole was concealed and a barren core was intentionally drilled off the anomaly. Meanwhile, the core of K-55-1 had been shipped to Utah for chemical assay which, when received in early December, revealed an average mineral content of 1.18 percent copper, 8.26 percent zinc, and 3.94 percent ounces of silver per ton over a length of 602 feet. These results were so remarkable that neither Clayton, an experienced geophysicist, nor four other TGS expert witnesses, had ever seen or heard of a comparable initial exploratory drill hole in a base metal deposit. . . .

During this period, from November 12, 1963 when K-55-1 was completed to March 31, 1964 when drilling was resumed, certain of the individual defendants and persons said to have received "tips" from them, purchased TGS stock or calls thereon. Prior to these transactions these persons had owned 1135 shares of TGS stock and possessed no calls; thereafter they owned a total of 8,235 shares and possessed 12,300 calls.

On February 20, 1964, also during this period, TGS issued stock options to 26 of its officers and employees whose salaries exceeded a specified amount, five of whom were the individual defendants Stephens, Fogarty, Mollison, Holyk and Kline. Of these, only Kline was unaware of the detailed results of K-55-1, but he, too, knew that a hole containing favorable bodies of copper and zinc ore had been drilled in Timmins. At this time, neither the TGS Stock Option Committee nor its Board of Directors had been informed of the results of K-55-1, presumably because of the pending land acquisition program which required confidentiality. All of the foregoing defendants accepted the options granted them.

When drilling was resumed on March 31, hole K-55-3 was commenced . . . . Daily progress reports of the drilling of this hole K-55-3 and of all subsequently drilled holes were sent to defendants Stephens and Fogarty (President and Executive Vice President of TGS) by Holyk and Mollison. . . . On April 7, drilling of a third hole, K-55-4 . . . was commenced and mineralization was encountered over 366 of its 579 foot length. . . . On the basis of these findings relative to the foregoing drilling results, the trial court concluded that . . . "There was real evidence that a body of commercially mineable ore might exist."

On April 8 TGS began with a second drill rig to drill another hole, K-55-6, 300 feet easterly of K-55-1. . . . On April 10, a third drill rig commenced drilling yet another hole, K-55-5. . . . By the evening of April 10 in this hole, too, substantial copper mineralization had been encountered over the last 42 feet of its 97 foot length.

Meanwhile rumors that a major ore strike was in the making had been circulating throughout Canada. On the morning of Saturday, April 11, Stephens at his home in Greenwich, Conn. read in the New York Herald Tribune and in the New York Times unauthorized reports of the TGS drilling which seemed to infer a rich strike from the fact that the drill cores had been flown to the United States for chemical assay. . . . With the aid of one Carroll, a public relations consultant, Fogarty drafted a press release designed to quell the rumors, which release after having been channeled through Stephens and Huntington, a TGS attorney, was issued at 3:00 P.M. on Sunday, April 12, and which appeared in the morning newspapers of general circulation on Monday, April 13. It read in pertinent part as follows:

. . .

During the past few days, the exploration activities of Texas Gulf Sulphur in the area of Timmins, Ontario, have been widely reported in the press, coupled with rumors of a substantial copper discovery there. These reports exaggerate the scale of operations, and mention plans and statistics of size and grade of ore that are without factual basis and have evidently originated by speculation of people not connected with TGS.

The facts are as follows. TGS has been exploring in the Timmins area for six years as part of its overall search in Canada and elsewhere for various minerals—lead, copper, zinc, etc. . . . Numerous prospects have been investigated by geophysical means and a large number of selected ones have been core-drilled. . . .

Most of the areas drilled in Eastern Canada have revealed either barren pyrite or graphite without value; a few have resulted in discoveries of small or marginal sulphide ore bodies.

Recent drilling on one property near Timmins has led to preliminary indications that more drilling would be required for proper evaluation of this prospect. The drilling done to date has not been conclusive, but the statements made by many outside quarters are unreliable and include information and figures that are not available to TGS.

The work done to date has not been sufficient to reach definite conclusions and any statement as to size and grade of ore would be premature and possibly misleading. When we have progressed to the point where reasonable and logical conclusions can be made, TGS will issue a definite statement to its stockholders and to the public in order to clarify the Timmins project.

The release purported to give the Timmins drilling results as of the release date, April 12. From Mollison Fogarty had been told of the developments through 7:00 P.M. on April 10, and of the remarkable discoveries made up to that time, detailed supra, which discoveries, according to the calculations of the experts who testified for the SEC at the hearing, demonstrated that TGS had already discovered 6.2 to 8.3 million tons of proven ore having gross assay values from $26 to $29 per ton. TGS experts, on the other hand, denied at the hearing

that proven or probable ore could have been calculated on April 11 or 12 because there was then no assurance of continuity in the mineralized zone.

The evidence as to the effect of this release on the investing public was equivocal and less than abundant.

While drilling activity ensued to completion, TGS officials were taking steps toward ultimate disclosure of the discovery. . . . An official detailed statement, announcing a strike of at least 25 million tons of ore, based on the drilling data set forth above, was read to representatives of American financial media from 10:00 A.M. to 10:10 or 10:15 A.M. on April 16, and appeared over Merrill Lynch's private wire at 10:29 A.M. and somewhat later than expected, over the Dow Jones ticker tape at 10:54 A.M.

Between the time the first press release was issued on April 12 and the dissemination of the TGS official announcement on the morning of April 16, the only defendants before us on appeal who engaged in market activity were Clayton and Crawford and TGS director Coates. Clayton ordered 200 shares of TGS stock through his Canadian broker on April 15, and the order was executed that day over the Midwest Stock Exchange. Crawford ordered 300 shares at midnight on 15th and another 300 shares at 8:30 A.M. the next day, and these orders were executed over the Midwest Exchange in Chicago at its opening on April 16. Coates left the TGS press conference and called his broker son-in-law Haemisegger shortly before 10:20 A.M. on the 16th and ordered 2,000 shares of TGS for family trust accounts of which Coates was a trustee but not a beneficiary; Haemisegger executed this order over the New York and Midwest Exchanges, and he and his customers purchased 1500 additional shares.

During the period of drilling Timmins the market price of TGS stock fluctuated but steadily gained overall. On Friday, November

8, when the drilling began, the stock closed at 17 3/8. . . . On April 16, the day of the official announcement of the Timmins discovery, the price climbed to a high of 37 and closed at 36 3/8. By May 15, TGS stock was selling at 58 1/4.

An insider is not, of course, always foreclosed from investing in his own company merely because he may be more familiar with company operations than are outside investors. An insider's duty to disclose information or his duty to abstain from dealing in his company's securities arises only in "those situations which are essentially extraordinary in nature and which are reasonably certain to have a substantial effect on the market price of the security if [the extraordinary situation is] disclosed."

Nor is an insider obligated to confer upon outside investors the benefit of his superior financial or other expert analysis by disclosing his educated guesses or predictions. . . .

As we stated in *List* v. *Fashion Park, Inc.,* 340 F.2d 457, 462. "The basic test of materiality . . . is whether a reasonable man would attach importance . . . in determining his choice of action in the transaction in question. This, of course, encompasses any fact . . . which in reasonable and objective contemplation might affect the value of the corporation's stock of securities . . . ." Thus, material facts include not only information of a company but also those facts which affect the probable future of the company and those which may affect the desire of investors to buy, sell, or hold the company's securities. . . .

Our survey of the facts found below conclusively establishes that knowledge of the results of the discovery hole, K-55-1, would have been important to a reasonable investor and might have affected the price of stock. . . .

Finally, a major factor in determining whether the K-55-1 discovery was a material fact is the importance attached to the drilling results by those who knew about it. In view of other unrelated recent developments favorably affecting TGS, participation by an informed person in a regular stock-purchase program, or even sporadic trading by an informed person, might lend only nominal support to the inference of the materiality of the K-55-1 discovery; nevertheless, the timing by those who knew of it of their stock purchases and their purchases of short-term calls—purchases in some cases by individuals who had never before purchased calls or even TGS stock—virtually compels the inference that the insiders were influenced by the drilling results. This insider trading activity, which surely constitutes highly pertinent evidence and the only truly objective evidence of the materiality of the K-55-1 discovery, was apparently disregarded by the court below in favor of the testimony of defendants, expert witnesses, all of whom "agreed that one drill core does not establish an ore body, much less a mine." . . .

It was the intent on Congress that all members of the investing public should be subject to identical market risks, which market risks include, of course, the risk that one's evaluative capacity or one's capital available to put at risk may exceed another's capacity or capital. The insiders here were not trading on an equal footing with the outside investors. . . .

We hold, therefore, that all transactions in TGS stock or calls by individuals apprised of the drilling results of K-55-1 were made in violation of Rule 10b-5. . . . The trial court also found . . . that Darke, after the drilling of K-55-1 had been completed and with detailed knowledge of the results thereof, told certain outside individuals that TGS "was a good buy." These individuals thereafter acquired TGS stock and calls. . . .

As Darke's "tippees" are not defendants in this action, we need not decide whether, if they acted with actual or constructive knowledge that the material information was undisclosed, their conduct is as equally violative of the Rule as the conduct of their insider source, though we note that it certainly could be equally reprehensible.

With reference to Huntington, . . . the evidence shows that he knew about and participated in TGS's land acquisition program which followed the receipt of the K-55-1 drilling results, and that on February 26, 1964 he purchased 50 shares of TGS stock. Later, on March 16, he helped prepare a letter for Dr. Holyk's signature in which TGS made a substantial offer for lands near K-55-1 and on the same day he, who had never before purchased calls on any stock, purchased a call on 100 shares of TGS stock. We are satisfied that these purchases in February and March coupled with his readily inferable and probably reliable understanding of the highly favorable nature of preliminary operations on the Kidd segment, demonstrate that Huntington possessed material inside information such as to make his purchase violative of the Rule and the Act.

Appellant Crawford, who ordered the purchase of TGS stock shortly before the TGS April 16 official announcement, and defendant Coates, who placed orders with and communicated the news to his broker immediately after the official announcement was read at the TGS-called press conference, concede that they were in possession of material information. They contend, however, that their purchases are not proscribed purchases for the news had already been effectively disclosed. We disagree

Crawford telephoned his orders to his Chicago broker about midnight on April 15 and again at 8:30 in the morning of the 16th, with instructions to buy at the opening of the Midwest Stock Exchange that morning. The trial court's finding that "he sought to, and did, 'beat the news' " . . . is well documented by the record. . . . Before insiders may act upon material information, such information must have

been effectively disclosed in a manner sufficient to insure its availability to the investing public. Particularly here, where a formal announcement to the entire financial news media had been promised in a prior official release known to the media, all insider activity must await dissemination of the promised official announcement.

Coates was absolved by the court below because his telephone order was placed shortly before 10:20 A.M. on April 16 which was after the announcement had been made even though the news could not be considered already a matter of public information. . . . The reading of a news release, which prompted Coates into action, is merely the first step in the process of dissemination required for compliance with the regulatory objective of providing all investors with an equal opportunity to make informed investment judgments. Assuming that the contents of the official release could instantaneously be acted upon, at the minimum Coates should have waited until the news could reasonably have been expected to appear over the media of widest circulation, the Dow Jones broad tape, rather than hastening to insure an advantage to himself and his broker son-in-law.

. . .

Coates, Crawford and Clayton, who ordered purchases before the news could be deemed disclosed, claim, nevertheless, that they were justified in doing so because they honestly believed that the news of the strike had become public at the time they placed their orders. However, whether the case before us is treated solely as an SEC enforcement proceeding or as a private action, proof of a specific intent to defraud is unnecessary. Thus, the beliefs of Coates, Crawford and Clayton that the news of the ore strike was sufficiently public at the time of their purchase orders are to no avail if those beliefs were not reasonable under the circumstances. . . .

. . .

On February 20, 1964, defendants Stephens, Fogarty, Mollison, Holyk and Kline accepted stock options issued to them and a number of other top officers of TGS, although not one of them had informed the Stock Option Committee of the Board of Directors of the Board of the results of K-55-1, which information we have held was then material. The SEC sought rescission of these options. In view of our conclusion as to materiality we hold that Stephens and Fogarty violated the Rule by accepting them.

Contrary to the belief of the trial court that Kline had no duty to disclose his knowledge of the Kidd project before accepting the stock option offered him we believe that he, a vice president, who had become the general counsel of TGS in January 1964, but who had been secretary of the corporation since January 1961 . . . was a member of top management and under a duty before accepting his option to disclose any material information he may have possessed, and, as he did not disclose such information to the Option Committee we direct rescission of the option he received. As to Holyk and Mollison, the SEC has not appealed the holding below that they, not being then members of top management (although Mollison was a vice president) had no duty to disclose their knowledge of the drilling before accepting their options. Therefore, the issue of whether, by accepting, they violated the Act, is not before us, and the holding below is undisturbed.

. . .

At 3:00 P.M. on April 12, 1964, evidently believing it desirable to comment upon the rumors concerning the Timmins project, TGS issued the press release quoted in pertinent part in the text. The SEC argued below and maintains on this appeal that this release painted a misleading and deceptive picture of the drilling progess at the time of its issuance, and hence violated Rule 10b-5(2). TGS relies on the holding of the court below that "The issuance of the release produced no unusual market action" and "In the absence of a showing that the purpose of the April 12 press release was to affect the market price of TGS stock to the advantage of TGS or its insiders, the issuance of the press release did not constitute a violation of Section 10(b) or Rule 10b-5 since it was not issued "in connection with the purchase or sale of any security" and, alternatively, "even if it had been established that the April 12 release was issued in connection with the purchase or sale of any security, the Commission has failed to demonstrate that it was false, misleading or deceptive." . . .

There is no indication that Congress intended that the corporations or persons responsible for the issuance of a misleading statement would not violate the section unless they engaged in related securities transactions or otherwise acted with wrongful motives; . . .

Accordingly, we hold that Rule 10b-5 is violated whenever assertions are made as here, in a manner reasonably calculated to influence the investing public, e.g., by means of the financial media, if such assertions are false or misleading or are so incomplete as to mislead irrespective of whether the issuance of the release was motivated by corporate officials for ulterior purposes. It seems clear, however, that if corporate management demonstrates that it was diligent in ascertaining that the information it published was the whole truth and that such diligently obtained information was disseminated in good faith, Rule 10b-5 would not have been violated.

. . .

Turning first to the question of whether the release was misleading, i.e., whether it conveyed to the public a false impression of the drilling situation at the time of its issuance, we note initially that the trial court did not actually decide this question. . . . we cannot, from the present record, by applying the standard Congress intended, definitively conclude that it was deceptive or misleading to the reasonable investor, or that he would have been misled by it. Accordingly, we remand that issue to the district court that took testimony and heard and saw the witnesses for a determination of the character of the release in the light of the facts existing at the time of the release, by applying the standard of whether the reasonable investor, in the exercise of due care, would have been misled by it.

In the event that it is found that the statement was misleading to the reasonable investor it will then become necessary to determine whether its issuance resulted from a lack of due diligence. . . .

MOORE, *Circuit Judge (dissenting) (with whom Chief Judge* LUMBARD *concurs):*

In their opinion, the majority have become so involved in usurping the function of the trial court, in selecting the witnesses they (at variance with the trial court) choose to believe, in forming their own factual conclusions from the evidence, in deciding with, of course, the benefit of the wisdom of hindsight, how they, had they been executives of Texas Gulf Sulphur Company (TGS), would have handled the publicity attendant to the exploration of the Timmins property, in determining (to their own satisfaction) the motives which prompted each of the individual defendants to buy TGS stock and in becoming mining engineering experts in their own right, that I find it desirable—in fact, essential—to state my opinion as to the fundamental jurisdiction of the Court of Appeals and the issues properly before us. Primarily, our task should be to review errors of law. Conversely, we are not a

jury of nine with no requirement of a unanimous verdict.

Assuming the majority's and the Commission's full disclosure theory, would the facts as then developed have given the buying or selling public the so-called advantages possessed by the insiders? TGS could have announced by November 15, 1963 that it had completed a first exploratory hole, the core of which by visual examination revealed over a length of 599 of 655 feet drilled, an average copper content of 1.15 percent, zinc 8.64 percent. . . . Such an announcement would, of course, have been of no value to anyone except possibly a few graduates of Institutes of Technology and they, as the expert witnesses here, would have recognized that one drill hole does not reveal a commercially profitable mine.

The final question to be answered is: were these officers and employees disqualified as the result of possessing information gleaned by the first drill core from purchasing TGS stock? . . .

There can be little doubt but that those familiar with the results of K-55-1 were influenced thereby in making their purchases. . . . Those who purchased were apparently willing on the basis of the inconclusive first hole and other information to risk a certain amount of their funds in TGS stock, hopeful that future developments would be favorable. Their motive for purchase does not establish the materiality of the facts which influenced them.

. . .

In summary, the most disturbing aspect of the majority opinion is its utterly unrealistic approach to the problem of the corporate press release. If corporations were literally to follow its implications, every press release would have to have the same SEC clearance as a prospectus. Even this procedure would not suffice if future events should prove the facts to have been over or understated—or too gloomy or optimistic—because the courts will always be ready and available to substitute their judgment for that of the business executives responsible therefor. . . . When and how are promising results to be disclosed? If they are not disclosed, the corporation is concealing information; if disclosed and hoped-for results do not materialize, there will always be those with the advantage of hindsight to brand them as false or misleading. . . .

Case Questions

1. Was it not hard for the defendants to argue the unimportance of the drilling results in light of their stock-buying activities? If you sat as a juror in this case, would their stock purchases have been decisive in reaching a decision?

2. In deciding cases after the fact, how can one avoid having judgment clouded by the wisdom of hindsight?

3. This decision was bitterly criticized by some when it was handed down. Does it appear to be an unreasonable decision?

Case Comment

Texas Gulf Sulphur later changed its name to Texasgulf Inc. and then in 1981 it was acquired by a French multinational, Société Nationale Elf Aquitaine. The latter company is 67 percent owned by the French government. While it may be true that one drill core does not establish an ore body, much less a mine, the discovery turned into a lucrative one. The Kidd Creek mine in Timmons, Ontario, in this case is among the richest base metal mines in the world.

Tipper and Tippee Liability

What is the liability of nontrading "tippers" and trading "tippees"? In Texas Gulf Sulphur a trading tipper, Drake, was held to have violated the law. The culpability of tippees was not determined although the court remarked that their conduct "could be equally reprehensible." The same court that decided *Texas Gulf Sulphur* provided answers in *Shapiro* v. *Merrill Lynch, Pierce, Fenner & Smith, Inc.*, 495 F 2d 228 (1974). Merrill Lynch, a prospective managing underwriter of a Douglas Aircraft debenture issue, divulged to some of its customers material adverse inside information regarding Douglas's earnings. Without disclosing this information these customers sold Douglas's common stock on a national securities exchange. As a result, Merrill Lynch received commissions, the customers minimized their losses, but the investing public who purchased Douglas stock during this same period sustained substantial losses.

The plaintiffs, although they purchased Douglas stock during this time period, did not purchase the actual stock sold by the Merrill Lynch customers. The plaintiffs sued both Merrill Lynch and its customers in a private damage action. The court held that the defendants violated Section 10(b) and Rule 10 b-5. The court held them liable for damages not only to the purchasers of the actual shares sold by the defendants, but to all persons who purchased stock in the open market without knowledge of the inside information. Merrill Lynch, the nontrading "tipper," was under a duty to the investing public not to recommend trading in Douglas stock without publicly disclosing the revised earnings figures in its possession. The trading "tippees" argued that they were unable to make effective public disclosure of information about a company with which they were not associated. The court rejected this argument and pointed out that the duty is not a naked one to disclose, but a duty to refrain from trading unless they do disclose.

In breaching their duty, the "tippers" and "tippees" incurred massive potential liability. Douglas common suffered a severe drop in its market price during June 1970 (the time at issue in the case). The number of persons who purchased in the open market during the requisite time period is probably substantial. The amount of a resulting judgment for damages does not change the application of the law. The court mentioned that, in deciding the case, it was not unmindful of the defendants' possible "Draconian liability."

The Merrill Lynch case should alert one to the potential application of the insider rules to more than just corporate employees. In addition to underwriters, banks, law firms, and accounting firms oftentimes have access to inside information by virtue of their work. In an effort to avoid becoming unnecessarily embroiled in litigation, one major accounting firm has imposed the following rules on all its employees:

1. Investments in companies that are clients of the firm are prohibited.

2. Investments in companies where an employee of the firm sits on the board of directors are prohibited.

3. All securities transactions by an employee, the employee's spouse, or the employee's dependants are to be reported to the firm.

Who Is an Insider for Purposes of Section 10(b)?

Cases such as *Texas Gulf* and *Merrill Lynch* would seem to indicate that any person who possesses material inside information cannot legally trade in that stock until and unless the information is disclosed. Subsequent Supreme Court decisions make clear that such an assumption is not always correct.

In *Chiarella* v. *U.S.*, 445 U.S. 222 (1980) the court set aside the criminal conviction of a printer for trading on the basis of nonpublic material information. The printer learned of corporate takeovers in his job in the composing room of a financial printing firm. He purchased stock in the target companies and sold the shares immediately after the takeover attempts were made public. The court held that the mere possession of such information does not create the duty to disclose it. Thus, with no duty to speak, and owing no fiduciary obligations to those he bought the stock from, his trading was legal. The decision created legal confusion because it appeared to indicate that the conviction could have been upheld if the SEC had proven a breach of duty to the acquiring corporation when he acted on information that it had supplied to his employer.

In the following case the Supreme Court clears up this confusion. It extends the *Chiarella* ruling and allows an even wider category of people to trade in stock without first disclosing nonpublic material information. One must read the case carefully, however, because the court does not permit every individual in every situation to use such information in trading securities.

DIRKS v. *SEC*
51 L.W. 5123 (1983)

JUSTICE POWELL *delivered the opinion of the Court.*

In 1973, Dirks was an officer of a New York broker-dealer firm who specialized in providing investment analysis of insurance company securities to institutional investors. On March 6, Dirks received information from Ronald Secrist, a former officer of Equity Funding of America. Secrist alleged that the assets of Equity Funding, a diversified corporation primarily engaged in selling life insurance and mutual funds, were vastly overstated as the result of fraudulent corporate practices. Secrist also stated that various regulatory agencies had failed to act on similar charges made by Equity Funding employees. He urged Dirks to verify the fraud and disclose it publicly.

Dirks decided to investigate the allegations. The senior management denied any wrongdoing, but certain corporation employees corroborated the charges of fraud. Neither Dirks nor his firm owned or traded any Equity Funding stock, but throughout his investigation he openly discussed the information he had obtained with a number of clients and investors. Some of these persons sold their holdings of Equity Funding securities, including five investment advisers who liquidated holdings of more than $16 million.

During the two-week period in which Dirks pursued his investigation and spread word of Secrist's charges, the price of Equity Funding stock fell from $26 per share to less than $15 per share. This led the New York Stock Exchange to halt trading on March 27.

The SEC began an investigation into Dirks' role in the exposure of the fraud. The SEC concluded: "Where 'tippees'—regardless of their motivation or occupation—come into possession of material information that they know is confidential and know or should know came from a corporate insider,' they must either publicly disclose that information or refrain from trading." Recognizing, however, that Dirks "played an important role in bringing [Equity Funding's] massive fraud to light," the SEC only censured him.

We were explicit in *Chiarella* in saying that there can be no duty to disclose where the person who has traded on inside information "was not [the corporation's] agent, . . . was not a fiduciary, [or] was not a person in whom the sellers [of the securities] had placed their trust and confidence."

Imposing a duty to disclose or abstain solely because a person knowingly receives material nonpublic information from an insider and trades on it could have an inhibiting influence on the role of market analysts, which the SEC itself recognizes is necessary to the preservation of a healthy market.

The conclusion that recipients of inside information do not invariably acquire a duty to disclose or abstain does not mean that such tippees always are free to trade on the information. The need for a ban on some tippee trading is clear. Not only are insiders forbidden by their fiduciary relationship from personally using undisclosed corporate information to their advantage, but they may not give such information to an outsider for the same improper purpose of exploiting the information for their personal gain. Similarly, the transactions of those who knowingly participate with the fiduciary in such a breach are "as forbidden" as transactions "on behalf of the trustee himself."

Thus, some tippees must assume an insider's duty to the shareholders not because they receive inside information, but rather because it has been made available to them improperly. Thus, a tippee assumes a fiduciary duty to the shareholders of a corporation not to trade on material nonpublic information only when the insider has breached his fiduciary duty to the shareholders by disclosing the information to the tippee and the tippee knows or should know that there has been a breach.

In determining whether a tippee is under an obligation to disclose or abstain, it thus is necessary to determine whether the insider's "tip" constituted a breach of the insider's fiduciary duty. All disclosures of confidential corporate information are not inconsistent with the duty insiders owe to shareholders. In contrast to the extraordinary facts of this case, the more typical situation in which there will be a question whether disclosure violates the insider's *Cady, Roberts* duty is when insiders disclose information to analysts. In some situations, the insider will act consistently with his fiduciary duty to shareholders, and yet release of the information may affect the market. For example, it may not be clear—either to the corporate insider or to the recipient analyst— whether the information will be viewed as ma-

terial nonpublic information. Corporate officials may mistakenly think the information already has been disclosed or that it is not material enough to affect the market. Whether disclosure is a breach of duty therefore depends in large part on the purpose of the disclosure. Thus, the test is whether the insider personally will benefit, directly or indirectly, from his disclosure. Absent some personal gain, there has been no breach of duty to stockholders. And absent a breach by the insider, there is no derivative breach.

Under the inside-trading and tipping rules set forth above, we find that there was no actionable violation by Dirks. It is undisputed that Dirks himself was a stranger to Equity Funding, with no preexisting fiduciary duty to its shareholders. He took no action, directly or indirectly, that induced the shareholders or officers of Equity Funding to repose trust or confidence in him. There was no expectation by Dirk's sources that he would keep their information in confidence. Nor did Dirks misappropriate or illegally obtain the information about Equity Funding.

It is clear that neither Secrist nor the other Equity Funding employees violated their *Cady, Roberts* duty to the corporation's shareholders by providing information to Dirks. The tippers received no monetary or personal benefit for revealing Equity Funding's secrets, nor was their purpose to make a gift of valuable information to Dirks. As the facts of this case clearly indicate, the tippers were motivated by a desire to expose the fraud. In the absence of a breach of duty to shareholders by the insiders, there was no derivative breach by Dirks.

We conclude that Dirks, in the circumstances of this case, had no duty to abstain from use of the inside information that he obtained.

Case Questions

1. Does this decision allow an individual with confidential information about a stock to legally trade that stock and never worry about liability under Section 10(b)?

2. Since Section 10(b) does not make activity such as Dirks's illegal, should the law be amended by Congress to outlaw it?

Case Note.   A federal grand jury indicted 22 persons for their role in the fraud, including many of Equity Funding's officers and directors. All defendants were found guilty, either by a plea of guilty or a conviction after trial.

SEC Enforcement of the Insider Trading Prohibitions

In 1981 when John Shad became chairman of the SEC and John Fedders became director of its enforcement section, they began a concentrated effort to halt insider trading abuses. Some individuals believe that such trading is so widespread and so easily hidden that the effort is doomed to failure. Shad and Fedders argue that the prevention of insider trading is crucial if the ordinary individual is to believe in the integrity of our capital market system. They also believe that such illegal trading can be discovered and halted through legal action. The SEC has brought insider trading cases against employees in the merger and acquisitions departments of investment banking firms, attorneys performing corporate takeover work for law firms, and brokers and accountants among others. In fiscal 1982 the SEC brought 20 insider cases; that is about 8 percent of its total cases for the year.

One obstacle to effective enforcement is the fact that trading on the basis of inside information is not illegal in some countries. Thus, an individual with such information might do the trading through several Caribbean nations or Switzerland. By executing the trades through a secret bank account and a broker in a country with stiff bank secrecy laws an individual may escape notice. The SEC is developing tactics to eliminate such loopholes. In 1981 Kuwait Petroleum Co., owned by the Kuwait government, announced the acquisition of Santa Fe International Corporation for $2.5 billion in cash. Prior to the announcement there had been active trading in Santa Fe options—contracts to buy Santa Fe stock at prices far above the then prevailing market price. The announcement of the merger caused the price of the options to skyrocket; some went from $37.50 to $1,925. As a result of this trading the SEC brought a number of insider trading cases. Some have been settled by the individuals denying violations of the law but agreeing to repay the profits they made on the transactions. In one case, the purchases were made by individuals who utilized foreign brokers. When the SEC was unable to obtain information on the clients because of the bank secrecy laws, they obtained court orders freezing $5 million of the profits from the trades that was located in the United States. The judge took the position that the foreign bank secrecy laws, while valid in the foreign country, did not apply in the United States. Under U.S. law insider trading is illegal and thus in this country the U.S. rules apply. Thus, while the bank in the foreign country did not have to reveal any information, the U.S. laws prevent the transfer of the funds outside our country until the SEC has the information it requires to determine whether a violation has occurred. This tactic of freezing funds in the U.S. generated by trading through a foreign bank and broker should cut down on such trading. What good are profits if one cannot lay hands on them?

In September of 1982 the SEC announced a new U.S.-Switzerland agreement designed to crack down on the use of Swiss banks for such trading. Under the agreement the SEC will request information from the Swiss. The Swiss bank will then freeze assets in the client's account equal to the alleged illegal trading profit and file a report with a special three-member Swiss commission. This commission will then make the determination as to whether the requested information shall be turned over to the SEC. If the information is denied, the decision can be appealed to the Swiss Banking Commission. The SEC hopes that the U.S. will also be able to negotiate such agreements with other foreign nations with bank secrecy laws.

In one of the settlements of the Sante Fe options case the federal judge heavily criticized the SEC for agreeing that the individual need only repay his profits. The judge wanted the SEC to pursue repayment of interest on the profits and criminal action against the individual. Under the current law criminal action is a possibility, but one need only repay the profits. Therefore if one trades illegally in inside information one usually need only repay the profits. Criminal action is unlikely because the burden of proof is much higher in criminal actions and prosecutors may also think it more important to concentrate on violent crime, not white collar crime. If one is not discovered, one can pocket the profits. To make violations of the law more costly, and create a deterrent effect, the SEC is seeking Congressional action to make violations punishable by repayment of up to three times the amount of the profit.

Both Section 10(b) and Rule 10b-5 leave a good deal unsaid and therefore the courts must provide answers. The statute and rule are both silent on the method of computing damages when violations occur. They are also silent as to what classes of individuals are entitled to recover for violations. We have seen that the SEC can institute legal action over alleged violations. A stockholder who bought stock from, or sold stock to, a person acting on inside information also has legal standing to bring suit. What of

Who May Recover for Section 10(b) and Rule 10b-5 Violations?

the corporation whose securities are traded on the basis of the material inside information; may a stockholder bring a derivative suit on behalf of the corporation against the trader? Since derivative suits are a matter of state corporation law, the answer to the question may vary from state to state. The next case makes that very point in its exploration of this legal area.

SCHEIN v. CHASEN

313 So. 2d 739 (1975) (Fla. S. Ct.)

ROBERTS, J.

This cause is before us for consideration of questions certified to us by the United States Court of Appeals for the Second Circuit pursuant to Rule 4.61, Florida Appellate Rules. The following questions have been certified:

> Are investors, who sell stock on the basis of inside information about the issuer corporation which they received from a stockbroker who in turn received the information from the president of the issuer corporation, liable to the corporation in a shareholder derivative suit under Florida law for the profits realized by the investors on the sale of that stock? Is the stockbroker, who relayed the material information from the president of the issuing corporation to the investors, jointly and severally liable with them for the profits they realized on the sale in a shareholder's derivative suit under Florida law?

The plaintiffs, appellants, Schein, Schein and Gregorio, are shareholders of Lum's, Inc., a Florida corporation (which has subsequent to the filing of their complaints been renamed Caesar's World, Inc.) and sue derivatively on behalf of Lum's, Inc. . . . Lehman Brothers (defendant-appellee) was a stock brokerage firm, and Benjamin Simon (defendant-appellee) was a registered representative employed by it in its Chicago office. Investors Diversified Services, Inc. (defendant-appellee) was the investment advisor for Investors Variable Payment Fund, Inc., and IDS New Dimensions Fund, Inc., two mutual funds based in Minneapolis. Eugene Sit . . . and James Jundt . . .

were employees of Investors Diversified Services, Inc. . . .

The only question before the United States Court of Appeals is the sufficiency of the complaints to state a cause of action under Florida law. . . .

In November of 1969 Chasen, who was president and chief operating officer of Lum's, addressed a seminar of about sixty members of the securities industry with reference to Lum's earning prospects for its fiscal year ending July 31, 1970. He informed them that Lum's earnings would be approximately $1.00 to $1.10 per share. On January 5, 1970, he learned that his estimate was too optimistic and that, in fact, Lum's earnings would be only approximately $.76 per share. Three days later, prior to announcing the information to the public, Chasen telephoned Simon in Chicago and told Simon that Lum's would not have as profitable a year as had been expected. He specified to Simon that earnings would be approximately $.76 per share rather than the $1.00 per share which he had earlier announced. Simon knew the information was confidential corporate property which Chasen had not given out publicly. Simon immediately telephoned this information to Sit, an employee of defendant Investors Diversified Services, Inc. (IDS), and Sit immediately telephoned it to Jundt, another employee of IDS. . . . Upon receiving the information Sit and Jundt directed the Funds to sell their entire stock holdings in Lum's and, on the morning of January 9, 1970, prior to any public announcement, Investors sold 43,000 shares of Lum's and Dimensions sold 40,000 shares. The sales were executed on the New

York Stock Exchange at about 10:30 A.M. at a price of approximately $17.50 per share. At 1:30 P.M. on the same day, the New York Stock Exchange halted further trading in Lum's stock pending a company announcement. At 2:45 P.M., Lum's issued a release which appeared on the Dow Jones News Wire Service and announced that the corporation's projected earnings would be lower than had been anticipated. When trading in Lum's was resumed on Monday, January 12, 1970, volume was heavy and the stock closed at a price of $14.00 per share—$3.50 per share lower than the Funds had realized from the sale of their shares on the previous Friday. . . .

Plaintiffs-appellants' theory of recovery is that the participants in this chain of wrongdoing are jointly and severally liable to the corporation under Florida law for misusing corporate information to their own advantage in violation of the duty they owed to Lum's, and that they must account to Lum's for the profits realized by the Mutual Funds. They do not allege in these complaints that defendants have violated any of the federal securities laws, and they concede that the substantive law of Florida governs the rights and liabilities of the parties. They urge, however, that inasmuch as there are no Florida cases directly in point, the Florida court, if it were deciding the case, would look to other jurisdictions and would take a particular and special interest in the decision of *Diamond* v. *Oreamuno*, . . . 24 N.Y. 2d 494, 301 N.Y.S. 2d 78, 248 N.E. 2d 910 (1969), a case which plaintiffs contend supports the position they urge on this appeal.

Defendants moved to dismiss the consolidated actions upon the ground that the complaints failed to state a claim upon which relief could be granted. . . .

The United States District Court considered the possibility that Florida courts might follow the rationale of the New York decision in *Diamond* v. *Oreamuno*, supra, and therefore considered whether defendants would be li-

able under the rationale of *Diamond* and concluded, as follows:

> It is clear that the complaints in these actions go far beyond the narrow holding of *Diamond*. In that case, the New York Court of Appeals held that a corporate fiduciary is liable for profits which he realizes from a sale of stock motivated by inside information received by him in his corporate position. None of the defendants in these actions fit into this mold. Chasen, as president and chief operating officer of Lum's was certainly a fiduciary of that corporation. None of the complaints, however, allege that he did anything more than pass the inside information to defendant Simon, and there are no allegations that Chasen sold any of his Lum's stock or derived any gain, monetary or otherwise, from the sales that ultimately occurred. On the other hand, the mutual fund defendants would have profited if, as alleged, they sold their 83,000 shares of Lum's stock on the basis of Chasen's inside information. It can scarcely be maintained, however, that the mutual fund defendants were officers or directors of Lum's or owed any fiduciary duties whatsoever to that corporation. The broker-dealer defendants fail to come within either of the *Diamond* perimeters as they were not fiduciaries of the corporation and did not profit by virtue of the sales.

With regard to Chasen, the District Court opined that as a corporate officer, he may come within the holding of *Diamond*, but that this question need not be reached because service of process on him was improper. The Circuit Court of Appeals by divided vote reversed the District Court and found that although Florida law was controlling, it could find none that was decisive, and, therefore, it turned to the law of New York, in particular *Diamond*, supra. The Circuit Court of Appeal stated its objective to be to interpret *Diamond* as the Florida Court would probably interpret it and apply it to the facts. . . . The Circuit Court opined that the cleansing effect of the *Diamond* rationale ought to reach third parties who, through breach of fiduciary relationship, become traders advantageously possessed of confidential insider knowledge. . . .

JUDGE KAUFMAN dissented to this decision and explained: . . .

The court holds today that a person with no relationship whatsoever—fiduciary or otherwise—to a corporation, who trades its shares on the basis of material inside information becomes, *ipso facto,* a fiduciary of the corporation whose shares he traded and, accordingly, may be required in a *shareholders' derivative action*—not a Section 10(b) or 16(b) action—to pay his profits to the corporation. . . .

It is important to note at the outset that the plaintiffs in these actions, shareholders of Lum's, do not claim to have suffered any damages themselves. Rather, these derivative suits are brought "on behalf of and for the benefit of Lum's." They seek to recover for Lum's treasury the windfall profit garnered by the IDS mutual funds, and assert that all defendants are jointly and severally liable for this amount. Thus, the proper method of analysis is not to focus on the unfairness of the mutual funds' profit at the expense of their purchasers—who have their own recourse for any wrongdoing—but on the strands of duty running to the corporation from the various individuals involved. . . .

Despite the manner in which the majority opinion convolutes the law and the facts in this case, a view that a tippee is cloaked with state law fiduciary obligations to the corporation whose shares he trades is an unknown and untenable legal concept. . . .

We quote with approval the dissent of Judge Kaufman and we hold it to be responsive and to be dispositive of the controlling questions posited by the United States Circuit Court of Appeals, which we answer in the negative. Not only will we not give the unprecedented expansive reading to *Diamond* sought by appellants but furthermore, we do not choose to adopt the innovative ruling of the New York Court of Appeals in *Diamond,* supra. We adhere to previous precedent established by the courts in this state that actual damage to the corporation must be alleged in the complaint to substantiate a stockholders' derivative action. . . . In *Talcott* v. *McDowell,* supra, the court opined:

> Thus, in order for a complaint to state a cause of action entitling the stockholder to relief, it must allege two distinct wrongs: the act whereby the corporation was caused to suffer damage, and a wrongful refusal by the corporation to seek redress for such act. . . .

We conclude that under the facts alleged in the complaint, Florida law does not permit the maintenance of shareholders' derivative suit on behalf of Lum's.

Case Questions

1. Can a corporation suffer damage in a form other than financial? Was there an injury to Lum's when Chasen passed confidential corporate property to an outsider, thereby violating his fiduciary duties?

2. Which decision is most appealing: (a) the innovative Court of Appeals decision with its resulting cleansing effect or (b) the traditional legalistic approach of Florida's highest court?

3. Since Section 10(b) and 16(b) do exist, does this decision weaken the drive against fraudulent stock activities?

What if fraudulent actions are taken, not in connection with the purchase or sale of securities, but rather to successfully discourage an individual from purchasing securities? In the case that follows the court holds that such conduct does not violate Section 10(b).

BLUE CHIP STAMPS v. MANOR DRUG STORES
421 U.S. 723 (1975)

MR. JUSTICE REHNQUIST *delivered the opinion of the Court.*

This case requires us to consider whether the offerees of a stock offering . . . may maintain a private cause of action for money damages where they allege that the offeror has violated the provisions of Rule 10b-5 of the Securities and Exchange Commission, but where they have neither purchased nor sold any of the offered shares. . . .

In 1963 the United States filed a civil antitrust action against Blue Chip Stamp Company ("Old Blue Chip"), a company in the business of providing trading stamps to retailers, and nine retailers who owned 90 percent of its shares. In 1967 the action was terminated by the entry of a consent decree. . . . The decree contemplated a plan of reorganization whereby Old Blue Chip was to be merged into a newly formed corporation "New Blue Chip." The holdings of the majority shareholders of Old Blue Chip were to be reduced, and New Blue Chip, one of the petitioners here, was required under the plan to offer a substantial number of its shares of common stock to retailers who had used the stamp service in the past but who were not shareholders in the old company. . . .

The reorganization plan was carried out, the offering was registered with the SEC as required by the 1933 Act, and a prospectus was distributed to all offerees. . . . Somewhat more than 50 percent of the offered units were actually purchased. In 1970, two years after the offering, respondent, a former user of the stamp service and therefore an offeree of the 1968 offering, filed this suit. . . .

Respondent's complaint alleged, *inter alia,* that the prospectus prepared and distributed by Blue Chip in connection with the offering was materially misleading in its overly pessimistic appraisal of Blue Chip's status and future prospects. It alleged that Blue Chip intentionally made the prospectus overly pessimistic in order to discourage respondent and other members of the allegedly large class whom it represents from accepting what was intended to be a bargain offer, so that the rejected shares might later be offered to the public at a higher price. The complaint alleged that class members because of and in reliance on the false and misleading prospectus failed to purchase the offered units. Respondents therefore sought on behalf of the alleged class some $21,400,000 in damages representing the lost opportunity to purchase the units; the right to purchase the previously rejected units at the 1968 price, and in addition, it sought some $25,000,000 in exemplary damages. . . .

Section 10(b) of the 1934 Act does not by its terms provide an express civil remedy for its violation. Nor does the history of this provision provide any indication that Congress considered the problem of private suits under it at the time of its passage. . . . Similarly there is no indication that the Commission in adopting Rule 10b-5 considered the question of private civil remedies under this provision. . . .

Despite the contrast between the provisions of Rule 10b-5 and the numerous carefully drawn express civil remedies provided in both the Acts of 1933 and 1934, it was held in 1946 . . . that there was an implied private right of action under the Rule. *Kardon* v. *National Gypsum Co.,* 69 F. Supp. 512 (1946). This Court had no occasion to deal with the subject until 20-odd years later, and at that time we confirmed with virtually no discussion the overwhelming consensus of the district courts and courts of appeals that such a cause of action did exist. . . . Such a conclusion was, of course, entirely consistent with the Court's recognition in *J. I. Case Corp.* v. *Borak,* 377 U.S. 426, 432 (1964), that private enforcement of

Commission rules may "[provide] a necessary supplement to Commission action."

Within a few years after the seminal *Kardon* decision, the Court of Appeals for the Second Circuit concluded that the plaintiff class for purposes of a private damage action under § 10(b) and Rule 10b-5 was limited to actual purchasers and sellers of securities. *Birnbaum* v. *Newport Steel Corp., supra.* . . .

As with *Kardon,* virtually all lower federal courts facing the issue in the hundreds of reported cases presenting this question over the past quarter century have reaffirmed *Birnbaum's* conclusion that the plaintiff class for purposes of § 10(b) and Rule 10b-5 private damage action is limited to purchasers and sellers of securities. . . .

In 1957 and again in 1959, the Securities and Exchange Commission sought from Congress amendment of § 10(b) to change its wording from "in connection with the purchase or sale of any security" to "in connection with the purchase or sale of, *or any attempt to purchase or sell,* any security." . . . Neither change was adopted by Congress.

The longstanding acceptance by the courts, coupled with Congress' failure to reject *Birnbaum's* reasonable interpretation of the wording of § 10(b), wording which is directed towards injury suffered "in connection with the purchase or sale" of securities, argues significantly in favor of acceptance of the *Birnbaum* rule by this Court. . . .

Available extrinsic evidence from the texts of the 1933 and 1934 Acts as to the congressional scheme in this regard, though not conclusive, supports the result reached by the *Birnbaum* court. The wording of § 10(b) directed at fraud "in connection with the purchase or sale" of securities stands in contrast with the parallel antifraud provision of the 1933 Act, § 17(a) . . . reaching fraud "in the offer or sale" of securities. When Congress wished to provide a remedy to those who neither purchase nor sell securities, it had little trouble in doing so expressly. . . .

When we deal with private actions under Rule 10b-5, we deal with a judicial oak which has grown from little more than a legislative acorn. Such growth may be quite consistent with the congressional enactment and with the role of the federal judiciary in interpreting it, . . . but it would by disingenuous to suggest that either Congress in 1934 or the Securities and Exchange Commission in 1942 foreordained the present state of the law with respect to Rule 10b-5. . . .

Three principal classes of potential plaintiffs are presently barred by the *Birnbaum* rule. First are potential purchasers of shares, . . . who allege that they decided not to purchase because of an unduly gloomy representation or the omission of favorable material which made the issue appear to be a less favorable investment vehicle than it actually was. Second are actual shareholders in the issuer who allege that they decided not to sell their shares because of an unduly rosy representation or a failure to disclose unfavorable material. Third are shareholders, creditors, and perhaps others related to an issuer who suffered loss in the value of their investment due to corporate or insider activities in connection with the purchase or sale of securities which violate Rule 10b-5. . . .

A great majority of the many commentators on the issue before us have taken the view that the *Birnbaum* limitation on the plaintiff class in Rule 10b-5 action for damages is an arbitrary restriction which unreasonably prevents some deserving plaintiffs from receiving damages which have in fact been caused by violations of Rule 10b-5. . . . We have no doubt that this is indeed a disadvantage of the *Birnbaum* rule, and if it had no countervailing advantages it would be undesirable as a matter of policy, however much it might be supported by precedent and legislative history. But we are of the opinion that there are countervailing advantages of the *Birnbaum* rule, purely as a matter of policy. . . .

There has been widespread recognition

that litigation under Rule 10b-5 presents a danger of vexatiousness different in degree and in kind from that which accompanies litigation in general. . . .

We believe that the concern expressed for the danger of vexatious litigation which could result from a widely expanded class of plaintiffs under Rule 10b-5 is founded in something more substantial than the common complaint of the many defendants who would prefer avoiding lawsuits entirely to either settling them or trying them. These concerns have two largely separate grounds.

The first of these concerns is that in the field of federal securities laws governing disclosure of information even a complaint which by objective standards may have very little chance of success at trial has a settlement value to the plaintiff out of any proportion to its prospect of success at trial so long as he may prevent the suit from being resolved against him by dismissal or summary judgment. . . .

The potential for possible abuse of the liberal discovery provisions of the federal rules may likewise exist in this type of case to a greater extent than they do in other litigation. The prospect of extensive deposition of the defendant's officers and associates and the concomitant opportunity for extensive discovery of business documents, is a common occurrence in this and similar types of litigation. . . .

Without the *Birnbaum* rule, an action under § 10b-5 will turn largely on which oral version of a series of occurrences the jury may decide to credit, and therefore no matter how improbable the allegations of the plaintiff, the case will be virtually impossible to dispose of prior to trial other than by settlement. . . .

The *Birnbaum* rule undoubtedly excludes plaintiffs who have in fact been damaged by violations of Rule 10b-5, and to that extent it is undesirable. . . .

In the absence of the *Birnbaum* doctrine, bystanders to the securities marketing process could await developments on the sidelines without risk, claiming that inaccuracies in disclosure caused nonselling in a falling market and that unduly pessimistic predictions by the issuer followed by a rising market caused them to allow retrospectively golden opportunities to pass. . . .

We therefore hold that respondent was not entitled to sue for violation of Rule 10b-5, and the judgment of the Court of Appeals is

Reversed.

MR. JUSTICE BLACKMUN, *with whom* MR. JUSTICE DOUGLAS *and* MR. JUSTICE BRENNAN *join, dissenting.*

Today the Court graves into stone *Birnbaum's* arbitrary principle of standing. . . . In so doing, the Court exhibits a preternatural solicitousness for corporate well-being and a seeming callousness toward the investing public quite out of keeping, it seems to me, with our own traditions and the intent of the securities laws. . . .

From a reading of the complaint in relation to the language of § 10(b) of the 1934 Act and of Rule 10b-5, it is manifest that plaintiffs have alleged the use of a deceptive scheme "in connection with the purchase or sale of any security." To my mind, the word "sale" ordinarily and naturally may be understood to mean not only a single, individualized act transferring property from one party to another, but also the generalized event of public disposal of property through advertisement, auction, or some other market mechanism. Here there is an obvious, indeed a court-ordered, "sale" of securities in the special offering of New Blue Chip shares and debentures to former users. Yet the Court denies these plaintiffs the right to maintain a suit under Rule 10b-5 because they do not fit into the mechanistic categories of either "purchaser" or "seller." This, surely, is an anomaly, for the very purpose of the alleged scheme was to inhibit these plaintiffs from ever acquiring the status of "purchaser." . . .

Case Questions

1. Does this decision indicate that the Supreme Court has a pro-business tilt?

2. Is it proper to have policy considerations as the determining factor in a case of this importance? Are policy considerations just another name for a judge's personal, political, social, and economic opinions?

3. When the Supreme Court is considering a case, what role should a concern over the judiciary's caseload (vexatious litigation) occupy?

The Burden of Proof in Securities Litigation

The plaintiff in a lawsuit has the burden of proving the allegations in the complaint. If the plaintiff fails to do so, the case will be lost. In criminal cases the prosecution must prove its case beyond a reasonable doubt. In civil litigation the normal burden is to prove one's case by a preponderance of the evidence. There is also a clear and convincing evidence standard that falls between these two. What burden of proof is required under the securities law? In the following case the Supreme Court decides that the individual suing under the securities laws must prove his case by a preponderance of the evidence. The Court also makes clear that a private person has an implied right of action under Section 10(b). It is a type of "catchall" provision that prohibits conduct of a broad general nature. The court determined that a plaintiff has the option of choosing to bring a suit alleging a violation of 10(b), or of another more specific provision of the securities statutes. Thus, the plaintiff is the one to select which section of the securities law he will attempt to prove (by a preponderance of the evidence) that the defendants have violated by their conduct.

HERMAN & MacLEAN v. *HUDDLESTON*
51 L.W. 4099 (1983)

(Authors' note Texas International Speedway, Inc. sold in excess of $4 million of securities through a public offer. The venture was not successful and the corporation entered bankruptcy about a year later. The plaintiffs brought suit on behalf of themselves and other purchasers of the securities. Most of the participants in the offering were alleged to have violated Section 10(b) of the '34 Act by engaging in a fraudulent scheme to misrepresent or conceal material facts regarding the corporation's financial condition. A jury rendered a verdict in favor of the plaintiffs and the Supreme Court upholds that verdict in this decision.)

JUSTICE MARSHALL *delivered the opinion of the Court.*

These consolidated cases raise two unresolved questions concerning Section 10(b) of the Securities Exchange Act of 1934. The first is whether purchasers of registered securities who allege they were defrauded by misrepresentations in a registration statement may maintain an action under Section 10(b) notwithstanding the express remedy for misstatements and omissions in registration statements provided by Section 11 of the Securities Act of 1933. The second question is whether persons seeking recovery under Section 10(b) must prove their cause of action by clear and convincing evidence rather than by a preponderance of the evidence.

The Acts created several express private rights of action, one of which is contained in Section 11 of the 1933 Act. In addition to the private actions created explicitly by the 1933 and 1934 Acts, federal courts have implied private remedies under other provisions of the two laws. Most significantly for present purposes, a private right of action under Section 10(b) of the 1934 Act and Rule 10b-5 has been consistently recognized for more than 35 years.

While some conduct actionable under Section 11 may also be actionable under Section 10(b), it is hardly a novel proposition that the Securities Exchange Act and the Securities Act "prohibit some of the same conduct."

Accordingly, we hold that the availability of an express remedy under Section 11 of the 1933 Act does not preclude defrauded purchasers of registered securities from maintaining an action under Section 10(b) of the 1934 Act.

In a typical civil suit for money damages, plaintiffs must prove their case by a preponderance of the evidence. Similarly, in an action by the SEC to establish fraud under Section 17(a) of the Securities Act, we have held that proof by a preponderance of the evidence suffices to establish liability. The same standard applies in administrative proceedings before the SEC and has been consistently employed by the lower courts in private actions under the securities laws.

A preponderance-of-the-evidence standard allows both parties to share the risk of error in roughly equal fashion. Any other standard expresses a preference for one side's interests. On the one hand, the defendants face the risk of opprobrium that may result from a finding of fraudulent conduct. On the other hand, the interests of plaintiffs in such suits are significant. Defrauded investors are among the very individuals Congress sought to protect in the securities laws. If they prove that it is more likely than not that they were defrauded, they should recover.

We therefore decline to depart from the preponderance-of-the-evidence standard generally applicable in civil actions.

Other Fraudulent Activities

The bulk of this chapter has concentrated on activities that are fraudulent, manipulative, or deceitful under Section 10(b) of the 1934 Act. However, there are other provisions of the securities statutes that deal with fraud, and the types of fraud are only limited by the imagination of persons with crooked tendencies. We will now examine two examples of other types of fraudulent activities. Notice in the following case that the individual was prosecuted criminally for his actions.

UNITED STATES v. *NAFTALIN*
441 U.S. 768 (1979)

(Author's note: Naftalin engaged in a fraudulent "short selling" scheme. He placed orders with five brokers to sell shares of stock that he believed had peaked in price and were entering a period of market decline. He did not own the stock and was gambling that the prices of the stocks would decline substantially before he was required to deliver them. He planned to make offsetting purchases at lower prices through other brokers. To avoid making a margin deposit with the selling brokers, he falsely indicated to them that he owned the stocks. Instead of falling, the prices of the stocks he sold rose sharply in price. Naftalin never delivered the securities and so the brokers that had "sold" the stock had to buy the stock on the open market, at the higher price, to meet their commitments. The investors to whom the stock was sold were thereby shielded from direct injury, but the five

brokers suffered substantial financial losses. Naftalin appealed his criminal conviction for violating Section 17 of the 1933 Act. He argued that the section applies solely to frauds against investors, and not those against brokers. The Supreme Court rejected his argument and upheld his conviction.)

MR. JUSTICE BRENNAN *delivered the opinion of the Court.*

The question presented in this case is whether § 17 (a)(1) of the Securities Act of 1933 prohibits frauds against brokers as well as investors. We hold that it does. . . .

Subsection (1) makes it unlawful for "any person in the offer or sale of any securities . . . *directly or indirectly* . . . to employ *any* device, scheme, or artifice to defraud . . . ." The statutory language does not require that the victim of the fraud be an investor—only that the fraud occur "in" an offer or sale.

An offer and sale clearly occurred here. Respondent placed sell orders with the brokers; the brokers, acting as agents, executed the orders; and the results were contracts of sale, which are within the statutory definition, . . . Moreover, the fraud occurred "in" the "offer" and "sale." . . . This language does not require that the fraud occur in any particular phase of the selling transaction. At the very least, an order to a broker to sell securities is certainly an "attempt to dispose" of them.

Thus, nothing in subsection (1) of § 17 (a) creates a requirement that injury occur to a purchaser. . . .

But neither this Court nor Congress has ever suggested that investor protection was the *sole* purpose of the Securities Act. As we have noted heretofore, the Act "emerged as part of the aftermath of the market crash in 1929." . . . Indeed, Congress' primary contemplation was that regulation of the securities markets might help set the economy on the road to recovery. . . . Prevention of frauds against investors was surely a key part of that program, but so was the effort "to achieve a high standard of business ethics . . . *in every facet of the securities industry.*" . . . Respondent's assertion that Congress' concern was limited to investors is thus manifestly inconsistent with the legislative history.

Moreover, the welfare of investors and financial intermediaries are inextricably linked—frauds perpetrated upon either business or investors can redound to the detriment of the other and to the economy as a whole. . . . Although investors suffered no immediate financial injury in this case because the brokers covered the sales by borrowing and then "buying in," the indirect impact upon investors may be substantial. . . . Losses suffered by brokers increase their cost of doing business, and in the long run investors pay at least part of this cost through higher brokerage fees. . . . Finally, while the investors here were shielded from direct injury, that may not always be the case. Had the brokers been insolvent or unable to borrow, the investors might well have failed to receive their promised shares. . . .

Case Question   1. Is short selling a riskier type of investing than the normal purchase of stock? Why?

Fraud can assume many forms. The Investment Advisors Act of 1940 prohibits practices that operate as a fraud or deceit on clients. An illustration of this type of illegal activity is contained in the Supreme Court decision in *SEC* v. *Capital Gains Research Bureau,* 375 U.S. 180

(1963). The publisher of two investment advisory services purchased shares of a particular security shortly before recommending it to readers of the service for long-term investment. This was done on six different occasions. Each time there was an increase in the market price and the volume of trading of the recommended security within a few days after the distribution of the service. Immediately thereafter, the publisher sold the securities at a profit. This was not disclosed to the clients or prospective clients of the service. Such an adviser may be motivated, either consciously or unconsciously, to recommend a given security, not because of its potential for a long-run price increase, but because of its potential for a short-run price increase in response to activity prompted by the recommendation. Thus, the court held that such activity by an adviser does operate as a fraud or deceit on a client and the SEC may enforce compliance with the law by obtaining an injunction requiring the adviser to make full disclosure of the practice to the clients.

Review Problems

1. A director of a company sells 3000 shares of his company's stock. Within six months he buys 2000 shares of this stock at a lower price for a trust. The director is a cotrustee of the trust, which was created by his mother many years ago for the benefit of his two sons, The "profit" from the transaction is $25,000. Has the director realized a profit that is recoverable by his company? [*CBI Industries* v. *Horton*, 51 L.W. 2040 (1982)]

   No — he is not owner or benefactor

2. Klawans purchased 9900 shares of stock of Williams-McWilliams Industries at various times between October 1, 1956, and January 17, 1957. These holdings amount to less than 10 percent of the corporation's stock and Klawans was neither a director nor officer during this time period. He became a director on March 18, 1957, about 60 days after the last purchase of stock. He made no further purchases but within 10 days of his election as director he sold 7900 shares at a profit. Thereafter, he sold the remaining shares at a loss. Under 16(b), do his profits belong to the corporation? *→Yes* If he is accountable for the profits, may he offset losses in transactions in the same stock within the six month period covered by the statute? [*Adler* v. *Klawans*, 267 F2d 840 (1959)] *↳No*

3. Oreamuno and Gonzalez are directors of Management Assistants, Inc. With their wives they own approximately 14 percent of the company's common stock. In August 1966 they learned that corporate earnings would be sharply reduced from earlier figures. This information did not become available to the other shareholders and investing public until October 18, 1966. In September 1966 Oreamuno sold 28,500 shares of common stock and Gonzalez sold 28,000 shares. The selling price was $23.75 a share; after release of the earnings report the stock fell to $11 per share. Diamond, another shareholder, now

brings a stockholders' derivative suit to recover the difference between the two prices. Neither Diamond nor the corporation purchased any of the shares that were sold. The corporation sustained no loss. Should Diamond's lawsuit be dismissed? Can the purchasers of the stock also bring suit? Do you think this potential double liability is a wise policy? [*Diamond* v. *Oreamuno*, 248 N.E. 2d 910 (1969)]

No — *exists, corp + purchasers.* / *Yes*

4. Crane Company makes a tender offer to the shareholders of Westinghouse Air Brake Company on April 6, 1968. Under the tender offer Crane acquired 32 percent of Air Brake's stock. However, prior to the offer, Air Brake's directors approved a merger with American Standard. After the tender offer expires, the Air Brake stockholders approve the merger. The merger is then consummated. Crane is a competitor of Standard. To avoid the antitrust problems inherent in having significant stock ownership in a competitor, Crane sells its stock during June 1968 at a profit of about $10 million. Standard now brings suit to recover these short-swing profits. Crane argues that the antitrust laws forced the sale and 16(b) does not govern such "forced" sales. It points out that 16(b) is aimed at trading abuses arising out of access to inside information. Although by statutory definition it is an insider, it is an outsider who failed in its takeover bid. Should Crane disgorge its short-swing profits? [*American Standard* v. *Crane*, 510 F.2d 1043 (1974)]

No, didn't have inside inform., forced sale

5. The Securities Exchange Act of 1934 holds certain insiders liable for short-swing profits under Section 16(b). Which of the following classes of people would not be insiders in relation to the corporation in which they own securities?

    (a) An executive vice president.
    (b) A major debenture holder. — *debt (creditor)*
    (c) An 11 percent owner, 8 percent of which is owned in his or her name and 3 percent in an irrevocable trust for his or her benefit for life.
    (d) A director who owns less than 10 percent of the shares of stock of the corporation.

(Adapted from CPA Exam Law Problem #1, Question #49, taken from the May 1979 exam. © American Institute of Certified Public Accountants, Inc., 1979.)

6. Whitworth has been charged by Bonanza Corporation with violating the Securities Exchange Act of 1934. Whitworth was formerly the president of Bonanza, but he was ousted as a result of a proxy battle. Bonanza seeks to recover from Whitworth any and all of his short-swing profits. Which of the following would be a valid defense to the charges?

    (a) Whitworth is a New York resident, Bonanza was incorporated in New York, and the transactions were all made through the New York Stock Exchange; therefore, an interstate commerce was not involved.

(b) Whitworth did not actually make use of any insider information in connection with the various stock transactions in question.

(c) All the transactions alleged to be in violation of the 1934 act were purchases made during February 1979 with the corresponding sales made in September 1979. *more than 6 mos. issue*

(d) Whitworth's motivation in selling the stock was solely a result of the likelihood that he would be ousted as president of Bonanza.

(Adapted from CPA Exam Law Problem #1, Question #32, © American Institute of Certified Public Accountants, Inc., 1979.)

7. Young owns 200 shares of stock of Victory Manufacturing Company. Victory is listed on a national stock exchange and has in excess of one million shares outstanding. Young claims that Truegood, a Victory director, has purchased and sold shares in violation of the insider trading provisions of the Securities Exchange Act of 1934. Young has threatened legal action. Which of the following statements is correct?

(a) Truegood will have a valid defense if he can show he did not have any insider information that influenced his purchases or sales.

(b) Young can sue Truegood personally, but his recovery will be limited to his proportionate share of Truegood's profits plus legal expenses. *belongs to corp.*

(c) In order to prevail, Young must sue for and on <u>behalf of the corporation</u> and establish that the transactions in question occurred within less than six months of each other and at a profit to Truegood.

(d) Since Young's stock ownership is less than 1 percent, his only recourse is to file a complaint with the SEC or obtain a sufficient number of shareholders to join him so that the 1 percent requirement is met. *not true @ all*

(Adapted from CPA Exam Law Problem #1, Question #33, taken from the November 1978 exam. © American Institute of Certified Public Accountants, Inc., 1978.)

8. Taylor is the executive Vice President for Marketing of Reflex Corporation and a member of the board of directors. On the basis of information obtained during the course of his duties, Taylor concluded that Reflex's profits would fall by 50 percent for the quarter and 30 percent for the year. He quietly contacted his broker and disposed of 10,000 shares of his Reflex stock at a profit, some of which he had acquired within six months of the sale. In fact, Reflex's profits did not fall, but its stock price declined for unrelated reasons. Taylor had also

Zippie

advised a friend to sell her shares and repurchase the stock later. She followed Taylor's advice, sold for $21, and subsequently repurchased an equal number of shares at $11. A shareholder has commenced a shareholder derivative action against Taylor and the friend for violation of the Securities Exchange Act of 1934. Will the suit be successful?   *Taylor – Yes, friend – No — prof. disagrees*

(Adapted from CPA Exam Law Problem #1, Question #27, taken from the November 1979 exam. © American Institute of Certified Public Accountants, Inc. 1979.)

9. A corporate shareholder holds 8 percent of the common stock of a company. The shareholder's <u>24</u>-year-old daughter is a stockbroker. Her firm issues a buy recommendation on the stock of the company in which her father holds an 8 percent interest. As a result of that recommendation, the daughter not only recommends the stock to her clients, but also purchases a 3 percent holding in the company herself. Is the shareholder father now covered by Section 16 as the beneficial owner of 11 percent of the stock?   *No – minor child only*

10. A corporate employee is given the title "vice president" as part of a corporate recognition program for sales achievement. The employee was one of about 50 to receive the title. The title did not bring with it any executive or policy-making duties. The employee then trades in his employer's stock within a six-month period and makes a profit of about $15,000. The employer now brings suit under Section 16 to recover the profits. Is this employee an "officer" and must he return the profit to the company? [*Merrill Lynch* v. *Livingston*, 566 F.2d 119, (1978)]   *No*

Liability of Directors and Attorneys Under the Securities Law

16

Currently there is extensive discussion and disagreement over what constitutes the proper role of directors, accountants, and attorneys under the securities laws. Are their duties restricted to serving their client corporation or do they also encompass a responsibility to the public and the SEC? The financial collapse of corporations caused by fraudulent activities, illegal political contributions, and the bribery of foreign officials all raise questions as to what the directors, accountants, and attorneys were doing when certain activities occurred. Did they have knowledge of what was taking place? If not, why not? Would a reasonable director, accountant, or attorney have uncovered the shenanigans? Do they have a duty of disclosure? If so, to whom does this duty run? The final answers to some of these queries remain unsettled. Yet in other areas the securities laws are specific as to the legal responsibility of various individuals. Let us now examine various aspects of these responsibilities.

Liability of the Board of Directors

Under state corporation law the directors owe a fiduciary duty to the corporation. In exercising their authority due care must be utilized. Directors meet their obligation when in good faith they exercise business judgment in making decisions regarding the corporation. The courts will not disturb their decision if any rational business purpose can be attributed to the directors' actions. Only in instances of fraud, bad faith, gross overreaching, or abuse of discretion will a court interfere with the directors' decision.

A fraudulent scheme carried out by a board of directors in violation of their fiduciary duties will not violate Section 10 of the 1934 Act unless their conduct can be fairly viewed as "manipulative or deceptive." This was the decision of the Supreme Court in *Santa Fe Industries* v. *Green,* 430 U.S. 462 (1977). In that case Santa Fe, which was the parent company of Kirby, used the Delaware short-form merger statute to merge with Kirby. The stockholders of the 5 percent minority interest in Kirby were notified the day after the merger became effective. They were offered $150 per share for their stock and advised of their right to attain an appraisal if dissatisfied with the price. Instead of pursuing their rights under state law, the shareholders brought an action against the directors under the federal securities law. They alleged that the stock had been fraudulently appraised in an effort to freeze out the minority shareholders at an inadequate price in violation of Section 10 and sought to set aside the merger and recover the fair value of their stock. The minority shareholders placed a value on their stock of at least $722 per share. Santa Fe fully complied with the provisions of the short-form merger statute. It did not make a "misstatement" or "omission" in the information statement that accompanied the notice of merger. With these facts the court said the directors' conduct was not deceptive or manipulative and not subject to a suit under the federal securities statutes. It pointed out that the corporate conduct of the directors in this instance is one traditionally left to state regulation.

Other provisions of the securities laws impose on the directors a more rigorous responsibility than does the general corporate law or common law. Yet a director does not bear absolute liability. The *BarChris* case that follows examines the liability of those that sign a materially false registration statement, including directors. Notice that a director incurs civil liability unless he can prove that (1) he relied on the authority of an expert and had no reasonable grounds to believe that the expert's statements were untrue or that (2) he made a reasonable investigation and had reasonable grounds to believe that the statements were true.

The director's liability does not vary according to whether his status is an inside or outside director. The judge in *BarChris* points out that the securities laws do not distinguish between the two. As you read the case, you will note that it deals with accountants' and underwriters' liability in addition to that of directors.

ESCOTT v. BARCHRIS CONSTRUCTION CORP.

283 F. Supp. 643 (1968)

MCLEAN, District Judge

This is an action by purchasers of 5½ percent convertible subordinated fifteen year debentures of BarChris Construction Corporation (BarChris). Plaintiffs purport to sue on their own behalf and "on behalf of all other and present and former holders" of the debentures. . . .

The action is brought under Section 11 of the Securities Act of 1933. . . . Plaintiffs allege that the registration statement with respect to these debentures filed with the Securities and Exchange Commission, which became effective on May 16, 1961, contained false statements and material omissions.

Defendants fall into three categories: (1) the persons who signed the registration statement; (2) the underwriters, consisting of eight investment banking firms, led by Drexel & Co. (Drexel); and (3) BarChris's auditors, Peat, Marwick, Mitchell & Co. (Peat, Marwick).

The signers, in addition to BarChris itself, were the nine directors of BarChris, plus its controller, who was not a director. . . .

On the main issue of liability, the questions to be decided are (1) did the registration statement contain false statements of fact, or did it omit to state facts which should have been stated in order to prevent it from being misleading; (2) if so, were the facts which were falsely stated or omitted "material" within the meaning of the Act; (3) if so, have defendants established their affirmative defense? . . .

At the time relevant here, BarChris was engaged primarily in the construction of bowling alleys. . . .

On October 29, 1962, it filed in this court a petition for an arrangement under Chapter XI of the Bankruptcy Act. . . .

The registration statement in its final form contained a prospectus as well as other information. . . .

For convenience, the various falsities and omissions . . . are recapitulated here. They were as follows:

1. *1960 Earnings*
   (a) *Sales*
As per prospectus	$9,165,320
Correct figure	8,511,420
Overstatement	$ 653,900
   (b) *Net Operating Income*
As per prospectus	$1,742,801
Correct figure	1,496,196
Overstatement	$ 246,605
   (c) *Earnings per Share*
As per prospectus	$ .75
Correct figure	.65
Overstatement	$ .10

2. *1960 Balance Sheet Current Assets*
As per prospectus	$4,524,021
Correct figure	3,914,332
Overstatement	609,689

3. *Contingent Liabilities as of December 31, 1960 on Alternative Method of Financing*
As per prospectus	$ 750,000
Correct figure	1,125,795
Understatement	$ 375,795
Capitol Lanes should have been shown as a direct liability	$ 325,000

4. *Contingent Liabilities as of April 30, 1961*
As per prospectus	$ 825,000
Correct figure	1,443,853
Understatement	$ 618,853
Capitol Lanes should have been shown as direct liability	$ 314,166

5. *Earnings Figures for Quarter ending March 31, 1961*
   (a) *Sales*
As per prospectus	$2,138,455
Correct figure	1,618,645
Overstatement	$ 519,810
   (b) *Gross Profit*
As per prospectus	$ 483,121
Correct figure	252,366
Overstatement	$ 230,755

6. *Backlog as of March 31, 1961*
As per prospectus	$6,905,000
Correct figure	2,415,000
Overstatement	$4,490,000

7. *Failure to Disclose Officers' Loans Outstanding and Unpaid on May 16, 1961*
	$ 386,615

8. *Failure to Disclose Use of Proceeds in Manner not Revealed in Prospectus*
Approximately	$1,160,000

9. *Failure to Disclose Cus-*
   tomers' Delinquencies in
   May 1961 and Bar-
   Chris's Potential Liability
   with Respect Thereto   Over $1,350,000

10. *Failure to Disclose the*
    Fact that BarChris was
    Already Engaged, and
    was about to be More
    Heavily Engaged, in the
    Operation of Bowling
    Alleys

It is a prerequisite to liability under Section 11 of the Act that the fact which is falsely stated in a registration statement, or the fact that is omitted when it should have been stated to avoid misleading, be "material." . . .

Early in the history of the Act, a definition of materiality was given . . . which is still valid today. A material fact was there defined as:

". . . a fact which if it had been correctly stated or disclosed would have deterred or tended to deter the average prudent investor from purchasing the securities in question." . . .

Judged by this test, there is no doubt that many of the misstatements and omissions in this prospectus were material. This is true of all of them which relate to the state of affairs in 1961. . . .

The misstatements and omissions pertaining to BarChris's status as of December 31, 1960, however, present a much closer question. . . . Would it have deterred the average prudent investor from purchasing these debentures if he had been informed that the 1960 sales were $8,511,420 rather than $9,165,320 . . . and that the earnings per share in 1960 were approximately 65 cents rather than 75 cents? . . . Would it have made a difference to an average prudent investor if he had known that in 1960 sales only 256 percent of 1959 sales, not 276 percent . . . and that earnings per share, while still approximately twice those of 1959, were not something more than

twice? These debentures were rated "B" by the investment rating services. They were thus characterized as speculative, as any prudent investor must have realized. It would seem that anyone interested in buying these convertible debentures would have been attracted primarily by the conversion feature, by the growth potential of the stock. The growth which the company enjoyed in 1960 over prior years was striking, even on the correct figures. It is hard to see how a prospective purchaser of this type of investment would have been deterred from buying if he had been advised of these comparatively minor errors in reporting 1960 sales and earnings.

Since no one knows what moves or does not move the mythical "average prudent investor," it comes down to a question of judgment, to be exercised by the trier of the fact as best he can in the light of all the circumstances. It is my best judgment that the average prudent investor would not have cared about there errors in the 1960 sales and earnings figures, regrettable though they may be. I therefore find that they were not material within the meaning of Section 11.

The same is true of the understatement of contingent liabilities in footnote 9 by approximately $375,000. . . .

This leaves for consideration the errors in the 1960 balance sheet figures which have previously been discussed in detail. . . .

There must be some point at which errors in disclosing a company's balance sheet position become material, even to a growth-oriented investor. On all the evidence I find that these balance sheet errors were material within the meaning of Section 11. . . .

The "Due Diligence" Defenses

Section 11(b) of the Act provides that:

". . . no person, other than the issuer, shall be liable . . . who shall sustain the burden of proof—

. . .

(3) that (A) as regards any part of the registration statement not purporting to be made on the authority of an expert . . . he had, after reasonable investigation, reasonable ground to believe and did believe, at the time such part of the registration statement became effective, that the statements therein were true and that there was no omission to state a material fact required to be stated therein or necessary to make the statements therein not misleading; . . . and (C) as regards any part of the registration statement purporting to be made on the authority of an expert (other than himself) . . . he had no reasonable ground to believe and did not believe, at the time such part of the registration statement became effective that the statements therein were untrue or that there was an omission to state a material fact required to be stated therein or necessary to make the statements therein not misleading . . .".

Section 11(c) defines "reasonable investigation" as follows:

"In determining . . . what constitutes reasonable investigation and reasonable ground for belief, the standard of reasonableness shall be that required of a prudent man in the management of his own property."

Every defendant, except BarChris itself, to whom as the issuer, these defenses are not available, and except Peat, Marwick, whose position rests on a different statutory provision, has pleaded these affirmative defenses. . . .

The only expert, in the statutory sense, was Peat, Marwick, and the only parts of the registration statement which purported to be made upon the authority of an expert were the portions which purported to be made on Peat, Marwick's authority. . . .

The registration statement contains a report of Peat, Marwick as independent public accountants dated February 23, 1961. This relates only to the consolidated balance sheet of BarChris and consolidated subsidiaries as of December 31, 1960, and the related statement of earnings and retained earnings for the five years then ended. This is all that Peat, Marwick purported to certify. It is perfectly clear that it did not purport to certify the 1961 figures, some of which are expressly stated in the prospectus to have been unaudited. . . .

I turn now to the question of whether defendants have proved their due diligence defenses.

Russo

Russo was, to all intents and purposes, the chief executive officer of BarChris. He was a member of the executive committee. He was familiar with all aspects of the business. . . .

In short, Russo knew all the relevant facts. He could not have believed that there were no untrue statements or material omissions in the prospectus. Russo has no due diligence defenses.

Vitolo and Pugliese

They were the founders of the business who stuck with it to the end. Vitolo was president and Pugliese was vice president. . . .

Vitolo and Pugliese are each men of limited education. It is not hard to believe that for them the prospectus was difficult reading, if indeed they read it at all. . . .

The liability of a director who signs a registration statement does not depend upon whether or not he read it or, if he did, whether or not he understood what he was reading.

And in any case, Vitolo and Pugliese were not as naive as they claim to be. They were members of BarChris's executive committee. At meetings of that committee BarChris's affairs were discussed at length. They must have known what was going on. . . .

They could not have believed that the registration statement was wholly true and that no material facts had been omitted. And in any case, there is nothing to show that they made any investigation of anything which they may not have known about or understood. They have not proved their due diligence defenses.

Kircher

Kircher was treasurer of BarChris and its chief financial officer. He is a certified public accountant and an intelligent man. He was thoroughly familiar with BarChris's financial affairs. . . .

Kircher worked on the preparation of the registration statement. . . . He read the prospectus and understood it. He knew what it said and what it did not say.

Kircher's contention is that he had never before dealt with a registration statement, that he did not know what it should contain, and that he relied wholly on Grant, Ballard and Peat, Marwick to guide him. He claims that it was their fault, not his, if there was anything wrong with it. He says that all the facts were recorded in BarChris's books where these "experts" could have seen them if they had looked. He says that he truthfully answered all their questions. In effect, he says that if they did not know enough to ask the right questions and to give him the proper instructions, that is not his responsibility. . . .

Kircher has not proved his due diligence defenses. . . .

. . .

Birnbaum

Birnbaum was a young lawyer, admitted to the bar in 1957, who, after brief periods of employment by two different law firms and an equally brief period of practicing in his own firm, was employed by BarChris as house counsel and assistant secretary in October 1960. . . .

One of Birnbaum's more important duties . . . was to keep the corporate minutes of Bar-Chris and its subsidiaries. This necessarily informed him to a considerable extent about the company's affairs. . . .

It seems probable that Birnbaum did not know of many of the inaccuracies in the prospectus. He must, however, have appreciated some of them. In any case, he made no investigation and relied on the others to get it right. . . . [H]e was entitled to rely upon Peat, Marwick for the 1960 figures, for as far as appears, he had no personal knowledge of the company's books of account or financial transactions. . . . As a lawyer, he should have known his obligations under the statute. . . . Birnbaum has not established his due diligence defenses except as to the audited 1960 figures.

Auslander

Auslander was an "outside" director, i.e., one who was not an officer of BarChris. . . . In February 1961 Vitolo asked him to become a director of BarChris. . . .

In February and early March 1961, before accepting Vitolo's invitation, Auslander made some investigation of BarChris. . . .

On March 3, 1961, Auslander indicated his willingness to accept a place on the board. Shortly thereafter, on March 14, Kircher sent him a copy of BarChris's annual report for 1960. Auslander observed that BarChris's auditors were Peat, Marwick. . . . He thought well of them.

Auslander was elected a director on April 17, 1961. . . . On May 10, 1961, he signed a signature page for the first amendment to the registration statement which was filed on May 11, 1961. This was a separate sheet without any document attached. Auslander did not know that it was a signature page for a registration statement. He vaguely understood that it was something "for the SEC."

Auslander attended a meeting of Bar-Chris's directors on May 15, 1961. At that meeting he, along with the other directors, signed the signature sheet for the second amendment which constituted the registration statement in its final form. Again, this was only a separate sheet without any document attached. Auslander never saw a copy of the registration statement in its final form.

At the May 15 directors' meeting, however, Auslander did realize that what he was signing was a signature sheet to a registration statement. This was the first time that he had appreciated that fact. A copy of the registration statement in its earlier form as amended on May 11, 1961 was passed around at the meeting. Auslander glanced at it briefly. He did not read it thoroughly. . . .

In considering Auslander's due diligence defenses, a distinction is to be drawn between the expertised and nonexpertised portions of the prospectus. As to the former, Auslander knew that Peat, Marwick had audited the 1960 figures. He believed them to be correct because he had confidence in Peat, Marwick. He had no reasonable ground to believe otherwise.

As to the non-expertised portions, however, Auslander is in a different position. . . . Auslander made no investigation of the accuracy of the prospectus. He relied on the assurance of Vitolo and Russo, and upon the information he had received in answer to his inquiries back in February and early March. These inquiries were general ones, in the nature of a credit check. The information which he received in answer to them was also general, without specific reference to the statements in the prospectus, which was not prepared until some time thereafter. . . .

Section 11 imposes liability in the first instance upon a director, no matter how new he is. He is presumed to know his responsibility when he becomes a director. He can escape liability only by using that reasonable care to investigate the facts which a prudent man would employ in the management of his own property. In my opinion, a prudent man would not act in an important matter without any knowledge of the relevant facts, in sole reliance upon representations of persons who are comparative strangers and upon general information which does not purport to cover the particular case. . . .

I find and conclude that Auslander has not established his due diligence defense with respect to the misstatements and omissions in those portions of the prospectus other than the audited 1960 figures.

Rose

Rose, another "outside" director, is in a position comparable to Auslander's. He is a civil engineer. Peat, Marwick were the auditors for his firm. . . .

Rose agreed to become a director and was elected on April 17, 1961, along with Auslander and the others. . . . He read the first (March 30) version of the registration statement for "about ten minutes."

On May 10, Rose signed a separate signature sheet for the first amendment. Unlike Auslander, Rose did know that the signature sheet pertained to a registration statement.

Rose attended the directors' meeting on May 15. He signed the signature sheet for the registration statement in its final form. The entire document was not submitted to the meeting.

Immediately prior to the May 15 meeting, Kircher told Rose that the progress of the company for the first quarter "was very much in line with the preceding year," but that BarChris expected to have a better year in 1961 than in 1960. At the meeting Rose inquired if the information in the registration statement was correct. Vitolo and Russo said it was. . . .

He made no investigation. He believed that the registration statement was true. The only basis for his belief was his reliance upon Peat, Marwick and upon the BarChris officers.

What has been said with respect to Auslander applies equally to Rose. He has not sustained the burden of proving his due diligence defense as to the portions of the registration statement other than the audited 1960 figures.

Grant

Grant became a director of BarChris in October 1960. His law firm was counsel to BarChris in matters pertaining to the registration of securities. . . .

Grant is sued as a director and as a signer of the registration statement. This is not an action against him for malpractice in his capacity as a lawyer. Nevertheless, in considering Grant's due diligence defenses, the unique position which he occupied cannot be disregarded. As the director most directly concerned with writing the registration statement and assuring its accuracy, more was required of him in the way of reasonable investigation than could fairly be expected of a director who had no connection with this work. . . .

I find that Grant honestly believed that the registration statement was true and that no material facts had been omitted from it. . . .

It is claimed that a lawyer is entitled to rely on the statements of his client and that to require him to verify their accuracy would set an unreasonably high standard. This is too broad a generalization. It is all a matter of degree. To require an audit would obviously be unreasonable. On the other hand, to require a check of matters easily verifiable is not unreasonable. Even honest clients can make mistakes. The statute imposes liability for untrue statements regardless of whether they are intentionally untrue. The way to prevent mistakes is to test oral information by examining the original written record.

Grant was entitled to rely on Peat, Marwick for the 1960 figures. . . . After making all due allowances for the fact that BarChris's officers misled him, there are too many instances in which Grant failed to make an inquiry which he could easily have made which,

if pursued, would have put him on his guard. In my opinion, this finding on the evidence in this case does not establish an unreasonably high standard in other cases for company counsel who are also directors. Each case must rest on its own facts. I conclude that Grant has not established his due diligence defenses except as to the audited 1960 figures.

The Underwriters and Coleman

The underwriters other than Drexel made no investigation of the accuracy of the prospectus. They all relied upon Drexel as the "lead" underwriter.

Drexel did make an investigation. The work was in charge of Coleman, a partner of the firm, assisted by Casperson, as associate. Drexel's attorneys acted as attorneys for the entire group of underwriters. Ballard did the work, assisted by Stanton.

On April 17, 1961 Coleman became a director of BarChris. He signed the first amendment to the registration statement filed on May 11 and the second amendment, constituting the registration statement in its final form, filed on May 16. He thereby assumed a responsibility as an underwriter.

The facts as to the extent of the investigation that Coleman made may be briefly summarized. He was first introduced to BarChris on September 15, 1960. Thereafter he familiarized himself with general conditions in the industry. . . . He also acquired general information on BarChris by reading the 1959 stock prospectus, annual reports for prior years, and an unaudited statement for the first half of 1960. . . .

The purpose of this preliminary investigation was to enable Coleman to decide whether Drexel would undertake the financing. . . .

Coleman continued his general investigation. He obtained a Dun & Bradstreet report on BarChris on March 16, 1961. He read BarChris's annual report for 1960 which was available in March.

By mid-March, Coleman was in a position to make more specific inquiries. Coleman attended three meetings to discuss the prospectus with BarChris's representatives. . . .

After Coleman was elected a director on April 17, 1961, he made no further independent investigation of the accuracy of the prospectus. He assumed that Ballard was taking care of this on his behalf as well as on behalf of the underwriters. . . .

Like Grant, Ballard, without checking, relied on the information which he got from Kircher. He also relied on Grant who, as company counsel, presumably was familiar with its affairs. . . .

In any event, it is clear that no effectual attempt at verification was made. The question is whether due diligence required that it be made. Stated another way, is it sufficient to ask questions, to obtain answers which, if true, would be thought satisfactory, and to let it go at that, without seeking to ascertain from the records whether the answers in fact are true and complete? . . .

The underwriters say that the prospectus is the company's prospectus, not theirs. Doubtless this is the way they customarily regard it. But the Securities Act makes no such distinction. The underwriters are just as responsible as the company if the prospectus is false. And prospective investors rely upon the reputation of the underwriters in deciding whether to purchase the securities. . . .

The purpose of Section 11 is to protect investors. To that end the underwriters are made responsible for the truth of the prospectus. In order to make the underwriters' participation in this enterprise of any value to the investors, the underwriters must make some reasonable attempt to verify the data submitted to them. They may not rely solely on the company's officers or on the company's counsel. A prudent man in the management of his own property would not rely on them.

It is impossible to lay down a rigid rule suitable for every case defining the extent to which such verification must go. It is a question of degree, a matter of judgment in each case. In the present case, the underwriters' counsel made almost no attempt to verify management's representations. I hold that that was insufficient.

On the evidence in this case, I find that the underwriters' counsel did not make a reasonable investigation of the truth of those portions of the prospectus which were not made on the authority of Peat, Marwick as an expert. Drexel is bound by their failure. It is not a matter of relying upon counsel for legal advice. Here the attorneys were dealing with matters of fact. Drexel delegated to them, as its agent, the business of examining the corporate minutes and contracts. It must bear the consequences of their failure to make an adequate examination.

The other underwriters, who did nothing and relied solely on Drexel and the lawyers, are also bound by it. It follows that although Drexel and the other underwriters believed that those portions of the prospectus were true, they had no reasonable ground for that belief, within the meaning of the statute. Hence, they have not established their due diligence defense, except as to the 1960 audited figures.

The same conclusions must apply to Coleman. He made no investigation after he became a director. When it came to verification, he relied upon his counsel to do it for him. Since counsel failed to do it, Coleman is bound by that failure. Consequently, in his case also, he has not established his due diligence defense except as to the audited 1960 figures.

Peat, Marwick

Section 11(b) provides:

Notwithstanding the provisions of subsection (a) no person . . . shall be liable as provided therein who shall sustain the burden of proof—

. . .

(3) that . . . (B) as regards any part of the registration statement purporting to be made upon his authority as an expert . . . (i) he had, after reasonable investigation, reasonable ground to believe and did believe, at the time such part of the registration statement became effective, that the statements therein were true and that there was no omission to state a material fact required to be stated therein or necessary to make the statements therein not misleading. . . .

This defines the due diligence defense for an expert. Peat, Marwick has pleaded it.

The part of the registration statement purporting to be made upon the authority of Peat, Marwick as an expert was, as we have seen, the 1960 figures. But because the statute requires the court to determine Peat, Marwick's belief, and the grounds thereof, "at the time such part of the registration statement became effective," for the purposes of this affirmative defense, the matter must be viewed as of May 16, 1961, and the question is whether at that time Peat, Marwick, after reasonable investigation, had reasonable ground to believe and did believe that the 1960 figures were true and that no material fact had been omitted from the registration statement which should have been included in order to make the 1960 figures not misleading. In deciding this issue, the court must consider not only what Peat, Marwick did in its 1960 audit, but also what it did in its subsequent "S-1 review." The proper scope of that review must also be determined. . . .

Most of the actual work was performed by a senior accountant, Berardi, who had junior assistants, one of whom was Kennedy.

Berardi was then about thirty years old. He was not yet a C.P.A. He had had no previous experience with the bowling industry. This was his first job as a senior accountant. He could hardly have been given a more difficult assignment.

After obtaining a little background information on BarChris by talking to Logan and reviewing Peat, Marwick's work papers on its 1959 audit, Berardi examined the results of test checks of BarChris's accounting procedures which one of the junior accountants had made, and he prepared an "internal control questionnaire" and an "audit program." Thereafter, for a few days subsequent to December 30, 1960, he inspected BarChris's inventories and examined certain alley construction. Finally, on January 13, 1961, he began his auditing work which he carried on substantially continuously until it was completed on February 24, 1961. Toward the close of the work, Logan reviewed it and made various comments and suggestions to Berardi. . . .

First and foremost is Berardi's failure to discover that Capitol Lanes had not been sold. This error affected both the sales figure and the liability side of the balance sheet.

As to factors' reserves, it is hard to understand how Berardi could have treated this item as entirely a current asset when it was obvious that most of the reserves would not be released within one year. If Berardi was unaware of that fact, he should have been aware of it.

Berardi erred in computing the contingent liability on Type B leaseback transactions at 25 percent. Berardi did not examine the documents which are in evidence which establish that BarChris's contingent liability on this type of transaction was in fact 100 percent. Berardi did not make a reasonable investigation in this instance.

. . .

The purpose of reviewing events subsequent to the date of a certified balance sheet (referred to as an S-1 review when made with reference to a registration statement) is to ascertain whether any material change has occurred in the company's financial position which should be disclosed in order to prevent the balance sheet figures from being misleading. The scope of such a review, under generally accepted auditing standards, is limited. It does not amount to a complete audit.

Peat, Marwick prepared a written program for such a review. I find that this program conformed a generally accepted auditing standards. . . .

Berardi made the S-1 review in May 1961. He devoted a little over two days to it, a total of 20½ hours. He did not discover any of the errors or omissions pertaining to the state of affairs in 1961 which I have previously discussed at length, all of which were material. The question is whether, despite his failure to find out anything, his investigation was reasonable within the meaning of the statute. . . .

He did not examine any "important financial records" other than the trial balance. As to minutes, he read only what minutes Birnbaum gave him, which consisted only of the board of directors' minutes of BarChris. . . .

In substance, what Berardi did is similar to what Grant and Ballard did. He asked questions, he got answers which he considered satisfactory, and he did nothing to verify them. For example, he obtained from Trilling a list of contracts. The list included Yonkers and Bridge. Since Berardi did not read the minutes of subsidiaries he did not learn that Yonkers and Bridge were intercompany sales.

Since he never read the prospectus, he was not even aware that there had ever been any problem about loans from officers.

There had been a material change for the worse in BarChris's financial position. That change was sufficiently serious so that the failure to disclose it made the 1960 figures misleading. Berardi did not discover it. As far as results were concerned, his S-1 review was useless.

Accountants should not be held to a standard higher than that recognized in their profession. I do not do so here. Berardi's review did not come up to that standard. He did not take some of the steps which Peat, Marwick's written program prescribed. He did not spend an adequate amount of time on a task of this magnitude. Most important of all, he was too easily satisfied with glib answers to his inquiries.

This is not to say that he should have made a complete audit. But there were enough danger signals in the materials which he did examine to require some further investigation on his part. Generally accepted accounting standards required such further investigation under these circumstances. It is not always sufficient merely to ask questions.

Here again, the burden of proof is on Peat, Marwick. I find that that burden has not been satisfied, I conclude that Peat, Marwick has not established its due diligence defense.

Case Questions

1. How does one explain the significant accounting errors in this case—incompetence? negligence? inexperience? or one of those things that inexplicably occur?

2. What lesson does this case hold for the individual who occupies a position on the board of numerous corporations?

3. How do sophisticated businessmen, underwriters, and lawyers get in the position of relying on another individual, with little or no personal verification, on matters as important as these? Is it practical to demand personal verification as an alternative to liability? Are there policy considerations supporting a strict standard of personal verification?

Checklist for Directors

What follows is a brief checklist of various requirements of the federal securities statutes, requirements of which any director of a publicly traded company should be aware. Some items on the list will be familiar, as we have already discussed them in some depth. Other topics will be discussed in greater detail in upcoming portions of the text.

Directors should make certain that they:

1. Do not engage in stock transactions that will generate illegal "short swing" profits in violation of Section 16 of the '34 Act. Any time there is a change in the beneficial holdings of a director, the director must file monthly a change of ownership report with the SEC. If a director should happen to beneficially own in excess of 5 percent of the company's shares, certain other reports are required of the director if there is a change in those stockholdings.

2. Do not trade a security on the basis of material inside information.

3. Do not disclose, even inadvertently, material information that others may use to trade in violation of the insider trading rules. Material information should be confined within the group of individuals who have a need to know it. Changes in dividend policies, significant discoveries, proposed mergers, or dramatic fluctuations in earnings can all be material. Their premature disclosure to corporate employees, personal friends, or favored members of the financial community are a potential trouble spot. While certain items must be reported to the SEC on a Form 8-K within a certain number of days of their occurrence, the corporation can generally decide the timing of significant events. Whereas silence may be a virtue, a corporate policy of full and fair disclosure on a timely basis is oftentimes a wise policy.

4. Adopt procedures to insure that such items as registration statements, proxy statements, reports to the SEC, press releases, and reports to shareholders contain accurate information. Material omissions or inaccuracies can lead to litigation and may result in liability for both the directors and the corporation.

5. Devise and enforce an internal accounting system that will reasonably insure that the corporation's books accurately reflect its transactions.

6. Construct a mechanism to prevent the company from offering or paying bribes in order to obtain, or retain, business.

Corporate Reporting

Since one purpose of the securities laws is disclosure, it should not be surprising that corporations must file a significant number of reports with the SEC. Under the '33 Act, an issuing company must file a registration statement prior to the public offering of its securities. The purpose is to provide disclosure of financial and other data on which investors can judge the security's merits. The investor must be supplied with a prospectus (selling circular) containing the salient data from the registration statement. (A copy of the prospectus is made a part of the registration statement.) The '34 Act requires corporations having their shares publicly traded on an exchange or having $1 million in assets and 500 or more shareholders to file a registration form with the Commission. This data is less extensive than that filed under the '33 Act. To keep this information current such companies must file periodic reports with the Commission.

A company's annual report is neither mandated by law nor cleared in advance by SEC. The SEC has a certain degree of indirect control over it, however, because of the Commission's control over the proxy solicitation process. Companies are required to file an annual report called the 10-K report with the Commission. It contains a great deal of technical information and includes a certified financial statement. It also contains a summary of prior years' financial information. It is a public document available from the SEC. Some companies include the 10-K in the annual shareholders' report. A majority of the board of directors must sign this document, just as they must sign the registration statement.

Other reports are required, only two of which we will mention. The first is the 10-Q report. It is a quarterly report filed with the Commission. By nature it is more of an interim or summary report. Its financial statements are unaudited. The second report is the 8-K. It must be filed for any month that observed the occurrence of significant events. For example, if a corporation had any unusual charges and credits to income, if the outside auditor was replaced in a dispute, or if there was a significant change in the company's assets through an acquisition or a sale, it must be reported in an 8-K.

Attorneys' Liability

In the famous words of Judge Friendly,[1] "the accountant's certificate and the lawyer's opinion can be instruments for inflicting pecuniary loss more potent than the chisel or the crowbar" in a society as complex as ours. Let us now scrutinize the obligations of the legal profession in federal securities matters.

The lawyer can encounter the federal securities laws in a variety of ways. It may be in connection with the preparation of a registration statement, either in the expertised portion by preparing for inclusion a legal opinion, or in the nonexpertised portion by generally overseeing its preparation and deciding what items should and should not be included and in what language. Or counsel may participate in the review of documents to be filed with the SEC or press releases for distribution to the media. The lawyer may prepare an opinion letter as to the legality of a proposed payment under the Foreign Corrupt Practices Act. Whatever the nature of the lawyer's activity, two basic questions arise: (1) to whom does the attorney owe a duty, and (2) what standard is to be used in measuring whether the attorney has breached that duty?

What makes the questions unusually sticky is the presence of the attorney-client privilege. Traditionally, the lawyer owes allegiance to the client. Communications between the lawyer and the client (even those involving past criminal activity by the client) are not to be disclosed without the client's permission. Under the lawyer's Code of Professional Responsibility, the lawyer may reveal an otherwise privileged communication if the client intends to commit a crime. But who is the attorney's client? Is it the corporation? The board of directors? The corporate officers? The shareholders? The SEC?

What is the law firm to do when an accounting firm approaches it and demands information on a mutual client, information the client refuses to supply? The accountants may claim that the information is necessary to ascertain the client's contingent liabilities. Without such data they cannot render a "clean opinion letter" or will become a likely candidate as a defendant in a subsequent shareholders' suit. The law firm, beyond citing attorney-client privilege, may claim that such information would be a practical invitation to a lawsuit or might aid an opponent in current litigation.

An equal number of questions are raised by the issue of what is the standard of care to be imposed on the attorney in the performance of legal work. Clearly, an attorney who violates the law will incur legal liability for that violation. Negligence in the performance of legal work will constitute malpractice, and the attorney will be liable to the client for any loss which results. However, will negligence make the attorney liable to an investor in the corporate securities or allow the SEC to obtain an injunction against such activity in the future? The answer will depend on the provision of the securities law that is allegedly violated. The Supreme Court has indicated, as we will see in the *Hochfelder* case, that more than mere negligence is required to violate Section 10(b)—scienter, or the intention to deceive, manipulate, or defraud, must be present.

In the following case a court finds the conduct of a law firm and two of its attorneys to have violated the securities law. This prestigious law firm was caught in a legal web through its representation of a client in a merger.

SEC v. NATIONAL STUDENT MARKETING CORP.
457 F. Supp. 682 (1978)

(Authors' note: Interstate National Corporation was merged into National Student Marketing Corp. in 1969. Proxy statements were used as part of the successful effort to secure shareholder approval of the proposed merger. A portion of the Interstate proxy material consisted of financial statements of National Student Marketing. The shareholders approved the merger at special shareholder meetings. The lawyers and some directors from the companies met to close the merger. A comfort letter from the outside auditors of National Student Marketing was delivered to the group by being dictated over the telephone. It indicated that significant adjustments should be reflected in the financial statements of National Student Marketing. This comfort letter did not meet the requirement of the merger agreement. The Interstate representatives considered the letter to be a serious matter. However, after discussing the matter they decided to

close the merger. Several days after the closing, a signed comfort letter was delivered to Interstate. It contained two additional paragraphs noting that the adjustments would result in a net loss for one time period and approximately a breakeven in earnings for a one-year period. The Interstate directors frequently discussed the matter, often consulting their lawyers. After approximately one week they decided to announce the completion of the merger. No effort was ever made to disclose the contents of the comfort letter to the former shareholders of Interstate, the SEC, or the general public. The SEC sought injunctions against various defendants as a result of their participation in alleged securities violations. The defendants included both corporations and certain of their officers and directors, an outside accounting firm and two of its partners, and the law firm of each corporation and some of their partners. Most defendants had reached out-of-court settlements with the SEC by the time of this trial. What follows is only that portion of the court's decision that involves the legal responsibility of lawyers who participate in such matters and issue legal opinions in connection with the transactions.)

PARKER, District Judge

The Commission contends that the attorneys should have refused to issue the opinions in view of the adjustments revealed by the unsigned comfort letter, and after receipt of the signed version, they should have withdrawn their opinion with regard to the merger and demanded resolicitation of the Interstate shareholders. If the Interstate directors refused, the attorneys should have withdrawn from the representation and informed the shareholders or the Commission. . . .

In the present case, the alleged misstatement or omission is the failure to disclose . . . to the Interstate shareholders . . . the adjustments contained in the unsigned comfort letter delivered at the October 31 closing. . . .

Initially, the sheer magnitude of the adjustments supports a finding that they were material. . . . The aggregate adjustments amounted to $884,000, thereby reducing the reported profit by 125 percent and resulting in a net loss for the nine-month period of approximately $180,000. Viewing these figures alone, it is difficult to imagine how the adjustments could not be material. . . .

Moreover, in this instance the Interstate shareholders were specifically informed of the importance of the NSMC financial statements by the proxy materials sent them in connection with the proposed merger. . . .

In summary, the Court concludes that the adjustments contained in the unsigned comfort letter would have altered the total mix of information available and would have assumed actual significance in the deliberations of the reasonable Interstate shareholder. . . .

In view of the obvious materiality of the information, especially to attorneys learned in securities law, the attorneys' responsibilities to their corporate client required them to take steps to ensure that the information would be disclosed to the shareholders. . . .

Contrary to the attorney defendants' contention, imposition of such a duty will not require lawyers to go beyond their accepted role in securities transactions, nor will it compel them to "err on the side of conservatism, . . . thereby inhibiting clients' business judgments and candid attorney-client communications." Courts will not lightly overrule an attorney's determination of materiality and the need for disclosure. However, where, as here, the significance of the information clearly removes any doubt concerning the materiality of the information, attorneys cannot rest on asserted "business judgments" as justification for their failure to make a legal decision pursuant to their fiduciary responsibilities to client shareholders.

Case Questions

1. How much trust would a client place in an attorney knowing that the attorney would reveal any securities law violations to the SEC?

2. What considerations could have led the lawyers in this instance to have remained silent about the comfort letter permitting the closing to proceed?

Case Note.   Despite the court's conclusion that violations of the securities laws had occurred, it denied the SEC's request for an injunction against the defendants. The court believed that an injunction was unnecessary to prevent further violations by the defendants.

Involved in this case was Lord, Bissel & Brook and two of its attorney partners. They represented Interstate in the merger. The law firm of White & Case and one of its partners represented National Student Marketing. They settled with the SEC on the eve of the trial. The partner denied any violation of the law but agreed to the issuance of an injunction and agreed not to practice before the SEC for a 180-day period. No injunction was issued against the law firm, but it did agree to comply with the law. [Fed. Sec. L. Rep. (CCH) ¶ 96,027 (1977)].

What routes are open to a lawyer, who bears significant responsibilities in carrying out a company's compliance with the disclosure requirements of the securities laws, when he or she becomes aware that the client company is engaged in a serious and continuing failure to satisfy the disclosure standards? The lawyer may not simply continue to aid the client in such activities. Professional standards require the lawyer to take prompt steps to halt the client's improper actions. The lawyer may meet with success by vigorously counselling compliance with the law. If that tactic is not successful, the lawyer might directly approach an officer, a director, or the entire board of directors in order to bring a halt to the illegal activities. If, after these steps have been taken, the company remains unwilling to comply with the law it may prove necessary for the lawyer to resign from representation of that client.

Both attorneys and accountants occupy a unique position as licensed professionals. They bear a twofold responsibility to their clients and to the public. The latter obligation can involve perplexing questions, and the exact parameters of their duty to the public remains in flux.

Statutory Liability for Securities Law Violations

Section 17 of the '33 Act contains a general fraud prohibition applicable to the sellers of securities. Section 10 and Rule 10-b-5 of the '34 Act prohibit the use of deceptive practices in the purchase and sale of securities. Section 16(b) outlaws short-swing profits. We have already examined these provisions in some depth. Several other possible sources of liability should be mentioned.

Under the '33 Act, Section 11 imposes civil liability on those participating in the preparation of a false registration statement. A purchaser who sustained a loss by reason of such misstatements or omissions can recover such losses plus attorneys' fees. The defendants are jointly and severally liable. Section 12(1) imposes liability on persons who offer or sell a security in violation of the registration and prospectus provisions of the statute. Section 12(2) imposes liability for the sale of a security, whether registered or exempt from registration, by means of a material misstatement or omission of a material fact. If the purchaser suffered any loss he or she may bring a private damage action to recover that loss.

Under the '34 Act, Section 9(e) imposes civil liability for manipulating the prices of securities. An individual who has been injured by such activities may recover losses plus attorneys' fees. Section 18 creates liability for any person who files any false document that is required to be filed by law. Any person who relied on that document, thereby suffering a loss, can recover that loss plus attorneys' fees.

Whenever the Commission believes that any provision has been or is about to be violated, it may seek injunctive relief [Section 20(b) of '33 Act and Section 21(e) of the '34 Act]. A willful violation of the '33 Act is a crime punishable by a fine not to exceed $5000 or a prison term not to exceed five years, or both (Section 24). A willful violation of the '34 Act is also punishable by a fine or jail term, or both. The maximum penalty varies according to the type of violation (Section 32).

Section 12(k) of the '34 Act allows the SEC to summarily suspend trading in any security for a period not exceeding 10 days if it believes the public interest and the protection of investors so requires. In *SEC* v. *Sloan*, 46 LW 4426 (1978), the Supreme Court held that this section does not allow the issuance of a series of consecutive suspension orders based on a single set of circumstances. The case was brought by a shareholder in a company when the SEC twice suspended trading in the company's shares in excess of one year by means of consecutive 10-day suspension orders. Despite the court's ruling, the SEC is not powerless. If the 10-day trading suspension does not solve the particular problem, the SEC can also seek injunctive relief from a federal court or utilize the available legal mechanisms to suspend or revoke the registration of the corporation's securities.

Review Problems

1. Violators of the federal antitrust laws may face civil suits seeking treble damages. Would the amendment of the securities laws to include a treble damage provision create a greater deterrent to violations by directors?

2. The directors of Clarion Corporation, their accountants, and their attorneys met to discuss the desirability of this highly successful corporation's going public. In this connection, the discussion turned to the potential liability of the corporation and the parties involved in the preparation and signing of the registration statement under the

Securities Act of 1933. Craft, Watkins, and Glenn are the largest shareholders. Craft is the Chairman of the Board, Watkins is the Vice Chairman, and Glenn is the Chief Executive Officer. It has been decided that they will sign the registration statement. There are two other directors who are also executives and shareholders of the corporation. All of the board members are going to have a percentage of their shares included in the offering. The firm of Witherspoon & Friendly, CPAs, will issue an opinion as to the financial statements of the corporation that will accompany the filing of the registration statement, and Blackstone & Abernathy, Attorneys-at-Law, will render legal services and provide any necessary opinion letters.

Discuss the types of potential liability and defenses pursuant to the Securities Act of 1933 that each of the above parties or classes of parties may be subject to as a result of going public.

(Adapted from CPA Exam, Law Problem #2, question #3 part b, taken from the May 1980 exam. © American Institute of Certified Public Accountants, Inc., 1980.)

3. A corporation has experienced a large increase in earnings. This increase has not yet been announced when the company announces a stock repurchase program. The stock is purchased on the open market at market prices. The company will use the stock in a stock incentive plan for certain high-level executives. After the desired number of shares are purchased, the earning results are announced and the market price of the stock spurts. Have the directors exposed themselves to any potential legal liability in approving the stock repurchase program?

4. High Baller was the largest trucking firm in the U.S. On February 1, 1968, Overdrive Express merged with it. However, poor planning, lack of capital, poor service, and executive in-fighting doomed the venture from the start. During 1970 it fell over the brink into bankruptcy. Several months after the merger, High Baller stock reached a high of $88.50; it dropped to a low of $10 a share in June 1970, just prior to the filing of the bankruptcy petition. Good-as-Gold, a prestigious investment banking and securities firm, handled the bulk of High Baller's securities offerings. A member of the firm sat on High Baller's board of directors. He was aware of High Baller's financial problems, and his investment banking firm had a buy recommendation on its stock. However, his firm quietly informed several favored clients to sell. The clients did so before the real bottom dropped out of the stock and prior to the filing of the bankruptcy petition.

As the company was financially declining, various officers and directors contrived various transactions with subsidiaries and improperly recorded revenue to give the impression that the company was financially sound. This fraudulent activity assumed massive proportions. The national accounting firm that handled High Baller's accounting work failed to ferret out the fraud. It conducted no search for fraud nor did it review the entire financial condition of the company. It confined its review to the legitimacy of certain transactions and accounts.

As the deepening financial plight of High Baller gradually came to the notice of the public, the stock began a sustained price decline. Some officers and directors sold their stock prior to and during this decline. Included in this group were the top officials of the finance department that dealt on a daily basis with the company's cash problems. Stock sales ranged from isolated, sporadic, and small to stunning examples of bailouts.

Not all the directors actively participated in the massive fraud scheme that preceded the company's financial collapse. The directors ranged in quality from the most sophisticated businessmen to individuals who obtained the position merely on the basis of their wealth and social status. The board consisted of both inside and outside directors. Some directors did not attend all board meetings; however, they were given the required legal notice. Some board members took an active part in the meetings, making numerous inquiries and requesting documentation from management. Others merely served as rubber stamps for the high company officers. A third small category often sat mute and would typically vote "present" on board resolutions.

Discuss the liability that the investment banking firm might incur in the situation outlined above.

5. In the hypothetical High Baller case what liability, if any, will the officers and directors bear who knew of, or took part in, juggling the corporate books?

6. Do the stock sales of officers and directors raise any legal questions in the High Baller incident? *10b + 10b-5 violations.*

7. Does the High Baller accounting firm appear to have met its legal obligations? *No*

8. Comment on whether the various categories of directors on the High Baller board have met their fiduciary obligations.

9. Would shareholders enjoy greater protection from fraudulent schemes if the law required the majority of a board of directors to be composed of outside directors?

10. Does society enjoy an overall benefit from the establishment and maintenance of the attorney-client privilege?

Endnote

1. *U.S.* v. *Benjamin,* 328 F.2d 854, 863 (1964).

Accountants and the Securities Law

The services that accountants provide to their clients usually fit within three categories: auditing, tax, and management consulting. This chapter focuses on the accounting profession's legal liability in the performance of its auditing function because it is the outside independent accountant's role in this process that generates the bulk of the lawsuits brought by corporate shareholders and creditors. Before examining the accountants' liability under the federal securities law, we will take a brief look at their liability under common law.

Accountants' Liability Under Common Law

If an accountant negligently performs work for a client and, as a result of that negligence, the client suffers a loss, the accountant is liable for that loss. The accountant has a contract (is in privity) with the client and has the obligation to perform the duties under that contract in a reasonable manner.

What obligation, if any, does the accountant owe to a third party who relies on the work supplied the client? It is not unexpected for a client to use the financial statements certified by an accountant in order to obtain a loan from a bank, convince a supplier to sell goods on credit, or persuade an individual to invest money in an enterprise. If those financial statements are false in significant respects and the result is a financial loss on the part of the third party, is the accountant liable to the third party with whom he is not in privity? If the loss was the result of a fraud on the third party perpetrated by both the client and the accountant, then the accountant is liable for his or her participation in the fraud. The answer to the question is less clear where the accountant did not engage in fraud but where the accounting work was performed in a negligent manner thereby allowing the client to successfully carry out a fraudulent scheme.

The traditional rule, established in *Ultramares* v. *Touche,* 174 N.E. 441 (1931), is that the accountant is not liable for ordinary negligence to a third person not in privity with him. In this case the New York court decided that the accountant's services were for the client and only incidentally for third parties. In that light, the court said that an accountant who commits a thoughtless slip should not be exposed to liability for an indeterminate amount for an indeterminate time to an indeterminate class of people. However, this doctrine is being eroded as other courts determine that the accountant's obligations extend beyond the client.

In *Aluma Kraft Mfg.* v. *Elmer Fox & Co.*, a Missouri court held that a negligent accountant is liable to a third party when he or she knows that an audit is to be used by the third party for its own benefit and guidance or where he or she knows the client intends to supply the accounting information to a third party for such a use. Aluma Kraft was to be acquired by another company through the purchase of 80 percent of its stock at book value. The outside auditing firm for Aluma Kraft prepared a profit and loss statement and a balance sheet. On the basis of these financial statements and the unqualified opinion of the auditing firm, the purchaser paid $229,090 for the stock. The purchaser subsequently sued the accountant alleging that the examination was not done in accordance with generally accepted auditing standards and that the accountant had failed to furnish an opinion in conformity with generally accepted accounting principles. The alleged result was that the book value of the stock was erroneously stated to be $150,000 in excess of its true value. The accounting firm attempted unsuccessfully to have the lawsuit against it dismissed on the grounds that the firm was not in privity with the purchaser. The court rejected the *Ultramares* decision and decided to follow more recent decisions holding an accountant liable for negligence as to those third persons for whose benefit and guidance the accountant intends to supply information.

Now let us turn to an examination of the liability borne by accountants under a variety of provisions of the federal securities statutes.

Accountants and the Federal Securities Law

The past decade has witnessed an increasing amount of litigation under the federal securities law with an outside independent accounting firm as a defendant. Plaintiffs in such lawsuits against the corporate auditor include shareholders, creditors, and the SEC. Naturally, the accounting profession deplores such developments. In some instances the profession believes it is being unfairly accused; that the SEC and investing public misunderstand its role. The annual audit of a publicly owned corporation plays a central role in the SEC regulatory scheme. CPAs regard such an audit as merely an affirmation that a company's transactions reflect generally accepted accounting standards. It does not mean that no fraud has occurred, since such a routine audit is not designed to ferret out fraud, particularly if management is intentionally lying to the auditors. Checking every transaction is a practical and financial impossibility. The SEC and stockholders view the accountant's role as encompassing more. The Commission is asserting that both the accounting and legal professions owe a duty beyond the one to their corporate client. The Commission has been pressuring the two professions to be more vigorous in their activities, to ask more searching questions and not to be satisfied by only verbal reassurances from top management.

Accounting Standards and Securities Liability

Despite the fact that a major goal of financial accounting is the provision of useful information to corporate management, shareholders, potential investors, and creditors, the objective of generally accepted accounting principles differs in some respects from that of the federal securities statutes. Thus, compliance with the standards of the profession does not automatically mean that an accountant will bear no liability under the securities law in connection with his or her work.

Under normal circumstances, an accountant will have no securities liability if the work performed does conform to the standards of the accounting profession. Refer back to the *BarChris* case in the preceding chapter. In that case the outside auditor, Peat, Marwick, was held liable for signing a registration statement that contained material misstatements and omissions. The judge stated that he was not holding the accounting firm to a higher standard than that of the profession. It was determined that the written program for conducting the S-1 review conformed to generally accepted auditing standards. However, their accountant performing the review had failed to carry out all the steps outlined in that program. It was this failure to perform all the work contained in the program that led to liability for the firm.

In the usual situation where the accountant has reason to doubt that the affairs of the corporation are being honestly conducted, the securities law can obligate the accountant to do more than merely meet the standards of the profession. In the following case the audit was done in conformance with generally accepted auditing standards, but the resulting financial statement was materially false. This led to the criminal conviction of the accountants.

UNITED STATES v. *SIMON*
425 F.2d 796 (1969)

Defendant Carl Simon was a senior partner, Robert Kaiser a junior partner, and Melvin Fishman a senior associate in the internationally known accounting firm of Lybrand, Ross Bros. & Montgomery. They stand convicted after trial . . . under three counts of an indictment charging them with drawing up and certifying a false or misleading financial statement of Continental Vending Machine Corporation (hereafter Continental) for the year ending September 30, 1962.

While every criminal conviction is important to the defendant, there is a special poignancy and a corresponding responsibility on reviewing judges when, as here, the defendants have been men of blameless lives and respected members of a learned profession.

This is no less true because the trial judge, wisely in our view, imposed no prison sentences.

The trial hinged on transactions between Continental and an affiliate, Valley Commercial Corporation (hereafter Valley). The dominant figure in both was Harold Roth, who was president of Continental, supervised the day-to-day operations of Valley, and owned about 25 percent of the stock of each company.

Valley, which was run by Roth out of a single office on Continental's premises, was engaged in lending money at interest to Continental and others in the vending machine business. Continental would issue negotiable notes to Valley, which would . . . use them as collateral for drawing on two lines of credit, of $1 million each, . . . and would then transfer to Continental the discounted amount of the notes. These transactions, beginning as early as 1956, gave rise to what is called "the Valley payable." By the end of fiscal 1962, the amount of this was $1,029,475, of which $543,345 was due within the year.

In addition to the Valley payable, there was what is known as the "Valley receivable," which resulted from Continental loans to Valley. Most of these stemmed from Roth's custom, dating from mid-1957, of using Continental and Valley as sources of cash to finance his transactions in the stock market. At the end of fiscal 1962, the amount of the Valley receivable was $3.5 million, and by February 15, 1963, the date of certification, it had risen to $3.9 million. The Valley payable could not be offset, or "netted," against the Valley receivable since, as stated, Continental's obligations to Valley were in the form of negotiable notes which Valley had endorsed in blank to the two banks and used as collateral to obtain the cash which it then lent to Continental.

By the certification date, the auditors had learned that Valley was not in a position to repay its debt, and it was accordingly arranged that collateral would be posted. Roth and members of his family transferred their equity in certain securities to Arthur Field, Continental's counsel, as trustee to secure Roth's debt to Valley and Valley's debt to Continental. Some 80 percent of these securities consisted of Continental stock and convertible debentures.

The 1962 financial statements of Continental, which were dismal by any standard, reported the status of the Valley transactions as follows:

. . .

NOTES TO CONSOLIDATED FINANCIAL STATEMENTS

2. The amount receivable from Valley Commercial Corp. (an affiliated company of which Mr. Harold Roth is an officer, director and stockholder) bears interest at 12 percent a year. Such amount, less the balance of the notes payable to that company, is secured by the assignment to the Company of Valley's equity in certain marketable securities. As of February 15, 1963, the amount of such equity at current market quotations exceeded the net amount receivable.

The case against the defendants can be best encapsulated by comparing what Note 2 stated and what the Government claims it would have stated if defendants had included what they knew:

The amount receivable from Valley Commercial Corp. (an affiliated company of which Mr. Harold Roth is an officer, director and stockholder), which bears interest at 12 percent a year, was uncollectible at September 30, 1962, since Valley had loaned approximately the same amount to Mr. Roth who was unable to pay. Since that date Mr. Roth and others have pledged as security for the repayment of his obligation to Valley and its obligation to Continental (now $3,900,000, against which Continental's liability to Valley cannot be offset) securities which, as of February 15, 1963, had a market value of $2,978,000. Approximately 80 percent of such securities are stock and convertible debentures of the Company.

Striking as the difference is, the latter version does not reflect the Government's further contention that in fact the market value of the pledged securities on February 15, 1963, was $1,978,000 rather than $2,978,000 due to liens of James Talcott, Inc. and Franklin for indebtedness other than Roth's of which defendants knew or should have known. . . .

The financial statements were mailed as part of Continental's annual report on February 20. By that time the market value of the collateral had declined some $270,000 from its February 15 value. The value of the collateral fell an additional $640,000 on February 21. When the market reopened on February 25 after the long Washington's birthday recess, it fell another $2 million and was worth only $395,000. The same day a Continental check to the Internal Revenue Service bounced. Two days later the Government padlocked the plant and the American Stock Exchange suspended trading in Continental stock. Investigations by the SEC and bankruptcy rapidly ensued.

The defendants called eight expert independent accountants, an impressive array of leaders of the profession. They testified generally that, except for the error with respect to netting, the treatment of the Valley receivable in Note 2 was in no way inconsistent with generally accepted accounting principles or generally accepted auditing standards, since it made all the informative disclosures reasonably necessary for fair presentation of the financial position of Continental as of the close of the 1962 fiscal year. Specifically, they testified that neither generally accepted accounting principles nor generally accepted auditing standards required disclosure of the make-up of the collateral or of the increase of the receivable after the closing date of the balance sheet, although three of the eight stated that in light of hindsight they would have preferred that the make-up of the collateral be disclosed. The witnesses likewise testified that disclosure of the Roth borrowings from Valley was not required, and seven of the eight were of the opinion that such disclosure would be inappropriate.

Defendants asked for two instructions which, in substance, would have told the jury that a defendant could be found guilty only if, according to generally accepted accounting principles, the financial statements as a whole did not fairly present the financial condition of Continental at September 30, 1962, and then only if his departure from accepted standards was due to willful disregard of those standards with knowledge of the falsity of the statements and an intent to deceive. The judge declined to give these instructions. Dealing with the subject in the course of his charge, he said that the "critical test" was whether the financial statement as a whole "fairly presented the financial position of Continental as of September 30, 1962, and whether it accurately reported the operations for fiscal 1962." If they did not, the basic issue became whether defendants acted in good faith. Proof of compliance with generally accepted standards was "evidence which may be very persuasive but not necessarily conclusive that he acted in good faith, and that the facts as certified were not materially false or misleading." . . .

We think the judge was right in refusing to make the accountants' testimony so nearly a complete defense. The critical test according to the charge was the same as that which the accountants testified was critical. We do not think the jury was also required to accept the accountants' evaluation whether a given fact was material to overall fair presentation, at least not when the accountants' testimony was not based on specific rules or prohibitions to which they could point, but only on the need for the auditor to make an honest judgment and their conclusion that nothing in the financial statements themselves negated the conclusion that an honest judgment had been made. Such evidence may be highly persuasive, but it is not conclusive, and so the trial judge correctly charged.

Defendants next contend that, particularly in light of the expert testimony, the evidence was insufficient to allow the jury to consider the failure to disclose Roth's borrowings from Valley, the make-up of the collateral, or the post-balance sheet increase in the Valley receivable. . . . We join defendants' counsel in assuming that the mere fact that a company has made advances to an affiliate does not ordinarily impose a duty on an accountant to investigate what the affiliate has done with them or even to disclose that the affiliate has made a loan to a common officer if this has come to his attention. But it simply cannot be true that an accountant is under no duty to disclose what he knows when he has reason to believe that, to a material extent, a corporation is being operated not to carry out its business in the interest of all the stockholders but for the private benefit of its president. Generally accepted accounting principles instruct an accountant what to do in the usual case where he has no reason to doubt that the affairs of the corporation are being honestly conducted. Once he has reason to believe that this basic assumption is false, an entirely different situation confronts him. Then, as the Lybrand firm stated in its letter accepting the Continental engagement, he must "extend his procedures to determine whether or not such suspicions are justified." If as a result of such an extension or, as here, without it, he finds his suspicions to be confirmed, full disclosure must be the rule, unless he has made sure the wrong has been righted and procedures to avoid a repetition have been established. At least this must be true when the dishonesty he has discovered is not some minor peccadillo but a diversion so large as to imperil if not destroy the very solvency of the enterprise. . . .

[W]e find it impossible to say that a reasonable jury could not be convinced beyond a reasonable doubt that the striking difference between what Note 2 said and what it needed to say in order to reveal the truth resulted not from mere carelessness but from design. That some other jury might have taken a more lenient view, as the trial judge said he would have done, is a misfortune for the defendants but not one within our power to remedy.

Case Questions

1. Was it, in your opinion, a wise decision not to impose prison sentences on the defendants?

2. White collar criminals receive more lenient treatment at the hands of judges than do other types of criminals. Rarely is a jail sentence imposed. What does this fact do to the concept of equal justice under law?

3. Congress passed the securities laws, which theoretically reflect the viewpoint and interests of all citizens. The accounting profession establishes the standard of generally accepted accounting principles. If compliance with these accounting principles constituted a complete defense in a case such as this, would not one small segment of society be determining the interpretation and applicability of national legislation?

Case Comment

President Richard Nixon granted a pardon to the defendants in the Simon litigation.

An individual can have both civil and criminal liability under the securities laws. The SEC recommends that the Justice Department press criminal charges when the SEC believes more than mere negligence is involved in a person's conduct. In the above case, the judge did not hand down a jail sentence. In the following one, the individuals were given jail sentences, in addition to a monetary fine, by the trial judge. Of course, the criminal conviction of an individual holding a license to practice a profession, such as an attorney or accountant, may also result in the loss of that license.

Besides being a second example of a criminal case, the *Natelli* case that follows shows how an accountant may be liable for an unaudited financial statement when he knows that it contains materially false information. It also introduces the troublesome issue of one's liability for following the orders of a superior.

U.S. v. NATELLI
527 F.2d 311 (1975)

GURFEIN, Circuit Judge

Anthony M. Natelli and Joseph Scansaroli appeal from judgments of conviction. . . . Judge Tyler imposed a one year sentence and a $10,000 fine upon Natelli, suspending all but 60 days of imprisonment, and a one year sentence and a $2,500 fine upon Scansaroli, suspending all but 10 days of the imprisonment.

Both appellants are certified public accountants. Natelli was the partner in charge of the Washington, D.C. office of Peat, Marwick, Mitchell & Co. ("Peat"), a large independent firm of auditors, and the engagement partner with respect to Peat's audit engagement for National Student Marketing Corporation ("Marketing"). Scansaroli was an employee of Peat, assigned as audit supervisor on that engagement. . . .

Count Two of the indictment charged that . . . four of Marketing's officers and the appellants, as independent auditors, "wilfully and knowingly made and caused to be made false and misleading statements with respect to material facts" in a proxy statement for Marketing. . . .

It was alleged that "as the defendants well knew but failed to disclose . . . (a) approximately one million dollars, or more than 20%, of the 1968 'net sales originally reported' has proven to be nonexistent by the time the proxy statement was filed and had been written off on [Marketing's] own internal books of account; (b) net sales and profits of 'pooled companies reflected retroactively' were substantially understated; and (c) net sales and profits of [Marketing] were substantially overstated."

Count Two charged further that the proxy statement also contained an unaudited statement of earnings for the nine months ended May 31, 1969 which was materially false and misleading in that it stated "net sales" as $11,313,569 and "net earnings" as $702,270, when, in fact, as the defendants well knew, "net sales" for the period were less than $10,500,000 and Marketing had no earnings at all.

As part of the proxy statement, appellants set about to draft a footnote purporting to reconcile the Company's prior reported net sales and earnings from the 1968 report with restated amounts resulting from pooled companies reflected retroactively. The earnings summary in the proxy statement included companies acquired after fiscal 1968 and their pooled earnings.

At Natelli's direction, Scansaroli subtracted the written-off Marketing sales from the 1968 sales figures for the seven later acquired pooled companies without showing any retroactive adjustment for Marketing's own fiscal 1968 figures. There was no disclosure in the footnote that over $1 million of previously reported 1968 sales of Marketing has been written off. All narrative disclosure in the footnote was striken by Natelli. This was a violation of Accounting Principles Board Opinion Number 9, which requires disclosure of prior adjustments which affect the net income of prior periods. . . .

It is hard to probe the intent of a defendant. Circumstantial evidence, particularly with proof of motive, where available, is often sufficient to convince a reasonable man of criminal intent beyond a reasonable doubt. When we deal with a defendant who is a professional accountant, it is even harder, at times, to distinguish between simple errors of judgment and errors made with sufficient criminal intent to support a conviction, especially when there is no financial gain to the accountant other than his legitimate fee. . . .

Honesty should have impelled appellants to disclose in the footnote which annotated their own audited statement for fiscal 1968 that substantial write-offs had been taken, after year end, to reflect a loss for the year. A simple desire to right the wrong that had been perpetrated on the stockholders and others by the false audited financial statement should have dictated that course. The failure to make open disclosure could hardly have been inadvertent, or a jury at least could so find, for appellants were themselves involved in determining the write-offs and their accounting treatment. The concealment of the retroactive adjustments to Marketing's 1968 year revenues and earnings could properly have been found

to have been intentional for the very purpose of hiding earlier errors. . . .

That the proxy statement did not contain a formal reaudit of fiscal 1968 is not determinative. The accountant has a duty to correct the earlier financial statement which he had audited himself and upon which he had issued his certificate, when he discovers "that the figures in the annual report were substantially false and misleading," and he has a chance to correct them. The accountant owes a duty to the public not to assert a privilege of silence until the next audited annual statement comes around in due time. Since companies were being acquired by Marketing for its shares in this period, Natelli had to know that the 1968 audited statement was being used continuously.

This raises the issue of the duty of the CPA in relation to an unaudited financial statement contained within a proxy statement where the figures are reviewed and to some extent supplied by the auditors. It is common ground that the auditors were "associated" with the statement and were required to object to anything they actually "knew" to be materially false. In the ordinary case involving an unaudited statement, the auditor would not be chargeable simply because he failed to discover the invalidity of booked accounts receivable, inasmuch as he had not undertaken an audit with verification. In this case, however, Natelli "knew" the history of post-period bookings and the dismal consequences later discovered. Was he under a duty in these circumstances to object or to go beyond the usual scope of an accountant's review and insist upon some independent verification? The American Institute of Certified Public Accountants, Statement of Auditing Standards No. 1 . . . recognizes that "if the certified public accountant concludes on the basis of facts known to him that unaudited financial statements with which he may become associated are not in conformity with generally accepted accounting principles, which include adequate disclosure, he should insist . . . upon appropriate revision. . . ."

We do not think this means, in terms of professional standards, that the accountant may shut his eyes in reckless disregard of his knowledge that highly suspicious figures, known to him to be suspicious, were being included in the unaudited earnings figures with which he was "associated" in the proxy statement. . . .

Scansaroli contends that there was insufficient evidence to prove beyond a reasonable doubt that (1) he participated in a criminal act with respect to the footnote or (2) that he made an accounting judgment permitting Marketing to include in sales certain contracts-in-progress with the requisite criminal intent. We hold that there was enough evidence to establish the former, but not the latter. For reasons relating to the form of the charge, we will reverse and remand for a new trial.

There is some merit to Scansaroli's point that he was simply carrying out the judgments of his superior Natelli. The defense of obedience to higher authority has always been troublesome. There is no sure yardstick to measure criminal responsibility except by measurement of the degree of awareness on the part of a defendant that he is participating in a criminal act, in the absence of physical coercion such as a soldier might face. Here the motivation to conceal undermines Scansaroli's argument that he was merely implementing Natelli's instructions, at least with respect to concealment of matters that were within his own ken.

We think the jury could properly have found him guilty on the specification relating to the footnote. Scansaroli himself wrote the journal entry in Marketing's books which improperly netted the tax credit with earnings, the true effect never being pointed out in the financial statement. This, with the background of Scansaroli's implication in preparation of the 1968 statement, could be found to have

been motivated by intent to conceal the 1968 overstatement of earnings.

Scansaroli participated in the decision to subtract in the proxy statement footnote $678,000 of written-off Marketing sales from the figures for later-acquired pooled companies instead of from its own figures, without further disclosure. Even if Scansaroli did not write the footnote, he supplied the misleading computations and subtractions though he was conscious of the true facts.

Having concluded that there was sufficient evidence to convict both appellants on the footnote specification, we turn to the nine-months earnings statement. . . .

With respect to the major item, the Eastern commitment, we think Scansaroli stands in a position different from that of Natelli. Natelli was his superior. He was the man to make the judgment whether or not to object to the last-minute inclusion of a new "commitment" in the nine-months statement. . . . Since in the hierarchy of the accounting firm it was not his responsibility to decide whether to book the Eastern contract, his mere adjustment of the figures to reflect it under orders was not a matter for his discretion. As we have seen, Natelli bore a duty in the circumstances to be suspicious of the Eastern commitment and to pursue the matter further. Scansaroli may also have been suspicious, but rejection of the Eastern contract was not within his sphere of responsibility. Absent such duty, he cannot be held to have acted in reckless disregard of the facts.

Appellants contend that the trial court erroneously instructed the jury on the issue of knowledge. We do not agree.

It was a balanced charge which made it clear that negligence or mistake would be insufficient to constitute guilty knowledge. Judge Tyler also carefully instructed the jury that "good faith, that is to say, an honest belief in the truth of the data set forth in the footnote and entries in the proxy statement, would constitute a complete defense here." On the other hand, "Congress equally could not have intended that men holding themselves out as members of these ancient professions [law and accounting] should be able to escape criminal liability on a plea of ignorance when they have shut their eyes to what was plainly to be seen or have represented a knowledge they knew they did not possess."

Case Question

1. Was the decision to uphold the conviction of the audit partner, while granting a new trial to the audit supervisor, a fair one? Would your answer be changed on learning that the Justice Department subsequently decided not to expend the time and resources necessary for a retrial of Scansaroli and dismissed the charges against him?

Case Comment

When National Student Marketing went public in 1968 its stock was priced at $1.50 per share. The following year saw it hit a high of $36.00. You have read how its financial collapse resulted in SEC-initiated action against both the law firms and accounting firm that were involved in its securities dealings. There were other legal actions. Cortes W. Randell, the president and founder of the company, plead guilty to several stock fraud charges. Stockholders of the company brought a civil suit against a number of defendants seeking monetary damages. The long, sad odyssey reached an end in 1982 after 12 years of litigation. In September of that year Peat, Marwick became the last defendant to reach an out-of-court settlement. It agreed to pay $6.5 million to the plaintiffs. In June 1982 the law firm of White & Case settled out of court with payment of about $2 million. All total there will be about $32 million to distribute to the former shareholders of the company, which was liquidated in 1980.

The thrust of our discussion in these chapters on the securities laws has involved civil and criminal action. The SEC can also use administrative proceedings to enforce the law. For example, in July 1975 the SEC settled administrative proceedings with the Peat, Marwick firm. The proceedings grew out of that accounting firm's role in auditing several clients, including National Student Marketing (see Chapter 16). As part of the settlement, Peat, Marwick was prohibited from accepting certain new clients for a six-month period.

Accountants and Section 10(b) of the '34 Act

Different provisions of the law can impose different obligations on an individual. We have seen in the *BarChris* case that an accountant is an expert who will not be held liable for a materially false registration statement if he can prove that he made a reasonable investigation that produced no reasonable grounds to disbelieve the information in that statement. In such a situation, the negligent performance of the audit function would fail to meet this reasonableness standard and the accountant would incur legal liability. This does not mean that every instance of negligent accounting work will constitute a violation of the securities law.

The *Hochfelder* case that follows involves a determination by the Supreme Court that an accounting firm bears no liability under Section 10(b) for the negligent conduct of an audit in a lawsuit for damages brought by a private party.

ERNST & ERNST v. HOCHFELDER
425 U.S. 185 (1976)

MR. JUSTICE POWELL *delivered the opinion of the Court.*

Petitioner, Ernst & Ernst, is an accounting firm. From 1946 through 1967 it was retained by First Securities Company of Chicago (First Securities), a small brokerage firm and member of the Midwest Stock Exchange and of the National Association of Securities Dealers, to perform periodic audits of the firm's books and records. In connection with these audits Ernst & Ernst prepared for filing with the Securities and Exchange Commission (the Commission) the annual reports required of First Securities under § 17(a) of the 1934 Act. . . It also prepared for First Securities responses to the financial questionnaires of the Midwest Stock Exchange (the Exchange).

Respondents were customers of First Securities who invested in a fraudulent securities scheme perpetrated by Leston B. Nay, president of the firm and owner of 92 percent of its stock. Nay induced the respondents to invest funds in "escrow" accounts that he represented would yield a high rate of return. Respondents did so from 1942 through 1966. . . . In fact, there were no escrow accounts as Nay converted respondents' funds to his own use immediately upon receipt. These transactions were not in the customary form of dealings between First Securities and its customers. The respondents drew their personal checks pay-

able to Nay or a designated bank for his account. No such escrow accounts were reflected on the books and records of First Securities, and none was shown on its periodic accounting to respondents in connection with their own investments. Nor were they included in First Securities' filings with the Commission or the Exchange.

This fraud came to light in 1968 when Nay committed suicide, leaving a note that described First Securities as bankrupt and the escrow accounts as "spurious." Respondents subsequently filed this action for damages against Ernst & Ernst. . . . The complaint charged that Nay's escrow scheme violated § 10(b) and Commission Rule 10b-5, and that Ernst & Ernst had "aided and abetted" Nay's violations by its "failure" to conduct proper audits of First Securities. As revealed through discovery, respondents' cause of action rested on a theory of negligent nonfeasance. The premise was that Ernst & Ernst had failed to utilize "appropriate auditing procedures" in its audits of First Securities, thereby failing to discover internal practices of the firm said to prevent an effective audit. The practice principally relied on was Nay's rule that only he could open mail addressed to him at First Securities or addressed to First Securities to his attention, even if it arrived in his absence. Respondents contended that if Ernst & Ernst had conducted a proper audit, it would have discovered this "mail rule." The existence of the rule then would have been disclosed is reports to the Exchange and to the Commission by Ernst &

Ernst as an irregular procedure that prevented an effective audit. This would have revealed the fraudulent scheme. Respondents specifically disclaimed the existence of fraud or intentional misconduct on the part of Ernst & Ernst.

After extensive discovery the District Court granted Ernst & Ernst's motion for summary judgment and dismissed the action. The court rejected Ernst & Ernst's contention that a cause of action for aiding and abetting a securities fraud could not be maintained under § 10(b) and Rule 10b-5 merely on allegations of negligence. It concluded, however, that there was no genuine issue of material fact with respect to whether Ernst & Ernst had conducted its audits in accordance with generally accepted auditing standards.

The Court of Appeals for the Seventh Circuit reversed and remanded, holding that one who breaches a duty of inquiry and disclosure owed another is liable in damages for aiding and abetting a third party's violation of Rule 10b-5 if the fraud would have been discovered or prevented but for the breach. . . . The court reasoned that Ernst & Ernst had a common-law and statutory duty of inquiry into the adequacy of First Securities' internal control system because it had contracted to audit First Securities and to prepare for filing with the Commission the annual report of its financial condition. . . . The Court further reasoned that respondents were beneficiaries of the statutory duty to inquire and the related duty to disclose any material irregularities that were discovered. The court concluded that there were genuine issues of fact as to whether Ernst & Ernst's failure to discover and comment upon Nay's mail rule constituted a breach of its duties of inquiry and disclosure, and whether inquiry and disclosure would have led to the discovery or prevention of Nay's fraud.

We granted certiorari to resolve the question whether a private cause of action for damages will lie under § 10(b) and Rule 10b-5 in the absence of any allegation of "scienter"—intent to deceive, manipulate, or defraud.[1] We conclude that it will not and therefore we reverse. . . .

Although § 10(b) does not by its terms create an express civil remedy for its violation, and there is no indication that Congress, or the Commission when adopting Rule 10b-5, contemplated such a remedy, the existence of a private cause of action for violations of the statute and the rule is now well established. . . . Courts and commentators long have differed with regard to whether scienter is a necessary element of such a cause of action, or whether negligent conduct alone is sufficient. . . .

Section 10(b) makes unlawful the use or employment of "any manipulative or deceptive device or contrivance" in contravention of Commission rules. The words "manipulative or deceptive" used in conjunction with "device or contrivance" strongly suggest that § 10(b) was intended to proscribe knowing or intentional misconduct. . . .

In its *amicus curiae* brief, however, the Commission contends that nothing in the language "manipulative or deceptive device or contrivance" limits its operation to knowing or intentional practices. . . . The argument simply ignores the use of the words "manipulative," "device," and "contrivance," terms that make unmistakable a congressional intent to proscribe a type of conduct quite different from negligence. Use of the word "manipulative" is especially significant. It is and was virtually a term of art when used in connection with securities markets. It connotes intentional or willful conduct designed to deceive or defraud investors by controlling or artificially affecting the price of securities.

In addition to relying upon the Commission's argument with respect to the operative language of the statute, respondents contend

---

[1] In this opinion the term "scienter" refers to a mental state embracing intent to deceive, manipulate, or defraud.

that since we are dealing with "remedial legislation," . . . it must be construed " 'not technically and restrictively, but flexibly to effectuate its remedial purposes.' " . . . They argue that the "remedial purposes" of the Acts demand a construction of § 10(b) that embraces negligence as a standard of liability. . . . In some circumstances and with respect to certain classes of defendants, Congress did create express liability predicated upon a failure to exercise reasonable care. . . . But in other situations good faith is an absolute defense. . . . And in still other circumstances Congress created express liability regardless of the defendant's fault. . . .

It is thus evident that Congress fashioned standards of fault in the express civil remedies in the 1933 and 1934 Acts on a particularized basis. . . . In view of the language of § 10(b) which so clearly connotes intentional misconduct, and mindful that the language of a statute controls when sufficiently clear in its context, . . . further inquiry may be unnecessary. We turn now, nevertheless, to the legislative history of the 1934 Act to ascertain whether there is support for the meaning attributed to § 10(b) by the Commission and respondents.

Although the extensive legislative history of the 1934 Act is bereft of any explicit explanation of Congress' intent, we think the relevant portions of that history support our conclusion that § 10(b) was addressed to practices that involve some element of scienter and cannot be read to impose liability for negligent conduct alone. . . .

The Commission argues that Congress has been explicit in requiring willful conduct when that was the standard of fault intended. . . .

The structure of the Acts does not support the Commission's argument. In each instance that Congress created express civil liability in favor of purchasers or sellers of securities it clearly specified whether recovery was to be premised on knowing or intentional

conduct, negligence, or entirely innocent mistake. . . .

We also consider it significant that each of the express civil remedies in the 1933 Act allowing recovery for negligent conduct . . . is subject to significant procedural restrictions not applicable under § 10(b). . . . We think these procedural limitations indicate that the judicially created private damage remedy under § 10(b)—which has no comparable restrictions—cannot be extended, consistently with the intent of Congress, to actions premised on negligent wrongdoing. . . . We would be unwilling to bring about this result absent substantial support in the legislative history, and there is none. . . .

When a statute speaks so specifically in terms of manipulation and deception, and of implementing devices and contrivances—the commonly understood terminology of intentional wrongdoing—and when its history reflects no more expansive intent, we are quite unwilling to extend the scope of the statute to negligent conduct. . . .

The judgment of the Court of Appeals is *Reversed.*

MR. JUSTICE STEVENS *took no part in the consideration or decision of this case.*

MR. JUSTICE BLACKMUN, *with whom* MR. JUSTICE BRENNAN *joins, dissenting.*

Once again—see *Blue Chip Stamps* v. *Manor Drug Stores,* 421 U.S. 723, . . . (1975)—the Court interprets § 10(b) of the Securities Exchange Act of 1934 . . . and . . . Rule 10b-5, . . . restrictively and narrowly and thereby stultifies recovery for the victim. This time the Court does so by confining the statute and the Rule to situations where the defendant has "scienter," that is, the "intent to deceive, manipulate, or defraud." Sheer negligence, the Court says, is not within the reach of the statute and the Rule, and was not contemplated when the great reforms of 1933, 1934, and 1942 were effectuated by Congress and the Commission.

Perhaps the Court is right, but I doubt it. . . . The Court's opinion, ante, to be sure, has a certain technical consistency about it. It seems to me, however, that an investor can be victimized just as much by negligent conduct as by positive deception, and that it is not logical to drive a wedge between the two, saying that Congress clearly intended the one but certainly not the other.

No one questions the fact that the respondents here were the victims of an intentional securities fraud practiced by Leston B. Nay. What is at issue, of course, is the petitioner-accountant firm's involvement and that firm's responsibility under Rule 10b-5. . . .

The critical importance of the auditing accountant's role in insuring full disclosure cannot be overestimated. The SEC has emphasized that in certifying statements the accountant's duty "is to safeguard the public interest, not that of his client." . . . In this light, the initial inquiry into whether Ernst & Ernst's preparation and certification of the financial statements of First Securities Company of Chicago were negligent, because of the failure to perceive Nay's extraordinary mail rule, and in other alleged respects, and thus whether Rule 10b-5 was violated, should not be thwarted.

But the Court today decides that it is to be thwarted; and so once again it rests with Congress to rephrase and to re-enact, if investor victims, such as these, are ever to have relief under the federal securities laws that I thought had been enacted for their broad, needed, and deserving benefit.

Case Questions

1. Is this decision technically correct yet violative of the law's spirit?

2. Was the paintiffs' decision to sue Ernst & Ernst influenced by the fact that Nay was deceased and First Securities bankrupt?

3. Can the legal rationale of this decision also be applied to situations where attorneys or underwriters were negligent in the performance of their duties?

The *Hochfelder* decision left open the question of whether the SEC is also required to prove scienter in the civil enforcement actions that it brings under Section 10(b). Subsequently the Supreme Court answered the question by determining that both private parties and the SEC must establish scienter in cases brought under this portion of the law. *Aaron* v. *SEC,* 446 U.S. 680 (1980).

Accountants' Liability to the Securities Investors Protection Corporation

Let us introduce a new element to the legal equation for accountants' legal liability. What if, instead of the SEC, the creditors, or the investors, the Securities Investors Protection Corporation (SIPC) sues the accountants in connection with their work for a client? As you will shortly read, the accountants avoid liability under another section of the law. Both *Hochfelder* and *Redington,* the case that follows, are significant decisions. They both severely limit the liability of accounting firms under the provisions of the federal securities statutes.

TOUCHE ROSS & CO. v. REDINGTON, TRUSTEE

442 U.S. 560 (1979)

(Authors' note: Touche Ross & Co., a certified public accounting firm, audited the books and records of Weis Securities, Inc. These audits were used in filing with the SEC annual reports of Weis's financial condition. The accounting firm also prepared responses to financial questionnaires required by the New York Stock Exchange of its members. When the financial condition of Weis became precarious the company was liquidated under the terms of Securities Investors Protection Act. SIPC advanced $14 million to the trustee to satisfy, up to the specified statutory limits, the claims of approximately 34,000 customers of Weis. This action was filed against Touche Ross to recover the money advanced by SIPC, to recover for the customers whose property the trustee was unable to return, and to recover funds on behalf of Weis itself. Section 17 of the '34 Act required Weis to file the documents audited by Touche Ross. The recovery of the money was sought because of the accounting firm's allegedly improper audit of Weis's financial statements. SIPC and the trustee argued that the accountants had breached duties it owed to them and that this misconduct prevented Weis's true financial condition from becoming known until it was too late to forestall liquidation or to lessen the adverse financial consequences to Weis's customers. The trial court dismissed the suit but the Court of Appeals reversed. It held that Section 17 does impose a duty on accountants and that a breach of this duty gives rise to an implied private right of action for damages. The Supreme Court then held that no implied cause of action exists.)

MR. JUSTICE REHNQUIST *delivered the opinion of the Court.*

Here we decided whether customers of securities brokerage firms that are required to file certain financial reports with regulatory authorities by § 17(a) of the Securities Exchange Act of 1934 . . . have an implied cause of action for damages under § 17(a) against accountants who audit such reports, based on misstatements contained in the reports.

As we recently have emphasized, "the fact that a federal statute has been violated and some person harmed does not automatically give rise to a private cause of action in favor of that person." Instead, our task is limited solely to determining whether Congress intended to create the private right of action asserted by SIPC and the Trustee.

In terms, § 17(a) simply requires broker-dealers and others to keep such records and file such reports as the Commission may prescribe. It does not, by its terms, purport to create a private cause of action in favor of anyone. It is true that in the past our cases have held that in certain circumstances a private right of action may be implied in a statute not expressly providing one.

The information contained in the § 17(a) reports is intended to provide the Commission, the Exchange, and other authorities with a sufficiently early warning to enable them to take appropriate action to protect investors before the financial collapse of the particular broker-dealer involved. But § 17(a) does not by any stretch of its language purport to confer private damages rights or, indeed, any remedy in the event the regulatory authorities are unsuccessful in achieving their objectives and the broker becomes insolvent before corrective steps can be taken. By its terms, § 17(a) is forward-looking not retrospective; it seeks to forestall insolvency, not to provide recompense after it has occurred.

Certainly, the mere fact that § 17(a) was designed to provide protection for brokers' customers does not require the implication of a private damages action in their behalf.

SIPC and the Trustee contend that the result we reach sanctions injustice. But even if that were the case, the argument is made in the wrong forum, for we are not at liberty to legislate. If there is to be a federal damages remedy under these circumstances, Congress must provide it.

MR. JUSTICE MARSHALL, *dissenting.*

A cause of action for damages here is also consistent with the underlying purposes of the legislative scheme. Because the SEC lacks the resources to audit all the documents that brokers file, it must rely on certification by accountants. Implying a private right of action would both facilitate the SEC's enforcement efforts and provide an incentive for accountants to perform their certification functions properly.

Case Questions

1. Why would Congress pass a federal statute and not allow a person harmed by a violation of that statute to sue for any resulting damages?
2. If the Court did determine that the statute provides, by implication, for a private right of action for damages, would the Court be engaging in legislating or mere judicial interpretation of a legislative act?
3. Is the result of this case a just one?

Liability of a Negligent Accountant to a Negligent Client

When an accountant fails to use professional care and skill in carrying out an audit he or she will have committed the tort of negligence or the tort of malpractice. The accountant will be liable to the client for any loss caused by that negligence. However, what if the top management of the client carried out a fraud that the accountant failed to detect? When the client sues the accountant for the loss that it has suffered, may the accountant use, as a defense to the charge of negligence, the negligence of the client that also contributed to the loss? The following case explores the issue and answers the question.

CENCO INC. v. SEIDMAN & SEIDMAN
686 F.2d 449 (7 Cir. 1982)

(Authors' note: Between 1970 and 1975 managerial employees, including the chairman and president plus a number of vice presidents, of Cenco Inc. engaged in a massive fraud. The fraud was discovered by a newly hired financial officer who reported his suspicions to the SEC. The independent auditor throughout the period of the fraud, Seidman & Seidman, either never discovered the fraud or if it did failed to report it. The fraud primarily involved the inflating of inventories. This increased the apparent worth of Cenco and the market price of its stock (which plummeted in excess of 75 percent when the fraud was revealed). The inflated stock was used to buy other companies. The inflated value of the inventories allowed it to borrow money at lower interest rates than if its true value were known, and to collect from its insurers inflated claims for inventory lost or destroyed. Thus, the fraud was designed not to steal from the company, but to aggrandize the company and those individuals perpetrating the fraud at the expense of outsiders. A class action suit was filed against Cenco, its corrupt managers, and Seidman & Seidman. Cenco filed a cross-claim against its codefendant Seidman & Seidman alleging it was liable for having failed to prevent the fraud by the managers. The accounting partnership filed a claim against Cenco alleging that it had been a victim of

the fraud and was entitled to damages. All the claims were settled out of court or dismissed except Cenco's claim that the independent auditors had breached their contract, committed malpractice, and engaged in fraud. The jury decided in favor of the accounting firm.)

POSNER, Circuit Judge

This brings us to the main issue in the case—whether the district judge gave erroneous instructions to the jury. The challenged instructions relate to the question whether Seidman was entitled to use the wrongdoing of Cenco's managers as a defense against the charges of breach of contract, professional malpractice, and fraud. Despite the plurality of charges it is one question because breach of contract, negligence, and fraud, when committed by auditors, are a single form of wrongdoing under different names. The contract in question here (really a series of contracts) consists of the letters between Seidman and Cenco outlining the terms of Seidman's annual retention to audit Cenco's books. The material part of the letters is the incorporation by reference of general accounting standards which, so far as pertinent to this case, require the auditor to use his professional skill to follow up any signs of fraud that he discovers in the audit. The tort of negligence in the context of auditing is likewise a failure to use professional care and skill in carrying out an audit. And if such care and skill are not used, then the audit reports to the client will contain misrepresentations, either negligent or, if the auditor knows that the representations in the reports are untruthful or is indifferent to whether or not they are truthful, fraudulent.

Because these theories of auditors' misconduct are so alike, the defenses based on misconduct of the audited firm or its employees are also alike, though verbalized differently. A breach of contract is excused if the promisee's hindrance or failure to cooperate prevented the promisor from performing the contract. The corresponding defense in the case of negligence is, of course, contributory negligence.

To determine the correctness of the instruction requires us to decide in what circumstances, if any, fraud by corporate employees is a defense in a suit by the corporation against its auditors for failure to prevent the fraud. Illinois precedent allows us to reject one extreme position on this question, which is that the employee's fraud is always attributed to the corporation by the principle of respondeat superior. This position, which would exonerate auditors from all liability for failing to detect and prevent frauds by employees of the audited company, was rejected in *Cereal Byproducts Co.* v. *Hall,* 8 Ill. App. 2d 331, 132 N.E.2d 27 (1956), where a company's independent auditors were held liable for negligently failing to detect embezzlement by the company's bookkeeper. Auditors are not detectives hired to ferret out fraud, but if they chance on signs of fraud they may not avert their eyes—they must investigate. The references to keeping an eye out for fraud that appear in the accounting standards incorporated (by reference) in the retention letters between Cenco and Seidman would have little point if not interpreted to impose a duty on auditors to follow up any signs of fraud that come to their attention.

But this does not tell us what the result should be if the fraud permeates the top management of the company and if, moreover, the managers are not stealing from the company—that is, from its current stockholders—but instead are turning the company into an engine of theft against outsiders—creditors, prospective stockholders, insurers, etc. On this question the Illinois cases on auditors' liability provide no guidance. In fact, to our knowledge the question has never been the subject of a reported case.

From the standpoint of deterrence, the

question is whether the type of fraud that engulfed Cenco between 1970 and 1975 will be deterred more effectively if Cenco can shift the entire cost of the fraud from itself (which is to say, from its stockholders' pockets) to the independent auditor who failed to prevent the fraud. We think not. Cenco's owners—the stockholders—hired managers (directly, in the case of the president and chairman, who were both members of the board of directors, indirectly in the case of the others) who turned out to be thoroughly corrupt and to corrupt the corporation so thoroughly that it caused widespread harm to outsiders. If Seidman had been a more diligent auditor, conceivably if it had been a more honest auditor, the fraud might have been nipped in the bud; and liability to Cenco will make Seidman, and firms like it, more diligent and honest in the future. But if the owners of the corrupt enterprise are allowed to shift the costs of its wrongdoing entirely to the auditor, their incentives to hire honest managers and monitor their behavior will be reduced.

Thus, not only were some of Cenco's owners dishonest (and, to repeat, to the extent they still own stock in Cenco they would benefit from any judgment in Cenco's favor against Seidman), but the honest owners, and their delegates—a board of directors on which dishonesty and carelessness were well represented—were slipshod in their oversight and

so share responsibility for the fraud that Seidman also failed to detect. In addition, the scale of the fraud—the number and high rank of the managers involved—both complicated the task of discovery for Seidman and makes the failure of oversight by Cenco's shareholders and board of directors harder to condone.

Fraud on behalf of a corporation is not the same thing as fraud against it. Fraud against the corporation usually hurts just the corporation; the stockholders are the principal if not only victims; their equities vis-à-vis a careless or reckless auditor are therefore strong. But the stockholders of a corporation whose officers commit fraud for the benefit of the corporation are beneficiaries of the fraud. Maybe not net beneficiaries, after the fraud is unmasked and the corporation is sued—that is a question of damages, and is not before us. But the primary costs of a fraud on the corporation's behalf are borne not by the stockholders but by outsiders to the corporation, and the stockholders should not be allowed to escape all responsibility for such a fraud, as they are trying to do in this case. . . .

[H]ere the uncontested facts show fraud permeating the top management of Cenco. In such a case the corporation should not be allowed to shift the entire responsibility for the fraud to its auditors.

Hence the challenged jury instruction was proper in the circumstances.

---

1. If the accounting firm did cause Cenco to suffer a loss, would it have been more equitable for the court to have required Seidman to pay Cenco the amount of that loss, minus that portion of the loss attributable to the corrupt Cenco management?

2. Does this decision mean that an outside auditor will never be liable to a client when corporate officials engage in fraudulent schemes?

3. Will this decision realistically cause shareholders to exercise a greater degree of care when voting for members of the board of directors and make them more diligent in supervising the conduct of corporate officers?

Case Questions

Case Comment

Individuals who had purchased Cenco stock during the period of the fraud brought a class action suit alleging violation of various federal securities laws. These claims were settled out of court. Cenco settled by paying $11 million and Seidman settled by paying $3.5 million in the class action. Thus, the trial involved just the company against the accountants.

Watchdog Audit Committees of Outside Directors

The legal qualifications necessary for membership on a board of directors are determined by state law. Most states merely require that a director be of legal age. The states allow the corporation to impose additional qualifications, such as being a stockholder, if it so desires. The SEC has no rules as to director qualifications.

Many corporate boards operate through a number of board committees. A common committee is an audit committee. It is usually designated to handle the relationship between the corporation and its outside independent accounting firm. Such an audit committee can serve as a buffer between the corporation and the accountants in settling disputes between management and the auditor as to the accounting treatment to be accorded a particular transaction, the adequacy of a financial statement, or the scope or procedure of an audit. Such a committee can enhance the independence of the accounting firm, particularly if a majority of the committee is made up of outside directors.

As of June 30, 1978, the New York Stock Exchange requires each domestic company with common stock listed on the Exchange to have, as a condition of listing, an audit committee composed solely of directors independent of management. A director who has a customary commercial, industrial, banking, or underwriting relationship with the corporation that is carried on in the ordinary course of business on an arms-length basis can be an independent director. However, a director who acts on a regular basis as an individual or representative of an organization serving as a professional advisor, legal counsel, or consultant to management will not be independent if the relationship is material to any of the involved parties.

The practice of requiring an audit committee composed of independent directors is controversial, and the other stock exchanges have declined to adopt such a rule for their listed companies.

The Foreign Corrupt Practices Act

One outgrowth of the investigations conducted by the Special Watergate Prosecutor in the early 1970s was the revelation that some corporations were expending corporate funds for illegal purposes. Naturally, the corporations also failed to disclose these expenditures to their shareholders and the government. These revelations led to a series of investigations by the SEC that resulted in the disclosure that substantial numbers of corporations had made questionable or illegal payments totalling several hundreds of millions of dollars to foreign government officials and politically well-connected individuals. Congressional hearings were conducted that resulted in the passage of the Foreign Corrupt Practices Act of 1977. The Act makes it a crime to bribe foreign officials to obtain or retain business. To aid enforcement, the law mandates the maintenance of internal accounting controls so that a company's books and records will accurately reflect its disposition of assets. Let us now examine more closely the provisions of this important and controversial law.

The Antibribery Provisions

It is unlawful for a U.S. citizen or U.S.-based company (including its agents) to use the mail, or any other instrumentality of interstate commerce, to corruptly offer or give anything of value to a foreign political party or any person, while having reason to know that a portion of the thing of value will be offered to a foreign official or political party, to influence any act or decision of that official in his official capacity, in order to assist in obtaining or retaining business for or with any person. The law makes a distinction between payments to public officials who exercise discretionary power and those who merely exercise ministerial functions. The former are illegal; the latter are exempted from the Act. Thus, paying a bribe to the minister of aviation so that he or she selects your firm, instead of a competitor's, to supply the national airline with a fleet of planes is criminal. If you have a shipload of fruit riding at anchor in a foreign harbor and slip some money to an official to expedite the processing of the shipment through customs, you have made a legal "grease payment."

Since the Foreign Corrupt Practices Act amends the Securities Exchange Act of 1934, one could easily be misled into believing that it is only applicable to companies subject to regulation by the SEC. In fact, the antibribery portion of the law applies to both privately held and publicly traded companies. A criminal conviction can lead to a fine of $1 million for a company and $10,000 or five years in jail, or both, for an individual who violated the law. If an individual is fined for his or her role in helping the company violate the law, the company cannot pay the fine, directly or indirectly.

The Accounting Provisions

There are two accounting-related provisions in the law. Companies subject to regulation by the SEC must (1) make and keep books, records, and accounts that, in reasonable detail, accurately and fairly reflect the transactions and dispositions of the firm's assets and (2) devise and maintain a system of internal accounting controls sufficient to provide reasonable assurances that (a) transactions are executed in accordance with management's authorization; (b) transactions are recorded so that financial statements may be prepared in conformity with generally accepted accounting principles and to maintain accountability for assets; (c) access to assets is allowed only in accordance with management's authorization; and (d) the recorded accountability for assets is compared with existing assets at reasonable intervals and appropriate action is taken with respect to any difference.

While these accounting sections are a part of a law that deals with foreign payoffs, they are not limited to companies engaged in international business. All companies that have issued securities subject to SEC regulation must comply with these provisions, even though they confine their operations to the United States and do not make illegal foreign bribery payments.

Enforcement of the Law

Enforcement of the law has been split between the Justice Department and the SEC. The Justice Department enforces the criminal portions of the antibribery statute. The SEC utilizes its normal civil enforcement mechanism to enforce the accounting provisions applicable to the companies under its jurisdiction. Because the law is relatively new there has not been a great number of enforcement actions brought as yet. However, an examination of several cases does provide a look at how the statute is being applied and provide guidance to those who must comply with its provisions.

In *SEC* v. *Aminex Resources*,[1] the company and some of its officers were charged with violations of the accounting provisions, not the bribery portions of the law. Allegedly more than $1 million in corporate funds were misappropriated by means of false documents and an inadequate internal accounting system. The case was settled with a consent decree. In *SEC* v. *International Systems & Controls Corp.*,[2] the company and certain of its officers were charged with a violation of both the antibribery and the accounting provisions of the law. Allegedly questionable and improper payments of almost $23 million were made to obtain business in a number of foreign countries, and then the payments were hidden in the books and records. In addition, it was alleged that the company lacked the accounting controls necessary to ensure that company transactions would be recorded properly. Again the case was settled by a consent decree. However, the consent decree was a sweeping one. It did not merely order the company and its officers to cease such conduct in the future. It also required the appointment of three independent directors, acceptable to the SEC, who would make up an audit committee; the appointment of an agent, acceptable to the SEC, who would investigate and report to the SEC certain fund transfers; and the filing of correct, amended SEC reports relative to foreign payments. The two officers agreed to reimburse the corporation for any funds deemed necessary by the audit committee and also agreed that they would not hold a position of officer or director of a publicly traded company unless it had an independent audit committee.

It is unclear as to whether a shareholder can bring a suit against a corporation for a violation of the statute. The law grants an express cause of action only to the Justice Department and the SEC. It will be for the courts to determine whether Congress intended a shareholder to have an implied private cause of action.

Controversy over the Law

There has been a substantial deal of controversy generated by the law. Some individuals regard the law as lacking the specificity required by such an important and far-reaching statute. They believe that one might in good faith attempt to comply with the law and then find oneself a defendant in a legal action under a liberal interpretation of the statute's provisions. Others believe the law is susceptible to vindicative application by a bureaucrat pursuing a company for a relatively small error in the corporate books. Such individuals believe the law should be amended to make only "material" errors in the books and records a violation. The most common criticism is that, no matter how well meaning the law is, it only hurts U.S. companies in the world market. Supporters of this view point out that in many parts of the world payoffs, bribes, and other forms of kickbacks are either not illegal or are such an acceptable way of doing business that the law winks at them. If we prevent our companies from playing by the rules in another country, we will simply lose the business to foreign companies that do not operate under the same legal constraints. Of course, the opposite argument is that a country with the stature of the United States should not determine its standards for doing business according to the lowest common denominator but should set a high standard and seek to raise the rest of the international community to that level through the negotiation of international treaties.

Review Problems

1. The representative of a U.S. company has become a personal friend of a member of the royal family in a Middle Eastern country. That family member also serves as the official in charge of his government's purchases from, among others, this U.S. company. The representative wishes to give an expensive golf club set to the member of the royal family as a birthday present. If such a present is given, will it be legal? If the representative is authorized to use corporate funds to purchase the gift, will it be legal? *Yes – not corrupt giving – no illegal intention*

2. The traditional common law rules regarding accountants' liability to third parties for negligence:
   (a) Remain substantially unchanged since their inception.
   (b) Were more stringent than the rules currently applicable.

(c) Are of relatively minor importance to the accountant.

(d) Have been substantially changed at both the federal and state levels.

(Adapted from CPA Exam Law Problem #2, Question #18, taken from the November 1975 exam. © American Institute of Certified Public Accountants, Inc., 1975.)

3. The CPA firm of Knox & Knox has been subpoenaed to testify and produce its correspondence and workpapers in connection with a lawsuit brought by a third party against one of their clients. Knox considers the subpoenaed documents to be privileged communication and therefore seeks to avoid admission of such evidence in the lawsuit. Is there any legal basis for Knox's objection to the subpoena of its working papers? *No CPA privilege*

w/p's belong to accts.

(Adapted from CPA Exam Law Problem #1, Question #2, taken from the May 1981 exam. © American Institute of Certified Public Accountants, Inc., 1981.)

4. Donalds & Company, CPAs, audited the financial statements included in the annual report submitted by Markum Securities, Inc., to the Securities and Exchange Commission. The audit was improper in several respects. Markum is now insolvent and unable to satisfy the claims of its customers. The customers have instituted legal action against Donalds on the basis of Section 10b and Rule 10b-5 of the Securities Exchange Act of 1934. What defense should be asserted by the accounting firm if it is to avoid liability?

Show no scienter reasonable basis not to have known

(Adapted from CPA Exam Law Problem #1, Question #4, taken from the May 1981 exam. © American Institute of Certified Public Accountants, Inc., 1981.)

5. Major, Major & Sharpe, CPAs, are the auditors of MacLain Industries. In connection with the public offering of $10 million of MacLain securities, Major expressed an unqualified opinion as to the financial statements. Subsequent to the offering, certain misstatements and omissions were revealed. Major has been sued by the purchasers of the stock offered pursuant to the registration statement, which included the financial statements audited by Major. In the ensuing lawsuit by the MacLain investors, Major will be able to avoid liability if it can prove what facts?

Hard time avoiding liab.

(Adapted from CPA Exam Law Problem #1, Question #3, taken from the May 1981 exam. © American Institute of Certified Public Accountants, Inc., 1981.)

6. The Foreign Corrupt Practices Act of 1977 prohibits the bribing of foreign officials. Which of the following statements correctly describes the Act's application to corporations engaging in such practices?

(a) It applies only to multinational corporations.

(b) It applies to all domestic corporations engaged in interstate commerce.

(c) It applies only to corporations whose securities are registered under the Securities Exchange Act of 1934.

(d) It applies only to corporations engaged in foreign commerce.

(Adapted from CPA Exam Law Problem #1, Question #44, taken from the November 1980 exam. © American Institute of Certified Public Accountants, Inc., 1980.)

7. Sharp, CPA, was engaged by Peters & Sons, a partnership, to give an opinion on the financial statements that were to be submitted to several prospective partners as part of a planned expansion of the firm. Sharp's fee was fixed on a per-diem basis. After a period of intensive work, Sharp completed about half of the necessary field work. Then, because of unanticipated demands on his time by other clients, Sharp was forced to abandon the work. The planned expansion of the firm failed to materialize because the prospective partners lost interest when the audit report was not promptly available. Sharp offered to complete the task at a later date. This offer was refused. Peters & Sons suffered damages of $4,000 as a result. Is Sharp liable for this loss? *Yes – malpractice of acct.*

(Adapted from CPA Exam Law Problem #1, Question #5, taken from the November 1977 exam. © American Institute of Certified Public Accountants, Inc., 1977.)

8. A third-party purchaser of securities has brought suit based on the Securities Act of 1933 against a CPA firm. Will the CPA firm prevail in the suit brought by the third party, even though the CPA firm issued an unqualified opinion on materially incorrect financial statements, if the firm can show that the third-party plaintiff did not rely on the audited financial statements? *No! Reliance has nothing to do c it.*

(Adapted from CPA Exam Law Problem #2, Question #19, taken from the November 1975 exam. © American Institute of Certified Public Accountants, Inc., 1975.)

9. Winslow Manufacturing, Inc., sought a $200,000 loan from National Lending Corporation. National Lending insisted that audited financial statements be submitted before it would extend credit. Winslow agreed to this and also agreed to pay the audit fee. An audit was performed by an independent CPA who submitted his report to Winslow to be used solely for the purpose of negotiating a loan from National. National, on reviewing the audited financial statements, decided in good faith not to extend the credit desired. Certain ratios, which as a matter of policy were used by National in reaching its decision, were deemed too low. Winslow used copies of the audited financial statements to obtain credit elsewhere. It was subsequently learned that the CPA, despite the exercise of reasonable care, had failed to discover a sophisticated embezzlement scheme by Winslow's chief accountant. Under these circumstances, what liability does the CPA have? *None – opinion said*

(Adapted from CPA Exam Law Problem #1, Question #3, taken from the November 1976 exam. © American Institute of Certified Public Accountants, Inc., 1976.)

10. Would the investing public be afforded an increased degree of protection if the SEC licensed the attorneys and accountants that practice before it?

Endnotes   1. Fed. Sec. L. Rep. (CCH) ¶ 96,352 (1978).
2. Fed. Sec. L. Rep. (CCH) ¶ 96,922 (1979).

Regulation of the Proxy Process and Tender Offers 18

A proxy is the device whereby a shareholder gives to another the right to vote his or her shares of stock. It is an agency relationship and, as such, it is revocable. A sample proxy is shown in Figure 18-1.

The proxy process is governed by the law of agency, the state's corporation statute, and the '34 Act. Our focus here will be on the regulatory process under Section 14(a) of the '34 Act. That section provides that it is unlawful for any person, by the use of the mails or by any means or instrumentality of interstate commerce or of any facility of a national securities exchange or otherwise, in contravention of such rules and regulations as the Commission may prescribe as necessary or appropriate in the public interest or for the protection of investors, to solicit or to permit the use of his name to solicit any proxy or consent or authorization in respect of any security (other than an exempted security) registered pursuant to Section 12 of this title. These regulations apply whether the proxy solicitation is for the election of directors or for approval of other corporate action.

Proxy Regulation

At one time the proxy process was rather staid. Occasionally, a bitter proxy battle occurred, when two or more groups struggled for control of a corporation, but these tended to be few in number. The late 1960s saw a dramatic change as social activist groups seized on the proxy process as a method of dramatizing their positions. A group called the Medical Committee for Human Rights sought to present a proposal to Dow Chemical shareholders to restrict the sale of napalm. The Project on Corporate Responsibility began its Campaign GM to include various proposals in the General Motors proxy statement. These and other such efforts led to extensive litigation over what is a proper subject for action by security holders. The result was the adoption of important amendments, which took effect January 1, 1973, to the proxy rules.

The proxy is accompanied by a proxy statement. Its contents are also highly regulated by Section 14. The shareholder votes by proxy and must

1 3733–08 5528231

GM

PROXY

The Items shown below are described and page referenced in the Table of Contents (page i) to the Proxy Statement. The Board of Directors Recommends a Vote AGAINST the following Stockholder Proposals:

	For	Against	Abstain			For	Against	Abstain			For	Against	Abstain
Item No. 4	☐	☐	☐		Item No. 5	☐	☐	☐		Item No. 6	☐	☐	☐

This proxy will be voted "AGAINST" Items 4 through 6 if no choice is specified.

FRED J NAFFZIGER & CAROL A
NAFFZIGER JT TEN
124 S GREENLAWN AVE
SOUTH BEND IND   46617

Dated: _____ , 1982

_____

_____
Signature of Stockholder

Please add your title if you are signing as Attorney, Administrator, Executor, Guardian, Trustee, or in any other representative capacity.

PLEASE MARK, SIGN, DATE AND RETURN THIS PROXY CARD PROMPTLY USING THE ENCLOSED ENVELOPE.

GENERAL MOTORS CORPORATION

Proxy Solicited by Board of Directors for Annual Meeting of Stockholders
Fisher Building, Detroit, Michigan, Friday, May 21, 1982, 9:00 A.M. Local Time

GM

PROXY

The undersigned authorizes Roger B. Smith, F. James McDonald, Howard H. Kehrl and F. Alan Smith, and each of them as the Proxy Committee, to vote the common stock of the undersigned upon the nominees for Director (A. L. Armstrong, C. B. Cleary, J. T. Connor, J. D. deButts, J. H. Evans, W. A. Fallon, C. T. Fisher, III, M. L. Goldberger, R. S. Hatfield, R. H. Herzog, J. J. Horan, R. R. Jensen, H. H. Kehrl, F. J. McDonald, W. E. McLaughlin, T. A. Murphy, E. C. Patterson, E. T. Pratt, Jr., G. P. Shultz, J. G. Smale, F. A. Smith, J. S. Smith, R. B. Smith, L. H. Sullivan, C. H. Townes), upon the other Items shown below and on the reverse side, *which are described and page referenced in the Table of Contents (page i) to the Proxy Statement,* and upon all other matters which may come before the 1982 Annual Meeting of Stockholders of General Motors Corporation, or any adjournment thereof.

You are encouraged to specify your choices by marking the appropriate boxes below, but you need not mark any boxes if you wish to vote in accordance with the Board of Directors' recommendations. The Proxy Committee cannot vote your shares unless you sign and return this card.

The Board of Directors Recommends a Vote FOR the following Board of Directors Proposals:

	For	Withheld			For	Against	Abstain
Item No. 1	☐	☐		Item No. 2	☐	☐	☐
For, except vote withheld from the following nominee(s):				Item No. 3	☐	☐	☐

_____

This proxy will be voted "FOR" Items 1 through 3 if no choice is specified.

```
SEE REVERSE
SIDE          ➤
```

FIGURE 18-1

be given the opportunity to vote "yes" or "no" on each item. The proxy statement is designed to provide the shareholder with sufficient information to cast an intelligent ballot. Even when management does not solicit proxies, it is still required by Section 14(c) to supply annually to the security holders information substantially equivalent to that which would be required in a proxy statement. The detailed regulation of the proxy process is set forth in Rule 14.

Shareholder Proposals[1]

Any security holder entitled to vote at a shareholders' meeting formerly was entitled to submit a proposal to be voted on by the shareholders. However, in August 1983 the SEC adopted new rules governing the submission of shareholder proposals. Under these changes the person wishing to present a proposal must have been a shareholder ~~for at least one year and must own a minimum of $1000 or 1 percent of the corporation's outstanding stock, whichever is less.~~ *no limit* He must submit his proposal accompanied by notice of his intention to present the proposal for action at the meeting. The management of the issuer shall set forth the proposal in its proxy statement and identify it in its proxy form so that the shareholders may vote on it. Management need not include the proposal unless it is received at the issuer's principal executive offices not less than 90 days in advance of the annual meeting date listed in the proxy statement for the last annual meeting. If that date is changed, the proposal must be received within a reasonable time. Excluded from these provisions are elections to office and counter proposals to matters to be submitted by management [Rule 14a-8(a)].

The proxy statement shall contain the name and address of the security holder making the proposal, or state that the issuer or Commission will furnish the information on request. If management opposes the proposal, it shall, at the request of the security holder, include in the proxy statement a statement of the security holder, in not more than 500 words, in support of the proposal [Rule 14a-8(b)]. ~~A stockholder is limited to making only one proposal to an issuer per year.~~

Improper Shareholder Proposals

Management may exclude a proposal under any of the following circumstances:

1. If the proposal as submitted is, under the laws of the issuer's domicile, not a proper subject for action by security holders; or

2. If the proposal relates to the redress of a personal claim or grievance against the issuer or any other person, or if it is designed to result in a benefit to the proponent or to further a personal interest, which benefit or interest is not shared with other security holders at large.

3. If the proposal relates to operations ~~which account for less than 5 percent of the issuer's total assets at the end of its most recent fiscal year, and for less than 5 percent of its net earnings and gross sales for its most recent fiscal year, and is not otherwise~~ significantly related to the issuer's business. *if economically racially, social cause*

4. If the proposal consists of a recommendation or request that the management take action with respect to a matter relating to the conduct of the ordinary business operations of the issuer.

Management may also omit the proposal if it was included at either of the last two annual meetings and the security holder failed without good cause to present the proposal for action. If substantially the same proposal has been previously presented in management's proxy statement within the preceding five calendar years, it may be omitted from any meeting held within the next three calendar years, provided that: (1) if submitted at only one meeting during the preceding period it received less than 5 percent of the total votes cast on the proposal; or (2) if submitted at two meetings, it received less than 8 percent of the votes at the time of its second submission; or (3) if submitted at three or more meetings, it received less than 10 percent of the vote at the time of its latest submission [Rule 14a-8(c)].

If management asserts that a proposal may properly be omitted, it must notify the Commission not later than 50 days prior to the date that the preliminary copies of the proxy materials are filed. The SEC requires advance filing of proxy material so that it may examine it for compliance with the applicable disclosure requirements. A copy of the proposal, with its supporting statement, is to be included accompanied by a statement of reasons why management deems omission to be proper in the particular case. At the same time, management must notify the security holder and supply him with a copy of the reasons for omission. [Rule 14a-8(d)] If the security holder wishes to dispute the omission, the SEC will determine the issue, with appeal to the courts being available.

Proxy Expenses

Who pays for the expense of a proxy fight and whose expenses are to be paid? Expenses incurred in a proxy fight can reach large sums. There is the expense of printing and mailing the items required under the proxy rules. There are newspaper ads, countermailings to reply to the oppositions, and even attorneys' fees. Often a professional proxy soliciting firm is hired to handle and manage the campaign and, of course, it must be paid. In one case, the following fees were incurred:

1. $106,000 incurred by the old board to defend its position.
2. $28,000 allowed by the new board to pay unreimbursed expenses of the old board.
3. $127,000 expenses incurred by the new board in waging their successful contest.

The shareholders ratified this action. These expenses were incurred at 1950s prices. The expenses today would be much greater. In upholding the payment of these expenses the court stated:

The rule then which we adopt is simply this: In a contest over policy, as compared to a purely personal power contest, corporate directors have the right to make reasonable and proper expenditures, subject to the scrutiny of the courts when duly challenged, from the corporate treasury for the purpose of persuading the stockholders of the correctness of their position and soliciting their support for policies which the directors believe, in all good faith, are in the best interests of the corporation. The stockholders, moreover, have the right to reimburse successful contestants for the reasonable and bona fide expenses incurred by them in any such policy contest, subject to like court scrutiny. That is not to say, however, that corporate directors can, under any circumstances, disport themselves in a proxy contest with the corporation's moneys to an unlimited extent. Where it is established that such moneys have been spent for personal power, individual gain or private advantage, and not in the belief that such expenditures are in the best interests of the stockholders and the corporation, or where the fairness and reasonableness of the amounts allegedly expended are duly and successfully challenged, the courts will not hesitate to disallow them. . . . [*Rosenfeld* v. *Fairchild Engine & Airplane Corp.*, 128 N.E. 2d 291 (1955) (N.Y. Ct. of App.).]

Case Questions

1. Does it appear odd that when the shareholders throw out the old board, thereby determining that its policies were not in the best interests of the corporation, they must pay the expenses of the discredited board?

2. Realistically, how can a court distinguish between instances where the directors are seeking personal power, as opposed to the corporation's best interests? In most situations will not the two elements be intertwined?

False or Misleading Proxy Statements

When one alleges that a proxy statement is materially false or misleading, what is the requisite burden of proof? The *TSC Industries* case that follows examines the question in the context of a proxy solicitation matter.

TSC INDUSTRIES v. NORTHWAY
426 U.S. 438 (1976)

(Authors' note: Northway, a shareholder of TSC, brought suit against National Industries and TSC Industries over the former's acquisition of the latter. National purchased 34 percent of TSC's voting securities from its founder and his family. The founder and his son resigned from the TSC board, and five National nominees were placed on the board. The TSC board subsequently approved a proposal to liquidate TSC and have its assets acquired by National in an exchange of stock. TSC and National issued a joint proxy statement to their shareholders recommending approval of the proposal. After the transaction was approved and consummated Northway instituted legal action alleging that the proxy statement was incomplete and materially misleading. The National nominees on the TSC board abstained when the board voted on the proposal. However, Northway claimed that the proxy material should have noted the fact that one nominee was the chairman of the board and another the chairman of the board's executive committee. Also, the material did not note that National might be deemed a parent of TSC and failed to disclose some unfavorable information about the proposal in a letter from an investment banking firm. The Supreme Court examined the entire proxy state-

ment and held that there was no evidence that the omissions were materially misleading as a matter of law thereby entitling the plaintiff to a summary judgment. What follows is the Court's discussion of what constitutes a material fact in a proxy statement.)

MR. JUSTICE MARSHALL *delivered the opinion of the Court.*

The proxy rules promulgated by the Securities and Exchange Commission under the Securities Exchange Act of 1934 bar the use of proxy statements that are false or misleading with respect to the presentation or omission of material facts. We are called upon to consider the definition of a material fact under those rules. . . .

As we have noted on more than one occasion, § 14(a) of the Securities Exchange Act "was intended to promote 'the free exercise of the voting rights of stockholders' by ensuring that proxies would be solicited with 'explanation to the stockholder of the real nature of the questions for which authority to cast his vote is sought.' "

Doubts as to the critical nature of the information misstated or omitted will be commonplace. And particularly in view of the prophylactic purpose of the Rule and the fact that the content of the proxy statement is within management's control, it is appropriate that these doubts be resolved in favor of those the statute is designed to protect.

We are aware, however, that the disclosure policy embodied in the proxy regulations is not without limit. Some information is of such dubious significance that insistence on its disclosure may accomplish more harm than good.

The general standard of materiality that we think best comports with the policies of Rule 14a-9 is as follows: An omitted fact is material if there is a substantial likelihood that a reasonable shareholder would consider it important in deciding how to vote. It does not require proof of a substantial likelihood that disclosure of the omitted fact would have caused the reasonable investor to change his vote. What the standard does contemplate is a showing of a substantial likelihood that, under all the circumstances, the omitted fact would have assumed actual significance in the deliberations of the reasonable shareholder. Put another way, there must be a substantial likelihood that the disclosure of the omitted fact would have been viewed by the reasonable investor as having significantly altered the "total mix" of information made available.

Case Questions

1. The proxy statement prominently displayed the fact that National owned 34 percent of the TSC stock and that 5 of the 10 TSC directors were National nominees. It also recited the positions of those National nominees with National. Knowing those facts, do you believe the Supreme Court made a reasonable decision in this case?

2. How is a court to know whether a reasonable shareholder would consider a particular fact important in deciding how to vote?

Tender Offers

Although defined neither by statute nor Commission rule, the term "tender offer" is generally understood to mean a public offer or solicitation to purchase securities during a given time at a given price. The tender offer can take three forms: (1) an offer for cash, (2) an offer to exchange for securities of another corporation, or (3) a combination of cash and securities.

Usually a tender offer consists not only of a direct communication to the shareholders, but also of a publicity campaign designed to convince the shareholders to tender their stock. This public campaign will consist of such activities as the placement of very large advertisements in the print media, *The Wall Street Journal* for example. At the opposite end of the spectrum is the private transaction in which a shareholder sells a controlling interest in a corporation to another person. The latter is not a tender offer requiring compliance with the tender offer rules. The line that divides a traditional tender offer from an unregulated sale of control is located at an uncertain position. When facing unconventional methods of acquiring controlling blocks of stock, the courts have said that the distinguishing characteristic of conduct subject to tender offer regulation is the exertion of pressure on the shareholders to make an ill-considered, hasty decision to sell. In *Wellman* v. *Dickinson*, 475 F.Supp. 783 (1979), a court determined that an intensive private solicitation of a controlling block of stock, with a premium offered for the shares and a strict time limitation on acceptance, constituted a tender offer.

Now let us examine the rules that govern tender offers.

Acquisition of 5 Percent or More of a Company's Securities

Section 13(d) of the '34 Act requires that any person acquiring directly or indirectly beneficial ownership of more than 5 percent of any registered equity security of a class file a report disclosing the acquisition. He or she must file a Schedule 13D with the SEC, the issuer of the security, and each exchange where the security is traded within 10 days of such acquisition. Schedule 13D requires such information as the identity of all persons on whose behalf the purchases have been made, the number of shares owned, the source and amount of the funds used in making the purchases, and the purpose in making the purchases. If the purpose is to acquire control of the issuer of the securities, then any plans to liquidate the issuer, sell its assets, merge it, or make any major change in its business or corporate structure must be disclosed. The purpose of this disclosure requirement is to supply public shareholders, facing a cash tender offer for their shares, with information regarding the qualifications and intentions of the offeror. This enables the incumbent management the opportunity to present its position to the shareholders. The legislation was drafted for the benefit of shareholders and not to aid or hamper either management or the corporate raider. Lacking such data a shareholder confronts several unknowns. He could simply sell his shares in the market. Or, he might await a more favorable tender offer. If one never appears, it may be too late to tender his shares. He might tender all of his shares in the hope that they will all be taken. Lastly, he might simply refuse the offer and continue to hold the stock. The decision is a hard one but the risks should be reduced if the stockholder has the Schedule 13D information to give some guidance.

Regulation of Tender Offers

It is unlawful for any person, directly or indirectly, to make a tender offer for any registered security if after consummation he or she would be the beneficial owner of more than 5 percent of that security, unless at the time the offer is first made such person has filed the requisite documents with the SEC. Section 14(d)(1) of the '34 Act requires the filing of the information specified in Section 13(d) and such other information as the Commission may prescribe by rule as in the public interest or for the protection of investors. Copies of all requests or invitations for tenders and advertisements making such a tender offer must also be filed with the Commission. Any additional material subsequent to the initial solicitation shall be filed not later than the time such material is first published or sent or given to security holders. Copies of all statements furnished to security holders and the Commission shall be sent to the issuer not later than the date such material is first published or sent or given to any security holder.

Tender offers that involve the offer of securities in exchange for the target company's securities must be registered under the terms of the '33 Act. Otherwise, the information that must be furnished the security holders, issuer, and Commission is similar to that required of a cash tender offer.

Communications by Management During the Tender Offer

The management of the company subject to the tender offer may support it, oppose it, or remain neutral. Management has no legal duty to comment on the offer. However, if management or any other person (such as a competing tender offeror) wishes to recommend acceptance or rejection of the offer, he must file a Schedule 14D with the Commission. Schedule 14D includes copies of all solicitations or recommendations to accept or reject the offer; the identity of the security involved and the name and address of the issuer; the reasons for recommending acceptance or rejection; the name, address, and relationship to the issuer or maker of the tender offer of the persons filing the schedule; and the identity of anyone retained by the person filing the schedule to engage in solicitation or make recommendations regarding the offer, accompanied by the terms of such employment [§ 14(d)(4)(a)]. This schedule must be filed at the time that copies are first published, sent or given to the security holders.

Management need not file this schedule if it is merely sending a "wait and see" communication. Such a communication is exempt under Rule 14(d)-2 if it only requests that the security holders defer making a decision while management studies the offer. To avoid undue stalling, management must communicate their recommendation at least 10 days prior to the expiration of the tender offer.

Withdrawal and Proration

Under Section 14(d)(5) the depositor of securities may withdraw them at any time until the expiration of 7 days after the time definitive copies of the offer are first published or sent or given to security holders, and at any time after 60 days from the date of the original tender offer. The effect of this provision is to create a minimum tender offer duration of 7 days.

Where the tender offer is for less than all the outstanding equity securities of a class, and where a greater number of securities is deposited within the first 10 days than the person is bound or willing to take up, the securities shall be taken up on a pro rata basis [14(d)(6)].

Fraudulent, Deceptive, or Manipulative Practices

Under Section 14(e) it is unlawful for any person to make any untrue statement of a material fact or omit to state any material fact necessary in order to make the statements made, in the light of the circumstances under which they are made, not misleading, or engage in any fraudulent, deceptive, or manipulative acts or practices, in connection with any tender offer or request or invitation for tenders, or any solicitation of security holders in opposition to or in favor of any such offer, request, or invitation.

Issuer's Tender Offer for its Own Securities

If the issuer is making a cash tender offer for its own securities it is exempt from the foregoing rules [§ 14(d)(8)]. However, the issuer must be cognizant of both Section 10(b) and Rule 10b-5. If all material information was not disclosed and the market price rises, individuals who tendered shares may sue.

Corporate Takeovers

When one company wishes to acquire a second company, one method of doing so is by utilizing a merger. If the boards of directors and shareholders of both corporations vote their approval, the merger will be consummated. However, if the board of directors of the target company opposes the takeover, no merger will occur. Under corporate law the board must approve such a proposal before the shareholders are allowed to vote on the matter.

Does this mean that only friendly takeovers occur? No. There are hostile acquisitions. If the directors of the target corporation, which is the object of the acquisition, resist the takeover, the acquiring company can resort to a tender offer. If a sufficient number of shares in the target company are tendered, the acquiring company votes them at a stockholders meeting to elect their own candidates to the board. Then this new board approves a merger, the acquiring company as the majority shareholder in the target corporation votes in favor of the proposal, the board of the acquiring company votes in favor of the proposal, the shareholders of the acquiring company vote their approval, and the merger is consummated.

Problems for the shareholders can arise if the acquiring company is interested only in a friendly merger. If the board rejects the merger proposal, the shareholders may miss out on a chance to receive a favorable price for their stock. If this does occur, may the shareholders successfully sue the directors for violations of the federal securities laws and a breach of their fiduciary duties under state law? The following case provides some answers.

PANTER v. MARSHALL FIELD & CO.
646 F.2d 271 (1981)

(Authors' note: In December 1977 the stock of Marshall Field was trading at about $22 per share. Carter Hawley Hale approached Field and proposed a merger offering $36 per share for Field stock. The Field directors rejected the proposal and filed suit against Carter to stop any merger. Shortly thereafter, Field announced expansion plans, including expansion into a shopping mall where Carter already had a department store. This created additional antitrust problems in any merger between the two department store chains. In February of 1978 Carter announced its intention to offer $42 in cash and stock for each Field share if the Field board would meet certain conditions. The directors of Field continued their opposition and Carter withdrew its proposed offer. Field stock, which had traded as high as $34 per share, dropped to $19. A class action lawsuit against Field and its directors was brought by some Field shareholders. They argued that they had been wrongfully deprived of an opportunity to dispose of their shares at a substantial premium over the market (with total damages in excess of $200 million) when the defendants successfully fended off the Carter takeover. The shareholders claimed the defendants'

actions violated the antifraud provisions of the federal securities laws and breached their fiduciary duties. After the presentation of the shareholders' case, the trial court judge found insufficient evidence to go to the jury and ruled in favor of the defendants. The Court of Appeals upheld that ruling. The court said that the Supreme Court had clearly ruled in Sante Fe Industries v. Green, 430 U.S. 462 (1977), that a breach of fiduciary duty by a director does not violate the federal securities laws. Deceptive actions by a director are necessary for his conduct to come within Section 10(b) of the securities provisions. The shareholders argued that the directors desired to perpetuate their control over Field and therefore adopted a policy of rejecting all acquisition offers for the company, regardless of the potential benefit of the offers to the shareholders. The court ruled that even if such a policy could be proved, or even if a failure by the directors to disclose the existence of such a policy could be proved, it would not constitute the element of manipulation or deception necessary for a securities law violation. The shareholders also argued that this policy of independence and the defensive acquisition of stores to create antitrust obstacles to a merger constituted a breach of fiduciary duty under the state corporate law. The court ruled that it did not.)

PELL, Circuit Judge

Under applicable Delaware corporate law, claims such as those made by the plaintiffs are analyzed under the "business judgment" rule.

However, rather than proceeding under the business judgment rule, the plaintiffs here seek to apply a different test in the takeover context, and propose that the burden be placed upon the directors to establish the compelling business purpose of any transaction which would have the effect of consolidating or retaining the directors' control. In light of the overwhelming weight of authority to the contrary, we refuse to apply such a novel rule to this case.

On the resistance to prior approaches, we have established above that evaluation and response to such approaches is within the scope of the directors' duties. The plaintiffs have presented no evidence of self-dealing, fraud, overreaching or other bad conduct sufficient to give rise to any reasonable inference that impermissible motives predominated in the board's consideration of the approaches. The desire to build value within the company, and the belief that such value might be diminished by a given offer is a rational business purpose. The record reveals that appropriate consideration was given to each individual approach made to Marshall Field & Company. . . . Therefore the presumption of good faith afforded by the business judgment rule applies, and the plaintiffs cannot survive the motion for directed verdict.

The plaintiffs also contend that the "defensive" acquisitions of the five Liberty House stores and the Galleria were imprudent, and designed to make Field's less attractive as an acquisition, as well as to exacerbate any antitrust problems created by the CHH merger. It is precisely this sort of Monday-morning-quarterbacking that the business judgment rule was intended to prevent. Again, the plaintiffs have brought forth no evidence of bad faith, overreaching, self-dealing or any other fraud necessary to shift the burden of justifying the transactions to the defendants. On the contrary, there was uncontroverted evidence that such expansion was reasonable and natural. Thus even if the desire to fend off CHH was among the motives of the board in entering the transactions, because the plaintiffs have failed to establish that such a motive was the sole or primary purpose, as has been required by Delaware law, . . . the mere allegation, or even some proof, that a given transaction was made on "unfavorable" terms does not meet the fairly stringent burden the business judgment rule imposes on plaintiffs.

To adopt the rule the plaintiffs seek to impose here would substantially obtenebrate the reasonableness of consideration by boards of directors of a tender offer, and is in direct conflict with the duty of directors to evaluate proposed business combinations on their merits and oppose those detrimental to the well-being of the corporation even if that is at the expense of the short term interests of individual shareholders.

The judgment of the district court is affirmed.

Case Question

1. Why didn't the shareholders sell their stock on the open market when the price of the Field stock had increased?

Case Comment

In March of 1982, the Field board accepted a merger offer of $25.50 a share from Batus Inc. (a subsidiary of a British concern, B.A.T. Industries). The merger was consummated after the per-share price was raised to $30 to ward off a potential hostile takeover by a group of private investors headed by Carl Icahn.

Panter v. *Marshall Field* is not the only court decision that grants almost complete immunity to directors. Other cases also exhibit a strong reluctance on the part of the judiciary to "second guess" the decisions of a board of directors. The result is to confer very broad discretion on the board in deciding whether to oppose a proposed takeover and in selecting appropriate defensive tactics. The result can also be that the shareholders miss a financial opportunity.

Defensive Strategies to Avoid a Takeover

We have already observed the tactics used by Marshall Field to avoid a takeover. A basic tactic is to sue your opponent arguing that the acquisition will violate the antitrust laws and that the mechanics of the takeover violate the federal securities laws. There are additional options that we will now examine.

The corporation can adopt a form of an antitakeover amendment. Such amendments make unfriendly takeovers extremely difficult. A typical one requires a super majority, perhaps 80 percent of the shares outstanding, for the approval of a merger. Sometimes these amendments are passed before a takeover threatens and are referred to as "shark repellent."

A "white knight" is the term given to a company that rescues the target company from its unfriendly suitor. The target company loses its independence, but at least it gets to choose with whom it will merge. The target seeks out a white knight who will outbid the unfriendly suitor in the tender offer battle. If a bidding war erupts with the appearance of the white knight, the shareholders of the target company stand to make a lot more money.

Frequently the white knight will desire an advantage over the competition and the target will want something that makes it less attractive to the unfriendly suitor. A lock-up device is just the answer. It takes the form of a contract between the target and the white knight. Typically the contract will involve the sale of a very valuable asset to the white knight. It would be a Pyrrhic victory for the unfriendly suitor to win control of a company whose prize asset has just been sold. Lock-ups are generally approved by the courts. One that wasn't involved a sale of *the* prize asset of the corporation that took effect only *if* a third party gained control of the target. See *Mobil* v. *Marathon*, 669 F.2d 366 (1981).

Sometimes the target will respond to a hostile takeover by mounting its own takeover of the acquiring company. See Step 2 in The Anatomy of a Complex Takeover chart in this chapter. This is often called the Pac Man strategy: Devour your opponent before it can get you.

Oftentimes the target company will grant "golden parachute" employment contracts to its management team. These lucrative arrangements guarantee the officer's salary and benefits for a given number of years in the event that control of the corporation shifts.

Saying nasty things about one's opponent may cause him to leave the scene if he does not enjoy the glare of adverse publicity. When Bendix acquired a stake in RCA, the latter's chairman publicly queried how, if the chairman of Bendix was unable to manage his own affairs, he could manage RCA's. In a similar type of dispute American Express sued McGraw-Hill for libel over some of the latter's comments. The suit was eventually voluntarily dismissed.

Finally, the management of the target company can embark on a "rule or ruin" strategy. Sometimes called a "scorched earth" policy, it involves the adoption of arrangements that could severely damage the corporation if there were a change in control. A bank loan might be negotiated specifying that a higher unfavorable interest rate will automatically be charged in the event of a control change. A collective bargaining agreement might be signed with the workforce that will require a significant wage increase in the event of a hostile takeover.

The following table briefly illustrates events that occurred in a takeover that generated a great deal of publicity.

Anatomy of a Complex Corporate Takeover

1. Bendix begins a hostile takeover of Martin Marietta in August 1982. It makes a tender offer for Marietta's stock at $43 per share.
2. Martin Marietta responds with a tender offer for a majority interest in Bendix at $75 per share.
3. Lawsuits by both parties are filed alleging violations of federal securities and various state laws.
4. United Technologies makes a tender offer for Bendix stock at $75. It announces an agreement with Martin Marietta to split up Bendix. Marietta will buy the aerospace and electronics portion of Bendix and United Technologies will retain the remainder of Bendix.
5. Bendix schedules a stockholders meeting to amend its charter in a manner to prevent a hostile takeover. The measures fail to pass.
6. Bendix acquires 70 percent of Marietta and Marietta acquires 50 percent of Bendix. The first stockholder to obtain a stockholders' meeting can vote their stock to throw out the board that controls the company, put in their new directors, and have the new directors cancel the company's bid for the opposing company.
7. Allied Corporation offers $85 per share for Bendix in a friendly takeover if United Technologies & Martin Marietta agree to halt their actions.
8. Bendix swaps 54 percent of Martin Marietta to Martin Marietta in return for Marietta's 50 percent interest in Bendix. The remainder of the Marietta stock acquired by Bendix goes to Allied.

9. In January 1983 the shareholders of Bendix and Allied approve the merger of Bendix into Allied. The acquisition is a $1.9 billion transaction that gives Allied the ownership of Bendix and 38% of Martin Marietta.

10. The expenses of the hostile takeover battle show in the financial results for the fourth quarter of 1982:

> Bendix shows a $19.3 million loss.
> Martin Marietta shows a loss of $2.4 million.
> Allied is profitable but suffers a 22 percent drop in earnings.

11. Shortly after the Allied acquisition is formally approved by the shareholders, both the chairman and president of Bendix resign. Their company has lost its independence, and they have lost a significant corporate role, but they have "golden parachutes" to cushion the fall.

State Antitakeover Statutes

While the federal government comprehensively regulates the issuance and trading of securities, the states do have a regulatory role. Notably, many states have passed "blue sky" laws to regulate securities transactions within their borders.

A number of years ago state legislatures began passing antitakeover statutes. The purpose was to prevent hostile takeovers of corporations incorporated or physically located within the state. A hostile takeover of such a company by a distant organization was considered detrimental to the interests of the state. A large distant organization may not be sensitive to local social and economic needs. Contributions to charities might be reduced or plants closed with a serious effect on the employment situation by executives who possess no ties to the community. On the other hand, the financial position and prestige of a state could be improved if it attracted corporations seeking refuge from hostile acquisitions.

These statutes, which exempt from regulation any takeover of which the target corporation approves, place serious obstacles in the path of a hostile takeover. Target corporations began to utilize them as another defensive tactic and potential acquiring corporations went to federal court to have them struck down as unconstitutional. The legal controversy was finally settled by the Supreme Court in 1982.

The *MITE* case that follows requires some explanation. In this case the Supreme Court declares the Illinois antitakeover statute unconstitutional under the Commerce Clause because it imposes an excessive burden on interstate commerce. When reading the case, you will see comments indicating that the Illinois law also conflicts with federal legislation (the Williams Act) and is therefore preempted under the Constitution's Supremacy Clause. Those comments are not the decision of the Court, because a majority of the Court does not agree with them. They were included because they demonstrate how state antitakeover statutes normally operate and how the tender offer process functions. Just remember that the law is held unconstitutional because it impermissibly interferes with interstate commerce.

EDGAR v. MITE CORPORATION
102 S.Ct. 2629 (1982)

MR. JUSTICE WHITE

The issue in this case is whether the Illinois Business Takeover Act is unconstitutional under the Supremacy and Commerce Clauses of the Federal Constitution.

Appellee MITE Corporation and its wholly-owned subsidiary, MITE Holdings, Inc., are corporations organized under the laws of Delaware with their principal executive offices in Connecticut. Appellant James Edgar is the Secretary of State of Illinois and is charged with the administration and enforcement of the Illinois Act.

On January 19, 1979, MITE initiated a cash tender offer for all outstanding shares of Chicago Rivet and Machine Co., a publicly held Illinois corporation, by filing a Schedule 14D-1 with the Securities and Exchange Commission in order to comply with the Williams Act. The Schedule 14D-1 indicated that MITE was willing to pay $28.00 per share for any and all outstanding shares of Chicago Rivet, a premium of approximately $4.00 over the then-prevailing market price. MITE did not comply with the Illinois Act, however, and commenced this litigation on the same day by filing an action in the United States District Court for the Northern District of Illinois. The complaint asked for a declaratory judgment that the Illinois Act was preempted by the Williams Act and violated the Commerce Clause.

The District Court entered final judgment on February 9, declaring that the Illinois Act was preempted by the Williams Act and that it violated the Commerce Clause.

The United States Court of Appeals for the Seventh Circuit affirmed.

We first address the holding that the Illinois Takeover Act is unconstitutional under the Supremacy Clause. We note at the outset that in passing the Williams Act, which is an amendment to the Securities and Exchange Act of 1934, Congress did not also amend § 28(a) of the 1934 Act, 15 U.S.C. § 78bb(a). In pertinent part, § 28(a) provides as follows:

> Nothing in this chapter shall affect the jurisdiction of the securities commission (or any agency or officer performing like functions) of any state over any security or any person insofar as it does not conflict with the provisions of this chapter or the rules and regulations thereunder.

Thus Congress did not explicitly prohibit states from regulating takeovers; it left the determination whether the Illinois statute conflicts with the Williams Act to the courts.

The issue thus is, whether the Illinois Act frustrates the objectives of the Williams Act in some substantial way.

The Williams Act, passed in 1968, was the congressional response to the increased use of cash tender offers in corporate acquisitions, a device that had "removed a substantial number of corporate control contests from the reach of existing disclosure requirements of the federal securities laws." The Williams Act filled this regulatory gap. The Act imposes several requirements.

There is no question that in imposing these requirements, Congress intended to protect investors. But it is also crystal clear that a major aspect of the effort to protect the investor was to avoid favoring either management or the takeover bidder.

To implement this policy of investor protection while maintaining the balance between management and the bidder, Congress required the latter to file with the Commission and furnish the company and the investor with all information adequate to the occasion. With that filing, the offer could go forward, stock could be tendered and purchased, but a stockholder was free within a specified time to withdraw his tendered shares. He was also protected if the offer was increased.

The Illinois Act requires a tender offeror to notify the Secretary of State and the target company of its intent to make a tender offer and the material terms of the offer 20 business days before the offer becomes effective. During that time, the offeror may not communicate its offer to the shareholders. Meanwhile, the target company is free to disseminate information to its shareholders concerning the impending offer. The contrast with the Williams Act is apparent. Under that Act, there is no precommencement notification requirement; the critical date is the date a tender offer is "first published or sent or given to security holders."

We agree with the Court of Appeals that by providing the target company with additional time within which to take steps to combat the offer, the precommencement notification provisions furnish incumbent management with a powerful tool to combat tender offers, perhaps to the detriment of the stockholders who will not have an offer before them during this period. These consequences are precisely what Congress determined should be avoided, and for this reason, the precommencement notification provision frustrates the objectives of the Williams Act.

For similar reasons, we agree with the Court of Appeals that the hearing provisions of the Illinois Act frustrate the congressional purpose by introducing extended delay into the tender offer process. The Illinois Act allows the Secretary of State to call a hearing with respect to any tender offer subject to the Act, and the offer may not proceed until the hearing is completed. The Secretary may call a hearing at any time prior to the commencement of the offer, and there is no deadline for the completion of the hearing. Although the Secretary is to render a decision within 15 days after the conclusion of the hearing, that period may be extended without limitation. Not only does the Secretary of State have the power to delay a tender offer indefinitely, but incumbent management may also use the hearing provisions of the Illinois Act to delay a tender

offer. The Secretary is required to call a hearing if requested to do so by, among other persons, those who are located in Illinois "as determined by post office address as shown on the records of the target company and who hold of record or beneficially, or both, at least 10% of the outstanding shares of any class of equity securities which is the subject of the takeover offer." Since incumbent management in many cases will control, either directly or indirectly, 10% of the target company's shares, this provision allows management to delay the commencement of an offer by insisting on a hearing.

As we have said, Congress anticipated investors and the takeover offeror be free to go forward without reasonable delay. The potential for delay provided by the hearing provisions upset the balance struck by Congress by favoring management at the expense of stockholders. We therefore agree with the Court of Appeals that these hearing provisions conflict with the Williams Act.

The Court of Appeals also concluded that the Illinois Act is preempted by the Williams Act insofar as it allows the Secretary of State of Illinois to pass on the substantive fairness of a tender offer. Under § 137.57.E of the Illinois law, the Secretary is required to deny registration of a takeover offer if he finds that the offer "fails to provide full and fair disclosure to the offerees . . . or that the take-over offer is inequitable. . . ." The Court of Appeals understood the Williams Act and its legislative history to indicate that Congress intended for investors to be free to make their own decisions. We agree.

The Commerce Clause provides that "Congress shall have Power . . . [t]o regulate Commerce . . . among the several states." U.S. Const., Art. 1, § 8, cl. 3. Not every exercise of state power with some impact on interstate commerce is invalid. A state statute must be upheld if it "regulates evenhandedly to effectuate a legitimate local public interest, and its effects on interstate commerce are only incidental . . . unless the burden imposed on such commerce is clearly excessive in relation to the putative local benefits." The Illinois Act violates these principles for two reasons. First, it directly regulates and prevents, unless its terms are satisfied, interstate tender offers which in turn would generate interstate transactions. Second, the burden the Act imposes on interstate commerce is excessive in light of the local interests the Act purports to further.

States have traditionally regulated intrastate securities transactions, and this Court has upheld the authority of states to enact "blue-sky" laws against Commerce Clause challenges on several occasions.

The Illinois Act differs substantially from state blue-sky laws in that it directly regulates transactions which take place across state lines, even if wholly outside the State of Illinois.

It is therefore apparent that the Illinois statute is a direct restraint on interstate commerce and that it has a sweeping extraterritorial effect. Furthermore, if Illinois may impose such regulations, so may other states; and interstate commerce in securities transactions generated by tender offers would be thoroughly stifled.

Appellant also contends that Illinois has an interest in regulating the internal affairs of a corporation incorporated under its laws. The Act applies to corporations that are not incorporated in Illinois and have their principal place of business in other states. Illinois has no interest in regulating the internal affairs of foreign corporations.

We conclude with the Court of Appeals that the Illinois Act imposes a substantial burden on interstate commerce which outweighs its putative local benefits. It is accordingly invalid under the Commerce Clause.

Case Question

1. If the various states were allowed to enact statutes similar to that of Illinois, how would the securities industry function in an efficient manner?

Securities and the Uniform Commercial Code

Article 8, "Investment Securities," of the Uniform Commercial Code governs securities. It does not regulate securities in the same manner as do the blue-sky or federal securities laws. Rather it regulates the mechanical process of negotiating and transferring securities. While securities are negotiable instruments they do not operate under the rules of Article 3 on commercial paper.

Transfer

A security that is delivered without an indorsement gives the purchaser the right to have the necessary indorsement supplied (8-307). The purchaser will not become a bona fide purchaser until the indorsement is supplied. A security can be indorsed in blank (including bearer) or with a special indorsement. Unless otherwise agreed the indorser assumes no obligation that the security will be honored by the issuer. An indorsement purporting to be only part of a security representing units intended by the issuer to be separately transferable is effective to the extent of the indorsement (8-308). Both physical delivery and indorsement are necessary to transfer (negotiate) a security (8-309). A purchaser who purchases for value in good faith and without notice of any adverse claim and who takes delivery of a security in bearer form or with an indorsement is a bona fide purchaser (8-302). A bona fide purchaser acquires the rights in the security that his transferor had or had actual authority to convey, and also takes the security free of any adverse claim (8-301).

Restrictions on Transfer

A corporation may place restrictions on the transfer of its stock if the state statute, corporate charter, or bylaws so provide. The courts will enforce such restrictions if they are reasonable. Typically such transfer restrictions appear only in close corporations. Oftentimes the restrictions will require that the corporation or other shareholders be given the first option to purchase such shares. Under the UCC, such restrictions, unless noted conspicuously on the security, will be ineffective except against a person with actual knowledge of it (8-204).

Warranties

A person who transfers a security to a purchaser for value warrants that the transfer is effective and rightful, that the security is genuine and has not been materially altered, and that he knows no fact that might impair the validity of the security. A person presenting a security for registration of transfer or for payment or exchange warrants to the issuer that he is entitled to the registration, payment, or exchange. A purchaser for value without notice who receives a new, reissued, or reregistered security on registration of transfer warrants only that he has no knowledge of any unauthorized signature in a necessary indorsement (8-306).

Wrongful Transfers

Any person against whom the transfer of a security is wrongful (for any reason) may reclaim possession of the security or obtain possession of a new security evidencing the same rights or have damages except against a bona fide purchaser (8-315). If the transfer is based on a forged indorsement, the owner may reclaim the security even from a bona fide purchaser, unless the bona fide purchaser has received a new, reissued, or reregistered security on registration of transfer (8-315, 8-311). Even in the latter case, the original owner of the security transferred by a forged indorsement is protected. On demand the issuer must issue a like security to the true owner unless such delivery would result in an overissue (8-404). Overissue means the issue of securities in excess of the amount which the issuer has corporate power to issue. If delivery would result in an overissue, then the owner can force the issuer to either purchase an identical security that is reasonably available for purchase or, if unavailable, to pay the owner the last price that the owner or last purchaser for value paid for it with interest from date of demand (8-104). The issuer's recourse is against the forger or the guarantor of the forger's signature.

There is a statute of frauds section applicable to investment securities (8-319). The provisions are similar to those applicable to the sale of goods, except that it is applicable regardless of the securities' value.

Registration

Whenever a security is presented to the issuer with a request to register transfer, the issuer must honor the request if (1) the security is properly indorsed, (2) reasonable assurance is given that the indorsements are genuine, (3) the issuer has no duty to inquire into adverse claims or has discharged such duty, (4) the applicable law relating to the collection of taxes has been complied with, and (5) it is a rightful transfer or is to a bona fide purchaser (8-401). The issuer may require a guarantee of the indorsement signature (8-402). The issuer has the duty to inquire into an adverse claim if he receives a written notification of an adverse claim at a time and in a manner that affords a reasonable opportunity to act prior to issuing the new security. The issuer can discharge this duty by any reasonable means, including notifying the adverse claimant that the transfer will be registered unless, within 30 days from the date of mailing the notification, either an appropriate restraining order is issued; or a sufficient indemnity bond is filed with the issuer to protect against any loss suffered by complying with the adverse claim (8-403).

If a security is lost, destroyed, or stolen, the issuer must issue a new security if the owner so requests before the issuer has notice that a bona fide purchaser has acquired the security, files a sufficient indemnity bond with the issuer, and satisfies any other reasonable requirement of the issuer (8-405).

Review Problems

1. Company X has steadily been losing ground in a competitive industry. This loss is reflected in a downward slide of the market price of its stock. One shareholder attributes the problems of the company to an entrenched inefficient management. Management learns that this shareholder-critic has recently begun purchasing additional stock. Her ownership now approaches 4 percent of the outstanding shares. With her wealth and the depressed price of the stock she can probably acquire in excess of 15 percent of the stock. This will probably give her control because the stock is so widely held. Management, in total, owns less than 1 percent. To stave her off, management is considering two courses of action. (1) Redemption of a large number of shares, thereby inflating her percentage ownership above 5 percent.

[handwritten margin notes: fraudulent, manipulative practices]

[handwritten margin notes: ok - show Business judgment reasoning]

This would necessitate her divulging her intentions in a Schedule 13D report. (2) Issuance of convertible debentures, to friends of management, in such an amount that if immediately converted the outstanding stock would double, thereby halving her percentage ownership. What do you think of such tactics? Would your views differ if (a) the redemption had been previously approved to obtain treasury stock for executive stock option plans or (b) additional financing was required for plant expansion and convertible debentures offered the most attractive feature?

2. Mosinee Paper Corporation has slightly more than 800,000 shares of common stock outstanding. It has only this one class of equity security and it is registered under terms of the '34 Act. Rondeau begins making large purchases of Mosinee stock in the over-the-counter market. By May 17, 1971, he had acquired 40,413 shares, which is in excess of 5 percent. He did not file a Schedule 13D but continued to purchase substantial blocks of stock. By July 30, 1971, he had acquired over 60,000 shares. On that date he received a letter from the chairman of the board stating that his activity had given rise to numerous rumors and was creating problems under the securities laws. Rondeau immediately stopped his purchase and consulted his attorney. On August 25, 1971, he filed a Schedule 13D. Mosinee seeks an injunction to prohibit him from voting or pledging his stock and from acquiring additional shares, requiring divestiture of the stock already owned, and for damages. Rondeau readily concedes his violation. He claims that it is merely a technical violation and proves that it was due to a lack of familiarity with the securities laws. He further claims that neither Mosinee nor its shareholders have been harmed. Would denial of the injunction be justified? [*Rondeau* v. *Mosinee Paper Corporation*, 422 U.S. 49 (1975)].

3. Is it appropriate that shareholders lack the absolute right to have their corporation adopt a stance on a political, racial, social, or religious cause?

4. Should a court enforce a restriction on the transfer of stock that requires a subsequent purchaser to be approved by the remaining shareholders?

[handwritten margin notes: family-owned closely-held]

5. Why would a corporation desire to restrict the free transfer of its stock? What disadvantages do stock transfer restrictions place on a corporation?

6. If a shareholder's proposal is one that management can properly exclude from the proxy form, yet is of a harmless nature, should management permit the matter to go before the shareholders?

7. A corporation is the target of an unfriendly takeover attempt by one of its own stockholders. When it appears that the corporation cannot remain independent, it seeks out a white knight. The target's board of directors issues a large block of stock to the white knight. The effect is to dilute the shareholdings of the unfriendly suitor and to help thwart the takeover. The chairman of the target company is to have a position in the corporation that results from the merger with the white knight. The unsuccessful shareholder–suitor now sues the directors of the target company, arguing that the issuance of the stock was improper because it was done only to affect the control of the corporation. The directors argue the business judgment rule in defense. Will the directors be victorious in the lawsuit? [*Treadway* v. *Care*, 638 F.2d 357 (1980)].

Yes

pg. 459

8. Shariff is a citizen of a foreign country. He has just purchased 6 percent of the outstanding common shares of Stratosphere Metals, Inc., a company listed on a national stock exchange. He has instructed the brokerage firm that quietly and efficiently handled the execution of the purchase order that he wants the securities to be held in street name. What are the legal implications of the above transactions? Shariff must:
   (a) Immediately have the securities registered in his own name and take delivery of them.
   (b) Sell the securities because he has violated the antifraud provisions of the Securities Exchange Act of 1934.
   (c) Notify Stratosphere Metals, Inc., of his acquisition and file certain information as to his identity and background with the SEC.
   (d) Notify the SEC and Stratosphere Metals, Inc., only if he acquires 10 percent or more of Stratosphere's common shares.

will go over 5% cut-off 8. 13(d)

(Adapted from CPA Exam Law Problem #1, Question #41, taken from the November 1980 exam. © American Institute of Certified Public Accountants, Inc., 1980.)

9. Section 5(c) of the '33 Act declares it unlawful for any person to make use of any means of communication in interstate commerce or of the mails to offer to sell or buy through the use of any prospectus or otherwise any security, unless a registration statement has been filed as to such security. SEC Rule 135 (a)(2) provides that it is not an offer to sell where a notice is communicated to any class of security holders of such issuer or of another issuer advising them that it proposes to offer its securities to them in exchange for other securities presently held by such security holders. Chris-Craft is battling Bangor Punta for Control of Piper Aircraft. The Piper family agrees to exchange their stock for Bangor Punta securities. Bangor Punta in turn will

attempt to gain control of Piper by acquiring in excess of 50 percent of Piper's outstanding stock. The management of both companies make this announcement through the issuance of a press release. The release mentions that Bangor Punta will make an exchange offer to all Piper shareholders for a package of Bangor Punta securities to be valued at not less than $80 per Piper share. The release mentions that a registration statement will be filed. Chris-Craft sues alleging, inter alia, that the press release is an unlawful offer to sell. Is it? [*Chris-Craft* v. *Bangor Punta*, 426 F. 2d 569, (1970), 430 U.S. 1 (1977)].

10. This chapter has illustrated the broad power bestowed on directors. When they exercise that power in takeover battles, the business judgment rule provides them with significant protection from shareholder lawsuits. Would the rights of shareholders be protected to a greater degree if the law removed the right of directors to take action in takeover battles, and instead provided that such struggles were to be decided solely by the results of a shareholder referendum?

A Business Organization's Duties to Its Employees and the Public

Part Six

The Employer-Employee Relationship

19

With the prominent role that organized labor occupies in our society today, it may be surprising to learn that the first federal labor law was not enacted until 1926. It was not until 1935 that Congress passed comprehensive legislation regulating the field of labor-management relations. Before examining the current state of labor law, let us first take a brief look into the past.

Early American labor law was common law that could be traced back to British roots. The law emphasized the rights of the employer and was hostile to the concept of unions. Concerted union action constituted a criminal conspiracy. Whereas one individual might ask the employer for improved wages and working conditions, if two or more such workers joined together in making a request it would be illegal. In the Philadelphia Cordwainer's case of 1806 a jury convicted a group of bootmakers of criminal conspiracy for their agreement not to work for any employer who paid less than a specified wage. It was not until 1842 that the threat of criminal prosecution for engaging in union activities was removed. In that year a court ruled that the formation of a union to achieve a closed shop, through its members' refusal to work for an employer who would not agree to hire only union members, was not criminal. The court ruled that the formation of the union did not have a criminal objective and it was not using criminal means to achieve its objective.

The civil law continued to place many obstacles in the path of the union movement. Many employers required their employees to sign "yellow dog" contracts. This was a form of employment contract where the employee agreed, as a condition of employment, not to join a union. If a union started an organizing attempt in the labor force of such an employer, the employer would fire any employee who had joined the union and seek an injunction against the union to prevent its interference with the contractual relationship between the employer and its employees. The threat of losing one's job combined with an injunction against the union

Historical Background of Labor Law

usually resulted in the failure of the unionization attempt. Today the yellow dog contract is against public policy and is unenforceable by a court.

The antitrust laws were also successfully wielded by employers in their opposition to unions. When a union called for a boycott of the employer's product, the employer's response was often to bring an antitrust suit against the union seeking to collect treble damages for the losses caused by the boycott. The Supreme Court upheld the legality of such suits as late as 1921. But the Norris-LaGuardia Act, passed in 1932, limited the power of federal courts to intervene in labor-management disputes. In 1935 Congress passed the Wagner Act. These two laws provide wide, but not complete, immunity to unions from the antitrust laws. Generally, unions will not violate the antitrust statutes if they are acting in their self-interest and do not combine their activities with a nonlabor group.

The National Labor Relations Act

Congress provided labor with broad rights and a significant mechanism to protect them when it passed the National Labor Relations Act (Wagner Act) in 1935. This was the first comprehensive federal labor law, and it was "pro-labor" legislation. It gave workers the right to organize and bargain collectively. To protect these rights it declared certain actions by an employer to be illegal (unfair labor practices). The National Labor Relations Board (NLRB) was created to administer the law. The NLRB fulfills two functions: (1) it administers the representation process, whereby employees vote as to whether they want a union to represent them in dealing with their employer; and (2) it investigates and prevents unfair labor practices.

Employee Rights and Union Elections

Labor law does not give rights to unions—it gives rights to employees. The employees have these rights whether they belong to a union or not. Since employees frequently exercise their rights through a union, people often incorrectly believe that it is the union that has the rights and that individuals who do not belong to a union lack such rights. Under the law employees have the right to form, join, or assist a labor organization; to bargain collectively through representatives of their own choosing; to engage in concerted activities (strikes, picketing, handbilling, etc.) for the purpose of collective bargaining, or for other mutual aid and protection; and the right to refrain from such activities in certain instances.

Notice that the law speaks of the rights of "employees." That is because there are two sides to the issue. Labor, the employees, makes up one side of the equation; the other side is made up of management. We are speaking of labor-management relations. They deal with each other in arms-length transactions across the bargaining table. There is an adversarial nature to the relationship under the law. A person is either on one side of the table as an employee or that person belongs elsewhere. If one does not come within the law's definition of an employee, one is not covered by the protections of the law. An employee is defined as everyone except agricultural workers, domestic servants, persons employed by a parent or spouse, independent contractors, supervisors, persons employed by employers that are subject to the Railway Labor Act (railroads and airlines), and local, state, or federal government employees (except the postal service).

Management personnel come within the term "supervisor." A supervisor is defined as a person who has the authority, in the interest of the employer, to hire, transfer, suspend, lay off, recall, promote, discharge, assign, reward, or discipline other employees, or responsibility to direct them, or to adjust their grievances, or effectively recommend such action if the exercise of such action requires the use of independent judgment, and is not merely carrying out the action in a routine or clerical capacity.

An election to determine whether the employees desire to have a union represent them will be conducted by the NLRB if an election petition is filed with it. The employer, the employees, or a labor organization can file a petition. If someone other than the employer files it, the petition must be supported by at least thirty percent of the employees. Once the NLRB determines that it has legal jurisdiction over the matter (that the workers are in fact employees under the law), it starts the election machinery. Sometimes all the parties agree on the issues and a consent election will be held. If that is not possible, the election will be a contested one. The NLRB then holds hearings to determine the appropriate bargaining unit, the eligibility of various employees to vote, and so forth. The NLRB will conduct the election by secret ballot. A majority vote of those actually voting, not those eligible to vote, will decide the outcome. See the following examples.

Example 1

Employees eligible to vote 100   Actually voted 80
Vote tally: No union 43   United Auto Workers Union 37
Result: no union representation

Example 2

Employees eligible to vote 100   Actually voted 80
Vote tally: No union 30   United Auto Workers 30   Brotherhood of
     Electrical Workers 20
Result: Runoff election between the two highest vote totals because no one
     choice received a majority
Runoff election: No union 28   United Auto Workers 52
Result: United Auto Workers will represent the employees

The Duty of Fair Representation

If the employees select a union to be their representative for collective bargaining purposes, that union will be the exclusive representative of all the employees in the bargaining unit. It will not represent only those employees who voted for it or become union members. The contract that it bargains with the employer in regard to wages, hours, and working conditions will be applicable to all the employees. An employee who disagrees with the union cannot obtain different terms from the employer for himself. The employer has signed a labor contract and must live up to its terms. Because of this legally imposed doctrine of exclusivity, the law has also created a counterbalancing obligation—the duty of fair representation. The union must represent everyone in the bargaining unit—union members, nonunion individuals, union members who belong to a dissident group, etc.—with fairness and in good faith. Fair representation and equal treatment are not the same. A union does not have to provide equal benefits to everyone. Differences that have a logical basis and a rational purpose are allowable. For instance, a union can negotiate a contract that provides higher wages to skilled workers than to nonskilled, longer vacation periods for workers with lengthy periods of employment, or a night shift differential to provide higher pay to those working what is generally considered to be a less attractive job shift. Such contractual terms are not unfair since everyone, men, women, blacks, whites, unionists, and nonunionists, have these terms apply to them. Each person will get the higher pay rate on obtaining a skilled job or qualify for the longer vacation when his or her length of service reaches the qualifying number of years. A breach of the duty of fair representation would be to exclude a group, such as women or nonunion individuals, from the skilled jobs or the night shift.

Operation of the grievance machinery in a contract will frequently lead to fair representation disputes. Most labor contracts have a grievance mechanism to handle disputes that arise between the parties to the contract. The grievance process will have several steps, or successively higher levels in the union-management hierarchy, at which a mutual attempt is made to settle the dispute. Often the process will culminate in an outside arbitrator being brought in to make a final and binding decision. A union cannot casually refuse to take a worker's grievance to arbitration or take it to arbitration with no investigation or preparation. This would be a breach of the duty of fair representation. Yet a union need not arbitrate every grievance. It will have met its duty if, after a thorough review, it declines to arbitrate the issue because the issue lacks merit under the contract. A union that breaches this duty can face unfair labor practices charges and a lawsuit for damages.

In the next case we observe a lawsuit brought against an employer alleging wrongful discharge, and against the union claiming a breach of duty of fair representation. In this case the union unsuccessfully attempted to avoid paying damages to the worker.

BOWEN v. *U.S. POSTAL SERVICE*
103 S. Ct. 588 (1983)

*(Authors' Note: Bowen was discharged after an al-
tercation with a fellow employee. He filed a grievance
with the union, and at each step of the grievance
process the responsible union officer recommended
pursuing it. For no apparent reason, the union's
national office refused to take the matter to arbitration. A jury determined that he had been wrongfully
discharged and that the union had breached its duty
of fair representation. His lost benefits and wages
totaled $52,954. It was determined that the employer
should pay $22,954 and the union the remaining
amount. The court decided the union should pay for
the time period following the date that Bowen would
have been reinstated if his grievance had been arbi-
trated. The union argued that it should have no
back-pay liability since it was the employer who made
the discharge decision.)*

JUSTICE POWELL *delivered the opinion of the Court.*

Of paramount importance is the right of the
employee, who has been injured by both the
employer's and the union's breach, to be made
whole. Were it not for the union's failure to
represent the employee fairly, the employer's
breach "could [have been] remedied through
the grievance process to the employee-
plaintiff's benefit."

It would indeed be unjust to prevent the
employee from recovering in such a situation.
It would be equally unjust to require the employer to bear the increase in the damages
caused by the union's wrongful conduct. It is
true that the employer discharged the employee wrongfully and remains liable for the
employee's backpay. The union's breach of its
duty of fair representation, however, caused
the grievance procedure to malfunction resulting in an increase in the employee's damages.
Even though both the employer and the union
have caused the damage suffered by the employee, the union is responsible for the increase in damages and, as between the two
wrongdoers, should bear its portion of the
damages.

Although each party participates in the
grievance procedure, the union plays a pivotal
role in the process since it assumes the responsibility of determining whether to press an employee's claims. The employer, for its part,
must rely on the union's decision not to pursue
an employee's grievance.

In the absence of damages apportionment
where the default of both parties contributes to
the employee's injury, incentives to comply with
the grievance procedure will be diminished.

Case Questions

1. Does the decision in this case illustrate an anti-union bias on the part of the
   Supreme Court?
2. In deciding whether to take a grievance to arbitration what type of factors will
   the union take into consideration?

Right-to-Work Laws

As a general proposition an employee will be free to join, or refrain from
joining, a union. There is an exception for what are called union security
clauses. Under certain circumstances the employer and the union can
agree to a union security clause. Such a clause may require the worker to
join the union within a certain number of days in order to remain employed. This is called a union shop provision. (Requiring a person to

belong to a union to be hired, called the closed shop, is illegal.) Or, they may agree to a provision that requires the worker to pay the union an amount equal to the union dues, while leaving the worker free not to join the union. This is called the agency shop. Unions believe that, because they must represent all the workers and all the workers receive the benefits of the contract, all the workers should financially contribute to the support of the union. Union opponents believe that if they do not want a union to represent them, they should not be forced to pay or join the union.

Thus, we see that one can join or not join a union, unless there is a form of a union security clause present. We now have arrived at another exception. If the state has passed a right-to-work law, an employee can never be forced to join or contribute to a union. A right-to-work law prohibits the requirement of union membership as a condition of employment. When Congress passed the Taft-Hartley Act in 1947 it included what is called Section 14(b)—the right-to-work provision. This provision allows the states to outlaw union security clauses within their borders. Twenty states have passed such laws.

not Indiana

Employer Unfair Labor Practices

To protect the rights given workers, Congress has prohibited certain conduct by the employer. Engaging in this prohibited activity constitutes an employer unfair labor practice. The employer is not to:

1. Interfere with, restrain, or coerce employees in the exercise of their rights.
2. Dominate or interfere with a labor organization.
3. Discriminate against an employee with the purpose of encouraging or discouraging membership in a labor organization.
4. Discriminate against an employee who has participated in a NLRB proceeding.
5. Refuse to bargain with the union.

Frequently action by an employer will violate more than one section of the law. If an employer fires an employee because the employee is trying to organize a union, the employer has violated both items 1 and 3 above. Threatening to fire a person for union activity is just as illegal as actually firing the person. Not only penalizing but rewarding an employee for certain activity can be illegal. Thus, if an employer who faces a union organizing campaign suddenly grants a wage increase and extended vacation time, he has committed unfair labor practices in violation of items 1 and 3 above. The employer in such an instance is just as effectively interfering with the free exercise of the employees' rights and attempting to discourage union membership by granting benefits as by voicing threats.

It is important to remember that it is the individual who possesses these labor law rights. He has these rights whether or not he belongs to a union.

In the next case an employee signed a petition seeking to have a former employee rehired. The signing of a petition is protected activity under the labor law. It is a concerted action by more than one person for the mutual aid of another and protection for themselves if they should ever find themselves in the same situation. The employer attempted to avoid the unfair labor practice charge by arguing that the signer, who was discharged for her action, was not an employee. If the woman had been management, she would not have had such protection and her discharge would not have violated the law. The employer lost the case.

NLRB v. HENDRICKS CO. RURAL ELEC. MEMBR. CORP.
102 S.Ct. 216 (1981)

JUSTICE BRENNAN *delivered the opinion of the Court.*

Mary Weatherman was the personal secretary to the general manager and chief executive officer of respondent Hendricks County Rural Electric Membership Corporation. . . . In May 1977 she signed a petition seeking reinstatement of a close friend and fellow employee, who had lost his arm in the course of employment with Hendricks, and had been dismissed. Several days later she was discharged.

Weatherman filed an unfair labor practice charge with the National Labor Relations Board. . . . Hendricks' defense, *inter alia,* was that Weatherman was denied the Act's protection because as a "confidential" secretary she was impliedly excluded from the Act's definition of "employee". . . . The Administrative Law Judge . . . rejected this argument. . . . He also determined that Hendricks had discharged Weatherman for activity—signing the petition—protected by § 7 of the Act. . . . The Board affirmed "the rulings, findings, and conclusions of the Administrative Law Judge," and ordered that Weatherman be reinstated with back pay. . . .

The employees covered by the Act were defined in § 2(3): "The term 'employee' shall include any employee . . . but shall not include any individual employed as an agricultural laborer, or in the domestic service of any family or person at his home, or any individual employed by his parent or spouse." Although the Act's express exclusions did not embrace confidential employees, the Board was soon faced with the argument that all individuals who had access to confidential information of their employers should be excluded, as a policy matter, from the definition of "employee." The Board rejected such an implied exclusion, finding it to have "no warrant under the Act." . . . But in fulfilling its statutory obligation to determine appropriate bargaining units, . . . for which broad discretion has been vested in the Board, . . . the Board adopted special treatment for the narrow group of employees with access to confidential, labor-relations information of the employer. The Board excluded these individuals from bargaining units composed of rank-and-file workers. . . . The Board's rationale was that management should not be required to handle labor relations matters through employees who are represented by the union with which the [c]ompany is required to deal and who in the normal performance of their duties may obtain advance information of the [c]ompany's position with regard to contract negotiations, the disposition of grievances, and other labor relations matters. . . .

The Court's ultimate task here is, of course, to determine whether the Board's "labor nexus" limitation on the class of confidential employees who, although within the definition of "employee," . . . may be denied inclusion in bargaining units has a reasonable basis in law. . . . Clearly the NLRB's longstanding practice of excluding from bargaining units only those confidential employees satisfying the Board's labor-nexus test, rooted firmly in the Board's understanding of the nature of the collective bargaining process, and Congress' acceptance of that practice, fairly demonstrates that the Board's treatment of confidential employees does indeed have a reasonable basis in law. . . .

In this Court respondent Hendricks does not argue that Weatherman came within the labor-nexus test as formulated by the Board, but rather concedes that Weatherman did not have confidential duties with respect to labor policies. . . . Because there is therefore no dispute in this respect, and in any event no suggestion that the Board's finding regarding labor nexus was not supported by substantial evidence, we conclude that the Court of Appeals erred in holding that the record did not support the Board's determination that Weatherman was not a confidential employee with a labor nexus. We therefore reverse the judgment of the Court of Appeals . . . insofar as enforcement of the Board's order was denied, and remand with direction to enter an order enforcing the Board's order.

Case Question   1. Does the decision in this case reflect a realistic common-sense method of determining which confidential employees enjoy the protection of labor law?

When an employer commits an unfair labor practice by discharging or otherwise penalizing an employee for the exercise of rights protected under the labor law, the NLRB has the power to remedy the situation. The employer is ordered to cease the improper activity and reinstate, with back pay, the individual to his or her previous position with the company. The NLRB order of reinstatement with back pay was upheld by the Supreme Court in the Hendricks case that you just read.

The Taft-Hartley Act

In 1947 Congress passed the Taft-Hartley Act (Labor Management Relations Act). This law significantly amended the National Labor Relations Act. It added union unfair labor practices to the law in an attempt to fairly balance the rights of employees and the employer. It created the Federal Mediation and Conciliation Service. This agency provides mediation, conciliation, and arbitration services to management and labor when they need assistance in settling a particularly difficult labor dispute. The law also created a mechanism for the President of the United States to enter labor disputes that so imperil the national health or safety as to constitute a national emergency. The right-to-work provision, which allows the states to banish union security clauses, it also contained in Taft-Hartley.

The law prohibits unions from engaging in certain types of conduct. A union that ignores these prohibitions commits a union unfair labor practice. A labor organization is not to:

1. Restrain or coerce employees in the exercise of their rights.
2. Cause or attempt to cause an employer to discriminate against an employee.
3. Refuse to bargain collectively with the employer.
4. Engage in secondary activity such as secondary strikes and boycotts.
5. Charge excessive or discriminatory membership fees.
6. Engage in certain types of featherbedding practices.

Because the labor law gives certain rights to employees, it is just as illegal for the union to interfere with the exercise of those rights as it is for the employer to do so. For example, a labor organization commits an unfair labor practice if it uses violence, or threats of violence, against employees who oppose the union. It is also illegal if the union attempts to get the employer to fire an employee who belongs to another union, or who engages in anti-union activity. The issue of excessive membership fees is not usually a problem. Most unions realize that charging union dues at an extremely high rate will simply discourage membership in the union and be self-defeating. A union engages in illegal featherbedding when it causes an employer to pay for services that are not performed. Hence, many practices that one might regard as featherbedding are not prohibited under the labor law. Consider a union that negotiates with an employer a contract that provides for the presence of an elevator operator in automatic elevators. Since the elevator is operated merely by pushing the button of the desired floor, one might consider the operator's presence unnecessary. In fact, the operator's presence may be of little value to the elevator's passengers, but the operator is providing a service and the contract provision is not illegal featherbedding.

Both the employer and the union have the obligation to bargain in good faith with respect to wages, hours, and other terms and conditions of employment. This obligates both parties to meet at reasonable times and confer in good faith concerning those subjects, or the negotiation of a collective bargaining agreement, or other questions that arise under a pre-existing agreement. However, the law provides that while they must bargain in good faith, neither party is compelled to agree to a proposal of the other, nor are they required to make a concession.

Good faith bargaining is evidenced by a serious attempt to negotiate a contract or settle a grievance. The parties will need to demonstrate that they have made a vigorous effort to reach an agreement. While neither party is obligated to make a concession to the other, total inflexibility by a party, with no willingness to engage in the give-and-take of negotiations, will call into question the good faith of that party. If the employer has information necessary for the bargaining process and the union requests such information, it must be supplied. The personnel office of the employer may have data on the racial, ethnic, or sexual makeup of the workforce that the union needs to fulfill its duty of fair representation in an arbitration or bargaining context.

Wages, hours, and working conditions are called mandatory subjects of bargaining. The union and the employer must bargain with regard to them. Included within these very broad topics are such items as pension and profit-sharing plans, vacations, insurance coverage, seniority provisions, discipline procedures, safety regulations, and break time for meals. If the parties wish to bargain over additional subjects they may generally do so, but one party cannot unilaterally force the other to bargain over these matters. These are called voluntary bargaining subjects. Benefits paid to already retired employees are a frequent subject of voluntary bargaining. There is a very limited number of topics, illegal subjects, over which the parties are forbidden to bargain. The demand that a person belong to a union to be hired is an example of such a forbidden subject.

The case that follows examines the difficult question of what employer decisions so directly affect the employees that they constitute a mandatory bargaining subject and what decisions are a function of owning the business and need not be bargained about, despite their impact on the employees.

FIRST NATIONAL MAINTENANCE v. NLRB

452 U.S. 666 (1981)

(Authors' note: First National Maintenance decided to cancel a maintenance contract with a Greenpark nursing home. The decision was purely a financial one. It discharged the employees used to staff the Greenpark operation and refused to bargain about the decision with the union recently selected by those employees. The union charged that this refusal constituted a violation of labor law.)

JUSTICE BLACKMUN *delivered the opinion of the Court.*

Must an employer, under its duty to bargain in good faith "with respect to wages, hours, and other terms and conditions of employment," . . . negotiate with the certified representative of its employees over its decision to close part of its business?

A fundamental aim of the National Labor Relations Act is the establishment and maintenance of industrial peace to preserve the flow of interstate commerce. *NLRB* v. *Jones & Laughlin Steel Corp.,* 301 U.S. 1 (1937). Central to achievement of this purpose is the promotion of collective bargaining as a method of defusing and channeling conflict between labor and management. Congress ensured that collective bargaining would go forward by creating the National Labor Relations Board and giving it the power to condemn as unfair labor practices certain conduct by unions and employees that it deemed deleterious to the process, including the refusal "to bargain collectively."

Although parties are free to bargain about any legal subject, Congress has limited the mandate or duty to bargain to matters of "wages, hours, and other terms and conditions of employment." A unilateral change as to a subject within this category violates the statutory duty to bargain and is subject to the Board's remedial order. Conversely, both employer and union may bargain to impasse over these matters and use the economic weapons at their disposal to attempt to secure their respective aims. Congress deliberately left the words "wages, hours, and other terms and conditions of employment" without further definition, for it did not intend to deprive the Board of the power further to define those terms in light of specific industrial practices.

Nonetheless, in establishing what issues must be submitted to the process of bargaining, Congress had no expectation that the elected union representative would become an equal partner in the running of the business enterprise in which the union's members are employed. Despite the deliberate open-endedness of the statutory language, there is an undeniable limit to the subjects about which bargaining must take place. . . .

Some management decisions, such as choice of advertising and promotion, product type and design, and financing arrangements, have only an indirect and attenuated impact on the employment relationship. Other management decisions, such as the order of succession of layoffs and recalls, production quotas, and work rules, are almost exclusively "an aspect of the relationship" between employer and employee. The present case concerns a third type of management decision, one that had a direct impact on employment, since jobs were inexorably eliminated by the termination, but had as its focus only the economic profitability of the contract with Greenpark, a concern under

these facts wholly apart from the employment relationship. This decision, involving a change in the scope and direction of the enterprise, is akin to the decision whether to be in business at all, "not in [itself] primarily about conditions of employment, though the effect of the decision may be necessarily to terminate employment." At the same time, this decision touches on a matter of central and pressing concern to the union and its member employees; the possibility of continued employment and the retention of the employees' very jobs. Nonetheless, in view of an employer's need for unencumbered decisionmaking, bargaining over management decisions that have a substantial impact on the continued availability of employment should be required only if the benefit, for labor-management relations and the collective bargaining process, outweighs the burden placed on the conduct of the business.

A union's interest in participating in the decision to close a particular facility or part of an employer's operations springs from its legitimate concern over job security. There is no dispute that the union must be given a significant opportunity to bargain about these matters of job security as part of the "effects" bargaining mandated by § 8(a)(5). And, under § 8(a)(5), bargaining over the effects of a decision must be conducted in a meaningful manner and at a meaningful time, and the Board may impose sanctions to insure its adequacy.

Moreover, the union's legitimate interest in fair dealing is protected by § 8(a)(3), which prohibits partial closings motivated by anti-union animus, when done to gain an unfair advantage.

Management's interest in whether it should discuss a decision of this kind is much more complex and varies with the particular circumstances. If labor costs are an important factor in a failing operation and the decision to close, management will have an incentive to confer voluntarily with the union to seek concessions that may make continuing the business profitable. At other times, management may have great need for speed, flexibility, and secrecy in meeting business opportunities and exigencies. It may face significant tax or securities consequences that hinge on confidentiality, the timing of a plant closing, or a reorganization of the corporate structure. The publicity incident to the normal process of bargaining may injure the possibility of a successful transition or increase the economic damage to the business. The employer also may have no feasible alternative to the closing, and even good-faith bargaining over it may be both futile and cause the employer additional loss.

We conclude that the harm likely to be done to an employer's need to operate freely in deciding whether to shut down part of its business purely for economic reasons outweighs the incremental benefit that might be gained through the union's participation in making the decision, and we hold that the decision itself is *not* part of § 8(d)'s "terms and conditions." . . . over which Congress has mandated bargaining.

JUSTICE BRENNAN, *with whom* JUSTICE MARSHALL *joins, dissenting.*

The Court bases its decision on a balancing test. It states that "bargaining over management decisions that have a substantial impact on the continued availability of employment should be required only if the benefit, for labor-management relations and the collective-bargaining process, outweighs the burden placed on the conduct of the business."

I cannot agree with this test, because it takes into account only the interests of *management;* it fails to consider the legitimate employment interests of the workers and their Union. I therefore agree with the Court of Appeals that employers presumptively have a duty to bargain over a decision to close an operation, and that this presumption can be rebutted by a showing that bargaining would be futile, that the closing was due to emergency financial circumstances, or that, for some other reason, bargaining would not further the purposes of the National Labor Relations Act.

Case Questions

1. How powerful a hand will a union hold in its bargaining with an employer over the "effects" of a partial closure, when the employer has already made the most significant decision to terminate operations? Would a strike by the union be an effective threat against the employer during this "effects" bargaining?

2. Viewing this decision from a labor-management perspective, does this decision enhance the collective bargaining process?

3. Is it illegal for a company to bargain with a union over the decision to partially close a business?

Strikes

If the parties have bargained in good faith without being able to achieve an agreement, the workers are free to go on strike. This is called an economic strike. The employer is free to lock out the employees in an effort to pressure them into a settlement. The strike and lockout are the economic weapons of the union and management. They are tactics that can be used to achieve goals that the parties have thus far been unable to obtain at the bargaining table. A strike is simply the cessation of work.

The striking employees have no legal right to reclaim their jobs. The employer may either temporarily or permanently replace them with other workers.

If an unfair labor practice by the employer has either caused the strike, or lengthened its duration, the legal situation is different. Such a strike is called an unfair labor practice strike. At the termination of the strike the striking workers have the right to return to their jobs. If the employer has hired strike replacements, the replacements cannot be retained in place of the strikers.

Since the employer will frequently find it to be in his self-interest to maintain production while bargaining continues, lockouts are not usually used by the employer. Likewise, the employer will often not hire replacements for the striking employees. Most strikes are of a relatively short duration and the employer knows that the strike will only be a temporary interruption. The problems and expenses in training a new group of employees is greater than the problems caused by a short strike.

If the parties have met all their obligations under the law but a strike results because an agreement has not been reached, the strike is legal. The employees stop working and begin to picket outside their employer's place of business. The idea is to put economic pressure on the employer by halting the work at his facility and by preventing others from doing business with him. The picketing is supposed to achieve the latter objective. The picket line is designed to convince people that they should not cross it to do business, make deliveries, etc. The pickets may not lawfully prevent persons physically from crossing the line. Its mere presence, however, may deter persons from crossing it. The strikers' dispute is with their employer, and their action is aimed directly at the employer. This is called a primary dispute. The fact that others may be affected by the picket line is only incidental.

Secondary Activity

It is an unfair labor practice for a union to engage in secondary activity. Secondary activity occurs when the union directly attempts to force a neutral third party to cease doing business with another. In a labor dispute it is part of the rules of the game for either party to directly exert whatever economic pressure it can on the other party. It goes beyond the rules when an attempt is made to use an outside neutral party as a lever in the dispute. Suppose a striking union approaches an important supplier of the struck employer and informs the supplier that, unless deliveries cease, his place of business will be picketed. This conduct by the union constitutes illegal secondary activity. The union has no direct labor dispute with the supplier. The supplier is a neutral in the dispute. The supplier is to make an independent decision whether or not the picket line at the employer's place of business is to be honored. He cannot be legally threatened with a picket line at his business if deliveries are not halted.

If another party is helping the employer in a direct manner to defeat the strike, that party is not a neutral and the union can legally picket it. Where a struck company arranged for some repair companies to perform repair work that it was legally obligated to perform for its customers, union picketing of the repair companies was held legal. In *NLRB* v. *Bus. Mach. & Office Appliance*, 228 F.2d 533 (1955), the court said that these repair companies were allies of the struck company and were performing work normally performed by the striking workers. Thus, they were not true neutrals to a labor dispute that the law is written to protect.

Legal issues of a secondary nature can easily flare up when more than one employer is located at one physical location—called a common situs. Company A may be working at a construction site. Likewise, Company B is working at that same site. If B's employees go on strike, may they picket at that construction site? Yes, so long as their employer is engaged in his normal business at that common situs and the picketing clearly discloses that the dispute is with Company B. Company A is not destined to have its operations at the site shut down by the picketing. Under the "separate gate doctrine" an entrance can be created for the exclusive use of the nonstruck companies. The union representing the striking employees of Company B cannot picket in front of this gate. Thus, persons can come to work and deliveries can be made to Company A without anyone having to cross a picket line.

Consumer Boycotts

Sometimes the union will attempt to increase the economic pressure on the employer by mounting a consumer boycott of the employer's product. Such an appeal to the public for a boycott is primary activity and is legal. The distribution of handbills, the placement of newspaper ads, or the conducting of a rally to call for such a boycott by the public constitute the exercise of one's free speech rights. However, questions of secondary activity arise if such a campaign is located at the place of business of a neutral party. Suppose a group of fruit packers strike their employer. The employer sells apples to retail stores. The union then pickets and passes out handbills in front of these retail stores. The signs and literature request only that the store customers refrain from purchasing their employer's apples. The pickets are not there when deliveries and pickups are made to the stores, nor are they present when the store employees come and go. Thus, the picketing does not prevent anyone from going to work or doing business with the retail stores, except insofar as some people do not buy the specific apples. The Supreme Court held this union action to be legal in *NLRB* v. *Fruit & Veg. Packers*, 377 U.S. 58 (1964). It was not held to be secondary action because the union was merely following the struck product and closely confined their action to the primary dispute with their employer. It would have been illegal if the union had asked the public not to shop at the store for any grocery products. This would constitute an illegal secondary boycott of the neutral retail stores.

Job-related injuries cost the workforce and the economy staggering amounts. These costs are both financial and social. The legal history of worker compensation for work-related injuries and of worker protection from unsafe working conditions is a sorry one. As the industrial revolution grew in this country the law did not develop a corresponding duty for employers to furnish a safe workplace. Indeed, the early common law provided the injured worker little chance for compensation. First, an injured worker put his job in jeopardy by suing or threatening to sue an employer who may have been neligent in providing faulty tools or an unsafe workplace. Similarly, witnesses, often fellow workers, were hesitant to testify against the employer.

Occupational Safety and Health

The greatest deterrents to compensation, however, were the legal defenses available to the employer. The early common law developed and established three rules ordinarily used by an employer: (1) if an injury was caused by *another employee*, the common law held that the employer was not liable—this was called the fellow-servant rule; (2) if the job was dangerous and had known risks, the employer could defend on the basis of the employee's "assumption of the risks" when he or she took the job; and (3) if the *employee's* lack of care played a part in the injury, then the employer could defend on the basis of contributory negligence. These defenses have been limited substantially today.

In response to a growing public awareness of both the cost to our society of work-related injuries and the increasing evidence that places of work once thought relatively safe (working in air-polluted factories, for example) do pose substantial threats to human life, Congress passed The Williams Steiger Occupational Safety and Health Act of 1970. This Act became effective April 28, 1971. The Act establishes the Occupational Safety and Health Administration. The public has adopted the abbreviation of OSHA to refer to both the Act and the administrative agency.

The Act applies to all persons engaged in a business affecting commerce who have employees. It does not cover those places of work already covered by the Coal Mine Health and Safety Act or the Atomic Energy Act. Also, municipal, county, state, and federal government workers are not directly covered by OSHA. Many states, however, do have occupational safety acts or plans that include municipal, county, and state employees.

The Act places two major duties on employers. First, employers must furnish to employees a place of employment that is *free* from *recognized hazards* that are *likely* to cause *death* or *serious physical harm*. This statement is referred to as the general duty clause of the Act, but it applies *only* where no specific safety standard promulgated under the Act is applicable. A second and related duty is for the employer to comply with all appropriate standards for safety. The Secretary of Labor and his agents have promulgated literally thousands of safety standards that apply to employers. Most of these safety standards were developed from earlier "national consensus standards" developed by nationally recognized standards producing organizations such as the American National Standards Institute and the National Fire Protection Association. These very specific safety standards cover subjects such as the proper construction and maintenance of equipment, machine guarding, and fire and injury prevention procedures. They also specify the type of personal protective equipment worn by employees and training requirements necessary to insure safe work practices.

In addition to complying with the two major duties above, employers with more than 10 employees must also keep substantial records and make reports on all work-related injuries and deaths. It must be remembered that the Act does not provide for compensation for injuries nor affect workers' compensation. It is not compensatory in concept. It is preventative.

To insure compliance with the standards promulgated by OSHA, the statute allows an inspector to enter any place of work at any reasonable time and in a reasonable manner. In *Marshall* v. *Barlow's Inc.*, 436 U.S. 307 (1978), the Supreme Court held this provision unconstitutional, as a violation of the Fourth Amendment's protection against unreasonable searches and seizures. The Court ruled that if the owner of the business does not give voluntary consent to such an inspection, OSHA must obtain a search warrant if it is to gain entry to the premise. The search warrant requirement does not place a serious obstacle in front of OSHA. Under the Court's decision, OSHA need not show probable cause in the criminal-law sense to obtain the warrant from a federal judge. It need meet only a lesser standard. If OSHA demonstrates that the business has been chosen on the basis of a general administrative plan for the enforcement of the Act derived from, for example, the dispersion of employees in various types of industries across a given area, the warrant is to be issued. Thus, a showing that reasonable legislative or administrative standards for conducting the inspection are satisfied with respect to the particular business will justify the grant of a warrant. Of course, if OSHA has specific evidence of an existing violation by a business, that evidence will justify the issuance of a search warrant and the entry into the business against the owner's wishes.

If on inspection a violation is believed to exist, a citation will be issued. The employer is given a reasonable time to remedy the situation (not longer than six months); if the citation or one of the safety standards used is believed unreasonable the employer may seek to appeal the citation or standard to an administrative law judge assigned to the case by the Occupational Safety and Health Commission; this appeal is an adversary one with the appealing party being opposed by the Secretary of Labor. The decision of this judge becomes final unless a member of the Commission agrees to hear an appeal to the full Commission. If the Commission rules against the employer, or if the Commission refuses to hear an appeal, the employer may appeal the case to the U.S. Court of Appeals for the circuit in which the violation allegedly occurred or where the party has his principal place of business.

Any employer who *willfully* and *repeatedly* violates the general duty clause may be assessed a civil penalty of not more than $10,000 for each violation; the fine is $1000 for a simple violation. However, any employer who fails to correct a violation may be assessed not over $1000 each day such failure continues.

The Act takes cognizance of the lack of protection afforded employees at common law who wished to charge their employers with maintaining unsafe work areas. Under the Act, an employee may report a violation of a standard to an area OSHA office on a complaint form that allows the reporter to remain anonymous. If there is an imminent danger alleged or if the complaint appears valid an inspection will follow within a reasonable time. If the employee wishes to reveal his identity, he may walk with the inspector during the visit to the work site. If he believes he has been discriminated against because he reported the company, he may file a complaint with OSHA and, if the charges are proven, he may be compensated.

At this early stage it is not easy to assess the impact of the Act. Since many cases have now reached the appellate court level it can be assumed that enforcement activity is well under way. Much of the litigation to date centers on the interpretations of the general duty clause. Although detailed safety standards are available and cover most usual employment circumstances, they cannot cover every situation. The general duty clause was intended to impose safety duties where no specific expressed standards were available. It should be noted that where a general duty clause violation is alleged, the common law fellow-servant rule and the defenses of assumption of risk and contributory negligence are not available to the employer.

Because this new law will grow and perhaps change by means of court interpretations of the general duty clause, we present here some of the decisions construing its meaning. As stated above, the general duty clause requires each employer to furnish employees a place of employment free from recognized hazards that might cause death or serious physical harm. Much litigation has focused on the meaning of the words "recognized hazards." Is an employer liable for a violation of the Act where injury was caused by an event it could not have foreseen? In one of the early cases a foreman of the employer was riding on the running board of a front-end loader as it descended a small hill at a construction site. The engine stalled, causing a loss of control over the vehicle and resulting in the death of the foreman. [*National Realty & Construction Co.* v. *OSAHRC*, 489 F. 2d 1257 (D.C. Cir., 1973).] The court held that the hazard of riding on heavy equipment was "recognized" and was "likely to cause death or serious physical harm" but held that there was no violation of the general duty clause because it was not shown what the employer could have done to eliminate the hazard. A violation of the clause does not exist when isolated and unpreventable accidents occur.

A similar result was reached when a new employee on the job only four days unexplainably cut a steel band around railroad ties that were being lifted into the air. He was killed when they fell on him. [*Brennan* v. *OSAHRC and Republic Creosoting Co.*, 487 F. 2d 438 (8th Cir., 1973).] In this case the result (the falling of the ties) was so obvious that no amount of training would have eliminated the hazard.

It is clear under some recent decisions that failure to properly train an employee may result in liability. In a 1974 decision a supervisor for an employer instructed employees to open elevator hoistway doors by tripping an emergency release device. This procedure led to an employee's stepping into an open elevator shaft and falling to his death. The Commission held this was a violation of the general duty clause because the employer had instructed a person to open the doors without giving him proper warning or training. (*National Cleaning Contractors, Inc.*, OSAHRC docket #4740, Nov., 1974). The employer does not have to be aware of the hazard to be liable; it is sufficient if the hazard would be recognizable by a prudent person.

A second line of decisions involves the liability of employers who request employees to work at a work site where employees of other employers are also working. It appears that liability is created even though the employer did not create the unsafe condition but required an employee to work where there was such a condition. One employer asserted in defense of an alleged violation that it was not responsible for the cleaning up of scrap lumber with protruding nails. Neither it nor its employees had any duty with regard to the lumber. The Commission found that the mere exposure of its employees to the hazard suffices regardless of who created the hazardous conditions. (*Johns Manville Sales Corp.*, OSAHRC docket #3163, Nov., 1974.) This decision and related ones establish the principle that a place of employment is any place the employer requires the employee to work.

It has been held that even where a general contractor promises subcontractors it will be solely responsible for the safety conditions on the job site, subcontractors will not be relieved from liability if the general duty clause is violated. [*Bayside Pipe Coats, Inc.*, OSAHRC #1953 (1974).]

In summary, the litigation prompted by OSHA has focused on the "recognized hazard" and "place of employment" phrases of the general duty clause. A recognized hazard (see the *American Smelting* decision below) is not one limited to detection by the human senses. Sensitive machines may be used. So, a violation of the general duty clause will exist if the hazard is (1) common knowledge or generally recognized in the particular industry in which it occurs and (2) detectable by the human senses or of such wide general recognition as a hazard in the industry that there are generally accepted tests for its existence that should be known to the employer.

The following case deals with two issues. The first is the definition of a recognized hazard and the second (less obvious) deals with violations that occur without obvious permanent injury to the employee. The Act deals with hazards that are causing, or are likely to cause, death or serious harm to employees.

AMERICAN SMELTING AND REFINING COMPANY v. OSAHRC
501 F2d 504 (C.A., 8 1974)

GIBSON, Circuit Judge

Petitioner, American Smelting and Refining Company, upon complaint of the United Steelworkers of America (Union), was charged with a violation of the Occupational Safety and Health Act of 1970, . . . in allowing the existence of a health hazard at its Omaha, Nebraska, plant. Specifically, Petitioner was charged with exposing its employees to hazardous airborne concentrations of lead. The Act's general purpose and its "general duty" clause evidence a clear Congressional purpose to provide employees a safe and nonhazardous environment in which business, including commercial and industrial corporations, is to be conducted.

The complaint of the Union about unsafe working conditions triggered an investigation of plant conditions and monitoring of the working environment present in the Petitioner's plant by personnel of the Secretary of Labor's office. The airborne lead concentrations within the plant varied depending on the type of industrial operation being performed in certain work areas, but the results obtained were adequate to indicate that long-range preventative engineering practices should be instituted within a six-month period, preceded by immediate administrative controls of approved respirators, rotation of employees, and any other appropriate measures.

The complaint and investigation, with its monitoring tests, resulted in a citation being issued. . . . After a hearing, the Administrative Law Judge on March 1, 1972, found that airborne concentrations in inorganic lead at American Smelting and Refining Company's Omaha plant presented "a recognized hazard that [was] likely to cause, if continued unabated, death or serious physical harm to employees, and as such, constituted a violation of Section 5(a)(1) [the general duty provision] of the Act." . . .

The petitioner, a New Jersey corporation, operates a lead refining plant in Omaha, Nebraska, and employs 390 to 400 workers there. Receiving lead bullion in solid blocks, the plant produces commercial grades of refined lead and lead alloys by separating impurities from the lead.

While inspecting the plant, the Secretary's representatives . . . observed that all but one of the employees had their company-supplied respirators hanging around their necks, rather than properly wearing them over their noses and mouths. After the tour of the plant, the representatives decided to take air samples of the melting, cupel, retort, and crane areas. Respondent chose seven employees and placed an air sampling pump on each employee. . . . The representatives activated the pumps on each of the seven workers, and the pumps were in place for approximately two hours and fifty-seven minutes. This period of time was sufficient to allow each worker to complete at least one complete cycle of his normal work throughout the plant. . . .

Relying on limited though express legislative history, the Petitioner argues that the general duty clause was not intended to cover hazards that can be detected only by testing devices. Since the airborne concentrations of lead in excess of .2 mg/M^3 were discovered by air sampling pumps instead of the human senses, Petitioner argues that no recognized hazard existed. In short, "recognized" only means recognized directly by human senses without the assistance of any technical instruments. . . .

We find Petitioner and Chairman Moran's views unpersuasive. Looking to the words of the Act itself, "recognized hazards" was enacted instead of "readily apparent hazards." From the commonly understood meanings of the terms themselves, "recognized" denotes a broader meaning than "readily apparent."

We further think that the purpose and intent of the Act is to protect the health of the workers and that a narrow construction of the general duty clause would endanger this purpose in many cases. To expose workers to health dangers that may not be emergency situations and to limit the general duty clause to dangers only detectable by the human senses seems to us to be a folly. Our technological age depends on instrumentation to monitor many conditions of industrial operations and the environment. Where hazards are recognized but not detectable by the senses, common sense and prudence demand that instrumentation be utilized. Certain kinds of health hazards, such as carbon monoxide and

asbestos poisoning, can only be detected by technical devices. . . . The Petitioner's contention, though advanced by arguable but loose legislative interpretation, would have us accept a result that would ignore the advances of industrial scientists, technologists, and hygienists, and also ignore the plain working, purpose, and intent of this Act. The health of workers should not be subjected to such a narrow construction. . . .

Most important in the Petitioner's view is a reliance on a biological monitoring program, which involves the testing of each employee's blood and urine to determine the concentration of lead. Dr. Nelson, the Petitioner's Director of Environmental Sciences, stated that this testing is "a far more effective way of securing the safety of employees." Dr. Kehoe prefers biological monitoring, since air measurement "is not a standard which we regard as crucial in relation to the individual." . . .

The biological monitoring did not eliminate or even reduce the hazard; it merely disclosed it. Although testing of the blood and urine is the most important test for each individual, the use of air sampling tests is the most efficient and practical way for the Secretary to check for a hazard likely to cause death or serious physical harm to the workers as a group. We think it also the most efficient manner for the employer to check the existence of a hazard. . . . Workers should not be subjected to hazardous concentrations of airborne lead; biological monitoring should complement an industrial hygiene program for clean or at least safe air, it is not a substitute for a healthful working environment.

In addition, the Petitioner knew or should have known that the respirators would not reduce the likelihood of serious physical harm to the employees. During the unannounced tour of the plant by the Secretary's representatives, only one employee was properly wearing his respirator. The reasonable inference is that employees rarely used the awkward and uncomfortable respirators. It was reasonably foreseeable to the Petitioner that the respirators would not be properly worn. We hold that there was adequate evidence on the record considered as a whole that the biological monitoring program would not prevent a likelihood of harm to employees.

Case Questions

1. Of what value was the biological monitoring system? It did not eliminate the hazard.
2. What are the duties of an employer when it finds that almost all of its employees do not use the safety devices provided?

The case that follows demonstrates the right to self-protection enjoyed by an employee when he or she faces the imminent risk of serious injury and there is not sufficient time to apprise OSHA of the danger.

WHIRLPOOL v. MARSHALL
445 U.S. 1 (1980)

(Authors' note: An overhead conveyor was used to transport components throughout a manufacturing plant. A wire mesh guard screen approximately 20 feet above the plant floor was used to protect employees from occasional falling objects. Maintenance employees spent several hours each week removing objects from the screen and performing work on the conveyors. Several employees had fallen through the screen, one to his death. About two weeks after the employee had fallen to his death a foreman directed two men to perform their normal maintenance duties on the screen. Claiming the screen was unsafe, they refused. They were sent home without being paid for the remaining six hours of their shift, and written reprimands were placed in their employment files. Subsequently the Secretary of Labor filed suit against the employer alleging that the action against the employees constituted discrimination in violation of the OSHA statute.)

MR. JUSTICE STEWART *delivered the opinion of the Court.*

The Occupational Safety and Health Act of 1970 (Act) prohibits an employer from discharging or discriminating against any employee who exercises "any right afforded by" the Act. The Secretary of Labor (Secretary) has promulgated a regulation providing that, among the rights that the Act so protects, is the right of an employee to choose not to perform his assigned task because of a reasonable apprehension of death or serious injury coupled with a reasonable belief that no less drastic alternative is available. The question presented in the case before us is whether this regulation is consistent with the Act.

The Act itself creates an express mechanism for protecting workers from employment conditions believed to pose an emergent threat of death or serious injury. Upon receipt of an employee inspection request stating reasonable grounds to believe that an imminent danger is present in a workplace, OSHA must conduct an inspection.

As this case illustrates . . . circumstances may sometimes exist in which the employee justifiably believes that the express statutory arrangement does not sufficiently protect him from death or serious injury. Such circumstances will probably not often occur, but such a situation may arise when (1) the employee is ordered by his employer to work under conditions that the employee reasonably believes pose an imminent risk of death or serious bodily injury, and (2) the employee has reason to believe that there is not sufficient time or opportunity either to seek effective redress from his employer or to apprise OSHA of the danger.

The regulation clearly conforms to the fundamental objective of the Act—to prevent occupational deaths and serious injuries. The Act, in its preamble, declares that its purpose and policy is "to assure so far as possible every working man and woman in the Nation safe and healthful working conditions and to *preserve* our human resources. . . ."

To accomplish this basic purpose, the legislation's remedial orientation is prophylactic in nature. . . . The Act does not wait for an employee to die or become injured. It authorizes the promulgation of health and safety standards and the issuance of citations in the hope that these will act to prevent deaths or injuries from ever occurring. It would seem anomalous to construe an Act so directed and constructed as prohibiting an employee, with no other reasonable alternative, the freedom to withdraw from a workplace environment that he reasonably believes is highly dangerous.

Moreover, the Secretary's regulation can be viewed as an appropriate aid to the full effectuation of the Act's "general duty" clause. That clause provides that "[e]ach employer . . . shall furnish to each of his employees employment and a place of employment which are free from recognized hazards that are causing or are likely to cause death or serious physical harm to his employees." . . . Since OSHA inspectors cannot be present around the clock in every workplace, the Secretary's regulation ensures that employees will in all circumstances enjoy the rights afforded them by the "general duty" clause.

The regulation thus on its face appears to further the overriding purpose of the Act, and rationally to complement its remedial scheme. In the absence of some contrary indication in the legislative history, the Secretary's regulation must, therefore, be upheld, particularly when it is remembered that safety legislation is to be liberally construed to effectuate the congressional purpose.

For these reasons we conclude that [the regulation] was promulgated by the Secretary in the valid exercise of his authority under the Act.

Case Question

1. If a person has fallen to his death from the screen, and the employer has not repaired or replaced the screen, is it not difficult to argue that an employee ordered to walk on the screen is unreasonably in fear of his safety?

The Employment Retirement Income Security Act of 1974

The Employment Retirement Income Security Act became law on Labor Day of 1974. It is a very complex piece of legislation and, like OSHA, is so new any statements about its value must be tenuous. We present here just a brief overview.

Many employers and most large corporations provide retirement plans of some kind for their employees. Usually the employee and employer both contribute to a fund that is administered for the benefit of the employee. Funds are invested conservatively so that slight growth in the fund can be expected. At retirement age, the employee typically could withdraw all or part of his share. However, at least three major events could disastrously alter the employee's hopes of a secure retirement: (1) the employee could be discharged or quit before any legal right to the retirement funds accrued; (2) the firm could fail and the retirement fund might be paid over to creditors; or (3) those in charge of the administration of the fund could abuse their position and either embezzle or squander the funds. This new legislation attempts to present such unfortunate results or at least minimize them. The Act primarily assures participants in a pension fund program that they will get what they planned on when they retire or quit. To achieve this, the act emphasizes (1) the vesting of rights in the fund, (2) insurance against company collapse, and (3) strict duties for the administrators of the fund.

The law does not require that a corporation have a pension plan. For those that do, however, the following requirements apply. First, the plan must cover all employees who are at least 25 years old and have one year of service. If the employee is to have an immediate vested right in the retirement benefits on payment to the fund, then three years of service may be required. Second, employers may choose one of three ways to let employees gain vested or guaranteed rights in the fund, which become payable at the retirement age provided in the plan or at age 65. The first of these is to provide that rights in the pension plan become nonforfeitable after 10 years of service, even if the employee quits. A second method of allowing a participant to gain vested or guaranteed rights in the plan is to provide that he be entitled to 25 percent of the accrued benefits after 5 years of service and this percentage increase to 50 percent after 10 years and 100 percent after 15 years. A third method of guaranteeing a worker benefits is to adopt the "rule of 45," which provides half of his benefits when the age of the worker and years of service total 45 (but a minimum of 5 years of service is required). For younger participants, the rule provides for full vesting after 15 years of service. These three methods just discussed provide a measure of protection for the employee against discharge or circumstances compelling one to quit.

Another objective of the Act is to protect employees' benefits when the corporation fails. A study by the Labor and Treasury Departments reveals that 1227 pension plans terminated in 1972 resulting in almost $50 million of lost benefits to approximately 20,000 participants. The Act creates a new Public Pension Benefit Guaranty Corporation, which guarantees workers through a scheme of insurance that they will receive the benefits they are entitled to if the company fails. The premiums for this insurance are about $1 per worker per year or 50 cents each for workers under more comprehensive multi-employer plans. The insurance will provide maximum benefits of the lesser of $750 per month or 100 percent of the employee's average wages for his best-paid five consecutive years of employment. This corporation could also seek to recover from the employer up to 30 percent of the collapsed firm's net worth if pension fund assets were insufficient to pay benefits.

Third, some of the Act's major provisions concern the standards to be observed by the fiduciaries administering the plan. Such fiduciaries are barred from engaging in such transactions as buying for the pension fund property they own personally. Pension funds holding stock and real property of the employer must reduce such holdings to 10 percent of the fund's total assets over the next 10 years.

To insure compliance with the terms of the Act, extensive reporting requirements must be met. Reports to employees, the Labor and Treasury Departments, and the Pension Benefit Guaranty Corporation are necessary. This reporting is designed to provide detailed information to the government as well as to participants in the plan.

Some authorities such as New York's Senator Jacob Javits declare that this Act is the first major achievement since Social Security to provide for the security of workers in retirement years. Although it is estimated that the Act will affect over 30 million persons presently covered by private pension plans, many view the Act as just one more costly type of interference from the federal government.

Review Problems

1. For the 14 years of its existence, a company has always granted wage and benefit increases on April 1. However, this time when it does so, a union is engaged in an organizational campaign among the company's employees. The union argues that the company action constitutes an unfair labor practice designed to coerce the employees in the exercise of their rights. The employer denies the charge, arguing that the increase is merely the continuation of a long-established practice and tradition. Is the employer's action legal?

2. A union calls a strike against its insurance company employer. A number of independent insurance agencies sell the policies written by the employer. In fact about 90 percent of their business comes from the sale of these policies. If the union asks the public not to buy its employer's insurance policies from these independent agencies, will it be guilty of illegal secondary activity?

3. In an effort to increase its chances in an organizational campaign, a member of the union proposes that the union promise to waive the first two months of union dues to any employee who votes for the union in the election. Is this marketing tactic legal?

4. A general contractor is unionized. A nonunion electrical subcontractor is also performing work at the construction site. The union strikes the general contractor because he will not replace the electrical sub-

contractor with an electrical firm that has a unionized workforce. Is this a legal strike? *No – secondary boycott arrangement*

5. The general manager of a plant suggests that the general managers of the employer's other four plants join in the formation of a union. This general managers' union would be used to increase their salaries and their management authority at their respective plants. As soon as the employer learns of this scheme, the manager that developed the idea is fired. Has the employer committed an unfair labor practice? *probably not – because gen. mngrs. + not employees under the act.*

6. A union negotiates a contract with a railroad. Under the contract work crews are to consist of five persons. Four are to perform the work; the fifth individual is to watch for trains so that none of the work crew will be struck and injured by a locomotive or the cars that it is pulling. Does the work crew provision of this contract constitute featherbedding under the federal labor law? *No – providing service even if of little value*

7. An employee, who is a member of a union, is fired by the employer. The reason for the discharge is the poor work performance of the employee. The union challenges the validity of the discharge by arguing that the employer was punishing the worker for being an active member of the union. The employer demonstrates that the worker does have a history of poor job performance, that the worker was warned several times of the need to improve, and that other employees guilty of the same offense have also been discharged. Has the employer committed an unfair labor practice? *No – fired for cause; must document*

8. Two separate unions are seeking to organize the employer's workforce. The employer hopes that one particular union will be successful. To that end, the employer allows the favored union to establish an organizing office in the plant and use the printing department to produce campaign literature at no charge. Do these actions by the employer create any legal difficulties? *Yes, interferring c rights of workers to use*

9. An employer unilaterally decides to subcontract out the maintenance work in the factory that is currently performed by unionized employees. When the union learns of the decision and demands to bargain over the matter, the employer informs the union that the matter is none of their business. Is the employer correct in this assertion? *No – mandatory subject of bargaining – not close but just subcontract.*

10. The United Auto Workers hold a bargaining conference composed of all the local unions that represent workers at Caterpillar Tractor, John Deere, International Harvester, and Allis Chalmers. At that conference the union establishes its bargaining goals and strategy. It decides to concentrate on first bargaining a contract with Caterpillar. It will then use that contract as a pattern and demand that the other companies sign a contract with the same wage and benefits package. All of the local unions vote in favor of this tactic. Are the UAW local unions violating the antitrust laws? *No – as long dont work c non-union group. acting in there benefit.*

20

Discrimination in Employment

The major employment discrimination legislation is contained in Title VII of the 1964 Civil Rights Act and its amendment by the 1972 Equal Employment Opportunity Act. Together they make it unlawful to discriminate on the basis of race, color, religion, sex, or national origin. The law applies to an employer in any industry affecting commerce who has 15 or more employees. It also applies to state and local governments and their political subdivisions.

Employees of the federal government are not covered by these laws, but the 1972 Act makes clear that they also have the right to equal employment opportunity. Each federal agency is required to be nondiscriminatory in employment. In 1979, responsibility for enforcement of equal opportunity in federal employment was transferred from the Civil Service Commission to the Equal Employment Opportunity Commission (EEOC).

The law also covers any union that operates a hiring hall or has 15 or more members.

Under the law it is an unlawful employment practice for an employer to fail or refuse to hire or to discharge any individual or otherwise to discriminate against any individual with respect to compensation, terms, conditions, or privileges of employment because of such individual's race, color, religion, sex, or national origin. It is unlawful for a labor organization to exclude or to expel from its membership, or otherwise to discriminate against, any individual because of race, color, religion, sex, or national origin. It is also unlawful for an employment agency to discriminate against an individual on any of these grounds. It is not enough for an organization to stop discriminatory practices. It must take affirmative action to remedy the effects of the past illegal practices.

This chapter is adapted from *A Basic Guide to Federal Labor Law: The Private Sector*, Second Edition, pp. 155–173. Copyright 1975, 1981, Frederick J. Naffziger and Keith Knauss.

634

Individuals are guaranteed the free exercise of religion, and the government is prohibited from establishing a religion, by the First Amendment to the U.S. Constitution. Because of this, a provision of the Civil Rights Act provides that it is not unlawful for a religious organization to hire employees of a particular religion to perform work connected with carrying on its activities. Thus, it is legal for a religion to hire only its members to teach in its parochial schools.

There is little protection, however, for individuals who find it impossible to work after sundown on Friday, or on Saturday, because of their religious beliefs. The statute does contain a provision that requires an employer to make a reasonable accommodation for the religious observance or practice of its employees. Consider the case of an individual whose religion views Saturday as the Sabbath and forbids work on the Sabbath. Suppose further that this person has insufficient seniority to bid for a shift that does not have Saturday work. What if the employee refuses to work on Saturday and is therefore discharged? In such a case, the union refused to allow any violation of the contract's seniority system. The company refused his request that he be allowed to work a four-day week or that he be replaced with a supervisor or other worker on the fifth day of his shift. It also refused to cover his position on Saturday by assigning overtime to another employee. Finally, because of the seniority provision in the collective bargaining agreement, it refused to work out a swap with another employee on a different shift. In exactly such an instance, the Supreme Court held that the employer had made a reasonable effort to accommodate the employee's religious practices. It said the adoption of any of the various alternatives proposed by the employee would have imposed an undue hardship on the employer. [*TWA* v. *Hardison*, 432 U.S. 63 (1977).]

It is illegal for an individual to be discriminated against because of his or her national origin. For instance, an employer could not legally refuse to hire German-Americans because he disliked people from Germany. It is not illegal to have a rule that only U.S. citizens will be hired. This is discrimination against aliens, but the discrimination is based on citizenship and not national origin. For example, under such a rule an individual from Germany would be eligible for employment so long as he or she was a U.S. citizen. [*Espinoza* v. *Farah*, 414 U.S. 86 (1973).]

Sex Discrimination

While it is illegal to discriminate against a man because of his sex, most sex discrimination cases involve allegations that a company and/or union has discriminated against a woman because of her sex.

What the Civil Rights Act makes illegal is the unequal treatment of men and women because of their sex—what the law calls disparate treatment. Thus, an employer would violate the law if it required the female employees to be married while allowing the male workers to be either married or unmarried. What makes this illegal is that one rule is enforced for members of one sex, while a different rule is applied to members of the opposite sex. Suppose a company has sexually segregated seniority lists and women are only eligible for jobs that require lifting 35 pounds or less. This is unlawful. All workers, regardless of their sex, must be afforded the opportunity to demonstrate their ability to perform more strenuous jobs on a regular basis. If a woman demonstrates the capability to perform a job requiring lifting items in excess of 35 pounds and desires that job, it cannot be denied her because she is a woman. [*Bowe* v. *Colgate Palmolive*, 416 F2d 711 (1970).]

Sometimes one encounters a rule that is facially neutral; in other words, on the surface it appears to treat all groups the same. Are these types of job qualifications legal? They are legal if they are neutral not only on their face but also in their effects. If they are neutral on their face but cause a disparate impact on a particular protected group, they are illegal. Minimum height and weight standards are good examples of a facially neutral rule. Alabama required that its prison guards have a minimum height of 5' 2" and a minimum weight of 120 pounds. If one takes all the individuals in the United States between the ages of 18 and 79, these restrictions exclude 41.13 percent of the female population from employment, while excluding less than 1 percent of the male population. In *Dothard* v. *Rawlinson*, 433 U.S. 321 (1977), the Supreme Court struck down this requirement as unlawful discrimination because it so disproportionately excluded women from employment.

What if a male supervisor conditions favorable job evaluations, provisions, or promotions for a female employee on her grant of sexual favors? The issue of sexual harassment on the job is being more frequently raised. If the subordinate employee's job status depends on a favorable response to the sexual demands, the employer will violate the law if it does not take prompt and appropriate remedial action after it learns of the incident. The same rule would also apply in the case of a female supervisor making sexual demands on a male subordinate.

The following case makes the important point that the discrimination laws do not prevent discrimination only in the original employment decision. Once an individual is on the job the law also protects the individual from discriminatory conduct. The case is a good example of disparate treatment of employees according to their sex.

EEOC v. BROWN & ROOT, INC.
30 FEP Cases 11 (1982)

RUBIN, Circuit Judge

The following facts are undisputed: Sarah Joan Boyes was employed by Brown & Root as an electrician's helper. Brown & Root is a construction company and Ms. Boyes was assigned to work on an overhead steel beam that was part of a structure being erected at Escatawpa, Missouri. She became paralyzed by fear and was unable to move, a condition known as "freezing." It was necessary physically to assist her to climb down. Brown & Root discharged Ms. Boyes from her job for the stated reason that she was "not capable of performing assigned work." After she was fired, another female worker was hired to fill the position of electrician's helper.

What is disputed is whether men who manifested the same acrophobia were also discharged. In opposition to the motion for summary judgment, the Equal Employment Opportunity Commission offered the affidavit of its investigator. To this were attached copies of statements taken from four male employees, each of whom stated that he or some other worker had at some prior time frozen on the beams, could not get down without help, and was not discharged. One statement referred also to a male worker who was kept on the ground because he was afraid of heights. There was also attached an "EEOC affidavit" from a male employee stating that he had "frozen" and had not been discharged. . . .

[T]he disputed issue was not whether Ms. Boyes was unable to work at heights, a fact that was, indeed, undisputed, or whether she was replaced by a male, another fact that was not disputed, but whether, had she been a man, she would have suffered dismissal as a result of her phobia. When an employment discrimination claim contends that a person was discharged from employment because of sex, race, age or some other reprobated reason, a prima facie case of discrimination is made if it is shown that (1) the person was a member of a protected minority; (2) the person was qualified for the job from which discharged; (3) the person was discharged; and (4) after the discharge, their employer filled the position with a nonminority. This showing, however, is not the only way to establish a prima facie case of discriminatory discharge.

If an employee is discharged under circumstances in which an employee of another sex would not have been discharged, an inference of discrimination arises irrespective of the gender of the employee's replacement. Punitive action against employees for violating work rules must not differentiate on the basis of sex or any of the other criteria reprobated by Title VII.

The summary judgment is reversed and the case remanded for further proceedings consistent with this opinion.

Case Questions

1. Since another female was hired to replace Ms. Boyes how can the company be viewed as discriminating against women?
2. Why would a company fire a woman for certain conduct when it did not fire men who engaged in the very same conduct?

The federal law does not prohibit discrimination against an individual on grounds of homosexuality. Some cities do have ordinances that prohibit various forms of discrimination against homosexuals.

Pregnancy and Sex Discrimination

In 1976, the Supreme Court ruled that an employer did not violate Title VII's ban on sex discrimination when it denied benefits for pregnancy-related disabilities under its disability income protection plan. The Court said that this did not constitute discrimination against a particular gender of people, that it merely removed one physical condition—pregnancy—

from the list of covered disabilities. It viewed pregnancy, which of course is confined only to women, as significantly different from the typically covered disease or disability and, thus, not merely a pretext for discrimination against women when a plan excluded it from coverage. This ruling is no longer in effect because Congress has amended the law. Let us now look at the situation as it is today.

The Pregnancy Disability Act of 1978 amends Title VII so as to forbid employment discrimination because of "pregnancy, childbirth, or related medical conditions." The law requires that employers make the necessary adjustments in their existing fringe benefit programs by April 29, 1979, so that pregnant workers would enjoy the same benefits as workers suffering other disabilities. The law does not require an employer to have a fringe benefit package or insurance program for disabilities. What the law requires is that when an employer does have such a program or package (as most employers do), then any woman unable to work for pregnancy-related reasons must receive the same disability benefits or sick leave as other employees receive when they are unable to work for medical reasons. If the employer furnishes health insurance, that insurance must cover expenses for pregnancy-related conditions on the very same basis as expenses for other medical conditions. Abortions are covered by the law. An employer cannot discriminate against a woman who has had an abortion. If fringe benefits, such as sick leave, are provided for medical reasons, they must also be provided for abortions. However, health insurance is required for abortions only where the life of the woman would be endangered if the fetus were carried to term or where medical complications arise from an abortion.

The idea of the law is to furnish the same treatment to women with pregnancy-related disabilities as is received by employees with other types of medical disabilities. If the employer furnishes sick leaves, leaves without pay, alternate job assignments, etc. to employees who are temporarily disabled, then the employer must make these same benefits available to a woman who is temporarily disabled by a condition related to pregnancy. These benefits must be supplied to both married and unmarried employees. If an employer requires all employees to submit a doctor's statement as to their inability to work, as a condition to receiving sick leave benefits, etc., then the employer can require the same statement from women who wish to qualify for those benefits for a pregnancy-related cause. An employer cannot impose a higher deductible for coverage of pregnancy-related disabilities than the deductible for the cost of other medical conditions. When the employee is reimbursed for pregnancy-related disabilities the basis must be the same as reimbursement for other medical costs. If the employer chooses to do so on a fixed basis, or on a percentage of the customary charge, that very same formula must be used in pregnancy situations. This law applies to state and local governments as well as to private employers.

On constitutional due process grounds, the Supreme Court has ruled that a woman cannot be forced by her employer to take a maternity leave at an arbitrary cutoff date such as the fourth or fifth month or pregnancy. She is entitled to work for as long as her doctor believes it to be medically safe. [*Cleveland Bd. of Education* v. *La Fleur*, 414 U.S. 632 (1974).] EEOC interprets the Pregnancy Disability Act to also permit the woman and her doctor to determine when she can no longer work. In 1977, the Supreme Court held that the denial of accumulated seniority to employees returning from pregnancy leave constitutes illegal sex discrimination. [*Nashville Gas Co.* v. *Satty*, 434 U.S. 136 (1977).]

On a topic somewhat related to pregnancy, the Supreme Court has held that a company violates the Civil Rights Act by rejecting women job applicants with preschool children when the company has no policy against hiring men with preschool children. [*Phillips* v. *Martin-Marietta*, 400 U.S. 542 (1971).]

Race and Color Discrimination

In its efforts to eliminate artificial or discriminatory barriers in the path of job applicants or employees, the law bars discrimination against an individual because of his or her color or race. The law does not guarantee any individual a job regardless of his or her qualifications. It seeks to provide everyone with equal employment opportunity. It is illegal to hire a lesser qualified white in place of a more qualified black. It is also illegal to hire a lighter skinned black over a more qualified but darker skinned black.

What we said earlier about facially neutral job qualifications and sex discrimination applies equally in cases of race discrimination. The '64 Act contains a provision that allows an employer to give and act on the results of any professionally developed ability test, provided that the test is not designed or used to discriminate because of race, color, religion, sex, or national origin. However, the Supreme Court has ruled that for such tests to be allowable, they must be "job-related." Suppose a company requires that an individual pass an aptitude test to be hired or to gain a job transfer. Also suppose that the tests do not measure the ability to perform a particular job and they render ineligible a markedly disproportionate number of blacks. Such tests, even though they are neutral on their face, do discriminate and do violate the 1964 Civil Rights Law. The tests are not job-related for they do not bear a demonstrable relationship to successful performance of the job. Some employees had never taken the tests, yet performed their jobs satisfactorily. [*Griggs* v. *Duke Power Co.*, 401 U.S. 424 (1971).] A person cannot be denied a job by an artificial, unnecessary, or discriminatory barrier.

Two issues of concern are dealt with in the next case. One examines the circumstances in which the remedy of back pay will be awarded because of discriminatory job practices. The second is a discussion of whether an employer's testing program is job-related.

ALBEMARLE PAPER COMPANY v. MOODY

422 U.S. 405 (1975)

MR. JUSTICE STEWART *delivered the opinion of the Court.*

These consolidated cases raise two important questions under Title VII of the Civil Rights Act of 1964, . . . as amended by the Equal Employment Opportunity Act of 1972, ... First: When employees or applicants for employment have lost the opportunity to earn wages because an employer has engaged in an unlawful discriminatory employment practice, what standards should a federal district court follow in deciding whether to award or deny backpay? Second: What must an employer show to establish that pre-employment tests racially discriminatory in effect, though not in intent, are sufficiently "job related" to survive challenge under Title VII? . . .

The respondents . . . are a certified class of present and former Negro employees at a paper mill in Roanoke Rapids, North Carolina; the petitioners . . . are the plant's owner, the Albemarle Paper Company, and the plant employees' labor union. . . .

The court refused . . . to award backpay to the plaintiff class for losses suffered under the "job seniority" program. The court explained:

> In the instant case there was no evidence of bad faith non-compliance with the Act. It appears that the company as early as 1964 began active recruitment of blacks for its Maintenance Apprenticeship Program. Certain lines of progression were merged on its own initiative, and as judicial decisions expanded the then existing interpretation of the Act, the defendants took steps to correct the abuses without delay. . . .

The court also refused to enjoin or limit Albemarle's testing program. . . .

It is true that backpay is not an automatic or mandatory remedy; like all other remedies under the Act, it is one which the courts "may" invoke. . . . The power to award backpay was bestowed by Congress, as part of a complex legislative design directed at an historic evil of national proportions. . . .

It is also the purpose of Title VII to make persons whole for injuries suffered on account of unlawful employment discrimination. This is shown by the very fact that Congress took care to arm the courts with full equitable powers. . . . Title VII deals with legal injuries of an economic character occasioned by racial or other antiminority discrimination. . . .

The "make whole" purpose of Title VII is made evident by the legislative history. The backpay provision was expressly modeled on the backpay provision of the National Labor Relations Act. Under that Act, "[m]aking the workers whole for losses suffered on account of an unfair labor practice is part of the vindication of the public policy which the Board enforces." . . . We may assume that Congress was aware that the Board, since its inception, has awarded backpay as a matter of course—not randomly or in the exercise of a standardless discretion, and not merely where employer violations are peculiarly deliberate, egregious or inexcusable. . . .

It follows that, given a finding of unlawful discrimination, backpay should be denied only for reasons which, if applied generally, would not frustrate the central statutory purposes of eradicating discrimination throughout the economy and making persons whole for injuries suffered through past discrimination. . . .

If backpay were awardable only upon a showing of bad faith, the remedy would become a punishment for moral turpitude, rather than a compensation for workers' injuries. This would read the "make whole" purpose right out of Title VII, for a worker's injury is no less real simply because his employer did not inflict it in "bad faith." Title VII is not concerned with the employer's "good intent or absence of discriminatory intent" for "Congress directed the thrust of the Act to the consequences of employment practices, not simply the motivation."

In *Griggs* v. *Duke Power Co.,* 401 U.S. 424, this Court unanimously held that Title VII forbids the use of employment tests that are discriminatory in effect unless the employer meets "the burden of showing that any given requirement [has] . . . a manifest relation to the employment in question." . . . This burden arises, of course, only after the complaining party or class has made out a prima facie case of discrimination—has shown that the tests in question select applicants for hire or promotion in a racial pattern significantly different from that of the pool of applicants. . . . If an employer does then meet the burden of proving that its tests are "job related," it remains open to the complaining party to show that other tests or selection devices, without a similarly undesirable racial effect, would also serve the employer's legitimate interest in "efficient and trustworthy workmanship." Such a showing would be evidence that the employer was using its tests merely as a "pretext" for discrimination. . . . In the present case, however, we are concerned only with the question whether Albemarle has shown its tests to be job related. . . .

Like the employer in *Griggs,* Albemarle uses two general ability tests, the Beta Examination, to test nonverbal intelligence, and the Wonderlic Test, . . . the purported measure of general verbal facility which was also involved in the *Griggs* case. . . .

Four months before this case went to trial, Albemarle engaged an expert in industrial psychology to "validate" the job relatedness of its testing program. He spent a half day at the plant and devised a "concurrent validation" study, which was conducted by plant officials, without his supervision. The expert then subjected the results to statistical analysis. . . .

The EEOC has issued "Guidelines" for employers seeking to determine, through professional validation studies, whether their employment tests are job related. . . . These guidelines draw upon and make reference to professional standards of test validation established by the American Psychological Association. The EEOC Guidelines are not administrative "regulations" promulgated pursuant to formal procedures established by the Congress. But, as this Court has heretofore noted, they do constitute "[t]he administrative interpretation of the Act by the enforcing agency," and consequently they are "entitled to great deference" . . . .

Measured against the Guidelines, Albemarle's validation study is materially defective in several respects:

1. Even if it had been otherwise adequate, the study would not have "validated" the Beta and Wonderlic test battery for all of the skilled lines of progression for which the two tests are, apparently, now required. The study showed significant correlations for the Beta Exam in only three of the eight lines. . . . The study . . . involved no analysis of the attributes of, or the particular skills needed in, the studied job groups. There is accordingly no basis for concluding that "no significant differences" exist among the lines of progression, or among distinct job groupings within the studied lines of progression. Indeed, the study's checkered results appear to compel the opposite conclusion.

2. The study compared test scores with subjective supervisorial rankings. While they allow the use of supervisorial rankings in test validation, the Guidelines quite plainly contemplate that the rankings will be elicited with far more care than was demonstrated here. Albemarle's supervisors were asked to rank employees by a "standard" that was ex-

tremely vague and fatally open to divergent interpretations. . . .

3. The company's study focused, in most cases, on job groups near the top of the various lines of progression. The fact that the best of those employees working near the top of a line of progression score well on a test does not necessarily mean that that test, or some particular cutoff score on the test, is a permissible measure of the minimal qualifications of new workers, entering lower level jobs.

4. Albemarle's validation study dealt only with job-experienced, white workers; but the tests themselves are given to new job applicants, who are younger, largely inexperienced, and in many instances nonwhite.

Accordingly, the judgment is vacated, and these cases are remanded to the District Court for proceedings consistent with this opinion.

Case Questions

1. Why did the District Court refuse to award back pay to the plaintiffs?
2. Under what circumstances will a court award back pay to a class of employees who have been discriminated against?

The testing area is somewhat confused today. What if a sufficiently validated test has a racially disproportionate impact? In a case that involved the due process clause of the Fifth Amendment, not Title VII of the Civil Rights Act, the Supreme Court faced such an issue. It held that as long as a racially discriminatory purpose was not proven, such a test was constitutional, even though four times as many blacks as whites failed the test. [*Washington* v. *Davis,* 426 U.S. 299 (1976).]

Bona Fide Occupational Qualifications

It is not an unlawful employment practice for an employer, union, or employment agency to judge an individual on his religion, sex, or national origin in those certain instances where religion, sex, or national origin is a bona fide occupational qualification, reasonably necessary to the normal operation of that particular enterprise. It is never permissible to discriminate on the basis of a person's race or color! What constitutes a bone fide occupational qualification (BFOQ)? May an airline restrict its flight cabin attendant jobs to females? Is being female a BFOQ for such a job if the passengers express overwhelming preference for female stewardesses? The answer to both questions is "no." Refusal to hire a male for such a position violates the Civil Rights Act. Being female is not a BFOQ in this instance. A male can perform the tasks of a flight cabin attendant just as well as a female. [*Diaz* v. *Pan Am,* 442 F2d 385 (1971).] Under guidelines on sex discrimination issued by the EEOC, the BFOQ exceptions are interpreted narrowly. For example, it gives the occupation of actor or actress as a legitimate BFOQ. These guidelines say that it is unlawful to refuse to hire a woman on the assumption that the turnover rate for women is higher than among men. It would also be unlawful to refuse to hire an individual on stereotyped sexual characterizations—that women are less capable of aggressive salesmanship or that men are less capable of assembling intricate equipment. The Supreme Court has held that being male is a BFOQ for a job as prison guard under a specific set of circumstances. The case was the Alabama one we mentioned earlier in the section on sex discrimination. The unique circumstances involved a maximum security prison suffering from such rampant violence that a court had held the conditions to be unconstitutional. Twenty percent of the male inmates were sex offenders and were scattered throughout the general prison population. The institution was understaffed and, because of dormitory-type living arrangements, the prisoners had access to the guards. The Court said such a factual situation directly links the sex of the prison guard to a security problem.

It is not unlawful for an employer to apply different standards of compensation, or different terms, conditions, or privileges of employment pursuant to a bona fide seniority or merit system, or a system that measures earnings by quantity or quality of production or to employees who work in different locations, provided that such differences are not the net result of an intention to unlawfully discriminate.

Quotas, Goals, and Reverse Discrimination

Quota systems are extremely controversial. Some individuals claim that affirmative action programs under the civil rights law constitute the imposition of a quota system. Others argue that a remedial quota program is necessary to offset the past discriminatory practices. The Civil Rights Act does not mandate a quota system. The Act also states that a union, employer, or employment agency is not required to grant preferential treatment to any individual or to any group because of the race, color, relation, sex, or national origin of such individual or group on account of an existing imbalance in the percentage of persons in the union, employed, or referred for employment. The Fourteenth Amendment to the U.S. Constitution guarantees persons equal protection of the laws. As jobs have become tight in times of economic stress, and women and minorities make some advances in employment, some white males believe that sex or color, not merit or ability, are being used to make hiring decisions. Hiring decisions are not necessarily going their way and they believe themselves to be the victims of reverse discrimination.

The first case to draw substantial publicity was in the educational arena. In 1973 and 1974 the University of California at Davis denied admission to its medical school to a white male by the name of Bakke. Each year there were 100 seats available in the entering class of medical students. Eighty-four of those were filled by a normal admission process; the remaining 16 seats were filled by a special minority admission process. Only members of minority races were eligible for consideration under the special admissions process. The two groups of applicants were rated separately, not against each other. Some of the students admitted through the special process had ratings below Bakke. In 1978, the Supreme Court, in a 5-4 decision, ordered Bakke's admission to medical school. It held that race, while it may be one of several factors considered in making admissions decisions, cannot be the sole decisive factor. [*University of California Regents* v. *Bakke*, 438 U.S. 265 (1978).]

Of much greater importance to the question of reverse discrimination in employment are two later decisions. The first one is *Kaiser Aluminum and Chemical Corp.* v. *Weber*, 443 U.S. 193 (1979). The United Steelworkers of America and the Kaiser Aluminum Company included an affirmative action plan in the collective bargaining agreement. That plan established a training program to train production workers to fill craft openings with the intention of eliminating a conspicuous racial imbalance in the craft positions. The program was to last until the percentage of black craft workers in a plant was commensurate with the percentage of blacks in the local labor force. Trainees for the craft positions were to be selected on the basis of seniority with the proviso that at least 50 percent of the trainees were to be black. During the plan's first year of operation seven blacks and six whites were selected. The most junior black trainee had less seniority than several white production workers whose bids for admission were rejected. One of those whites, Brian Weber, filed suit alleging that he had been illegally discriminated against because of his race. In a 5-2 decision the Supreme Court rejected Weber's argument. It held that Title VII does not condemn all private, voluntary, race-conscious affirmative action plans. It said the prohibition against race discrimination must be read against a legislative intent to open opportunities for blacks in occupations traditionally closed to them. It said that Congress said that nothing in Title VII "shall be interpreted to *require* any employer . . . to grant preferential treatment . . . to any group because of race . . . of such . . . group on account of" a de facto racial imbalance in the employer's workforce. This means, in the Court's view, that while Congress will not *require* such action, it will *permit* such action. It held that this type of affirmative action plan was permissible (by implication some may be impermissible). It noted that the purpose of the plan was to break down old patterns of racial discrimination (at the plant in question, only 1.83 percent of the skilled crafts were held by blacks) and that it was structured to open employment opportunities in occupations traditionally closed to blacks. It noted further that the plan did not require the discharge of white workers and their replacement with new black hires and that the program was not an absolute bar to whites, since half of those admitted to the program were white. Finally, it pointed out that the plan was temporary in nature to simply eliminate a manifest racial imbalance and was not intended to maintain a racial balance.

In 1976, the Court did hold that Title VII prohibits racial discrimination against white persons, as well as that against nonwhites. In that case an employer had cargo stolen by three employees. Two of the employees involved, who were white, were fired as a result. The black employee involved was not fired. The white workers involved sued the employer and union involved. They won reinstatement and back pay. The Court noted that theft is a proper reason for the discharge of an employee, but all employees must be judged by the same standards in discharge cases. It is improper to make discharge decisions according to the race of the employee involved. [*McDonald* v. *Santa Fe Trail*, 427 U.S. 273 (1976).]

The second case where the Supreme Court faced an important reverse discrimination issue is *Fullilove* v. *Klutznick*, 48 LW 4979 (1980). It involved a challenge to a 10 percent set-aside program in a 1977 public works law. The law stated that at least 10 percent of federal funds granted for local public works projects must be used to secure services or supplies from businesses owned by minority group members. It defined minority group members as U.S. citizens "who are Negroes, Spanish-speaking, Orientals, Indians, Eskimos, and Aleuts." A group of nonminority contractors, alleging that they had suffered economic injury due to enforcement of the law, challenged it, arguing that it violated the equal protection clause of the Fourteenth Amendment and the equal protection component of the due process clause of the Fifth Amendment. The Court ruled that the law does not violate the Constitution in a 6-3 decision. The Court said that a proper constitutional objective of Congress is the elimination of barriers to minority firm access to public contracts. Since the purpose of the program is remedial (the removal of the effects of prior discrimination) there is no requirement that Congress act in a wholly "color-blind" fashion. The Court said such a program is not defective even though it may deny contracting opportunities to nonminority firms who have not themselves discriminated in the past. Congress, in the Court's view, had provided a reasonable assurance that the application of racial or ethnic criteria would be narrowly limited to accomplishing proper remedial objectives. The Court said the law could be viewed as a pilot project, appropriately limited in extent and duration and subject to reassessment and reevaluation by Congress prior to any extension or reenactment.

What about reverse discrimination on the basis of sex? That question is faced in the following case, not in the context of the employment discrimination laws, but under the equal protection clause of the Constitution.

MISSISSIPPI UNIVERSITY FOR WOMEN v. *HOGAN*
102 S.Ct. 3331 (1982)

JUSTICE O'CONNOR *delivered the opinion of the Court.*

This case presents the narrow issue of whether a state statute that excludes males from enrolling in a state-supported professional nursing school violates the Equal Protection Clause of the Fourteenth Amendment.

The facts are not in dispute. In 1884, the Mississippi legislature created the Mississippi Industrial Institute and College for the Education of White Girls of the State of Mississippi, now the oldest state-supported all-female college in the United States. The school, known today as Mississippi University for Women (MUW), has from its inception limited its enrollment to women.

Respondent, Joe Hogan, is a registered nurse but does not hold a baccalaureate degree in nursing. Since 1974, he has worked as a nursing supervisor in a medical center in Columbus, the city in which MUW is located. In 1979, Hogan applied for admission to the MUW School of Nursing's baccalaureate program. Although he was otherwise qualified, he was denied admission to the School of Nursing solely because of his sex. School officials informed him that he could audit the courses in which he was interested, but could not enroll for credit.

We begin our analysis aided by several firmly-established principles. Because the challenged policy expressly discriminates among applicants on the basis of gender, it is subject to scrutiny under the Equal Protection Clause of the Fourteenth Amendment. That this statute discriminates against males rather than against females does not exempt it from scrutiny or reduce the standard of review. Our decisions also establish that the party seeking to uphold a statute that classifies individuals on the basis of their gender must carry the burden of showing an "exceedingly persuasive justification" for the classification. The burden is met only by showing at least that the classification serves "important governmental objectives and that the discriminatory means employed" are "substantially related to the achievement of those objectives."

The State's primary justification for maintaining the single-sex admissions policy of MUW's School of Nursing is that it compensates for discrimination against women and, therefore, constitutes educational affirmative action. As applied to the School of Nursing, we find the State's argument unpersuasive.

In limited circumstances, a gender-based classification favoring one sex can be justified if it intentionally and directly assists members of the sex that is disproportionately burdened.

In fact, in 1970, the year before the School of Nursing's first class enrolled, women earned 94 percent of the nursing baccalaureate degrees conferred in Mississippi and 98.6 percent of the degrees earned nationwide.

Rather than compensate for discriminatory barriers faced by women, MUW's policy of excluding males from admission to the School of Nursing tends to perpetuate the stereotyped view of nursing as an exclusively woman's job. By assuring that Mississippi allots more openings in its state-supported nursing schools to women than it does to men, MUW's admissions policy lends credibility to the old view that women, not men, should become nurses, and makes the assumption that nursing is a field for women a self-fulfilling prophecy. Thus, we conclude that, although the State recited a "benign, compensatory purpose," it failed to establish that the alleged objective is the actual purpose underlying the discriminatory classification.

The policy is invalid also because it fails the second part of the equal protection test, for the State has made no showing that the gender-based classification is substantially and directly related to its proposed compensatory objective. To the contrary, MUW's policy of permitting men to attend classes as auditors fatally undermines its claim that women, at least those in the School of Nursing, are adversely affected by the presence of men.

MUW permits men who audit to participate fully in classes. Additionally, both men and women take part in continuing education courses offered by the School of Nursing, in which regular nursing students also can enroll.

Thus, considering both the asserted interest and the relationship between the interest and the methods used by the State, we conclude that the State has fallen far short of establishing the "exceedingly persuasive justification" needed to sustain the gender-based classification. Accordingly, we hold that MUW's policy of denying males the right to enroll for credit in its School of Nursing violates the Equal Protection Clause of the Fourteenth Amendment.

JUSTICE POWELL, *with whom Justice Rehnquist joins, dissenting.*

The Court's opinion bows deeply to conformity. Left without honor—indeed, held unconstitutional—is an element of diversity that has characterized much of American education and enriched much of American life. The Court in effect holds today that no State now may provide even a single institution of higher learning open only to women students.

A constitutional case is held to exist solely because one man found it inconvenient to travel to any of the other institutions made available to him by the State of Mississippi. In essence he insists that he has a right to attend a college in his home community. This simply is not a sex discrimination case. The Equal Protection Clause was never intended to be applied to this kind of case.

Case Questions

1. If a university demonstrated that business is a traditional field of men's study and that eighty percent of the business degrees conferred in the last quarter century were granted men, could that university start a business school which restricted admission to women only?

2. Is the dissent correct in its assessment that a mere situation of travel inconvenience was inflated to a matter of constitutional proportions?

Seniority Systems and Civil Rights

Naturally, seniority is critical in the workplace. The last-hired, first-fired formula is the traditional one used to determine layoffs. As we all know, it is used in all types of areas of importance to workers. Job bids, order of recalls, shift selections, bumping rights, and vacation are just a few of them.

What happens when an individual has low seniority because he or she was the target of illegal discrimination? The Supreme Court has ruled that retroactive seniority can be granted an employee to cure the effects of prior discrimination. [*Franks* v. *Bowman Transportation Co.*, 424 U.S. 747 (1976).] Back pay can also be granted such an employee, even where there is an absence of bad faith on the employer's part. [*Albemarle Paper Co.* v. *Moody*, 422 U.S. 405 (1975).] The Supreme Court has even gone so far as to rule that an individual who has not formally applied for a job can be granted retroactive seniority so long as the individual can meet the burden of proving that he or she would have applied for the job had it not been for the illegal discriminatory practices. [*Teamsters* v. *U.S.*, 431 U.S. 324 (1977).] Such a case might arise where an employer had a sign posted at the employment office saying "whites only" or where it was publicly known in the community that an employer never hired women and thus women in the area knew there was no use in applying.

What if an employer and a union discriminated against certain groups prior to passage of the 1964 Civil Rights Act, but then halted their discrimination once it became a violation of federal law? The question arises in the application of seniority provisions of collective bargaining agreements. The seniority system can carry forward the effects of the past discrimination. Title VII provides that "Notwithstanding any other provisions . . . it shall not be an unlawful employment practice for an employer to apply different standards of compensation, or different terms, conditions, or privileges of employment pursuant to a bona fide seniority . . . system, ..." The issue was litigated against a company and union that discriminated against blacks and Spanish-surnamed individuals. The Supreme Court ruled in *Teamsters* v. *U.S.* that a bona fide seniority system does not become unlawful simply because it may perpetuate pre-Title VII discrimination. The Court said the provision quoted above was an indication by Congress that it did not intend to make it illegal for employees with vested seniority rights to continue to exercise those rights, even at the expense of pre-Civil Rights Act discrimination targets. The victim of discrimination prior to the effective date of the law is entitled to no seniority. A victim of seniority after the law became effective is entitled to retroactive seniority to make him or her whole. Notice the law speaks of "bona fide" seniority systems. To be bona fide a seniority system must apply equally to all racial, sexual, ethnic, and religious groups. It must be negotiated and maintained free from any illegal purpose. If it meets these standards, it will be bona fide and thus not rendered illegal by the mere fact that it extends no retroactive seniority to victims of discrimination prior to the Act.

Another idea of what constitutes a bona fide seniority system is provided by a 1980 Supreme Court decision. A multiemployer brewery industry collective bargaining agreement provided greater benefits, with respect to hiring and layoffs, to "permanent" rather than "temporary" employees. To qualify as a permanent employee it was necessary that a temporary employee work a minimum of 45 weeks in a single calendar year. A black challenged the provision arguing that it had precluded him from achieving a reasonable opportunity to gain permanent status and was not a bona fide seniority system component. The Court upheld the validity of the system. It noted that the fact that two parallel seniority ladders, one allocating benefits for permanent employees and another for temporary employees, were created does not prevent it from being a proper seniority system. The 45-week requirement serves a needed function of determining eligibility for the permanent seniority ladder and focuses on length of employment, as does any seniority system. The Court distinguished it from criteria such as educational standards, aptitude tests, or physical tests that can give effect to subjectivity. Finally, the system rewards employment longevity with greater benefits and generally operates so that the more seniority a temporary employee gains the greater is the likelihood that he or she will reach the 45-week requirement. [*California Brewers Association* v. *Bryant,* 48 L.W. 4156 (1980).]

It is also an unlawful employment practice for an employer, union, or employment agency to discriminate against any person because that person has opposed any practice made an unlawful employment practice by the Civil Rights Law, or because that person has made a charge, testified, assisted, or participated in any manner in an investigation, proceeding, or hearing under the law. In *McDonnell Douglas* v. *Green*, 411 U.S. 792 (1972), the Supreme Court ordered a lower court to determine a company's motivation in refusing to rehire a properly discharged employee. If the refusal was based on the former employee's impermissible activity, it would be legal; if it was based on the discharged employee's civil rights activities against the company, the refusal to rehire would be unlawful.

Finally, it is an unlawful employment practice for an employer, union, or employment agency to print or publish or cause to be printed or published any notice or advertisement relating to employment indicating any preference, limitation, specification, or discrimination, based on race, color, religion, sex, or national origin, except that such a notice or advertisement may indicate a preference, limitation, specification, or discrimination based on religion, sex, or national origin when religion, sex, or national origin is a bona fide occupational qualification for employment. The Supreme Court, in *Pittsburgh Press Co.*, 93 S. Ct. 2553 (1973), has held that it is not a violation of the First Amendment to prohibit a newspaper from carrying job want ads by sex.

Assorted Provisions

Compliance with the 1964 and 1972 laws is enforced through the Equal Employment Opportunity Commission (EEOC). It consists of five members appointed by the President with the consent of the Senate. No more than three members can be of the same political party, and they serve five-year terms. There is a General Counsel who conducts any necessary litigation under the law. This position is also filled by a Presidential appointment, with the Senate's consent, and the term of office is four years. Like the NLRB, the EEOC has numerous offices throughout the United States.

Charges of discrimination can be brought to the EEOC by the aggrieved individual, a person acting *on behalf* of the aggrieved individual (such as a union), or a Commission member. A charge must be filed within 180 days of the alleged discrimination. If a state or local government EEOC-type agency exists, the EEOC defers the charge to that agency for 60 days. If the case is not resolved within 60 days or if the state or local agency waives jurisdiction, the EEOC resumes jurisdiction.

The organization charged with employment discrimination is notified within 10 days of the filing of the charge. Efforts are then made to resolve the problem informally. If these efforts fail, the EEOC decides whether a complete investigation and formal conciliation efforts are called for. If a full investigation is carried out, the EEOC will continue conciliation efforts. All of these activities are conducted confidentially.

The Equal Employment Opportunity Commission

Should conciliation prove impossible, the EEOC may sue the charged party in an effort to remedy an alleged unlawful practice in private employment. If the charged party is a government or any of its political subdivisions, the EEOC refers the case to the U.S. Justice Department, which can sue the governmental body. The EEOC can also bring class action suits.

The person filing charges, the charging party, is free to sue the charged party if (1) the EEOC dismisses the complaint; (2) more than 180 days have passed since the charge was filed; (3) the EEOC, or the Justice Department in cases involving governmental units, decides not to sue; or (4) a written request is made to the EEOC for a "right to sue letter" prior to the expiration of 180 days from the filing of the charge, and the EEOC sends such a letter with a certification that it will be unable to complete its processing of the charge within 180 days of the filing of the charge. Once the charging party receives the right to sue, the suit must be filed within 80 days.

Since many persons who file charges end up having to sue, it is important to know that if they bring a lawsuit and are successful in proving that he or she was the victim of illegal discrimination, the court can, and usually does, order the defendant (charged party) to pay the reasonable attorney's fees of the plaintiff (charging party).

The EEOC now enforces both the Equal Pay Act and the Age Discrimination Act, in addition to the '64 and '72 civil rights statutes. In the past, the Secretary of Labor enforced the equal pay and age discrimination laws. However, in 1978 President Carter shifted enforcement to the EEOC. Both of these encourage the voluntary settlement of disputes and require that a voluntary settlement be attempted before a lawsuit may be filed. If EEOC declines to bring a lawsuit, the private individual may do so. Again, if the suit is successful, the plaintiff can collect not only the amount of damages caused by the discrimination, but also reasonable attorney's fees.

The Equal Pay Act   The year 1963 saw the enactment of the Equal Pay Act. It amended Section 6 of the Fair Labor Standards Act and outlawed wage discrimination based on the employee's sex. The concept that a man, because of his role in society, should be paid more than a woman for doing the same job is declared unlawful. Every employee covered by the federal minimum wage law is protected by the Equal Pay Act. On July 1, 1972, the Act's protection was extended to executive, administrative, and professional employees and to outside sales personnel who previously had been exempt from coverage.

The Act prohibits an employer from discriminating "between employees on the basis of sex by paying wages to employees at a rate less than the rate at which he pays wages to employees of the opposite sex for equal work on jobs the performance of which requires equal skill, effort, and responsibility, and which are performed under similar working conditions." Equal work does not mean that the jobs be identical, only that they be substantially equal. Artificial job classifications that do not substantially differ from genuine ones cannot be created to avoid the operation of the law. If unlawful wage differentials do exist, the employer cannot eliminate them by reducing wage rates. The employer must raise the pay rate of those being discriminated against to the higher wage level of those performing equal work. The law prohibits a union from causing or attempting to cause an employer to discriminate as to wage rates. There are four exceptions to the mandate of equal pay for equal work: where different payment to employees of opposite sexes "is made pursuant to (i) a seniority system; (ii) a merit system; (iii) a system which measures earnings by quantity or quality of production; or (iv) a differential based on any other factor other than sex." Once it is shown that an employer pays workers of one sex more than workers of the opposite sex for equal work, the burden shifts to the employer to show that the differential is justified under one of these exceptions.

Litigation under the Act has been significant. The amount of money involved can be large. In the Wheaton Glass case, which we will discuss shortly, the court ordered the employer to pay $901,062 in back pay to women inspector-packers. It is also noteworthy that in cases under the Equal Pay Act and the Age Discrimination Act the court can order the company to pay the reasonable attorney's fees of the employees.

Let us take a brief look at three important cases to see how the courts are applying the law. In *Schultz* v. *Wheaton Glass Co.*, 421 F.2d 259 (1970), the employer paid its female selector-packers $2.14 per hour while paying its male selector-packers $2.355 per hour. The company denied that the men and women performed equal work and claimed that, in any event, the pay differential was based on a factor other than sex. During periodic oven shutdowns, the male workers could be assigned to perform the duties of snap-up boys, who were paid $2.16 per hour. The court said that the company failed to explain why the availability of men to perform work that pays 2 cents per hour more than women receive should result in overall payment to men of 21 and ½ cents more than women for their common work. The court said the jobs of male and female selector-packers are substantially equal and that therefore the employer had violated the Act.

What is a factor other than sex that can justify a wage differential? We receive a good answer in *Hodgson* v. *Robert Hall Clothes*, 473 F.2d 589 (1973). Robert Hall had men staff its men's department while all the sales personnel in the women's department were women. These sales personnel performed equal work, yet the salesmen received higher salaries than did the saleswomen. Each received a base salary plus incentive payments based on the garment sold. Robert Hall said this wage differential was based not on sex, but on economic factors, i.e., the higher profitability of the men's department. The court held that this economic benefit to Robert Hall can be used to justify a wage differential. It also said that Robert Hall proved that it received the economic benefits on which it based its salary differentials. Robert Hall showed that for every year of the store's operation, the men's department was substantially more profitable than the women's department. The court pointed out that while it may require equal effort to sell two different shoes for $10, if the employer receives a $4 dollar profit on one pair as opposed to a $2 dollar profit on the other, the employer can pay a higher wage to the person selling the pair yielding the higher profit.

Another factor other than sex which allows some individuals to receive a higher wage than others is participation in a bona fide training program. Of course, if participants in the program are of only one sex, that will raise the legal issue of sex discrimination under Title VII and also make the program immediately suspect as to whether it is in fact a bona fide training program. For those interested in this area a case worth reading is *Hodgson* v. *Behrens Drug Co.*, 475 F.2d 1041 (1973), where the court held the training program not to be a bona fide one.

In our last case, the Supreme Court held an employer in violation of the Act for paying a higher base wage to male night-shift inspectors than it paid to female inspectors performing the same tasks on the day shift, where the higher wage was paid in addition to a night shift differential paid to all employees for night work. [*Corning Glass Works* v. *Brennan*, 417 U.S. 188 (1974).]

The most recent issue in the equal pay area is whether the law requires an employer to pay equal wages to employees of different sexes who perform not equal work but jobs of "comparable worth." One case, *Lemons* v. *City & County of Denver*, 48 LW 2716 (1980), says that Title VII of the Civil Rights Act does not require such equal pay for jobs of "comparable worth." The language of the Equal Pay Act does not seem to require it either. However, the Supreme Court, in *County of Washington* v. *Gunther*, 452 U.S. 161 (1981), has held that if the male and female jobs are not equal (thereby removing the case from the equal pay law), but the employer intentionally pays lower wages to women than men, a case may be properly brought under the 1964 Civil Rights Law.

Finally, it is important to recognize that this law mandates equal pay for men as well as women. If a woman is being paid more money than a man performing the same job, and the pay differential does not come under one of the law's exceptions, then the employer must raise the man's salary to the higher level of the woman's.

Age Discrimination

In 1967, Congress passed the Age Discrimination in Employment Act and then made significant amendments to it in 1978. The law prohibits discrimination against individuals who are at least 40 years of age but less than 70 years of age on account of their age by employers, labor organizations, and employment agencies. Executive Order 11141 forbids age discrimination by those holding federal contracts. These laws do not require that persons between the ages of 40 and 70 must be hired. Instead, they say that a refusal to hire them cannot be based on their age.

The law governs employers engaged in an industry affecting commerce who have 20 or more employees. It governs unions that either operate a hiring hall or have 25 or more members. Employment agencies are covered regardless of their size or the number of persons placed. If the employment agency regularly procures employees for an employer, it will be covered, even if it is not paid for its services. State and local government agencies are covered employers. Most, but not all, employees of the federal government enjoy the protection of the Act. In fact, the 1978 amendments eliminate the mandatory retirement age of 70 for most federal employees.

Under the 1967 Age Discrimination Act it is unlawful for an employer to fail or refuse to hire or to discharge any individual or otherwise discriminate against any individual with respect to his or her compensation, terms, conditions, or privileges of employment because of such individual's age, or to reduce the wage rate of any employee (irrespective of his or her age) in order to comply with the Act. It is unlawful for a union to exclude or to expel from its membership, or otherwise to discriminate against, any individual because of his or her age, or to cause or attempt to cause an employer to discriminate against an individual in violation of this section. It shall be unlawful for an employment agency to fail or refuse to refer for employment, or otherwise to discriminate against, any individual because of such individual's age, or to classify or refer for employment any individual on the basis of such individual's age. It is permissible to take action based on a person's age where age is a bona fide occupational qualification (BFOQ) reasonably necessary to the normal operation of the particular business, or where the differentiation is based on reasonable factors other than age, or to observe the terms of a bona fide seniority system. The original law allowed an employer to require mandatory retirement of an individual under the age of 65 if it were according to the terms of a bona fide employee benefit plan such as a retirement, pension, or insurance plan, which was not a subterfuge to evade the purpose of the Act. The 1978 Amendments removed this provision.

We began this section with the comment that the law prohibits discrimination against individuals between the ages of 40 and 70. Naturally, like most laws, there are some exceptions. The law does permit an employer to compulsorily retire certain executives at age 65. If the person was a bona fide executive or in a high-level policymaking position for the two-year period immediately before retirement, and is entitled to a pension of at least $27,000, that person can be forced to retire at age 65. A college or university can require a tenured professor to retire at age 65 until July 1, 1982. After that date, tenured professors will enjoy protection until age 70.

Let us look at the BFOQ exception in the law. The most important case in this area involves Greyhound Lines. Greyhound declined to consider applications for intercity bus drivers from individuals 35 years of age or older. The Secretary of Labor alleged that this violated the Act. Greyhound argued that age was a BFOQ for such drivers. Greyhound won the case. The court showed great concern for the passenger safety issue. It pointed out that more was involved than simply the safety of the employee. It held that for the age limitation to be valid, Greyhound must demonstrate that it has a rational basis in fact to believe that elimination of its maximum hiring age will increase the likelihood of risk of harm to its passengers. It said that Greyhound need only show a minimal increase of risk of harm—that one more person's safety would be jeopardized. The government had argued that applicants 40 to 65 years of age should be judged on the basis of their "functional age" (ability to perform the job), rather than their chronological age. The court rejected this by saying that it is not clear that functional age is readily determinable and that it is questionable whether Greyhound could practically scrutinize their continued fitness on a frequent and regular basis. The court ruled that Greyhound had proved its case by proving three things: (1) rigors of extra board assignments (the type of driving required of new employees), (2) degenerative physical and sensory changes brought on by the aging process beginning in the late thirties, and (3) statistical evidence showing that its safest drivers had 16 to 20 years of experience and were between 50 and 55 years of age. This could not be attained by hiring applicants 40 years of age or over. [*Hodgson* v. *Greyhound Lines,* 499 F.2d 859 (1974).] On January 20, 1975, the Supreme Court refused to hear an appeal of the case.

In another case, this one involving a test pilot, a court ruled that age is not a BFOQ for test pilots where the employer's evidence related to changes that accompany the aging process in the general population, while the employee's evidence tended to show that the aging process occurs more slowly and to a lesser degree among pilots and where the accident rate actually decreased with age. [*Houghton* v. *McDonnell Douglas,* 553 F.2d 561 (1971).]

Age is not a BFOQ when it comes to jobs such as tellers, as exemplified in the following factual situation. Between June 12, 1968, and July 14, 1969, the defendant employer hired 35 tellers or teller trainees, none of whom was over 40 years of age. When two women applied, both of whom were over 40, the personnel manager wrote in his notes: "too old for teller" and "wants teller, too old." On December 3, 1968, a request was placed with an employment agency for teller trainees and the employer specified applicants to be female, moderately intelligent, with or without experience, and ages 21–24. The court concluded that the ADEA has been violated. [*Hodgson* v. *First Federal Savings & Loan*, 455 F.2d 818 (1972).]

Since newspapers' classified ads jobs sections serve as a source for potential jobs, the Act devotes attention to such ads and also to job referrals. In relevant part, it provides that:

> It shall be unlawful for an employer, labor organization, or employment agency to print or publish, or cause to be printed or published, any notice or advertisement relating to employment by such an employer or membership in or any classification or referral for employment by such a labor organization, or relating to any classification or referral for employment by such an employment agency, indicating any preference, limitation, specification, or discrimination, based on age.

In developing guidelines for this portion of the Act, the Department of Labor interpreted such words and phrases as "young," "boy," "girl," "age 25 to 35," "recent college graduate" to be illegal. Likewise, phrases such as "retired person" or "Social Security recipient," that indicate a preference for individuals over 70, are considered impermissible by the Department of Labor. However, the federal courts do not regard all such phrases to be a *per se* violation. In *Hodgson* v. *Approved Personnel Service, Inc.*, 44 L.W. 2208 (1975), the Fourth Circuit decided that such phrases must be judged by reading them in context. The respondent employment agency used such terms as a part of its job ads over a period of three and a half years. The Secretary of Labor had maintained that these were "trigger words" that constituted a *per se* violation when present in a job ad. Instead, the court concluded that such a term as "junior" executive or secretary in many contexts refers to the duties to be performed by the employee rather than age. On the other hand, the court ruled that the terms "girl" or "career girl" implied youth and therefore violate the Act.

Before Congress amended the law to include state and local government employees, there was a legal challenge to state laws that mandated early retirement. A Massachusetts state policeman argued that a state law requiring state police to retire at the age of 50, when other state employees could work beyond that year, denied him equal protection of the law in violation of the Fourteenth Amendment. In *Mass. Bd. of Retirement* v. *Murgia*, 427 U.S. 307 (1976), the Supreme Court upheld the constitutionality of the Massachusetts law.

After Congress amended the law, various states challenged the constitutionality of the amendment. They argued that the Constitution does not grant Congress the power to regulate the States in regard to such matters. In the following case the Supreme Court decided that Congress does have such power and that the states must abide by the age discrimination law.

EEOC v. WYOMING
103 S.Ct. 1054 (1983)

(Authors' note: Bill Crump, a supervisor in the Wyoming Game and Fish Department, was involuntarily retired at age 55 under the provisions of Wyoming law. EEOC challenged the retirement as being in violation of the Age Discrimination Act. Wyoming argued that Congress violated the Tenth Amendment when it applied the Act to the States. Wyoming supported its argument by pointing to the Supreme Court's decision in the National League of Cities case where the Congressional extension of the wage and hour law to the states was declared unconstitutional.)

JUSTICE BRENNAN *delivered the opinion of the Court.*

The question presented in this case is whether Congress acted constitutionally when, in 1974, it extended the definition of "employer" under § 11(b) of the Act to include state and local governments.

National League of Cities v. *Usery* struck down Congress's attempt to extend the wage and hour provisions of the Fair Labor Standards Act to state and local governments.

The management of state parks is clearly a traditional state function. As we have already emphasized, however, the purpose of the doctrine of immunity articulated in *National League of Cities* was to protect States from federal intrusions that might threaten their "separate and independent existence." We conclude that the degree of federal intrusion in this case is sufficiently less serious than it was in *National League of Cities* so as to make it unnecessary for us to override Congress's express choice to extend its regulatory authority to the States.

In this case, appellees claim no substantial stake in their retirement policy other than "assur[ing] the physical preparedness of Wyoming game wardens to perform their duties." Under the ADEA, however, the State may still, at the very least, assess the fitness of its game wardens and dismiss those wardens whom it reasonably finds to be unfit. Put another way, the Act requires the State to achieve its goals in a more individualized and careful manner than would otherwise be the case, but it does not require the State to abandon those goals, or to abandon the public policy decisions underlying them.

Perhaps more important, appellees remain free under the ADEA to continue to do *precisely what they are doing now,* if they can demonstrate that age is a "bona fide" occupational qualification" for the job of game warden. Thus, . . . even the State's discretion to achieve its goals *in the way it thinks best* is not being overridden entirely, but is merely being tested against a reasonable federal standard.

Finally, the Court's concern in *National League of Cities* was not only with the effect of the federal regulatory scheme on the particular decisions it was purporting to regulate, but also with the potential impact of that scheme on the States' ability to structure operations and set priorities over a wide range of decisions. In this case, we cannot conclude from the nature of the ADEA that it will have either a director or an obvious negative effect on state finances.

The extension of the ADEA to cover state and local governments, both on its face and as applied in this case, was a valid exercise of Congress's powers under the Commerce Clause.

Case Questions   1. Does this decision mean that Wyoming must retain on the payroll all game wardens who are 55 years of age and older?

2. Should Congress have the power to interfere in the employer-employee relationship between a state and one of its citizens?

As noted earlier, the Secretary of Labor used to enforce this law, whereas today EEOC has the enforcement power. EEOC is empowered to make investigations and require the keeping of records necessary for administration of the Act. Voluntary settlement of disputes is encouraged. In fact, before EEOC can sue, it must attempt to reach a voluntary elimination of the discrimination.

An individual cannot file a private lawsuit until 60 days after he or she has filed a charge with EEOC alleging unlawful discrimination. The charge must be filed within 180 days after the alleged unlawful practice occurred. If a state agency has the power to enforce age discrimination cases, the charge must be filed within 300 days of the alleged occurrence, or within 30 days after receipt by the individual of notice of termination of proceedings under state law, whichever is earlier. After a charge is filed with EEOC, the persons named in the charge are notified and an attempt is made to reach a voluntary settlement of the case. If voluntary settlement proves impossible, then the EEOC or the individual can bring suit. The lawsuit must be filed within two years of the violation, or three years if the violation was willful. The time period during which the EEOC is attempting to reach a voluntary settlement is not counted in the two- or three-year period. In legal language, the conciliation tolls the statute of limitations. If the EEOC brings the lawsuit, the right of the individual to sue is terminated. The 1978 amendments make clear that an individual is entitled to a jury trial in age discrimination cases. An individual that has been the victim of illegal discrimination is entitled to monetary damages and equitable relief, and a court *must* award him or her reasonable attorney's fees. Of course, if the EEOC brings the lawsuit, the individual will have no legal fees.

The Rehabilitation Act of 1973 was passed by Congress and signed by the President as part of the federal effort to remove discriminatory barriers to employment. Section 504 of the Act provides in pertinent part:

Discrimination Against the Handicapped

> No otherwise qualified handicapped individual in the United States . . . shall, solely by reason of his handicap, be excluded from participation in, be denied the benefits of, or be subjected to discrimination under any program or activity receiving Federal financial assistance. . . .

Section 503 of the Act requires those receiving federal contracts in excess of $2500 to take affirmative action to employ and advance in employment qualified handicapped persons. Section 501 bars federal agencies from discriminating against handicapped individuals in the employment process. Handicapped can mean either a physical or mental impairment that substantially limits a person's activity. The Office of Federal Contract Compliance Programs (OFCCP) in the U.S. Department of Labor enforces Section 503 through an administrative process. If that office determines that a violation has occurred, there are three sanctions that can be imposed on the federal contractor: (1) debarment from future federal contracts, (2) cancellation of a current contract, and (3) withholding progress payments due on current contracts. If that office decides to take no action, even though they believe a violation has occurred, can the aggrieved individual bring a private suit to collect damages? The answer is unclear. Originally the courts seemed to answer "no." However, Congress amended the law in 1978 (Rehabilitation, Comprehensive Services & Developmental Disabilities Act of 1978). One of the amendments specifies that the prevailing party in a lawsuit, other than the United States, may be provided with reasonable attorney's fees by the court. If Congress is saying the winner of the lawsuit can recover their legal fees, it seems only logical that Congress is saying that a private individual can bring a lawsuit in the first place. However, a 1980 court decision seems to indicate otherwise. It will take some time before we know the correct answer to the question.

It should be noted that the first section quoted, Section 504, does not speak in terms of employment. Instead it speaks of those receiving federal financial assistance. The applicability of this section has also resulted in mixed results from the courts. It also will require future litigation before one can definitely say what that section means, to whom it applies, and who can bring a lawsuit for any violation.

Office of Federal Contract Compliance Programs

Executive Order 11246 forbids discrimination by contractors and subcontractors that do business with the federal government. While this executive order resembles in many respects the provisions of the Civil Rights Act, there are some differences. An important difference is its requirement that those covered by the order take affirmative action to remove employment barriers to minorities and women. For example, in the famous "Philadelphia Plan," contractors were required to meet an affirmative action plan that established goals for hiring minority workers based on that minority group's percentage of representation in the construction industry in a given geographical area. Any bidder on construction contracts in excess of $10,000 must certify that it will take the necessary affirmative action and see that its subcontractors do likewise. Those who are not in the construction industry, but do business with the federal government, are also covered by the order. If the employer has 50 or more employees and a contract in excess of $50,000, it must adopt a written affirmative action plan. Such a plan must establish goals and timetables for achieving those minority and women hiring goals.

The Office of Federal Contract Compliance Programs (OFCCP) in the U.S. Department of Labor enforces Executive Order 11246. Responsibility for compliance has been assigned to certain other federal agencies in some specific industries. The idea is that certain agencies will be more familiar with programs in certain industries. For example, the Defense Department has compliance responsibilities for contractors performing defense contracts. OFCCP normally leaves administration of cases within these industries to the specific federal agency, but it can take over responsibility if it so desires. OFCCP has several remedies available to it in the case of noncompliance. It can debar the contractor from future federal contracts, cancel current contracts, or withhold installment payments due on current contracts.

Review Problems

1. As a member of one of the world's major religions, Jim has the religious obligation to pray five times daily. Three of the prayer times cause no difficulty as they occur either when he is off the job or on lunch break. Two of the times, however, fall during his work shift. Jim works in a food processing plant. He stands at the end of a conveyor belt where he picks up bottles of salad dressing and places them in cardboard boxes. The conveyor belt is part of a continuous operation that operates around the clock. The belt itself is only stopped for lunch breaks and for a short period during the change in work shifts. Jim wants the conveyor belt to be halted for about ten minutes twice during his shift so that he can pray, or he desires another job in the plant that allows him the prayer time. What is the employer's obligation in this situation? *Reasonable adjust if possible – otherwise no obligation*

2. The personnel director of a company is faced with making a payroll cutback of approximately $70,000. Instead of discharging three employees in their late 20's, who earn a total of $70,000, the director decides to eliminate the positions of two individuals in their 50's, whose salaries total that amount. Is the director's action on safe legal ground? *Surface – age discrimination*

3. A union is on strike against an employer. The union pays strike benefits to its members. However, to qualify for these benefits a member must pull picket duty a minimum of 10 hours per week. The employer's plant is located in a tough part of town. Consequently, the union leadership decrees that the women members will be exempt from night picket duty. Is this exemption legal? *No – sex discrim. against males*

4. A U.S. company has operations in a foreign country that discriminates against women and members of certain religious groups. A properly qualified woman fills out an application for a position in that country. The company hires her and instructs her to report for work in the country the following month. However, she is unable to report for work when the country refuses to grant her the visa that is necessary for entry. Is this woman the victim of illegal discrimination? *No – country can keep her out.*

5. An oil company has operations in South America. The prevailing mores and cultural customs of Latin America are such that customers and oil distributors would not regard it as desirable to deal with a woman in a high-level management position. In fact, they might find it offensive. Thus, when the position of director of international operations becomes vacant, the company states that being male is a BFOQ for the job. Is the company claim a valid one? *No, stereotypes + prejud of customers don't matt*

6. A woman is an operator in the rolling mill portion of a steel plant. Such an operator performs her job in the very small confines of a control booth high above the plant floor. At the eight-month point of her pregnancy, the operator is too large to gain access into the control booth. Thus, the employer informs her that it will be necessary for her to begin her pregnancy leave. Is the employer's action legal? *yes-can't* What if the employer allowed overweight male operators to transfer to another job when they found it impossible to squeeze into the control booth? *Then discrimination*

7. Should Congress pass legislation mandating equal pay for individuals who hold jobs of comparable worth to the employer? Is the position of police officer of comparable worth to that of a fire fighter?

8. An employer regards marriage as a sign of stability and therefore hires only married individuals. In that company, singles need not apply, and on divorce, the employee will be discharged. The employer will allow employees to retain their job on the death of a spouse. Is such an employment standard permissible?

probably ok surviving spouses could be a problem.

9. There is a job vacancy in a plant. A woman has the most seniority and is informed that the job is hers, if she can demonstrate her ability to perform each task of the job classification. She adequately performs each task except one. She is unable to dismantle a machine by grasping a major section of it, lowering it four feet to the ground, and then replacing it. The machine section weighs 200 pounds, and it must be removed twice a year for the proper maintenance of the equipment. When denied the job, she points out the fact that, while the job description calls for the machine operator to perform this task, the past male operator was assisted by two to three co-workers when maintenance was necessary. The company will not accept her argument and gives the job to another person. Has this woman been treated legally? *No - description isn't accurate*

10. A male and female employee are engaging in an illicit affair with each other. When their supervisor learns of it, disciplinary action is recommended. The woman is discharged and the letter of dismissal cites "immoral behavior unbecoming an employee." A letter of reprimand is placed in the male employee's personnel file, but he is allowed to retain his job because, in the words of his boss, "any number of red blooded males do what he did." Is this sex discrimination or the reasonable exercise of discretion by an employer? *NO WAY*

Business Organization Duties to the Public

21

The modern business corporation in America today is by far the dominant form of business organization in terms of productive assets owned. Its ascendancy has been followed by increasing government attempts, primarily at the federal level, to impose on it and other forms of business organizations new legal duties intended to protect or serve the corporation's major constituencies. These attempts have been sometimes crude and often costly. With the election of President Reagan, a process of retreat from such attempts, or at least a retrenchment, is under way. But, like it or not, federal regulation is here to stay.

The cost to business organizations of "federal regulation" is substantial and is likely to remain so. Business organizations are spending millions of dollars to alter their management structures and productive processes in order to achieve compliance with this federal legislation. For example, on December 15, 1975, *Newsweek* Magazine (p. 45) reported that in 1975, Goodyear Tire and Rubber Company spent the following amounts to achieve compliance with federal regulations:

Environmental costs (capital, equipment, manpower, etc.)	$17.2 million
Occupational safety and health	6.9 million
Motor vehicle safety standards (equipment and testing of tires)	3.4 million
Personnel and administration	2.5 million
Total	$30.0 million

So far in this text we have examined federal legislation as it applies to two major constituencies of the business corporation: the shareholders and the stocktrading public (the Federal Security Laws), and the employees (the Wagner Act, the Equal Pay Act, the 1967 Civil Rights Act, OSHA, etc.). This chapter presents material on the law protecting two more constituencies. The first is the consuming public—those who buy consumer goods. The second is the public in general and its (our) right to a pollution-free environment. So, this chapter focuses on the law compensating or protecting the consuming public from defective products. This area of law is also known as products liability law or, in more general terms, consumer law. A second focus will be on the broad outlines of environmental law.

The common law and federal statutory law in these two areas is relatively new. Its application in many areas has not been attempted before. Therefore, until a body of case law develops adding stability and clarity to the application of the legislation (with regard to Consumer Product Safety Commission rules and regulations especially) it will be subject to varying interpretation and even, perhaps, substantial alteration by Congress or administrative agencies.

While the impact of recent federal legislation on business organizations is analyzed and evaluated by social and economic commentators and scholars, it seems clear that not all the activity, products, or services generated by these organizations can be subject to legislation. There remain significant issues about the conduct of business organizations, megacorporations in particular, that are unresolved by legislative act. These issues are often lumped into one vaguely defined area called "social responsibility." This area of dimly perceived and debatable duties is the subject of the final portion of this chapter.

Products Liability Law

The duties creating liability for producing a defective product are now an unclear mix of state and federal-level duties. The law of products liability has, until very recently, been created by state legislatures and courts, and thus state law is still most important in providing a remedy to an injured consumer. Therefore we begin our examination of products liability law at the state level and then explain when, how, and why the federal government became involved. Also, we find it convenient to divide the common law principles discussed into two groups: those arising from contract law and those arising from tort law. We will present the material in that order.

Contract Liability Through Warranty: State Law

The Uniform Commercial Code (UCC) is a comprehensive piece of legislation that, in its Article 2, covers contracts for the sale of goods. Contracts for services are not covered. Work on this legislation began in the 1940s, and by 1968, only Louisiana had not adopted most portions of the code in its state legislative scheme. This is the legislation referred to in Chapter 1 that supplanted much of the common law of contracts.

One of the firmly entrenched common law concepts was *caveat emptor* (buyer beware). This phrase stood for the legal principle that the buyer of a product had a duty to inspect and try out the product before purchase. If the buyer satisfied this duty or failed to exercise the privilege of a thorough inspection, and then purchased a product that subsequently failed, it was the purchaser's loss. Although there are some vestiges of this principle in today's court opinions, generally speaking it is in a state of sharp descent. As a result of the increasing complexity of consumer goods, the principle simply was no longer fair. It was impossible to tell before purchase, for example, if a complex piece of machinery such as an automobile could not only fulfill all of the expectations of the purchaser but would also last a reasonable length of time. More and more consumers were led to rely on the seller's assertions of performances and the seller's judgment in selecting the goods for the purchaser's needs.

The UCC recognizes this shift in consumer reliance by providing that a seller of goods may be liable for breach of warranty in three circumstances.

Section 2-313 of Article 2 of the UCC provides:

(1) Express warranties by the seller are created as follows:
    (a) Any affirmation of fact or promise made by the seller to the buyer which relates to the goods and becomes part of the basis of the bargain creates an express warranty that the goods shall conform to the affirmation or promise.
    (b) Any description of the goods which is made part of the basis of the bargain creates an express warranty that the goods shall conform to the description.
    (c) Any sample or model which is made part of the basis of the bargain creates an express warranty that the whole of the goods shall conform to the sample or model.
(2) It is not necessary to the creation of an express warranty that the seller use formal words such as "warranty" or "guarantee" or that he have a specific intention to make a warranty, but an affirmation merely of the value of the goods or a statement purporting to be merely the seller's opinion or commendation of the goods does not create a warranty.

If a consumer *relies* on a promise of the seller or manufacturer that is made on the packaging material or in advertising materials or made by the selling agent at the time of sale, and the item fails to fulfill that promise, the buyer is given a cause of action against the seller or manufacturer based on Section 2-313 for a breach of the promise.

Section 2-314 provides:

(1) Unless excluded or modified . . . a warranty that the goods shall be merchantable is implied in a contract for their sale if the seller is a merchant with respect to goods of that kind. Under this section the serving for value of food or drink to be consumed either on the premises or elsewhere is a sale.
(2) Goods to be merchantable must be at least such as
    (a) pass without objection in the trade under the contract description; and
    (b) in the case of fungible goods, are of fair average quality within the description; and
    (c) are fit for the ordinary purposes for which such goods are used, and

    (d) run, within the variations permitted by the agreement, of even kind, quality and quantity within each unit and among all units involved; and

    (e) are adequately contained, packaged, and labeled as the agreement may require; and

    (f) conform to the promises or affirmations of fact made on the container or label if any.

  (3) Unless excluded or modified . . . other implied warranties may arise from course of dealings or usage of trade.

Section 2-315 provides:

consumer puts himself in hands of merchant to help select product.

Where the seller at the time of contracting has reason to know any particular purpose for which the goods are required and that the buyer is relying on the seller's skill or judgment to select or furnish suitable goods, there is unless excluded or modified under the next section an implied warranty that the goods <u>shall be fit for such purpose.</u>

Now that these three sections are before you, several differences in their terms should be noted. First observe that Sections 2-313 and 2-315 apply to *sellers* of goods and Section 2-314 applies to sellers who are merchants. The term "merchant" as it is used here is narrower than the term seller and refers to a person, a corporation, or other legal entity who deals in goods of the kind sold or holds itself out as having knowledge or skill peculiar to the goods involved. [UCC § 2-104(1)]. A seller is anyone who is selling. Second, note that in both Sections 2-314 and 2-315 the words "unless excluded or modified" appear.

Exclusion or Modification of Warranties

Section 2-316 provides for the exclusion or modification of warranties. Somewhat simplified, this section provides that if an *express warranty* is made under Section 2-313 and then an attempt to exclude or modify the warranty is made by the seller, it will not be allowed because such an attempt is inconsistent with the making of the *express warranty*. Thus *express warranties* may not be excluded or modified once they are made. The Section further provides that to exclude or modify the *implied warranty of merchantability* (§ 2-314), the language so used must mention merchantability and must be conspicuous. To exclude or modify the implied warranty of fitness for a particular purpose (§ 2-315) there must be a writing and the language must be conspicuous. The UCC further provides in Section 2-316 that the expression "as is" or "with all faults" or other language commonly used to exclude warranties does operate to exclude implied warranties. If the packaging states "there are no warranties which extend beyond the description on the face hereof" this will operate to exclude all warranties of fitness. There are also other provisions relating to the waiver of warranties, but the point is that the waiver and modification provisions are present in the UCC, and they are often used by manufacturers and sellers so that little protection is afforded the consumer. This is especially true where all the manufacturers in a market adopt the same waiver and modification provisions. (See the *Henningen* case.) The potential abuse of the waiver and modification section of the UCC is one of the major reasons for the passage of recent federal legislation dealing with warranties. Before we proceed to a discussion of this legislation, however, a second problem area of the UCC must be identified.

The warranty provisions already discussed do not differentiate between the various levels of distribution for a product. Typically an item is produced and packaged by a manufacturer, shipped to a wholesaler, which distributes to a retailer, which sells to a consumer. At each level, title to the goods may change hands so that a "sale of goods" has taken place. If there is a breach of a warranty, against whom may the consumer bring suit? The code itself does not answer this question. One might argue that a consumer could sue his or her seller, that the seller could sue its seller, and so on up the chain until the manufacturer or the one responsible for the breach is ultimately liable. This result would not only cause a needless multiplicity of lawsuits but might result in difficulties if one of the sellers is insolvent. Nevertheless, some courts have read the UCC as compelling this result. However, the better view is that such a result is not required nor was it intended by the drafters of the UCC.[1] Most recent cases have allowed an injured consumer to sue the manufacturer based on warranties made by it. This result not only places liability on those who are ultimately responsible for the breach, but is fair in light of the massive advertising campaigns by many manufacturers inducing consumers to buy.

A related problem is to whom the warranties extend. A suggested version of Section 2-318 of the UCC provides in part that:

> A seller's warranty whether express or implied extends to any natural person who is in the family or household of his buyer or who is a guest in his home if it is reasonable to expect that such person may use, consume or be affected by the goods. . . .

Some courts have reasoned that since the UCC, Article 2, is concerned with contracts, recovery for a breach of warranty may only be awarded to one contracting with ("in privity with") a seller and that Section 2-318 was intended to expand this scope of liability. Thus Section 2-318 limited liability to buyers, family or household members, and guests of the buyer.[2] This result has been criticized by some authorities[3] who argue that Section 2-318 was to be only a partial statement of those to whom the warranties extended. Indeed, bystanders injured by defective products have recovered in some states.[4]

In concluding this section we present one of the leading cases in the product liability field. This case illustrates not only how major manufacturers attempted to withdraw warranties once made, but also that in some cases courts will provide a measure of flexibility in the law to protect those at the mercy of massive concentrations of economic power. The case was decided under the Uniform Sale of Goods Law, the UCC's predecessor. This does not alter the viability of the court's reasoning. Under the UCC, this case would probably be decided the same way. Also, note that as a result of the inadequate protection provided by the UCC warranty provisions, two results have been manifest. The first, already noted, is that Congress has passed new federal laws on warranties. The second is that tort law has developed and expanded its concept of negligent design and strict liability to provide remedies where the UCC might not. Both of these subjects are discussed in greater detail following this case.

HENNINGSEN v. BLOOMFIELD MOTORS, INC. and CHRYSLER CORPORATION
32 N.J. 358, 161 A.2d 69 (Sup. Ct. of N.J., 1960)

FRANCIS, J.

Plaintiff, Clause H. Henningsen, purchased a Plymouth automobile, manufactured by defendant Chrysler Corporation, from defendant Bloomfield Motors, Inc. His wife, plaintiff Helen Henningsen, was injured while driving it and instituted suit against both defendants to recover damages on account of her injuries. . . . The complaint was predicated upon breach of express and implied warranties and upon negligence. At the trial the negligence counts were dismissed by the court and the cause was submitted to the jury for determination solely on the issues of implied warranty of merchantability. Verdicts were returned against both defendants and in favor of the plaintiffs. Defendants appealed. . . .

The facts are not complicated, but a general outline of them is necessary to an understanding of the case.

On May 7, 1955 Mr. and Mrs. Henningsen visited the place of business of Bloomfield Motors, Inc., an authorized De Soto and Plymouth dealer, to look at a Plymouth. . . . They were shown a Plymouth which appealed to them and the purchase followed. The record indicates that Mr. Henningsen intended the car as a Mother's Day gift to his wife. He said

the intention was communicated to the dealer. When the purchase order or contract was prepared and presented, the husband executed it alone. His wife did not join as a party.

The purchase order was a printed form of one page. On the front it contained blanks to be filled in with a description of the automobile to be sold, the various accessories to be included, and the details of the financing. . . .

The reverse side of the contract contains 8-½ inches of fine print. . . . The page is headed "Conditions" and contains ten separate paragraphs consisting of 65 lines in all. . . . In the seventh paragraph, about two-thirds of the way down the page, the warranty, which is the focal point of the case, is set forth. It is as follows:

> 7. It is expressly agreed that there are no warranties, express or implied, made by either the dealer or the manufacturer on the motor vehicle, chassis, or parts furnished hereunder except as follows.
> The manufacturer warrants each new motor vehicle (including original equipment placed thereon by the manufacturer except tires), chassis or parts manufactured by it to be free from defects in material or workmanship under normal use and service. Its obligation under this warranty being limited to making good at its factory any part or parts thereof which shall, within ninety (90) days after delivery of such vehicle to the original purchaser or before such vehicle has been driven 4,000 miles, whichever event shall first occur, be re-

turned to it with transportation charges pre-paid and which its examination shall disclose to its satisfaction to have been thus defective; *this warranty being expressly in lieu of all other warranties expressed or implied and all other obligations or liabilities on its part,* . . . * * *. (Emphasis ours.)

[The car] had no servicing and no mishaps of any kind before the event of May 19. That day, Mrs. Henningsen drove to Asbury Park. On the way down and in returning, the car performed in normal fashion until the accident occurred.

She was proceeding north on Route 36 in Highlands, New Jersey, at 20–22 miles per hour. The highway was paved and smooth, and contained two lanes for northbound travel. She was riding in the right hand lane. Suddenly she heard a loud noise "from the bottom, by the hood." It "felt as if something cracked." The steering wheel spun in her hands; the car veered sharply to the right and crashed into a highway sign and a brick wall. No other vehicle was in any way involved. A bus operator driving in the left-hand lane testified that he observed plaintiffs' car approaching in normal fashion in the opposite direction; "all of a sudden [it] veered at 90 degrees . . . and right into this wall." As a result of the impact, the front of the car was so badly damaged that it was impossible to determine if any of the parts of the steering wheel mechanism or workmanship or assembly were defective or improper prior to the accident. The condition was such that the collision insurance carrier, after inspection, declared the vehicle a total loss. It had 468 miles on the speedometer at the time.

* * *

The Claim of Implied Warranty Against the Manufacturer

In the ordinary case of sale of goods by description an implied warranty of merchantability is an integral part of the transaction. . . . If the buyer, expressly or by implication, makes known to the seller the particular purpose for which the article is required and it appears that he has relied on the seller's skill or judgment, an implied warranty arises of reasonable fitness for that purpose. . . . The former type of warranty simply means that the thing sold is reasonably fit for the general purpose for which it is manufactured and sold. . . .

The uniform act codified, extended and liberalized the common law of sales. The motivation in part was to ameliorate the harsh doctrine of *caveat emptor,* and in some measure to impose a reciprocal obligation on the seller to beware. The transcendent value of the legislation, particularly with respect to implied warranties, rests in the fact that obligations on the part of the seller were imposed by operation of law, and did not depend on their existence upon express agreement of the parties. And of tremendous significance in a rapidly expanding commercial society was the recognition of the right to recover damages on account of personal injuries arising from breach of warranty. . . . Recovery of damages does not depend upon proof of negligence or knowledge of the defect.

As the Sales Act and its liberal interpretation by the courts threw this protective cloak about the buyer, the decisions in various jurisdictions revealed beyond doubt that many manufacturers took steps to avoid these ever increasing warranty obligations. Realizing that the act governed the relationship of buyer and seller, they undertook to withdraw from actual and direct contractual contact with the buyer. They ceased selling products to the consuming public through their own employees and making contracts of sale in their own names. Instead, a system of independent dealers was established; their products were sold to dealers who in turn dealt with the buying public, ostensibly solely in their own personal capacity as sellers. In the past in many instances, manufacturers were able to transfer to the dealers burdens imposed by the act and thus achieved a large measure of immunity for themselves. But, as will be noted in more detail hereafter, such marketing practices, coupled with the advent of large scale advertising by manufacturers to promote the purchase of these goods from dealers by members of the public, provided a basis upon which the existence of express or implied warranties were predicated, even though the manufacturer was not a party to the contract of sale.

With these considerations in mind, we come to a study of the express warranty on the reverse side of the purchase order signed by Clause Henningsen. . . .

The terms of the warranty are a sad commentary upon the automobile manufacturers' marketing practices. . . .

The manufacturer agrees to replace defective parts for 90 days after the sale or until the car has been driven 4,000 miles, whichever is first to occur, *if the part is sent to the factory, transportation charges prepaid, and if examination discloses to its satisfaction that the part is defective.* It is difficult to imagine a greater burden on the consumer, or less satisfactory remedy. Aside from imposing on the buyer the trouble of removing and shipping the part, the maker has sought to retain the uncontrolled discretion to decide the issue of defectiveness. Some courts have removed much of the force of that reservation by declaring that the purchaser is not bound by the manufacturer's decision. . . .

The matters referred to represent only a small part of the illusory character of the security presented by the warranty. Thus far the analysis has dealt only with the remedy provided in the case of a defective part. What relief is provided when the breach of the warranty results in personal injury to the buyer? [A]s we have said above, the law is clear that such damages are recoverable under an ordinary warranty. The right exists whether the warranty sued on is express or implied. . . . And, of course, it has long since been settled that where the buyer or a member of his family

driving with his permission suffers injuries because of negligent manufacture or construction of the vehicle, the manufacturer's liability exists. . . . But in this instance, after reciting that defective parts will be replaced at the factory, the alleged agreement relied upon by Chrysler provides that the manufacturer's "obligation under this warranty" is limited to that undertaking; further, that such remedy is "in lieu of all other warranties, express or implied, and all other obligations or liabilities on its part." The contention has been raised that such language bars any claim for personal injuries which may emanate from a breach of the warranty. . . .

Putting aside for the time being the problem of the efficacy of the disclaimer provisions contained in the express warranty, a question of first importance to be decided is whether an implied warranty of merchantability by Chrysler Corporation accompanied the sale of the automobile to Clause Henningsen.

Chrysler points out that an implied warranty of merchantability is an incident of a contract of sale. It conceded, of course, the making of the original sale to Bloomfield Motors, Inc., but maintains that this transaction marked the terminal point of its contractual connection with the car. Then Chrysler urges that since it was not a party to the sale by the dealer to Henningsen, there is no privity of contract between it and the plaintiffs, and the absence of this privity eliminates any such implied warranty.

There is no doubt that under early common-law concepts of contractual liability only those persons who were parties to the bargain could sue for breach of it. In more recent times a noticeable disposition has appeared in a number of jurisdictions to break through the narrow barrier of privity when dealing with sales of goods in order to give realistic recognition to a universally accepted fact. The fact is that the dealer and the ordinary buyer do not, and are not expected to, buy goods, whether they be foodstuffs or automobiles, exclusively for their own consumption or use. Makers and manufacturers know that and advertise and market their products on that assumption; witness, the "family" car, the baby foods, etc. . . . With the advent of mass-marketing, the manufacturer became remote from the purchaser, sales were accomplished through intermediaries, and the demand for the product was created by advertising media. In such an economy it became obvious that the consumer was the person being cultivated. . . .

Accordingly, we hold that under modern marketing conditions, when a manufacturer puts a new automobile in the stream of trade and promotes its purchase by the public, an implied warranty that it is reasonably suitable for use as such accompanies it into the hands of the ultimate purchaser. Absence of agency between the manufacturer and the dealer who makes the ultimate sale is immaterial.

The Effect of the Disclaimer and Limitation of Liability Clauses on the Implied Warranty of Merchantability

The task of the judiciary is to administer the spirit as well as the letter of the law. On issues such as the present one, part of that burden is to protect the ordinary man against the loss of important rights through what, in effect, is the unilateral act of the manufacturer. The status of the automobile industry is unique. Manufacturers are few in number and strong in bargaining position. In the matter of warranties on the sales of their products, the Automotive Manufacturers Association has enabled them to present a united front. From the standpoint of the purchaser, there can be no arms length negotiating on the subject. Because his capacity for bargaining is so grossly unequal, the inexorable conclusion which follows is that he is not permitted to bargain at all. He must take or leave the automobile on the warranty terms dictated by the maker. He cannot turn to a competitor for better security.

Public policy is a term not easily defined. Its significance varies as the habits and needs of a people may vary. It is not static and the field of application is an ever increasing one. A contract, or a particular provision therein, valid in one era may be wholly opposed to the public policy of another. . . . Courts keep in mind the principle that the best interests of society demand that persons should not be unnecessarily restricted in their freedom to contract. But they do not hesitate to declare void as against public policy contractual provisions which clearly tend to the injury of the public in some way. . . .

Public policy at a given time finds expression in the Constitution, the statutory law and judicial decisions. In the area of sale of goods, the legislative will has imposed an implied warranty of merchantability as a general incident of sale of an automobile by description. The warranty does not depend upon the affirmative intention of the parties. It is a child of the law; it annexes itself to the contract because of the very nature of the transaction. The judicial process has recognized a right to recover damages for personal injuries arising from a breach of that warranty. The disclaimer of the implied warranty and exclusion of all obligations except those specifically assumed by the express warranty signify a studied effort to frustrate that protection. . . . The lawmakers did not authorize the automobile manufacturer to use its grossly disproportionate bargaining power to relieve itself from liability and to impose on the ordinary buyer, who in effect has no real freedom of choice, the grave danger of injury to himself and others that attends the sale of such a dangerous instrumentality as a defectively made automobile. In the framework of this case, illuminated as it is by the facts and the many decisions noted, we are of the opinion that Chrysler's attempted disclaimer of an implied warranty of merchantability and of the obligations arising therefrom is so inimical to the public good as to compel an adjudication of its invalidity. . . .

Under all of the circumstances outlined above, the judgment in favor of the plaintiffs and against the defendants is affirmed.

Case Questions

1. Define the "implied warranty" created by the court. Under what circumstances will a court be likely to create such a warranty?
2. Under what circumstances will a court consider limiting or voiding a written waiver of warranties made by a consumer?

Federal Warranty Legislation

The average consumer does not know the meaning of the words "express warranty" or "warranty of merchantability" or "warranty of fitness for a particular purpose." Moreover, if a consumer is educated enough to understand and be able to apply these rules, there is the chance that access to the legal system will prove too costly to redress the breach of such a warranty. Or, there is always the chance that the manufacturer has waived or modified the warranties when and if made. Consumer dissatisfaction with both their inability to understand the complex warranty provisions of the UCC and their reluctance to enforce breaches are two of the major reasons for the passage of the Consumer Product Warranty and Federal Trade Commission Improvements Act (also called the Magnuson—Moss Warranty—Federal Trade Commission Improvement Act), which became law on July 4, 1975.[5]

The Act seeks to regulate written product warranties and service contracts provided by manufacturers and suppliers. Also, the Act places some of the burden of enforcement and promulgation of warranty standards on the Federal Trade Commission. The Act does not alter the warranties of merchantability or fitness for a particular purpose created by the UCC; nor is it applicable when no warranties are made. It is applicable when a warranty is made and the cost of the item purchased exceeds $15.00.

At least three definitions are important under this Act. This applies to written warranties and defines these as any affirmation of fact, promise, or undertaking in writing that becomes part of the basis of the bargain. So, if the promise made is relied on to the extent that it forms part of the basis of the bargain, then the provisions of the Act apply if the product was distributed in or affected interstate commerce. Remember, this last requirement exists for all federal legislation. Second, the product sold must be bought by a *consumer,* who is defined as any person who buys a consumer product for purposes other than resale, or any person to whom the product is transferred during the warranty period. Third, the Act defines a consumer product as any tangible personal property normally used for personal, family, or household purposes. Contracts for the service of consumer products are also covered.

The items and persons covered by the act are extensive. We will not go into detail but will present here only an overview of the legislation. Fundamentally, the act attempts to compel sellers of consumer products to make clear to consumers the warranties made and the process that must be followed to claim a breach of the warranty. The Act also imposes certain minimum standards in the making of warranties and, finally, requires the FTC to prosecute violators and promulgate added rules and regulations for the implementation of the Act.

The one who makes a warranty (called a warrantor) is required to fully and conspicuously disclose the terms and limitations of the warranty to the consumer *before* the sale. Some of the items that warrantors should disclose are, among others, the following:[6]

1. A clear identification of the names and addresses of warrantors.
2. The identity of the party or parties to whom the warranty is extended.
3. The products or parts covered.
4. A statement as to what the warrantor will do, at whose expense the work will be done, and the period of time the warranty will last, assuming that the product fails to conform to the written warranty.
5. A statement of what the consumer must do and the expenses he will bear.
6. A statement of the exceptions and exclusions from the terms of the warranty.
7. The step-by-step procedure consumers must take in order to obtain performance of any obligation under the warranty.
8. Information about the availability and required usage by the consumer of any informal—dispute settlement procedure.
9. A brief summary of the legal remedies available to the consumer.
10. The time during which the warrantor will fulfill its obligations under the warranty.

Further, the Act stipulates that written warranties be conspicuously designated as either (1) a full warranty—with the duration of the warranty stated; or (2) a limited warranty. A full (e.g., two-year) warranty must conform to certain federal minimum content standards. These substantive standards state that:[7]

1. Any defects, malfunctions, or inability to conform to the terms of a written warranty must be corrected by the warrantor without charge and within a reasonable length of time.

2. The warrantor cannot limit the period of time within which implied warranties will be effective with respect to the consumer product.

3. The warrantor cannot limit or exclude consequential damages on a consumer product unless noted conspicuously on the face of the warranty.

4. The warrantor must allow the consumer to choose between a refund of the purchase price or replacement of the defective product or part whenever a reasonable number of attempts to remedy the defect or malfunction has occurred.

A "limited warranty" need not satisfy these standards but it must be conspicuously labeled as such. Remember that a warranty is any statement of fact, promise, or undertaking. So, a statement such as "satisfaction guaranteed" or the like is neither a full or limited warranty (it is sometimes referred to as seller's puffing). These "designation" requirements just referred to apply to goods costing more than $15.00. Do not confuse this with the "disclosure" requirements that are applicable to written warranties on consumer products costing more than $5.00.

Perhaps the most significant provision of the act is the one limiting the use of written warranties to disclaim the implied warranties created in law by the UCC. This is the practice revealed by the manufacturer of Plymouth in the *Henningsen* case. The Act provides that a written warranty may not be used to impose any limitation on the duration of implied warranties.[8] If a written warranty of reasonable duration is given, however, an implied warranty may be limited to the same time period. Moreover, the Act is clear in its statement that a supplier may not disclaim or modify an implied warranty when either a written warranty is given or a service contract is entered into at the time of sale or written 90 days thereafter.[9]

The remedy provisions of the Act are also noteworthy. If the Act applies to a warrantor and a breach of the warranty occurs, the warrantor or his designated representative must remedy the defect within a reasonable time and without charge. The term "without charge" means that the warrantor may not assess the consumer for any costs the warrantor or his representative incur in connection with the required remedy.[10]

In the provision referred to as an "anti-lemon" provision, the consumer may receive a refund or replacement if the warrantor does not remedy the defect after a reasonable number of attempts.[11] What is "reasonable" in this case awaits definition by the FTC.

Enforcement of the Act's provisions are divided between the consumer and the government. If informal attempts to settle disputed claims are not sufficient the individual may seek redress in the courts. If there are at least 100 named plaintiffs and the claims of each exceed $25 and the aggregate of all claims, exclusive of interest and costs, exceeds $50,000, class actions are authorized.[12] If repeated violations are evident or if a warrantor fails to comply with a cease and desist order of the FTC, then either the FTC or the Justice Department may bring an action in the district court asking for an injunction. Persons or corporations knowingly violating a cease and desist order declaring conduct to be unfair and deceptive are subject to a civil penalty not exceeding $10,000 for each violation.[13]

Finally, considerable responsibility is placed on the FTC for developing efficient remedies (especially for the anti-lemon provisions) and in promulgating minimum requirements for informal dispute settlement and for developing other standards needed for the accomplishment of the Act's objectives. Only if the consumer and the FTC accept the responsibilities placed on them by the Act (no amount of legislation can make a consumer pursue remedies if he or she simply is not interested or does not take the time) will the Act achieve its objectives of attempting to hold sellers liable for the warranties they make.

Tort Liability Through Negligent Design and Strict Liability

In this section of the chapter we again return to a brief presentation of state law. An entirely separate set of legal principles that provide remedies to a consumer injured by a defectively produced product are provided by the application of tort law. These tort remedies may be sought in the same trial in which the breach of the contract-warranty remedies are also alleged. It is good to argue the tort duties even in those cases where the application of current warranty law would be applicable because the warranty arguments may fail because of some technicality. For example, it may be that the manufacturer had successfully modified or waived the warranty, or perhaps the express warranty relied on did not form the basis of the bargain. More importantly, tort law provides a remedy to those who would be denied a remedy by some courts because they were not in privity with—had not contracted with—the manufacturer.

Tort law has developed two lines of analysis. These lines are not clear and appear to overlap in many instances. The older of the two holds simply that a manufacturer has a duty to design a product reasonably fit for its intended use. Proving negligent design, however, was, and continues to be, a substantial problem. What if, for example, all of the manufacturers in the market producing the defective product used the same design and manufacturing methods? How is the standard of "reasonableness" to be derived? Moreover, how is a plaintiff to show the negligent design was *the cause* of the defect resulting in injury? One of the most interesting cases in this area, *Larsen* v. *General Motors*, is used to illustrate that in some circumstances a manufacturer may be liable for a negligently designed part of an automobile where such design would expose a person to unreasonable risk or injury. In this case, can you discern how the court arrives at its decision that the negligently designed steering mechanism posed an unreasonable risk of injury?

Because of the problems of proof, tort law has developed a second line of analysis for defective products that is less rigorous. This developing line of analysis is based on the "strict" liability of a manufacturer. This principle is well stated by the *Restatement of Torts, Second,* § 402A, 1965, which provides:

> (1) One who sells any product in a defective condition unreasonably dangerous to the user or consumer or to his property is subject to liability for physical harm thereby caused to the ultimate user or consumer, or to his property, if
> > (a) the seller is engaged in the business of selling such a product, and
> > (b) it is expected to and does reach the user or consumer without substantial change in the condition in which it is sold.
> (2) The rule stated in Sub-section (1) applies although
> > (a) the seller has exercised all possible care in the preparation and sale of his product, and
> > (b) the user or consumer has not bought the product from or entered into any contractual relation with the seller.

Note that this principle imposes liability on a seller without regard to fault or negligence. The key words in the statement are "unreasonably dangerous." The types of products that can be classified as unreasonably dangerous have been steadily expanding. In the nineteenth century courts held that weapons (guns), poisons, and scaffolding, if created with a defect, would create strict liability for the manufacturer. In the twentieth century courts have expanded the classification of unreasonably dangerous products to include automobiles and consumer items such as power tools. (See the *Greenman* case.)

The definition of which products are unreasonably dangerous varies from state to state, so differing results in the application of the principle of strict liability can be expected.

We have reproduced two famous products liability cases. The first, the *Larsen* case, presents the outlines of a negligent design cause of action. The second, the *Greenman* case, exemplifies the application of strict liability together with warranty arguments. Also note in the *Greenman* case those products that have been termed "unreasonably dangerous," thus allowing recovery based on strict liability.

LARSEN v. *GENERAL MOTORS*
391 F 2d 495 (8 Cir 1968)

The driver of a 1963 Chevrolet Corvair claims injury as a result of the alleged negligent design of the automobile's steering assembly. The alleged design defect did not cause the acci-

dent. There was a head-on collision with the impact occurring on the left front corner of the car. This caused a severe rearward thrust of the steering mechanism into the plaintiff's head. The solid steering shaft extended without interruption from a point 2.7 inches in front of the leading surface of the front tire to a position directly in front of the driver. The District Court dismissed the complaint ruling that the manufacturer has no legal duty to make a vehicle that would protect the plaintiff from injury in the event of a head-on collision.

The plaintiff does not contend that the design caused the accident but that because of the design he received injuries he would not have otherwise received or, in the alternative, his injuries would not have been as severe.

General Motors contends that it has no duty to produce a vehicle in which it is safe to collide or which is accident proof or incapable of injurious misuse. It views its duty as extending only to producing a vehicle that is reasonably fit for its intended use or for the purpose for which it was made and that is free from hidden defects; and that the intended use of a vehicle and the purpose for which it is manufactured do not include its participation in head-on collisions or any other type of impact, regardless of the manufacturer's ability to foresee that such collisions may occur.

The plaintiff maintains that General Motors' view of its duty is too narrow and restrictive and that an automobile manufacturer is under a duty to use reasonable care in the design of the automobile to make it safe to the user for its foreseeable use and that its intended use or purpose is for travel on the streets and highways, including the possibility of impact or collision with other vehicles or stationary objects. . . .

Accepting . . . the principle that a manufacturer's duty of design and construction extends to producing a product that is reasonably fit for its intended use and free of hidden defects that could render it unsafe for such use, the issue narrows on the proper interpretation of "intended use." Automobiles are made for use on the roads and highways in transporting persons and cargo to and from various points. This intended use cannot be carried out without encountering in varying degrees the statistically proved hazard of injury-producing impacts of various types. The manufacturer should not be heard to say that it does not intend its product to be involved in any accident when it can easily foresee and when it knows that the probability over the life of its product is high, that it will be involved in some type of injury-producing accident. O'Connell, in his article "Taming the Automobile," 58 *Nw. U.L. Rev.* 299, 348 (1963), cites that between one-fourth to two-thirds of all automobiles during their use at some time are involved in an accident producing injury or death.

We think the "intended use" construction urged by General Motors is much too narrow and unrealistic. Where the manufacturer's negligence in design causes an unreasonable risk to be imposed upon the user of its product, the manufacturer should be liable for the injury caused by its failure to exercise reasonable care in the design. These injuries are readily foreseeable as an incident to the normal and expected use of an automobile. While automobiles are not made for the purpose of colliding with each other, a frequent and inevitable contingency of normal automobile use will result in collisions and injury-producing impacts. No rational basis exists for limiting recovery to situations where the defect in design or manufacture was the causative factor of the accident, as the accident and the resulting injury, usually caused by the so-called "second collision" of the passenger with the interior part of the automobile, all are foreseeable. Where the injuries or enhanced injuries are due to the manufacturer's failure to use reasonable care to avoid subjecting the user of its products to an unreasonable risk of injury, general negligence principles should be applicable. The sole function of an automobile is not just to provide a means of transportation, it is to provide a means of safe transportation, or as safe as is reasonably possible under the present state of the art. . . .

The duty of reasonable care in design should be viewed in light of the risk. While all risks cannot be eliminated nor can a crash-proof vehicle be designed under the present state of the art, there are many common-sense factors in design, which are or should be well known to the manufacturer that will minimize or lessen the injurious effects of a collision. The standard of reasonable care is applied in many other negligence situations and should be applied here.

The courts . . . have held that a manufacturer of automobiles is under a duty to construct a vehicle that is free of latent and hidden defects. We can perceive of no significant difference in imposing a common law duty of a reasonable standard of care in design the same as in construction. A defect in either can cause severe injury or death and a negligent design defect should be actionable. Any design defect not causing the accident would not subject the manufacturer to liability for the entire damage, but the manufacturer should be liable for that portion of the damage or injury caused by the defective design over and above the damage or injury that probably would have occurred as a result of the impact or collision absent the defective design. . . .

If, because of the alleged undisclosed defect in design of the 1963 Corvair steering assembly, an extra hazard is created over and above the normal hazard, General Motors should be liable for this unreasonable hazard.

Case Questions

1. Does the GM position on their legal and financial responsibility to automobile accident victims expose them to valid social criticism?

2. Is GM's defense a wise one from an economic perspective? What would be your position in light of the following statistics: new cars sold in excess of 11 million per year, 1972 automobile accident deaths of 56,600, and disabling injuries of 2.1 million? Would your opinion differ on learning that in 1970 the "big three" automakers had revenue in excess of $40.7 billion and profits exceeding $1.1 billion? Does ownership of GM stock or a GM automotive product color your view?

3. If the safety of the user is to be a concern of the manufacturer, where is the line to be drawn? Was the court's decision, in extending liability beyond accident causing defects, a wise one? Who is to draw the line? Is such a decision exclusively within the realm of the legislative branch?

4. Is the best legal defense to a lawsuit necessarily the preferable one from a public relations or social point of view?

GREENMAN v. YUBA POWER PRODUCTS, INC.
59 Cal. 2d 57, (S. Ct., Cal., 1963)

TRAYNOR, Justice

Plaintiff brought this action for damages against the retailer and the manufacturer of a Shopsmith, a combination power tool that could be used as a saw, drill, and wood lathe. He saw a Shopsmith demonstrated by the retailer and studied a brochure prepared by the manufacturer. He decided he wanted a Shopsmith for his home workshop, and his wife bought and gave him one for Christmas in 1955. In 1957 he bought the necessary attachments to use the Shopsmith as a lathe for turning a large piece of wood he wished to make into a chalice. After he had worked on the piece of wood several times without difficulty, it suddenly flew out of the machine and struck him on the forehead, inflicting serious injuries. About ten and a half months later, he gave the retailer and the manufacturer written notice of claimed breaches of warranties and filed a complaint against them alleging such breaches and negligence.

After a trial before a jury, the court ruled that there was no evidence that the retailer was negligent or had breached any express warranty and that the manufacturer was not liable for the breach of any implied warranty. Accordingly, it submitted to the jury only the cause of action alleging breach of implied warranties against the retailer and the causes of action alleging negligence and breach of express warranties against the manufacturer. The jury returned a verdict for the retailer against plaintiff and for plaintiff against the manufacturer in the amount of $65,000. The trial court denied the manufacturer's motion for a new trial and entered judgment on the verdict. The manufacturer and plaintiff appeal. Plaintiff seeks a reversal of the part of the judgment in favor of the retailer, however, only in the event that the part of the judgment against the manufacturer is reversed.

Plaintiff introduced substantial evidence that his injuries were caused by defective design and construction of the Shopsmith. His expert witnesses testified that inadequate set screws were used to hold parts of the machine together so that normal vibration caused the tailstock of the lathe to move away from the piece of wood being turned permitting it to fly out of the lathe. They also testified that there were other more positive ways of fastening the parts of the machine together, the use of which would have prevented the accident. The jury could therefore reasonably have concluded that the manufacturer negligently constructed the Shopsmith. The jury could also reasonably have concluded that statements in the manufacturer's brochure were untrue, that they con-

stituted express warranties[1] and that plaintiff's injuries were caused by their breach.

The manufacturer contends, however, that plaintiff did not give it notice of breach of warranty within a reasonable time and that therefore his cause of action for breach of warranty is barred by section 1769 of the Civil Code. Since it cannot be determined whether the verdict against it was based on the negligence or warranty cause of action or both, the manufacturer concludes that the error in presenting the warranty cause of action to the jury was prejudicial.

Section 1769 of the Civil Code provides: "In the absence of express or implied agreement of the parties, acceptance of the goods by the buyer shall not discharge the seller from liability in damages or other legal remedy for breach of any promise or warranty in the contract to sell or the sale. But, if, after acceptance of the goods, the buyer fails to give notice to the seller of the breach of any promise or warranty within a reasonable time after the buyer knows, or ought to know of such breach, the seller shall not be liable therefor."

Like other provisions of the uniform sales act (Civ. Code. §§ 1721–1800), section 1769 deals with the rights of the parties to a contract of sale or a sale. It does not provide that notice must be given of the breach of a warranty that arises independently of a contract of sale between the parties. Such warranties are not imposed by the sales act, but are the product of common-law decisions that have recognized them in a variety of situations. . . .

We conclude, therefore, that even if plaintiff did not give timely notice of breach of war-

---

[1] In this respect the trial court limited the jury to a consideration of two statements in the manufacturer's brochure: (1) "WHEN SHOPSMITH IS IN HORIZONTAL POSITION— Rugged construction of frame provides rigid support from end to end. Heavy centerless-ground steel tubing insures perfect alignment [sic] of components." (2) "SHOPSMITH maintains its accuracy because every component has positive locks that hold adjustments through rough or precision work."

ranty to the manufacturer, his cause of action based on the representations contained in the brochure was not barred.

Moreover, to impose strict liability on the manufacturer under the circumstances of this case, it was not necessary for plaintiff to establish an express warranty as defined in section 1732 of the Civil Code.[2] A manufacturer is strictly liable in tort when an article he places on the market, knowing that it is to be used without inspection for defects, proves to have a defect that causes injury to a human being. Recognized first in the case of unwholesome food products, such liability has now been extended to a variety of other products that create as great or greater hazards if defective. *Peterson* v. *Lamb Rubber Co.*, 54 Cal. 2d 339, 347 [grinding wheel]; *Vallis* v. *Canada Dry Ginger Ale, Inc.*, 190 Cal. App. 2d 35, 42–44 [bottle]; *Jones Burgermeister Brewing Corp.*, 198 Cal. App. 2d 198, 204 [bottle]; *Gottsdanker* v. *Cutter Laboratories*, 182 Cal. App. 2d 602, 607 [vaccine]; *McQuaide* v. *Bridgport Brass Co.*, D.C. 190 F. Supp. 252, 254 [insect spray]; *Bowles* v. *Zimmer Manufacturing Co.*, 7 Cir., 277 F.2d 868, 875 [surgical pin]; *Thompson* v. *Reedman D.C.*, 199 F. Supp. 120, 121 [automobile]; *Chapman* v. *Brown*. D.C. 198 F. Supp. 78, 118, 119, affd. *Brown* v. *Chapman*, 9 Cir., 304 F. 2d 149 [skirt]; *B.F. Goodrich Co.* v. *Hammond*, 10 Cir., 269 F. 2d 501, 504 [automobile tire]; *Markovich* v. *McKesson and Robbins, Inc.*, 106 Ohio App. 265 [home permanent]; *Graham* v. *Bottenfield's Inc.*, 176 Kan. 68 [Hair dye]; *General Motors Corp.* v. *Dodson*, 47 Tenn. App. 438 [automobile]; *Henningsen* v. *Bloomfield Motors, Inc.*, 32 N.J. 358 [automobile]; *Hinton* v. *Republic Aviation Corporation*, D.C., 180 F. Supp. 31, 33 [airplane].

[2] Any affirmation of fact or any promise by the seller relating to the goods is an express warranty if the natural tendency of such affirmation or promise is to induce the buyer to purchase the goods, and if the buyer purchases the goods relying thereon. No affirmation of the value of the goods, nor any statement purporting to be a statement of the seller's opinion only shall be construed as a warranty.

Although in these cases strict liability has usually been based on the theory of an express or implied warranty running from the manufacturer to the plaintiff, the abandonment of the requirement of a contract between them, the recognition that the liability is not assumed by agreement but imposed by law . . . and the refusal to permit the manufacturer to define the scope of its own responsibility for defective products . . . make clear that the liability is not one governed by the law of contract warranties but by the law of strict liability in tort. Accordingly, rules defining and governing warranties that were developed to meet the needs of commercial transactions cannot properly be invoked to govern the manufacturer's liability to those injured by their defective products unless those rules also serve the purposes for which such liability is imposed.

[T]he purpose of such [strict] liability is to insure that the costs of injuries resulting from defective products are borne by the manufacturers that put such products on the market rather than by the injured persons who are powerless to protect themselves. Sales warranties serve this purpose fitfully at best. . . . In the present case, for example, plaintiff was able to plead and prove an express warranty only because he read and relied on the representations of the Shopsmith's ruggedness contained in the manufacturer's brochure. Implicit in the machine's presence on the market, however, was a representation that it would safely do the jobs for which it was built. Under these circumstances, it should not be controlling whether plaintiff selected the machine because of the statements in the brochure, or because of the machine's own appearance of excellence that belied the defect lurking beneath the surface, or because he merely assumed that it would safely do the jobs it was built to do. It should not be controlling whether the details of the sales from manufacturer to retailer and from retailer to plaintiff's wife were such that one or more of the implied warranties of the sales act arose. . . . "The remedies of injured consumers ought not to be made to depend upon the intricacies of the law of sales." *Ketterer* v. *Armour & Co.*, D.C., 200 F. 323, 333; *Klein* v. *Duchess Sandwich Co.*, 14 Cal. 2d 272. To establish the manufacturer's liability it was sufficient that plaintiff proved that he was injured while using the Shopsmith in a way it was intended to be used as a result of a defect in design and manufacture of which plaintiff was not aware. . . .

The judgment is affirmed.

---

1. What are the policy reasons for the doctrine of strict liability?
2. Note that the judge writing this opinion is the same one who was in favor of an expanding definition of inherent authority in Chapter 4. Is Judge Traynor consistent in arguing for strict liability and an expanded scope of circumstances in which the principle of inherent authority will be applied?

Recent Judicial Developments in Product Liability Law: The *Sindell* Case

The image of the typical product liability case is one of some commonly viewed product, such as an automobile, causing severe injury (as in the *Henningsen* case) because of a defect. However, in the very near future this image may change substantially. Because of the new understanding and knowledge about the drugs and chemicals in our environment, the courts are being pressed to develop new legal theories to provide remedies for injured consumers. There is no more important case in this area than the *Sindell* case produced below. The new legal theory of market-share liability is so radical that assessment of it is very difficult. Before we explore this assessment, we present a portion of this case.

SINDELL v. *ABBOTT LABORATORIES*
607 P.2d 924 (S. Ct., Calif., 1980)

MOSK, Justice

This case involves a complex problem both timely and significant: may a plaintiff, injured as the result of a drug administered to her mother during pregnancy, who knows the type of drug involved but cannot identify the manufacturer of the precise product, hold liable for her injuries a maker of a drug produced from an identical formula?

Plaintiff Judith Sindell brought an action against eleven drug companies . . . on behalf of herself and other women similarly situated. The complaint alleges as follows:

Between 1941 and 1971, defendants were engaged in the business of manufacturing, promoting, and marketing diethylstilbestrol (DES), a drug which is a synthetic compound of the female hormone estrogen. The drug was administered to plaintiff's mother and the mothers of the class she represents, for the purpose of preventing miscarriage. In 1947, the Food and Drug Administration authorized the marketing of DES as a miscarriage preventative, but only on an experimental basis, with a requirement that the drug contain a warning label to that effect.

DES may cause cancerous vaginal and cervical growths in the daughters exposed to it before birth, because their mothers took the drug during pregnancy. The form of cancer from which these daughters suffer is known as adenocarcinoma, and it manifests itself after a minimum latent period of 10 or 12 years. It is a fast-spreading and deadly disease, and radical surgery is required to prevent it from spreading. DES also causes adenosis, precancerous vaginal and cervical growths which may spread to other areas of the body. The treatment for adenosis is cauterization, surgery, or cryosurgery. Women who suffer from this condition must be monitored by biopsy or colposcopic examination twice a year, a painful and expensive procedure. Thousands of women whose mothers received DES during pregnancy are unaware of the effects of the drug.

In 1971, the Food and Drug Administration ordered defendants to cease marketing and promoting DES for the purpose of preventing miscarriages, and to warn physicians and the public that the drug should not be used by pregnant women because of the danger to their unborn children.

During the period defendants marketed DES, they knew or should have known that it was a carcinogenic substance, that there was a grave danger after varying periods of latency it would cause cancerous and precancerous growths in the daughters of the mothers who took it, and that it was ineffective to prevent miscarriage. Nevertheless, defendants continued to advertise and market the drug as a miscarriage preventative. They failed to test DES for efficacy and safety; the tests performed by others, upon which they relied, indicated that it was not safe or effective. In violation of the authorization of the Food and Drug Administration, defendants marketed DES on an unlimited basis rather than as an experimental drug, and they failed to warn of its potential danger.

Because of defendants' advertised assurances that DES was safe and effective to prevent miscarriage, plaintiff was exposed to the drug prior to her birth. She became aware of the danger from such exposure within one year of the time she filed her complaint. As a result of the DES ingested by her mother, plaintiff developed a malignant bladder tumor which was removed by surgery. She suffers from adenosis and must constantly be monitored by biopsy or colposcopy to insure early warning of further malignancy.

The first cause of action alleges that defendants were jointly and individually negligent in that they manufactured, marketed and promoted DES as a safe and efficacious drug to prevent miscarriage, without adequate testing or warning, and without monitoring or reporting its effects.

* * *

Other causes of action are based upon theories of strict liability, violation of express and implied warranties, false and fraudulent representations, misbranding of drugs in violation of federal law, conspiracy and "lack of consent."

Each cause of action alleges that defendants are jointly liable because they acted in concert, on the basis of express and implied agreements, and in reliance upon and ratification and exploitation of each other's testing and marketing methods.

Plaintiff seeks compensatory damages of $1 million and punitive damages of $10 million for herself. For the members of her class, she prays for equitable relief in the form of an order that defendants warn physicians and others of the danger of DES and the necessity of performing certain tests to determine the presence of disease caused by the drug, and that they establish free clinics in California to perform such tests.

* * *

This case is but one of a number filed throughout the country seeking to hold drug manufacturers liable for injuries allegedly resulting from DES prescribed to the plaintiffs' mothers since 1947. According to a note in the Fordham Law Review, estimates of the number of women who took the drug during pregnancy range from 1½ million to 3 million. Hundreds, perhaps thousands, of the daughters of these women suffer from adenocarcinoma, and the incidence of vaginal adenosis among them is 30 to 90 percent. (Comment, *DES and a Proposed Theory of Enterprise Liability* (1978) 46 Fordham L.Rev. 963, 964–967 [hereafter Fordham Comment].) Most of the cases are still pending. With two exceptions, those that have been decided resulted in judgments in favor of the drug company defendants because of the failure of the plaintiffs to identify the manufacturer of the DES prescribed to their mothers. The same result was reached in a recent California case. (*McCreery* v. *Eli Lilly & Co.* (1978) 87 Cal.App.3d 77, 82–84, 150 Cal. Rptr. 730.) The present action is another attempt to overcome this obstacle to recovery.

* * *

In our contemporary complex industrialized society, advances in science and technology create fungible goods which may harm consumers and which cannot be traced to any specific producer. The response of the courts can be either to adhere rigidly to prior doctrine, denying recovery to those injured by such products, or to fashion remedies to meet these changing needs. Just as Justice Traynor in his landmark concurring opinion in *Escola* v. *Coca Cola Bottling Company* (1944) 24 Cal.2d 453, 467–468, 150 P.2d 436, recognized that in an era of mass production and complex marketing methods the traditional standard of negligence was insufficient to govern the obligations of manufacturer to consumer, so should we acknowledge that some adaptation of the rules of causation and liability may be appropriate in these recurring circumstances.

* * *

The most persuasive reason for finding plaintiff states a cause of action is that . . . as between an innocent plaintiff and negligent defendants, the latter should bear the cost of the injury. Here, . . . plaintiff is not at fault in failing to provide evidence of causation, and although the absence of such evidence is not attributable to the defendants either, their conduct in marketing a drug the effects of which are delayed for many years played a significant role in creating the unavailability of proof.

From a broader policy standpoint, defendants are better able to bear the cost of injury resulting from the manufacture of a defective product. As was said by Justice Traynor in *Escola*, "[t]he cost of an injury and the loss of time or health may be an overwhelming misfortune to the person injured, and a needless one, for the risk of injury can be insured by the manufacturer and distributed among the public as a cost of doing business." (24 Cal.2d p. 462, 150 P.2d p. 441; see also Rest.2d Torts, § 402A, com. c, pp. 349–350.) The manufacturer is in the best position to discover and guard against defects in its products and to warn of harmful effects; thus, holding it liable for defects and failure to warn of harmful effects will provide an incentive to product safety. . . . These considerations are particularly significant where medication is involved, for the consumer is virtually helpless to protect himself from serious, sometimes permanent, sometimes fatal, injuries caused by deleterious drugs.

Where, as here, all defendants produced a drug from an identical formula and the manufacturer of the DES which caused plaintiff's injuries cannot be identified through no fault of plaintiff, a modification of the rule [requiring causation] . . . is warranted. . . .

[W]e hold it to be reasonable in the present context to measure the likelihood that any of the defendants supplied the product which allegedly injured plaintiff by the percentage which the DES sold by each of them for the purpose of preventing miscarriage bears to the entire production of the drug sold by all for that purpose. Plaintiff asserts in her briefs that Eli Lilly and Company and 5 or 6 other companies produced 90 percent of the DES marketed. If at trial this is established to be the fact, then there is a corresponding likelihood that this comparative handful of producers manufactured the DES which caused plaintiff's injuries, and only a 10 percent likelihood that the offending producer would escape liability.

If plaintiff joins in the action the manufacturers of a substantial share of the DES which her mother might have taken, the injustice of shifting the burden of proof to defendants to demonstrate that they could not have made the substance which injured plaintiff is significantly diminished. While 75 to 80 percent of the market is suggested as the requirement by the Fordham Comment (at p. 996), we hold only that a substantial percentage is required.

The presence in the action of a substantial share of the appropriate market also provides a ready means to apportion damages among the defendants. Each defendant will be held liable for the proportion of the judgment represented by its share of that market unless it demonstrates that it could not have made the product which caused plaintiff's injuries. In the present case, as we have seen, one DES manufacturer was dismissed from the action upon filing a declaration that it had not manufactured DES until after plaintiff was born. Once plaintiff has met her burden of joining the required defendants, they in turn may cross-complaint against other DES manufacturers, not joined in the action, which they can

allege might have supplied the injury-causing product.

Under this approach, each manufacturer's liability would approximate its responsibility for the injuries caused by its own products. Some minor discrepancy in the correlation between market share and liability is inevitable; therefore, a defendant may be held liable for a somewhat different percentage of the damage than its share of the appropriate market would justify. It is probably impossible, with the passage of time, to determine market share with mathematical exactitude. . . .

We are not unmindful of the practical problems involved in defining the market and determining market share, but these are largely matters of proof which properly cannot be determined at the pleading stage of these proceedings. Defendants urge that it would be both unfair and contrary to public policy to hold them liable for plaintiff's injuries in the absence of proof that one of them supplied the drug responsible for the damage. Most of their arguments, however, are based upon the assumption that one manufacturer would be held responsible for the products of another or for those of all other manufacturers if plaintiff ultimately prevails. But under the rule we adopt, each manufacturer's liability for an injury would be approximately equivalent to the damages caused by the DES it manufactured.

The judgments are reversed.

BIRD, C.J., *and* NEWMAN *and* WHITE, JJ., *concur.*

RICHARDSON, *Justice, dissenting.*

I respectfully dissent. In these consolidated cases the majority adopts a wholly new theory which contains these ingredients: The plaintiffs were not alive at the time of the commission of the tortious acts. They sue a generation later. They are permitted to receive substantial damages from multiple defendants without any proof that any defendant caused or even probably caused plaintiffs' injuries.

Although the majority purports to change only the required burden of proof by shifting it from plaintiffs to defendants, the effect of its holding is to guarantee that plaintiffs will prevail on the causation issue because defendants are no more capable of disproving factual causation than plaintiffs are of proving it. "Market share" liability thus represents a new high water mark in tort law. The ramifications seem almost limitless, a fact which prompted one recent commentator, in criticizing a substantially identical theory, to conclude that "Elimination of the burden of proof as to identification [of the manufacturer whose drug injured plaintiff] would impose a liability which would exceed absolute liability." (Coggins, *Industry-Wide Liability* (1979) 13 Suffolk L.Rev. 980, 998, fn. omitted; see also, pp. 1000–1001.) In my view, the majority's departure from traditional tort doctrine is unwise.

* * *

The majority's decision effectively makes the entire drug industry (or at least its California members) an insurer of all injuries attributable to defective drugs of uncertain or unprovable origin, including those injuries manifesting themselves a generation later, and regardless of whether particular defendants had any part whatever in causing the claimed injury. Respectfully, I think this is unreasonable overreaction for the purpose of achieving what is perceived to be a socially satisfying result.

Finally, I am disturbed by the broad and ominous ramifications of the majority's holding. The law review comment, which is the wellspring of the majority's new theory, conceding the widespread consequences of industry-wide liability, openly acknowledges that "The DES cases are only the tip of an iceberg." (Comment, *DES and a Proposed Theory of Enterprise Liability* (1978) 46 Fordham L.Rev. 963, 1007.) Although the pharmaceutical drug industry may be the first target of this new sanction, the majority's reasoning has equally threatening application to many other areas of business and commercial activities.

Given the grave and sweeping economic, social, and medical effects of "market share" liability, the policy decision to introduce and define it should rest not with us, but with the Legislature which is currently considering not only major statutory reform of California product liability law in general, but the DES problem in particular. . . . which would establish and appropriate funds for the education, identification, and screening of persons exposed to DES, and would prohibit health care and hospital service plans from excluding or limiting coverage to persons exposed to DES.) An alternative proposal for administrative compensation, described as "a limited version of no-fault products liability" has been suggested by one commentator. (*Coggins*, supra, 13 Suffolk L.Rev. at pp. 1019–1021.) Compensation under such a plan would be awarded by an administrative tribunal from funds collected "via a tax paid by all manufacturers." (P. 1020, fn. omitted.) In any event, the problem invites a legislative rather than an attempted judicial solution.

I would affirm the judgments of dismissal. CLARK and MANUEL, JJ., concur.

The U.S. Supreme Court has refused to hear this case, thus leaving standing the decision reproduced in part above. The impact of market-share liability and even its limits are very difficult to assess. One product liability lawyer has posed this case, in a slightly exaggerated form: suppose a person is walking along a beach and slices his foot on a bottle opener. The design of the opener is predictably dangerous to such walkers, but he cannot identify the producer. So, under *Sindell's* reasoning, he could sue all makers of such can openers.[14] Perhaps another application of *Sindell* better highlights the complexity of these issues. In a federal court in Des Moines, nine people are suing for wrongful death and/or injury that resulted from a fire in a local department store in 1978. They claim the deaths and injuries were caused by the emission of a gas from polyvinyl chloride that insulated the store's electrical wires. Dozens of companies manufactured the chemical, making identification impossible. So, the plaintiffs are suing 31 of the manufacturers and each is asking $13 million in damages.[15]

Summary of *Sindell* and Related Theories

The new applications of market-share liability are only dimly perceived at this point. Remember that, for the most part, product liability law based on contract and tort theories is state law. So far only California has adopted this principle, but there is a widespread interest in it. The impact of *Sindell* is this: an essential element of any plaintiff's cause of action for negligence or strict liability is that there be some reasonable connection between the negligent manufacture or design, or causing the defect and unreasonably dangerous quality of the product produced by the defendant, *and* the damage suffered by the plaintiff. In short, the defendant must have caused the damage. *Sindell* relieved the plaintiff of proving exactly which defendant caused the injury when (1) the identification of the manufacturer is impossible through no fault of the plaintiff, (2) the product is fungible (exactly like every other product made by all the defendants), and (3) the plaintiff joined enough defendants so that a "substantial percentage" of the market for that product is represented. In addition, the court held that once these elements of the case are established, a defendant could be held liable for the injury claimed. This liability is measured by first taking the total injury claimed by the plaintiff. Then a given defendant's liability is measured by the proportion of that total represented by its share of sales in that market at the time of the injury unless it can demonstrate that it could not have made the product that caused the plaintiff's injury.[16] That is, if a particular defendant had 10 percent of the sales in the market for DES, it would pay 10 percent of the judgment.

There are three other legal theories that have been proposed by scholars and picked up by courts for use when plaintiffs cannot establish causation. In our commercial society dominated by three or more sellers or manufacturers in a market, these theories will become more prominent in years to come. Briefly stated, these theories, like the one applied in

Sindell, all result in lessening the burden of proving causation when it would be impossible or unfair to the plaintiff to have this burden.

1. Alternative liability. This theory was first used when a plaintiff was shot by one of two other hunters and he could not prove which one. The court reasoned that it would be fair to shift the burden of causation to the defendants because they were in a far better position to identify the real wrongdoer than was the injured plaintiff. The basic reasoning of this case was used in *Sindell.*[17]

2. Concert of action. Under this theory, multiple defendants may be held liable for the acts or omissions of one of the defendants if there is a common design among the defendants creating an unreasonable risk. The usual example given is that of an illegal drag race between two cars where one of the cars causes injury to a third party. All of the racers may be held liable.[18]

3. Enterprise liability. This theory is very similar to the concert of action theory but lessens the burden of the plaintiffs in proving a common design. The common design of the defendant is inferred because of the defendants' mutual adherence to an industry-wide standard relating to the production of the injury-producing product.

The number and quality of legal principles available to plaintiffs and to defendants in a product liability case are proliferating almost as fast as the number of new categories of consumer products! It is understandable if you are mildly confused by the various remedies available to plaintiffs and the defenses that can be used by the defendants. There are numerous suggestions for reform that are being seriously discussed. For example, with regard to the concept of market-share liability, it is suggested that the aggregate amount of harm should be estimated and all defendants should contribute to this aggregate in proportion to their sales of the product (for example, DES). Each plaintiff's share of the aggregate would be determined by the proportion that the plaintiff's injuries bore to the total.[19]

These new legal theories are not the only solution to a problem as pervasive and as complex as the one posed by the prevalence of readily available products capable of doing harm. There are numerous suggestions for legislative solutions, some of which will be explained in the next section.

Recent State and Federal Legislation on Product Safety

There are two important and lingering problems associated with a discussion of product liability law based on contract and tort theories. The first is that despite a relatively rapid growth of these theories (and that announced in the *Sindell* case), there is no evidence that business organizations are providing the public with safer products. We do not intend to fault the manufacturer for this; perhaps the reason is an increased consumer appetite for complex consumer products. Nevertheless, we as a commercial society should address the question of whether there is a way to insure a supply of safer consumer products.

A second and related problem is that the remedies for defective products discussed thus far exist only when a claim is worth pursuing. As one of the cases in this section states, in recent years there have been an average of 77,000 injuries from walk-behind lawnmowers. Of these injuries, an estimated 9,900 involved the amputation of at least one finger or toe and 11,400 involved fractures. Most of these injuries did not result in a lawsuit. So, the burden for many, probably most, consumer injuries from defective products falls on the consumer. The solution is not to develop new or "better" legal theories that provide remedies for injury, but to seek a way to provide safer products. Generally, this search ends with proposed legislation.

There is also the perspective of the manufacturer. Although Article 2 of the UCC and the warranties created therein are uniformly interpreted and applied by the states, the conceptions of negligence and strict liability are not uniform. Business organizations have to face numerous different legal theories and interpretations of those theories depending on how many states they do business in. This has resulted in pressure by manufacturers for uniform legislation, as well as other pressure to cope with what is perceived to be a legal system on the verge of being out of control regarding plaintiffs who are injured by defective products, and who are recovering judgments that threaten the economic viability of firms.

Since the response by manufacturers leading to the perceived need for uniform legal theories, usually in the form of legislation applicable to product safety cases, is in direct response to the material presented in the last section, we first present an explanation of two recent developments in the legislative arena that will become more prominent in the near future.

Proposed Legislation.   In this section, we first discuss legislation that has been only proposed, not passed, to help deal more efficiently with what some people have described as a product liability crisis. Following this discussion, we provide an explanation of legislation that has been passed.

The proposed legislation that is of the most significance exists in two areas. The first is the attempt by the federal government to bring about a measure of uniformity and consistent treatment to product liability claims by promoting a Model Uniform Product Liability Act (MUPLA). The second is the adoption in about 17 states of "statutes of repose."

The Model Uniform Product Liability Act.   The MUPLA was published by the Department of Commerce on October 31, 1979.[20] It was the result of a process begun by President Ford in 1976 to clarify and stabilize the proliferation of the law applicable to products liability. The Commerce Department provides the Act so that state legislatures may use it as a model for refining their own approach to product liability law. In this section, we will explain just the highlights. The Act is rather comprehensive: it deals with the creation of the cause of action, the defenses available, and the measures of damages in product liability cases.

The MUPLA preempts the UCC and common law theories discussed in the first part of this chapter: breach of warranty, negligence, and strict liability. It replaces these principles with a single "product liability claim." This claim may be asserted by injured consumers, bystanders, or their estates and does not depend on a contractual relationship with a seller. So, the Act opts for more of a negligence approach than one based on contract. The essence of the cause of action is liability created because of defective construction, defective design, or inadequate warnings or instructions. The term "defect" is the heart of this cause of action, but it is not defined. Rather, factors are listed that the jury or judge as a fact-finder will consider.

A *defective construction* case allows the trier of fact to evaluate whether the injury-causing product deviates from the product seller's own standards. The *design defect* case is more difficult, and the trier of fact is instructed to consider whether another design should have been used in light of:

1. The likelihood at the time of manufacture that the product would cause the harm suffered by the claimant.

2. The seriousness of that harm.

3. The technological feasibility of manufacturing a product designed so as to have prevented the claimant's harm.

4. The relative costs of producing, distributing, and selling such an alternative design.

5. The new or additional harms that may result from such an alternative design.[21]

The defenses available to a defendant center on the comparative responsibility of the plaintiff. The fact-finder may determine the total amount of damages and then deduct from this an amount equal to what the plaintiff contributed to his or her own injury because of conduct that was not similar to that which would have been used by a prudent person. That is, the Act allows recovery for injury from a defective product reduced by the amount of money that approximates the percentage of injury caused by the plaintiff by not using the product as a prudent person would. The Act differentiates between failing to act as an ordinary prudent person would act and acting unreasonably. A claimant who is aware of the defect yet persists in voluntarily and unreasonably using it, may be barred from recovery. Also barred from recovery is the plaintiff who misuses a product in a way that the product seller could not have reasonably anticipated and whose injuries would never have occurred but for the misuse.

Physical, emotional, and economic damages are recoverable under the Act, but unless an express warranty is given, damages for loss of the use of the product (lost profits) are not recoverable. Also, damages for pain and suffering cannot exceed $25,000 unless the case involves permanent disfigurement, mental illness, or loss of a bodily function.

This Act has caused much discussion and debate. As of 1982, the Act was being given serious consideration by a few states. The concepts of a type of unified product liability claim and the use of comparative fault are new to this area of the law, and it is too early to judge whether the MUPLA will be of lasting value.

Statutes of Repose: One Response to the Problem of Latent Defects in Products.   Another legislative solution at the proposal stage in many state legislatures is the passage of "statutes of repose." Statutes of repose are urged by insurance companies and manufacturers to help them assess the possible losses due to defective products. These statutes create a time period after which a product goes into repose (a period of permanent rest). Any injury caused by the product after the period has ended is not actionable. The time period would be measured from either the date of manufacture or the date of sale for use, and not from the time of infliction of the actual harm. These statutes favor merchants and the insurance industry, and do not favor injured plaintiffs whose injuries fall outside the period. Some have argued that the Act favors all consumers since it is guessed that product liability insurance premiums will fall if these acts are passed, thus resulting in lower consumer prices.

The major item of debate is the length of the time period. It must be sufficiently long to allow a reasonable time for aggrieved parties to discover a product's defects, and sufficiently short to eliminate uncertainty concerning exposure to liability. Proposed time periods range from 8 to 10 years.[22]

Existing Consumer Product Safety Legislation: Introduction.

In 1970, a major study of consumer product safety sponsored by the federal government found that 20 million Americans were injured each year as a result of incidents connected with consumer products.[23] Of this total, 110,000 were *permanently disabled* and 30,000 were killed. The study estimated that the annual cost to the nation of product-related injuries might exceed $5.5 billion.[24] These statistics *excluded* injuries caused by food, drugs, cosmetics, motor vehicles, and some other causes of consumer injury.

The 1981 Annual Report of the Consumer Product Safety Commission (CPSC) reveals that this record has not improved. In 1981, an estimated 36 million Americans were injured and 30,000 killed in incidents involving consumer products. The cost of these injuries to our economy in medical costs and lost earnings is $12.5 billion annually.[25] The types of consumer products that cause the most injuries are portrayed in Figure 21-1 below.

The fact that 514,000 Americans were estimated to have been injured by bicycles during the time period is not as noteworthy as the estimated 129,000 injuries resulting from glass bottles and jars and the 23,000 injuries resulting from TV sets, refrigerators, and freezers. We all know of the dangers and risks involved in riding a bicycle, but the threat to us from glass bottles and jars, TV sets, refrigerators, and freezers is less foreseeable. The statistics reveal that almost every consumer product may be dangerous if it is not properly made or if it is not properly used. A crucial question is whether the traditional legal theories of breach of warranty, negligence, and strict liability, together with the forces that economic theory has assumed to be at work in the retail marketplace, provide our society with reasonably safe products. If we consider the activity of both federal and state governments in the areas of consumer product safety, the answer to this question must be a resounding "no!" Why?

First, an injured consumer must be aware of his or her legal right to sue the sellers and producers of a defective product. Second, he or she must have sustained sufficient damage so that an attorney will find the

Product Group	National Estimate in Thousands
Stairs—(including folding stairs)	683
Bicycles and bicycle accessories	514
Baseball, activity and related equipment	446
Football, activity and related equipment	443
Basketball	422
Skating	237
Nails, carpet tacks, screws and thumbtacks	220
Glass doors, windows and panels	196
Playground equipment	162
Glass bottles and jars	129
Power home workshop saws	73
Power lawn mowers	63
Chain saws	62
Television sets	23
Refrigerators and freezers	23

1981 Annual Report, Part Two, U.S. Consumer Product Safety Commission, Appendix A, pp. 2–3.

FIGURE 21-1   Consumer products injuries by product groups (estimated number of injuries associated with consumer products requiring emergency room treatment: October 1, 1979 to September 30, 1980—a partial listing).

promise of an adequate fee in the case. Probably the most serious limitation on recovery of damages to consumers is the cost of trial. Some experts say it hardly pays to go to trial for less than $5,000 to $10,000.[26] Moreover, at the trial, the plaintiff usually runs a substantial risk that one of the defenses available to the seller or manufacturer may be successfully asserted. Even in the best of circumstances, a product liability case is a financially bruising, onerous undertaking for both client and lawyer.[27]

Only the most serious product liability cases are litigated. A survey of 276 persons living in Denver and Boston who had reported injuries to the Food and Drug Administration showed that only 4 percent contacted an attorney to investigate initiating a claim for injury.[28] Another study revealed that some manufacturers do not even respond to letters claiming compensation because they know that over two thirds will never pursue their claim further.[29] As for the others, let us assume that a plaintiff does recover a substantial judgment for injury due to a defective power saw. How does the manufacturer respond? More likely than not, the manufacturer will have insurance that will cover most, if not all, of the claim and thereby lessen some of the incentive to design a safer product.

Even where there is money recovery, there is no coherent or organized effort to publicize the name of a manufacturer held liable so that consumers could *in the future* select safer products over those produced by manufacturers with bad safety records.

The legal theories discussed in the first part of this chapter provide legal remedies for only a few of the most seriously injured consumers. These remedies do little to assure the public that in the future it will be able to select safer products. For these reasons, Congress and most state legislatures have passed consumer product legislation.

Since 1966, Congress has passed six acts that govern some aspect of product safety or product design. Also, the Federal Trade Commission and the Consumer Affairs Section within the Antitrust Division of the Justice Department have become much more active in pressing the interests of consumers. In the sections that follow, we will explain some of this recent federal legislation and regulation.

The Consumer Product Safety Act of 1972. The Consumer Product Safety Act of 1972[30] created the Consumer Product Safety Commission (CPSC), which was activated as an independent federal regulatory agency on May 14, 1973. The CPSC is becoming one of the most powerful regulatory agencies in the federal government. It has jurisdiction over every consumer product except automobiles, food, and a few other items regulated by older federal agencies. The basic idea behind the creation of the CPSC was to bring order to an increasingly confusing mish-mash of federal and state consumer regulatory bodies.

The commission is to collect and disseminate information relating to injuries and to conduct investigations and tests on consumer products and their use. When a consumer product creates a hazard of injury or illness, the CPSC may develop consumer product safety standards. These standards must be set forth in performance requirements. If the CPSC finds that an unreasonable risk exists and that no standard will provide protection, it may ban a product. It has banned such products as garments containing asbestos, some baby cribs, some drain cleaners, assorted types of fireworks, furniture painted with lead paint, some kinds of lawn darts, and self-pressurized products containing vinyl chloride.[31]

Since 1973, the CPSC has taken a number of major regulatory actions that have been responsible for keeping millions of hazardous products off the market. Also, by 1979, the Commission had received more than 650 reports from manufacturers, distributors, and retailers indicating possible safety-related product defects. These reports resulted in recall actions affecting more than 60 million potentially hazardous product units.[32]

In recent years, and especially since 1980 and the election of President Reagan (elected on campaign promises of less regulation), the CPSC has narrowed the number of consumer product targets. In 1980, it focused on standards and regulation of:

1. Unvented gas-fired space heaters, which caused at least 50 deaths per year.
2. Formaldehyde, after receiving 1,500 formal complaints involving 4,000 people.
3. Asbestos, now known as a carcinogen. The CPSC is engaged in developing standards that would result in banning asbestos paper in consumer products.[33]

One of the most important activities of the CPSC is to develop data banks on consumer injuries. In order to find out what products are involved in accidents, the Commission has established a network of hospital emergency rooms which report daily to Washington headquarters. National estimates can be derived from these reports. More than two million accident reports have been logged since 1973. In addition, the Commission has conducted more than 40,000 in-depth accident investigations to collect more detailed information about the involvement of consumer products in accidents and injuries. The case that follows reveals the work and impact of the CPSC.

SOUTHLAND MOWER COMPANY v. CONSUMER PRODUCT SAFETY COMMISSION
619 F.2d 499 (5th Cir., 1980)

GEE, Circuit Judge

Approximately 77,000 people are injured each year in the United States by contacting the blades of walk-behind power mowers. Of these injuries, an estimated 9,900 involve the amputation of at least one finger or toe, 11,400 involve fractures, 2,400 involve avulsions (the tearing of flesh or a body part), 2,300 involve contusions, and 51,400 involve lacerations. The annual economic cost inflicted by the 77,000 yearly blade-contact injuries has been estimated to be about $253 million. This figure does not include monetary compensation for pain and suffering or for the lost use of amputated fingers and toes.

To reduce these blade-contact injuries, the Consumer Product Safety Commission ("CPSC" or "the Commission") promulgated a Safety Standard for Walk-Behind Power Lawn Mowers, . . . pursuant to section 7 of the Consumer Product Safety Act ("CPSA" or "the Act"), ... In the present case we consider petitions by the Outdoor Power Equipment Institute ("OPEI"), manufacturers of power lawn mowers, and an interested consumer to review the Safety Standard for Walk-Behind Power Lawn Mowers.

The standard consists of three principal provisions: a requirement that rotary walk-behind power mowers pass a foot-probe test, . . . a requirement that rotary machines have a blade-control system that will stop the mower blade within three seconds after the operator's hands leave their normal operating position, . . . and a requirement, applicable to both rotary and reel-type mowers, that the product have a label of specified design to warn of the danger of blade contact. . . .

OPEI challenges the legality of the standard by contending that it includes nonconsumer products within its scope of regulation, as well as unique consumer products not proven to present the same hazards as typical consumer lawn mowers. OPEI also argues that substantial evidence on the record as a whole does not support the Commission's determination that the foot-probe and shielding requirements "are reasonably necessary to reduce or eliminate an unreasonable risk of injury" associated with walk-behind power lawn mowers.

* * *

The CPSC may regulate only "consumer products.". . .

OPEI asserts that the Commission exceeded its statutory authority by attempting to regulate lawn mowers that are not consumer products and by failing to exclude "unique"

products, such as high-wheel and three- or five-wheel mowers, that differ significantly from the typical mower used by consumers and that allegedly were not shown by substantial evidence to need regulation in order to eliminate or reduce an unreasonable risk of harm. We find, however, that the safety regulation's coverage is not impermissibly broad. The standard expressly states that: "Except as provided in paragraph (c) of this section, all walk-behind rotary and reel-type power lawn mowers manufactured or imported on or after the effective date of the standard are subject to the requirements of this standard *if they are 'consumer products'.* . . ." Thus, if a lawn mower is not customarily produced or distributed for sale to, or use or consumption by, or enjoyment of, a consumer, it is *ab initio* not covered by the standard.

The Commission may treat "a range of similar products as a single product class" if they "exhibit . . . sufficient *similarity of functional and risk characteristics.*" . . . The task of evaluating function and risk factors to determine product classification for purposes of inclusion within a safety standard "is committed primarily to the judgment of the Commission.". . . However, the Commission does have "a responsibility to justify application of the standard to a product or product use that, according to the facts elicited in the course of rulemaking, *exhibits significantly dissimilar functional or risk characteristics when compared with the other products covered by the standard.*". . .

In the present case no evidence was introduced to show that the so-called "unique design" or "specialty" mowers were *significantly* dissimilar in function or risk characteristics from the typical walk-behind power lawn mower studied by the Commission. As the Commission determined, these mowers have rotating, hardcutting blades that produce the hazards addressed by the safety standard. Thus, the unique design machines are part of the general product category of walk-behind power lawn mowers, and in the absence of any evidence pointing to features differentiating their risk or function characteristics for purposes of protecting consumers from blade-contact injuries, the Commission properly included them in the standard. . . .

The standard mandates that walk-behind power rotary mowers pass a foot-probe test designed to assure that the machine guards the operator's feet against injuries caused by contact with the moving blade. The test requires that a probe simulating a human foot be inserted along the rear 120 degrees of the mower and at the discharge chute without coming into contact with the blade when inserted. . . .

OPEI does not deny that a foot-probe test for the rear area of the mower is reasonably necessary to reduce injuries. Rather, it asserts that application of the test to the discharge chute is not supported by substantial record evidence. It alleges that the injury data does not show that foot injuries occur at that location and that it would be theoretically impossible for an operator to suffer a foot injury at the discharge chute while holding the "deadman's" blade-control switch on the mower handle.

The Act requires that safety standards be supported by "substantial evidence on the record as a whole.". . . The foot-probe provision can be sustained only if the record contains " 'such relevant evidence as a reasonable mind might accept as adequate to support a conclusion' " that an unreasonable risk of foot injury exists from blade-contact at the discharge chute, that the foot-probe test will ameliorate it, and that the benefits of this proposed reform make it reasonable in light of the burdens it imposes on product manufacturers and consumers. . . .

The determination of whether an unreasonable risk of discharge-chute injury exists involves "a balancing test like that familiar in tort law: The regulation may issue if the severity of the injury that may result from the prod-uct, factored by the likelihood of the injury, offsets the harm the regulation imposes upon manufacturers and consumers.". . . Thus, under the unreasonable risk balancing test, even a very remote possibility that a product would inflict an extremely severe injury could pose an "unreasonable risk of injury" if the proposed safety standard promised to reduce the risk effectively without unduly increasing the product's price or decreasing its availability or usefulness. . . . Conversely, if the potential injury is less severe, its occurrence must be proven more likely in order to render the risk unreasonable and the safety standard warranted.

In the present case, the discharge-chute probe is intended to reduce the risk of such injuries as amputation of toes, fractures of bones in the feet or toes, avulsions, deep lacerations, and contusions. While the seriousness of these injuries cannot be gainsaid, it does not rise to the level of gravity that would render almost any risk, however remote, unreasonable if the risk could be reduced effectively by the proposed regulation. Substantial evidence that such injury is significantly likely to occur is therefore necessary to sustain this portion of the lawn mower safety standard.

Our examination of the record has failed to reveal substantial evidence that injury at the discharge chute was sufficiently probable that it made the risk addressed by the foot probe of this area unreasonable. In a study of 36 blade-contact foot injuries conducted for the CPSC by the National Electronic Injury Surveillance System (NEISS), one injury occurred when the operator inserted his foot into the blade path at the discharge chute while holding the mower handle. This injury represented almost three percent of the blade-contact foot injuries in the sample. However, the study did not involve a random sample, and it is not possible to extrapolate the percentage of total blade-contact injuries represented by discharge-chute incidents involving the operator's feet from the limited information furnished in the record. In any event, trustworthy statistical inferences cannot be drawn from a single incident of discharge-chute injury. Without reliable evidence of the likely number of injuries that would be addressed by application of the foot-probe test to the discharge chute, we are unable to agree that this provision is reasonably necessary to reduce or prevent an unreasonable risk of injury. . . .

Our conclusion that substantial evidence fails to justify this provision is not altered by the fact that the industry's voluntary standard, . . . requires probing of the discharge chute. . . . A private industry safety standard cannot, by itself, provide sufficient support for a Commission regulation. " 'While such private standards may tend to show the reasonableness of similar Commission standards, they do not prove the *need* for such provisions.' ". . . We therefore vacate that part of the standard requiring the discharge-chute area of power lawn mowers to pass a foot-probe test.

* * *

The second key element of the standard requires a blade-control system that (1) will prevent the blade from rotating unless the operator activates a control, (2) allows the blade to be driven only if the operator remains in continuous contact with the "deadman's" control, and (3) causes the blade to stop moving within three seconds after the deadman's control is released. . . .

The blade-control system is intended to protect the operator against blade-contact injuries to both hands and feet by stopping the blade before the operator can contact it after he or she leaves the normal operating position and thus releases the deadman's control. The Commission estimates that the blade-control provisions will eliminate approximately 46,500 operator blade-contact injuries a year. This figure represents approximately 60 percent of all blade-contact injuries and nearly 80 percent of all injuries claimed to be reduced by the standard. As OPEI acknowledges, the blade-contact requirements thus are the "centerpiece" of the Commission's strategy for reducing blade-control injuries.

Perhaps as befits its importance in the regulatory scheme promulgated by the Commission, the blade-control system is vigorously attacked by both OPEI and consumer proponents of stricter safety requirements. OPEI asserts that the blade-control system provision is expressed as a design requirement, rather than as a performance requirement, in violation of the Act. It argues that a number of alternative requirements are available that are less design restrictive and more performance oriented than the blade-stop criterion and that the Commission therefore erred in adopting the blade-stop approach. OPEI further contends that the standard is unreasonable because it requires the use of mechanisms that allegedly are not safe or reliable. And, OPEI claims, the three-second stopping time is unreasonably short. In contrast, consumer advocate John O. Hayward maintains that the three-second blade-stopping time is too lax and that substantial evidence demonstrates that only a two-second or shorter blade-stopping time is justified.

The CPSA directs that a safety standard's provisions "shall, whenever feasible, be expressed in terms of performance requirements.". . . The statutory preference for performance requirements is rooted in the belief that this mode of regulation stimulates product innovation, promotes the search for cost-effective means of compliance, and fosters competition by offering consumers a range of choices in the marketplace, while design-restrictive rules tend to freeze technology, stifle research aimed at better and cheaper compliance measures, and deprive consumers of the opportunity to choose among competing designs. . . .

Although only a limited number of designs can satisfy the blade-stop provision, we find this part of the standard is nonetheless a performance requirement. While the standard mandates that mower blades stop within a specified time period, it does not dictate a specific means of fulfilling this condition. Manufacturers are neither formally nor practically restricted to employing a particular design, since two existing mechanisms, a blade-disengagement system employing a brake-clutch device and an engine-stop system, are capable of passing the blade-stop test. . . .

* * *

We turn now to the issue of whether substantial evidence supports the selection of three seconds as the time limit within which blades must stop. The Commission based the three-second blade-stop time limit primarily upon four time-motion studies of operator-blade access time. These experiments were designed to measure the interval between the moment the operator released the deadman's control and the instant he or she reached the mower blade. One study of operator-blade access data collected at the University of Iowa in 1971 and analyzed by the National Bureau of Standards in 1975 showed that operators reached the blade hazard point after moving directly to it from the mower's rear in times ranging from 2.0 to 3.5 seconds. A second operator-blade access study, using 100 subjects ranging in age from 16–62 with a mean age of 35, was conducted by Consumer's Union at Eckerd College in St. Petersburg, Florida, on March 5–7, 1975. The participants were tested using a reaction-time device designed to simulate a walk-behind power lawn mower. Each participant underwent 25 trials, for a total of 2,500 time-motion incidents. A December 7, 1976, summary of this Eckerd College Study reported that operator access time ranged from 1.66 to 4.90 seconds for normal, as opposed to intentionally fast, movements. This summary cited data from trials using 12 and 15

subjects, aged 18–21. The Final Report on the Eckerd College Study, issued in May 1977, shows operator access time for the 100 participants as ranging from .6 to 3.3 seconds. The discrepancy is not explained. . . .

In setting the blade-stop time, the Commission considered not only the time in which an operator could reach the blade after releasing the deadman's control but also the incremental cost of successively faster blade-stop times. The record contains substantial evidence that the cost of blade-stop mechanisms varies inversely with the length of time in which the device stops the blade, so that a three-second blade-stop requirement will be cheaper to implement than a one- or two-second time limit.

We find that the three-second blade-stop requirement is not too lax, contrary to petitioner Hayward's claim. The three-second measure will protect consumers against many, although certainly not all, blade-contact injuries. While the Commission may not rely upon mere "common sense" or speculation to establish the *existence* of an *unreasonable risk* of injury, it may exercise considerable discretion in determining an appropriate *remedy*. The Commission was entitled to consider the incremental cost of requiring a shorter blade-stop time in rejecting a one- or two-second blade-stop solution. The standard need not guarantee protection for all consumers; it is sufficient that it promises greater safety for consumers and is reasonably necessary to *reduce* the risk of blade-contact injuries.

Correspondingly, we find no merit in OPEI's contention that the requirement of a three-second stopping time is unreasonably demanding. OPEI strenuously urges that the empirical studies cannot support a three-second blade-stop limit because they unrealistically fail to account for such psychological factors as a person's fear of a noisily operating machine and resulting reluctance to approach it. . . .

* * *

We are also unpersuaded by OPEI's contention that current technology is inadequate safely to achieve a three-second blade-stop time. . . .

Extensive evidence that available brake-clutch technology can produce lawn mowers capable of three-second blade stops overcomes the doubt expressed by some commentators as to their ability to provide a safe and reliable three-second blade-stop mechanism. One clutch manufacturer introduced empirical data showing that its brake-clutch mechanism was durable and reliable. In actual mowing tests, three of its units successfully completed over 250 field test hours, and in laboratory testing, several mower units completed 250 hours of operation without blade-stop failure and without increased wear on the engine or crankshaft. . . .

Most convincing proof that safe and reliable three-second blade-stop mowers are currently feasible is the fact that, at the time the standard was issued, at least two mower manufacturers were currently producing and marketing mowers that had a brake-clutch mechanism complying with the standard. As one of these manufacturers declared, that such mowers are offered for sale demonstrates their manufacturer's belief in the safety and reliability of this type of brake-clutch mechanism. . . .

This evidence provides substantial support for the Commission's judgment that technology is available to design, produce, and assemble brake-clutch power lawn mowers that are unlikely to fail in an unsafe manner. . . .

* * *

In the preceding discussion, we have examined the petitioners' challenges to specific provisions of the standard and have found several of the complaints unfounded. However, OPEI also contends that the standard as a whole is not supported by substantial record evidence. It claims that the Commission based its determination that the standard was "rea-sonably necessary" and would produce a net benefit to society upon a document, "Economic Impact of Blade Contact Requirements for Power Mowers" ("the economic report"), which was unreliable because its methodology was fatally flawed, and its findings had never been exposed to public scrutiny in the administrative rulemaking process. Petitioner Hayward also criticizes the Commission's evaluation of the standard's net social benefit. He argues that the CPSC undervalued the safety benefits of the standard by erroneously failing to place a monetary value on the pain and suffering inflicted by the injuries that the rule was expected to reduce.

* * *

We have carefully scrutinized the record and find that substantial evidence supports the conclusion that the safety benefits expected from the standard bear a reasonable relationship to its costs and make the standard reasonably necessary and in the public interest. The cost-benefit analysis contained in the final economic report and adopted by the standard, . . . is not methodologically flawed. The Commission estimated that the regulations would raise the retail price of a complying lawn mower $35, costing the consumer $4.40 per year over the projected eight-year life of the mower. Total yearly compliance costs were believed to be $189 million for 5.4 million mower units (1978 production estimate). Blade-contact injuries were calculated to cost $253 million annually, exclusive of pain and suffering. Since, as we have noted, there are approximately 77,000 blade-contact injuries from walk-behind power mowers each year, each injury costs about $3,300, without counting the cost of pain and suffering. Currently there are some 40 million mowers in use by consumers, so that a consumer has about one chance in 500 ($\frac{1}{520}$) of incurring an injury costing $3,300, exclusive of pain and suffering. The standard's injury cost associated with each mower without the safety features is thus $6.35 per year. The Commission anticipated that implementation of the standard would reduce this injury cost by 83 percent, for an annual savings of $5.30 per mower, exclusive of the savings of pain and suffering costs. Because the standard would result in a net benefit of $.90, a mower meeting the standard's safety requirements would represent a worthwhile investment for the consumer, and the standard's implementation is in the best interests of society.

* * *

In summary, the standard's scope and its

requirements that mowers pass a rear foot-probe test, shield-strength and obstruction tests, satisfy a three-second blade-stop criterion, and carry a prescribed warning label are upheld. The Commission's conclusion that the standard is reasonably necessary and in the public interest is also valid. The standard's requirement that mowers pass a discharge chute foot-probe test is not justified by substantial evidence on the record as a whole and is therefore vacated.

Affirmed in part, vacated in part.

Motor Vehicle Safety Legislation.   Automobiles and other motor vehicles are not subject to regulation by the CPSC. The impact on our society of the automobile is so pervasive and so deep that its design, production, and operation are governed by the Department of Transportation and one of its administrative agencies, the National Highway Traffic Safety Administration (NHTSA). In this section, we will review and explain the key features of this agency.

The National Traffic and Motor Vehicle Safety Act[34] and the Highway Safety Act[35] were both enacted in 1966. They were passed to provide an impetus to reduce the number of highway deaths and injuries. Approximately 50,000 people die in motor vehicle accidents each year. The deaths for 1979 (51,083) were 7 percent higher than in 1977. Today, motor vehicle accidents are the largest single killer of Americans under the age of 50.[36] Although the total number of deaths is going up, automobiles are becoming safer. Since 1966, the fatality rate measured in the number of deaths per 100 million miles driven has been reduced by 39 percent. This has come about through enforcement of the 55-mile-per-hour speed limit and through mandated attention to safety design. This record exists despite large increases in traffic since 1966 (motor vehicle registration is up 67 percent), increases in licensed drivers (up 42 percent) and increases in vehicle miles driven (up 65 percent).[37] In other words, it is fair to assert that since the enactment of federally mandated motor vehicle standards, the number of highway deaths per mile driven (the fatality rate) has dropped. But, the overall number of deaths has increased.

Contributing to the overall steadily increasing death toll was the increase in the number of heavy trucks, vans, light trucks, and multipurpose vehicles. These are not subject to many of the federal safety requirements that apply to passenger cars.

The National Highway Traffic Safety Administration (NHTSA) was established as an administrative agency in 1970. It was created to carry out the Congressional mandate in other acts to reduce the mounting deaths, injuries, and economic loss from traffic accidents. The Administration is implementing motor vehicle safety programs to (1) reduce the occurrence of highway crashes, (2) reduce the severity of injuries in such crashes as do occur, (3) improve survivability and injury recovery by better postcrash measures, (4) reduce the economic losses in crashes, (5) conduct a consumer information study to determine motor vehicle damage susceptibility, degree of crashworthiness, and ease of diagnosis and repair, and (6) establish safeguards for the protection of purchasers of motor vehicles having altered or reset odometers.

Under the NHTSA's program, Federal Motor Vehicle Safety Standards are issued that prescribe safety features and levels of safety-related performance for vehicles and motor vehicle equipment. Damage susceptibility, crashworthiness, and ease of repair are to be studied and reported to the Congress and public. The Administration establishes safeguards to protect purchasers of motor vehicles from vehicles with altered or reset odometers. The Administration conducts an intensive testing program to determine whether vehicles and equipment comply with applicable standards. It also investigates reports of safety-related defects and can require a manufacturer of motor vehicles or motor vehicle equipment to take corrective action.

NHTSA also develops and promulgates mandatory automotive fuel economy standards for passenger cars and light trucks for model years 1978 and after, and administers the fuel economy regulatory program. Finally, it has the duty to establish rules for the collection and reporting of information required concerning manufacturers' technological alternatives and corporate economic capabilities in meeting fuel economy standards.[38]

One of the major controversies created by NHTSA was the promulgation of an order requiring vehicles to be equipped with a passive restraint device. This order was entirely consistent with NHTSA's Congressional mandate to reduce automobile deaths and injuries. By one estimate, about one half of the vehicle occupant deaths and serious injuries could have been avoided by using occupant restraint systems such as safety belts or air bags.[39] Recent studies of accident victims show that 9 out of 10 were *not* wearing their seat belts.[40] In the case that is reproduced below, there is more evidence that when used properly, restraint devices in autos drastically reduce death and injury. This single issue, whether the government should require auto manufacturers to install devices to protect occupants, is one of the best examples for raising and discussing the complex issue of government involvement with business organizations. Should the federal government act as a parent and attempt to protect consumers when, it appears, they will not protect themselves? Our free-market traditions would cause us to answer this question "no." Yet the government does have a duty to act to protect the public health and safety. You should form your own opinion about this important question. The answers will not be easy nor will they be comfortable for many of us. The process of providing an answer, though, involves the law as it works through the administrative process. The following case highlights some of the crucial issues in the government's attempt to reach a solution to the problem of automobile safety.

CHRYSLER CORPORATION v. DEPARTMENT OF TRANSPORTATION
472 F.2d 659 (6th Cir., 1972)

JOHN W. PECK, Circuit Judge

The petitioners, major domestic and foreign manufacturers of automobiles, have petitioned this Court for a review of an order of the National Highway Traffic Safety Administration of the Department of Transportation, adopted pursuant to the National Traffic and Motor Vehicle Safety Act of 1966. . . . The Automobile Safety Act of 1966 was enacted as a response to the alarming number of deaths and injuries resulting from automobile accidents. Its expressed purpose is "[T]o reduce traffic accidents and deaths and injuries to persons resulting from traffic accidents.". . . In achieving this goal, two courses of action are open to the Agency. . . . It can act to prevent accidents, or it can act to prevent injuries in the event of accidents. Standard 208 is designed to accomplish the latter.

It is now established that most injuries caused by the impact of the automobile passenger with the steering wheel and column, the dashboard, the windshield, and other interior protrusions, can be prevented or at least ameliorated by safety-oriented vehicle design, and much attention has recently been devoted to the problem of the "second collision."

While many injuries of this sort can be prevented by the elimination from the interior surfaces of hard projections or sharp edges . . . , and by the use of energy absorbing steering columns . . . , and by the application of energy absorbing materials to reduce impact forces at probable points of contact in the event of rapid deceleration, . . . the most serious injuries can be prevented only by an occupant restraint device which absorbs the high deceleration forces while firmly preventing the passenger from being thrown against the inside of the vehicle or from being ejected out of it. The idea is to assure that when the car stops dead, the passengers don't.

The standard under review requires the petitioners to build into their vehicles by a specified date a specified quantum of "passive protection" through the use of "passive restraint devices." A passive restraint is defined as a protective occupant restraint device which does not depend for its effectiveness upon any action taken by the occupants beyond that necessary to operate the vehicle. . . . An active restraint is a device which is not effective unless some action is taken by the occupants, the most familiar example of which is the fastening of a seat belt.

An "airbag" is a passive inflatable occupant restraint system. The term "airbag" is used generally to designate the entire system of apparatus in which a sensor, activated by the deceleration force of a collision, causes an explosive charge of compressed gas (or a gas generator) to rapidly inflate a large bag which restrains the occupant as he moves toward the windshield, dashboard or steering wheel of the car, and then deflates itself. This entire cycle, including the deflation, is completed in less than one-half second. Although the safety standard under review does not by its terms specify that airbags be used to meet the specified injury criteria, the petitioners unanimously contend that because the injury criteria of Standard 208 were established with the airbag in mind that the airbag is the only device which can be reasonably expected to satisfy these criteria, and that therefore, the standard is in reality an airbag requirement standard. Although nothing in the record justifies disagreement with the petitioners on this point, for the purposes of this opinion we do not find it necessary to distinguish between the airbag and any other form of passive restraint.

* * *

The petitioners' first argument is that the Automobile Safety Act of 1966 does not authorize the Agency to establish a safety standard which requires the improvement of existing technology, and that the Agency may only establish performance requirements which can be met with devices which, at the time of the rulemaking, are developed to the point that they may be readily installed. The Agency's response is that inasmuch as the technology of airbags is fully developed, and inasmuch as airbags are presently readily available to all manufacturers, this issue is not properly before the Court in this case. The Agency also contends that, even if that were not so, one of the prime purposes of the Act is to require automobile manufacturers to develop safety technology not presently existing.

The explicit purpose of the Act, as amplified in its legislative history, is to enable the Federal government to impel automobile manufacturers to develop and apply new technology to the task of improving the safety design of automobiles as readily as possible. The Senate Report, in a section entitled "Purpose and Need," states:

"[T]his legislation reflects the faith that the restrained and responsible exercise of Federal authority can channel the creative energies and vast technology of the automobile industry into a vigorous and competitive effort to improve the safety of vehicles.". . .

The same report continues:

"While the bill reported by the committee authorizes the Secretary to make grants or award contracts for research in certain cases, a principal aim is to encourage the auto industry itself to engage in greater auto safety and safety-related research." . . .

There is no suggestion in the Act that developed technology be in use by an automobile manufacturer or that any given procedure be an established industry practice prior to its incorporation into a federal motor vehicle safety standard. If the Agency were so limited, it would have little discretion to accomplish its primary mission of reducing the deaths and injuries resulting from highway accidents.

In fact, specific efforts by the Automobile Manufacturers Association to tie the rate of innovation imposed by safety standards to the pace of innovation of the manufacturers were rejected by the House Committee on Interstate and Foreign Commerce, and the reported bill proposed that safety standards be "practicable, meet the need for motor vehicle safety, and be stated in objective terms."

* * *

If the Agency were limited to issuing standards only on the basis of devices already in existence, there would be no need for the Agency to give any consideration to the manufacturers' technological ability to achieve a stated goal. Under this proposed interpretation, the Agency would be unable to require technological improvements of any kind unless manufacturers voluntarily made these improvements themselves. This is precisely the situation that existed prior to the passage of the Act, and we decline to eviscerate this important legislation by the adoption of this proposed interpretation. As it stands, the Act is reasonable, and the power of the Agency to "channel the creative energies and vast technology of the automobile industry into a vigorous and competitive effort to improve the safety of vehicles" fully meets the need for motor vehicle safety.

We do not intend to suggest that the Agency might impose standards so demanding as to require a manufacturer to perform the impossible, or impose standards so imperative as to put a manufacturer out of business. But it is clear from the Act and its legislative history that the Agency may issue standards requiring future levels of motor vehicle performance which manufacturers could not meet unless they diverted more of their resources to producing additional safety technology than they might otherwise do. . . .

* * *

Since we have rejected the petitioners' contention that nonexisting technology may not be the subject of motor vehicle safety standards, and in view of the present state of the art of passive inflatable occupant restraint systems, we conclude that Standard 208 is practicable as that term is used in this legislation.

The petitioners contend that Standard 208 does not meet the need for motor vehicle safety because belts offer better protection to occupants than do airbags. The Agency defends the standard by contending that airbags offer better protection to occupants than do belts. The record supports the conclusion that each type of occupant restraint offers protection in a slightly different form for differing impact situations. Neither is clearly superior to the other in every respect. Consequently, we conclude that the Agency's decision to abandon active restraints in favor of passive restraints was a proper exercise of its administrative discretion.

Paramount among the Agency's considerations in deciding to require all occupant restraint systems to be fully passive was the factor of low belt usage. It is uncontested that active restraints are not extensively used. The record indicates that usage rates for lap belts are about 20 to 30%, and for the lap and shoulder harness combination about 1 to 5%; it is projected that devices (or laws) to encourage or to force belt usage will not increase usage rates above 60%. . . .

It is conceded that belts, when used, are extremely effective. The conclusive evidence on this point is a study of more than 28,000 accident cases in Sweden which showed that no occupant wearing a combined lap belt and shoulder harness was fatally injured in any accident occurring at speeds below 60 miles per hour. On the other hand, while belts are superior to airbags in some respects, most notably in rollovers and multiple impact situations, airbags have advantages over belts in other equally important respects. For example, airbags spread crash deceleration forces over most of the whole body, while belts concentrate them on the narrow area of the rigid belt. . . .

We conclude that the issue of the relative effectiveness of active as opposed to passive restraints is one which has been duly delegated to the Agency, with its expertise, to make; we find that the Agency's decision to require passive restraints is supported by substantial evidence, and we cannot say on the basis of the record before us that this decision does not meet the need for motor vehicle safety.

We now turn to the final major substantive argument presented by the petitioners: that Standard 208 fails to meet the statutorily required criteria of objectivity. The necessity for objective certainty in the performance requirements of safety standards was clearly recognized by Congress in the Safety Act. The Act provides, as noted above, that "standard[s] shall be practicable, shall meet the need for motor vehicle safety, and shall be stated in objective terms." . . .

The importance of objectivity in safety standards cannot be overemphasized. The Act puts the burden upon the manufacturer to assure that his vehicles comply under pain of substantial penalties. In the absence of objectively defined performance requirements and test procedures, a manufacturer has no assurance that his own test results will be duplicated in tests conducted by the Agency. Accordingly, such objective criteria are absolutely necessary so that "the question of whether there is compliance with the standard can be answered by objective measurement and without recourse to any subjective determination."

Objective, in the context of this case, means that tests to determine compliance must be capable of producing identical results when test conditions are exactly duplicated, that they be decisively demonstrable by performing a rational test procedure, and that compliance is based upon the readings obtained from measuring instruments as opposed to the subjective opinions of human beings. . . .

The record supports the conclusions that the test procedures and the test device specified by Standard 208 are not objective in at least the following respects: (1) The absence of an adequate flexibility criteria for the dummy's neck; the existing specifications permit the neck to be very stiff, or very flexible, or somewhere in between, significantly affecting the resultant forces measured on the dummy's head. (2) Permissible variations in the test procedure for determining thorax dynamic spring rate (force deflection characteristics of the dummy's chest) permit considerable latitude in chest construction which could produce wide variations in maximum chest deceleration between two different dummies, each of which meets the literal requirements of SAE J963. (3) The absence of specific, objective specifications for construction of the dummy's head permits significant variation in forces imparted to the accelerometer by which performance is to be measured.

* * *

The petitioners' principal procedural arguments can be consolidated into the assertion that the Agency has acted arbitrarily, capriciously, irresponsibly and unlawfully by requir-

ing manufacturers to comply with Standard 208 by a fixed date while it has consistently been issuing a rapid succession of final orders, each of which has been incomplete in several significant respects, (several have been coupled with proposed rulemaking to fill in missing parts), thereby constantly changing the basic requirements of the standard (performance criteria and test procedures), and more proposed changes are still pending. The Agency's response is that its actions in this regard reflect the extreme flexibility which is the very purpose of delegated rulemaking authority. We agree. The Safety Act gives the Secretary the authority "to issue, amend, and revoke such rules and regulations as he deems necessary to carry out [the Act].". . . This broad delegation of rulemaking authority allows the Agency to amend its safety standards in those complex and technical respects which are brought to its attention as a result of petitions for reconsideration filed by "interested persons." In this way the Act contemplates that a safety standard might evolve through a series of industry-suggested and agency-adopted amendments, as has been done in this case. This procedure is consistent with one of the central purposes of the Act that the automobile industry be encouraged to develop new and improved safety technology.

* * *

The proceeding is remanded to the Agency with instructions that any further specifications for test devices be made in objective terms which will assure comparable results among testing agencies, and that the effective date for the implementation of passive restraints be delayed until a reasonable time after such test specifications are issued.

The problem of motor vehicle safety has many dimensions. Safety in the design of such vehicles is one very important dimension but there are others, such as the regulation of driver skill through state licensing schemes, highway construction, weather monitoring, etc. Many of these dimensions of the problem are beyond the federal government. The responsibility for them rests with the states or with the individual consumer. One of the most important questions is how much information about a vehicle and its operation the average consumer can be required to know and understand. When defects are exposed, should it be the consumer's duty to act accordingly? Clearly, some of this burden has been removed from the consumer. Not only may NHTSA mandate some safety design features, but it may (directly or indirectly) pressure manufacturers to recall defective products. For example, in the three-month period July 1, 1981, to September 30, 1981, domestic manufacturers of road vehicles recalled 563,821 vehicles and foreign manufacturers recalled 600,637.[41] But many lesser known safety-related defects were probably observed by consumers and disregarded. The law cannot reach every instance of damage or injury caused by a defective design or part. The responsibility for dangerous and defective products must be shared by both the manufacturer and the consumer.

Summary of Consumer Law

The topic of consumer law is much broader than the material in the first part of this chapter would lead you to believe, although this material is the core of the area. For example, we did not discuss the Federal Trade Commission. The Federal Trade Commission regulates deceptive trade practices of merchants as well as applies consumer-oriented statutes that regulate the labeling and packaging of goods, and it prevents price discrimination and supervises the Debt Collection Act of 1977, the Export Trade Act, and many others.

The law that surrounds the duties of business organizations to provide safe products to the public is diverse, complex, and growing rapidly. Numerous approaches have been tried both to provide compensation for injured consumers and to help assure the public of a supply of relatively safe products. These approaches range from the application of contract and tort law to recent federal and state legislative initiatives. Currently there does not appear to be one dominant theory or approach to this pervasive and complex problem.

The same may be said about the second major category of duties from the business organization to the public. This area of recent and rapidly changing and growing duties involves environmental protection.

Business organizations have been subject to both federal and state laws intending to protect the environment since the late nineteenth century. However, these laws were not enforced and, until very recently, legal policy regarding the business organization and the environment was at best fragmented. Today, some states have very active environmental pro-

Recent Federal Environmental Protection Laws

tection agencies, but for the sake of simplicity and uniformity, we will focus only on *federal* efforts to protect the environment.

The National Environmental Policy Act

The federal effort may be exemplified by analyzing one piece of legislation, The National Environmental Policy Act, and two administrative agencies: the Council on Environmental Quality (CEQ) and the Environmental Protection Agency (EPA). The National Environmental Policy Act (NEPA) became law January 1, 1970.[42] The purpose of the statute was to declare a national environmental policy that would encourage harmony between humans and the environment by promoting efforts to eliminate damage to the environment and biosphere. In general, the statute attempts to accomplish this rather broadly stated objective by requiring *federal agencies* to create environmental impact statements under some circumstances and by creating the Council on Environmental Quality. The primary duties under NEPA are not on business organizations directly, but are on federal agencies that plan to disturb the environment. Since federal agencies hire private-sector employers to accomplish much of their work, they and their employees are indirectly concerned, and they should have a basic understanding of NEPA requirements. In order to insure that environmental values are considered at all levels in the decision-making process of the federal bureaucracy, the statute requires the preparation of an impact statement by each federal agency that proposes legislation and/or any other major federal action having a significant effect on the quality of the environment. This detailed environmental impact statement must include:[43]

1. The environmental impact of the proposed action.
2. Any adverse environmental effects that cannot be avoided should the proposal be implemented.
3. Alternatives to the proposed action.
4. The relationship between local short-term uses by man and the maintenance and enhancement of long-term productivity.
5. Any irreversible and irretrievable commitments of resources that would be involved in the proposed action should it be implemented.

The question of when these impact statements must be submitted is not defined clearly by the Act. The CEQ, however, has issued some guidelines that require an impact statement where the proposed federal action is likely to be highly controversial or the environment, even in a very limited geographic area, may be significantly affected.[44]

The litigation that has arisen under the provisions of the Act has been concerned primarily with proper procedures for filing the impact statements and the content of the statements themselves. There can be little doubt that the courts have not backed off in requiring the federal government to strictly adhere to the Congressional intent of the Act. We have reproduced excerpts from one of the early decisions (1971) under the Act emphasizing the necessity for strict compliance. The opinion also illustrates how the Act was intended to protect the environment by requiring a deliberate, conscious weighing by decision makers of the adverse environmental impact of the activity against the benefits to be derived. This decision applies to the Atomic Energy Commission, which today is the Nuclear Regulatory Commission. The decision affects business organizations because every time they contract with the federal government to build a structure that would have an impact on the environment, an environmental impact statement must be prepared.

CALVERT CLIFFS' COORD. COM. v. UNITED STATES A. E. COMM'N
449 F 2d 1109 (D.C.C.A., 1971)

WRIGHT, Circuit Judge

These cases are only the beginning of what promises to become a flood of new litigation—litigation seeking judicial assistance in protecting our natural environment. Several recently enacted statutes attest to the commitment of the Government to control, at long last, the destructive engine of material "progress." But it remains to be seen whether the promise of this legislation will become a reality. Therein lies the judicial role. In these cases, we must for the first time interpret the broadest and perhaps most important of the recent statutes: the National Environmental Policy Act of 1969 (NEPA). We must assess claims that one of the agencies charged with its administration has failed to live up to the congressional mandate. Our duty, in short, is to see that important legislative purposes, heralded in the halls of Congress, are not lost or misdirected in the vast hallways of the federal bureaucracy.

NEPA, like so much other reform legislation of the last forty years, is cast in terms of a general mandate and broad delegation of authority to new and old administrative agencies. It takes the major step of requiring all federal agencies to consider values of environmental preservation in their spheres of activity, and it prescribes certain procedural measures to ensure that those values are in fact fully respected. Petitioners argue that rules recently adopted by the Atomic Energy Commission to govern consideration of environmental matters fail to satisfy the rigor demanded by NEPA. The Commission, on the other hand, contends that the vagueness of the NEPA mandate and delegation leaves much room for discretion and that the rules challenged by petitioners fall well within the broad scope of the Act. We find the policies embodied in NEPA to be a good deal clearer and more demanding than does the Commission. We conclude that the Commission's procedural rules do not comply with the congressional policy. Hence we remand these cases for further rule making. . . .

Perhaps the greatest importance of NEPA is to require the Atomic Energy Commission and other agencies to *consider* environmental issues just as they consider other matters within their mandates. This compulsion is most plainly stated in Section 102. There, "Congress authorizes and directs that, to the fullest extent possible: (1) the policies, regulations, and public laws of the United States shall be interpreted and administered in accordance with the policies set forth in this Act . . . ," Congress also "authorizes and directs" that "(2) all agencies of the Federal Government shall" follow certain rigorous procedures in considering environmental values. . . . In general, all agencies must use a "systematic, interdisciplinary approach" to environmental planning and evaluation "in decision making which may have an impact on man's environment." In order to include all possible environmental factors in the decisional equation, agencies must "identify and develop methods and procedures . . . which will insure that presently unquantified environmental amenities and values may be given appropriate consideration in decision making along with economic and technical considerations." "Environmental amenities" will often be in conflict with "economic and technical considerations." To "consider" the former "along with" the latter must involve a balancing process. In some instances environmental costs may outweigh economic and technical benefits and in other instances they may not. But NEPA mandates a rather finely tuned and "systematic" balancing analysis in each instance.

To ensure that the balancing analysis is carried out and given full effect, Section 102 (2) (C) requires that responsible officials of all agencies prepare a "detailed statement" covering the impact of particular actions on the environment, the environmental costs which might be avoided, and alternative measures which might alter the cost-benefit equation. The apparent purpose of the "detailed statement" is to aid in the agencies' own decision making process and to advise other interested agencies and the public of the environmental consequences of planned federal action. Beyond the "detailed statement," Section 102 (2) (1) requires all agencies specifically to "study, develop, and describe appropriate alternatives to recommended courses of action in any proposal which involves unresolved conflicts concerning alternative uses of available resources." This requirement, like the "detailed statement" requirement, seeks to ensure that

each agency decision maker has before him and takes into proper account all possible approaches to a particular project (including total abandonment of the project) which would alter the environmental impact and the cost-benefit balance. Only in that fashion is it likely that the most intelligent, optimally beneficial decision will ultimately be made. . . .

We conclude, then, that Section 102 of NEPA mandates a particular sort of careful and informed decision-making process and creates judicially enforceable duties. . . .

In the cases before us now, we do not have to review a particular decision by the Atomic Energy Commission granting a construction permit or an operating license. Rather, we must review the Commission's recently promulgated rules which govern consideration of environmental values in all such individual decisions. The rules were devised strictly in order to comply with the NEPA procedural requirements but petitioners argue that they fall far short of the congressional mandate. . . .

The question here is whether the Commission is correct in thinking that its NEPA responsibilities may "be carried out in toto outside the hearing process"—whether it is enough that environmental data and evaluations merely "accompany" an application through the review process, but receive no consideration whatever from the hearing board.

We believe that the Commission's crabbed interpretation of NEPA makes a mockery of the Act. What possible purpose could there be in the Section 102 (2) (C) requirement (that the "detailed statement" accompany proposals through agency review processes) if "accompany" means no more than physical proximity—mandating no more than the physical act of passing certain folders and papers, unopened, to reviewing officials along with other folders and papers? What possible purpose could there be in requiring the "detailed statement" to be before hearing boards, if the boards are free to ignore entirely the contents of the statement? NEPA was meant to do more than regulate the flow of papers in the federal bureaucracy. The word "accompany" in Section 102 (2) (C) must not be read so narrowly as to make the Act ludicrous. It must, rather, be read to indicate a congressional intent that environmental factors, as compiled in the "detailed statement," be considered through agency review processes.

Beyond Section 102 (2) (C), NEPA requires that agencies consider the environmental impact of their actions "to the fullest extent possible." The Act is addressed to agencies as a whole, not only to their professional staffs. Compliance to the "fullest" possible extent would seem to demand that environmental issues be considered at every important stage in the decision making process concerning a particular action at every stage where an overall balancing of environmental and non-environmental factors is appropriate and where alterations might be made in the proposed action to minimize environmental costs. . . .

NEPA mandates a case-by-case balancing judgment on the part of federal agencies. In each individual case, the particular economic and technical benefits of planned action must be assessed and then weighed against the environmental costs; alternatives must be considered which would effect the balance of values. The magnitude of possible benefits and possible costs may lie anywhere on a broad spectrum. Much will depend on the particular magnitudes involved in particular cases. In some cases, the benefits will be great enough to justify a certain quantum of environmental costs; in other cases, they will not be so great and the proposed action may have to be abandoned or significantly altered so as to bring the benefits and costs into a proper balance. The point of the individualized balancing analysis is to ensure that, with possible alterations the optimally beneficial action is finally taken. . . .

We hold that, in the . . . respects detailed above, the Commission must revise its rules governing consideration of environmental issues. We do not impose a harsh burden on the Commission. For we require only an exercise of substantive discretion which will protect the environment "to the fullest extent possible." No less is required if the grand congressional purposes underlying NEPA are to become a reality.

Remanded for proceedings consistent with this opinion.

---

1. List the duties placed by NEPA on federal agencies.
2. What has the Atomic Energy Commission done to impose the consideration of potential adverse environmental alteration on those who have received construction permits *before* NEPA's effective date?

Case Questions

Council on Environmental Quality

Title I of NEPA covers the declaration of a national environmental policy and the requirement of the creation of impact statements to be used in the decision-making process concerning almost all federal actions affecting the environment. Title II creates the Council on Environmental Quality (CEQ) and gives it the following functions (a partial listing only):[45]

1. "to assist and advise the President in the preparation of the Environmental Quality Report . . ." This report is submitted to Congress before July 1 of each year and is to include a current evaluation of the status and condition of the major environmental assets of the nation (land, water, air and depletable resources).
2. "to gather authoritative information concerning the conditions and trends in the quality of the environment . . ."
3. "to review and appraise the various programs and activities of the Federal Government in light of the policy set forth in Title I . . ."
4. "to develop and recommend to the President national policies to foster and promote the improvement of environmental quality . . ."

In summary, NEPA was established to oversee the development of a national environmental policy and to make sure that, within reason, the nation's most powerful producer and consumer, the federal government, conformed to that policy.

Environmental Protection Agency

The Environmental Protection Agency (EPA) was created by executive order and began operation on December 2, 1970.[46] The EPA cooperates closely with the CEQ but pursues different objectives. The EPA coordinates enforcement of federal laws, rules, and regulations as they affect the *private sector*. More specifically, the EPA is responsible for conducting research and demonstrations, for establishing and enforcing environmental standards, for monitoring pollution and, perhaps most importantly, for working with state and local governments in their attempt to enforce state and local laws.

In fact, it is the policy of the EPA to leave pollution control enforcement to the states where the states have effective environmental laws. However, it is difficult for states to effectively attack major environmental polluters of the air and water, or users of pesticides or producers of radiation and noise, because these substances seldom stay within state boundary lines.

Below we have presented what may become a very important case concerning the enforcement ability of the EPA (the conditions under which the EPA may enter or view a business organization). We have followed this case with an explanation of the main areas of enforcement for the EPA. Please remember that environmental protection is a relatively new area for the legal system. Procedures and standards for judicial review, measures of damages, and effective remedies are just emerging. Generalization, therefore, is difficult, but rapid development in the substantive areas under the EPA's jurisdiction is expected.

DOW CHEMICAL CO. v. U.S.
ENVIRONMENTAL PROTECTION AGENCY
— F.Supp. — (1982), Civil No. 78-10044

HARVEY, District Judge

This case involves a constitutional and statutory challenge to the use of warrantless aerial photography of a chemical manufacturing plant by the Environmental Protection Agency (EPA). . . .

The Dow Chemical Company owns and operates a 2000 acre manufacturing plant in Midland, Michigan. . . .

In September of 1977, EPA made an on-site inspection of the power houses at Dow's plant. After the inspection EPA requested, and later received schematic drawings of the power houses from Dow.

In December of 1977 EPA again contacted Dow and requested a subsequent entry for purposes of inspecting the power houses. Prior to making this request EPA had already begun preparations for a planned enforcement action against Dow. EPA informed Dow that as part of the inspection it would be taking photographs of the Dow layout and facility. Dow objected to EPA's intention to take photographs and therefore denied EPA's request for entry. In response, EPA suggested to Dow that it would consider seeking a search warrant to gain entrance to the plant.

Rather than institute a civil action or seek a search warrant, EPA decided to obtain aerial photographs of Dow's facility.

The Court has carefully examined all of the photographs and has been struck by their vivid detail and resolution. When enlarged . . . and viewed under magnification, it is possible to discern equipment, pipes, and power lines as small as 1/2 inch in diameter. Many of these minute, but observable items are located in *interior* regions of the plant which are surrounded by buildings and other structures which make observation from anywhere but *directly above*, a near physical impossibility.

Dow was not aware of the EPA flyover either before or during its occurrence. When it subsequently became aware of this event a few weeks later, from sources other than EPA, Dow immediately instituted this action.

Dow asserts that *Barlow's*, wherein the Court held that a warrantless administrative inspection under the Occupational Safety and Health Act, violated the Fourth Amendment, controls this case.

Unlike the government's control over the alcohol, firearms, and mining industries, the chemical industry is not "pervasively regulated" by EPA under the Clean Air Act. EPA's authority to regulate entities such as Dow is more closely akin to the authority of the Department of Labor under OSHA which the Supreme Court reviewed in *Barlow's*.

The inescapable conclusion of the foregoing judicial and legislative pronouncements is that the holding and rationale of *Barlow's* controls this case. Therefore, EPA's warrantless aerial search of Dow's plant cannot withstand Fourth Amendment scrutiny.

In the typical administrative inspection case the Court's Fourth Amendment inquiry would halt at this point. This case, however, is not "typical" in any sense of the word. We are not here dealing with an ordinary *on-site* administrative search, neither are we faced with one of the more common Fourth Amendment challenges. Indeed, the Court's research suggests that, considering the facts before it, it is venturing into uncharted constitutional territory.

This Fourth Amendment analysis, as applied to this case, focuses on the question of whether Dow had a reasonable expectation of privacy which was violated by EPA's flyover and photography of Dow's plant.

While the expectation of privacy that the

owner of commercial property enjoys "differs significantly from the sanctity accorded an individual's home," it is clear that a commercial establishment may possess a protectable privacy expectation under the Fourth Amendment.

The Fourth Amendment should not be read as to require the citizens or businesses of this nation to take unreasonable measures to protect themselves from surreptitious governmental searches. This Court is not prepared to conclude that Dow must build a dome over its entire plant before it can be said to have manifested or exhibited an expectation of privacy.

As stated previously the Court would agree that Dow could not possess a reasonable expectation of privacy in its *entire* plant. It may, however, exhibit such an expectation with respect to internal areas of the plant.

Having examined the photographs, the Court is unable to agree with EPA's position that "the camera can't see what the eye can't see." On the contrary, when flying at 1,200 or 5,000 feet, the eye can discern only the basic sizes, shapes, outlines, and colors of the objects below. In this case, the finest precision aerial camera available was used to take the EPA photographs. The camera successfully captured vivid images of Dow's plant which EPA could later analyze under enlarged and magnified conditions. In doing so, the camera saw a great deal more than the human eye could ever see. The Court therefore would agree with Dow that the use of a sophisticated aerial camera is, at a minimum, on a par with other methods of visually enhanced surveillance in terms of its intrusiveness.

In this age of ever-advancing and potentially unlimited technology the government should be made aware that it does not possess carte blanche authority to utilize sophisticated surveillance methods to keep watch over citizens or businesses not suspected of any criminal activity.

A final argument raised by EPA, which, at first blush, is not without a good deal of merit, is that the public interest in effective pollution control outweighs any privacy expectation which Dow may have.

A . . . reason militating against EPA's position is that it is difficult to justify a need for the agency to conduct *warrantless* aerial searches. It appears to the Court that *at a minimum,* an *ex parte* warrant procedure would best strike the balance between Dow's expectation of privacy and EPA's asserted need to conduct surprise inspections of this sort.

Section 114(a)(2)(A) [of the Clean Air Act] grants to EPA, or its "authorized representative":

—a right of entry;
—to, upon, or through any premises;
—upon presentation of credentials.

An analysis of each of these phrases compels the conclusion that aerial surveillance and photography by EPA is not authorized under the statute, even by reasonable implication.

A "right of entry" cannot be viewed as synonymous with a "right to search." Had Congress intended that EPA be allowed to use aerial search techniques, it could have considered granting the agency a broad "right to search," or could have specifically enumerated aerial surveillance as among the permissible methods of monitoring and inspection. But a "right of entry," in literal terms, is something quite different. The noun "entry" denotes the physical act of admission or ingress into a given area. The fact that Congress used the phrase "right of entry," suggests to this Court a common sense interpretation, leading to the conclusion that EPA's intended inspection authority is land-based.

In summary, the Court concludes that the EPA flyover and aerial photography of Dow's plant constituted an unreasonable search in violation of the Fourth Amendment. In addition, the Court finds that EPA exceeded its statutory authority under Section 114 of the Clean Air Act in using this method of inspection.

IT IS HEREBY ORDERED AND ADJUDGED that EPA is permanently enjoined and restrained from conducting future aerial surveillance and photograph of the Dow Chemical manufacturing facility in Midland, Michigan, without first seeking judicial oversight which, *at a minimum,* will require EPA to secure an ex parte search warrant.

Case Question

1. In the *Barlow* case, which this decision refers to, the Supreme Court ruled that if the owner of a business does not consent to an inspection by the Occupational Safety & Health Administration, a search warrant is necessary to gain entry to the premises. For a search warrant to be issued the agency need only show that the business has been chosen for inspection on the basis of a general administrative plan for enforcement of the statute. Since a search warrant for an administrative inspection can be obtained so easily, why did not EPA get a search warrant and then take the aerial photos?

Clean Air Legislation

The federal legislation on air quality is comprehensive. It began with the Air Pollution Act of 1955,[47] which authorized the first federally funded air pollution research. The Motor Vehicle Pollution Control Act of 1965[48] gave the federal government the authority to set standards for emission discharges into the air by automobiles. The Air Quality Act of 1967[49] established comprehensive federal research in air pollution, and the Clean Air Act of 1970[50] set up a new system of national air quality standards and provided for the establishment of new auto pollution levels. This 1970 Act was the first to provide for national, uniform air quality standards based on geographic regions.

No act has created more controversy and difficulty for the EPA than the Clean Air Act. Although the National Motor Vehicle Emissions Standards Act recognized in 1965 that pollution from motor vehicles could only be handled by federal (national) standards, it was the 1970 Act that accelerated the schedule for emission controls. It required that by 1975 new autos had to show a 90 percent reduction in hydrocarbon and carbon emissions over 1970 models. Also, the 1970 law prohibited the sale of a new car unless it was certified by the EPA as having complied with emission standards. This Act has been revised several times and is currently (1982) undergoing another major revision.

Congress gave the EPA special powers in the 1970 Act. It was specifically granted:

1. The power to require those firms under review to give all necessary information.

2. The emergency authority under which it could suspend the imposition of emission standards.

Also, the Act provided that willful violators of EPA regulations could be denied federal contract awards.

Most enforcement of the 1970 Act is not accomplished in court. The Administrator of the EPA notifies a polluter that there is a violation of the law, issues an order to stop the pollution, and, if this fails, may seek court action for an injunction. A noteworthy provision of the 1970 Act is that when certain conditions are met, private citizens may bring legal action against polluters. A clear violation of a standard or EPA order must be alleged and notice must be given both the polluter and the EPA. Citizens may also bring an action against the Administrator of the EPA if he or she fails to perform an act required under the law.

Clean Water Legislation

Early attempts at controlling water pollution by legislation in 1886 and 1899 were unsuccessful because those in charge of enforcing the law did not enforce it. It was not until recently that enforcement of such legislation was forthcoming.

The Federal Water Pollution Control Act (FWPCA) was passed in 1948, amended in 1956, and again in 1972.[51] The 1972 amendments restructured the authority for water pollution control and consolidated this authority in the Administrator of the EPA.

The objective of the recent water pollution amendments to the FWPCA is to restore and then maintain the chemical, physical, and biological integrity of the nation's navigable waters. A primary goal is the elimination of the discharge of all pollutants into the navigable waters of the U.S. by 1985. This is only a goal, not, at this date, a requirement.

A second goal is to achieve an interim level of water quality that would provide for the protection of fish, shellfish, wildlife, and recreation areas by 1983.

The 1972 amendments changed the thrust of the EPA's efforts in water quality control from the promulgation of water quality standards to effluent limitations of pollutants being discharged from any discernible, confined, and separate means of conveyance. Generally, the emphasis was less on setting standards for and measuring pollutants in a given body of water, and more on identifying the major polluters. Again, state enforcement techniques and efforts are respected by the EPA.

Under present legislation the Administrator of the EPA is directed to publish a list of toxic pollutants and effluent limitations for these pollutants. Such limitations may constitute an absolute prohibition against discharging.

Enforcement of the various water pollution laws is accomplished in much the same manner as air pollution enforcement. Informal attempts to reach a resolution are stressed with the ultimate remedy of an injunction being provided by the court system. Also, private suits against water polluters are allowed in some instances.

Solid Waste, Pesticides, Radiation, and Noise Legislation

Since 1965, federal legislation aimed at controlling the interstate effects of solid waste disposal, the use of pesticides, and radiation and noise has received increasing attention. Again, legislation places the enforcement of federal laws in these areas within the jurisdiction of the EPA. The mandate of the EPA in each case is much the same. It is to conduct research, develop standards, and enforce its rules and regulations as well as enforce the substantial provisions of other federal legislation in these areas.

In summary, it is difficult to assess the EPA's impact at this point. The history of "regulating" conduct through federal administrative agencies is one characterized by some successes but more failures. In no small sense, the success of the agency will depend on the attitude and abilities of the Administrator and those he or she hires as well as the money provided by Congress for agency operation.

In conclusion of this section, we again stress the risks of including new legislation in a textbook. The rules and regulations made by the appropriate administrative agencies and court interpretation of the legislation may substantially change some of the material. However, the broad range of circumstances in which new duties have been imposed cannot be ignored in a book for the student of business organizations. For the most part, these legislative duties are here to stay.

Thus far in the chapter we have presented material outlining the circumstances in which the enforcement machinery of federal administrative agencies and the court system may be used to impose duties on business organizations that are producers and polluters. However, many activities of business organizations that have undesirable effects on human welfare remain beyond the reaches of the law. Recently, because of disclosures made during the Watergate proceedings about unethical corporate conduct (some of it illegal), the public consciousness about such activity has been aroused. This conduct by business organizations (primarily corporations), which violates no expressed or recognized legal duty yet appears to most persons to be beyond the rules of "fair play," has created the fundamental question of whether or not business organizations should exercise a measure of "social responsibility."

Most humans recognize that they are subject to some social control that is beyond the formal enforcing structure of the legal system. They

**Social
Responsibilities
of American
Business
Organizations**

obey these codes of conduct because they perceive that it is in their best interests *as humans* to do so. Also, responsibility for such an act by a single person can be relatively easily affixed on the perpetrator of the act. Accountability is not much of a problem when focusing on the acts of an individual human. In applying the concept of "social responsibility" to a business organization, however, at least two formidable obstacles are presented.

First, affixing responsibility for an act done in the name of an organization is not the same as affixing it on a human. In a business organization, the human responsibility for a decision is diffused. For example, Ralph Nader attempted for years to determine what person at General Motors was responsible for designing the Corvair automobile. No satisfactory answer has been found.

If the human accountability for corporate decisions is obfuscated then what means of enforcement would be effective? Fines against the business organizations hurt the shareholders more than those actually responsible for the decision prompting the fine—the managers.

A second formidable obstacle is again presented by the very nature of the business organization. By definition, the objective of business organizations is to earn a profit, not, as is true of humans, to maximize one's total welfare. Thus when the task of making a profit conflicts with the proposed course of action that would maximize some other objective, the conventional wisdom dictates that business organizations must opt for the profit-maximizing opportunity. This view is most eloquently stated by Professor Milton Friedman, noted conservative economist. He argued that when a corporation spends time or effort on what is "socially" desirable and thereby sacrifices an economic opportunity to earn profit, it is engaging in an undesirable infringement on the political process and misleading the shareholders.[52] Social decisions, he asserts, should be made by either individual humans or, where the need is greater, by the elected politicians whose express task is to protect the public welfare. Moreover, when business organizations make social decisions what standards are to be applied? He continues that if, at the expense of corporate profits, the managers of a corporation decide to hire "hardcore" unemployed instead of better qualified workers, the corporation would be spending someone else's money—the shareholders', to the extent this reduced profits—for a general social interest.

In summary, Friedman's doctrine is that business organizations, especially large corporations, are chartered by the state to make a profit, and the general welfare is best served when each corporation acts to maximize this objective. Certainly our perceptions of this restatement of Adam Smith's invisible hand moving in the economy vary with the times. Nevertheless, Friedman's logic is in accord with our capitalistic tradition. It presents a modern-day manifestation of the reasoning found in the *Dodge* v. *Ford Motor Co.* opinion discussed in the first chapter on corporation law.

In that case, you will recall, the court sided with the Dodge brothers and compelled Henry Ford to continue to pay massive dividends to the shareholders rather than spend some of the great quantities of revenues on employee and customer benefits.

On the other hand, the Friedman view appears to some to be simplistic. The question of when profits should be sacrificed to achieve a socially desirable result is, perhaps, one of the most important and complex questions facing the directors of large corporations. Certainly, there is precedent, both legal and otherwise, for corporate acts of compassion and humanity. For example, recall the logic and language of the court in the *A. P. Smith Mfg. Co.* v. *Barlow* case also in the first chapter on corporation law. There, a court recognized that a corporate donation of $1,500 dollars to Princeton University was permissible and even desirable because so much of the wealth today is generated by this form of organization that some commitment to its "social environment" should be allowed.

If these questions of the existence of social responsibilities and human accountability for corporate acts are still being formulated, one can hardly expect answers. We provide none here. One can recognize with some satisfaction that business organization duties to end discrimination in employment, to provide adequate retirement security, to provide safe products and nonpolluting manufacturing processes have recently been formally recognized by Congress. However, the struggle to develop the appropriate balance between profits and the needs of human welfare continues. This struggle can be most dramatically highlighted by the litigation involving the Reserve Mining Company. The following reproduced portions of this litigation are used to illustrate the complex nature of the balance being sought. Following this we cite another example that can be used to raise issues of corporate social responsibility. Finally, we present an analysis of these two examples and close with one scholar's approach and solution to this complex set of issues and questions in the area of the social responsibility of business.

The Reserve Mining Litigation

The litigation involving the Reserve Mining Company at Silver Bay, Minnesota, is extremely complex. The plaintiffs were the cities of Duluth, Minnesota, and Superior, Wisconsin; and the states of Minnesota, Wisconsin, and Michigan as well as the federal government and numerous environmental groups. The defendants were, among others, Reserve Mining Company, Armco Steel Corporation, and Republic Steel Corporation. At issue was Reserve Mining's pollution of Lake Superior. The case was tried in the U.S. District Court at Duluth. After nine and one-half months of trial, the district judge, Judge Lord, ordered Reserve Mining to cease its discharge into Lake Superior as of 12:01 a.m., April 21, 1974. The opinion accompanying this order is reproduced below. Not quite two days later the Eighth Circuit Court of Appeals stayed (suspended) the order of the District Court closing Reserve Mining pending a full hearing by the Circuit Court on a motion to suspend the stay. On May 15, 1974, the Circuit Court continued its stay until June 4, 1974. On this latter date the Circuit Court of Appeals granted a 70-day continuation on Reserve's taking prompt steps to abate its discharge into air and water. The Circuit Court remanded part of the case back to the District Court and set out a procedure by which Reserve was to submit plans for abating its discharges. On August 3, 1974, the District Court again found the attempts by Reserve to abate its discharge inadequate and suggested to the Circuit Court that the stay of the initial temporary injunction be lifted. Meanwhile, the first order of the Circuit Court staying the District Court injunction against continued discharge reached the U.S. Supreme Court on appeal. The Supreme Court decision was announced October 11, 1974. The decision follows.

On March 14, 1975, the Circuit Court reached its decision on the merits of the case and held that Reserve was guilty of creating a risk to the public health of sufficient gravity to be legally cognizable and that an abatement order on reasonable grounds might be issued, but the evidence did not require that Reserve immediately terminate its operations. Reserve and its parent companies were to be given a reasonable opportunity to convert its taconite operations to on-land disposal and to restrict air emissions.

The record is silent as to the activities of the parties between the spring of 1975 and November of 1975. It is safe to assume that the pollution continued while the feasibility of various on-land disposal sites was explored. In November of 1975, the state of Minnesota asked the trial court to order the U.S. Corps of Engineers to supply filtered water to the city of Duluth, Minnesota, which draws its drinking water from Lake Superior. The result of this proceeding was that Judge Lord ordered Reserve Mining to pay $100,000 to cover the cost of this filtration. Reserve Mining appealed this decision based on three alleged errors: the fact that (1) it had no notice that it might be fined; (2) that Judge Lord exhibited prejudice toward it; and (3) that Judge Lord violated an earlier appellate court order that recognized state jurisdiction over the issue of the disposal cite. On January 6, 1976, the appellate court removed Judge Lord from the case based on the arguments of Reserve.[53] The order of removal cites the following as evidence of judicial prejudice.[54]

> . . . the trial judge announced on the record that witnesses called by Reserve could not be believed, that in every instance Reserve Mining Company hid the evidence, misrepresented, delayed and frustrated the ultimate conclusions, and that he did not have 'any faith' in witnesses to be called by Reserve.

Indeed, such statements are out of the ordinary for a trial judge. But so is the nature of the threat posed to the public by Reserve. On February

21, 1976, Judge Edward Devitt, the apparent replacement for Judge Lord, heard arguments by the U.S. Government that Reserve should be required to pay $288,800 expended by the U.S. Army Corps of Engineers for filtration of water. The court agreed that Reserve should be liable for the expenses of filtration and ordered the parties to meet promptly to agree on the correctness of the amount sought.[55]

U.S. v. RESERVE MINING
6 ERC 1449 (D. Ct., Minn., 1974)

Action for injunctive relief to abate mining company's discharges of taconite tailings into air and into Lake Superior.

Injunctive relief granted. . . .

LORD, J.

This action for injunctive relief is before the Court after 139 days of trial, which included testimony from well over 100 witnesses, over 1,621 exhibits, and over 18,000 pages of transcript. Of necessity, it will require several weeks before the Court will be able to set forth in writing its detailed findings of fact and conclusions of law. Inasmuch as the case deals with issues concerning public health, the ultimate resolution of the problem should not be delayed by this procedural matter. The Court has carefully considered all of the evidence and hereto sets forth its essential findings of fact and conclusions of law to be refined and supplemented at a later date.

Findings of Fact

1. Reserve Mining Company (Reserve) is set up and run for the sole benefit of its owners, Armco Steel Corporation (Armco) and Republic Steel Corporation (Republic), and acts as a mere instrumentality or agent of its parent corporations. Reserve is run in such a manner as to pass all its profits to the parents.

2. Reserve acting as an instrumentality and agent for Armco and Republic discharges large amounts of minute amphibole fibers into Lake Superior and into the air of Silver Bay daily.

3. The particles when deposited into the water are dispersed throughout Lake Superior and into Wisconsin and Michigan.

4. The currents in the lake, which are largely influenced by the discharge, carry many of the fibers in a southwesterly direction toward Duluth and are found in substantial quantities in the Duluth drinking water.

5. Many of these fibers are morphologically and chemically identical to amosite asbestos and an even larger number are similar to amosite asbestos.

6. Exposure to these fibers can produce asbestosis, mesothelioma, and cancer of the lung, gastrointestinal tract and larynx.

7. Most of the studies dealing with this problem are concerned with the inhalation of fibers; however, the available evidence indicates that the fibers pose a risk when ingested as well as when inhaled.

8. The fibers emitted by the defendant into Lake Superior have the potential for causing great harm to the health of those exposed to them.

9. The discharge into the air substantially endangers the health of the people of Silver Bay and surrounding communities as far away as the eastern shore in Wisconsin.

10. The discharge into the water substantially endangers the health of the people who procure their drinking water from the western arm of Lake Superior including

the communities of Beaver Bay, Two Harbors, Cloquet, Duluth, and Superior, Wisconsin.

11. The present and future industrial standard for a safe level of asbestos fibers in the air is based on the experience related to asbestosis and not to cancer. In addition its formulation was influenced more by technological limitations than health considerations.

12. The exposure of a non-worker populace cannot be equated with industrial exposure if for no other reason than the environmental exposure, as contrasted to a working exposure, is for every hour of every day.

13. While there is a dose-response relationship associated with the adverse effects of asbestos exposure and may be therefore a threshold exposure value below which no increase in cancer would be found, this exposure threshold is not now known. . . .

Memorandum

It has been clearly established in this case that Reserve's discharge creates a serious health hazard to the people exposed to it. The exact scope of this potential health hazard is impossible to accurately quantify at this time. Significant increase in diseases associated with asbestos exposure do not develop until fifteen to twenty years after the initial exposure to the fibers. The state of the scientific and medical knowledge available in this area is in its early stages and there is insufficient knowledge upon which to base an opinion as to the magnitude of the risks associated with this exposure. The fact that few fibers have been found in the tissue of certain deceased Duluth residents may indicate that the general contamination in the community of Duluth has not yet reached alarming proportions. Unfortunately, the real answer to the problem will not be available until some ten to twenty years from this date when the health experience of those exposed to the fibers emitted from Reserve's plant is reviewed. At present the Court is faced with a situation where a commercial industry is daily exposing thousands of people to substantial quantities of a known human carcinogen. Emphasis is placed upon the fact that the Court is not dealing with a situation in which a substance causes cancer in experimental animals where the effect on humans is largely speculative. Fibers identical and similar to those emitted from Reserve's plant have been directly associated with a marked increase in the incidence of cancer in humans.

The Court has been constantly reminded that a curtailment in the discharge may result in a severe economic blow to the people of Silver Bay, Babbit and others who depend on Reserve directly or indirectly for their livelihood. Certainly unemployment in itself can result in an unhealthy situation. At the same time, however, the Court must consider the people downstream from the discharge. Under no circumstances will the Court allow the people of Duluth to be continuously and indefinitely exposed to a known human carcinogen in order that the people in Silver Bay can continue working at their jobs.

Naturally the Court would like to find a middle ground that would satisfy both considerations. If an alternate method of disposal is available that is economically feasible, could be speedily implemented and took into consideration the health questions involved, the Court might be disposed to fashion a remedy that would permit the implementation of such a system. However, if there is no alternative method available, the Court has no other choice but to immediately curtail the discharge and stop the contamination of the water supply of those downstream from the plant.

With these considerations in mind, the Court on February 5, 1974, took the unusual step of relating to the parties the Court's view of the evidence to date concerning the public health issue. The Court had heard in one form or another from substantially all of the world's experts in the area. The Court was led to believe by Reserve that little had been done in the way of devising an alternative method of disposing of the tailings on land and, in fact, that Reserve knew of no feasible way to accomplish such a system. At that time, it was Reserve's posture in this litigation that the only feasible alternative to the present discharge was the creation of a pipe system that would carry the tailings to the bottom of the lake. If, in fact, the deep pipe system was unacceptable, the Court was led to believe that Reserve had no alternative method for disposing of the tailings. Hence the Court found it essential that Reserve's attention be focused directly on the problem and a possible on land disposal alternative be developed as quickly as possible.

The Court was at one and the same time hearing a motion for a temporary restraining order and a permanent injunction. The reluctance of the Court to make a formal ruling on the temporary restraining order at an early time was done out of caution with the anticipation of hearing from more of the world's experts. It was after hearing all of this evidence that the Court gave its tentative findings on the health issue with the caveat that further evidence would be taken. The statement was made with a view toward giving Reserve an impetus to start resolving its problem and to give Duluth and the Lake Shore communities time to seek clean water. It did not have the desired effect in either instance.

As it turned out, after days of testimony on the underwater disposal alternative proposed by Reserve, it became clear to the Court that this alternative in no way lessened the public health threat and possibly created additional problems relating to public health. The Court's findings in this regard turned out to be superfluous in that later testimony by representatives of Armco, half owner of Reserve,

indicated that Armco had long since disregarded this underwater disposal system on the basis of engineering infeasibility alone, without any regard to its effect on the lake or public health. Upon further inquiry to officers of Armco and Republic, who also serve on the Board of Directors of Reserve, it appeared that several plans had been developed dealing with the possibility of on land disposal. Although these plans had been asked for by plaintiffs by way of interrogatories and by the Court by direct order, they were not produced nor mentioned until the representatives of Armco and Republic were deposed on March 1, 1974. The Court is apprised that defendants' failure to produce these plans for on land disposal will be the subject matter for motions by the plaintiffs to collect costs involved in the litigation so this matter will be dealt with at that time. The Court has stated on the record and will repeat here that Reserve's insistence on advocating the underwater disposal system which had been deemed infeasible by one of its owners and the failure to timely produce the documents dealing with possible on land disposal systems has substantially delayed the outcome of this litigation in a situation where a speedy resolution is essential.

The Court refers to this history in the case only to point out that since February 5, defendants were informed that the present method of discharge would stop and that if they chose to keep Reserve in operation they had to come up with an on land disposal alternative that would satisfy the health problems created by the present discharge in the air and water. It was the Court's fervent wish that the health hazard could be abated without the economic problems that would be imposed upon the people in the North Shore communities if Reserve in fact closed down permanently. The documents of Reserve's parent companies indicate that they have known for some time that they would have to make modifications in their discharge. . . . Even when faced with the evidence in this case that their discharge creates a substantial threat to the health of the people exposed to it, defendants are reluctant to curtail their discharge until the latest possible moment, presumably in order to prolong the profitability of the present discharge.

It was not until a few days ago that there was any indication to this Court that Reserve had a feasible plan for the disposal of taconite tailings on land. The testimony in the case by Reserve and representations by Reserve's counsel indicated that they not only had no such plan but that the engineering problems of such a system were insurmountable. The plaintiffs, on the other hand, introduced testimony indicating that on land disposal is feasible. Reserve took issue with this testimony even after the major engineering problems were solved and maintained that it would simply be too expensive to change their method of disposal to on land.

The evidence in the case indicates that the daily profit in the operation at Reserve is in the neighborhood of $60,000.00 per day. Each year that the plant remains in operation there is a 90 percent return on owner's equity. In other words, for every dollar Armco and Republic initially invested in Reserve, they get back ninety cents each year the plant remains in operation.

This is not to say that the companies could not afford to make modifications. The testimony adduced at trial was to the effect that (with product improvement) Reserve, Republic and Armco could afford at the very least a $180,000,000 to $200,000,000 capital outlay with reasonably associated operating costs without substantially changing their economic situation as to profitability, intraindustry position, interest coverage, bond rating, etc. This figure should come as no shock to the defendant. Their own documents, recently discovered, support this fact. In this area it should be noted that any reduction in the royalty rate paid by Reserve or the interest rate, by such devices as revenue bonds or industrial bonds,

would make even larger capital outlays, with accompanying operating expenses, possible. . . . The evidence is clear that Republic and Armco are two of the largest corporations in this country. They are prosperous now and would remain prosperous even after the necessary alterations are made. Defendants have had the means to implement a feasible, economical alternative. It was their choice whether they would make the investment or abandon their employees and the State of Minnesota.

It should be noted in this regard that the State of Minnesota is here in the posture of asking the Court for fines and penalties as well as injunctive relief. Reserve on the other hand still has outstanding counterclaims against the state. It would, therefore, be inappropriate and premature for this governmental unit to subsidize the company before these matters are decided by the Court.

Today, April 20, 1974, the chief executive officers of both Armco and Republic have testified that they are unwilling to abate the discharge and bring their operation into compliance with applicable Minnesota regulations in an acceptable manner. They proposed a plan for an on land disposal site in the Palisades Creek area adjacent to the Silver Bay plant. Although this particular plan was in existence for several years it was not brought forward until the latest stages of this proceeding. The plan, which has been rejected by the plaintiffs because it is not environmentally sound, is totally unacceptable to the Court because of the conditions imposed with it. . . .

Defendants have the economic and engineering capability to carry out an on land disposal system that satisfies the health and environmental considerations raised. For reasons unknown to this Court they have chosen not to implement such a plan. In essence they have decided to continue exposing thousands daily to a substantial health risk in order to maintain the current profitability of the present operation and delay the capital outlay (with its concommitant profit) needed to institute modifications. The Court has no other alternative but to order an immediate halt to the discharge with threatens the lives of thousands. In that defendants have no plan to make the necessary modifications, there is no reason to delay any further the issuance of the injunction.

Up until the time of writing this opinion the Court has sought to exhaust every possibility in an effort to find a solution that would alleviate the health threat without a disruption of operations at Silver Bay. Faced with the defendants' intransigence, even in the light of the public health problem, the Court must order an immediate curtailment of the discharge.

THEREFORE, IT IS ORDERED

1) That the discharge from the Reserve Mining Company into Lake Superior be enjoined as of 12:01 A.M., April 21, 1974.

2) That the discharge of amphibole fibers from the Reserve Mining Company into the air be enjoined as of 12:01 A.M., April 21, 1974 until such time as defendants prove to the Court that they are in compliance with all applicable Minnesota Regulations. . . .

U.S. v. RESERVE MINING
7 ERC 1113 (U.S. Sup. Ct., 1974)

The respective applications for an order vacating or modifying the stay order of the United States Court of Appeals for the Eighth Circuit, presented to MR. JUSTICE BLACKMUN and by him referred to the Court, are each denied. Four Justices, however, state explicitly that these denials are without prejudice to the applicants' renewal of their applications to vacate if the litigation has not been finally decided by the Court of Appeals by January 31, 1975.

MR. JUSTICE DOUGLAS, *dissenting*.

I would vacate the stay issued by the Court of Appeals.

Judge Lord made detailed findings as to the health hazards of the respondent's discharges into the air and into the waters of Lake Superior, . . . The Court of Appeals disagreed with Judge Lord's conclusion but it stopped short of holding that his findings were "clearly erroneous" within the meaning of Rule 52 (a) of the Rules of Civil Procedure. Even in its view, the issue, however, was close or rather neatly balanced. It therefore decided that being a "court of law" it was "governed by rules of proof" and that "unknowns may not be sub-stituted for proof of a demonstrable hazard to the public health."

That position, however, with all respect makes "maximizing profits" the measure of the public good, not health of human beings or life itself. Property is, of course, protected under the Due Process Clause of the Fifth Amendment against federal intrusion. But so is life and liberty. Where the scales are so evenly divided, we cannot say that the findings on health were "clearly erroneous" nor am I able to discover how "maximizing profits" becomes a governing principle overriding the health hazards. If equal justice is the federal standard, we should be as alert to protect people and their rights as the Court of Appeals was to protect "maximizing profits." If, as the Court of Appeals indicates, there is doubt, it should be resolved in favor of humanity, lest in the end our judicial system be part and parcel of a regime that makes people, the sovereign power in this Nation, the victims of the great God Progress which is behind the stay permitting this vast pollution of Lake Superior and its environs. I am not aware of a constitutional principle that allows either private or public enterprises to despoil any part of the domain that belongs to all of the people. Our guiding principle should be Mr. Justice Holmes' dictum that our waterways, great and small, are treasures, not garbage dumps or cesspools.

Case Questions

1. Who owns Reserve Mining? From the limited information available do you think it would be fair to impose responsibility for the acts of pollution on any human in the form of a fine or imprisonment? If so, which person?

2. Assume an employee of Reserve who must breathe the polluted air of Silver Bay every day wishes to object to his employer's acts. What are his remedies? What are the remedies of the residents of the city of Duluth?

3. Do Reserve or the owners of Reserve make a product that can be identified as having been made by them so that concerned consumers might bring some form of pressure to bear on them in the form of a boycott?

4. Each year Reserve returns to its owners 90 percent of their initial investment. Is Reserve too profitable? How would Milton Friedman view this case? Is Reserve being socially responsible by maximizing its profit?

5. Is Reserve Mining beyond the law?

Ford Motor Company and the Pinto Gas-Tank Litigation

The managers of business organizations, and megacorporations especially, seldom do wrong or injure people or the environment intentionally. We must assume that these managers are law-abiding, humane individuals. From the Reserve Mining litigation comes this quote from H. S. Taylor, Mines Engineer of Reserve (at 412 F. Supp. 709, 1976): "This company will be a responsible company and we will recognize our legal liabilities."

Managers want to be "responsible." But, what does this word mean? Does it mean a commitment to a principle of "doing good" or a commitment to an approach of balancing costs against what may be perceived as "doing good"? Henry Ford II would answer the question this way:

> In our national effort to solve common problems caused by our private choices we have spent too much time on moralistic and ideological disputes and too little time seeking practical compromises. Our real task is to find the best balance between benefits to people as citizens and costs to people as consumers. (From "The High Cost of Regulation," *Newsweek*, p. 15, March 20, 1978.)

Before we present our analysis of this difficult set of issues labeled "social responsibility," consider the following account of the facts taken from a lawsuit against Ford Motor Company.

The Ford Motor Company designed, produced, and marketed the Pinto automobile beginning in 1970. The gas tank in the Pinto was located behind the rear axle; it was only 3¼ inches behind the differential housing.[56] In rear-end collisions the gas tank would be pushed into the differential housing, which would work like a can opener on the tank. Ford Motor Company produced a movie for its own use which showed a Pinto backing into a wall at 20 miles per hour. In the film the gas tank of the car ruptured with such force, according to one observer, that "it looked like a fireman had stuck a hose inside the car and turned it on." Apparently the gas tank was shoved into the housing, which split the tank and literally threw the liquid substance into the passenger compartment. The location of the tank was not substantially changed until 1977.

In 1971 Lily Gray was driving a Pinto with Richard Grimshaw riding as a passenger. The car stalled on the freeway and was struck from behind by another car. Lily Gray died of burns suffered when the passenger compartment exploded in flames, and Grimshaw was burned over 90 percent of his body; he required over 60 operations in the next seven years to repair some of the damage done.

Grimshaw and a representative of the estate of Lily Gray sued Ford. The trial was held in late 1977. After the evidence was heard a jury returned for the plaintiffs the largest single award of damages in U.S. history at that time. It awarded Grimshaw $3.5 million to compensate him for his injury and $125 million in punitive damages. The punitive damage award was so large that after the trial, the judge proposed reducing the award to $6.3 million.

Observers explained that the reason for this large punitive damage award was the fact that the evidence at the trial made it clear that Ford management knew of the dangerous tank design and produced the car anyway. One juror commented that, "Ford knew people would be killed."

It appears that Ford carefully assessed the savings that would result from this particular design. Ford's own documents revealed that Ford management calculated they could save $20.9 million if they delayed making gas-tank alterations for two years. Also, the cost of the possible lawsuits could be calculated and then set against the projected savings. From the testimony at the Grimshaw trial it appears another juror reasoned that Ford could have saved as much as $100 million by not installing safer tanks, which would have cost $10 to $15 more per car. Some of the jurors reasoned that to punish Ford, the punitive damage award should exceed the total savings resulting from the gas tank design. Thus, the jury settled on $125 million.

It is estimated that Ford will report 1977 fourth-quarter profits of from $380 million to $395 million. The jury's punitive damage award is about equal to one month's profit for Ford.

How can this behavior be considered socially responsible or desirable? Consider the possible answers to these questions:

1. Do you think the engineers who designed the location for the gas tank and the tank itself and who presumably knew better than anyone the consequences of this design made the decision to use that particular design? (It appears from the reports of the Grimshaw trial that at least one Ford engineer was a critic of the Pinto fuel-tank design.)

2. In what way can those in Ford who are responsible for the adoption of the Pinto fuel-tank design be held accountable for this decision? Should they be held accountable?

3. In this case what standards are to be used to define "reasonably pru-

dent" behavior of management? (To adopt an analogy from tort law, one may not be held liable for negligence if one is acting as a reasonably prudent person would under the circumstances.)

4. Assume that the large award of punitive damages is not altered on appeal. Who ultimately would bear the cost of the punitive damage award assuming that the prices of automobiles are not subject to substantial competitive market conditions? Are there market inducements for socially desirable behavior? Trace the effects of this payment. Who ultimately will bear the cost of this penalty?

An Analysis of the "Social Responsibility" Debate[57]

How is this undesirable corporate behavior to be explained? This section is a search for a rational explanation of and a possible remedy for such behavior. The thesis will be advanced that our ideas about what is socially, economically, and legally desirable are founded on tradition, and that these tradition-bound ideas have failed to account for the impact on our society of the modern corporation, and particularly, the impact caused by the structure of the modern corporation. This failure presents us with a paradox. We must assume that the managements of Reserve Mining and Ford believe they are acting in a socially desirable manner when they seek to maximize their profit—profit-maximizing acts are consistent with our whole prevailing social ideology, which predicts that the general welfare of our society is served by such activity. Yet it is the pursuit of profit by large corporations that, more than any other single source, threatens both our environment and our bodily safety.

A resolution of the paradox, it will be argued, does not involve the standard of profit. Instead, the resolution lies in directing our attention to the structure of the modern corporation. This structure, which facilitates profit maximization, minimizes the perception of the hard-to-measure costs to our society of the production of a good. We must increase the perception or awareness by corporate management of the full impact of their decisions.

The examination of this thesis will be presented in two parts. The first examines the nature of our current ideology defining socially desirable commercial behavior. The second part makes some suggestions for confronting the threats to our present society posed by the modern megacorporation.

On the Significance of Conventional Wisdom

> The first requirement of an understanding of contemporary economic and social life is a clear view of the relation between events and the ideas which interpret them.
>
> J.K. Galbraith, *The Affluent Society* 3rd ed., p. 6 (1976).

In the 1950s, noted Harvard economist John Kenneth Galbraith suggested the term "conventional wisdom" as a key to understanding current social and economic phenomena.[58] Conventional wisdom associates truth with that which is acceptable and familiar. Our American notions about what is socially, economically, or legally desirable are organized around and based on what the community *as a whole* finds acceptable or convenient. We approve of and promote that which we best understand. Over time the competition between the old policies and the new is usually resolved in favor of the former because the strategic advantage lies with that which has always existed. The accepted ideas become increasingly elaborate as the entire business-government-education complex devotes more and more resources to justifying established, accepted, self-serving ideas and practices. The conventional wisdom develops a literature, even a mystique, and ultimately becomes more or less synonymous with sound scholarship; thus, its position becomes virtually impregnable.[59]

Conventional wisdom dictates that the best method for the distribution of most industrial goods in the American economy is to allow purchasers and sellers to bargain freely in an established market for the goods. If there are many sellers and purchasers in the market, the price of the good sold will tend toward the cost of the last good provided to the market, and unreasonable or monopolistic profits will be eliminated. Movement of resources between markets is assured by assuming that where some markets are more profitable than others, they will attract resources. This results in more sellers and ultimately a lower priced good. When a market becomes unprofitable, resources will leave. This flow of resources to and from industrial markets resulting in lower prices of the goods produced is caused by each individual pursuing his or her own selfish desire to maximize return on investment. No central authority is needed to guarantee the maximization of society's welfare. It is done by an "invisible hand" guided only by individual greed. One must admit there is a ring of "truth" to this widely accepted and simplistically beautiful model of how our economy should be organized.

The conventional wisdom recognizes several corollaries to this general theory. The role of government is not to interfere with the industrial markets because this "distorts" the markets and inevitably results in inefficiencies. However, the government does have a role to play. It is to ensure, through its laws, that the "invisible hand" first recognized by Adam Smith continues to move freely. Thus, even most conservatives believe that government legitimately passes and enforces laws protecting the competitiveness of markets.

The more fundamental corollary equates the maximization of total welfare with profit. Conventional wisdom acknowledges that the participants in every industrial market have a duty to act in a socially responsible way. This duty is perceived by most participants, and is discharged by acting in a way that maximizes profit. When the duty to make a profit conflicts with a proposed course of action that would serve some other objective, the conventional wisdom dictates that the participant must choose the profit-maximizing opportunity. This is especially true when a *corporation* is making the decisions, because corporate management has a duty to the owners of the enterprise to earn a return on their investment.

Conventional wisdom accommodates itself not to an ever-changing reality, but to the believer's desired view of the world. So, the conventional wisdom is not threatened by new ideas—they can be rationalized and reconciled in terms of the believer's values and perceptions of reality. The real threat to the conventional wisdom is the march of events.[60]

Conventional Wisdom and the Rise of the Modern Corporation

> The corporation has, in fact, become both a method of property tenure and a means of organizing economic life. Grown to tremendous proportions, there may be said to have evolved a "corporate system"—as there was once a feudal system—which has attracted to itself a combination of attributes and powers, and has attained a degree of prominence entitling it to be dealt with as a major social institution. A. Berle and G. Means, *The Modern Corporation and Private Property*, 1 (1932).

The conventional, simplistic model of how our economy operates or should operate to distribute industrial goods has failed to account for the rise of the modern corporate enterprise. The older conventional wisdom was based on the writings of Adam Smith. Adam Smith's philosophy and economics were based on the observation that humans are at once selfish (individualistic) and social beings. They desire to, on the one hand, maximize their own wealth and, on the other, seek approbation. He reconciled these two competing notions by asserting that the reason humans work is to gain the favor of others. He said:

> For to what purpose is all the toil and bustle of this world? What is the end of avarice and ambition, of the pursuit of wealth, of power, and pre-eminence? . . . what are the advantages we propose by that great purpose of human life which we call bettering our condition? *To be observed, to be attended to, to be taken notice of with sympathy, . . . and approbation, are all the advantages which we can propose to derive from it.*[61] (emphasis added)

Since commercial activity was brought about by individuals who were desiring to be well thought of in a public sense, the individuals would self-regulate their commercial activity so as not to inflict damage on others or invoke the public wrath. Smith again states:

> In the race for wealth, and honours . . . [he] may run as hard as he can and strain every nerve and every muscle, in order to outstrip all his competitors. But if he should jostle, or throw down any of them, the indulgence of the spectators is entirely at an end. It is a violation of fair play, which they cannot admit of.[62]

Sellers in the markets of the eighteenth and early nineteenth centuries were mostly single individuals who most probably produced the product and marketed it. Then it was appropriate to build a theory on the assumptions that a seller (as a human) (1) had complete information about the entire production and distribution process and market conditions, and (2) owned the assets of production or, at least, had some property at risk in the venture. *Such a seller would be particularly sensitive to the quantitative and qualitative demands of the "spectators" associated with the market.* In many instances such a seller would adjust both the products produced and general commercial conduct in response to those viewing or trading in the market for the product. The response could be predicted because the seller could be identified by those in the market and held *personally accountable* for the undesirable commercial activity.

While the traders in most industrial markets today differ radically from those of the 19th century, the prevailing social theory is still based on the conventional wisdom, which assumes all traders are human beings rather than corporations. For example, when the noted economist Paul Samuelson is introducing the general idea of perfect competition in his best selling textbook he states:

> Perfect competition exists *only* in the case where no *farmer, businessman* or *laborer* is a big enough part of the total market to have any personal influence on market price.[63] (emphasis added)

By defining the ideal model of perfect competition in terms of a human actor ("farmer," "businessman," "laborer"), Samuelson is contributing to the perpetuation of the myth that significant traders are human (indeed today, there are human traders, but they are not significant in terms of the total value of manufactured goods).

The conventional assumption about the character of sellers in most industrial markets in this country is inaccurate, and it may result in a condition that seriously threatens our welfare. American corporate enterprise accounts for most of the total value of manufactured goods produced and sold in this country. The structure of large corporations (especially the largest 200 corporations) differs drastically from the so-called rational decision-makers in the conventional model. Most large corporations are broken into many divisions and subsidiaries that separate the designer from the producer, the producer from the distributor, and the distributor from the seller; and they are directed by a team of managers who control the enterprise but do not own it. *The decision makers are effectively insulated from both the market and the shareholder-owners.* In this relative isolation, the decision-makers still behave as Adam Smith suggested: they attempt to maximize profit. But, and this is where the failure of our social theory is apparent, the conventional view assumed the event producing the profit was to be evaluated together with other alternatives that would satisfy the "spectators." A decision depended on a perception of how others in the market or associated with it would view those responsible for producing the product. As the human decision-makers of the twentieth century have withdrawn from direct contact with the production process and the market, they have had to rely more on the objective standard of profit to judge performance. The more subtle, human, subjective responses by those in the market cannot be measured and have thus been minimized in corporate decision-making.

We are not ignoring the fact that major corporate decisions are based on a "cost-benefit" analysis approach. The point is that in today's corporate boardrooms, the perception of what is a cost and what is a benefit is not an accurate one. In numerous situations, intuitive, humane judgments that were possible under the commercial circumstances of the nineteenth century are replaced by a framework for decision making that overemphasizes profit. Profit is overemphasized because the decision makers are so removed from the production process and the market that they cannot judge the product's impact in any other terms than conventionally recognized costs. Thus, well-meaning, sensitive people overemphasize profit because they cannot perceive the results of the decision. The consequences of this overemphasis are apparent every time one picks up a newspaper, book, or scholarly journal on commercial behavior. This overemphasis helps to explain the "rational" behavior of both Reserve Mining and Ford.

Confronting the Modern Corporation. The traditional, individual-centered model of a market economy used to explain and understand how goods and services are distributed in this country has failed to account for some significant activity of the modern corporate enterprise. This failure has been recognized by many. However, the response has been to enact enormous amounts of federal legislation applicable to business conduct. Most of this legislation focuses on corporate conduct but does not address the central problem of the manner in which today's significant corporate sellers make decisions.

The image we must focus on in constructing a social theory (and legislation) for confronting the less desirable effects of the large corporate enterprise on our society is one based on the reality of the current decision making process of the largest 200 corporations. More precisely, we must focus on the fact that significant corporate decisions are made in a corporate boardroom in which sit 15 to 25 individuals looking at sheets of paper on which numerous figures portray the outcomes of many possible choices. These sheets of paper are summaries of other long and complex reports generated as the result of meetings at the lower divisional or subsidiary level; and the people in those meetings discuss reports from the departmental level, etc. In almost every instance involving a matter of choice, the more profitable alternative is favored. By the time the issues are presented to the body that has the legal responsibility for managing the corporation (the board of directors), many alternatives have already been evaluated and excluded. Because the information reaching the board has been carefully selected at each level with a view toward the most profitable alternative and because the board is substantially removed from the market and the production facility, the board will amost always opt for the more profitable alternative. How else can one explain the conduct of Reserve and Ford?

· A reasonable solution would be based on altering the information flow within these large corporations so that the decisional structure of the corporation would more closely conform to the perspective of the rational decision maker in the conventional model. Responsible behavior begins with perception. The responsible person observes and accounts for phenomena the irresponsible person ignores.[64]

There have been a number of suggestions for changing corporate perception. However, only the one cogently advanced by Professor Christopher Stone of the University of Southern California Law School in his book, *Where the Law Ends*, seems to confront the image of corporate decision making that we should be concerned about. Professor Stone suggests federal legislation to alter the structure of the board of directors of large corporations. He recommends that:

1. Interested or inside directors—those who have a position with management—should be eliminated in corporations of major impact, i.e., corporations over $50 million in sales;

2. A percentage of the board (either two persons or 10 percent of the directors, whichever is larger) could neither personally own stock nor be a director or officer of a firm that owned shares in the company.

3. The functions of directors should be defined and standards for holding directors liable for neglect of duty should be developed.

4. Directors should be given a full-time staff accountable to them and not to management. This staff should take steps to ensure that the directors get all relevant information on choices confronting the board.

In addition to the above Stone would require by federal law the selection of General Public Directors (GPDs) and Special Public Directors (SPDs). Every manufacturing corporation would have to have 10 percent of its directors be GPDs for every billion dollars in sales or assets. This means the 14 largest corporations would have all GPDs. GPDs would be selected not by shareholders but by a Federal Corporation Commission or, perhaps, an agency like the SEC and would have, among others, the following duties:

1. To check corporate compliance with all applicable federal and state laws.

2. To serve as a monitor on internal information and other systems.

3. To serve as a "hot line" to employees who have vital information.

4. To prepare impact studies on proposed major corporate actions.

5. In general, to be "probing and vigilant."

Corporations engaged in a critical area of social concern—those depending on rapid technological innovation the impact of which is difficult to assess, or those likely to pollute or affect the physical or social environment—would be assigned SPDs. SPDs are directors who have special backgrounds or training in science, foreign affairs, etc. If a corporation is delinquent or in violation of some federal regulatory agency's rules, an SPD would be assigned to bring about reform from within.

These proposals may seem drastic, but the remedy must be in direct proportion to the threat posed. The examples of Reserve and Ford show the threat to be substantial. The threat is all the more insidious when one realizes we have no established social ideology to explain the paradox presented in the first portion of this section on social responsibility. The corporation has replaced the *individual* (human) as a significant seller, but the entire elaborate social ideology (primarily economics and law) still assumes that individuals are the primary actors in our society. At the very least we should begin, as students of economics, law, and business conduct, to focus on the less desirable impact on our society of its predominant institution, the modern corporation.

Review Problems

1. Define each of the following and then explain the differences between them. Include a statement of the circumstances in which each may be excluded or modified.
   (a) Express warranty
   (b) Implied warranty of merchantability
   (c) Implied warranty of fitness for a particular purpose
   (d) Warranty of title

2. Assume that you have been asked to draft the warranty language that will go on the packaging and instructions of a superlight, small automobile-shaped vehicle that will be powered by pedaling much as a bicycle is powered. Discuss what you would attempt to do and why.

3. In a series of short paragraphs explain in your own words why the tort theories of negligence and strict liability have seen such rapid growth in their application to product liability cases. Why would an injured plaintiff prefer these tort theories over a claim for damages based on warranty theories?

4. John wanted to buy a new electric drill. He saw an advertisement in the local newspaper that said Sears was having a special sale on ". . . 1/2-inch electric drills, reduced 20 percent to $15." John went to Sears

to buy the drill but was very interested in whether or not the drill was double-insulated. A double-insulated drill has special wiring in it so that if a short develops the drill will not shock the user. John was interested in this feature because he often worked in his basement where the floor was damp as the result of leaky plumbing and there was a substantial risk of electrocution. John asked the salesperson at Sears, "Do you have double-insulated drills?" The salesperson replied, "We have just what you want," and got for John one of the drills on sale. She said, "This drill is double-insulated." John then said, "Fine, I'll take it," and handed her his Sears credit card. The salesperson made out the appropriate sales slip and John left with the drill.

Answer the following questions in a series of short paragraphs by first defining the legal principle used and then picking out the circumstances of the factual pattern which would be appropriate for applying the principle.

(a) Did Sears make an express warranty? *Yes* *1) ad 2) clerk said*

(b) Did Sears make an implied warranty of merchantability? *yes – didn't disclaim*

(c) Did Sears make an implied warranty of fitness for a particular purpose? *Yes but maybe, didn't get real specific on use of drill*

(d) Did Sears make any other warranties? *Yes, warranty of title – Sears owes item sold to Sears. Consumer takes free of lien under U.C.C.*

5. In the question above, assume that John took the drill home and let his daughter use it in the basement one day, where she was injured because the drill was not double-insulated. If Sears were sued for the injuries based on a warranty theory, what might Sears argue? Would Sears be successful? *Probably not ←* *→ Privity – which state in?* What if John <u>had sold the drill</u> before using it to a friend of his visiting from another state and the friend was injured in his (the friend's) home because the drill was not double-insulated? *→ Privity breakdown* What would Sears argue in response to a claim for injury based on warranty theories? Would Sears be successful this time?

6. If the packaging and instructions for the drill that John purchased said in plain and conspicuous language:

   For one year from the date of purchase, Sears will repair or replace this drill free of charge if defective in material or workmanship.

   And, in larger type it added:

   SEARS WILL NOT BE LIABLE FOR LOSS OR DAMAGE TO PROPERTY OR ANY INCIDENTAL OR CONSEQUENTIAL LOSS OR EXPENSE FROM PROPERTY DAMAGE DUE DIRECTLY TO DEFECTS IN THE DRILL.

Assume all of the information in Question 4 above is true and that after John purchased the drill he was severely injured when he was using the drill in his basement, which at the time was dry. Also assume that the drill was not properly double-insulated. As a result of this defect, the drill exploded and caught John's basement on fire, resulting in $5000 damage to the basement and personal injury to John. Does the above language on the packaging and directions limit John's measure of recovery to the value of the drill? What additional circumstances might help John's case? *[handwritten: Unconscionability, conspicuous]*

[handwritten margin note: Possibly does]

7. Assume the facts in Questions 4 and 6 to be true; what theories of liability should John argue and which would he probably be successful with? *[handwritten: Use negligent design + strict liability]*

8. X's father took a drug for a skin disease he had before X was born. It is now discovered that the drug rendered the offspring of the father extremely susceptible to various kinds of skin cancer. X's father is now deceased but X's relatives can remember the name of the drug. Outline the remedy that X may have if he lived in California.

[handwritten margin note: mkt. share liability]

9. Write a short but concise paragraph explaining the attempts of Congress to establish and provide for enforcement of environmental policy. Have such efforts been successful?

10. Derive your own definition of "social responsibility" as applied to business organizations.

Endnotes

1. R.J. Nordstrom, *Law of Sales*, p. 284 (1970).
2. *Ibid.*, p. 280.
3. *Ibid.*
4. *Ibid.*
5. Pub. L. No. 93-637; 101 et seq. (Jan. 4, 1975). (15 U.S.C.A. § 2301 *et seq*).
6. *Ibid.*, § 102(a).
7. *Ibid.*, § 104(a)(1).
8. *Ibid.*, § 104(a)(2).
9. *Ibid.*, § 108(a).
10. *Ibid.*, § 104(a)(1).
11. *Ibid.*, § 101.
12. *Ibid.*, § 110(d).
13. *Ibid.*, § 204(b).
14. Reported in *The Wall Street Journal*, December 30, 1980, Col. 6, p. 1.
15. *Ibid.*
16. See "The DES Cases and Liability Without Causation," 19 *Am. Bus. L.J.* 511 (1982).
17. See *Summers* v. *Tice*, 199 P. 2d 1 (1948) and *Restatement (Second) of Torts*, Sec. 433B(3) (1965).
18. Comment on Clause (a), Illustration 2, *Restatement (Second) of Torts*, Sec. 876 (1979).
19. Refining Market Share Liability: *Sindell* v. *Abbott Laboratories, 33 Stan. L. Rev.* 937, 943 (1981).
20. Model Uniform Product Liability Act, reprinted in 44 *Fed. Reg.* 62, 714 (1979); and see Dworkin, Product Liability Reform and the Model Uniform Product Liability Act, 60 *Nebraska L. Rev.* 50 (1981).

21. MUPLA, Section 104(B).

22. "Limiting Liability: Products Liability and a Statute of Repose," 32 *Baylor L. Rev.,* 137, 145 (1980).

23. The term "consumer products" in this context includes all retail products used by consumers in and around the household *except* food, drugs, cosmetics, motor vehicles, firearms, insecticides, and cigarettes.

24. *Final Report of the National Commission on Product Safety,* Washington, D.C.: U.S. Government Printing Office, June 1970, p. 1.

25. 1981 Annual Report, U.S. Consumer Product Safety Commission (FY. 1980, p. 13).

26. *Final Report, supra,* note 24 at p. 74.

27. *Ibid.,* p. 73.

28. *Ibid.,* p. 74.

29. *Ibid.*

30. 15 U.S.C.A. Sec. 2051 *et seq.*

31. U.S. Consumer Product Safety Commission, 1979 *Annual Report,* Appendix L.

32. Pamphlet: U.S. Consumer Product Safety Commission 1979, p. 2.

33. C.P.S.C. 1981 *Annual Report,* Part I, p. 9.

34. 15 U.S.C.A. Sec. 1381 *et seq.*

35. 23 U.S.C.A. Sec. 401 *et seq.*

36. Motor Vehicle Safety 1979: "A Report on Activities Under the National Traffic and Motor Vehicle Act of 1966 . . . .," p.14 (1981).

37. *Ibid.,* iii.

38. U.S. Government Manual, 408 (1980).

39. Motor Vehicle Safety, 1979, *supra,* p. 14.

40. *Ibid.*

41. *Safety Related Recall Campaigns for Motor Vehicles and Motor Vehicle Equipment, Including Tires,* July 1, 1981–September 30, 1981, U. S. Department of Transportation, p. v (1982).

42. 42 U.S.C.A. § 4321 *et seq.* (1970).

43. 42 U.S.C.A. § 4332 (2)(c).

44. 36 Fed Reg. 7724 (1971).

45. 42 U.S.C.A. § 4344.

46. Much of the information in this section was taken from *The Challenge of the Environment: A Primer on EPA's Statutory Authority,* 1972, U.S.G.P.O.

47. 42 U.S.C.A. § 1857 *et seq.* (1955).

48. 42 U.S.C.A. § 1857b-1 to 1857b-8 (1965).

49. 42 U.S.C.A. § 1857 (2) (1967).

50. 42 U.S.C.A. § 1857 as amended (1970).

51. 33 U.S.C.A. § 1155 *et seq.* as amended (1972).

52. *The New York Times Magazine,* pp. 32–33 (Sept. 13, 1970).

53. 44 LW 2306 (1976).

54. *Ibid.,* citing transcript of November 14, 1975 hearings at 2–5, 56, and 109.

55. Environ. Repr., Current Developments, 1873 (March 5, 1976).

56. These facts and those that follow were taken from "Why the Pinto Jury Felt Ford Deserved $125 Million Penalty," *The Wall Street Journal,* Feb. 14, 1978, p. 1, Col. 6.

57. Much material in this section and the final portion of this chapter is taken from A. Wolfe, "The Modern Corporation and the Failure of Social Theory," a chapter printed

in *Business Law, Key Issues and Concepts,* Edited by T. Dunfee and D. Reitzel, at p. 37 to 48 (1978).

58. J. Galbraith, *The Affluent Society,* (1958, 3rd ed. 1976).

59. *Ibid.,* p. 9 (3rd ed., 1976).

60. *Ibid.,* p. 11.

61. A. Smith, *An Inquiry into the Nature and Causes of the Wealth of Nations* 1776 (R. Campbell and A. Skinner ed.; 1976, Vol 1, pp. 9–10 of the General Introduction.

62. *Ibid.,* p. 10.

63. P. Samuelson, *Economics, An Introductory Analysis,* 41 (7th ed., 1967). There are parts of this text devoted to a discussion of corporations, but none contradict the point illustrated by this quote.

64. This thought and the solution herein proposed are based on C. Stone, *Where the Law Ends—The Social Control of Corporate Behavior,* 1976. Stone is also responsible for the observation that our law ignores or has failed to develop principles of liability holding corporate management personally accountable for their decisions. The reason for this, he argues, is that law has traditionally focused on humans as primary actors in our society, not on corporations as the primary actors.

American Business Organizations in the Political and International Environment

22

This chapter is divided into two parts, reflecting very important dimensions of the modern American business organization and the megacorporation especially. As the role of both state and federal governments has increased in the business environment, we see that the national response has been a corresponding increased interest by the business community in government. If business organizations are conceived of as legal people, do these entities have the same right to participate in the political process (lobbying especially) as natural people? What are and what should be the limits on this participation? These and related questions are examined in the first part of the chapter.

The second part of the chapter outlines some of the basic concerns of those doing business outside this country.

The Bill of Rights prohibits the federal government from enacting laws that abridge the freedom of speech or interfere with the people's right to peaceably assemble and petition the government for a redress of grievances. The Supreme Court has ruled that these restrictions on the federal government also apply to the states through the Fourteenth Amendment. It is not only the individual person who enjoys these protections. The corporate entity also shares this constitutional shield.

Business Organizations and the Political Process

The First Amendment and the Corporation

The freedom of speech provision of the First Amendment is designed to protect public discussion of all issues of concern to the public. The speaker is not to be restrained in such speech or punished for the words spoken. (Speech that presents a clear and present danger, such as shouting "Fire!" in a crowded theater, is subject to regulation. Also defamatory speech can subject the speaker to liability for the damage caused by the false statements. But these are exceptions to the general rule.) The right to free speech does not depend on the nature of the speaker. If speech is protected by the First Amendment, it is protected regardless of whether the speaker is an individual or a corporation.

In *First National Bank of Boston* v. *Bellotti,* 435 U.S. 765 (1978), the Supreme Court struck down a Massachusetts law limiting corporate speech. The law in question made it a crime for a corporation to make contributions or expenditures to influence the vote on a ballot measure except one that materially affected the property, business, or assets of the corporation. The law specified that questions concerning the taxation of income, property, or transactions of individuals do not materially affect the corporation. In holding this provision to be in violation of the First Amendment the Court concluded that the nature of the speech in question was the type protected. The Court stated that nowhere in the law is there a provision that speech sheds that protection once it is shown that the speaker is a corporation. The bank had challenged the law because it wished to oppose a measure that would have allowed the imposition of a graduated income tax on individuals.

Bellotti was the first in a series of cases that consider free speech rights within a corporate context. The Supreme Court faced the question in a different setting in *Consolidated Edison* v. *Public Service Commission,* 447 U.S. 530 (1980). Consolidated Edison included a pro-nuclear-power leaflet in each customer's electric bill. The New York Public Service Commission then banned the inclusion of bill inserts that discuss political matters. The Commission did allow bill inserts that discuss topics that are not controversial issues of public policy. The Court held the regulation unconstitutional as a direct infringement of the utility's freedom of speech. It pointed out that in the *Bellotti* decision it had rejected the contention that a state could confine corporate speech to specific issues. When protected speech is involved the government cannot regulate the message, ideas, subject matter, or the content of a speaker's message.

If the state cannot prohibit corporate speech, may it limit in some manner the amount of speech? For instance, if the state cannot prohibit corporate contributions to influence the vote of the public on a ballot measure, may the state place a dollar limitation on such contributions? In the following case the Supreme Court answers that question with a resounding "no." Notice that the organization involved in the case is not a corporation but an unincorporated organization. One has free speech rights whether one is an individual, corporation, labor union, partnership, or unincorporated organization.

CITIZENS AGAINST RENT CONTROL v. *BERKELEY*

102 S.Ct. 434 (1981)

CHIEF JUSTICE BURGER *delivered the opinion of the Court.*

The issue on appeal is whether a limitation of $250 on contributions to committees formed to support or oppose ballot measures violates the First Amendment.

Appellant Citizens Against Rent Control is an unincorporated association formed to oppose a ballot measure at issue in the April 19, 1977 election. The ballot measure would have imposed rent control on many of Berkeley's rental units. To make its views on the ballot measure known, Citizens Against Rent Control raised more than $108,000 from approximately 1,300 contributors. It accepted nine contributions over the $250 limit. Those nine contributions totaled $20,850, or $18,600 more than if none of the contributions exceeded $250.

We begin by recalling that the practice of persons sharing common views banding together to achieve a common end is deeply embedded in the American political process.

The Court has long viewed the First Amendment as protecting a market place for the clash of different views and conflicting ideas. That concept has been stated and restated almost since the Constitution was drafted. The voters of the City of Berkeley adopted the challenged ordinance which places restrictions on that market place.

The Court has acknowledged the importance of freedom of association in guaranteeing the right of people to make their voices heard on public issues. . . .

More recently the Court stated, "The First Amendment protects political association as well as political expression." *Buckley* v. *Valeo,* 424 U.S. 1 (1976).

There are, of course, some activities, legal if engaged in by one, yet illegal if performed in concert with others, but political expression is not one of them. To place a spartan limit—or indeed any limit—on individuals wishing to band together to advance their views on a ballot measure, while placing none on individuals acting alone, is clearly a restraint on the right of association.

Buckley identified a single narrow exception to the rule that limits on political activity were contrary to the First Amendment. The exception relates to the perception of undue influence of large contributors to a candidate. . . .

Buckley thus sustained limits on contributions to candidates and their committees.

Federal courts of appeals have recognized that *Buckley* does not support limitations on contributions to committees formed to favor or oppose ballot measures.

In *First National Bank* v. *Bellotti,* 435 U.S. 765 (1978), we held that a state could not prohibit corporations any more than it could preclude individuals from making contributions or expenditures advocating views on ballot measures.

Whatever may be the state interest or degree of interest in regulating and limiting contributions to or expenditures of a candidate or a candidate's committees there is no significant state or public interest in curtailing debate and discussion of a ballot measure. Placing limits on contributions which in turn limit expenditures plainly impairs freedom of expression. The integrity of the political system will be adequately protected if contributors are identified in a public filing revealing the amounts contributed; if it is thought wise, legislation can outlaw anonymous contributions.

Case Question   1. Does this decision prevent the government from placing dollar limitations on what a contributor may give to a candidate for public office?

Commercial Speech and Corporations

One can divide speech into a variety of categories. There is actual verbal speech and there is symbolic speech, such as a work of art or a physical gesture, which can be just as powerful a method of communication as the spoken or written word. Also there is a type of speech that enjoys the full protection of the First Amendment, which is what we have been discussing, and a type of speech that receives less than full protection. Advertising, which is speech devoted to a commercial purpose, enjoys lesser protection under the First Amendment. Commercial speech is a blend of information and a sales pitch. Commercial speech may be banned by the government if it is deceptive or is related to illegal activity. Such speech may also be regulated if it intrudes on a captive audience. Thus, the government can prevent false advertising or prohibit a company from using a loud soundtruck to broadcast advertisements in a residential neighborhood between the hours of 9 P.M. and 6 A.M.

When commercial speech is not deceptive or somehow related to illegal activity, the government must show a substantial interest that will be achieved if its restriction is to be upheld. The more vital the governmental interest, the greater the permissible degree of regulation.

Suppose a state utility commission totally banned utilities from engaging in promotional advertising and justified its regulation on the state's interest in energy conservation. Does such a regulation violate the free speech rights of the utilities? The government may regulate it, if it shows a governmental interest and the regulation is carefully designed to achieve the state's goal of protecting the interest. Energy conservation is a worthy goal and any advertising designed to increase electrical consumption will thwart the achievement of that goal. Note, however, that the utility commission has totally banned promotional advertising. A utility cannot advertise devices that would reduce energy consumption. It is for the latter reason that the Supreme Court in *Central Hudson Gas & Elec.* v. *Public Service Comm. of N.Y.*, 447 U.S. 557 (1980) declared such a regulation unconstitutional. The state's interest is an important one, but the regulation chosen to promote that interest was too broad. A more limited regulation could have served the state's interest in energy conservation and would have been constitutional. The commission could have regulated the format and content of the utilities' advertisements by requiring that they include information about the relative efficiency and expense of the offered service, under current conditions and for the foreseeable future. A regulation of the latter nature would achieve the state's goal and be reasonably related to the achievement of that goal.

Another example of an overly broad regulation of commercial

speech involved a Virginia state law. Virginia prohibited pharmacists from advertising the prices of prescription drugs. In *Virginia Pharmacy Bd. v. Virginia Citizens Commerce Council,* 425 U.S. 746 (1976), the Supreme Court declared this regulation of commercial speech to be a violation of First Amendment rights.

Corporate Lobbying

Lobbying is a constitutionally protected activity. We began this section by noting that the Bill of Rights grants the people the right to petition the government for a redress of grievances. Lobbying, be it conducted by an individual, group, or corporation, is a form of petitioning for a redress of grievances.

The federal government requires that lobbyists register with it. Many states also require lobbyists to register. However, these laws typically contain major loopholes and are therefore considered by some to be ineffectual. It is possible for an individual to be engaged in conduct that an ordinary person would consider lobbying activity, and yet that conduct may not be covered by the relevant lobbying statute.

Lobbying assumes many forms. It is not confined to buttonholing legislators in the halls of Congress and attempting to convince them to vote a certain way when the issue appears for action on the floor. It may involve the actual drafting of legislation for the legislator to introduce as a bill. It may involve the preparation of data and the authorship of written arguments for the legislator to use in support of, or opposition to, a bill in committee or on the floor of Congress. It can be alerting a legislator to the positive or negative impact that a particular piece of proposed legislation will have on the voters back home. It might involve the generation of a groundswell of support or opposition to a measure back in the legislator's home district. It may involve having important contributors to the legislator's campaign coffers place personal phone calls expressing their views of an issue. It may be an invitation to speak before an influential group of individuals. Such an invitation gives the legislator political exposure and a most important political commodity, news coverage.

Lobbying occurs not only within the legislative branch of government. It is rampant within the executive branch and within the regulatory agencies. If the president or a governor sponsors legislation, one can expect broad support for that proposal within the ranks of those legislators who belong to the same political party as the president or governor. Thus, a successful effort in convincing the executive branch to propose legislation will give it instant credibility. The executive also possesses important appointive powers. Strenuous lobbying is devoted to getting the right person appointed to administer a government department or agency. The individual appointed can establish an agenda or emphasize certain areas of responsibility that will have a great effect on the regulated industry.

Once Congress passes a law and establishes a regulatory agency to enforce that legislation, the lobbying focus may shift to the agency. The agency has important powers in drafting the regulations that will carry out the legislation. Thus, opposing special interest groups will array their lobbying tactics against each other in an attempt to get a regulation that favors their position.

The Freedom of Information Act

An important tool for a lobbyist at the federal level is the Freedom of Information Act (FOIA). FOIA prevents an administrative agency from conducting its affairs in secret. A lobbyist is thus able to know if an agency is contemplating action that may harm the lobbyist's client. It also allows the lobbyist to keep an eye on the opposition by engaging in a legal form of industrial espionage. FOIA requires federal administrative agencies to make their documents public on request. There is a time period within which the documents must be furnished after a request. If the agency refuses, the person making the request may bring suit in the federal courts. If the court determines that the documents were wrongfully withheld, the agency must not only disclose the documents but also pay the legal fees of the person who made the request.

Certain categories of documents are exempt from disclosure. Included in the list of exemptions are national security documents, documents containing trade secrets, internal agency documents related to the proposed adoption of a course of action, law enforcement files that would disclose confidential sources or hamper current enforcement actions, documents protected from disclosure by other laws, documents that would invade a person's privacy, such as certain medical information, and certain data relative to financial entities.

Lobbying and the Judiciary

While one can end up in jail for contempt of court for approaching a judge in an attempt to obtain a favorable court ruling, lobbying does occur in the judicial arena. If the judges mount the bench through the electoral process, a person or group can engage in the campaign to elect a candidate who shares their political, economic, or social background. If an individual becomes a judge through the appointive process, one lobbies the person with the power of appointment in an effort to see that the desired individual gets appointed.

Litigation is also a powerful weapon in the lobbyist's arsenal. If the legislature passes legislation that is unfavorable to one's position, an interested party may challenge the law in court. The law may be held unconstitutional. If an administrative agency enacts a rule of regulation that one has unsuccessfully opposed, one can take the agency to court. The agency may have adopted the regulation in contravention of the agency rules or may have abused its discretion in the adoption of the regulation. A lawsuit can be the last resort of the lobbyist or the affected party.

The Corporation and Political Contributions

A legal distinction is made between financial contributions to a campaign in opposition to, or support of, a ballot measure and contributions to a candidate for public office or the candidate's campaign committee. We have already observed in the *Citizens Against Rent Control* case that the First Amendment prohibits the government from either preventing or limiting the amount of money that a corporation may contribute to a ballot measure campaign. The government can and does place limitations on contributions to candidates.

The Watergate scandal of the 1970s resulted in the enactment of a number of legislative reforms. One major reform focused on the financial methods for political campaigns. The law regulated the financing process. The constitutionality of the law was challenged on First Amendment grounds. In *Buckley* v. *Valeo*, 424 U.S. 1 (1976), the Supreme Court upheld portions of the law while striking down other portions. The Court created a single narrow exception to the general rule that governmental limits on political activity are contrary to the First Amendment. Because large contributions to a candidate for public office can be donated with the expectation of a political *quid pro quo,* with all the dangers that such a situation poses for our system of representative democracy, the Court upheld the limitations on contributions to candidates and their political committees.

The law allows an individual to contribute a maximum of $1000 to a candidate for federal office but allows a political group to contribute $5000. A contribution up to this limit can be made in the primary campaign and again in the general election campaign. The law prohibits a corporation or a labor union from contributing funds from their treasury to a candidate. However, the law does allow them to form political action committees (PACs), which can raise funds and make contributions. A PAC is the campaign finance organ of a special interest group. Individuals that share common beliefs and goals form a PAC and then solicit contributions to it. Corporate PACs can solicit funds from their shareholders and management personnel. Labor unions solicit donations from their members. These contributions are then pooled and theoretically contributed to candidates who share the philosophy of the PAC. However, campaign records demonstrate that incumbent candidates, regardless of their party affiliation or philosophical outlook, receive the majority of the PAC money. It is not unusual to find a conservative PAC making the maximum contribution to a liberal member of the opposite party, who has no serious opposition in the election, when that candidate holds a position of important legislative power.

At the federal level, the PACs focus on the races for the Senate and the House. Candidates running for President do not have as great a need for PAC money because they can qualify for public financing of their campaigns. On the state level, each state establishes it own rules governing contributions for state office. Some states do not place a cap on the dollar amount they may be contributed by a PAC. Activity by PACs at the state level is increasing at a fast pace.

The substantial role currently occupied by PACs in financing campaigns has generated controversy. The campaign limits originally placed on financial contributions were designed to reform the election process by preventing a large contributor from gaining undue influence over an elected official. Yet it appears to some observers that the law in fact did not improve matters but made them worse. The special interest groups can target their contributions to a relatively small group of incumbents who hold positions of power over legislative matters of concern to that interest group. This can give them influence greatly out of proportion to the number of members in the population at large. For example, there are not a large number of dairy farmers in the United States, yet the dairy industry has continued to benefit from special interest legislation tailored to meet its needs. It is not coincidental that the Associated Milk Producers Inc., a dairy farm cooperative of about 35,000 members, has one of the wealthiest and most active PACs. It is not uncommon for a PAC to contribute $1 million or $1½ million to candidates in an election campaign.

In 1983 there were approximately 3500 PACs. Some of them represent specific industries (SixPAC for the beer distributors) or unions (United Auto Workers PAC). Ideological PACs also exist (NickPAC for the National Conservative PAC or the NOWPAC for the National Organization for Women).

Funds from PACs are a very significant source of campaign funds for political candidates. Candidates are able to raise more money from PACs than they can obtain from their own political party. PAC contributions in the 1980 congressional elections were approximately $55 million and in the 1982 election reached $87.3 million. A number of proposals have been suggested to limit the special–interest danger inherent in PACs. Some would place a limit on the total amount a candidate could accept from PACs. Others would channel the PAC money into the major political parties and have the party distribute the funds to its candidates. Ideally, the party would have broader interests that would better reflect the national interest than the narrow interest of a particular PAC. Since the public funds the presidental campaigns, it has been suggested that the public financing of congressional campaigns would eliminate special interest influence. Public financing, however, is frequently attacked as favoring the better known incumbent over the lesser known challenger.

Unless the current system is altered by Congress, PACs will continue to grow in influence. Corporations will continue to expand their fundraising efforts for existing PACs and continue to create new ones. Whether or not such political donations advance the interest of the shareholders or the nation is debatable—and the debate will continue.

The Corporation and the International Business Environment

Today it is not just the large multinational corporations, such as General Motors, International Telephone & Telegraph, IBM, Toyota, Unilever, and Royal Dutch Shell, that engage in commercial transactions that extend across national boundaries. Many relatively small corporations will furnish services, purchase goods, and sell products in more than one country. Crossing a border can yield substantial opportunities for generating additional profits, but it also involves operating within a very different legal milieu. Management of a corporation must plan carefully before starting the foreign transaction because new and different risks accompany such an undertaking.

In the time when the large colonial powers ruled the world, international business was a simple proposition. International trade was normally limited to exporting raw materials and agricultural products back to the colonial power. To engage in such activities one needed only the permission of the colonial power. Its legal system governed any controversies that might arise and its military power protected the enterprise from the natives and from foreign powers.

Today the situation is very different and more complex. Instead of being confined to the extractive industries within a group of colonies, commerce encompasses diverse international trade involving manufacturing, communications, and financial transactions within what are now sovereign nations. Such an environment includes not only the normal business risks but also political and legal risks.

International Business Risks

The greatest political risk facing the international enterprise is the possibility that one's assets may be expropriated. Expropriation may assume the form of outright confiscation with no compensation being paid for the assets. Or, if compensation is paid, the host country may dictate the formula by which compensation is to be calculated. Expropriation is a risk not only in the less developed countries. It can occur in the industrialized nations too. For instance, when the Socialist Party of Francois Mitterrand was elected in the early 1980s France began a program of nationalization of both domestic and foreign business. Financial risks are inherent in dealing with a foreign currency. Not only can there be the normal fluctuations in the value of one currency relative to another, but there may also occur the shock of a major currency revaluation. The Mexican devaluation of the peso and the concurrent imposition of currency controls in 1982 played havoc with those engaged in business within that country. Doing business in a foreign country also means conducting affairs in an alien culture, a culture that can have very different values from the society of the corporation's home country.

Foreign Risk or "Political Risk" Insurance

A corporation need not make foreign investments totally exposed to the risks inherent in war, expropriation, or currency regulations that limit the return of foreign earnings. The corporation can acquire a degree of protection by obtaining "political risk" insurance. The major industrial nations, whose corporations engage in the bulk of foreign investments, all have a form of insurance protection to guard against the significant foreign investment risks. Some nations provide such insurance to their corporations doing business anywhere in the world, whereas other nations limit the insurance coverage to enterprises in the less developed countries.

United States corporations can obtain insurance coverage from the Overseas Private Investment Corporation (OPIC). OPIC provides protection for investments made in those countries that have signed a bilateral investment treaty with the United States. The U.S. has such treaties with in excess of 100 foreign nations. Coverage for a variety of types of investments is available. The premium rate can vary according to the value of the investment. Retroactive coverage is not available, as the insurance will only be issued for projects that have the advance approval of both OPIC and the foreign government. Obviously, OPIC requires the corporation that has suffered the loss to make a good faith effort to obtain compensation from the foreign nation before it will cover the loss.

The Legal Complexities of International Business

When a Texas corporation does business in Illinois there exists the possibility that the law of one sovereign state may conflict with that of the other. There is also the possibility that the laws of those states may be in conflict with the law of the federal government. Such a conflict of laws within the United States does not pose insurmountable legal problems. There exists a legal mechanism to solve jurisdictional disputes of this nature. As you learned in Chapter 2, the Constitution of the United States contains the commerce clause and the supremacy clause. The commerce clause gives Congress the right to regulate commerce between and among the states and between the states and foreign nations. The supremacy clause provides that, whenever a properly enacted federal law conflicts with a state statute, the federal law is controlling. The Supreme Court provides a final determination of such legal disputes and its decision is binding on the parties.

When a Texas corporation does business in a foreign nation there can exist a conflict between the U.S. corporation and the foreign government about their respective legal rights and obligations. How is such a dispute settled? Again the Constitution of the United States has a provision that specifies that a treaty between the United States and a foreign government is a part of United States law. Thus, if the dispute in question is covered by a treaty, the U.S. courts can interpret and enforce the terms of that treaty. However, if there is no treaty between America and the foreign country, of if the treaty does not govern the issue in dispute, the parties confront legal uncertainty. Each party may pursue its claim in its home country under different laws with different results, and there is no umpire to settle the matter with finality. To avoid such problems the parties will frequently insert a choice-of-laws provision in their contract. Such a provision will specify the law of the particular country that is to be applied to disputes that arise between the parties under that contract. Another device utilized to avoid such problems is the insertion of an arbitration clause in the contract. Such a clause will specify that any dispute under the contract is to be settled through arbitration with the decision of the arbitrator to be final and binding on the parties. The clause will provide the mechanism to be used in selecting the arbitrator.

In the case that follows we observe a contract between an American corporation and a German corporation that contains a forum selection clause. The clause specifies that any contractual disputes are to be litigated in London, England. When a dispute arises the American company attempts to avoid litigation in the neutral country and instead have the lawsuit in America. The Supreme Court discusses the growth in international business and the fact that sophisticated businessmen negotiated the forum selection clause in reaching its decision.

M/S BREMEN v. ZAPATA OFF-SHORE COMPANY
92 S.Ct. 1907 (1972)

MR. CHIEF JUSTICE BURGER *delivered the opinion of the Court.*

In November 1967, respondent Zapata, a Houston-based American corporation, contracted with petitioner Unterweser, a German corporation, to tow Zapata's ocean-going, self-elevating drilling rig Chaparral from Louisiana to a point off Ravenna, Italy, in the Adriatic Sea, where Zapata had agreed to drill certain wells.

The contract submitted by Unterweser contained the following provision, which is at issue in this case: "Any dispute arising must be treated before the London Court of Justice."

After reviewing the contract and making several changes, but without any alteration in the forum-selection or exculpatory clauses, a Zapata vice president executed the contract and forwarded it to Unterweser in Germany, where Unterweser accepted the changes, and the contract became effective.

On January 5, 1968, Unterweser's deep sea tug Bremen departed Venice, Louisiana, with the Chaparral in tow bound for Italy. On January 9, while the flotilla was in international waters in the middle of the Gulf of Mexico, a severe storm arose. The sharp roll of the Chaparral in Gulf waters caused its elevator legs, which had been raised for the voyage, to break off and fall into the sea, seriously damaging the Chaparral. In this emergency situation Zapata instructed the Bremen to tow its damaged rig to Tampa, Florida, the nearest port of refuge.

On January 12, Zapata, ignoring its contract promise to litigate "any dispute arising" in the English courts, commenced a suit in admiralty in the United States District Court at Tampa, seeking $3,500,000 damages against Unterweser . . . and the Bremen . . . , alleging negligent towage and breach of contract. Unterweser responded by invoking the forum clause of the towage contract, and moved to dismiss for lack of jurisdiction. . . .

We hold, with the six dissenting members of the Court of Appeals, that far too little weight and effect were given to the forum clause in resolving this controversy. For at least two decades we have witnessed an expansion of overseas commercial activities by business enterprises based in the United States. The barrier of distance that once tended to confine a business concern to a modest territory no longer does so. Here we see an American company with special expertise contracting with a foreign company to tow a complex machine thousands of miles across seas and oceans. The expansion of American business and industry will hardly be encouraged if, notwithstanding solemn contracts, we insist on a parochial concept that all disputes must be resolved under our laws and in our courts.

We cannot have trade and commerce in world markets and international waters exclusively on our terms, governed by our laws, and resolved in our courts.

The choice of that forum was made in an arm's-length negotiation by experienced and sophisticated businessmen, and absent some compelling and countervailing reason it should be honored by the parties and enforced by the courts.

There are compelling reasons why a freely negotiated private international agreement, unaffected by fraud, undue influence, or overweening bargaining power, such as that involved here, should be given full effect.

Thus, in the light of present-day commercial realities and expanding international trade we conclude that the forum clause should control absent a strong showing that it should be set aside.

We note, however, that there is nothing in the record presently before us that would support a refusal to enforce the forum clause.

Case Questions

1. The parties could have selected any number of neutral countries in which to litigate their disputes. Was England possibly chosen because of its long history as a seafaring nation?

2. What possible danger would American business face if the Supreme Court had ruled that the American courts should ignore the forum selection clause?

The International Court of Justice at The Hague is not available to rule on international legal disputes within a commercial context. The Court is an arm of the United Nations that was created to adjudicate disputes arising between nations. The Court has no power to force a nation to abide by its decision, so a country can decide not to abide by a decision. Remember the Iranian government's decision to ignore the Court's ruling that the holding of the American hostages in Tehran was in violation of international law.

Foreign nations can enact laws that act as incentives to foreign investment as well as regulations that restrict business activities within the host country. Normally, a corporation does not complain about incentive legislation, but willingly seeks to take advantage of its provisions. Typical of this type of legislation are regulations yielding tax breaks, tariff protection, waiver of import duties, and government-provided loans.

Corporations are less happy with restrictive legislation but have no choice other than to comply if they wish to do business in that nation. Such restrictions take the form of one or all of the following: (1) governmental approval to do business in the country, (2) a prohibition against foreign enterprises engaging in certain activities within the country, (3) requirements that the foreign ownership in the project not exceed 49 percent, (4) requirements that the workforce employ specified percentages of the native population and that the manufactured product contain a certain percentage of locally produced materials, and (5) the imposition of various financial controls to insure that the profits generated in the host country remain there for the continued development of the country.

An additional source of conflict is the attempt by a government to apply its laws extraterritorially. For instance, the Arab League Boycott is an attempt by the Arab governments to insure that no Israeli products gain entry to the Arab countries and to prevent companies that have a major presence in Israel from doing business in the Arab world. The Arab governments attempt to apply the boycott regulations to any corporations with which they deal. At the very same time, the U.S. government makes it illegal for an American corporation to comply with the boycott provisions. A second example is the U.S. Foreign Corrupt Practices Act. This law makes it a crime to pay a bribe to a foreign official to obtain or retain business. Yet in the foreign country where the bribe is offered, the bribery may be an acceptable way of doing business.

A Comparative Legal View

An examination of several specific differences in the legal treatment of business by foreign nations will be helpful in understanding the uniqueness of American law. In the U.S. the board of directors of a corporation has the exclusive authority to manage the corporation. Labor law requires the corporation to bargain with its employees with respect to wages, hours, and working conditions if the employees select a labor organization to represent them. The labor organization has no legal right to participate in the management of the corporation. Let us contrast this corporate scheme to a European country, which has its corporations operate under a codetermination law. Under the German law of Mitbestimmung the shareholders in corporations that have in excess of 2000 employees (a separate law applies to companies in the coal and steel industries) elect only one half the board of directors (the supervisory board). The remaining members of the board are elected by the employees. The union that represents the employees is guaranteed either two or three of the employee board seats, depending on the size of the board. The remaining employee board seats are allocated among the wage earners, the salaried employees, and the leading management according to their percentage in the workforce. The chairman and vice chairman are elected by a two-thirds majority vote of the board. If a two-thirds majority does not develop after two ballots, the shareholder representatives on the board select the chairman and the vice chairman is chosen by the employee board of representatives.

A two-tiered board system also exists in Germany. The second board (the managing board) is selected by the preceding board with a two-thirds majority vote. If a two-thirds vote cannot be mustered a mediation committee is chosen. The recommendation of the committee is put to a vote of the board and, if a two-thirds vote again proves impossible, the chairman appoints the members of this lower board. Thus, the employee in the large German corporation is given a role in corporate governance. While it is still possible for the shareholders to wield ultimate control (interestingly the shareholders, and not the board, declare the dividends at the annual meeting), the employees do have a greater formal role than in the American system.

Let us shift our focus to a country where religion occupies a central position in the legal system. Saudi Arabia is an Islamic nation where the principles of the Muslim faith regulate both personal and commercial matters. Thus, a corporation must be prepared to have its operations halt five times a day as the faithful fulfill their prayer obligations to Allah. The work week consists of Saturday through Wednesday, and no business is transacted on religious holidays. There is no patent law to protect inventions, and interest on loans is technically prohibited. Labor unions do not exist, women are not employed in the workforce, and employees are paid both by their job classification and their national origin. Individuals who run afoul of the law are subject to the ancient Islamic laws on punishment for criminal offenses, i.e. loss of a hand for theft and decapitation for the crime of murder.

Whenever a corporation ventures into a foreign country it must comply with the law of the host country. As we have observed, those laws can be very different from our own. It is extremely important that a company considering the initiation of foreign operations obtain competent legal advice in advance. Such advice will greatly enhance the wisdom of management's decisions relative to international operations.

Corporate Responsibility and the Employee's Duty of Loyalty and Obedience: A Preliminary Inquiry

Phillip I. Blumberg*

APPENDIX A

I. Introduction

The nature of the American corporate world is changing, reflecting changing concepts of the objectives, role and responsibilities of business. The public corporation as a social and economic organization is undergoing a process of re-examination which has not yet run its course, and the ultimate outcome of which one may still not safely predict. There is general acceptance of the concept of corporate social responsibility with the major public corporation assuming a role of increasing significance in social problem solving. Although highly controversial and not generally accepted, there is also increasing expression of a new view of the large American corporation as a social institution to achieve social objectives, rather than as an economic institution to be operated for economic objectives for the benefit of shareholders. It is inevitable, therefore, that as a corollary, new views will also emerge with respect to the changing relationship between the corporation and the groups vitally affected by it, particularly its employees, as well as such other groups as consumers, suppliers, and the public generally.

II. Three Recent Developments

This article constitutes a preliminary inquiry into aspects of a problem that the author believes will become an area of dynamic change in the corporate organization and in time will produce significant change in established legal concepts. It is concerned with the impact of the new view of the corporation upon traditional concepts of the duties of loyalty and obedience of the employee to his employer, firmly recognized in the law of agency. This impact has been illustrated by a number of recent developments, which have a common core: the right of the employee of the large public corporation to take action adverse to the interests of his

*Dean and Professor of Law, University of Connecticut; this edited article is from 24 Oklahoma Law Review 279, © Oklahoma Law Review 1971; reprinted with permission; the footnotes have been renumbered and many have been eliminated.

employer in response to the employee's view as to the proper social responsibility of his corporate employer.

A. The "Public Interest Disclosure" Proposal

The outstanding example, which will serve as the major topic of this article, is the recent appeal of Mr. Ralph Nader that "professional" employees of corporations, as well as of government, disclose to private agencies information about their "employers' policies or practices that they consider harmful to public or consumer interests." Mr. Nader simultaneously announced the establishment of a "Clearing House for Professional Responsibility" to solicit and receive such reports and to encourage what Mr. Nader termed "responsible whistle-blowing" by scientists, engineers, and other professional employees, and to protect employees acting as informants or tipsters from retaliation by employers. Mr. Nader originally stated his program in terms of professionalism: professional ethics should take precedence over loyalty to employers when the public interest is at stake. Although this initial statement rested on an appeal to a professional responsibility, Mr. Nader's broad reference to harm to "public or consumer interests" was apparently restricted to cases where the employer's behavior was "illegal, hazardous, or unconscionable."

Subsequently, Mr. Nader substantially broadened the scope of his appeal for disclosure of confidential information by employees. He included all employees, not merely professional employees, and extended the area of disclosure to a wide range of information, going far beyond the original restrictions of unprofessional conduct or "illegal, hazardous, or unconscionable" behavior. . . .

* * *

Thus, the test has become a personal decision by each employee "where responsibility to society transcends responsibility to his organization." It is clear that Mr. Nader wishes to encourage the "corporate leak" to facilitate efforts of so-called "public interest" organizations in publicizing actions by the major power centers in the society—whether governmental or corporate—not deemed to be in the public interest.

In brief, any person in any organization, who disagrees with a decision of his superiors in the social or environmental area is encouraged to continue the campaign (which he lost, or in which he did not have an opportunity to participate within his own organization) in the public arena via disclosure to a "public interest" organization.

Mr. James M. Roche, Chairman of General Motors Corporation, promptly attacked the proposal, stating:

> Some of the enemies of business now encourage an employee to be disloyal to the enterprise. They want to create suspicion and disharmony and pry into the proprietary interests of the business. However this is labelled—industrial

espionage, whistle blowing or professional responsibility—it is another tactic for spreading disunity and creating conflict.[1]

Thus, the question arises: What is the duty of the employee to his employer? To what extent, if any, has a heightened sense of a responsibility to society—on the employee level as well as on the corporate level—changed the nature of the employee's obligations to his employer?

B. Eastern Air Lines

[An] example involves Eastern Air Lines. The airline's procedure required pilots shortly after takeoff to jettison in the atmosphere about three gallons of excess fuel in holding tanks remaining from the previous run. A senior pilot of thirty years experience had repeatedly requested the draining of the tanks on the ground by mechanics because of his concern of the impact of the practice on air pollution. Eastern management had refused. The pilot thereupon violated the regulation and had the kerosene drained while on the ground. Eastern maintained that "each of its 3,700 pilots cannot make his own rules" and discharged the pilot. After considerable publicity (and pressure from the Airline Pilots Association), Eastern reinstated the pilot. It subsequently went further and announced that it was endeavoring to have manufacturers develop engines to eliminate the problem by allowing excess fuel to return to the regular fuel tanks.

* * *

Still another reflection of changing views . . . of loyalty and obedience of employees is the following glimpse of the corporate future depicted in Mr. Anthony Athos' article in the *Harvard Business Review* entitled "Is the Corporation Next to Die?"

> "Within five years a president of a major corporation will be locked out of his office by his junior executives," remarked George Koch, president of the Grocery Manufacturers Association, not long ago. The very idea would have seemed outrageous and impossible only a few years ago . . . the situation is rapidly becoming ripe for the kind of action Koch predicts.[2]

The foregoing illustrations of the present and possible future world of the corporate employee require a reexamination of the traditional fundamental concepts of the employer-employee relationship: the employee's duties of loyalty and obedience to the employer, and the employer's freedom to discharge an employee. They reflect a new view of responsibility—a view that the employee's duty as a citizen transcends his duties as employee. . . . These examples may also involve a different concept, the

[1] The *New York Times,* March 26, 1971 at 53, col. 5.
[2] Anthony Athos, "Is the Corporation Next to Die," *Harv. Bus. Rev.,* Mar.-Apr., 1970, at 49–50.

view that employees should play a part in the corporate decision-making process, at least in issues of public concern involving questions of corporate social responsibility. . . .

III. The Restatement of Agency

A review of the relevant provisions of the *Restatement of Agency* provides an obvious starting point for consideration of the new view of the role and duties of the employee.

A. The Duty of Obedience

Section 383 and *Section 385* state the agent's duty to obey the principal. Section 385(1) imposes upon the agent "a duty to obey all reasonable directions" of the principal. Comment *a* points out:

> In determining whether or not the orders of the principal to the agent are reasonable . . . *business or professional ethics* . . . are considered. (emphasis added)

Comment *a* continues:

> In no event would it be implied that an agent has a duty to perform acts which . . . are *illegal or unethical* . . . (emphasis added)

Thus, Comment *a* expressly excludes matters contrary to "business or professional ethics" or "illegal or unethical" acts from those which an agent would be required to perform. This frees the agent from participation in such behavior and authorizes him to withdraw from the agency relation if the principal persists.

* * *

[E]xcept in the single area of "crime," the *Restatement* provides no support for the view that the employee may disclose nonpublic information about his employer acquired as a result of the employment relationship in order to promote the superior interest of society. While prohibiting affirmative acts of the employee such as disclosure, the *Restatement* relieves the employee of any duty to obey or act for the employer not only in the case of "crime" or "illegality" but also in case of "unethical acts" or acts "contrary to public policy" or constituting a tort.

The duties of obedience, loyalty, and confidentiality enunciated by the *Restatement* and the carefully circumscribed privileged exceptions clearly proscribe the "public interest disclosure" proposal suggested by Mr. Nader. We must recognize, however, that the *Restatement* drawn from the common-law cases is drafted in terms of economic activity, economic motivation, and economic advantage and formulates duties of loyalty and obedience for the agent to prevent the agent's own economic interests from impairing his judgment, zeal, or single-minded devotion to the furtherance of his principal's economic interests. The reference in section 395, Comment *f* permitting the agent to disclose confidential information concerning a criminal act committed or planned by the principal is the sole exception to a system of analysis that is otherwise exclusively concerned with matters relating to the economic position of the parties. Thus, the question may fairly be asked to what extent the *Restatement* and the common-law decisions are useful in the analysis of a proposal that rests on the concept of an agent's primary obligation as a citizen to the society, transcending his economic duty to the principal.

Are doctrines resting on a policy of protecting the economic position of the principal against impairment by reason of an agent's effort to achieve economic gain properly applicable to the employee who releases non-public information about his employer without intent to obtain economic advantage for himself—and in fact at considerable economic risk to himself—and motivated by a desire to promote the public good rather than to injure the principal (although such injury may in fact result)?

The duties of loyalty and obedience on the part of the agent are unquestionably central to the agency relationship, irrespective of economic considerations. But these duties, as the *Restatement* itself recognizes, have limitations. To paraphrase Mr. Justice Frankfurter's well-known admonition: To say that an agent has duties of loyalty and obedience only begins analysis; it gives direction to further inquiry. It is thus not enough to say that the agent has duties of loyalty and obedience which will be impaired. One must inquire more deeply and ascertain the outer perimeters of the agent's obligations by balancing the conflicting considerations. On this critical question of how far the duties of loyalty and obedience extend, the *Restatement* enunciating the traditional rules in their economic setting provides limited guidance.

* * *

Presumably, the basis for the proposal for unauthorized disclosure of corporate conduct that is regarded as socially irresponsible rests on a judgment as to the crucial social importance of controlling the important centers of power in the nation. The disclosure proposal would appear to be another variation on Mr. Nader's theme that the large public corporation is a political institution in which forces not represented in the traditional decision-making process of the corporation, such as the public generally, should participate in the decision-making process. This theme was clearly articulated in Campaign GM where its counsel acknowledged that a major objective of the Campaign was to involve the public—not merely shareholders—in the corporate decision. When the references to "professionalism" or "illegal, hazardous or unconscionable" activity are removed, this is the real basis of the proposal that corporate employees become informers, ready to act whenever they believe their responsibility to society requires disclosure of aspects of their employer's activities which they

VII. The View of the Corporation as a Political Institution

do not deem to be in the public interest. Emphasizing the view that the public corporation is a political institution, Mr. Nader has also called for "the popularization" of the corporation and the election of 5 directors out of 20 by the public—not shareholders—in a national election. The adaptation of the tolerated, if not accepted, practice of the government "leak" to corporate affairs is a simple corollary of this view.

Even without accepting the implications that Mr. Nader draws from the conclusion, it is clear that his view of the large public corporation as a political institution is in many respects sound. The tremendous concentration of economic power, the lack of accountability of management as a result of the separation of ownership and control, the increasing involvement of the large corporation in social problem-solving, the interrelationship between major corporations and the government arising from the billions of government funds spent for defense and space, the interrelationship between many major corporations, universities, and the government in connection with the employment of the billions of government funds spent for research and development all support the view that in many respects the corporation has become a political institution.

Finally, the politicalization of the voting processes of the major corporation, symbolized by Campaign GM and other "public interest" groups, reflects the changed nature of the corporate institution.

If the validity of the disclosure proposal rests on the changing nature of the major public corporation into a political institution with governmentlike qualities, it becomes appropriate to review the duties of obedience, loyalty, and confidentiality of the government employee.

VIII. The Government Employee

The cases involving the discharge or suspension of government employees for public criticism of the policies or administration of the governmental agencies in which they have been employed provide insight into the degree of importance to be accorded to the employee's duties of obedience and loyalty. The problem presented is the extent to which the government employee loses his constitutional right to free speech with respect to issues of public importance because he has accepted public employment.

In the leading case of *Pickering v. Board of Education,* the Supreme Court held that in the absence of

> proof of false statements knowingly or recklessly made by him, a teacher's exercise of his right to speak on issues of public importance may not furnish the basis for his dismissal from public employment.[3]

The Court made it plain that

> teachers may [not] constitutionally be compelled to relinquish the First Amendment rights they would otherwise enjoy as citizens to comment on

[3] 391 U.S. 563, 574 (1968).

matters of public interest in connection with the operation of the public schools in which they work.[4]

In reaching its conclusion, the Court recognized that it had

> to arrive at a balance between the interests of the teacher, as a citizen, in commenting on matters of public concern and the interest of the State, as an employer, in promoting the efficiency of the public services it performs through its employees.[5]

The significance of the *Pickering* decision is the relatively unimportant role it assigned to "the interest of the State, as an employer" and to the teacher's duty of loyalty and obedience to the school board and the superintendent of schools. The Court left no doubt that in the balance of interests, freedom of speech for government employees was deemed so important that it outweighed any general duty of loyalty and obedience to the public employer, and that . . . even false statements were protected so long as they were not "knowingly or recklessly made."

Thus, the Court emphasized the degree of intimacy of relationship required before the government employee's right of free public comment would be lost. It stated:

> Appellant's employment relationships with the Board and, to a somewhat lesser extent, with the superintendent are not the kind of close working relationships for which it can persuasively be claimed that personal loyalty and confidence are necessary to their proper functioning.[6]

Thus, with respect to the balance between the private employee's position as a citizen and the private employer's claim to loyalty and obedience, the *Pickering* case supports the view that traditional concepts as to loyalty and obedience may have to yield to permit employees to fulfill their role as citizens. This is the foundation for the disclosure proposal—the importance to the nation of encouraging citizens interested in working for a better society to place their interests as citizens above the interests of their employer. If governmental agencies may, notwithstanding such public criticism by government employees, function effectively in the view of the Court, why should not the major corporation be able to do the same? With increasing recognition of the "blurring" of the line of difference between the so-called "public" and "private" sectors and the increasing resemblance of employee relations in government service to those in private industry, the implications of the *Pickering* decision for the major public corporation become even more pronounced.

*   *   *

It is possible, however, to argue for a less restricted standard for disclosure of corporate employees than that applicable to government

---

[4]*Id.* at 568.
[5]*Id.*
[6]*Id.* at 570.

employees. In democratic society, the existence of the opposition party provides a counter-balance to the administration, and the opposition may be relied upon to look after the public interest in any controversy. The public employee need not feel that he must act to protect the public interest himself. In the corporation run by management not effectively subject to shareholder control, appeal by an employee to the public generally may be the only available alternative for the protection of the public interest, and the forces for disclosure may therefore be stronger. Further, unlike government, the corporation has institutional objectives other than the promotion of the public interest and disclosure may be essential to protect the public interest.

In addition to the question of the applicable rules, one must not lose sight of the practicalities of the situation. Notwithstanding statute and agency regulations, governmental "leaks" have persisted and appear to play a role of some usefulness in the shaping of opinion and the determination of public policy. Government personnel involved may be disciplined in the rare cases where they are identified, but if the political considerations involved are important enough, the political groups whose ends have been served by the "leak" support their source.

* * *

In short, the major corporation may well anticipate an unhappy future where corporate "leaks" in the area of social responsibility will become not uncommon, and the corporation, like the government, will have to learn to live with this unwelcome development.

IX. The Changing Role of the Corporate Employee

Underlying the problem is the concept of the proper position of the employee of the major corporation. In the balance of the conflicting rights of the government employee as citizen and the objective of government for efficient administration, the courts have placed a lesser value on the traditional duties of loyalty and obedience and have subordinated these duties to the employee's right of free speech in order to enable the employee to play a role as a citizen in matters of public controversy. Similarly, one may inquire whether, in time, erosion of the traditional employer-employee relation and the traditional concepts of loyalty and obedience will not also occur within the major American corporation.

A. The Developing Law

The basic problem goes to the employer's right of discharge of an employee who is publicly acting contrary to the interests of the employer: the Polaroid worker picketing in protest of Polaroid's alleged involvement with apartheid; the Eastern Air Line pilot disobeying standard operating procedures for dumping excess kerosene in the atmosphere instead of draining it on the ground; the automobile worker who protests the shipment of allegedly unsafe cars from his employer's factory; or the employee who "leaks" non-public information in accordance with the "public interest disclosure" proposal.

At common law, the employer's freedom to discharge was absolute. Over the years, this right of discharge has been increasingly restricted by statute and by collective bargaining agreements, but the basic principle of the employer's legal right to discharge, although challenged on the theoretical level, is still unimpaired.

In an illuminating article,[7] Dean Blades has re-examined the traditional concept of employment at will and the employer's traditional power to discharge the employee at any time for any reason (or indeed for no reason) and has suggested that in time the doctrine—already hedged in by statute and collective bargaining agreements—will be modified, possibly by the legislatures, perhaps by the courts, to protect the employee against discharge for exercise of those personal rights which have no legitimate connection with the employment relationship.

B. The Dynamics of the Public Climate

As one moves from the theoretical level to the practical level, one may inquire whether the employer's right of discharge has not already been impaired at least in those cases where public sympathy is squarely behind the employee, as in the case of the Eastern Air Lines pilot who placed his concern with air pollution above obedience to company regulations. The rules of law may condemn such activity as a clear breach of the duty of loyalty and obedience. The corporation may be tempted to exercise its right of discharge, but its freedom of action (without regard to obligations under any union contract) will be severely restricted by the climate of public opinion which may well have been significantly influenced by the publicity attending the affair.

* * *

At this stage, whatever the traditional legal doctrines, the corporation's right of discharge may be illusory. The major corporation must recognize that it has become a public institution and must respond to the public climate of opinion. Thus, whether or not the major corporation, in the law of the future comes to be regarded as a quasi-governmental body for some purpose, it operates today as a political as well as economic institution, subject to political behavior by those affected by it and to public debate over those of its actions which attain public visibility.

The "corporate leak" will join the "government leak" and serve the

---

[7]Dean Blades, *Employment at Will* v. *Individual Freedom: Or Limiting the Abusive Exercise of Employer Power,* 67 Colum. L. Rev. 1404 (1967).

same political purposes. Whatever the incidental cost, business will survive, as has government, and indeed wrongful though it may be, the possibility of such a "leak" may serve a useful therapeutic or preventive function. . . .

Fortune . . . reports:

> Both reporters and professional politicians find him [Mr. Nader] extremely useful. "Nader has become the fifth branch of government if you count the press as fourth," says a Senate aide who has worked with Nader often in drafting legislation. "He knows all the newspaper deadlines and how to get in touch with anybody anytime. By his own hard work he has developed a network of sources in every arm of government. And believe me, no Senator turns down those calls from Ralph. He will say he's got some stuff and it's good, and the Senator can take the credit."[8]

Once the duty of loyalty yields to the primacy of what the individual in question regards as the "public interest," the door is open to widespread abuse.

In a society accustomed to governmental "leaks"—deliberately instigated by an administration as trial balloons as well as by bureaucrats dissatisfied with administrative decision—extension of the conduct described above to the corporate area will be merely more of the same, part of a tolerated pattern in a political world, embracing the major corporation as well as government. At the same time, it sharply poses the question of the desirability of encouraging the spread of such patterns of violation of the concepts of loyalty and obedience from government to major business. The proposal for disclosure to private groups—however disinterested their objective or public-spirited their purpose—seems an excessive and dangerous response to the problem of subordinating to social controls the tremendous economic and social power of the major public corporations.

In brief, unauthorized disclosure of confidential information presents serious problems for any organization; the matter can hardly be allowed to rest on each individual employee's decision as to the nature of his responsibilities to society and to his employer.

C. Alternatives to Unauthorized Disclosure

Other alternatives to reach the same objective without the same corrosive effect on personnel and the same potential for private abuse are available. These involve the use of governmental machinery with governmental safeguards with respect to the use of information received.

1. Traditional doctrines of agency law recognize the privilege of employees to report violations of law to proper governmental authorities. Private vigilante efforts should not be essential to achieve effective admin-

---

[8] Armstrong, "The Passion That Rules Ralph Nader," *Fortune,* May 1971 at 144, 145.

istration. "Public interest" groups would seem better advised to continue to concentrate their attention on improving the efficiency and effectiveness of the regulatory processes.

2. Another alternative is to extend further the growing statutory and administrative requirements of disclosure of conduct in areas of social responsibility. Examples include the Employer Information Report EEO-1 on minority employment practices filed with the Federal Equal Employment Opportunity Commission. . . . Enforcement of such matters by public agencies under public standards and with public personnel and safeguards would serve the basic object without the serious disadvantages involved in the "public-interest disclosure" proposal.

3. Still another alternative is the development of the so-called social audit or a systematic quantitative (and possibly qualitative) review of a corporation's activities in the area of social responsibility. This proposal, suggested almost 20 years ago, has been gathering increasing attention and strength with a number of institutions and corporations endeavoring to develop a satisfactory methodology. Such disclosure and evaluation seem an inevitable product of the forces making for greater corporate participation in the solution of social and environmental problems.

D. Protection Against Discharge

Another aspect of the proposal for a "public interest clearing house" has considerable merit. This is the objective to provide protection through exposure to public opinion for corporate employees discharged for refusal to participate in illegal, immoral, or unprofessional acts. Involving no breach of confidentiality, this is a laudable effort to translate into reality the theoretical legal rights of the employee recognized at common law and in the *Restatement of Agency* in the face of the grave economic inequality between the individual employee and the giant corporate employer. Such an effort should receive the support of all interested in raising the standards of industrial morality.

The related objective of assuring employee rights to participate in the public discussion of corporate conduct, including that of their employer, may also be achieved through extension of employee protection in collective bargaining agreements. . . .

An example of the power of the trade union is provided by Mr. Nader:

> For example, the Fisher Body inspector who, five years ago, turned over information to me about defective welding of Chevrolet bodies, after the plant manager and all his other bosses told him to forget it, is still on the job. Why? Because he is a union member. Had he been an engineer, or a scientist, or a lawyer or any nonunion person, G.M. could have showed him the door at 5 p.m. and he would have had no rights.

Statutory relief is another possible method to achieve appropriate protection for the rights of employees covering unionized and non-unionized employees alike. Anti-discrimination employment statutes already prohibit discrimination on the basis of "race, color, religion, sex, or national origin," age, or union membership. They might well be extended to make unlawful discrimination for political, social, or economic views.

X. Conclusion

The duties of loyalty and obedience are essential in the conduct of any enterprise—public or private. Yet, they do not serve as a basis to deprive government employees of their rights as citizens to participate in public debate and criticism of their governmental employer and should not be utilized to deprive corporate employees of similar rights.

As employee attitudes and actions reflect the increased public concern with social and environmental problems and the proper role of the corporation in participating in their solution, traditional doctrines of the employee's duties of loyalty and obedience and the employer's right of discharge will undergo increasing change. The pressure of "public interest" stockholder groups for increased corporate social responsibility will also be reflected by employees. At some point in the process, disagreement with management policies is inevitable. When the employees persist in their disagreement and the disagreement becomes public, an erosion of the traditional view of the duties of loyalty and obedience will have occurred. Yet this hardly seems a fundamental problem for the corporation or undesirable from the point of view of the larger society. The real question is to establish civilized perimeters of permissible conduct that will not silence employees from expressing themselves on the public implications of their employers' activities in the social and environmental arena and at the same time will not introduce elements of breach of confidentiality and impairment of loyalty that will materially impair the functioning of the corporation itself. A balancing of interests, not a blind reiteration of traditional doctrines, is required. It is hoped that this preliminary review will suggest some possible solutions to the problem.

Uniform Partnership Act*

PART I Preliminary Provisions

§ 1. Name of Act. This Act may be cited as Uniform Partnership Act.

§ 2. Definition of Terms. In this Act, "Court" includes every court and judge having jurisdiction in the case.

"Business" includes every trade, occupation, or profession.

"Person" includes individuals, partnerships, corporations, and other associations.

"Bankrupt" includes bankrupt under the Federal Bankruptcy Act or insolvent under any state insolvent act.

"Conveyance" includes every assignment, lease, mortgage, or encumbrance.

"Real property" includes land and any interest or estate in land.

§ 3. Interpretation of Knowledge and Notice. (1) A person has "knowledge" of a fact within the meaning of this Act not only when he has actual knowledge thereof, but also when he has knowledge of such other facts as in the circumstances shows bad faith.

(2) A person has "notice" of a fact within the meaning of this Act when the person who claims the benefit of the notice:

(a) States the fact to such person, or

(b) Delivers through the mail, or by other means of communication, a written statement of the fact to such person or to a proper person at his place of business or residence.

*Reprinted with permission from the National Conference of Commissioners on Uniform State Laws.

§ 4. Rules of Construction. (1) The rule that statutes in derogation of the common law are to be strictly construed shall have no application to this Act.

(2) The law of estoppel shall apply under this Act.

(3) The law of agency shall apply under this Act.

(4) This Act shall be so interpreted and construed as to effect its general purpose to make uniform the law of those states which enact it.

(5) This Act shall not be construed so as to impair the obligations of any contract existing when the Act goes into effect, nor to affect any action or proceedings begun or right accrued before this Act takes effect.

§ 5. Rules for Cases not Provided for in this Act. In any case not provided for in this Act the rules of law and equity, including the law merchant, shall govern.

PART II Nature of a Partnership

§ 6. Partnership Defined. (1) A partnership is an association of two or more persons to carry on as co-owners a business for profit.

(2) But any association formed under any other statute of this state, or any statute adopted by authority, other than the authority of this state, is not a partnership under this act, unless such association would have been a partnership in this state prior to the adoption of this act; but this act shall apply to limited partnerships except in so far as the statutes relating to such partnerships are inconsistent herewith.

§ 7.   Rules for Determining the Existence of a Partnership.   In determining whether a partnership exists, these rules shall apply:

(1) Except as provided by § 16 persons who are not partners as to each other are not partners as to third persons.

(2) Joint tenancy, tenancy in common, tenancy by the entireties, joint property, common property, or part ownership does not of itself establish a partnership, whether such co-owners do or do not share any profits made by the use of the property.

(3) The sharing of gross returns does not of itself establish a partnership, whether or not the persons sharing them have a joint or common right or interest in any property from which the returns are derived.

(4) The receipt by a person of a share of the profits of a business is prima facie evidence that he is a partner in the business, but no such inference shall be drawn if such profits were received in payment:

(a) As a debt by installments or otherwise,

(b) As wages of an employee or rent to a landlord,

(c) As an annuity to a widow or representative of a deceased partner,

(d) As interest on a loan, though the amount of payments vary with the profits of the business,

(e) As the consideration for the sale of a good-will of a business or other property by installments or otherwise.

§ 8. Partnership Property.   (1) All property originally brought into the partnership stock or subsequently acquired by purchase or otherwise, on account of the partnership, is partnership property.

(2) Unless the contrary intention appears, property acquired with partnership funds is partnership property.

(3) Any estate in real property may be acquired in the partnership name. Title so acquired can be conveyed only in the partnership name.

(4) A conveyance to a partnership in the partnership name, though without words of inheritance, passes the entire estate of the grantor unless a contrary intent appears.

PART III   Relations of Partners to Persons Dealing With the Partnership

§ 9.   Partner Agent of Partnership as to Partnership Business.   (1) Every partner is an agent of the partnership for the purpose of its business, and the act of every partner, including the execution in the partnership name of any instrument, for apparently carrying on in the usual way the business of the partnership of which he is a member binds the partnership, unless the partner so acting has in fact no authority to act for the partnership in the particular matter, and the person with whom he is dealing has knowledge of the fact that he has no such authority.

(2) An act of a partner which is not apparently for the carrying on of the business of the partnership in the usual way does not bind the partnership unless authorized by the other partners.

(3) Unless authorized by the other partners or unless they have abandoned the business, one or more but less than all the partners have no authority to:

(a) Assign the partnership property in trust for creditors or on the assignee's promise to pay the debts of the partnership,

(b) Dispose of the good-will of the business,

(c) Do any other act which would make it impossible to carry on the ordinary business of a partnership,

(d) Confess a judgment,

(e) Submit a partnership claim or liability to arbitration or reference.

(4) No act of a partner in contravention of a restriction on authority shall bind the partnership to persons having knowledge of the restriction.

§ 10.   Conveyance of Real Property of the Partnership.   (1) Where title to real property is in the partnership name, any partner may convey title to such property by a conveyance executed in the partnership name; but the partnership may recover such property unless the partner's act binds the partnership under the provisions of paragraph (1) of § 9 or unless such property has been conveyed by the grantee or a person claiming through such grantee to a holder for value without knowledge that the partner, in making the conveyance, has exceeded his authority.

(2) Where title to real property is in the name of the partnership, a conveyance executed by a partner, in his own name, passes the equitable interest of the partnership, provided the act is one within the authority of the partner under the provisions of paragraph (1) of § 9.

(3) Where title to real property is in the name

of one or more but not all the partners, and the record does not disclose the right of the partnership, the partners in whose name the title stands may convey title to such property, but the partnership may recover such property if the partners' act does not bind the partnership under the provisions of paragraph (1) of § 9, unless the purchaser or his assignee, is a holder for value, without knowledge.

(4) Where the title to real property is in the name of one or more or all the partners, or in a third person in trust for the partnership, a conveyance executed by a partner in the partnership name, or in his own name, passes the equitable interest of the partnership, provided the act is one within the authority of the partner under the provisions of paragraph (1) of § 9.

(5) Where the title to real property is in the names of all the partners a conveyance executed by all the partners passes all their rights in such property.

§ 11.   Partnership Bound by Admission of Partner.
An admission or representation made by any partner concerning partnership affairs within the scope of his authority as conferred by this Act is evidence against the partnership.

§ 12.   Partnership Charged with Knowledge of or Notice to Partner.
Notice to any partner of any matter relating to partnership affairs, and the knowledge of the partner acting in the particular matter, acquired while a partner or then present to his mind, and the knowledge of any other partner who reasonably could and should have communicated it to the acting partner, operate as notice to or knowledge of the partnership, except in the case of a fraud on the partnership committed by or with the consent of that partner.

§ 13.   Partnership Bound by Partner's Wrongful Act.
Where, by any wrongful act or omission of any partner acting in the ordinary course of the business of the partnership or with the authority of his co-partners, loss or injury is caused to any person, not being a partner in the partnership, or any penalty is incurred, the partnership is liable therefor to the same extent as the partner so acting or omitting to act.

§ 14.   Partnership Bound by Partner's Breach of Trust.
The partnership is bound to make good the loss:

(a) Where one partner acting within the scope of his apparent authority receives money or property of a third person and misapplies it; and

(b) Where the partnership in the course of its business receives money or property of a third person and the money or property so received is misapplied by any partner while it is in the custody of the partnership.

§ 15.   Nature of Partner's Liability.
All partners are liable:

(a) Jointly and severally for everything chargeable to the partnership under §§ 13 and 14.

(b) Jointly for all other debts and obligations of the partnership; but any partner may enter into a separate obligation to perform a partnership contract.

§ 16.   Partner by Estoppel.
(1) When a person, by words spoken or written or by conduct, represents himself, or consents to another representing him to any one, as a partner in an existing partnership or with one or more persons not actual partners, he is liable to any such person to whom such representation has been made, who has, on the faith of such representation, given credit to the actual or apparent partnership, and if he has made such representation or consented to its being made in a public manner he is liable to such person, whether the representation has or has not been made or communicated to such person so giving credit by or with the knowledge of the apparent partner making the representation or consenting to its being made:

(a) When a partnership liability results, he is liable as though he were an actual member of the partnership.

(b) When no partnership liability results, he is liable jointly with the other persons, if any, so consenting to the contract or representation as to incur liability, otherwise separately.

(2) When a person has been thus represented to be a partner in an existing partnership, or with one or more persons not actual partners, he is an agent of the persons consenting to such representation to bind them to the same extent and in the same manner as though he were a partner in fact, with respect to persons who rely upon the representation. Where all the members of the existing partnership consent to the representation, a partnership act or obligation results; but in all other cases it is the

joint act or obligation of the person acting and the persons consenting to the representation.

§ 17.   Liability of Incoming Partner.   A person admitted as a partner into an existing partnership is liable for all the obligations of the partnership arising before his admission as though he had been a partner when such obligations were incurred, except that this liability shall be satisfied only out of partnership property.

PART IV   Relations of Partners to One Another

§ 18.   Rules Determining Rights and Duties of Partners.   The rights and duties of the partners in relation to the partnership shall be determined, subject to any agreement between them, by the following rules:

(a) Each partner shall be repaid his contributions, whether by way of capital or advances to the partnership property and share equally in the profits and surplus remaining after all liabilities, including those to partners, are satisfied; and must contribute towards the losses, whether of capital or otherwise, sustained by the partnership according to his share in the profits.

(b) The partnership must indemnify every partner in respect of payments made and personal liabilities reasonably incurred by him in the ordinary and proper conduct of its business, or for the preservation of its business or property.

(c) A partner, who in aid of the partnership makes any payment or advance beyond the amount of capital which he agreed to contribute, shall be paid interest from the date of the payment or advance.

(d) A partner shall receive interest on the capital contributed by him only from the date when repayment should be made.

(e) All partners have equal rights in the management and conduct of the partnership business.

(f) No partner is entitled to remuneration for acting in the partnership business, except that a surviving partner is entitled to reasonable compensation for his services in winding up the partnership affairs.

(g) No person can become a member of a partnership without the consent of all the partners.

(h) Any difference arising as to ordinary matters connected with the partnership business may be decided by a majority of the partners; but no act in contravention of any agreement between the partners may be done rightfully without the consent of all the partners.

§ 19.   Partnership Books.   The partnership books shall be kept, subject to any agreement between the partners, at the principal place of business of the partnership, and every partner shall at all times have access to and may inspect and copy any of them.

§ 20.   Duty of Partners to Render Information.   Partners shall render on demand true and full information of all things affecting the partnership to any partner or the legal representative of any deceased partner or partner under legal disability.

§ 21.   Partner Accountable as a Fiduciary.   (1) Every partner must account to the partnership for any benefit, and hold as trustee for it any profits derived by him without the consent of the other partners from any transaction connected with the formation, conduct, or liquidation of the partnership or from any use by him of its property.

(2) This section applies also to the representatives of a deceased partner engaged in the liquidation of the affairs of the partnership as the personal representatives of the last surviving partner.

§ 22.   Right to an Account.   Any partner shall have the right to a formal account as to partnership affairs:

(a) If he is wrongfully excluded from the partnership business or possession of its property by his co-partners,

(b) If the right exists under the terms of any agreement,

(c) As provided by § 21,

(d) Whenever other circumstances render it just and reasonable.

§ 23.   Continuation of Partnership Beyond Fixed Term.   (1) When a partnership for a fixed term or particular undertaking is continued after the termination of such term or particular undertaking without any express agreement, the rights and duties of the partners remain the same as they were at such termination, so far as is consistent with a partnership at will.

(2) A continuation of the business by the partners or such of them as habitually acted therein during the term, without any settlement or liquidation of the partnership affairs, is prima facie evidence of a continuation of the partnership.

PART V Property Rights of a Partner

§ 24. Extent of Property Rights of a Partner. The property rights of a partner are (1) his rights in specific partnership property, (2) his interest in the partnership, and (3) his right to participate in the management.

§ 25. Nature of a Partner's Right in Specific Partnership Property. (1) A partner is co-owner with his partners of specific partnership property holding as a tenant in partnership.

(2) The incidents of this tenancy are such that:

(a) A partner, subject to the provisions of this Act and to any agreement between the partners, has an equal right with his partners to possess specific partnership property for partnership purposes; but he has no right to possess such property for any other purpose without the consent of his partners.

(b) A partner's right in specific partnership property is not assignable except in connection with the assignment of rights of all the partners in the same property.

(c) A partner's right in specific partnership property is not subject to attachment or execution, except on a claim against the partnership. When partnership property is attached for a partnership debt the partners, or any of them, or the representatives of a deceased partner, cannot claim any right under the homestead or exemption laws.

(d) On the death of a partner his right in specific partnership property vests in the surviving partner or partners, except where the deceased was the last surviving partner, when his right in such property vests in his legal representative. Such surviving partner or partners, or the legal representative of the last surviving partner, has no right to possess the partnership property for any but a partnership purpose.

(e) A partner's right in specific partnership property is not subject to dower, curtesy, or allowances to widows, heirs, or next of kin.

§ 26. Nature of Partner's Interest in the Partnership. A partner's interest in the partnership is his share of the profits and surplus, and the same is personal property.

§ 27. Assignment of Partner's Interest. (1) A conveyance by a partner of his interest in the partnership does not of itself dissolve the partnership, nor, as against the other partners in the absence of agreement, entitle the assignee, during the continuance of the partnership to interfere in the management or administration of the partnership business or affairs, or to require any information or account of partnership transactions, or to inspect the partnership books; but it merely entitles the assignee to receive in accordance with his contract the profits to which the assigning partner would otherwise be entitled.

(2) In case of a dissolution of the partnership, the assignee is entitled to receive his assignor's interest and may require an account from the date only of the last account agreed to by all the partners.

§ 28. Partner's Interest Subject to Charging Order. (1) On due application to a competent court by any judgment creditor of a partner, the court which entered the judgment, order, or decree, or any other court, may charge the interest of the debtor partner with payment of the unsatisfied amount of such judgment debt with interest thereon; and may then or later appoint a receiver of his share of the profits, and of any other money due or to fall due to him in respect of the partnership, and make all other orders, directions, accounts and inquiries which the debtor partner might have made, or which the circumstances of the case may require.

(2) The interest charged may be redeemed at any time before foreclosure, or in case of a sale being directed by the court may be purchased without thereby causing a dissolution:

(a) With separate property, by any one or more of the partners, or

(b) With partnership property, by any one or more of the partners with the consent of all the partners whose interests are not so charged or sold.

(3) Nothing in this Act shall be held to deprive a partner of his right, if any, under the exemption laws, as regards his interest in the partnership.

PART VI   Dissolution and Winding Up

§ 29.   Dissolution Defined.   The dissolution of a partnership is the change in the relation of the partners caused by any partner ceasing to be associated in the carrying on as distinguished from the winding up of the business.

§ 30.   Partnership Not Terminated by Dissolution.   On dissolution the partnership is not terminated, but continues until the winding up of partnership affairs is completed.

§ 31.   Causes of Dissolution.   Dissolution is caused:

(1) Without violation of the agreement between the partners:

(a) By the termination of the definite term or particular undertaking specified in the agreement,

(b) By the express will of any partner when no definite term or particular undertaking is specified,

(c) By the express will of all the partners who have not assigned their interests or suffered them to be charged for their separate debts, either before or after the termination of any specified term or particular undertaking.

(d) By the expulsion of any partner from the business bona fide in accordance with such a power conferred by the agreement between the partners;

(2) In contravention of the agreement between the partners, where the circumstances do not permit a dissolution under any other provision of this section, by the express will of any partner at any time;

(3) By any event which makes it unlawful for the business of the partnership to be carried on or for the members to carry it on in partnership;

(4) By the death of any partner;

(5) By the bankruptcy of any partner or the partnership;

(6) By decree of court under § 32.

§ 32.   Dissolution by Decree of Court.   (1) On application by or for a partner the court shall decree a dissolution whenever:

(a) A partner has been declared a lunatic in any judicial proceeding or is shown to be of unsound mind,

(b) A partner becomes in any other way incapable of performing his part of the partnership contract,

(c) A partner has been guilty of such conduct as tends to affect prejudicially the carrying on of the business,

(d) A partner wilfully or persistently commits a breach of the partnership agreement, or otherwise so conducts himself in matters relating to the partnership business that it is not reasonably practicable to carry on the business in partnership with him,

(e) The business of the partnership can only be carried on at a loss,

(f) Other circumstances render a dissolution equitable.

(2) On the application of the purchaser of a partner's interest under §§ 27 or 28:

(a) After the termination of the specified term or particular undertaking,

(b) At any time if the partnership was a partnership at will when the interest was assigned or when the charging order was issued.

§ 33.   General Effect of Dissolution on Authority of Partner.   Except so far as may be necessary to wind up partnership affairs or to complete transactions begun but not then finished, dissolution terminates all authority of any partner to act for the partnership,

(1) With respect to the partners,

(a) When the dissolution is not by the act, bankruptcy or death of a partner; or

(b) When the dissolution is by such act, bankruptcy or death of a partner, in cases where § 34 so requires.

(2) With respect to persons not partners, as declared in § 35.

§ 34.   Right of Partner to Contribution From Co-partners After Dissolution.   Where the dissolution is caused by the act, death or bankruptcy of a partner, each partner is liable to his co-partners for his share of any liability created by any partner acting for the partnership as if the partnership had not been dissolved unless:

(a) The dissolution being by act of any partner,

the partner acting for the partnership had knowledge of the dissolution, or

(b) The dissolution being by the death or bankruptcy of a partner, the partner acting for the partnership had knowledge or notice of the death or bankruptcy.

§ 35. Power of Partner to Bind Partnership to Third Persons After Dissolution.

(1) After dissolution a partner can bind the partnership except as provided in Paragraph (3)

(a) By any act appropriate for winding up partnership affairs or completing transactions unfinished at dissolution;

(b) By any transaction which would bind the partnership if dissolution had not taken place, provided the other party to the transaction:

(I) Had extended credit to the partnership prior to dissolution and had no knowledge or notice of the dissolution; or

(II) Though he had not so extended credit, had nevertheless known of the partnership prior to dissolution, and, having no knowledge or notice of dissolution, the fact of dissolution had not been advertised in a newspaper of general circulation in the place (or in each place if more than one) at which the partnership business was regularly carried on.

(2) The liability of a partner under paragraph (1b) shall be satisfied out of partnership assets alone when such partner had been prior to dissolution:

(a) Unknown as a partner to the person with whom the contract is made; and

(b) So far unknown and inactive in partnership affairs that the business reputation of the partnership could not be said to have been in any degree due to his connection with it.

(3) The partnership is in no case bound by any act of a partner after dissolution:

(a) Where the partnership is dissolved because it is unlawful to carry on the business, unless the act is appropriate for winding up partnership affairs; or

(b) Where the partner has become bankrupt; or

(c) Where the partner has no authority to wind up partnership affairs; except by a transaction with one who:

(I) Had extended credit to the partnership

prior to dissolution and had no knowledge or notice of his want of authority; or

(II) Had not extended credit to the partnership prior to dissolution, and, having no knowledge or notice of his want of authority, the fact of his want of authority has not been advertised in the manner provided for advertising the fact of dissolution in paragraph (1bII).

(4) Nothing in this section shall affect the liability under § 16 of any person who after dissolution represents himself or consents to another representing him as a partner in a partnership engaged in carrying on business.

§ 36. Effect of Dissolution on Partner's Existing Liability.

(1) The dissolution of the partnership does not of itself discharge the existing liability of any partner.

(2) A partner is discharged from any existing liability upon dissolution of the partnership by an agreement to that effect between himself, the partnership creditor and the person or partnership continuing the business; and such agreement may be inferred from the course of dealing between the creditor having knowledge of the dissolution and the person or partnership continuing the business.

(3) Where a person agrees to assume the existing obligations of a dissolved partnership, the partners whose obligations have been assumed shall be discharged from any liability to any creditor of the partnership who, knowing of the agreement, consents to a material alteration in the nature or time of payment of such obligations.

(4) The individual property of a deceased partner shall be liable for all obligations of the partnership incurred while he was a partner but subject to the prior payment of his separate debts.

§ 37. Right to Wind Up.

Unless otherwise agreed the partners who have not wrongfully dissolved the partnership or the legal representative of the last surviving partner, not bankrupt, has the right to wind up the partnership affairs; provided, however, that any partner, has legal representative or his assignee, upon cause shown, may obtain winding up by the court.

§ 38. Rights of Partners to Application of Partnership Property.

(1) When dissolution is caused in any way, except in contravention of the partnership agreement, each partner as against his

co-partners and all persons claiming through them in respect of their interests in the partnership, unless otherwise agreed, may have the partnership property applied to discharge its liabilities, and the surplus applied to pay in cash the net amount owing to the respective partners. But if dissolution is caused by expulsion of a partner, bona fide under the partnership agreement and if the expelled partner is discharged from all partnership liabilities, either by payment or agreement under § 36 (2), he shall receive in cash only the net amount due him from the partnership.

(2) When dissolution is caused in contravention of the partnership agreement the rights of the partners shall be as follows:

(a) Each partner who has not caused dissolution wrongfully shall have:

(I) All the rights specified in paragraph (1) of this section, and

(II) The right, as against each partner who has caused the dissolution wrongfully, to damages for breach of the agreement.

(b) The partners who have not caused the dissolution wrongfully, if they all desire to continue the business in the same name, either by themselves or jointly with others, may do so, during the agreed term for the partnership and for that purpose may possess the partnership property, provided they secure the payment by bond approved by the court, or pay to any partner who has caused the dissolution wrongfully, the value of his interest in the partnership at the dissolution, less any damages recoverable under clause (2aII) of the section, and in like manner indemnify him against all present or future partnership liabilities.

(c) A partner who has caused the dissolution wrongfully shall have:

(I) If the business is not continued under the provisions of paragraph (2b) all the rights of a partner under paragraph (1), subject to clause (2aII), of this section,

(II) If the business is continued under paragraph (2b) of this section the right as against his co-partners and all claiming through them in respect of their interests in the partnership, to have the value of his interest in the partnership, less any damages caused to his co-partners by the dissolution, ascertained and paid him in cash, or the payment secured by bond approved by the court, and to be released from all existing liabilities of the partnership; but in ascertaining the value of the partner's interest the value of the good-will of the business shall not be considered.

§ 39.   Rights Where Partnership is Dissolved for Fraud or Misrepresentation.   Where a partnership contract is rescinded on the ground of the fraud or misrepresentation of one of the parties thereto, the party entitled to rescind is, without prejudice to any other right, entitled:

(a) To a lien on, or right of retention of, the surplus of the partnership property after satisfying the partnership liabilities to third persons for any sum of money paid by him for the purchase of an interest in the partnership and for any capital or advances contributed by him; and

(b) To stand, after all liabilities to third persons have been satisfied, in the place of the creditors of the partnership for any payments made by him in respect of the partnership liabilities; and

(c) To be indemnified by the person guilty of the fraud or making the representation against all debts and liabilities of the partnership.

§ 40.   Rules for Distribution.   In settling accounts between the partners after dissolution, the following rules shall be observed, subject to any agreement to the contrary:

(a) The assets of the partnership are:

(I) The partnership property,

(II) The contributions of the partners necessary for the payment of all the liabilities specified in clause (b) of this paragraph,

(b) The liabilities of the partnership shall rank in order of payment, as follows:

(I) Those owing to creditors other than partners,

(II) Those owing to partners other than for capital and profits,

(III) Those owing to partners in respect of capital,

(IV) Those owing to partners in respect of profits.

(c) The assets shall be applied in the order of their declaration in clause (a) of this paragraph to the satisfaction of the liabilities.

(d) The partners shall contribute, as provided

by § 18 (a) the amount necessary to satisfy the liabilities; but if any, but not all, of the partners are insolvent, or, not being subject to process, refuse to contribute, the other partners shall contribute their share of the liabilities, and, in the relative proportions in which they share the profits, the additional amount necessary to pay the liabilities.

(e) An assignee for the benefit of creditors or any person appointed by the court shall have the right to enforce the contributions specified in clause (d) of this paragraph.

(f) Any partner or his legal representative shall have the right to enforce the contributions specified in clause (d) of this paragraph, to the extent of the amount which he has paid in excess of his share of the liability.

(g) The individual property of a deceased partner shall be liable for the contributions specified in clause (d) of this paragraph.

(h) When partnership property and the individual properties of the partners are in possession of a court for distribution, partnership creditors shall have priority on partnership property and separate creditors on individual property, saving the rights of lien or secured creditors as heretofore.

(i) Where a partner has become bankrupt or his estate is insolvent the claims against his separate property shall rank in the following order:

(I) Those owing to separate creditors,

(II) Those owing to partnership creditors,

(III) Those owing to partners by way of contribution.

§ 41. Liability of Persons Continuing the Business in Certain Cases.

(1) When any new partner is admitted into an existing partnership, or when any partner retires and assigns (or the representative of the deceased partner assigns) his rights in partnership property to two or more of the partners, or to one or more of the partners and one or more third persons, if the business is continued without liquidation of the partnership affairs, creditors of the first or dissolved partnership are also creditors of the partnership so continuing the business.

(2) When all but one partner retire and assign (or the representative of a deceased partner assigns) their rights in partnership property to the remaining partner, who continues the business without liquidation of partnership affairs, either alone or with others, creditors of the dissolved partnership are also creditors of the person or partnership so continuing the business.

(3) When any partner retires or dies and the business of the dissolved partnership is continued as set forth in paragraphs (1) and (2) of this section, with the consent of the retired partners or the representative of the deceased partner, but without any assignment of his right in partnership property, rights of creditors of the dissolved partnership and of the creditors of the person or partnership continuing the business shall be as if such assignment had been made.

(4) When all the partners or their representatives assign their rights in partnership property to one or more third persons who promise to pay the debts and who continue the business of the dissolved partnership, creditors of the dissolved partnership are also creditors of the person or partnership continuing the business.

(5) When any partner wrongfully causes a dissolution and the remaining partners continue the business under the provisions of § 38 (2b), either alone or with others, and without liquidation of the partnership affairs, creditors of the dissolved partnership are also creditors of the person or partnership continuing the business.

(6) When a partner is expelled and the remaining partners continue the business either alone or with others, without liquidation of the partnership affairs, creditors of the dissolved partnership are also creditors of the person or partnership continuing the business.

(7) The liability of a third person becoming a partner in the partnership continuing the business, under this section, to the creditors of the dissolved partnership shall be satisfied out of partnership property only.

(8) When the business of a partnership after dissolution is continued under any conditions set forth in this section the creditors of the dissolved partnership, as against the separate creditors of the retiring or deceased partner or the representative of the deceased partner, have a prior right to any claim of the retired partner or the representative of the deceased partner against the person or partnership

continuing the business, on account of the retired or deceased partner's interest in the dissolved partnership or on account of any consideration promised for such interest or for his right in partnership property.

(9) Nothing in this section shall be held to modify any right of creditors to set aside any assignment on the ground of fraud.

(10) The use by the person or partnership continuing the business of the partnership name, or the name of a deceased partner as part thereof, shall not of itself make the individual property of the deceased partner liable for any debts contracted by such person or partnership.

§ 42. Rights of Retiring or Estate of Deceased Partner When the Business is Continued. When any partner retires or dies, and the business is continued under any of the conditions set forth in § 41 (1, 2, 3, 5, 6), or § 38 (2b), without any settlement of accounts as between him or his estate and the person or partnership continuing the business,

unless otherwise agreed, he or his legal representative as against such persons or partnership may have the value of his interest at the date of dissolution ascertained, and shall receive as an ordinary creditor an amount equal to the value of his interest in the dissolved partnership with interest, or, at his option or at the option of his legal representative, in lieu of interest, the profits attributable to the use of his right in the property of the dissolved partnership; provided that the creditors of the dissolved partnership as against the separate creditors, or the representative of the retired or deceased partner, shall have priority on any claim arising under this section, as provided by § 41 (8) of this Act.

§ 43. Accrual of Actions. The right to an account of his interest shall accrue to any partner, or his legal representative, as against the winding up partners or the surviving partners or the person or partnership continuing the business, at the date of dissolution, in the absence of any agreement to the contrary.

Selected Portions of the Uniform Limited Partnership Act*

(Note: This Act has been superseded by the Uniform Limited Partnership Act (1976) adopted by the National Conference of Commissioners on Uniform State Laws in August, 1976. The text of the revised Act is printed following this Act.)

§ 1. Limited Partnership Defined. A limited partnership is a partnership formed by two or more persons under the provisions of § 2, having as members one or more general partners and one or more limited partners. The limited partners as such shall not be bound by the obligations of the partnership.

§ 2. Formation. (1) Two or more persons desiring to form a limited partnership shall:

(a) Sign and swear to a certificate, which shall state:

I. The name of the partnership,

II. The character of the business,

III. The location of the principal place of business,

IV. The name and place of residence of each member; general and limited partners being respectively designated,

V. The term for which the partnership is to exist,

VI. The amount of cash and a description of and the agreed value of the other property contributed by each limited partner,

VII. The additional contributions, if any, agreed to be made by each limited partner and the times at which or events on the happening of which they shall be made,

VIII. The time, if agreed upon, when the contribution of each limited partner is to be returned,

IX. The share of the profits or the other compensation by way of income which each limited partner shall receive by reason of his contribution,

X. The right, if given, of a limited partner to substitute an assignee as contributor in his place, and the terms and conditions of the substitution,

XI. The right, if given, of the partners to admit additional limited partners,

XII. The right, if given, of one or more of the limited partners to priority over other limited partners, as to contributions or as to compensation by way of income, and the nature of such priority,

XIII. The right, if given, of the remaining general partner or partners to continue the business on the death, retirement or insanity of a general partner, and

XIV. The right, if given, of a limited partner to demand and receive property other than cash in return for his contribution.

(b) File for record the certificate in the office of [here designate the proper office].

(2) A limited partnership is formed if there has been substantial compliance in good faith with the requirements of paragraph (1).

§ 3. Business Which May Be Carried On. A limited partnership may carry on any business

*Reprinted with permission from the National Conference of Commissioners on Uniform State Laws.

which a partnership without limited partners may carry on, except [here designate the business to be prohibited].

§ 4. Character of Limited Partner's Contribution. The contributions of a limited partner may be cash or other property, but not services.

§ 5. A Name Not to Contain Surname of Limited Partner; Exceptions. (1) The surname of a limited partner shall not appear in the partnership name, unless:

(a) It is also the surname of a general partner, or

(b) Prior to the time when the limited partner became such the business had been carried on under a name in which his surname appeared.

(2) A limited partner whose name appears in a partnership name contrary to the provisions of paragraph (1) is liable as a general partner to partnership creditors who extend credit to the partnership without actual knowledge that he is not a general partner.

§ 6. Liability for False Statements in Certificate. If the certificate contains a false statement, one who suffers loss by reliance on such statement may hold liable any party to the certificate who knew the statement to be false:

(a) At the time he signed the certificate, or

(b) Subsequently, but within a sufficient time before the statement was relied upon to enable him to cancel or amend the certificate, or to file a petition for its cancellation or amendment as provided in § 25 (3).

§ 7. Limited Partner Not Liable to Creditors. A limited partner shall not become liable as a general partner unless, in addition to the exercise of his rights and powers as a limited partner, he takes part in the control of the business.

§ 8. Admission of Additional Limited Partners. After the formation of a limited partnership, additional limited partners may be admitted upon filling an amendment to the original certificate in accordance with the requirements of § 25.

§ 9. Rights, Powers and Liabilities of a General Partner. (1) A general partner shall have all the rights and powers and be subject to all the restrictions and liabilities of a partner in a partnership without limited partners, except that without the

written consent or ratification of the specific act by all the limited partners, a general partner or all of the general partners have no authority to:

(a) Do any act in contravention of the certificate,

(b) Do any act which would make it impossible to carry on the ordinary business of the partnership,

(c) Confess a judgment against the partnership,

(d) Possess partnership property, or assign their rights in specific partnership property, for other than a partnership purpose,

(e) Admit a person as a general partner,

(f) Admit a person as a limited partner, unless the right so to do is given in the certificate,

(g) Continue the business with partnership property on the death, retirement or insanity of a general partner, unless the right so to do is given in the certificate.

§ 10. Rights of a Limited Partner. (1) A limited partner shall have the same rights as a general partner to:

(a) Have the partnership books kept at the principal place of business of the partnership, and at all times to inspect and copy any of them;

(b) Have on demand true and full information of all things affecting the partnership, and a formal account of partnership affairs whenever circumstances render it just and reasonable, and

(c) Have dissolution and winding up by decree of court.

(2) A limited partner shall have the right to receive a share of the profits or other compensation by way of income, and to the return of his contribution as provided in §§ 15 and 16.

§ 11. Status of Person Erroneously Believing Himself a Limited Partner. A person who has contributed to the capital of a business conducted by a person or partnership erroneously believing that he has become a limited partner in a limited partnership, is not, by reason of his exercise of the rights of a limited partner, a general partner with the person or in the partnership carrying on the business, or bound by the obligations of such person or partnership; provided that on ascertaining the mistake he promptly renounces his interest in the profits of the business, or other compensation by way of income.

§ 12. One Person both General and Limited Partner. (1) A person may be a general partner and a limited partner in the same partnership at the same time.

(2) A person who is a general, and also at the same time a limited partner, shall have all the rights and powers and be subject to all the restrictions of a general partner; except that, in respect to his contribution, he shall have the rights against the other members which he would have had if he were not also a general partner.

§ 13. Loans and Other Business Transactions with Limited Partner. (1) A limited partner also may loan money to and transact other business with the partnership, and, unless he is also a general partner, receive on account of resulting claims against the partnership, with general creditors, a pro rata share of the assets. No limited partner shall in respect to any such claim:

(a) Receive or hold as collateral security any partnership property, or

(b) Receive from a general partner or the partnership any payment, conveyance, or release from liability, if at the time the assets of the partnership are not sufficient to discharge partnership liabilities to persons not claiming as general or limited partners,

(2) The receiving of collateral security, or a payment, conveyance, or release in violation of the provisions of paragraph (1) is a fraud on the creditors of the partnership.

§ 15. Compensation of Limited Partner. A limited partner may receive from the partnership the share of the profits or the compensation by way of income stipulated for in the certificate; provided, that after such payment is made, whether from the property of the partnership or that of a general partner, the partnership assets are in excess of all liabilities of the partnership except liabilities to limited partners on account of their contributions and to general partners.

§ 16. Withdrawal or Reduction of Limited Partner's Contribution. (1) A limited partner shall not receive from a general partner or out of partnership property any part of his contribution until:

(a) All liabilities of the partnership, except liabilities to general partners and to limited partners on account of their contributions, have been paid or there remains property of the partnership sufficient to pay them,

(b) The consent of all members is had, unless the return of the contribution may be rightfully demanded under the provisions of paragraph (2), and

(c) The certificate is cancelled or so amended as to set forth the withdrawal or reduction.

(2) Subject to the provisions of paragraph (1) a limited partner may rightfully demand the return of his contribution

(a) On the dissolution of a partnership, or

(b) When the date specified in the certificate for its return has arrived, or

(c) After he has given six months' notice in writing to all other members, if no time is specified in the certificate either for the return of the contribution or for the dissolution of the partnership,

(3) In the absence of any statement in the certificate to the contrary or the consent of all members, a limited partner, irrespective of the nature of his contribution, has only the right to demand and receive cash in return for his contribution.

(4) A limited partner may have the partnership dissolved and its affairs wound up when

(a) He rightfully but unsuccessfully demands the return of his contribution, or

(b) The other liabilities of the partnership have not been paid, or the partnership property is insufficient for their payment as required by paragraph (1a) and the limited partner would otherwise be entitled to the return of his contribution.

§ 17. Liability of Limited Partner to Partnership. (1) A limited partner is liable to the partnership:

(a) For the difference between his contribution as actually made and that stated in the certificate as having been made, and

(b) For any unpaid contribution which he agreed in the certificate to make in the future at the time and on the conditions stated in the certificate.

(2) A limited partner holds as trustee for the partnership:

(a) Specific property stated in the certificate as contributed by him, but which was not contributed or which has been wrongfully returned, and

(b) Money or other property wrongfully paid or conveyed to him on account of his contribution.

(3) The liabilities of a limited partner as set forth in this section can be waived or compromised only by the consent of all members; but a waiver or compromise shall not affect the right of a creditor of a partnership, who extended credit or whose claim arose after the filing and before a cancellation or amendment of the certificate, to enforce such liabilities.

(4) When a contributor has rightfully received the return in whole or in part of the capital of his contribution, he is nevertheless liable to the partnership for any sum, not in excess of such return with interest, necessary to discharge its liabilities to all creditors who extended credit or whose claims arose before such return.

§ 18.   Nature of Limited Partner's Interest in Partnership.   A limited partner's interest in the partnership is personal property.

§ 19.   Assignment of Limited Partner's Interest.   (1) A limited partner's interest is assignable.

(2) A substituted limited partner is a person admitted to all the rights of a limited partner who has died or has assigned his interest in a partnership.

(3) An assignee, who does not become a substituted limited partner, has no right to require any information or account of the partnership transactions or to inspect the partnership books; he is only entitled to receive the share of the profits or other compensation by way of income, or the return of his contribution, to which his assignor would otherwise be entitled.

(4) An assignee shall have the right to become a substituted limited partner if all the members (except the assignor) consent thereto or if the assignor, being thereunto empowered by the certificate, gives the assignee that right.

(5) An assignee becomes a substituted limited partner when the certificate is appropriately amended in accordance with § 25.

(6) The substituted limited partner has all the rights and powers, and is subject to all the restrictions and liabilities of his assignor, except those liabilities of which he was ignorant at the time he became a limited partner and which could not be ascertained from the certificate.

(7) The substitution of the assignee as a limited partner does not release the assignor from liability to the partnership under §§ 6 and 17.

§ 20.   Effect of Retirement, Death or Insanity of a General Partner.   The retirement, death or insanity of a general partner dissolves the partnership, unless the business is continued by the remaining general partners:

(a) Under a right so to do stated in the certificate, or

(b) With the consent of all members.

§ 21.   Death of Limited Partner.   (1) On the death of a limited partner his executor or administrator shall have all the rights of a limited partner for the purpose of settling his estate, and such power as the deceased had to constitute his assignee a substituted limited partner.

(2) The estate of a deceased limited partner shall be liable for all his liabilities as a limited partner.

§ 22.   Rights of Creditors of Limited Partner. (1) On due application to a court of competent jurisdiction by any judgment creditor of a limited partner, the court may charge the interest of the indebted limited partner with payment of the unsatisfied amount of the judgment debt; and may appoint a receiver, and make all other orders, directions, and inquiries which the circumstances of the case may require.

(2) The interest may be redeemed with the separate property of any general partner, but may not be redeemed with partnership property.

(3) The remedies conferred by paragraph (1) shall not be deemed exclusive of others which may exist.

(4) Nothing in this act shall be held to deprive a limited partner of his statutory exemption.

§ 23.   Distribution of Assets.   (1) In settling accounts after dissolution the liabilities of the partnership shall be entitled to payment in the following order:

(a) Those to creditors, in the order of priority as provided by law, except those to limited partners on account of their contributions, and to general partners,

(b) Those to limited partners in respect to their share of the profits and other compensation by way of income on their contributions,

(c) Those to limited partners in respect to the capital of their contributions,

(d) Those to general partners other than for capital and profits,

(e) Those to general partners in respect to profits,

(f) Those to general partners in respect to capital.

(2) Subject to any statement in the certificate or to subsequent agreement, limited partners share in the partnership assets in respect to their claims for capital, and in respect to their claims for profits or for compensation by way of income on their contributions respectively, in proportion to the respective amounts of such claims.

Selected Portions of the Uniform Limited Partnership Act* (1976)

ARTICLE 1 General Provisions

§ 101. Definitions. As used in this Act, unless the context otherwise requires:

(1) "Certificate of limited partnership" means the certificate referred to in Section 201, and the certificate as amended.

(2) "Contribution" means any cash, property, services rendered, or a promissory note or other binding obligation to contribute cash or property or to perform services, which a partner contributes to a limited partnership in his capacity as a partner.

(3) "Event of withdrawal of a general partner" means an event that causes a person to cease to be a general partner as provided in Section 402.

(4) "Foreign limited partnership" means a partnership formed under the laws of any State other than this State and having as partners one or more general partners and one or more limited partners.

(5) "General partner" means a person who has been admitted to a limited partnership as a general partner in accordance with the partnership agreement and named in the certificate of limited partnership as a general partner.

(6) "Limited partner" means a person who has been admitted to a limited partnership as a limited partner in accordance with the partnership agreement and named in the certificate of limited partnership as a limited partner.

(7) "Limited partnership" and "domestic limited partnership" means a partnership formed by 2 or more persons under the laws of this State and having one or more general partners and one or more limited partners.

(8) "Partner" means a limited or general partner.

(9) "Partnership agreement" means any valid agreement, written or oral, of the partners as to the affairs of a limited partnership and the conduct of its business.

(10) "Partnership interest" means a partner's share of the profits and losses of a limited partnership and the right to receive distributions of a partnership assets.

(11) "Person" means a natural person, partnership, limited partnership (domestic or foreign), trust, estate, association, or corporation.

(12) "State" means a state, territory, or possession of the United States, the District of Columbia, or the Commonwealth of Puerto Rico.

§ 102. Name. The name of each limited partnership as set forth in its certificate of limited partnership:

(1) shall contain without abbreviation the words "limited partnership";

(2) may not contain the name of a limited partner unless (i) it is also the name of a general partner or the corporate name of a corporate general partner, or (ii) the business of the limited partnership had been carried on under that name before the admission of that limited partner;

(3) may not contain any word or phrase indicating or implying that it is organized other than for a purpose stated in its certificate of limited partnership;

*Reprinted with permission from the National Conference of Commissioners on Uniform State Laws.

(4) may not be the same as, or deceptively similar to, the name of any corporation or limited partnership organized under the laws of this State or licensed or registered as a foreign corporation or limited partnership in this State; and

(5) may not contain the following words [here insert prohibited words].

§ 103.   Reservation of Name.

(a) The exclusive right to the use of a name may be reserved by:

(1) any person intending to organize a limited partnership under this Act and to adopt that name;

(2) any domestic limited partnership or any foreign limited partnership registered in this State which, in either case, intends to adopt that name;

(3) any foreign limited partnership intending to register in this State and adopt that name; and

(4) any person intending to organize a foreign limited partnership and intending to have it register in this State and adopt that name.

(b) The reservation shall be made by filing with the Secretary of State an application, executed by the applicant, to reserve a specified name. If the Secretary of State finds that the name is available for use by a domestic or foreign limited partnership, he shall reserve the name for the exclusive use of the applicant for a period of 120 days. Once having so reserved a name, the same applicant may not again reserve the same name until more than 60 days after the expiration of the last 120-day period for which that applicant reserved that name. The right to the exclusive use of a reserved name may be transferred to any other person by filing in the office of the Secretary of State a notice of the transfer, executed by the applicant for whom the name was reserved and specifying the name and address of the transferee.

§ 104.   Specified Office and Agent.   Each limited partnership shall continuously maintain in this State:

(1) an office, which may but need not be a place of its business in this State, at which shall be kept the records required by Section 105 to be maintained; and

(2) an agent for service of process on the limited partnership, which agent must be an individual resident of this State, a domestic corporation, or a foreign corporation authorized to do business in this State.

§ 105.   Records to be Kept.   Each limited partnership shall keep at the office referred to in Section 104(1) the following: (1) a current list of the full name and last known business address of each partner set forth in alphabetical order, (2) a copy of the certificate of limited partnership and all certificates of amendment thereto, together with executed copies of any powers of attorney pursuant to which any certificate has been executed, (3) copies of the limited partnership's federal, state and local income tax returns and reports, if any, for the 3 most recent years, and (4) copies of any then effective written partnership agreements and of any financial statements of the limited partnership for the 3 most recent years. Those records are subject to inspection and copying at the reasonable request, and at the expense, of any partner during ordinary business hours.

§ 106.   Nature of Business.   A limited partnership may carry on any business that a partnership without limited partners may carry on except [here designate prohibited activities].

§ 107.   Business Transactions of Partner with Partnership.   Except as provided in the partnership agreement, a partner may lend money to and transact other business with the limited partnership and, subject to other applicable law, has the same rights and obligations with respect thereto as a person who is not a partner.

ARTICLE 2   Formation: Certificate of Limited Partnership

§ 201.   Certificate of Limited Partnership.

(a) In order to form a limited partnership two or more persons must execute a certificate of limited partnership. The certificate shall be filed in the office of the Secretary of State and set forth:

(1) the name of the limited partnership;

(2) the general character of its business;

(3) the address of the office and the name and address of the agent for service of process required to be maintained by Section 104;

(4) the name and the business address of each partner (specifying separately the general partners and limited partners);

(5) the amount of cash and a description and statement of the agreed value of the other property

or services contributed by each partner and which each partner has agreed to contribute in the future;

(6) the times at which or events on the happening of which any additional contributions agreed to be made by each partner are to be made;

(7) any power of a limited partner to grant the right to become a limited partner to an assignee of any part of his partnership interest, and the terms and conditions of the power;

(8) if agreed upon, the time at which or the events on the happening of which a partner may terminate his membership in the limited partnership and the amount of, or the method of determining, the distribution to which he may be entitled respecting his partnership interest, and the terms and conditions of the termination and distribution;

(9) any right of a partner to receive distributions of property, including cash from the limited partnership;

(10) any right of a partner to receive, or of a general partner to make, distributions to a partner which include a return of all or any part of the partner's contribution;

(11) any time at which or events upon the happening of which the limited partnership is to be dissolved and its affairs wound up;

(12) any right of the remaining general partners to continue the business on the happening of an event of withdrawal of a general partner; and

(13) any other matters the partners determine to include therein.

(b) A limited partnership is formed at the time of the filing of the certificate of limited partnership in the office of the Secretary of State or at any later time specified in the certificate of limited partnership if, in either case, there has been substantial compliance with the requirements of this section.

§ 207.   Liability for False Statement in Certificate.   If any certificate of limited partnership or certificate of amendment or cancellation contains a false statement, one who suffers loss by reliance on the statement may recover damages for the loss from:

(1) any person who executes the certificate, or causes another to execute it on his behalf, and knew, and any general partner who knew or should have known, the statement to be false at the time the certificate was executed; and

(2) any general partner who thereafter knows or should have known that any arrangement or other fact described in the certificate has changed, making the statement inaccurate in any respect within a sufficient time before the statement was relied upon reasonably to have enabled that general partner to cancel or amend the certificate, or to file a petition for its cancellation or amendment under Section 205.

§ 208.   Notice.   The fact that a certificate of limited partnership is on file in the office of the Secretary of State is notice that the partnership is a limited partnership and the persons designated therein as limited partners are limited partners, but it is not notice of any other fact.

§ 209.   Delivery of Certificates to Limited Partners.   Upon the return by the Secretary of State pursuant to Section 206 of a certificate marked "Filed," the general partners shall promptly deliver or mail a copy of the certificate of limited partnership and each certificate to each limited partner unless the partnership agreement provides otherwise.

ARTICLE 3   Limited Partners

§ 301.   Admission of Additional Limited Partners.

(a) After the filing of a limited partnership's original certificate of limited partnership, a person may be admitted as an additional limited partner:

(1) in the case of a person acquiring a partnership interest directly from the limited partnership, upon the compliance with the partnership agreement or, if the partnership-agreement does not so provide, upon the written consent of all partners; and

(2) in the case of an assignee of a partnership interest of a partner who has the power, as provided in Section 704, to grant the assignee the right to become a limited partner, upon the exercise of that power and compliance with any conditions limiting the grant or exercise of the power.

(b) In each case under subsection (a), the person acquiring the partnership interest becomes a limited partner only upon amendment of the certificate of limited partnership reflecting that fact.

§ 302.   Voting.   Subject to Section 303, the

partnership agreement may grant to all or a specified group of the limited partners the right to vote (on a per capita or other basis) upon any matter.

§ 303. Liability to Third Parties.

(a) Except as provided in subsection (d), a limited partner is not liable for the obligations of a limited partnership unless he is also a general partner or, in addition to the exercise of his rights and powers as a limited partner, he takes part in the control of the business. However, if the limited partner's participation in the control of the business is not substantially the same as the exercise of the powers of a general partner, he is liable only to persons who transact business with the limited partnership with actual knowledge of his participation in control.

(b) A limited partner does not participate in the control of the business within the meaning of subsection (a) solely by doing one or more of the following:

(1) being a contractor for or an agent or employee of the limited partnership or of a general partner;

(2) consulting with and advising a general partner with respect to the business of the limited partnership;

(3) acting as surety for the limited partnership;

(4) approving or disapproving an amendment to the partnership agreement; or

(5) voting on one or more of the following matters;

(i) the dissolution and winding up of the limited partnership;

(ii) the sale, exchange, lease, mortgage, pledge, or other transfer of all or substantially all of the assets of the limited partnership other than in the ordinary course of its business;

(iii) the incurrence of indebtedness by the limited partnership other than in the ordinary course of its business;

(iv) a change in the nature of the business; or

(v) the removal of a general partner.

(c) The enumeration in subsection (b) does not mean that the possession or exercise of any other powers by a limited partner constitutes participation by him in the business of the limited partnership.

(d) A limited partner who knowingly permits his name to be used in the name of the limited partnership, except under circumstances permitted by Section 102(2)(i), is liable to creditors who extend credit to the limited partnership without actual knowledge that the limited partner is not a general partner.

§ 304. Person Erroneously Believing Himself Limited Partner.

(a) Except as provided in subsection (b), a person who makes a contribution to a business enterprise and erroneously but in good faith believes that he has become a limited partner in the enterprise is not a general partner in the enterprise and is not bound by its obligations by reason of making the contribution, receiving distributions from the enterprise, or exercising any rights of a limited partner, if, on ascertaining the mistake, he:

(1) causes an appropriate certificate of limited partnership or a certificate of amendment to be executed and filed; or

(2) withdraws from future equity participation in the enterprise.

(b) A person who makes a contribution of the kind described in subsection (a) is liable as a general partner to any third party who transacts business with the enterprise (i) before the person withdraws and an appropriate certificate is filed to show withdrawal, or (ii) before an appropriate certificate is filed to show his status as a limited partner and, in the case of an amendment, after expiration of the 30-day period for filing an amendment relating to the person as a limited partner under Section 202, but in either case only if the third party actually believed in good faith that the person was a general partner at the time of the transaction.

§ 305. Information. Each limited partner has the right to:

(1) inspect and copy any of the partnership records required to be maintained by Section 105; and

(2) obtain from the general partners from time to time upon reasonable demand (i) true and full information regarding the state of the business and financial condition of the limited partnership, (ii) promptly after becoming available, a copy of the limited partnership's federal, state and local income tax returns for each year, and (iii) other information regarding the affairs of the limited partnership as is just and reasonable.

ARTICLE 4   General Partners

§ 401. Admission of Additional General Partners. After the filing of a limited partnership's original certificate of limited partnership, additional general partners may be admitted only with the specific written consent of each partner.

§ 402. Events of Withdrawal. Except as approved by the specific written consent of all partners at the time, a person ceases to be a general partner of a limited partnership upon the happening of any of the following events:

(1) the general partner withdraws from the limited partnership as provided in Section 602;

(2) the general partner ceases to be a member of the limited partnership as provided in Section 702;

(3) the general partner is removed as a general partner in accordance with the partnership agreement;

(4) unless otherwise provided in the certificate of limited partnership, the general partner: (i) makes an assignment for the benefit of creditors; (ii) files a voluntary petition in bankruptcy; (iii) is adjudicated a bankrupt or insolvent; (iv) files a petition or answer seeking for himself any reorganization, arrangement, composition, readjustment, liquidation, dissolution or similar relief under any statute, law, or regulation; (v) files an answer or other pleading admitting or failing to contest the material allegations of a petition filed against him in any proceeding of this nature; or (vi) seeks, consents to, or acquiesces in the appointment of a trustee, receiver, or liquidator of the general partner or of all or any substantial part of his properties;

(5) unless otherwise provided in the certificate of limited partnership, [120] days after the commencement of any proceeding against the general partner seeking reorganization, arrangement, composition, readjustment, liquidation, dissolution or similar relief under any statute, law, or regulation, the proceeding has not been dismissed, or if within [90] days after the appointment without his consent or acquiescence of a trustee, receiver, or liquidator of the general partner or of all or any substantial part of his properties, the appointment is not vacated or stayed or within [90] days after the expiration of any such stay, the appointment is not vacated;

(i) his death; or

(ii) the entry by a court of competent jurisdiction adjudicating him incompetent to manage his person or his estate;

(7) in the case of a general partner who is acting as a general partner by virtue of being a trustee of a trust, the termination of the trust (but not merely the substitution of a new trustee);

(8) in the case of a general partner that is a separate partnership, the dissolution and commencement of winding up of the separate partnership;

(9) in the case of a general partner that is a corporation, the filing of a certificate of dissolution, or its equivalent, for the corporation or the revocation of its charter; or

(10) in the case of an estate, the distribution by the fiduciary of the estate's entire interest in the partnership.

§ 403. General Powers and Liabilities. Except as provided in this Act or in the partnership agreement, a general partner of a limited partnership has the rights and powers and is subject to the restrictions and liabilities of a partner in a partnership without limited partners.

§ 404. Contributions by General Partner. A general partner of a limited partnership may make contributions to the partnership and share in the profits and losses of, and in distributions from, the limited partnership as a general partner. A general partner also may make contributions to and share in the profits, losses, and distributions as a limited partner. A person who is both a general partner and a limited partner has the rights and powers, and is subject to the restrictions and liabilities, of a general partner and, except as provided in the partnership agreement, also has the powers, and is subject to the restrictions, of a limited partner to the extent of his participation in the partnership as a limited partner.

§ 405. Voting. The partnership agreement may grant to all or certain identified general partners the right to vote (on a per capita or any other basis), separately or with all or any class of the limited partners, on any matter.

ARTICLE 5   Finance

§ 501. Form of Contribution. The contribution of a partner may be in cash, property, or services rendered, or a promissory note or other obligation to contribute cash or property or to perform services.

§ 502.   Liability for Contribution.

(a) Except as provided in the certificate of limited partnership, a partner is obligated to the limited partnership to perform any promise to contribute cash or property or to perform services, even if he is unable to perform because of death, disability or any other reason. If a partner does not make the required contribution of property or services, he is obligated at the option of the limited partnership to contribute cash equal to that portion of the value (as stated in the certificate of limited partnership) of the stated contribution that has not been made.

(b) Unless otherwise provided in the partnership agreement, the obligation of a partner to make a contribution or return money or other property paid or distributed in violation of this Act may be compromised only by consent of all the partners. Notwithstanding the compromise, a creditor of a limited partnership who extends credit, or whose claim arises, after the filing of the certificate of limited partnership or an amendment thereto which, in either case, reflects the obligation, and before the amendment or cancellation thereof to reflect the compromise, may enforce the original obligation.

§ 503.   Sharing of Profits and Losses.

The profits and losses of a limited partnership shall be allocated among the partners, and among classes of partners, in the manner provided in the partnership agreement. If the partnership agreement does not so provide, profits and losses shall be allocated on the basis of the value (as stated in the certificate of limited partnership) of the contributions made by each partner to the extent they have been received by the partnership and have not been returned.

§ 504.   Sharing of Distributions.

Distributions of cash or other assets of a limited partnership shall be allocated among the partners, and among classes of partners, in the manner provided in the partnership agreement. If the partnership agreement does not so provide, distributions shall be made on the basis of the value (as stated in the certificate of limited partnership) of the contributions made by each partner to the extent they have been received by the partnership and have not been returned.

ARTICLE 6   Distributions and Withdrawal

§ 601.   Interim Distributions.

Except as provided in this Article, a partner is entitled to receive distributions from a limited partnership before his withdrawal from the limited partnership and before the dissolution and winding up thereof:

(1) to the extent and at the times or upon the happening of the events specified in the partnership agreement; and

(2) if any distribution constitutes a return of any part of his contribution under Section 608(c), to the extent and at the times or upon the happening of the events specified in the certificate of limited partnership.

§ 602.   Withdrawal of General Partner.

A general partner may withdraw from a limited partnership at any time by giving written notice to the other partners, but if the withdrawal violates the partnership agreement, the limited partnership may recover from the withdrawing general partner damages for breach of the partnership agreement and offset the damages against the amount otherwise distributable to him.

§ 603.   Withdrawal of Limited Partner.

A limited partner may withdraw from a limited partnership at the time or upon the happening of events specified in the certificate of limited partnership and in accordance with the partnership agreement. If the certificate does not specify the time or the events upon the happening of which a limited partner may withdraw or a definite time for the dissolution and winding up of the limited partnership, a limited partner may withdraw upon not less than 6 months' prior written notice to each general partner at his address on the books of the limited partnership at its office in this State.

§ 604.   Distribution Upon Withdrawal.

Except as provided in this Article, upon withdrawal any withdrawing partner is entitled to receive any distribution to which he is entitled under the partnership agreement and, if not otherwise provided in the agreement, he is entitled to receive, within a reasonable time after withdrawal, the fair value of his interest in the limited partnership as of the date of withdrawal based upon his right to share in distributions from the limited partnership.

§ 605.   Distribution in Kind.

Except as provided in the certificate of limited partnership, a partner, regardless of the nature of his contribution, has no right to demand and receive any distribution from a limited partnership in any form other than cash. Except as provided in the partnership agreement, a partner may not be compelled to accept a distribution of any asset in kind from a limited partnership to the extent that the percentage of the asset distributed to him exceeds a percentage of that asset which is equal to the percentage in which he shares in distributions from the limited partnership.

§ 606. Right to Distribution. At the time a partner becomes entitled to receive a distribution, he has the status of, and is entitled to all remedies available to, a creditor of the limited partnership with respect to the distribution.

§ 607. Limitations on Distribution. A partner may not receive a distribution from a limited partnership to the extent that, after giving effect to the distribution, all liabilities of the limited partnership, other than liabilities to partners on account of their partnership interests, exceed the fair value of the partnership assets.

§ 608. Liability Upon Return of Contribution.

(a) If a partner has received the return of any part of his contribution without violation of the partnership agreement or this Act, he is liable to the limited partnership for a period of one year thereafter for the amount of the returned contribution, but only to the extent necessary to discharge the limited partnership's liabilities to creditors who extended credit to the limited partnership during the period the contribution was held by the partnership.

(b) If a partner has received the return of any part of his contribution in violation of the partnership agreement or this Act, he is liable to the limited partnership for a period of 6 years thereafter for the amount of the contribution wrongfully returned.

(c) A partner receives a return of his contribution to the extent that a distribution to him reduces his share of the fair value of the net assets of the limited partnership below the value (as set forth in the certificate of limited partnership) of his contribution which has not been distributed to him.

ARTICLE 7   Assignment of Partnership Interests

§ 701. Nature of Partnership Interest. A partnership interest is personal property.

§ 702. Assignment of Partnership Interest. Except as provided in the partnership agreement, a partnership interest is assignable in whole or in part. An assignment of a partnership interest does not dissolve a limited partnership or entitle the assignee to become or to exercise any rights of a partner. An assignment entitles the assignee to receive, to the extent assigned, only the distribution to which the assignor would be entitled. Except as provided in the partnership agreement, a partner ceases to be a partner upon assignment of all his partnership interest.

§ 703. Rights of Creditor. On application to a court of competent jurisdiction by any judgment creditor of a partner, the court may charge the partnership interest of the partner with payment of the unsatisfied amount of the judgment with interest. To the extent so charged, the judgment creditor has only the rights of an assignee of the partnership interest. This Act does not deprive any partner of the benefit of any exemption laws applicable to his partnership interest.

§ 704. Right of Assignee to Become Limited Partner.

(a) An assignee of a partnership interest, including an assignee of a general partner, may become a limited partner if and to the extent that (1) the assignor gives the assignee that right in accordance with authority described in the certificate of limited partnership, or (2) all other partners consent.

(b) An assignee who has become a limited partner has, to the extent assigned, the rights and powers, and is subject to the restrictions and liabilities, of a limited partner under the partnership agreement and this Act. An assignee who becomes a limited partner also is liable for the obligations of his assignor to make and return contributions as provided in Article 6. However, the assignee is not obligated for liabilities unknown to the assignee at the time he became a limited partner and which could not be ascertained from the certificate of limited partnership.

(c) If an assignee of a partnership interest becomes a limited partner, the assignor is not released from his liability to the limited partnership under Sections 207 and 502.

§ 705.   Power of Estate of Deceased or Incompetent Partner.   If a partner who is an individual dies or a court of competent jurisdiction adjudges him to be incompetent to manage his person or his property, the partner's executor, administrator guardian, conservator, or other legal representative may exercise all the partner's rights for the purpose of settling his estate or administering his property, including any power the partner had to give an assignee the right to become a limited partner. If a partner is a corporation, trust, or other entity and is dissolved or terminated, the powers of that partner may be exercised by its legal representative or successor.

ARTICLE 8   Dissolution

§ 801.   Nonjudicial Dissolution.   A limited partnership is dissolved and its affairs shall be wound up upon the happening of the first to occur of the following:

(1) at the time or upon the happening of events specified in the certificate of limited partnership;

(2) written consent of all partners;

(3) an event of withdrawal of a general partner unless at the time there is at least one other general partner and the certificate of limited partnership permits the business of the limited partnership to be carried on by the remaining general partner and that partner does so, but the limited partnership is not dissolved and is not required to be wound up by reason of any event of withdrawal, if, within 90 days after the withdrawal, all partners agree in writing to continue the business of the limited partnership and to the appointment of one or more additional partners if necessary or desired; or

(4) entry of a decree of judicial dissolution under Section 802.

§ 802.   Judicial Dissolution.   On application by or for a partner the [here designate the proper court] court may decree dissolution of a limited partnership whenever it is not reasonably practicable to carry on the business in conformity with the partnership agreement.

§ 803.   Winding Up.   Except as provided in the partnership agreement, the general partners who have not wrongfully dissolved a limited partnership or, if none, the limited partners, may wind up the limited partnership's affairs; but the [here designate the proper court] court may wind up the limited partnership's affairs upon application of any partner, his legal representative, or assignee.

§ 804.   Distribution of Assets.   Upon the winding up of a limited partnership, the assets shall be distributed as follows:

(1) to creditors, including partners who are creditors, to the extent permitted by law, in satisfaction of liabilities of the limited partnership other than liabilities for distributions to partners under Section 601 or 604;

(2) except as provided in the partnership agreement, to partners and former partners in satisfaction of liabilities for distributions under Section 601 or 604; and

(3) except as provided in the partnership agreement, to partners *first* for the return of their contributions and *secondly* respecting their partnership interests, in the proportions in which the partners share in distributions.

Selected Portions of the Model Business Corporation Act

As Revised Through August 1977 And Amendments Through October 12, 1981
Prepared by the
Committee on Corporate Laws (Section
of Corporation, Banking and Business Law)
of the
AMERICAN BAR ASSOCIATION

Note: The following printing incorporates all amendments by the Committee through August, 1977. For convenience of reference, subsequent amendments are set forth separately at the end of the fully incorporated text. The separate amendments so set forth include amendments adopted through October 12, 1981. (The most recent amendment was adopted by the Committee on June 20, 1980.) Not included are proposed amendments which have not yet been officially adopted by the Committee. All proposed amendments and information regarding their final adoption are published in The Business Lawyer. Annotations may be found in the Model Business Corporation Act Annotated edited by the Committee on Corporate Laws and published

Authors' note concerning the Model Business Corporation Act: The Model Business Corporation Act is undergoing almost yearly amendment. The selected portions below are the latest that we could get (Summer, 1983). However, the value in the sections below is not the fact that they are current. Many state legislatures vary the provisions below. We have reproduced here most of the major provisions of the current model act so that you may appreciate how comprehensive this act is and get a general idea of how most states would probably treat a subject of corporation law. For a more thorough answer to any particular corporation-law question you may have, we direct your attention to your state's own system of corporation law. The most recent version of the Model Business Corporation Act may be found in the volumes of Martindale-Hubbell.

for the American Bar Foundation by West Publishing Company. The text of the Act has not been submitted either to the House of Delegates of the American Bar Association or the National Conference of Commissioners on Uniform State Laws for approval. . . .

This Act should be distinguished from the Model Business Corporation Act promulgated in 1928 as the "Uniform Business Corporation Act" by the Conference of Commissioners on Uniform State Laws which in 1943 was renamed "Model Business Corporation Act" and in 1957 was withdrawn.

§ 2. Definitions. As used in this Act, unless the context otherwise requires, the term:

(a) "Corporation" or "domestic corporation" means a corporation for profit subject to the provisions of this Act, except a foreign corporation.

(b) "Foreign corporation" means a corporation for profit organized under laws other than the laws of this State for a purpose or purposes for which a corporation may be organized under this Act.

(c) "Articles of incorporation" means the original or restated articles of incorporation or articles of consolidation and all amendments thereto including articles of merger.

(d) "Shares" means the units into which the proprietary interests in a corporation are divided.

(e) "Subscriber" means one who subscribes for shares in a corporation, whether before or after incorporation.

(f) "Shareholder" means one who is a holder of record of shares in a corporation. If the articles of incorporation or the by-laws so provide, the board of directors may adopt by resolution a procedure whereby a shareholder of the corporation may certify in writing to the corporation that all or a portion of the shares registered in the name of such shareholder are held for the account of a specified person or persons. The resolution shall set forth (1) the classification of shareholder who may certify, (2) the purpose or purposes for which the certification may be made, (3) the form of certification and information to be contained therein, (4) if the certification is with respect to a record date or closing of the stock transfer books, the time after the record date or closing of the stock transfer books within which the certification must be received by the corporation and (5) such other provisions with respect to the procedure as are deemed necessary or desirable. Upon receipt by the corporation of a certification complying with the procedure, the persons specified in the certification shall be deemed, for the purpose or purposes set forth in the certification, to be the holders of record of the number of shares specified in place of the shareholder making the certification.

(g) "Authorized shares" means the shares of all classes which the corporation is authorized to issue.

(h) "Treasury shares" means shares of a corporation which have been issued, have been subsequently acquired by and belong to the corporation, and have not, either by reason of the acquisition or thereafter, been cancelled or restored to the status of authorized but unissued shares. Treasury shares shall be deemed to be "issued" shares, but not "outstanding" shares.

(i) "Net assets" means the amount by which the total assets of a corporation exceed the total debts of the corporation.

(j) "Stated capital" means, at any particular time, the sum of (1) the par value of all shares of the corporation having a par value that have been issued, (2) the amount of the consideration received by the corporation for all shares of the corporation without par value that have been issued, except such part of the consideration therefor as may have been allocated to capital surplus in a manner permitted by law, and (3) such amounts not included in clauses (1) and (2) of this paragraph as have been transferred to stated capital of the corporation, whether upon the issue of shares as a share dividend or otherwise, minus all reductions from such sum as have been effected in a manner permitted by law. Irrespective of the manner of designation thereof by the laws under which a foreign corporation is organized, the stated capital of a foreign corporation shall be determined on the same basis and in the same manner as the stated capital of a domestic corporation, for the purpose of computing fees, franchise taxes and other charges imposed by this Act.

(k) "Surplus" means the excess of the net assets of a corporation over its stated capital.

(l) "Earned surplus" means the portion of the surplus of a corporation equal to the balance of its net profits, income, gains and losses from the date of incorporation, or from the latest date when a deficit was eliminated by an application of its capital surplus or stated capital or otherwise, after deducting subsequent distributions to shareholders and transfers to stated capital and capital surplus to the extent such distributions and transfers are made out of earned surplus. Earned surplus shall include also any portion of surplus allocated to earned surplus in mergers, consolidations or acquisitions of all or substantially all of the outstanding shares or of the property and assets of another corporation, domestic or foreign.

(m) "Capital surplus" means the entire surplus of a corporation other than its earned surplus.

(n) "Insolvent" means inability of a corporation to pay its debts as they become due in the usual course of its business.

(o) "Employee" includes officers but not directors. A director may accept duties which make him also an employee.

§ 3. Purposes. Corporations may be organized under this Act for any lawful purpose or purposes, except for the purpose of banking or insurance.

§ 4. General Powers. Each corporation shall have power:

(a) To have perpetual succession by its corporate name unless a limited period of duration is stated in its articles of incorporation.

(b) To sue and be sued, complain and defend, in its corporate name.

(c) To have a corporate seal which may be altered at pleasure, and to use the same by causing it, or a facsimile thereof, to be impressed or affixed or in any other manner reproduced.

(d) To purchase, take, receive, lease, or otherwise acquire, own, hold, improve, use and otherwise deal in and with, real or personal property, or any interest therein, wherever situated.

(e) To sell, convey, mortgage, pledge, lease, exchange, transfer and otherwise dispose of all or any part of its property and assets.

(f) To lend money and use its credit to assist its employees.

(g) To purchase, take, receive, subscribe for, or otherwise acquire, own, hold, vote, use, employ, sell, mortgage, lend, pledge, or otherwise dispose of, and otherwise use and deal in and with, shares or other interests in, or obligations of, other domestic or foreign corporations, associations, partnerships or individuals, or direct or indirect obligations of the United States or of any other government, state, territory, governmental district or municipality or of any instrumentality thereof.

(h) To make contracts and guarantees and incur liabilities, borrow money at such rates of interest as the corporation may determine, issue its notes, bonds, and other obligations, and secure any of its obligations by mortgage or pledge of all or any of its property, franchises and income.

(i) To lend money for its corporate purposes, invest and reinvest its funds, and take and hold real and personal property as security for the payment of funds so loaned or invested.

(j) To conduct its business, carry on its operations and have offices and exercise the powers granted by this Act, within or without this State.

(k) To elect or appoint officers and agents of the corporation, and define their duties and fix their compensation.

(l) To make and alter by-laws, not inconsistent with its articles of incorporation or with the laws of this State, for the administration and regulation of the affairs of the corporation.

(m) To make donations for the public welfare or for charitable, scientific or educational purposes.

(n) To transact any lawful business which the board of directors shall find will be in aid of governmental policy.

(o) To pay pensions and establish pension plans, pension trusts, profit sharing plans, stock bonus plans, stock option plans and other incentive plans for any or all of its directors, officers and employees.

(p) To be a promoter, partner, member, associate, or manager of any partnership, joint venture, trust or other enterprise.

(q) To have and exercise all powers necessary or convenient to effect its purposes.

§ 6. Right of Corporation to Acquire and Dispose of its Own Shares. A corporation shall have the right to purchase, take, receive or otherwise acquire, hold, own, pledge, transfer or otherwise dispose of its own shares, but purchases of its own shares, whether direct or indirect, shall be made only to the extent of unreserved and unrestricted earned surplus available therefor, and, if the articles of incorporation so permit or with the affirmative vote of the holders of a majority of all shares entitled to vote thereon, to the extent of unreserved and unrestricted capital surplus available therefor.

To the extent that earned surplus or capital surplus is used as the measure of the corporation's right to purchase its own shares, such surplus shall be restricted so long as such shares are held as treasury shares, and upon the disposition or cancellation of any such shares the restriction shall be removed pro tanto.

Notwithstanding the foregoing limitation, a corporation may purchase or otherwise acquire its own shares for the purpose of:

(a) Eliminating fractional shares.

(b) Collecting or compromising indebtedness to the corporation.

(c) Paying dissenting shareholders entitled to payment for their shares under the provisions of this Act.

(d) Effecting, subject to the other provisions of this Act, the retirement of its redeemable shares by redemption or by purchase at not to exceed the redemption price.

No purchase of or payment for its own shares shall be made at a time when the corporation is insolvent or when such purchase or payment would make it insolvent.

§ 7. Defense of Ultra Vires. No act of a corporation and no conveyance or transfer of real or personal property to or by a corporation shall be invalid by reason of the fact that the corporation was without capacity or power to do such act or to make or receive such conveyance or transfer, but such lack of capacity or power may be asserted:

(a) In a proceeding by a shareholder against the corporation to enjoin the doing of any act or the transfer of real or personal property by or to the corporation. If the unauthorized act or transfer sought to be enjoined is being, or is to be, performed or made pursuant to a contract to which the corporation is a party, the court may, if all of the parties to the contract are parties to the proceeding and if it deems the same to be equitable, set aside and enjoin the performance of such contract, and in so doing may allow to the corporation or to the other parties to the contract, as the case may be, compensation for the loss or damage sustained by either of them which may result from the action of the court in setting aside and enjoining the performance of such contract, but anticipated profits to be derived from the performance of the contract shall not be awarded by the court as a loss or damage sustained.

(b) In a proceeding by the corporation, whether acting directly or through a receiver, trustee, or other legal representative, or through shareholders in a representative suit, against the incumbent or former officers or directors of the corporation.

(c) In a proceeding by the Attorney General, as provided in this Act, to dissolve the corporation, or in a proceeding by the Attorney General to enjoin the corporation from the transaction of unauthorized business.

§ 8.   Corporate Name.

The corporate name:

(a) Shall contain the word "corporation," "company," "incorporated" or "limited," or shall contain an abbreviation of one of such words.

(b) Shall not contain any word or phrase which indicates or implies that it is organized for any purpose other than one or more of the purposes contained in its articles of incorporation.

(c) Shall not be the same as, or deceptively similar to, the name of any domestic corporation existing under the laws of this State or any foreign corporation authorized to transact business in this State, or a name the exclusive right to which is, at the time, reserved in the manner provided in this Act, or the name of a corporation which has in ef-

fect a registration of its corporate name as provided in this Act, except that this provision shall not apply if the applicant files with the Secretary of State either of the following: (1) the written consent of such other corporation or holder of a reserved or registered name to use the same or deceptively similar name and one or more words are added to make such name distinguishable from such other name, or (2) a certified copy of a final decree of a court of competent jurisdiction establishing the prior right of the applicant to the use of such name in this State.

A corporation with which another corporation, domestic or foreign, is merged, or which is formed by the reorganization or consolidation of one or more domestic or foreign corporations or upon a sale, lease or other disposition to or exchange with, a domestic corporation of all or substantially all the assets of another corporation, domestic or foreign, including its name, may have the same name as that used in this State by any of such corporations if such other corporation was organized under the laws of, or is authorized to transact business in, this State.

§ 12.   Registration Office and Registered Agent.

Each corporation shall have and continuously maintain in this State:

(a) A registered office which may be, but need not be, the same as its place of business.

(b) A registered agent, which agent may be either an individual resident in this State whose business office is identical with such registered office, or a domestic corporation, or a foreign corporation authorized to transact business in this State, having a business office identical with such registered office.

§ 14.   Service of Process on Corporation.

The registered agent so appointed by a corporation shall be an agent of such corporation upon whom any process, notice or demand required or permitted by law to be served upon the corporation may be served.

Whenever a corporation shall fail to appoint or maintain a registered agent in this State, or whenever its registered agent cannot with reasonable diligence be found at the registered office, then the Secretary of State shall be an agent of such corporation upon whom any such process, notice, or demand may be served. Service on the Secretary of State of any such process, notice, or demand shall be made by delivering to and leaving with him, or with any clerk having charge of the corporation department of his office, duplicate copies of such process, notice or demand. In the event any such process, notice or demand is served on the Secretary of State, he shall immediately cause one of the copies thereof to be forwarded by registered mail, addressed to the corporation at its registered office. Any service so had on the Secretary of State shall be returnable in not less than thirty days.

The Secretary of State shall keep a record of all processes, notices and demands served upon him under this section, and shall record therein the time of such service and his action with reference thereto.

Nothing herein contained shall limit or affect the right to serve any process, notice or demand required or permitted by law to be served upon a corporation in any other manner now or hereafter permitted by law.

§ 15. Authorized Shares.

§ 15. Authorized Shares. Each corporation shall have power to create and issue the number of shares stated in its articles of incorporation. Such shares may be divided into one or more classes, any or all of which classes may consist of shares with par value or shares without par value, with such designations, preferences, limitations, and relative rights as shall be stated in the articles of incorporation. The articles of incorporation may limit or deny the voting rights of or provide special voting rights for the shares of any class to the extent not inconsistent with the provisions of this Act.

Without limiting the authority herein contained, a corporation, when so provided in its articles of incorporation, may issue shares of preferred or special classes:

(a) Subject to the right of the corporation to redeem any of such shares at the price fixed by the articles of incorporation for the redemption thereof.

(b) Entitling the holders thereof to cumulative, noncumulative or partially cumulative dividends.

(c) Having preference over any other class or classes of shares as to the payment of dividends.

(d) Having preference in the assets of the corporation over any other class or classes of shares upon the voluntary or involuntary liquidation of the corporation.

(e) Convertible into shares of any other class or into shares of any series of the same or any other class, except a class having prior or superior rights and preferences as to dividends or distribution of assets upon liquidation, but shares without par value shall not be converted into shares with par value unless that part of the stated capital of the corporation represented by such shares without par value is, at the time of conversion, at least equal to the aggregate par value of the shares into which the shares without par value are to be converted or the amount of any such deficiency is transferred from surplus to stated capital.

§ 18. Consideration for Shares. Shares having a par value may be issued for such consideration expressed in dollars, not less than the par value thereof, as shall be fixed from time to time by the board of directors.

Shares without par value may be issued for such consideration expressed in dollars as may be fixed from time to time by the board of directors unless the articles of incorporation reserve to the shareholders the right to fix the consideration. In the event that such right be reserved as to any shares, the shareholders shall, prior to the issuance of such shares, fix the consideration to be received for such shares, by a vote of the holders of a majority of all shares entitled to vote thereon.

Treasury shares may be disposed of by the corporation for such consideration expressed in dollars as may be fixed from time to time by the board of directors.

That part of the surplus of a corporation which is transferred to stated capital upon the issuance of shares as a share dividend shall be deemed to be the consideration for the issuance of such shares.

In the event of the issuance of shares upon the conversion or exchange of indebtedness or shares, the consideration for the shares so issued shall be (1) the principal sum of, and accrued interest on, the indebtedness so exchanged or converted, or the stated capital then represented by the shares so exchanged or converted, and (2) that part of surplus, if any, transferred to stated capital upon the issuance of shares for the shares so exchanged or converted, and (3) any additional consideration paid to the corporation upon the issuance of shares for the indebtedness or shares so exchanged or converted.

§ 19. Payment for Shares. The consideration for the issuance of shares may be paid, in whole or in part, in cash, in other property, tangible or intangible, or in labor or services actually performed for the corporation. When payment of the consideration for which shares are to be issued shall have been received by the corporation, such shares shall be deemed to be fully paid and non-assessable.

Neither promissory notes nor future services shall constitute payment or part payment for the issuance of shares of a corporation.

In the absence of fraud in the transaction, the judgment of the board of directors or the shareholders, as the case may be, as to the value of the consideration received for shares shall be conclusive.

§ 20.   **Stock Rights and Options.**   Subject to any provisions in respect thereof set forth in its articles of incorporation, a corporation may create and issue, whether or not in connection with the issuance and sale of any of its shares or other securities, rights or options entitling the holders thereof to purchase from the corporation shares of any class or classes. Such rights or options shall be evidenced in such manner as the board of directors shall approve and, subject to the provisions of the articles of incorporation, shall set forth the terms upon which, the time or times within which and the price or prices at which such shares may be purchased from the corporation upon the exercise of any such right or option. If such rights or options are to be issued to directors, officers or employees as such of the corporation or of any subsidiary thereof, and not to the shareholders generally, their issuance shall be approved by the affirmative vote of the holders of a majority of the shares entitled to vote thereon or shall be authorized by and consistent with a plan approved or ratified by such a vote of shareholders. In the absence of fraud in the transaction, the judgment of the board of directors as to the adequacy of the consideration received for such rights or options shall be conclusive. The price or prices to be received for any shares having a par value, other than treasury shares to be issued upon the exercise of such rights or options, shall not be less than the par value thereof.

§ 21.   **Determination of Amount of Stated Capital.**   In case of the issuance by a corporation of shares having a par value, the consideration received therefor shall constitute stated capital to the extent of the par value of such shares, and the ex-

cess, if any, of such consideration shall constitute capital surplus.

In case of the issuance by a corporation of shares without par value, the entire consideration received therefor shall constitute stated capital unless the corporation shall determine as provided in this section that only a part thereof shall be stated capital. Within a period of sixty days after the issuance of any shares without par value, the board of directors may allocate to capital surplus any portion of the consideration received for the issuance of such shares. No such allocation shall be made of any portion of the consideration received for shares without par value having a preference in the assets of the corporation in the event of involuntary liquidation except the amount, if any, of such consideration in excess of such preference.

If shares have been or shall be issued by a corporation in merger or consolidation or in acquisition of all or substantially all of the outstanding shares or of the property and assets of another corporation, whether domestic or foreign, any amount that would otherwise constitute capital surplus under the foregoing provisions of this section may instead be allocated to earned surplus by the board of directors of the issuing corporation except that its aggregate earned surplus shall not exceed the sum of the earned surpluses as defined in this Act of the issuing corporation and of all other corporations, domestic or foreign, that were merged or consolidated or of which the shares or assets were acquired.

The stated capital of a corporation may be increased from time to time by resolution of the board of directors directing that all or part of the surplus of the corporation be transferred to stated capital. The board of directors may direct that the amount of the surplus so transferred shall be deemed to be stated capital in respect of any designated class of shares.

§ 22.   **Expenses of Organization, Reorganization and Financing.**   The reasonable charges and expenses of organization or reorganization of a corporation, and the reasonable expenses of and compensation for the sale or underwriting of its shares, may be paid or allowed by such corporation out of the consideration received by it in payment for its shares without thereby rendering such shares not fully paid or assessable.

§ 23. Certificates Representing Shares. The shares of a corporation shall be represented by certificates signed by the president or a vice president and the secretary or an assistant secretary of the corporation, and may be sealed with the seal of the corporation or a facsimile thereof. The signatures of the president or vice president and the secretary or assistant secretary upon a certificate may be facsimiles if the certificate is manually signed on behalf of a transfer agent or a registrar, other than the corporation itself or an employee of the corporation. In case any officer who has signed or whose facsimile signature has been placed upon such certificate shall have ceased to be such officer before such certificate is issued, it may be issued by the corporation with the same effect as if he were such officer at the date of its issue.

Every certificate representing shares issued by a corporation which is authorized to issue shares of more than one class shall set forth upon the face or back of the certificate, or shall state that the corporation will furnish to any shareholder upon request and without charge, a full statement of the designations, preferences, limitations, and relative rights of the shares of each class authorized to be issued, and if the corporation is authorized to issue any preferred or special class in series, the variations in the relative rights and preferences between the shares of each such series so far as the same have been fixed and determined and the authority of the board of directors to fix and determine the relative rights and preferences of subsequent series.

Each certificate representing shares shall state upon the face thereof:

(a) That the corporation is organized under the laws of this State.

(b) The name of the person to whom issued.

(c) The number and class of shares, and the designation of the series, if any, which such certificate represents.

(d) The par value of each share represented by such certificate, or a statement that the shares are without par value.

No certificate shall be issued for any share until such share is fully paid.

§ 25. Liability of Subscribers and Shareholders. A holder of or subscriber to shares of a corporation shall be under no obligation to the corporation or its creditors with respect to such shares other than the obligation to pay to the corporation the full consideration for which such shares were issued or to be issued.

Any person becoming an assignee or transferee of shares or of a subscription for shares in good faith and without knowledge or notice that the full consideration therefor has not been paid shall not be personally liable to the corporation or its creditors for any unpaid portion of such consideration.

An executor, administrator, conservator, guardian, trustee, assignee for the benefit of creditors, or receiver shall not be personally liable to the corporation as a holder of or subscriber to shares of a corporation but the estate and funds in his hands shall be so liable.

No pledgee or other holder of shares as collateral security shall be personally liable as a shareholder.

§ 26. Shareholders' Preemptive Rights. The shareholders of a corporation shall have no preemptive right to acquire unissued or treasury shares of the corporation, or securities of the corporation convertible into or carrying a right to subscribe to or acquire shares, except to the extent, if any, that such right is provided in the articles of incorporation.

Alternative § 26A. Shareholders' Preemptive Rights. Except to the extent limited or denied by this section or by the articles of incorporation, shareholders shall have a preemptive right to acquire unissued or treasury shares or securities convertible into such shares or carrying a right to subscribe to or acquire shares.

Unless otherwise provided in the articles of incorporation,

(a) No preemptive right shall exist

(1) to acquire any shares issued to directors, officers or employees pursuant to approval by the affirmative vote of the holders of a majority of the shares entitled to vote thereon or when authorized by and consistent with a plan theretofore approved by such a vote of shareholders; or

(2) to acquire any shares sold otherwise than for cash.

(b) Holders of shares of any class that is preferred or limited as to dividends or assets shall not be entitled to any preemptive right.

(c) Holders of shares of common stock shall

not be entitled to any preemptive right to shares of any class that is preferred or limited as to dividends or assets or to any obligations, unless convertible into shares of common stock or carrying a right to subscribe to or acquire shares of common stock.

(d) Holders of common stock without voting power shall have no preemptive right to shares of common stock with voting power.

(e) The preemptive right shall be only an opportunity to acquire shares or other securities under such terms and conditions as the board of directors may fix for the purpose of providing a fair and reasonable opportunity for the exercise of such right.

§ 27.   By-Laws.   The initial by-laws of a corporation shall be adopted by its board of directors. The power to alter, amend or repeal the by-laws or adopt new by-laws, subject to repeal or change by action of the shareholders, shall be vested in the board of directors unless reserved to the shareholders by the articles of incorporation. The by-laws may contain any provisions for the regulation and management of the affairs of the corporation not inconsistent with law or the articles of incorporation.

§ 28.   Meetings of Shareholders.   Meetings of shareholders may be held at such place within or without this State as may be stated in or fixed in accordance with the by-laws. If no other place is stated or so fixed, meetings shall be held at the registered office of the corporation.

An annual meeting of the shareholders shall be held at such time as may be stated in or fixed in accordance with the by-laws. If the annual meeting is not held within any thirteen-month period the Court of . . . may, on the application of any shareholder, summarily order a meeting to be held.

A special meeting of the shareholders may be called by the board of directors, the holders of not less than one-tenth of all the shares entitled to vote at the meeting, or such other persons as may be authorized in the articles of incorporation or the by-laws.

§ 29.   Notice of Shareholders' Meetings. Written notice stating the place, day and hour of the meeting and, in case of a special meeting, the purpose or purposes for which the meeting is called, shall be delivered not less than ten nor more than fifty days before the date of the meeting, either personally or by mail, by or at the direction of the president, the secretary, or the officer or persons calling

the meeting, to each shareholder of record entitled to vote at such meeting. If mailed, such notice shall be deemed to be delivered when deposited in the United States mail addressed to the shareholder at his address as it appears on the stock transfer books of the corporation, with postage thereon prepaid.

§ 30.   Closing of Transfer Books and Fixing Record Date.   For the purpose of determining shareholders entitled to notice of or to vote at any meeting of shareholders or any adjournment thereof, or entitled to receive payment of any dividend, or in order to make a determination of shareholders for any other proper purpose, the board of directors of a corporation may provide that the stock transfer books shall be closed for a stated period but not to exceed, in any case, fifty days. If the stock transfer books shall be closed for the purpose of determining shareholders entitled to notice of or to vote at a meeting of shareholders, such books shall be closed for at least ten days immediately preceding such meeting. In lieu of closing the stock transfer books, the by-laws, or in the absence of an applicable by-law the board of directors, may fix in advance a date as the record date for any such determination of shareholders, such date in any case to be not more than fifty days and, in case of a meeting of shareholders, not less than ten days prior to the date on which the particular action, requiring such determination of shareholders, is to be taken. If the stock transfer books are not closed and no record date is fixed for the determination of shareholders entitled to notice of or to vote at a meeting of shareholders, or shareholders entitled to receive payment of a dividend, the date on which notice of the meeting is mailed or the date on which the resolution of the board of directors declaring such dividend is adopted, as the case may be, shall be the record date for such determination of shareholders. When a determination of shareholders entitled to vote at any meeting of shareholders has been made as provided in this section, such determination shall apply to any adjournment thereof.

§ 31.   Voting Record.   The officer or agent having charge of the stock transfer books for shares of a corporation shall make a complete record of the shareholders entitled to vote at such meeting or any adjournment thereof, arranged in alphabetical order, with the address of and the number of shares held by each. Such record shall be produced and kept open at the time and place of the meeting and shall be subject to the inspection of any shareholder during the whole time of the meeting for the purposes thereof.

Failure to comply with the requirements of this section shall not affect the validity of any action taken at such meeting.

An officer or agent having charge of the stock transfer books who shall fail to prepare the record of shareholders, or produce and keep it open for inspection at the meeting, as provided in this section, shall be liable to any shareholder suffering damage on account of such failure, to the extent of such damage.

§ 32.   Quorum of Shareholders.   Unless otherwise provided in the articles of incorporation, a majority of the shares entitled to vote, represented in person or by proxy, shall constitute a quorum at a meeting of shareholders, but in no event shall a quorum consist of less than one-third of the shares entitled to vote at the meeting. If a quorum is present, the affirmative vote of the majority of the shares represented at the meeting and entitled to vote on the subject matter shall be the act of the shareholders, unless the vote of a greater number or voting by classes is required by this Act or the articles of incorporation or by-laws.

§ 33.   Voting of Shares.   Each outstanding share, regardless of class, shall be entitled to one vote on each matter submitted to a vote at a meeting of shareholders, except as may be otherwise provided in the articles of incorporation. If the articles of incorporation provide for more or less than one vote for any share, on any matter, every reference in this Act to a majority or other proportion of shares shall refer to such a majority or other proportion of votes entitled to be cast.

Neither treasury shares, nor shares held by another corporation if a majority of the shares entitled to vote for the election of directors of such other corporation is held by the corporation, shall be voted at any meeting or counted in determining the total number of outstanding shares at any given time.

A shareholder may vote either in person or by proxy executed in writing by the shareholder or by his duly authorized attorney-in-fact. No proxy shall be valid after eleven months from the date of its execution, unless otherwise provided in the proxy.

[Either of the following prefatory phrases may be inserted here: "The articles of incorporation may provide that" or "Unless the articles of incorporation otherwise provide"] . . . at each election for directors every shareholder entitled to vote at such election shall have the right to vote, in person or by proxy, the number of shares owned by him for as many persons as there are directors to be elected and for whose election he has a right to vote, or to cumulate his votes by giving one candidate as many votes as the number of such directors multiplied by the number of his shares shall equal, or by distributing such votes on the same principle among any number of such candidates.

Shares standing in the name of another corporation, domestic or foreign, may be voted by such officer, agent or proxy as the by-laws of such other corporation may prescribe, or, in the absence of such provision, as the board of directors of such other corporation may determine.

Shares held by an administrator, executor, guardian or conservator may be voted by him, either in person or by proxy, without a transfer of such shares into his name. Shares standing in the name of a trustee may be voted by him, either in person or by proxy, but no trustee shall be entitled to vote shares held by him without a transfer of such shares into his name.

Shares standing in the name of a receiver may be voted by such receiver, and shares held by or under the control of a receiver may be voted by such receiver without the transfer thereof into his name if authority so to do be contained in an appropriate order of the court by which such receiver was appointed.

A shareholder whose shares are pledged shall be entitled to vote such shares until the shares have been transferred into the name of the pledgee, and thereafter the pledgee shall be entitled to vote the shares so transferred.

On and after the date on which written notice of redemption of redeemable shares has been mailed to the holders thereof and a sum sufficient to redeem such shares has been deposited with a bank or trust company with irrevocable instruction and authority to pay the redemption price to the holders thereof upon surrender of certificates therefor, such shares shall not be entitled to vote on any matter and shall not be deemed to be outstanding shares.

§ 34.   Voting Trusts and Agreements Among Shareholders.   Any number of shareholders of a corporation may create a voting trust for the purpose of conferring upon a trustee or trustees the right to vote or otherwise represent their shares, for a period of not to exceed ten years, by entering into a written voting trust agreement specifying the terms and conditions of the voting trust, by depositing a counterpart of the agreement with the corporation at its registered office, and by transferring their shares to such trustee or trustees for the purposes of the agreement. Such trustee or trustees shall keep a record of the holders of voting trust certificates evidencing a beneficial interest in the voting trust, giving the names and addresses of all such holders and the number and class of the shares in respect of which the voting trust certificates held by each are issued, and shall deposit a copy of such record with the corporation at its registered office. The counterpart of the voting trust agreement and the copy of such record so deposited with the corporation shall be subject to the same right of examination by a shareholder of the corporation, in person or by agent or attorney, as are the books and records of the corporation, and such counterpart and such copy of such record shall be subject to examination by any holder of record of voting trust certificates, either in person or by agent or attorney, at any reasonable time for any proper purpose.

Agreements among shareholders regarding the voting of their shares shall be valid and enforceable in accordance with their terms. Such agreements shall not be subject to the provisions of this section regarding voting trusts.

§ 35.   Board of Directors.   All corporate powers shall be exercised by or under authority of, and the business and affairs of a corporation shall be managed under the direction of, a board of directors except as may be otherwise provided in this Act or the articles of incorporation. If any such provision is made in the articles of incorporation, the powers and duties conferred or imposed upon the board of directors by this Act shall be exercised or performed to such extent and by such person or persons as shall be provided in the articles of incorporation. Directors need not be residents of this State or shareholders of the corporation unless the articles of incorporation or by-laws so require. The articles of incorporation or by-laws may prescribe other qualifications for directors. The board of directors shall have authority to fix the compensation of directors unless otherwise provided in the articles of incorporation.

A director shall perform his duties as a director, including his duties as a member of any committee of the board upon which he may serve, in good faith, in a manner he reasonably believes to be in the best interests of the corporation, and with such care as an ordinarily prudent person in a like position would use under similar circumstances. In performing his duties, a director shall be entitled to rely on information, opinions, reports or statements, including financial statements and other financial data, in each case prepared or presented by:

(a) one or more officers or employees of the corporation whom the director reasonably believes to be reliable and competent in the matters presented.

(b) counsel, public accountants or other persons as to matters which the director reasonably believes to be within such person's professional or expert competence, or

(c) a committee of the board upon which he does not serve, duly designated in accordance with a provision of the articles of incorporation or the by-laws, as to matters within its designated authority, which committee the director reasonably believes to merit confidence,

but he shall not be considered to be acting in good faith if he has knowledge concerning the matter in question that would cause such reliance to be unwarranted. A person who so performs his duties shall have no liability by reason of being or having been a director of the corporation.

A director of a corporation who is present at a meeting of its board of directors at which action on any corporate matter is taken shall be presumed to have assented to the action taken unless his dissent shall be entered in the minutes of the meeting or unless he shall file his written dissent to such action with the secretary of the meeting before the adjournment thereof or shall forward such dissent by registered mail to the secretary of the corporation immediately after the adjournment of the meeting. Such right to dissent shall not apply to a director who voted in favor of such action.

§ 36.   Number and Election of Directors.
The board of directors of a corporation shall consist

of one or more members. The number of directors shall be fixed by, or in the manner provided in, the articles of incorporation or the by-laws, except as to the number constituting the initial board of directors, which number shall be fixed by the articles of incorporation. The number of directors may be increased or decreased from time to time by amendment to, or in the manner provided in, the articles of incorporation or the by-laws, but no decrease shall have the effect of shortening the term of any incumbent director. In the absence of a by-law providing for the number of directors, the number shall be the same as that provided for in the articles of incorporation. The names and addresses of the members of the first board of directors shall be stated in the articles of incorporation. Such persons shall hold office until the first annual meeting of shareholders, and until their successors shall have been elected and qualified. At the first annual meeting of shareholders and at each annual meeting thereafter the shareholders shall elect directors to hold office until the next succeeding annual meeting, except in case of the classification of directors as permitted by this Act. Each director shall hold office for the term for which he is elected and until his successor shall have been elected and qualified.

§ 37.   Classification of Directors.

When the board of directors shall consist of nine or more members, in lieu of electing the whole number of directors annually, the articles of incorporation may provide that the directors be divided into either two or three classes, each class to be as nearly equal in number as possible, the term of office of directors of the first class to expire at the first annual meeting of shareholders after their election, that of the second class to expire at the second annual meeting after their election, and that of the third class, if any, to expire at the third annual meeting after their election. At each annual meeting after such classification the number of directors equal to the number of the class whose term expires at the time of such meeting shall be elected to hold office until the second succeeding annual meeting, if there be two classes, or until the third succeeding annual meeting, if there be three classes. No classification of directors shall be effective prior to the first annual meeting of shareholders.

§ 38.   Vacancies.

Any vacancy occurring in the board of directors may be filled by the affirmative vote of a majority of the remaining directors though less than a quorum of the board of directors. A director elected to fill a vacancy shall be elected for the unexpired term of his predecessor in office. Any directorship to be filled by reason of an increase in the number of directors may be filled by the board of directors for a term of office continuing only until the next election of directors by the shareholders.

§ 39.   Removal of Directors.

At a meeting of shareholders called expressly for that purpose, directors may be removed in the manner provided in this section. Any director or the entire board of directors may be removed, with or without cause, by a vote of the holders of a majority of the shares then entitled to vote at an election of directors.

In the case of a corporation having cumulative voting, if less than the entire board is to be removed, no one of the directors may be removed if the votes cast against his removal would be sufficient to elect him if then cumulatively voted at an election of the entire board of directors, or, if there be classes of directors, at an election of the class of directors of which he is a part.

Whenever the holders of the shares of any class are entitled to elect one or more directors by the provisions of the articles of incorporation, the provisions of this section shall apply, in respect to the removal of a director or directors so elected, to the vote of the holders of the outstanding shares of that class and not to the vote of the outstanding shares as a whole.

§ 40.   Quorum of Directors.

A majority of the number of directors fixed by or in the manner provided in the by-laws or in the absence of a by-law fixing or providing for the number of directors, then of the number stated in the articles of incorporation, shall constitute a quorum for the transaction of business unless a greater number is required by the articles of incorporation or the by-laws. The act of the majority of the directors present at a meeting at which a quorum is present shall be the act of the board of directors, unless the act of a greater number is required by the articles of incorporation or the by-laws.

§ 41.   Director Conflicts of Interest.

No contract or other transaction between a corporation and

one or more of its directors or any other corporation, firm, association or entity in which one or more of its directors are directors or officers or are financially interested, shall be either void or voidable because of such relationship or interest or because such director or directors are present at the meeting of the board of directors or a committee thereof which authorizes, approves or ratifies such contract or transaction or because his or their votes are counted for such purpose, if:

(a) the fact of such relationship or interest is disclosed or known to the board of directors or committee which authorizes, approves or ratifies the contract or transaction by a vote or consent sufficient for the purpose without counting the votes or consents of such interested directors; or

(b) the fact of such relationship or interest is disclosed or known to the shareholders entitled to vote and they authorize, approve or ratify such contract or transaction by vote or written consent; or

(c) the contract or transaction is fair and reasonable to the corporation.

Common or interested directors may be counted in determining the presence of a quorum at a meeting of the board of directors or a committee thereof which authorizes, approves or ratifies such contract or transaction.

§ 42. Executive and Other Committees.

If the articles of incorporation or the by-laws so provide, the board of directors, by resolution adopted by a majority of the full board of directors, may designate from among its members an executive committee and one or more other committees each of which, to the extent provided in such resolution or in the articles of incorporation or the by-laws of the corporation, shall have and may exercise all the authority of the board of directors, except that no such committee shall have authority to (i) declare dividends or distributions, (ii) approve or recommend to shareholders actions or proposals required by this Act to be approved by shareholders, (iii) designate candidates for the office of director, for purposes of proxy solicitation or otherwise, or fill vacancies on the board of directors or any committee thereof, (iv) amend the by-laws, (v) approve a plan of merger not requiring shareholder approval, (vi) reduce earned or capital surplus, (vii) authorize or approve the reacquisition of shares unless pursuant

to a general formula or method specified by the board of directors, or (viii) authorize or approve the issuance or sale of, or any contract to issue or sell, shares or designate the terms of a series of a class of shares, provided that the board of directors, having acted regarding general authorization for the issuance or sale of shares, or any contract therefor, and, in the case of a series, the designation thereof, may, pursuant to a general formula or method specified by the board by resolution or by adoption of a stock option or other plan, authorize a committee to fix the terms of any contract for the sale of the shares and to fix the terms upon which such shares may be issued or sold, including, without limitation, the price, the dividend rate, provisions for redemption, sinking fund, conversion, voting or preferential rights, and provisions for other features of a class of shares, or a series of a class of shares, with full power in such committee to adopt any final resolution setting forth all the terms thereof and to authorize the statement of the terms of a series for filing with the Secretary of State under this Act.

Neither the designation of any such committee, the delegation thereto of authority, nor action by such committee pursuant to such authority shall alone constitute compliance by any member of the board of directors, not a member of the committee in question, with his responsibility to act in good faith, in a manner he reasonably believes to be in the best interests of the corporation, and with such care as an ordinarily prudent person in a like position would use under similar circumstances.

§ 43. Place and Notice of Directors' Meetings; Committee Meetings.

Meetings of the board of directors, regular or special, may be held either within or without this State.

Regular meetings of the board of directors or any committee designated thereby may be held with or without notice as prescribed in the by-laws. Special meetings of the board of directors or any committee designated thereby shall be held upon such notice as is prescribed in the by-laws. Attendance of a director at a meeting shall constitute a waiver of notice of such meeting, except where a director attends a meeting for the express purpose of objecting to the transaction of any business because the meeting is not lawfully called or convened. Neither the business to be transacted at, nor the purpose of, any regular or special meeting of the board of directors or any committee designated thereby need be specified in the notice or waiver of notice of such meeting unless required by the by-laws.

Except as may be otherwise restricted by the articles of incorporation or by-laws, members of the board of directors or any committee designated thereby may participate in a meeting of such board or committee by means of a conference telephone or similar communications equipment by means of which all persons participating in the meeting can hear each other at the same time and participation by such means shall constitute presence in person at a meeting.

§ 44.   Action by Directors Without a Meeting. Unless otherwise provided by the articles of incorporation or by-laws, any action required by this Act to be taken at a meeting of the directors of a corporation, or any action which may be taken at a meeting of the directors or of a committee, may be taken without a meeting if a consent in writing, setting forth the action so taken, shall be signed by all of the directors, or all of the members of the committee, as the case may be. Such consent shall have the same effect as a unanimous vote.

§ 45.   Dividends.   The board of directors of a corporation may, from time to time, declare and the corporation may pay dividends in cash, property, or its own shares, except when the corporation is insolvent or when the payment thereof would render the corporation insolvent or when the declaration or payment thereof would be contrary to any restriction contained in the articles of incorporation, subject to the following provisions:

(a) Dividends may be declared and paid in cash or property only out of the unreserved and unrestricted earned surplus of the corporation, except as otherwise provided in this section.

[Alternative] (a) Dividends may be declared and paid in cash or property only out of the unreserved and unrestricted earned surplus of the corporation, or out of the unreserved and unrestricted net earnings of the current fiscal year and the next preceding fiscal year taken as a single period, except as otherwise provided in this section.

(b) If the articles of incorporation of a corporation engaged in the business of exploiting natural resources so provide, dividends may be declared and paid in cash out of the depletion reserves, but each such dividend shall be identified as a distribution of such reserves and the amount per share paid from such reserves shall be disclosed to the shareholders receiving the same concurrently with the distribution thereof.

(c) Dividends may be declared and paid in its own treasury shares.

(d) Dividends may be declared and paid in its own authorized and unissued shares out of any unreserved and unrestricted surplus of the corporation upon the following conditions:

(1) If a dividend is payable in its own shares having a par value, such shares shall be issued at not less than the par value thereof and there shall be transferred to stated capital at the time such dividend is paid an amount of surplus equal to the aggregate par value of the shares to be issued as a dividend.

(2) If a dividend is payable in its own shares without par value, such shares shall be issued at such stated value as shall be fixed by the board of directors by resolution adopted at the time such dividend is declared, and there shall be transferred to stated capital at the time such dividend is paid an amount of surplus equal to the aggregate stated value so fixed in respect of such shares; and the amount per share so transferred to stated capital shall be disclosed to the shareholders receiving such dividend concurrently with the payment thereof.

(e) No dividend payable in shares of any class shall be paid to the holders of shares of any other class unless the articles of incorporation so provide or such payment is authorized by the affirmative vote or the written consent of the holders of at least a majority of the outstanding shares of the class in which the payment is to be made.

A split-up or division of the issued shares of any class into a greater number of shares of the same class without increasing the stated capital of the corporation shall not be construed to be a share dividend within the meaning of this section.

§ 46.   Distributions from Capital Surplus. The board of directors of a corporation may, from time to time, distribute to its shareholders out of capital surplus of the corporation a portion of its assets, in cash or property, subject to the following provisions:

(a) No such distribution shall be made at a time when the corporation is insolvent or when such distribution would render the corporation insolvent.

(b) No such distribution shall be made unless the articles of incorporation so provide or such distribution is authorized by the affirmative vote of the holders of a majority of the outstanding shares of each class whether or not entitled to vote thereon by the provisions of the articles of incorporation of the corporation.

(c) No such distribution shall be made to the holders of any class of shares unless all cumulative dividends accrued on all preferred or special classes of shares entitled to preferential dividends shall have been fully paid.

(d) No such distribution shall be made to the holders of any class of shares which would reduce the remaining net assets of the corporation below the aggregate preferential amount payable in event of involuntary liquidation to the holders of shares having preferential rights to the assets of the corporation in the event of liquidation.

(e) Each such distribution, when made, shall be identified as a distribution from capital surplus and the amount per share disclosed to the shareholders receiving the same concurrently with the distribution thereof.

The board of directors of a corporation may also, from time to time, distribute to the holders of its outstanding shares having a cumulative preferential right to receive dividends, in discharge of their cumulative dividend rights, dividends payable in cash out of the capital surplus of the corporation, if at the time the corporation has no earned surplus and is not insolvent and would not thereby be rendered insolvent. Each such distribution when made, shall be identified as a payment of cumulative dividends out of capital surplus.

§ 47.   Loans to Employees and Directors.
A corporation shall not lend money to or use its credit to assist its directors without authorization in the particular case by its shareholders, but may lend money to and use its credit to assist any employee of the corporation or of a subsidiary, including any such employee who is a director of the corporation, if the board of directors decides that such loan or assistance may benefit the corporation.

§ 48.   Liabilities of Directors in Certain
Cases.   In addition to any other liabilities, a director shall be liable in the following circumstances unless he complies with the standard provided in this Act for the performance of the duties of directors:

(a) A director who votes for or assents to the declaration of any dividend or other distribution of the assets of a corporation to its shareholders contrary to the provisions of this Act or contrary to any restrictions contained in the articles of incorporation, shall be liable to the corporation, jointly and severally with all other directors so voting or assenting, for the amount of such dividend which is paid or the value of such assets which are distributed in excess of the amount of such dividend or distribution which could have been paid or distributed without a violation of the provisions of this Act or the restrictions in the articles of incorporation.

(b) A director who votes for or assents to the purchase of the corporation's own shares contrary to the provisions of this Act shall be liable to the corporation, jointly and severally with all other directors so voting or assenting, for the amount of consideration paid for such shares which is in excess of the maximum amount which could have been paid therefor without a violation of the provisions of this Act.

(c) A director who votes for or assents to any distribution of assets of a corporation to its shareholders during the liquidation of the corporation without the payment and discharge of, or making adequate provision for, all known debts, obligations, and liabilities of the corporation shall be liable to the corporation, jointly and severally with all other directors so voting or assenting, for the value of such assets which are distributed, to the extent that such debts, obligations and liabilities of the corporation are not thereafter paid and discharged.

Any director against whom a claim shall be asserted under or pursuant to this section for the payment of a dividend or other distribution of assets of a corporation and who shall be held liable thereon, shall be entitled to contribution from the shareholders who accepted or received any such dividend or assets, knowing such dividend or distribution to have been made in violation of this Act, in proportion to the amounts received by them.

Any director against whom a claim shall be asserted under or pursuant to this section shall be entitled to contribution from the other directors who voted for or assented to the action upon which the claim is asserted.

§ 49. Provisions Relating to Actions by Shareholders.

No action shall be brought in this State by a shareholder in the right of a domestic or foreign corporation unless the plaintiff was a holder of record of shares or of voting trust certificates therefor at the time of the transaction of whch he complains, or his shares or voting trust certificates thereafter devolved upon him by operation of law from a person who was a holder of record at such time.

In any action hereafter instituted in the right of any domestic or foreign corporation by the holder or holders of record of shares of such corporation or of voting trust certificates therefor, the court having jurisdiction, upon final judgment and a finding that the action was brought without reasonable cause, may require the plaintiff or plaintiffs to pay to the parties named as defendant the reasonable expenses, including fees of attorneys, incurred by them in the defense of such action.

In any action now pending or hereafter instituted or maintained in the right of any domestic or foreign corporation by the holder or holders of record of less than five per cent of the outstanding shares of any class of such corporation or of voting trust certificates therefor, unless the shares or voting trust certificates so held have a market value in excess of twenty-five thousand dollars, the corporation in whose right such action is brought shall be entitled at any time before final judgment to require the plaintiff or plaintiffs to give security for the reasonable expenses, including fees of attorneys, that may be incurred by it in connection with such action or may be incurred by other parties named as defendant for which it may become legally liable. Market value shall be determined as of the date that the plaintiff institutes the action or, in the case of an intervenor, as of the date that he becomes a party to the action. The amount of such security may from time to time be increased or decreased, in the discretion of the court, upon showing that the security provided has or may become inadequate or is excessive. The corporation shall have recourse to such security in such amount as the court having jurisdiction shall determine upon the termination of such action, whether or not the court finds the action was brought without reasonable cause.

§ 50. Officers.

The officers of a corporation shall consist of a president, one or more vice presidents as may be prescribed by the by-laws, a secretary, and a treasurer, each of whom shall be elected by the board of directors at such time and in such manner as may be prescribed by the by-laws. Such other officers and assistant officers and agents as may be deemed necessary may be elected or appointed by the board of directors or chosen in such other manner as may be prescribed by the by-laws. Any two or more offices may be held by the same person, except the offices of president and secretary.

All officers and agents of the corporation, as between themselves and the corporation, shall have such authority and perform such duties in the management of the corporation as may be provided in the by-laws, or as may be determined by resolution of the board of directors not inconsistent with the by-laws.

§ 51. Removal of Officers.

Any officer or agent may be removed by the board of directors whenever in its judgment the best interests of the corporation will be served thereby, but such removal shall be without prejudice to the contract rights, if any, of the person so removed. Election or appointment of an officer or agent shall not of itself create contract rights.

§ 53. Incorporators.

One or more persons, or a domestic or foreign corporation, may act as incorporator or incorporators of a corporation by signing and delivering in duplicate to the Secretary of State articles of incorporation for such corporation.

§ 54. Articles of Incorporation.

The articles of incorporation shall set forth:

(a) The name of the corporation.

(b) The period of duration, which may be perpetual.

(c) The purpose or purposes for which the corporation is organized which may be stated to be, or to include, the transaction of any or all lawful business for which corporations may be incorporated under this Act.

(d) The aggregate number of shares which the

corporation shall have authority to issue; if such shares are to consist of one class only, the par value of each of such shares, or a statement that all of such shares are without par value; or, if such shares are to be divided into classes, the number of shares of each class, and a statement of the par value of the shares of each such class or that such shares are to be without par value.

(e) If the shares are to be divided into classes, the designation of each class and a statement of the preferences, limitations and relative rights in respect of the shares of each class.

(f) If the corporation is to issue the shares of any preferred or special class in series, then the designation of each series and a statement of the variations in the relative rights and preferences as between series insofar as the same are to be fixed in the articles of incorporation, and a statement of any authority to be vested in the board of directors to establish series and fix and determine the variations in the relative rights and preferences as between series.

(g) If any preemptive right is to be granted to shareholders, the provisions therefor.

(h) Any provision, not inconsistent with law, which the incorporators elect to set forth in the articles of incorporation for the regulation of the internal affairs of the corporation, including any provision restricting the transfer of shares and any provision which under this Act is required or permitted to be set forth in the by-laws.

(i) The address of its initial registered office, and the name of its initial registered agent at such address.

(j) The number of directors constituting the initial board of directors and the names and addresses of the persons who are to serve as directors until the first annual meeting of shareholders or until their successors be elected and qualify.

(k) The name and address of each incorporator.

It shall not be necessary to set forth in the articles of incorporation any of the corporate powers enumerated in this Act.

§ 55. Filing of Articles of Incorporation.
Duplicate originals of the articles of incorporation shall be delivered to the Secretary of State. If the Secretary of State finds that the articles of incorporation conform to law, he shall, when all fees have been paid as in this Act prescribed:

(a) Endorse on each of such duplicate originals the word "Filed," and the month, day and year of the filing thereof.

(b) File one of such duplicate originals in his office.

(c) Issue a certificate of incorporation to which he shall affix the other duplicate original.

The certificate of incorporation, together with the duplicate original of the articles of incorporation affixed thereto by the Secretary of State, shall be returned to the incorporators or their representative.

§ 56. Effect of Issuance of Certificate of Incorporation.
Upon the issuance of the certificate of incorporation, the corporate existence shall begin, and such certificate of incorporation shall be conclusive evidence that all conditions precedent required to be performed by the incorporators have been complied with and that the corporation has been incorporated under this Act, except as against this State in a proceeding to cancel or revoke the certificate of incorporation or for involuntary dissolution of the corporation.

§ 57. Organization Meeting of Directors.
After the issuance of the certificate of incorporation an organization meeting of the board of directors named in the articles of incorporation shall be held, either within or without this State, at the call of a majority of the directors named in the articles of incorporation, for the purpose of adopting by-laws, electing officers and transacting such other business as may come before the meeting. The directors calling the meeting shall give at least three days' notice thereof by mail to each director so named, stating the time and place of the meeting.

§ 58. Right to Amend Articles of Incorporation.
A corporation may amend its articles of incorporation, from time to time, in any and as many respects as may be desired, so long as its articles of incorporation as amended contain only such provisions as might be lawfully contained in original articles of incorporation at the time of making such amendment, and, if a change in shares or the rights of shareholders, or an exchange, reclassification or

cancellation of shares or rights of shareholders is to be made, such provisions as may be necessary to effect such change, exchange, reclassification or cancellation.

In particular, and without limitation upon such general power of amendment, a corporation may amend its articles of incorporation, from time to time, so as:

(a) To change its corporate name.

(b) To change its period of duration.

(c) To change, enlarge or diminish its corporate purposes.

(d) To increase or decrease the aggregate number of shares, or shares of any class, which the corporation has authority to issue.

(e) To increase or decrease the par value of the authorized shares of any class having a par value, whether issued or unissued.

(f) To exchange, classify, reclassify or cancel all or any part of its shares, whether issued or unissued.

(g) To change the designation of all or any part of its shares, whether issued or unissued, and to change the preferences, limitations, and the relative rights in respect of all or any part of its shares, whether issued or unissued.

(h) To change shares having the par value, whether issued or unissued, into the same or a different number of shares without par value, and to change shares without par value, whether issued or unissued, into the same or a different number of shares having a par value.

(i) To change the shares of any class, whether issued or unissued, and whether with or without par value, into a different number of shares of the same class or into the same or a different number of shares, either with or without par value, of other classes.

(j) To create new classes of shares having rights and preferences either prior and superior or subordinate and inferior to the shares of any class then authorized, whether issued or unissued.

(k) To cancel or otherwise affect the right of the holders of the shares of any class to receive dividends which have accrued but have not been declared.

(l) To divide any preferred or special class of shares, whether issued or unissued, into series and fix and determine the designations of such series and the variations in the relative rights and preferences as between the shares of such series.

(m) To authorize the board of directors to establish, out of authorized but unissued shares, series of any preferred or special class of shares and fix and determine the relative rights and preferences of the shares of any series so established.

(n) To authorize the board of directors to fix and determine the relative rights and preferences of the authorized but unissued shares of series theretofore established in respect of which either the relative rights and preferences have not been fixed and determined or the relative rights and preferences theretofore fixed and determined are to be changed.

(o) To revoke, diminish, or enlarge the authority of the board of directors to establish series out of authorized but unissued shares of any preferred or special class and fix and determine the relative rights and preferences of the shares of any series so established.

(p) To limit, deny or grant to shareholders of any class the preemptive right to acquire additional or treasury shares of the corporation, whether then or thereafter authorized.

§ 60. Class Voting on Amendments. The holders of the outstanding shares of a class shall be entitled to vote as a class upon a proposed amendment, whether or not entitled to vote thereon by the provisions of the articles of incorporation, if the amendment would:

(a) Increase or decrease the aggregate number of authorized shares of such class.

(b) Increase or decrease the par value of the shares of such class.

(c) Effect an exchange, reclassification or cancellation of all or part of the shares of such class.

(d) Effect an exchange, or create a right of exchange, of all or any part of the shares of another class into the shares of such class.

(e) Change the designations, preferences, limitations or relative rights of the shares of such class.

(f) Change the shares of such class, whether with or without par value, into the same or a different number of shares, either with or without par value, of the same class or another class or classes.

(g) Create a new class of shares having rights

and preferences prior and superior to the shares of such class, or increase the rights and preferences or the number of authorized shares, of any class having rights and preferences prior or superior to the shares of such class.

(h) In the case of a preferred or special class of shares, divide the shares of such class into series and fix and determine the designation of such series and the variations in the relative rights and preferences between the shares of such series, or authorize the board of directors to do so.

(i) Limit or deny any existing preemptive rights of the shares of such class.

(j) Cancel or otherwise affect dividends on the shares of such class which have accrued but have not been declared.

§ 69. Reduction of Stated Capital in Certain Cases.

A reduction of the stated capital of a corporation, where such reduction is not accompanied by any action requiring an amendment of the articles of incorporation and not accompanied by a cancellation of shares, may be made in the following manner:

(A) The board of directors shall adopt a resolution setting forth the amount of the proposed reduction and the manner in which the reduction shall be effected, and directing that the question of such reduction be submitted to a vote at a meeting of shareholders, which may be either an annual or a special meeting.

(B) Written notice, stating that the purpose or one of the purposes of such meeting is to consider the question of reducing the stated capital of the corporation in the amount and manner proposed by the board of directors, shall be given to each shareholder of record entitled to vote thereon within the time and in the manner provided in this Act for the giving of notice of meetings of shareholders.

(C) At such meeting a vote of the shareholders entitled to vote thereon shall be taken on the question of approving the proposed reduction of stated capital, which shall require for its adoption the affirmative vote of the holders of a majority of the shares entitled to vote thereon.

When a reduction of the stated capital of a corporation has been approved as provided in this section, a statement shall be executed in duplicate by the corporation by its president or a vice president and by its secretary or an assistant secretary, and verified by one of the officers signing such statement, and shall set forth:

(a) The name of the corporation.

(b) A copy of the resolution of the shareholders approving such reduction, and the date of its adoption.

(c) The number of shares outstanding, and the number of shares entitled to vote thereon.

(d) The number of shares voted for and against such reduction, respectively.

(e) A statement of the manner in which such reduction is effected, and a statement, expressed in dollars, of the amount of stated capital of the corporation after giving effect to such reduction.

Duplicate originals of such statement shall be delivered to the Secretary of State. If the Secretary of State finds that such statement conforms to law, he shall, when all fees and franchise taxes have been paid as in this Act prescribed:

(1) Endorse on each of such duplicate originals the word "Filed," and the month, day and year of the filing thereof.

(2) File one of such duplicate originals in his office.

(3) Return the other duplicate original to the corporation or its representative.

Upon the filing of such statement, the stated capital of the corporation shall be reduced as therein set forth.

No reduction of stated capital shall be made under the provisions of this section which would reduce the amount of the aggregate stated capital of the corporation to an amount equal to or less than the aggregate preferential amounts payable upon all issued shares having a preferential right in the assets of the corporation in the event of involuntary liquidation, plus the aggregate par value of all issued shares having a par value but no preferential right in the assets of the corporation in the event of involuntary liquidation.

§ 70. Special Provisions Relating to Surplus and Reserves.

The surplus, if any, created by or arising out of a reduction of the stated capital of a corporation shall be capital surplus.

The capital surplus of a corporation may be

increased from time to time by resolution of the board of directors directing that all or a part of the earned surplus of the corporation be transferred to capital surplus.

A corporation may, by resolution of its board of directors, apply any part or all of its capital surplus to the reduction or elimination of any deficit arising from losses, however incurred, but only after first eliminating the earned surplus, if any, of the corporation by applying such losses against earned surplus and only to the extent that such losses exceed the earned surplus, if any. Each such application of capital surplus shall, to the extent thereof, effect a reduction of capital surplus.

A corporation may, by resolution of its board of directors, create a reserve or reserves out of its earned surplus for any proper purpose or purposes, and may abolish any such reserve in the same manner. Earned surplus of the corporation to the extent so reserved shall not be available for the payment of dividends or other distributions by the corporation except as expressly permitted by this Act.

§ 71. Procedure for Merger. Any two or more domestic corporations may merge into one of such corporations pursuant to a plan of merger approved in the manner provided in this Act.

The board of directors of each corporation shall, by resolution adopted by each such board, approve a plan of merger setting forth:

(a) The names of the corporations proposing to merge, and the name of the corporation into which they propose to merge, which is hereinafter designated as the surviving corporation.

(b) The terms and conditions of the proposed merger.

(c) The manner and basis of converting the shares of each corporation into shares, obligations or other securities of the surviving corporation or of any other corporation or, in whole or in part, into cash or other property.

(d) A statement of any changes in the articles of incorporation of the surviving corporation to be effected by such merger.

(e) Such other provisions with respect to the proposed merger as are deemed necessary or desirable.

§ 72. Procedure for Consolidation. Any two or more domestic corporations may consolidate into a new corporation pursuant to a plan of consolidation approved in the manner provided in this Act.

The board of directors of each corporation shall, by a resolution adopted by each such board, approve a plan of consolidation setting forth:

(a) The names of the corporations proposing to consolidate, and the name of the new corporation into which they propose to consolidate, which is hereinafter designated as the new corporation.

(b) The terms and conditions of the proposed consolidation.

(c) The manner and basis of converting the shares of each corporation into shares, obligations or other securities of the new corporation or of any other corporation or, in whole or in part, into cash or other property.

(d) With respect to the new corporation, all of the statements required to be set forth in articles of incorporation for corporations organized under this Act.

(e) Such other provisions with respect to the proposed consolidation as are deemed necessary or desirable.

§ 73. Approval by Shareholders. The board of directors of each corporation in the case of a merger or consolidation, and the board of directors of the corporation the shares of which are to be acquired in the case of an exchange, upon approving such plan of merger, consolidation or exchange, shall, by resolution, direct that the plan be submitted to a vote at a meeting of its shareholders, which may be either an annual or a special meeting. Written notice shall be given to each shareholder of record, whether or not entitled to vote at such meeting, not less than twenty days before such meeting, in the manner provided in this Act for the giving of notice of meetings of shareholders, and, whether the meeting be an annual or a special meeting, shall state that the purpose or one of the purposes is to consider the proposed plan of merger, consolidation or exchange. A copy or a summary of the plan of merger, consolidation or exchange, as the case may be, shall be included in or enclosed with such notice.

At each such meeting, a vote of the shareholders shall be taken on the proposed plan. The plan shall be approved upon receiving the affirmative vote of the holders of a majority of the shares entitled to vote thereon of each such corporation, unless any class of shares of any such corporation is entitled to vote thereon as a class, in which event, as to such corporation, the plan shall be approved upon receiving the affirmative vote of the holders of a majority of the shares of each class of shares entitled to vote thereon as a class and of the total shares entitled to vote thereon. Any class of shares of any such corporation shall be entitled to vote as a class if any such plan contains any provision which, if contained in a proposed amendment to articles of incorporation, would entitle such class of shares to vote as a class and, in the case of an exchange, if the class is included in the exchange.

After such approval by a vote of the shareholders of each such corporation, and at any time prior to the filing of the articles of merger, consolidation or exchange, the merger, consolidation or exchange may be abandoned pursuant to provisions therefor, if any, set forth in the plan.

§ 74.   Articles of Merger, Consolidation or Exchange.

Upon such approval, articles of merger, articles of consolidation or articles of exchange shall be executed in duplicate by each corporation by its president or a vice president and by its secretary or an assistant secretary, and verified by one of the officers of each corporation signing such articles, and shall set forth:

(a) The plan of merger, consolidation or exchange.

(b) As to each corporation the shareholders of which were required to vote thereon, the number of shares outstanding, and, if the shares of any class were entitled to vote as a class, the designation and number of outstanding shares of each such class.

(c) As to each corporation the shareholders of which were required to vote thereon, the number of shares voted for and against such plan, respectively, and, if the shares of any class were entitled to vote as a class, the number of shares of each such class voted for and against such plan, respectively.

(d) As to the acquiring corporation in a plan of exchange, a statement that the adoption of the plan and performance of its terms were duly approved by its board of directors and such other requisite corporate action, if any, as may be required of it.

Duplicate originals of the articles of merger,

consolidation or exchange shall be delivered to the Secretary of State. If the Secretary of State finds that such articles conform to law, he shall, when all fees and franchise taxes have been paid as in this Act prescribed:

(1) Endorse on each of such duplicate originals the word "Filed," and the month, day and year of the filing thereof.

(2) File one of such duplicate originals in his office.

(3) Issue a certificate of merger, consolidation or exchange to which he shall affix the other duplicate original.

The certificate of merger, consolidation or exchange together with the duplicate original of the articles affixed thereto by the Secretary of State, shall be returned to the surviving, new or acquiring corporation, as the case may be, or its representative.

§ 75.   Merger of Subsidiary Corporation.

Any corporation owning at least ninety per cent of the outstanding shares of each class of another corporation may merge such other corporation into itself without approval by a vote of the shareholders of either corporation. Its board of directors shall, by resolution, approve a plan of merger setting forth:

(A) The name of the subsidiary corporation and the name of the corporation owning at least ninety per cent of its shares, which is hereinafter designated as the surviving corporation.

(B) The manner and basis of converting the shares of the subsidiary corporation into shares, obligations or other securities of the surviving corporation or of any other corporation or, in whole or in part, into cash or other property.

A copy of such plan of merger shall be mailed to each shareholder of record of the subsidiary corporation.

Articles of merger shall be executed in duplicate by the surviving corporation by its president or a vice president and by its secretary or an assistant secretary, and verified by one of its officers signing such articles, and shall set forth:

(a) The plan of merger;

(b) The number of outstanding shares of each class of the subsidiary corporation and the number of such shares of each class owned by the surviving corporation; and

(c) The date of the mailing to shareholders of the subsidiary corporation of a copy of the plan of merger.

On and after the thirtieth day after the mailing of a copy of the plan of merger to shareholders of the subsidiary corporation or upon the waiver thereof by the holders of all outstanding shares duplicate originals of the articles of merger shall be delivered to the Secretary of State. If the Secretary of State finds that such articles conform to law, he shall, when all fees and franchise taxes have been paid as in this Act prescribed:

(1) Endorse on each of such duplicate originals the word "Filed," and the month, day and year of the filing thereof.

(2) File one of such duplicate originals in his office, and

(3) Issue a certificate of merger to which he shall affix the other duplicate original.

The certificate of merger, together with the duplicate original of the articles of merger affixed thereto by the Secretary of State, shall be returned to the surviving corporation or its representative.

§ 78. Sale of Assets in Regular Course of Business and Mortgage or Pledge of Assets. The sale, lease, exchange, or other disposition of all, or substantially all, the property and assets of a corporation in the usual and regular course of its business and the mortgage or pledge of any or all property and assets of a corporation whether or not in the usual and regular course of business may be made upon such terms and conditions and for such consideration, which may consist in whole or in part of cash or other property, including shares, obligations or other securities of any other corporation, domestic or foreign, as shall be authorized by its board of directors; and in any such case no authorization or consent of the shareholders shall be required.

§ 79. Sale of Assets Other Than in Regular Course of Business. A sale, lease, exchange, or other disposition of all, or substantially all, the property and assets, with or without the good will, of a corporation, if not in the usual and regular course of its business, may be made upon such terms and conditions and for such consideration, which may consist in whole or in part of cash or other property, including shares, obligations or other securities of

any other corporation, domestic or foreign, as may be authorized in the following manner:

(a) The board of directors shall adopt a resolution recommending such sale, lease, exchange, or other disposition and directing the submission thereof to a vote at a meeting of shareholders, which may be either an annual or a special meeting.

(b) Written notice shall be given to each shareholder of record, whether or not entitled to vote at such meeting, not less than twenty days before such meeting, in the manner provided in this Act for the giving of notice of meetings of shareholders, and, whether the meeting be an annual or a special meeting, shall state that the purpose, or one of the purposes is to consider the proposed sale, lease, exchange, or other disposition.

(c) At such meeting the shareholders may authorize such sale, lease, exchange, or other disposition and may fix, or may authorize the board of directors to fix, any or all of the terms and conditions thereof and the consideration to be received by the corporation therefor. Such authorization shall require the affirmative vote of the holders of a majority of the shares of the corporation entitled to vote thereon, unless any class of shares is entitled to vote thereon as a class, in which event such authorization shall require the affirmative vote of the holders of a majority of the shares of each class of shares entitled to vote as a class thereon and of the total shares entitled to vote thereon.

(d) After such authorization by a vote of shareholders, the board of directors nevertheless, in its discretion, may abandon such sale, lease, exchange, or other disposition of assets, subject to the rights of third parties under any contracts relating thereto, without further action or approval by shareholders.

§ 80. Right of Shareholders to Dissent. Any shareholder of a corporation shall have the right to dissent from any of the following corporate actions:

(a) Any plan of merger or consolidation to which the corporation is a party; or

(b) Any sale or exchange of all or substantially all of the property and assets of the corporation not made in the usual and regular course of its business, including a sale in dissolution, but not including a sale pursuant to an order of a court having jurisdiction in the premises or a sale for cash on terms requiring that all or substantially all of the net proceeds of sale be distributed to the shareholders in accordance with their respective interests within one year after the date of sale.

(c) Any plan of exchange to which the corporation is a party as the corporation the shares of which are to be acquired.

A shareholder may dissent as to less than all of the shares registered in his name. In that event, his rights shall be determined as if the shares as to which he has dissented and his other shares were registered in the names of different shareholders.

This section shall not apply to the shareholders of the surviving corporation in a merger if a vote of shareholders of such corporation is not necessary to authorize such merger. Nor shall it apply to the holders of shares of any class or series if the shares of such class or series were registered on a national securities exchange on the date fixed to determine the shareholders entitled to vote at the meeting of shareholders at which the plan of merger, consolidation or exchange or the proposed sale or exchange of property and assets is to be acted upon unless the articles of incorporation of the corporation shall otherwise provide.

§ 82. Voluntary Dissolution by Incorporators.
A corporation which has not commenced business and which has not issued any shares, may be voluntarily dissolved by its incorporators at any time in the following manner:

(a) Articles of dissolution shall be executed in duplicate by a majority of the incorporators, and verified by them, and shall set forth:

(1) The name of the corporation.

(2) The date of issuance of its certificate of incorporation.

(3) That none of its shares has been issued.

(4) That the corporation has not commenced business.

(5) That the amount, if any, actually paid in on subscriptions for its shares, less any part thereof disbursed for necessary expenses, has been returned to those entitled thereto.

(6) That no debts of the corporation remain unpaid.

(7) That a majority of the incorporators elect that the corporation be dissolved.

(b) Duplicate originals of the articles of dissolution shall be delivered to the Secretary of State. If the Secretary of State finds that the articles of dissolution conform to law, he shall, when all fees and franchise taxes have been paid as in this Act prescribed:

(1) Endorse on each of such duplicate originals the word "Filed," and the month, day and year of the filing thereof.

(2) File one of such duplicate originals in his office.

(3) Issue a certificate of dissolution to which he shall affix the other duplicate original.

The certificate of dissolution, together with the duplicate original of the articles of dissolution affixed thereto by the Secretary of State, shall be returned to the incorporators or their representative. Upon the issuance of such certificate of dissolution by the Secretary of State, the existence of the corporation shall cease.

§ 83. Voluntary Dissolution by Consent of Shareholders.
A corporation may be voluntarily dissolved by the written consent of all of its shareholders.

Upon the execution of such written consent, a statement of intent to dissolve shall be executed in duplicate by the corporation by its president or a vice president and by its secretary or an assistant secretary, and verified by one of the officers signing such statement, which statement shall set forth:

(a) The name of the corporation.

(b) The names and respective addresses of its officers.

(c) The names and respective addresses of its directors.

(d) A copy of the written consent signed by all shareholders of the corporation.

(e) A statement that such written consent has been signed by all shareholders of the corporation or signed in their names by their attorneys thereunto duly authorized.

§ 84. Voluntary Dissolution by Act of Corporation.
A corporation may be dissolved by the act of the corporation, when authorized in the following manner:

(a) The board of directors shall adopt a resolution recommending that the corporation be dissolved, and directing that the question of such dissolution be submitted to a vote at a meeting of shareholders, which may be either an annual or a special meeting.

(b) Written notice shall be given to each shareholder of record entitled to vote at such meeting within the time and in the manner provided in this Act for the giving of notice of meetings of shareholders, and, whether the meeting be an annual or special meeting, shall state that the purpose, or one of the purposes, of such meeting is to consider the advisability of dissolving the corporation.

(c) At such meeting a vote of shareholders entitled to vote thereat shall be taken on a resolution to dissolve the corporation. Such resolution shall be adopted upon receiving the affirmative vote of the holders of a majority of the shares of the corporation entitled to vote thereon, unless any class of shares is entitled to vote thereon as a class, in which event the resolution shall be adopted upon receiving the affirmative vote of the holders of a majority of the shares of each class of shares entitled to vote thereon as a class and of the total shares entitled to vote thereon.

(d) Upon the adoption of such resolution, a statement of intent to dissolve shall be executed in duplicate by the corporation by its president or a vice president and by its secretary or an assistant secretary, and verified by one of the officers signing such statement, which statement shall set forth:

(1) The name of the corporation.

(2) The names and respective addresses of its officers.

(3) The names and respective addresses of its directors.

(4) A copy of the resolution adopted by the shareholders authorizing the dissolution of the corporation.

(5) The number of shares outstanding, and, if the shares of any class are entitled to vote as a class, the designation and number of outstanding shares of each such class.

(6) The number of shares voted for and against the resolution, respectively, and, if the shares of any class are entitled to vote as a class, the number of shares of each such class voted for and against the resolution, respectively.

§ 94. Involuntary Dissolution. A corpora-

tion may be dissolved involuntarily by a decree of the . . . court in an action filed by the Attorney General when it is established that:

(a) The corporation has failed to file its annual report within the time required by this Act, or has failed to pay its franchise tax on or before the first day of August of the year in which such franchise tax becomes due and payable; or

(b) The corporation procured its articles of incorporation through fraud; or

(c) The corporation has continued to exceed or abuse the authority conferred upon it by law; or

(d) The corporation has failed for thirty days to appoint and maintain a registered agent in this state; or

(e) The corporation has failed for thirty days after change of its registered office or registered agent to file in the office of the Secretary of State a statement of such change.

§ 95. Notification to Attorney General. The Secretary of State, on or before the last day of December of each year, shall certify to the Attorney General the names of all corporations which have failed to file their annual reports or to pay franchise taxes in accordance with the provisions of this Act, together with the facts pertinent thereto. He shall also certify, from time to time, the names of all corporations which have given other cause for dissolution as provided in this Act, together with the facts pertinent thereto. Whenever the Secretary of State shall certify the name of a corporation to the Attorney General as having given any cause for dissolution, the Secretary of State shall concurrently mail to the corporation at its registered office a notice that such certification has been made. Upon the receipt of such certification, the Attorney General shall file an action in the name of the State against such corporation for its dissolution. Every such certificate from the Secretary of State to the Attorney General pertaining to the failure of a corporation to file an annual report or pay a franchise tax shall be taken and received in all courts as prima facie evidence of the facts therein stated. If, before action is filed, the corporation shall file its annual report or pay its franchise tax, together with all penalties thereon, or shall appoint or maintain a registered agent as provided in this Act, or shall file with the Secretary of State the required statement of change of registered office or registered agent, such fact shall be forthwith certified by the Secretary of State to the Attorney General and he shall not file an action against such corporation for such cause. If, after action is filed, the corporation shall file its annual report or pay its franchise tax, together with all penalties thereon, or shall appoint or maintain a registered agent as provided in this Act, or shall file with the Secretary of State the required statement of change of registered office or registered agent, and shall pay the costs of such action, the action for such cause shall abate.

§ 106.   Admission of Foreign Corporation. No foreign corporation shall have the right to transact business in this State until it shall have procured a certificate of authority so to do from the Secretary of State. No foreign corporation shall be entitled to procure a certificate of authority under this Act to transact in this State any business which a corporation organized under this Act is not permitted to transact. A foreign corporation shall not be denied a certificate of authority by reason of the fact that the laws of the state or country under which such corporation is organized governing its organization and internal affairs differ from the laws of this State, and nothing in this Act contained shall be construed to authorize this State to regulate the organization or the internal affairs of such corporation.

Without excluding other activities which may not constitute transacting business in this State, a foreign corporation shall not be considered to be transacting business in this State, for the purposes of this Act, by reason of carrying on in this State any one or more of the following activities:

(a) Maintaining or defending any action or suit, or any administrative or arbitration proceeding, or effecting the settlement thereof or the settlement of claims or disputes.

(b) Holding meetings of its directors or shareholders or carrying on other activities concerning its internal affairs.

(c) Maintaining bank accounts.

(d) Maintaining offices or agencies for the transfer, exchange and registration of its securities, or appointing and maintaining trustees or depositaries with relation to its securities.

(e) Effecting sales through independent contractors.

(f) Soliciting or procuring orders, whether by mail or through employees or agents or otherwise, where such orders require acceptance without this State before becoming binding contracts.

(g) Creating as borrower or lender, or acquiring, indebtedness or mortgages or other security interests in real or personal property.

(h) Securing or collecting debts or enforcing any rights in property securing the same.

(i) Transacting any business in interstate commerce.

(j) Conducting an isolated transaction completed within a period of thirty days and not in the course of a number of repeated transactions of like nature.

§ 107.   Powers of Foreign Corporation. A foreign corporation which shall have received a certificate of authority under this Act shall, until a certificate of revocation or of withdrawal shall have been issued as provided in this Act, enjoy the same, but no greater, rights and privileges as a domestic corporation organized for the purposes set forth in the application pursuant to which such certificate of authority is issued; and, except as in this Act otherwise provided, shall be subject to the same duties, restrictions, penalties and liabilities now or hereafter imposed upon a domestic corporation of like character.

§ 124.   Transacting Business Without Certificate of Authority. No foreign corporation transacting business in this State without a certificate of authority shall be permitted to maintain any action, suit or proceeding in any court of this State, until such corporation shall have obtained a certificate of authority. Nor shall any action, suit or proceeding be maintained in any court of this State by any successor or assignee of such corporation on any right, claim or demand arising out of the transaction of business by such corporation in this State, until a certificate of authority shall have been obtained by such corporation or by a corporation which has acquired all or substantially all of its assets.

The failure of a foreign corporation to obtain a certificate of authority to transact business in this State shall not impair the validity of any contract or act of such corporation, and shall not prevent such corporation from defending any action, suit or proceeding in any court of this State.

A foreign corporation which transacts business in this State without a certificate of authority shall be liable to this State, for the years or parts thereof during which it transacted business in this State without a certificate of authority, in an amount equal to all fees and franchise taxes which would have been imposed by this Act upon such corporation had it duly applied for and received a certificate of authority to transact business in this State as required by this Act and thereafter filed all reports required by this Act, plus all penalties imposed by this Act for failure to pay such fees and franchise taxes. The Attorney General shall bring proceedings to recover all amounts due this State under the provisions of this Section.

§ 125.   Annual Report of Domestic and Foreign Corporations.   Each domestic corporation, and each foreign corporation authorized to transact business in this State, shall file, within the time prescribed by this Act, an annual report setting forth:

(a) The name of the corporation and the state or country under the laws of which it is incorporated.

(b) The address of the registered office of the corporation in this State, and the name of its registered agent in this State at such address, and, in case of a foreign corporation, the address of its principal office in the state or country under the laws of which it is incorporated.

(c) A brief statement of the character of the business in which the corporation is actually engaged in this State.

(d) The names and respective addresses of the directors and officers of the corporation.

(e) A statement of the aggregate number of shares which the corporation has authority to issue, itemized by classes, par value of shares, shares without par value, and series, if any, within a class.

(f) A statement of the aggregate number of issued shares, itemized by classes, par value of shares, shares without par value, and series, if any, within a class.

(g) A statement, expressed in dollars, of the amount of stated capital of the corporation, as defined in this Act.

(h) A statement, expressed in dollars, of the value of all the property owned by the corporation, wherever located, and the value of the property of the corporation located within this State, and a statement, expressed in dollars, of the gross amount of business transacted by the corporation for the twelve months ended on the thirty-first day of December preceding the date herein provided for the filing of such report and the gross amount thereof transacted by the corporation at or from places of business in this State. If, on the thirty-first day of December preceding the time herein provided for the filing of such report, the corporation had not been in existence for a period of twelve months, or in the case of a foreign corporation had not been authorized to transact business in this State for a period of twelve months, the statement with respect to business transacted shall be furnished for the period between the date of incorporation or the date of its authorization to transact business in this State, as the case may be, and such thirty-first day of December. If all the property of the corporation is located in this State and all of its business is transacted at or from places of business in this State, or if the corporation elects to pay the annual franchise tax on the basis of its entire stated capital, then the information required by this subparagraph need not be set forth in such report.

(i) Such additional information as may be necessary or appropriate in order to enable the Secretary of State to determine and assess the proper amount of franchise taxes payable by such corporation.

Such annual report shall be made on forms prescribed and furnished by the Secretary of State and the information therein contained shall be given as of the date of the execution of the report, except as to the information required by subparagraphs (g), (h) and (i) which shall be given as of the close of business on the thirty-first day of December next preceding the date herein provided for the filing of such report. It shall be executed by the corporation by its president, a vice president, secretary, an assistant secretary, or treasurer, and verified by the officer executing the report, or, if the corporation is in the hands of a receiver or trustee, it shall be executed on behalf of the corporation and verified by such receiver or trustee.

§ 135.   Penalties Imposed Upon Corporations.   Each corporation, domestic or foreign, that fails or refuses to file its annual report for any year within the time prescribed by this Act shall be subject to a penalty of ten per cent of the amount of the franchise tax assessed against it for the period beginning July 1 of the year in which such report should have been filed. Such penalty shall be assessed by the Secretary of State at the time of the assessment of the franchise tax. If the amount of the franchise tax as originally assessed against such corporation be thereafter adjusted in accordance with the provisions of this Act, the amount of the penalty shall be likewise adjusted to ten percent of the amount of the adjusted franchise tax. The amount of the franchise tax and the amount of the penalty shall be separately stated in any notice to the corporation with respect thereto.

If the franchise tax assessed in accordance with the provisions of this Act shall not be paid on or before the thirty-first day of July, it shall be deemed to be delinquent, and there shall be added a penalty of one percent for each month or part of month that the same is delinquent, commencing with the month of August.

Each corporation, domestic or foreign, that fails or refuses to answer truthfully and fully within the time prescribed by this Act interrogatories propounded by the Secretary of State in accordance with the provisions of this Act, shall be deemed to be guilty of a misdemeanor and upon conviction thereof may be fined in any amount not exceeding five hundred dollars.

§ 136.   Penalties Imposed Upon Officers and Directors.   Each officer and director of a corporation, domestic or foreign, who fails or refuses within the time prescribed by this Act to answer truthfully and fully interrogatories propounded to him by the Secretary of State in accordance with the provisions of this Act, or who signs any articles, statement, report, application or other document filed with the Secretary of State which is known to such officer or director to be false in any material respect, shall be deemed to be guilty of a misdemeanor, and upon conviction thereof may be fined in any amount not exceeding . . . . dollars.

§ 145.   Action by Shareholders Without a Meeting.   Any action required by this Act to be taken at a meeting of the shareholders of a corporation, or any action which may be taken at a meeting of the shareholders, may be taken without a meeting if a consent in writing, setting forth the action so taken, shall be signed by all of the shareholders entitled to vote with respect to the subject matter thereof.

Such consent shall have the same effect as a unanimous vote of shareholders, and may be stated as such in any articles or document filed with the Secretary of State under this Act.

§ 146.   Unauthorized Assumption of Corporate Powers.   All persons who assume to act as a corporation without authority so to do shall be jointly and severally liable for all debts and liabilities incurred or arising as a result thereof.

AMENDMENTS SUBSEQUENT TO AUGUST 1977

Amendments Adopted September 24, 1977

§ 81.   Rights of Dissenting Shareholders. Amended to read:

Any shareholder electing to exercise such right of dissent shall file with the corporation, prior to or at the meeting of shareholders at which such proposed corporate action is submitted to a vote, a written objection to such proposed corporate action. If such proposed corporate action be approved by the required vote and such shareholder shall not have voted in favor thereof, such shareholder may, within ten days after the date on which the vote was taken or if a corporation is to be merged without a vote of its shareholders into another corporation, any of its shareholders may, within fifteen days after the plan of such merger shall have been mailed to such shareholders, make written demand on the corporation, or, in the case of merger or consolidation, on the surviving or new corporation, domestic or foreign, for payment of the fair value of such shareholder's shares, and, if such proposed corporate action is effected, such corporation shall pay to such shareholder, upon the determination of the fair value, by agreement or judgment as provided herein, and, in the case of shares represented by certificates, the surrender of such certificates, the fair value thereof as of the day prior to the date on which the vote was taken approving the proposed corporate action, excluding any appreciation or depreciation in anticipation of such corporate action. Any shareholder failing to make demand within the ten-day period shall be bound by the terms of the proposed corporate action. Any shareholder making such demand shall thereafter be entitled only to payment as in this section provided and shall not be entitled to vote or to exercise any other rights of a shareholder.

[no changes in second and third paragraphs]

If within thirty days after the date on which such corporate action was effected the fair value of such shares is agreed upon between any such dissenting shareholder and the corporation, payment therefor shall be made within ninety days after the date on which such corporate action was effected, and, in the case of shares represented by certificates, upon surrender of such certificates. Upon payment of the agreed value the dissenting shareholder shall cease to have any interest in such shares.

If within such period of thirty days a dissenting shareholder and the corporation do not so agree, then the corporation, within thirty days after receipt of written demand from any dissenting shareholder given within sixty days after the date on which such corporate action was effected, shall, or at its election at any time within such period of sixty days may, file a petition in any court of competent jurisdiction in the county in this State where the registered office of the corporation is located requesting that the fair value of such shares be found and determined. If, in the case of a merger or consolidation, the surviving or new corporation is a foreign corporation without a registered office in this State, such petition shall be filed in the county where the registered office of the domestic corporation was last located. If the corporation shall fail to institute the proceeding as herein provided, any dissenting shareholder may do so in the name of the corporation. All dissenting shareholders, wherever residing, shall be made parties to the proceeding as an action against their shares quasi in rem. A copy of the petition shall be served on each dissenting shareholder who is a resident of this State and shall be served by registered or certified mail on each dissenting shareholder who is a nonresident. Service on nonresidents shall also be made by publication as provided by law. The jurisdiction of the court shall be plenary and exclusive. All shareholders who are parties to the proceeding shall be entitled to judgment against the corporation for the amount of the fair value of their shares. The court may, if it so elects, appoint one or more persons as appraisers to receive evidence and recommend a decision on the question of fair value. The appraisers shall have such power and authority as shall be specified in the order of their appointment or an amendment thereof. The judgment shall be payable to the holders of uncertificated shares immediately but to the holders of shares represented by certificates only upon and concurrently with the surrender to the corporation of such certificates. Upon payment of the judgment, the dissenting shareholder shall cease to have any interest in such shares.

[no changes in sixth and seventh paragraphs]

Upon receiving a demand for payment from any dissenting shareholder the corporation shall make an appropriate notation thereof in its shareholder records. Within twenty days after demanding payment for his shares, each holder of shares represented by certificates demanding payment shall submit such certificates to the corporation for notation thereon that such demand has been made. His failure to do so shall, at the option of the corporation, terminate his rights under this section unless a court of competent jurisdiction, for good and sufficient cause shown, shall otherwise direct. If uncertificated shares for which payment has been demanded or shares represented by a certificate on which notation has been so made shall be transferred, any new certificate issued therefor shall bear similar notation together with the name of the original dissenting holder of such shares, and a transferee of any such shares shall acquire by such transfer no rights in the corporation other than those which the original dissenting shareholder had after making demand for payment of the fair value thereof.

[no changes in final paragraph]

§ 80. Right of Shareholders to Dissent and Obtain Payment for Shares.

(a) Any shareholder of a corporation shall have the right to dissent from, and obtain payment for his shares in the event of, any of the following corporate actions:

(1) Any plan of merger or consolidation to which the corporation is a party, except as provided in subsection (c);

(2) Any sale or exchange of all or substantially all of the property and assets of the corporation not

made in the usual or regular course of its business, including a sale in dissolution, but not including a sale pursuant to an order of a court having jurisdiction in the premises or a sale for cash on terms requiring that all or substantially all of the net proceeds of sale be distributed to the shareholders in accordance with their respective interests within one year after the date of sale;

(3) Any plan of exchange to which the corporation is a party as the corporation the shares of which are to be acquired;

(4) Any amendment of the articles of incorporation which materially and adversely affects the rights appurtenant to the shares of the dissenting shareholder in that it—

(i) alters or abolishes a preferential right of such shares;

(ii) creates, alters or abolishes a right in respect of the redemption of such shares, including a provision respecting a sinking fund for the redemption or repurchase of such shares;

(iii) alters or abolishes a preemptive right of the holder of such shares to acquire shares of other securities;

(iv) excludes or limits the right of the holder of such shares to vote on any matter, or to cumulate his votes, except as such right may be limited by dilution through the issuance of shares or other securities with similar voting rights; or

(5) Any other corporate action taken pursuant to a shareholder vote with respect to which the articles of incorporation, the bylaws, or a resolution of the board of directors directs that dissenting shareholders shall have a right to obtain payment for their shares.

(b) (1) A record holder of shares may assert dissenters' rights as to less than all of the shares registered in his name only if he dissents with respect to all the shares beneficially owned by any one person, and discloses the name and address of the person or persons on whose behalf he dissents. In that event, his rights shall be determined as if the shares as to which he has dissented and his other shares were registered in the names of different shareholders.

(2) A beneficial owner of shares who is not the record holder may assert dissenters' rights with respect to shares held on his behalf, and shall be treated as a dissenting shareholder under the terms of this section and Section 81 if he submits to the corporation at the time of or before the assertion of these rights a written consent of the record holder.

(c) The right to obtain payment under this section shall not apply to the shareholders of the surviving corporation in a merger if a vote of the shareholders of such corporation is not necessary to authorize such merger.

(d) A shareholder of a corporation who has a right under this section to obtain payment for his shares shall have no right at law or in equity to attack the validity of the corporate action that gives rise to his right to obtain payment, nor to have the action set aside or rescinded, except when the corporate action is unlawful or fraudulent with regard to the complaining shareholder or to the corporation.

§ 81. Rights of Dissenting Shareholders. Amended to read:

§ 81. Procedures for Protection of Dissenters' Rights.

(a) As used in this section—

(1) "Dissenter" means a shareholder or beneficial owner who is entitled to and does assert dissenters' rights under Section 80, and who has performed every act required up to the time involved for the assertion of such rights.

(2) "Corporation" means the issuer of the shares held by the dissenter before the corporate action, or the successor by merger or consolidation of that issuer.

(3) "Fair value" of shares means their value immediately before the effectuation of the corporate action to which the dissenter objects, excluding any appreciation or depreciation in anticipation of such corporate action unless such exclusion would be inequitable.

(4) "Interest" means interest from the effective date of the corporate action until the date of payment, at the average rate currently paid by the corporation on its principal bank loans, or, if none, at such rate as is fair and equitable under all the circumstances.

(b) If a proposed corporate action which would give rise to dissenters' rights under Section 80(a) is submitted to a vote at a meeting of shareholders, the notice of meeting shall notify all shareholders that they have or may have a right to dissent and obtain payment for their shares by complying with the terms of this Section, and shall be accompanied by a copy of Sections 80 and 81 of this Act.

(c) If the proposed corporate action is submitted to a vote at a meeting of shareholders, any shareholder who wishes to dissent and obtain payment for his shares must file with the corporation, prior to the vote, a written notice of intention to demand that he be paid fair compensation for his shares if the proposed action is effectuated, and shall refrain from voting his shares in approval of such action. A shareholder who falls in either respect shall acquire no right to payment for his shares under this section or Section 80.

(d) If the proposed corporate action is approved by the required vote at a meeting of shareholders, the corporation shall mail a further notice to all shareholders who gave due notice of intention to demand payment and who refrained from voting in favor of the proposed action. If the proposed corporate action is to be taken without a vote of shareholders, the corporation shall send to all shareholders who are entitled to dissent and demand payment of their shares a notice of the adoption of the plan of corporate action. The notice shall (1) state where and when a demand for payment must be sent and certificates of certificated shares must be deposited in order to obtain payment, (2) inform holders of uncertificated shares to what extent transfer of shares will be restricted from the time that demand for payment is received, (3) supply a form for demanding payment which includes a request for certification of the date on which the shareholder, or the person on whose behalf the shareholder dissents, acquired beneficial ownership of the shares, and (4) be accompanied by a copy of Sections 80 and 81 of this Act. The time set for the demand and deposit shall be not less than 30 days from the mailing of the notice.

(e) A shareholder who fails to demand payment, or fails (in the case of certificated shares) to deposit certificates, as required by a notice pursuant to subsection (d) shall have no right under this section or Section 80 to receive payment for his shares. If the shares are not represented by certificates, the corporaton may restrict their transfer from the time of receipt of demand for payment until effectuation of the proposed corporate action, or the release of restrictions under the terms of subsection (f). The dissenter shall retain all other rights of a shareholder until these rights are modified by effectuation of the proposed corporate action.

(f) (1) Within 60 days after the date set for demanding payment and depositing certificates, if the corporation has not effectuated the proposed corporate action and remitted payment for shares pursuant to paragraph (3), it shall return any certificates that have been deposited, and release uncertificated shares from any transfer restrictions imposed by reason of the demand for payment.

(2) When uncertificated shares have been released from transfer restrictions, and deposited certificates have been returned, the corporation may at any later time send a new notice conforming to the requirements of subsection (d), with like effect.

(3) Immediately upon effectuation of the proposed corporate action, or upon receipt of demand for payment if the corporate action has already been effectuated, the corporation shall remit to dissenters who have made demand and (if their shares are certificated) have deposited their certificates the amount which the corporation estimates to be the fair value of the shares, with interest if any has accrued. The remittance shall be accompanied by—

(i) the corporation's closing balance sheet and statement of income for a fiscal year ending not more than 16 months before the date of remittance, together with the latest available interim financial statements;

(ii) a statement of the corporation's estimate of fair value of the shares; and

(iii) a notice of the dissenter's right to demand supplemental payment, accompanied by a copy of Sections 80 and 81 of this Act.

(g) (1) If the corporation fails to remit as required by subsection (f), or if the dissenter believes that the amount remitted is less than the fair value of his shares, or that the interest is not correctly determined, he may send the corporation his own estimate of the value of the shares or of the interest, and demand payment of the deficiency.

(2) If the dissenter does not file such an estimate within 30 days after the corporation's mailing of its remittance, he shall be entitled to no more than the amount remitted.

(h) (1) Within 60 days after receiving a demand for payment pursuant to subsection (g), if any such demands for payment remain unsettled, the corporation shall file in an appropriate court a petition requesting that the fair value of the shares and interest thereon be determined by the court.

(2) An appropriate court shall be a court of competent jurisdiction in the county of this state where the registered office of the corporation is located. If, in the case of a merger or consolidation or exchange of shares, the corporation is a foreign corporation without a registered office in this state, the petition shall be filed in the county where the registered office of the domestic corporation was last located.

(3) All dissenters, wherever residing, whose demands have not been settled shall be made parties to the proceeding as in an action against their shares. A copy of the petition shall be served on each such dissenter; if a dissenter is a nonresident, the copy may be served on him by registered or certified mail or by publication as provided by law.

(4) The jurisdiction of the court shall be plenary and exclusive. The court may appoint one or more persons as appraisers to receive evidence and recommend a decision on the question of fair value. The appraisers shall have such power and authority as shall be specified in the order of their appointment or in any amendment thereof. The dissenters shall be entitled to discovery in the same manner as parties in other civil suits.

(5) All dissenters who are made parties shall be entitled to judgment for the amount by which the fair value of their shares is found to exceed the amount previously remitted, with interest.

(6) If the corporation fails to file a petition as provided in paragraph (1) of this subsection, each dissenter who made a demand and who has not already settled his claim against the corporation shall be paid by the corporation the amount demanded by him, with interest, and may sue therefor in an appropriate court.

(i) (1) The costs and expenses of any proceeding under subsection (h), including the reasonable compensation and expenses of appraisers appointed by the court, shall be determined by the court and assessed against the corporation, except that any part of the costs and expenses may be apportioned and assessed as the court may deem equitable against all or some of the dissenters who are parties and whose action in demanding supplemental payment the court finds to be arbitrary, vexatious, or not in good faith.

(2) Fees and expenses of counsel and of experts for the respective parties may be assessed as the court may deem equitable against the corporation and in favor of any or all dissenters if the corporation failed to comply substantially with the requirements of this section, and may be assessed against either the corporation or a dissenter, in favor of any other party, if the court finds that the party against whom the fees and expenses are assessed acted arbitrarily, vexatiously, or not in good faith in respect to the rights provided by this Section and Section 80.

(3) If the court finds that the services of counsel for any dissenter were of substantial benefit to other dissenters similarly situated, and should not be assessed against the corporation, it may award to these counsel reasonable fees to be paid out of the amounts awarded to the dissenters who were benefitted.

(j) (1) Notwithstanding the foregoing provisions of this section, the corporation may elect to withhold the remittance required by subsection (f) from any dissenter with respect to shares of which the dissenter (or the person on whose behalf the dissenter acts) was not the beneficial owner on the date of the first announcement to news media or to shareholders of the terms of the proposed corporate action. With respect to such shares, the corporation shall, upon effectuating the corporate action, state to each dissenter its estimate of the fair value of the shares, state the rate of interest to be used (explaining the basis thereof) and offer to pay the resulting amounts on receiving the dissenter's agreement to accept them in full satisfaction.

(2) If the dissenter believes that the amount offered is less than the fair value of the shares and interest determined according to this section, he may within 30 days after the date of mailing of the corporation's offer, mail the corporation his own estimate of fair value and interest, and demand their payment. If the dissenter fails to do so, he shall be entitled to no more than the corporation's offer.

(3) If the dissenter makes a demand as provided in paragraph (2), the provisions of subsections (h) and (i) shall apply to further proceedings on the dissenter's demand. [*See* subsections (c) and (d), *supra*.]

Amendment Adopted on September 23, 1978

§ 52. Books and Records.

Amended to read:

§ 52. Books and Records: Financial Reports to Shareholders; Examination of Records. Each corporation shall furnish to its shareholders annual financial statements, including at least a balance sheet as of the end of each fiscal year and a statement of income for such fiscal year, which shall be prepared on the basis of generally accepted accounting principles, if the corporation prepares financial statements for such fiscal year on that basis for any purpose, and may be consolidated statements of the corporation and one or more of its subsidiaries. The financial statements shall be mailed by the corporation to each of its shareholders within 120 days after the close of each fiscal year and, after such mailing and upon written request, shall be mailed by the corporation to any shareholder (or holder of a voting trust certificate for its shares) to whom a copy of the most recent annual financial statements has not previously been mailed. In the case of statements audited by a public accountant, each copy shall be accompanied by a report setting forth his opinion thereon; in other cases, each copy shall be accompanied by a statement of the president or the person in charge of the corporation's financial accounting records (1) stating his reasonable belief as to whether or not the financial statements were prepared in accordance with generally accepted accounting principles and, if not, describing the basis of presentation, and (2) describing any respects in which the financial statements were not prepared on a basis consistent with those prepared for the previous year.

Amendment Adopted on June 20, 1980

Section 5 of the Model Business Corporation Act is amended to read as follows:

§ 5. Indemnification of Directors and Officers.

(a) As used in this section:

(1) *Director* means any person who is or was a director of the corporation and any person who, while a director of the corporation, is or was serving at the request of the corporation as a director, officer, partner, trustee, employee or agent of another foreign or domestic corporation, partnership, joint venture, trust, other enterprise or employee benefit plan.

(2) *Corporation* includes any domestic or foreign predecessor entity of the corporation in a merger, consolidation or other transaction in which the predecessor's existence ceased upon consummation of such transaction.

(3) *Expenses* include attorneys' fees.

(4) *Official capacity* means

(A) when used with respect to a director, the office of director in the corporation, and

(B) when used with respect to a person other than a director, as contemplated in subsection (i), the elective or appointive office in the corporation held by the officer or the employment or agency relationship undertaken by the employee or agent in behalf of the corporation, but in each case does not include service for any other foreign or domestic corporation or any partnership, joint venture, trust, other enterprise, or employee benefit plan.

(5) *Party* includes a person who was, is, or is threatened to be made, a named defendant or respondent in a proceeding.

(6) *Proceeding* means any threatened, pending or completed action, suit or proceeding, whether civil, criminal, administrative or investigative.

(b) A corporation shall have power to indemnify any person made a party to any proceeding by reason of the fact that he is or was a director if

(1) he conducted himself in good faith; and

(2) he reasonably believed

(A) in the case of conduct in his official capacity with the corporation, that his conduct was in its best interests, and

(B) in all other cases, that his conduct was at least not opposed to its best interests; and

(3) in the case of any criminal proceeding, he had no reasonable cause to believe his conduct was unlawful.

Indemnification may be made against judgments, penalties, fines, settlements and reasonable expenses, actually incurred by the person in connection with the proceeding; except that if the proceeding was by or in the right of the corporation, indemnification may be made only against such reasonable expenses and shall not be made in respect of any proceeding in which the person shall have been adjudged to be liable to the corporation. The termination of any proceeding by judgment, order, settlement, conviction, or upon a plea of nolo contendere or its equivalent, shall not, of itself, be determinative that the person did not meet the requisite standard of conduct set forth in this subsection (b).

(c) A director shall not be indemnified under subsection (b) in respect of any proceeding charging improper personal benefit to him, whether or not involving action in his official capacity, in which he shall have been adjudged to be liable on the basis that personal benefit was improperly received by him.

(d) Unless limited by the articles of incorporation,

(1) a director who has been wholly successful, on the merits or otherwise, in the defense of any proceeding referred to in subsection (b) shall be indemnified against reasonable expenses incurred by him in connection with the proceeding; and

(2) a court of appropriate jurisdiction, upon application of a director and such notice as the court shall require, shall have authority to order indemnification in the following circumstances:

(A) if it determines a director is entitled to reimbursement under clause (1), the court shall order indemnification, in which case the director shall also be entitled to recover the expenses of securing such reimbursement; or

(B) if it determines that the director is fairly and reasonably entitled to indemnification in view of all the relevant circumstances, whether or not he has met the standard of conduct set forth in subsection (b) or has been adjudged liable in the circumstances described in subsection (c), the court may order such indemnification as the court shall deem proper, except that indemnification with respect to any proceeding by or in the right of the corporation or in which liability shall have been adjudged in the circumstances described in subsection (c) shall be limited to expenses.

A court of appropriate jurisdiction may be the same court in which the proceeding involving the director's liability took place.

(e) No indemnification under subsection (b) shall be made by the corporation unless authorized in the specific case after a determination has been made that indemnification of the director is permissible in the circumstances because he has met the standard of conduct set forth in subsection (b). Such determination shall be made:

(1) by the board of directors by a majority vote of a quorum consisting of directors not at the time parties to the proceeding; or

(2) if such a quorum cannot be obtained, then by a majority vote of a committee of the board, duly designated to act in the matter by a majority vote of the full board (in which designation directors who are parties may participate), consisting solely of two or more directors not at the time parties to the proceeding; or

(3) by special legal counsel, selected by the board of directors or a committee thereof by vote as set forth in clauses (1) or (2) of this subsection (e), or, if the requisite quorum of the full board cannot be obtained therefor and such committee cannot be established, by a majority vote of the full board (in which selection directors who are parties may participate); or

(4) by the shareholders.

Authorization of indemnification and determination as to reasonableness of expenses shall be made in the same manner as the determination that indemnification is permissible, except that if the determination that indemnification is permissible is made by special legal counsel, authorization of indemnification and determination as to reasonableness of expenses shall be made in a manner specified in clause (3) in the preceding sentence for the selection of such counsel. Shares held by directors who are parties to the proceeding shall not be voted on the subject matter under this subsection (e).

(f) Reasonable expenses incurred by a director who is a party to a proceeding may be paid or reimbursed by the corporation in advance of the final disposition of such proceeding upon receipt by the corporation of

(1) a written affirmation by the director of his good faith belief that he has met the standard of conduct necessary for indemnification by the corporation as authorized in this section, and

(2) a written undertaking by or on behalf of the director to repay such amount if it shall ultimately be determined that he has not met such standard of conduct, and

after a determination that the facts then known to those making the determination would not preclude indemnification under this section. The undertaking required by clause (2) shall be an unlimited general obligation of the director but need not be secured and may be accepted without reference to financial ability to make repayment. Determinations and authorizations of payments under this subsection (f) shall be made in the manner specified in subsection (e).

(g) No provision for the corporation to indemnify or to advance expenses to a director who is made a party to a proceeding, whether contained in the articles of incorporation, the by-laws, a resolution of shareholders or directors, an agreement or otherwise (except as contemplated by subsection (j)), shall be valid unless consistent with this section or, to the extent that indemnity hereunder is limited by the articles of incorporation, consistent therewith. Nothing contained in this section shall limit the corporation's power to pay or reimburse expenses incurred by a director in connection with his appearance as a witness in a proceeding at a time when he has not been made a named defendant or respondent in the proceeding.

(h) For purposes of this section, the corporation shall be deemed to have requested a director to serve an employee benefit plan whenever the performance by him of his duties to the corporation also imposes duties on, or otherwise involves services by, him to the plan or participants or beneficiaries of the plan; excise taxes assessed on a director with respect to an employee benefit plan pursuant to applicable law shall be deemed "fines"; and action taken or omitted by him with respect to an employee benefit plan in the performance of his duties for a purpose reasonably believed by him to be in the interest of the participants and beneficiaries of the plan shall be deemed to be for a purpose which is not opposed to the best interests of the corporation.

(i) Unless limited by the articles of incorporation,

(1) an officer of the corporation shall be indemnified as and to the extent provided in subsection (d) for a director and shall be entitled to the same extent as a director to seek indemnification pursuant to the provisions of subsection (d);

(2) a corporation shall have the power to indemnify and to advance expenses to an officer, employee or agent of the corporation to the same extent that it may indemnify and advance expenses to directors pursuant to this section; and

(3) a corporation, in addition, shall have the power to indemnify and to advance expenses to an officer, employee or agent who is not a director to such further extent, consistent with law, as may be provided by its articles of incorporation, by-laws, general or specific action of its board of directors, or contract.

(j) A corporation shall have power to purchase and maintain insurance on behalf of any person who is or was a director, officer, employee or agent of the corporation, or who, while a director, officer, employee or agent of the corporation, is or was serving at the request of the corporation as a director, officer, partner, trustee, employee or agent of another foreign or domestic corporation, partnership, joint venture, trust, other enterprise or employee benefit plan, against any liability asserted against him and incurred by him in any such capacity or arising out of his status as such, whether or not the corporation would have the power to indemnify him against such liability under the provisions of this section.

(k) Any indemnification of, or advance of expenses to, a director in accordance with this section, if arising out of a proceeding by or in the right of the corporation, shall be reported in writing to the shareholders with or before the notice of the next shareholders' meeting.

Review Problems

A substantial drawback to current instructional efforts at the university level is that the information learned is too often fragmented by our desire to categorize bodies of knowledge. This makes instruction relatively easy by providing manageable units of knowledge. However, most problems in reality do not come in defined categories. For example, managers seldom are informed of a problem in a business by reference to the traditional compartments of knowledge. Problems do not come labeled: this is a cost accounting problem; or, this is a marketing channels problem; or, this is an agency law problem. Only after serious analysis and consultation can a problem be so classified; and even when it is, it may often require the application of principles from all of those areas.

Review Problems

The student of the law of business organizations will almost never be presented with a problem clearly designated as a "corporation law" problem, for example. To acquaint the student with some of the problems he or she might face as a manager of a business organization we have presented below some review problems which are not labled by the principles which must be applied. We start with relatively easy review questions and end with complex ones. In the more difficult problems the student is advised to first list the "legal" issues as you see them. Then recall and define the legal principle which you believe to be applicable. Finally, in a concisely worded paragraph or two, explain how the principle might be applied by a court. There may be no obvious or correct solution. The most important task here is to correctly recall, define and apply the legal principle.

Some of the questions are direct quotes from or adaptations of problems from the Uniform CPA Examinations copyrighted by the American Institute of Certified Public Accountants, Inc., and are reproduced here with their permission. These questions are identified by designating them,

817

"CPA Exam Question" followed by the number of the question and the month, day and year they appeared on the exam.

The remainder of the review questions are fictional and were created only for purposes of review.

Indicate whether the answer for questions 1 and 9 is true or false. Then in a short paragraph give the reasons for your answer.

1. Adaptation of CPA Exam Question 3, November 5, 1971

Peters, Long and Tyler formed a general merchandising partnership. Cash capital contributions were $50,000 from Peters, and $25,000 each from Long and Tyler. The partnership agreement provides that the partners are to share profits and losses in proportion to capital contribution balances and that the partnership is to have a duration of ten years. After the partnership was established, the partners decided to admit Kramer as a partner if he would make a capital contribution of $25,000 and Kramer agreed to this. At the time of Kramer's admission, the partnership agreement was amended to provide that no partner shall make any contract for the firm involving more than $50,000 without the express consent of all other partners.

a. If the partnership makes a profit of $100,000 during its first year of operations, Peters is entitled to $50,000.

b. If the partnership agreement were silent on the subject of the division of profits, the answer to the question above would be different.

c. If a judgment is entered against the partnership, each of the partners would be personally liable for the full amount thereof and the judgment creditor could proceed to collect from any one of them.

d. In the question above, the judgment creditor must first exhaust the assets of the partnership before he can proceed against the individual assets of the partners.

e. If Tyler should die, the partnership would be dissolved as a matter of law.

f. Any one of the partners may retire from the business at any time and dissolve the partnership without liability.

g. Kramer's admission required the dissolution of the old partnership and the formation of a new partnership.

h. Kramer would be liable personally for obligations of the partnership incurred prior to his admission.

i. If Kramer is liable for partnership obligations incurred prior to his admission to the firm, such obligations could be collected out of both his partnership and personal assets.

**2. Adaptation of CPA Exam Question 27,
   May 9, 1975**

Head is a crane operator for Magnum Construction Corporation. One day while operating the crane he negligently swung the crane into another building, which caused extensive damage to the other building and the crane. The accident also resulted in fracturing Head's elbow and dislocating his hip. In this situation,

a. Head is liable for the damages he caused to the crane and the building.
b. Magnum's liability is limited to the damage to the building only if Head was acting within the scope of his authority.
c. Magnum will not be liable for damage to the building if Head's negligence was in clear violation of Magnum's safety standards and the rules regarding operation of the crane.

**3. Adaptation of CPA Exam Question 30,
   May 9, 1975**

The ratification doctrine

a. Is not applicable to situations where the party claiming to act as the agent for another has no express or implied authority to do so.
b. Is designed to apply to situations where the principal was originally incompetent to have made the contract himself, but who, upon becoming competent, ratifies.
c. Requires the principal to ratify the entire act of the agent and the ratification is retroactive.
d. Applies only if the principal expressly ratifies in writing the contract made on his behalf within a reasonable time.

**4. Adaptation of CPA Exam Question 31,
   May 9, 1975**

Normally a principal will not be liable to a third party

a. On a contract signed on his behalf by an agent who was expressly forbidden by the principal to make it and where the third party was unaware of the agent's limitation.
b. On a contract made by his agent and the principal is not disclosed, unless the principal ratifies it.
c. For torts committed by an independent contractor if they are within the scope of the contract.
d. On a negotiable instrument signed by the agent in his own name without revealing he signed in his agency capacity.

5. Adaptation of CPA Exam Question 23, May 9, 1975

The partnership of Baker, Green, and Madison is insolvent. The partnership's liabilities exceed its assets by $123,000. The liabilities include a $25,000 loan from Madison. Green is personally insolvent, his personal liabilities exceed his personal assets by $13,500. Green has filed a voluntary petition in bankruptcy. Under these circumstances, partnership creditors

a. Must proceed jointly against the partnership and all the general partners so that losses may be shared equitably among the partners.

b. Rank first in payment and all (including Madison) will share proportionately in the partnership assets to be distributed.

c. Will have the first claim to partnership property to the exclusion of the personal creditors of Green.

d. Have the right to share pro rata with Green's personal creditors Green's personal assets.

6. Adaptation of CPA Exam Question 24, May 9, 1975

Jack Gordon, a general partner of Visions Unlimited, is retiring. He sold his partnership interest to Don Morrison for $80,000. Gordon assigned to Morrison all his rights, title, and interests in the partnership and named Morrison as his successor partner in Visions. In this situation

a. The assignment to Morrison dissolves the partnership.

b. Absent any limitation regarding the assignment of a partner's interest, Gordon is free to assign it at his will.

c. Morrison is entitled to an equal voice and vote in the management of the partnership, and he is entitled to exercise all the rights and privileges that Gordon had.

d. Morrison does not have the status of a partner, but he can, upon demand, inspect the partnership accounting records.

7. Adaptation of CPA Exam Question 25, May 9, 1975

Morton, a senior staff member of Wilcox & Southern, CPAs, has been offered the opportunity to become a junior partner of the firm. However, to be admitted to the partnership he must contribute $30,000 to the partnership's capital, and he does not have that amount of money. It is estimated that the partnership interest in question is worth at least

$100,000. The partnership agreement is silent on assignment of a partner's interest. Morton accepts the offer and becomes a junior partner.

a. Morton could assign his partnership interest to a bank or other lending institution as security for a loan to acquire his partnership interest.

b. Morton is personally liable for all debts of the partnership, past and present, unless the partnership agreement provides otherwise.

c. Since Morton is only a junior partner with very little say in the management of the firm and the selection of clients, he has the legal status of a quasi limited partner.

d. If Morton pledged his partnership interest as security for a loan to acquire his partnership interest, the transaction created a subpartnership between himself and the lending institution.

8. Adaptation of CPA Exam Question 26, May 9, 1975

Menlow Corporation dismissed Gibson, its purchasing agent, for incompetence. It published a notice in the appropriate trade journals which stated: "This is to notify all parties concerned that Gibson is no longer employed by the Menlow Corporation and the corporation assumes no further responsibility for his acts." Gibson called on several of Menlow's suppliers with whom he had previously dealt, and when he found one who was unaware of his dismissal, he would place a substantial order for merchandise to be delivered to a warehouse in which he had rented space. Menlow had rented warehouse space in the past when its storage facilities were crowded. Gibson also called on several suppliers with whom Menlow had never dealt; he would present one of his old business cards to the secretary and then make purchases on open account in the name of Menlow. Gibson then sold all the merchandise delivered to the warehouse and absconded with the money. In this situation,

a. Gibson had continuing express authority to make contracts on Menlow's behalf with suppliers with whom he had previously dealt as Menlow's agent, if they were unaware of his dismissal.

b. The suppliers who previously had no dealings with Menlow cannot enforce the contracts against Menlow even if the suppliers were unaware of Gibson's lack of authority.

c. Menlow is liable on the Gibson contracts to all suppliers who had dealt with Gibson in the past as Menlow's agent.

d. Constructive notice via publication in the appropriate trade journals is an effective notice to all third parties regardless of whether they had dealt with Gibson or read the notice.

9. Adaptation of CPA Exam Question 3, May 11, 1973

A. The examination of the financial statements of the Franklin Grocery Company revealed the following dispute relating to a balance due on open account. The item in dispute was a certain quantity of canned goods allegedly purchased by the Birch Steamship Company. On October 10, 1972, Arthur Snead, one of Franklin's salesmen, called upon Birch Steamship to solicit business. He had done business for several years with Ken Small, one of Birch Steamship's purchasing agents. Upon asking for Small at the receptionist's desk, he was told that Small was not there. The receptionist then called James Drew, another purchasing agent. She informed Drew that Arthur Snead of Franklin Grocery was looking for Small. Drew told the secretary that Small was at pier 30 supervising the loading of provisions. Snead found Small at pier 30 and took the disputed order for the canned goods, which were duly shipped to Birch Steamship. Unknown to Snead, Small had been relieved of his position as purchasing agent due to incompetency. Small obtained possession of the canned goods shipped to Birch Steamship and sold them. Birch refuses to pay.

1. Small had no express authority to make the purchase on Birch Steamship's behalf.
2. Small had the apparent authority to bind Birch Steamship.
3. To defeat Franklin Grocery, Birch Steamship must show knowledge by Franklin of Small's dismissal as a purchasing agent.
4. A publication in local papers and trade publications of the removal of Small as a purchasing agent would give effective notice to new suppliers of Birch Steamship.
5. Birch Steamship is liable on the contract made by Small as its purported agent.
6. Had Birch Steamship learned of the unauthorized contract made on its behalf by Small, it could have ratified the transaction.

B. During your examination of the financial statements of Bonanza Development Corporation, you reviewed certain land transactions involving John Walters as agent for Bonanza. Bonanza feared the price of land would skyrocket if it became known that it was trying to purchase a large number of tracts of land to develop a shopping center. It, therefore, instructed Walters not to disclose to prospective sellers that he was acting as an agent on its behalf. The agreement between Walters and Bonanza was in writing and signed by both parties.

1. Bonanza is an undisclosed principal.
2. Unless Bonanza ratifies the contracts made by Walters, it has no liability thereon.

3. Walters has committed a fraud in failing to notify prospective buyers of the fact he is acting as Bonanza's agent.

4. Bonanza cannot enforce the contracts made by Walters secretly on its behalf.

5. Walters will not be entitled to the commissions agreed to by Bonanza in that he has entered into an illegal bargain.

6. If Walters gave the usual warranties in connection with the purchase of the land, Bonanza would be liable on them even though Walters was not authorized to make them.

C. Your client, Sanitary Dairies, Inc., had employed Harold Stone as a milk-truck driver. Stone negligently ran the truck into the car of Ronald Green, injuring Green, his wife, and damaging Green's car. Stone was also injured in the collision.

1. If Stone had never had a previous accident, Sanitary Dairies would not be liable.

2. Stone can avoid liability in that he was engaged in the performance of his principal's business.

3. Had Stone left his assigned route in order to pick up his wife and take her shopping, Sanitary Dairies would not be liable.

4. Stone has breached one of his duties to his principal.

D. Charles Golden, a promoter, contacted an inventor, a plant owner, and several investors to join him in creating the Meglo Corporation. Golden made several contracts on behalf of the corporation prior to its coming into existence. The principals other than Golden subsequently decided to disassociate themselves from Golden and the contracts that he made and independently created the Meglo Corporation. You have been engaged as the CPA for Meglo.

1. Meglo is liable on the contracts made by Golden on behalf of the corporation.

2. Golden was the agent for a nonexistent principal.

3. The ratification doctrine does not apply to the contracts made by Golden on Meglo's behalf.

4. Golden is a principal.

10. CPA Exam Question 6, May 11, 1973

A. Charles Meskill has decided to invest $600,000 in a new business venture. Meskill will be joined by two, possibly three, former business associates. He has purchased the patent rights to a revolutionary adhesive substance known as "sticko." In connection with the transaction, he is considering the various forms of business organization he might use in establishing the business. You have been engaged to study the accounting and business problems he should consider in choosing to operate as a general partnership, limited partnership, or corporation. Meskill requests specific advice on the following aspects as they relate to the operation of a business as one of these three forms of business organization: 1) personal liability in the event the venture proves to be a disaster; 2) the borrowing capacity of the entity; 3) requirements for doing a multi-state business; 4) the liability of the entity for the acts of its agents; and 5) the recognition of the entity for income tax purposes and major income tax considerations in selecting one of the three forms of business organizations.

Required:

Discuss the various legal implications of each specific aspect for which Meskill seeks advice for operating a business in the above mentioned forms of business organization.

B. Selecting the general partnership versus the corporation as a form of business organization requires consideration of: 1) the right to compensation for services rendered; 2) the fiduciary duty; and 3) management prerogatives.

Required:

Compare and contrast the rights and responsibilities of a common stockholder with a general partner for each of the three areas stated above.

11. CPA Exam Question 4, May 11, 1973

A. Parker Pastry, Inc., is a closely held corporation. Curtis and Smith, two of Parker's directors, together own 55 percent of the corporation's outstanding stock. Devlin, an elderly retired executive, owns 25 percent of Parker's outstanding stock. The remaining 20 percent of the outstanding stock is held by five other unrelated persons. There have been no ownership changes in recent years. Parker's stock has no par value and a present book value of $50 per share.

Baxter Bakeries Corp. is a large, publicly held corporation whose stock is traded on a national securities exchange. The Baxter stock has a par value of $75 per share and is presently being traded at about $100 per share.

Baxter is seeking control of Parker. For tax reasons, Baxter must acquire 80 percent of Parker's stock to make the acquisition economically feasible. It is not interested at this time in acquiring more than this 80 percent. Baxter's president proposes to Curtis and Smith that Baxter exchange one share of its stock for one share of Parker stock provided that no less than 80 percent nor more than 85 percent of Parker's stock is thus acquired by Baxter.

Without revealing Baxter's offer, Curtis and Smith purchase the Parker stock owned by Devlin at book value. Thereafter, Smith and Curtis deliver their now 80 percent of Parker's outstanding stock to Baxter in exchange for Baxter stock.

Required:

What right does Devlin have against Curtis and Smith under the federal Securities Exchange Act of 1934? Explain.

B. In order for Baxter to acquire the Parker stock, as described in part A. above, Baxter was required to deliver 30,000 of its shares in exchange for the Parker stock. Baxter had 12,000 shares in its treasury and was currently authorized by its charter to issue 100,000 additional shares. The Baxter directors formally authorized the delivery of the 12,000 treasury shares and the issuance of 18,000 additional shares to acquire the Parker stock. As the auditor of Baxter's financial statements, you are concerned about the contingency that Baxter might incur a liability from stockholders' objections to this Board action. Baxter stockholders might argue that the exchange was unfair, considering the fact that the Parker stock had a book value of $50 per share and was being exchanged for Baxter stock on a share-for-share basis.

Required:

1. Was the action of Baxter's directors proper? Explain.

2. Could any Baxter stockholder successfully assert a preemptive right to acquire any of the shares to be delivered by Baxter? Explain.

C. The 12,000 Baxter shares delivered equally to Curtis and Smith, as described in part B. above, had been issued originally in connection with a public offering registered under the federal Securities Act of 1933. The 18,000 newly issued shares had not been registered by Baxter.

Shortly after acquiring his Baxter shares, Curtis sold them to the public in a regular stock exchange transaction, a plan he had in mind at the time he acquired the shares. Smith retained his shares for several years, having viewed his acquisition as an investment. Smith then sold his stock to the public in a regular stock exchange transaction in order to meet unexpected financial reverses. At the time of their respective sales, neither Curtis nor Smith was employed by Baxter in any capacity and neither owned 10 percent of Baxter's stock. Neither Curtis nor Smith registered their sales with the Securities and Exchange Commission.

Required:

Will persons who purchased Curtis' and Smith's stock have any rights against Baxter under the federal Securities Act of 1933? Explain.

D. Several years after acquiring 80 percent of the stock of Parker, Baxter decided to merge Parker into itself. Under applicable state law, the merger required approval of only two-thirds of the Parker shares. Baxter voted its 80 percent of Parker's stock in favor of the merger which provided that each minority stockholder of Parker receive one share of Baxter stock in exchange for three shares of Parker stock. In connection with your examination of Baxter's financial statements, you have discovered that some of the minority stockholders voted against the merger. You are concerned that Baxter properly disclose in its financial statements the liability, if any, to the minority stockholders voting against the merger.

Required:

1. What are the rights of Parker stockholders who oppose the merger?
2. What steps must a stockholder ordinarily take to protect his rights in these circumstances?

12. CPA Exam Question 5, November 7, 1975

A. Boswell Realty Corporation, whose sole business is land development, purchased a large tract of land on which it intended to construct a high-rise apartment-house complex. In order to finance the construction, Boswell offered to sell $3,000,000 worth of shares in Boswell Realty to about 1,000 prospective investors located throughout the United States.

Required:

1. Discuss the implications of the Securities Act of 1933 to Boswell's offering to sell shares in the corporation.
2. The Securities Act of 1933 is considered a disclosure statute. Briefly describe the means provided and the principal types of information required to accomplish this objective of disclosure.
3. If an investor acquires shares of stock in Boswell Realty Corporation, is his interest real or personal property? Explain.

B. Taylor Corporation, incorporated and doing business in Delaware, is a manufacturing company whose securities are registered on a national securities exchange. On February 6, 1975, one of Taylor's engineers disclosed to management that he had discovered a new product which he believed would be quite profitable to the corporation. Messrs. Jackson and Wilson, the corporation's president and treasurer and members of its board of directors, were very impressed with the prospects of the new product's profitability. Because the corporation would need additional capital to finance the development, production, and marketing of the new product, the board of directors proposed that the corporation issue an additional 100,000 shares of common stock.

Wilson was imbued with such confidence in the corporation's prospects that on February 12, 1975, he purchased on the open market 1,000 shares of the corporation's common stock at $10 per share. This was before news of the new product reached the public in late February and caused a rise in the market price to $30 per share. Jackson did not purchase any shares in February because he had already purchased 600 shares of the corporation's common stock on January 15, 1975, for $10 per share.

In late February, when the market price of the corporation's common stock was $30 per share, Wilson approached two insurance companies to discuss the proposed issuance of an additional 100,000 shares of common stock. In March, Wilson reported to the board of directors that negotiations had been successful and one of the insurance companies had agreed to purchase the entire 100,000 shares for $3,000,000. The insurance company signed an investment letter, and a legend restricting transfers was imprinted on the face of each certificate issued to it. Moreover, the appropriate stock-transfer instructions were given to the corporation's stock-transfer agent.

Due to unexpected expenses arising from a fire in his home, on April 16, 1975, Jackson sold at $35 per share on the open market the 600 shares of stock he purchased in January. Wilson continues to hold his 1,000 shares.

What questions arising out of the federal securities laws are suggested by these facts? Discuss.

13. Adaptation of CPA Exam Question 4, May 9, 1975

Byron Corporation acquired more than 70 percent of the outstanding common stock of Sage, Inc., during the last twelve months; most of the shares were purchased from five of Sage's directors who owned approximately 60 percent of Sage's outstanding common stock which they sold to Byron. These five individuals were on the board of directors of both Sage and Byron for many years and still remain on both boards. Also, Byron utilized its ownership control to elect the remaining members of the board of directors and its own slate of officers of Sage.

You have just begun your first examination of the financial statements of Burke Corporation. Your examination is for the year ended December 31, 1974. Burke has never been audited before and is not subject to the Securities Act of 1933 or the Securities Exchange Act of 1934.

You have extracted the following information from Burke's general ledger and the corporation's Articles of Incorporation.

Stockholder's Equity

8%, cumulative, nonvoting preferred stock; par value, $100 per share; authorized, issued, and outstanding, 10,000 shares; liquidation preference, $115 per share aggregating $1,150,000	$1,000,000
Common stock; par value, $10 per share: authorized, 100,000 shares; issued and outstanding 10,000 shares	100,000
Additional paid-in capital	50,000
Retained earnings	110,000
Total	$1,260,000

Your preliminary inquiry has revealed the following information:

- Burke was incorporated in 1965 in a state which had adopted the Model Business Corporation Act.

- No dividends have been declared or paid on the preferred stock for 1973 and 1974. Dividends on the preferred stock had been declared and paid in all prior years. The preferred stock was issued six years ago at par to a group of local investors different from the common stockholders.

- Dividends of $20,000 were declared and paid on the common stock in both 1973 and 1974. Annual dividends have been declared and paid on the 10,000 shares of common stock outstanding since Burke's incorporation. The common stock is closely held and most of the common stockholders are members of the board of directors, officers, or employees.

- Burke's net income was $50,000 and $40,000 for 1973 and 1974, respectively. The $110,000 balance of retained earnings at December 31, 1974, was after closing the books on that date.

- Burke is and has been solvent since its incorporation.

Required:
Discuss the legal implications of the above facts to Burke, its directors, and its stockholders.

14. In 1971, S learned that A, B, and C were planning to form a corporation for the purpose of manufacturing and marketing a line of novelty-type items to wholesale outlets. S had patented a self-locking gas tank cap, but lacked the financial backing to market it profitably. He negotiated with A, B, and C, who agreed to purchase the patent rights for $5,000 to be paid in cash and 200 shares of $100 par value preferred stock in the corporation to be formed. The agreement was signed in December, 1971. The corporation was formed and properly registered with the Secretary of State in January, 1972 and S's stock was issued to him in the Spring of 1972 but the corporation has refused to pay the $5,000 cash and to declare dividends although the business grew very profitable due to the value of S's patent. What are S's rights?

15. C, the president of C Corp. is a good friend of yours and asked you to buy a few of the common shares of C Corp. when the initial issue came out. This you did. Shortly thereafter, he asked you if you would be willing to stand for election to the board. At first you refused, but he finally won out by convincing you that all you had to do was to sign the annual report; you did not have to attend lengthy board meetings or make any decisions or read any of the financial statements. Based upon C's assertions above you accepted the nomination and were elected to the board. You attended no meetings and did not read any of the corporate reports. You did feel some responsibility to the other shareholders and from time to time you questioned C about the company. You always relied upon C's verbal responses to your questions as to the financial condition of the company.

At the end of your second year on the board you were horrified to learn that the corporation had filed for bankruptcy. It was revealed that during the last year's operation, your friend, C, received a loan of $10,000 from the company which was secured by some of the company's most valuable and liquid assets. His drinking problem, of which you were aware, had caused his competent sales force to quit and he replaced it with dishonest men interested in looting the company. In 1970 net profits of the C Corp. were $25,000, in 1971 they were $150 and in 1972 the corporation was unable to meet some of its obligations as they became due.

A minority shareholder sues you and the president, C, for the recovery of the $10,000 loan, and for $50,000 he alleges is due for mismanagement.

a. Decide the case against the president. What are the legal cause(s) of action, the defenses and how much should be recovered?

b. Decide the case against yourself; what are the causes of action, the defenses and will recovery be successful?

16. As president of C Corp. discussed above, C hired a supposed super salesman, S, to develop the Chicago sales region. His official title was general agent and salesman. C furnished him with a list of potential customers in the region and told him to do everything he could to increase the business of C Corp. This was in 1966. On his first visit to Chicago S discovered that Y Corp. of Indianapolis, Indiana was a close competitor of C Corp. in the region. S, therefore, adopted a strategy of relating the falsified results of a test that was conducted by one of the consumer agencies which revealed that Y Corp.'s products had been declared unsafe and had been or would soon be banned. Soon the word that S was spreading took effect. The sales of Y Corp. dropped off sharply and the sales of C Corp. zoomed upward.

Y Corp. received word that S was spreading false and malicious information about the company's product which was an obvious tort (civil wrong) called intentional disparaging of another's product. As soon as C Corp.'s president found out about this he fired S. Soon thereafter Y Corp. sues C Corp. for $250,000 in lost business.

Describe the circumstances or facts that must be established in order to hold C Corp. liable for the $250,000.

17. Y Corporation, an engine manufacturer, desired to enter the boat building business. It decided upon a vote of 5 to 2 of the board to form a subsidiary corporation to engage in that business and sell its motors to the subsidiary. Thereupon it formed the Z Yacht Company for the purpose, with an initial capitalization of $250,000 and loaned the Yacht Company $750,000 secured by promissory notes.

A was the Vice President in charge of development for the Y Corporation and was appointed by the board to develop the Z Yacht Company. He moved his office from the Y corporation headquarters into the building which Z Yacht Company rented for its operation. A hired a chief naval architect, N, to do all of the designing and A promised to pay him a salary of $20,000 per year plus 10 percent of the Z Yacht Company profits arising from the sale of the new boats, plus he was promised stock options in Y Corp. A also acted as the chief purchasing agent and ordered raw materials from creditors, C, D, and E for a total of $220,000 of which $120,000 was paid in cash and the balance was to be paid upon the sale of boats. Another supplier, F, decided not to do business with A and Z Yacht Company because he just didn't ". . . like the looks of the situation."

Y Corporation provided $250,000 worth of motors for no cash payment to Z Yacht Company. The agreement between Y and Z was that Y would be paid as soon as the boats were sold.

In order to impress the prospective purchasers of the yachts A bought a Cadillac convertible special monarch deluxe for $20,000 on credit from Kady, the local Cadillac dealer and he signed the security agreement and purchase contract in his capacity as a representative of Z Yacht Company.

Unfortunately, A was much better at developing sales campaigns for new products than he was at developing a new manufacturing company. Most of the cash in the company *was* paid out for exorbitant salaries and huge promotional parties. Within a short time from the period when all of the above arrangements were made, the Z Yacht Company filed for bankruptcy. N had been paid only for the first two months of work, then was not paid for the next three months time he put in; C, D, E and Kady were never paid and neither was Y. What are the rights and remedies of N, C, D, E, Kady and Y? Who gets what from whom and why based upon what possible legal agreements?

Deciding whether or not a party will ultimately prevail in the courts is not as important as recognizing and discussing all legal issues. If you think a fact which is not stated is important, state what it is, and that you are assuming its existence.

18.   Three engineers who lived in San Francisco designed and made, in their spare time, a People Powered Car (hereafter, "PPC") which was propelled by pumping pedals much like a bicycle. They were so impressed with the ease by which PPC's could be manufactured that they formed the PPC Company to manufacture and market the PPC's. This company sold shares to the public on the west coast. An elderly retired man, R, purchased some shares.

Having raised $500,000 by the sale of stock, PPC Company began business and the three engineers, A, B, and C, were elected directors along with D & E. D & E were very wealthy businessmen who bought large amounts of stock because PPC looked like a sure thing. However, they never took an interest in the business and rarely came to board meetings. They left the enterprise to A, B, and C, to operate. Unfortunately, A, B, and C were much better engineers than businessmen. At their first board meeting, they hired O as president of the company. O was a hot-shot-promoter type who had just been discharged from the Detroit fraternity of top automobile manufacturing managers for questionable deals. O was given the express assignment of developing the marketing and promotion for the PPC as well as overseeing staff operations. A, B, and C were to concentrate on manufacturing, research and development.

O realized when he was hired that $500,000 in paid-in capital was not going to take the company far. He negotiated an unsecured loan from L lending institution for one million dollars. This was possible because he altered the books of the corporation to make it appear five million dollars was paid in, instead of $500,000. O reported at the next board meeting that this loan had been received. A, B, and C said nothing; D, who was present, was reading the Wall Street Journal and not paying attention. O asked for a vote of approval and it passed unanimously. (E was absent).

Surprised with the easy affirmation by the board obtained for the loan, O transferred to the PPC Company for a very small price the ownership of his home and his two family autos. He did this because he was expecting to be sued, individually, by all of his Detroit creditors for debts incurred there. Again, the board acquiesced to this transaction upon O's pointing out that his home and cars were used sometimes to entertain business clients, and thus the PPC Company benefited.

O entered into a contract to purchase a $250,000 airplane for the corporation. O signed the name of the PPC Company on the contract. The seller of the airplane, S, asked O if he were authorized to make the purchase. O said he was authorized to enter into all contracts which concerned the marketing of the PPC. He used the plane a few times to fly from coast to coast to promote the sale of the PPC. The first time the directors learned of the airplane, they held a special board meeting and passed a resolution directing O to cancel the airplane contract because it was unauthorized. O does this, S repossesses the plane and sues PPC Company for breach of contract.

Meanwhile, A, in his capacity as Vice President for Development, hired N to test drive all of the PPC's which were manufactured. He was instructed to drive each one around town, up and down hills and to maintain a speed of 30 m.p.h. for three minutes on each car. While going down a steep hill, N lost control of the PPC and it ran over T, standing on the sidewalk. T sues N and PPC Company for $500,000 because both of his legs were broken.

Sales of the PPC never developed. GM and Ford began to manufacture much smaller autos and the consumers opted for these or motorcycles. The roof began to fall in. L demanded a $125,000 payment which was due, O had judgments of $80,000 against him in Detroit and PPC Company already faced two large law suits from S and T; and R has demanded the PPC Company sue O for fraud.

Write a well organized essay answer explaining the legal liability, if any, of PPC Company to L, Detroit creditors of O, S, and T.

Deciding whether or not a party will ultimately prevail in the courts is not as important as recognizing and discussing all legal issues. If you think a fact which is not stated is important state the fact and that you are assuming its existence.

19. X is a large shareholder in the Midwest Real Estate Development Corporation (hereafter referred to as, "The Corp."), its president and chairman of the Board of Directors. The Corp. is a publicly held corporation with its shares being traded on the American Stock Exchange. The activities of the Corp. primarily include the purchase of large tracts of real estate in the Midwest and the development of them into condominiums, large apartment complexes and shopping centers. The Corp. has been very successful. It is now the largest real estate development firm between Chicago and Cleveland and it's branching out into the manufacturing of preconstructed housing modules which will be built in a large 50,000 square foot plant and delivered to construction sites.

X's uncle, Y, is President of an Elkhart, Indiana firm which, in the past, has concentrated on constructing recreational vehicles. The name of this corporation is Mooncraft International (hereafter called "Moon"). Moon is very research oriented for a firm of its size and employs several ex-NASA metallurgical engineers to research and develop new materials for recreational vehicle construction. In January of 1973, Moon's engineers discovered a process which combines aluminum, fiberglass, soybeans and water into a building material which is as strong as steel, as workable as wood and has better insulating qualities than any commercially available insulation material. It can be made into sheets (up to 5 inches thick), beams, tubes, posts, or almost any shape. This substance can be manufactured at 1/2 the cost of an equal amount of other building material and is 2/3 the cost of wood. In February, 1973, Moon secured patents on the primary process and the related processes required to manufacture this material.

Moon was controlled by Y and other members of his family; about 20 percent of Moon was owned by persons unrelated to Y in any way. X has purchased 10 percent of Moon for his wife who sat on Moon's Board of Directors.

The discovery of this material had not been made public. In March, 1973, X and Y had preliminary discussions about the Corp's acquiring a controlling interest in Moon from Y and members of his family. On March 30, 1973, the Corp., through its president X, and Y and Y's family agreed in a lengthy contract entitled, "Memorandum of Understanding" that the Corp. would acquire about 80 percent of the stock of Moon which was held by Y, his family and X's wife for $30 per share. The book value of the stock was $10 per share and the 20 percent that was owned by the public had never traded at more than $15 per share. Of course, the Memorandum was to be voted on at the Corp's board meeting on April 10.

The proposal passed the April 10 board meeting. A provision in the Memorandum which was not specifically pointed out at this meeting nor was it discussed, states, "36. Until the final date of sale, Moon reserves the right to sell licenses to produce under the new patents to whomever it selects." The patent was owned by Moon and was, at this point, a major asset.

On April 10, X purchased 500 shares of the Corp. for his two sons and then did the same thing on April 12 for his two daughters.

On April 11, the Corp. issued an announcement to the public which states, "The Midwest Real Estate Development Corporation has made arrangements to purchase Mooncraft International, an Elkhart, Indiana firm which manufactures recreational vehicles."

On April 20 Moon gave a license to produce the material for the next fifteen years to a new corporation (Called "New Corp.") owned by X and Y and their families.

Assume:

1. You have owned shares of Moon since 1970 and you were not offered $50/share for your stock.

2. The common stock of the Corp. sold for about $8 per share from 1971 to April 27, 1973. You owned some shares of the Corp. and sold them for $8.25 on April 15, 1973. Between April 27, 1973 and August 1, 1973 the price of the Corp.'s common went from $8.25 to $48.00/ share. This was due to the publicity given to the new building material and process in July and July, 1973.

3. Assume New Corp. is sold in July by X and Y for 1000 percent profit to a firm which plans to develop and expand activities in the Midwest.

Write a well organized essay about the legal problems you discern in the above problem. Specifically, what remedies do you have? What breaches of duty do you see? Where is the legal liability and to whom? If you see an issue but feel uncomfortable about reaching a definite conclusion you may argue both sides of the issue.

20. Additrol (hereafter "A") is a midwest corporation which manufactures additives for engine oil and gasoline. These additives are combined with the refined gas and oil and are intended to make the automobile engine run without knocking. A is publicly owned and its shares are traded on the American Stock Exchange. Last year, the gross sales amounted to 77 million dollars, and the company earned almost 9.5 million dollars net profit.

A was founded by the Smith family, and currently 30 percent of the outstanding shares are owned by the Smith family giving them voting control of A. They usually can elect three out of five directors. Bob Smith is Chairman of the Board and his brother, Carl, is President and Chief Executive Officer of A.

A's competitors are Standard Oil of New Jersey and Gulf Oil, each of which manufactures additives for their own refined gas and oil as well as sell these additives to other major refiners. A can maintain its competitiveness only by expanding large amounts for research and development. Much of A's success has been attributed to its ability to develop patents for new additives. After a patent is received A then sells a license to produce the substance to other manufacturers.

In March of 1973, an inventor, "I" approached Carl Smith with an idea of making a chemical compound out of clay which would eliminate much of the smoke (produced by the internal combustion engine) when added to the gas supply. Carl referred the matter to his research staff and they recommended A buy the complete rights to develop the idea of I. Carl took the matter to a board meeting and suggested A buy the concept from I. Although all of the five directors were notified, only two of the Smith directors and two of the others attended. The others, named "C" and "D," were very perceptive businessmen and could see that in the near future the price of crude oil was going to double. This made them fear that the long-run outlook for the additive market which was directly linked to the automobile market was rather speculative. These directors believed that the resources of A should be directed into developing large batteries or energy storing cells which could be used in electric cars. Therefore, they voted against the proposal of Carl's that I's invention be purchased by A. Therefore, the matter failed because it did not receive a majority vote. It would be three months until the next board meeting and Bob and Carl thought they should not wait. Together, they personally purchased the rights to the development of I's idea for $500,000.

A month later, the price of oil began to climb. Since most of the additives were derivatives from petroleum, A's costs began to climb. Most oil companies had the market leverage to raise prices, and most raised their prices more than their costs were rising; therefore, they showed large profits. A, however, was a family-run corporation and they had refused to promote good managers to top positions in the corporation. Their profits did not rise and it was felt that at last Standard Oil and Gulf were going to squeeze A out of the market. At the next board meeting in June, Bob and Carl made an impassioned plea for A to buy the rights for I's invention from them. This time, all of the Smith family directors were present and the vote was 3 to 2 to buy I's invention from Bob and Carl for

1 million dollars. It was made clear that Bob and Carl were the present owners.

The 1 million dollars was paid in July, August, and September; and, by September it was realized that A was going to show a loss for the first time in 20 years due in part to the large cash payment to Bob and Carl.

On August 30, 1973, the shares of A were selling at $25 per share. By September 15, Bob and Carl had information to indicate that due to their rising costs and their inability to raise the selling price of their product and due to a severe lack of cash, A was approaching insolvency. They each sold 10,000 shares of A on September 16 at $24 per share. The third quarter earnings report was made public on September 30, indicating a severe loss. The selling price of A's shares dropped to $15 per share as soon as the market absorbed the news of the loss.

Shortly thereafter, Bob and Carl agreed to sell their remaining shares to a subsidiary of ITT for $25 per share. This sale was to take place November 3, 1973 and this sale would give ITT voting control of A. ITT was really after A's patents and, in particular, they were most interested in I's invention. A had put much money into the development of I's concept and it now appeared, at least in the short run, that I's invention was truly miraculous.

Shortly before the sale of Bob and Carl's shares to ITT was finalized, Carl Smith, as president, sold on behalf of the corporation an "irrevocable" license to use I's invention to Family Corporation owned by Bob and Carl and recently formed just to own the license. The contract price was $25,000. At this time, one of the chief assets which A owned was I's invention. Bob and Carl insist that the $25,000 was needed to keep A in operation.

Write a well organized essay about the legal issues you discern in the above fact pattern. After discussing the causes of action, if any, describe the *remedies* available. What defenses may be argued and do you anticipate that they will be successful? If you see an issue but feel uncomfortable about reaching a definite conclusion you may argue both sides of the issue. Finally, be sure to discuss the manner in which D may seek a remedy.

G Glossary of Legal Terms

AB INITIO, Latin From the beginning. An agreement or act may be illegal ab initio.

ABSOLUTE/STRICT LIABILITY Tort liability imposed without regard to fault.

ACCOUNTING As used in this text, refers to a remedy available to a partner which compels disclosure to the partner of all financial matters of the partnership. A complete statement of all accounts.

ACTUAL AUTHORITY A classification of authority in which a principal expressly or impliedly authorizes an agent to act for the principal.

ACTUAL NOTICE Notice or knowledge of an event actually received.

ADJUDICATION The rendering of a judgment in a court case.

ADMINISTRATIVE AGENCY A federal or state unit invested by the legislature or executive with rule making and enforcing authority.

ADMINISTRATOR A person appointed by a probate court to wind up the affairs of a deceased person when the deceased left no will or, if a will existed, it did not name an executor.

AEQUITAS, Latin A term usually denoting equity law or equitable principles.

AFFIDAVIT A written declaration of facts made voluntarily and confirmed by an oath of the party making it.

AGENCY A consensual, fiduciary relation between two persons, created by law by which one, the principal, has a right to control the conduct of the agent, and the agent has the power to affect the legal relations of the principal.

AGENT The legal entity acting for another in the agency relationship.

ANSWER A pleading document usually submitted by the defendant in which the party asserts matters of fact as a defense to facts asserted in a complaint or petition.

APPARENT AUTHORITY An agent's power to affect the legal relations of a principal arising from the principal's manifestation of authority to the third person and the latter's reasonable reliance on the manifestation.

APPELLANT (also sometimes called PETITIONER) The party initiating the appeal from one court to another.

APPELLATE COURT A court with three or more judges sitting in judgment on appeals to it from a lower appellate court or other tribunal of original jurisdiction.

APPELLEE (sometimes also called RESPONDENT) The party in an appellate case against whom the appeal is taken. The one responding to the appellant.

ARTICLES OF INCORPORATION The articles of incorporation is the document filed with the secretary of state to incorporate an enterprise. It establishes the basic structure and conduct of the corporation. It is also called the charter or certificate of incorporation.

ASSAULT An intentional, unlawful threat of injury to another by the use of force under such circumstances as create a well founded fear of injury to the one threatened.

ASSUMPSIT An older form of a cause of action based primarily upon a promise implied in the law.

ASSUMPTION OF RISK A defense in a tort action available to employers which permits the employer to avoid liability to an injured employee caused by the employer or one of its other agents on the basis that the injured employee knowingly undertook a dangerous task and therefore agreed that the risk of injury was his own.

ATTACHMENT The act of a sheriff, marshall or other officer of the court in seizing a person's property by authority of a court order. The property is usually sold by the sheriff or marshall.

AUDIT The process of investigating and reporting on an organization's financial accounts.

AUTHORITY A broad legal term denoting some of the circumstances in which courts will hold the principal liable for an agent's promises or acts made for the principal. (See specific types of authority—express, implied, apparent, estoppel, inherent, incidental).

BALANCE SHEET A financial statement showing the assets, liabilities and owners' equity of a business organization as of a certain date.

BATTERY A forceful unlawful touching of another person without the consent of the injured person.

BLUE SKY LAWS State securities law statutes.

BONA FIDE, Latin In good faith.

BONA FIDE OCCUPATIONAL QUALIFICATION (BFOQ) An exception to Title VII of the 1964 Civil Rights Act allowing employment discrimination when it is reasonably necessary in the normal operation of the enterprise. Discrimination based upon race can never be a bona fide occupational qualification.

BOND A corporate debt instrument which matures at a specified date in the future and usually provides for the regular payment of interest until the maturity date. A bondholder is a creditor of the corporation.

BREACH OF DUTY See CAUSE OF ACTION.

BRIEF Appellate A formal legal document setting forth the detailed legal arguments made to an appellate court.

Study an informal method of student note taking on appellate cases.

BY-LAWS The document containing the detailed requirements that regulate the internal affairs of the corporation. They are subordinate to the articles.

CAPACITY The legal ability to act as defined primarily by state statute.

CAPITAL SURPLUS Capital derived from the sale of stock at a price in excess of its par or stated value. It is also called paid-in surplus.

CAUSE OF ACTION The heart of the plaintiff's case composed of at least two elements: the assertion of the existence of a legal duty and its breach.

CAVEAT EMPTOR, Latin Let the buyer beware.

CERTIORARI A discretionary writ of review. Usually filed with an appellate court asking that court to review judicial actions.

CHANCERY Equity, the system of jurisprudence administered by a court of equity.

CHATTEL Personal property, moveables.

CHOSE IN ACTION A cause of action for the return of personal property held by another.

CIRCUMSTANTIAL AUTHORITY Authority of an agent to act created by circumstances. (See APPARENT, INHERENT AUTHORITY AND ESTOPPEL.)

CIVIL LAW The system of jurisprudence indicating the private rights and remedies of citizens in contrast to those which are public, the violation of which is prosecuted under the criminal law.

CLASS ACTION A type of civil case in which one person sues or is sued as a representative of a class of persons. It will be allowed if 1) the class is so numerous joinder of all is impracticable, 2) there are questions of fact and law common to all, 3) the claims asserted are typical of those assertable by the class, 4) the representative will fairly represent the class, and 5) such a method of trying the case is superior to others.

CLOSE CORPORATIONS A corporation that has a small number of shareholders.

COMMON LAW That body of law which derives its authority from usage and customs and is expressed in judicial opinions, not legislative acts.

COMPLAINT The formal document filed by a plaintiff to initiate the trial of a civil case.

CONDITION PRECEDENT Describes an event which must occur before other acts or promises become legally operative.

CONSIDERATION That exchange of promises

or value which will support an enforceable contract.

CONSIGNMENT   The act or process of allowing another to hold your goods for sale, storage or shipment.

CONSOLIDATION   An alteration of corporate structure whereby corporations A and B will cease to exist and will be replaced by a new corporation C.

CONSTRUCTIVE NOTICE   A form of notice of an event or information which the law implies in circumstances in which actual notice is impracticable.

CONTRIBUTORY NEGLIGENCE   A defense to a negligence case in some jurisdictions in which recovery for injury caused by a defendant's negligence will be denied if the injured party was negligent in causing the injury.

CONVERSION   A tort in which one exercises unauthorized control over the personal property of another to the owner's damage.

COOPERATIVE ASSOCIATION   A form of business organization formed primarily to provide an economic service to its members.

CORPORATION   A legal entity created, most often, by state statute which provides for the limited liability of its owners and for perpetual existence.

COUNTER CLAIM   A cause of action asserted by a defendant against another party in a law suit, usually the plaintiff.

COVENANT   An agreement or promise.

CRIMINAL LAW   That system of jurisprudence which is prosecuted by governmental personnel and is intended to punish the wrongful intent of the defendant. Imprisonment or a fine are the possible results.

CUMULATIVE PREFERRED STOCK   If dividends are not paid on the stock they are not lost but will cumulate until paid.

CUMULATIVE VOTING   Allows a shareholder to multiply the number of votes given him by his shares times the number of directors to be elected. It is designed to allow minority shareholders to gain representation on the board.

DEBENTURE   An unsecured corporate debt instrument.

DECEIT   (See MISREPRESENTATION)

DE FACTO, Latin   In fact, in actuality.

DEFAMATION   The tort of injuring a person's character, fame or reputation by publishing or speaking falsely about the person.

DEFAULT JUDGMENT   A judgment rendered when one of the parties fails to respond or appear before the court.

DEFENDANT   The party being sued in a court case.

DE JURE CORPORATION   A legally formed corporation, one formed in compliance with the state statute.

DELEGATION, of authority   A grant of authority by an agent to another agent with the permission or knowledge of the principal.

DEMURRER   An older form of pleading usually used by the defendant to challenge the legal sufficiency of the plaintiff's complaint; this pleading is construed to mean that the party using it admits the facts alleged but asserts they have no legal consequences.

DEPOSITION   The written testimony of a party or a witness taken out of court but under oath.

DERIVATIVE SUIT   A lawsuit brought by a shareholder on behalf of the corporation for damage suffered by the corporation. Also called a representative suit. The recovery goes to the corporation.

DESCENT   Hereditary succession of property.

DIRECTED VERDICT   A verdict entered by the court when one of the parties has made a motion for the directed verdict and the judge believes, after resolving all inferences against the moving party, that reasonable minds could reach but one conclusion and that is in favor of the moving party.

DIRECTORS AND OFFICERS INSURANCE   Insurance purchased by the corporation to indemnify directors and officers for the expense of defending their actions in a lawsuit against them arising because of corporate business. Also called D & O insurance.

DISCLOSED PRINCIPAL   A principal which can be identified by a third party.

DISCOVERY   Procedure a set of procedures available for use in the trial of a case which enable all parties to obtain all relevant evidence from the other parties.

Devices (See DEPOSITION, INTERROGA-TORIES)

DISMISSAL WITH PREJUDICE Dismissal of a case under circumstances in which the issues presented may not be litigated again.

DISSENT AND APPRAISAL A remedy available to a shareholder that objects to a merger or other special corporate transaction as defined by state statute. The corporation must purchase the dissenting shareholder's stock for its agreed upon or appraised value.

DISSOLUTION Corporation The termination of the corporation's legal existence.

Partnership the change in the relation of the partners caused by any partner ceasing to be associated in the carrying on of the business. This change usually terminates the authority of the partners to act for the partnership in the usual course of business.

DIVERSITY JURISDICTION The power of federal district courts to hear a dispute based upon a breach of state law if it is between residents of different states and the amount in controversy exceeds $10,000.

DIVIDEND An amount of money or other property set aside out of corporate profits by the board of directors for payment to the shareholders.

DUE PROCESS The exercise of the powers of government as the settled maxims of law permit. Basic procedural and substantive rights of individuals as expressed in the U. S. and state constitutions as interpreted by the courts.

EARNED SURPLUS The profit derived from the operation of the corporation. Accountants sometimes call it retained earnings.

EQUITY LAW, EQUITABLE PRINCIPLES That body of law which relies for its authority upon the conscience of the chancellor or judge.

ESTOPPEL A bar raised by the law which stops a party from alleging or from denying facts when, if allowed, it would permit the party to work an injustice by allowing the allegation or denial.

EX PARTE, Latin By or for one party only.

EXPRESS AUTHORITY Authority of an agent based upon explicit instructions either oral or written.

EXPRESSED WARRANTY Any affirmation of fact made by a seller of goods to the buyer which relates to the goods and becomes part of the basis of the bargain.

FALSE IMPRISONMENT A tort committed when one intentionally restrains another against the latter's will.

FELLOW-SERVANT RULE The rule relieving a master of liability for injury to a servant caused through the negligence of a fellow servant.

FELONY A criminal offense that carries a penitentiary or a death sentence. It is a more serious crime than a misdemeanor.

FIDUCIARY An individual who, because of the relationship of trust and confidence that he enjoys with another person, is in the position of a trustee. The law demands the utmost good faith and loyalty from the fiduciary in fulfilling his duties. The work is used as both a noun and an adjective.

GRAVAMEN The significant portion of a legal complaint or charge.

IMPLIED AUTHORITY That authority which the law recognizes the agent has which is reasonably necessary to carry out the expressed authority of the principal. It may also be referred to as incidental authority.

IMPLIED WARRANTY OF FITNESS FOR A PARTICULAR PURPOSE A warranty (guarantee or promise) that is implied in a contract for the sale of goods by the U.C.C., § 2-315, which provides that where the seller at the time of contracting has reason to know any particular purpose for which the goods are required and that the buyer is relying on the seller's skill or judgment to select or furnish suitable goods, then the goods sold shall be fit for such purpose.

IMPLIED WARRANTY OF MERCHANTABILITY The warranty (guarantee) automatically created by the U.C.C., § 2-314, when a merchant sells an item of personal property. Under this warranty the item is guaranteed to be of fair average quality and fit for the ordinary purpose for which such goods are used.

INCIDENTAL AUTHORITY (See IMPLIED AUTHORITY)

INCOME STATEMENT The accounting statement that reports the revenues and expenses of an enterprise for a period of time.

INDEMNITY   A duty requiring one person to make good any loss incurred by another while acting at the request or for the benefit of the former.

INDEPENDENT CONTRACTOR   A person who performs a task according to his own methods and judgment. His employer exercises no control over him except as to the resulting product.

INHERENT AUTHORITY   The power of an agent derived not from the principal's authority but from the position of the agent in the principal's business together with reasonable reliance by a third party upon the power which usually accompany the position.

INJUNCTION   An order issued by a court of equity that orders a person to do or cease doing a particular activity.

INSIDE DIRECTOR   A director that is also a corporate employee.

INSTRUCTION, from judge   The statement made by the trial judge to the jury informing them of the applicable law they are to use in their deliberations.

INTER ALIA, Latin   Among other things.

INTERESTED DIRECTOR   A director who has a personal interest in a matter to be considered by the board.

INTERLOCKING DIRECTORATE   A situation where one individual sits on the board of directors of two or more corporations which do business with one another or are otherwise connected.

INTERMEDIATE APPELLATE COURT   The court to which decisions of a trial court or an administrative agency are appealed. It is the court just below the highest appellate court of the jurisdiction, usually called the supreme court.

INTERROGATORIES   Written questions directed to a witness or a party to a lawsuit. The questions must be answered in writing and under oath. Interrogatories form one part of the pre-trial discovery process.

JOINT OBLIGATIONS   Obligations or liability that is incurred by two or more persons. Their liability is undivided and they must be sued jointly. They do not bear individual liability as do persons who have joint and several liability.

JOINT AND SEVERAL LIABILITY   Liability incurred by two or more persons who may then be sued individually or as a group.

JOINT VENTURE   A combination of two or more legal persons to conduct a profit making enterprise. Usually the combination involves a single business transaction. Although the parties incur joint liability, it is distinguished from a partnership by its limited nature and scope.

JUDGMENT   The official judicial determination upon the issues in a lawsuit.

JUDGMENT CREDITOR   A creditor who has established, through court action, the existence, and non-payment of a debt owed by his debtor.

JUDGMENT NOTWITHSTANDING THE VERDICT   Also called JUDGMENT N.O.V. Judgment entered by a court that overturns or reverses the verdict of the jury. Judgment N.O.V.'s are quite rare and only granted when absolutely no legal basis exists for the jury's decision.

JUDGMENT ON THE PLEADINGS   Judgment entered by the court in favor of a party based only upon the pleadings filed before a trial. It will be granted only where there is no genuine issue as to any material fact and the moving party is entitled to a judgment as a matter of law. It accomplishes the same purpose as summary judgment.

JURISDICTION   The "power" of a court to hear and decide a lawsuit. It is contrasted to venue which refers to the geographical location where the lawsuit is brought.

LACHES   An equitable doctrine that bars a person from enforcing a claim. This doctrine is utilized when the person has delayed enforcing his claim for such an unreasonable period of time that the adverse party's cause has been unfairly prejudiced.

LAW   As used in this text means a statement of the circumstances when courts or law enforcement agencies will act.

LEGAL DUTY   An obligation that is imposed by either a state or federal statute, an administrative agency or an appellate court relying upon the common law.

LEGISLATURE   The branch of government that passes the statutes.

LIABILITY   An extremely broad legal term

meaning an obligation, debt, unliquidated claim, legal responsibility, or the possibility of incurring the judgment of a court.

LIBEL Written defamation. Oral defamation is called slander.

LIMITED LIABILITY Liability the extent of which is in some measure limited, not absolute. Oftentimes limited liability is used in a context meaning a person's financial liability has a ceiling. Most often applied to shareholders of corporations to limit their liability to corporate creditors to the amount of money promised or paid into the corporation in exchange for the shares.

LIMITED PARTNERSHIP A partnership consisting of one or more general partners, with the normal partnership rights and liabilities, and one or more limited partners, who do not conduct the partnership business and whose liability is limited to the extent of their capital contribution.

LITIGANT A party to a lawsuit.

LOANED/BORROWED SERVANT A servant who is loaned by his master to another. The borrower is liable for acts of the servant performed in his employment if he has direct control over the servant.

MASTER The principal that engages another, called a servant, to perform services on his behalf and who exercises control over the physical acts of the servant. In the area of contracts the usual terms are principal-agent, whereas when tort law is involved the terms used respectively are master-servant.

MATERIAL INFORMATION A technical term used in the application of the federal securities laws to denote information about corporate activities which would cause a reasonably prudent investor in the securities market to either buy, sell or refrain from buying or selling.

MERGER An alteration of corporate structure where corporation A and B are combined. Corporation A ceases to exist while B, the surviving corporation, will continue in operation.

MISDEMEANOR A criminal offense that is not as serious as a felony. Typically the penalty is a fine and/or imprisonment in a facility other than a penitentiary.

MISREPRESENTATION A misstatement, either by word or conduct, of fact. Sometimes the word "fraud" is used to indicate an intentional misstatement while misrepresentation is used to indicate non-willful misstatements.

MOTION TO DISMISS FOR FAILURE TO STATE A CLAIM. A procedural device whereby a litigant admits the facts stated in the opponent's pleading, but asserts that they are insufficient in law to support the legal action. This motion accomplishes the same purpose as the older pleading called a demurrer.

MUNICIPAL CORPORATION A public corporation organized under congressional or legislative authority to carry out political or governmental purposes. Cities and towns are prime examples.

NEGLIGENCE The failure to exercise the ordinary care that a reasonable person would exercise under those circumstances. An act of negligence may be one of commission or omission.

NOTICE, KNOWLEDGE Knowledge of, or information about, the existence of facts. Notice can be either actual or constructive.

ORDINANCE Those statutes created by the legislative arm of a municipal corporation.

OUTSIDE DIRECTOR A director who is not an employee of the corporation.

PARTIALLY DISCLOSED PRINCIPAL The situation where a person knows that he is dealing with an agent, thereby knowing the existence of the principal but not his identity.

PARTNERSHIP An organization of two or more persons to carry on as co-owners a business for profit.

PARTNERSHIP INTEREST A technical term used by the U.P.A., § 26 to refer to a partner's right to share in the profits of the firm.

PARTNERSHIP PROPERTY Assets or property of any kind that belongs to the partnership. Partnership property is not the property of individual partners.

PETITIONER The person who files a petition with a court. The person opposing the petition is called the "respondent." Sometimes used as a synonym for appellant.

PLAINTIFF The person who initiates a lawsuit by filing a complaint.

PLEADINGS A term designating both the complaint filed by the plaintiff and the answer filed by the defendant in a lawsuit plus supplementary documents which are the formal allegations or denials forming the basis of the suit.

POLICE POWER   The inherent power of a state to enact legislation necessary for the protection of the public's safety, health and welfare.

PRE-EMPTIVE RIGHTS   The right of a shareholder to purchase his pro rata share of any newly authorized and issued shares of the corporation.

PREFERRED STOCK   Stock that is entitled to certain preferences, usually in the payment of dividends, over that of common stock. Oftentimes, preferred stock will not have voting rights and will be preferred over common upon the liquidation of the corporation.

PRIMA FACIE, Latin   On its face. Evidence sufficient to establish one's claim unless rebutted by the opposing party.

PRINCIPAL   The person who engages another (called an agent) to act for him and upon his behalf.

PRINCIPLE   A basic truth or rule.

PRIVITY   A relationship between two or more persons that is mutual or successive, i.e., seller—buyer, heir—ancestor, etc.; historically, it denoted a relationship between contracting parties that was necessary in order to support a suit based upon a breach of contract.

PROMOTER   The individual that performs all the items necessary for incorporation.

PROPRIETORSHIP   The form of business organization that is owned and operated by a single owner. The owner is called the "sole proprietor."

PUBLIC CORPORATION   A corporation organized by Congress or a state to carry out a governmental purpose. (See MUNICIPAL CORPORATION.) A corporation serving the public interest, such as a railroad or utility, is sometimes called a public or public service corporation. A publicly held corporation is a private corporation whose shares are owned by members of the general public.

PUBLIC POLICY   A very broad term usually denoting the legal duties of persons to the community as expressed in legislative and judicial pronouncements.

RATIFICATION   A person's approval of a prior act which was done on his behalf but was not binding on him when done. One cannot ratify an act unless he has knowledge of all the material facts.

RESPONDEAT SUPERIOR, Latin   Let the master answer. This doctrine makes a master liable for the acts of his servant committed within the course and scope of the servant's employment. It includes liability for acts incidental to acts within the scope of employment.

RESPONDENT   The person who is the opposing party in a court petition or appellate proceeding.

RESTATEMENT OF THE LAW (of Agency, of Negligence, etc.)   A compilation of legal principles published by the American Law Institute which represent a desired statement of the law.

RESTRICTIVE COVENANT   Usually refers to an expressed promise made by an employee not to compete with the employer in a defined geographical area and in a defined line of work after the employment is terminated.

SECTION 1244 STOCK   Stock issued by a corporation which meets the requirements of Section 1244 of the Internal Revenue Code which allows the loss sustained upon sale of the stock to be treated as an ordinary loss of the individual up to $25,000.

SERVANT   A person acting on behalf of, and controlled by, another called a master.

SERVICE OF PROCESS   The delivery of the legal papers in a lawsuit (usually the complaint) to the correct person.

SHOP RIGHTS   The nonexclusive royalty-free license enjoyed by an employer in an employee's invention when the employer's time, tools or services were used in developing the invention.

SHORT SALE   selling short   The sale of shares of stock by a seller who does not own them. At a later date the seller replaces the shares by purchasing them on the open market, hopefully at a lower price than he sold them for, thereby making a profit.

SHORT SWING PROFITS   Profits realized by a director, officer or beneficial owner of more than 10 percent of any class of stock from transactions in his corporation's stock within any period of less than six months. Under § 16(b) of the Securities Exchange Act of 1934 such profits belong to the corporation.

SLANDER Oral defamation. Defamation that is published in written form is called libel.

SPECIFIC PERFORMANCE Performance of a contract according to its exact literal terms. It is an extraordinary legal remedy ordered by a court only when money damages are inadequate compensation for the breach of the contract.

STATUTE, STATUTORY LAW A law enacted by a legislature.

STATUTE OF LIMITATIONS Statutes or laws prescribing the time within which legal action must be instituted upon certain claims or forever be barred from bringing suit.

STOCK OPTION A form of corporate compensation that grants an executive the right to purchase a given number of corporate shares within a specified future period at a specified price.

STOCK SPLIT A device designed to reduce the per share market price of a stock thereby increasing demand and broadening the number of shareholders. If stock is priced at $400 per share it is relatively unattractive to small investors. If a 4 for 1 stock split occurs, four shares valued at $100 per share will be issued for each one share of the previous stock.

STRIKE SUIT A stockholder's derivative suit wholly lacking in merit.

SUB AGENTS An agent appointed by another agent who is empowered to perform acts undertaken by the appointing agent for the principal but for whose conduct the principal remains primarily liable.

SUBCHAPTER S CORPORATIONS A corporation with 25 or fewer shareholders who are individuals or estates (not partnerships or corporations) with one class of stock and which meet the other requirements of Sections 1371–1379 of the Internal Revenue Code. These sections allow the qualifying corporation to elect to avoid paying any corporate tax on its income and instead have the shareholders taxed on the taxable income of the corporation in proportion to their shareholdings. If the corporation has a net operating loss, it can be deducted directly by the shareholders against their individual incomes.

SUBSIDIARY A corporation substantially owned and controlled by another corporation called the parent corporation.

SUMMONS A writ directing the sheriff to notify the defendant that a lawsuit has been filed against him and that he has a certain number of days to answer or have judgment entered against him.

SURETY A person who serves as an insurer of the debt or obligation of his principal. The surety's liability is contingent on default by the principal.

TENDER OFFER An offer to buy shares directed at the shareholders of a target company over which the offeror is seeking to gain control. Federal securities laws govern such offers.

THIRD PARTY A person that is not a party to the immediate contract, relationship, matter or transaction.

TIPPEE The recipient of material corporate information.

TIPPER The individual who passes material information affecting the price of a corporation's securities to another, called a tippee.

TORT A civil wrong or injury committed by one person against another. Assault, battery, slander, and negligence are just some examples of a tort.

TRADE MARK, TRADE NAME A trade mark is a symbol, emblem, or words attached to goods to identify them as the product of a specific manufacturer. A trade name is a name used to identify a specific business.

TRADE SECRET Any formula, pattern, device or compilation of information which is used in one's business, and which gives him an opportunity to obtain an advantage over competitors who do not know or use it.

TREASURY STOCK Stock that has been repurchased by the issuing corporation.

TRESPASS A non-consensual transgression against another's person or property.

UNDERWRITER An individual or company whose business is the distribution of securities for sale. The term can have a more technical definition under the federal securities law which regulates the activities of the defined underwriters.

UNDISCLOSED PRINCIPAL The situation

where a person lacks the knowledge that the one with whom he is dealing is not acting on his own behalf but is an agent of another. The existence and the identity of the principal is unrevealed.

ULTRA VIRES, Latin   Beyond the powers. An act outside the powers granted a corporation in its articles.

VERDICT   The formal decision rendered by the jury in a lawsuit.

VICARIOUS LIABILITY   Liability which the law imposes upon one for the illegal acts of another. In agency law vicarious liability is accomplished by the application of the common law doctrine of Respondeat Superior.

VOIRE DIRE   The process of questioning prospective jurors to determine their objectivity and the presence or lack of bias or prejudice.

WAIVER   The voluntary relinquishing of one's legal rights or claims.

WARRANTY   An expressed or implied legal guarantee or promise that certain specified facts are true.

Index

Accountants' legal liability:
  accounting standards and the securities
    laws, 562-569
  under common law, 560-561
  for negligence to a negligent client,
    575-577
  foreign corrupt practices act, 578-581
  relationship to audit committee, 578
  under Section 10(b), 569-573
  under securities law, 561-562
  to SIPC, 573-575
Age discrimination:
  applied to states, 655
  bfoqs, 653-654
  generally, 652-657
  job advertisements, 655
Agency:
  coupled with an interest, 195
  creation, 79-82
  defined, 48, 79
  delegation, 190
  husband and wife, 106-107
  operation, 182-183
  scope of employment, 162-163
  termination, 195-201
  type of business organization, 48
Agent:
  contractual liability of, 134-136
  duties of, 82-86
  general and special, 119
Answer, 16
Apparent authority:
  generally, 119-120
  tort liability for, 167-168
Appeals:
  courts of, 21
  process, 21
  study of appellate cases, 24, 28-29

Appellant, 21
Appellee, 22
Articles of incorporation:
  amendment, 446
  generally, 292
  specimen, 292-294
Assault, 144
Attorneys' liability under securities law,
    generally, 553-556
Authority:
  actual, 114
  circumstantial, 119
  to commit a tort, 144-145
  for other types, *see individual headings,*
    e.g., Express authority

Battery, 144
Blue Sky Laws, generally, 477-478
Board of directors, *see* Directors
Bonds, generally, 323-324
Briefing cases, generally, 26-27
Business organizations:
  generally, 46-47
  types, 46-49
By-laws, generally, 295

Capacity:
  to form a partnership, 209
  of principal and agent, 106
Cause of action, 27-28
Certificate of incorporation, *see* Articles
    of incorporation
Charter, *see* Articles of incorporation
Circumstantial authority, generally,
    119-130
Civil law, 8-9
Civil Rights:
  age discrimination, *see* Age Discrimination

Civil Rights (*Continued*)
   backpay, 639-642
   bona fide occupational qualifications
      (bfoqs), 642-643
   Civil Rights Act of 1964, 634
   color discrimination, 639-642
   Equal Employment Opportunity Act,
      634
   Equal Employment Opportunity Com-
      mission (EEOC), 649-650
   equal pay, *see* Equal Pay Act
   handicapped discrimination, 657-658
   national origin discrimination, 635
   office of federal contract compliance,
      658
   pregnancy discrimination, 637-639
   quotas, 643-647
   race discrimination, 639-642
   religious discrimination, 635
   reverse discrimination, 643-647
   seniority systems, 647-649
   sex discrimination, 635-639
   testing, 639-642
Civil trial process, outlined, 11-23
Class actions, 16-17
Close corporations:
   defined, 337
   generally, 337-345
   oppression of minority interests, 462
   special statutory provisions, 342-345
Clubs, members' liability, 50-51
Commodity Futures Trading Commission,
      generally, 499
Common law, 16
Complaint, 11-12
Consolidation, generally, 446-447
Consumer Product Safety Commission,
      generally, 688-691
Consumer Product Warrant Act (Magnuson-
      Moss Act), generally, 670-673
Contracts, generally, 113
Cooperatives, generally, 63-64
Corporate entity:
   defective incorporation, 296
   disregard of, 297-304
   nature of, 273-276
   powers of, 310-311
Corporate Takeovers:
   anatomy of, 597
   defenses, 596-597
   generally, 593-596
Corporation law:
   generally, 273-276

historical note, 276-280
Corporations:
   advantages of corporate form, 59, 69,
      286-287
   business judgment rule, 397
   by-laws, *see* By-laws
   capital structure, 323-328
   characteristics, 58-59
   close, *see* Close corporations
   compared with other business organiza-
      tions, 58, 69
   consolidation, *see* Consolidation
   constitutional law, 281, 285-286
   criminal liability of, 389-396
   control, 321-323
   de facto, 296
   de jure, 296
   directors, *see* Directors
   dissolution, 464-466
   dividends, *see* Dividends
   first amendment rights, 735-741
   foreign, 304-306
   incorporation, 286-287
   lobbying, 739-740
   merger, *see* Merger
   municipal, 61
   officers, *see* Officers
   piercing the veil, 297-303
   political contributions, 741-743
   powers of, 308-309
   public *vs.* private, 61
   purposes, 310-311
   restrictions on, 61-62
   sale of assets, *see* Sale of assets
   social responsibility of, 724
   structural changes, 445-470
   Subchapter S, 60-61
   subsidiaries, *see* Subsidiaries
   tender offers, *see* Tender offers
   ultra vires, 309
   value structure of, 102
   varieties of, 261
Crimes:
   defined, 8, 389-396
   felony, 9
   misdemeanor, 9
Cumulative voting, generally, 332-334

Deceit, 144
Defamation, 144
Delegation, of agency duties, 190
Demurrer, *see* Motion to dismiss
Deposition, 18

Derivative suits:
  costs, 350
  defined, 349
  demand on directors and shareholders,
    350
  indemnification, 350
  security for expenses, 350
Directed verdict, motion for, 20
Directors:
  audit committees, 578
  authority, 356-359
  business judgment, defense of, 397
  committees of, 360-362
  compensation, 380-381
  election, 332-334, 356
  executive committees, 360
  fiduciary duties, 399, 417-418, 459
  indemnification of, 414
  informal action, 358
  inside, 362
  insurance, *see* Directors' and officers'
    insurance
  interested, 419-420
  interlocking, 419-422
  liability for impermissible dividends,
    366-367
  liability under securities laws, 541-543
  management by, 355-356, 358
  meetings, 358-359
  outside, 362
  qualifications of, 362-363
  removal, 359-360
  statutory liabilities of, 398-399
Directors' and officers' insurance, generally,
  416
Discovery, 17-18
Discrimination, *see* Civil rights
Dissolution of corporation:
  involuntary, 465-466
  voluntary, 464
Dissolution of partnership, *see* Partnership
Diversity jurisdiction, explained, 10-11
Dividends:
  directors' discretion, 363, 368-369
  forms of, 367-368
  impermissible, 366-367
  nimble dividends, 365-366
  payment of, 368
  policy considerations, 363
  shareholders' rights to, 363-369
  sources of, 363-365
  statutory limitations, 363-366
  stock dividends, 367-368

Earned surplus, 365
Educational objectives, of the book, 23-24
Employees, fiduciary duties of, 82-90
Employment Retirement Income Security
  Act (ERISA), generally, 630-632
Environmental protection:
  Council on Environmental Quality
    (CEQ), 704, 707
  Environmental Protection Agency
    (EPA), 704, 708
  National Environmental Policy Act
    (NEPA), 704
  Reserve Mining litigation, 715-721
Equal Pay Act:
  comparable worth, 652
  exceptions to, 651
  generally, 650-652
Equity law, 6-7
Estoppel:
  creation of agency by, 80
  defined, 80, 123-124
Express authority, generally, 114-115

False imprisonment, 144
Federalism, 32-33
Fiduciary duties:
  breach of, 99-101
  care, 82-90
  control, sale of, 433-434
  corporate opportunities, 427-433
  defined, 82-83
  employees, 82-90
  generally, 85-86
  insider trading, *see* Insider trading
  interested directors, *see* Directors
  interlocking directors, *see* Directors
  partners as fiduciaries, 226
  remedies for breach, 99-101
Foreign corporations, *see* Corporations
Foreign Corrupt Practices Act:
  accounting provisions, 579-580
  antibribery provisions, 579
  controversy over the law, 581
  enforcement, 580
Foreign operations, *see* International
  Business
Fourteenth Amendment, to U.S.
  Constitution, 34-35
Franchises, generally, 67
Freedom of Information Act, generally, 740

Husband and wife, as agents for one
  another, 106-107

Implied authority, 115
Incorporation, *see* Corporations
Independent contractor, generally, 151
Inherent authority, generally, 127-128
Insider trading:
  burden of proof, 534-535
  common law rule (special circumstances
    doctrine), 511
  generally, 504
  materiality, 513-515
  other fraudulent activities, 535-537
  Rule 10b-5, 510-522
  sale of control, *see* Sale of control
  S.E.C. enforcement, 526-527
  Section 16b, 504-510
  tippee liability, 522-523
  tipper liability, 522-523
  who can recover for violations, 527-534
  who is an insider, 523-526
Instructional objectives, generally, 23-24
Instructions, judicial, 20
International business:
  business risks, 743-744
  comparative legal view, 747-748
  legal complexities of, 744-747
  political risk insurance, 744
Interrogatories, 18
Interstate commerce, 41

Joint and several liability, of partners,
    247, 264
Joint venture, generally, 58, 229
Judgment N.O.V., 21
Judgment on pleadings, 18
Judicial system, generally, 9
Jury trial, generally, 19-20

Labor Law:
  bargaining, 617-620
  consumer boycotts, 622
  discrimination, *see* Civil Rights
  duty of fair representation, 612
  elections, 610-611
  employee rights, 610
  employer unfair labor practices, 614-615
  historical background, 609
  management (supervisors), 611
  National Labor Relations Act, 610
  occupational safety and health, 623-630
  pension plans, 630-632
  right to work laws, 613
  secondary activity, 621
  strikes, 620

Taft-Hartley Act, 616
  union unfair labor practices, 617
Law, 3
Loaned or borrowed servant, generally,
    191
Licenses, from state, 39
Limited partnership:
  control by a partner, 230-231
  corporate general partner, 232
  creation, 229-230
  dissolution, 233, 262
  generally, 57-58

Management, *see* Officers; Directors
Master:
  defined, 151
  liability of, 151-175
Materiality, under federal securities laws,
    513-515
Merger:
  de facto, 450-453
  dissent and appraisal rights, 447-450
  generally, 446-459
  shareholder vote, 447-450
  short form, 454
Motions:
  for directed verdict, 20
  to dismiss for failure to state a claim, 17
  generally, 17
  for judgment N.O.V., 21

Negligence:
  generally, 20
  in product design, 673
Non-servant agent, 157-158
Notice:
  of agency termination, 199-200
  given to an agent, 182-183
  of partnership dissolution, 264-265

Occupational safety and health, generally,
    623-630
Officers:
  authority, 374-375
  compensation, 380-381
  fiduciary duties, 397-414, 417
  indemnification of, 414-415
  insiders under Section 16(b), 504-506
  liability for torts and crimes, 389-414,
    408-410
  president, 374
  secretary, 374
  treasurer, 374

vice-president, 374

Partners:
  expulsion, 224
  incoming, 255
  interest in partnership, 223
  joint and several liability of, 247, 264
  liability upon dissolution, 263
  property, 220-221
  right to manage, 223
Partnership:
  advantages, 56-57
  agreement, sample of, 211, 217-219
  capacity, 209
  capital, 220
  compared with other business organiza-
    tions, 56-57, 69
  contract liability, 239
  corporations as partners, 225
  creation of, 211-212
  crimes, liability for, 251
  definition, 208
  dissolution, 257-258, 261, 264-265
  legal character, 208
  liability for negligent operation of auto,
    247
  property, 220
  right to an account, 215
  tort liability, 243-244, 251-252
  trading and non trading, 240
  winding up, 261
Patent law, generally, 90-91
Payment, to agent, 182-183
Pensions, see Employee Retirement
  Income Security Act
Petition, see Complaint
Petitioner, see Appellant
Police power, of the states, 33-35
Power of attorney, generally, 80
Preemptive rights, see Shareholders
Preferred stock, generally, 326-328
Principal:
  disclosed, 135
  duties, 104-105
  liability:
    contract, 113-138
    loaned or borrowed servant, 191-192
    on public policy or statute, 173-174
    sub-agents, 186
    tort, 144-175
    vicarious, 147-163
  partially disclosed, 135
  undisclosed, 135

Product liability:
  federal warranty legislation, 670-673
  generally, 662-666
  negligent design, 673
  recent developments, 679, 684-687
  strict liability, 673-674
  U.C.C. warranties, 662-666
Professional corporations, generally, 62
Promoters:
  contracts by, 289
  generally, 287-288
  secret profits by, 288-289
Proprietorship:
  compared to other business organiza-
    tions, 55, 69
  generally, 54
Proxies:
  costs, 588-589
  forms of, 335
  generally, 334-335
  misleading statements, 589-590
  regulation under federal securities laws,
    585-590
  revocability, 335
  shareholder proposals, 587-588
  solicitation, 585-586
  specimen, 335, 586

Ratification:
  of agent's contracts, 130-132
  creation of agency by, 80
Registration of securities, see Securities
  regulation
Remedies, for breach of fiduciary duties,
  99-101
Reorganization, corporate, see Merger;
  Consolidation
Respondeat superior, generally, 148
Respondent, see Appellee
Restatement of the law, 77
Restrictions on business organizations:
  federal, 33, 41
  state, 39-40
Restrictive covenant, generally, 95-96
Rules:
  application, 7-8
  individual, 5
  judicial, 6
  legislative, 4

Sale of assets, generally, 447-448
Sale of control, liability of shareholder
  seller, 433-434

Scope of employment, generally, 161
Securities and Exchange Commission, generally, 480-481
Securities Investors Protection Corporation (SIPC), generally, 498-499
Securities regulation:
    fraudulent activities, 496-498, 535-537
    generally, 478-479
    going public, 481-483, 488, 490
    insider trading, *see* Insider trading
    intrastate offerings, 495
    liability for violations, 556-557
    nonpublic (private) offerings, 491-493
    public offerings, 488
    registration of securities, 488-490, 603
    Regulations A and D, 495-496
    regulation of proxies, 585-590
    regulation of tender offers, 592-593
    Rule 144, 493
    Rule 147, 495
    Securities Act of 1933, 479-480
    securities checklist for directors, 551-552
    Securities Exchange Act of 1934, 480
    securities exempt from registration, 490
    shelf registration, *see* Shelf Registration
    state antitakeover laws, 598-601
    state regulation, *see* Blue Sky Laws
    takeovers of corporations, 593-598
    U.C.C. rules, 601-603
    underwriting, 489
    what is a security, 483-488
Servant:
    generally, 151-175
    loaned or borrowed, 191-192
Shareholders:
    agreements, 341-342
    cumulative voting, 332-334
    derivative suits, 348-350
    fiduciary duties, 433-434, 462
    inspection rights, 345-346
    liabilities:
        debts of corporation, 297, 304, 323
        piercing the corporate veil, 297-298, 303
        subscription agreements, 324
    meetings, 331
    oppression of minority interests, 462
    power of, 321-323
    preemptive rights, 336-337
    proxies, *see* Proxies
    right of dissent and appraisal, 447-450
    voting trusts, 335-336

Shelf registration, of securities, 489-490
Shop rights doctrine, generally, 423
Social responsibilities of business, generally, 713-730
Stock:
    common, 326-328
    dividends, *see* Dividends
    nonvoting, 324-326
    no par, 325
    par value, 325
    preemptive rights, 336
    preferred, 326-328
    registration, 488-490, 603
    restriction on transfer of, 602
    Section 1244, 60
    specimen, 325
    splits, 368
    subscriptions, 324
    treasury stock, 325
    voting, 335
    watered, 288
Strict liability, *see* Product liability
Sub-agents, generally, 186-187
Subsidiaries:
    generally, 297-298
    liability of parent, 298
Summary judgment, *see* Judgment on the pleadings
Summons, 16

Tender offers, regulation of, *see* Securities regulation
Termination:
    of agency, *see* Agency
    of partnerships, *see* Partnership
Third party, 113
Tort:
    defined, 113, 143
    types, 143-144
Trade marks and names, generally, 39-40
Trade secrets, generally, 90-92
Trial process, explained, 11-23

Underwriters, *see* Securities Regulation
Unincorporated organizations, generally, 49
Uniform Partnership Act, 207. *See also* Appendix

Voting trusts, *see* Shareholders

Warranties, *see* Product liability